Saab 9-3
Owners Workshop Manual

M R Storey

Models covered

(5569 - 368)

Saloon, Estate (SportWagon) & Convertible
Petrol: 2.0 litre (1998cc) turbo
Turbo-diesel: 1.9 litre (1910cc)

Does NOT cover 1.8 litre or 2.8 litre petrol engines, or 2.0 litre A20NFT petrol engine introduced during 2011
Does NOT cover 'BioPower' models or 'XWD' models

ABCDE
FGHIJ
KL

A book in the **Haynes Owners Workshop Manual Series**

ISBN **978 1 78521 372 4**

British Library Cataloguing in Publication Data
A catalogue record for this book is available from the British Library.

Printed in India

Haynes Group Limited
Sparkford, Yeovil, Somerset BA22 7JJ, England

Haynes North America, Inc
2801 Townsgate Road, Suite 340, Thousand Oaks, CA 91361

Disclaimer

There are risks associated with automotive repairs. The ability to make repairs depends on the individual's skill, experience and proper tools. Individuals should act with due care and acknowledge and assume the risk of performing automotive repairs.

The purpose of this manual is to provide comprehensive, useful and accessible automotive repair information, to help you get the best value from your vehicle. However, this manual is not a substitute for a professional certified technician or mechanic.

This repair manual is produced by a third party and is not associated with an individual vehicle manufacturer. If there is any doubt or discrepancy between this manual and the owner's manual or the factory service manual, please refer to the factory service manual or seek assistance from a professional certified technician or mechanic.

Even though we have prepared this manual with extreme care and every attempt is made to ensure that the information in this manual is correct, neither the publisher nor the author can accept responsibility for loss, damage or injury caused by any errors in, or omissions from, the information given.

Contents

Contents

The original Saab 9-3 was first introduced in the UK in March 1998, as a replacement for the Saab 900. This manual covers the third generation 9-3 introduced in October 2007. Like the previous model it is based on the General Motors Epsilon platform, also shared by the Vauxhall Vectra, and is available as a 4-door Saloon, 5-door Estate, or 2-door Convertible. Engines covered by this manual are the 2.0 litre turbocharged petrol engine (note that this manual does not include the A20NFT 2.0 litre petrol engines fitted to a few of the very last cars to be produced) and the 1.9 litre turbo-diesel engine. The diesel engines are either SOHC 8v (Z19DT) engines or DOHC 16v engines (Z19DTR and DTH). The diesel engines were developed in conjunction with Fiat, and all share a similar cylinder block with belt-driven camshaft(s). The petrol engine has two chain-driven overhead camshafts (DOHC) with 16 valves acting on hydraulic tappets, and 2 integral balancer shafts.

Standard equipment includes power-assisted steering, anti-lock brakes, remote deadlock central locking, twin front and side airbags, inflatable side curtain, electric windows and mirrors, and climate control. Optional extras include an electric sunroof, electric front seats, leather upholstery and CD autochanger.

Models may be fitted with a five- or 6-speed manual transmission or five- or 6-speed automatic transmission mounted on the left-hand side of the engine.

All models have front-wheel-drive with fully-independent front and rear suspension, incorporating struts, gas-filled shock absorbers, and coil springs.

As most owners and potential owners will be aware, Saab ceased production of motor vehicles in 2011. A new company (Saab Automobile Parts AB) has been formed to ensure the supply of parts for all Saab models. The company has the backing of the Swedish government. The reference section at the end of this manual has further information (see *Buying spare parts*).

For the home mechanic, the Saab 9-3 is a relatively straightforward vehicle to maintain and repair, since design features have been incorporated to reduce the actual cost of ownership to a minimum, and most of the items requiring frequent attention are easily accessible.

Your Saab 9-3 manual

The aim of this manual is to help you get the best value from your vehicle. It can do so in several ways. It can help you decide what work must be done (even should you choose to get it done by a garage), provide information on routine maintenance and servicing, and give a logical course of action and diagnosis when random faults occur. However, it is hoped that you will use the manual by tackling the work yourself. On simpler jobs, it may even be quicker than booking the car into a garage and going there twice, to leave and collect it. Perhaps most important, a lot of money can be saved by avoiding the costs a garage must charge to cover its labour and overheads.

The manual has drawings and descriptions to show the function of the various components, so that their layout can be understood. Then the tasks are described and photographed in a clear step-by-step sequence.

References to the 'left' or 'right' are in the sense of a person in the driver's seat, facing forward.

Acknowledgements

Thanks are also due to Draper Tools Limited, who provided some of the workshop tools, and to all those people at Sparkford who helped in the production of this manual.

Working on your car can be dangerous. This page shows just some of the potential risks and hazards, with the aim of creating a safety-conscious attitude.

General hazards

Scalding

• Don't remove the radiator or expansion tank cap while the engine is hot.

• Engine oil, transmission fluid or power steering fluid may also be dangerously hot if the engine has recently been running.

Burning

• Beware of burns from the exhaust system and from any part of the engine. Brake discs and drums can also be extremely hot immediately after use.

Crushing

• When working under or near a raised vehicle, always supplement the jack with axle stands, or use drive-on ramps. ***Never venture under a car which is only supported by a jack.***

• Take care if loosening or tightening high-torque nuts when the vehicle is on stands. Initial loosening and final tightening should be done with the wheels on the ground.

Fire

• Fuel is highly flammable; fuel vapour is explosive.

• Don't let fuel spill onto a hot engine.

• Do not smoke or allow naked lights (including pilot lights) anywhere near a vehicle being worked on. Also beware of creating sparks (electrically or by use of tools).

• Fuel vapour is heavier than air, so don't work on the fuel system with the vehicle over an inspection pit.

• Another cause of fire is an electrical overload or short-circuit. Take care when repairing or modifying the vehicle wiring.

• Keep a fire extinguisher handy, of a type suitable for use on fuel and electrical fires.

Electric shock

• Ignition HT and Xenon headlight voltages can be dangerous, especially to people with heart problems or a pacemaker. Don't work on or near these systems with the engine running or the ignition switched on.

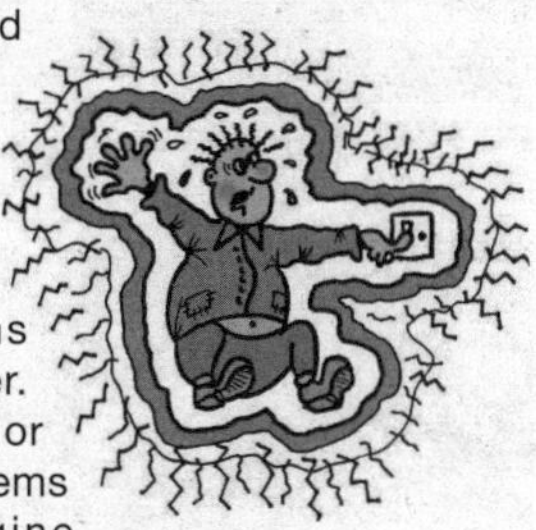

• Mains voltage is also dangerous. Make sure that any mains-operated equipment is correctly earthed. Mains power points should be protected by a residual current device (RCD) circuit breaker.

Fume or gas intoxication

• Exhaust fumes are poisonous; they can contain carbon monoxide, which is rapidly fatal if inhaled. Never run the engine in a confined space such as a garage with the doors shut.

• Fuel vapour is also poisonous, as are the vapours from some cleaning solvents and paint thinners.

Poisonous or irritant substances

• Avoid skin contact with battery acid and with any fuel, fluid or lubricant, especially antifreeze, brake hydraulic fluid and Diesel fuel. Don't syphon them by mouth. If such a substance is swallowed or gets into the eyes, seek medical advice.

• Prolonged contact with used engine oil can cause skin cancer. Wear gloves or use a barrier cream if necessary. Change out of oil-soaked clothes and do not keep oily rags in your pocket.

• Air conditioning refrigerant forms a poisonous gas if exposed to a naked flame (including a cigarette). It can also cause skin burns on contact.

Asbestos

• Asbestos dust can cause cancer if inhaled or swallowed. Asbestos may be found in gaskets and in brake and clutch linings. When dealing with such components it is safest to assume that they contain asbestos.

Special hazards

Hydrofluoric acid

• This extremely corrosive acid is formed when certain types of synthetic rubber, found in some O-rings, oil seals, fuel hoses etc, are exposed to temperatures above 4000C. The rubber changes into a charred or sticky substance containing the acid. *Once formed, the acid remains dangerous for years. If it gets onto the skin, it may be necessary to amputate the limb concerned.*

• When dealing with a vehicle which has suffered a fire, or with components salvaged from such a vehicle, wear protective gloves and discard them after use.

The battery

• Batteries contain sulphuric acid, which attacks clothing, eyes and skin. Take care when topping-up or carrying the battery.

• The hydrogen gas given off by the battery is highly explosive. Never cause a spark or allow a naked light nearby. Be careful when connecting and disconnecting battery chargers or jump leads.

Air bags

• Air bags can cause injury if they go off accidentally. Take care when removing the steering wheel and trim panels. Special storage instructions may apply.

Diesel injection equipment

• Diesel injection pumps supply fuel at very high pressure. Take care when working on the fuel injectors and fuel pipes.

Warning: Never expose the hands, face or any other part of the body to injector spray; the fuel can penetrate the skin with potentially fatal results.

Remember...

DO

• Do use eye protection when using power tools, and when working under the vehicle.

• Do wear gloves or use barrier cream to protect your hands when necessary.

• Do get someone to check periodically that all is well when working alone on the vehicle.

• Do keep loose clothing and long hair well out of the way of moving mechanical parts.

• Do remove rings, wristwatch etc, before working on the vehicle – especially the electrical system.

• Do ensure that any lifting or jacking equipment has a safe working load rating adequate for the job.

DON'T

• Don't attempt to lift a heavy component which may be beyond your capability – get assistance.

• Don't rush to finish a job, or take unverified short cuts.

• Don't use ill-fitting tools which may slip and cause injury.

• Don't leave tools or parts lying around where someone can trip over them. Mop up oil and fuel spills at once.

• Don't allow children or pets to play in or near a vehicle being worked on.

The following pages are intended to help in dealing with common roadside emergencies and breakdowns. You will find more detailed fault finding information at the back of the manual, and repair information in the main chapters.

If your car won't start and the starter motor doesn't turn

- ☐ If it's a model with automatic transmission, make sure the selector is in P or N.
- ☐ Open the bonnet and make sure that the battery terminals are clean and tight.
- ☐ Switch on the headlights and try to start the engine. If the headlights go very dim when you're trying to start, the battery is probably flat. Get out of trouble by jump starting (see next page) using a friend's car.

If your car won't start even though the starter motor turns as normal

- ☐ Is there fuel in the tank?
- ☐ Is there any moisture on electrical components under the bonnet? Switch off the ignition, then wipe off any obvious dampness with a dry cloth. Spray a water-repellent aerosol product (WD-40 or equivalent) on ignition and fuel system electrical connectors.

1 Unscrew the 2 fasteners, remove the battery cover, and check that the battery cables are securely connected.

2 Check that the combustion detection module wiring is securely connected.

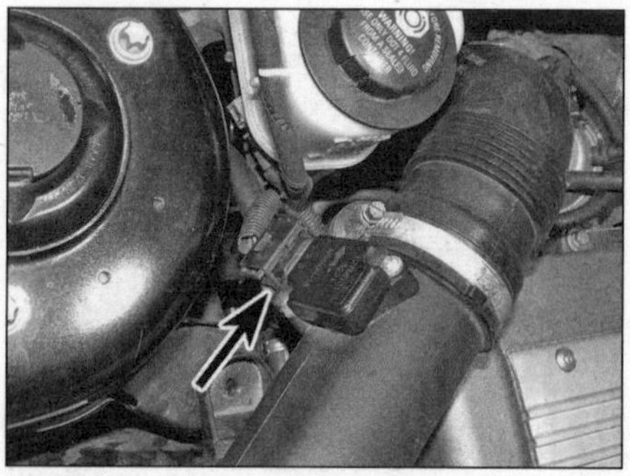

3 Check that the mass airflow meter wiring is securely connected.

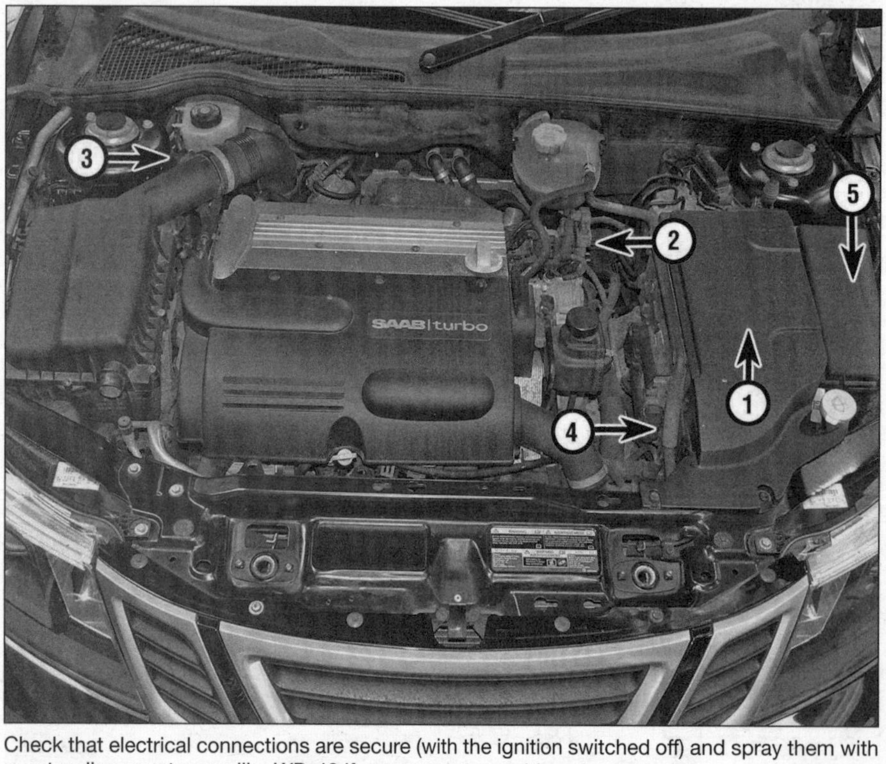

Check that electrical connections are secure (with the ignition switched off) and spray them with a water-dispersant spray like WD-40 if you suspect a problem due to damp.

4 Check the engine wiring loom multiplugs for security.

5 Check that none of the engine compartment fuses have blown.

Jump starting

HAYNES HiNT *Jump starting will get you out of trouble, but you must correct whatever made the battery go flat in the first place. There are three possibilities:*

***1** The battery has been drained by repeated attempts to start, or by leaving the lights on.*

***2** The charging system is not working properly (alternator drivebelt slack or broken, alternator wiring fault or alternator itself faulty).*

***3** The battery itself is at fault (electrolyte low, or battery worn out).*

When jump-starting a car, observe the following precautions:

✓ Before connecting the booster battery, make sure that the ignition is switched off.

Caution: Remove the key in case the central locking engages when the jump leads are connected

✓ Ensure that all electrical equipment (lights, heater, wipers, etc) is switched off.

✓ Take note of any special precautions printed on the battery case.

✓ Make sure that the booster battery is the same voltage as the discharged one in the vehicle.

✓ If the battery is being jump-started from the battery in another vehicle, the two vehicles MUST NOT TOUCH each other.

✓ Make sure that the transmission is in neutral (or PARK, in the case of automatic transmission).

HAYNES HiNT *Budget jump leads can be a false economy, as they often do not pass enough current to start large capacity or diesel engines. They can also get hot.*

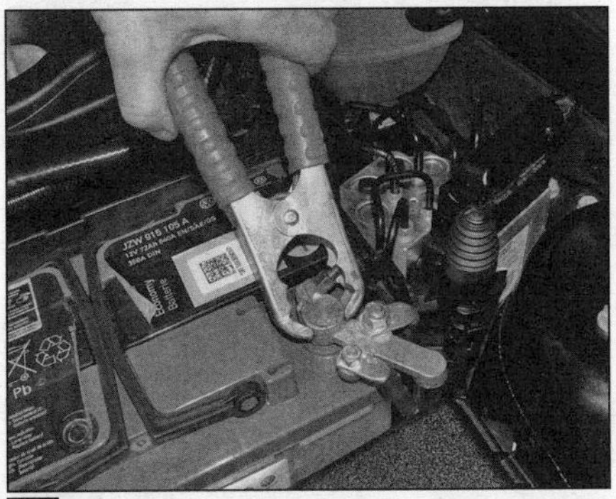

1 Connect one end of the red jump lead to the positive (+) terminal of the flat battery

2 Connect the other end of the red lead to the positive (+) terminal of the booster battery.

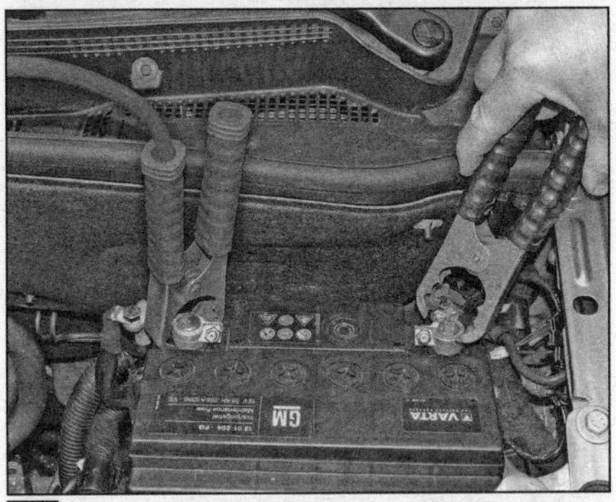

3 Connect one end of the black jump lead to the negative (-) terminal of the booster battery

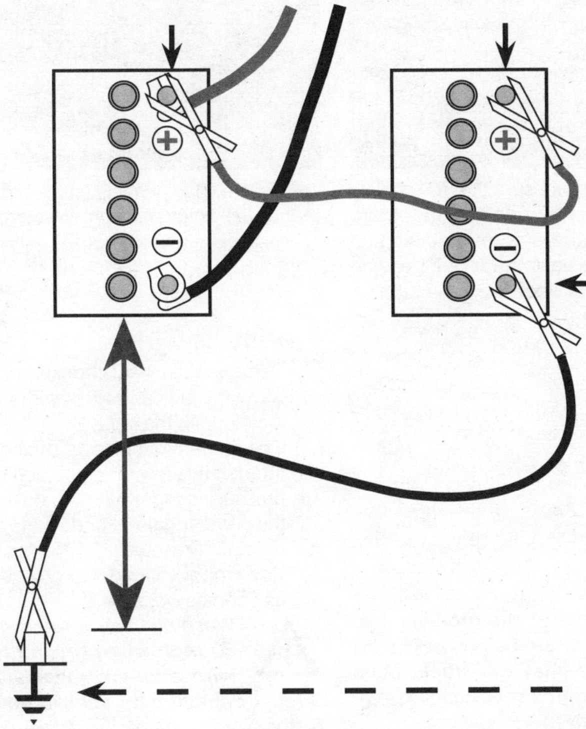

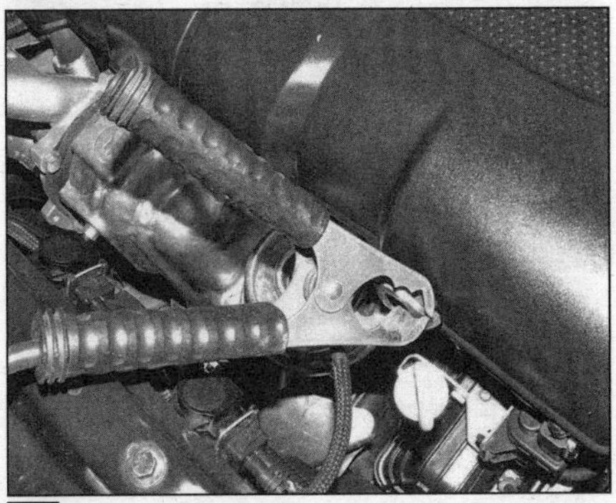

4 Connect the other end of the black jump lead to a bolt or bracket on the engine block, well away from the battery, on the vehicle to be started.

5 Make sure that the jump leads will not come into contact with the fan, drive-belts or other moving parts of the engine.

6 Start the engine using the booster battery and run it at idle speed. Switch on the lights, rear window demister and heater blower motor, then disconnect the jump leads in the reverse order of connection. Turn off the lights etc.

Wheel changing

Warning: Do not change a wheel in a situation where you risk being hit by other traffic. On busy roads, try to stop in a lay-by or a gateway. Be wary of passing traffic while changing the wheel – it is easy to become distracted by the job in hand.

Preparation

☐ When a puncture occurs, stop as soon as it is safe to do so.
☐ Park on firm level ground, if possible, and well out of the way of other traffic.
☐ Use hazard warning lights if necessary.
☐ If you have one, use a warning triangle to alert other drivers of your presence.
☐ Apply the handbrake and engage first or reverse gear (or Park on models with automatic transmission).
☐ Chock the wheel diagonally opposite the one being removed – a couple of large stones will do for this.
☐ If the ground is soft, use a flat piece of wood to spread the load under the jack.

Changing the wheel

1 Remove the luggage compartment cover and then unscrew the plastic retaining nut. Lift out the spare wheel and place it beneath the sill as a precaution against the jack failing. Note that the spare wheel may be of the 'space saver' type.

2 The jack and wheel removal tools are stored beneath the spare wheel. Lift the tools from place.

3 Where fitted, pull the wheel trim from the wheel. Before you raise the car, loosen each wheel bolt by half a turn only. On models with alloy wheels, use the special adapter.

4 Locate the jack head in the rectangular rubber pad below the reinforced jacking points (indicated by the arrows in the sill), nearest the wheel to be changed. Turn the handle until the base of the jack touches the ground then make sure that the base is located directly below the sill. Raise the vehicle until the wheel is clear of the ground.

5 If the tyre is flat make sure that the vehicle is raised sufficiently to allow the spare wheel to be fitted. Remove the bolts and lift the wheel from the vehicle. Place it beneath the sill in place of the spare as a precaution against the jack failing.

6 Fit the spare wheel, then insert each of the wheel bolts and tighten them moderately using the wheelbrace.

7 Lower the vehicle to the ground, then finally tighten the wheel bolts in a diagonal sequence. Note that the wheel bolts should be tightened to the specified torque at the earliest opportunity.

Finally . . .

☐ Remove the wheel chocks.
☐ Stow the jack and tools in the correct locations in the car.
☐ Check the tyre pressure on the wheel just fitted. If it is low, or if you don't have a pressure gauge with you, drive slowly to the nearest garage and inflate the tyre to the right pressure.
☐ Have the damaged tyre or wheel repaired as soon as possible.

Warning: You should not exceed 50 mph when driving the vehicle with a space saver spare wheel fitted – consult your vehicle handbook for further information.

Identifying leaks

Puddles on the garage floor or drive, or obvious wetness under the bonnet or underneath the car, suggest a leak that needs investigating. It can sometimes be difficult to decide where the leak is coming from, especially if an engine undershield is fitted. Leaking oil or fluid can also be blown rearwards by the passage of air under the car, giving a false impression of where the problem lies.

Warning: Most automotive oils and fluids are poisonous. Wash them off skin, and change out of contaminated clothing, without delay.

HAYNES HiNT *The smell of a fluid leaking from the car may provide a clue to what's leaking. Some fluids are distinctively coloured. It may help to remove the engine undershield, clean the car carefully and to park it over some clean paper overnight as an aid to locating the source of the leak.*
Remember that some leaks may only occur while the engine is running.

Sump oil

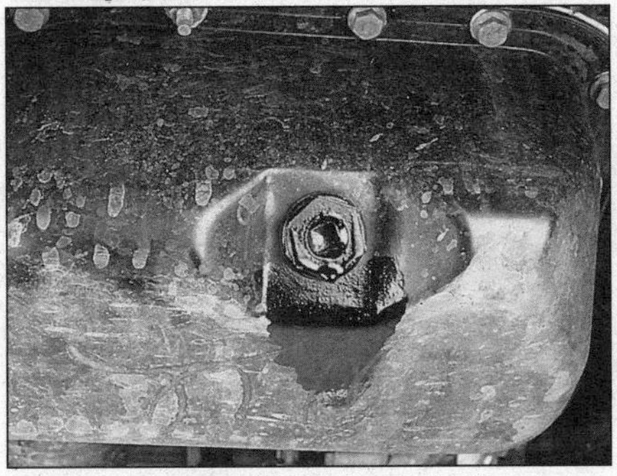

Engine oil may leak from the drain plug...

Oil from filter

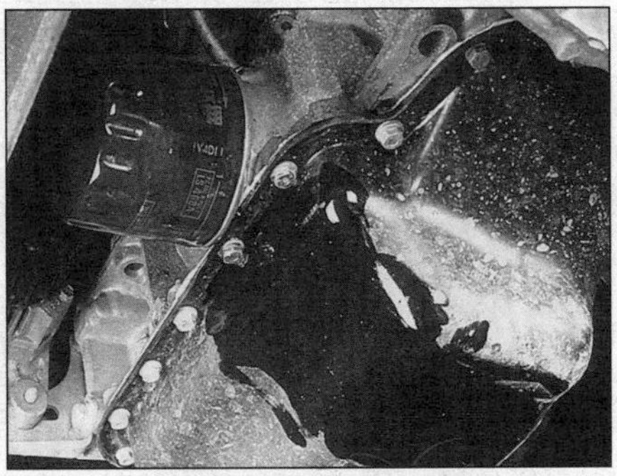

...or from the base of the oil filter.

Gearbox oil

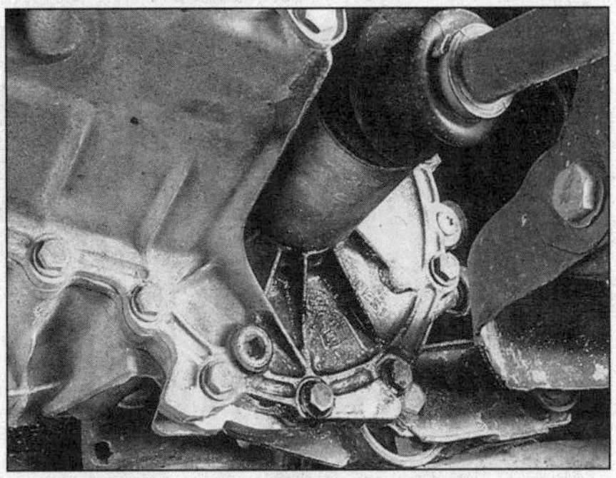

Gearbox oil can leak from the seals at the inboard ends of the driveshafts.

Antifreeze

Leaking antifreeze often leaves a crystalline deposit like this.

Brake fluid

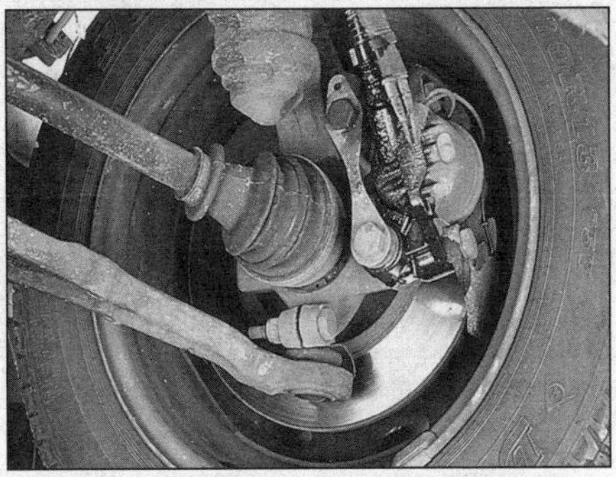

A leak occurring at a wheel is almost certainly brake fluid.

Power steering fluid

Power steering fluid may leak from the pipe connectors on the steering rack.

Towing

When all else fails, you may find yourself having to get a tow home – or of course you may be helping somebody else. Long-distance recovery should only be done by a garage or breakdown service. For shorter distances, DIY towing using another car is easy enough, but observe the following points:

☐ The front towing eye is located alongside the spare wheel, and is inserted behind a cover on the right-hand side of the front bumper. Prise out the cover and screw in the towing eye. Note the towing eye has a ***left-hand*** thread.

☐ The rear towing eye is provided beneath the rear of the vehicle.

☐ Use a proper tow-rope – they are not expensive. The vehicle being towed must display an ON TOW sign in its rear window. Only attach the tow-rope to the towing eyes provided.

☐ Always turn the ignition key to the 'on' position when the vehicle is being towed, so that the steering lock is released, and that the direction indicator and brake lights will work.

☐ Before being towed, release the handbrake and select neutral on the transmission. On models with automatic transmission, special precautions apply, as follows (if in doubt, do not tow, or transmission damage may result):

a) *The car may only be towed in the forward direction.*
b) *The gear selector lever must be in the N position.*
c) *The vehicle must not be towed at a speed exceeding 30 mph, nor for a distance of more than 30 miles.*

☐ Note that greater-than-usual pedal pressure will be required to operate the brakes, since the vacuum servo unit is only operational with the engine running.

☐ Since the power steering will not be functional, greater-than-usual steering effort will also be required.

☐ The driver of the car being towed must keep the tow-rope taut at all times to avoid snatching.

☐ Make sure that both drivers know the route before setting off.

☐ Only drive at moderate speeds and keep the distance towed to a minimum. Drive smoothly and allow plenty of time for slowing down at junctions.

☐ The driver of the towing vehicle must accelerate very gently from a standstill and must bear in mind the aditional length of the vehicle being towed when pulling out at junctions, roundabouts, etc.

Introduction

There are some very simple checks which need only take a few minutes to carry out, but which could save you a lot of inconvenience and expense.

These checks require no great skill or special tools, and the small amount of time they take to perform could prove to be very well spent, for example:

☐ Keeping an eye on tyre condition and pressures, will not only help to stop them wearing out prematurely, but could also save your life.

☐ Many breakdowns are caused by electrical problems. Battery-related faults are particularly common, and a quick check on a regular basis will often prevent the majority of these.

☐ If your car develops a brake fluid leak, the first time you might know about it is when your brakes don't work properly. Checking the level regularly will give advance warning of this kind of problem.

☐ If the oil or coolant levels run low, the cost of repairing any engine damage will be far greater than fixing the leak, for example.

Underbonnet check points

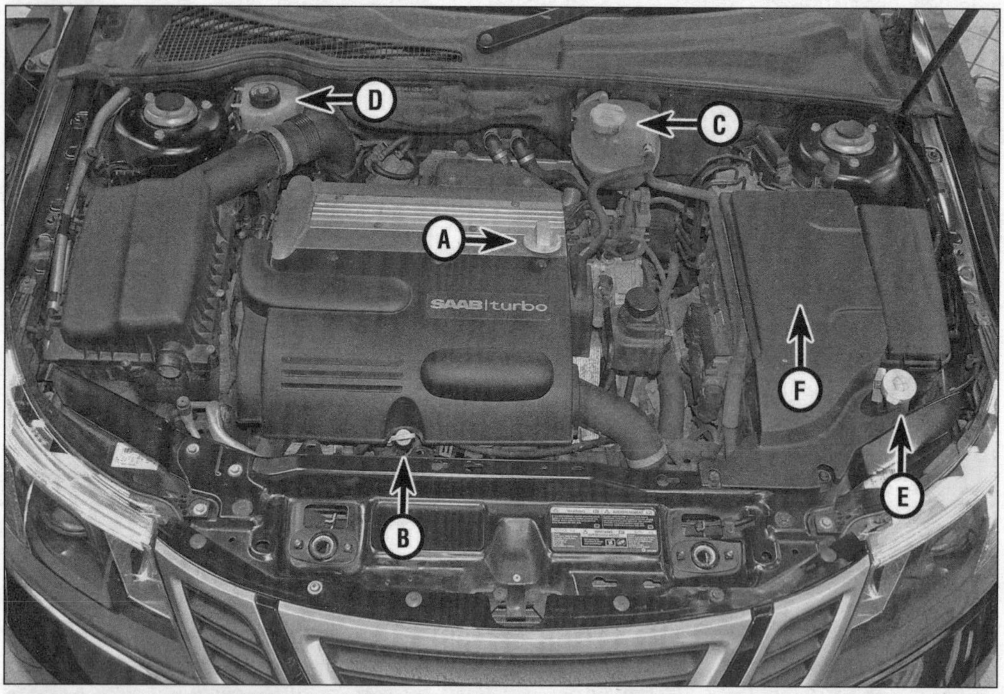

◀ **Petrol engines**

A *Engine oil filler cap*
B *Engine oil level dipstick*
C *Coolant reservoir (expansion tank)*
D *Brake (and clutch) fluid reservoir*
E *Washer fluid reservoir*
F *Battery*

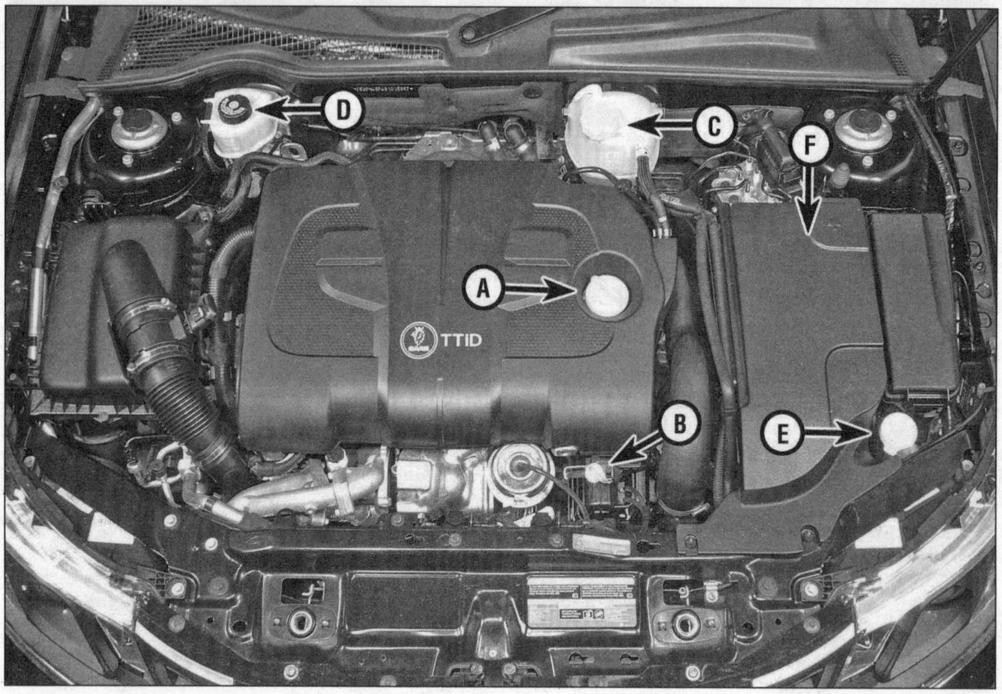

◀ **Diesel engines**

A *Engine oil filler cap*
B *Engine oil level dipstick*
C *Coolant reservoir (expansion tank)*
D *Brake (and clutch) fluid reservoir*
E *Washer fluid reservoir*
F *Battery*

Engine oil level

Before you start

✔ Make sure that the car is on level ground.
✔ Check the oil level with the engine at operating temperature, and between 2 and 5 minutes after the engine has been switched off.

> HAYNES HiNT *If the oil is checked immediately after driving the vehicle, some of the oil will remain in the upper engine components, resulting in an inaccurate reading on the dipstick.*

The correct oil

Modern engines place great demands on their oil. It is very important that the correct oil for your car is used (see *Lubricants and fluids*).

Car care

- If you have to add oil frequently, you should check whether you have any oil leaks. Place some clean paper under the car overnight, and check for stains in the morning. If there are no leaks, then the engine may be burning oil.
- Always maintain the level between the upper and lower dipstick marks (see photo 3). If the level is too low, severe engine damage may occur. Oil seal failure may result if the engine is overfilled by adding too much oil.

1 On all models, the dipstick is located on the front of the engine, and the oil filler cap is on the top of the engine (see *Underbonnet check points* for exact location). Withdraw the dipstick.

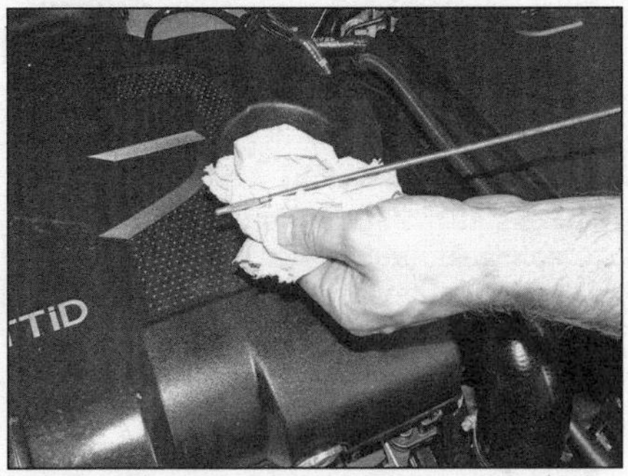

2 Using a clean rag or paper towel, remove all oil from the dipstick. Insert the clean dipstick into the tube and then withdraw it again.

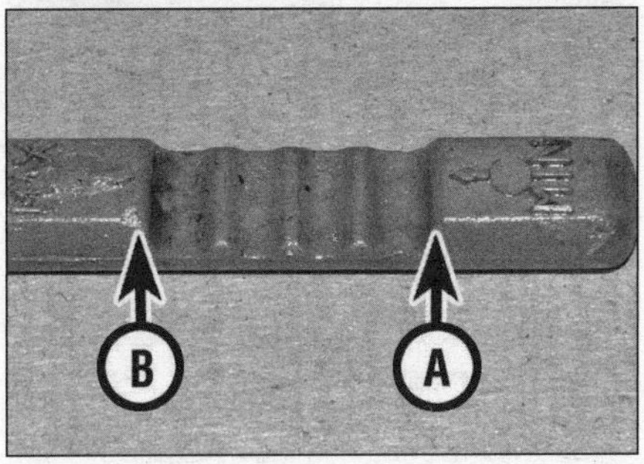

3 Note the oil level on the end of the dipstick (petrol model shown) which should be between the upper mark (B) and lower mark (A). Approximately 1.0 litre of oil will raise the level from the lower mark to the upper mark.

4 Oil is added through the filler cap hole. Unscrew the cap and withdraw it. Top-up the level. A funnel may help to reduce spillage. Add the oil slowly, checking the level on the dipstick often. Do not overfill. Refit the cap on completion.

Coolant level

> ***Warning: Do not attempt to remove the expansion tank pressure cap when the engine is hot, as there is a very great risk of scalding. Do not leave open containers of coolant about, as it is poisonous.***

Car care

- With a sealed-type cooling system, adding coolant should not be necessary on a regular basis. If frequent topping-up is required, it is likely there is a leak. Check the radiator, all hoses and joint faces for signs of staining or wetness, and rectify as necessary.
- It is important that antifreeze is used in the cooling system all year round, not just during the winter months. Don't top up with water alone, as the antifreeze will become diluted.

1 The coolant level varies with the temperature of the engine. When the engine is cold, the coolant level should be on or slightly above the KALT/COLD mark on the side of the tank. When the engine is hot, the level will rise.

2 If topping-up is necessary, wait until the engine is cold. Slowly unscrew the expansion tank cap, to release any pressure present in the cooling system, and remove it.

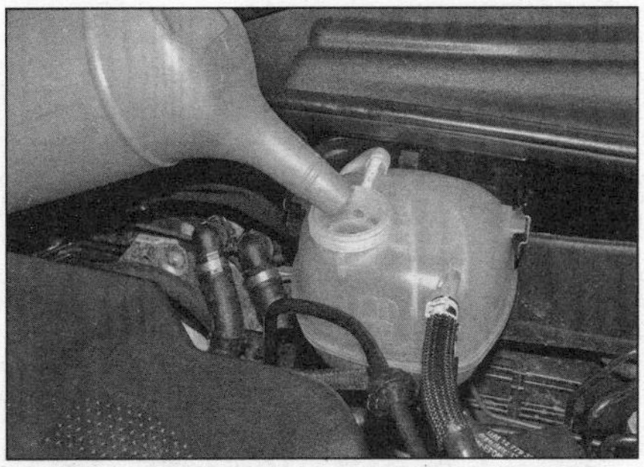

3 Top-up the level by adding a mixture of water and antifreeze to the expansion tank. A funnel may help to reduce spillage. Refit the cap and tighten it securely.

Brake (and clutch) fluid level

Note: *On manual transmission models, the fluid reservoir also supplies the clutch master cylinder with fluid.*

Before you start

✔ Make sure that the car is on level ground.

✔ Cleanliness is of great importance when dealing with the braking system, so take care to clean around the reservoir cap before topping-up. Use only clean brake fluid.

Safety first!

- If the reservoir requires repeated topping-up, this is an indication of a fluid leak somewhere in the system, which should be investigated immediately. Note that the level will drop naturally as the brake pad linings wear, but must never be allowed to fall below the MIN mark.
- If a leak is suspected, the car should not be driven until the braking system has been checked. Never take any risks where brakes are concerned.

Warning: Brake fluid can harm your eyes and damage painted surfaces, so use extreme caution when handling and pouring it. Do not use fluid which has been standing open for some time, as it absorbs moisture from the air, which can cause a dangerous loss of braking effectiveness.

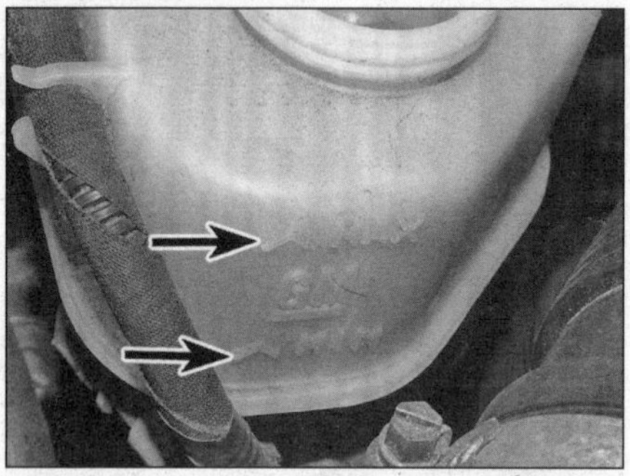

1 The MIN and MAX marks are indicated on the front of the reservoir located in the right-hand rear corner of the engine compartment. The fluid level must always be kept between the marks.

2 If topping-up is necessary, first wipe clean the area around the filler cap to prevent dirt entering the hydraulic system. Unscrew the cap and place it on an absorbent rag.

3 Carefully add fluid, taking care not to spill it onto the surrounding components. Use only the specified fluid; mixing different types can cause damage to the system. After topping-up to the correct level, securely refit the cap and wipe off any spilt fluid.

Washer fluid level

- Screenwash additives not only keep the windscreen clean during bad weather, they also prevent the washer system freezing in cold weather – which is when you are likely to need it most. Don't top-up using plain water, as the screenwash will become diluted, and will freeze in cold weather.
- Check the operation of the windscreen and rear window washers. Adjust the nozzles using a pin if necessary, aiming the spray to a point slightly above the centre of the swept area.

Warning: On no account use engine coolant antifreeze in the screen washer system – this may damage the paintwork.

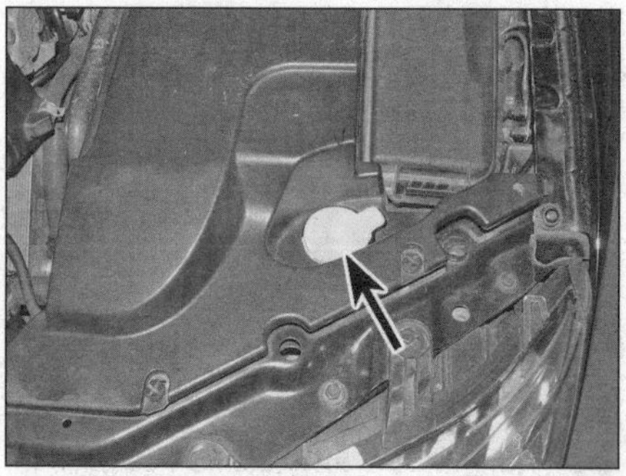

1 The reservoir for the windscreen and rear window (where applicable) washer systems is located on the front left-hand corner of the engine compartment. If topping-up is necessary, open the cap.

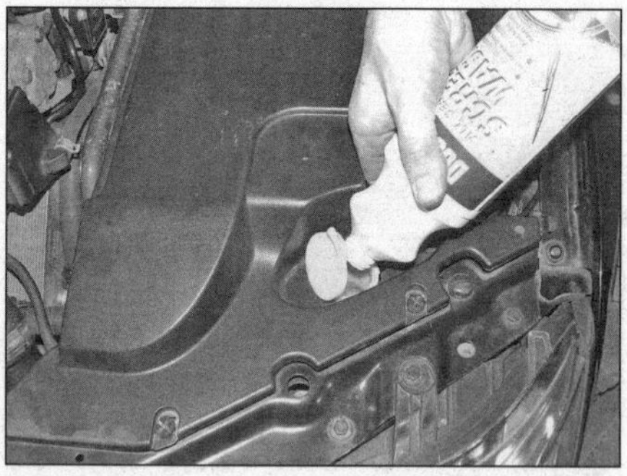

2 When topping-up the reservoir a screenwash additive should be added in the quantities recommended on the bottle.

Electrical systems

✔ Check all external lights and the horn. Refer to Chapter 12, Section 2 for details if any of the circuits are found to be inoperative.

✔ Visually check all accessible wiring connectors, harnesses and retaining clips for security, and for signs of chafing or damage.

HAYNES HiNT ***If you need to check your brake lights and indicators unaided, back up to a wall or garage door and operate the lights. The reflected light should show if they are working properly.***

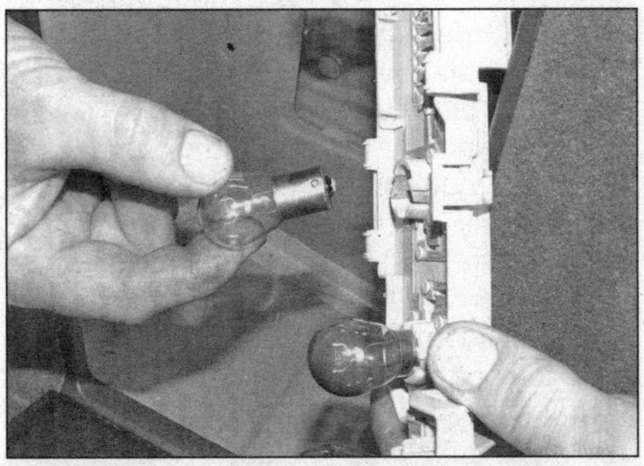

1 If a single indicator light, brake light or headlight has failed, it is likely that a bulb has blown and will need to be renewed. Refer to Chapter 12, Section 7 for details. If both brake lights have failed, it is possible that the switch has failed (see Chapter 9, Section 17).

2 If more than one indicator light or headlight has failed, it is likely that either a fuse has blown or that there is a fault in the circuit (see Chapter 12, Section 2 and 3). The main fuses are accessed by removing a cover on the driver's end of the facia. Additional fuses and relays are located in the left-hand side of the engine compartment, and the left-hand side of the luggage compartment.

3 To renew a blown fuse, remove it using the plastic tool provided. Fit a new fuse of the same rating, available from car accessory shops. If the fuse blows repeatedly, refer to Chapter 12, Section 2 to locate the fault

Battery

Caution: Before carrying out any work on the vehicle battery, read the precautions given in 'Safety first!' at the start of this manual.

✔ Make sure that the battery tray is in good condition, and that the clamp is tight. Corrosion on the tray, retaining clamp and the battery itself can be removed with a solution of water and baking soda. Thoroughly rinse all cleaned areas with water. Any metal parts damaged by corrosion should be covered with a zinc-based primer, then painted.

✔ Periodically (approximately every three months), check the charge condition of the battery as described in Chapter 5A, Section 3.

✔ If the battery is flat, and you need to jump start your vehicle, see *Roadside repairs*.

HAYNES HiNT

Battery corrosion can be kept to a minimum by applying a layer of petroleum jelly to the clamps and terminals after they are reconnected.

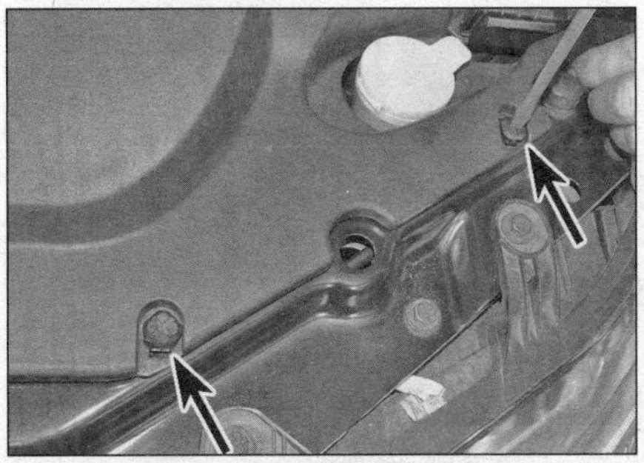

1 The battery is located at the front, left-hand side of the engine compartment. Rotate the fasteners anti-clockwise and remove the battery cover.

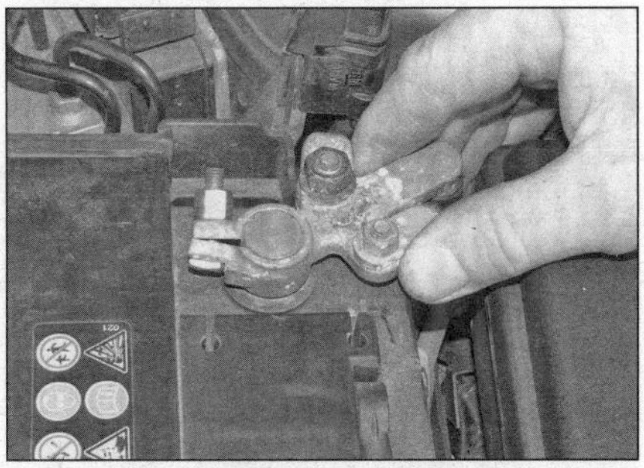

2 Check the tightness of battery clamps to ensure good electrical connections. You should not be able to move them. Also check each cable for cracks and frayed conductors.

3 If corrosion (white, fluffy deposits) is evident, remove the cables from the battery terminals, clean them with a small wire brush, then refit them. Automotive stores sell a tool for cleaning the battery post ...

4 ... as well as the battery cable clamps.

Tyre condition and pressure

It is very important that tyres are in good condition, and at the correct pressure - having a tyre failure at any speed is highly dangerous.
Tyre wear is influenced by driving style - harsh braking and acceleration, or fast cornering, will all produce more rapid tyre wear. As a general rule, the front tyres wear out faster than the rears. Interchanging the tyres from front to rear ("rotating" the tyres) may result in more even wear. However, if this is completely effective, you may have the expense of replacing all four tyres at once!
Remove any nails or stones embedded in the tread before they penetrate the tyre to cause deflation. If removal of a nail does reveal that the tyre has been punctured, refit the nail so that its point of penetration is marked. Then immediately change the wheel, and have the tyre repaired by a tyre dealer.
Regularly check the tyres for damage in the form of cuts or bulges, especially in the sidewalls. Periodically remove the wheels, and clean any dirt or mud from the inside and outside surfaces. Examine the wheel rims for signs of rusting, corrosion or other damage. Light alloy wheels are easily damaged by "kerbing" whilst parking; steel wheels may also become dented or buckled. A new wheel is very often the only way to overcome severe damage.
New tyres should be balanced when they are fitted, but it may become necessary to re-balance them as they wear, or if the balance weights fitted to the wheel rim should fall off. Unbalanced tyres will wear more quickly, as will the steering and suspension components. Wheel imbalance is normally signified by vibration, particularly at a certain speed (typically around 50 mph). If this vibration is felt only through the steering, then it is likely that just the front wheels need balancing. If, however, the vibration is felt through the whole car, the rear wheels could be out of balance. Wheel balancing should be carried out by a tyre dealer or garage.

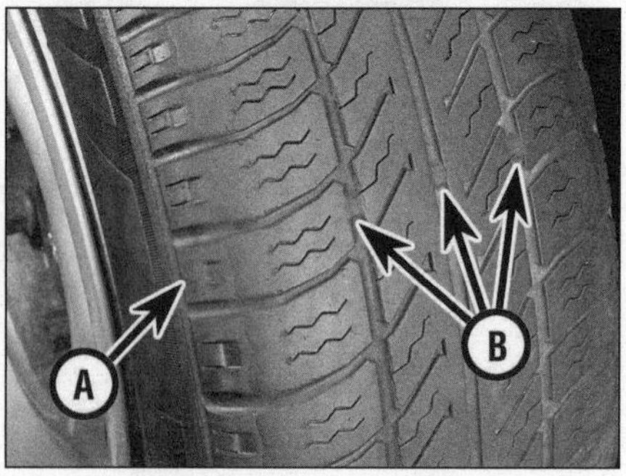

1 *Tread Depth - visual check*
The original tyres have tread wear safety bands (B), which will appear when the tread depth reaches approximately 1.6 mm. The band positions are indicated by a triangular mark on the tyre sidewall (A).

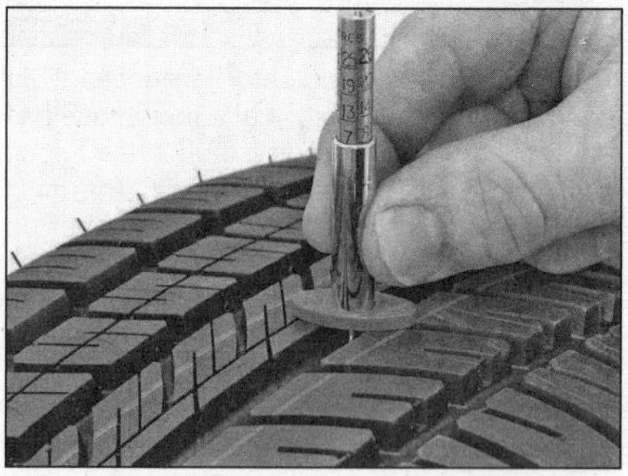

2 *Tread Depth - manual check*
Alternatively, tread wear can be monitored with a simple, inexpensive device known as a tread depth indicator gauge.

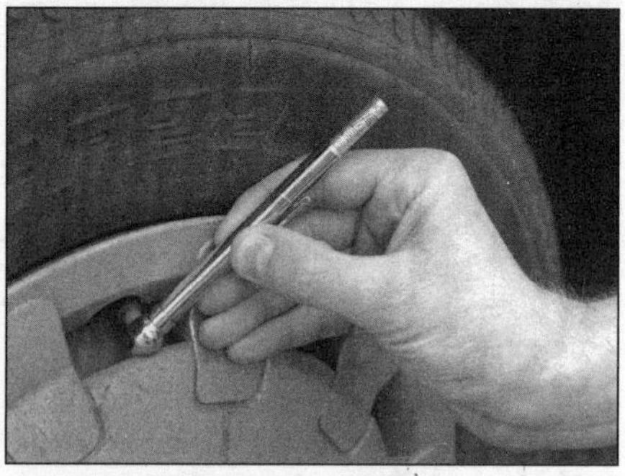

3 *Tyre Pressure Check*
Check the tyre pressures regularly with the tyres cold. Do not adjust the tyre pressures immediately after the vehicle has been used, or an inaccurate setting will result.

Tyre tread wear patterns

Shoulder Wear

Underinflation (wear on both sides)
Under-inflation will cause overheating of the tyre, because the tyre will flex too much, and the tread will not sit correctly on the road surface. This will cause a loss of grip and excessive wear, not to mention the danger of sudden tyre failure due to heat build-up.
Check and adjust pressures
Incorrect wheel camber (wear on one side)
Repair or renew suspension parts
Hard cornering
Reduce speed!

Centre Wear

Overinflation
Over-inflation will cause rapid wear of the centre part of the tyre tread, coupled with reduced grip, harsher ride, and the danger of shock damage occurring in the tyre casing.
Check and adjust pressures

If you sometimes have to inflate your car's tyres to the higher pressures specified for maximum load or sustained high speed, don't forget to reduce the pressures to normal afterwards.

Uneven Wear

Front tyres may wear unevenly as a result of wheel misalignment. Most tyre dealers and garages can check and adjust the wheel alignment (or "tracking") for a modest charge.
Incorrect camber or castor
Repair or renew suspension parts
Malfunctioning suspension
Repair or renew suspension parts
Unbalanced wheel
Balance tyres
Incorrect toe setting
Adjust front wheel alignment
Note: *The feathered edge of the tread which typifies toe wear is best checked by feel.*

Wiper blades

Check the condition of the wiper blades; if they are cracked or show any signs of deterioration, or if the glass swept area is smeared, renew them. For maximum clarity of vision, wiper blades should be renewed annually.

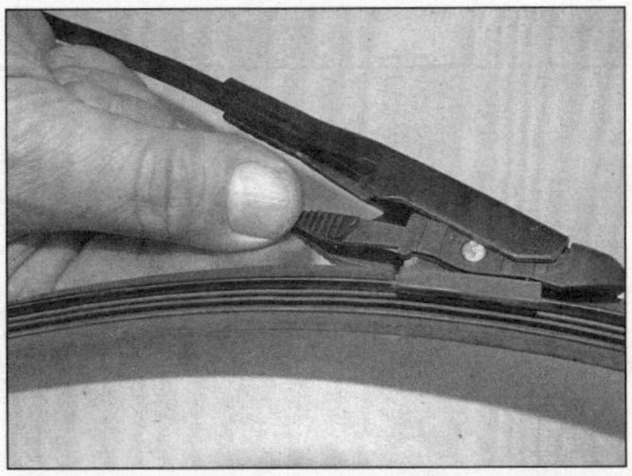

1 Position the wiper blades in the vertical position by switching off the ignition and removing the key. Press down the wiper switch within 16 seconds and the wipers will park in the vertical position. Left the blade away from the windscreen and depress the locking tab to release the wiper blade from the wiper arm. Rotate the blade and unhook it from the wiper arm.

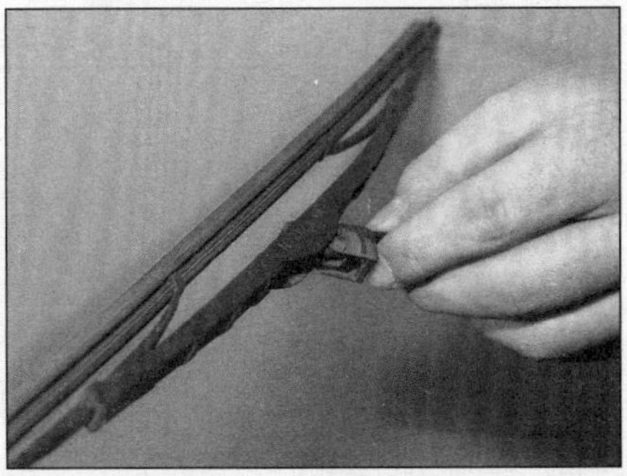

2 Don't forget to check the tailgate wiper blade as well on Estate models. The blade is clipped onto the arm.

Lubricants and fluids

Engine	
Petrol	Saab Turbo Engine Oil or any fully synthetic oil with viscosity 0W-30 or 0W-40 to specification GM-LL-A-025
Diesel*	
Z19DT and Z19DTH engines	Saab Turbo Engine Oil or any synthetic engine oil with viscosity 0W-30, 0W-40, 5W-30 or 5W-40 to specification GM-LL-B-025
Z19DTR engine	Saab Turbo Engine Oil or any synthetic engine oil with viscosity 0W-40 to specification GM-LL-B-025 (GM 93 165 386)
Cooling system	Saab original coolant/antifreeze only
Manual gearbox	Saab synthetic manual gearbox oil MTF 0063, part no 93 165 290
Automatic transmission	
5-speed	Saab automatic transmission fluid 3309
6-speed	AW-1 part no 93 165 147
Power steering reservoir	Saab power steering fluid part no 93 160 548
Convertible roof fluid reservoir	Saab power steering fluid CHF 11S
Brake fluid reservoir	Hydraulic fluid to DOT 4

** For details of engine code location, see 'Vehicle identification' in the Reference Chapter.*

Tyre pressures (cold)

Note: *Pressures apply to original-equipment tyres, and may vary if any other make or type of tyre is fitted; check with the tyre manufacturer or supplier for correct pressures if necessary. Pressures are also given on the passenger's glovebox lid.*

Tyre size	Front	Rear
195/65 R15	33 psi (2.3 bar)	33 psi (2.3 bar)
215/60 R15	35 psi (2.4 bar)	32 psi (2.2 bar)
215/55 R16	32 psi (2.2 bar)	32 psi (2.2 bar)
225/45 R17	35 psi (2.4 bar)	35 psi (2.4 bar)
235/45 R17	35 psi (2.4 bar)	35 psi (2.4 bar)
225/45 R18	35 psi (2.4 bar)	35 psi (2.4 bar)

Chapter 1 Part A:
Routine maintenance and servicing – petrol models

Contents

Degrees of difficulty

Easy, suitable for novice with little experience	**Fairly easy,** suitable for beginner with some experience	**Fairly difficult,** suitable for competent DIY mechanic	**Difficult,** suitable for experienced DIY mechanic	**Very difficult,** suitable for expert DIY or professional

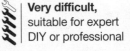

Lubricants and fluids

Refer to the end of *Weekly checks* on page 0•16

Capacities

Engine oil	
Drain and refill, with filter change	6.0 litres
Between dipstick MAX and MIN markings	1.0 litres
Cooling system	
All models	7.1 litres
Transmission	
Manual (drain and refill):	
5-speed	1.8 litres
6-speed	3.0 litres
Automatic:	
Drain and refill	2.8 litres
Total from dry (including torque converter and cooler)	7.0 litres
Fuel tank	
All models	58.0 litres

Cooling system

Antifreeze mixture:*	
50% antifreeze	Protection down to -37°C
55% antifreeze	Protection down to -45°C

*** Note:** *Refer to antifreeze manufacturer for latest recommendations. Saab antifreeze coolant is premixed.*

Ignition system

Firing order	1 – 3 – 4 – 2
Spark plugs:	
Type	NGK PFR 6T-10G
Electrode gap	0.9 to 1.0 mm

Brakes

Brake pad friction material minimum thickness	2.0 mm
Disc minimum thickness:	
Front	22.0 mm (288 mm dia.) or 25.0 mm (302 or 314 mm dia.)
Rear	10.0 mm (solid) or 18.0 mm (ventilated)

Remote control battery

Type	CR2032

Tyre pressures

Refer to the end of *Weekly checks* on page 0•16

Torque wrench settings

	Nm	lbf ft
Automatic transmission drain plug:		
5-speed	40	30
6-speed	45	33
Automatic transmission filler plug (6-speed only)	30	22
Engine oil sump drain plug	25	18
Front chassis reinforcement bolts (Convertible only)	50	37
Ignition coil screws	20	15
Manual transmission level/filler plug	50	37
Spark plugs	27	20
Wheel bolts	110	81

The maintenance intervals in this manual are provided with the assumption that you will be carrying out the work yourself. These are the minimum maintenance intervals recommended by the manufacturer for vehicles driven daily. If you wish to keep your vehicle in peak condition at all times, you may wish to perform some of these procedures more often. We encourage frequent maintenance, because it enhances the efficiency, performance and resale value of your vehicle.

If the vehicle is driven in dusty areas, used to tow a trailer, or driven frequently at slow speeds (idling in traffic) or on short journeys, more frequent maintenance intervals are recommended.

When the vehicle is new, it should be serviced by a dealer service department (or other workshop recognised by the vehicle manufacturer as providing the same standard of service) in order to preserve the warranty. The vehicle manufacturer may reject warranty claims if you are unable to prove that servicing has been carried out as and when specified, using only original equipment parts or parts certified to be of equivalent quality.

All Saab models are equipped with a service interval display (or Saab Information Display – SID) on the facia, which will indicate TIME FOR SERVICE when a service is due. However, Saab point out that, 'due to the relationship between time and mileage, some operating conditions will make annual service more suitable'.

Every 250 miles or weekly

☐ Refer to *Weekly checks*

Every 6000 miles or 6 months

☐ Engine oil and filter – renewal (Section 3)

Note: *Saab recommend that the engine oil and filter are changed every 18 000 miles. However, oil and filter changes are good for the engine and we recommend that they are renewed more frequently, especially if the vehicle is used on a lot of short journeys.*

After first 6000 miles and thereafter every 12 000 miles or 12 months

Note: *The 12 000 mile intervals start at 18 000 miles, ie, at 18 000 miles, 30 000 miles, 42 000 miles, 54 000 miles, etc.*

☐ Service indicator – resetting (Section 4)
☐ Hoses and fluids – leak check (Section 5)
☐ Steering and suspension components – check (Section 6)
☐ Brake pad wear and disc check (Section 7)
☐ Handbrake – check and adjustment (Section 8)
☐ Seat belt condition – check (Section 9)
☐ Airbag system – check (Section 10)
☐ Headlight beam alignment – check (Section 11)
☐ Power steering fluid level – check (Section 12)
☐ Road test (Section 13)
☐ Coolant antifreeze concentration – check (Section 14)
☐ Driveshaft joints and gaiters – check (Section 15)
☐ Exhaust system – check (Section 16)
☐ Hinges and locks – lubrication (Section 17)
☐ Pollen air filter – renewal (Section 18)
☐ Plenum chamber drain hose – clean (Section 19)
☐ Auxiliary drivebelt condition – check (Section 20)

Every 36 000 miles

Note: *The 36 000 mile intervals start at 42 000 miles, ie, at 42 000 miles, 78 000 miles, 114 000 miles, etc.*

☐ Air filter element – renewal (Section 21)
☐ Manual transmission fluid level – check (Section 22)
☐ Fuel filter – renewal (Section 23)

Every 60 000 miles

Note: *The 60 000 mile intervals start at 66 000 miles, ie, at 66 000 miles, 126 000 miles, etc.*

☐ Spark plugs – renewal (Section 24)
☐ Automatic transmission fluid – renewal (Section 25)
☐ Auxiliary drivebelt – renewal (Section 26)

Every 3 years

☐ Coolant – renewal (Section 27)

Note: *This work is not included in the Saab schedule, and should not be required if the recommended Saab antifreeze/inhibitor is used.*

Every 4 years

☐ Brake fluid – renewal (Section 28)
☐ Remote control battery – renewal (Section 29)

Underbonnet view

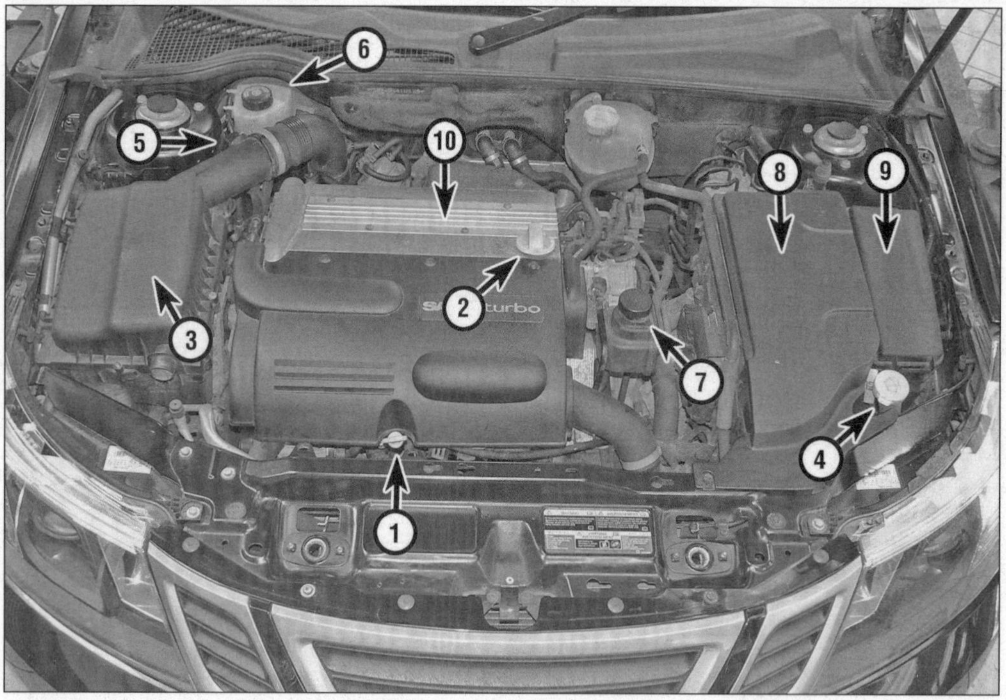

1 *Engine oil level dipstick*
2 *Engine oil filler cap*
3 *Air cleaner assembly*
4 *Screen washer fluid reservoir*
5 *Airflow meter*
6 *Brake (and clutch) fluid reservoir*
7 *Power steering fluid reservoir*
8 *Battery*
9 *Fusebox*
10 *Ignition coils/spark plugs cover*

Front underbody view

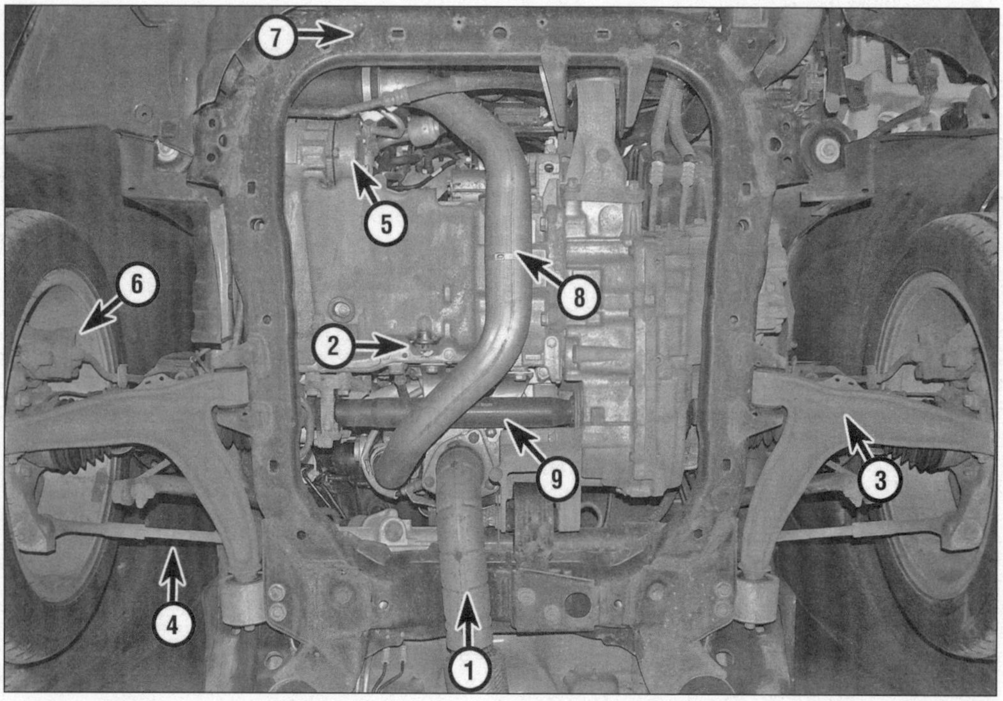

1 *Front exhaust pipe*
2 *Engine oil sump plug*
3 *Lower control arm*
4 *Steering track rod*
5 *Air conditioning compressor*
6 *Brake caliper*
7 *Front subframe*
8 *Turbocharger air charge pipe*
9 *Intermediate driveshaft*

Rear underbody view

1 *Exhaust pipe*
2 *Charcoal canister*
3 *Lower transverse link arm*
4 *Toe-in link arm*
5 *Trailing arm*
6 *Handbrake cable*
7 *Shock absorber*
8 *Anti-roll bar*
9 *Fuel tank*

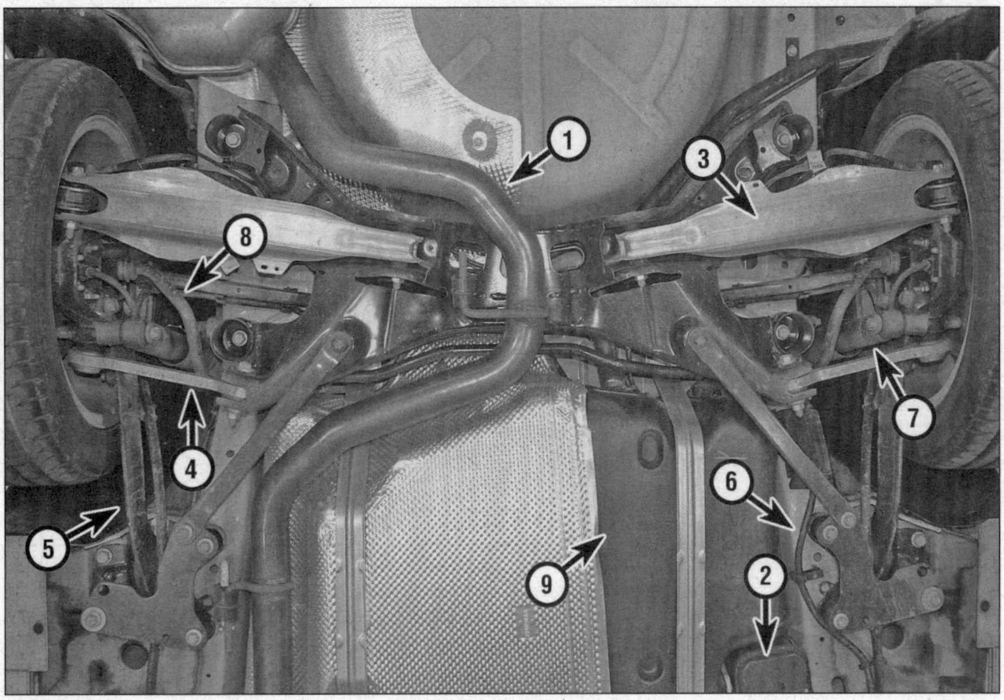

Maintenance procedures

1 General information

This Chapter is designed to help the home mechanic maintain his/her vehicle for safety, economy, long life and peak performance.

The Chapter contains a master maintenance schedule, followed by Sections dealing specifically with each task in the schedule. Visual checks, adjustments, component renewal and other helpful items are included. Refer to the accompanying illustrations of the engine compartment and the underside of the vehicle for the locations of the various components.

Servicing your vehicle in accordance with the mileage/time maintenance schedule and the following Sections will provide a planned maintenance programme, which should result in a long and reliable service life. This is a comprehensive plan, so maintaining some items, but not others, at the specified service intervals will not produce the same results.

As you service your vehicle, you will discover that many of the procedures can – and should – be grouped together, because of the particular procedure being performed, or because of the close proximity of two otherwise-unrelated components to one another. For example, if the vehicle is raised for any reason, the exhaust system could be inspected at the same time as the suspension and steering components.

The first step in this maintenance programme is to prepare yourself before the actual work begins. Read through all the Sections relevant to the work to be carried out, then make a list and gather together all the parts and tools required. If a problem is encountered, seek advice from a parts specialist, or a dealer service department.

2 Regular maintenance

If, from the time the vehicle is new, the routine maintenance schedule is followed closely, and frequent checks are made of fluid levels and high-wear items, as suggested throughout this manual, the engine will be kept in relatively good running condition, and the need for additional work will be minimised.

It is possible that there will be times when the engine is running poorly due to the lack of regular maintenance. This is even more likely if a used vehicle, which has not received regular and frequent maintenance checks, is purchased. In such cases, additional work may need to be carried out, outside of the regular maintenance intervals.

If engine wear is suspected, a compression test (refer to Chapter 2A, Section 2) will provide valuable information regarding the overall performance of the main internal components. Such a test can be used as a basis to decide on the extent of the work to be carried out. If, for example, a compression test indicates serious internal engine wear, conventional maintenance as described in this Chapter will not greatly improve the performance of the engine, and may prove a waste of time and money, unless extensive overhaul work (Chapter 2D) is carried out first.

The following series of operations are those most often required to improve the performance of a generally poor-running engine:

Primary operations

a) Clean, inspect and test the battery ('Weekly checks' and Chapter 5A, Section 3)
b) Check all the engine-related fluids ('Weekly checks').
c) Check the condition and tension of the auxiliary drivebelt (Section 26).
d) Renew the spark plugs (Section 24).
e) Check the condition of the air filter element, and renew if necessary (Section 21).
f) Renew the fuel filter (Section 23).
g) Check the condition of all hoses, and check for fluid leaks (Section 5).

Secondary operations

If the above operations do not prove fully effective, carry out the following secondary operations:

a) Check the charging system (Chapter 5A, Section 3).
b) Check the ignition system (Chapter 5B, Section 2).
c) Check the fuel system (Chapter 4A, Section 9).

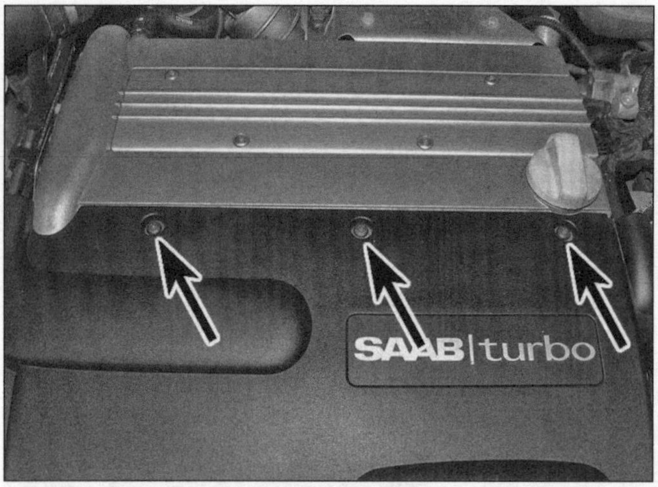

3.3 Undo the 3 Torx screws (arrowed) and remove the plastic cover

3.4a The oil filter housing is located at the front left-hand end of the engine (arrowed)

Every 6000 miles or 6 months

3 Engine oil and filter – renewal

1 Frequent oil changes are the most important preventative maintenance the DIY home mechanic can give the engine, because ageing oil becomes diluted and contaminated, which leads to premature engine wear.

2 Before starting this procedure, gather together all the necessary tools and materials. Also make sure that you have plenty of clean rags and newspapers handy, to mop-up any spills. Ideally, the engine oil should be warm, as it will drain better, and more built-up sludge will be removed with it. Take care, however, not to touch the exhaust or any other hot parts of the engine when working under the vehicle. To avoid any possibility of scalding, and to protect yourself from possible skin irritants and other harmful contaminants in used engine oils, it is advisable to wear gloves when carrying out this work.

3 Undo the 3 Torx screws and remove the plastic cover from the top of the engine **(see illustration)**.

4 The filter is located at the front of the engine. Use a special 32 mm oil filter removal socket or a 32 mm spanner to slacken the filter cover **(see illustrations)**.

5 Apply the handbrake, then jack up the front of the vehicle and support it on axle stands (see *Jacking and vehicle support*).

6 The engine oil drain plug is located on the rear of the sump; slacken the plug about half a turn. Position the draining container under the drain plug, then remove the plug completely – recover the sealing washer **(see illustrations)**.

7 Allow some time for the old oil to drain, noting that it may be necessary to reposition the container as the oil flow slows to a trickle.

8 After all the oil has drained, wipe off the drain plug with a clean rag. Clean the area around the drain plug opening, and refit the plug with a new sealing washer. Tighten the plug to the specified torque.

9 Lower the vehicle to the ground, then completely unscrew and remove the oil filter cover along with the filter element **(see illustration)**. Discard the cover O-ring seal, a new one must be fitted.

3.4b Unscrew the filter cover using a 32 mm filter removal socket ...

3.4c ... or use a 32 mm spanner

3.6a Sump drain plug (arrowed)

3.6b Renew the plug sealing washer

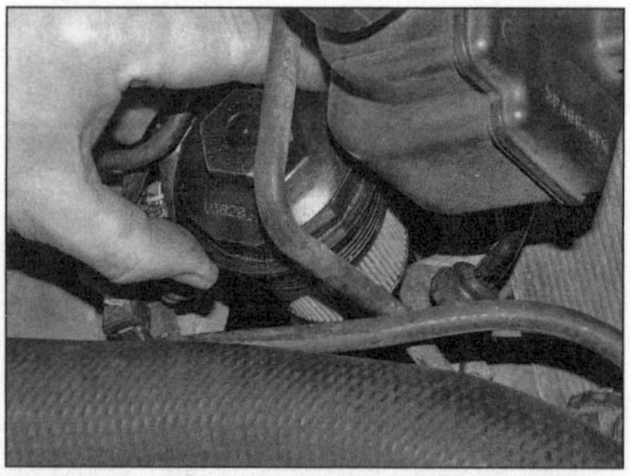
3.9 Unscrew and remove the filter cover along with the element

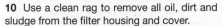

3.11 Fit the new element and O-ring seal (arrowed) to the filter cover

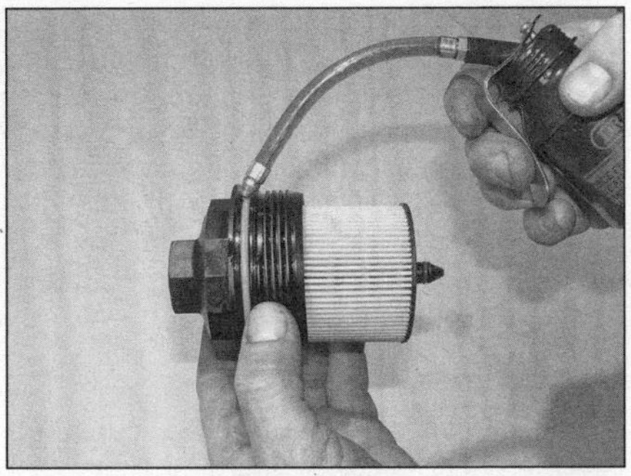

3.12a Apply a little engine oil to the O-ring

3.12b Tighten the filter cover securely

10 Use a clean rag to remove all oil, dirt and sludge from the filter housing and cover.

11 Fit the new filter element and O-ring seal to the filter cover **(see illustration)**.

12 Apply a light coating of clean engine oil to the O-ring seal on the filter cover, then fit the element and cover into the housing, and tighten it securely **(see illustrations)**.

13 Remove the oil filler cap and withdraw the level dipstick from the tube. Fill the engine, using the correct oil (see *Lubricants and fluids*). An oil can spout or funnel may help to reduce spillage. Pour in half the specified quantity of oil first, then wait a few minutes for the oil to run to the sump. Continue adding oil a small quantity at a time until the level is up to the lower mark on the dipstick. Adding a further 1.0 litre will bring the level up to the upper mark on the dipstick. Insert the dipstick, and refit the filler cap **(see illustrations)**.

14 Start the engine and run it for a few minutes; check for leaks around the oil filter seal and the sump drain plug. Note that there may be a delay of a few seconds before the oil pressure warning light goes out when the engine is first started, as the oil circulates through the engine oil galleries and the new oil filter, before the pressure builds-up.

3.13a Pull the engine oil level dipstick from the front of the engine

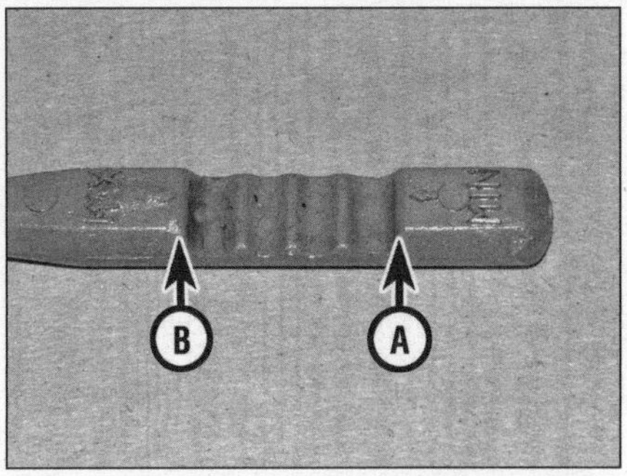

3.13b Oil level dipstick maximum and minimum marks (arrowed)

15 Switch off the engine, and wait a few minutes for the oil to settle in the sump once more. With the new oil circulated and the filter completely full, recheck the level on the dipstick, and add more oil as necessary.

16 Dispose of the used engine oil safely, in accordance with the guidance given in *General repair procedures*.

Every 12 000 miles

Note: *The 12 000 mile intervals start at 18 000 miles, ie, at 18 000 miles, 30 000 miles, 42 000 miles, 54 000 miles, etc.*

4 Service indicator – resetting

1 The SID (Saab Information Display) system incorporates a service interval indicator. When the distance covered between services approaches the next service, a visual message is displayed **(see illustration)**. The service indicator is manually reset after the vehicle has been serviced. The indicator can also be reset at any time using the Saab diagnostic tool.

2 Turn the ignition key to the ON position and select SETTINGS, using the INFO button. Hold the SET button until an audible warning is heard.

3 Select TIME FOR SERVICE using the INFO button and then hold the SET button until an audible warning is heard.

4 Select YES using the INFO switch and then briefly press the SET button.

5 Turn the ignition off. The indicator is now reset.

5 Hoses and fluids – leak check

Cooling system

Warning: Refer to the safety information given in 'Safety first!' and Chapter 3, Section 1 before disturbing any of the cooling system components.

1 Carefully check the radiator and heater coolant hoses along their entire length. Renew any hose which is cracked, swollen or which shows signs of deterioration. Cracks will show up better if the hose is squeezed. Pay close attention to the clips that secure the hoses to the cooling system components. Hose clips that have been overtightened can pinch and puncture hoses, resulting in cooling system leaks.

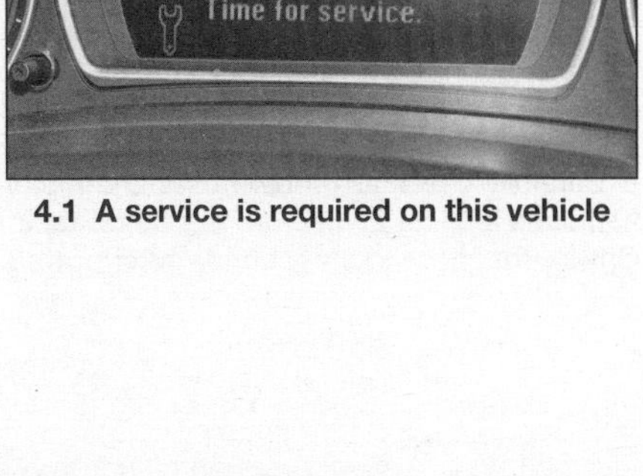

4.1 A service is required on this vehicle

A leak in the cooling system will usually show up as white- or antifreeze-coloured deposits on the area adjoining the leak.

2 Inspect all the cooling system components (hoses, joint faces, etc) for leaks. Where any problems of this nature are found on system components, renew the component or gasket with reference to Chapter 3 **(see Haynes Hint)**.

Fuel system

Warning: Refer to the safety information given in 'Safety first!' and Chapter 4A, Section 1 before disturbing any of the fuel system components.

3 Petrol leaks can be difficult to pinpoint, unless the leakage is significant and hence easily visible. Fuel tends to evaporate quickly once it comes into contact with air, especially in a hot engine bay. Small drips can disappear before you get a chance to identify the point of leakage. If you suspect that there is a fuel leak from the area of the engine bay, leave the vehicle overnight then start the engine from cold, with the bonnet open. Metal components tend to shrink when they are cold, and rubber seals and hoses tend to harden, so any leaks will be more apparent whilst the engine is warming-up from a cold start.

4 Check all fuel lines at their connections to the fuel rail, fuel pressure regulator and fuel filter. Examine each rubber fuel hose along its length for splits or cracks. Check for leakage from the crimped joints between rubber and metal fuel lines. Examine the unions between the metal fuel lines and the fuel filter housing. Also check the area around the fuel injectors for signs of O-ring leakage.

5 To identify fuel leaks between the fuel tank and the engine bay, the vehicle should be raised and securely supported on axle stands (see *Jacking and vehicle support*). Inspect the petrol tank and filler neck for punctures, cracks and other damage. The connection between the filler neck and tank is especially critical. Sometimes a rubber filler neck or connecting hose will leak due to loose retaining clamps or deteriorated rubber.

6 Carefully check all rubber hoses and metal fuel lines leading away from the petrol tank. Check for loose connections, deteriorated hoses, kinked lines, and other damage. Pay particular attention to the vent pipes and hoses, which often loop up around the filler neck and can become blocked or kinked, making tank filling difficult. Follow the fuel supply and return lines to the front of the vehicle, carefully inspecting them all the way for signs of damage or corrosion. Renew damaged sections as necessary.

Engine oil

7 Inspect the area around the camshaft cover, cylinder head, oil filter and sump joint faces. Bear in mind that, over a period of time, some very slight seepage from these areas is to be expected – what you are really looking for is any indication of a serious leak caused by gasket failure. Engine oil seeping from the base of the timing chain cover or the transmission bellhousing may be an indication of crankshaft or transmission input shaft oil seal failure. Should a leak be found, renew the failed gasket or oil seal by referring to the appropriate Chapters in this manual.

Automatic transmission fluid

8 Where applicable, check the hoses leading to the transmission fluid cooler at the front of the engine bay for leakage. Look for deterioration caused by corrosion and damage from grounding, or debris thrown up from the road surface. Automatic transmission fluid is a thin oil and is usually red in colour.

Power-assisted steering fluid

9 Examine the hose running between the fluid reservoir and the power steering pump, and the return hose running from the steering rack to the fluid reservoir. Also examine the high pressure supply hose between the pump and the steering rack.

10 Check the condition of each hose carefully. Look for deterioration caused by corrosion and damage from grounding, or debris thrown up from the road surface.

11 Pay particular attention to crimped unions, and the area surrounding the hoses that are secured with adjustable worm-drive clips. Like automatic transmission fluid, PAS fluid is a thin oil, and is usually red in colour.

Air conditioning refrigerant

Warning: Refer to the safety information given in 'Safety first!' and Chapter 3, Section 8 regarding the dangers of disturbing any of the air conditioning system components.

12 The air conditioning system is filled with a liquid refrigerant, which is retained under high pressure. If the air conditioning system is opened and depressurised without the aid of specialised equipment, the refrigerant will immediately turn into gas and escape into the atmosphere. If the liquid comes into contact with your skin, it can cause severe frostbite. In addition, the refrigerant contains substances which are environmentally damaging; for this reason, it should not be allowed to escape into the atmosphere in an uncontrolled fashion.

13 Any suspected air conditioning system leaks should be immediately referred to a Saab dealer or air conditioning specialist. Leakage will be shown up as a steady drop in the level of refrigerant in the system.

14 Note that water may drip from the condenser drain pipe, underneath the car, immediately after the air conditioning system has been in use. This is normal, and should not be cause for concern.

Brake fluid

Warning: Refer to the safety information given in 'Safety first!' and Chapter 9, Section 2 regarding the dangers of handling brake fluid.

15 With reference to Chapter 9, Section 10, examine the area surrounding the brake pipe unions at the master cylinder for signs of leakage. Check the area around the base of fluid reservoir, for signs of leakage caused by seal failure. Also examine the brake pipe unions at the ABS hydraulic unit.

16 If fluid loss is evident, but the leak cannot be pinpointed in the engine bay, the brake calipers and underbody brake lines should be carefully checked with the vehicle raised and supported on axle stands (see *Jacking and vehicle support*). Leakage of fluid from the braking system is a serious fault that must be rectified immediately.

17 Brake/clutch hydraulic fluid is a toxic substance with a watery consistency. New fluid is almost colourless, but it becomes darker with age and use.

Unidentified fluid leaks

18 If there are signs that a fluid of some description is leaking from the vehicle, but you cannot identify the type of fluid or its exact origin, park the vehicle overnight and slide a large piece of card underneath it. Providing that the card is positioned in roughly the right location, even the smallest leak will show up on the card. Not only will this help you to pinpoint the exact location of the leak, it should be easier to identify the fluid from its colour. Bear in mind, though, that the leak may only be occurring when the engine is running!

Vacuum hoses

19 Although the braking system is hydraulically-operated, the brake servo unit amplifies the effort applied at the brake pedal by making use of the vacuum in the inlet manifold generated by the engine. Vacuum is ported to the servo by means of a large-bore hose. Any leaks that develop in this hose will reduce the effectiveness of the braking system, and may affect the running of the engine.

20 In addition, a number of the underbonnet components, particularly the emission control components, are driven by vacuum supplied from the inlet manifold via narrow-bore hoses. A leak in a vacuum hose means that air is being drawn into the hose (rather than escaping from it) and this makes leakage very difficult to detect. One method is to use an old length of vacuum hose as a kind of stethoscope – hold one end close to (but not in!) your ear and use the other end to probe the area around the suspected leak. When the end of the hose is directly over a vacuum leak, a hissing sound will be heard clearly through the hose. Care must be taken to avoid contacting hot or moving components when testing in this manner, as the engine must be running. Renew any vacuum hoses that are found to be defective.

6 Steering and suspension components – check

Front suspension and steering

1 Raise the front of the vehicle, and securely support it on axle stands (see *Jacking and vehicle support*).

2 Visually inspect the balljoint dust covers and the steering rack-and-pinion gaiters for splits, chafing or deterioration. Any wear of these components will cause loss of lubricant, together with dirt and water entry, resulting in rapid deterioration of the balljoints or steering gear.

3 Check the power steering fluid hoses for chafing or deterioration, and the pipe and hose unions for fluid leaks. Also check for signs of fluid leakage under pressure from the steering gear rubber gaiters, which would indicate failed fluid seals within the steering gear.

4 Grasp the roadwheel at the 12 o'clock and 6 o'clock positions, and try to rock it **(see illustration)**. Very slight free play may be felt, but if the movement is appreciable, further investigation is necessary to determine the source. Continue rocking the wheel while an assistant depresses the footbrake. If the movement is now eliminated or significantly reduced, it is likely that the hub bearings are at fault. If the free play is still evident with the footbrake depressed, then there is wear in the suspension joints or mountings.

5 Now grasp the wheel at the 9 o'clock and 3 o'clock positions, and try to rock it as before. Any movement felt now may again be caused by wear in the hub bearings or the steering track rod balljoints. If the outer balljoint is worn, the visual movement will be obvious. If the inner joint is suspect, it can be felt by placing a hand over the rack-and-pinion rubber gaiter and gripping the track rod. If the wheel is now rocked, movement will be felt at the inner joint if wear has taken place.

6 Using a large screwdriver or flat bar, check for wear in the suspension mounting bushes by levering between the relevant suspension component and its attachment point. Some movement is to be expected, as the mountings are made of rubber, but excessive wear should be obvious. Also check the condition of any visible rubber bushes, looking for splits, cracks or contamination of the rubber.

7 With the car standing on its wheels, have an assistant turn the steering wheel back-and-forth, about an eighth of a turn each way. There should be very little, if any, lost movement between the steering wheel and roadwheels. If this is not the case, closely observe the joints and mountings previously described. In addition, check the steering column universal joints for wear, and also check the rack-and-pinion steering gear itself.

8 The front suspension mountings should be checked for tightness.

Rear suspension

9 Chock the front wheels, then jack up the rear of the vehicle and support securely on axle stands (see *Jacking and vehicle support*).

10 Working as described previously for the front suspension, check the rear hub bearings, the suspension bushes and the strut or shock absorber mountings (as applicable) for wear.

11 The rear suspension mountings should be checked for tightness.

Shock absorber

12 Check for any signs of fluid leakage around the shock absorber bodies, or from the rubber gaiters around the piston rods. Should any fluid be noticed, the shock absorber is defective internally, and should be renewed. **Note:** *Shock absorbers should always be renewed in pairs on the same axle.*

13 The efficiency of the shock absorber may be checked by bouncing the vehicle at each corner. Generally speaking, the body will return to its normal position and stop after being depressed. If it rises and returns on a rebound, the shock absorber is probably suspect. Also examine the shock absorber upper and lower mountings for any signs of wear.

Removable towbar attachment

14 Where applicable, clean the coupling pin then apply a little grease to the socket. Make sure that the removable towbar attachment fits easily to its mounting and locks correctly in position.

7 Brake pad wear and disc check

1 The work described in this Section should be carried out at the specified intervals, or whenever a defect is suspected in the braking system. Any of the following symptoms could indicate a potential brake system defect:

a) The vehicle pulls to one side when the brake pedal is depressed.

b) The brakes make squealing, scraping or dragging noises when applied.

c) Brake pedal travel is excessive, or pedal feel is poor.

d) The brake fluid requires repeated topping-up. Note that, because the hydraulic clutch shares the same fluid as the braking system (see Chapter 6, Section 2), this problem could be due to a leak in the clutch system.

6.4 Check for wear in the hub bearings by grasping the wheel and trying to rock it

Front disc brakes

2 Apply the handbrake, then loosen the front wheel bolts. Jack up the front of the vehicle, and support it on axle stands (see *Jacking and vehicle support*).

3 For better access to the brake calipers, remove the wheels.

4 Look through the inspection window in the caliper, and check that the thickness of the friction lining material on each of the pads is not less than the recommended minimum thickness given in the Specifications **(see Haynes Hint)**.

HAYNES HiNT

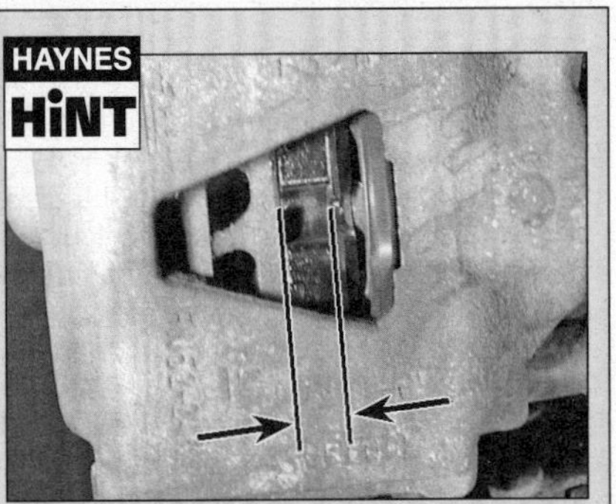

For a quick check, then thickness of the friction material remaining on the inner brake pad can be measured through the aperture in the caliper body.

HAYNES HiNT

Bear in mind that the lining material is normally bonded to a metal backing plate. To differentiate between the metal and the lining material, it is helpful to turn the disc slowly at first – the edge of the disc can then be identified, with the lining material on each pad either side of it, and the backing plates behind.

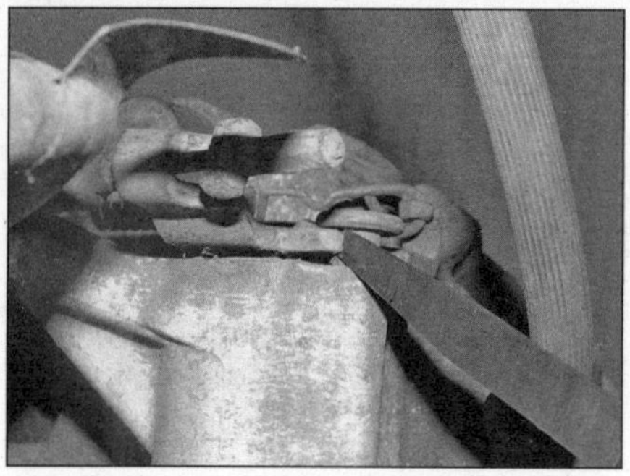

8.3 Insert a 1.0 mm feeler gauge between the caliper lever and the stop

5 If it is difficult to determine the exact thickness of the pad linings, or if you are at all concerned about the condition of the pads, then remove them from the calipers for further inspection (refer to Chapter 9, Section 4 and 5).

6 Check the other caliper in the same way.

7 If any one of the brake pads has worn down to, or below, the specified limit, all four pads at that end of the car must be renewed as a set. If the pads on one side are significantly more worn than the other, this may indicate that the caliper pistons have partially seized – refer to the brake pad renewal procedure in Chapter 9, Section 4 and 5, and push the pistons back into the caliper to free them.

8 Measure the thickness of the discs with a micrometer, if available, to make sure that they still have service life remaining. Do not be fooled by the lip of rust which often forms on the outer edge of the disc, which may make the disc appear thicker than it really is – scrape off the loose rust if necessary, without scoring the disc friction (shiny) surface.

9 If any disc is thinner than the specified minimum thickness, renew both (refer to Chapter 9, Section 8 and 9).

10 Check the general condition of the discs. Look for excessive scoring and discolouration caused by overheating. If these conditions exist, remove the relevant disc and have it resurfaced or renewed (refer to Chapter 9, Section 8 and 9).

11 Make sure that the handbrake is firmly applied, then check that the transmission is in neutral. Spin the wheel, and check that the brake is not binding. Some drag is normal with a disc brake, but it should not require any great effort to turn the wheel – also, do not confuse brake drag with resistance from the transmission.

12 Before refitting the wheels, check all brake lines and hoses (refer to Chapter 9, Section 3). In particular, check the flexible hoses in the vicinity of the calipers, where they are subjected to most movement. Bend them between the fingers (but do not actually bend them double, or the casing may be damaged) and check that this does not reveal previously-hidden cracks, cuts or splits.

13 On completion, refit the wheels and lower the car to the ground. Tighten the wheel bolts to the specified torque.

Rear disc brakes

14 Loosen the rear wheel bolts, then chock the front wheels. Jack up the rear of the car, and support it on axle stands. Release the handbrake and remove the rear wheels.

15 The procedure for checking the rear brakes is much the same as described in paragraphs 2 to 13 above. Check that the rear brakes are not binding, noting that transmission resistance is not a factor on the rear wheels. Abnormal effort may indicate that the handbrake needs adjusting – see Chapter 9, Section 13.

8 Handbrake – check and adjustment

1 Chock the front wheels, then jack up the rear of the vehicle and support on axle stands (see *Jacking and vehicle support*).

2 Fully release the handbrake lever.

3 Check that the distance between the handbrake cable arm and the brake caliper is 1.0 mm **(see illustration)**. If not, adjust the handbrake as described in Chapter 9, Section 13.

4 Fully apply the handbrake lever, and check that both rear wheels are locked when attempting to turn them by hand.

5 Lower the vehicle to the ground.

9 Seat belt condition – check

1 Working on each seat belt in turn, carefully examine the seat belt webbing for cuts, or for any signs of serious fraying or deterioration. Pull the belt all the way out, and examine the full extent of the webbing.

2 Fasten and unfasten the belt, ensuring that the locking mechanism holds securely, and releases properly when intended. Check also that the retracting mechanism operates correctly when the belt is released.

3 Check the security of all seat belt mountings and attachments which are accessible, without removing any trim or other components from inside the vehicle.

4 Check the function of the seat belt reminder lamp.

10 Airbag system – check

1 The following work can be carried out by the home mechanic, however, if an electronic fault is apparent, it will be necessary to take the car to a Saab dealer or specialist, who will have the necessary diagnostic equipment to extract fault codes from the system.

2 Turn the ignition switch to the drive position (ignition warning lights on), and check that the SRS (Supplementary Restraint System) warning light is illuminated for 3 to 4 seconds. After this period the light should go out, indicating that the system has been checked and is functioning correctly.

3 If the warning light remains on or refuses to light, have the system checked by a Saab dealer or specialist.

4 Visually examine the steering wheel centre pad and the passenger airbag module for external damage. Also check the exterior of the front seats around the side airbag locations. If damage is evident, consult a Saab dealer or specialist.

5 In the interests of safety, make sure that there are no loose items inside the car which could be thrown onto the airbag modules in the event of an accident.

11 Headlight beam alignment – check

Refer to Chapter 12, Section 8 for details

12 Power steering fluid level – check

1 The power steering fluid reservoir is located on the left-hand side of the engine compartment between the battery and the cylinder head **(see illustration)**. The fluid level should be checked with the engine stopped.

2 Unscrew the filler cap from the top of the reservoir, and wipe all fluid from the cap dipstick with a clean rag. Refit the filler cap,

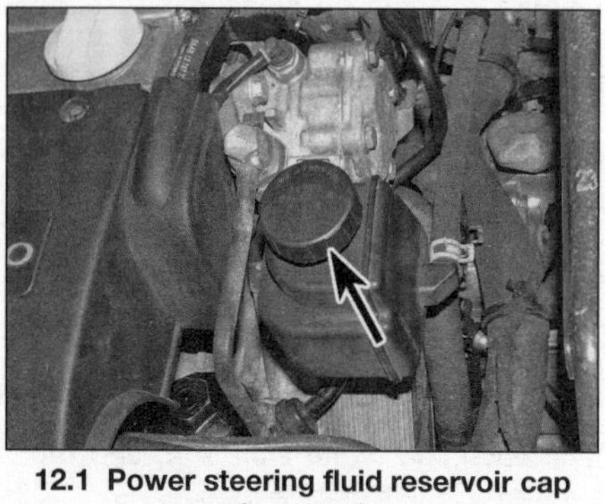

12.1 Power steering fluid reservoir cap (arrowed)

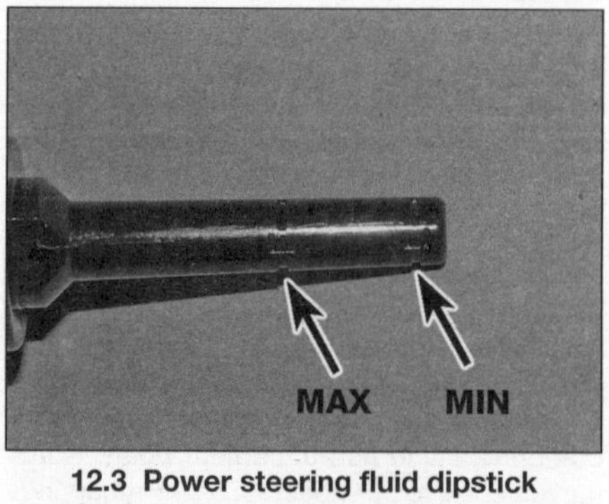

12.3 Power steering fluid dipstick maximum and minimum marks (arrowed)

then remove it again. Note the fluid level on the dipstick.

3 When the engine is cold, the fluid level should be between the upper MAX and lower MIN marks on the dipstick. Where only one mark is provided, the level should be between the bottom of the dipstick and the mark **(see illustration)**.

4 Top-up the fluid level using the specified type of fluid (do not overfill the reservoir), then refit and tighten the filler cap.

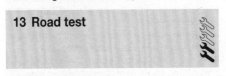

13 Road test

Instruments and electrical equipment

1 Check the operation of all instruments and electrical equipment.

2 Make sure that all instruments read correctly, and switch on all electrical equipment in turn to check that it functions properly. Check the function of the heating, air conditioning and automatic climate control systems.

Steering and suspension

3 Check for any abnormalities in the steering, suspension, handling or road 'feel'.

4 Drive the vehicle, and check that there are no unusual vibrations or noises.

5 Check that the steering feels positive, with no excessive 'sloppiness', or roughness, and check for any suspension noises when cornering, or when driving over bumps. Check that the power steering system operates correctly.

Drivetrain

6 Check the performance of the engine, clutch (manual transmission), transmission and driveshafts. Check that the turbo boost pressure needle moves up to the upper limit during sharp acceleration. The needle may occasionally enter the red zone for an instant, but if this happens frequently, or for extended periods, a problem may exist within the turbo boost control mechanism (see Chapter 4A, Section 10).

7 Listen for any unusual noises from the engine, clutch (manual transmission) and transmission.

8 Make sure that the engine runs smoothly when idling, and that there is no hesitation when accelerating.

9 On manual transmission models, check that the clutch action is smooth and progressive, that the drive is taken up smoothly, and that the pedal travel is correct. Also listen for any noises when the clutch pedal is depressed. Check that all gears can be engaged smoothly, without noise, and that the gear lever action is smooth and not abnormally vague or 'notchy'.

10 On automatic transmission models, make sure that all gearchanges occur smoothly without snatching, and without an increase in engine speed between changes. Check that all the gear positions can be selected with the vehicle at rest. If any problems are found, they should be referred to a Saab dealer.

11 Listen for a metallic clicking sound from the front of the vehicle, as the vehicle is driven slowly in a circle with the steering on full lock. Carry out this check in both directions. If a clicking noise is heard, this indicates wear in a driveshaft joint, in which case, refer to Chapter 8, Section 3.

Braking system

12 Make sure that the vehicle does not pull to one side when braking, and that the wheels do not lock when braking hard.

13 Check that there is no vibration through the steering when braking.

14 Check that the handbrake operates correctly, without excessive movement of the lever, and that it holds the vehicle stationary on a slope.

15 Test the operation of the brake servo unit as follows. With the engine off, depress the footbrake four or five times to exhaust the vacuum, then start the engine while holding the brake pedal depressed. As the engine starts, there should be a noticeable 'give' in the brake pedal as vacuum builds-up. Allow the engine to run for at least two minutes, and then switch it off. If the brake pedal is now depressed again, it should be possible to detect a 'hiss' from the servo as the pedal is depressed. After about four or five applications, no further sound should be heard, and the pedal should feel considerably harder.

14 Coolant antifreeze concentration – check

1 The cooling system should be filled with the recommended antifreeze and corrosion protection fluid. Over a period of time, the concentration of fluid may be reduced due to topping-up (this can be avoided by topping-up with the correct antifreeze mixture) or fluid loss. If loss of coolant has been evident, it is important to make the necessary repair before adding fresh fluid. The exact mixture of antifreeze-to-water which you should use depends on the relative weather conditions. The mixture should contain at least 40% antifreeze, but not more than 70%. Consult the mixture ratio chart on the antifreeze container before adding coolant. Use antifreeze which meets the vehicle manufacturer's specifications. Note that antifreeze coolant available from Saab dealers is premixed with water at the correct ratio.

2 With the engine cold, carefully remove the cap from the expansion tank. If the engine is not completely cold, place a cloth rag over the cap before removing it, and remove it slowly to allow any pressure to escape.

3 Antifreeze checkers are available from car accessory shops. Draw some coolant from the expansion tank and observe how many plastic balls are floating in the checker **(see illustration)**. Usually, 2 or 3 balls must be floating for the correct concentration of antifreeze, but follow the manufacturer's instructions.

14.3 Follow the instructions supplied with the antifreeze checker

4 If the concentration is incorrect, it will be necessary to either withdraw some coolant and add undiluted antifreeze, or alternatively drain the old coolant and add fresh coolant of the correct concentration.

15 Driveshaft joints and gaiters – check

1 With the front of the vehicle raised and securely supported on stands, turn the steering onto full lock then slowly rotate the roadwheel. Inspect the condition of the outer constant velocity (CV) joint rubber gaiters while squeezing the gaiters to open out the folds **(see illustration)**. Check for signs of cracking, splits or deterioration of the rubber which may allow the grease to escape and lead to water and grit entry into the joint. Also check the security and condition of the retaining clips. Repeat these checks on the inner CV joints. If any damage or deterioration is found, the gaiters should be renewed as described in Chapter 8, Section 4.

2 At the same time check the general condition of the CV joints themselves by first holding the driveshaft and attempting to rotate the wheel.

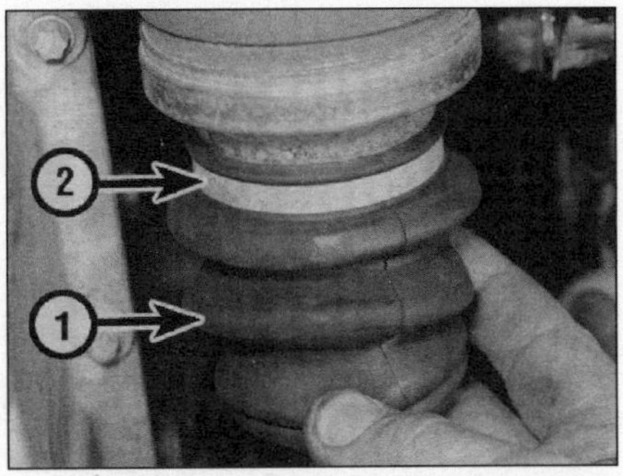

15.1 Check the condition of the driveshaft gaiters (1) and the retaining clips (2)

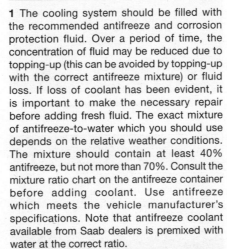

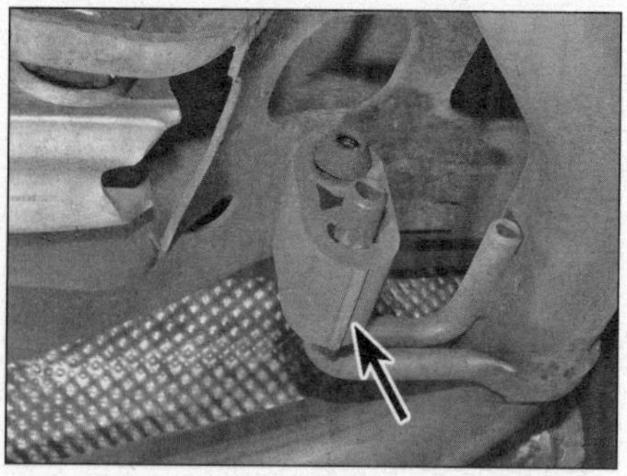

16.2 Check the condition of the exhaust rubber mountings

Repeat this check by holding the inner joint and attempting to rotate the driveshaft. Any appreciable movement indicates wear in the joints, wear in the driveshaft splines or a loose driveshaft retaining nut.

16 Exhaust system – check

1 With the engine cold, check the complete exhaust system, from its starting point at the engine to the end of the tailpipe. If necessary, raise the front and rear of the vehicle and support it on axle stands (see *Jacking and vehicle support*). Remove any engine undershields as necessary for full access to the exhaust system.
2 Check the exhaust pipes and connections for evidence of leaks, severe corrosion, and damage. Make sure that all brackets and mountings are in good condition and that all relevant nuts and bolts are tight **(see illustration)**. Leakage at any of the joints or in other parts of the system will usually show up as a black sooty stain in the vicinity of the leak.
3 Rattles and other noises can often be traced to the exhaust system, especially the brackets and rubber mountings. Try to move the pipes and silencers. If the components are able to come into contact with the body or suspension parts, secure the system with new mountings. Otherwise separate the joints (if possible) and twist the pipes as necessary to provide additional clearance.

17 Hinges and locks – lubrication

1 Work around the vehicle and lubricate the hinges of the bonnet, doors and tailgate with a light machine oil.
2 Lightly lubricate the two bonnet release locks with a smear of grease.
3 Check carefully the security and operation of all hinges, latches and locks. Check that the central locking system operates correctly.
4 Check the condition and operation of the bonnet and boot lid/tailgate struts, renewing them if either is leaking or no longer able to support the bonnet/tailgate.

18 Pollen air filter – renewal

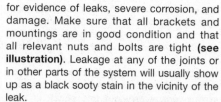

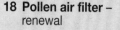

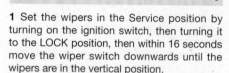

1 Set the wipers in the Service position by turning on the ignition switch, then turning it to the LOCK position, then within 16 seconds move the wiper switch downwards until the wipers are in the vertical position.
2 Open the bonnet, remove the clip securing the left-hand side of the scuttle trim panel **(see illustration)**.
3 Pull the bulkhead rubber seal upwards from the left-hand side **(see illustration)**.
4 Lift the left-hand end of the scuttle trim panel, then fold it over the right-hand side.
5 Remove the water barrier. Note that the water barrier is not fitted to all models.
6 Release the 2 retaining clips and lift the filter from place **(see illustrations)**.
7 Fit the new element using a reversal of the removal procedure. Note the arrow indicating direction of airflow **(see illustration)**.

19 Plenum chamber drain hose – clean

1 Remove the pollen filter element as described in Section 18.
2 Lift the drain hose from place and clean it **(see illustration)**.
3 Refit the drain hose, making sure that it is secure.

18.2 Press in the centre pin and prise out the plastic clip

18.3 Pull the rubber seal upwards

18.6a Release the 2 clips (arrowed) ...

18.6b ... and lift the pollen filter from place

18.7 The arrow indicates direction of airflow

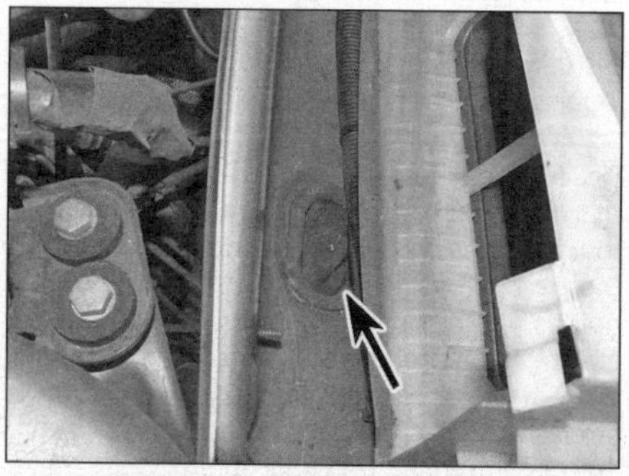

19.2 Check the plenum chamber drain hose (arrowed) is clear

20 Auxiliary drivebelt condition – check

1 On all engines, a single, multi-grooved auxiliary drivebelt is used to transmit drive from the crankshaft pulley to the alternator and the refrigerant compressor. The drivebelt is tensioned automatically by a spring-loaded tensioner pulley.

2 For better access to the drivebelt, apply the handbrake then jack up the front of the car and support it on axle stands (see *Jacking and vehicle support*). Remove the right-hand front roadwheel, then remove the plastic liner from under the right-hand wheel arch to expose the crankshaft pulley **(see illustration)**.

3 Using a suitable socket and extension bar fitted to the crankshaft pulley bolt, rotate the crankshaft so that the entire length of the drivebelt can be examined. Examine the drivebelt for cracks, splitting, fraying, or other damage. Check also for signs of glazing (shiny patches) and for separation of the belt plies. Renew the belt if worn or damaged.

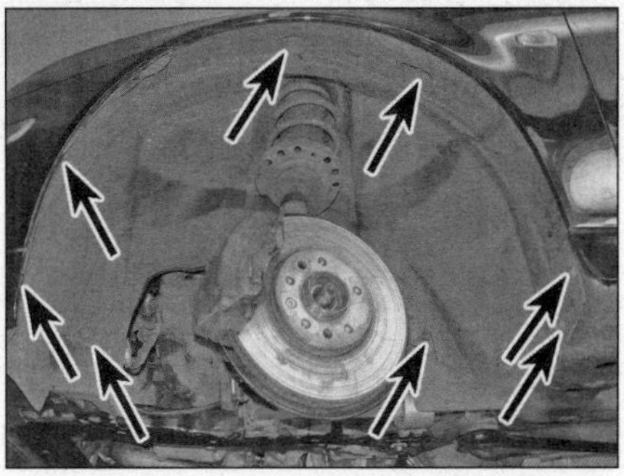

20.2 Wheel arch liner fasteners (arrowed)

Every 36 000 miles

Note: *The 36 000 mile intervals start at 42 000 miles, ie, at 42 000 miles, 78 000 miles, 114 000 miles, etc.*

21 Air filter element – renewal

1 The air cleaner is located on the front right-hand corner of the engine compartment, and the air inlet is taken from the front of the car behind the radiator grille area.

2 Disconnect the mass airflow sensor wiring plug **(see illustration)**.

3 Release the clamp and disconnect the outlet hose from the air filter cover **(see illustration)**.

4 Undo the Torx screws and remove the air filter cover **(see illustration)**.

5 Lift out the air cleaner filter element, noting which way round it is fitted **(see illustration)**.

6 Wipe clean the inner surfaces of the cover and main housing, then locate the new element in the housing, making sure that the sealing lip is correctly engaged with the edge of the housing.

7 Refit the cover, and secure with the clips.

8 Reconnect the air outlet hose and secure it by tightening the hose clip.

9 Reconnect the mass airflow sensor wiring plug.

21.2 Disconnect the mass airflow sensor wiring plug (arrowed)

21.3 Slacken the hose clamp (arrowed)

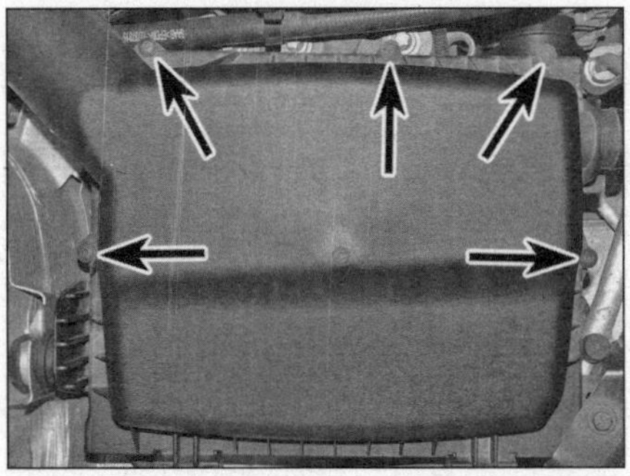

21.4 Air filter cover Torx screws (arrowed)

21.5 Lift the air filter element from place

22 Manual transmission fluid level – check

Note: *There is no requirement in the Saab service schedule to check the transmission fluid level. However, we consider it prudent to carry out the following procedure on 5-speed transmissions at the mileage specified in the schedule at the start of this Chapter.*

5-speed transmission

1 Take the car on a short journey to warm the transmission up to normal operating temperature. Position the car over an inspection pit, or alternatively jack up the front and rear of the car and support on axle stands (see *Jacking and vehicle support*). Whichever method is used, make sure that the car is level for checking the fluid level later.

2 Position a suitable container beneath the transmission, then unscrew the filler/level plug located on the left-hand side of the transmission casing **(see illustration)**.

3 The fluid level should be up to the bottom of the filler/level plug hole. If necessary, add

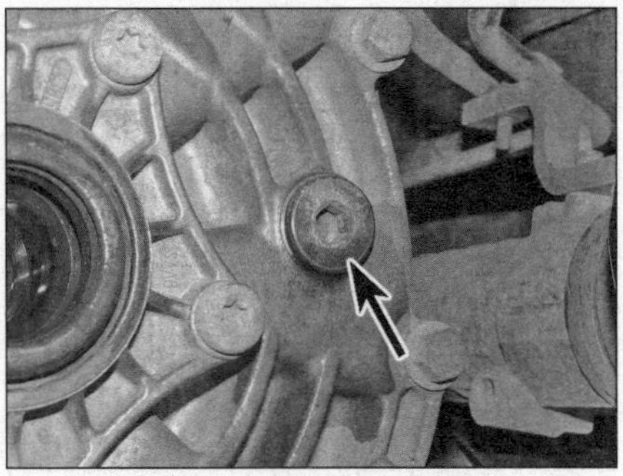

22.2 Oil level plug (arrowed) – 5-speed transmission

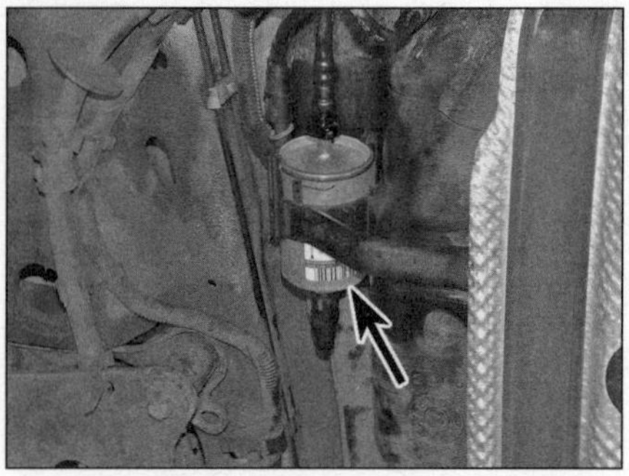

23.1 The fuel filter (arrowed) is located on the right-hand side of the fuel tank

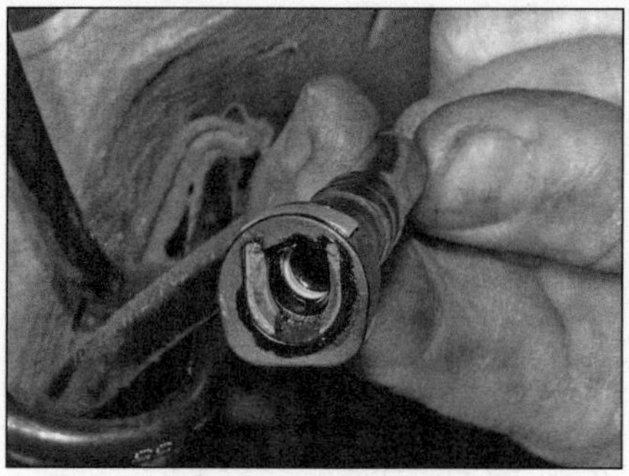

23.5a Depress the blue tab (arrowed) to release the front coupling

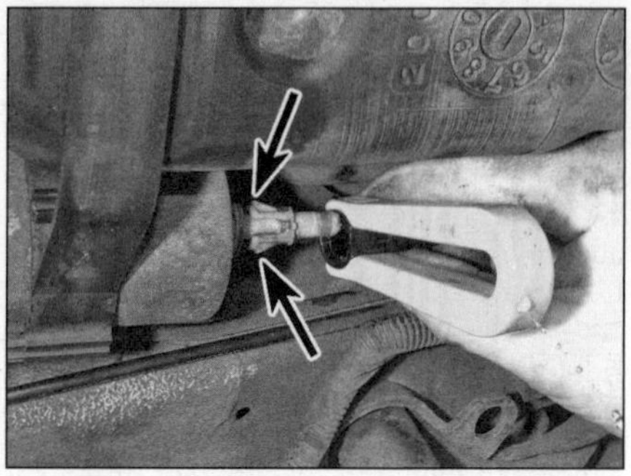

23.5b Squeeze together both clips (arrowed) to release the rear coupling

23.6 Filter retaining clip (arrowed)

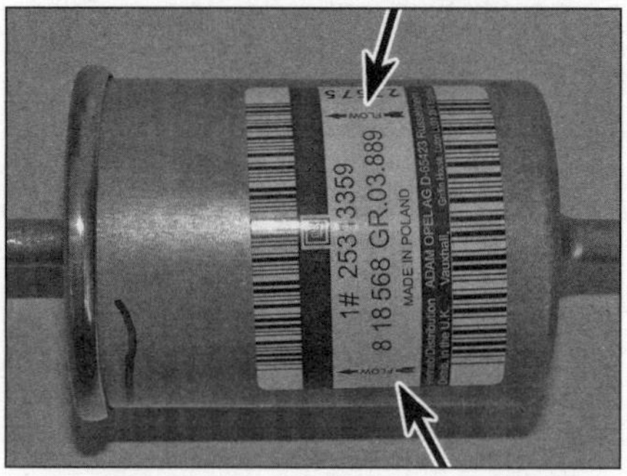

23.7 Ensure the arrows on the filter point to the front of the car (arrowed)

the specified fluid until it begins to run out of the hole.

4 Refit the filler/level plug and tighten it to the specified torque.

5 Lower the vehicle to the ground.

6-speed transmission

6 No level plug is fitted to the 6-speed transmission casing, nor is there any requirement in the Saab service schedule to check or change the fluid. If it is necessary to ensure the transmission has the correct quantity of fluid, it will need to be drained and refilled as described in Chapter 7A, Section 2.

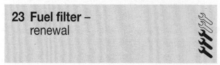

23 Fuel filter – renewal

Warning: Before carrying out the following operation, refer to the precautions given in 'Safety first!' at the beginning of this manual, and follow them implicitly. Petrol is a highly-dangerous and volatile liquid, and the precautions necessary when handling it cannot be overstressed.

1 On all models, the fuel filter is mounted adjacent to the fuel tank underneath the rear of the car **(see illustration)**.

2 Depressurise the fuel system with reference to Chapter 4A, Section 5.

3 Chock the front wheels, then jack up the rear of the car and support on axle stands (see *Jacking and vehicle support*).

4 Position a small container or cloth rags beneath the filter to catch spilt fuel.

5 Disconnect the fuel pipes from the filter and plug the openings to prevent contamination. To release the front coupling, depress the blue section and pull the coupling apart. The rear coupling is release by depressing the clip on each side together **(see illustrations)**.

6 Release the clip and push the filter from the bracket, noting the direction of the arrow marked on the filter body **(see illustration)**.

7 Locate the new filter in the retaining clip. Make sure that the direction of flow arrow on the filter body is pointing towards the outlet which leads to the engine compartment **(see illustration)**.

8 Reconnect the fuel pipes to the filter.

9 Wipe away any excess fuel, then lower the car to the ground.

10 Start the engine, and check the filter hose connections for leaks.

11 The old filter should be disposed of safely, bearing in mind that it will be highly inflammable.

Every 60 000 miles

Note: *The 60 000 mile intervals start at 66 000 miles, ie, at 66 000 miles, 126 000 miles, etc.*

24 Spark plugs – renewal

Note: *The spark plugs must be renewed at the specified interval. An annual inspection of the spark plugs is recommended. This is best performed when the oil and filter are changed.*

1 The correct functioning of the spark plugs is vital for the correct running and efficiency of the engine. It is essential that the plugs fitted are appropriate for the engine. If this type is used and the engine is in good condition, the spark plugs should not need attention between scheduled renewal intervals.

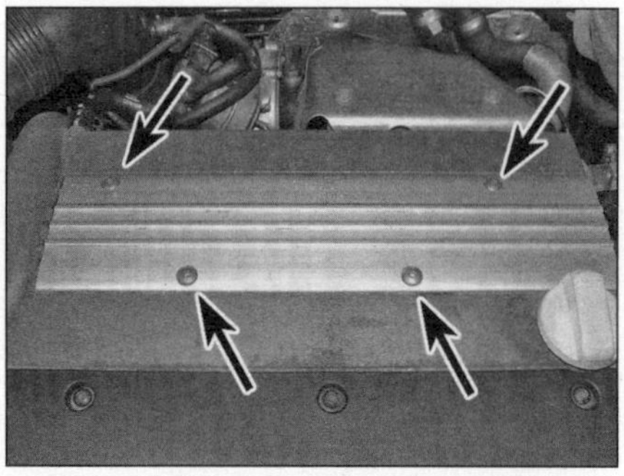

24.2 Undo the Torx screws securing the cover (arrowed)

2 Undo the screws and remove the cover over the ignition coils on the top of the engine **(see illustration)**.

3 Starting at No 1 cylinder (right-hand end), undo the bolts, lift up the ignition coil and move it to one side. Repeat on the remaining cylinders **(see illustration)**.

4 It is advisable to remove the dirt from the spark plug recesses using a clean brush, vacuum cleaner or compressed air before removing the plugs, to prevent dirt dropping into the cylinders.

24.3 Undo the bolts and pull up the ignition coils

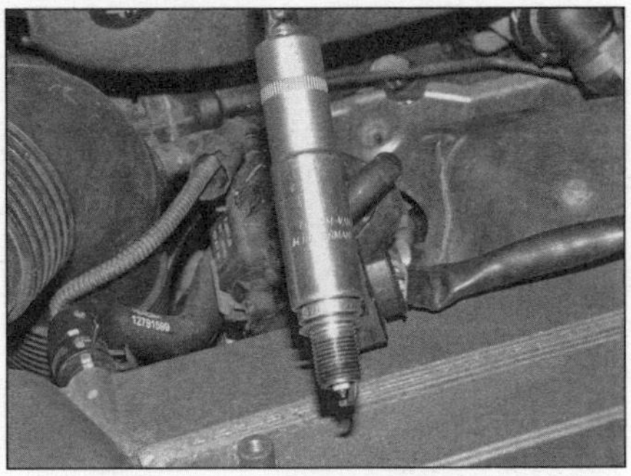

24.5 Unscrew the spark plugs

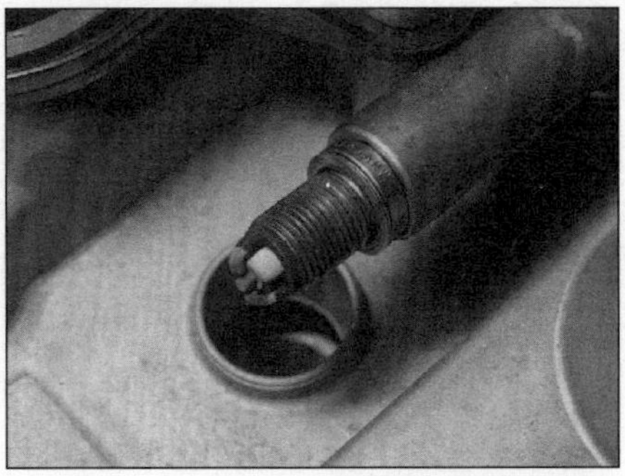

24.10a The gap of the multi-electrode plugs (where fitted) must not be adjusted

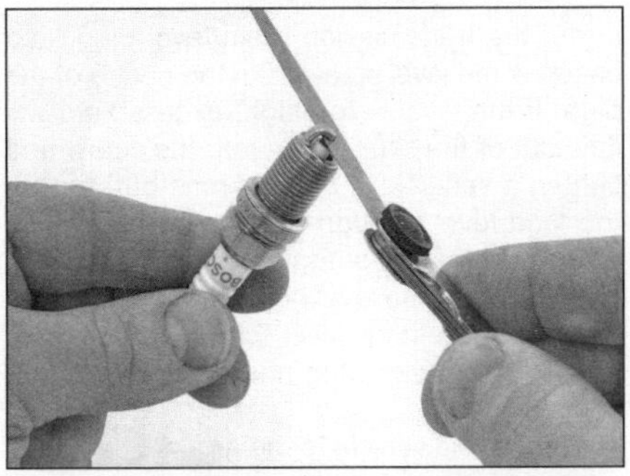

24.10b If single electrode plugs are fitted, check the electrode gap using a feeler gauge ...

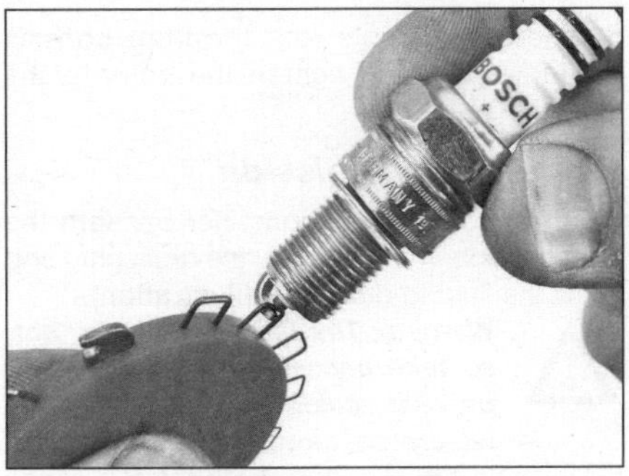

24.10c ... or a wire gauge ...

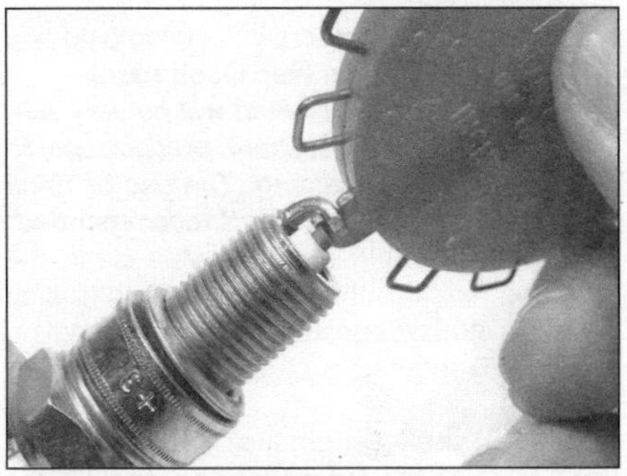

24.10d ... and if necessary, adjust the gap by bending the electrode

5 Unscrew the plugs using a spark plug spanner, suitable box spanner or a deep socket and extension bar **(see illustration)**. Keep the socket aligned with the spark plug – if it is forcibly moved to one side, the ceramic insulator may be broken off. As each plug is removed, examine it as follows.

6 Examination of the spark plugs will give a good indication of the condition of the engine. If the insulator nose of the spark plug is clean and white, with no deposits, this is indicative of a weak mixture or too hot a plug (a hot plug transfers heat away from the electrode slowly, a cold plug transfers heat away quickly).

7 If the tip and insulator nose are covered with hard black-looking deposits, then this is indicative that the mixture is too rich. Should the plug be black and oily, then it is likely that the engine is fairly worn, as well as the mixture being too rich.

8 If the insulator nose is covered with light tan to greyish-brown deposits, then the mixture is correct, and it is likely that the engine is in good condition.

9 The electrode gap is of considerable importance as, if it is too large or too small, the size of the spark and its efficiency will be seriously impaired. The gap should be set to the value given in the Specifications.

10 To set the gap, measure it with a feeler blade or wire gauge and then bend open, or close, the outer plug electrode until the correct gap is achieved. The centre electrode should never be bent, as this will crack the insulator and cause plug failure, if nothing worse. If using feeler blades, the gap is correct when the appropriate-size blade is a firm sliding fit. Note that some models may be fitted with multi-electrode spark plugs – no attempt to adjust the electrode gap should be made on this type of spark plug **(see illustrations)**.

11 Special spark plug electrode gap adjusting tools are available from most motor accessory shops, or from some spark plug manufacturers.

HAYNES HiNT

It is very often difficult to insert spark plugs into their holes without cross-threading them. To avoid this possibility, fit a short length of rubber hose over the end of the spark plug. The flexible hose acts as a universal joint to help align the plug with the plug hole. Should the plug begin to cross-thread, the hose will slip on the spark plug, preventing damage to the aluminium cylinder head.

12 Before fitting the spark plugs, check that the threaded connector sleeves are tight, and that the plug exterior surfaces and threads are clean. It is very often difficult to insert spark plugs into their holes without cross-threading them **(see Haynes Hint)**.

13 Remove the rubber hose (if used), and tighten the plug to the specified torque (see Specifications) using the spark plug socket and a torque wrench. Refit the remaining plugs in the same way.

14 Refit the ignition coils, and tighten the retaining screws to the specified torque.

15 Refit the cover over the ignition coils, and tighten the retaining screws securely.

25 Automatic transmission fluid – renewal

1 Take the car on a short journey to warm the transmission up to normal operating temperature. Position the car over an inspection pit, or alternatively jack up the front and rear of the car and support on axle stands (see *Jacking and vehicle support*). Whichever method is used, make sure that the car is level for checking the fluid level later.

5-speed transmission

2 On Convertible models, undo the bolts and remove the front chassis reinforcement **(see illustration)**.

3 Position a suitable container beneath the

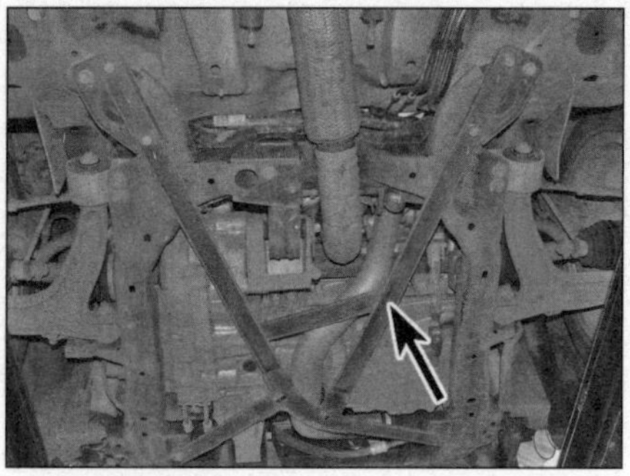

25.2 Front chassis reinforcement (arrowed) – Convertible models

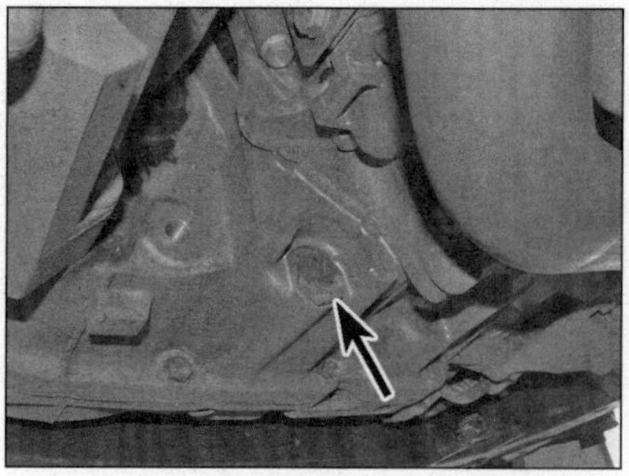

25.3 Fluid drain plug (arrowed) – 5 speed transmission

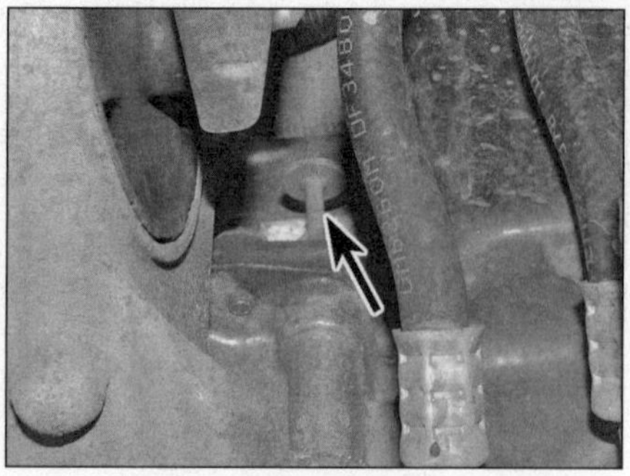

25.5 Fluid level dipstick (arrowed) – viewed from underneath

transmission, then unscrew the drain plug and allow the fluid to drain **(see illustration)**.

Warning: The fluid will be very hot, so take necessary precautions to prevent scalding. The use of thick waterproof gloves is recommended.

4 With all the fluid drained, wipe clean the plug and refit it to the automatic transmission housing. Where applicable fit a new sealing washer. Tighten the plug to the specified torque.

5 Remove the level dipstick (located on the front face of the transmission), and fill the automatic transmission with the specified grade and quantity of fluid through the dipstick hole **(see illustration)**. The use of a funnel and length of hose will make the task much easier. Use the low temperature set of dipstick markings first, then take the car for a run. With the fluid at operating temperature, recheck the fluid level using the high temperature set of dipstick markings. Note that the difference between the COLD and HOT dipstick markings is approximately 0.3 litres.

6 Where applicable refit the front chassis reinforcement and tighten the bolts to the specified torque.

6-speed transmission

7 Position a suitable container beneath the transmission, then unscrew the drain plug and allow the fluid to drain **(see illustration)**.

Warning: The fluid will be very hot, so take necessary precautions to prevent scalding. The use of thick waterproof gloves is recommended.

8 Unscrew the filler plug from the top of the casing and add approximately 3 litres of new fluid **(see illustration)**.

9 Lower the vehicle to the ground.

10 Run the engine until the fluid temperature is approximately 30° to 45°C, then move the selector lever through positions P to D, and back again, with the footbrake depressed. Allow the selector lever to rest in each position for 2 seconds. Repeat this procedure twice.

11 Raise the vehicle again, place a receptacle under the transmission drain/level plug, and unscrew the level screw from the centre of the plug. If the level is too high, excess fluid will flow out of the level hole – refit the screw and tighten it securely. If no fluid runs out, top-up the fluid level through the filler plug hole on the top of the transmission casing, until fluid emerges from the level hole. Allow the excess to drain and refit the level screw securely.

12 Refit the filler plug and tighten it to the specified torque.

13 Lower the vehicle to the ground.

26 Auxiliary drivebelt – renewal

1 On all engines, a single, multi-grooved auxiliary drivebelt is used to transmit drive from the crankshaft pulley to the alternator and the refrigerant compressor. The drivebelt is tensioned automatically by a spring-loaded tensioner pulley.

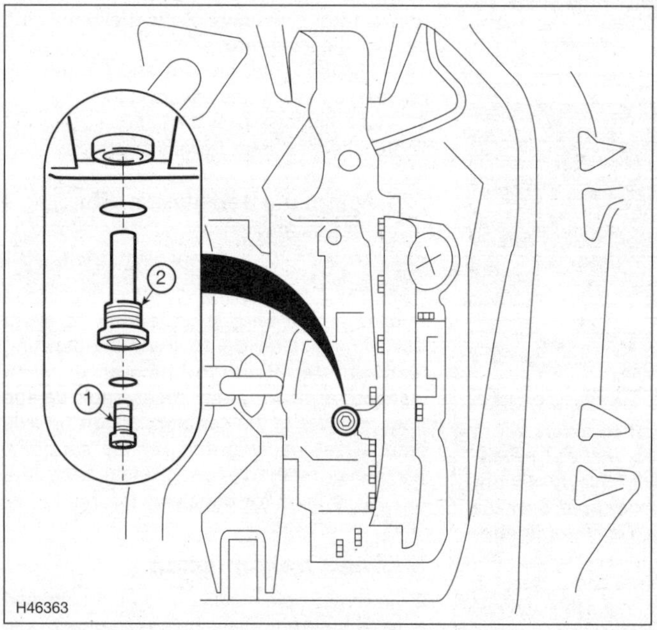

25.7 Transmission fluid level checking plug (1) and drain plug (2) – 6-speed transmission

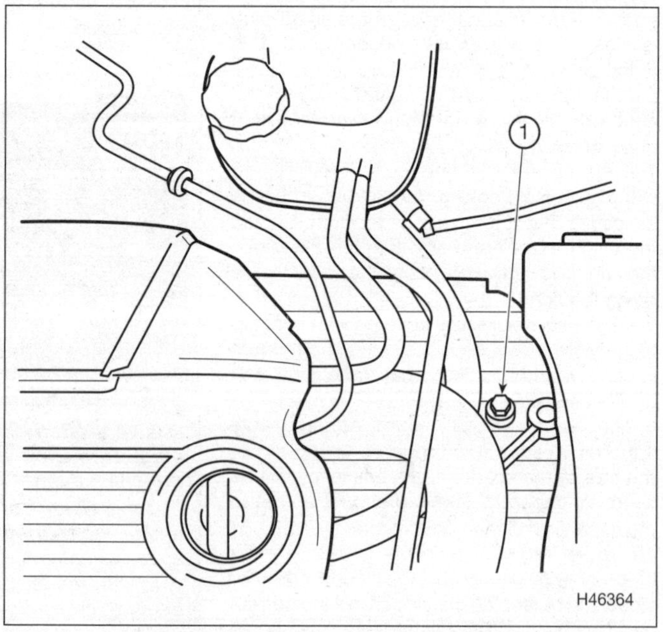

25.8 Transmission fluid filler plug (1)

26.3a We made a tool using flat steel bar, 3 mm thick, 25 mm wide, and two 8 mm bolts with 25 mm between centres

26.3b The bolts engage with the hole in the end of the tensioner, allowing the arm to be levered anti-clockwise

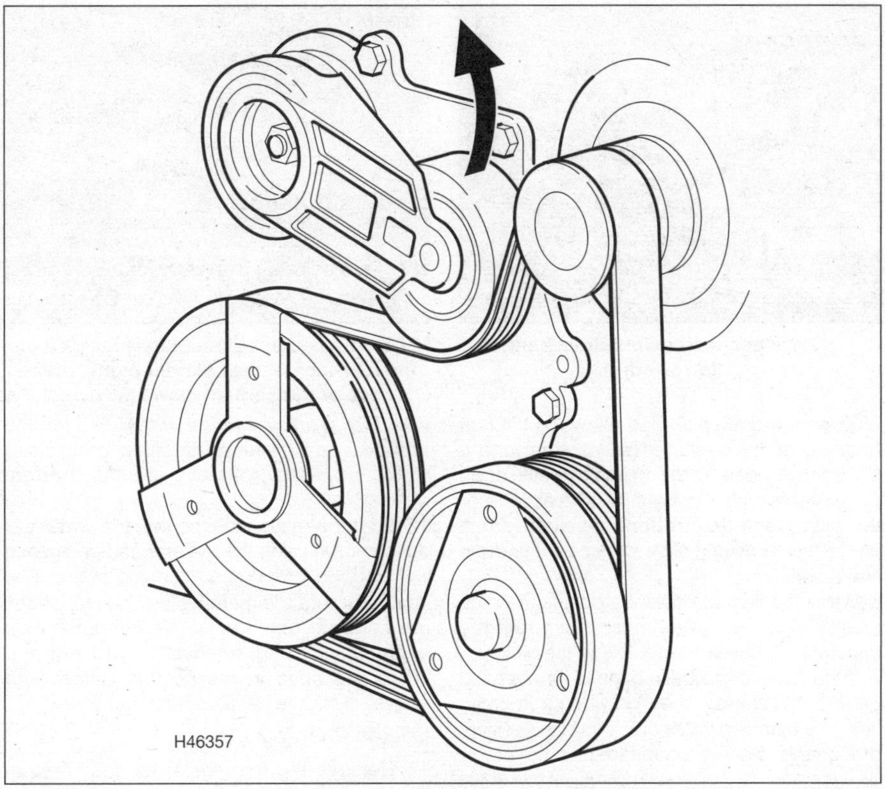

26.4 Fit the new belt around the pulleys

2 For better access to the drivebelt, apply the handbrake then jack up the front of the car and support it on axle stands (see *Jacking and vehicle support*). Remove the right-hand front roadwheel, then remove the plastic liner from under the right-hand wheel arch to expose the crankshaft pulley **(see illustrations 20.2)**.

3 The tensioner pulley spring must now be compressed. Saab special tool No 86 12 798 is available, which engages in the 10 mm square hole in the tensioner arm. In the absence of the Saab tool, fabricate a homemade equivalent similar to the one shown **(see illustration)**. Engage the tool with the tensioner arm, then rotate the arm anti-clockwise and manoeuvre the belt from the pulleys **(see illustration)**.

4 Locate the new drivebelt over all the pulleys, making sure that the multi-grooved side is correctly engaged with the grooves on the pulleys **(see illustration)**.

5 Compress the tensioner spring using the method employed earlier, the locate the new drivebelt over the pulleys, making sure the multi-grooved side is correctly engaged with the grooves on the pulleys.

6 Ensure that the belt is correctly seated on all the pulleys, then start the engine and allow it to idle for a few minutes. This will allow the tensioner to settle in position and distribute the tension evenly throughout the belt. Stop the engine and check once again that the belt is correctly seated on all the pulleys.

7 On completion, refit the plastic wheel arch liner and roadwheel, and then lower the car to the ground.

Every 3 years

27 Coolant – renewal

Note: *This work is not included in the Saab schedule, and should not be required if the recommended Saab antifreeze/inhibitor is used.*

Warning: Do not allow antifreeze to come in contact with your skin or painted surfaces of the vehicle. Flush contaminated areas immediately with plenty of water. Don't store new coolant, or leave old coolant lying around, where it's accessible to children or pets – they're attracted by its sweet smell. Ingestion of even a small amount of coolant can be fatal. Wipe up garage-floor and drip-pan spills immediately. Keep antifreeze containers covered, and repair cooling system leaks as soon as they're noticed.

Warning: Never remove the expansion tank filler cap when the engine is running, or has just been switched off, as the cooling system will be hot, and the consequent escaping steam and scalding coolant could cause serious injury.

Warning: Wait until the engine is cold before starting these procedures.

Cooling system draining

1 With the engine completely cold, remove the expansion tank filler cap. Turn the cap anti-clockwise, wait until any pressure remaining in the system is released, then unscrew it and lift it off.

2 Raise the front of the vehicle and support it on axle stands (see *Jacking and vehicle support*).

3 Undo the screws and remove the undershield beneath the radiator. Note the retaining screws in the wheel arch liner.

4 Attach a hose to the drain plug on the right-hand side of the radiator, and position the other end of the hose in a suitable container.

27.4 Open the coolant drain plug (arrowed)

27.5 The coolant drain plug is located on the rear face of the cylinder block, at the base of the coolant pump (arrowed)

Slacken the drain plug and allow the coolant to drain into the container **(see illustration)**.

5 Attach a hose to the cylinder block drain plug, located on the right-hand rear face of the block **(see illustration)**. Open the drain plug a few turns and allow the coolant to drain into a container.

6 When the flow of coolant stops, tighten the drain plugs, remove the hoses, and refit the undershield. Lower the vehicle to the ground.

7 If the coolant has been drained for a reason other than renewal, then provided it is clean and less than two years old, it can be re-used, though this is not recommended.

Cooling system flushing

8 If coolant renewal has been neglected, or if the antifreeze mixture has become diluted, then in time the cooling system may gradually lose efficiency, as the coolant passages become restricted due to rust, scale deposits and other sediment. The cooling system efficiency can be restored by flushing the system clean.

9 The radiator should be flushed independently of the engine, to avoid unnecessary contamination.

Radiator flushing

10 Disconnect the top and bottom hoses and any other relevant hoses from the radiator, with reference to Chapter 3, Section 3.

11 Insert a garden hose into the radiator top inlet. Direct a flow of clean water through the radiator, and continue flushing until clean water emerges from the radiator bottom outlet.

12 If after a reasonable period, the water still does not run clear, the radiator can be flushed with a good proprietary cleaning agent. It is important that the manufacturer's instructions are followed carefully. If the contamination is particularly bad, remove the radiator and insert the hose in the bottom outlet, and reverse-flush the radiator, then refit it.

Engine flushing

13 Remove the thermostat as described in Chapter 3, Section 4, then temporarily refit the thermostat cover. If the radiator top hose has been disconnected, temporarily reconnect the hose.

14 With the top and bottom hoses disconnected from the radiator, insert a garden hose into the radiator top hose. Direct a clean flow of water through the engine, and continue flushing until clean water emerges from the radiator bottom hose.

15 On completion of flushing, refit the thermostat and reconnect the hoses with reference to Chapter 3, Section 4.

Cooling system filling

16 Before attempting to fill the cooling system, make sure that all hoses and clips are in good condition, and that the clips are tight. Note that an antifreeze mixture must be used all year round, to prevent corrosion of the engine components.

17 Make sure that the air conditioning (A/C) or automatic climate control (ACC) is switched off. This is to prevent the air conditioning system starting the radiator cooling fan before the engine is at normal temperature when refilling the system.

18 Remove the expansion tank filler cap and slowly fill the system until the coolant level reaches the MAX mark on the side of the expansion tank.

19 Refit and tighten the expansion tank filler cap.

20 Start the engine and set the heater to hot, then run the engine until it reaches normal operating temperature (until the cooling fan cuts in and out). Running the engine at varying speeds will allow the engine to warm-up quickly.

21 Stop the engine, and allow it to cool, then recheck the coolant level with reference to *Weekly checks*. Top-up the level if necessary and refit the expansion tank filler cap.

Antifreeze mixture

22 Always use an ethylene-glycol based antifreeze which is suitable for use in mixed-metal cooling systems. The quantity of antifreeze and levels of protection are given in the Specifications.

23 Before adding antifreeze, the cooling system should be completely drained, preferably flushed, and all hoses checked for condition and security.

24 After filling with antifreeze, a label should be attached to the expansion tank, stating the type and concentration of antifreeze used, and the date installed. Any subsequent topping-up should be made with the same type and concentration of antifreeze.

Caution: Do not use engine antifreeze in the windscreen/tailgate washer system, as it will cause damage to the vehicle paintwork. A screenwash additive should be added to the washer system in the quantities stated on the bottle.

Every 4 years

28.0 A brake fluid tester can be used to test the water content of the brake fluid

28 Brake fluid – renewal

Warning: Brake hydraulic fluid can harm your eyes and damage painted surfaces, so use extreme caution when handling and pouring it. Do not use fluid that has been standing open for some time, as it absorbs moisture from the air. Excess moisture can cause a dangerous loss of braking effectiveness.

Note: *If no equipment is available for testing the quality of the brake fluid, it is recommended that the brake fluid is renewed every 2 years* ***(see illustration)***.

1 The procedure is similar to that for the bleeding of the hydraulic system as described in Chapter 9, Section 2.

2 Working as described in Chapter 9, Section 2, open the first bleed screw in the sequence, and pump the brake pedal gently until nearly all the old fluid has been emptied from the master cylinder reservoir. Top-up to the MAX level with new fluid, and continue pumping until only the new fluid remains in the reservoir, and new fluid can be seen emerging from the bleed screw. Tighten the screw, and top the reservoir level up to the MAX level line.

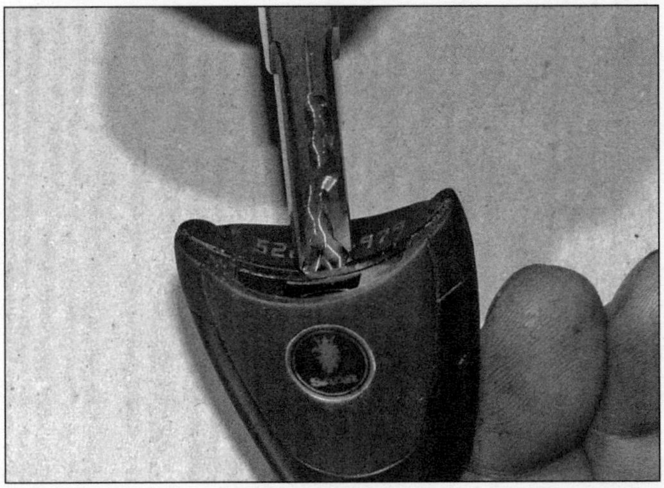

29.2 **Insert the end of the key into the small a lot, and twist apart the two halves**

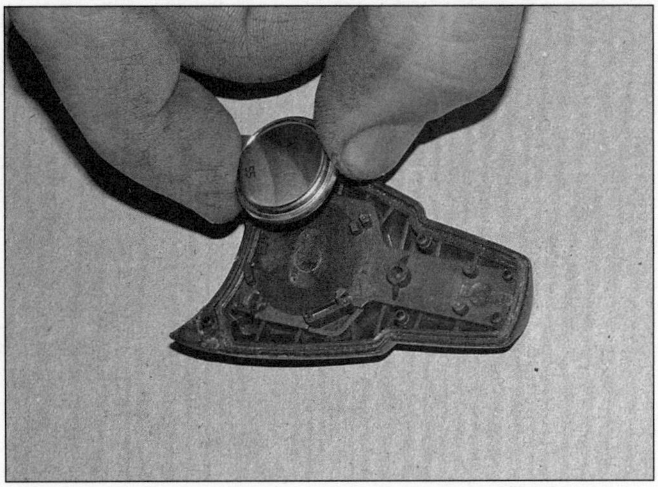

29.4 **Insert the battery with the positive (+) side down**

3 Work through all the remaining bleed screws in the sequence until new fluid can be seen at all of them. Be careful to keep the master cylinder reservoir topped-up to above the MIN level at all times, or air may enter the system and greatly increase the length of the task.
4 When the operation is complete, check that all bleed screws are securely tightened, and that their dust caps are refitted. Wash off all traces of spilt fluid, and recheck the master cylinder reservoir fluid level.
5 Check the operation of the brakes before taking the car on the road.

29 Remote control battery – renewal

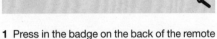

1 Press in the badge on the back of the remote control and pull out the emergency key.
2 Insert the end of the key into the small hole, then twist it to separate the 2 halves of the control **(see illustration)**.
3 Note how it's fitted, then remove the battery from the control. **Note:** *Avoid touching the battery contacts or remote control circuitry with bare fingers.*
4 Insert the new battery (positive side down), and clip together the two halves of the control **(see illustration)**.
5 It is now necessary to synchronise the control with the receiver, by inserting the key into the ignition switch. If the vehicle is locked, unlock it with the emergency key (the alarm will sound), insert the remote control into the ignition switch and turn it on. This will synchronise the components, and turn off the alarm siren.

Notes

Chapter 1 Part B:
Routine maintenance and servicing – diesel models

Contents

Section number

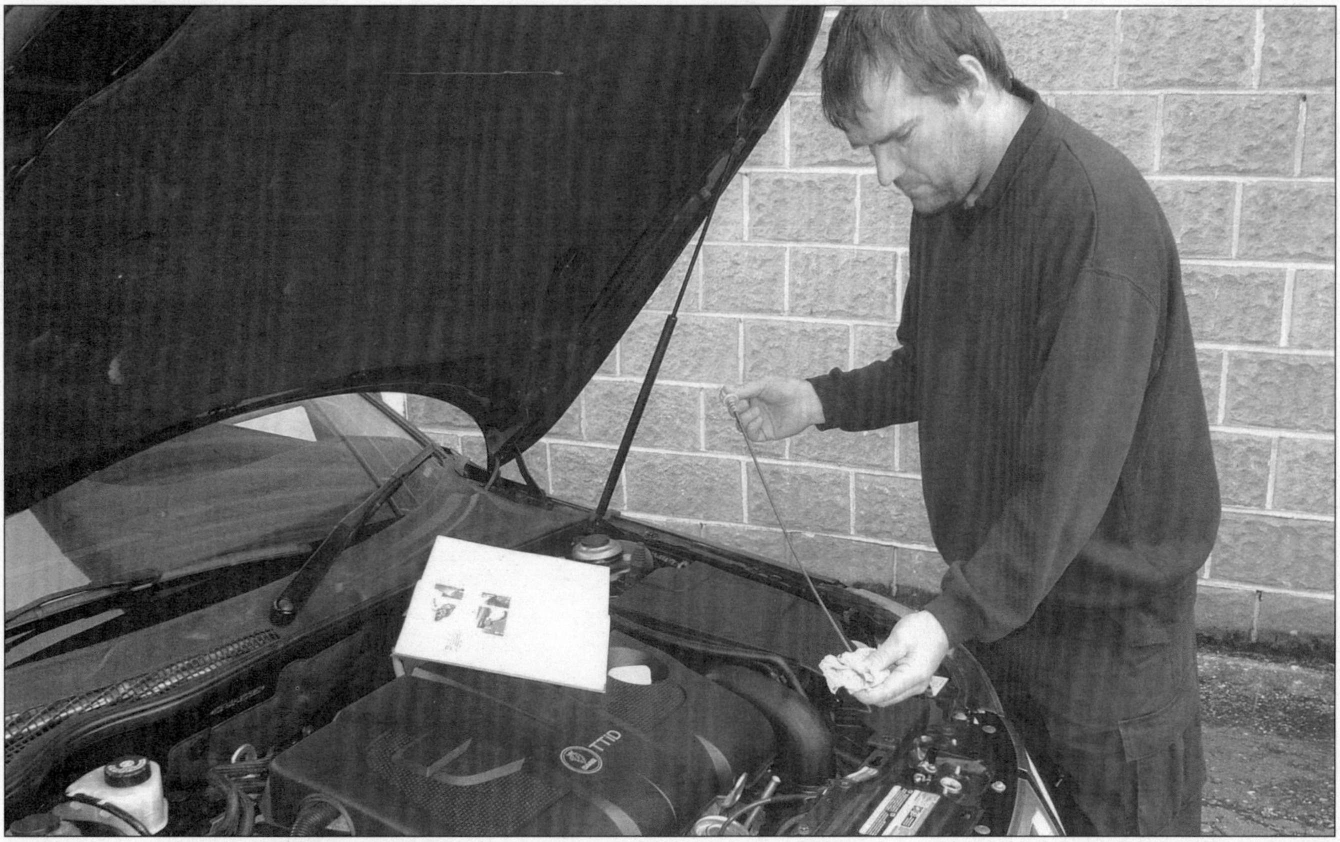

Degrees of difficulty

Easy, suitable for novice with little experience	**Fairly easy,** suitable for beginner with some experience	**Fairly difficult,** suitable for competent DIY mechanic	**Difficult,** suitable for experienced DIY mechanic	**Very difficult,** suitable for expert DIY or professional

Lubricants and fluids

See end of *Weekly checks* on page 0•16

Capacities

Engine oil	
Drain and refill, with filter change	4.3 litres
Between dipstick MAX and MIN markings	1.0 litres
Cooling system	7.2 litres
Transmission	
Manual (drain and refill):	
5-speed	1.8 litres
6-speed	3.0 litres
Automatic:	
Drain and refill	2.8 litres
Total from dry (including torque converter and cooler)	7.0 litres
Fuel tank	
All models	58.0 litres

Cooling system

Antifreeze mixture:*	
50% antifreeze	Protection down to -37°C
55% antifreeze	Protection down to -45°C

* **Note:** *Refer to antifreeze manufacturer for latest recommendations. Saab antifreeze coolant is premixed.*

Brakes

Brake pad friction material minimum thickness:	
Front	2.0 mm
Rear	2.0 mm
Front disc minimum thickness	22.0 mm (288 mm dia.) or 25.0 mm (302 or 314 mm dia.)
Rear disc minimum thickness	10.0 mm (solid) or 18.0 mm (ventilated)

Remote control battery

Type	CR2032

Tyre pressures

See end of *Weekly checks* on page 0•16

Torque wrench settings	Nm	lbf ft
Automatic transmission drain plug:		
5-speed	40	30
6-speed	45	33
Automatic transmission filler plug (6-speed only)	30	22
Engine oil filter cover	25	18
Engine oil sump drain plug	25	18
Front chassis reinforcement bolts (Convertible only)	50	37
Fuel filter	20	15
Manual transmission level/filler plug	50	37
Wheel bolts	110	81

The maintenance intervals in this manual are provided with the assumption that you will be carrying out the work yourself. These are the minimum maintenance intervals recommended by the manufacturer for vehicles driven daily. If you wish to keep your vehicle in peak condition at all times, you may wish to perform some of these procedures more often. We encourage frequent maintenance, because it enhances the efficiency, performance and resale value of your vehicle.

If the vehicle is driven in dusty areas, used to tow a trailer, or driven frequently at slow speeds (idling in traffic) or on short journeys, more frequent maintenance intervals are recommended.

When the vehicle is new, it should be serviced by a dealer service department (or other workshop recognised by the vehicle manufacturer as providing the same standard of service) in order to preserve the warranty. The vehicle manufacturer may reject warranty claims if you are unable to prove that servicing has been carried out as and when specified, using only original equipment parts or parts certified to be of equivalent quality.

All models are equipped with a service interval display. When a service is due the Saab Information Display (SID) will display a spanner symbol and the text TIME FOR SERVICE. However, Saab point out that, 'due to the relationship between time and mileage, some operating conditions will make annual service more suitable'.

Where a diesel particle filter (DPF) is fitted it is essential that the vehicle is driven at motorway speeds for a least 25 minutes every 1000 miles. This will enable the engine management system to clean the accumulated soot from the DPF. This procedure is called 'regeneration' and if regeneration does not take place the DPF will become blocked and will require renewal.

Every 250 miles or weekly

☐ Refer to *Weekly checks*

Every 6000 miles or 6 months

☐ Engine oil and filter – renewal (Section 3)

Note: *Saab recommend that the engine oil and filter are changed every 18 000 miles. However, oil and filter changes are good for the engine and we recommend that they are renewed more frequently, especially if the vehicle is used on a lot of short journeys.*

After first 6000 miles and thereafter every 12 000 miles or 12 months

Note: *The 12 000 mile intervals start at 18 000 miles, ie, at 18 000 miles, 30 000 miles, 42 000 miles, 54 000 miles, etc.*

☐ Service indicator – resetting (Section 4)
☐ Hoses and fluids – leak check (Section 5)
☐ Steering and suspension components – check (Section 6)
☐ Brake pad wear and disc check (Section 7)
☐ Handbrake – check and adjustment (Section 8)
☐ Seat belt condition – check (Section 9)
☐ Airbag system – check (Section 10)
☐ Headlight beam alignment – check (Section 11)
☐ Power steering fluid level – check (Section 12)
☐ Road test (Section 13)
☐ Coolant antifreeze concentration – check (Section 14)
☐ Driveshaft joints and gaiters – check (Section 15)
☐ Exhaust system – check (Section 16)
☐ Hinges and locks – lubrication (Section 17)
☐ Pollen air filter – renewal (Section 18)
☐ Plenum chamber drain hose – clean (Section 19)
☐ Auxiliary drivebelt condition – check (Section 20)
☐ Fuel filter – renewal (Section 21)

Every 36 000 miles

Note: *The 36 000 mile intervals start at 42 000 miles, ie, at 42 000 miles, 78 000 miles, 114 000 miles, etc.*

☐ Valve clearances – check and adjustment (8v engine only) (Section 22)
☐ Air filter element – renewal (Section 23)
☐ Manual transmission fluid level – check (Section 24)

Every 48 000 miles

Note: *The 48 000 mile intervals start at 54 000 miles, ie, at 54 000 miles, 102 000 miles, etc.*

☐ Timing belt – renewal (Section 25)

Note: *Saab recommend that the interval for timing belt renewal is 72 000 miles or 6 years. However, if the vehicle is used mainly for short journeys or a lot of stop-start driving it is recommended that the renewal interval is shortened. The actual belt renewal interval is very much up to the individual owner but, bearing in mind that severe engine damage will result if the belt breaks in use, we recommend you err on the side of caution.*

Every 60 000 miles

Note: *The 60 000 mile intervals start at 66 000 miles, ie, at 66 000 miles, 126 000 miles, etc.*

☐ Timing belt – renewal (Section 25)

Note: *Saab recommend that the interval for timing belt renewal is 72 000 miles or 6 years. However, if the vehicle is used mainly for short journeys or a lot of stop-start driving it is recommended that the renewal interval is shortened. The actual belt renewal interval is very much up to the individual owner but, bearing in mind that severe engine damage will result if the belt breaks in use, we recommend you err on the side of caution.*

☐ Automatic transmission fluid – renewal (Section 26)
☐ Auxiliary drivebelt – renewal (Section 27)

Every 3 years

☐ Coolant – renewal (Section 28)

Note: *This work is not included in the Saab schedule, and should not be required if the recommended Saab antifreeze/inhibitor is used.*

Every 4 years

☐ Brake fluid – renewal (Section 29)
☐ Remote control battery – renewal (Section 30)

Underbonnet view

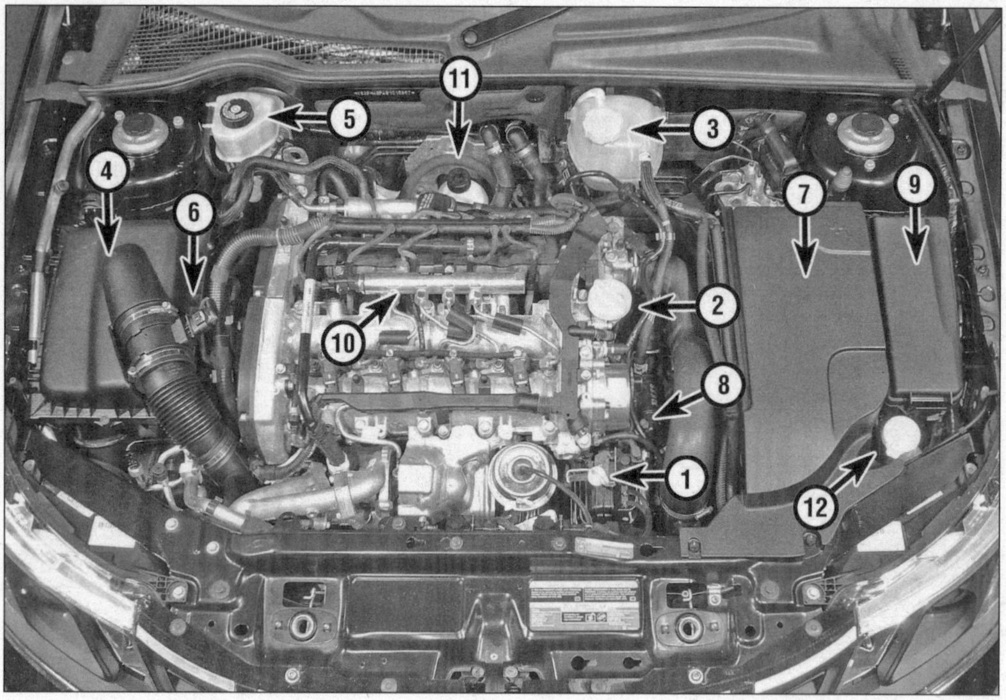

1. Engine oil level dipstick
2. Engine oil filler cap
3. Coolant expansion tank
4. Air cleaner assembly
5. Brake (and clutch) fluid reservoir
6. Mass airflow meter
7. Battery
8. Coolant bleed screw
9. Fusebox
10. Common (fuel) rail
11. Power steering fluid reservoir
12. Screen washer fluid reservoir

Front underbody view

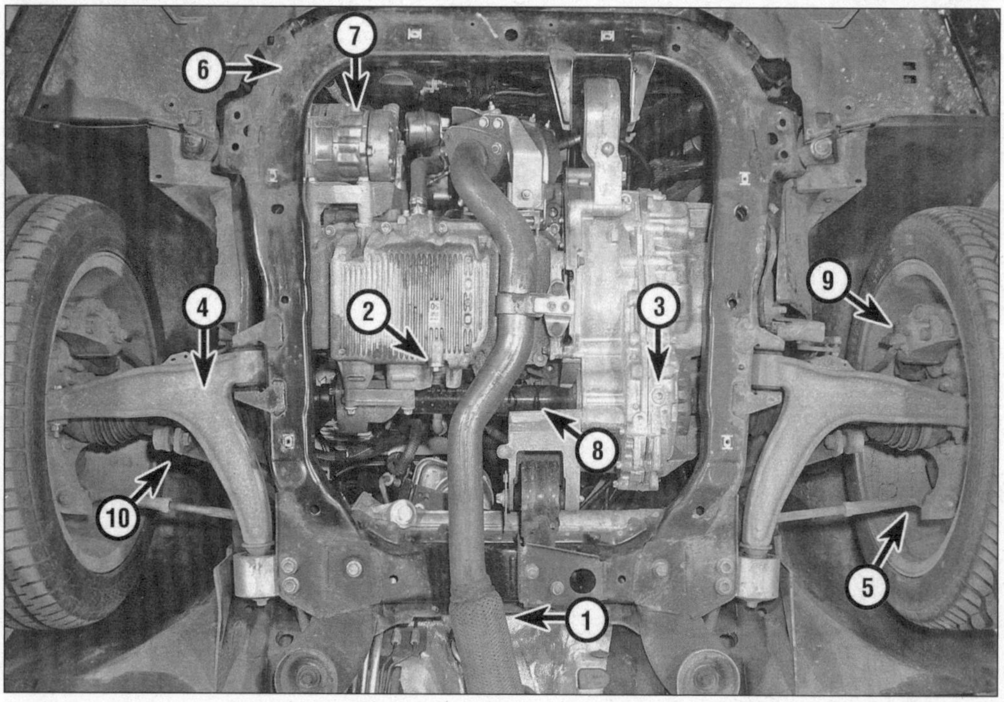

1. Exhaust pipe
2. Engine oil sump drain plug
3. Transmission fluid drain plug
4. Front lower arm
5. Steering track rod
6. Front subframe
7. Air conditioning compressor
8. Intermediate driveshaft
9. Brake caliper
10. Anti-roll bar

Rear underbody view

1 Exhaust pipe
2 Lower transverse arm
3 Toe-in link arm
4 Fuel filter
5 Handbrake cable
6 Trailing arm
7 Fuel tank
8 Shock absorber
9 Anti-roll bar
10 Jacking points

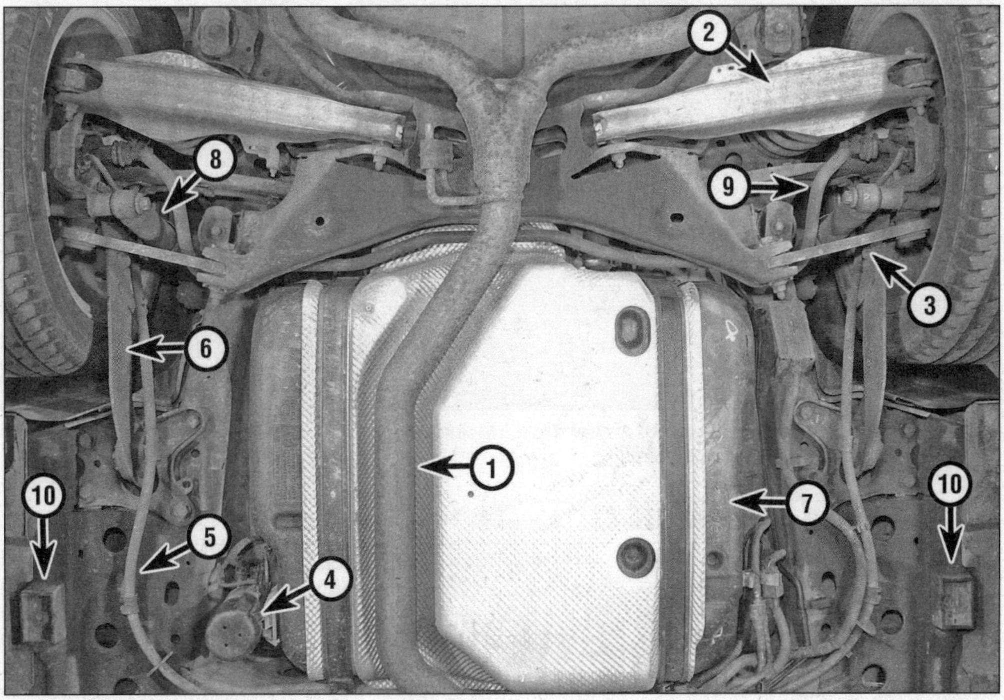

Maintenance procedures

1 General information

This Chapter is designed to help the home mechanic maintain his/her vehicle for safety, economy, long life and peak performance.

The Chapter contains a master maintenance schedule, followed by Sections dealing specifically with each task in the schedule. Visual checks, adjustments, component renewal and other helpful items are included. Refer to the accompanying illustrations of the engine compartment and the underside of the vehicle for the locations of the various components.

Servicing your vehicle in accordance with the mileage/time maintenance schedule and the following Sections will provide a planned maintenance programme, which should result in a long and reliable service life. This is a comprehensive plan, so maintaining some items, but not others, at the specified service intervals will not produce the same results.

As you service your vehicle, you will discover that many of the procedures can – and should – be grouped together, because of the particular procedure being performed, or because of the close proximity of two otherwise-unrelated components to one another. For example, if the vehicle is raised for any reason, the exhaust system could be inspected at the same time as the suspension and steering components.

The first step in this maintenance programme is to prepare yourself before the actual work begins. Read through all the Sections relevant to the work to be carried out, then make a list and gather together all the parts and tools required. If a problem is encountered, seek advice from a parts specialist, or a dealer service department.

2 Regular maintenance

If, from the time the vehicle is new, the routine maintenance schedule is followed closely, and frequent checks are made of fluid levels and high-wear items, as suggested throughout this manual, the engine will be kept in relatively good running condition, and the need for additional work will be minimised.

It is possible that there will be times when the engine is running poorly due to the lack of regular maintenance. This is even more likely if a used vehicle, which has not received regular and frequent maintenance checks, is purchased. In such cases, additional work may need to be carried out, outside of the regular maintenance intervals.

If engine wear is suspected, a compression test (refer to Chapter 2B, Section 2 or Chapter 2C, Section 2) will provide valuable information regarding the overall performance of the main internal components. Such a test can be used as a basis to decide on the extent of the work to be carried out. If, for example, a compression test indicates serious internal engine wear, conventional maintenance as described in this Chapter will not greatly improve the performance of the engine, and may prove a waste of time and money, unless extensive overhaul work (Chapter 2D) is carried out first.

The following series of operations are those most often required to improve the performance of a generally poor-running engine:

Primary operations

a) Clean, inspect and test the battery ('Weekly checks' and Chapter 5A, Section 3)
b) Check all the engine-related fluids ('Weekly checks').
c) Check the condition and tension of the auxiliary drivebelt (Section 20).
d) Check the condition of the air filter element, and renew if necessary (Section 23).
e) Renew the fuel filter (Section 21).
f) Check the condition of all hoses, and check for fluid leaks (Section 5).

Secondary operations

If the above operations do not prove fully effective, carry out the following secondary operations:

a) Check the charging system (Chapter 5A, Section 5).
b) Check the fuel system (Chapter 4B, Section 9).

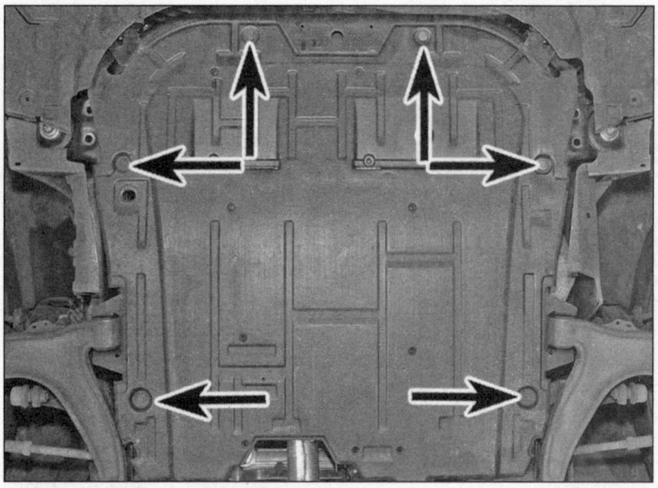

3.4 Undo the screws (arrowed) and remove the engine undershield

3.5a The engine oil drain plug is located at the rear of the sump (arrowed)

Every 6000 miles or 6 months

3 Engine oil and filter – renewal

1 Frequent oil changes are the most important preventative maintenance the DIY home mechanic can give the engine, because ageing oil becomes diluted and contaminated, which leads to premature engine wear.

2 Before starting this procedure, gather together all the necessary tools and materials. Also make sure that you have plenty of clean rags and newspapers handy, to mop-up any spills. Ideally, the engine oil should be warm, as it will drain better, and more built-up sludge will be removed with it. Take care, however, not to touch the exhaust or any other hot parts of the engine when working under the vehicle. To avoid any possibility of scalding, and to protect yourself from possible skin irritants and other harmful contaminants in used engine oils, it is advisable to wear gloves when carrying out this work.

3.5b Unscrew the plug and allow the oil to drain

3.7 Refit the drain plug with a new sealing washer

3 Apply the handbrake, then jack up the front of the vehicle and support it on axle stands (see *Jacking and vehicle support*).

4 Undo the fasteners and remove the engine undershield **(see illustration)**.

5 The engine oil drain plug is located on the rear of the sump; slacken the plug about half a turn. Position the draining container under the drain plug, then remove the plug completely – recover the sealing washer **(see illustrations)**.

6 Allow some time for the old oil to drain, noting that it may be necessary to reposition the container as the oil flow slows to a trickle.

7 After all the oil has drained, wipe off the drain plug with a clean rag. Clean the area around the drain plug opening, and refit the plug with a new O-ring seal. Tighten the plug to the specified torque **(see illustration)**.

8 Position the container under the oil filter housing, then slacken the filter housing cap a few turns, using a 32 mm socket (DT and DTH engines) or a suitable special oil filter removal tool (DTR engines) and allow the oil to drain into the container. To prevent the oil contacting the exhaust system, attach a length of hose to the drain tube on the filter housing **(see illustrations)**.

9 When the oil has finished draining,

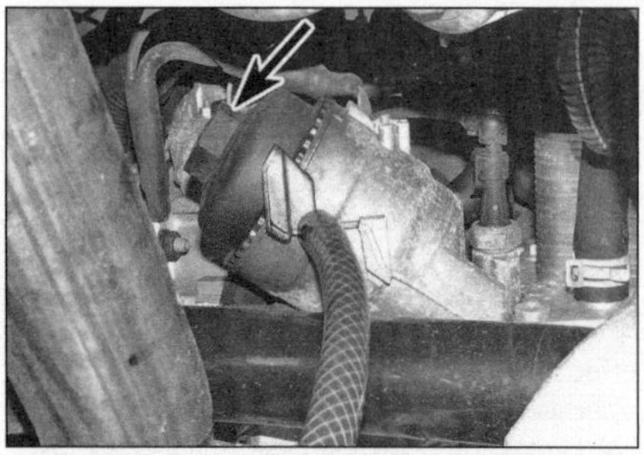

3.8a Attach a length of hose to the spout on the oil filter housing. Unscrew the cap (arrowed) a few turns with a 32 mm socket ...

3.8b ... or a suitable oil filter removal tool

3.8c Allow the oil to drain from the housing before removing the cap

3.11a The new oil filter and O-rings for the DT and DTH engines ...

3.11b ... and for the DTR engines

3.11c Fit the new filter into the housing ...

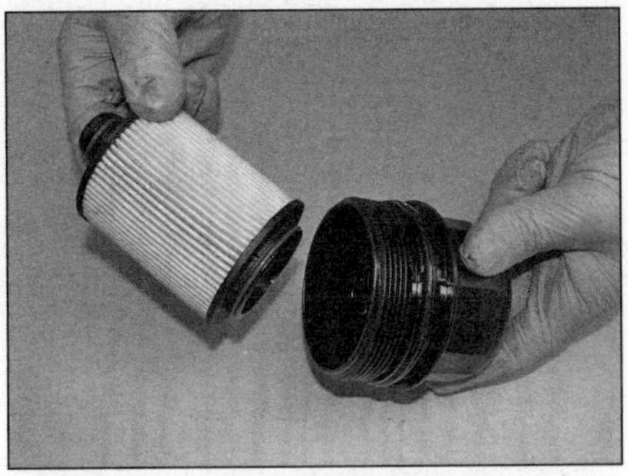

3.11d ... or to the cap on DTR engines

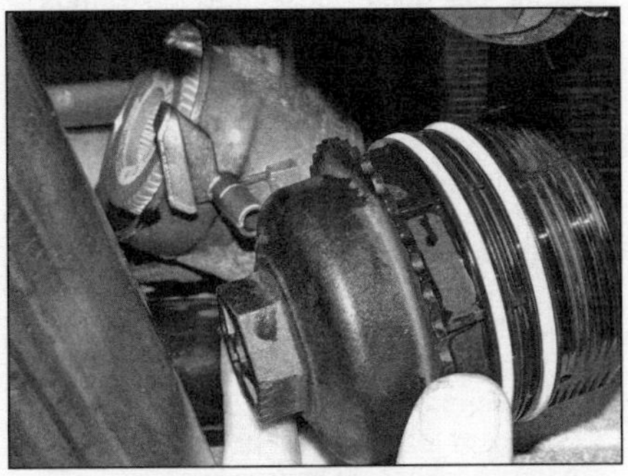

3.12 Fit the cap with the O-rings to the housing

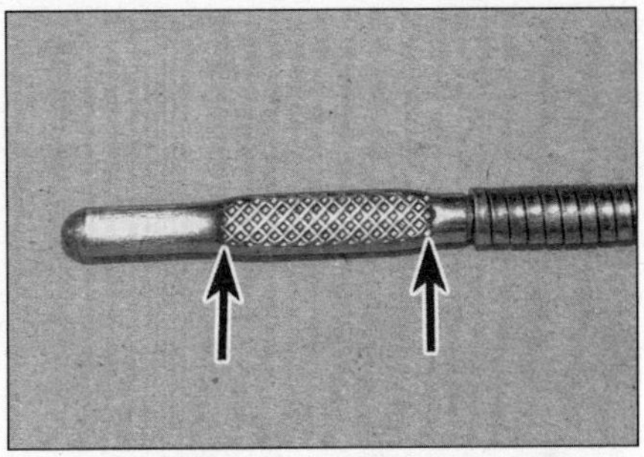

3.13 The difference between the upper and lower marks on the dipstick is approximately 1.0 litre

completely unscrew and remove the oil filter cover along with the filter element. Discard the cover O-ring seals, new ones must be fitted.

10 Use a clean rag to remove all oil, dirt and sludge from the filter housing and cover.

11 Fit the new filter element to the filter housing, and the O-ring seals to the filter cover **(see illustrations)**.

12 Apply a light coating of clean engine oil to the O-ring seal on the filter cover, then fit the element and cover into the housing, and tighten it to the specified torque **(see illustration)**. Lower the vehicle to the ground.

13 Remove the oil filler cap and withdraw the level dipstick from the tube. Fill the engine, using the correct oil (see *Lubricants and fluids*). An oil can spout or funnel may help to reduce spillage. Pour in half the specified quantity of oil first, then wait a few minutes for the oil to run to the sump. Continue adding oil a small quantity at a time until the level is up to the lower mark on the dipstick. Adding a further 1.0 litre will bring the level up to the upper mark on the dipstick. Insert the dipstick, and refit the filler cap **(see illustration)**.

14 Start the engine and run it for a few minutes; check for leaks around the oil filter seal and the sump drain plug. Note that there may be a delay of a few seconds before the oil pressure warning light goes out when the engine is first started, as the oil circulates through the engine oil galleries and the new oil filter, before the pressure builds-up.

15 Switch off the engine, and wait a few minutes for the oil to settle in the sump once more. With the new oil circulated and the filter completely full, recheck the level on the dipstick, and add more oil as necessary.

16 Refit the engine undershield.

17 Dispose of the used engine oil safely, in accordance with the guidance given in *General repair procedures*.

After first 6000 miles and thereafter every 12 000 miles

Note: *The 12 000 mile intervals start at 18 000 miles, ie, at 18 000 miles, 30 000 miles, 42 000 miles, 54 000 miles, etc.*

4 Service indicator – resetting

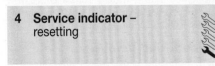

1 The SID (Saab Information Display) system incorporates a service interval indicator **(see illustration)**. When the distance covered between services approaches the next service, a visual message is displayed. The service indicator is manually reset after the vehicle has been serviced. The indicator can also be reset at any time using the Saab diagnostic tool.

2 Turn the ignition key to the ON position and select SETTINGS, using the INFO button. Hold the SET button until an audible warning is heard.

3 Select TIME FOR SERVICE using the INFO button and then hold the SET button until an audible warning is heard.

4 Select YES using the INFO switch.

5 Press and hold the brake pedal and then briefly press the SET button.

6 Turn the ignition off and release the brake pedal. The indicator is now reset.

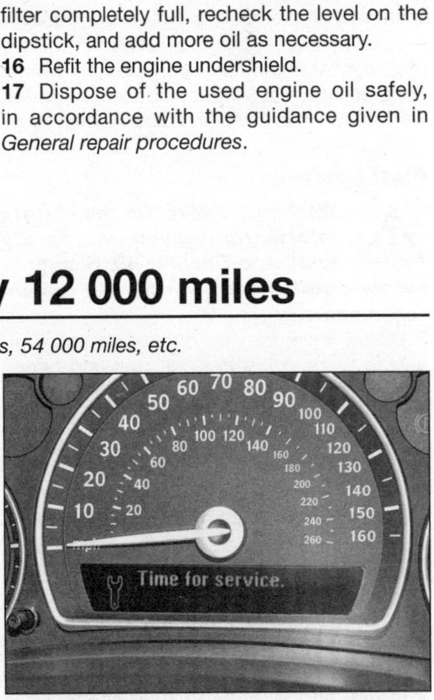

4.1 A service is required on this vehicle

HAYNES HINT

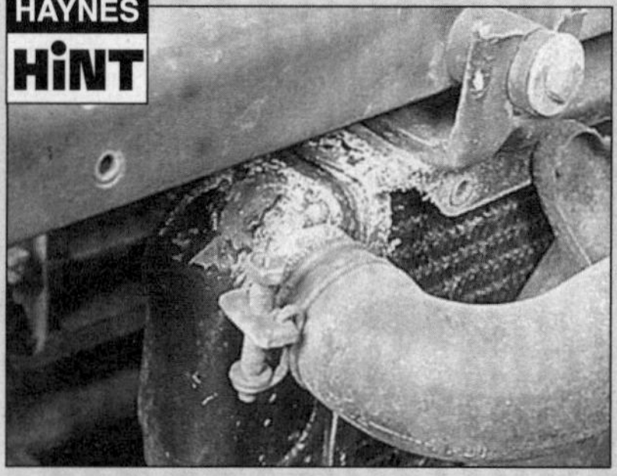

A leak in the cooling system will usually show up as white- or antifreeze-coloured deposits on the area adjoining the leak.

5 Hoses and fluids – leak check

Cooling system

Warning: Refer to the safety information given in 'Safety first!' and Chapter 3, Section 1 before disturbing any of the cooling system components.

1 Carefully check the radiator and heater coolant hoses along their entire length. Renew any hose which is cracked, swollen or which shows signs of deterioration. Cracks will show up better if the hose is squeezed. Pay close attention to the clips that secure the hoses to the cooling system components. Hose clips that have been overtightened can pinch and puncture hoses, resulting in cooling system leaks.

2 Inspect all the cooling system components (hoses, joint faces, etc) for leaks. Where any problems of this nature are found on system components, renew the component or gasket with reference to Chapter 3 **(see Haynes Hint).**

Fuel system

Warning: Refer to the safety information given in 'Safety first!' and Chapter 4B, Section 1 before disturbing any of the fuel system components.

3 Diesel leaks can be difficult to pinpoint, unless the leakage is significant and hence easily visible. Fuel tends to evaporate once it comes into contact with air, especially in a hot engine bay. Small drips can disappear before you get a chance to identify the point of leakage. If you suspect that there is a fuel leak from the area of the engine bay, leave the vehicle overnight then start the engine from cold, with the bonnet open. Metal components tend to shrink when they are cold, and rubber seals and hoses tend to harden, so any leaks will be more apparent whilst the engine is warming-up from a cold start.

4 Check all fuel lines at their connections to the fuel pump, common rail and fuel filter. Examine each rubber fuel hose along its length for splits or cracks. Check for leakage from the crimped joints between rubber and metal fuel lines. Examine the unions between the metal fuel lines and the fuel filter housing. Also check the area around the fuel injectors for signs of O-ring leakage.

5 To identify fuel leaks between the fuel tank and the engine bay, the vehicle should be raised and securely supported on axle stands (see *Jacking and vehicle support*). Inspect the fuel tank and filler neck for punctures, cracks and other damage. The connection between the filler neck and tank is especially critical. Sometimes a rubber filler neck or connecting hose will leak due to loose retaining clamps or deteriorated rubber.

6 Carefully check all rubber hoses and metal fuel lines leading away from the fuel tank. Check for loose connections, deteriorated hoses, kinked lines, and other damage. Pay particular attention to the vent pipes and hoses, which often loop up around the filler neck and can become blocked or kinked, making tank filling difficult. Follow the fuel supply and return lines to the front of the vehicle, carefully inspecting them all the way for signs of damage or corrosion. Renew damaged sections as necessary.

Engine oil

7 Inspect the area around the camshaft cover, cylinder head, oil filter and sump joint faces. Bear in mind that, over a period of time, some very slight seepage from these areas is to be expected – what you are really looking for is any indication of a serious leak caused by gasket failure. Engine oil seeping from the base of the timing chain cover or the transmission bellhousing may be an indication of crankshaft or transmission input shaft oil seal failure. Should a leak be found, renew the failed gasket or oil seal by referring to the appropriate Chapters in this manual.

Automatic transmission fluid

8 Where applicable, check the hoses leading to the transmission fluid cooler at the front of the engine bay for leakage. Look for deterioration caused by corrosion and damage from grounding, or debris thrown up from the road surface. Automatic transmission fluid is a thin oil and is usually red in colour.

Power-assisted steering fluid

9 Examine the hose running between the fluid reservoir and the power steering pump, and the return hose running from the steering rack to the fluid reservoir. Also examine the high pressure supply hose between the pump and the steering rack.

10 Check the condition of each hose carefully. Look for deterioration caused by corrosion and damage from grounding, or debris thrown up from the road surface.

11 Pay particular attention to crimped unions, and the area surrounding the hoses that are secured with adjustable worm-drive clips. Like automatic transmission fluid, PAS fluid is a thin oil, and is usually red in colour.

Air conditioning refrigerant

Warning: Refer to the safety information given in 'Safety first!' and Chapter 3, Section 8 regarding the dangers of disturbing any of the air conditioning system components.

12 The air conditioning system is filled with a liquid refrigerant, which is retained under high pressure. If the air conditioning system is opened and depressurised without the aid of specialised equipment, the refrigerant will immediately turn into gas and escape into the atmosphere. If the liquid comes into contact with your skin, it can cause severe frostbite. In addition, the refrigerant contains substances which are environmentally damaging; for this reason, it should not be allowed to escape into the atmosphere in an uncontrolled fashion.

13 Any suspected air conditioning system leaks should be immediately referred to a Saab dealer or air conditioning specialist. Leakage will be shown up as a steady drop in the level of refrigerant in the system.

14 Note that water may drip from the condenser drain pipe, underneath the car, immediately after the air conditioning system has been in use. This is normal, and should not be cause for concern.

Brake fluid

Warning: Refer to the safety information given in 'Safety first!' and Chapter 9, Section 2 regarding the dangers of handling brake fluid.

15 With reference to Chapter 9, Section 7, examine the area surrounding the brake pipe unions at the master cylinder for signs of leakage. Check the area around the base of fluid reservoir, for signs of leakage caused by seal failure. Also examine the brake pipe unions at the ABS hydraulic unit.

16 If fluid loss is evident, but the leak cannot be pinpointed in the engine bay, the brake calipers and underbody brake lines should be carefully checked with the vehicle raised and supported on axle stands (see *Jacking and vehicle support*). Leakage of fluid from the braking system is a serious fault that must be rectified immediately.

17 Brake/clutch hydraulic fluid is a toxic substance with a watery consistency. New fluid is almost colourless, but it becomes darker with age and use.

Unidentified fluid leaks

18 If there are signs that a fluid of some description is leaking from the vehicle, but you cannot identify the type of fluid or its exact origin, park the vehicle overnight and slide a large piece of card underneath it. Providing that the card is positioned in roughly the right location, even the smallest leak will show up on the card. Not only will this help you to pinpoint the exact location of the leak, it should be easier to identify the fluid from its colour. Bear in mind, though, that the leak may only be occurring when the engine is running!

Vacuum hoses

19 Although the braking system is hydraulically-operated, the brake servo unit amplifies the effort applied at the brake pedal by making use of the vacuum in the inlet manifold generated by the engine. Vacuum is ported to the servo by means of a large-bore hose. Any leaks that develop in this hose will reduce the effectiveness of the braking system, and may affect the running of the engine.

20 In addition, a number of the underbonnet components, particularly the emission control components, are driven by vacuum supplied from the inlet manifold via narrow-bore hoses. A leak in a vacuum hose means that air is being drawn into the hose (rather than escaping from it) and this makes leakage very difficult to detect. One method is to use an old length of vacuum hose as a kind of stethoscope – hold one end close to (but not in!) your ear and use the other end to probe the area around the suspected leak. When the end of the hose is directly over a vacuum leak, a hissing sound will be heard clearly through the hose. Care must be taken to avoid contacting hot or moving components when testing in this manner, as the engine must be running. Renew any vacuum hoses that are found to be defective.

6 Steering and suspension components – check

Front suspension and steering

1 Raise the front of the vehicle, and securely support it on axle stands (see *Jacking and vehicle support*).

2 Visually inspect the balljoint dust covers and the steering rack-and-pinion gaiters for splits, chafing or deterioration. Any wear of these components will cause loss of lubricant, together with dirt and water entry, resulting in rapid deterioration of the balljoints or steering gear.

3 Check the power steering fluid hoses for chafing or deterioration, and the pipe and hose unions for fluid leaks. Also check for signs of fluid leakage under pressure from the steering gear rubber gaiters, which would indicate failed fluid seals within the steering gear.

4 Grasp the roadwheel at the 12 o'clock and 6 o'clock positions, and try to rock it **(see illustration)**. Very slight free play may be felt, but if the movement is appreciable, further investigation is necessary to determine the source. Continue rocking the wheel while an assistant depresses the footbrake. If the movement is now eliminated or significantly reduced, it is likely that the hub bearings are at fault. If the free play is still evident with the footbrake depressed, then there is wear in the suspension joints or mountings.

5 Now grasp the wheel at the 9 o'clock and 3 o'clock positions, and try to rock it as before. Any movement felt now may again be caused by wear in the hub bearings or the steering track rod balljoints. If the outer balljoint is worn, the visual movement will be obvious. If the inner joint is suspect, it can be felt by placing a hand over the rack-and-pinion rubber gaiter and gripping the track rod. If the wheel is now rocked, movement will be felt at the inner joint if wear has taken place.

6 Using a large screwdriver or flat bar, check for wear in the suspension mounting bushes by levering between the relevant suspension component and its attachment point. Some movement is to be expected, as the mountings are made of rubber, but excessive wear should be obvious. Also check the condition of any visible rubber bushes, looking for splits, cracks or contamination of the rubber.

7 With the car standing on its wheels, have an assistant turn the steering wheel back-and-forth, about an eighth of a turn each way. There should be very little, if any, lost movement between the steering wheel and roadwheels. If this is not the case, closely observe the joints and mountings previously described. In addition, check the steering column universal joints for wear, and also check the rack-and-pinion steering gear itself.

8 The front suspension mountings should be checked for tightness.

Rear suspension

9 Chock the front wheels, then jack up the rear of the vehicle and support securely on axle stands (see *Jacking and vehicle support*).

10 Working as described previously for the front suspension, check the rear hub bearings, the suspension bushes and the strut or shock absorber mountings (as applicable) for wear.

11 The rear suspension mountings should be checked for tightness.

Shock absorber

12 Check for any signs of fluid leakage around the shock absorber bodies, or from the rubber gaiters around the piston rods. Should any fluid be noticed, the shock absorber is defective internally, and should be renewed. **Note:** *Shock absorbers should always be renewed in pairs on the same axle.*

13 The efficiency of the shock absorber may be checked by bouncing the vehicle at each corner. Generally speaking, the body will return to its normal position and stop after being depressed. If it rises and returns on a rebound, the shock absorber is probably suspect. Also examine the shock absorber upper and lower mountings for any signs of wear.

Removable towbar attachment

14 Where applicable, clean the coupling pin then apply a little grease to the socket. Make sure that the removable towbar attachment fits easily to its mounting and locks correctly in position.

6.4 Check for wear in the hub bearings by grasping the wheel and trying to rock it

7 Brake pad wear and disc check

1 The work described in this Section should be carried out at the specified intervals, or whenever a defect is suspected in the braking system. Any of the following symptoms could indicate a potential brake system defect:

a) The vehicle pulls to one side when the brake pedal is depressed.
b) The brakes make squealing, scraping or dragging noises when applied.
c) Brake pedal travel is excessive, or pedal feel is poor.
d) The brake fluid requires repeated topping-up. Note that, because the hydraulic clutch shares the same fluid as the braking system (see Chapter 6, Section 2), this problem could be due to a leak in the clutch system.

Front disc brakes

2 Apply the handbrake, then loosen the front wheel bolts. Jack up the front of the vehicle, and support it on axle stands (see *Jacking and vehicle support*).

3 For better access to the brake calipers, remove the wheels.

4 Look through the inspection window in the caliper, and check that the thickness of the friction lining material on each of the pads is not less than the recommended minimum thickness given in the Specifications **(see Haynes Hint)**.

HAYNES HiNT

For a quick check, the thickness of friction material remaining on the inner brake pad can be measured through the aperture in the caliper body.

HAYNES HiNT ***Bear in mind that the lining material is normally bonded to a metal backing plate. To differentiate between the metal and the lining material, it is helpful to turn the disc slowly at first – the edge of the disc can then be identified, with the lining material on each pad either side of it, and the backing plates behind.***

5 If it is difficult to determine the exact thickness of the pad linings, or if you are at all concerned about the condition of the pads, then remove them from the calipers for further inspection (refer to Chapter 9, Section 4 or 5).
6 Check the other caliper in the same way.
7 If any one of the brake pads has worn down to, or below, the specified limit, all four pads at that end of the car must be renewed as a set. If the pads on one side are significantly more worn than the other, this may indicate that the caliper pistons have partially seized – refer to the brake pad renewal procedure in Chapter 9, Section 4 or 5, and push the pistons back into the caliper to free them.
8 Measure the thickness of the discs with a micrometer, if available, to make sure that they still have service life remaining. Do not be fooled by the lip of rust which often forms on the outer edge of the disc, which may make the disc appear thicker than it really is – scrape off the loose rust if necessary, without scoring the disc friction (shiny) surface.
9 If any disc is thinner than the specified minimum thickness, renew both (refer to Chapter 9, Section 8 or 9).
10 Check the general condition of the discs. Look for excessive scoring and discolouration caused by overheating. If these conditions exist, remove the relevant disc and have it resurfaced or renewed (refer to Chapter 9, Section 8 or 9).
11 Make sure that the handbrake is firmly applied, then check that the transmission is in neutral. Spin the wheel, and check that the brake is not binding. Some drag is normal with a disc brake, but it should not require any great effort to turn the wheel – also, do not confuse brake drag with resistance from the transmission.
12 Before refitting the wheels, check all brake lines and hoses (refer to Chapter 9, Section 3). In particular, check the flexible hoses in the vicinity of the calipers, where they are subjected to most movement. Bend them between the fingers (but do not actually bend them double, or the casing may be damaged) and check that this does not reveal previously-hidden cracks, cuts or splits.
13 On completion, refit the wheels and lower the car to the ground. Tighten the wheel bolts to the specified torque.

Rear disc brakes

14 Loosen the rear wheel bolts, then chock the front wheels. Jack up the rear of the car, and support it on axle stands. Release the handbrake and remove the rear wheels.

8.3 Insert a 1.0 mm feeler gauge between the caliper lever and the stop

15 The procedure for checking the rear brakes is much the same as described in paragraphs 2 to 13 above. Check that the rear brakes are not binding, noting that transmission resistance is not a factor on the rear wheels. Abnormal effort may indicate that the handbrake needs adjusting – see Chapter 9, Section 13.

8 Handbrake – check and adjustment

1 Chock the front wheels, then jack up the rear of the vehicle and support on axle stands (see *Jacking and vehicle support*).
2 Fully release the handbrake lever.
3 Check that the distance between the handbrake cable arm and the brake caliper is 1.0 mm **(see illustration)**. If not, adjust the handbrake as described in Chapter 9, Section 13.
4 Fully apply the handbrake lever, and check that both rear wheels are locked when attempting to turn them by hand.
5 Lower the vehicle to the ground.

9 Seat belt condition – check

1 Working on each seat belt in turn, carefully examine the seat belt webbing for cuts, or for any signs of serious fraying or deterioration. Pull the belt all the way out, and examine the full extent of the webbing.

12.1 The electro-hydraulic power steering fluid reservoir is located behind the engine (arrowed)

2 Fasten and unfasten the belt, ensuring that the locking mechanism holds securely, and releases properly when intended. Check also that the retracting mechanism operates correctly when the belt is released.
3 Check the security of all seat belt mountings and attachments which are accessible, without removing any trim or other components from inside the vehicle.
4 Check the function of the seat belt reminder lamp.

10 Airbag system – check

1 The following work can be carried out by the home mechanic, however, if an electronic fault is apparent, it will be necessary to take the car to a Saab dealer or specialist, who will have the necessary diagnostic equipment to extract fault codes from the system.
2 Turn the ignition switch to the drive position (ignition warning lights on), and check that the SRS (Supplementary Restraint System) warning light is illuminated for 3 to 4 seconds. After this period the light should go out, indicating that the system has been checked and is functioning correctly.
3 If the warning light remains on or refuses to light, have the system checked by a Saab dealer or specialist.
4 Visually examine the steering wheel centre pad and the passenger airbag module for external damage. Also check the exterior of the front seats around the side airbag locations. If damage is evident, consult a Saab dealer or specialist.
5 In the interests of safety, make sure that there are no loose items inside the car which could be thrown onto the airbag modules in the event of an accident.

11 Headlight beam alignment – check

Refer to Chapter 12, Section 8 for details.

12 Power steering fluid level – check

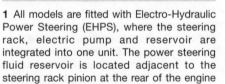

1 All models are fitted with Electro-Hydraulic Power Steering (EHPS), where the steering rack, electric pump and reservoir are integrated into one unit. The power steering fluid reservoir is located adjacent to the steering rack pinion at the rear of the engine compartment **(see illustration)**.
2 The fluid level should be checked with the engine stopped. Unscrew the filler cap from the top of the reservoir, and wipe all fluid from the cap dipstick with a clean rag. Refit the filler cap, then remove it again. Note the fluid level on the dipstick **(see illustration)**.

3 When the engine is cold, the fluid level should be between the upper MAX and lower MIN marks on the dipstick. Where only one mark is provided, the level should be between the bottom of the dipstick and the mark **(see illustration)**.

4 Top-up the fluid level using the specified type of fluid (do not overfill the reservoir), then refit and tighten the filler cap.

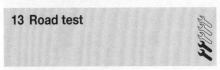

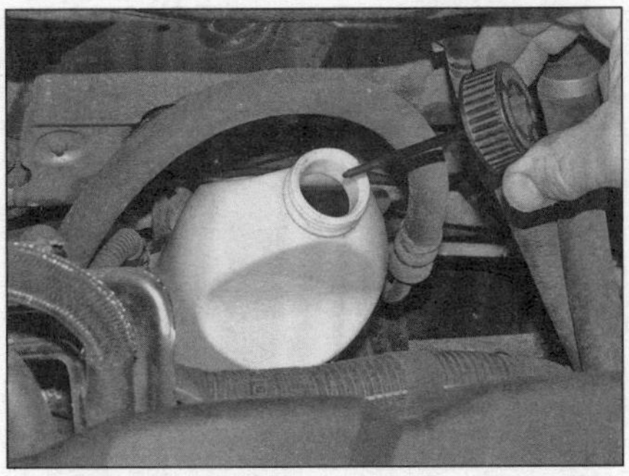

12.2 Unscrew the filler cap – the level dipstick is integral with the cap

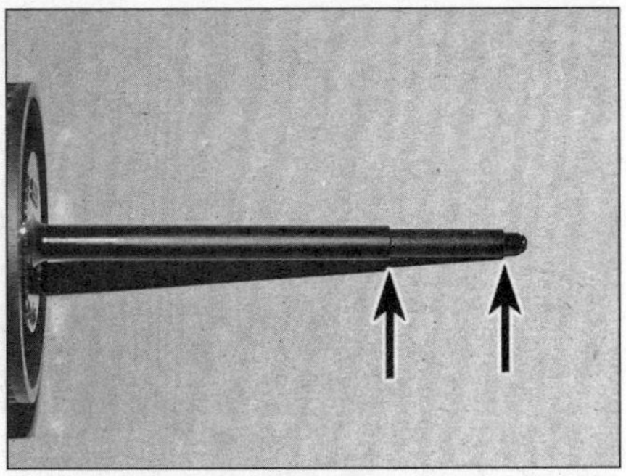

12.3 Fluid level upper and lower marks (arrowed)

13 Road test

Instruments and electrical equipment

1 Check the operation of all instruments and electrical equipment.

2 Make sure that all instruments read correctly, and switch on all electrical equipment in turn to check that it functions properly. Check the function of the heating, air conditioning and automatic climate control systems.

Steering and suspension

3 Check for any abnormalities in the steering, suspension, handling or road 'feel'.

4 Drive the vehicle, and check that there are no unusual vibrations or noises.

5 Check that the steering feels positive, with no excessive 'sloppiness', or roughness, and check for any suspension noises when cornering, or when driving over bumps. Check that the power steering system operates correctly.

Drivetrain

6 Check the performance of the engine, clutch (manual transmission), transmission and driveshafts. Check that the turbo boost pressure needle moves up to the upper limit during sharp acceleration. The needle may occasionally enter the red zone for an instant, but if this happens frequently, or for extended periods, a problem may exist within the turbo boost control mechanism (see Chapter 4B, Section 9).

7 Listen for any unusual noises from the engine, clutch (manual transmission) and transmission.

8 Make sure that the engine runs smoothly when idling, and that there is no hesitation when accelerating.

9 On manual transmission models, check that the clutch action is smooth and progressive, that the drive is taken up smoothly, and that the pedal travel is correct. Also listen for any noises when the clutch pedal is depressed. Check that all gears can be engaged smoothly, without noise, and that the gear lever action is smooth and not abnormally vague or 'notchy'.

10 On automatic transmission models, make sure that all gearchanges occur smoothly without snatching, and without an increase in engine speed between changes. Check that all the gear positions can be selected with the vehicle at rest. If any problems are found, they should be referred to a Saab dealer.

11 Listen for a metallic clicking sound from the front of the vehicle, as the vehicle is driven slowly in a circle with the steering on full lock. Carry out this check in both directions. If a clicking noise is heard, this indicates wear in a driveshaft joint, in which case, refer to Chapter 8, Section 3.

Braking system

12 Make sure that the vehicle does not pull to one side when braking, and that the wheels do not lock when braking hard.

13 Check that there is no vibration through the steering when braking.

14 Check that the handbrake operates correctly, without excessive movement of the lever, and that it holds the vehicle stationary on a slope.

15 Test the operation of the brake servo unit as follows. With the engine off, depress the footbrake four or five times to exhaust the vacuum, then start the engine while holding the brake pedal depressed. As the engine starts, there should be a noticeable 'give' in the brake pedal as vacuum builds-up. Allow the engine to run for at least two minutes, and then switch it off. If the brake pedal is now depressed again, it should be possible to detect a 'hiss' from the servo as the pedal is depressed. After about four or five applications, no further sound should be heard, and the pedal should feel considerably harder.

14 Coolant antifreeze concentration – check

1 The cooling system should be filled with the recommended antifreeze and corrosion protection fluid. Over a period of time, the concentration of fluid may be reduced due to topping-up (this can be avoided by topping-up with the correct antifreeze mixture) or fluid loss. If loss of coolant has been evident, it is important to make the necessary repair before adding fresh fluid. The exact mixture of antifreeze-to-water which you should use depends on the relative weather conditions. The mixture should contain at least 40% antifreeze, but not more than 70%. Consult the mixture ratio chart on the antifreeze container before adding coolant. Use antifreeze which meets the vehicle manufacturer's specifications. Note that antifreeze coolant available from Saab dealers is premixed with water at the correct ratio.

2 With the engine cold, carefully remove the cap from the expansion tank. If the engine is not completely cold, place a cloth rag over the cap before removing it, and remove it slowly to allow any pressure to escape.

3 Antifreeze checkers are available from car accessory shops. Draw some coolant from the expansion tank and observe how many plastic balls are floating in the checker. Usually, 2 or 3 balls must be floating for the correct concentration of antifreeze, but follow the manufacturer's instructions **(see illustration)**.

4 If the concentration is incorrect, it will be necessary to either withdraw some coolant and add undiluted antifreeze, or alternatively drain the old coolant and add fresh coolant of the correct concentration.

15 Driveshaft joints and gaiters – check

1 With the front of the vehicle raised and securely supported on stands, turn the steering onto full lock then slowly rotate the roadwheel. Inspect the condition of the outer constant velocity (CV) joint rubber gaiters while squeezing the gaiters to open out the folds

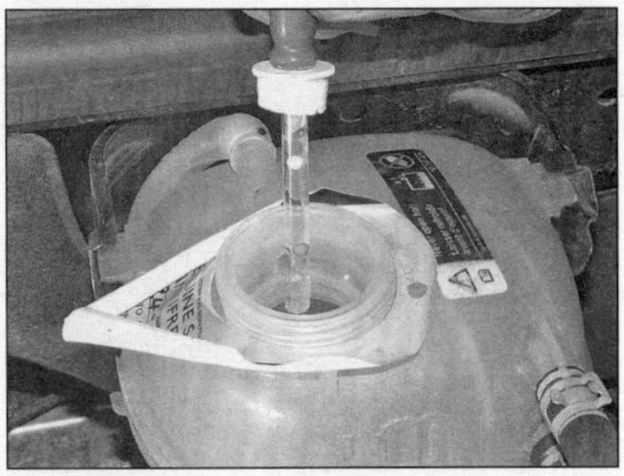

14.3 Follow the manufacturer's instructions when using an antifreeze checker

15.1 Check the condition of the driveshaft gaiters (1) and the retaining clips (2)

18.2 Push in the centre pin and prise out the plastic clip securing the scuttle trim panel

(see illustration). Check for signs of cracking, splits or deterioration of the rubber which may allow the grease to escape and lead to water and grit entry into the joint. Also check the security and condition of the retaining clips. Repeat these checks on the inner CV joints. If any damage or deterioration is found, the gaiters should be renewed as described in Chapter 8, Section 4.

2 At the same time check the general condition of the CV joints themselves by first holding the driveshaft and attempting to rotate the wheel. Repeat this check by holding the inner joint and attempting to rotate the driveshaft. Any appreciable movement indicates wear in the joints, wear in the driveshaft splines or a loose driveshaft retaining nut.

16 Exhaust system – check

1 With the engine cold, check the complete exhaust system, from its starting point at the engine to the end of the tailpipe. If necessary, raise the front and rear of the vehicle and support it on axle stands (see *Jacking and vehicle support*). Remove any engine undershields as necessary for full access to the exhaust system.

2 Check the exhaust pipes and connections for evidence of leaks, severe corrosion, and damage. Make sure that all brackets and mountings are in good condition and that all relevant nuts and bolts are tight. Leakage at any of the joints or in other parts of the system will usually show up as a black sooty stain in the vicinity of the leak.

3 Rattles and other noises can often be traced to the exhaust system, especially the brackets and rubber mountings. Try to move the pipes and silencers. If the components are able to come into contact with the body or suspension parts, secure the system with new mountings. Otherwise separate the joints (if possible) and twist the pipes as necessary to provide additional clearance.

17 Hinges and locks – lubrication

1 Work around the vehicle and lubricate the hinges of the bonnet, doors and tailgate with a light machine oil.

2 Lightly lubricate the two bonnet release locks with a smear of grease.

3 Check carefully the security and operation of all hinges, latches and locks. Check that the central locking system operates correctly.

4 Check the condition and operation of the bonnet and boot/tailgate struts, renewing them if either is leaking or no longer able to support the bonnet/tailgate.

18 Pollen air filter – renew

1 Set the wipers in the Service position by turning on the ignition switch, then turning it to the LOCK position, then move the wiper switch downwards until the wipers are in the vertical position.

2 Open the bonnet, remove the clips securing the left-hand side of the scuttle trim panel **(see illustration)**. On Convertible models, also remove the clip at the corner of the panel.

3 Pull the bulkhead rubber seal upwards from the left-hand side **(see illustration)**.

4 Lift up the foam block, and lift the front edge of the scuttle trim panel, then fold it over the right-hand side.

5 Remove the water barrier. Note that the water barrier is not fitted to all models.

6 Release the 2 retaining clips and lift the filter from place **(see illustrations)**.

18.3 Pull the rubber bulkhead seal upwards

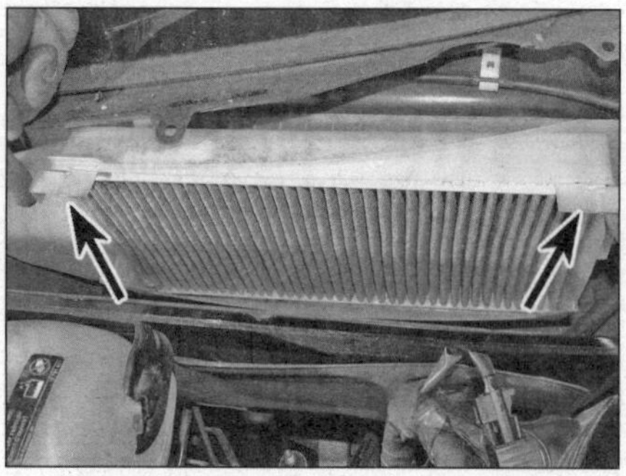

18.6a Lift up the 2 clips (arrowed) ...

18.6b ... and lift the filter from place

18.7 The arrow indicates airflow

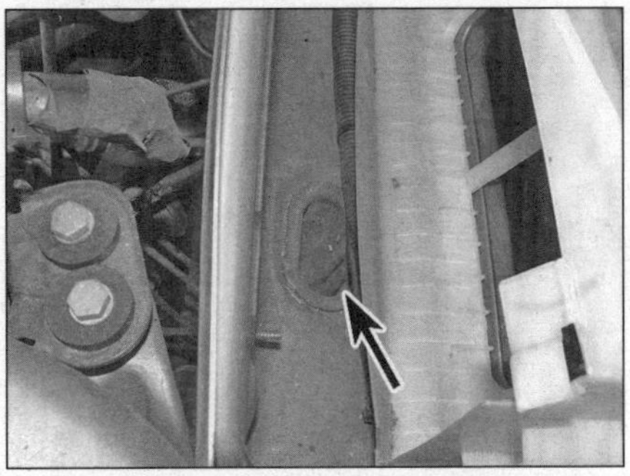
19.2 Check the plenum chamber drain hole (arrowed) is clear

20.2 Remove the wheel arch liner to expose the crankshaft pulley and auxiliary belt

7 Fit the new element using a reversal of the removal procedure **(see illustration)**.

19 Plenum chamber drain hose – clean

1 Remove the pollen filter element as described in Section 18.
2 Lift the drain hose from place and clean it **(see illustration)**.
3 Refit the drain hose, making sure that it is secure.

20 Auxiliary drivebelt condition – check

1 On all engines, a single, multi-grooved auxiliary drivebelt is used to transmit drive from the crankshaft pulley to the alternator, power steering pump (if applicable) and the refrigerant compressor. The drivebelt is tensioned automatically by a spring-loaded tensioner pulley.
2 For better access to the drivebelt, apply the handbrake then jack up the front of the car and support it on axle stands (see *Jacking and vehicle support*). Remove the right-hand front roadwheel, then remove the plastic liner from under the right-hand wheel arch to expose the crankshaft pulley **(see illustration)**.

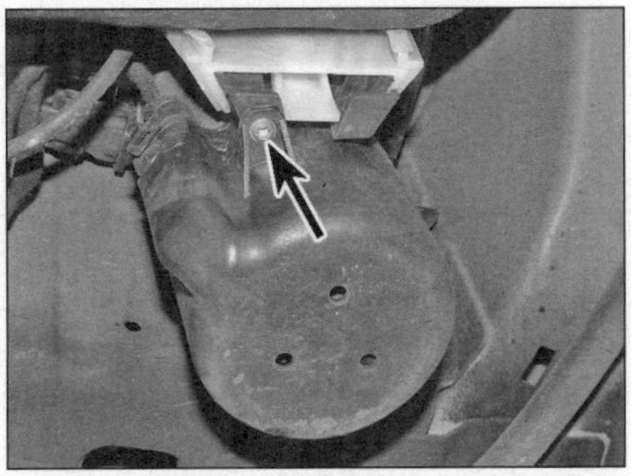
21.2 Undo the Torx screw (arrowed) and lower the plastic cover

3 Using a suitable socket and extension bar fitted to the crankshaft pulley bolt, rotate the crankshaft so that the entire length of the drivebelt can be examined. Examine the drivebelt for cracks, splitting, fraying, or other damage. Check also for signs of glazing (shiny patches) and for separation of the belt plies. Renew the belt if worn or damaged.

21 Fuel filter – renewal

Warning: Absolute cleanliness must be observed during this procedure. Even the smallest particle of dirt could cause extensive damage to the fuel system.

21.3a Disconnect the sensor wiring plug (arrowed) ...

1 The fuel filter is attached to the left-hand side of the fuel tank under the vehicle. One of two types may be fitted.
2 Where fitted, undo the Torx screw and pull down the protective cover on the base of the filter **(see illustration)**.
3 Disconnect the water sensor wiring plug then unscrew the sensor from the base of the filter **(see illustrations)**. Some models do not have the sensor fitted, on these slacken the drain plug. Be prepared for fuel spillage – position a container under the filter to catch the fuel.
4 Unscrew the filter cartridge (or cap) from the housing, using a strap wrench, filter removal tool or suitable socket **(see illustration)**.

21.3b ... then unscrew the sensor and allow the filter to drain

21.4 Using a filter removal tool to unscrew the filter

21.5a Lubricate the filter seal with clean fuel ...

21.5b ... and screw it into position

Recover the seal on models fitted with the paper type filter.

5 Lubricate the new filter seal (or the new O-ring on the paper type filter) with a little clean diesel fuel, then screw the new filter into position **(see illustrations)**. On the paper insert type filter fit the new filter to the cap and screw it into position. Tighten the filter to the specified torque.

6 Where fitted screw the water sensor into the base of the new filter, ensuring the rubber seal is fitted.

7 Reconnect the water sensor wiring plug, refit the cover and tighten the retaining screw.

8 Start the engine, and check the filter for leaks.

9 The old filter should be disposed of safely.

Every 36 000 miles

Note: *The 36 000 mile intervals start at 42 000 miles, ie, at 42 000 miles, 78 000 miles, 114 000 miles, etc.*

22 Valve clearances – check and adjustment

Note: *This procedure only applies to 1.9 litre SOHC 8v engines. The 1.9 litre DOHC 16v engine is equipped with hydraulic tappets, which are maintenance-free.*

1 Refer to Chapter 2B, Section 10 for the procedure description.

23 Air filter element – renewal

1 The air cleaner is located on the front right-hand corner of the engine compartment.

2 Slide out the locking catch, depress the clip, and disconnect the mass airflow sensor wiring plug **(see illustration)**.

3 Release the clamp and disconnect the outlet hose from the mass airflow sensor **(see illustration)**.

4 Undo the 5 Torx screws and remove the air filter cover **(see illustration)**.

5 Lift out the air cleaner filter element, noting which way round it is fitted **(see illustration)**.

6 Wipe clean the inner surfaces of the cover and main housing, then locate the new element in the housing, making sure that the sealing lip is correctly engaged with the edge of the housing **(see illustration)**.

7 Refit the cover, and securely tighten the Torx screws.

8 Reconnect the air outlet hose and secure it by tightening the hose clip.

9 Reconnect the mass airflow sensor wiring plug.

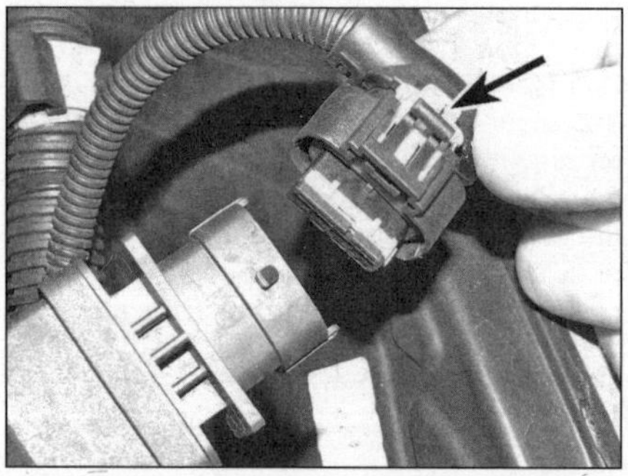

23.2 Slide out the yellow locking catch (arrowed), depress the clip and disconnect the airflow sensor wiring plug

23.3 Slacken the air outlet hose clamp (arrowed)

24 Manual transmission fluid level – check

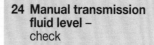

Note: *There is no requirement in the Saab service schedule to check the transmission fluid level. However, we consider it prudent to carry out the following procedure on 5-speed transmissions at the mileage specified in the schedule at the start of this Chapter.*

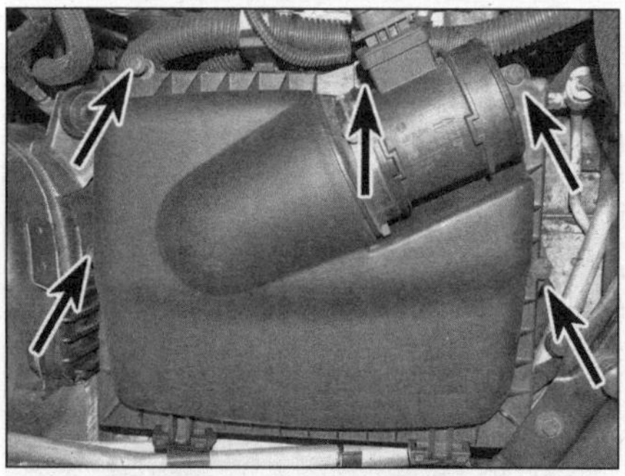

23.4 The filter cover is secured by 5 Torx screws (arrowed)

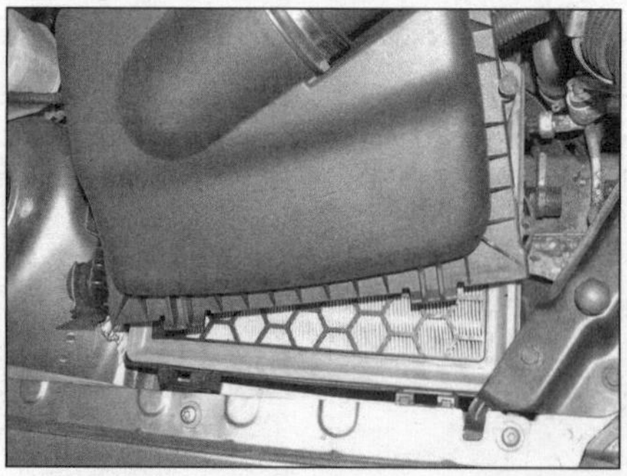

23.5 Lift off the cover and remove the element

23.6 Fit the new element with the rubber seal uppermost

5-speed transmission

1 Take the car on a short journey to warm the transmission up to normal operating temperature. Position the car over an inspection pit, or alternatively jack up the front and rear of the car and support on axle stands (see *Jacking and vehicle support*). Whichever method is used, make sure that the car is level for checking the fluid level later. Undo the fasteners and remove the engine undershield **(see illustration 3.4)**.

2 Position a suitable container beneath the transmission, then unscrew the filler/level plug located on the left-hand side of the transmission casing **(see illustration)**.

3 The fluid level should be up to the bottom of the filler/level plug hole. If necessary, add the specified fluid until it begins to run out of the hole.

4 Refit the filler/level plug and tighten it to the specified torque.

5 Lower the vehicle to the ground.

6-speed transmission

6 No level plug is fitted to the 6-speed transmission casing, nor is there any requirement in the Saab service schedule to check or change the fluid. If it is necessary to ensure the transmission has the correct quantity of fluid, it will need to be drained and refilled as described in Chapter 7A, Section 2.

24.2 Unscrew the filler/level plug (arrowed) - 5-speed transmission

Every 48 000 miles

Note: *The 48 000 mile intervals start at 54 000 miles, ie, at 54 000 miles, 102 000 miles, etc.*

25 Timing belt renewal

1 Refer to Chapter 2B, Section 7 (SOHC 8v engines) or Chapter 2C, Section 6 (DOHC 16v engines) as applicable.

Every 60 000 miles

Note: *The 60 000 mile intervals start at 66 000 miles, ie, at 66 000 miles, 126 000 miles, etc.*

26 Automatic transmission fluid – renewal

1 Take the car on a short journey to warm the transmission up to normal operating temperature. Position the car over an inspection pit, or alternatively jack up the front and rear of the car and support on axle stands (see *Jacking and vehicle support*). Whichever method is used, make sure that the car is level for checking the fluid level later. Undo the fasteners and remove the engine undershield.

5-speed transmission

2 On Convertible models, undo the bolts and remove the front chassis reinforcement **(see illustration)**.

3 Position a suitable container beneath the transmission, then unscrew the drain plug and allow the fluid to drain **(see illustration)**.

Warning: The fluid will be very hot, so take necessary precautions to prevent scalding. The use of thick waterproof gloves is recommended.

4 With all the fluid drained, wipe clean the plug and refit it to the automatic transmission housing. Where applicable fit a new sealing washer. Tighten the plug to the specified torque.

5 Remove the level dipstick, and fill the automatic transmission with the specified

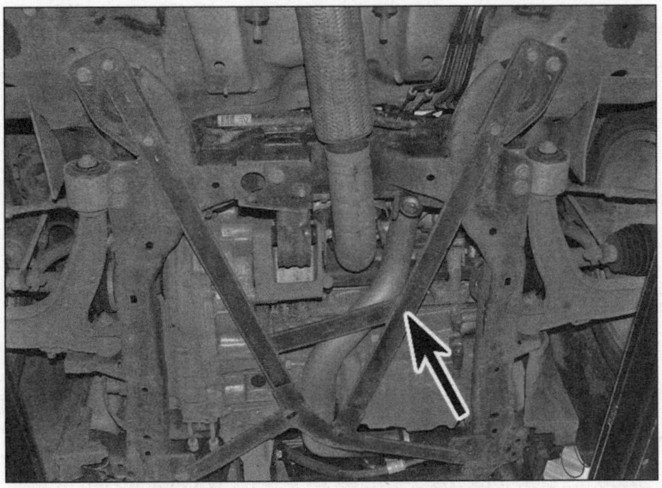

26.2 Front chassis reinforcement (arrowed) – Convertible models

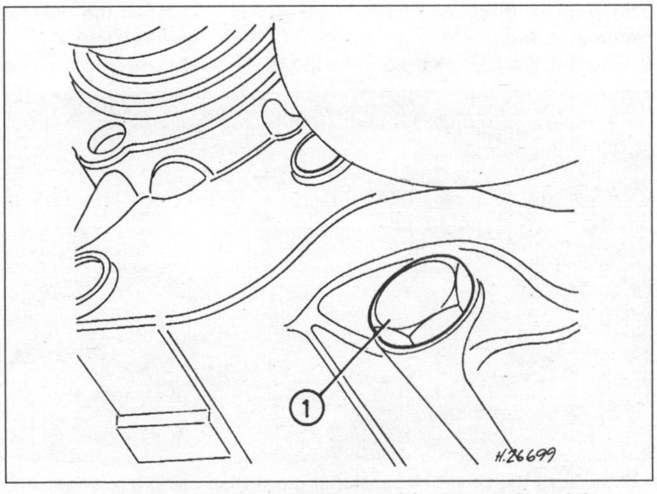

26.3 Transmission fluid drain plug (1) – 5-speed models

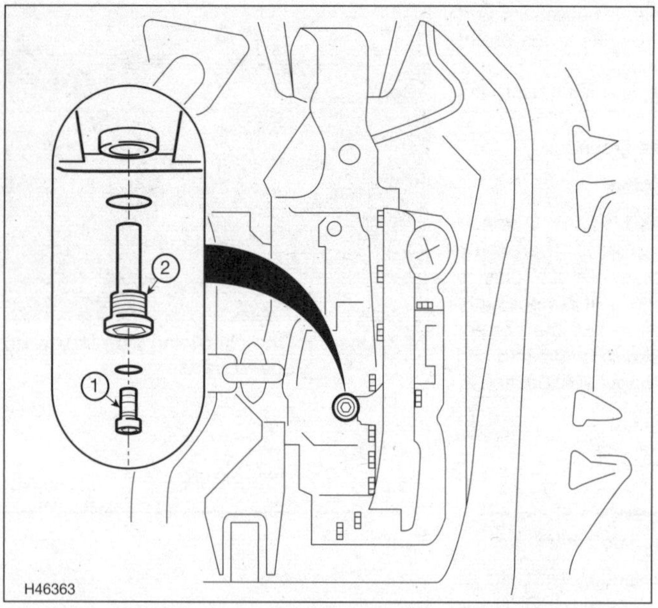

26.7 Transmission fluid level checking plug (1) and drain plug (2) – 6-speed transmissions

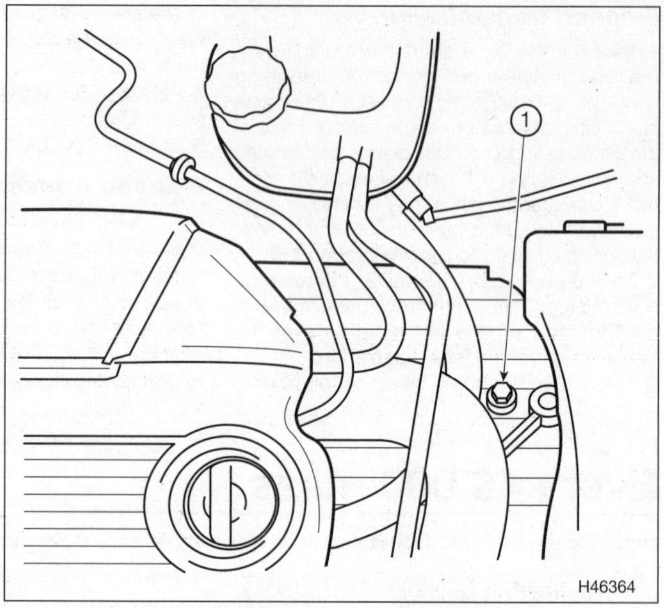

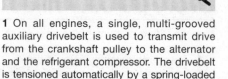

26.8 Transmission fluid filler plug (1)

grade and quantity of fluid through the dipstick hole. The use of a funnel and length of hose will make the task much easier. Use the low temperature set of dipstick markings first, then take the car for a run. With the fluid at operating temperature, recheck the fluid level using the high temperature set of dipstick markings. Note that the difference between the COLD and HOT dipstick markings is approximately 0.3 litres.

6 Where applicable refit the front chassis reinforcement and tighten the bolts to the specified torque.

6-speed transmission

7 Position a suitable container beneath the transmission, then unscrew the drain plug and allow the fluid to drain **(see illustration)**.

Warning: The fluid will be very hot, so take necessary precautions to prevent scalding. The use of thick waterproof gloves is recommended.

8 Unscrew the filler plug from the top of the casing and add approximately 3 litres of new fluid **(see illustration)**.

9 Lower the vehicle to the ground.

10 Run the engine until the fluid temperature is approximately 30° to 45°C, then move the selector lever through positions P to D, and back again, with the footbrake depressed. Allow the selector lever to rest in each position for 2 seconds. Repeat this procedure twice.

11 Raise the vehicle again, place a receptacle under the transmission drain/level plug, and unscrew the level screw from the centre of the plug. If the level is too high, excess fluid will flow out of the level hole – refit the screw and tighten it securely. If no fluid runs out, top-up the fluid level through the filler plug hole on the top of the transmission casing, until fluid emerges from the level hole. Allow the excess to drain and refit the level screw securely.

12 Refit the filler plug and tighten it to the specified torque.

13 Lower the vehicle to the ground.

27 Auxiliary drivebelt – renewal

1 On all engines, a single, multi-grooved auxiliary drivebelt is used to transmit drive from the crankshaft pulley to the alternator and the refrigerant compressor. The drivebelt is tensioned automatically by a spring-loaded tensioner pulley.

2 For better access to the drivebelt, apply the handbrake then jack up the front of the car and support it on axle stands (see *Jacking and vehicle support*). Remove the right-hand front roadwheel, then remove the plastic liner from under the right-hand wheel arch to expose the crankshaft pulley.

3 The tensioner pulley spring must now be compressed and locked in position. Using a spanner or socket and bar, rotate the tensioner clockwise, then insert a locking pin/5 mm drill bit once the holes in the arm and body align, to lock the tensioner in place **(see illustrations)**.

27.3a Turn the drivebelt tensioner clockwise using a spanner on the pulley centre bolt (arrowed) ...

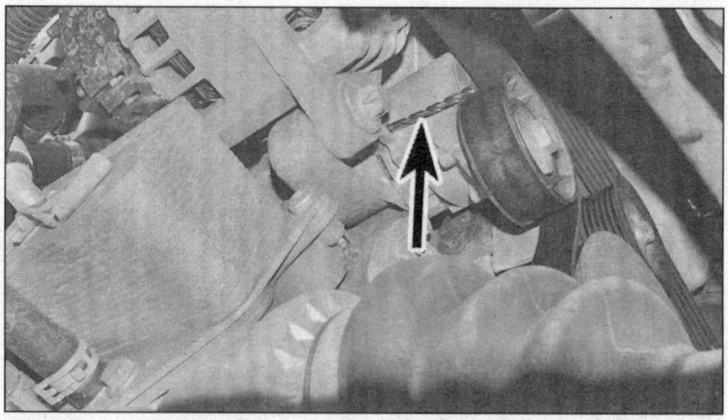

27.3b ... then lock the tensioner by inserting a locking pin or drill bit (arrowed) through the special hole

4 Slip the drivebelt from the pulleys, then remove it from the engine compartment from the right-hand wheel arch. If the belt is to be re-used, mark its direction of rotation.
5 Locate the drivebelt over all the pulleys, making sure that the multi-grooved side is correctly engaged with the grooves on the pulleys **(see illustration)**.
6 Compress the tensioner spring and withdrawn the locking pin/drill bit. Slowly release the tensioner, allowing it to apply pressure to the rear surface of drivebelt.
7 Ensure that the belt is correctly seated on all the pulleys, then start the engine and allow it to idle for a few minutes. This will allow the tensioner to settle in position and distribute the tension evenly throughout the belt. Stop the engine and check once again that the belt is correctly seated on all the pulleys.
8 On completion, refit the plastic wheel arch liner and roadwheel, and then lower the car to the ground.

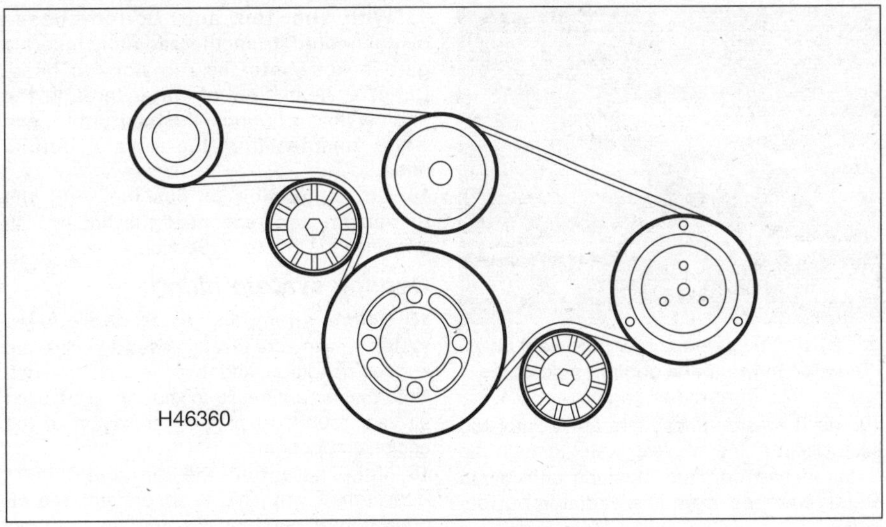

27.5 Auxiliary drivebelt routing

Every 3 years

28 Coolant – renewal

Note: *This work is not included in the Saab schedule, and should not be required if the recommended Saab antifreeze/inhibitor is used.*

Warning: Do not allow antifreeze to come in contact with your skin or painted surfaces of the vehicle. Flush contaminated areas immediately with plenty of water. Don't store new coolant, or leave old coolant lying around, where it's accessible to children or pets – they're attracted by its sweet smell. Ingestion of even a small amount of coolant can be fatal. Wipe up garage-floor and drip-pan spills immediately. Keep antifreeze containers covered, and repair cooling system leaks as soon as they're noticed.

Warning: Never remove the expansion tank filler cap when the engine is running, or has just been switched off, as the cooling system will be hot, and the consequent escaping steam and scalding coolant could cause serious injury.

Warning: Wait until the engine is cold before starting these procedures.

Cooling system draining

1 With the engine completely cold, remove the expansion tank filler cap. Turn the cap anti-clockwise, wait until any pressure remaining in the system is released, then unscrew it and lift it off.
2 Raise the front of the vehicle and support it on axle stands (see *Jacking and vehicle support*).
3 Undo the screws and remove the undershield beneath the radiator. Note the retaining screws in the wheel arch liner **(see illustrations)**.
4 Attach a hose to the drain plug on the right-hand side of the radiator, and position the other end of the hose in a suitable container. Slacken the drain plug and allow the coolant to drain into the container **(see illustration)**.
5 When the flow of coolant stops, tighten the drain plug, remove the hose, and refit the undershield. Lower the vehicle to the ground.
6 If the coolant has been drained for a reason other than renewal, then provided it is clean and less than two years old, it can be re-used, though this is not recommended.

Cooling system flushing

7 If coolant renewal has been neglected, or if the antifreeze mixture has become diluted, then in time the cooling system may gradually lose efficiency, as the coolant passages become restricted due to rust, scale deposits and other sediment. The cooling system efficiency can be restored by flushing the system clean.
8 The radiator should be flushed independently of the engine, to avoid unnecessary contamination.

Radiator flushing

9 Disconnect the top and bottom hoses and any other relevant hoses from the radiator, with reference to Chapter 3, Section 3.

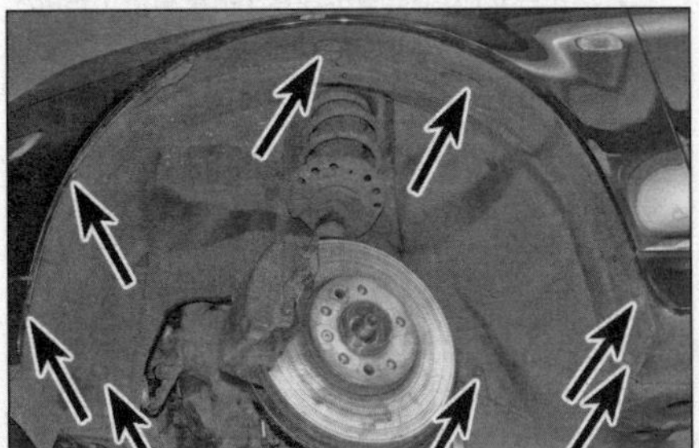
28.3a Wheel arch liner screws/nuts (arrowed)

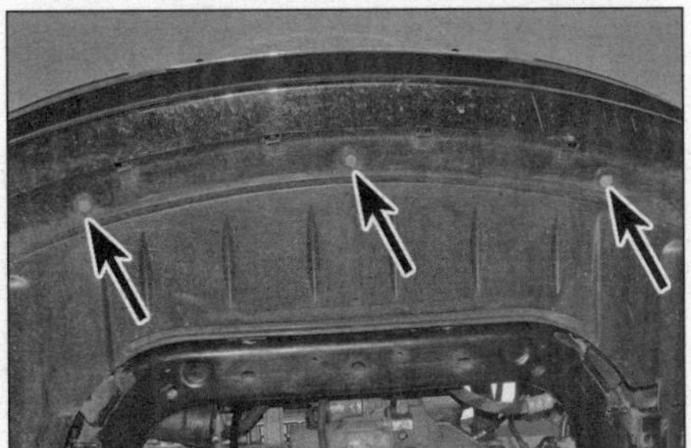
28.3b Radiator undershield central bolts (arrowed)

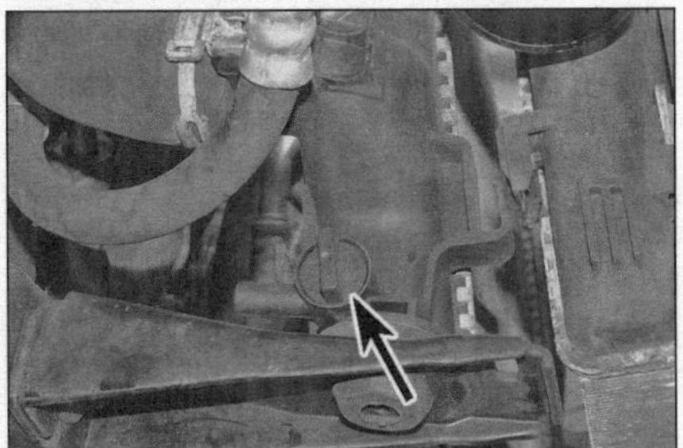
28.4 The drain plug (arrowed) is located on the right-hand end of the radiator

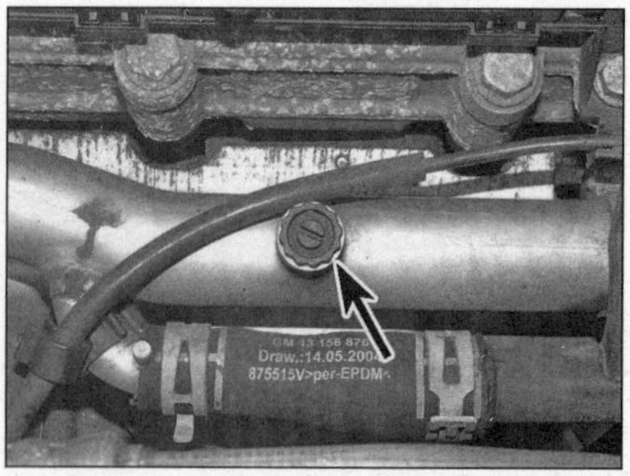

28.18 The bleed screw (arrowed) is located in the metal coolant pipe at the front of the engine

10 Insert a garden hose into the radiator top inlet. Direct a flow of clean water through the radiator, and continue flushing until clean water emerges from the radiator bottom outlet.

11 If after a reasonable period, the water still does not run clear, the radiator can be flushed with a good proprietary cleaning agent. It is important that the manufacturer's instructions are followed carefully. If the contamination is particularly bad, remove the radiator and insert the hose in the bottom outlet, and reverse-flush the radiator, then refit it.

Engine flushing

12 Remove the thermostat housing as described in Chapter 3, Section 4. If the radiator top hose has been disconnected, temporarily reconnect the hose.

13 With the top and bottom hoses disconnected from the radiator, insert a garden hose into the radiator top hose. Direct a clean flow of water through the engine, and continue flushing until clean water emerges from the radiator bottom hose.

14 On completion of flushing, refit the thermostat and reconnect the hoses with reference to Chapter 3, Section 4.

Cooling system filling

15 Before attempting to fill the cooling system, make sure that all hoses and clips are in good condition, and that the clips are tight. Note that an antifreeze mixture must be used all year round, to prevent corrosion of the engine components.

16 Make sure that the air conditioning is switched off. This is to prevent the air conditioning system starting the radiator cooling fan before the engine is at normal temperature when refilling the system.

17 Remove the expansion tank filler cap and slowly fill the system until the coolant level reaches 30 mm above the MAX mark on the side of the expansion tank.

18 Undo the bleed screw in the coolant pipe at the front of the engine (Z19DT and Z19DTH engines) **(see illustration)** or on the thermostat housing (Z19DTR engines). Allow any trapped air to escape, and close the bleed screw once bubble-free coolant emerges from the pipe.

19 Check the coolant level, top-up if necessary, then refit and tighten the expansion tank filler cap.

20 Start the engine and set the heater to hot, then run the engine until it reaches normal operating temperature (until the cooling fan cuts in and out). Running the engine at varying speeds will allow the engine to warm-up quickly.

21 Stop the engine, and allow it to cool, then recheck the coolant level with reference to *Weekly checks*. Top-up the level if necessary and refit the expansion tank filler cap.

Antifreeze mixture

22 Always use an ethylene-glycol based antifreeze which is suitable for use in mixed-metal cooling systems. The quantity of antifreeze and levels of protection are given in the Specifications.

23 Before adding antifreeze, the cooling system should be completely drained, preferably flushed, and all hoses checked for condition and security.

24 After filling with antifreeze, a label should be attached to the expansion tank, stating the type and concentration of antifreeze used, and the date installed. Any subsequent topping-up should be made with the same type and concentration of antifreeze.

Caution: Do not use engine antifreeze in the windscreen/tailgate washer system, as it will cause damage to the vehicle paintwork. A screenwash additive should be added to the washer system in the quantities stated on the bottle.

Every 4 years

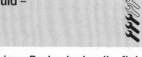

29 Brake fluid – renewal

Warning: Brake hydraulic fluid can harm your eyes and damage painted surfaces, so use extreme caution when handling and pouring it. Do not use fluid that has been standing open for some time, as it absorbs moisture from the air. Excess moisture can cause a dangerous loss of braking effectiveness.

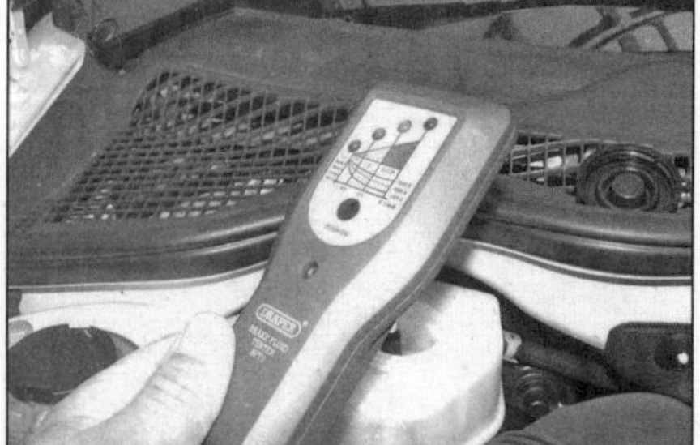

29.0 A brake fluid tester can be used to test the water content of the brake fluid

Note: *If no equipment is available for testing the quality of the brake fluid, it is recommended that the brake fluid is renewed every 2 years* ***(see illustration).***

1 The procedure is similar to that for the bleeding of the hydraulic system as described in Chapter 9, Section 2.

2 Working as described in Chapter 9, Section 2, open the first bleed screw in the sequence, and pump the brake pedal gently until nearly all the old fluid has been emptied from the master cylinder reservoir. Top-up to the MAX level with new fluid, and continue pumping until only the new fluid remains in the reservoir, and new fluid can be seen emerging from the bleed screw. Tighten the screw, and top the reservoir level up to the MAX level line.

3 Work through all the remaining bleed screws in the sequence until new fluid can be seen at all of them. Be careful to keep the master cylinder reservoir topped-up to above the MIN level at all times, or air may enter the system and greatly increase the length of the task.

4 When the operation is complete, check that all bleed screws are securely tightened, and that their dust caps are refitted. Wash off all traces of spilt fluid, and recheck the master cylinder reservoir fluid level.

5 Check the operation of the brakes before taking the car on the road.

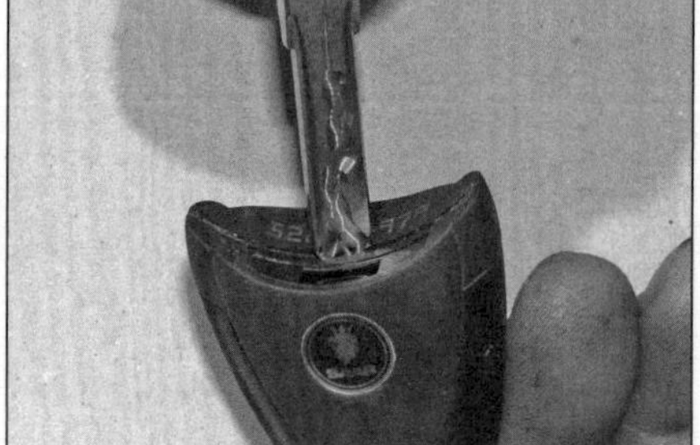

30.2 Insert the end of the key into the small slot, and twist the two halves apart

30 Remote control battery – renewal

1 Press in the badge on the back of the remote control and pull out the emergency key.

2 Insert the end of the key into the small hole, then twist it to separate the 2 halves of the control **(see illustration)**.

3 Note how it's fitted (positive side down), then remove the battery from the control. **Note:** *Avoid touching the battery contacts or remote control circuitry with bare fingers.*
4 Insert the new battery, and clip together the two halves of the control **(see illustration)**.
5 It is now necessary to synchronise the control with the receiver, by inserting the key into the ignition switch. If the vehicle is locked, unlock it with the emergency key (the alarm will sound), insert the remote control into the ignition switch and turn it on. This will synchronise the components, and turn off the alarm siren.

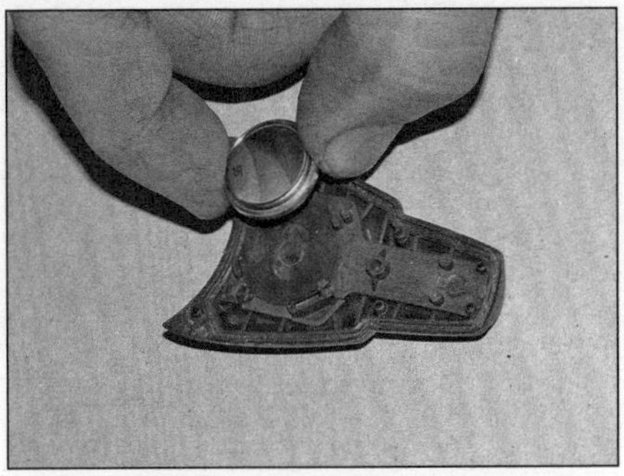

30.4 Insert the new battery positive (+) side down

Notes

Chapter 2 Part A:
Petrol engine in-car repair procedures

Contents

Degrees of difficulty

Easy, suitable for novice with little experience	**Fairly easy,** suitable for beginner with some experience	**Fairly difficult,** suitable for competent DIY mechanic	**Difficult,** suitable for experienced DIY mechanic	**Very difficult,** suitable for expert DIY or professional

Specifications

General

Engine type	Four-cylinder, in-line, water-cooled. Chain-driven, 16 valve, DOHC (double overhead camshaft), aluminium alloy cylinder head and engine block
Designation:	
1998 cc 110 kW turbocharged	B207E
1998 cc 129 kW turbocharged	B207L
1998 cc 154 kW turbocharged	B207R
Bore	86.00 mm
Stroke	86.00 mm
Direction of crankshaft rotation	Clockwise (viewed from right-hand side of vehicle)
No 1 cylinder location	At timing chain end of engine
Compression ratio	9.5 : 1
Minimum compression pressure	12.4 bar
Maximum power/torque:	
B207E	110 kW @ 3500 rpm/240 Nm
B207L	129 kW @ 5800 rpm/265 Nm
B207R	154 kW @ 5300 rpm/300 Nm

Camshafts

Drive	Chain from crankshaft
Number of bearings	6 per camshaft
Camshaft bearing journal diameter (outside diameter)	26.935 to 26.960 mm
Endfloat (without camshaft sprocket)	0.104 to 0.177 mm
Camshaft lobe lift:	
Intake	9.7 mm
Exhaust	9.9 mm

Lubrication system

Oil pump type	Bi-rotor type in timing cover, driven off the crankshaft
Minimum oil pressure at 80°C:	
Crankcase	2.0 bar at 1000 rpm
Cylinder head	0.8 bar at 1000 rpm
Oil pressure warning switch operating pressure	0.3 bar
Pressure release valve opens at	5.0 bar
Oil cooler thermostat starts to open at	107°C approximately

Torque wrench settings	Nm	lbf ft
Air conditioning compressor	24	18
Alternator	20	15
Auxiliary belt tensioner	50	37
Balance shaft chain guide bolts	10	7
Balance shaft chain sprocket centre bolt:		
Stage 1	8	6
Stage 2	Angle-tighten a further 30°	
Balance shaft chain tensioner	10	7
Balance shaft retaining bolts	10	7
Big-end bearing cap:*		
Stage 1	25	18
Stage 2	Angle-tighten a further 100°	
Camshaft bearing cap:		
M6	8	6
M8	22	16
Camshaft sprockets:		
Stage 1	85	63
Stage 2	Angle-tighten a further 30°	
Coolant pump:		
Long bolt	25	18
Short bolts	20	15
Coolant pump sprocket	8	6
Crankshaft pulley bolt:*		
Stage 1	100	74
Stage 2	Angle-tighten a further 75°	
Cylinder head bolts:*		
Stage 1	30	22
Stage 2	Angle-tighten a further 150°	
Stage 3	Angle-tighten a further 15°	
Cylinder head cover	10	7
Cylinder head to timing cover	35	26
Driveplate to crankshaft:*		
Stage 1	65	48
Stage 2	Angle-tighten a further 40°	
Engine mountings:		
RH mounting bracket to engine	93	69
RH mounting pad to engine bracket:		
Stage 1	70	52
Stage 2	Angle-tighten a further 60°	
RH mounting pad to body:		
Stage 1	40	30
Stage 2	Angle-tighten a further 60°	
LH mounting pad to body:		
Stage 1	15	11
Stage 2	Angle-tighten a further 30°	
LH mounting bracket to manual transmission:		
Stage 1	35	26
Stage 2	Angle-tighten a further 90°	
LH mounting bracket to automatic gearbox	93	69
LH mounting pad to bracket:		
Stage 1	70	52
Stage 2	Angle-tighten a further 45°	
Rear torque arm to sump	37	27
Rear torque arm to subframe:		
Stage 1	60	44
Stage 2	Angle-tighten a further 90°	
Torque arm bracket to transmission	80	59
Torque arm to subframe:		
Stage 1	60	44
Stage 2	Angle-tighten a further 90°	
Torque arm to transmission bracket:		
Stage 1	70	52
Stage 2	Angle-tighten a further 90°	
Engine oil drain plug	25	18
Flywheel:*		
Stage 1	65	48
Stage 2	Angle-tighten a further 40°	

Torque wrench settings

	Nm	lbf ft
Front chassis reinforcement bolts (Convertible only)	50	37
Main bearing intermediate section to cylinder block:		
M8	25	18
M10:		
Stage 1	20	15
Stage 2	Angle-tighten a further 70°	
Stage 3	Angle-tighten a further 15°	
Oil cooler thermostat	40	30
Oil cooler unit:		
To cylinder head	12	9
To cylinder block	22	16
Oil filter cap	25	18
Oil pick-up pipe	12	9
Oil pressure switch	18	13
Oil pressure relief valve plug	40	30
Oil pump cover	6	4
Piston cooling jet	15	11
Power steering pump	22	16
Roadwheel bolts	110	81
Sump:		
To crankcase	22	16
To transmission	70	52
Sump baffle	12	9
Thermostat housing	10	7
Timing chain:		
Guide bolt	10	7
Guide plug	25	18
Tensioner	75	55
Tensioner guide bolt	10	7
Timing cover	20	15
Vacuum pump	22	16

** Do not re-use*

1 General information

How to use this Chapter

Repair operations that can be carried out with the engine in the vehicle are described in Part A (petrol engines), Part B (1.9 litre SOHC diesel engines) and Part C (1.9 litre DOHC diesel engines). Part D covers the removal of the engine/transmission as a unit, and describes the engine dismantling and overhaul procedures.

In Parts A, B and C, the assumption is made that the engine is installed in the vehicle, with all ancillaries connected. If the engine has been removed for overhaul, the preliminary dismantling information which precedes each operation may be ignored.

Note that, while it may be possible to overhaul items such as the piston/connecting rod assemblies while the engine is in the car, such tasks are not normally carried out as separate operations. Usually, several additional procedures (including the cleaning of components and of oilways) have to be carried out, and these are more easily carried out with the engine removed from the vehicle. For this reason, all such tasks are classed as major overhaul procedures, and are described in Part D of this Chapter.

Engine description

The engine is of in-line four-cylinder, double-overhead camshaft (DOHC), 16-valve type, mounted transversely at the front of the car with the transmission attached to its left-hand end. The Saab 9-3 is fitted with 1998 cc engine which has balance shafts integral with the cylinder block, to smooth out vibrations. All engines are controlled by full engine management systems; see Chapter 4A, Section 4 for further details.

The crankshaft runs in five main bearings. Thrustwashers are fitted to the centre main bearing to control crankshaft endfloat. The main bearing caps are not separate, but are integrated into a common intermediate section/bearing ladder clamped between the sump and the engine block.

The connecting rods rotate on horizontally-split bearing shells at their big-ends. The pistons are attached to the connecting rods by fully-floating gudgeon pins, which are retained in the pistons by circlips. The aluminium-alloy pistons are fitted with three piston rings – two compression rings and an oil control ring.

The cylinder block is of aluminium, and the cylinder bores steel liners pressed into the cylinder block. The intake and exhaust valves are closed by coil springs, and operate in guides pressed into the cylinder head; the valve seat inserts are also pressed into the cylinder head, and can be renewed separately if worn. There are four valves per cylinder.

The camshafts are driven by a single-row timing chain, and they operate the 16 valves via hydraulic cam followers. The hydraulic cam followers maintain a predetermined clearance between the cam lobe and the end of the valve stem, using hydraulic chambers and a tension spring. The followers are fed with oil from the main engine lubrication circuit.

The balance shafts are driven in counter-rotation by a small single-row chain from a sprocket on the front of the crankshaft, that also drives the coolant pump. The balance shaft chain run is controlled by three fixed guide rails. The chain is located on the inside of the main camshaft timing chain, with its tension being controlled by a dedicated spring-loaded tensioner.

The engine/transmission assembly is supported on an hydraulic-type rubber mounting on the right-hand side, a rubber mounting on the left-hand side, and two torque arms underneath the engine/transmission assembly.

Lubrication is by means of a bi-rotor oil pump, driven from the front of the crankshaft and located in the timing cover. A relief valve in the timing cover limits the oil pressure at high engine speeds by returning excess oil to the sump. Oil is drawn from the sump through a strainer and, after passing through the oil pump, is forced through an externally-mounted filter and oil cooler (on certain models) into galleries in the cylinder block/crankcase. From there, the oil is distributed to the crankshaft (main bearings), balance shafts, camshaft bearings and hydraulic cam followers. It also lubricates the water-cooled turbocharger and the crankcase-mounted piston cooling jets. The big-end bearings are supplied with oil via internal drillings in the crankshaft, while the camshaft lobes and valves are lubricated by splash, as are all other engine components.

Repairs with engine in car

The following work can be carried out with the engine in the car:

a) Compression pressure – testing.
b) Cylinder head cover – removal and refitting.
c) Camshaft oil seals – renewal.
d) Camshafts – removal, inspection and refitting.
e) Cylinder head – removal and refitting.
f) Cylinder head and pistons – decarbonising (refer to Chapter 2D, Section 7).
g) Sump – removal and refitting.
h) Oil pump – removal, overhaul and refitting.
i) Crankshaft oil seals – renewal.
j) Flywheel/driveplate – removal, inspection and refitting.
k) Engine/transmission mountings – inspection and renewal.

2 Compression test – description and interpretation

1 When engine performance is down, or if misfiring occurs which cannot be attributed to the ignition or fuel systems, a compression test can provide diagnostic clues as to the engine's condition. If the test is performed regularly, it can give warning of trouble before any other symptoms become apparent.

2 The engine must be fully warmed-up to normal operating temperature, the battery must be fully-charged, and all the spark plugs must be removed (Chapter 1A, Section 24). The aid of an assistant will also be required.

3 Disable the ignition system by removing relay No 8 from the engine compartment electrical box.

4 Fit a compression tester to the No 1 cylinder spark plug hole – the type of tester which screws into the plug thread must be used to obtain accurate readings.

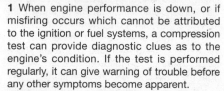

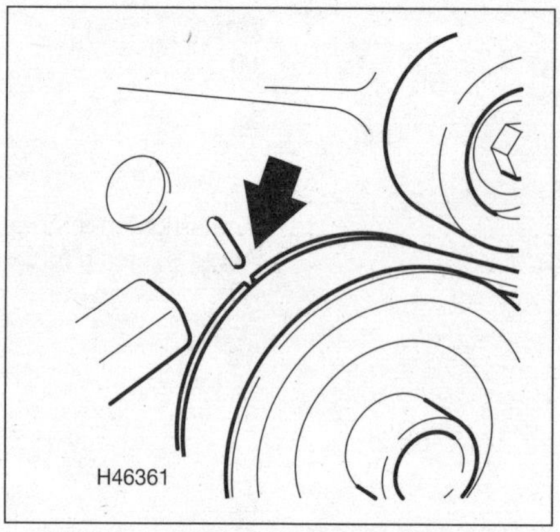

3.4 Crankshaft pulley and timing chain cover timing marks (arrowed)

5 Have the assistant depress the accelerator pedal fully, and crank the engine on the starter motor; after one or two revolutions, the compression pressure should build-up to a maximum figure, and then stabilise. Record the highest reading obtained.

6 Repeat the test on the remaining cylinders, recording the pressure in each.

7 All cylinders should produce very similar pressures; a difference of more than 2 bars between any two cylinders indicates a fault. Note that the compression should build-up quickly in a healthy engine; low compression on the first stroke, followed by gradually-increasing pressure on successive strokes, indicates worn piston rings. A low compression reading on the first stroke, which does not build-up during successive strokes, indicates leaking valves or a blown head gasket (a cracked cylinder head could also be the cause). Deposits on the undersides of the valve heads can also cause low compression.

8 Compare the readings obtained with those given in the Specifications.

9 If the pressure in any cylinder is low, carry out the following test to isolate the cause. Introduce a teaspoonful of clean oil into that cylinder through its spark plug hole, and repeat the test.

10 If the addition of oil temporarily improves the compression pressure, this indicates that bore or piston wear is responsible for the pressure loss. No improvement suggests that leaking or burnt valves, or a blown head gasket, may be to blame.

11 A low reading only from two adjacent cylinders is almost certainly due to the head gasket having blown between them; the presence of coolant in the engine oil will confirm this.

12 On completion of the test, refit the spark plugs and the relay.

3 Top dead centre (TDC) for No 1 piston – locating

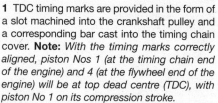

1 TDC timing marks are provided in the form of a slot machined into the crankshaft pulley and a corresponding bar cast into the timing chain cover. **Note:** *With the timing marks correctly aligned, piston Nos 1 (at the timing chain end of the engine) and 4 (at the flywheel end of the engine) will be at top dead centre (TDC), with piston No 1 on its compression stroke.*

2 For access to the crankshaft pulley bolt, jack up the front of the car and support on axle stands (see *Jacking and vehicle support*). Remove the right-hand front wheel, then remove the screws/nuts and detach the right-hand wheel arch liner. To access the crankshaft pulley bolt, bend up the metal bracket on the lower edge of the inner wing a little.

3 Remove the cylinder head cover with reference to Section 4.

4 Using a socket on the crankshaft pulley, turn the engine until the TDC slot in the crankshaft pulley is aligned with the slot on the timing cover **(see illustration)**. No 1 piston (at the timing chain end of the engine) will be at the top of its compression stroke. At this point the lobes on the inlet and exhaust camshafts on cylinder No 1 will be pointing upwards and towards the centre of the cylinder head. The compression stroke can be confirmed by removing the No 1 spark plug, and checking for compression with the wooden handle of a screwdriver over the plug hole as the piston approaches the top of its stroke. No compression indicates that the cylinder is on its exhaust stroke and is therefore one crankshaft revolution out of alignment.

5 Remove the camshaft bearing caps from the intake and exhaust camshaft over No 1 cylinder. Press Saab special tools No 83 96 046 (B207E or L engines) or No 83 96 079 (B207R engine) onto the bearing cap positions. The tools are designed to accommodate the lobes of the camshaft, and lock them in their reference position. Gently press the tools into place, if necessary rotate the crankshaft slightly until the tools fit correctly. Once fully fitted, insert the bolts supplied with the tools, and tighten them to lock the camshafts in place **(see illustrations)**. Check the crankshaft pulley mark still aligns with the mark on the timing chain cover.

3.5a Fit the Saab special tools (arrowed) over the camshaft lobes of No 1 cylinder

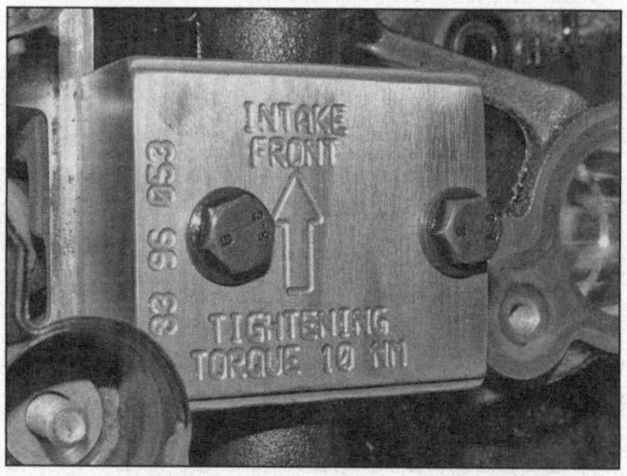

3.5b The tools are marked INTAKE or EXHAUST, and the arrow points towards the timing chain

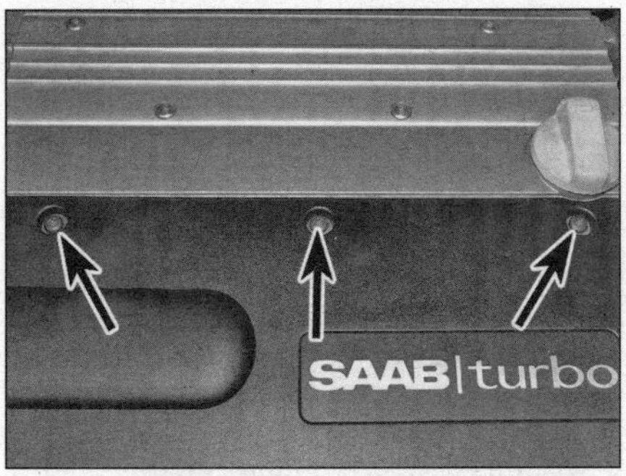

4.1 Undo the 3 Torx screws and remove the plastic cover (arrowed)

4 Cylinder head cover – removal and refitting

Removal

1 Open the bonnet, undo the 3 Torx screws and remove the engine top cover **(see illustration)**.

2 Remove the air filter assembly as described in Chapter 4A, Section 2.

3 Depressurise the fuel system by pressing in the centre of the valve on the fuel supply pipe, then undo the unions and disconnect the fuel pipes **(see illustrations)**. Plug the openings to prevent contamination.

4 Undo the 2 bolts and detach the pipe/hose bracket from the right-hand of the cylinder head cover **(see illustration)**.

5 Remove the ignition coils as described in Chapter 5B, Section 4.

6 Release the clamp and disconnect the engine breather hose from the cylinder head cover **(see illustration)**.

7 Disconnect the combustion detection module (CDM), crankshaft position and coolant temperature sensor wiring plugs, then undo the nuts and lift the cable duct from place. Release the cable-ties and detach the wiring loom from the bracket at the right-hand side of the cylinder head.

8 Detach the earth lead from the left-hand side of the camshaft cover **(see illustration)**.

9 Undo the 2 bolts at the top and move the heat shield over the turbocharger rearwards a little. If removing the cylinder head, lift the heat shield to release the clip at the rear and remove it **(see illustration)**.

10 Undo the bolts and remove the cylinder head cover. If the cover is stuck, tap it gently with the palm of your hand to free it.

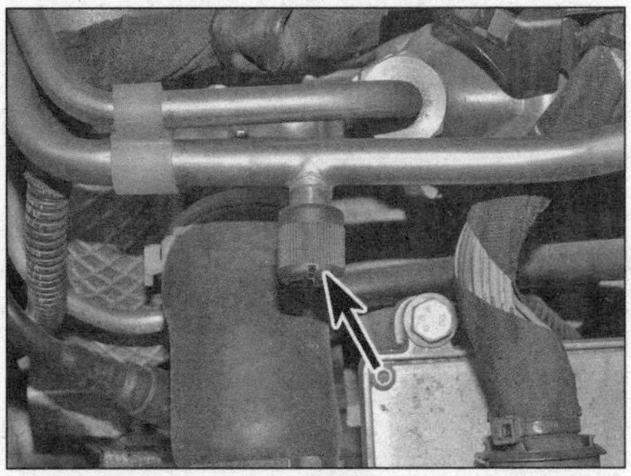

4.3a Unscrew the plastic cap (arrowed) ...

4.3b ... then depress the centre of the valve to depressurise the fuel system (arrowed)

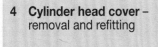

4.3c Undo the fuel supply and return unions (arrowed)

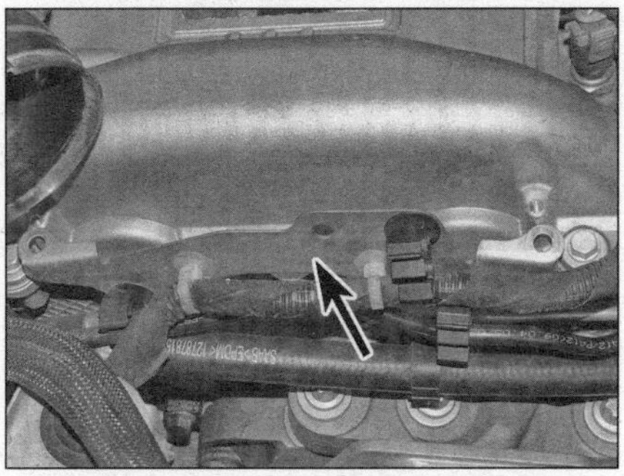

4.4 Detach the pipe bracket (arrowed) from the cylinder head cover

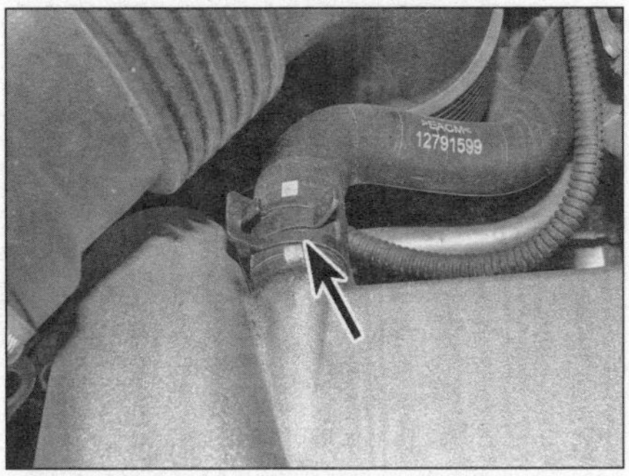

4.6 Release the clamp and disconnect the breather hose (arrowed)

Refitting

11 Clean the contact surfaces of the cylinder head cover and cylinder head. Locate the narrower edges of the seals securely in the grooves in the cylinder head cover **(see illustrations)**.

4.8 Disconnect the earth lead from the left-hand end of the cylinder head (arrowed)

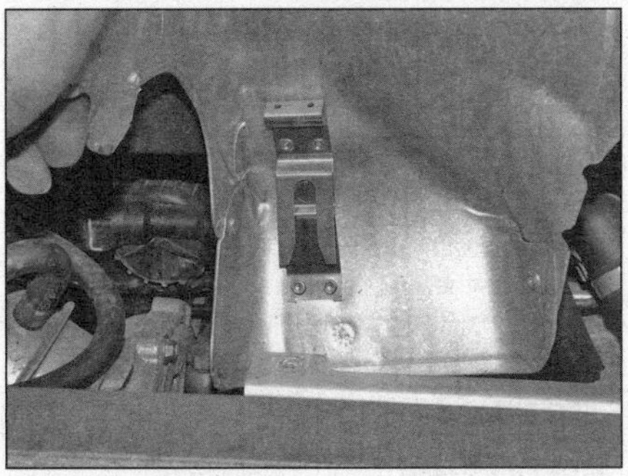

4.9 Lift the heat shield to release the clip

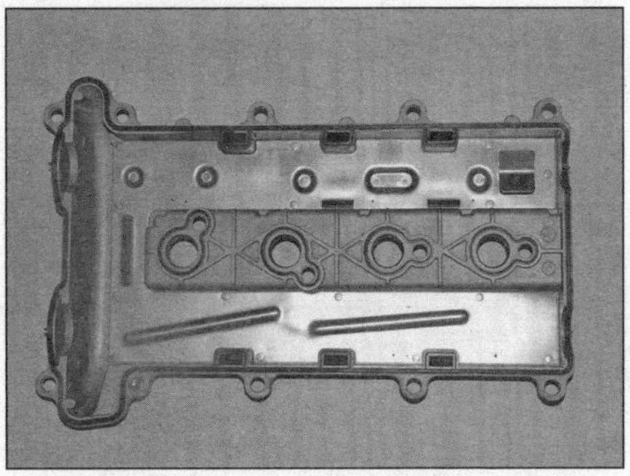

4.11a Fit new seals to the cylinder head cover ...

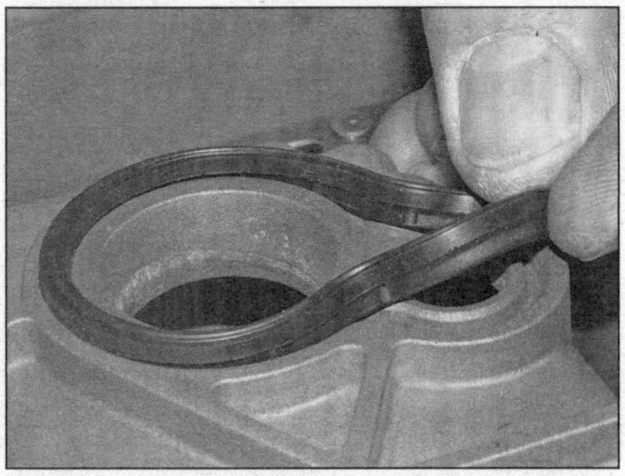

4.11b ... ensuring the narrower edge of the seals locates in the cover's grooves

5.3 Unscrew the timing chain tensioner hexagon cap from the rear left-hand corner of the cylinder head

12 Refit the cylinder head cover, and insert the securing bolts. Tighten the bolts progressively and evenly until all the bolts are tightened to the specified torque.

13 Refit the turbocharger heat shield.

14 Reconnect the crankcase breather hose to the cylinder head cover.

15 Refit the earth lead and cable guide.

16 Refit the ignition coils as described in Chapter 5B, Section 4.

17 The remainder of refitting is a reversal of removal.

5 Camshafts and hydraulic cam followers – removal, inspection and refitting

Removal

1 Set the engine at TDC on No 1 cylinder, as described in Section 3, but do not fit the camshaft locking tools.

5.4 Prevent the camshaft from rotating using a spanner on the hexagonal section of the camshafts

2 Undo the bolts and detach the vacuum and power steering pumps from the ends of the camshafts – refer to Chapter 9, Section 12 or Chapter 10, Section 18 as applicable.

3 Slowly undo the hexagon cap, and remove the timing chain tensioner **(see illustration)**.

4 Undo the camshaft sprockets retaining bolts, counter-holding the camshafts with an open-ended spanner on the hexagonal sections **(see illustration)**.

5 Secure the timing chain to the sprockets using cable-ties, then lower the sprockets and chain from the camshafts.

6 Check that the camshaft bearing caps and the camshafts are identified for position. They have stamped markings on the caps – do not mix up these when refitting, 1 to 5 for the intake side and 6 to 10 for the exhaust side. The bearing caps at the flywheel/driveplate end, are marked Ex and I for exhaust and intake camshafts.

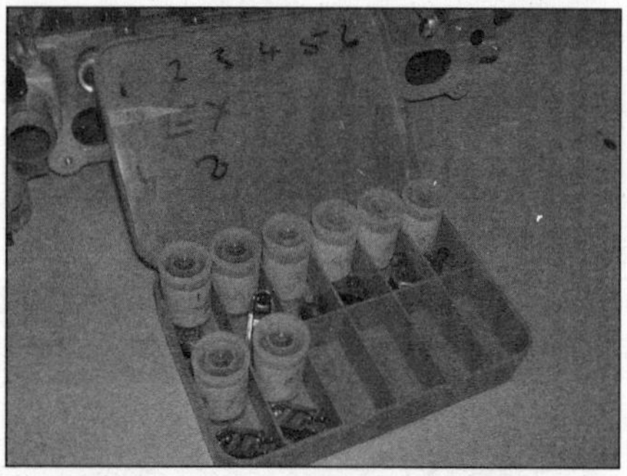

5.8a Use a container to keep the followers and hydraulic tappets in order

5.8b Keep the hydraulic tappets in labelled containers with clean engine oil

5.12a Insert the tappets into their original positions ...

5.12b ... followed by the cam followers

7 Progressively unscrew the bearing cap bolts, so that the caps are not stressed unduly by the valve springs. Ensure that the bearing caps closest to the open valves are removed last, to avoid stressing the camshaft unduly. Fully remove the bolts and lift off the caps, then lift the camshafts from the cylinder head. Keep the camshafts carefully identified for location.

8 Obtain sixteen small, clean plastic containers, and number them 1i to 8i (intake) and 1e to 8e (exhaust). Alternatively, divide a larger container into sixteen compartments, similarly marked for the intake and exhaust camshafts. Withdraw each cam follower and hydraulic tappet in turn, and place it in its respective container **(see illustrations)**. Do not interchange the cam followers or tappets. To prevent the oil draining from the hydraulic tappets, pour fresh oil into the containers until it covers them.

Caution: Take great care to avoid scratching the cylinder head bores as the followers are withdrawn.

Inspection

9 Examine the camshaft bearing surfaces and cam lobes for signs of wear ridges and scoring. Renew the camshaft if any of these conditions are apparent. Examine the condition of the bearing surfaces on the camshaft journals, in the camshaft bearing caps, and in the cylinder head. If the head or cap bearing surfaces are worn excessively, the cylinder head will need to be renewed. If the necessary measuring equipment is available, camshaft bearing journal wear can be checked by direct measurement and comparison with the specifications given.

10 Camshaft endfloat can be measured by locating each camshaft in the cylinder head, refitting the sprockets, and using feeler blades between the shoulder on the front of the camshaft and the front bearing surface on the cylinder head.

11 Check the hydraulic tappets where they contact the bores in the cylinder head for wear, scoring and pitting. Occasionally, a hydraulic tappet may be noisy and require renewal, and this will have been noticed when the engine was running. It is not easy to check a tappet for internal damage or wear once it has been removed; if there is any doubt, the complete set of tappets should be renewed.

Refitting

12 Lubricate the bores for the hydraulic tappets in the cylinder head, and the tappets themselves, then insert them in their original positions, followed by the cam followers **(see illustrations)**.

13 Lubricate the bearing surfaces of the camshafts in the cylinder head.

14 Locate the camshafts in their correct positions in the cylinder head, so that the

5.14 The intake camshaft is marked K

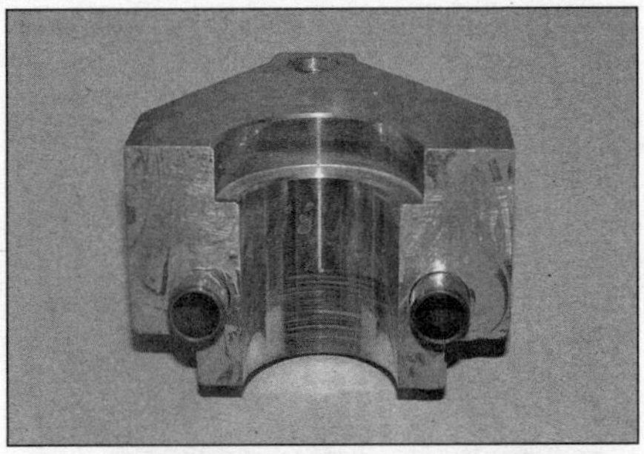

5.16 Apply a layer of sealant to the bearing caps at the flywheel/driveplate end, and check the dowels are still in place

5.20a Remove the circlip from the end of the tensioner ...

camshaft lobes for No 1 cylinder are pointing upwards. The intake camshaft is marked K and the exhaust is marked L **(see illustration)**.

15 Check that the crankshaft pulley is still in the TDC position – see Section 3.

16 Apply a thin layer of sealant to the cylinder head mating surface at the flywheel/driveplate end of the intake and exhaust bearing caps **(see illustration)**. **Note:** *Ensure the locating dowels are in place on these bearing caps.*

17 Lubricate the bearing surfaces in the bearing caps, then locate them in their correct positions and insert the retaining bolts. Progressively tighten the bolts to the specified torque. **Note:** *Do not fit No 1 cylinder camshaft bearing caps at this stage, to facilitate the fitting of the camshaft locking tools described in the next paragraph.*

18 Refit the camshaft locking tools, as described in Section 3.

19 Locate the sprockets on the camshafts, fitting the exhaust one first, followed by the intake one. Do not fully-tighten the bolts at this stage.

20 Remove the circlip and pull the piston from the timing chain tensioner. Using a flat-bladed screwdriver, rotate the timing chain piston tensioner clockwise until it engages in the tensioned position. Refit the piston into the tensioner, and refit the circlip **(see illustrations)**. Note that if the O-ring is damaged, the complete tensioner must be renewed.

21 Fit the timing chain tensioner, and tighten it to the specified torque. Note that the groove in the end of the tensioner must be vertical when fitting **(see illustration)**.

22 Fully-tighten the camshaft sprocket retaining bolts to the specified torque, while holding them stationary with a spanner on the hexagon sections, then cut the cable-ties securing the chain to the sprockets.

23 Activate the chain tensioner by pressing the chain/guide onto the tensioner to release the piston **(see illustration)**. Check the tensioner is released.

24 Remove the camshaft locking tools and refit the camshaft bearing caps Nos 2 and 7.

25 Using a socket on the crankshaft pulley, rotate the engine two complete turns clockwise, then check that the TDC timing marks on the crankshaft pulley and timing chain cover are still correctly aligned.

26 Check the camshaft locking tools can be fitted as described in Section 3. If the timing is correct, refit the Nos 2 and 7 bearing caps and tighten the retaining bolts to the specified torque.

27 Refit the power steering and vacuum pumps, using new seals/gaskets, and tighten the fasteners to the specified torques.

28 Refit the cylinder head cover as described in Section 4.

29 Refit the wheel arch liner and roadwheel, tightening the bolts to the specified torque.

5.20b ... and pull the tensioner piston from the body

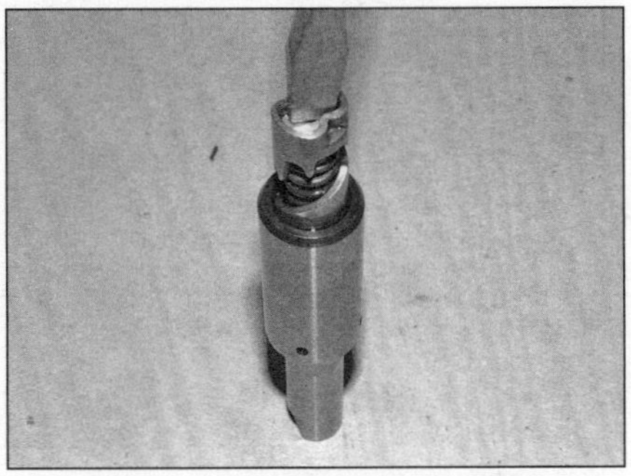

5.20c Push and twist the piston clockwise ...

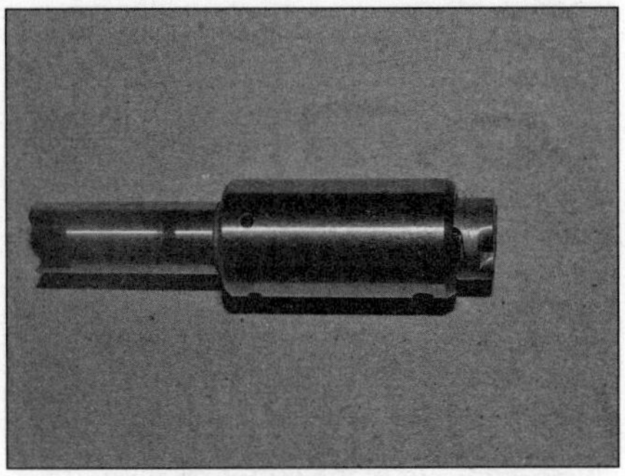

5.20d ... until it locks in the tensioned position

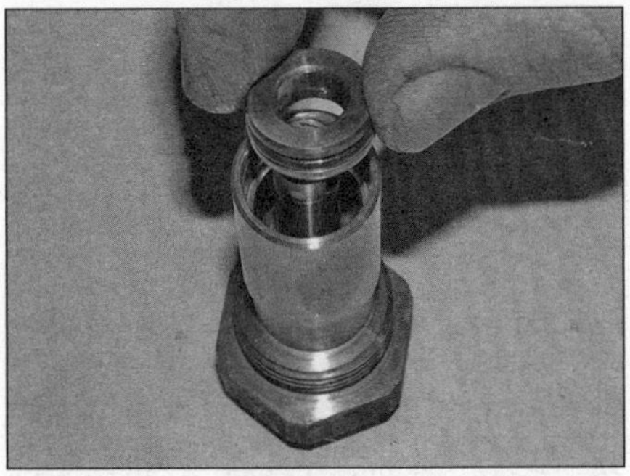

5.20e Check the O-ring seal, and refit the circlip

5.21 The groove in the end of the tensioner (arrowed) must be vertical

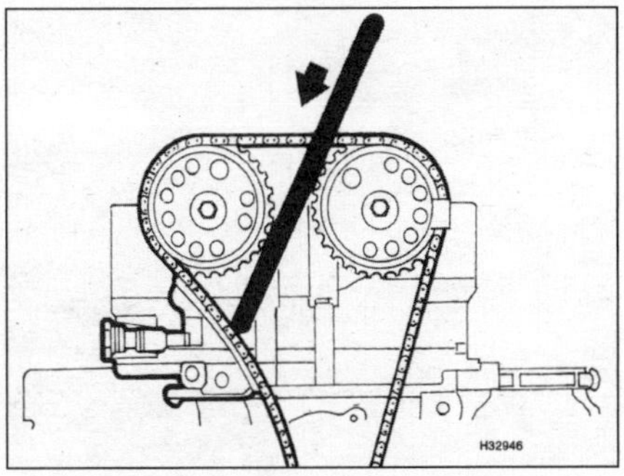

5.23 Press a bar/screwdriver against the tensioner rail to release the tensioner piston

6.3 Slide out the red locking catches and disconnect the oxygen sensor wiring plugs (arrowed)

6.5 Turbocharger oil feed pipe banjo bolt (arrowed)

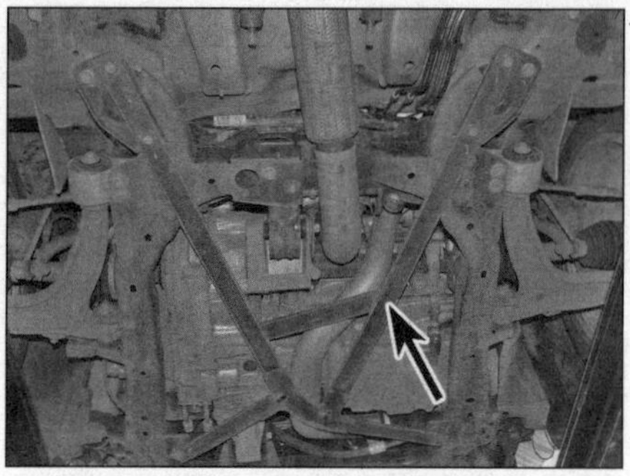

6.7 Front chassis reinforcement (arrowed) – Convertible models

6.8 Turbocharger pipe retaining bolts (arrowed)

6 Cylinder head – removal and refitting

Removal

1 Disconnect the battery negative lead as described in Chapter 5A, Section 4.

2 Drain the cooling system as described in Chapter 1A, Section 27.

3 Disconnect the oxygen sensors wiring plugs, located at the left-hand end of the cylinder head **(see illustration)**.

4 Set the crankshaft at TDC on No 1 cylinder, as described in Section 3.

5 Undo the banjo bolt, and disconnect the oil supply pipe from the turbocharger **(see illustration)**. Be prepared for oil spillage and recover the copper sealing washers.

6 Undo the nuts securing the catalytic converter to the turbocharger, undo the two nuts and two bolts, then remove the support bracket from the cylinder block, and detach the converter from the turbocharger – see Chapter 4A, Section 16.

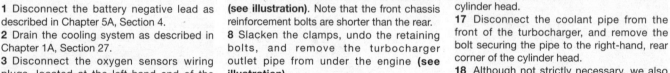

6.9 Undo the coolant pipe banjo bolt (arrowed)

7 On Convertible models, undo the bolts and remove the front chassis reinforcement **(see illustration)**. Note that the front chassis reinforcement bolts are shorter than the rear.

8 Slacken the clamps, undo the retaining bolts, and remove the turbocharger outlet pipe from under the engine **(see illustration)**.

9 Undo the banjo bolt, and detach the coolant pipe from the rear of the turbocharger **(see illustration)**.

10 Undo the fasteners and remove the bracket between the exhaust manifold and the cylinder block.

11 Undo the fasteners and disconnect the oil return pipe from the turbocharger. Take care not to kink or twist the pipe, as this may result in internal damage.

12 Disconnect the wiring from the starter motor.

13 Note their fitted positions, then disconnect the wiring from the turbocharger solenoid valve, air conditioning pressure sensor, coolant temperature sensor, engine management ECM (see Chapter 4A, Section 10), bypass solenoid valve, throttle body, intake manifold pressure sensor, atmospheric pressure sensor, combustion detection module (CDM), oil pressure sensor, and the earth connection adjacent to the engine management ECM.

14 Slacken the clamp, disconnect the vacuum hoses, and remove the plastic air intake hose from the turbocharger.

15 Release the clamp and disconnect the coolant hose from the right-hand end of the cylinder head.

16 Slacken the clamp and disconnect the coolant hose at the front left-hand end of the cylinder head.

17 Disconnect the coolant pipe from the front of the turbocharger, and remove the bolt securing the pipe to the right-hand, rear corner of the cylinder head.

18 Although not strictly necessary, we also disconnected the carbon canister hose at the quick-release connector in front of the cylinder head, and the turbo coolant hose, so that we could move all the pipework at the right-hand end of the engine out of the way.

19 Support the engine with a trolley jack under the engine sump, then undo the bolts and remove the right-hand engine mounting assembly.

20 Remove the CDM, then disconnect the servo vacuum hose at the vacuum pump, and vacuum hose from the turbocharger bypass valve **(see illustrations)**.

21 Undo the bolts and detach the power steering pump from the end of the intake camshaft.

22 Slowly undo the hexagon cap, and remove the timing chain tensioner **(see illustration 5.3)**.

23 Undo and remove the camshaft sprockets retaining bolts, counter-holding the camshafts with an open-ended spanner on the hexagonal sections **(see illustration 5.4)**.

24 Secure the timing chain to the intake camshaft sprocket using a cable-tie, then remove the exhaust camshaft sprocket, and

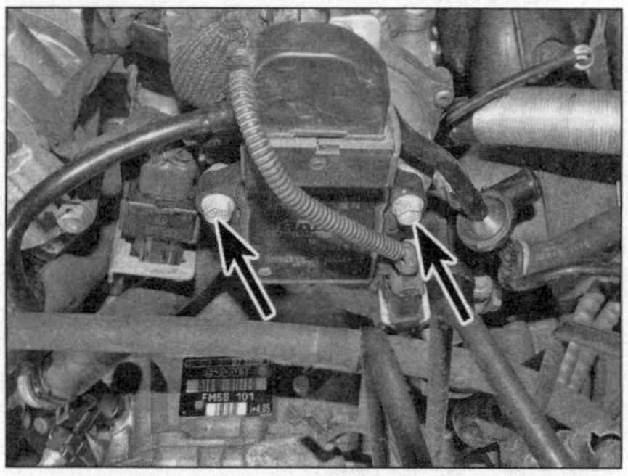

6.20a Undo the CDM retaining bolts (arrowed) ...

6.20b ... depress the release button (arrowed) and disconnect the vacuum hose from the pump

6.25 Undo the plug, then undo the bolt securing the top of the chain guide (arrowed)

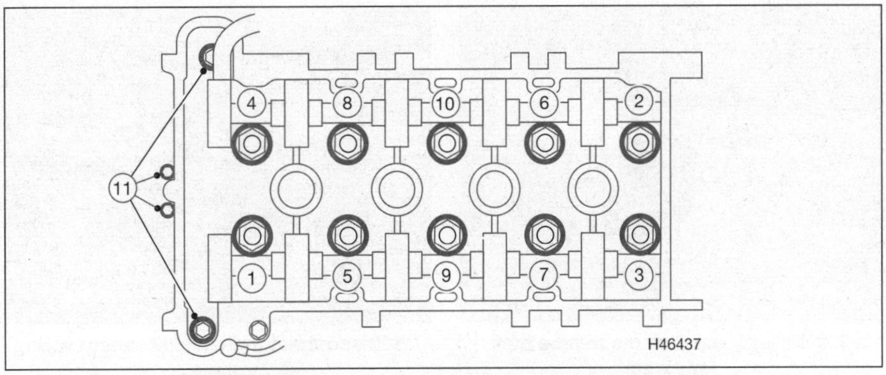

6.26 Cylinder head bolt slackening sequence

lower the intake camshaft sprocket and chain from the camshaft.

25 Undo the plug from the timing chain cover, then remove the bolt securing the top of the chain guide **(see illustration)**.

26 Working in sequence, gradually and evenly slacken and remove the cylinder head bolts **(see illustration)**.

27 Make a final check to ensure all relevant wiring and coolant hoses have been disconnected.

28 With all the cylinder head bolts removed, check that the timing chain is positioned so that the pivoting chain guide will not obstruct removal of the head. Lift the cylinder head directly from the top of the cylinder block and place it on a clean workbench, without damaging the mating surface. Enlist the help of an assistant, since the cylinder head is quite heavy. If the cylinder head is stuck, try rocking it slightly to free it from the gasket – do not insert a screwdriver or similar tool between the gasket joint, otherwise the gasket mating faces will be damaged. The head is located on dowels, so do not try to free it by tapping it sideways.

29 Remove the gasket from the top of the block, noting the two locating dowels. If the locating dowels are a loose fit, remove them and store them with the head for safe-keeping **(see illustration)**. Do not discard the gasket – it may be needed for identification purposes.

30 If the cylinder head is to be dismantled for overhaul, remove the intake and exhaust manifolds as described in Chapter 4A, Section 14 and 15, and the camshafts as described in Section 5 of this Chapter.

Preparation for refitting

31 The mating faces of the cylinder head and cylinder block must be perfectly clean before refitting the head. Use a hard plastic or wood scraper to remove all traces of gasket and carbon; also clean the piston crowns. Take particular care during the cleaning operations, as the soft aluminium alloy is damaged easily. Also, make sure that the carbon is not allowed to enter the oil and water passages – this is particularly important for the lubrication system, as carbon could block the oil supply to the engine's components. Using adhesive tape and paper, seal the water, oil and bolt holes in the cylinder block. After cleaning each piston, use a small brush to remove all traces of grease and carbon from the gap, then wipe away the remainder with a clean rag. Clean all the pistons in the same way.

32 Check the mating surfaces of the cylinder block and the cylinder head for nicks, deep scratches and other damage. If slight, they may be removed carefully with a file, but if excessive, machining may be the only alternative to renewal.

33 If warpage of the cylinder head gasket surface is suspected, use a straight-edge to check it for distortion. Refer to Chapter 2D, Section 7 if necessary.

34 Check the condition of the cylinder head bolts, and particularly their threads. Wash the bolts in suitable solvent, and wipe them dry. Check each for any sign of visible wear or damage, renewing any bolt if necessary. Measure the length of each bolt, and compare with the length of a new bolt. Although Saab do not specify that the bolts must be renewed, it is strongly recommended that the bolts are renewed as a complete set if the engine has completed a high mileage.

Refitting

35 Where removed, refit the camshafts with reference to Section 5, and the intake and exhaust manifolds with new gaskets as described in Chapter 4A, Section 14 and 15.

36 Ensure the crankshaft is positioned at TDC on No 1 cylinder, and the camshafts are locked using the special tools, as described in Section 3.

37 Wipe clean the mating surfaces of the cylinder head and cylinder block/crankcase. Clean away all oil from the bolt holes in the cylinder block. Check that the two locating dowels are in position on the cylinder block.

38 Position a new gasket on the cylinder block surface, making sure that it is fitted the correct way round, and pull the exhaust camshaft sprocket, timing chain and chain guides up through the gasket.

39 Carefully lower the cylinder head onto the block, aligning it with the locating dowels, and feeding the exhaust camshaft sprocket, chain and chain guides through the head as it is lowered.

40 Insert the bolts into the cylinder head and finger-tighten them. Take care not to drop the bolts into position, as the threads in the cylinder block are easily damaged.

41 Working progressively and in sequence,

6.29 Check the dowels (arrowed) are in place

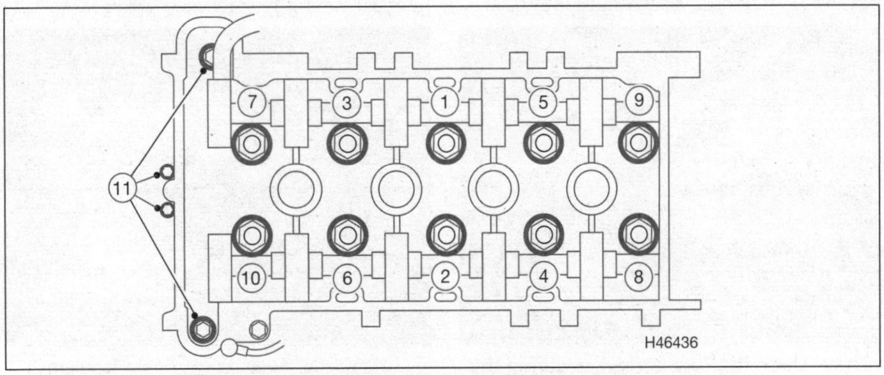

6.41 Cylinder head bolt tightening sequence

7.4 Oil level dipstick guide tube bolt (arrowed)

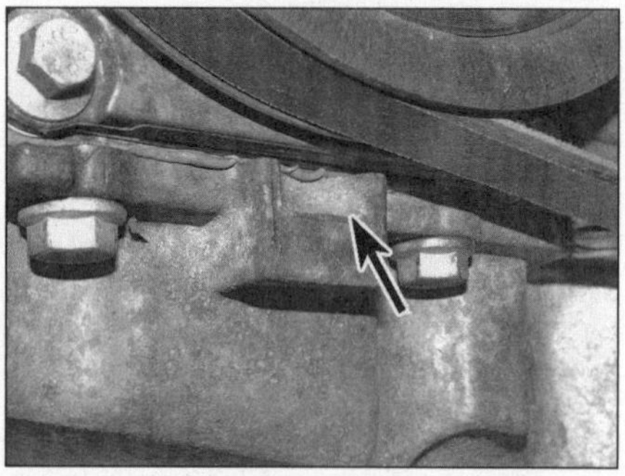

7.10 Insert a screwdriver between the sump and timing cover (arrowed)

tighten the cylinder head bolts to their Stage 1 torque setting, using a torque wrench **(see illustration)**.

42 Using the same sequence, tighten the cylinder head bolts to their Stage 2 and Stage 3 angle-tighten settings.

43 Finally, tighten the 4 bolts securing the cylinder head to the timing cover to their specified torque.

44 Move the intake side timing chain guide into position, insert the retaining bolt through the hole in the timing cover, and tighten it to the specified torque **(see illustration 6.25)**.

45 Engage the intake camshaft sprocket with the timing chain, and position the sprockets on the camshafts. Insert the retaining bolts but do not tighten them yet. Check that the timing chain is correctly located on the guides and sprockets.

46 Check the crankshaft is still positioned at TDC for No 1 cylinder, as described in Section 3.

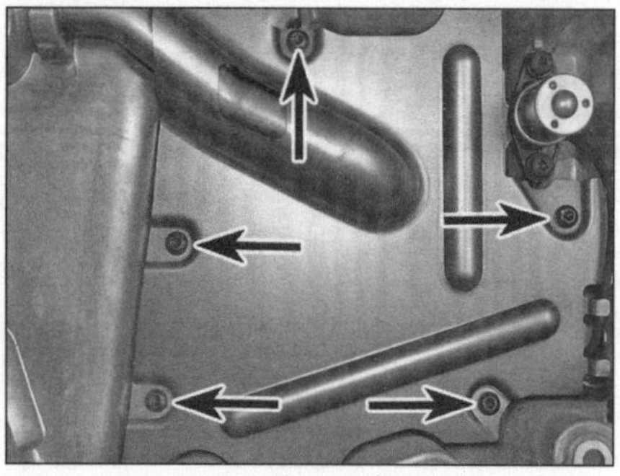

7.11a Undo the Torx screws securing the baffle plate (arrowed)

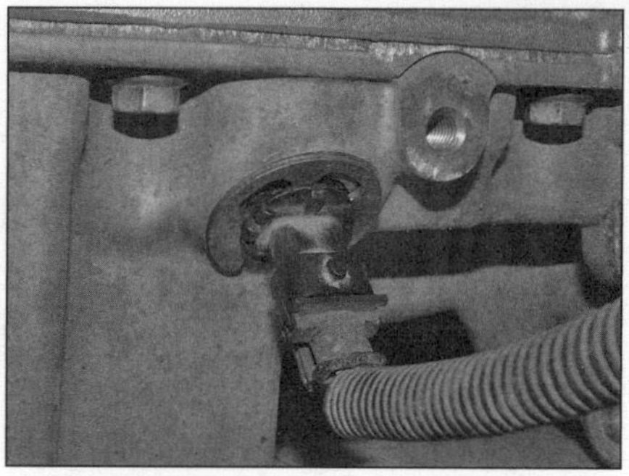

7.5 Disconnect the oil level sensor wiring plug

47 Remove the circlip and pull the piston from the timing chain tensioner. Using a flat-bladed screwdriver, rotate the timing chain tensioner piston clockwise until it engages in the tensioned position. Refit the piston into the tensioner, and refit the circlip **(see illustrations 5.20a to 5.20e)**. Note that if the tensioner sealing washer is damaged, the complete tensioner must be renewed.

48 Fit the timing chain tensioner, and tighten it to the specified torque. Note that the groove in the end of the tensioner must be vertical when fitting **(see illustration 5.21)**.

49 Fully-tighten the camshaft sprocket retaining bolts to the specified torque, while holding them stationary with a spanner on the hexagon sections, then cut the cable-tie securing the chain to the sprocket.

50 Activate the chain tensioner by pressing the chain/guide onto the tensioner to release the piston **(see illustration 5.23)**. Check the tensioner is released.

51 Remove the camshaft locking tools and refit the camshaft bearing caps Nos 2 and 7.

52 Using a socket on the crankshaft pulley, rotate the engine two complete turns clockwise, then check that the TDC timing marks on the crankshaft pulley and timing chain cover are still correctly aligned.

53 Remove the camshaft bearing caps from Nos 2 and 7 and check that the camshaft locking tools can be fitted as described in Section 3. If the timing is correct, refit the Nos 2 and 7 bearing caps and tighten the retaining bolts to the specified torque.

54 The remainder of refitting is a reversal of removal, noting the following points:

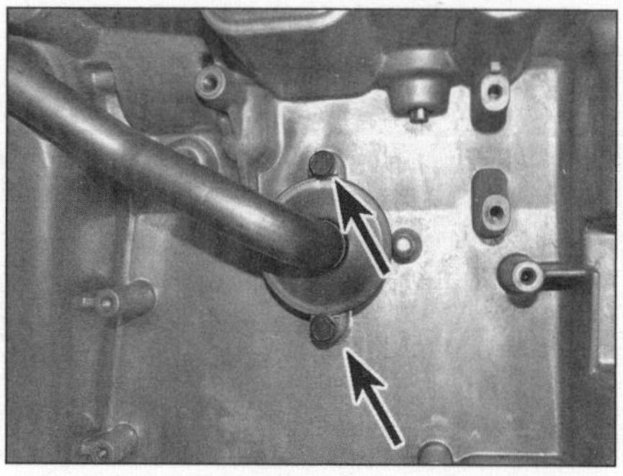

7.11b Oil pick-up retaining screws (arrowed)

a) Tighten all fasteners to the specified torque where given.
b) Refit the power steering pump using a new seal.
c) Renew any turbocharger outlet ducting clamps if they show any sign of damage or corrosion.
d) Top-up the coolant as described in Chapter 1A, Section 27.
e) Reconnect the battery negative lead as described in Chapter 5A, Section 4.

7 Sump – removal and refitting

Removal

1 Slacken the right-hand front roadwheel bolts. Firmly apply the handbrake, then jack up the front of the car and support it on axle stands (see *Jacking and vehicle support*). Remove the roadwheel.

2 Undo the fasteners and remove the right-hand front wheel arch liner. On Convertible models, undo the bolts and remove the front chassis reinforcement **(see illustration 6.7)**. Note that the front chassis reinforcement bolts are shorter than the ones at the rear.

3 Drain the engine oil, clean and refit the engine oil drain plug with a new seal, and tighten it to the specified torque. If the engine is nearing its service interval when the oil and filter are due for renewal, it is recommended that the filter is also removed, and a new one fitted. After reassembly, the engine can then be refilled with fresh oil. Refer to Chapter 1A, Section 3 for further information.

4 Undo the 3 Torx screws, remove the plastic cover on the top of the engine, then remove the oil level dipstick, undo the dipstick tube retaining bolt, detach the electrical connector from the bracket on the tube, then unclip the tube from the sump **(see illustration)**.

5 Disconnect the oil level sensor wiring plug (where fitted) from the sump **(see illustration)**.

6 Slacken the clamps, undo the retaining bolt, and remove the charge air pipe from under the engine **(see illustration 6.8)**.

7 Remove the lower bolt securing the air conditioning compressor to the sump.

8 On early vehicles undo the bolts and remove the rear engine torque arm.

9 Progressively unscrew and remove the bolts securing the sump to the cylinder block, leaving one or two bolts in position to prevent the sump falling.

10 Remove the remaining bolts, and lower the sump to the ground. Break the joint by inserting a screwdriver between the sump and timing cover below the crankshaft pulley **(see illustration)**.

11 While the sump is removed, take the opportunity to unscrew the baffle plate Torx screws, remove the plate, undo the 2 screws and remove the oil pump pick-up/strainer. Check the oil pump pick-up/strainer for signs of clogging or damage **(see illustrations)**.

Refitting

12 Clean all traces of sealant from the mating surfaces of the cylinder block/crankcase and sump, then use a clean rag to wipe out the sump and the engine's interior.

13 Where removed, refit the pick-up/strainer (with a new O-ring seal) and baffle plate to the sump, then tighten the bolts to the specified torque. Ensure the level sensor cable is correctly routed **(see illustrations)**.

14 Ensure that the sump and cylinder block/ crankcase mating surfaces are clean and dry, then apply a bead of suitable sealant (Saab part No 90 543 772 or Loctite 5900) approximately 2 mm thick to the sump flange **(see illustrations)**.

15 Offer up the sump and refit the retaining bolts securing the sump to the crankcase, tightening them progressively to the specified torque, then fit the sump-to-transmission bolts, again, tightening them to the specified torque. When lifting the sump make sure that the sealant is not disturbed.

16 The remainder of refitting is a reversal of removal, noting the following points:

a) Tighten all fasteners to the specified torque where given.

b) Fit a new oil filter element, and refill the engine with new oil as described in Chapter 1A, Section 3.

c) Start the engine and check for leaks before venturing out onto the road.

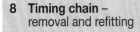

8 Timing chain – removal and refitting

Removal

1 Set the engine at TDC on No 1 cylinder, as described in Section 3.

2 Slacken the right-hand front roadwheel bolts, raise the front of the vehicle (see *Jacking and vehicle support*) and support it securely on axle stands. Remove the roadwheel.

3 Undo the fasteners and remove the right-hand front wheel arch liner. On Convertible models, undo the bolts and remove the front chassis reinforcement **(see illustration 6.7)**. Note that the front chassis reinforcement bolts are shorter than the rear.

4 Remove the auxiliary drivebelt as described in Chapter 1A, Section 26, then undo the bolt and remove the belt tensioner assembly **(see illustration)**.

5 Unscrew the timing chain tensioner from the rear of the engine **(see illustration)**.

6 Support the engine from underneath using a trolley jack, then undo the bolts and remove the right-hand engine mounting assembly **(see illustration 14.10)**.

7 Temporarily remove the camshaft locking tools.

8 Lower the right-hand of the engine approximately 30 mm, then unscrew the bolt and remove the crankshaft pulley **(see illustrations)**. Prevent the crankshaft from rotating using Saab tools No 83 95 360 and 8396210 or a suitable equivalent.

9 Undo the bolts and remove the timing chain cover **(see illustration)**. Be prepared for oil spillage.

10 Cut off the part of the timing chain cover gasket that fits around the engine mounting, and remove the gasket.

11 Undo the plug covering the intake side timing chain guide upper bolt, then unscrew the bolt **(see illustration 6.25)**.

12 Undo the lower chain guide bolt, and

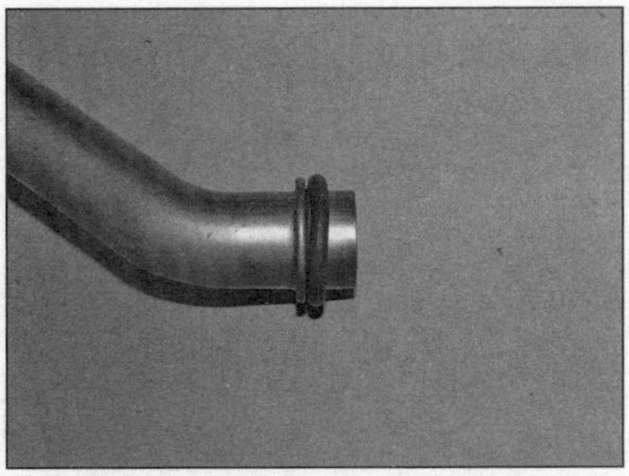

7.13a Renew the pick-up O-ring seal

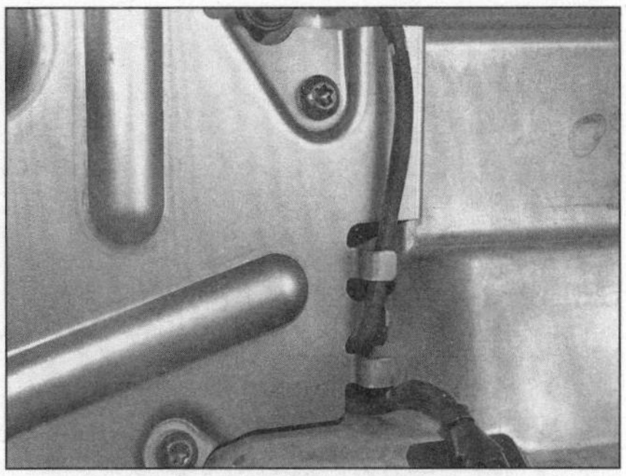

7.13b Ensure the level sensor cable is correctly routed

7.14a Apply a continuous bead of silicone sealant around the sump flange ...

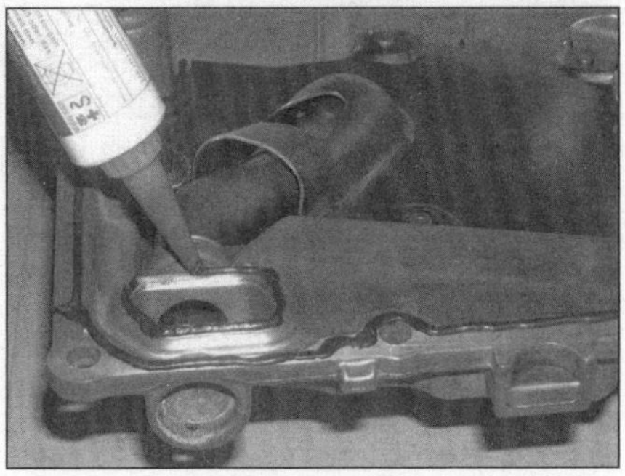

7.14b ... and also around the oil intake pipe area

8.4 Undo the bolt and remove the auxiliary drivebelt tensioner

8.5 Unscrew the tensioner from the right-hand rear corner of the cylinder head

8.8a Slacken the pulley bolt whilst preventing the pulley from rotating with a suitable tool ...

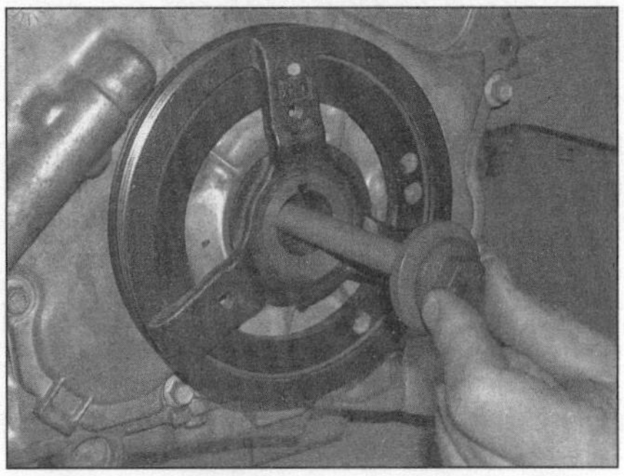

8.8b ... discard it – a new one must be fitted

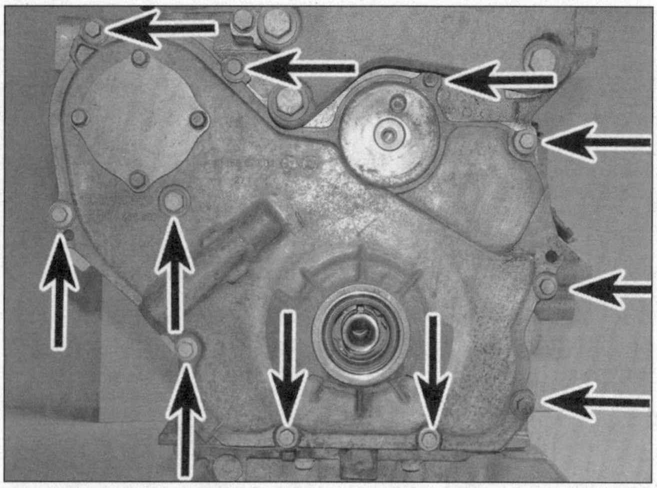

8.9 Timing chain cover bolts (arrowed)

8.12 Chain guide lower bolt (arrowed)

remove the chain guide downwards **(see illustration)**.

13 Disengage the timing chain from the crankshaft sprocket, then undo the retaining bolts, remove the camshaft sprockets and lift the chain and sprockets from the engine. Prevent the camshafts from rotating using a spanner the hexagonal sections **(see illustration)**.

14 Remove the bolt and lift the tensioner guide upwards from position **(see illustration)**. If either of the chain guides show signs of excessive wear or damage, they must be renewed.

Refitting

15 Refit the tensioner guide to the cylinder block, then engage the intake camshaft sprocket with the chain, and lower the chain into position. Fit the sprocket to the intake camshaft and finger-tighten the sprocket retaining bolt.

16 Engage the chain with the crankshaft sprocket, and refit the chain guide on the intake side. Tighten the chain guide lower bolt to the specified torque.

17 Engage the exhaust camshaft sprocket with the chain, and refit the sprocket to the camshaft. Only finger-tighten the sprocket retaining bolt at this stage.

18 Refit the chain guide upper bolt and tighten it to the specified torque.

19 Refit the plug over the chain guide upper bolt, and tighten it to the specified torque.

20 Remove the circlip and pull the piston from the timing chain tensioner. Using a flat-bladed screwdriver, rotate the timing chain tensioner piston clockwise until it engages in the tensioned position. Refit the piston into the tensioner, and refit the circlip **(see illustrations 5.20a to 5.20e)**. Note that if the O-ring seal is damaged, the complete tensioner must be renewed.

21 Fit the timing chain tensioner, and tighten it to the specified torque. Note that the groove in the end of the tensioner must be vertical when fitting **(see illustration 5.21)**.

22 Activate the chain tensioner by pressing the chain/guide onto the tensioner to release the piston **(see illustration 5.23)**. Check the tensioner is released.

23 Ensure the crankshaft is still positioned at TDC on No 1 cylinder, and refit the camshaft locking tools as described in Section 3.

24 Fit the new gasket for the timing cover, cutting away the part of the gasket that fits around the engine mounting **(see illustration)**.

25 Prise/press the oil crankshaft oil seal from the timing cover, then refit the timing cover, and tighten the bolts to the specified torque.

26 Fit a new crankshaft oil seal to the timing cover, as described in Section 12.

27 Refit the crankshaft pulley using a new retaining bolt, and tighten it to the specified torque **(see illustrations)**. Hold the crankshaft stationary using the same method employed during removal. Note that the flats on the pulley hub must align with the oil pump drive flats.

28 Check the crankshaft is still positioned at TDC on No 1 cylinder, then tighten the camshaft sprocket bolts to 30 Nm (22 lbf ft).

29 Remove the camshaft locking tools, then fully-tighten the camshaft sprocket retaining bolts to the specified torque, while holding them stationary with a spanner on the hexagon sections.

8.13 Use an open-ended spanner to counter-hold the camshafts

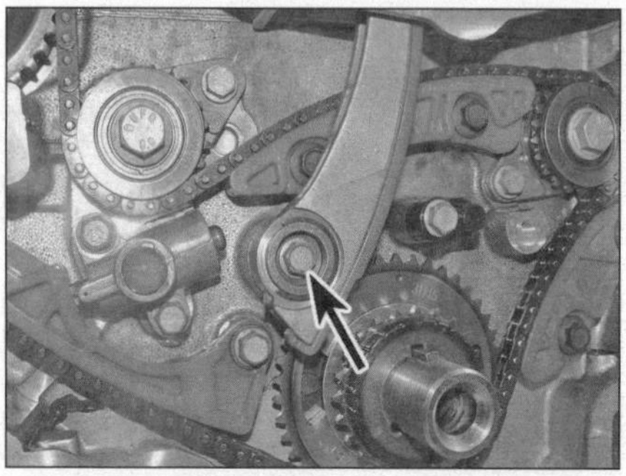

8.14 Tensioner guide bolt (arrowed)

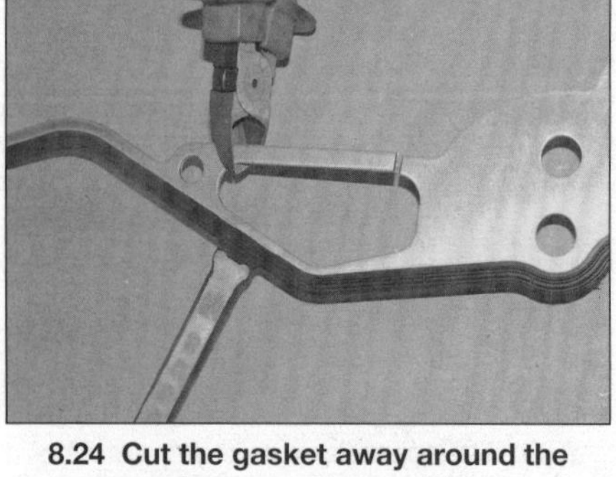

8.24 Cut the gasket away around the engine mounting position

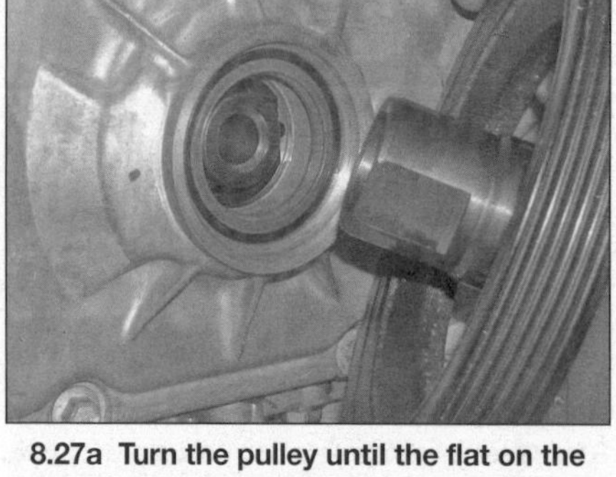

8.27a Turn the pulley until the flat on the centre hub engages with the oil pump drive

8.27b Tighten the pulley bolt accurately using an angle-gauge

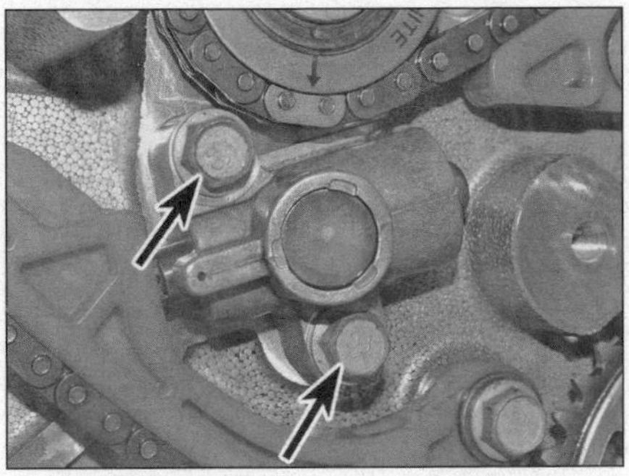

9.2a Undo the 2 bolts securing the balance chain tensioner (arrowed)

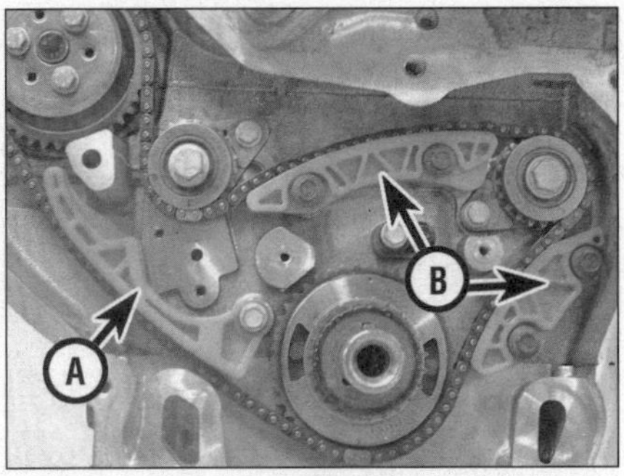

9.2b Balance chain tensioner rail (A) and guide rails (B)

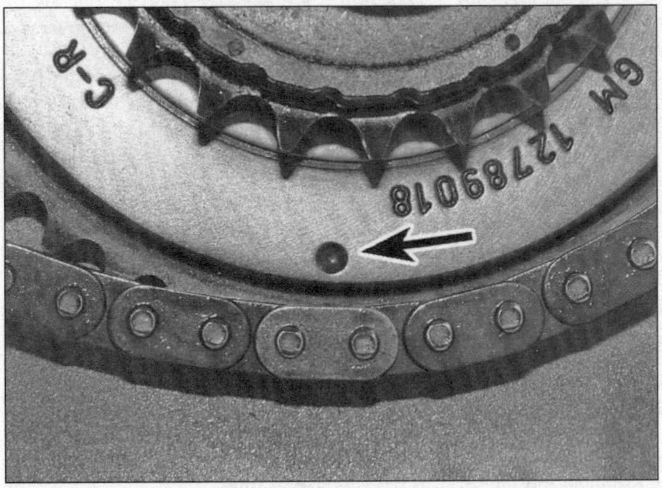

9.4a The silver-coloured chain links align with the timing mark dot on the crankshaft sprocket (arrowed) ...

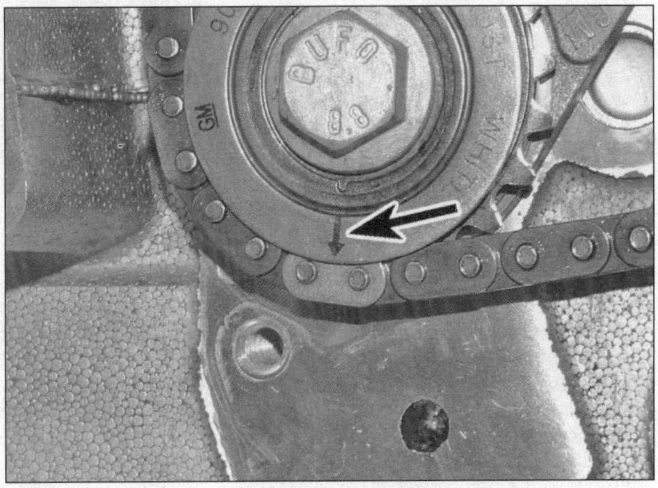

9.4b ... and the timing arrow on the exhaust side balance shaft sprocket (arrowed)

30 Refit the camshaft bearing caps Nos 2 and 7.

31 Using a socket on the crankshaft pulley, rotate the engine two complete turns clockwise, then check that the TDC timing marks on the crankshaft pulley and timing chain cover are still correctly aligned.

32 Remove the camshaft bearing caps from Nos 2 and 7 and check that the camshaft locking tools can be fitted as described in Section 3.

33 If the timing is correct, refit the Nos 2 and 7 bearing caps and tighten the retaining bolts to the specified torque.

34 The remainder of refitting is a reversal of removal, ensuring all fasteners are tightened to the specified torque.

9 Balance shafts and chain – removal and refitting

Chain

Removal

1 Remove the timing chain as described in Section 8.

2 Undo the bolts and remove the chain tensioner, and guide rails **(see illustrations)**.

3 Remove the chain from the sprockets.

Refitting

4 Three of the chain side-plate links are colour-coded to correspond with the crankshaft and balance shaft sprockets **(see illustrations)**. Refit the chain so that:

a) The silver-coloured link aligns with the mark on the crankshaft sprocket.

b) The silver-coloured link aligns with the mark on the exhaust side balance shaft sprocket.

c) The copper-coloured link aligns with the mark on the intake side balance shaft sprocket.

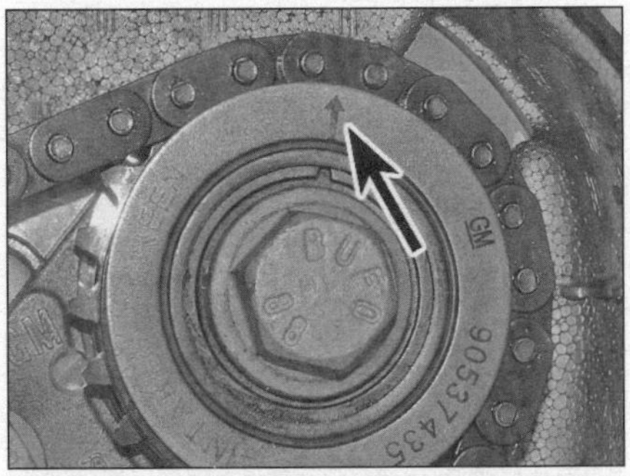

9.4c The copper-coloured chain link aligns with the timing arrow on the intake side balance shaft sprocket (arrowed)

5 Refit the chain guide rails, apply a little thread-locking compound, and tighten the retaining bolts to the specified torque.

6 Turn the tensioner plunger clockwise approximately 45° and push it back into the tensioner housing. Lock it in position using a 1.0 mm drill bit or pin inserted through the holes **(see illustration)**.

7 Refit the tensioner, apply a little thread-locking compound to the retaining bolts, and tighten them to the specified torque.

8 Remove the drill bit or pin from the tensioner.

9 Refit the timing chain as described in Section 8.

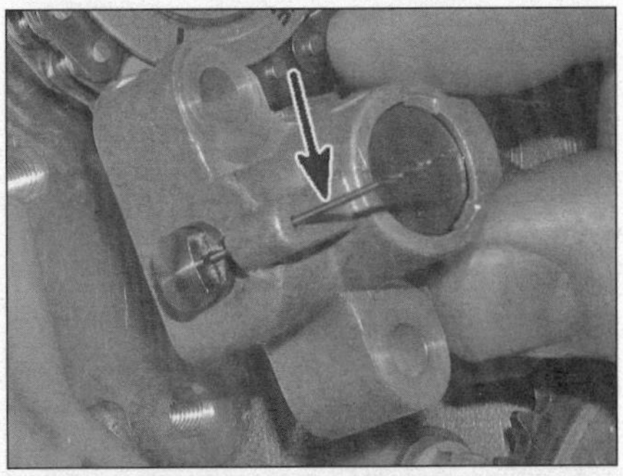

9.6 1.0 mm dill bit (arrowed) used to lock the tensioner piston in place

Balance shafts

Removal

10 Remove the balance shaft chain as previously described in this Section.

11 Undo the retaining bolt and pull the balance shaft(s) from the cylinder block **(see illustrations)**. Note that if the sprockets are removed, mark the shafts to identify the intake side shaft from the exhaust side shaft.

Refitting

12 Refitting is a reversal of removal, remembering to tighten the retaining bolt(s) to the specified torque.

9.11a Undo the retaining bolt (arrowed) …

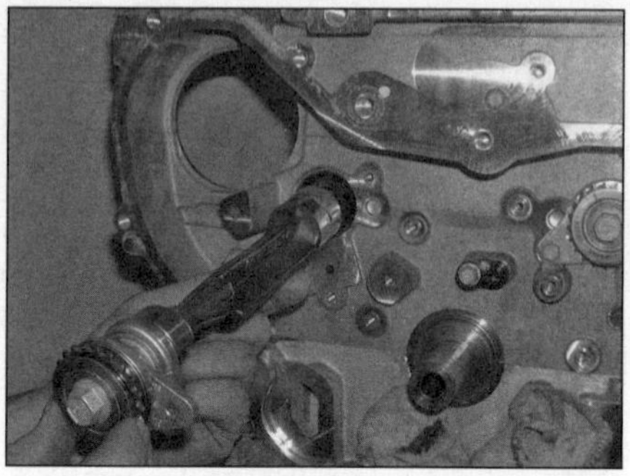

9.11b … and withdraw the balance shaft assembly

10 Oil pump – removal, inspection and refitting

Removal

1 Slacken the right-hand front roadwheel bolts, raise the front of the vehicle (see *Jacking and vehicle support*) and support it securely on axle stands. Remove the roadwheel.

2 Undo the fasteners and remove the right-hand front wheel arch liner. On Convertible models, undo the bolts and remove the front chassis reinforcement **(see illustration 6.7)**. Note that the front chassis reinforcement bolts are shorter than the rear.

3 Remove the auxiliary drivebelt as described in Chapter 1A, Section 26, then undo the bolt and remove the belt tensioner assembly **(see illustration 8.4)**.

4 Undo the 3 Torx screws and remove the plastic cover from the top of the engine.

5 Remove the air cleaner housing as described in Chapter 4A, Section 2.

6 Undo bolts and remove the turbocharger upper heat shield **(see illustration 4.9)**.

7 Support the engine from underneath using a trolley jack, then undo the bolts and remove the right-hand engine mounting assembly.

8 Lower the right-hand of the engine approximately 30 mm, then unscrew the bolt and remove the crankshaft pulley **(see illustrations 8.8a and 8.8b)**. Prevent the crankshaft from rotating using Saab tool No 83 95 360 and 83 96 210, or alternative.

9 Undo the bolts and remove the timing chain cover **(see illustration 8.9)**. Be prepared for oil spillage.

10 Cut off the part of the timing chain cover gasket that fits around the engine mounting, and remove the gasket.

11 Undo the cover bolts and lift out the oil pump gears. Note the marks on the gears to aid refitting **(see illustrations)**.

12 If required, slowly unscrew the plug, and withdraw the oil pressure relief valve spring and piston **(see illustrations)**.

10.11a Undo the screws and lift off the pump cover plate

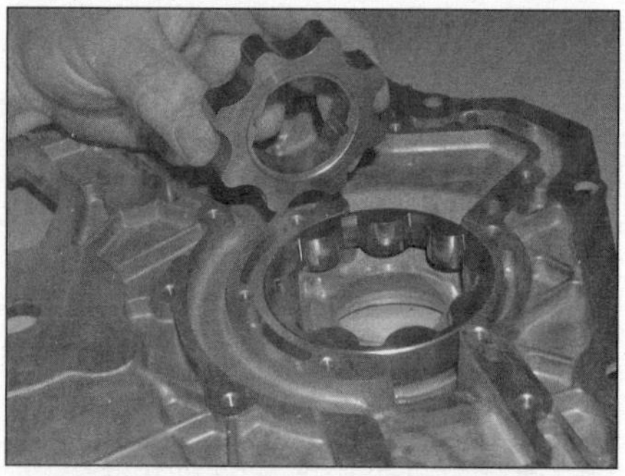

10.11b Lift out the inner and outer rotors

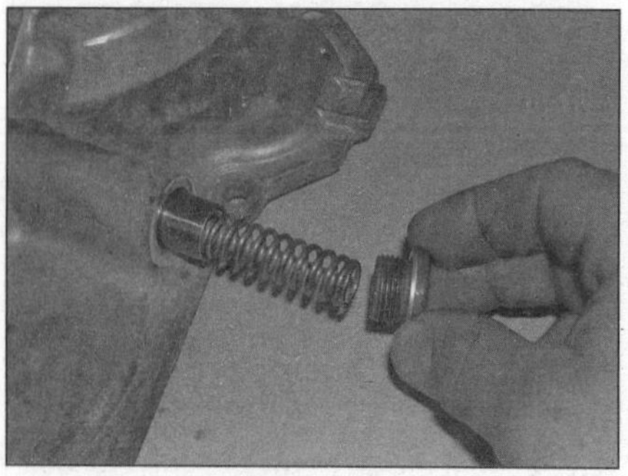

10.12a Unscrew the oil pressure relief valve plug …

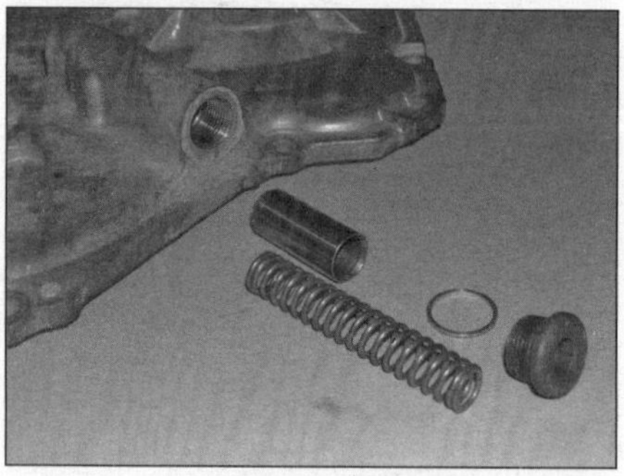

10.12b … and remove the oil pressure valve spring and plunger

Refitting

13 Examine the oil pump and pressure relief valve components for signs of wear or damage. As no technical details for the components are provided by the manufacturer, consult a Saab dealer or specialist with regard to new parts.

14 Fit the oil pump gears into position, ensuring the marks on the gears are orientated as before removal.

15 Lubricate the rotors with fresh engine oil.

16 Ensure the mating faces are clean, then refit the oil pump cover and tighten the bolts to the specified torque.

17 Fit the oil pressure relief valve piston and spring, then refit the plug using a new seal. Tighten the plug to the specified torque.

18 Fit the new gasket for the timing cover, cutting away the part of the gasket that fits around the engine mounting **(see illustration 8.24)**.

19 Prise/press the oil crankshaft oil seal from the timing cover, then refit the timing cover, and tighten the bolts to the specified torque.

20 Fit a new crankshaft oil seal to the timing cover, as described in Section 12.

21 Refit the crankshaft pulley using a new retaining bolt, and tighten it to the specified torque. Hold the crankshaft stationary using the same method employed during removal.

22 The remainder of refitting is a reversal of removal, ensuring all fasteners are tightened to the specified torque where given.

11 Oil pressure warning light switch – removal and refitting

Removal

1 The oil pressure switch is screwed into the front of the cylinder block, adjacent to the oil filter **(see illustration)**. First jack up the front of the car, and support on axle stands (see *Jacking and vehicle support*).

2 Release the retaining clip and disconnect the wiring plug from the switch.

3 Unscrew the switch from the cylinder block; be prepared for slight loss of oil. If the switch is to be left removed for any length of time, plug the hole, to prevent the entry of debris.

Refitting

4 Wipe clean the threads of the switch and the location aperture. Do not insert tools or wire into the hole at the tip of the switch in an attempt to clean it out, as this may damage the internal components.
5 Insert the switch into the cylinder block and tighten it to the specified torque.
6 Reconnect the switch wiring plug.
7 Start the engine and check for leakage, then lower the car to the ground. Check the engine oil level and top-up if necessary (see *Weekly checks*).

12 Crankshaft oil seals – renewal

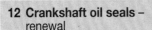

Right-hand oil seal

1 Apply the handbrake, then slacken the right-hand front roadwheel bolts, jack up the front of the car and support on axle stands (see *Jacking and vehicle support*). Remove the right-hand front wheel, undo the securing screws and withdraw the wheel arch liner.
2 Remove the auxiliary drivebelt with reference to Chapter 1A, Section 26.
3 Unscrew and remove the centre bolt from the crankshaft pulley. To do this, the crankshaft must be held stationary using one of the following methods. On manual transmission models, have an assistant depress the brake pedal and engage 4th gear. Alternatively, remove the flywheel cover plate or starter motor as described in Chapter 5A, Section 10, then insert a flat-bladed screwdriver through the bellhousing and jam the starter ring gear to prevent the crankshaft turning. On automatic transmission models, use the latter method only.
4 Pull the crankshaft pulley from the end of the crankshaft. If it is tight, careful use of two levers may be required.
5 Note the fitted depth of the oil seal in its housing, then using a screwdriver, carefully

11.1 Oil pressure warning switch

prise the oil seal from the oil pump casing **(see illustration)**.
6 Clean the seating in the oil pump casing, then lubricate the lips of the new oil seal with petroleum jelly, and locate it squarely on the oil pump casing. Make sure that the closed side is facing outwards. Using a suitable tubular drift (such as a socket) which bears only on the hard outer edge of the seal, tap the seal into position to the same depth in the casing as the original was prior to removal **(see illustration)**.
7 Locate the crankshaft pulley and hub on the end of the crankshaft. Insert the centre bolt and tighten it to the specified torque, holding the crankshaft stationary using one of the methods described in paragraph 3.
8 Refit the auxiliary drivebelt with reference to Chapter 1A, Section 26, then refit the engine mounting assembly.
9 Refit the wheel arch liner, and tighten the screws.
10 Refit the right-hand front wheel, and lower the car to the ground.

Left-hand oil seal

11 Remove the flywheel/driveplate as described in Section 13.
12 Make a note of the fitted depth of the seal in its housing (just below flush). Punch or drill two small holes opposite each other in the seal. Thread a self-tapping screw into each hole, and pull on the screw heads with pliers to extract the seal. Alternatively, use a screwdriver to prise out the oil seal **(see illustrations)**.
13 Clean the seal housing, and polish off any burrs or raised edges which may have caused the seal to fail in the first place. **Note:** *Insulation tape can be put around the crankshaft flange to help fit the seal.*
14 Lubricate the lips of the new seal with petroleum jelly, and carefully locate the seal on the end of the crankshaft. Ensure the lips of the seal locate around the shoulder of the crankshaft **(see illustration)**.
15 Where available, using a suitable tubular drift which bears only on the hard outer edge of the seal, drive the seal into position to the same depth in the housing as the original was prior to removal.
16 If insulation tape was used around the crankshaft flange, remove it, taking care not to damage the oil seal. Wipe clean the oil seal, then refit the flywheel/driveplate as described in Section 13.

12.5 Carefully prise the oil seal from the timing cover

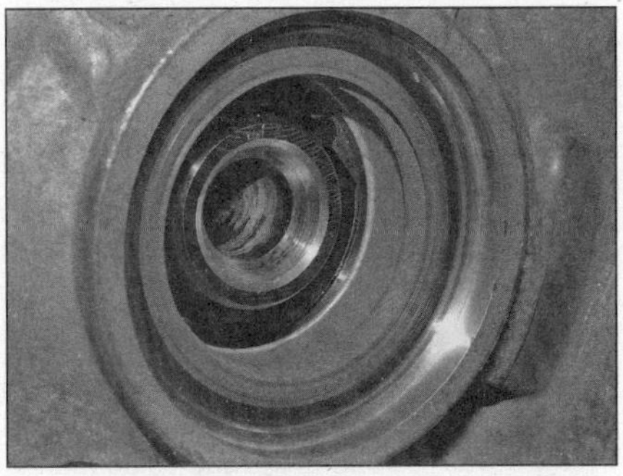

12.6 Ensure the seal is fitted to its original depth

12.12a Using a pair of pliers and a screw to remove the left-hand oil seal ...

12.12b ... or carefully prise the seal from place with a screwdriver

12.14 Ease the oil seal over the end of the crankshaft

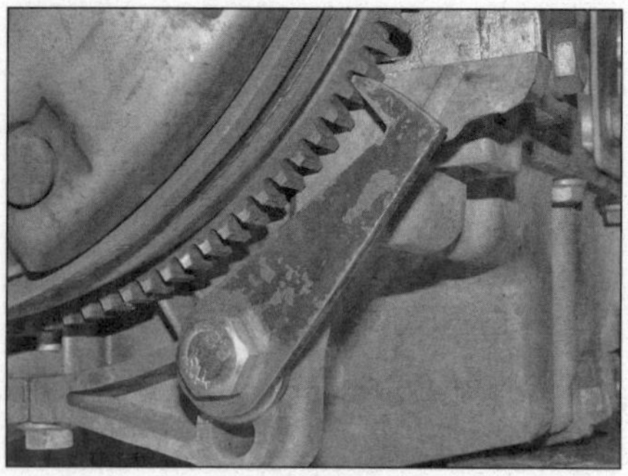

13.4 Lock the flywheel/driveplate ring gear

13 Flywheel/driveplate – removal, inspection and refitting

Removal

1 Remove the transmission as described in Chapter 7A, Section 7 or Chapter 7B, Section 9.
2 On manual transmission models, remove the clutch assembly as described in Chapter 6, Section 5.
3 Use a centre-punch or paint to make alignment marks on the flywheel/driveplate and crankshaft, to ensure correct alignment during refitting.
4 Prevent the flywheel/driveplate from turning by locking the ring gear teeth, or by bolting a strap between the flywheel/driveplate and the cylinder block/crankcase **(see illustration)**. Slacken the bolts evenly until all are free.
5 Remove each bolt in turn, and ensure that new ones are obtained for reassembly; these bolts are subjected to severe stresses, and so must be renewed, regardless of their apparent condition, whenever they are disturbed.
6 Withdraw the flywheel/driveplate from the end of the crankshaft. **Note:** *Take care when removing the flywheel/driveplate as it is a very heavy component.*

Inspection

7 Clean the flywheel/driveplate to remove grease and oil. Inspect the surface for cracks, rivet grooves, burned areas and score marks. Light scoring can be removed with emery cloth. Check for cracked and broken ring gear teeth. Lay the flywheel/driveplate on a flat surface, and use a straight-edge to check for warpage.
8 Clean and inspect the mating surfaces of the flywheel/driveplate and the crankshaft. If the crankshaft left-hand oil seal is leaking, renew it (see Section 12) before refitting the flywheel/driveplate.
9 While the flywheel/driveplate is removed, carefully clean its inboard (right-hand) face. Thoroughly clean the threaded bolt holes in the crankshaft – this is important, since if old sealer remains in the threads, the bolts will settle over a period and will not retain their correct torque wrench settings.
10 Where a dual mass flywheel is fitted it

13.11 The flywheel and crankshaft mounting holes will only align in one position

must be renewed if there is any evidence of fluid or grease on the flywheel or clutch components. The following procedures are given for guidance only. If in doubt as to the condition of the flywheel a professional inspection is recommended. If the assembly passes all the checks listed and there was no juddering from the clutch when taking up the drive, the flywheel can be refitted. However if the vehicle has covered a high mileage and especially if the vehicle is on its second new clutch, then it would be prudent to renew the dual mass flywheel.

Warpage

Check the drive surface for any signs of warpage or damage. The flywheel will normally warp like a bowl – ie, higher at the circumference. If the warpage is more than 4.0 mm consider renewing the flywheel.

Free rotational movement

This is the distance the drive surface of the flywheel can be turned independently of the flywheel primary element, using finger pressure only. Move the drive surface in one direction and make a mark where the locating pin aligns with the flywheel edge. Move the drive surface in the other direction (finger pressure only) and make another mark. The total of free movement should not exceed 10 mm. If it is more consider renewing the flywheel.

Total rotational movement

This is the total distance the drive surface can be turned independently of the flywheel primary elements. Insert two bolts into the clutch pressure/plate damper unit mounting holes and, with the crankshaft flywheel held stationary, use a pry bar between the bolts and use some effort to move the drive surface fully in one direction. Make a mark where the locating pin aligns with the flywheel edge. Now force the drive surface fully in the opposite direction, and make another mark. The total rotational movement should not exceed 44.0 mm. If it does have the flywheel professionally inspected.

Lateral movement

The lateral movement (up and down) of the drive surface in relation to the primary element of the flywheel should not exceed 2.0 mm, if it does the flywheel may need renewing. This can be checked by pressing the drive surface down on one side into the flywheel (flywheel horizontal) and making an alignment mark between the drive surface and the inner edge of the primary elements. Now press down on the opposite side of the drive surface and make another mark above the original one. The difference between the two marks is the lateral movement.

Refitting

11 On refitting, fit the flywheel/driveplate to the crankshaft so that all bolt holes align – it will fit only one way – check this using the marks made on removal. Apply suitable thread-locking compound to the threads of the new bolts then insert them **(see illustration)**.
12 Lock the flywheel/driveplate by the method used on dismantling. Working in a diagonal sequence to tighten them evenly, and increasing to the final amount in three stages, tighten the new bolts to the specified torque wrench setting.
13 The remainder of reassembly is the reverse of the removal procedure, referring to the relevant text for details where required.

14 Engine/transmission mountings – inspection and renewal

Inspection

1 For improved access, raise the front of the car and support it securely on axle stands (see *Jacking and vehicle support*).
2 The engine mountings are located at the front right-hand side, above the left-hand side of the transmission, and at the rear of the engine. The right-hand mounting is a rubber/hdraulic type, incorporating an inner chamber filled with oil. Vibration damping is progressive depending on the load applied, and works for both horizontal and vertical movement.
3 Check the mounting rubbers to see if they are cracked, hardened or separated from the metal at any point; renew the mounting if any such damage or deterioration is evident.
4 Check that all the mounting's fasteners are securely tightened.
5 Using a large screwdriver or a crowbar, check for wear in the mounting by carefully levering against it to check for freeplay. Where this is not possible, enlist the aid of an assistant to move the engine/transmission back-and-forth, or from side-to-side, while you watch the mounting. While some freeplay is to be expected even from new components, excessive wear should be obvious. If excessive freeplay is found, check first that the fasteners are securely tightened, then if necessary renew any worn components as described below.

Renewal

Right-hand engine mounting

6 Apply the handbrake, then jack up the front

of the car and support on axle stands (see *Jacking and vehicle support*).

7 On Convertible models, undo the bolts and remove the front chassis reinforcement **(see illustration 6.7)**. Note that the front bolts are shorter than the rear ones.

8 Place a trolley jack under the engine sump, and take the weight of the engine. Use a block of wood between the jack head and the sump to spread the load and prevent any damage.

9 Remove the air cleaner assembly as described in Chapter 4A, Section 2.

10 Make alignment marks between the engine mounting pad, the vehicle body, and the mounting bracket to aid reassembly **(see illustration)**.

11 Undo the retaining bolts and remove the mounting. If necessary, unbolt the bracket from the front of the cylinder block.

12 Fit the new mountings using a reversal of the removal procedure, making sure that the bolts are tightened to the correct torque.

Left-hand engine/ transmission mounting

13 Apply the handbrake, then jack up the front of the car and support on axle stands (see *Jacking and vehicle support*).

14 On Convertible models, undo the bolts and remove the front chassis reinforcement **(see illustration 6.7)**. Note that the front bolts are shorter than the rear ones.

15 Position a trolley jack underneath the transmission and raise the jack head until it is just taking the combined weight of the engine and transmission. On models with automatic transmission, ensure that the jack head does not bear on the underside of the transmission sump.

16 Remove the battery and battery tray as described in Chapter 5A, Section 4.

14.10 Right-hand engine mounting assembly

14.17 Undo the bolt and disconnect the earth lead (arrowed)

14.22a Left-hand rear torque arm ...

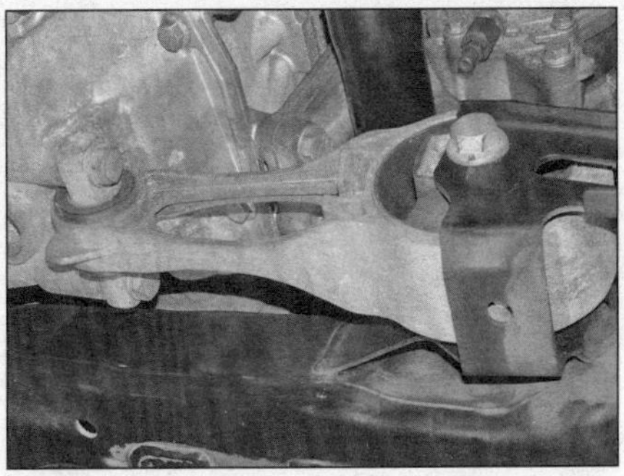

14.22b ... and right-hand rear torque arm

17 Undo the bolt and disconnect the earth lead from the mounting **(see illustration)**.

18 Undo the bolts and remove the mounting.

19 If required, undo the bolts and remove the bracket.

20 Fit the new mounting using a reversal of the removal procedure, making sure that the bolts are tightened to the correct torque.

Torque arms

21 Apply the handbrake, then jack up the front of the car and support on axle stands (see *Jacking and vehicle support*).

22 Undo the bolts and remove the torque arm from position **(see illustrations)**.

23 Fit the new mounting using a reversal of the removal procedure, making sure that the nuts/bolts are tightened to the correct torque.

Notes

Chapter 2 Part B:
Diesel SOHC engine in-car repair procedures

Contents

Degrees of difficulty

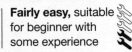

Easy, suitable for novice with little experience	**Fairly easy,** suitable for beginner with some experience	**Fairly difficult,** suitable for competent DIY mechanic	**Difficult,** suitable for experienced DIY mechanic	**Very difficult,** suitable for expert DIY or professional

Specifications

General

Engine type	Four-cylinder, in-line, water-cooled. Single overhead camshaft, belt-driven
Manufacturer's engine code*	Z19DT
Bore	82.0 mm
Stroke	90.4 mm
Capacity	1910 cc
Output:	
Torque	280 Nm @ 2000 rpm
Power	88 kW @ 4000 rpm
Compression ratio	18.0:1
Firing order	1-3-4-2 (No 1 cylinder at timing belt end of engine)
Direction of crankshaft rotation	Clockwise (viewed from timing belt end of engine)

* *For details of engine code location, see 'Vehicle identification' in the Reference Chapter.*

Compression pressures

Pressure	25 to 32 bar
Maximum difference between any two cylinders	1.5 bar

Valve clearances

Intake and exhaust (engine cold)	0.30 to 0.40 mm

Lubrication system

Minimum oil pressure at 80°C:	
At idle speed	1.0 bar
At 4000 rpm	4.0 bar
Oil pump type	Rotor-type, driven by crankshaft pulley/vibration damper from crankshaft

Torque wrench settings

	Nm	lbf ft
Air conditioning compressor mounting bracket to cylinder block/sump	50	37
Air conditioning compressor to bracket	24	18
Auxiliary drivebelt idler pulley bolt	25	18
Auxiliary drivebelt tensioner assembly bolts	50	37
Camshaft bearing cap bolts	15	11
Camshaft cover bolts	10	7
Camshaft sprocket bolt*	120	89
Connecting rod big-end bearing cap bolt:*		
Stage 1	25	18
Stage 2	Angle-tighten a further 60°	
Crankshaft oil seal housing	9	7
Crankshaft pulley/vibration damper bolts	25	18
Crankshaft sprocket bolt*†	340	251
Cylinder head bolts:*		
Stage 1	20	15
Stage 2	65	48
Stage 3	Angle-tighten a further 90°	
Stage 4	Angle-tighten a further 90°	
Stage 5	Angle-tighten a further 90°	
Engine mountings:		
Front mounting/torque link bracket to transmission	80	59
Front mounting/torque link to subframe:		
Stage 1	60	44
Stage 2	Angle-tighten a further 90°	
Left-hand:		
Mounting-to-body bolts	20	15
Mounting bracket to transmission bracket	55	41
Transmission bracket to transmission	55	41
Rear mounting/torque link bracket to transmission	80	59
Rear mounting/torque link to subframe	60	44
Rear mounting/torque link to transmission bracket	80	59
Right-hand:		
Engine bracket-to-engine bolts	55	41
Lower bolts (M8)	25	18
Upper bolts (M10)	50	37
Mounting-to-body bolts:		
Stage 1	40	30
Stage 2	Angle-tighten a further 60°	
Mounting-to-engine bracket bolts	50	37
Engine-to-transmission unit bolts:		
M10 bolts	40	30
M12 bolts	60	44
Flywheel bolts*	160	118
High-pressure fuel pump sprocket nut*	50	37
Intermediate shaft bearing housing support bracket bolts	55	41
Main bearing cap bolts:*		
Stage 1	25	18
Stage 2	Angle-tighten a further 100°	
Oil filter housing to cylinder block	50	37
Oil pump housing to cylinder block	9	7
Oil pump pick-up/strainer bolts	9	7
Roadwheel bolts	110	81
Sump bolts:		
M6 bolts	9	7
M8 bolts	25	18
M10 bolts	40	30
Sump drain plug	25	18
Timing belt idler pulley bolt	50	37
Timing belt tensioner bolt	25	18
Timing belt upper cover bolts:		
M6 bolts	9	7
M8 bolts	25	18

** Do not re-use*
† Left-hand thread

1 General information

How to use this Chapter

This Chapter describes the repair procedures which can reasonably be carried out on the engine while it remains in the vehicle. If the engine has been removed from the vehicle and is being dismantled as described in Chapter 2D, any preliminary dismantling procedures can be ignored.

Note that, while it may be possible physically to overhaul items such as the piston/connecting rod assemblies while the engine is in the vehicle, such tasks are not usually carried out as separate operations, and usually require the execution of several additional procedures (not to mention the cleaning of components and of oilways); for this reason, all such tasks are classed as major overhaul procedures, and are described in Chapter 2D.

Chapter 2D describes the removal of the engine/transmission unit from the vehicle, and the full overhaul procedures which can then be carried out.

Engine description

The 1.9 litre SOHC diesel engine is an eight-valve, in-line four-cylinder, single overhead camshaft engine. The engine is mounted transversely at the front of the car, with the transmission on its left-hand end.

The crankshaft is supported within the cylinder block on five shell-type main bearings. Thrustwashers are fitted to number 3 main bearing, to control crankshaft endfloat.

The connecting rods rotate on horizontally-split bearing shells at their big-ends. The pistons are attached to the connecting rods by gudgeon pins, which are retained by circlips. The aluminium-alloy pistons are fitted with three piston rings – two compression rings and scraper-type oil control ring.

The camshaft runs directly in the cylinder head, and is driven by the crankshaft via a toothed composite rubber timing belt (which also drives the high-pressure fuel pump and the coolant pump). The camshaft operates each valve via a camshaft follower with adjustment shim.

Lubrication is by pressure-feed from a rotor-type oil pump, which is mounted on the right-hand end of the crankshaft. The pump draws oil through a strainer located in the sump, and then forces it through an externally mounted full-flow cartridge-type filter. The oil flows into galleries in the cylinder block/crankcase, from where it is distributed to the crankshaft (main bearings) and camshaft. The big-end bearings are supplied with oil via internal drillings in the crankshaft, while the camshaft bearings also receive a pressurised supply. The camshaft lobes and valves are lubricated by splash, as are all other engine components.

A semi-closed crankcase ventilation system is employed; crankcase fumes are drawn from the oil separator (integral with the camshaft cover), and passed via a hose to the intake manifold.

Operations with engine in car

The following operations can be carried out without having to remove the engine from the car.

a) Removal and refitting of the camshaft cover.
b) Adjustment of the valve clearances.
c) Removal and refitting of the cylinder head.
d) Removal and refitting of the timing belt, tensioner, idler pulleys and sprockets.
e) Renewal of the camshaft oil seal.
f) Removal and refitting of the camshaft and followers.
g) Removal and refitting of the sump.
*h) Removal and refitting of the connecting rods and pistons.**
i) Removal and refitting of the oil pump.
j) Removal and refitting of the oil filter housing.
k) Renewal of the crankshaft oil seals.
l) Renewal of the engine mountings.
m) Removal and refitting of the flywheel.

** Although the operation marked with an asterisk can be carried out with the engine in the car (after removal of the sump), it is preferable for the engine to be removed, in the interests of cleanliness and improved access. For this reason, the procedure is described in Chapter 2D, Section 9.*

2 Compression and leakdown tests – description and interpretation

Compression test

Note: *A compression tester specifically designed for diesel engines must be used for this test because of the higher pressures involved.*

Note: *The battery must be in a good state of charge, the air filter must be clean, and the engine should be at normal operating temperature.*

1 When engine performance is down, or if misfiring occurs which cannot be attributed to the fuel system, a compression test can provide diagnostic clues as to the engine's condition. If the test is performed regularly, it can give warning of trouble before any other symptoms become apparent.

2 The tester is connected to an adapter which screws into the injector holes. It is unlikely to be worthwhile buying such a tester for occasional use, but it may be possible to borrow or hire one – if not, have the test performed by a Saab dealer, or suitably-equipped garage. If the necessary equipment is available, proceed as follows.

3 Remove the fuel injectors as described in Chapter 4B, Section 12.

4 Screw the compression tester adapter in to the fuel injector hole of No 1 cylinder.

5 With the help of an assistant, crank the engine on the starter motor; after a few revolutions, the compression pressure should build-up to a maximum figure, and then stabilise. Record the highest reading obtained.

6 Repeat the test on the remaining cylinders, recording the pressure in each.

7 All cylinders should produce very similar pressures; any difference greater than the maximum figure given in the Specifications indicates the existence of a fault. Note that the compression should build-up quickly in a healthy engine; low compression on the first stroke, followed by gradually-increasing pressure on successive strokes, indicates worn piston rings. A low compression reading on the first stroke, which does not build-up during successive strokes, indicates leaking valves or a blown head gasket (a cracked head could also be the cause). **Note:** *The cause of poor compression is less easy to establish on a diesel engine than on a petrol one. The effect of introducing oil into the cylinders ('wet' testing) is not conclusive, because there is a risk that the oil will sit in the recess on the piston crown instead of passing to the rings.*

8 On completion of the test, refit the fuel injectors as described in Chapter 4B, Section 12.

Leakdown test

9 A leakdown test measures the rate at which compressed air fed into the cylinder is lost. It is an alternative to a compression test, and in many ways it is better, since the escaping air provides easy identification of where pressure loss is occurring (piston rings, valves or head gasket).

10 The equipment needed for leakdown testing is unlikely to be available to the home mechanic. If poor compression is suspected, have the test performed by a Saab dealer, or suitably-equipped garage.

3 Top dead centre (TDC) for No 1 piston – locating

Note: *To accurately determine the TDC position for No 1 piston, it will be necessary to use Saab special tool 32 025 009 (or a suitable equivalent) to set the crankshaft at the TDC position* ***(see illustration)****.*

1 In its travel up and down its cylinder bore, Top Dead Centre (TDC) is the highest point that each piston reaches as the crankshaft rotates. While each piston reaches TDC both at the top of the compression stroke and again at the top of the exhaust stroke, for the purpose of timing the engine, TDC refers to the piston position of No 1 cylinder at the top of its compression stroke.

3.0 Saab special tool 32 025 009 (or equivalent) is required to set the TDC position for No 1 cylinder

3.5 Undo the central mounting bolt (arrowed) and remove the auxiliary drivebelt tensioner assembly

2 Number 1 piston (and cylinder) is at the right-hand (timing belt) end of the engine, and its TDC position is located as follows. Note that the crankshaft rotates clockwise when viewed from the right-hand side of the car.

3 Remove the engine oil filler cap, undo the two retaining bolts, release the hose support clip, then lift off the plastic cover over the top of the engine. Refit the oil filler cap.

4 Remove the crankshaft pulley/vibration damper as described in Section 6.

5 Undo the central mounting bolt, and remove the auxiliary drivebelt tensioner assembly from the engine **(see illustration)**.

6 Remove the air cleaner assembly and air intake duct as described in Chapter 4B, Section 3.

7 Undo the fasteners and remove the engine undershield, then place a trolley jack beneath the right-hand end of the engine with a block of wood on the jack head. Raise the jack until it is supporting the weight of the engine.

8 Mark the bolt positions for correct refitting, then undo the three bolts securing the right-hand engine mounting to the engine bracket, and the three bolts securing the mounting to the body. Remove the mounting **(see illustration)**.

9 Unclip the wiring harness from the top and side of the upper timing belt cover. Unscrew the six retaining bolts and lift off the upper timing belt cover **(see illustration)**.

10 Using a socket and extension bar on the crankshaft sprocket bolt, rotate the crankshaft in the normal direction of rotation until the mark on the camshaft sprocket is aligned with the pointer on the camshaft cover **(see illustration)**.

11 Unscrew the bolt from the lower left-hand side of the oil pump housing and screw in the fastening stud of Saab special tool 32 025 009 **(see illustration)**.

12 Fit the positioning ring of tool 32 025 009 over the fastening stud and engage it with the crankshaft sprocket. Ensure that the hole in the positioning ring engages with the lug on the sprocket. Secure the tool in position with the retaining bolt and nut **(see illustration)**.

13 With the crankshaft positioning ring in place, and the mark on the camshaft sprocket aligned with the pointer on the camshaft cover, the engine is positioned with No 1 piston at TDC on compression.

3.8 Remove the right-hand engine mounting

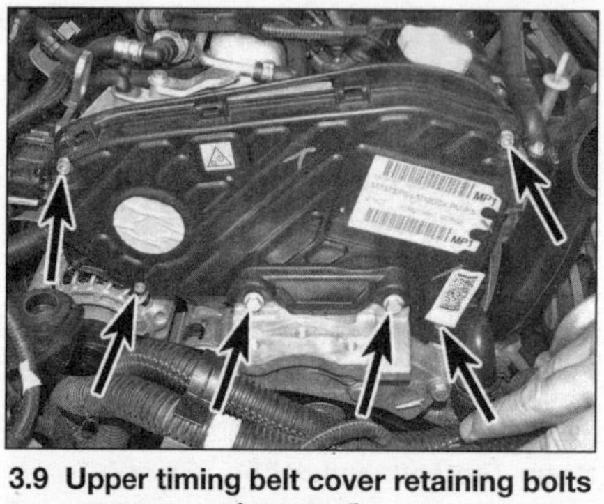

3.9 Upper timing belt cover retaining bolts (arrowed)

3.10 Rotate the crankshaft to align the mark on the camshaft sprocket (arrowed) with the pointer on the camshaft cover

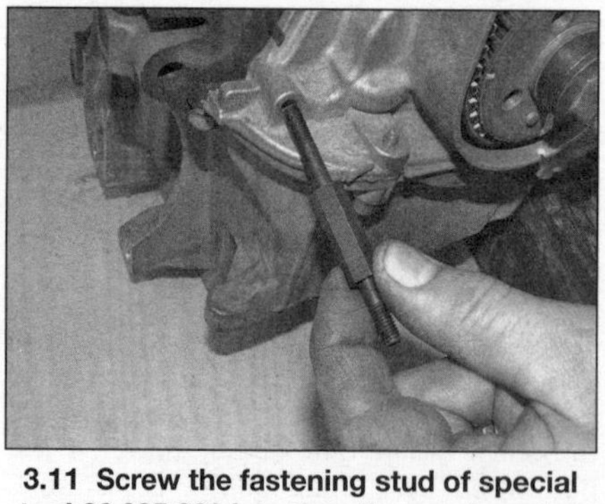

3.11 Screw the fastening stud of special tool 32 025 009 into the oil pump housing

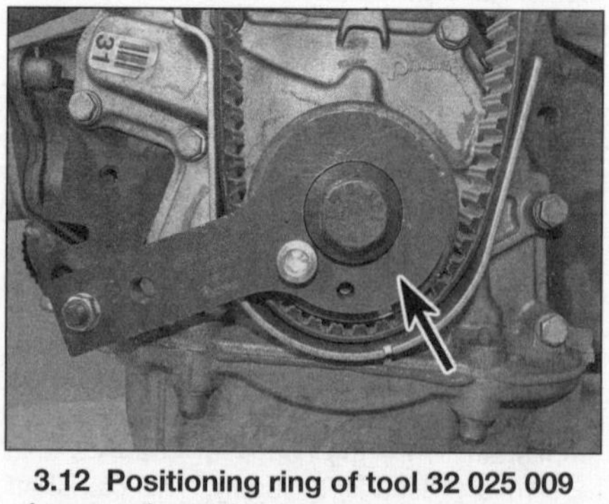

3.12 Positioning ring of tool 32 025 009 (arrowed) attached to the fastening stud and crankshaft sprocket

5.2 Undo the retaining bolt(s) to release the vacuum lines from the camshaft cover

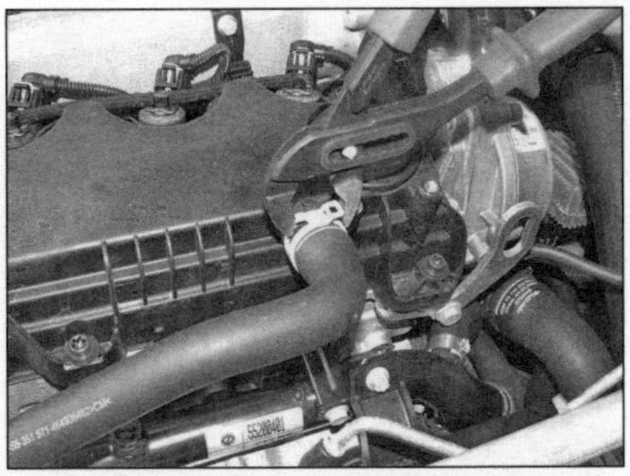
5.3a Release the retaining clips and disconnect the breather hoses from the front ...

5.3b ... and rear of the camshaft cover

5.5 Undo the 7 bolts (arrowed) securing the camshaft cover to the cylinder head

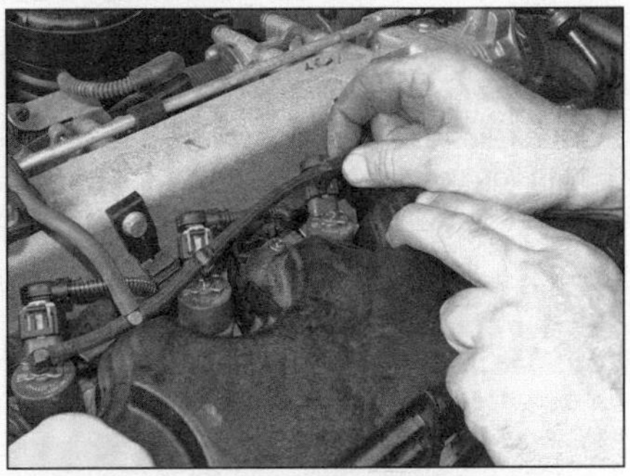
5.6 Move the lead-off hose assembly rearward, then lift the camshaft cover from the cylinder head

5.7 Fit the seal to the camshaft cover groove

4 Valve timing – checking and adjustment

1 Position No 1 cylinder at TDC on its compression stroke as described in Section 3.

2 With the crankshaft positioning ring in place, check that the mark on the camshaft sprocket is aligned with the pointer on the camshaft cover; if so, the valve timing is correct **(see illustration 3.10)**.

3 If the mark on the camshaft sprocket is not aligned with the pointer on the camshaft cover, readjust the timing belt position as described in Section 7.

5 Camshaft cover – removal and refitting

Removal

1 Remove the engine oil filler cap, undo the two retaining bolts, release the hose support clip, then undo the two bolts and lift off the plastic cover over the top of the engine. Refit the oil filler cap.

2 Undo the retaining bolt(s) to release the vacuum lines running over the top of the camshaft cover **(see illustration)**.

3 Release the retaining clips and disconnect the breather hoses from the front and rear of the camshaft cover **(see illustrations)**.

4 Disconnect the fuel leak-off hose connection at No 2 and No 3 injector by extracting the locking clip and lifting out the hose fitting. Refit the locking clips to the injectors after disconnecting the hose fitting.

5 Undo the seven retaining bolts securing the camshaft cover to the cylinder head **(see illustration)**.

6 Carefully move the disconnected leak-off hose assembly rearward, then lift the camshaft cover from the cylinder head **(see illustration)**.

Refitting

7 Ensure the cover and cylinder head surfaces are clean and dry then fit the seal to the cover groove **(see illustration)**.

8 Move the leak-off hose assembly to the rear and carefully lower the cover into position. Screw in the retaining bolts and lightly tighten them. Once all bolts are hand-tight, go around and tighten them all to the specified torque setting.

9 Reconnect the leak-off hose fittings to the injectors by pushing in the locking clip, attaching the fitting, then releasing the locking clip. Ensure that each fitting is securely connected and retained by the clip.

10 Reconnect the breather hoses to the cover.

11 Refit and tighten the bolts securing the vacuum lines.

12 Refit the plastic cover to the top of the engine, tighten the two retaining bolts and resecure the hose.

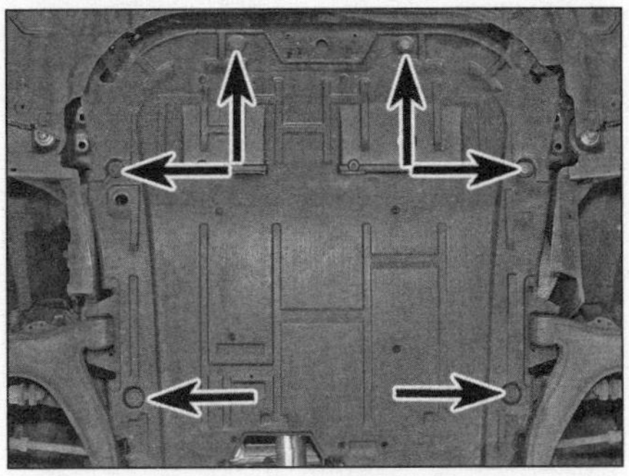
6.1 Engine undershield bolts (arrowed)

6 Crankshaft pulley/ vibration damper – removal and refitting

Removal

1 Apply the handbrake, then jack up the front of the vehicle and support it on axle stands (see *Jacking and vehicle support)*. Remove the right-hand front roadwheel, then undo the bolts and remove the engine undershield for access to the crankshaft pulley **(see illustration)**.

2 Remove the auxiliary drivebelt as described in Chapter 1B, Section 27. Prior to removal, mark the direction of rotation on the belt to ensure the belt is refitted the same way around.

3 Undo the four bolts securing the pulley to the crankshaft sprocket and remove the pulley from the sprocket **(see illustration)**.

Refitting

4 Locate the crankshaft pulley on the sprocket, ensuring that the hole on the rear face of the pulley engages with the lug on the sprocket.
5 Refit the four retaining bolts and tighten them progressively to the specified torque.
6 Refit the auxiliary drivebelt as described in Chapter 1B, Section 27 using the mark made prior to removal to ensure the belt is fitted the correct way around.
7 Refit the roadwheel and engine undershield, then lower the car to the ground and tighten the wheel bolts to the specified torque.

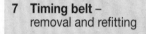

7 Timing belt – removal and refitting

Note: *Saab special tool 32 025 009 or an equivalent will be required.*
Note: *The timing belt must be removed and refitted with the engine cold.*

Removal

1 Position No 1 cylinder at TDC on its compression stroke as described in Section 3.
2 Undo the retaining bolt and remove the auxiliary drivebelt idler pulley from the engine bracket **(see illustration)**.
3 Undo the two lower bolts, and the three upper bolts, and remove the engine bracket from the engine **(see illustrations)**.

6.3 Crankshaft pulley/vibration damper retaining bolts (arrowed)

4 Undo the nut and bolt and remove the crankshaft positioning tool (32 025 009) from the crankshaft sprocket.
5 Slacken the timing belt tensioner retaining bolt and allow the tensioner to retract, relieving the tension on the timing belt.
6 Slide the timing belt from its sprockets and remove it from the engine. If the belt is to be re-used, use white paint or similar to mark the direction of rotation on the belt.
Caution: Do not rotate the crankshaft or camshafts until the timing belt has been refitted.
7 Check the timing belt carefully for any signs of uneven wear, splitting or oil contamination, and renew it if there is the slightest doubt about its condition. If the engine is undergoing an overhaul and is approaching the specified interval for belt renewal (see Chapter 1B, Section 25) renew the belt as a matter of course, regardless of its apparent condition. If signs of oil contamination are found, trace the source of the oil leak and rectify it, then wash down the engine timing belt area and all related components to remove all traces of oil.

Refitting

8 On reassembly, thoroughly clean the timing belt sprockets and tensioner/idler pulleys.
9 Place the timing belt in position over the crankshaft sprocket. If the original belt is being refitted, ensure that the arrow mark made on removal points in the normal direction of rotation, as before.
10 Check that the camshaft and crankshaft are still correctly positioned with No 1 piston at TDC on compression as described in Section 3, and refit the crankshaft positioning tool.
11 Fit the timing belt over the crankshaft, camshaft and fuel pump sprockets and around the idler pulleys, ensuring that the belt front run is taut (ie, all slack is on the tensioner side of the belt), then fit the belt over the coolant pump sprocket and tensioner pulley **(see illustration)**. Do not twist the belt sharply while refitting it. Ensure that the belt teeth are correctly seated centrally in the sprockets, and that the timing mark on the camshaft sprocket remains in alignment.
12 Screw in a suitable bolt, approximately 50 mm in length, into the threaded hole directly below the timing belt tensioner. Using a screwdriver resting on the bolt as a pivot, move the adjusting lever on the tensioner until the tensioner pointer is aligned with the mark on the backplate. Hold the tensioner in this position and tighten the tensioner retaining bolt **(see illustrations)**.

7.2 Undo the bolt (arrowed) and remove the auxiliary drivebelt idler pulley from the engine mounting bracket

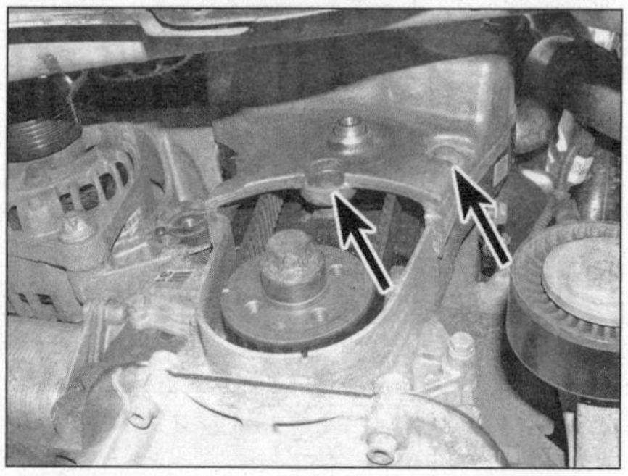

7.3a Undo the 2 lower bolts (arrowed) ...

7.3b ... and the 3 upper bolts (arrowed) ...

7.3c ... and remove the mounting bracket from the engine

7.11 Timing belt routing

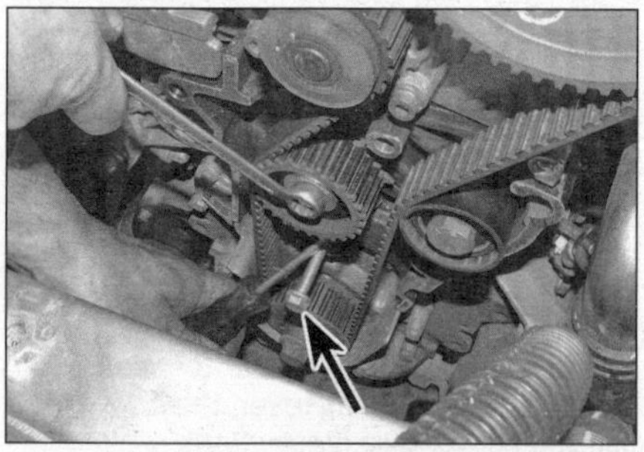

7.12a Using a screwdriver resting on a pivot bolt (arrowed), move the adjusting lever on the tensioner ...

7.12b … until the tensioner pointer (arrowed) is aligned with the mark on the backplate

13 Remove the crankshaft positioning tool.

14 Using a socket on the crankshaft sprocket bolt, rotate the crankshaft smoothly through two complete turns (720°) in the normal direction of rotation to settle the timing belt in position. At the end of the second turn, align the mark on the camshaft sprocket with the pointer on the camshaft cover.

15 Refit the positioning ring of tool (32 025 009) over the fastening stud and engage it with the crankshaft sprocket. Ensure that the hole in the positioning ring engages with the lug on the sprocket. Secure the tool in position with the retaining bolt and nut.

16 Slacken the timing belt tensioner retaining bolt and, using a screwdriver resting on the pivot bolt as before, move the adjusting lever on the tensioner until the tensioner pointer is once again aligned with the mark on the backplate. Hold the tensioner in this position and tighten the tensioner retaining bolt to the specified torque.

17 Remove all the positioning tools and again rotate the crankshaft smoothly through two complete turns (720°) in the normal direction of rotation. Check that the timing belt tensioner pointer is still aligned with the mark on the backplate. If not, repeat the procedure described in paragraph 16.

18 When all is correct, remove the tensioner position pivot bolt. Refit the bolt removed from the oil pump housing and tighten it to the specified torque.

19 Place the engine bracket in position and refit the two lower bolts, and the three upper bolts. Tighten the bolts to the specified torque. Refit the auxiliary drivebelt idler pulley to the engine bracket and tighten the retaining bolt to the specified torque.

20 Refit the upper timing belt cover and tighten the retaining bolts to the specified torque. Clip the wiring harness back into position.

21 Place the right-hand engine mounting assembly in position and refit the three bolts securing the mounting to the body. Tighten the bolts/nut to the specified torque. Align the mounting in its original position, then tighten the three mounting bracket bolts to the specified torque. Remove the jack from under the engine.

22 Refit the air cleaner assembly and air intake duct as described in Chapter 4B, Section 3.

23 Place the auxiliary drivebelt tensioner assembly in position ensuring that the locating peg on the tensioner mounting surface engages correctly with the corresponding hole in the mounting bracket. Tighten the tensioner central mounting bolt to the specified torque.

24 Refit the crankshaft pulley/vibration damper as described in Section 6, then refit the auxiliary drivebelt as described in Chapter 1B, Section 27.

25 Refit the plastic cover to the top of the engine and tighten the retaining bolts.

26 Refit the roadwheel and engine undershield, then lower the car to the ground and tighten the wheel bolts to the specified torque.

8 Timing belt sprockets, tensioner and idler pulley – removal and refitting

Note: *Certain special tools will be required for the removal and refitting of the sprockets. Read through the entire procedure to familiarise yourself with the work involved, then either obtain the manufacturer's special tools, or use the alternatives described.*

Camshaft sprocket

Note: *A new sprocket retaining bolt will be required for refitting.*

Removal

1 Remove the timing belt as described in Section 7.

2 It will now be necessary to hold the camshaft sprocket to enable the retaining bolt to be removed. Saab special tools 32 025 008-1 are available for this purpose, however, a home-made tool can easily be fabricated **(see Tool Tip)**.

3 Engage the tool with the holes in the camshaft sprocket, taking care not to damage the camshaft sensor located behind the sprocket

4 Unscrew the retaining bolt and remove the sprocket from the end of the camshaft.

Refitting

5 Prior to refitting, check the oil seal for signs of damage or leakage. If necessary, renew as described in Section 9.

8.12a Remove the bolt and washer …

TOOL TIP

To make a sprocket holding tool, obtain two lengths of steel strip about 6 mm thick by about 30 mm wide or similar, one 600 mm long, the other 200 mm long (all dimensions are approximate). Bolt the two strips together to form a forked end, leaving the bolt slack so the shorter strip can pivot freely. At the other end of each 'prong' of the fork, fit a nut and bolt to allow the tool to engage with the spokes in the sprocket.

6 Refit the sprocket to the camshaft end, aligning its cut-out with the locating peg, and fit the new retaining bolt.

7 Retain the sprocket using the holding tool, and tighten the retaining bolt to the specified torque.

8 Refit the timing belt as described in Section 7.

Crankshaft sprocket

Note: *The crankshaft sprocket retaining bolt is extremely tight. Ensure that the holding tool used to prevent rotation as the bolt is slackened is of sturdy construction and securely attached.*

Note: *A new sprocket retaining bolt will be required for refitting.*

Removal

9 Remove the timing belt as described in Section 7.

10 It will now be necessary to hold the crankshaft sprocket to enable the retaining bolt to be removed. Saab special tools 32 025 006 and 83 95 360 are available for this purpose, however, a home-made tool similar to that described in paragraph 2 can easily be fabricated.

11 Using the crankshaft pulley retaining bolts, securely attach the tool to the crankshaft sprocket. With the help of an assistant, hold the sprocket stationary and unscrew the retaining bolt. **Note:** *The sprocket retaining bolt has a* ***left-hand thread*** *and is unscrewed by turning it clockwise.*

12 Remove the bolt and washer and slide the sprocket off the end of the crankshaft **(see illustrations)**. Note that a new bolt will be required for refitting.

8.12b ... and slide the sprocket off the end of the crankshaft

Refitting

13 Align the sprocket location key with the crankshaft groove and slide the sprocket into position. Fit the new retaining bolt and washer.

14 Hold the sprocket stationary using the holding tool and tighten the retaining bolt to the specified torque, remembering it has a **left-hand thread**. Remove the holding tool.

15 Refit the timing belt as described in Section 7.

High-pressure fuel pump sprocket

Note: *A new sprocket retaining nut will be required for refitting.*

Removal

16 Remove the timing belt as described in Section 7.

8.18 Engage the holding tool with the holes in the fuel pump sprocket and undo the retaining nut

17 It will now be necessary to hold the fuel pump sprocket to enable the retaining nut to be removed. Saab special tools 32 025 019 and 83 95 360 are available for this purpose, however, a home-made tool similar to that described in paragraph 2 can easily be fabricated.

18 Engage the tool with the holes in the fuel pump sprocket and undo the sprocket retaining nut **(see illustration)**.

19 Attach a suitable puller to the threaded holes in the fuel pump sprocket using bolts and washers similar to the arrangement shown **(see illustration)**.

20 Tighten the puller centre bolt to release the sprocket from the taper on the pump shaft. Once the taper releases, remove the puller and withdraw the sprocket. Collect the Woodruff key from the pump shaft **(see illustrations)**.

8.19 Use a suitable puller to release the fuel pump sprocket taper

Refitting

21 Clean the fuel pump shaft and the sprocket hub ensuring that all traces of oil or grease are removed.

22 Refit the Woodruff key to the pump shaft, then locate the sprocket in position. Fit the new retaining nut.

23 Hold the sprocket stationary using the holding tool and tighten the retaining nut to the specified torque. Remove the holding tool.

24 Refit the timing belt as described in Section 7.

8.20a Once the taper releases, withdraw the sprocket ...

8.20b ... and collect the Woodruff key from the pump shaft

8.26 Slacken and remove the retaining bolt and remove the timing belt tensioner assembly

8.27 The slot on the tensioner backplate must locate over the peg (arrowed) on the engine bracket

Tensioner assembly

Removal

25 Remove the timing belt as described in Section 7.

26 Slacken and remove the retaining bolt and remove the tensioner assembly from the engine **(see illustration)**.

Refitting

27 Fit the tensioner to the engine, making sure that the slot on the tensioner backplate is correctly located over the peg on the engine bracket **(see illustration)**.

28 Clean the threads of the retaining bolt. Screw in the retaining bolt, set the tensioner in the retracted position and tighten the retaining bolt.

29 Refit the timing belt as described in Section 7.

Idler pulley

Removal

30 Remove the timing belt as described in Section 7.

31 Slacken and remove the retaining bolt and remove the idler pulley from the engine.

Refitting

32 Refit the idler pulley and tighten the retaining bolt to the specified torque.

33 Refit the timing belt as described in Section 7.

9 Camshaft oil seal – renewal

1 Remove the camshaft sprocket as described in Section 8.
2 Carefully punch or drill a small hole in the oil seal. Screw in a self-tapping screw, and pull on the screw with pliers to extract the seal.
3 Clean the seal housing, and polish off any burrs or raised edges which may have caused the seal to fail in the first place.
4 Lubricate the lips of the new seal with silicone paste (Saab No 90 167 353), and press it into position using a suitable tubular drift (such as a socket) which bears only on the hard outer edge of the seal. Take care not to damage the seal lips during fitting; note that the seal lips should face inwards.
5 Refit the camshaft sprocket as described in Section 8.

10 Valve clearances – checking and adjustment

Note: *Saab special tools 32 025 035 and 32 025 036 (or suitable equivalents) will be required if adjustment is necessary.*

Checking

1 The importance of having the valve clearances correctly adjusted cannot be overstressed, as they vitally affect the performance of the engine. The engine must be cold for the check to be accurate. The clearances are checked as follows.
2 Apply the handbrake, then jack up the front of the vehicle and support it on axle stands (see *Jacking and vehicle support*). Remove the right-hand front roadwheel, then undo the ten bolts and remove the engine undershield for access to the crankshaft pulley.
3 Remove the camshaft cover as described in Section 5.
4 Using a socket and extension on the crankshaft pulley bolt, rotate the crankshaft in the normal direction of rotation (clockwise when viewed from the right-hand end of the engine) until camshaft lobes 1 and 6 are pointing upward **(see illustration)**.
5 On a piece of paper, draw the outline of the engine with the cylinders numbered from the timing belt end. Show the position of each valve, together with the specified valve clearance. Note that the clearance for both the intake and exhaust valves is the same.
6 With the cam lobes positioned as described in paragraph 4, using feeler blades, measure the clearance between the base of camshaft lobes 1 and 6 and the adjustment shim located on the top of the camshaft follower **(see illustration)**. Record the clearances on the paper.
7 Rotate the crankshaft until camshaft lobes 5 and 8 are pointing upward. Measure the

10.4 Camshaft positioned with No 1 and No 6 cam lobes (arrowed) pointing upwards

clearance between the base of the camshaft lobes and the shims on their followers and record the clearances on the paper.
8 Rotate the crankshaft until camshaft lobes 4 and 7 are pointing upward. Measure the clearance between the base of the camshaft lobes and the shims on their followers and record the clearances on the paper.
9 Rotate the crankshaft until camshaft lobes 2 and 3 are pointing upward. Measure the clearance between the base of the camshaft lobes and the shims on their followers and record the clearances on the paper.
10 If all the clearances are correct, refit the camshaft cover as described in Section 5. Refit the roadwheel and engine undershield, then lower the car to the ground and tighten the wheel bolts to the specified torque.
11 If any clearance measured is not correct, adjustment must be carried out as described in the following paragraphs.

Adjustment

12 Rotate the crankshaft clockwise until camshaft lobes 1 and 6 are once again pointing upward. With the camshaft in this position, valve No 1 and valve No 6 can be adjusted as follows.
13 Rotate the follower until the groove on its upper edge is facing towards the front of the engine **(see illustration)**.
14 Insert Saab special tool 32 025 035 between the base of the camshaft lobe and the shim, and lever downward to open the valve. Now insert Saab special tool 32 25 036

10.13 Rotate the follower until the groove (arrowed) is facing towards the front of the engine

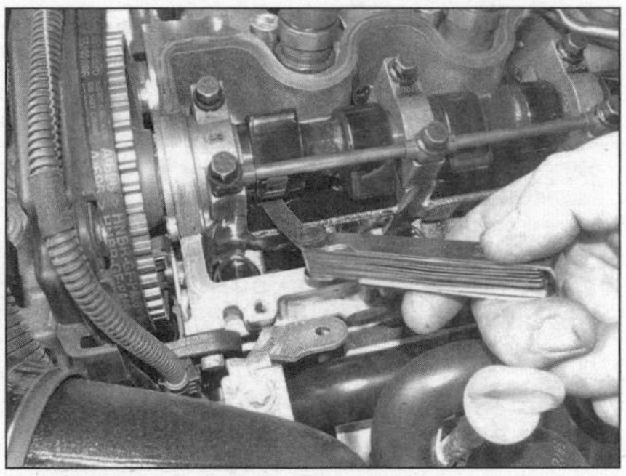

10.6 Valve clearance measurement

between the edge of the follower and the base of the camshaft to hold the valve open. Take care when doing this as it is possible for the valve to contact the piston. If any resistance is felt as the valve is opened, remove the tool and rotate the crankshaft slightly to move the piston down its bore.
15 Using a small screwdriver inserted in the groove on the edge of the follower, lift up the shim, then slide it out from between the follower and camshaft.
16 Clean the shim, and measure its thickness with a micrometer. The shims carry thickness markings, but wear may have reduced the original thickness, so be sure to double-check **(see illustration)**.
17 Add the measured clearance of the valve to the thickness of the original shim then subtract the specified valve clearance from this figure. This will give you the thickness of the shim required. For example:

Measured valve clearance	*0.45 mm*
Plus thickness of the original shim	*2.70 mm*
Equals	*3.15 mm*
Minus clearance required	*0.35 mm*
Thickness of shim required	*2.80 mm*

18 Obtain the correct thickness of shim required and lubricate it with clean engine oil. With the valve still held open with the special tool, slide the shim into position, with the thickness number downwards, ensuring it is correctly located.
19 Using the first special tool, lever down on the shim and remove the second special tool.

10.16 The thickness of each shim should be stamped on one of its surfaces

Allow the valve to close and remove the first special tool. Check that the valve clearance is within limits.

HAYNES HiNT ***It may be possible to correct the clearances by moving the shims around between the valves, but don't rotate the crankshaft with any shims missing. Keep a note of all the shim thicknesses to assist valve clearance adjustment when they need to be done again.***

20 Rotate the crankshaft clockwise until camshaft lobes 5 and 8 are once again pointing upward. Adjust No 5 and No 8 valve clearances as described in paragraphs 13 to 19.

21 Rotate the crankshaft clockwise until camshaft lobes 4 and 7 are once again pointing upward. Adjust No 4 and No 7 valve clearances as described in paragraphs 13 to 19.

22 Rotate the crankshaft clockwise until camshaft lobes 2 and 3 are once again pointing upward. Adjust No 2 and No 3 valve clearances as described in paragraphs 13 to 19.

23 On completion, refit the camshaft cover as described in Section 5. Refit the roadwheel and engine undershield, then lower the car to the ground and tighten the wheel bolts to the specified torque.

11 Camshaft and followers – removal, inspection and refitting

Removal

1 Remove the timing belt as described in Section 7.

2 Remove the camshaft sprocket as described in Section 8.

3 Remove the camshaft cover as described in Section 5.

4 Remove the braking system vacuum pump as described in Chapter 9, Section 12.

5 Check for identification markings on the camshaft bearing caps. If no markings can be seen, make suitable identification marks on the caps, to indicate their number and which way round they are fitted.

6 Working in a spiral pattern from the outside inwards, slacken the twelve camshaft bearing cap retaining bolts by half a turn at a time, to relieve the pressure of the valve springs on the bearing caps gradually and evenly **(see illustration)**. Once the valve spring pressure has been relieved, the bolts can be fully unscrewed and removed.

Caution: If the bearing cap bolts are carelessly slackened, the bearing caps might break. If any bearing cap breaks then the complete cylinder head assembly must be renewed; the bearing caps are matched to the head and are not available separately.

7 Carefully release the oil supply pipe from its location in the cylinder head, then lift the pipe off the bearing caps **(see illustration)**.

8 Remove the bearing caps, then lift the camshaft out of the cylinder head and slide off the oil seal.

9 Obtain eight small, clean plastic containers, and label them for identification. Alternatively, divide a larger container into compartments. Lift the followers and shims out from the top of the cylinder head and store each one in its respective fitted position. Make sure the followers and shims are not mixed up, to ensure the valve clearances remain correct on refitting.

Inspection

10 Examine the camshaft bearing surfaces and cam lobes for signs of wear ridges and scoring. Renew the camshaft if any of these conditions are apparent. Examine the condition of the bearing surfaces both on the camshaft journals and in the cylinder head. If the head bearing surfaces are worn excessively, the cylinder head will need to be renewed.

11 Check the camshaft followers and their bores in the cylinder head for signs of wear or damage. If any follower is thought to be faulty or is visibly worn it should be renewed.

Refitting

12 Commence refitting by turning the crankshaft anti-clockwise by 90°. This will position all the pistons half-way down their bores, and prevent any chance of the valves touching the piston crowns as the camshaft is being fitted.

13 Lubricate the camshaft followers with clean engine oil and carefully insert each one (together with its adjusting shim) into its original location in the cylinder head.

14 Lubricate the camshaft follower shims, and the bearing journals with clean engine oil, then lay the camshaft in position.

15 Apply a smear of sealant to the mating surfaces of both the No 1 and No 5 camshaft bearing caps. Using the marks made on removal as a guide, refit the camshaft bearing caps in their original locations on the cylinder head.

16 Carefully engage the oil supply pipe into its location in the cylinder head, then place the pipe in position on the bearing caps.

17 Refit the bearing cap retaining bolts and tighten them by hand until they just contact the bearing caps.

18 Working in a spiral pattern from the centre outwards, tighten the bolts by half a turn at a time to gradually impose the pressure of the valve springs on the bearing caps. Repeat this sequence until all bearing caps are in contact with the cylinder head then go around and tighten the camshaft bearing cap bolts to the specified torque.

Caution: If the bearing cap bolts are carelessly tightened, the bearing caps might break. If any bearing cap breaks then the complete cylinder head assembly must be renewed; the bearing caps are matched to the head and are not available separately.

19 Fit a new camshaft oil seal as described in Section 9.

11.6 Camshaft bearing cap retaining bolts (arrowed)

11.7 Carefully release the oil pipe (arrowed) from its location in the cylinder head

20 Refit the braking system vacuum pump as described in Chapter 9, Section 12.
21 Refit the camshaft cover as described in Section 5.
22 Refit the camshaft sprocket as described in Section 8. Rotate the camshaft until the mark on the camshaft sprocket is aligned with the pointer on the camshaft cover (see Section 3).
23 Turn the crankshaft clockwise by 90° to bring No 1 and 4 pistons to approximately the TDC position.
24 Refit the timing belt as described in Section 7.
25 If any new components have been fitted, check, and if necessary adjust, the valve clearances as described in Section 10.

12 Cylinder head – removal and refitting

Note: *New cylinder head bolts will be required on refitting.*

Removal

1 Disconnect the battery negative terminal as described in Chapter 5A, Section 4.
2 Drain the cooling system as described in Chapter 1B, Section 28.
3 Remove the timing belt as described in Section 7.
4 Disconnect the wiring harness connectors from the following components with reference to the Chapters indicated:

a) Coolant temperature sensor (Chapter 3, Section 6).
b) Fuel pressure sensor (Chapter 4B, Section 9).
c) Fuel pressure regulating valve (Chapter 4B, Section 9).
d) Throttle valve module (Chapter 4B, Section 9).
e) Fuel injectors (Chapter 4B, Section 12).
f) Air conditioning compressor (Chapter 3, Section 9).
g) EGR valve (Chapter 4C, Section 3).
h) Intake air pressure sensor (Chapter 4B, Section 9).
i) High-pressure fuel pump (Chapter 4B, Section 10).
j) Camshaft sensor (Chapter 4B, Section 9).

5 Undo the wiring harness support bracket bolts, release the retaining clips and move the harness to one side **(see illustration)**.
6 Remove the intake and exhaust manifolds as described in Chapter 4B, Section 13 and 17.
7 Remove the camshaft cover as described in Section 5.
8 Remove the braking system vacuum pump as described in Chapter 9, Section 12.
9 Make a final check to ensure that all relevant hoses, pipes and wires have been disconnected.
10 Working in the **reverse** of the tightening sequence **(see illustration 12.28)**, progressively slacken the cylinder head bolts by half a turn at a time, until all bolts can be unscrewed by hand. Note that an M14 RIBE socket bit will be required to unscrew the bolts. Remove the cylinder head bolts and recover the washers.
11 Engage the help of an assistant and lift the cylinder head from the cylinder block. Take care as it is a bulky and heavy assembly.
Caution: Do not lay the head on its lower mating surface; support the head on wooden blocks, ensuring each block only contacts the head mating surface.
12 Remove the gasket and keep it for identification purposes (see paragraph 19).
13 If the cylinder head is to be dismantled for overhaul, then refer to Chapter 2D, Section 6.

Preparation for refitting

14 The mating faces of the cylinder head and cylinder block/crankcase must be perfectly clean before refitting the head. Use a hard plastic or wood scraper to remove all traces of gasket and carbon; also clean the piston crowns. Take particular care, as the surfaces are damaged easily. Also, make sure that the carbon is not allowed to enter the oil and water passages – this is particularly important for the lubrication system, as carbon could block the oil supply to any of the engine's components. Using adhesive tape and paper, seal the water, oil and bolt holes in the cylinder block/crankcase. To prevent carbon entering the gap between the pistons and bores, smear a little grease in the gap. After cleaning each piston, use a small brush to remove all traces of grease and carbon from the gap, then wipe away the remainder with a clean rag. Clean all the pistons in the same way.
15 Check the mating surfaces of the cylinder block/crankcase and the cylinder head for nicks, deep scratches and other damage. If slight, they may be removed carefully with a file, but if excessive, machining may be the only alternative to renewal.
16 Ensure that the cylinder head bolt holes in the crankcase are clean and free of oil. Syringe or soak up any oil left in the bolt holes. This is most important in order that the correct bolt tightening torque can be applied and to prevent the possibility of the block being cracked by hydraulic pressure when the bolts are tightened.
17 The cylinder head bolts must be discarded and renewed, regardless of their apparent condition.

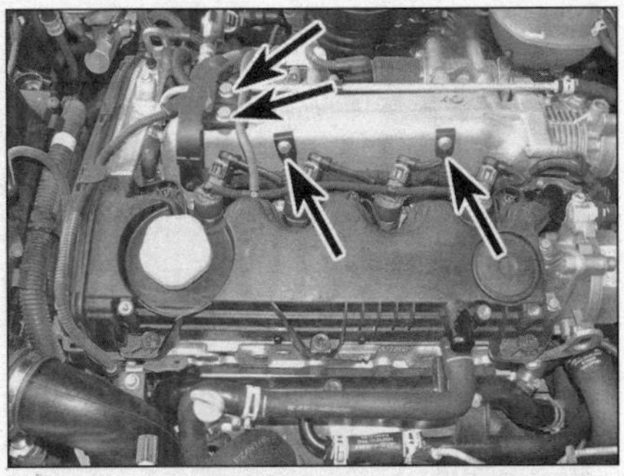

12.5 Undo the support bracket bolts (arrowed), release the retaining clips and move the wiring harness to one side

18 If warpage of the cylinder head gasket surface is suspected, use a straight-edge to check it for distortion. Refer to Chapter 2D, Section 7 if necessary.
19 On this engine, the cylinder head-to-piston clearance is controlled by fitting different thickness head gaskets. The gasket thickness can be determined by looking at the holes stamped on the edge of the gasket **(see illustration)**.

Number of holes	Gasket thickness
No holes	0.77 to 0.87 mm
One hole	0.87 to 0.97 mm
Two holes	0.97 to 1.07 mm

The correct thickness of gasket required is selected by measuring the piston protrusions as follows.
20 Mount a dial test indicator securely on the block so that its pointer can be easily pivoted between the piston crown and block mating surface. Turn the crankshaft to bring No 1 piston roughly to the TDC position. Move the dial test indicator probe over and in contact with No 1 piston. Turn the crankshaft back-and-forth slightly until the highest reading is shown on the gauge, indicating that the piston is at TDC.
21 Zero the dial test indicator on the gasket surface of the cylinder block then carefully move the indicator over No 1 piston. Measure its protrusion at the highest point between the valve cut-outs, and then again at its highest point between the valve cut-outs at 90° to the first measurement **(see illustration)**. Repeat this procedure with No 4 piston.

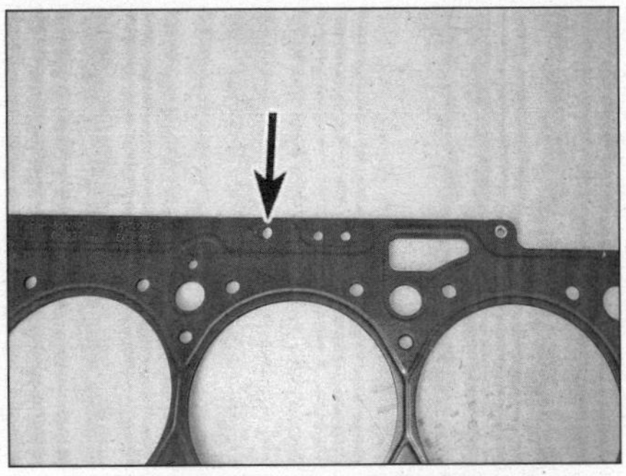

12.19 Cylinder head gasket thickness identification hole (arrowed)

12.21 Using a dial test indicator to measure piston protrusion

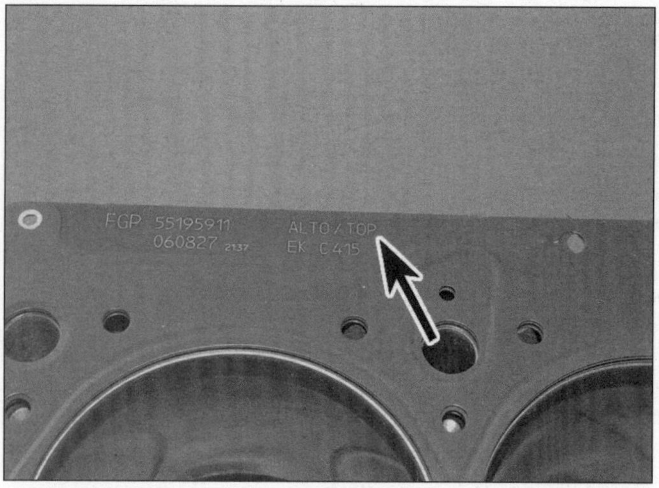

12.24 Place the new gasket in position with the words ALTO/TOP (arrowed) uppermost

12.28 Cylinder head bolt tightening sequence

22 Rotate the crankshaft half a turn (180°) to bring No 2 and 3 pistons to TDC. Ensure the crankshaft is accurately positioned then measure the protrusions of No 2 and 3 pistons at the specified points. Once all pistons have been measured, rotate the crankshaft to position all the pistons at their mid-stroke.

23 Select the correct thickness of head gasket required by determining the largest amount of piston protrusion, and using the following guide.

Piston protrusion measurement	Gasket thickness required
0.020 to 0.100 mm	0.77 to 0.87 mm (no holes)
0.101 to 0.200 mm	0.87 to 0.97 mm (one hole)
0.201 to 0.295 mm	0.97 to 1.07 mm (two holes)

Refitting

24 Wipe clean the mating surfaces of the cylinder head and cylinder block/crankcase. Place the new gasket in position with the words ALTO/TOP uppermost **(see illustration)**.

25 If not already done, rotate the crankshaft to position all the pistons at their mid-stroke.

26 With the aid of an assistant, carefully refit the cylinder head assembly to the block, aligning it with the locating dowels.

27 Apply a thin film of engine oil to the bolt threads and the underside of the bolt heads. Carefully enter each new cylinder head bolt into its relevant hole (do not drop them in). Screw all bolts in, by hand only, until finger-tight.

28 Working progressively in sequence, tighten the cylinder head bolts to their Stage 1 torque setting, using a torque wrench and suitable socket **(see illustration)**. Working again in the same sequence, go around and tighten all bolts through the specified Stage 2 torque setting.

29 Once all bolts have been tightened to the Stage 2 torque, working again in the same sequence, go around and tighten all bolts through the specified Stage 3 angle, then through the specified Stage 4 angle, and finally through the specified Stage 5 angle using an angle-measuring gauge.

30 Refit the braking system vacuum pump as described in Chapter 9, Section 12.

31 Refit the camshaft cover as described in Section 5.

32 Refit the intake and exhaust manifolds as described in Chapter 4B, Section 13 and 17.

33 Reconnect the wiring harness connectors to the components listed in paragraph 4, then refit the wiring harness support bracket bolts, and secure the harness with the retaining clips.

34 Refit the timing belt as described in Section 7.

35 On completion, reconnect the battery negative terminal, then refill the cooling system as described in Chapter 1B, Section 28.

13 Sump – removal and refitting

Removal

1 Disconnect the battery negative terminal as described in Chapter 5A, Section 4.

2 Apply the handbrake, then jack up the front of the vehicle and support it on axle stands (see *Jacking and vehicle support*). Remove the right-hand front roadwheel, then remove the engine undershield **(see illustration 6.1)**.

3 Remove the right-hand driveshaft and the intermediate shaft as described in Chapter 8, Section 2 and 5.

4 Undo the three bolts securing the intermediate shaft bearing housing support bracket to the cylinder block and remove the support bracket **(see illustration)**.

5 Remove the exhaust system as described in Chapter 4B, Section 18.

6 Undo the three bolts and remove the support bracket from the catalytic converter and sump.

7 Remove the crankshaft pulley/vibration damper as described in Section 6.

8 Disconnect the wiring connector from the air conditioning compressor. Undo the three bolts securing the air conditioning compressor to the mounting bracket and suitably support the compressor on the front subframe.

9 Undo the four bolts securing the compressor mounting bracket to the cylinder block and sump **(see illustration)**. Unclip the wiring harness and remove the mounting bracket.

10 Drain the engine oil as described in Chapter 1B, Section 3. When the oil has completely drained, refit the drain plug with new sealing washer, and tighten to the specified torque.

11 Undo the upper bolt securing the oil

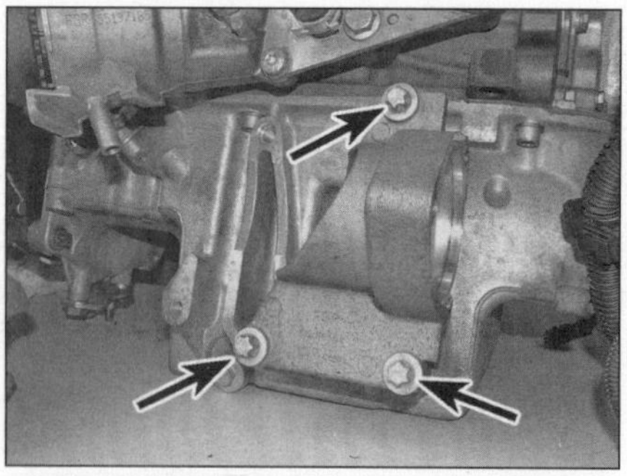

13.4 Intermediate shaft bearing housing support bracket retaining bolts (arrowed)

13.9 Air conditioning compressor mounting bracket retaining bolts (arrowed)

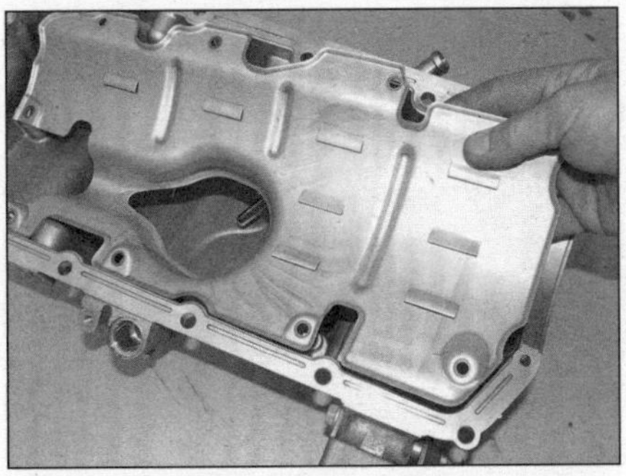

13.17 Remove the oil baffle plate from the inside of the sump

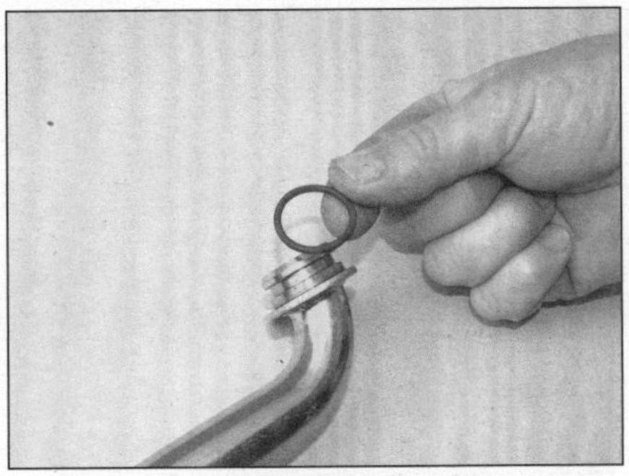

13.18 Renew the pick-up/strainer sealing ring prior to refitting

13.21 Apply a continuous bead of silicone sealing compound to the sump flange

dipstick guide tube to the coolant pipe. Undo the lower bolt securing the guide tube to the sump flange, then unclip the wiring harness and withdraw the tube from the sump flange sealing grommet.

12 Disconnect the wiring connector from the oil level sensor, then release the retaining clip and disconnect the oil return hose.

13 Undo the two bolts securing the sump flange to the transmission bellhousing.

14 Using a socket and extension on the crankshaft pulley bolt, rotate the crankshaft in the normal direction of rotation (clockwise when viewed from the right-hand end of the engine) until the opening in the flywheel is positioned to allow access to one of the rear sump retaining bolts. Undo and remove the bolt, then rotate the crankshaft again until the flywheel allows access to the second rear retaining bolt. Undo and remove the bolt.

15 Progressively slacken and remove the remaining twelve bolts securing the sump to the base of the cylinder block and oil pump housing. Using a wide-bladed scraper or similar tool inserted between the sump and cylinder block, carefully break the joint to release the sump.

16 Manoeuvre the sump out from under the car. Clearance is extremely limited between the sump and subframe, and it may be necessary to release the oil pump pick-up/strainer, by undoing its two retaining bolts, to enable the sump to be removed.

17 If required, undo the retaining bolts and remove the oil baffle plate from inside the sump **(see illustration)**.

18 While the sump is removed, take the opportunity to check the oil pump pick-up/strainer for signs of clogging or splitting. If not already done, unbolt the oil pump pick-up/strainer and remove it from the engine along with its sealing ring. The strainer can then be cleaned easily in solvent or renewed. Renew the pick-up/strainer sealing ring prior to refitting **(see illustration)**.

Refitting

19 Thoroughly clean the sump and remove all traces of silicone sealer and oil from the mating surfaces of the sump and cylinder block. If removed, refit the oil baffle plate and tighten its retaining bolts securely.

20 If clearance allows, refit the oil pump pick-up/strainer using a new sealing ring, and tighten its two retaining bolts securely. If it was necessary to unbolt the pick-up/strainer to allow the sump to be removed, place the unit in position and loosely screw in the bolt securing it to the main bearing cap. It must still be possible for the forward end of the pipe to be moved to the rear as the sump is refitted.

21 Apply a continuous bead of silicone sealing compound (available from your Saab dealer) at approximately 1.0 mm from the inner edge of the sump **(see illustration)**. The bead of sealant should be between 2.0 and 2.5 mm in diameter.

22 Locate the sump over the pick-up/strainer then, where applicable, fit the forward end of the pick-up/strainer to the oil pump housing and fit the retaining bolt. Tighten both retaining bolts securely.

23 Engage the sump with the cylinder block and loosely refit all the retaining bolts.

24 Working out from the centre in a diagonal sequence, progressively tighten the bolts securing the sump to the cylinder block and oil pump housing. Tighten all the bolts to their specified torque setting.

25 Tighten the two bolts securing the sump flange to the transmission bellhousing to their specified torque settings.

26 Reconnect the wiring connector to the oil level sensor, then refit the oil return hose and secure with the retaining clip.

27 Refit the oil dipstick guide tube and secure with the two bolts tightened securely.

28 Locate the air conditioning compressor mounting bracket in position and refit the four retaining bolts. Tighten the bolts to the specified torque. Clip the wiring harness back into position on the bracket.

29 Position the air conditioning compressor on the mounting bracket. Fit and tighten the three retaining bolts to the specified torque, then reconnect the compressor wiring connector.

30 Refit the crankshaft pulley/vibration damper as described in Section 6.

31 Refit the catalytic converter support bracket and securely tighten the three bolts.

32 Refit the exhaust system as described in Chapter 4B, Section 18.

33 Position the intermediate shaft bearing housing support bracket on the cylinder block and secure with the three retaining bolts tightened to the specified torque.

34 Refit the intermediate shaft and right-hand driveshaft as described in Chapter 8, Section 5 and 2.

35 Refit the roadwheel and engine undershield, then lower the car to the ground and tighten the wheel bolts to the specified torque.

36 Fill the engine with fresh engine oil as described in Chapter 1B, Section 3.

37 On completion, reconnect the battery negative terminal.

14 Oil pump – removal, overhaul and refitting

Removal

1 Remove the timing belt as described in Section 7.

2 Remove the crankshaft sprocket as described In Section 8.

3 Remove the sump and oil pump pick-up/strainer as described in Section 13.

4 Slacken and remove the seven retaining bolts then slide the oil pump housing assembly off of the end of the crankshaft **(see illustration)**. Remove the housing gasket and discard it.

Overhaul

5 Undo the retaining screws and lift off the

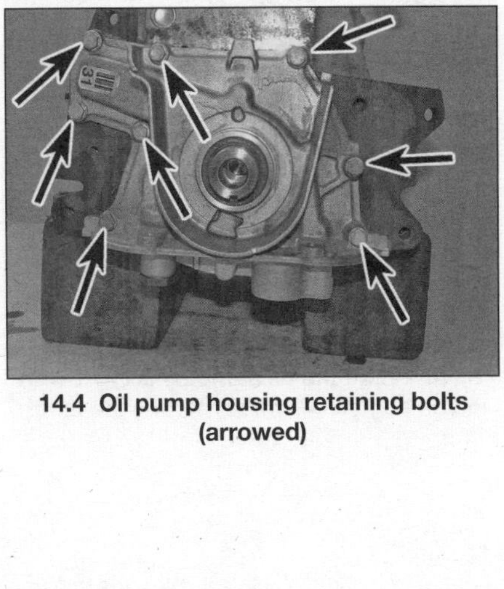

14.4 Oil pump housing retaining bolts (arrowed)

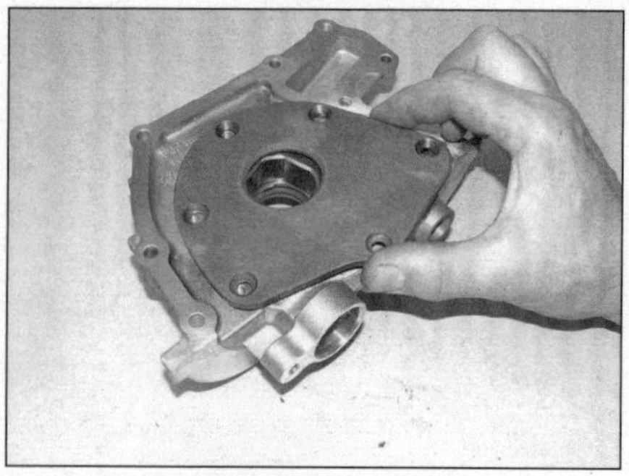

14.5 Undo the retaining screws and lift off the oil pump cover

14.6 Oil pump inner and outer rotor identification dots (arrowed)

14.8a Unscrew the oil pressure relief valve bolt ...

14.8b ... and withdraw the spring ...

14.8c ... and plunger

pump cover from the rear of the housing **(see illustration)**.

6 Check the inner and outer rotors for identification dots indicating which way round they are fitted **(see illustration)**. If no marks are visible, use a suitable marker pen to mark the surface of both the pump inner and outer rotors.

7 Lift out the inner and outer rotors from the pump housing.

8 Unscrew the oil pressure relief valve bolt from the base of the housing, and withdraw the spring and plunger, noting which way around the plunger is fitted **(see illustrations)**. Remove the sealing washer from the valve bolt.

9 Clean the components, and carefully examine the rotors, pump body and relief valve plunger for any signs of scoring or wear. If any damage or wear is noticed, it will be necessary to renew the complete pump assembly.

10 If the pump is satisfactory, reassemble the components in the reverse order of removal, noting the following.

a) *Ensure both rotors are fitted the correct way around.*
b) *Fit a new sealing ring to the pressure relief valve bolt and securely tighten the bolt.*
c) *Apply a little locking compound to the threads, and securely tighten the pump cover screws.*
d) *On completion prime the oil pump by filling it with clean engine oil whilst rotating the inner rotor* ***(see illustration)****.*

Refitting

11 Prior to refitting, carefully lever out the crankshaft oil seal using a flat-bladed screwdriver. Fit the new oil seal, ensuring its sealing lip is facing inwards, and press it squarely into the housing using a tubular drift which bears only on the hard outer edge of the seal. Press the seal into position so that it is flush with the housing and lubricate the oil seal lip with clean engine oil.

12 Ensure the mating surfaces of the oil pump and cylinder block are clean and dry.

13 Fit a new gasket to the oil pump housing and bend down the tabs on the edge of the gasket to retain it on the pump housing **(see illustration)**.

14 Locate the pump housing over the end of the crankshaft and into position on the cylinder block.

15 Refit the pump housing retaining bolts and tighten them to the specified torque.

16 Refit the oil pump pick-up/strainer and sump as described in Section 13.

17 Refit the crankshaft sprocket as described in Section 8.

18 Refit the timing belt as described in Section 7.

19 On completion, fit a new oil filter and fill the engine with clean oil as described in Chapter 1B, Section 3.

15 Oil filter housing – removal and refitting

Removal

1 The oil filter housing with integral oil cooler is located at the rear of the cylinder block, above the right-hand driveshaft.

2 Disconnect the battery negative terminal as described in Chapter 5A, Section 4.

3 Apply the handbrake, then jack up the front of the vehicle and support it on axle stands *(see Jacking and vehicle support)*. Remove the right-hand front roadwheel, then undo the ten bolts and remove the engine undershield.

4 Drain the cooling system as described in Chapter 1B, Section 28.

5 Remove the engine oil filter element as described in Chapter 1B, Section 3.

6 Remove the right-hand driveshaft and the intermediate shaft as described in Chapter 8, Section 2 and 5.

7 Undo the three bolts securing the

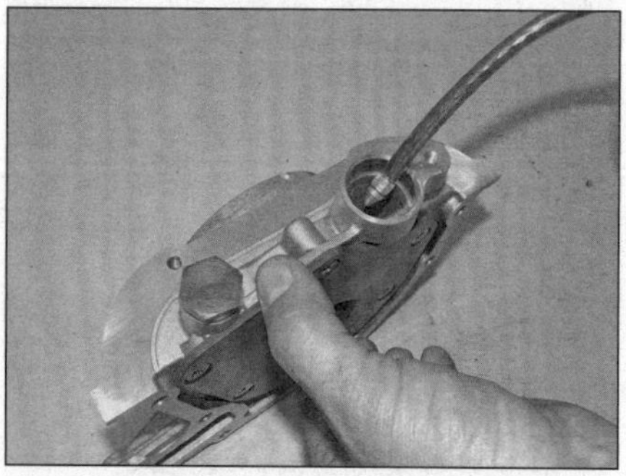

14.10 Prime the oil pump by filling it with clean engine oil whilst rotating the inner rotor

14.13 Bend down the tabs on the edge of the gasket to retain it on the oil pump housing

15.10 Oil filter housing retaining bolts (arrowed)

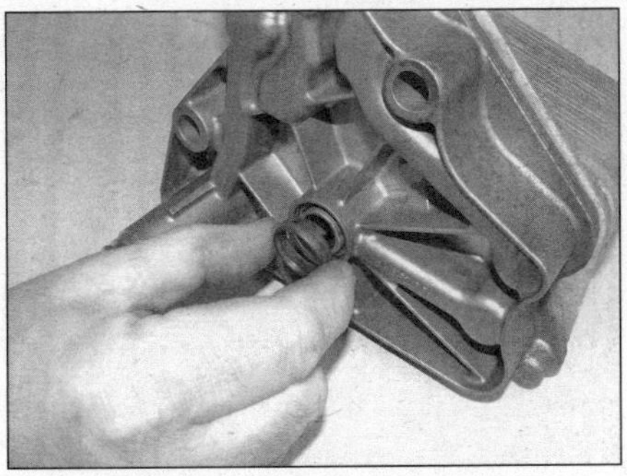

15.11a Fit a new sealing ring to the oil filter housing supply channel ...

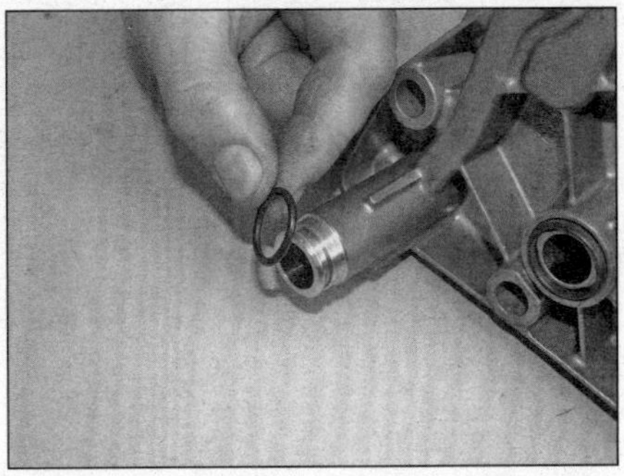

15.11b ... and to the return channel

intermediate shaft bearing housing support bracket to the cylinder block and remove the support bracket **(see illustration 13.4)**.

8 Disconnect the wiring connector from the oil pressure switch.

9 Release the retaining clips and disconnect the two coolant hoses from the oil cooler on the oil filter housing.

10 Undo the three retaining bolts and remove the oil filter housing from the cylinder block **(see illustration)**. Recover the two rubber seals from the rear of the housing. Note that new seals will be required for refitting.

Refitting

11 Thoroughly clean the oil filter housing, then fit the two new sealing rings **(see illustrations)**.

12 Position the oil filter housing on the cylinder block and refit the retaining bolts. Tighten the bolts to the specified torque.

13 Refit the two coolant hoses and secure with their retaining clips. Reconnect the oil pressure switch wiring connector.

14 Position the intermediate shaft bearing housing support bracket on the cylinder block and secure with the three retaining bolts tightened to the specified torque.

15 Refit the intermediate shaft and right-hand driveshaft as described in Chapter 8, Section 5 and 2.

16 Fit a new oil filter element as described in Chapter 1B, Section 3.

17 Refit the roadwheel and engine undershield, then lower the car to the ground and tighten the wheel bolts to the specified torque.

18 Refill the cooling system as described in Chapter 1B, Section 28.

19 Check, and if necessary, top-up the engine oil as described in Weekly checks.

20 On completion, reconnect the battery negative terminal.

16 Crankshaft oil seals – renewal

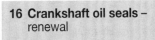

Right-hand (timing belt end)

1 Remove the crankshaft sprocket as described in Section 8.

2 Carefully punch or drill a small hole in the oil seal. Screw in a self-tapping screw and pull on the screw with pliers to extract the seal **(see illustration)**.

3 Clean the seal housing and polish off any burrs or raised edges which may have caused the seal to fail in the first place.

4 Lubricate the lips of the new seal with clean engine petroleum jelly and ease it into position on the end of the shaft. Press the seal squarely into position until it is flush with the housing. If necessary, a suitable tubular drift which bears only on the hard outer edge of the seal can be used to tap the seal into position **(see illustration)**. Take great care not to damage the seal lips during fitting and ensure that the seal lips face inwards.

5 Wash off any traces of oil, then refit the crankshaft sprocket as described in Section 8.

Left-hand (flywheel end)

6 Remove the flywheel as described in Section 17.

7 Remove the sump as described in Section 13.

8 Undo the five bolts and remove the oil seal housing. Note that the oil seal and the housing are a single assembly.

9 Clean the crankshaft and polish off any burrs or raised edges which may have caused the seal to fail in the first place.

10 Position the new oil seal housing, complete with seal over the crankshaft and into position on the cylinder block **(see illustration)**. Note that the new oil seal housing is supplied with a protector sleeve over the oil seal. Leave the sleeve in position as the housing is fitted.

11 Refit the five retaining bolts and tighten to the specified torque.

12 Remove the protector sleeve from the housing **(see illustration)**.

13 Refit the sump as described in Section 13.

14 Refit the flywheel as described in Section 17.

16.2 Screw in a self-tapping screw and pull on the screw with pliers to extract the oil seal

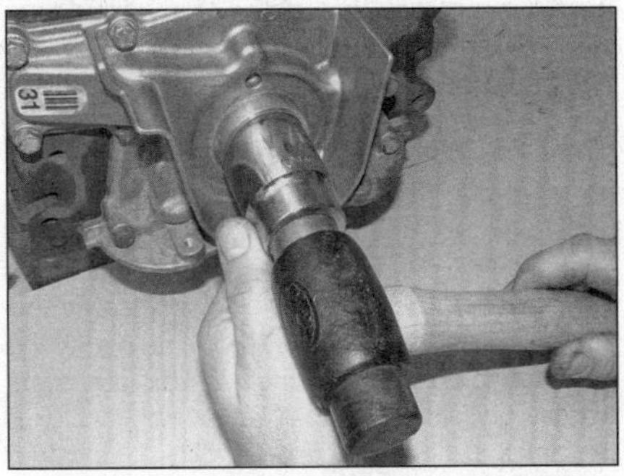

16.4 Use a socket as a tubular drift to fit the new oil seal

16.10 Fit the new oil seal housing, with integral oil seal over the crankshaft

16.12 After fitting, remove the protector sleeve from the housing

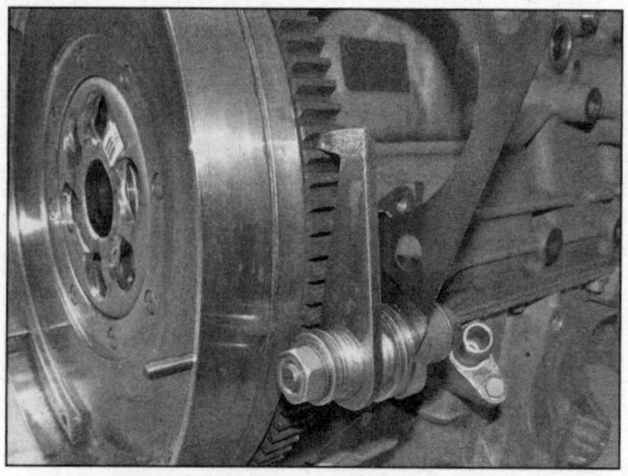

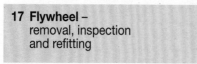

17.2 Prevent the flywheel from turning by locking the ring gear teeth

17 Flywheel – removal, inspection and refitting

Note: *New flywheel retaining bolts will be required on refitting.*

Removal

1 Remove the transmission as described in Chapter 7A, Section 7, then remove the clutch assembly as described in Chapter 6, Section 5.
2 Prevent the flywheel from turning by locking the ring gear teeth with a similar arrangement to that shown **(see illustration)**.
3 Slacken and remove the retaining bolts and remove the flywheel **(see illustration)**. Do not drop it, as it is very heavy.

17.3 Flywheel retaining bolts (arrowed)

Inspection

4 If there is any doubt about the condition of the flywheel, seek the advice of a Saab dealer or engine reconditioning specialist. They will be able to advise if it is possible to recondition it or whether renewal is necessary.
5 Where a dual mass flywheel is fitted it must be renewed if there is any evidence of fluid or grease on the flywheel or clutch components. The following procedures are given for guidance only. If in doubt as to the condition of the flywheel a professional inspection is recommended. If the assembly passes all the checks listed and there was no juddering from the clutch when taking up the drive, the flywheel can be refitted. However if the vehicle has covered a high mileage and especially if the vehicle is on its second new clutch, then it would be prudent to renew the dual mass flywheel.

Warpage

Check the drive surface for any signs of warpage or damage. The flywheel will normally warp like a bowl – ie, higher at the circumference. If the warpage is more than 4.0 mm consider renewing the flywheel.

Free rotational movement

This is the distance the drive surface of the flywheel can be turned independently of the flywheel primary element, using finger pressure only. Move the drive surface in one direction and make a mark where the locating pin aligns with the flywheel edge. Move the drive surface in the other direction (finger pressure only) and make another mark. The total of free movement should not exceed 10 mm. If it is more consider renewing the flywheel.

Total rotational movement

This is the total distance the drive surface can be turned independently of the flywheel primary elements. Insert two bolts into the clutch pressure/plate damper unit mounting holes and with the crankshaft flywheel held stationary user a pry bar between the bolts and use some effort to move the drive surface fully in one direction. Make a mark where the locating pin aligns with the flywheel edge. Now force the drive surface fully in the opposite direction, and make another mark. The total rotational movement should not exceed 44.0 mm. If it does have the flywheel professionally inspected.

Lateral movement

The lateral movement (up and down) of the drive surface in relation to the primary element of the flywheel should not exceed 2.0 mm, if it does the flywheel may need renewing. This can be checked by pressing the drive surface down on one side into the flywheel (flywheel horizontal) and making an alignment mark between the drive surface and the inner edge of the primary elements. Now press down on the opposite side of the drive surface and make another mark above the original one. The difference between the two marks is the lateral movement.

Refitting

6 Clean the mating surfaces of the flywheel and crankshaft.

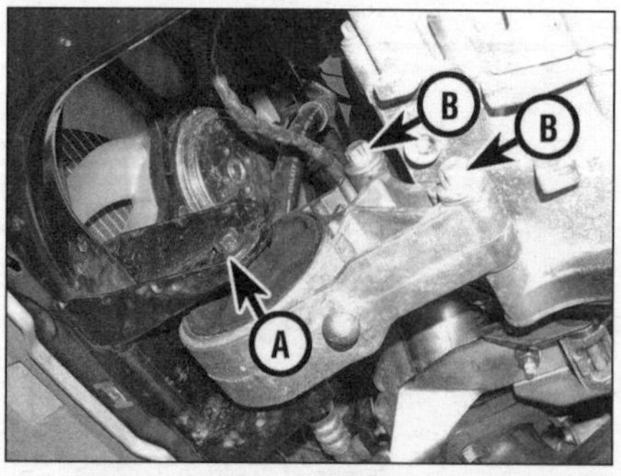

18.6 Front mounting/torque link through-bolt (A) and mounting bracket-to-transmission bolts (B)

7 Offer up the flywheel and engage it over the positioning dowel on the crankshaft. Apply a drop of locking compound to the threads of each new flywheel retaining bolt (unless they are precoated) and install the new bolts.
8 Lock the flywheel by the method used on removal then, working in a diagonal sequence, evenly and progressively tighten the retaining bolts to the specified torque.
9 Refit the clutch as described in Chapter 6, Section 5, then remove the locking tool, and refit the transmission as described in Chapter 7A, Section 7.

18 Engine/transmission mountings – inspection and renewal

Inspection

1 If improved access is required, firmly apply the handbrake, then jack up the front of the car and support it securely on axle stands (see *Jacking and vehicle support)*.
2 Check the mounting rubber to see if it is cracked, hardened or separated from the metal at any point; renew the mounting if any such damage or deterioration is evident.
3 Check that all the mounting's fasteners are securely tightened; use a torque wrench to check if possible.
4 Using a large screwdriver or a pry bar, check for wear in the mounting by carefully levering against it to check for free play; where this is not possible, enlist the aid of an assistant to move the engine/transmission unit back-and-forth, or from side-to-side, while you watch the mounting. While some free play is to be expected even from new components, excessive wear should be obvious. If excessive free play is found, check first that the fasteners are correctly secured, then renew any worn components as described below.

Renewal

Note: *Before slackening any of the engine mounting bolts/nuts, the relative positions of the mountings to their various brackets should be marked to ensure correct alignment upon refitting.*

Front mounting/torque link

5 Apply the handbrake, then jack up the front of the vehicle and support it on axle stands (see *Jacking and vehicle support)*. Undo the fasteners and remove the engine undershield **(see illustration 6.1)**.
6 Slacken and remove the nut securing the mounting to the subframe bracket. Withdraw the through-bolt **(see illustration)**.
7 Undo the bolts securing the mounting bracket to the transmission, then manoeuvre the mounting and bracket out of position.
8 Check all components for signs of wear or damage, and renew as necessary.
9 Locate the mounting in the subframe, refit the through-bolt and nut, then tighten the nut finger-tight at this stage.

10 Refit the mounting bracket to the transmission and tighten its bolts to the specified torque.
11 Tighten the through-bolt nut to the specified torque.
12 On completion, refit the engine undershield, and lower the vehicle to the ground.

Rear mounting/torque link

13 Apply the handbrake, then jack up the front of the vehicle and support it on axle stands (see *Jacking and vehicle support*). Undo the fasteners and remove the engine undershield **(see illustration 6.1)**.
14 Undo the three bolts securing the mounting bracket to the transmission and the through-bolt securing the mounting to the bracket **(see illustration)**. If improved access is required, remove the front section of the exhaust pipe as described in Chapter 4B, Section 18.
15 Undo the nuts and remove the two bolts securing the mounting to the subframe **(see illustration)**. Manoeuvre the mounting and bracket out from under the car.
16 Refit the bracket to the transmission and tighten the bolts to the specified torque.
17 Locate the new mounting in position. Insert the bolts and tighten the bolt/nuts to the specified torque.
18 On completion, refit the engine undershield and lower the vehicle to the ground.

Right-hand mounting

19 Apply the handbrake, then jack up the front of the vehicle and support it on axle stands (see *Jacking and vehicle support*). Undo the fasteners and remove the engine undershield **(see illustration 6.1)**.
20 Remove the air cleaner as described in Chapter 4B, Section 2.
21 Place a trolley jack beneath the right-hand end of the engine with a block of wood on the jack head. Raise the jack until it is supporting the weight of the engine.
22 Mark the position of the three bolts securing the mounting bracket to the engine bracket and undo the bolts. Undo the three bolts securing the mounting to the body

18.14 Rear mounting/torque link through-bolt (arrowed)

18.22a Right-hand mounting bracket-to-engine bracket bolts (arrowed) ...

and remove the mounting assembly **(see illustrations)**.
23 Place the mounting assembly in position and refit the two bolts and the nut securing the mounting to the body. Tighten the bolts/nut to the specified torque. Align the mounting in its original position, then tighten the three mounting bracket bolts to the specified torque.
24 Remove the support jack, then refit the air cleaner as described in Chapter 4B, Section 2.
25 On completion, refit the engine undershield, and lower the vehicle to the ground.

Left-hand mounting

26 Remove the battery and battery box as described in Chapter 5A, Section 4.
27 Place a trolley jack beneath the

18.15 Rear mounting/torque link bracket-to-subframe mounting bolt nuts (arrowed)

18.22b ... and mounting-to-body retaining bolts (arrowed)

transmission with a block of wood on the jack head. Raise the jack until it is supporting the weight of the engine/transmission unit.
28 Using a Torx socket, unscrew the three bolts securing the mounting bracket to the transmission bracket **(see illustration)**.
29 Undo the four bolts securing the mounting to the body and the three bolts securing the transmission bracket to the transmission **(see illustration)**. Remove the mounting assembly from the car.
30 Locate the mounting brackets in position then insert the bolts and tighten them to the specified torque.
31 Remove the support jack from under the transmission.
32 Refit the battery box and battery as described in Chapter 5A, Section 4.

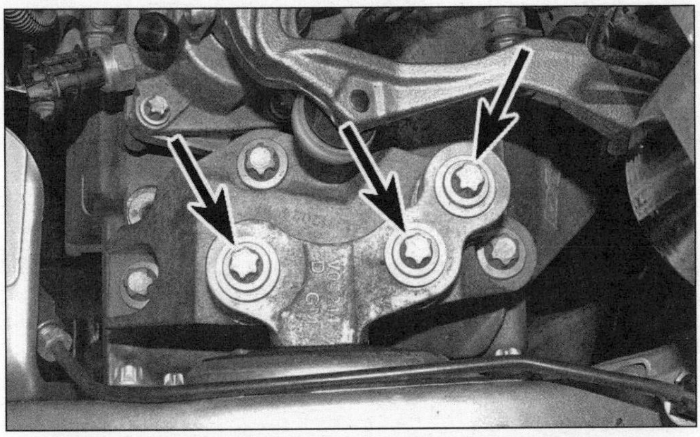

18.28 Left-hand mounting bracket-to-transmission bracket retaining bolts (arrowed)

18.29 Left-hand mounting-to-body retaining bolts (arrowed) – shown with the engine/transmission removed

Chapter 2 Part C:
Diesel DOHC engine in-car repair procedures

Contents

Degrees of difficulty

Easy, suitable for novice with little experience	**Fairly easy,** suitable for beginner with some experience	**Fairly difficult,** suitable for competent DIY mechanic	**Difficult,** suitable for experienced DIY mechanic	**Very difficult,** suitable for expert DIY or professional

Specifications

General

Engine type	Four-cylinder, in-line, water-cooled. Double overhead camshaft, belt-driven
Manufacturer's engine codes*	Z19DTH and Z19DTR
Bore	82.0 mm
Stroke	90.4 mm
Capacity	1910 cc
Compression ratio:	
Z19DTH engine	17.5:1
Z19DTR engine	16.5:1
Output:	
Z19DTH:	
Torque	320 Nm @ 2000 rpm
Power	110 kW @ 4000 rpm
Z19DTR:	
Torque	400Nm @ 2000 rpm
Power	180 kW @ 4000 rpm
Firing order	1-3-4-2 (No 1 cylinder at timing belt end of engine)
Direction of crankshaft rotation	Clockwise (viewed from timing belt end of engine)

** For details of engine code location, see 'Vehicle identification' in the Reference Chapter.*

Compression pressures

Compression	25 to 32 bar
Maximum difference between any two cylinders	1.5 bar

Lubrication system

Minimum oil pressure at 80°C:	
At idle speed	1.0 bar
At 4000 rpm	4.0 bar
Oil pump type	Rotor-type, driven by crankshaft pulley/vibration damper from crankshaft

Torque wrench settings

Torque wrench settings	Nm	lbf ft
Air conditioning compressor mounting bracket to cylinder block/sump	50	37
Air conditioning compressor to bracket	24	18
Auxiliary drivebelt idler pulley bolt	25	18
Auxiliary drivebelt tensioner assembly bolts	50	37
Camshaft drivegear bolts*	120	89
Camshaft housing bolts	25	18
Camshaft housing closure bolt	16	12
Camshaft sprocket bolt*	120	89
Connecting rod big-end bearing cap bolt:*		
Stage 1	25	18
Stage 2	Angle-tighten a further 60°	
Crankshaft oil seal housing	9	7
Crankshaft pulley/vibration damper bolts	25	18
Crankshaft sprocket bolt*†	360	266
Cylinder head bolts:*		
Stage 1	20	15
Stage 2	65	48
Stage 3	Angle-tighten a further 90°	
Stage 4	Angle-tighten a further 90°	
Stage 5	Angle-tighten a further 90°	
Driveplate bolts*	160	118
Engine mountings:		
Front mounting/torque link bracket to transmission	80	59
Front mounting/torque link to subframe	80	59
Left-hand:		
Mounting-to-body bolts	20	15
Mounting bracket to transmission bracket	55	41
Transmission bracket to transmission	55	41
Rear mounting/torque link bracket to transmission	80	59
Rear mounting/torque link to subframe	60	44
Rear mounting/torque link to transmission bracket	80	59
Right-hand:		
Engine bracket-to-engine bolts	55	41
Lower bolts (M8)	25	18
Upper bolts (M10)	50	37
Mounting-to-body bolts/nut	55	41
Mounting-to-engine bracket bolts	55	41
Engine-to-transmission unit bolts:		
M10 bolts	40	30
M12 bolts	60	44
Flywheel bolts*	160	118
High-pressure fuel pump sprocket nut*	50	37
Intermediate shaft bearing housing support bracket bolts	55	41
Main bearing cap bolts:*		
Stage 1	25	18
Stage 2	Angle-tighten a further 100°	
Oil filler housing bolts	9	7
Oil filter housing to cylinder block	50	37
Oil pump housing to cylinder block	9	7
Oil pump pick-up/strainer bolts	9	7
Roadwheel bolts	110	81
Sump bolts:		
M6 bolts	9	7
M8 bolts	25	18
M10 bolts	40	30
Sump drain plug	20	15
Timing belt idler pulley bolt	50	37
Timing belt tensioner bolt	25	18
Timing belt upper cover bolts:		
M6 bolts	9	7
M8 bolts	25	18

** Do not re-use*
† Left-hand thread

1 General information

How to use this Chapter

This Chapter describes the repair procedures which can reasonably be carried out on the engine while it remains in the vehicle. If the engine has been removed from the vehicle and is being dismantled as described in Chapter 2D, any preliminary dismantling procedures can be ignored.

Note that, while it may be possible physically to overhaul items such as the piston/connecting rod assemblies while the engine is in the vehicle, such tasks are not usually carried out as separate operations, and usually require the execution of several additional procedures (not to mention the cleaning of components and of oilways); for this reason, all such tasks are classed as major overhaul procedures, and are described in Chapter 2D.

Chapter 2D describes the removal of the engine/transmission unit from the vehicle, and the full overhaul procedures which can then be carried out.

Engine description

The 1.9 litre DOHC diesel engine is of the sixteen-valve, in-line four-cylinder, double overhead camshaft type, mounted transversely at the front of the car, with the transmission on its left-hand end.

The crankshaft is supported within the cylinder block on five shell-type main bearings. Thrustwashers are fitted to number 3 main bearing, to control crankshaft endfloat.

The connecting rods rotate on horizontally-split bearing shells at their big-ends. The connecting rods are forged on the Z19DTH engine and cast on the Z19DTR engine. The pistons are attached to the connecting rods by gudgeon pins, which are retained by circlips. The gudgeon pins are reinforced on the Z19DTR engines. The aluminium-alloy pistons are fitted with three piston rings – two compression rings and scraper-type oil control ring.

The camshafts are situated in a separate housing bolted to the top of the cylinder head. The exhaust camshaft is driven by the crankshaft via a toothed composite rubber timing belt (which also drives the high-pressure fuel pump and the coolant pump). The exhaust camshaft drives the intake camshaft via a spur gear. Each cylinder has four valves (two intake and two exhaust), operated via followers which are supported at their pivot ends by hydraulic self-adjusting tappets. One camshaft operates the intake valves, and the other operates the exhaust valves. Note that the camshaft housing on the Z19DTR is of a different design as it supplies oil for the high-pressure turbocharger.

The intake and exhaust valves are each closed by a single valve spring, and operate in guides pressed into the cylinder head.

Lubrication is by pressure-feed from a rotor-type oil pump, which is mounted on the right-hand end of the crankshaft. The pump draws oil through a strainer located in the sump, and then forces it through an externally mounted full-flow cartridge-type filter. The oil flows into galleries in the cylinder block/crankcase, from where it is distributed to the crankshaft (main bearings) and camshafts. The big-end bearings are supplied with oil via internal drillings in the crankshaft, while the camshaft bearings also receive a pressurised supply. The camshaft lobes and valves are lubricated by splash, as are all other engine components.

A semi-closed crankcase ventilation system is employed; crankcase fumes are drawn from the oil separator attached to the cylinder block via a hose to the camshaft housing. The fumes are then passed via a hose to the intake manifold.

Operations with engine in car

The following operations can be carried out without having to remove the engine from the car:

a) Removal and refitting of the cylinder head.
b) Removal and refitting of the timing belt, tensioner, idler pulleys and sprockets.
c) Renewal of the camshaft oil seal.
d) Removal and refitting of the camshaft housing.
e) Removal and refitting of the camshafts and followers.
f) Removal and refitting of the sump.
*g) Removal and refitting of the connecting rods and pistons.**
h) Removal and refitting of the oil pump.
i) Removal and refitting of the oil filter housing.
j) Renewal of the crankshaft oil seals.
k) Renewal of the engine mountings.
l) Removal and refitting of the flywheel/driveplate.

** Although the operation marked with an asterisk can be carried out with the engine in the car (after removal of the sump), it is preferable for the engine to be removed, in the interests of cleanliness and improved access. For this reason, the procedure is described in Chapter 2D, Section 9.*

2 Compression and leakdown tests – description and interpretation

Compression test

Note: *A compression tester specifically designed for diesel engines must be used for this test because of the higher pressures involved.*

Note: *The battery must be in a good state of charge, the air filter must be clean, and the engine should be at normal operating temperature.*

1 When engine performance is down, or if misfiring occurs which cannot be attributed to the fuel system, a compression test can provide diagnostic clues as to the engine's condition. If the test is performed regularly, it can give warning of trouble before any other symptoms become apparent.

2 The tester is connected to an adapter which screws into the glow plug holes. It is unlikely to be worthwhile buying such a tester for occasional use, but it may be possible to borrow or hire one – if not, have the test performed by a Saab dealer, or suitably-equipped garage. If the necessary equipment is available, proceed as follows.

3 Remove the glow plugs as described in Chapter 5A, Section 16.

4 Screw the compression tester adapter in to the glow plug hole of No 1 cylinder.

5 With the help of an assistant, crank the engine on the starter motor; after one or two revolutions, the compression pressure should build-up to a maximum figure, and then stabilise. Record the highest reading obtained.

6 Repeat the test on the remaining cylinders, recording the pressure in each.

7 All cylinders should produce very similar pressures; any difference greater than the maximum figure given in the Specifications indicates the existence of a fault. Note that the compression should build-up quickly in a healthy engine; low compression on the first stroke, followed by gradually-increasing pressure on successive strokes, indicates worn piston rings. A low compression reading on the first stroke, which does not build-up during successive strokes, indicates leaking valves or a blown head gasket (a cracked head could also be the cause). **Note:** *The cause of poor compression is less easy to establish on a diesel engine than on a petrol one. The effect of introducing oil into the cylinders ('wet' testing) is not conclusive, because there is a risk that the oil will sit in the recess on the piston crown instead of passing to the rings.*

8 On completion of the test refit the glow plugs as described in Chapter 5A, Section 16.

Leakdown test

9 A leakdown test measures the rate at which compressed air fed into the cylinder is lost. It is an alternative to a compression test, and in many ways it is better, since the escaping air provides easy identification of where pressure loss is occurring (piston rings, valves or head gasket).

10 The equipment needed for leakdown testing is unlikely to be available to the home mechanic. If poor compression is suspected, have the test performed by a Saab dealer, or suitably-equipped garage.

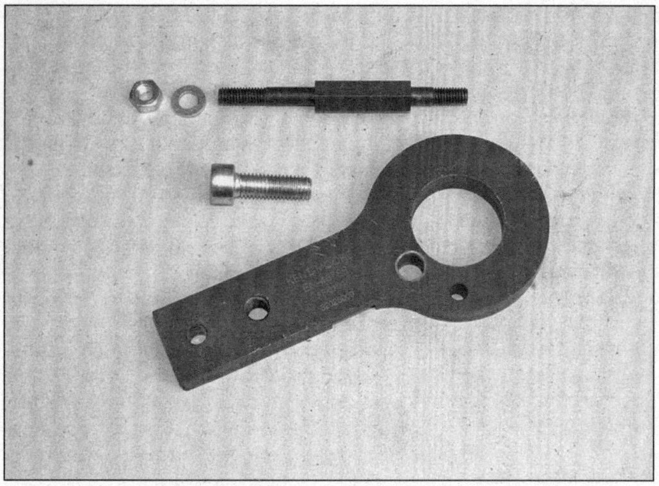

3.0a Saab special tool 32 025 009 (or equivalent) is required to set the TDC position for No 1 piston ...

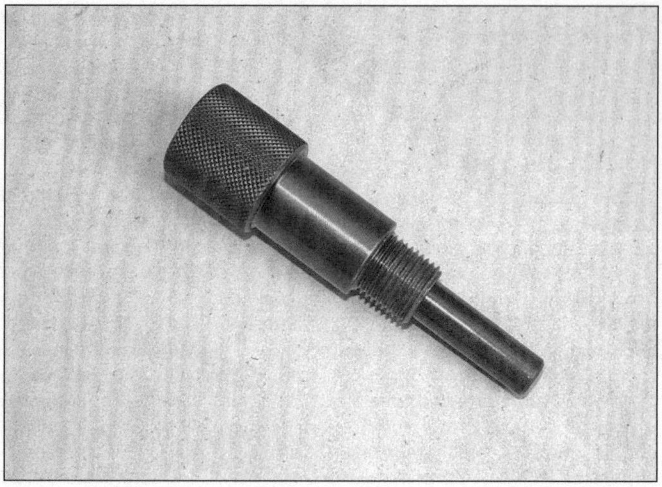

3.0b ... together with Saab special tool 32 025 008 (or equivalent) to set the camshaft position

3 Top dead centre (TDC) for No 1 piston – locating

Note: *To accurately determine the TDC position for No 1 piston, it will be necessary to use Saab special tool 32 025 009 (or suitable equivalent) to set the crankshaft at the TDC position, together with the camshaft positioning tool, Saab special tool 32 025 008 (or suitable equivalent)* ***(see illustrations).***

1 In its travel up-and-down its cylinder bore, Top Dead Centre (TDC) is the highest point that each piston reaches as the crankshaft rotates. While each piston reaches TDC both at the top of the compression stroke and again at the top of the exhaust stroke, for the purpose of timing the engine, TDC refers to the piston position of No 1 cylinder at the top of its compression stroke.

2 Number 1 piston (and cylinder) is at the right-hand (timing belt) end of the engine, and its TDC position is located as follows. Note that the crankshaft rotates clockwise when viewed from the right-hand side of the car.

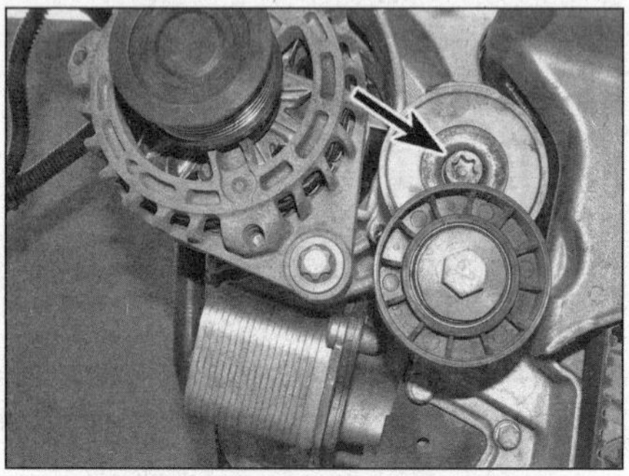

3.5 Undo the central mounting bolt (arrowed), and remove the auxiliary drivebelt tensioner assembly

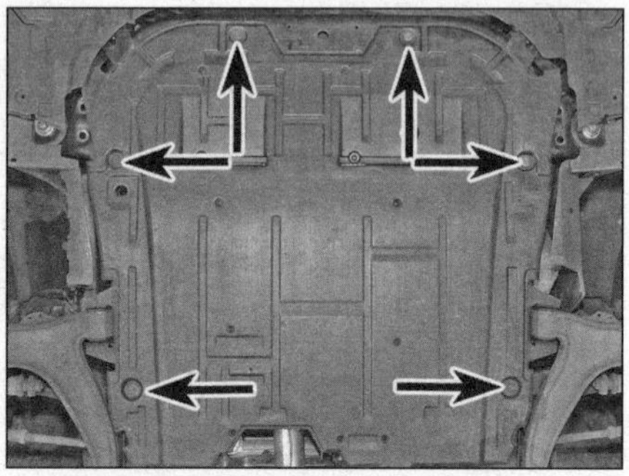

3.7 Engine undershield retaining screws (arrowed)

3 Disconnect the battery negative terminal as described in Chapter 5A, Section 4, then lift off the plastic cover over the top of the engine.

4 Remove the crankshaft pulley/vibration damper as described in Section 5.

5 Undo the central mounting bolt, and remove the auxiliary drivebelt tensioner assembly from the engine **(see illustration)**.

6 Remove the air cleaner assembly and air intake duct as described in Chapter 4B, Section 3.

7 Remove the engine undershield, then place a trolley jack beneath the right-hand end of the engine with a block of wood on the jack head. Raise the jack until it is supporting the weight of the engine **(see illustration)**.

8 Mark the bolt positions for correct refitting, then undo the three bolts securing the right-hand engine mounting to the engine bracket, and the three bolts securing the mounting to the body. Remove the mounting **(see illustration)**.

9 Release the retaining clip securing the engine breather hose to the breather pipe adjacent to the engine oil dipstick. Undo the two bolts securing the breather pipe to the cylinder head, and disconnect the pipe from the hose **(see illustration)**.

10 Undo the bolt and release the engine oil dipstick guide tube from the coolant pipe **(see illustration)**.

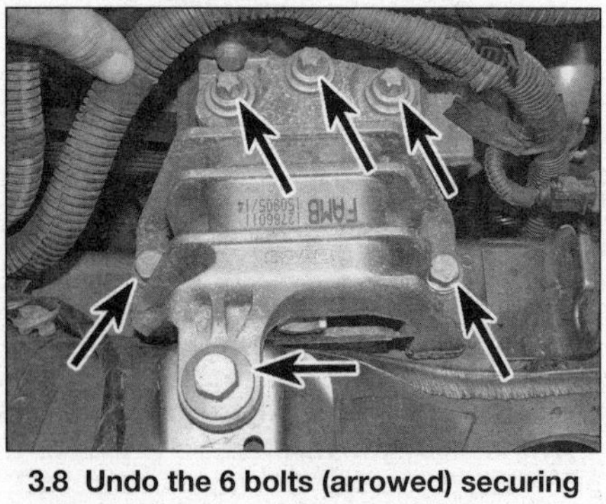

3.8 Undo the 6 bolts (arrowed) securing the engine mounting to the body and engine bracket

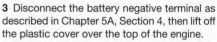

3.9 Engine breather pipe retaining bolts (arrowed)

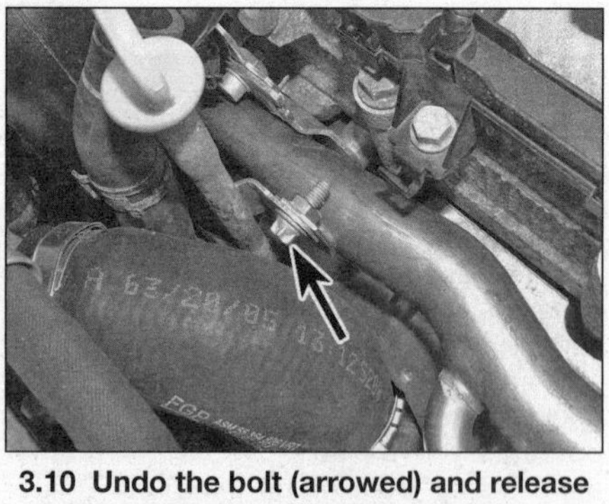

3.10 Undo the bolt (arrowed) and release the engine oil dipstick guide tube from the coolant pipe

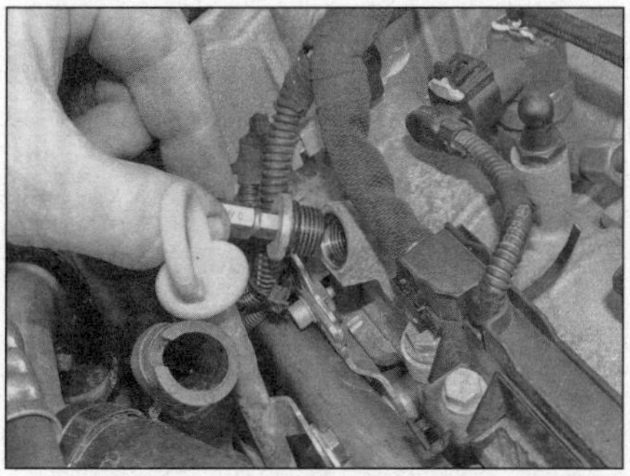

3.11 Unscrew the closure bolt from the valve timing checking hole in the camshaft housing

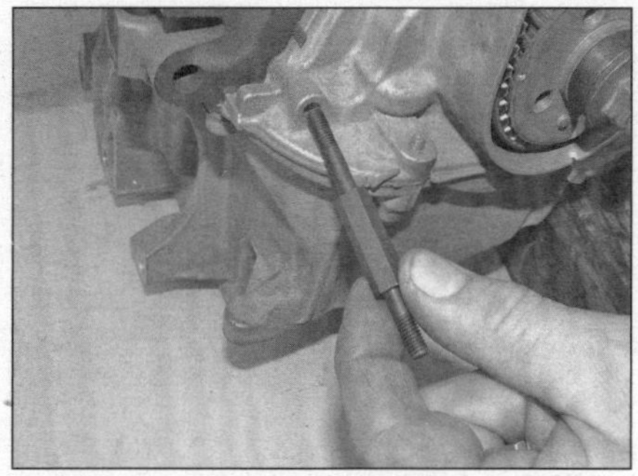

3.14 Screw the fastening stud of special tool 32 025 009 into the oil pump housing

3.15 Positioning ring of tool 32 025 009 (arrowed) attached to the fastening stud and crankshaft sprocket

11 Unscrew the closure bolt from the valve timing checking hole in the camshaft housing **(see illustration)**.

12 Screw the camshaft positioning tool (Saab special tool 32 025 008) into the valve timing checking hole.

13 Using a socket and extension bar on the crankshaft sprocket bolt, rotate the crankshaft in the normal direction of rotation until the spring-loaded plunger of the positioning tool slides into engagement with the slot in the camshaft. There will be an audible click from the tool when this happens.

14 Unscrew the bolt from the lower left-hand side of the oil pump housing and screw in the fastening stud of Saab special tool 32 025 009 **(see illustration)**.

15 Fit the positioning ring of tool 32 025 009 over the fastening stud and engage it with the crankshaft sprocket. Ensure that the hole in the positioning ring engages with the lug on the sprocket. Secure the tool in position with the retaining bolt and nut **(see illustration)**.

16 With the crankshaft positioning ring in place and the camshaft positioning tool engaged with the slot in the camshaft, the engine is positioned with No 1 piston at TDC on compression.

4 Valve timing – checking and adjustment

Note: *To check and adjust the valve timing, it will be necessary to use Saab special tool 32 025 009 (or suitable equivalent) to set the crankshaft at the TDC position. Additionally, it will be necessary to use Saab special tools 32 025 008 (or suitable equivalents) to lock the camshafts in the TDC position.*

Checking

1 Disconnect the battery negative terminal (refer Chapter 5A, Section 4), then lift off the plastic cover over the top of the engine.

2 Release the retaining clip securing the engine breather hose to the breather pipe adjacent to the engine oil dipstick. Undo the two bolts securing the breather pipe to the cylinder head, and disconnect the pipe from the hose **(see illustration 3.9)**.

3 Undo the bolt and release the engine oil dipstick guide tube from the coolant pipe **(see illustration 3.10)**.

4 Unscrew the closure bolt from the valve timing checking hole in the exhaust side of camshaft housing **(see illustration 3.11)**.

5 Screw the exhaust camshaft positioning tool (Saab special tool 32 025 008) into the valve timing checking hole.

6 Unscrew the closure bolt from the valve timing checking hole in the intake side of the camshaft housing. The closure bolt is located below the fuel pressure regulating valve on the fuel rail.

7 Screw the intake camshaft positioning tool (Saab special tool 32 025 008) into the valve timing checking hole.

8 Using a socket and extension bar on the crankshaft sprocket bolt, rotate the crankshaft in the normal direction of rotation until the spring-loaded plungers of the positioning tools slide into engagement with the slots in the camshafts. There will be an audible click from the tools when this happens.

9 Remove the crankshaft pulley/vibration damper as described in Section 5.

10 Unscrew the bolt from the lower left-hand side of the oil pump housing and screw in the fastening stud of Saab special tool 32 025 009 **(see illustration 3.14)**.

11 Fit the positioning ring of tool 32 025 009 over the fastening stud and engage it with the crankshaft sprocket. Ensure that the hole in the positioning ring engages with the lug on the sprocket. Secure the tool in position with the retaining bolt and nut **(see illustration 3.15)**.

12 If it is not possible to fit the positioning ring of tool 32 025 009 as described, or if the camshaft positioning tools did not engage with the camshaft slots, adjust the valve timing as follows.

Adjustment

13 Remove the timing belt as described in Section 6.

14 Using a socket and extension bar on the crankshaft sprocket bolt, rotate the crankshaft anti-clockwise by 90°. This will position all the pistons half-way down their bores, and prevent any chance of the valves touching the piston crowns during the following procedure.

15 Remove the intake and exhaust camshaft positioning tools from the valve timing checking holes.

16 Using a suitable tool engaged with the timing belt sprocket on the exhaust camshaft, rotate the sprocket approximately 90° clockwise **(see Tool Tip in Section 7)**. Take care not to damage the camshaft sensor with the tool as the sprocket is rotated.

17 Screw the intake camshaft positioning tool (Saab special tool 32 025 008) into the valve timing checking hole.

18 Rotate the camshaft sprocket clockwise until the spring-loaded plunger of the positioning tool slides into engagement with the slot in the intake camshaft. There will be an audible click from the tool when this happens.

19 Release the two retaining clips and disconnect the charge air hose from the throttle body/housing, and intercooler charge air pipe.

20 Release the clip and disconnect the crankcase ventilation hose from the engine oil filler housing.

21 Disconnect the wiring connector from the coolant temperature sensor, then undo the three retaining bolts and remove the oil filler housing.

22 Remove the braking system vacuum pump as described in Chapter 9, Section 12.

23 Working through the oil filler housing aperture, and using the holding tool to prevent rotation of the camshaft, slacken the intake camshaft drivegear retaining bolt. Working through the vacuum pump aperture, slacken the exhaust camshaft drivegear retaining bolt in the same way.

24 Screw the exhaust camshaft positioning tool (Saab special tool 32 025 008) into the valve timing checking hole.

25 Rotate the camshaft sprocket clockwise until the spring-loaded plunger of the positioning tool slides into engagement with the slot in the exhaust camshaft. There will be an audible click from the tool when this happens.

26 Hold the camshaft sprocket with the tool and tighten both drivegear retaining bolts to the specified torque.

27 Remove the positioning tool from the intake camshaft and refit the closure bolt. Tighten the bolt to the specified torque.

28 Refit the oil filler housing to the camshaft housing using a new gasket, refit the retaining bolts and tighten the bolts to the specified torque. Reconnect the coolant temperature sensor wiring connector, and reconnect the crankcase ventilation hose.

29 Refit the braking system vacuum pump as described in Chapter 9, Section 12.

30 Refit the charge air hose to the throttle body/housing, and intercooler charge air pipe and secure with the retaining clips.

31 Refit the timing belt as described in Section 6.

5 Crankshaft pulley/ vibration damper – removal and refitting

Removal

1 Apply the handbrake, then jack up the front of the vehicle and support it on axle stands (see *Jacking and vehicle support*). Remove the right-hand front roadwheel, then undo the bolts and remove the engine undershield for access to the crankshaft pulley **(see illustration 3.7)**.

2 Remove the auxiliary drivebelt as described in Chapter 1B, Section 27. Prior to removal, mark the direction of rotation on the belt to ensure the belt is refitted the same way around.

3 Undo the four bolts securing the pulley to the crankshaft sprocket and remove the pulley from the sprocket **(see illustration)**.

5.3 Crankshaft pulley/vibration damper retaining bolts (arrowed)

Refitting

4 Locate the crankshaft pulley on the sprocket, ensuring that the hole on the rear face of the pulley engages with the lug on the sprocket.

5 Refit the four retaining bolts and tighten them progressively to the specified torque.

6 Refit the auxiliary drivebelt as described in Chapter 1B, Section 27 using the mark made prior to removal to ensure the belt is fitted the correct way around.

7 Refit the roadwheel and engine undershield, then lower the car to the ground and tighten the wheel bolts to the specified torque.

6 Timing belt – removal and refitting

Note: *The timing belt must be removed and refitted with the engine cold.*

Removal

1 Position No 1 cylinder at TDC on its compression stroke as described in Section 3.

2 Unclip the wiring harness from the side of the upper timing belt cover. Unscrew the seven retaining bolts and lift off the upper timing belt cover **(see illustration)**.

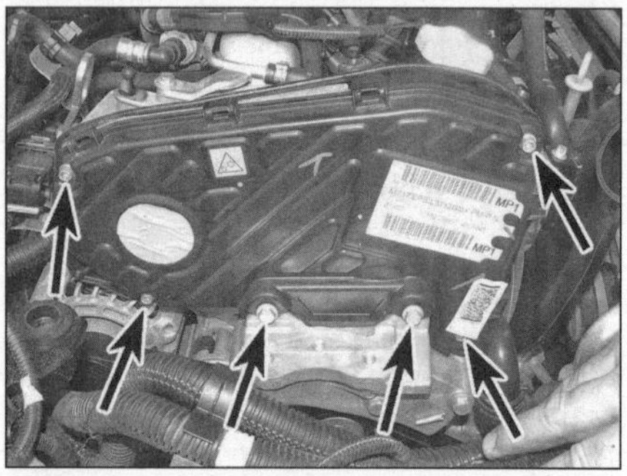

6.2 Upper timing belt cover retaining bolts (arrowed)

3 Undo the retaining bolt and remove the auxiliary drivebelt idler pulley from the engine bracket **(see illustration)**.

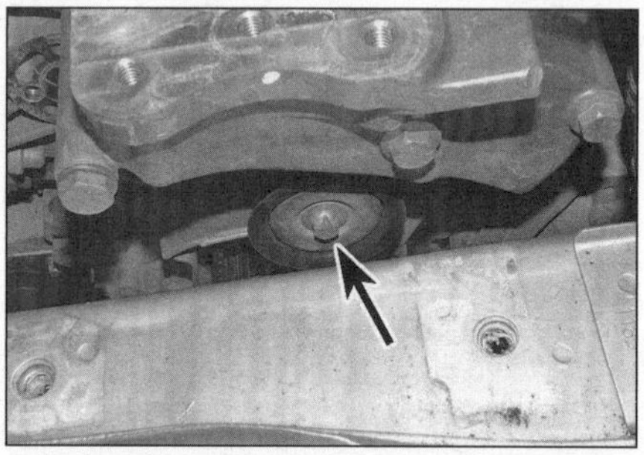

6.3 Undo the bolt (arrowed) and remove the auxiliary drivebelt idler pulley from the engine bracket

4 Undo the two lower bolts, and the three upper bolts, and remove the engine bracket from the engine **(see illustrations)**.

6.4a Undo the two lower bolts (arrowed) ...

6.4b ... and the three upper bolts (arrowed) ...

6.4c ... and remove the bracket from the engine

5 Undo the nut and bolt and remove the crankshaft positioning tool (32 025 009) from the crankshaft sprocket.

6 Slacken the timing belt tensioner retaining bolt and allow the tensioner to retract, relieving the tension on the timing belt.

7 Slide the timing belt from its sprockets and remove it from the engine. If the belt is to be re-used, use white paint or similar to mark the direction of rotation on the belt. Do not rotate the crankshaft or camshafts until the timing belt has been refitted.

8 Check the timing belt carefully for any signs of uneven wear, splitting or oil contamination, and renew it if there is the slightest doubt about its condition. If the engine is undergoing an overhaul and is approaching the specified interval for belt renewal (see Chapter 1B, Section 25) renew the belt as a matter of course, regardless of its apparent condition. If signs of oil contamination are found, trace the source of the oil leak and rectify it, then wash down the engine timing belt area and all related components to remove all traces of oil.

Refitting

9 On reassembly, thoroughly clean the timing belt sprockets and tensioner/idler pulleys.

10 Place the timing belt in position over the crankshaft sprocket. If the original belt is being refitted, ensure that the arrow mark made on removal points in the normal direction of rotation, as before.

11 Check that the camshaft and crankshaft are still positioned with No 1 piston at TDC on compression as described in Section 3, and with the camshaft positioning tool still in place. Now refit the crankshaft positioning tool.

12 Fit the timing belt over the crankshaft, camshaft and fuel pump sprockets and around the idler pulleys, ensuring that the belt front run is taut (ie, all slack is on the tensioner side of the belt), then fit the belt over the coolant pump sprocket and tensioner pulley. Do not twist the belt sharply while refitting it. Ensure that the belt teeth are correctly seated centrally in the sprockets. Note that the marks on the new belt correspond to the marks on the crankshaft and camshaft sprockets.
13 Screw in a suitable bolt, approximately 50 mm in length, into the threaded hole directly below the timing belt tensioner. Using a screwdriver resting on the bolt as a pivot, move the adjusting lever on the tensioner until the tensioner pointer is aligned with the mark on the backplate. Hold the tensioner in this position and tighten the tensioner retaining bolt **(see illustrations)**.
14 Remove the crankshaft and camshaft positioning tools.
15 Using a socket on the crankshaft sprocket bolt, rotate the crankshaft smoothly through two complete turns (720°) in the normal direction of rotation to settle the timing belt in position. Stop rotating the crankshaft just before completing the second turn.
16 Refit the camshaft positioning tool and continue turning the crankshaft until the camshaft positioning tool engages.
17 Refit the positioning ring of tool 32 025 009 over the fastening stud and engage it with the crankshaft sprocket. Ensure that the hole in the positioning ring engages with the lug on the sprocket. Secure the tool in position with the retaining bolt and nut.
18 Slacken the timing belt tensioner retaining bolt and, using a screwdriver resting on the pivot bolt as before, move the adjusting lever on the tensioner until the tensioner pointer is once again aligned with the mark on the backplate. Hold the tensioner in this position and tighten the tensioner retaining bolt to the specified torque.
19 Remove all the positioning tools and again rotate the crankshaft smoothly through two complete turns (720°) in the normal direction of rotation. Check that the timing belt tensioner pointer is still aligned with the mark on the backplate. If not, repeat the procedure described in paragraph 18.
20 When all is correct, remove the tensioner position pivot bolt. Refit the bolt removed from the oil pump housing and tighten it to the specified torque. Refit the closure plug to the camshaft housing and tighten to the specified torque.
21 Place the engine bracket in position and refit the two lower bolts, and the three upper bolts. Tighten the bolts to the specified torque. Refit the auxiliary drivebelt idler pulley to the engine bracket and tighten the retaining bolt to the specified torque.
22 Refit the upper timing belt cover and tighten the retaining bolts to the specified torque. Clip the wiring harness back into position.

6.13a Use a screwdriver resting on a pivot bolt (arrowed), to move the adjusting lever on the tensioner ...

23 Place the right-hand engine mounting assembly in position and refit the three bolts securing the mounting to the body. Tighten the bolts/nut to the specified torque. Align the mounting in its original position, then tighten the three mounting bracket bolts to the specified torque. Remove the jack from under the engine.
24 Refit the air cleaner assembly and air intake duct as described in Chapter 4B, Section 3.
25 Place the auxiliary drivebelt tensioner assembly in position ensuring that the locating peg on the tensioner mounting surface engages correctly with the corresponding hole in the mounting bracket. Tighten the tensioner central mounting bolt to the specified torque.
26 Refit the crankshaft pulley/vibration damper as described in Section 5, then refit the auxiliary drivebelt as described in Chapter 1B, Section 27.
27 Move the engine oil dipstick guide tube back into position. Refit the bolt securing the guide tube to the coolant pipe and tighten the bolt securely.

TOOL TiP

To make a sprocket holding tool, obtain two lengths of steel strip about 6 mm thick by about 30 mm wide or similar, one 600 mm long, the other 200 mm long (all dimensions are approximate). Bolt the two strips together to form a forked end, leaving the bolt slack so the shorter strip can pivot freely. At the other end of each 'prong' of the fork, fit a nut and bolt to allow the tool to engage with the spokes in the sprocket.

6.13b ... until the tensioner pointer (arrowed) is aligned with the mark on the backplate

28 Attach the engine breather hose to the breather pipe and secure with the retaining clip. Secure the breather pipe to the cylinder head with the two bolts securely tightened.
29 Refit the plastic cover to the top of the engine.
30 Refit the roadwheel and engine undershield, then lower the car to the ground and tighten the wheel bolts to the specified torque.

7 Timing belt sprockets, tensioner and idler pulley – removal and refitting

Note: *Certain special tools will be required for the removal and refitting of the sprockets. Read through the entire procedure to familiarise yourself with the work involved, then either obtain the manufacturer's special tools, or use the alternatives described.*

Camshaft sprocket

Note: *A new sprocket retaining bolt will be required for refitting.*

Removal

1 Remove the timing belt as described in Section 6, then remove camshaft positioning tool from the valve timing checking hole.
2 It will now be necessary to hold the camshaft sprocket to enable the retaining bolt to be removed. Saab special tool 32 025 035 is available for this purpose, however, a home-made tool can easily be fabricated **(see Tool Tip)**.
3 Engage the tool with the holes in the camshaft sprocket, taking care not to damage the camshaft sensor located behind the sprocket
4 Unscrew the retaining bolt and remove the sprocket from the end of the camshaft.

Refitting

5 Prior to refitting check the oil seal for signs of damage or leakage. If necessary, renew as described in Section 8.
6 Refit the sprocket to the camshaft end, aligning its cut-out with the locating peg, and fit the new retaining bolt finger-tight only at this stage. Final tightening is carried out after the timing belt has been fitted and tensioned.
7 Refit the camshaft positioning tool to the

7.14a Remove the bolt and washer ...

valve timing checking hole. If necessary, rotate the camshaft slightly, by means of the sprocket, until the tool audibly engages.

8 Proceed with the timing belt refitting procedure as described in Section 6, paragraphs 9 to 14.

9 Retain the camshaft sprocket using the holding tool, and tighten the retaining bolt to the specified torque.

10 Continue with the timing belt refitting procedure as described in Section 6, paragraphs 15 to 30.

Crankshaft sprocket

Note: *The crankshaft sprocket retaining bolt is extremely tight. Ensure that the holding tool used to prevent rotation as the bolt is slackened is of sturdy construction and securely attached.*

Note: *A new sprocket retaining bolt will be required for refitting.*

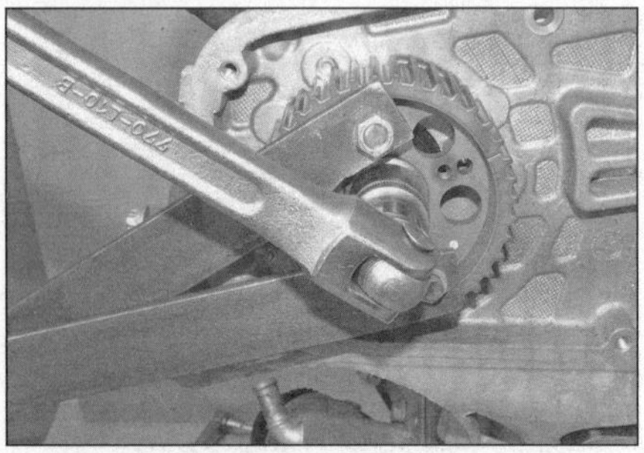

7.20 Engage the holding tool with the holes in the fuel pump sprocket and undo the retaining nut

7.22a Once the taper releases, withdraw the sprocket ...

7.14b ... and slide the sprocket off the end of the crankshaft

Removal

11 Remove the timing belt as described in Section 6.

12 It will now be necessary to hold the crankshaft sprocket to enable the retaining bolt to be removed. Saab special tools 32 025 006 and 83 95 360 are available for this purpose, however, a home-made tool similar to that described in paragraph 2, can easily be fabricated.

13 Using the crankshaft pulley retaining bolts, securely attach the tool to the crankshaft sprocket. With the help of an assistant, hold the sprocket stationary and unscrew the retaining bolt. **Note:** *The sprocket retaining bolt has a* ***left-hand thread*** *and is unscrewed by turning it clockwise.*

14 Remove the bolt and washer and slide the sprocket off the end of the crankshaft **(see illustrations)**. Note that a new bolt will be required for refitting.

7.21 Use a suitable puller to release the fuel pump sprocket taper

7.22b ... and collect the Woodruff key from the pump shaft

Refitting

15 Align the sprocket location key with the crankshaft groove and slide the sprocket into position. Fit the new retaining bolt and washer.

16 Hold the sprocket stationary using the holding tool and tighten the retaining bolt to the specified torque, remembering it has a **left-hand thread**. Remove the holding tool.

17 Refit the timing belt as described in Section 6.

High-pressure fuel pump sprocket

Note: *A new sprocket retaining nut will be required for refitting.*

Removal

18 Remove the timing belt as described in Section 6.

19 It will now be necessary to hold the fuel pump sprocket to enable the retaining nut to be removed. Saab special tools 32 025 019 and 83 95 360 are available for this purpose, however, a home-made tool similar to that described in paragraph 2, can easily be fabricated.

20 Engage the tool with the holes in the fuel pump sprocket and undo the sprocket retaining nut **(see illustration)**. Note that a new nut will be required for refitting.

21 Attach a suitable puller to the threaded holes in the fuel pump sprocket using bolts and washers similar to the arrangement shown **(see illustration)**.

22 Tighten the puller centre bolt to release the sprocket from the taper on the pump shaft. Once the taper releases, remove the puller and withdraw the sprocket. Collect the Woodruff key from the pump shaft **(see illustrations)**.

Refitting

23 Clean the fuel pump shaft and the sprocket hub ensuring that all traces of oil or grease are removed.

24 Refit the Woodruff key to the pump shaft, then locate the sprocket in position. Fit the new retaining nut.

25 Hold the sprocket stationary using the holding tool and tighten the retaining nut to the specified torque. Remove the holding tool.

26 Refit the timing belt as described in Section 6.

Tensioner assembly

Removal

27 Remove the timing belt as described in Section 6.

28 Slacken and remove the retaining bolt and remove the tensioner assembly from the engine **(see illustrations)**.

Refitting

29 Fit the tensioner to the engine, making sure that the slot on the tensioner backplate is correctly located over the peg on the engine bracket **(see illustration)**.

30 Clean the threads of the retaining bolt and apply thread-locking compound to the bolt threads. Screw in the retaining bolt, set the tensioner in the retracted position and tighten the retaining bolt.

31 Refit the timing belt as described in Section 6.

Idler pulley

Removal

32 Remove the timing belt as described in Section 6.

33 Slacken and remove the retaining bolt and remove the idler pulley from the engine **(see illustration)**.

Refitting

34 Refit the idler pulley and tighten the retaining bolt to the specified torque.

35 Refit the timing belt as described in Section 6.

7.28a Slacken and remove the retaining bolt ...

7.28b ... and remove the timing belt tensioner assembly

7.29 The slot on the tensioner backplate must locate over the peg (arrowed) on the engine bracket

7.33 Slacken and remove the retaining bolt and remove the idler pulley from the engine

8 Camshaft oil seal – renewal

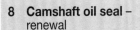

1 Remove the camshaft sprocket as described in Section 7.

2 Carefully punch or drill a small hole in the oil seal. Screw in a self-tapping screw, and pull on the screw with pliers to extract the seal.

3 Clean the seal housing, and polish off any burrs or raised edges which may have caused the seal to fail in the first place.

4 Lubricate the lips of the new seal with clean engine oil, and press it into position using a suitable tubular drift (such as a socket) which bears only on the hard outer edge of the seal. Take care not to damage the seal lips during fitting; note that the seal lips should face inwards.

5 Refit the camshaft sprocket as described in Section 7.

9 Camshaft housing – removal and refitting

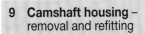

Removal

1 Remove the timing belt as described in Section 6.

2 Disconnect the wiring harness connectors from the following components **(see illustrations)**:

a) Fuel injectors.

b) Fuel pressure regulating valve.

c) Fuel pressure sensor.

d) Camshaft sensor.

e) Air conditioning compressor.

9.2a Disconnect the wiring plugs at the fuel injectors ...

9.2b ... fuel pressure regulating valve ...

9.2c ... fuel pressure sensor ...

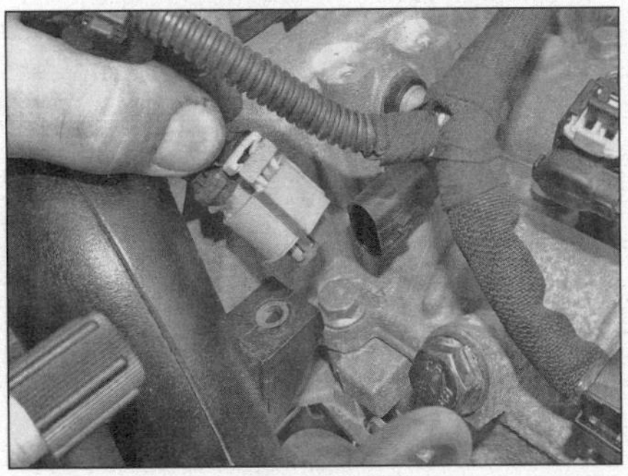

9.2d ... camshaft sensor ...

9.2e ... and air conditioning compressor (arrowed)

9.3a Undo the two bolts (arrowed) securing the wiring harness guide to the camshaft housing ...

9.3b ... and move the harness to one side

9.4a Disconnect the two vacuum hoses (arrowed) from the pipe assembly ...

9.4b ... then undo the two retaining bolts (arrowed) and move the pipe assembly to one side

9.5 Remove the oil supply hose from the camshaft housing

3 Release the air conditioning compressor wiring harness from the clip on the oil dipstick guide tube. Undo the two bolts securing the plastic wiring harness guide to the camshaft housing and move the disconnected wiring harness to one side **(see illustrations)**.

4 Disconnect the two vacuum hoses from the vacuum pipe assembly on top of the camshaft housing. Undo the two retaining bolts and move the pipe assembly to one side **(see illustrations)**.

5 Remove the fuel injectors and the fuel rail as described in Chapter 4B, Section 11 and 12. On DTR engines remove the wiring loom from the fuel injectors and then remove the upper turbocharger oil supply pipe **(see illustration)**.

6 Release the two retaining clips and disconnect the charge air hose from the throttle body/housing, and intercooler charge air pipe **(see illustration)**.

7 Disconnect the vacuum hose quick-release fitting from the braking system vacuum pump **(see illustration)**.

8 Release the clip and disconnect the crankcase ventilation hose from the engine oil filler housing **(see illustration)**.

9 Undo the retaining bolts and remove the two engine lifting brackets from the left-hand end of the camshaft housing. Undo the bolt securing the turbocharger charge air pipe to the right-hand end of the camshaft housing

10 Working in a spiral pattern from the outside inwards, progressively slacken, then remove, the sixteen bolts securing the camshaft housing to the cylinder head. Ensure that the housing releases evenly from the cylinder block.

11 Lift the camshaft housing off the cylinder head and recover the gasket **(see illustration)**.

12 Thoroughly clean the mating faces of the cylinder head, camshaft housing and vacuum pump and obtain a new gasket for refitting.

Refitting

13 Check that all the hydraulic tappets and rocker arms are correctly positioned in the cylinder head and none have been disturbed.

14 Commence refitting by turning the crankshaft anti-clockwise by 90°. This will position all the pistons half-way down their bores, and prevent any chance of the valves touching the piston crowns as the camshaft housing is being fitted.

15 Place a new gasket on the cylinder head, then locate the camshaft housing in position aligning it with the locating dowels.

16 Refit the sixteen camshaft housing retaining bolts. Progressively screw in the bolts to gradually draw the housing down and into contact with the cylinder head.

9.6 Release the retaining clips and remove the charge air hose (arrowed)

9.7 Depress the clip and disconnect the vacuum hose quick-release fitting from the braking system vacuum pump

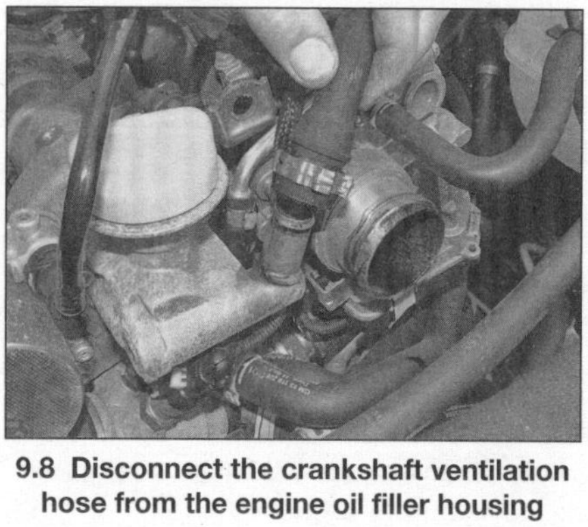

9.8 Disconnect the crankshaft ventilation hose from the engine oil filler housing

9.11 Lift the camshaft housing off the cylinder head and recover the gasket

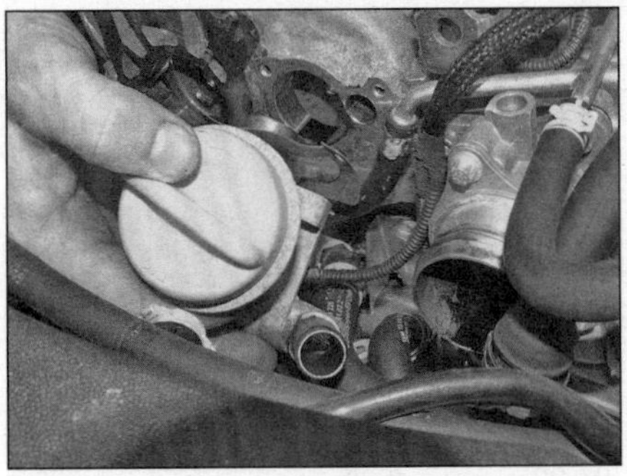

10.3 Undo the 3 bolts and remove the oil filler housing

10.8a Slacken the intake camshaft drivegear retaining bolt ...

10.8b ... and the exhaust camshaft drivegear retaining bolt

17 Working in a spiral pattern from the inside outwards, progressively tighten the sixteen bolts to the specified torque.

18 Refit the two engine lifting brackets to the left-hand end of the camshaft housing and tighten the retaining bolts securely. Refit and tighten the charge air pipe retaining bolt.

19 Reconnect the crankcase ventilation hose to the engine oil filler housing.

20 Reconnect the vacuum hose quick-release fitting to the braking system vacuum pump ensuring that the fitting audibly engages.

21 Refit the charge air hose to the throttle body/housing and intercooler charge air pipe, and secure with the retaining clips.

22 Refit the fuel rail and fuel injectors as described in Chapter 4B, Section 11 and 12.

23 Place the vacuum pipe assembly in position on the top of the camshaft housing and refit the two retaining bolts. Tighten the bolts securely, then reconnect the two vacuum hoses.

24 Lay the plastic wiring harness guide in position on the camshaft housing, then refit and tighten the two retaining bolts.

25 Reconnect the wiring harness connectors to the components listed in paragraph 2, ensuring that the harness is secured by all the relevant retaining clips.

26 Turn the crankshaft clockwise by 90° to bring No 1 and 4 pistons to approximately the TDC position.

27 Refit the timing belt as described in Section 6.

10 Camshafts – removal, inspection and refitting

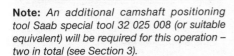

Note: *An additional camshaft positioning tool Saab special tool 32 025 008 (or suitable equivalent) will be required for this operation – two in total (see Section 3).*

Removal

1 Carry out the operations described in Section 9, paragraphs 1 to 8.

2 Remove the braking system vacuum pump as described in Chapter 9, Section 12.

3 Disconnect the wiring connector from the coolant temperature sensor, then undo the three retaining bolts and remove the oil filler housing **(see illustration)**.

4 Undo the retaining bolt and remove the camshaft sensor from the right-hand end of the camshaft housing.

5 Before removing the camshaft housing completely, the retaining bolts for the camshaft drivegears and sprocket should be slackened as follows.

6 Remove the exhaust camshaft positioning tool from the valve timing checking hole.

7 It will be necessary to hold the camshaft sprocket to enable the drivegear and sprocket retaining bolts to be slackened. A home-made tool can easily be fabricated **(see Tool Tip in Section 7)**.

8 Working through the oil filler housing aperture, and using the holding tool to prevent rotation of the camshaft, slacken the intake camshaft drivegear retaining bolt. Working through the vacuum pump aperture, slacken the exhaust camshaft drivegear retaining bolt in the same way **(see illustrations)**.

9 Again, using the holding tool, slacken the camshaft sprocket retaining bolt.

10 Continue with the camshaft housing removal procedure as described in Section 9, paragraphs 9 to 11.

11 With the camshaft housing placed upside-down on the bench, unscrew and remove the previously-slackened retaining bolt, and remove the timing belt sprocket from the exhaust camshaft.

12 At the other end of the housing, unscrew and remove the two previously-slackened retaining bolts, and lift off the drivegears from the intake and exhaust camshafts **(see illustrations)**.

13 Carefully prise out the exhaust camshaft oil seal with a screwdriver or similar hooked tool. Carefully withdraw the exhaust camshaft out from the timing belt end of the camshaft housing **(see illustration)**.

10.12a Unscrew and remove the two previously-slackened retaining bolts ...

10.12b ... then lift out the exhaust camshaft drivegear ...

10.12c ... and the intake camshaft drivegear

10.13 Withdraw the exhaust camshaft ...

10.14 ... and intake camshaft from the housing

14 Using a wooden dowel or similar, carefully tap the end of the intake camshaft toward the timing belt end of the housing, to release the blanking cap. Remove the cap, then carefully withdraw the intake camshaft from the housing **(see illustration)**.

Inspection

15 Examine the camshaft bearing surfaces and cam lobes for signs of wear ridges and scoring. Renew the camshaft(s) if any of these conditions are apparent. Examine the condition of the bearing surfaces in the camshaft housing. If the any wear or scoring is evident, the camshaft housing will need to be renewed.

16 If either camshaft is being renewed, it will be necessary to renew all the rocker arms and tappets for that particular camshaft also (see Section 11).

17 Check the condition of the camshaft

10.22 Refit the camshaft positioning tool to the valve timing checking hole of the exhaust camshaft

drivegears and sprocket for chipped or damaged teeth, wear ridges and scoring. Renew any components as necessary.

Refitting

18 Prior to refitting, thoroughly clean all components and dry with a lint-free cloth. Ensure that all traces of oil and grease are removed from the contact faces of the drivegears, sprocket and camshafts.

19 Lubricate the camshaft bearing journals in the camshaft housing and carefully insert the intake and exhaust camshafts.

20 Ensuring that the contact faces are clean and dry, refit the drivegear to each camshaft. Note that the gear with the vacuum pump drive dogs is fitted to the exhaust camshaft, and the plain gear is fitted to the intake camshaft.

21 Screw in a new drivegear retaining bolt for each camshaft and tighten both bolts finger-tight only at this stage.

22 Refit the camshaft positioning tool to the valve timing checking hole of the exhaust camshaft. If necessary, rotate the exhaust camshaft slightly, until the tool audibly engages **(see illustration)**.

23 Unscrew and remove the closure bolt from the intake camshaft side of the camshaft housing and fit a second camshaft positioning tool **(see illustrations)**. If necessary, rotate the camshaft slightly, until the tool audibly engages.

24 With both camshafts locked by means of the positioning tools, tighten both drivegear retaining bolts to the specified torque **(see illustration)**. It may be beneficial to have an assistant securely support the camshaft housing as the bolts are tightened.

25 Remove the positioning tool from the intake camshaft and refit the closure bolt. Tighten the bolt to the specified torque.

26 Fit a new intake camshaft blanking cap to the timing belt end of the camshaft housing and tap it into position until it is flush with the outer face of the housing, using a suitable socket or tube, or a wooden block **(see illustrations)**.

27 Similarly, fit a new exhaust camshaft oil seal to the timing belt end of the camshaft housing and tap it into position until it is flush with the outer face of the housing, using a suitable socket or tube, or a wooden block **(see illustration)**.

28 Refit the timing belt sprocket to the exhaust camshaft, aligning its cut-out with the locating peg, and fit the new retaining bolt finger-tight only at this stage. Final tightening

10.23a Unscrew the closure bolt from the intake camshaft side of the housing ...

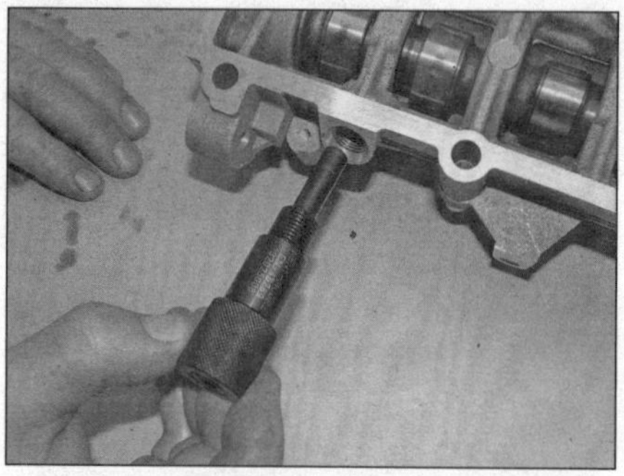

10.23b ... and fit a camshaft positioning tool for the intake camshaft

10.24 With both camshafts locked, tighten both drivegear retaining bolts to the specified torque

10.26a Fit a new intake camshaft blanking cap to the camshaft housing ...

10.26b ... and tap it into position until it is flush with the outer face of the housing

10.27 Similarly, fit a new exhaust camshaft oil seal to the camshaft housing

is carried out after the timing belt has been fitted and tensioned.

29 Refit the camshaft sensor to the camshaft housing and tighten the retaining bolt securely.

30 Refit the oil filler housing to the camshaft housing using a new gasket, refit the retaining bolts and tighten the bolts to the specified torque. Reconnect the coolant temperature sensor wiring connector.

31 Refit the braking system vacuum pump as described in Chapter 9, Section 12.

32 Thoroughly clean the mating faces of the cylinder head and camshaft housing.

33 Refit the camshaft housing to the cylinder head as described in Section 9, paragraphs 13 to 26.

34 Commence refitting of the timing belt as described in Section 6, paragraphs 9 to 14.

35 Retain the camshaft sprocket using the holding tool, and tighten the retaining bolt to the specified torque.

36 Continue refitting of the timing belt as described in Section 6, paragraphs 15 to 30.

11 Camshaft followers and hydraulic tappets – removal, inspection and refitting

Removal

1 Remove the camshaft housing as described in Section 9.

2 Obtain sixteen small, oil-tight clean plastic containers, and number them intake 1 to 8 and exhaust 1 to 8; alternatively, divide a larger container into sixteen compartments and number each compartment accordingly.

3 Withdraw each camshaft follower and hydraulic tappet in turn, unclip the follower from the tappet, and place them in their respective container **(see illustrations)**. Do not interchange the followers and tappets, or the rate of wear will be much increased. Fill each container with clean engine oil and ensure that the tappet is submerged.

Inspection

4 Examine the followers and hydraulic tappet bearing surfaces for wear ridges and scoring. Renew any follower or tappet on which these conditions are apparent.

5 If any new hydraulic tappets are obtained, they should be immersed in a container of clean engine oil prior to refitting.

Refitting

6 Liberally oil the cylinder head hydraulic tappet bores and the tappets. Working on one assembly at a time, clip the follower back onto the tappet, then refit the tappet to the cylinder head, ensuring that it is refitted to its original bore. Lay the follower over its respective valve **(see illustrations)**.

7 Refit the remaining tappets and followers in the same way.

8 With all the tappets and followers in place,

11.3a Withdraw each camshaft follower ...

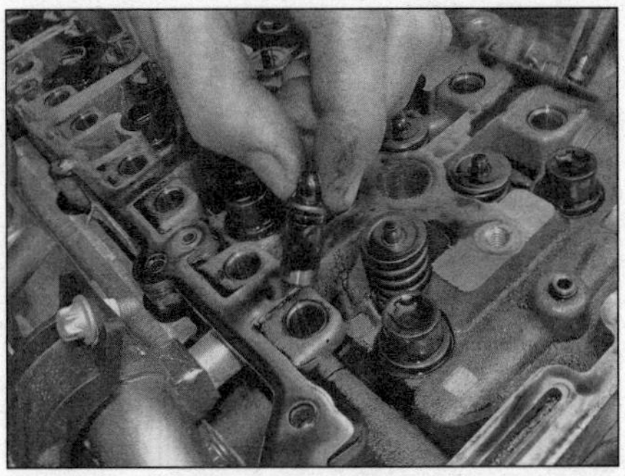

11.3b ... and hydraulic tappet in turn, then place them in their respective container

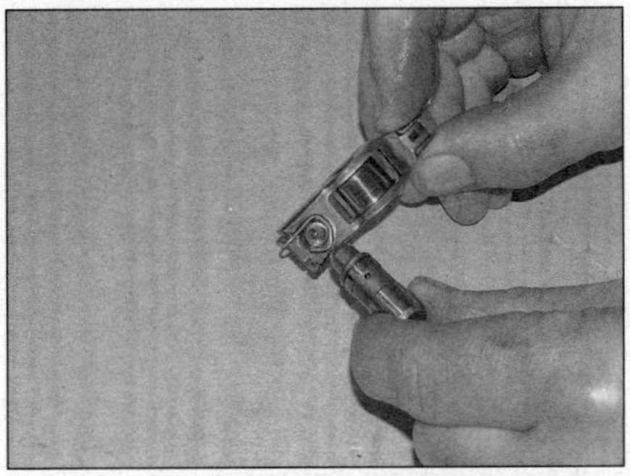

11.6a Clip the follower back onto the tappet ...

11.6b ... then refit the tappet to its original bore, and lay the follower over its respective valve

refit the camshaft housing as described in Section 9.

12 Cylinder head – removal and refitting

Note: *New cylinder head bolts will be required for refitting.*

Removal

1 Disconnect the battery negative terminal as described in Chapter 5A, Section 4.

2 Drain the cooling system as described in Chapter 1B, Section 28.

3 Remove the camshaft housing as described in Section 9.

4 Remove the camshaft followers and hydraulic tappets as described in Section 11.

5 Remove the intake and exhaust manifolds as described in Chapter 4B, Section 13 and 17.

6 Release the clips and disconnect the remaining two coolant hoses at the thermostat housing, and the coolant hose at the EGR valve heat exchanger **(see illustration)**.

7 Release the coolant pipe from the stud at the base of the thermostat housing **(see illustration)**.

8 Undo the bolt securing the high-pressure fuel pump mounting bracket to the cylinder head **(see illustration)**.

9 Make a final check to ensure that all relevant hoses, pipes and wires have been disconnected.

10 Working in the **reverse** of the tightening sequence **(see illustration 12.27)**,

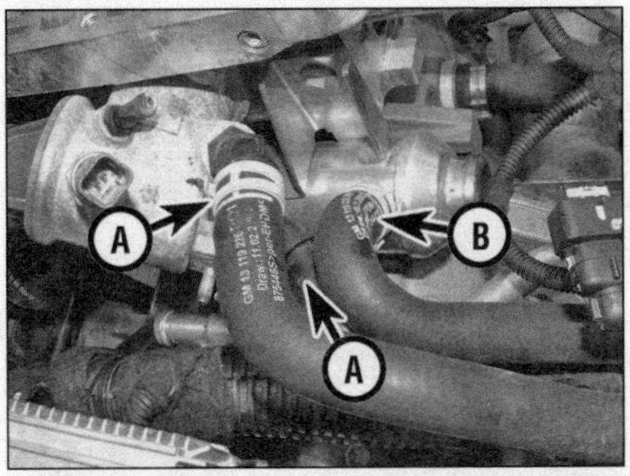

12.6 Disconnect the coolant hoses at the thermostat housing (A), and at the EGR valve heat exchanger (B)

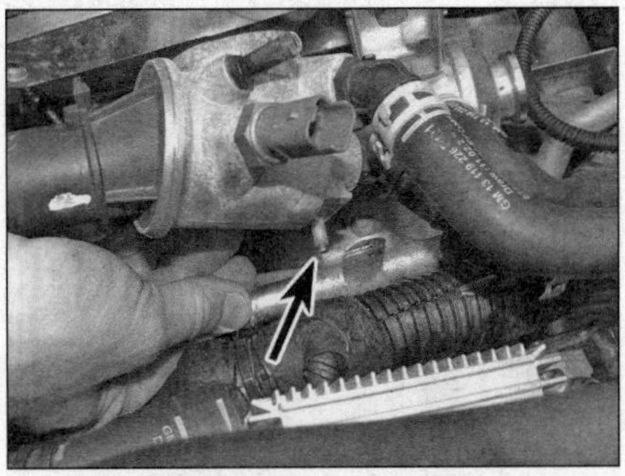

12.7 Release the coolant pipe from the stud (arrowed) at the base of the thermostat housing

12.8 Undo the bolt (arrowed) securing the high-pressure fuel pump mounting bracket to the cylinder head

progressively slacken the cylinder head bolts by half a turn at a time, until all bolts can be unscrewed by hand. Note that an M14 RIBE socket bit will be required to unscrew the bolts. Remove the cylinder head bolts and recover the washers.

11 Engage the help of an assistant, if necessary, and lift the cylinder head from the cylinder block **(see illustration)**.

Caution: Do not lay the head on its lower mating surface; support the head on wooden blocks, ensuring each block only contacts the head mating surface.

12 Remove the gasket and keep it for identification purposes (see paragraph 19).

13 If the cylinder head is to be dismantled for overhaul, then refer to Chapter 2D.

Preparation for refitting

14 The mating faces of the cylinder head and cylinder block/crankcase must be perfectly clean before refitting the head. Use a hard plastic or wood scraper to remove all traces of gasket and carbon; also clean the piston crowns. Take particular care, as the surfaces are damaged easily. Also, make sure that the carbon is not allowed to enter the oil and water passages – this is particularly important for the lubrication system, as carbon could block the oil supply to any of the engine's components. Using adhesive tape and paper, seal the water, oil and bolt holes in the cylinder block/crankcase. To prevent carbon entering the gap between the pistons and bores, smear a little grease in the gap. After cleaning each piston, use a small brush to remove all traces of grease and carbon from the

12.11 Lift the cylinder head from the cylinder block

gap, then wipe away the remainder with a clean rag. Clean all the pistons in the same way.

15 Check the mating surfaces of the cylinder block/crankcase and the cylinder head for nicks, deep scratches and other damage. If slight, they may be removed carefully with a file, but if excessive, machining may be the only alternative to renewal.

16 Ensure that the cylinder head bolt holes in the crankcase are clean and free of oil. Syringe or soak up any oil left in the bolt holes. This is most important in order that the correct bolt tightening torque can be applied and to prevent the possibility of the block being cracked by hydraulic pressure when the bolts are tightened.

17 The cylinder head bolts must be discarded and renewed, regardless of their apparent condition.

18 If warpage of the cylinder head gasket surface is suspected, use a straight-edge to check it for distortion. Refer to Chapter 2D if necessary.

19 On this engine, the cylinder head-to-piston clearance is controlled by fitting different thickness head gaskets. The gasket thickness can be determined by looking at the holes stamped on the edge of the gasket **(see illustration)**.

Number of holes	Gasket thickness
No holes	*0.77 to 0.87 mm*
One hole	*0.87 to 0.97 mm*
Two holes	*0.97 to 1.07 mm*

The correct thickness of gasket required is selected by measuring the piston protrusions as follows.

20 Mount a dial test indicator securely on the block so that its pointer can be easily pivoted between the piston crown and block mating surface. Turn the crankshaft to bring No 1 piston roughly to the TDC position. Move the dial test indicator probe over and in contact with No 1 piston. Turn the crankshaft back-and-forth slightly until the highest reading is shown on the gauge, indicating that the piston is at TDC.

21 Zero the dial test indicator on the gasket surface of the cylinder block then carefully move the indicator over No 1 piston. Measure its protrusion at the highest point between the valve cut-outs, and then again at its highest point between the valve cut-outs at 90° to the first measurement **(see illustration)**. Repeat this procedure with No 4 piston.

22 Rotate the crankshaft half a turn (180°) to bring No 2 and 3 pistons to TDC. Ensure the crankshaft is accurately positioned then measure the protrusions of No 2 and 3 pistons at the specified points. Once all pistons have been measured, rotate the crankshaft to position all the pistons at their mid-stroke.

23 Select the correct thickness of head gasket required by determining the largest amount of piston protrusion, and using the following guide.

Piston protrusion measurement	Gasket thickness required
0.020 to 0.100 mm	*0.77 to 0.87 mm (no holes)*
0.101 to 0.200 mm	*0.87 to 0.97 mm (one hole)*
0.201 to 0.295 mm	*0.97 to 1.07 mm (two holes)*

Refitting

24 Wipe clean the mating surfaces of the cylinder head and cylinder block/crankcase. Place the new gasket in position with the words ALTO/TOP uppermost **(see illustration)**.

25 Carefully refit the cylinder head assembly to the block, aligning it with the locating dowels.

26 Apply a thin film of engine oil to the bolt threads and the underside of the bolt heads. Carefully enter each new cylinder head bolt into its relevant hole (do not drop them in). Screw all bolts in, by hand only, until finger-tight.

27 Working progressively in sequence, tighten the cylinder head bolts to their Stage 1

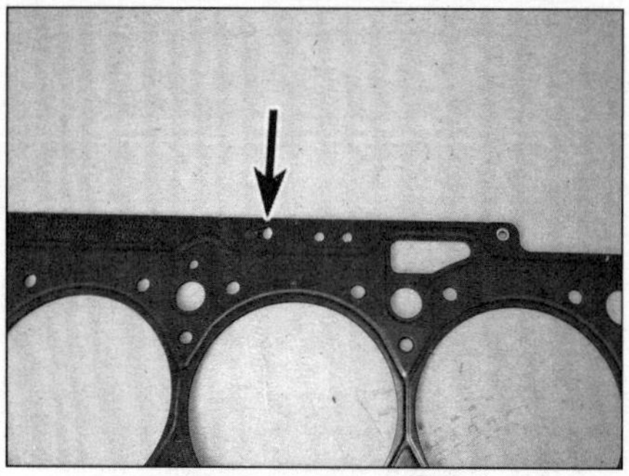

12.19 Cylinder head gasket thickness identification holes (arrowed)

12.21 Use a dial test indicator to measure piston protrusion

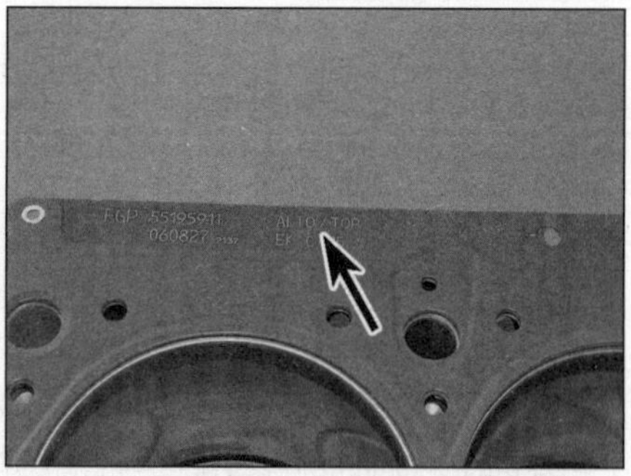

12.24 Place the new gasket in position with the words ALTO/TOP uppermost (arrowed)

12.27 Cylinder head bolt tightening sequence

13.4 Intermediate shaft bearing housing support bracket retaining bolts (arrowed)

torque setting, using a torque wrench and suitable socket **(see illustration)**. Working again in the same sequence, go around and tighten all bolts through the specified Stage 2 torque setting.

28 Once all bolts have been tightened to the Stage 2 torque, working again in the same sequence, go around and tighten all bolts through the specified Stage 3 angle, then through the specified Stage 4 angle, and finally through the specified Stage 5 angle using an angle-measuring gauge.

29 Refit the bolt securing the high-pressure fuel pump mounting bracket to the cylinder head and tighten the bolt securely.

30 Engage the coolant pipe with the stud on the thermostat housing, then reconnect the coolant hoses to the thermostat housing and EGR valve heat exchanger.

31 Refit the intake and exhaust manifolds as described in Chapter 4B, Section 13 and 17.

32 Refit the camshaft followers and hydraulic tappets as described in Section 11.

33 Refit the camshaft housing as described in Section 9.

34 On completion, reconnect the battery negative terminal, then refill the cooling system as described in Chapter 1B, Section 28.

13 Sump – removal and refitting

Removal

1 Disconnect the battery negative terminal as described in Chapter 5A, Section 4.

2 Apply the handbrake, then jack up the front of the vehicle and support it on axle stands (see *Jacking and vehicle support*). Remove the right-hand front roadwheel, then undo the bolts and remove the engine undershield **(see illustration 3.7)**.

3 Remove the right-hand driveshaft and the intermediate shaft as described in Chapter 8, Section 2 and 5.

4 Undo the three bolts securing the intermediate shaft bearing housing support bracket to the cylinder block and remove the support bracket **(see illustration)**.

5 Remove the exhaust system as described in Chapter 4B, Section 18.

6 Undo the three bolts and remove the support bracket from the catalytic converter and sump.

7 Remove the crankshaft pulley/vibration damper as described in Section 5.

8 Disconnect the wiring connector from the air conditioning compressor. Undo the three bolts securing the air conditioning compressor to the mounting bracket and suitably support the compressor on the front subframe.

9 Undo the four bolts securing the compressor mounting bracket to the cylinder block and sump **(see illustration)**. Unclip the wiring harness and remove the mounting bracket.

10 Drain the engine oil as described in Chapter 1B, Section 3. When the oil has completely drained, refit the drain plug with new sealing washer, and tighten to the specified torque.

11 Undo the upper bolt securing the oil dipstick guide tube to the coolant pipe. Undo the lower bolt securing the guide tube to the sump flange, then unclip the wiring harness and withdraw the tube from the sump flange sealing grommet.

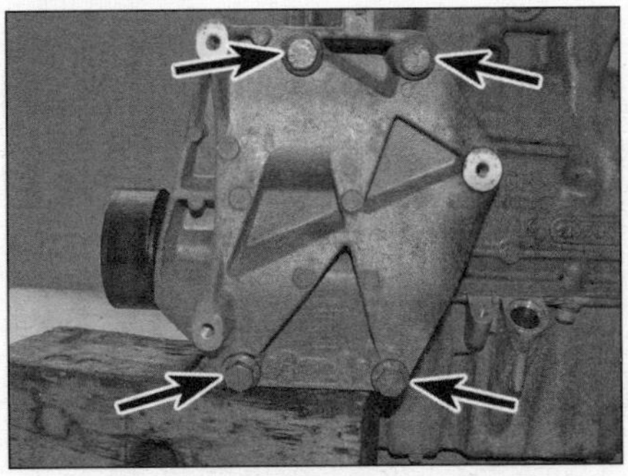

13.9 Air conditioning compressor mounting bracket retaining bolts (arrowed)

12 Disconnect the wiring connector from the oil level sensor, then release the retaining clip and disconnect the oil return hose.

13 Undo the two bolts securing the sump flange to the transmission bellhousing.

14 Using a socket and extension on the crankshaft pulley bolt, rotate the crankshaft in the normal direction of rotation (clockwise when viewed from the right-hand end of the engine) until the opening in the flywheel is positioned to allow access to one of the rear sump retaining bolts. Undo and remove the bolt, then rotate the crankshaft again until the flywheel allows access to the second rear retaining bolt. Undo and remove the bolt.

15 Progressively slacken and remove the remaining twelve bolts securing the sump to the base of the cylinder block and oil pump housing. Using a wide-bladed scraper or similar tool inserted between the sump and cylinder block, carefully break the joint to release the sump.

16 Manoeuvre the sump out from under the car. Clearance is extremely limited between the sump and subframe, and it may be necessary to release the oil pump pick-up/strainer, by undoing its two retaining bolts, to enable the sump to be removed.

17 If required, undo the retaining bolts and remove the oil baffle plate from inside the sump **(see illustration)**.

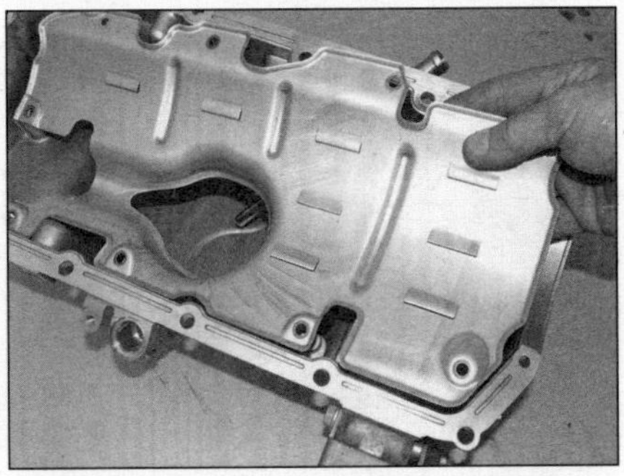

13.17 Remove the oil baffle plate from inside the sump

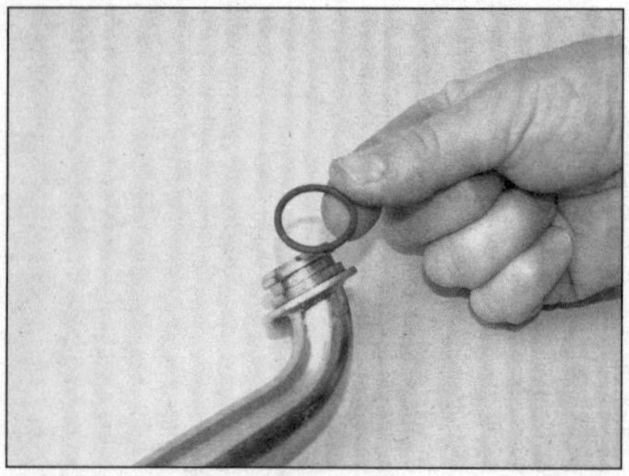

13.18 Renew the pick-up/strainer sealing ring prior to refitting

13.21 Apply a continuous bead of silicone sealing compound to the sump flange

18 While the sump is removed, take the opportunity to check the oil pump pick-up/strainer for signs of clogging or splitting. If not already done, unbolt the oil pump pick-up/strainer and remove it from the engine along with its sealing ring. The strainer can then be cleaned easily in solvent or renewed. Renew the pick-up/strainer sealing ring prior to refitting **(see illustration)**.

Refitting

19 Thoroughly clean the sump and remove all traces of silicone sealer and oil from the mating surfaces of the sump and cylinder block. If removed, refit the oil baffle plate and tighten its retaining bolts securely.

20 If clearance allows, refit the oil pump pick-up/strainer using a new sealing ring, and tighten its two retaining bolts securely. If it was necessary to unbolt the pick-up/strainer to allow the sump to be removed, place the unit in position and loosely screw in the bolt securing it to the main bearing cap. It must still be possible for the forward end of the pipe to be moved to the rear as the sump is refitted.

21 Apply a continuous bead of silicone sealing compound (90 543 772 – available from your Saab dealer) at approximately 1.0 mm from the inner edge of the sump **(see illustration)**. The bead of sealant should be between 2.0 and 2.5 mm in diameter.

22 Locate the sump over the pick-up/strainer then, where applicable, fit the forward end of the pick-up/strainer to the oil pump housing and fit the retaining bolt. Tighten both retaining bolts securely.

23 Engage the sump with the cylinder block and loosely refit all the retaining bolts.

24 Working out from the centre in a diagonal sequence, progressively tighten the bolts securing the sump to the cylinder block and oil pump housing. Tighten all the bolts to their specified torque setting.

25 Tighten the two bolts securing the sump flange to the transmission bellhousing to their specified torque settings.

26 Reconnect the wiring connector to the oil level sensor, then refit the oil return hose and secure with the retaining clip.

27 Refit the oil dipstick guide tube and secure with the two bolts tightened securely.

28 Locate the air conditioning compressor mounting bracket in position and refit the four retaining bolts. Tighten the bolts to the specified torque. Clip the wiring harness back into position on the bracket.

29 Position the air conditioning compressor on the mounting bracket. Fit and tighten the three retaining bolts to the specified torque, then reconnect the compressor wiring connector.

30 Refit the crankshaft pulley/vibration damper as described in Section 5.

31 Refit the catalytic converter support bracket and securely tighten the three bolts.

32 Refit the exhaust system as described in Chapter 4B, Section 18.

33 Position the intermediate shaft bearing housing support bracket on the cylinder block and secure with the three retaining bolts tightened to the specified torque.

34 Refit the intermediate shaft and right-hand driveshaft as described in Chapter 8, Section 2 and 5.

35 Refit the roadwheel and engine undershield, then lower the car to the ground and tighten the wheel bolts to the specified torque.

36 Fill the engine with fresh engine oil as described in Chapter 1B, Section 3.

37 On completion, reconnect the battery negative terminal as described in Chapter 5A, Section 4.

14 Oil pump – removal, overhaul and refitting

Removal

1 Remove the timing belt as described in Section 6.

2 Remove the crankshaft sprocket as described In Section 7.

3 Remove the sump and oil pump pick-up/strainer as described in Section 13.

4 Slacken and remove the seven retaining bolts then slide the oil pump housing assembly off of the end of the crankshaft **(see illustration)**. Remove the housing gasket and discard it.

Overhaul

5 Undo the retaining screws and lift off the pump cover from the rear of the housing **(see illustration)**.

6 Check the inner and outer rotors for identification dots indicating which way round they are fitted **(see illustration)**. If no marks are visible, use a suitable marker pen to mark the surface of both the pump inner and outer rotors.

7 Lift out the inner and outer rotors from the pump housing.

8 Unscrew the oil pressure relief valve bolt from the base of the housing and withdraw the spring and plunger, noting which way around the plunger is fitted **(see illustrations)**. Remove the sealing washer from the valve bolt.

9 Clean the components, and carefully examine the rotors, pump body and relief valve plunger for any signs of scoring or wear. If any damage or wear is noticed, it will be necessary to renew the complete pump assembly.

14.4 Oil pump housing retaining bolts (arrowed)

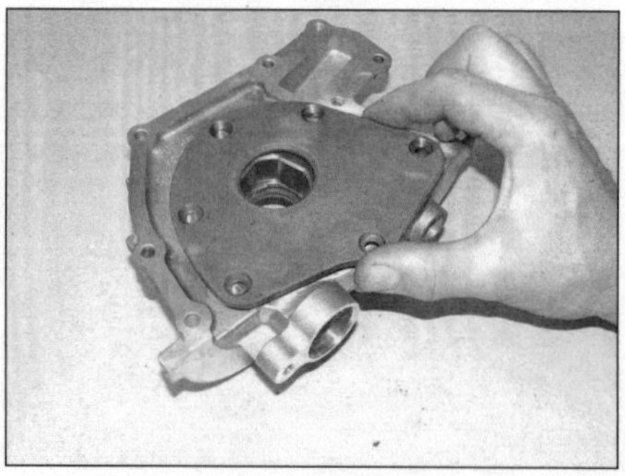

14.5 Undo the retaining screws and lift off the oil pump cover

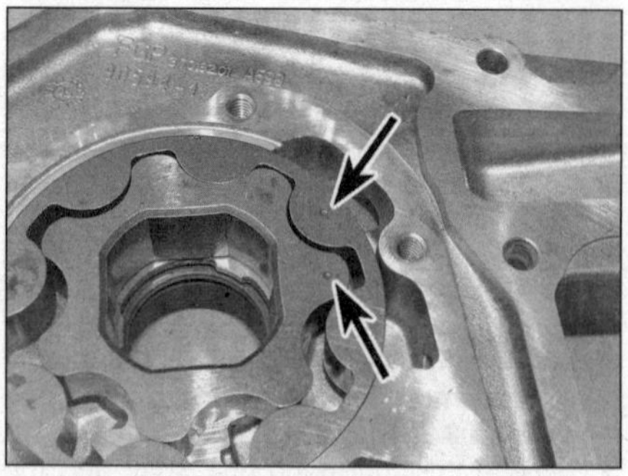

14.6 Oil pump inner and outer rotor identification dots (arrowed)

14.8a Unscrew the oil pressure relief valve bolt ...

14.8b ... then withdraw the spring ...

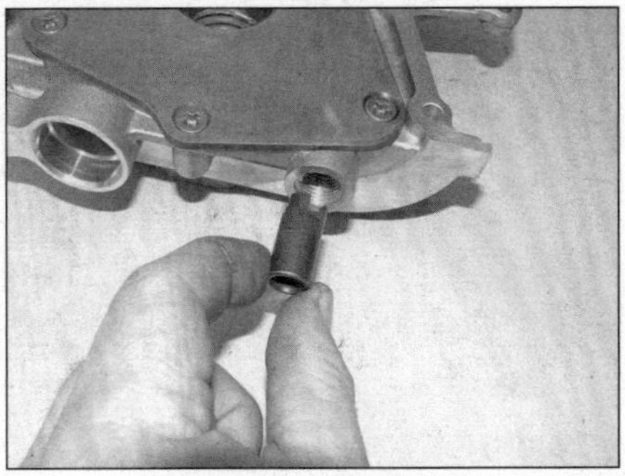

14.8c ... and plunger

10 If the pump is satisfactory, reassemble the components in the reverse order of removal, noting the following.

a) Ensure both rotors are fitted the correct way around.

b) Fit a new sealing ring to the pressure relief valve bolt and securely tighten the bolt.

c) Apply a little locking compound to the threads, and securely tighten the pump cover screws.

*d) On completion prime the oil pump by filling it with clean engine oil whilst rotating the inner rotor **(see illustration)**.*

Refitting

11 Prior to refitting, carefully lever out the crankshaft oil seal using a flat-bladed screwdriver. Fit the new oil seal, ensuring its sealing lip is facing inwards, and press it squarely into the housing using a tubular drift which bears only on the hard outer edge of the seal. Press the seal into position so that it is flush with the housing and lubricate the oil seal lip with clean engine oil.

12 Ensure the mating surfaces of the oil pump and cylinder block are clean and dry.

13 Fit a new gasket to the oil pump housing and bend down the tabs on the edge of the gasket to retain it on the pump housing **(see illustration)**.

14 Locate the pump housing over the end of the crankshaft and into position on the cylinder block.

15 Refit the pump housing retaining bolts and tighten them to the specified torque.

16 Refit the oil pump pick-up/strainer and sump as described in Section 13.

17 Refit the crankshaft sprocket as described in Section 7.

18 Refit the timing belt as described in Section 6.

19 On completion, fit a new oil filter and fill the engine with clean oil as described in Chapter 1B, Section 3.

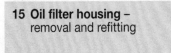

15 Oil filter housing – removal and refitting

Removal

1 The oil filter housing with integral oil cooler is located at the rear of the cylinder block, above the right-hand driveshaft.

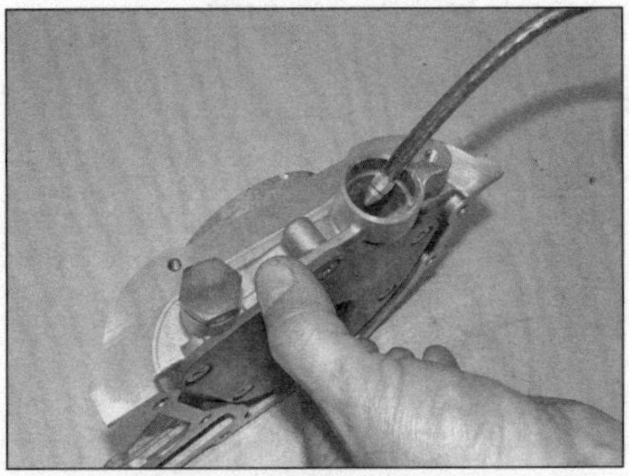

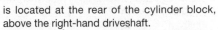

14.10 Prime the oil pump by filling it with clean engine oil whilst rotating the inner rotor

2 Disconnect the battery negative terminal as described in Chapter 5A, Section 4.

3 Apply the handbrake, then jack up the front of the vehicle and support it on axle stands (see *Jacking and vehicle support*). Remove the right-hand front roadwheel, then undo the bolts and remove the engine undershield **(see illustration 3.7)**.

4 Drain the cooling system as described in Chapter 1B, Section 28.

5 Remove the engine oil filter element as described in Chapter 1B, Section 3.

6 Remove the right-hand driveshaft and the intermediate shaft as described in Chapter 8, Section 2 and 5.

7 Undo the three bolts securing the intermediate shaft bearing housing support bracket to the cylinder block and remove the support bracket **(see illustration 13.4)**.

15.10 Oil filter housing retaining bolts (arrowed)

14.13 Bend down the tabs on the edge of the gasket to retain it on the oil pump housing

8 Disconnect the wiring connector from the oil pressure switch.

9 Release the retaining clips and disconnect the two coolant hoses from the oil cooler on the oil filter housing.

10 Undo the three retaining bolts and remove the oil filter housing from the cylinder block **(see illustration)**. Recover the two rubber seals from the rear of the housing. Note that new seals will be required for refitting.

Refitting

11 Thoroughly clean the oil filter housing, then fit the two new sealing rings **(see illustrations)**.

12 Position the oil filter housing on the cylinder block and refit the retaining bolts. Tighten the bolts to the specified torque.

13 Refit the two coolant hoses and secure

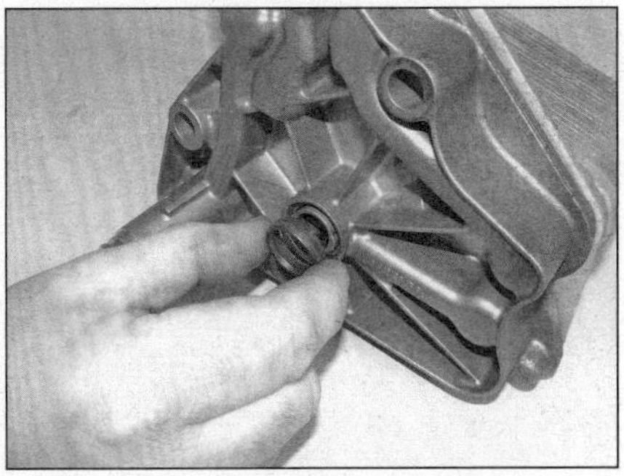

15.11a Fit a new sealing ring to the oil filter housing supply channel ...

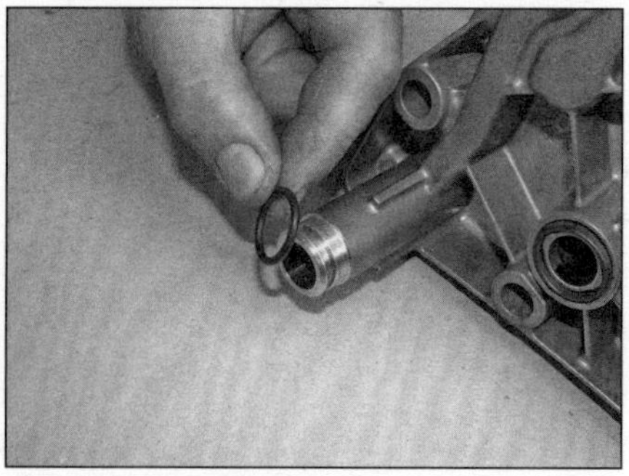

15.11b ... and to the return channel

with their retaining clips. Reconnect the oil pressure switch wiring connector.

14 Position the intermediate shaft bearing housing support bracket on the cylinder block and secure with the three retaining bolts tightened to the specified torque.

15 Refit the intermediate shaft and right-hand driveshaft as described in Chapter 8, Section 2 and 5.

16 Fit a new oil filter element as described in Chapter 1B, Section 3.

17 Refit the roadwheel and engine undershield, then lower the car to the ground and tighten the wheel bolts to the specified torque.

18 Refill the cooling system as described in Chapter 1B, Section 28.

19 Top-up the engine oil as described in *Weekly checks*.

20 On completion, reconnect the battery negative terminal as described in Chapter 5A, Section 4.

16 Crankshaft oil seals – renewal

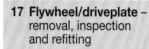

Right-hand (timing belt end)

1 Remove the crankshaft sprocket as described in Section 7.

2 Carefully punch or drill a small hole in the oil seal. Screw in a self-tapping screw and pull on the screw with pliers to extract the seal **(see illustration)**.

3 Clean the seal housing and polish off any burrs or raised edges which may have caused the seal to fail in the first place.

4 Lubricate the lips of the new seal with clean engine oil and ease it into position on the end of the shaft. Press the seal squarely into position until it is flush with the housing. If necessary, a suitable tubular drift which bears only on the hard outer edge of the seal, can be used to tap the seal into position **(see illustration)**. Take great care not to damage the seal lips during fitting and ensure that the seal lips face inwards.

5 Wash off any traces of oil, then refit the crankshaft sprocket as described in Section 7.

Left-hand (flywheel/driveplate end)

6 Remove the flywheel/driveplate as described in Section 17.

7 Remove the sump as described in Section 13.

8 Undo the five bolts and remove the oil seal housing. Note that the oil seal and the housing are a single assembly.

9 Clean the crankshaft and polish off any burrs or raised edges which may have caused the seal to fail in the first place.

10 Position the new oil seal housing, complete with seal over the crankshaft and into position on the cylinder block **(see illustration)**. Note that the new oil seal housing is supplied with a protector sleeve over the oil seal. Leave the sleeve in position as the housing is fitted.

11 Refit the five retaining bolts and tighten to the specified torque.

12 Remove the protector sleeve from the housing **(see illustration)**.

13 Refit the sump as described in Section 13.

14 Refit the flywheel/driveplate as described in Section 17.

17 Flywheel/driveplate – removal, inspection and refitting

Note: *New flywheel/driveplate retaining bolts will be required on refitting.*

Removal

Manual transmission models

1 Remove the transmission as described in Chapter 7A, Section 7 then remove the clutch assembly as described in Chapter 6, Section 5.

2 Prevent the flywheel from turning by locking the ring gear teeth with a similar arrangement to that shown **(see illustration)**.

3 Slacken and remove the retaining bolts and remove the flywheel **(see illustration)**. Do not drop it, as it is very heavy.

16.2 Screw in a self-tapping screw and pull on the screw with pliers to extract the oil seal

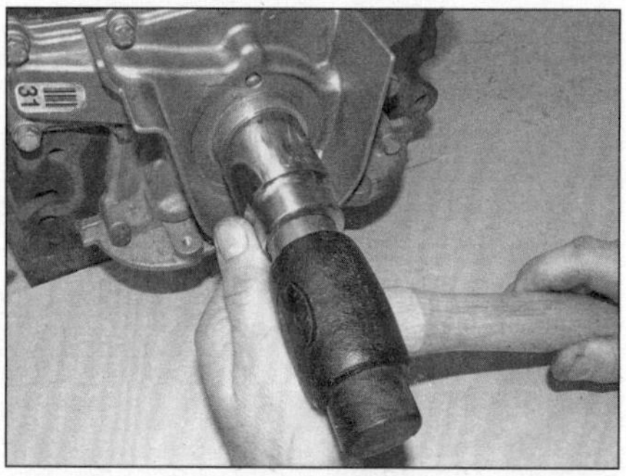

16.4 Use a socket as a tubular drift to fit the new oil seal

16.10 Fit the new housing with integral oil seal over the crankshaft

16.12 After fitting, remove the protector sleeve from the housing

17.2 Prevent the flywheel from turning by locking the ring gear teeth

17.3 Flywheel retaining bolts (arrowed)

Automatic transmission models

4 Remove the transmission as described in Chapter 7B, Section 9 then remove the driveplate as described in paragraphs 2 and 3.

Inspection

5 If there is any doubt about the condition of the flywheel/driveplate, seek the advice of a Saab dealer or engine reconditioning specialist. They will be able to advise if it is possible to recondition it or whether renewal is necessary.

6 Where a dual mass flywheel is fitted it must be renewed if there is any evidence of fluid or grease on the flywheel or clutch components. The following procedures are given for guidance only. If in doubt as to the condition of the flywheel a professional inspection is recommended. If the assembly passes all the checks listed and there was no juddering from the clutch when taking up the drive, the flywheel can be refitted. However if the vehicle has covered a high mileage and especially if the vehicle is on its second new clutch, then it would be prudent to renew the dual mass flywheel.

Warpage

Check the drive surface for any signs of warpage or damage. The flywheel will normally warp like a bowl – ie, higher at the circumference. If the warpage is more than 4.0 mm consider renewing the flywheel.

Free rotational movement

This is the distance the drive surface of the flywheel can be turned independently of the flywheel primary element, using finger pressure only. Move the drive surface in one direction and make a mark where the locating pin aligns with the flywheel edge. Move the drive surface in the other direction (finger pressure only) and make another mark. The total of free movement should not exceed 10 mm. If it is more consider renewing the flywheel.

Total rotational movement

This is the total distance the drive surface can be turned independently of the flywheel primary elements. Insert two bolts into the clutch pressure/plate damper unit mounting holes and with the crankshaft flywheel held stationary user a pry bar between the bolts and use some effort to move the drive surface fully in one direction. Make a mark where the locating pin aligns with the flywheel edge. Now force the drive surface fully in the opposite direction, and make another mark. The total rotational movement should not exceed 44.0 mm. If it does have the flywheel professionally inspected.

Lateral movement

The lateral movement (up and down) of the drive surface in relation to the primary element of the flywheel should not exceed 2.0 mm, if it does the flywheel may need renewing. This can be checked by pressing the drive surface down on one side into the flywheel (flywheel horizontal) and making an alignment mark between the drive surface and the inner edge of the primary elements. Now press down on the opposite side of the drive surface and make another mark above the original one. The difference between the two marks is the lateral movement.

Refitting

Manual transmission models

7 Clean the mating surfaces of the flywheel and crankshaft.

8 Offer up the flywheel and engage it over the positioning dowel on the crankshaft. Apply a drop of locking compound to the threads of each new flywheel retaining bolt (unless they are precoated) and install the new bolts.

9 Lock the flywheel by the method used on removal then, working in a diagonal sequence, evenly and progressively tighten the retaining bolts to the specified torque.

10 Refit the clutch as described in Chapter 6, Section 5, then remove the locking tool, and refit the transmission as described in Chapter 7A, Section 7.

Automatic transmission models

11 Refit the driveplate as described in paragraphs 7 to 9.

12 Remove the locking tool, and refit the transmission as described in Chapter 7B, Section 9.

18 Engine/transmission mountings – inspection and renewal

Refer to Chapter 2B, Section 18.

Chapter 2 Part D:
Engine removal and overhaul procedures

Contents

Degrees of difficulty

Easy, suitable for novice with little experience

Fairly easy, suitable for beginner with some experience

Fairly difficult, suitable for competent DIY mechanic

Difficult, suitable for experienced DIY mechanic

Very difficult, suitable for expert DIY or professional

Specifications

Engine identification

Engine type	**Manufacturer's engine code**
2.0 litre (1998 cc) DOHC 16-valve petrol engine	B207E, L and R
1.9 litre (1910 cc) diesel engine:	
SOHC 8-valve	Z19DT
DOHC 16-valve	Z19DTH and DTR

Petrol engines (B207)

Cylinder head

Maximum gasket face distortion	0.15 mm
Height	129.0 mm

Valves and guides	**Intake**	**Exhaust**
Stem diameter	5.9625 ± 0.0075 mm	5.953 ± 0.007 mm
Valve head diameter	35.1 ± 0.15 mm	30.1 ± 0.15 mm
Valve length	102.27 ± 0.15 mm	100.96 mm
Guide-to-valve stem maximum play (measure with valve raised 3 mm)	0.030 to 0.057 mm	0.040 to 0.066 mm
Guide length (intake and exhaust)	36.0 ± 0.05 mm	
Guide internal diameter (intake and exhaust)	9.976 to 9.991 mm	
Valve spring free length (intake and exhaust)	42.8 ± 0.5 mm	

Cylinder block

Maximum gasket face distortion	0.15 mm
Bore	85.992 to 86.008 mm
Maximum oversize	0.125 mm

Crankshaft and bearings

Number of main bearings	5
Main bearing journal diameter	55.994 to 56.008 mm
Big-end journal diameter	49.000 to 49.014 mm
Crankshaft endfloat	0.040 to 0.372 mm

Pistons and piston rings

Piston diameter (9.0 mm from base)	85.961 to 85.979 mm
Number of rings (per piston)	2 compression, 1 oil control
Ring end gap:	
Top compression	0.15 to 0.35 mm
Second compression	0.40 to 0.60 mm
Oil control	0.25 to 0.75 mm

Torque wrench settings	Refer to Chapter 2A, Specifications.

SOHC diesel engines (Z19DT)

Note: *Where specifications are given as N/A, no information was available at the time of writing. Refer to your Saab dealer for the latest information available.*

Cylinder head

Maximum gasket face distortion	0.10 mm
Cylinder head height	140.85 to 141.15 mm

Valves and guides	**Intake**	**Exhaust**
Stem diameter	7.974 to 7.992 mm	7.974 to 7.992 mm
Valve head diameter	35.5 mm	34.5 mm
Valve length	115 mm	115 mm
Maximum permissible valve stem play in guide	N/A	
Valve clearances (cold) (intake and exhaust)	0.30 to 0.40 mm	
Valve spring free length (intake and exhaust)	53.9 mm	

Cylinder block

Maximum gasket face distortion	0.15 mm
Cylinder bore diameter	82.000 to 82.030 mm
Maximum cylinder bore ovality	0.050 mm
Maximum cylinder bore taper	0.005 mm

Crankshaft and bearings

Number of main bearings	5
Main bearing journal diameter	59.855 to 60.000 mm
Big-end bearing journal diameter	50.660 to 50.805 mm
Crankshaft endfloat	0.049 to 0.211 mm

Pistons and piston rings

Piston diameter	81.920 to 81.950 mm
Number of rings (per piston)	2 compression, 1 oil control
Ring end gap:	
Top compression	0.25 to 0.35 mm
Second compression	0.25 to 0.50 mm
Oil control	0.25 to 0.50 mm

Torque wrench settings	Refer to Chapter 2B, Specifications.

DOHC diesel engines (Z19DTH and DTR)

Note: *Where specifications are given as N/A, no information was available at the time of writing. Refer to your Saab dealer for the latest information available.*

Cylinder head		
Maximum gasket face distortion	0.10 mm	
Cylinder head height	105.95 to 107.05 mm	
Valves and guides (DTH)	**Intake**	**Exhaust**
Stem diameter	5.982 to 6.000 mm	5.972 to 5.990 mm
Valve head diameter	29.489 mm	27.491 mm
Valve length	107.95 mm	107.95 mm
Maximum permissible valve stem play in guide	N/A	
Valve spring free length (intake and exhaust)	43.1 mm	
Valves and guides (DTR)	**Intake**	**Exhaust**
Stem diameter	4.982 to 5.000 mm	4.972 to 4.999 mm
Valve head diameter	27.700 to 28.000 mm	24.200 to 24.500 mm
Valve length	107.2 mm	106.7 mm
Maximum permissible valve stem play in guide	N/A	
Valve clearances	Automatic adjustment by hydraulic cam followers	
Valve spring free length (intake and exhaust)	44.1 mm	
Cylinder block		
Maximum gasket face distortion	0.15 mm	
Cylinder bore diameter	82.000 to 82.030 mm	
Maximum cylinder bore ovality	0.050 mm	
Maximum cylinder bore taper	0.005 mm	
Crankshaft and bearings		
Number of main bearings	5	
Main bearing journal diameter	59.855 to 60.000 mm	
Big-end bearing journal diameter	50.660 to 50.805 mm	
Crankshaft endfloat	0.049 to 0.211 mm	
Pistons and piston rings		
Piston diameter	81.920 to 81.950 mm	
Number of rings (per piston)	2 compression, 1 oil control	
Ring end gap:		
Top compression	0.20 to 0.35 mm	
Second compression	0.60 to 0.80 mm	
Oil control	0.25 to 0.50 mm	
Torque wrench settings	Refer to Chapter 2C, Specifications.	

1 General information

Included in this Chapter are details of removing the engine/transmission from the car and general overhaul procedures for the cylinder head, cylinder block/crankcase and all other engine internal components.

The information given ranges from advice concerning preparation for an overhaul and the purchase of parts, to detailed step-by-step procedures covering removal, inspection, renovation and refitting of engine internal components.

After Section 5, all instructions are based on the assumption that the engine has been removed from the car. For information concerning in-car engine repair, as well as the removal and refitting of those external components necessary for full overhaul, refer to Chapter 2A, 2B or 2C (as applicable) and to Section 5. Ignore any preliminary dismantling operations described in Chapter 2A, 2B or 2C that are no longer relevant once the engine has been removed from the car.

Apart from torque wrench settings, which are given at the beginning of Chapter 2A, 2B or 2C (as applicable), all specifications relating to engine overhaul are at the beginning of this Chapter.

2 Engine overhaul – general information

It is not always easy to determine when, or if, an engine should be completely overhauled, as a number of factors must be considered.

High mileage is not necessarily an indication that an overhaul is needed, while low mileage does not preclude the need for an overhaul. Frequency of servicing is probably the most important consideration. An engine which has had regular and frequent oil and filter changes, as well as other required maintenance, should give many thousands of miles of reliable service. Conversely, a neglected engine may require an overhaul very early in its life.

Excessive oil consumption is an indication that piston rings, valve seals and/or valve guides are in need of attention. Make sure that oil leaks are not responsible before deciding that the rings and/or guides are worn. Have a compression test performed (refer to Chapter 2A, Section 2 for petrol engines and to Chapter 2B, Section 2 or Chapter 2C, Section 2 for diesel engines), to determine the likely cause of the problem.

Check the oil pressure with a gauge fitted in place of the oil pressure switch and compare it with that specified. If it is extremely low, the main and big-end bearings, and/or the oil pump, are probably worn out.

Loss of power, rough running, knocking or metallic engine noises, excessive valve gear noise, and high fuel consumption may also point to the need for an overhaul, especially if they are all present at the same time. If a complete service does not cure the situation, major mechanical work is the only solution.

A full engine overhaul involves restoring all internal parts to the specification of a new engine. During a complete overhaul, the pistons and the piston rings are renewed, and the cylinder bores are reconditioned. New main and big-end bearings are generally fitted; if necessary, the crankshaft may be reground, to compensate for wear in the journals. The valves are also serviced as well, since they are usually in less-than-perfect condition at this point. Always pay careful attention to the condition of the oil pump when overhauling the engine, and renew it if there is any doubt as to its serviceability. The end result should be an as-new engine that will give many trouble-free miles.

Critical cooling system components such as the hoses, thermostat and coolant pump should be renewed when an engine is overhauled. The radiator should also be checked carefully, to ensure that it is not clogged or leaking.

Before beginning the engine overhaul, read through the entire procedure, to familiarise yourself with the scope and requirements of the job. Check on the availability of parts and make sure that any necessary special tools and equipment are obtained in advance. Most work can be done with typical hand tools, although a number of precision measuring tools are required for inspecting parts to determine if they must be renewed.

The services provided by an engineering machine shop or engine reconditioning specialist will almost certainly be required, particularly if major repairs such as crankshaft regrinding or cylinder reboring are necessary. Apart from carrying out machining operations, these establishments will normally handle the inspection of parts, offer advice concerning reconditioning or renewal and supply new components such as pistons, piston rings and bearing shells. It is recommended that the establishment used is a member of the Federation of Engine Re-Manufacturers, or a similar society.

Always wait until the engine has been completely dismantled, and until all components (especially the cylinder block/crankcase and the crankshaft) have been inspected, before deciding what service and repair operations must be performed by an engineering works. The condition of these components will be the major factor to consider when determining whether to overhaul the original engine, or to buy a reconditioned unit. Do not, therefore, purchase parts or have overhaul work done on other components until they have been thoroughly inspected. As a general rule, time is the primary cost of an overhaul, so it does not pay to fit worn or sub-standard parts.

As a final note, to ensure maximum life and minimum trouble from a reconditioned engine, everything must be assembled with care, in a spotlessly-clean environment.

3 Engine removal – methods and precautions

If you have decided that the engine must be removed for overhaul or major repair work, several preliminary steps should be taken.

Engine/transmission removal is extremely complicated and involved on these vehicles. It must be stated, that unless the vehicle can be positioned on a ramp, or raised and supported on axle stands over an inspection pit, it will be very difficult to carry out the work involved.

Cleaning the engine compartment and engine/transmission before beginning the removal procedure will help keep tools clean and organised.

An engine hoist will also be necessary. Make sure the equipment is rated in excess of the combined weight of the engine and transmission. Safety is of primary importance, considering the potential hazards involved in removing the engine/transmission from the car.

The help of an assistant is essential. Apart from the safety aspects involved, there are many instances when one person cannot simultaneously perform all of the operations required during engine/transmission removal.

Plan the operation ahead of time. Before starting work, arrange for the hire of or obtain all of the tools and equipment you will need. Some of the equipment necessary to perform engine/transmission removal and installation safely (in addition to an engine hoist) is as follows: a heavy duty trolley jack, complete sets of spanners and sockets as described in the rear of this manual, wooden blocks, and plenty of rags and cleaning solvent for mopping-up spilled oil, coolant and fuel. If the hoist must be hired, make sure that you arrange for it in advance, and perform all of the operations possible without it beforehand. This will save you money and time.

Plan for the car to be out of use for quite a while. An engineering machine shop or engine reconditioning specialist will be required to perform some of the work which cannot be accomplished without special equipment. These places often have a busy schedule, so it would be a good idea to consult them before removing the engine, in order to accurately estimate the amount of time required to rebuild or repair components that may need work.

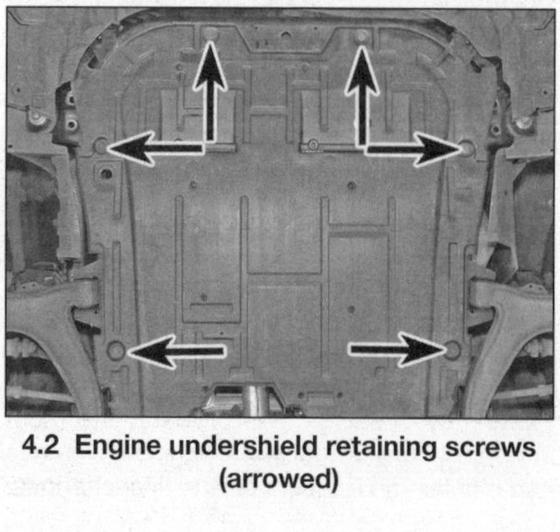

4.2 Engine undershield retaining screws (arrowed)

During the engine/transmission removal procedure, it is advisable to make notes of the locations of all brackets, cable-ties, earthing points, etc, as well as how the wiring harnesses, hoses and electrical connections are attached and routed around the engine and engine compartment. An effective way of doing this is to take a series of photographs of the various components before they are disconnected or removed; the resulting photographs will prove invaluable when the engine/transmission is refitted.

Always be extremely careful when removing and refitting the engine/transmission. Serious injury can result from careless actions. Plan ahead and take your time, and a job of this nature, although major, can be accomplished successfully.

On all 9-3 models, the engine must be removed complete with the transmission as an assembly. There is insufficient clearance in the engine compartment to remove the engine leaving the transmission in the vehicle. It is possible to remove the engine after the transmission has been removed. The assembly is removed by raising the front of the vehicle, and lowering the assembly from the engine compartment.

4 Engine and transmission unit – removal, separation and refitting

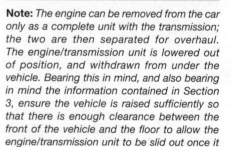

Note: *The engine can be removed from the car only as a complete unit with the transmission; the two are then separated for overhaul. The engine/transmission unit is lowered out of position, and withdrawn from under the vehicle. Bearing this in mind, and also bearing in mind the information contained in Section 3, ensure the vehicle is raised sufficiently so that there is enough clearance between the front of the vehicle and the floor to allow the engine/transmission unit to be slid out once it has been lowered out of position.*

Note: *Such is the complexity of the power unit arrangement on these vehicles, and the variations that may be encountered according to model and optional equipment fitted, that the following should be regarded as a guide to the work involved, rather than a step-by-step procedure. Where differences are encountered, or additional component disconnection or removal is necessary, make notes of the work involved as an aid to refitting.*

Removal

1 Have the air conditioning system fully discharged by an air conditioning specialist.

2 Position the vehicle as described in Section 3, paragraph 2, and remove both front roadwheels. Remove both wheel arch liner inner covers. Undo the screws and remove the engine undershield where fitted **(see illustration)**.

3 Remove the bonnet and the front bumper as described in Chapter 11, Section 8 and 6.

4 Remove the plastic cover from the top of the engine.

5 Remove the battery and battery box as described in Chapter 5A, Section 4.

6 Carry out the following operations as described in Chapter 1A or 1B, as applicable:

a) Drain the engine oil.

b) Drain the cooling system.

c) Remove the auxiliary drivebelt.

7 Remove the air cleaner assembly and intake ducts as described in Chapter 4A, Section 2 or Chapter 4B, Section 3, as applicable.

8 Remove the intercooler and air ducting as described in Chapter 4A, Section 13 or Chapter 4B, Section 15.

9 Remove the radiator as described in Chapter 3, Section 3.

10 Disconnect the brake vacuum servo hose from the vacuum pump.

11 On automatic transmission models, disconnect the TCM (Transmission control module) wiring plug (see Chapter 7B, Section 8).

12 Lift off the cover from the engine compartment fuse/relay box, and unscrew the two Torx screws securing the upper section of the fuse/relay box to the lower section. Disconnect the battery positive cable. Undo the bolt securing the engine wiring harness block connector to the fuse/relay box upper section. Remove the engine harness clamp from the body and earth cables, then move the harness to one side **(see illustrations)**.

13 Release the retaining clips and disconnect the coolant hoses at the cooling system

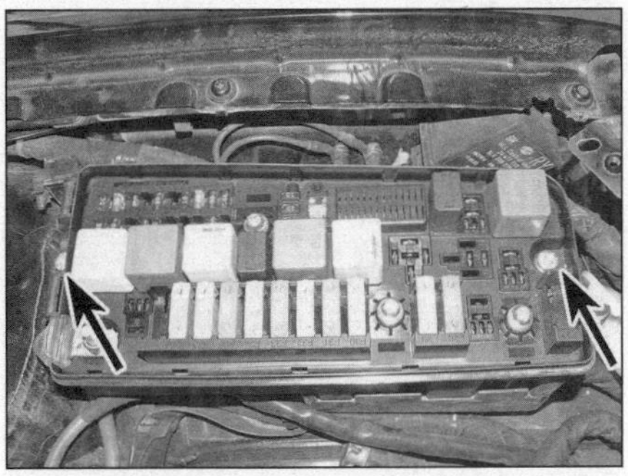

4.12a Undo the screws (arrowed) securing the upper half of the fusebox to the lower half

expansion tank. Disconnect the wiring connector then remove the expansion tank from its mounting bracket.

14 Disconnect the wiring block connector from the left-hand side of the engine compartment, beneath the battery tray, attached to the chassis leg **(see illustrations)**. Release the wiring harness from the retaining clips so that it is free to be removed with the engine.

15 Remove the air conditioning system compressor as described in Chapter 3, Section 9.

16 On Convertible models, undo the bolts and remove the front chassis reinforcement **(see illustration)**.

Petrol engine models

17 Depressurise the fuel system with reference to Chapter 4A, Section 5, then disconnect the fuel supply and return pipes

4.12b Undo the screw securing the engine wiring harness connector block to the fusebox

from the fuel rail, then release the hoses from the clips on the camshaft cover. Be prepared for fuel spillage, and take adequate precautions. Clamp or plug the open unions, to minimise further fuel loss.

18 Disconnect the fuel evaporation purge hose.

Diesel engine models

19 Disconnect the wiring plug and remove the turbo solenoid valve.

20 Disconnect the fuel supply and return pipes **(see illustrations)**. Suitably cover or plug the open hose connections to prevent dirt entry.

21 Working under the front, right-hand side of the car, release the locking lever catch, then lift the locking levers and disconnect the two wiring connectors from the engine management system ECM **(see illustration)**.

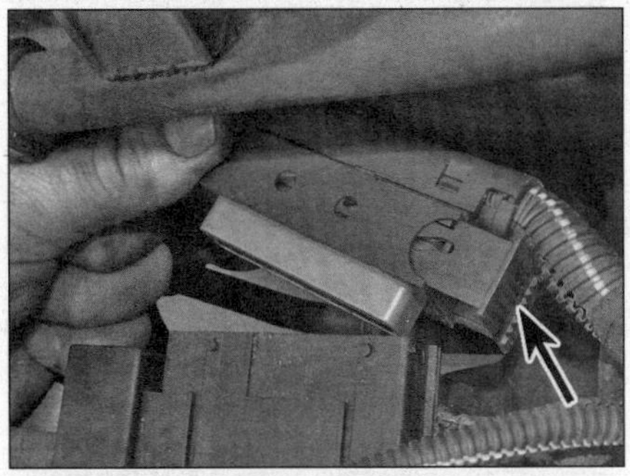

4.14a Slide out the locking catch (arrowed) and disconnect the cooling fan wiring plug ...

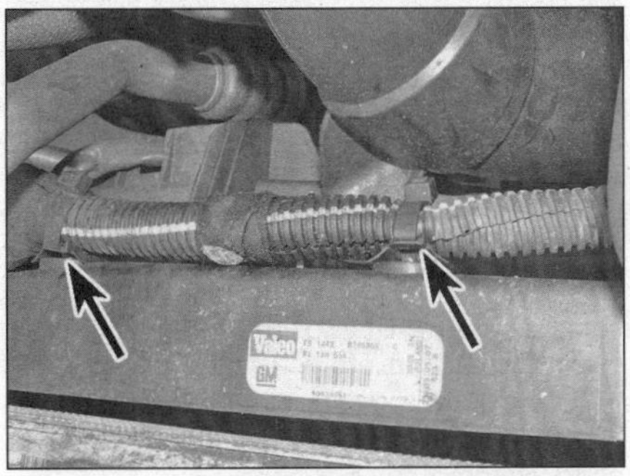

4.14b ... then release the wiring harness from the clips (arrowed)

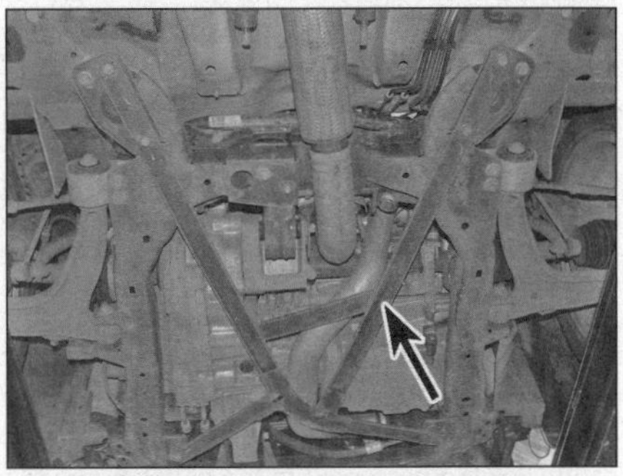

4.16 Front chassis reinforcement (arrowed) – Convertible models

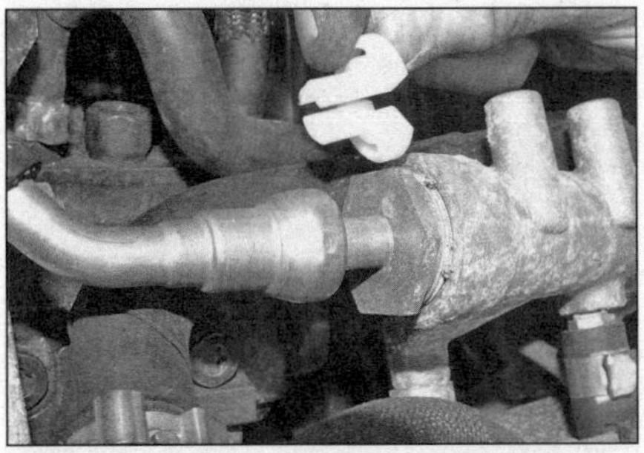

4.20a Fit a release tool around the pipe, slide it into the coupling to release the locking clips, and disconnect the fuel return ...

4.20b ... and supply coupling (arrowed)

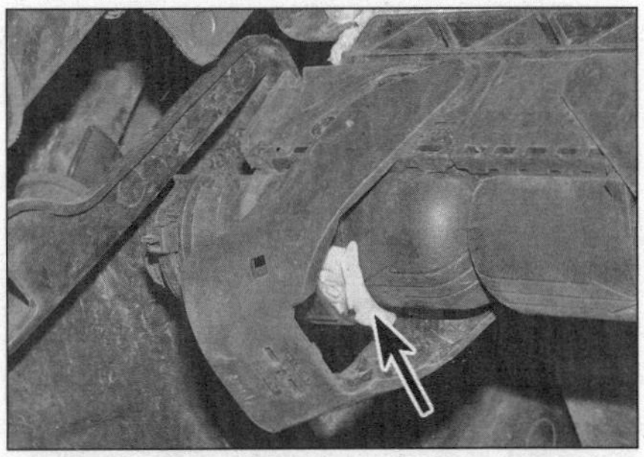

4.21 Pull out the locking clip (arrowed), pull down the locking bar and disconnect the ECM wiring plugs

4.22a Prise out the locking clips ...

4.22b ... and disconnect the heater hoses

All models

22 Using a small screwdriver, lift up the wire clips securing the two heater hoses to the heater matrix pipe stubs, and disconnect the hoses from the stubs **(see illustrations)**.

23 On manual transmission models, using a suitable forked tool, release the gearchange selector cable end fittings from the transmission selector levers. Pull back the retaining sleeves and detach the outer cables from the mounting bracket on the transmission – see Chapter 7A, Section 4.

24 On automatic transmission models, use a forked tool or flat-bladed screwdriver, and carefully lever the gear selector inner cable end fitting off the balljoint on the selector lever position switch. Pull back the retaining sleeve and detach the outer cable from the mounting bracket on the transmission.

25 Drain the manual transmission oil or automatic transmission fluid as described in Chapter 7A, Section 2 or Chapter 7B, Section 2, as applicable.

26 Remove both driveshafts as described in Chapter 8, Section 2.

27 Position the steering with the front roadwheels straight-ahead, and lock the steering by removing the ignition key.

28 On manual transmission models, remove the filler cap from the brake/clutch fluid reservoir on the bulkhead, then tighten it onto a piece of polythene. This will reduce the loss of fluid when the clutch hydraulic hose is disconnected. Alternatively, fit a hose clamp to the flexible hose next to the clutch hydraulic connection on the transmission housing.

29 Place some cloth rags beneath the clutch hydraulic hose, then prise out the retaining clip a little, and detach the hose end fitting. Re-insert the retaining clip back into position in the end fitting. Discard the sealing ring from the fitting on the bellhousing; a new sealing ring must be used on refitting. Plug/cover both the end fitting and hose end to minimise fluid loss and prevent the entry of dirt into the hydraulic system. ***Note:*** *Whilst the hose is disconnected, do not depress the clutch pedal.*

30 On automatic transmission models, unscrew the central retaining bolt (or nut) and detach the fluid cooler pipes from the transmission. Suitably cover the pipe ends and plug the transmission orifices to prevent dirt entry.

31 Attach a suitable hoist and lifting tackle to the engine lifting brackets on the cylinder head, and support the weight of the engine/transmission.

32 Remove the front subframe as described in Chapter 10, Section 23.

33 Detach the earth cable at the left-hand end of the gearbox casing **(see illustration)**.

34 Mark the position of the three bolts securing the right-hand engine mounting bracket to the engine bracket and undo the bolts **(see illustration)**.

35 Mark the position of the three bolts securing the left-hand engine mounting to the transmission bracket, then (if required) undo the bolts and remove the mounting **(see illustration)**. Where fitted, disconnect the earth lead from the mounting.

36 Make a final check to ensure that all relevant pipes, hoses, wires, etc, have been disconnected, and that they are positioned clear of the engine and transmission.

37 With the help of an assistant, carefully lower the engine/transmission assembly to the ground. Make sure that the surrounding components in the engine compartment are not damaged. Ideally, the assembly should be lowered onto a trolley jack or low platform with castors, so that it can easily be withdrawn from under the car.

38 Ensure that the assembly is adequately supported, then disconnect the engine hoist and lifting tackle, and withdraw the engine/transmission assembly from under the front of the vehicle.

39 Clean away any external dirt using paraffin or a water-soluble solvent and a stiff brush.

40 With reference to Chapter 7A, Section 7 or Chapter 7B, Section 9, unbolt the transmission from the engine. Carefully withdraw the transmission from the engine. On manual transmission models, ensure that its weight is not allowed to hang on the input shaft while engaged with the clutch friction disc. On automatic transmission models, ensure that the torque converter is removed together with the transmission so that it remains engaged with the oil pump. Note that the transmission locates on dowels positioned in the rear of the cylinder block.

Refitting

41 With reference to Chapter 7A, Section 7 or Chapter 7B, Section 9, refit the transmission to the engine and tighten the bolts to the specified torque.

42 With the front of the vehicle raised and supported on axle stands, move the engine/transmission assembly under the vehicle, ensuring that the assembly is adequately supported.

43 Reconnect the hoist and lifting tackle to the engine lifting brackets, and carefully raise the engine/transmission assembly up into the engine compartment with the help of an assistant.

44 Reconnect the right- and left-hand engine/transmission mountings and tighten the bolts to the specified torque given in Chapter 2A, 2B or 2C as applicable. Ensure that the marks made on removal are correctly aligned when tightening the retaining bolts.

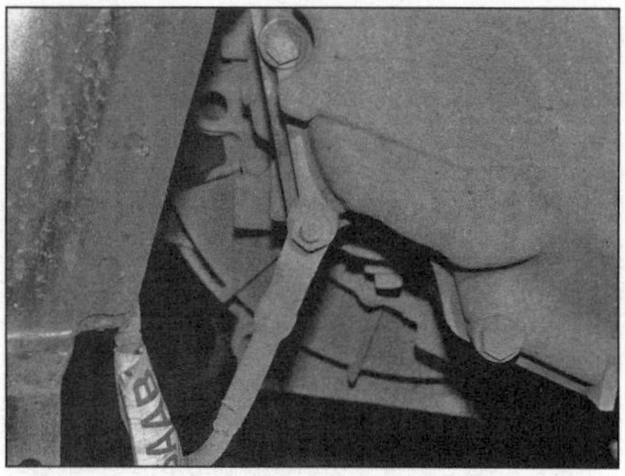

4.33 Disconnect the earth lead from the gearbox casing

4.34 Right-hand engine mounting bolts

4.35 Disconnect the earth lead from the transmission mounting

45 Refit the front subframe as described in Chapter 10, Section 23.
46 Disconnect the hoist and lifting tackle from the engine lifting brackets.
47 The remainder of refitting is a reversal of removal, noting the following points:

- *a) On automatic transmission models, reconnect the fluid cooler pipes together with new O-ring seals to the transmission.*
- *b) On manual transmission models, reconnect and bleed the clutch hydraulic connection at the transmission with reference to Chapter 6, Section 2.*
- *c) Make a final check to ensure that all relevant hoses, pipes and wires have been correctly reconnected.*
- *d) Refill the engine with oil with reference to Chapter 1A, Section 3 or Chapter 1B, Section 3, as applicable.*
- *e) Refill the transmission with correct quantity and type of fluid, as described in Chapter 7A, Section 2 or Chapter 7B, Section 2.*
- *f) Refill and bleed the cooling system with reference to Chapter 1A, Section 27 or Chapter 1B, Section 28, as applicable.*
- *g) Have the air conditioning system evacuated, charged and leak-tested by the specialist who discharged it.*

5 Engine overhaul – dismantling sequence

1 It is much easier to dismantle and work on the engine if it is mounted on a portable engine stand. These stands can often be hired from a tool hire shop. Before the engine is mounted on a stand, the flywheel/driveplate should be removed, so that the stand bolts can be tightened into the end of the cylinder block/crankcase.
2 If a stand is not available, it is possible to dismantle the engine with it blocked up on a sturdy workbench, or on the floor. Be extra careful not to tip or drop the engine when working without a stand.
3 If you are going to obtain a reconditioned engine, all the external components must be removed first, to be transferred to the new engine (just as they will if you are doing a complete engine overhaul yourself). These components include the following:

- *a) Engine wiring harness and supports.*
- *b) Alternator and air conditioning compressor mounting brackets (as applicable).*
- *c) Coolant pump (where applicable) and intake/outlet housings.*
- *d) Dipstick tube.*
- *e) Fuel system components.*
- *f) All electrical switches and sensors.*
- *g) Intake and exhaust manifolds and, where fitted, the turbocharger.*
- *h) Oil filter and oil cooler/heat exchanger.*
- *i) Flywheel/driveplate.*

Note: *When removing the external components from the engine, pay close attention to details that may be helpful or important during refitting. Note the fitted position of gaskets, seals, spacers, pins, washers, bolts, and other small items.*
4 If you are obtaining a 'short' engine (which consists of the engine cylinder block/crankcase, crankshaft, pistons and connecting rods all assembled), then the cylinder head, sump, oil pump, and timing belt/chain (as applicable) will have to be removed also.
5 If you are planning a complete overhaul, the engine can be dismantled, and the internal components removed, in the order given below.

Petrol engines

- *a) Intake and exhaust manifolds (see Chapter 4A, Section 14 and 15).*
- *b) Timing chain, sprockets, tensioner and idler pulleys (see Chapter 2A, Section 8).*
- *c) Coolant pump (see Chapter 3, Section 7).*
- *d) Cylinder head (see Chapter 2A, Section 6).*
- *e) Flywheel/driveplate (see Chapter 2A, Section 13).*
- *f) Sump (see Chapter 2A, Section 7).*
- *g) Oil pump (see Chapter 2A, Section 10).*
- *h) Pistons/connecting rod assemblies (see Section 9).*
- *i) Crankshaft (see Section 10).*

Diesel engines

- *a) Intake and exhaust manifolds (see Chapter 4B, Section 13 and 17).*
- *b) Timing belt, sprockets, tensioner and idler pulleys (see Chapter 2B, Section 7 and 8 or Chapter 2C, Section 6 and 7).*
- *c) Coolant pump (see Chapter 3, Section 7).*
- *d) Cylinder head (see Chapter 2B, Section 12 or Chapter 2C, Section 12).*
- *e) Flywheel/driveplate (see Chapter 2B, Section 17 or Chapter 2C, Section 17).*
- *f) Sump (see Chapter 2B, Section 13 or Chapter 2C, Section 13).*
- *g) Oil pump (see Chapter 2B, Section 14 or Chapter 2C, Section 14).*
- *h) Piston/connecting rod assemblies (see Section 9).*
- *i) Crankshaft (see Section 10).*

6 Before beginning the dismantling and overhaul procedures, make sure that you have all of the correct tools necessary. See *Tools and working facilities* for further information.

6.2 Use a valve spring compressor to compress the valve spring to relieve the pressure on the collets

6 Cylinder head – dismantling

Note: *New and reconditioned cylinder heads are available from the manufacturer, and from engine overhaul specialists. Due to the fact that some specialist tools are required for the dismantling and inspection procedures, and new components may not be readily available, it may be more practical and economical for the home mechanic to purchase a reconditioned head rather than to dismantle, inspect and recondition the original head. A valve spring compressor tool will be required for this operation.*
1 With the cylinder head removed as described in Chapter 2A, 2B or 2C, clean away all external dirt, and remove the following components as applicable, if not already done:

- *a) Manifolds (see Chapter 4A, Section 14 and 15 or Chapter 4B, Section 13 and 17).*
- *b) Spark plugs (petrol engines – see Chapter 1A, Section 24).*
- *c) Glow plugs (diesel engines – see Chapter 5A, Section 16).*
- *d) Camshafts and associated valve train components (see Chapter 2A, 2B or 2C).*
- *e) Fuel injectors (diesel engines – see Chapter 4B, Section 12).*
- *f) Engine lifting brackets.*

2 To remove a valve, fit a valve spring compressor tool. Ensure that the arms of the compressor tool are securely positioned on the head of the valve and the spring cap **(see illustration)**. The valves are deeply-recessed on petrol engines, and a suitable extension piece may be required for the spring compressor.
3 Compress the valve spring to relieve the pressure of the spring cap acting on the collets.

> **HAYNES HINT** ***If the spring cap collets stick to the valve stem, support the compressor tool, and give the end a light tap with a soft-faced mallet to help free the collets.***

4 Extract the two split collets by hooking them out using a small screwdriver, then slowly release the compressor tool **(see illustration)**.

6.4 Extract the two split collets by hooking them out using a small screwdriver

6.5a Remove the valve spring cap ...

6.5b ... and the spring ...

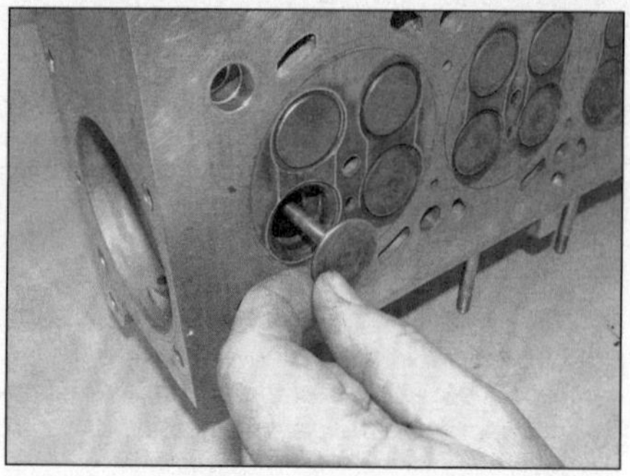

6.5c ... then withdraw the valve through the combustion chamber

6.5d Use pliers to remove the valve stem oil seal, which also incorporates the spring seat on most models

5 Remove the valve spring cap, the spring and lower cap (diesel exhaust valve only), then withdraw the valve through the combustion chamber. Using pliers, remove the valve stem oil seal, which also incorporates the spring seat on most engines **(see illustrations)**. If the spring seat is not part of the valve stem oil seal, hook it out using a small screwdriver.

6 Repeat the procedure for the remaining valves, keeping all components in strict order so that they can be refitted in their original positions, unless all the components are to be renewed. If the components are to be kept and used again, place each valve assembly in a labelled polythene bag or a similar small container **(see illustration)**. Note that as with cylinder numbering, the valves are normally numbered from the timing chain (or timing belt) end of the engine. Make sure that the valve components are identified as Intake and Exhaust, as well as numbered.

7 Cylinder head and valves – cleaning and inspection

1 Thorough cleaning of the cylinder head and valve components, followed by a detailed inspection, will enable you to decide how much valve service work must be carried out during the engine overhaul. **Note:** *If the engine has been severely overheated, it is best to assume that the cylinder head is warped – check carefully for signs of this.*

6.6 Place each valve assembly in a labelled polythene bag or similar container

Cleaning

2 Scrape away all traces of old gasket material from the cylinder head.

3 Scrape away the carbon from the combustion chambers and ports, then wash the cylinder head thoroughly with paraffin or a suitable solvent.

4 Scrape off any heavy carbon deposits that may have formed on the valves, then use a power-operated wire brush to remove deposits from the valve heads and stems.

Inspection

Note: *Be sure to perform all the following inspection procedures before concluding that the services of a machine shop or engine overhaul specialist are required. Make a list of all items that require attention.*

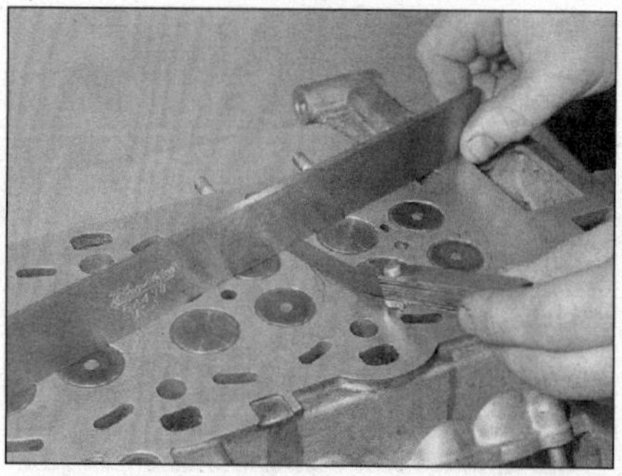

7.6 Use a straight-edge and feeler gauge to check cylinder head surface distortion

Cylinder head

5 Inspect the head very carefully for cracks, evidence of coolant leakage, and other damage. If cracks are found, a new cylinder head should be obtained.

6 Use a straight-edge and feeler gauge blade to check that the cylinder head surface is not distorted **(see illustration)**. If it is, it may be possible to resurface it, provided that the cylinder head is not reduced to less than the minimum specified height.

7 Examine the valve seats in each of the combustion chambers. If they are severely pitted, cracked or burned, then they will need to be recut by an engine overhaul specialist. If they are only slightly pitted, this can be removed by grinding-in the valve heads and seats with fine valve-grinding compound, as described below.

8 If the valve guides are worn, indicated by a side-to-side motion of the valve, oversize valve guides are available, and valves with oversize stems can be fitted. This work is best carried out by an engine overhaul specialist. A dial gauge may be used to determine whether the amount of side play of a valve exceeds the specified maximum.

9 Check the tappet bores in the cylinder head for wear. If excessive wear is evident, the cylinder head must be renewed. Also check the tappet oil holes in the cylinder head for obstructions.

Valves

10 Examine the head of each valve for pitting, burning, cracks and general wear, and check the valve stem for scoring and wear ridges. Rotate the valve, and check for any obvious indication that it is bent. Look for pitting and excessive wear on the tip of each valve stem. Renew any valve that shows any such signs of wear or damage.

11 If the valve appears satisfactory at this stage, measure the valve stem diameter at several points using a micrometer **(see illustration)**. Any significant difference in the readings obtained indicates wear of the valve stem. Should any of these conditions be apparent, the valve(s) must be renewed.

12 If the valves are in satisfactory condition, they should be ground (lapped) into their respective seats, to ensure a smooth gas-tight seal. If the seat is only lightly pitted, or if it has been recut, fine grinding compound only should be used to produce the required finish. Coarse valve-grinding compound should not be used unless a seat is badly burned or deeply pitted; if this is the case, the cylinder head and valves should be inspected by an expert to decide whether seat recutting, or even the renewal of the valve or seat insert, is required.

13 Valve grinding is carried out as follows. Place the cylinder head upside-down on a bench, with a block of wood at each end to give clearance for the valve stems.

14 Smear a trace of the appropriate grade of valve-grinding compound on the seat face, and press a suction grinding tool onto the valve head. With a semi-rotary action, grind the valve head to its seat, lifting the valve occasionally to redistribute the grinding compound **(see illustration)**. A light spring placed under the valve head will greatly ease this operation.

15 If coarse grinding compound is being used, work only until a dull, matt even surface is produced on both the valve seat and the valve, then wipe off the used compound and repeat the process with fine compound. When a smooth unbroken ring of light grey matt finish is produced on both the valve and seat, the grinding operation is complete. Do not grind in the valves any further than absolutely necessary, or the seat will be prematurely sunk into the cylinder head.

16 When all the valves have been ground-in, carefully wash off all traces of grinding

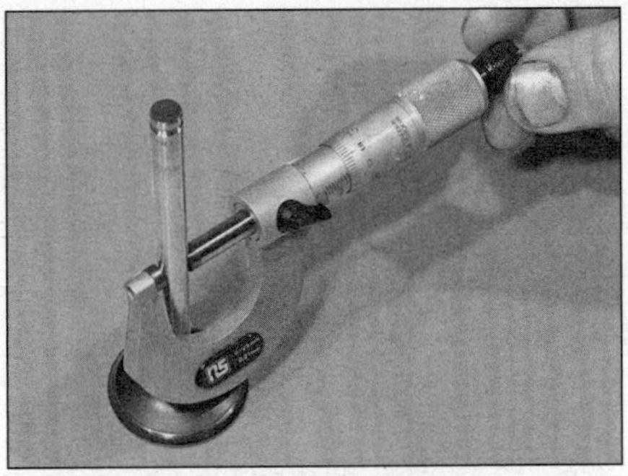

7.11 Use a micrometer to measure valve stem diameter

compound using paraffin or a suitable solvent before reassembly of the cylinder head.

Valve components

17 Examine the valve springs for signs of damage and discoloration; if possible; also compare the existing spring free length with new components.

18 Stand each spring on a flat surface, and check it for squareness. Measure the length of the springs un-compressed (free length) and compare with the dimension given in the Specifications. If any of the springs are damaged, distorted or have lost their tension, obtain a complete new set of springs.

8 Cylinder head – reassembly

1 Lubricate the stems of the valves, and

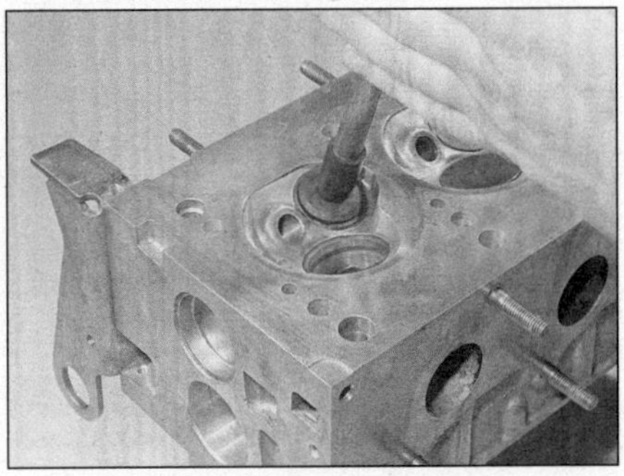

7.14 Grinding-in a valve

insert them into their original locations **(see illustration)**. If new valves are being fitted, insert them into the locations to which they have been ground.

2 Working on the first valve, refit the spring seat if it is not an integral part of the valve stem oil seal. Dip the new valve stem seal in fresh engine oil, then carefully locate it over the valve and onto the guide. Take care not to damage the seal as it is passed over the valve stem. Use a suitable socket or metal tube to press the seal firmly onto the guide. **Note:** *If genuine seals are being fitted, use the oil seal protector which is supplied with the seals; the protector fits over the valve stem and prevents the oil seal lip being damaged on the valve **(see illustrations)**.*

3 Locate the spring on the seat and fit the spring cap **(see illustration)**.

4 Compress the valve spring, and locate the split collets in the recess in the valve stem

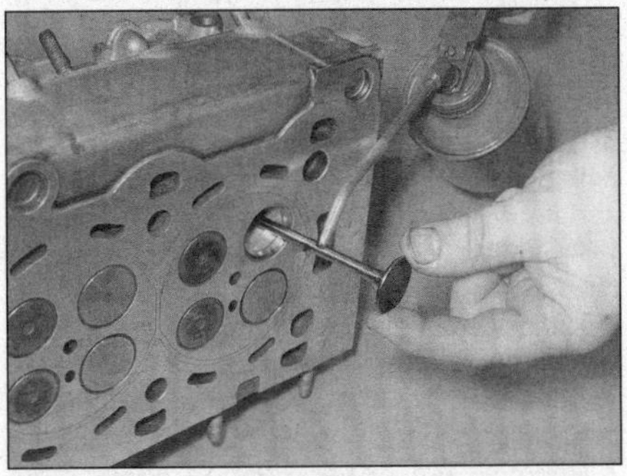

8.1 Lubricate the valve stem with engine oil and insert the valve into the correct guide

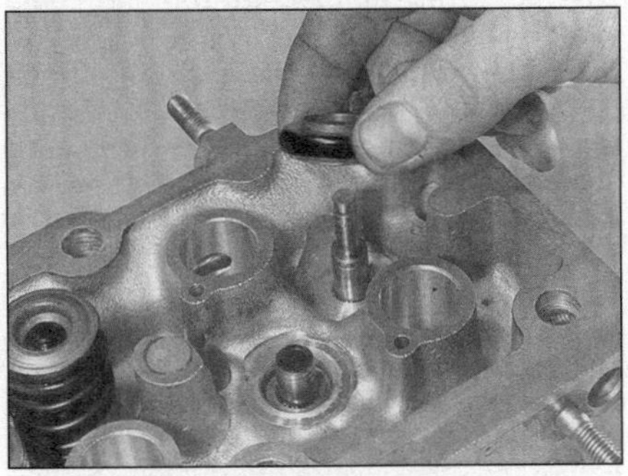

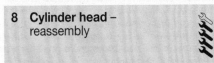

8.2a Fit the spring seat ...

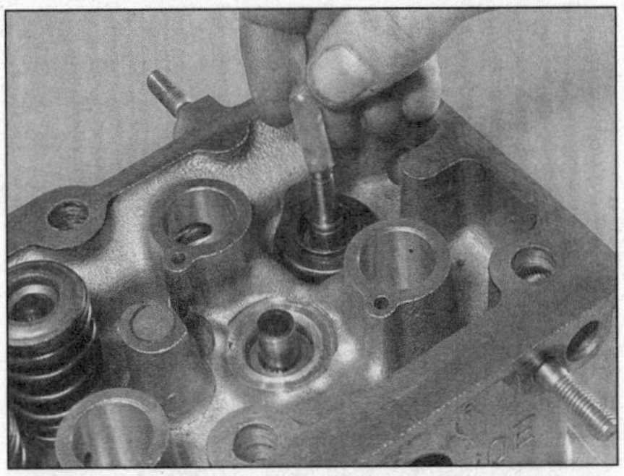

8.2b ... then fit the seal protector (where supplied) to the valve ...

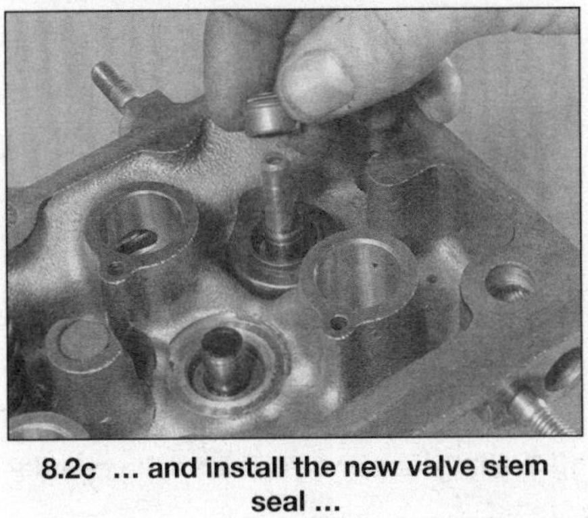

8.2c ... and install the new valve stem seal ...

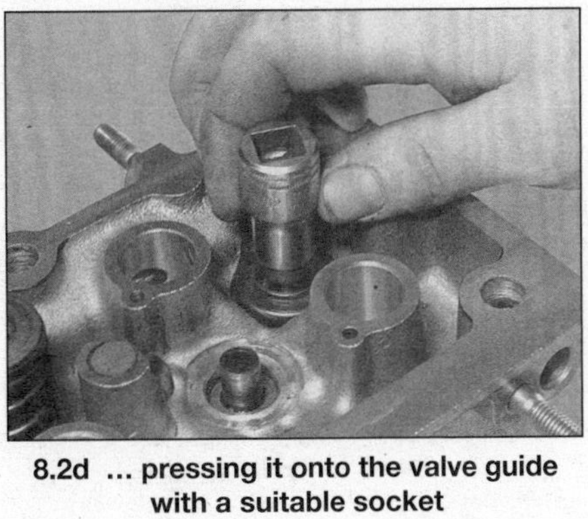

8.2d ... pressing it onto the valve guide with a suitable socket

8.3 Refit the valve spring and fit the spring cap

8.4 Compress the valve and locate the collets in the recess on the valve stem

(see illustration and Haynes Hint). Release the compressor, then repeat the procedure on the remaining valves.

5 With all the valves installed, support the cylinder head on blocks on the bench and, using a hammer and interposed block of wood, tap the end of each valve stem to settle the components.

6 Refit the components removed in Section 6, paragraph 1.

9 Pistons/connecting rods – removal

Note: *New connecting rod big-end cap bolts will be needed on refitting.*

1 Referring to Chapter 2A, 2B or 2C, remove the cylinder head and sump. Where fitted, unbolt the pick-up/strainer from the base of the oil pump.

2 If there is a pronounced wear ridge at the top of any bore, it may be necessary to remove it with a scraper or ridge reamer, to avoid piston damage during removal. Such a ridge indicates excessive wear of the cylinder bore.

3 If the connecting rods and big-end caps are not marked to indicate their positions in the cylinder block (ie, marked with cylinder numbers), suitably mark both the rod and cap with quick-drying paint or similar. Note which side of the engine the marks face and accurately record this also. There may not be any other way of identifying which way round the cap fits on the rod, when refitting.

HAYNES HINT

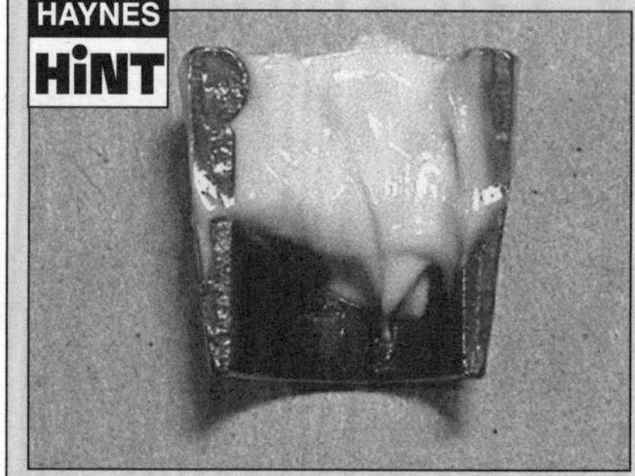

Use a little dab of grease to hold the collets in position on the valve stem when while the spring compressor is released.

4 Turn the crankshaft to bring pistons 1 and 4 to BDC (bottom dead centre).

5 Unscrew the bolts from No 1 piston big-end bearing cap, then take off the cap and recover the bottom half-bearing shell. If the bearing shells are to be re-used, tape the cap and the shell together.

Caution: On some engines, the connecting rod/bearing cap mating surfaces are not machined flat; the big-end bearing caps are 'cracked' off from the rod during production and left untouched to ensure the cap and rod mate perfectly. Where this type of connecting rod is fitted, great care must be taken to ensure the mating surfaces of the cap and rod are not marked or damaged in anyway. Any damage to the mating surfaces will adversely affect the strength of the connecting rod and could lead to premature failure.

6 Using a hammer handle, push the piston up through the bore, and remove it from the top of the cylinder block. Recover the bearing shell, and tape it to the connecting rod for safe-keeping.

7 Loosely refit the big-end cap to the connecting rod, and secure with the nuts/bolts – this will help to keep the components in their correct order.

8 Remove No 4 piston assembly in the same way.

9 Turn the crankshaft through 180° to bring pistons 2 and 3 to BDC, and remove them in the same way.

10 Crankshaft – removal

Note: *New main bearing bolts will be required on refitting.*

Petrol engines

1 Working as described in Chapter 2A, Section 13 and 10, remove the flywheel and the oil pump.

2 Remove the piston and connecting rod assemblies as described in Section 9. If no work is to be done on the pistons and connecting rods, unbolt the caps and push the pistons far enough up the bores that the connecting rods are positioned clear of the crankshaft journals.

3 Before removing the crankshaft, check the endfloat using a dial gauge in contact with the end of the crankshaft. Push the crankshaft fully one way, and then zero the gauge. Push the crankshaft fully the other way, and check the endfloat **(see illustration)**. The result should be compared with the specified limit, and will give an indication as to the size of the main bearing shell thrust journal width which will be required for reassembly.

4 If a dial gauge is not available, a feeler gauge can be used to measure crankshaft endfloat. Push the crankshaft fully towards one end of the crankcase, and insert a feeler gauge between the thrust flange of the main bearing shell and the machined surface of the crankshaft web **(see illustration)**. Before measuring, ensure that the crankshaft is fully forced towards one end of the crankcase, to give the widest possible gap at the measuring location. **Note:** *Measure at the bearing with the thrustwasher (see Section 17).*

5 Evenly and progressively slacken the cylinder block lower casing retaining bolts and remove the casing from the cylinder block **(see illustration)**. Lift the lower main bearing shells from the casing. If the locating dowels are a loose fit, remove them and store them with the casing for safe-keeping.

6 Carefully lift out the crankshaft, taking care not to displace the upper main bearing shells.

7 Recover the upper bearing shells from the cylinder block, and tape them to their respective caps for safe-keeping.

10.3 Check the crankshaft endfloat using a dial gauge ...

10.4 ... or feeler gauge

10.5 Lift the lower casing from the cylinder block

Diesel engines

8 Working as described in Chapter 2B or 2C (as applicable), remove the flywheel/driveplate, oil pump and the crankshaft left-hand oil seal housing.

9 Remove the piston and connecting rod assemblies as described in Section 9. If no work is to be done on the pistons and connecting rods, unbolt the caps and push the pistons far enough up the bores that the connecting rods are positioned clear of the crankshaft journals.

10 Before removing the crankshaft, check the endfloat as described in paragraphs 3 and 4.

11 Check the main bearing caps for identification markings. Normally, No 1 bearing cap (timing belt end) is not marked and the remaining caps are numbered I, II, III, IIII. The lug at the base of the cap is used to identify the intake manifold side of the engine **(see illustrations)**. If the bearing caps are not marked, using a hammer and punch or a suitable marker pen, number the caps from 1 to 5 from the timing belt end of the engine and mark each cap to indicate its correct fitted direction to avoid confusion on refitting.

12 Working in a diagonal sequence, evenly and progressively slacken the ten main bearing cap retaining bolts by half a turn at a time until all bolts are loose. Remove all the bolts.

13 Carefully remove each cap from the cylinder block, ensuring that the lower main bearing shell remains in position in the cap.

14 Carefully lift out the crankshaft, taking care not to displace the upper main bearing shells.

15 Recover the upper bearing shells and the thrustwashers from the cylinder block, and tape them to their respective caps for safe-keeping.

11 Cylinder block – cleaning and inspection

Cleaning

1 For complete cleaning, remove all external components (senders, sensors, brackets, oil pipes, coolant pipes, etc) from the cylinder block.

2 Scrape all traces of gasket and/or sealant from the cylinder block and lower casing (where applicable), taking particular care not to damage the cylinder head and sump mating faces.

3 Remove all oil gallery plugs, where fitted. The plugs are usually very tight – they may have to be drilled out and the holes retapped. Use new plugs when the engine is reassembled. On diesel engines, undo the retaining bolts and remove the piston oil spray nozzles from inside the cylinder block **(see illustration)**.

4 If the block and lower casing (where applicable) are extremely dirty, they should be steam-cleaned.

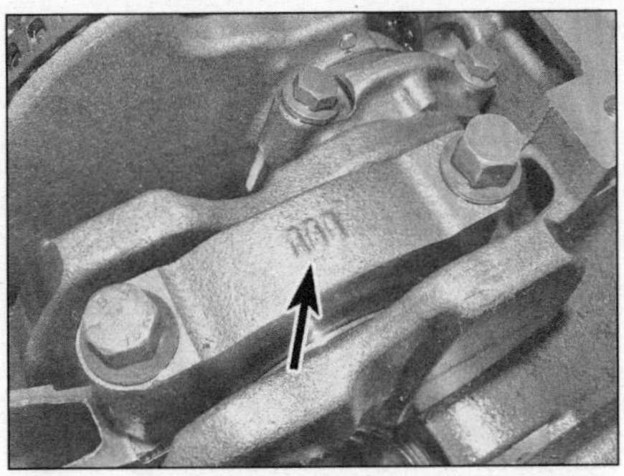

10.11a Main bearing cap identification marks (arrowed) ...

5 If the components have been steam-cleaned, clean all oil holes and oil galleries one more time on completion. Flush all internal passages with warm water until the water runs clear. Dry the block and, where necessary, the lower casing thoroughly and wipe all machined surfaces with a light oil. If you have access to compressed air, use it to speed-up the drying process, and to blow out all the oil holes and galleries.

> ⚠ ***Warning: Wear eye protection when using compressed air.***

6 If the block and lower casing are relatively clean, an adequate cleaning job can be achieved with hot soapy water and a stiff brush. Take plenty of time, and do a thorough job. Regardless of the cleaning method used, be sure to clean all oil holes and galleries very thoroughly, dry everything completely, and coat all cast-iron machined surfaces with light oil.

7 The threaded holes in the cylinder block must be clean, to ensure accurate torque readings when tightening fixings during reassembly. Run the correct-size tap (which can be determined from the size of the relevant bolt) into each of the holes to remove rust, corrosion, thread sealant or other contamination, and to restore damaged threads. If possible, use compressed air to clear the holes of debris produced by this operation. Do not forget to clean the threads of all bolts and nuts which are to be re-used, as well.

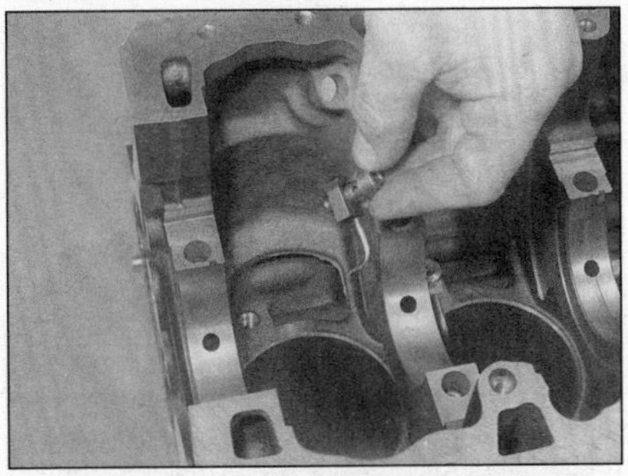

11.3 On diesel engines, unscrew the retaining bolts and remove the piston oil spray nozzles from the cylinder block

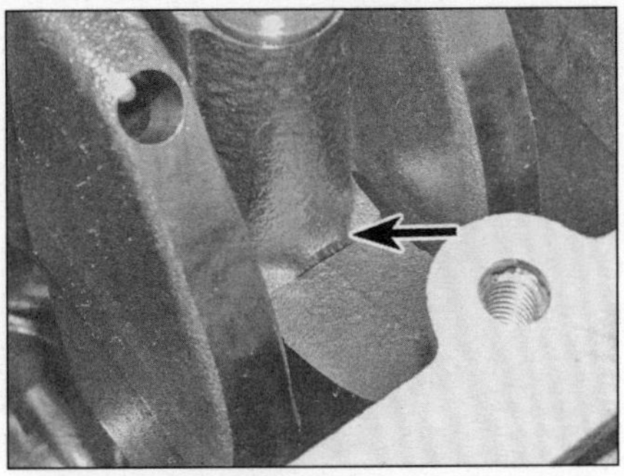

10.11b ... and the lug at the base of the cap (arrowed) is used to identify the intake manifold side of the engine – diesel engines

8 Where applicable, apply suitable sealant to the new oil gallery plugs, and insert them into the relevant holes in the cylinder block. Tighten the plugs securely. On diesel engines, refit the oil spray nozzles into the block and secure with the retaining bolts tightened securely.

9 If the engine is to be left dismantled for some time, cover the cylinder block with a large plastic bag to keep it clean and prevent corrosion. Where applicable, refit the lower casing and tighten the bolts finger-tight.

Inspection

10 Visually check the block for cracks, rust and corrosion. Look for stripped threads in the threaded holes. It's also a good idea to have the block checked for hidden cracks by an engine reconditioning specialist that has the equipment to do this type of work, especially if the vehicle had a history of overheating or using coolant. If defects are found, have the block repaired, if possible, or renewed.

11 If in any doubt as to the condition of the cylinder block, have it inspected and measured by an engine reconditioning specialist. If the bores are worn or damaged, they will be able to carry out any necessary reboring (where possible), and supply appropriate oversized pistons, etc.

12 Pistons/connecting rods – inspection

1 Before the inspection process can begin, the piston/connecting rod assemblies must be cleaned, and the original piston rings removed from the pistons. **Note:** *Always use new piston rings when the engine is reassembled.*

2 Carefully expand the old rings over the top of the pistons. The use of two or three old feeler gauges will be helpful in preventing the rings dropping into empty grooves **(see illustration)**. Take care, however, as piston rings are sharp.

3 Scrape away all traces of carbon from the top of the piston. A hand-held wire brush, or a piece of fine emery cloth, can be used once the majority of the deposits have been scraped away.

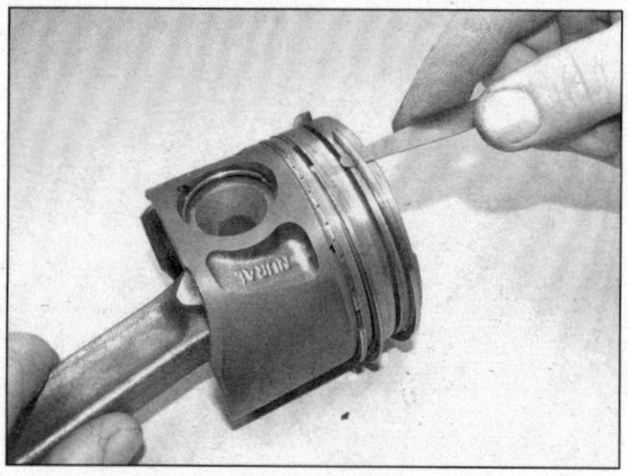

12.2 Use a feeler blade to remove a piston ring

4 Remove the carbon from the ring grooves in the piston, using an old ring. Break the ring in half to do this (be careful not to cut your fingers – piston rings are sharp). Be very careful to remove only the carbon deposits – do not remove any metal, and do not nick or scratch the sides of the ring grooves.

5 Once the deposits have been removed, clean the piston/connecting rod assembly with paraffin or a suitable solvent, and dry thoroughly. Make sure that the oil return holes in the ring grooves are clear.

6 If the pistons and cylinder bores are not damaged or worn excessively, and if the cylinder block does not need to be rebored, the original pistons can be refitted. Normal piston wear shows up as even vertical wear on the piston thrust surfaces, and slight looseness of the top ring in its groove. New piston rings should always be used when the engine is reassembled.

7 Carefully inspect each piston for cracks around the skirt, at the gudgeon pin bosses, and at the piston ring lands (between the ring grooves).

8 Look for scoring and scuffing on the thrust faces of the piston skirt, holes in the piston crown, and burned areas at the edge of the crown. If the skirt is scored or scuffed, the engine may have been suffering from overheating, and/or abnormal combustion ('pinking') which caused excessively-high operating temperatures. The cooling and lubrication systems should be checked thoroughly. A hole in the piston crown, or burned areas at the edge of the piston crown indicates that abnormal combustion (pre-ignition, 'pinking', knocking or detonation) has been occurring. If any of the above problems exist, the causes must be investigated and corrected, or the damage will occur again.

9 Corrosion of the piston, in the form of pitting, indicates that coolant has been leaking into the combustion chamber and/or the crankcase. Again, the cause must be corrected, or the problem may persist in the rebuilt engine.

10 If in any doubt as to the condition of the pistons and connecting rods, have them inspected and measured by an engine reconditioning specialist. If new parts are required, they will be able to supply and fit appropriate-sized pistons/rings, and rebore (where possible) or hone the cylinder block.

13.8 Transfer the crankshaft speed/position sensor pulse pick-up ring to the new crankshaft

13 Crankshaft – inspection

1 Clean the crankshaft using paraffin or a suitable solvent, and dry it, preferably with compressed air if available. Be sure to clean the oil holes with a pipe cleaner or similar probe, to ensure that they are not obstructed.

Warning: Wear eye protection when using compressed air.

2 Check the main and big-end bearing journals for uneven wear, scoring, pitting and cracking.

3 Big-end bearing wear is accompanied by distinct metallic knocking when the engine is running (particularly noticeable when the engine is pulling from low revs), and some loss of oil pressure.

4 Main bearing wear is accompanied by severe engine vibration and rumble – getting progressively worse as engine revs increase – and again by loss of oil pressure.

5 Check the bearing journal for roughness by running a finger lightly over the bearing surface. Any roughness (which will be accompanied by obvious bearing wear) indicates that the crankshaft requires regrinding.

6 If the crankshaft has been reground, check for burrs around the crankshaft oil holes (the holes are usually chamfered, so burrs should not be a problem unless regrinding has been carried out carelessly). Remove any burrs with a fine file or scraper, and thoroughly clean the oil holes as described previously.

7 Have the crankshaft journals measured by an engine reconditioning specialist. If the crankshaft is worn or damaged, they may be able to regrind the journals and supply suitable undersize bearing shells. If no undersize shells are available and the crankshaft has worn beyond the specified limits, it will have to be renewed. Consult your Saab dealer or engine reconditioning specialist for further information on parts availability.

8 If a new crankshaft is to be fitted, undo the screws securing the crankshaft speed/position sensor pulse pick-up ring to the crankshaft, and transfer the ring to the new crankshaft **(see illustration)**.

14 Main and big-end bearings – inspection

1 Even though the main and big-end bearings should be renewed during the engine overhaul, the old bearings should be retained for close examination, as they may reveal valuable information about the condition of the engine.

2 Bearing failure occurs because of lack of lubrication, the presence of dirt or other foreign particles, overloading the engine, or corrosion **(see illustration)**. If a bearing fails, the cause must be found and eliminated before the engine is reassembled, to prevent the failure from happening again.

3 To examine the bearing shells, remove them from the cylinder block, the main bearing caps or cylinder block lower casing, the connecting rods and the big-end bearing caps, and lay them out on a clean surface in the same order as they were fitted to the engine. This will enable any bearing problems to be matched with the corresponding crankshaft journal.

4 Dirt and other foreign particles can enter the engine in a variety of ways. Contamination may be left in the engine during assembly, or it may pass through filters or the crankcase ventilation system. Normal engine wear produces small particles of metal, which can eventually cause problems. If particles find their way into the lubrication system, it is likely that they will eventually be carried to the bearings. Whatever the source, these foreign particles often end up embedded in the soft bearing material, and are easily recognised. Large particles will not embed in the bearing,

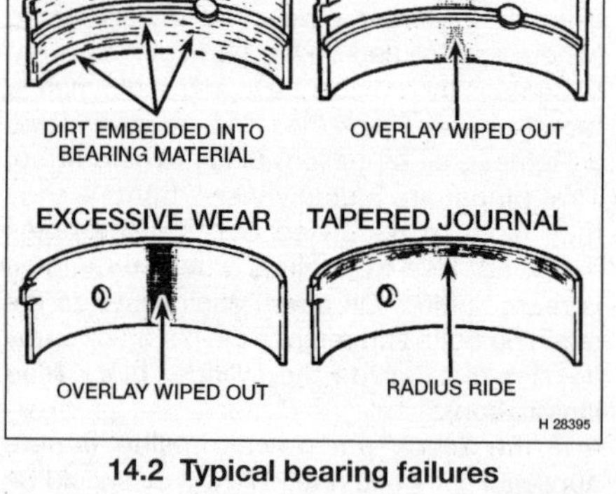

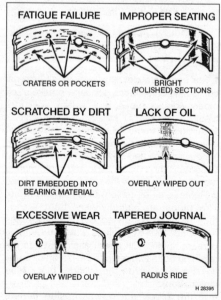

14.2 Typical bearing failures

and will score or gouge the bearing and journal. To prevent possible contamination, clean all parts thoroughly, and keep everything spotlessly-clean during engine assembly. Once the engine has been installed in the vehicle, ensure that engine oil and filter changes are carried out at the recommended intervals.

5 Lack of lubrication (or lubrication breakdown) has a number of interrelated causes. Excessive heat (which thins the oil), overloading (which squeezes the oil from the bearing face), and oil leakage (from excessive bearing clearances, worn oil pump or high engine speeds) all contribute to lubrication breakdown. Blocked oil passages, which may be the result of misaligned oil holes in a bearing shell, will also starve a bearing of oil and destroy it. When lack of lubrication is the cause of bearing failure, the bearing material is wiped or extruded from the steel backing of the bearing. Temperatures may increase to the point where the steel backing turns blue from overheating.

6 Driving habits can have a definite effect on bearing life. Full-throttle, low-speed operation (labouring the engine) puts very high loads on bearings, which tends to squeeze out the oil film. These loads cause the bearings to flex, which produces fine cracks in the bearing face (fatigue failure). Eventually the bearing material will loosen in places, and tear away from the steel backing. Regular short journeys can lead to corrosion of bearings, because insufficient engine heat is produced to drive off the condensed water and corrosive gases which form inside the engine. These products collect in the engine oil, forming acid and sludge. As the oil is carried to the bearings, the acid attacks and corrodes the bearing material.

7 Incorrect bearing installation during engine assembly will also lead to bearing failure. Tight-fitting bearings leave insufficient bearing lubrication clearance, and will result in oil starvation. Dirt or foreign particles trapped behind a bearing shell results in high spots on the bearing which can lead to failure.

8 Do not touch any shell's bearing surface with your fingers during reassembly; there is a risk of scratching the delicate surface, or of depositing particles of dirt on it.

9 As mentioned at the beginning of this Section, the bearing shells should be renewed as a matter of course during engine overhaul; to do otherwise is false economy.

15 Engine overhaul – reassembly sequence

1 Before reassembly begins, ensure that all necessary new parts have been obtained (particularly gaskets, and various bolts which must be renewed), and that all the tools required are available. Read through the entire procedure to familiarise yourself with the work involved, and to ensure that all items necessary for reassembly of the engine are to hand. In addition to all normal tools and materials, a thread-locking compound will be required. A tube of suitable sealant will be required to seal certain joint faces which are not fitted with gaskets.

2 In order to save time and avoid problems, engine reassembly can be carried out in the following order:

Petrol engines

a) Piston rings (see Section 16).
b) Crankshaft (see Section 17).
c) Piston/connecting rod assemblies (see Section 18).
d) Oil pump (see Chapter 2A, Section 10).
e) Sump (see Chapter 2A, Section 7).
f) Flywheel (see Chapter 2A, Section 13).
g) Cylinder head (see Chapter 2A, Section 6).
h) Coolant pump (see Chapter 3, Section 7).
i) Timing chain and sprockets (see Chapter 2A, Section 8).
j) Intake and exhaust manifolds (see Chapter 4A, Section 14 and 15).

Diesel engines

a) Piston rings (see Section 16).
b) Crankshaft (see Section 17).
c) Pistons/connecting rod assemblies (see Section 18).
d) Cylinder head (see Chapter 2B, Section 12 or Chapter 2C, Section 12).
e) Oil pump (see Chapter 2B, Section 14 or Chapter 2C, Section 14).
f) Sump (see Chapter 2B, Section 13 or Chapter 2C, Section 13).
g) Flywheel/driveplate (see Chapter 2B, Section 17 or Chapter 2C, Section 17).
h) Coolant pump (see Chapter 3, Section 7).
i) Timing belt, sprockets, tensioner and idler pulleys (see Chapter 2B, Section 7 and 8 or Chapter 2C, Section 6 and 7).
j) Intake and exhaust manifolds (see Chapter 4B, Section 13 and 17).

16 Piston rings – refitting

1 Before refitting the new piston rings, the ring end gaps must be checked as follows.

2 Lay out the piston/connecting rod assemblies and the new piston ring sets, so that the ring sets will be matched with the same piston and cylinder during the end gap measurement and subsequent engine reassembly.

3 Insert the top ring into the first cylinder, and push it down the bore slightly using the top of the piston. This will ensure that the ring remains square with the cylinder walls. Push the ring down into the bore until it is positioned 15 to 20 mm down from the top edge of the bore, then withdraw the piston.

4 Measure the end gap using feeler gauges, and compare the measurements with the figures given in the Specifications **(see illustration)**.

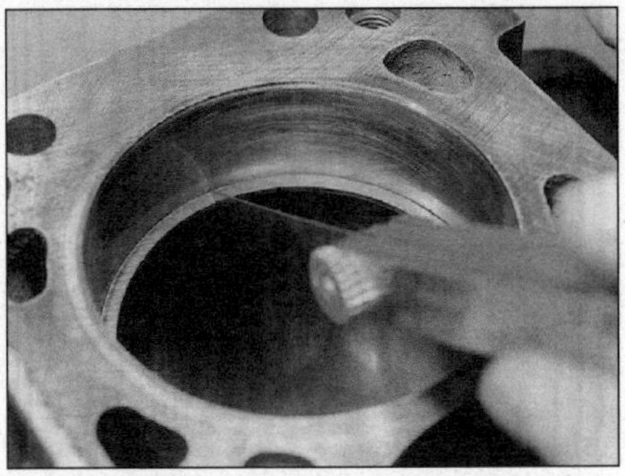

16.4 Measure the piston ring end gap using a feeler gauge

5 If the gap is too small (unlikely if genuine Saab parts are used), it must be enlarged or the ring ends may contact each other during engine operation, causing serious damage. Ideally, new piston rings providing the correct end gap should be fitted, but as a last resort, the end gap can be increased by filing the ring ends very carefully with a fine file. Mount the file in a vice equipped with soft jaws, slip the ring over the file with the ends contacting the file face, and slowly move the ring to remove material from the ends – take care, as piston rings are sharp, and are easily broken.

6 With new piston rings, it is unlikely that the end gap will be too large. If they are too large, check that you have the correct rings for your engine and for the particular cylinder bore size.

7 Repeat the checking procedure for each ring in the first cylinder, and then for the rings in the remaining cylinders. Remember to keep rings, pistons and cylinders matched up.

8 Once the ring end gaps have been checked and if necessary corrected, the rings can be fitted to the pistons.

9 The oil control ring (lowest one on the piston) is composed of three sections, and should be installed first. Fit the lower steel ring, then the spreader ring, followed by the upper steel ring **(see illustrations)**.

10 With the oil control ring components installed, the second (middle) ring can be fitted. It is usually stamped with a mark (TOP) which must face up, towards the top of the piston. **Note:** *Always follow the instructions supplied with the new piston ring sets – different manufacturers may specify different*

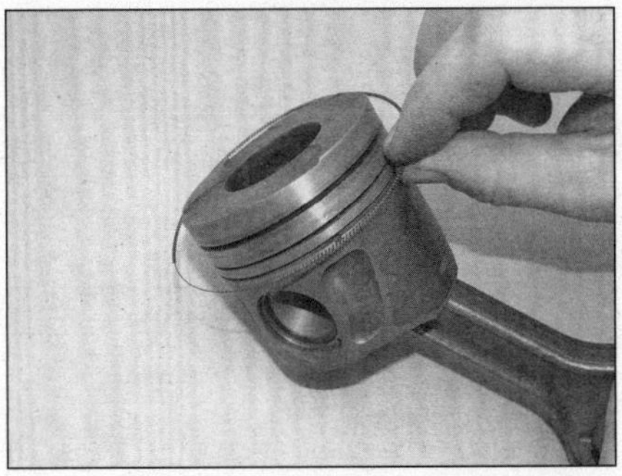

16.9a Fit the oil control spreader ring

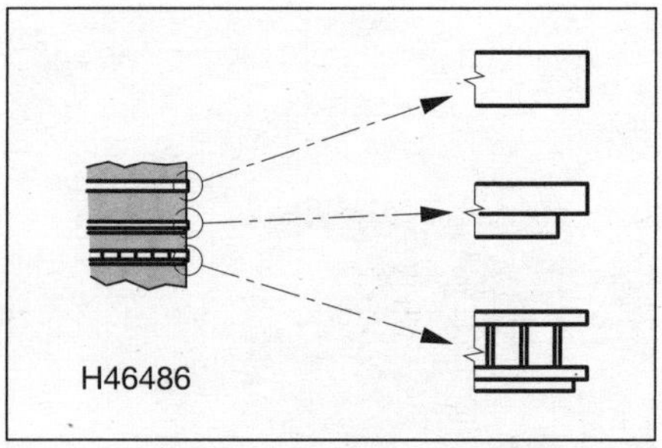

16.9b Cross-sectional view of piston rings

1 Top compression ring
2 2nd compression ring
3 Oil control ring

procedures. Do not mix up the top and middle rings, as they have different cross-sections. Using two or three old feeler blades, as for removal of the old rings, carefully slip the ring into place in the middle groove.

11 Fit the top ring in the same manner, ensuring that, where applicable, the mark on the ring is facing up. If a stepped ring is being fitted, fit the ring with the smaller diameter of the step uppermost.

12 Repeat the procedure for the remaining pistons and rings.

17 Crankshaft – refitting

Note: *It is recommended that new main bearing shells are fitted regardless of the condition of the original ones.*

1 Refitting the crankshaft is the first step in the engine reassembly procedure. It is assumed at this point that the cylinder block, cylinder block lower casing (where applicable) and crankshaft have been cleaned, inspected and repaired or reconditioned as necessary.

2 Position the cylinder block with the sump/lower casing mating face uppermost.

3 Clean the bearing shells and the bearing recesses in both the cylinder block and the lower casing/caps. If new shells are being fitted, ensure that all traces of the protective grease are cleaned off using paraffin. Wipe the shells dry with a clean lint-free cloth.

4 Note that the crankshaft endfloat is controlled by thrustwashers located on one of the main bearing shells. The thrustwashers may be separate or incorporated into, or attached to, the bearing shells themselves.

5 If the original bearing shells are being re-used, they must be refitted to their original locations in the block and lower casing, or caps.

6 Fit the upper main bearing shells in place in the cylinder block, ensuring that the tab on each shell engages in the notch in the cylinder block **(see illustration)**. Where separate thrustwashers are fitted, use a little grease to stick them to each side of their respective bearing upper location; ensure that the oilway grooves on each thrustwasher face outwards (away from the block).

Petrol engines

7 Liberally lubricate each bearing shell in the cylinder block, and lower the crankshaft into position.

8 If necessary, seat the crankshaft using light taps from a soft-faced mallet on the crankshaft balance webs.

9 Fit the bearing shells into the cylinder block lower casing.

10 Ensure that the cylinder block and lower casing mating surfaces are clean and dry, then apply a 2 to 5 mm diameter bead of sealant (available from Saab dealers) to the groove in the cylinder block **(see illustration)**.

11 Locate the lower casing over the crankshaft and onto the cylinder block.

12 Fit the twenty new M10 bolts and the ten M8 bolts and tighten the bolts as far as possible by hand.

13 Working in a diagonal sequence from the centre outwards, tighten the twenty M10 lower casing bolts to the specified Stage 1 torque setting.

14 Once all M10 bolts are tightened to the specified Stage 1 torque, go around again and tighten them through the specified Stage 2 angle then go around once more and tighten them through the specified Stage 3 angle. It is recommended that an angle-measuring gauge is used during the final stages of the tightening, to ensure accuracy **(see illustration)**. If a gauge is not available, use white paint to make alignment marks between the bolt head and casing prior to tightening; the marks can then be used to check that the bolt has been rotated through the correct angle.

15 After tightening all the M10 bolts, tighten the M8 bolts to the specified torque, working in a diagonal sequence from the centre outwards.

16 Check that the crankshaft is free to rotate smoothly; if excessive pressure is required to turn the crankshaft, investigate the cause before proceeding further.

17 Check the crankshaft endfloat with reference to Section 10.

18 Refit/reconnect the piston connecting rod assemblies to the crankshaft as described in Section 18.

19 Referring to Chapter 2A, fit a new left-hand crankshaft oil seal, then refit the sump, flywheel/driveplate, cylinder head, and the timing chains and sprockets.

Diesel engines

20 Liberally lubricate each bearing shell in the cylinder block, and lower the crankshaft into position.

21 If necessary, seat the crankshaft using light taps from a soft-faced mallet on the crankshaft balance webs.

22 Fit the bearing shells into the bearing caps.

23 Lubricate the bearing shells in the bearing caps, and the crankshaft journals, then fit the caps ensuring they are fitted to their correct locations and the right way around. Fit and tighten the new bolts as far as possible by hand.

24 Working in a spiral pattern from the centre outwards, tighten the main bearing cap bolts to the specified Stage 1 torque setting.

25 Once all bolts are tightened to the specified Stage 1 torque, go around again and tighten all bolts through the specified Stage 2 angle. It is recommended that an angle-measuring gauge is used during the final stages of the tightening, to ensure accuracy. If a gauge is not available, use white paint to make alignment marks between the bolt head and cap prior to tightening; the marks can then be used to check that the bolt has been rotated through the correct angle.

26 Check that the crankshaft is free to rotate smoothly; if excessive pressure is required

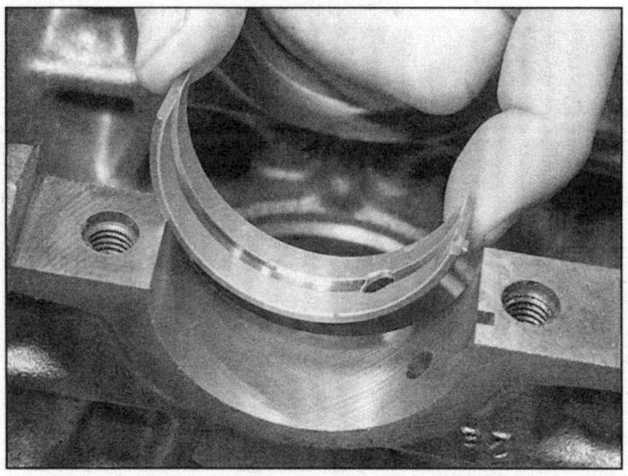

17.6 Fit the main bearing shell to the cylinder block

17.10 Apply a continuous bead of sealant (arrowed) to the groove in the cylinder block

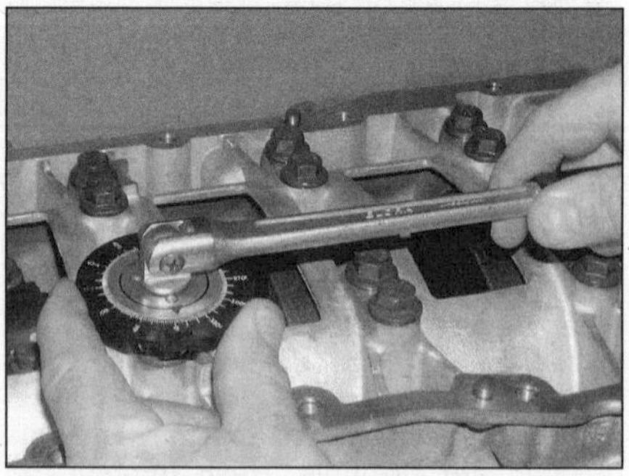

17.14 Tighten the cylinder block lower casing bolts through the specified angles

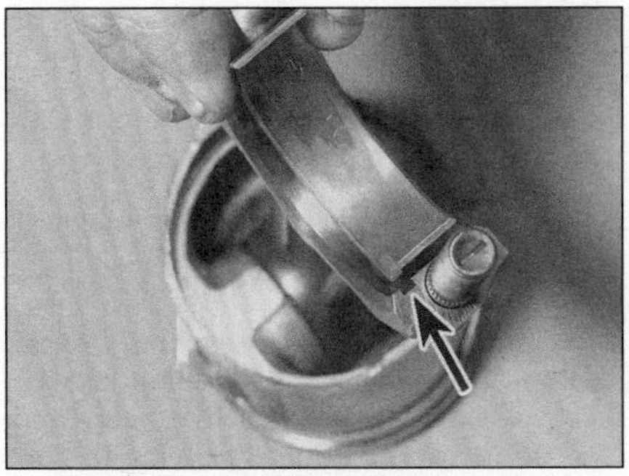

18.2 Fit the bearing shells making sure their tabs are correctly located in the connecting rod/cap groove (arrowed)

to turn the crankshaft, investigate the cause before proceeding further.

27 Check the crankshaft endfloat with reference to Section 10.

28 Refit/reconnect the piston connecting rod assemblies to the crankshaft as described in Section 18.

29 Referring to Chapter 2B or 2C, fit a new left-hand crankshaft oil seal/housing, then refit the oil pump, sump, flywheel/driveplate, cylinder head, timing belt sprocket(s) and fit a new timing belt.

18 Pistons/connecting rods – refitting

Note: *It is recommended that new big-end bearing shells are fitted regardless of the condition of the original ones.*

1 Clean the backs of the big-end bearing shells and the recesses in the connecting rods and big-end caps. If new shells are being fitted, ensure that all traces of the protective grease are cleaned off using paraffin. Wipe the shells, caps and connecting rods dry with a lint-free cloth.

2 Press the bearing shells into their locations, ensuring that the tab on each shell engages in the notch in the connecting rod and cap **(see illustration)**. If there is no tab on the bearing shell (and no notch in the rod or cap) position the shell equidistant from each side of the rod and cap. If the original bearing shells are being

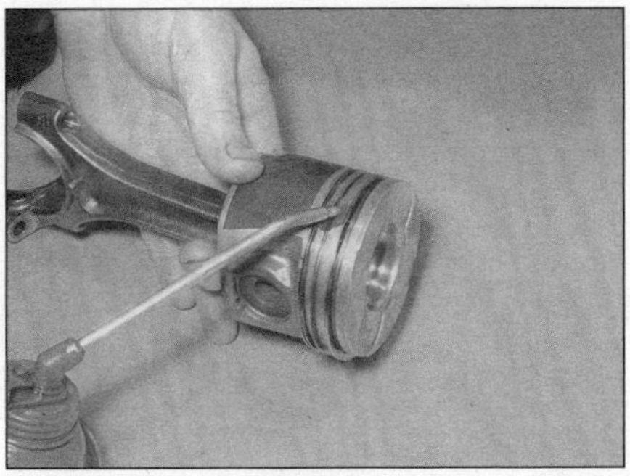

18.3 Lubricate the piston rings with clean engine oil

used ensure they are refitted in their original locations.

3 Lubricate the bores, the pistons and piston rings then lay out each piston/connecting rod assembly in its respective position **(see illustration)**.

Petrol engines

4 Lubricate No 1 piston and piston rings, and check that the ring gaps are correctly positioned. The gaps in the upper and lower steel rings of the oil control ring should be offset by 25 to 50 mm to the right and left of the spreader ring gap. The two upper compression ring gaps should be offset by 180° to each other **(see illustration)**.

5 Fit a ring compressor to No 1 piston, then insert the piston and connecting rod into the cylinder bore so that the base of the compressor stands on the block. With the crankshaft big-end bearing journal positioned at its lowest point, tap the piston carefully into the cylinder bore with the wooden handle of a hammer, and at the same time guide the connecting rod onto the bearing journal. Note that the arrow on the piston crown must point towards the timing chain end of the engine **(see illustrations)**.

6 Liberally lubricate the bearing journals and bearing shells, and fit the bearing cap in its original location (the bearing tab notch in cap and connecting rod must butt up against each other).

7 Screw in the new bearing cap retaining bolts, and tighten both bolts to the specified Stage 1

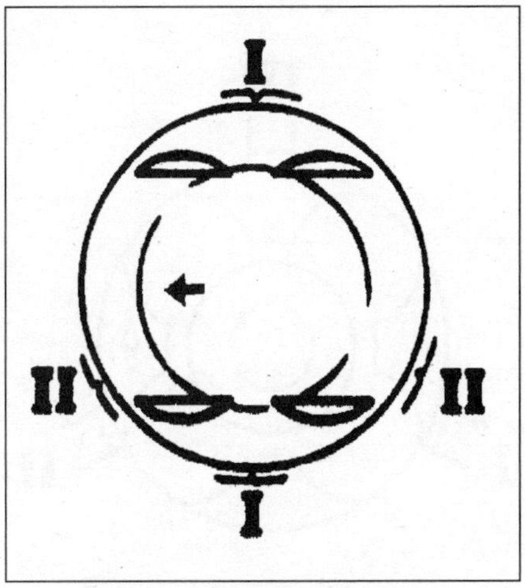

18.4 Piston ring end gap positions – petrol engines

I Top and second compression rings
II Oil control ring side rails

torque setting then tighten them through the specified Stage 2 angle. It is recommended that an angle-measuring gauge is used during the final stage of the tightening, to ensure accuracy. If a gauge is not available, use white paint to make alignment marks between the bolt head and cap prior to tightening; the marks can then be used to check that the bolt has been rotated through the correct angle.

8 Refit the remaining three piston and connecting rod assemblies in the same way.

9 Rotate the crankshaft, and check that it turns freely, with no signs of binding or tight spots.

10 Refit the oil pump pick-up/strainer, sump and the cylinder head as described in Chapter 2A.

Diesel engines

11 Lubricate No 1 piston and piston rings, and space the ring gaps uniformly around the piston at 120° intervals **(see illustration)**.

12 Fit a ring compressor to No 1 piston, then insert the piston and connecting rod into the cylinder bore so that the base of the compressor stands on the block. The cut-out on the piston skirt must be on the same side

18.5a With the piston ring end gaps correctly spaced, fit the ring compressor

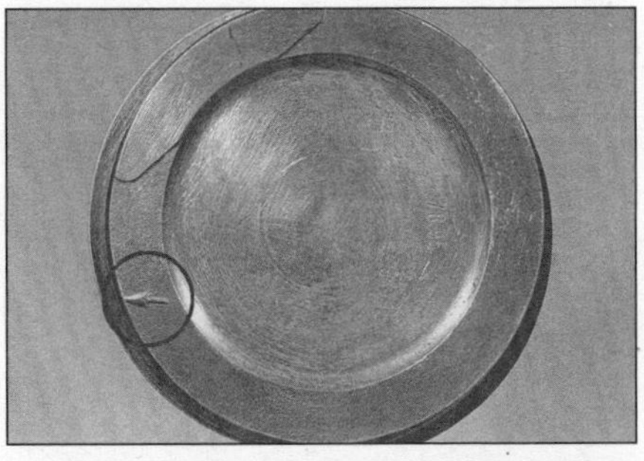

18.5b Ensure the arrow on the piston crown (circled) is pointing towards the timing chain end of the engine – petrol engines

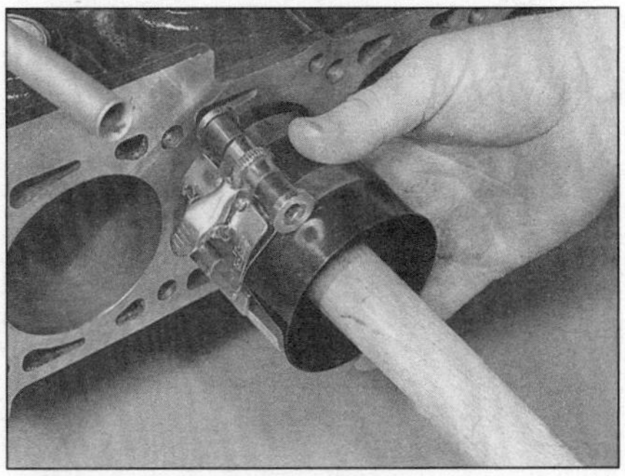

18.5c Tap the piston gently into the bore using a handle of a hammer

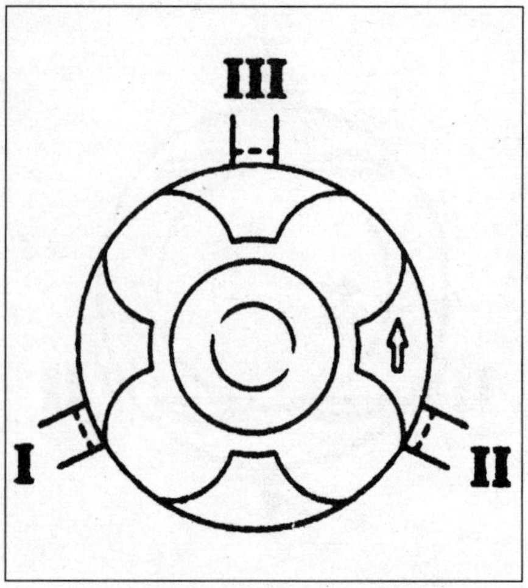

18.11 Piston ring end gap positions – diesel engines

I Top compression ring
II Second compression ring
III Oil control ring

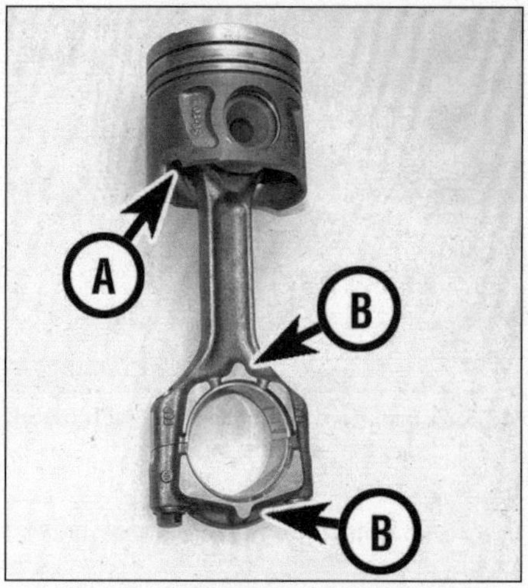

18.12 The cut-out on the piston skirt (A) must be on the same side as the oil spray jet, and the lugs on the cap and rod (B) must be toward the timing belt end of the engine – diesel engines

as the oil spray jet, and the lugs on the cap and rod must be toward the timing belt end of the engine **(see illustration)**.

13 With the crankshaft big-end bearing journal positioned at its lowest point, tap the piston carefully into the cylinder bore with the wooden handle of a hammer, and at the same time guide the connecting rod onto the bearing journal.

14 Liberally lubricate the bearing journals and bearing shells, and fit the bearing cap in its original location.

15 Screw in the new bearing cap retaining bolts, and tighten both bolts to the specified Stage 1 torque setting then tighten them through the specified Stage 2 angle. It is recommended that an angle-measuring gauge is used during the final stage of the tightening, to ensure accuracy. If a gauge is not available, use white paint to make alignment marks between the bolt head and cap prior to tightening; the marks can then be used to check that the bolt has been rotated through the correct angle.

16 Refit the remaining three piston and connecting rod assemblies in the same way.

17 Rotate the crankshaft, and check that it turns freely, with no signs of binding or tight spots.

18 Refit the oil pump pick-up/strainer, sump and the cylinder head as described in Chapter 2B or 2C.

19 Engine – initial start-up after overhaul

1 With the engine refitted in the vehicle, double-check the engine oil and coolant levels. Make a final check that everything has been reconnected, and that there are no tools or rags left in the engine compartment.

2 Start the engine, noting that this may take a little longer than usual. Make sure that the oil pressure warning light goes out.

3 While the engine is idling, check for fuel, water and oil leaks. Don't be alarmed if there are some odd smells and smoke from parts getting hot and burning off oil deposits.

4 Assuming all is well, run the engine until it reaches normal operating temperature, then switch off the engine.

5 After a few minutes, recheck the oil and coolant levels as described in *Weekly checks*, and top-up as necessary.

6 Note that there is no need to retighten the cylinder head bolts once the engine has first run after reassembly.

7 If new pistons, rings or crankshaft bearings have been fitted, the engine must be treated as new, and run-in for the first 600 miles. Do not operate the engine at full-throttle, or allow it to labour at low engine speeds in any gear. It is recommended that the oil and filter be changed at the end of this period.

Chapter 3
Cooling, heating and air conditioning systems

Contents

Degrees of difficulty

Easy, suitable for novice with little experience	**Fairly easy,** suitable for beginner with some experience	**Fairly difficult,** suitable for competent DIY mechanic	**Difficult,** suitable for experienced DIY mechanic	**Very difficult,** suitable for expert DIY or professional

Specifications

Engine identification

Engine type	**Manufacturer's engine code**
2.0 litre (1998 cc) DOHC 16-valve petrol engine	B207E, L and R
1.9 litre (1910 cc) diesel engine:	
SOHC 8-valve	Z19DT
DOHC 16-valve	Z19DTH and DTR

General

Expansion tank cap opening pressure	1.4 to 1.5 bars

Thermostat

Opening temperature:	
Petrol models	82°C ± 2°C
Diesel models	88°C ± 2°C

Electric cooling fan

Cut-in temperature:	**Petrol models**	**Diesel models**
Stage 1	100° ± 2°C	98° ± 2°C
Stage 2	108° ± 2°C	101° ± 2°C
Stage 3	114° ± 2°C	103° ± 2°C
Stage 4	120° ± 2°C	105° ± 2°C
Cut-out temperature	Not available	Not available

Coolant temperature sensor

Resistance:	
-30°C	26 kohms
-10°C	9.4 kohms
0°C	5.9 kohms
20°C	2.5 kohms
40°C	1.8 kohms
60°C	596 ohms
80°C	323 ohms
100°C	187 ohms

Refrigerant

Refrigerant type	R123a
Refrigerant quantity	680 gms
Compressor oil – type	PAG (164759106)
Compressor oil quantity (new compressor)	135 ml ± 15ml
Compressor oil (to be added per component):	
Draining of the refrigerant	15ml
Split A/C hose	30ml
Hose renewal	15ml
Condenser renewal	30ml
Evaporator renewal	30ml
Receiver drier renewal	30ml
Expansion valve renewal	15ml
Compressor renewal	70ml

Torque wrench settings

Torque wrench settings	Nm	lbf ft
Air conditioning pipe connection nut at bulkhead	15	11
Chassis reinforcement bolts (Convertible only)	50	37
Compressor	24	18
Compressor oil drain plug	30	22
Compressor refrigerant pipe connections	18	13
Condenser refrigerant pipe connections	18	13
Coolant pump:		
Petrol engines	22	16
Short bolts	20	15
Long bolts	25	18
Diesel engines	25	18
Coolant temperature sensor:		
Petrol engines	15	11
Diesel engines	22	16
Expansion valve screws	15	11
Thermostat housing:		
Petrol engines	8	6
Diesel engines	25	18

1 General information and precautions

General information

The cooling system is of pressurised type, comprising a water pump driven by the balancer shaft chain (petrol engines) or timing belt (diesel engines), a crossflow radiator, electric cooling fan, a thermostat, heater matrix and all associated hoses. The expansion tank is located in the engine compartment. The water pump is bolted to the cylinder block.

The system functions as follows. Cold coolant in the bottom of the radiator passes through the bottom hose to the water pump, where it is pumped around the cylinder block and head passages. After cooling the cylinder bores, combustion surfaces and valve seats, the coolant reaches the underside of the thermostat, which is initially closed. The coolant passes through the heater, and is returned to the water pump. On petrol models, a small proportion of coolant is channelled from the cylinder head through the throttle body, and a further amount is channelled through the turbocharger.

When the engine is cold, the coolant circulates only through the cylinder block, cylinder head, throttle body, heater and turbocharger, as applicable. When the coolant reaches a predetermined temperature, the thermostat opens, and the coolant passes through the top hose to the radiator. As the coolant circulates through the radiator, it is cooled by the inrush of air when the car is in forward motion, and also by the action of the electric cooling fan when necessary. Upon reaching the bottom of the radiator, the coolant has now cooled, and the cycle is repeated.

When the engine is at normal operating temperature, the coolant expands, and some of it is displaced into the expansion tank. Coolant collects in the tank, and is returned to the radiator when the system cools.

Two four-speed electric cooling fans are mounted on the rear of the radiator, and are controlled by the engine management ECM. At a predetermined coolant temperature, the ECM actuates the fans via a relay.

Precautions

Warning: Do not attempt to remove the expansion tank filler cap, or to disturb any part of the cooling system, while the engine is hot, as there is a high risk of scalding. If the expansion tank filler cap must be removed before the engine and radiator have fully cooled (even though this is not recommended), the pressure in the cooling system must first be relieved. Cover the cap with a thick layer of cloth, to avoid scalding, and slowly unscrew the filler cap until a hissing sound is heard. When the hissing has stopped, indicating that the pressure has reduced, slowly unscrew the filler cap until it can be removed; if more hissing sounds are heard, wait until they have stopped before unscrewing the cap completely. At all times, keep well away from the filler cap opening, and protect your hands.

Warning: Do not allow antifreeze to come into contact with your skin, or with the painted surfaces of the vehicle. Rinse off spills immediately, with plenty of water. Never leave antifreeze lying around in an open container, or in a puddle in the driveway or on the garage floor. Children and pets are attracted by its sweet smell, but antifreeze can be fatal if ingested.

Warning: If the engine is hot, the electric cooling fan may start rotating even if the engine is not running. Be careful to keep your hands, hair and any loose clothing well clear when working in the engine compartment.

Warning: Refer to Section 8 for precautions to be observed when working on models with air conditioning.

2 Cooling system hoses – disconnection and renewal

1 The number, routing and pattern of the hoses will vary according to the model, but the same basic procedure applies. Before commencing work, make sure that the new hoses are to hand, along with new hose clips if needed. It is good practice to renew the hose clips at the same time as the hoses.

2 Drain the cooling system, as described in Chapter 1A, Section 27 or Chapter 1B, Section 28, saving the coolant if it is fit for re-use. Squirt a little penetrating oil onto the hose clips if they are corroded.

3 Loosen and release the hose clips from the hose concerned.

4 Unclip any wires, cables or other hoses which may be attached to the hose being removed. Make notes for reference when reassembling if necessary. The hoses can be removed with relative ease when new, however on an older vehicle they may be stuck to the outlet.

5 If a hose proves stubborn, try to release it by rotating it before attempting to work it off. Take care not to damage the pipe stubs or hoses. Note in particular that the radiator hose stubs are fragile; do not use excessive force when attempting to remove the hoses.

6 Before fitting the new hose, smear the stubs with washing-up liquid or a suitable rubber lubricant to aid fitting. Do not use oil or grease, which may attack the rubber.

7 Fit the hose clips over the ends of the hose, then fit the hose to the stub. Work the hose into position. When satisfied, locate and tighten the hose clips.

8 Refill the cooling system as described in Chapter 1A, Section 27 or Chapter 1B, Section 28. Run the engine, and check that there are no leaks.

9 Top-up the coolant level if necessary (see *Weekly checks*).

3 Radiator – removal, inspection and refitting

Note: *If the reason for removing the radiator is to cure a leak, bear in mind that minor leaks can often be cured using a radiator sealant added to the coolant.*

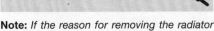

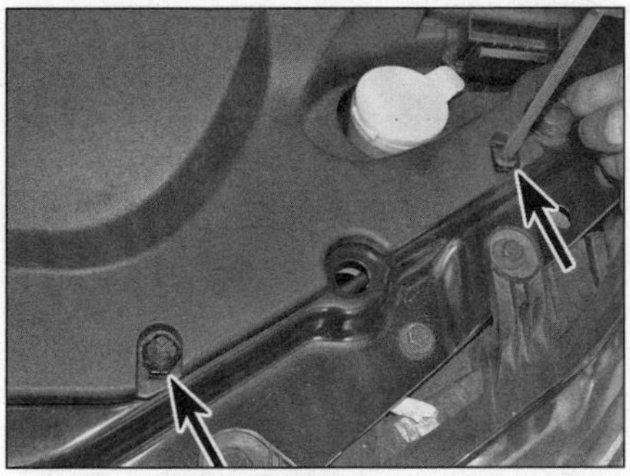

3.3a Rotate the fasteners (arrowed) anti-clockwise ...

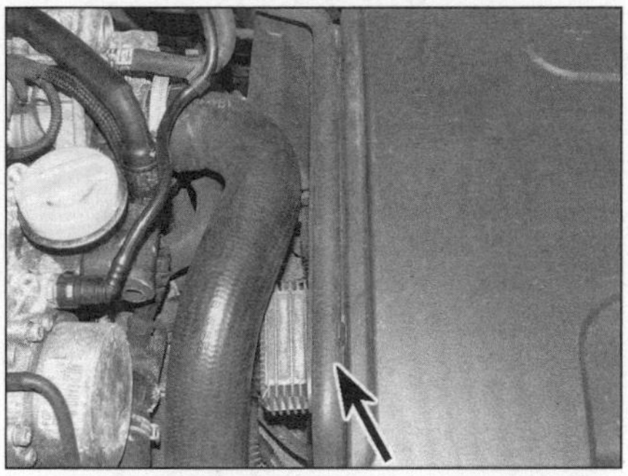

3.3b ... and unclip the coolant hose (arrowed)

Removal

1 Apply the handbrake, then jack up the front of the vehicle and support it on axle stands (see *Jacking and vehicle support*). Remove the plastic cover from the top of the engine.

2 Drain the cooling system as described in Chapter 1A, Section 27 or Chapter 1B, Section 28. If the coolant is relatively new or in good condition, drain it into a clean container for re-use.

3 Remove the battery cover, unclip the cables and unclip the coolant pipe (where fitted) **(see illustrations)**.

Petrol models

4 Slacken the clamp and disconnect the charge air pipe from the throttle body, then detach the pipe from the mounting on the cooling fan shroud **(see illustration)**. Disconnect the pressure/temperature sensor wiring plug from the pipe as it's withdrawn.

5 Undo the retaining bolts and remove the undershield beneath the radiator **(see illustration)**.

6 Slacken the clamps, undo the mounting bolts, and remove the charge air pipes either side of the intercooler.

7 Remove the 2 bolts securing the air conditioning receiver/drier to the radiator **(see illustration 9.108)**.

8 Slacken the clamp and disconnect the upper cooling hose and expansion tank hose from the radiator **(see illustrations)**.

9 On models with automatic transmission, remove the dust shield, and disconnect the transmission fluid cooling pipes from the radiator.

10 Remove the cooling fan shroud upper mounting bolts **(see illustration)**.

3.4 Slacken the clamp, and undo the retaining bolt (arrowed)

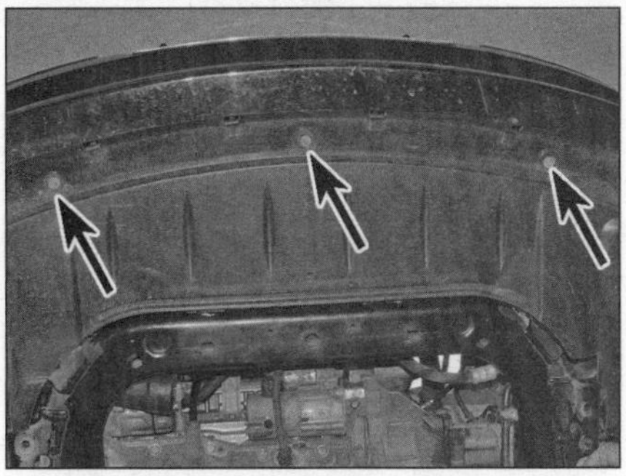

3.5 Undo the 3 screws in the centre securing the radiator undershield (arrowed)

3.8a Disconnect the radiator upper hose ...

3.8b ... and expansion tank hose (arrowed)

3.10 Undo the cooling fan shroud upper bolt each side (arrowed)

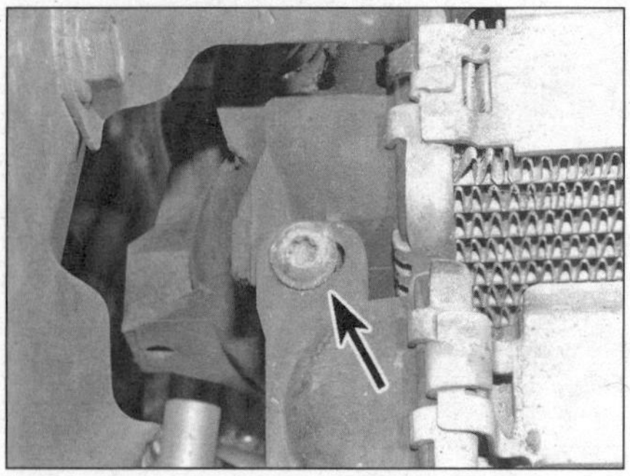

3.11 Intercooler-to-radiator mounting bolt (arrowed)

3.15 Radiator lower mounting bolt (arrowed)

11 Remove the intercooler-to-radiator upper mounting bolts **(see illustration)**.

12 Using straps, cables-ties or similar, suspend the cooling fan shroud and intercooler from the bonnet slam panel.

13 Working underneath the vehicle, slacken the clamps and disconnect the radiator lower hose.

14 Unhook the intercooler, condenser and cooling fan shroud from the radiator.

15 Undo the bolts securing the radiator lower mounting to the subframe **(see illustration)**.

16 Carefully lower the radiator from place, taking care not to damage the cooling fins as it's lowered. If required, remove the rubber mountings from the radiator.

Diesel models

17 Undo the bolts and remove the radiator undershield.

18 Slacken the clamps, undo the mounting bolts, and remove the charge air pipe from the left-hand side of the radiator.

19 Remove the front bumper cover as described in Chapter 11, Section 6.

20 Remove the headlights as described in Chapter 12, Section 6.

21 Undo the bolts securing the air conditioning pipe and boost pressure valve to the bonnet slam panel **(see illustrations)**.

22 Undo the bolts/nuts, disconnect the horn wiring plug and remove the bonnet slam panel **(see illustrations)**.

23 Undo the retaining bolts, release any retaining clips, and remove the charge air pipe from the intercooler and turbocharger.

24 Slacken the clamp and disconnect the radiator upper hose **(see illustration)**.

25 Disconnect the expansion hose from the left-hand upper edge of the radiator **(see illustration)**.

26 On automatic transmission models remove the upper oil cooler pipe. On DTR models remove the crankcase ventilation pipe **(see illustration)**.

27 Disconnect the cooling fan wiring plug at the fan shroud, then undo the 2 retaining bolts and lift the fan shroud upwards to disengage the lower lugs. Secure the fans to the engine lifting eyes with suitable straps.

28 Remove the cover from the right-hand side of the radiator, then undo the mounting bolts and remove the air intake ducting **(see illustration)**.

29 Slacken the clamps and remove the charge air pipe from the right-hand side of the radiator. On models fitted with the DTR engine remove the metal pipe as well as the rigid plastic intake pipe.

30 Undo the 2 bolts securing the air conditioning receiver/drier to the radiator **(see illustration 9.108)**.

3.21a Undo the bolt (arrowed) securing the air conditioning pipe ...

3.21b ... and the 2 securing the turbocharger boost pressure valve

3.22a Undo the bonnet slam panel bolts at the top (right-hand bolts arrowed) ...

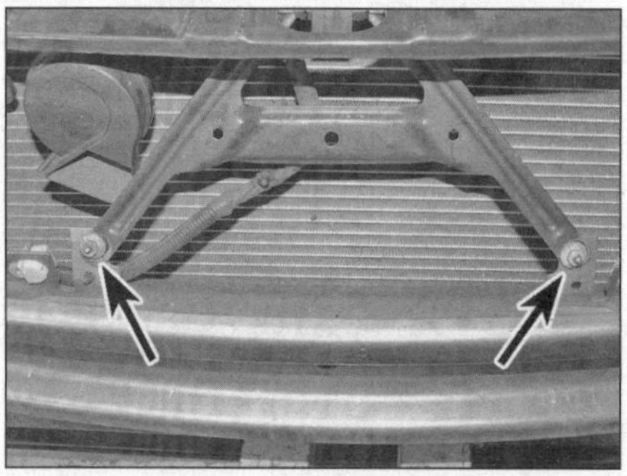

3.22b ... and the nuts at the centre (arrowed)

3.24 Release the upper radiator hose clip (arrowed)

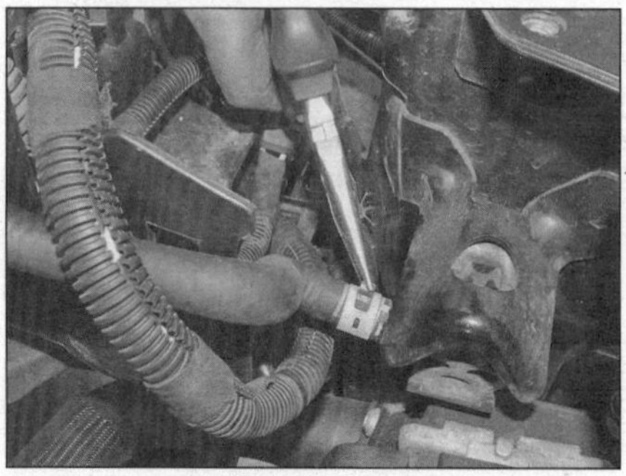

3.25 Disconnect the coolant expansion hose from the radiator

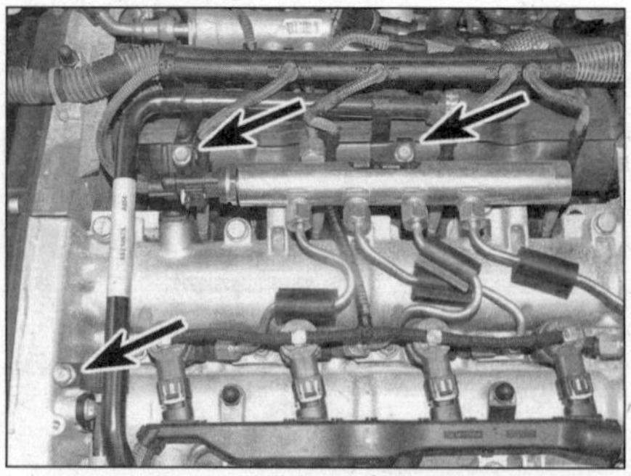

3.26 Remove the breather pipe mounting bolts (arrowed)

3.28 Remove the cover (arrowed) from the lower, right-hand side of the radiator

3.31 Release the lower radiator hose clip (arrowed)

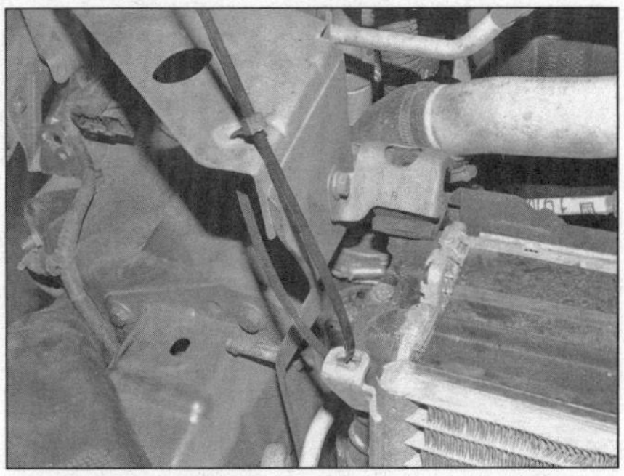

3.32a Use cable-ties (or similar) to suspend the intercooler and condenser from the vehicle body

3.32b Remove the plastic strip from the top of the radiator/intercooler

3.33 Undo the bolt each side (right-hand bolt arrowed) securing the radiator lower mountings to the subframe

3.34 Lower the radiator

31 Slacken the clamp and disconnect the radiator lower hose **(see illustration)**.

32 Suspend the intercooler and condenser from the vehicle body using straps, cable-ties or similar, then undo the bolts securing the intercooler to the radiator, and remove the plastic strip on the top of the radiator/intercooler **(see illustrations)**.

33 Undo the bolts securing the radiator lower mountings to the subframe **(see illustration)**.

34 Lower the radiator downwards **(see illustration)**.

Inspection

35 If the radiator has been removed due to suspected blockage, reverse-flush it as described in Chapter 1A, Section 27 or Chapter 1B, Section 28. Clean dirt and debris from the radiator fins, using an airline or a soft brush.

36 If necessary, a radiator specialist can perform a flow test on the radiator, to establish whether an internal blockage exists. A leaking radiator must be referred to a specialist for permanent repair. Do not attempt to weld or solder a leaking radiator. If the radiator is to be sent for repair, or is to be renewed, remove the cooling fan thermostatic switch.

37 Inspect the condition of the upper and lower radiator mounting rubbers, and renew them if necessary.

Refitting

38 Refitting is a reversal of removal, but note the following additional points.

a) Fill the cooling system as described in Chapter 1A, Section 27 or Chapter 1B, Section 28.

b) Tighten all nuts and bolts to the specified torque where given.

c) Check and if necessary top-up the fluid level in the automatic transmission with reference to Chapter 1A, Section 25 or Chapter 1B, Section 26.

d) Finally, check the cooling system for leaks.

4 Thermostat – removal, testing and refitting

Petrol models

Removal

1 The thermostat is located on the left-hand end of the cylinder head. First, drain the cooling system as described in Chapter 1A, Section 27. If the coolant is relatively new or in good condition, drain it into a clean container for re-use.

2 Disconnect the coolant level sensor, then pull the coolant expansion tank upwards and move it to one side **(see illustration)**.

3 Depress the release tab, and disconnect the vacuum servo hose from the pump at the left-hand end of the cylinder head.

4 Undo the 3 retaining bolts and move the thermostat cover to one side **(see illustration)**.

5 Remove the thermostat **(see illustration)**. Recover the sealing ring.

Testing

Note: *Frankly, if there is any question about the operation of the thermostat,*

4.2 Pull out the base of the coolant expansion tank, then pull it upwards from the bracket

4.4 Undo the 3 bolts and remove the thermostat cover

4.5 Pull the thermostat from the housing

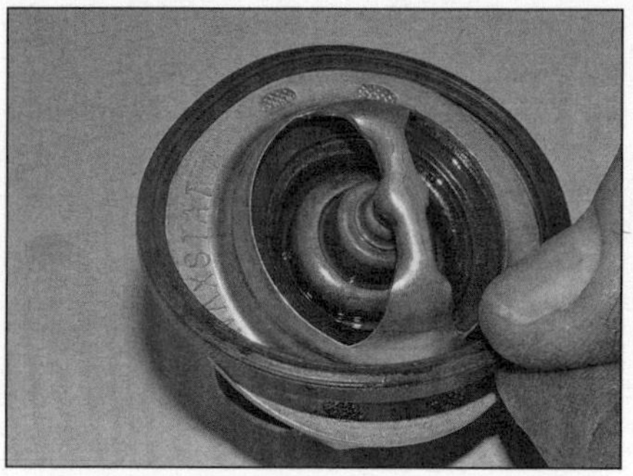

4.10 Renew the sealing ring around the thermostat

it's best to renew it – they are not usually expensive items. Testing involves heating in, or over, an open pan of boiling water, which carries with it the risk of scalding. A thermostat which has seen more than five years' service may well be past its best already.

6 A rough test of the thermostat may be made by suspending it with a piece of string in a container full of water. Heat the water to boiling point and check that the thermostat opens. If not, renew it.

7 If a thermometer is available, the precise opening temperature of the thermostat may be determined and compared with the figures given in the Specifications. The opening temperature is normally marked on the thermostat.

8 A thermostat which fails to close as the water cools must also be renewed.

Refitting

9 Clean the surfaces of the thermostat housing, cover and cylinder head. Smear a little petroleum jelly on the new sealing ring.

10 Locate the sealing ring around the thermostat, and refit it into the housing **(see illustration)**.

11 Refit the thermostat housing and tighten the bolts to the specified torque.

12 The remaining refitting procedure is a reversal of removal, but refill and bleed the cooling system with reference to Chapter 1A, Section 27.

Diesel models

Removal – Z19DT

13 The thermostat is located on the left-hand end of the cylinder head, and is integral with the housing. First, drain the cooling system as described in Chapter 1B, Section 28. If the coolant is relatively new or in good condition, drain it into a clean container for re-use.

14 Remove the EGR cooler as described in Chapter 4C, Section 3.

15 Loosen the clips and disconnect the hoses from the thermostat housing. Unbolt the thermostat housing. Clean away all traces of gasket from the housing and cylinder head.

Removal – Z19DTH and Z19DTR

16 The thermostat is located on the left-hand end of the cylinder head, and is integral with the housing. First, drain the cooling system as described in Chapter 1B, Section 28. If the coolant is relatively new or in good condition, drain it into a clean container for re-use.

17 Remove the plastic cover from the top of the engine.

18 Slacken the clamps, undo the retaining bolt, and remove the charge air pipe from the throttle body **(see illustration)**.

19 On the DTH engine disconnect the coolant temperature sensor wiring plug.

20 Place a clean cloth below the housing, remove the clamps and disconnect the hoses from the thermostat housing.

21 Undo the 2 retaining bolts (DTH engine) or 3 bolts (DTR engine) and remove the thermostat housing **(see illustration)**.

4.18 Release the clamps and remove the charge air pipe

4.21 Remove the thermostat

Testing

22 Refer to paragraphs 6 to 8, but note that the complete housing must be renewed if the thermostat proves to be faulty.

Refitting

23 Refitting is a reversal of removal, but fit a new gasket and tighten the mounting bolts to the specified torque. Refill and bleed the cooling system with reference to Chapter 1B, Section 28.

5 Electric cooling fan – testing, removal and refitting

Testing

1 Current supply to the cooling fan is controlled by the engine management ECM. The module is supplied with information of the coolant temperature sensor, air conditioning pressure, vehicle speed and outside temperature. Models with air conditioning are fitted with two cooling fans.

2 If the fan does not appear to work, first check that the wiring plug located near the cooling fan is intact. Check the maxi fuses numbers 36 and 35 in the underbonnet fusebox. If the fuses and wiring are in good condition the system should be checked for fault codes. A Saab dealer or suitably-equipped specialist should carry out a diagnostic check to locate the fault.

3 If the wiring is in good condition, use a voltmeter to check that 12 volts is reaching the motor when the engine temperature dictates. The motor itself can be checked by disconnecting it from the wiring loom, and connecting a 12 volt supply directly to it.

Removal

4 Apply the handbrake, then jack up the front of the vehicle and support it on axle stands (see *Jacking and vehicle support*). Remove the plastic cover from the top of the engine.

Petrol models

5 Remove the battery cover and battery box as described in Chapter 5A, Section 4.

6 Slacken the clamp and disconnect the charge air pipe from the throttle body, then detach the pipe from the mounting on the cooling fan shroud **(see illustration 3.4)**. Disconnect the pressure/temperature sensor wiring plug from the pipe as it's withdrawn.

7 Undo the retaining bolts and remove the undershield beneath the radiator **(see illustration 3.5)**.

8 Disconnect the bonnet release cable at the junction adjacent to the fusebox, then undo the bolts and remove the bonnet slam panel.

9 Slacken the clamps, undo the mounting bolts, and remove the charge air pipes either side of the intercooler.

10 Lift the upper radiator cover, then undo and remove the radiator upper mountings

(see illustration). Move the radiator forwards a little.

11 On models with automatic transmission, disconnect the quick-release connector and detach the transmission fluid upper cooling pipe from the radiator. Be prepared for fluid spillage.

12 Remove the cooling fan shroud mounting bolts, and lift it from place **(see illustration)** complete with the cooling fan(s). Remove the fan or fans from the cowling.

Diesel models

13 Undo the bolts and remove the radiator undershield.

14 Slacken the clamps, undo the mounting bolt, and remove the charge air pipe from the left-hand side of the radiator.

15 Remove the right-hand headlight as described in Chapter 12, Section 6.

16 Undo the bolts securing the air conditioning pipe and boost pressure valve to the bonnet slam panel **(see illustrations 3.21a and 3.21b)**.

17 Undo the bolts/nuts, disconnect the horn wiring plug, and remove the bonnet slam panel **(see illustrations 3.22a and 3.22b)**.

18 Undo the clamps, release any retaining clips, and remove the charge air pipe from the intercooler pipe and turbocharger.

19 Support the radiator with a suitable strap. Undo the retaining bolts and remove the radiator lower mountings **(see illustrations)**.

20 Disconnect the cooling fan wiring plug at the fan shroud, release the wiring harness clips, then undo the 2 retaining Torx screws and lift the fan shroud upwards **(see illustrations)**.

21 If required, disconnect the wiring plugs, undo the Torx screw and remove the fan relay unit from the shroud **(see illustrations)**.

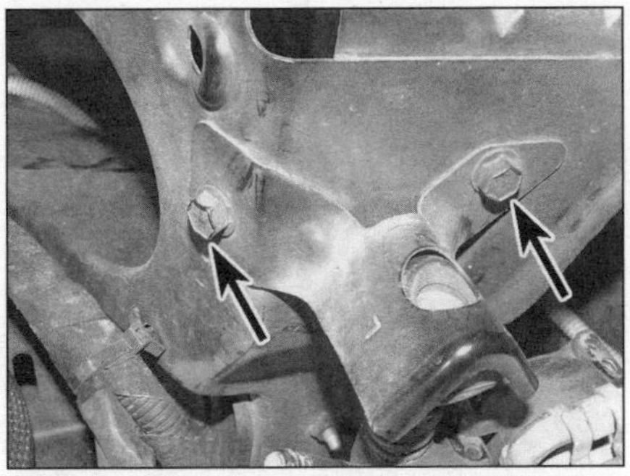

5.10 Undo the bolts (arrowed) and remove the radiator upper mounting brackets

5.12 Cooling fan upper mounting bolt (arrowed)

5.19a Support the radiator assembly ...

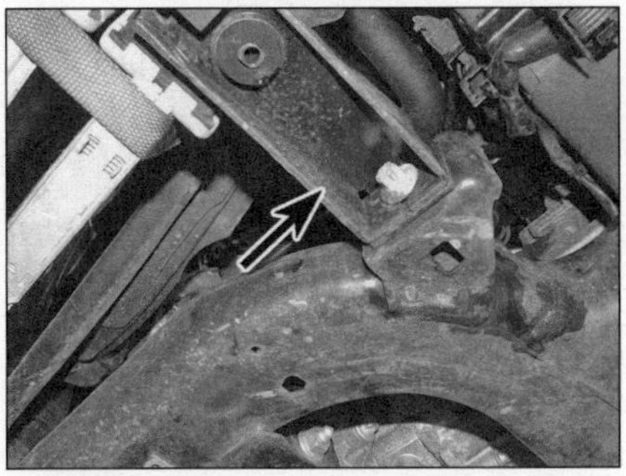

5.19b ... and remove the lower support brackets (arrowed)

Refitting

22 Refitting is a reversal of removal but tighten the mounting bolts securely.

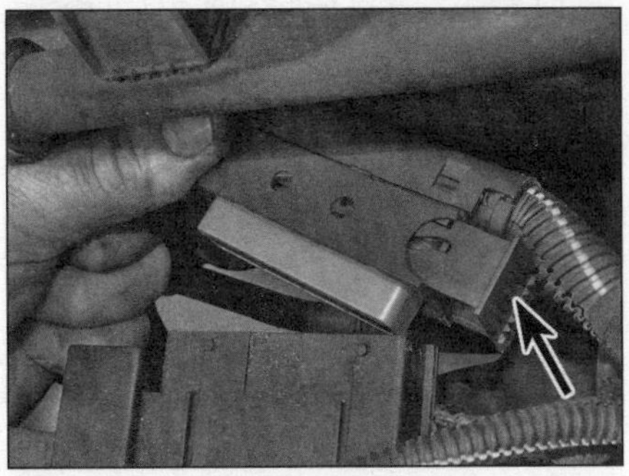

5.20a Slide out the locking catch (arrowed) and disconnect the cooling fan wiring plug at the top of the shroud ...

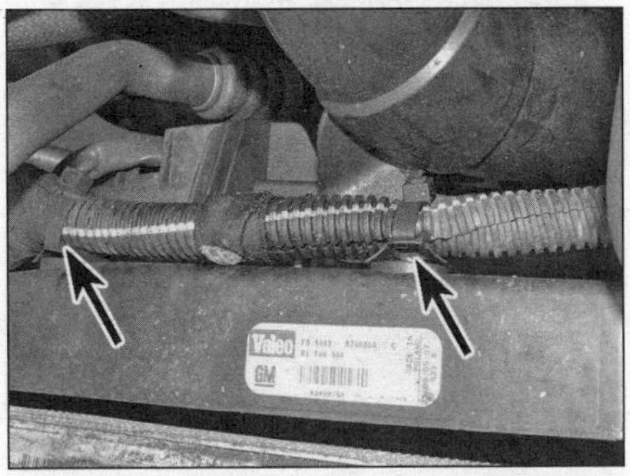

5.20b ... then release the wiring harness clips (arrowed)

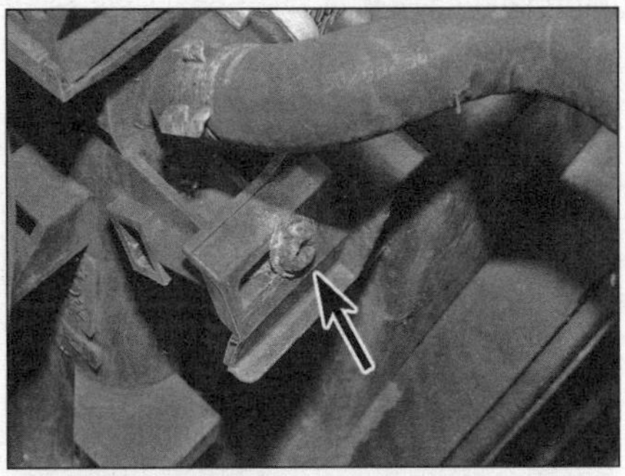

5.20c Undo the Torx screw each side (left-hand screw arrowed) securing the fan shroud to the radiator

5.20d Rotate the fan and remove it

5.21a Remove the control unit ...

5.21b ... and if required the fans can be removed from the shroud (arrowed)

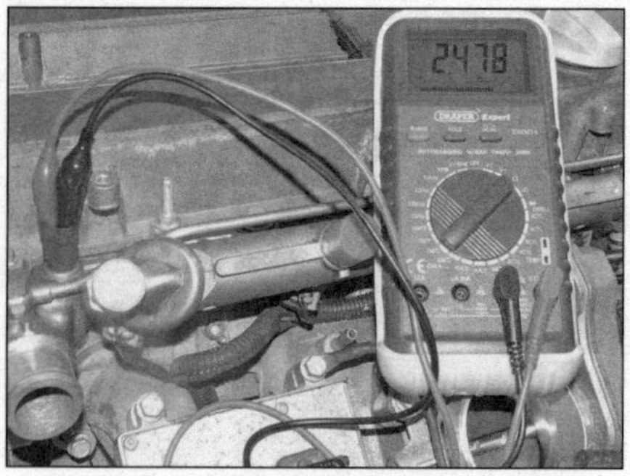

6.2 Measure the resistance of the temperature sensor with a digital multimeter

6 Coolant temperature sensor – testing, removal and refitting

Testing

1 On petrol engines, the coolant temperature sensor is located in the upper front right-hand corner of the engine. On diesel engines, the coolant temperature sensor is located on the thermostat housing on the left-hand end of the cylinder head. The resistance of the sensor varies according to the temperature of the coolant.

2 To test the sensor, disconnect the wiring at the plug then connect an ohmmeter to the sensor **(see illustration)**.

3 Determine the temperature of the coolant, then compare the resistance with the information given in the Specifications. If

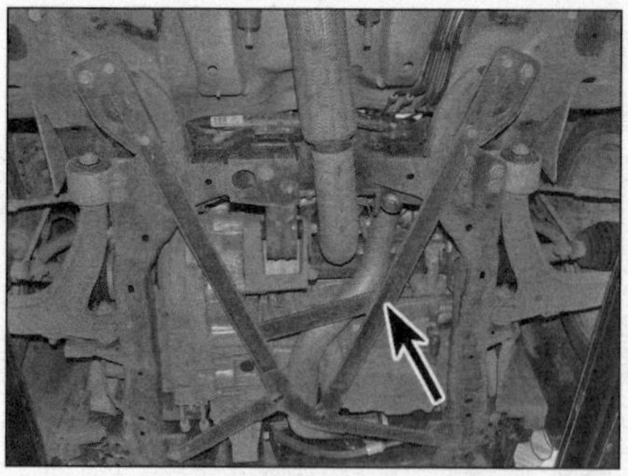

7.3 Front chassis reinforcement (arrowed) – Convertible models

the reading is incorrect, the sender must be renewed.

Removal and refitting

4 Refer to Chapter 4A, Section 10 or Chapter 4B, Section 9, as applicable.

7 Coolant pump – removal and refitting

Removal

1 Drain the cooling system as described in Chapter 1A, Section 27 or Chapter 1B, Section 28. If the coolant is relatively new or in good condition, drain it into a clean container and re-use it.

Petrol models

2 Apply the handbrake, then jack up the front of the vehicle and support it on axle stands (see *Jacking and vehicle support*). Remove the engine top cover, and the right-hand front roadwheel and wheel arch liner.

3 On Convertible models, undo the bolts and remove the front chassis reinforcement **(see illustration)**.

4 Working at the left-hand end of the cylinder head, disconnect the oxygen sensors and temperature sensor wiring plugs **(see illustration)**.

5 Remove the air cleaner complete with mass airflow meter as described in Chapter 4A, Section 2.

6 Remove the air intake from the turbocharger.

7 Remove the coolant pump upper bolt **(see illustration)**.

8 Undo the fasteners and remove the heat shield over the turbocharger.

9 Remove the catalytic converter with reference to Chapter 4A, Section 16.

10 Remove the auxiliary drivebelt as described in Chapter 1A, Section 26.

11 Remove the turbocharger coolant pipe from the thermostat housing and turbocharger **(see illustration)**.

12 Undo the bolts securing the thermostat housing **(see illustration)**.

13 Remove the coolant pump lower mounting bolt from the timing cover/engine block **(see illustration)**.

14 Undo the 4 bolts securing the coolant pump cover to the timing cover **(see illustration)**.

15 Fit Saab special tool 83 96 103 to secure

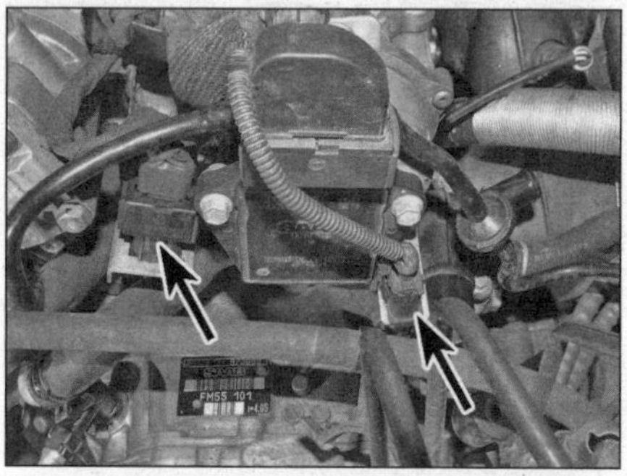

7.4 Oxygen sensors and temperature sensor wiring plugs (arrowed)

7.7 Coolant pump upper bolt (arrowed)

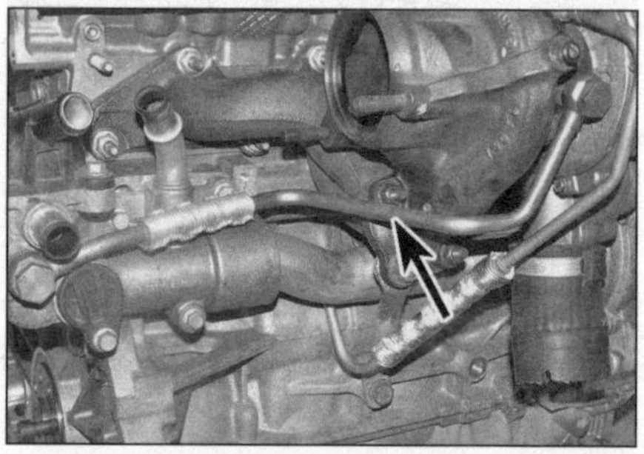

7.11 Remove the coolant pipe from the thermostat housing to the turbocharger (arrowed)

7.12 Thermostat housing bolts (arrowed)

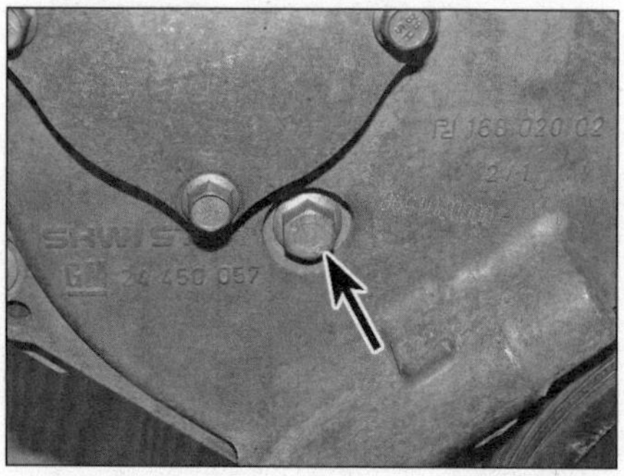

7.13 Coolant pump lower mounting bolt (arrowed)

7.14 Remove the 4 bolts securing the access cover

7.15a Saab special tool attached to the timing cover and the coolant pump drive sprocket

7.15b Homemade tool holding the coolant pump drive sprocket stationary

7.15c Unscrew the 2 remaining bolts securing the coolant pump to the sprocket

7.17a Pull the coolant pipe from the rear of the pump ...

7.17b ... then undo the bolts ...

7.17c ... and remove the pump

the coolant pump drive sprocket in position **(see illustration)**. In the absence of the special tool, fabricate an equivalent using a length of flat metal bar and two threaded rods screwed into the sprocket. First unscrew one of the sprocket bolts, taking care not to drop it into the timing case, then bolt the tool into position to hold the sprocket. With the tool in position, unscrew the remaining bolts from the sprocket **(see illustrations)**.

16 If using the Saab tool, undo and remove the coolant pump drive sprocket bolts.

17 Undo the 2 bolts on the rear of the coolant pump, move the thermostat housing (and coolant pipe) to one side, and remove the pump **(see illustrations)**.

Diesel models

18 Remove the timing belt as described in Chapter 2B, Section 7 or Chapter 2C, Section 6 as applicable.

19 On Z19DT engines, remove the camshaft sprocket as described in Chapter 2B, Section 8, then undo the bolt and remove the camshaft position sensor.

20 On all diesel engines, undo the Allen screws and remove the coolant pump **(see illustration)**.

Refitting

21 Refitting is a reversal of removal, but note the following additional points:

a) Clean the pump and block contact faces.
*b) Fit new O-rings, and apply a little petroleum jelly to them to aid seating **(see illustration)**.*
c) On diesel engines, apply a little thread-locking compound to the coolant pump retaining bolts.
d) On Z19DT diesel engines, apply a little thread-locking compound to the camshaft position sensor retaining bolt.
e) Tighten all nuts/bolts to the specified torque where given.
f) Refill and bleed the cooling system with reference to Chapter 1A, Section 27 or Chapter 1B, Section 28.

8 Climate control systems – general information

1 All models feature a fully Automatic Climate Control (ACC) system which maintains the temperature inside the car at a selected temperature, regardless of the temperature outside the car. The heating/ventilation unit is common to all versions, and consists of air ducting from the centrally-located heater assembly to a central vent and two side vents, with an extension leading from the bottom of the heater through the centre console to the rear passenger footwell areas. A five-speed heater blower motor is fitted.

2 The heating and ventilation controls are mounted in the centre of the facia. Electrically-controlled flap valves are contained in the air distribution housing, to divert the air to the various ducts and vents.

3 Cold air enters the system through the grille at the bottom of the windscreen. If required, the airflow is boosted by the blower, and then flows through the various ducts, according to the settings of the controls. Stale air is expelled through ducts at the rear of the vehicle behind the rear bumper. If warm air is required, the cold air is passed over the heater matrix, which is heated by the engine coolant.

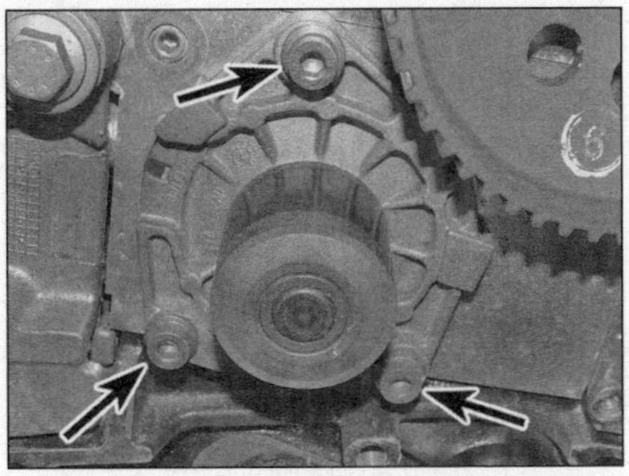
7.20 Undo the three coolant pump Hex screws (arrowed)

7.21 Renew the coolant pump O-ring seals

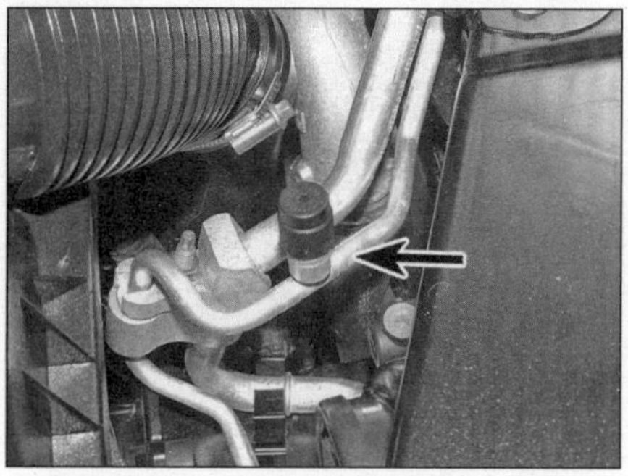

8.10a The high pressure service port (arrowed) ...

8.10b ... and the low pressure port (arrowed)

4 A recirculation switch enables the outside air supply to be closed off, while the air inside the vehicle is recirculated. This can be useful to prevent unpleasant odours entering from outside the vehicle, but should only be used briefly, as the recirculated air inside the vehicle will soon become stale.

5 A solar sensor located on top of the facia panel detects increased solar radiation, and increases the speed of the blower motor. This is necessary in order to increase the throughput of air in the vehicle.

Air conditioning

6 Air conditioning enables the temperature of air inside the car to be lowered, and also dehumidifies the air, which makes for rapid demisting and increased comfort.

7 The cooling side of the system works in the same way as a domestic refrigerator. Refrigerant gas is drawn into a belt-driven compressor, and passes into a condenser mounted in front of the radiator, where it loses heat and becomes liquid. The liquid passes through a receiver and expansion valve to an evaporator, where it changes from liquid under high pressure to gas under low pressure. This change is accompanied by a drop in temperature, which cools the evaporator. The refrigerant returns to the compressor, and the cycle begins again.

8 Air drawn through the evaporator passes to the air distribution unit. The air conditioning system is switched on with the switch located on the heater panel.

9 The compressor operation is controlled by an electromagnetic clutch on the drive pulley. Any problems with the system should be referred to a Saab dealer or specialist.

10 The air conditioning refrigerant circuit service ports are located at the front right-hand corner of the engine compartment **(see illustrations)**.

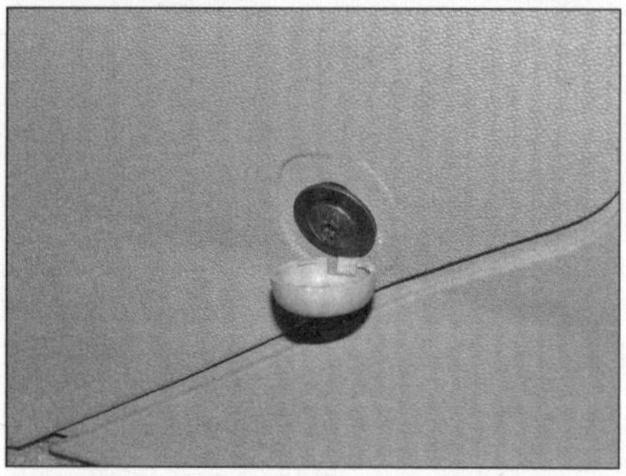

9.3a Prise off the cap and undo the Torx screw ...

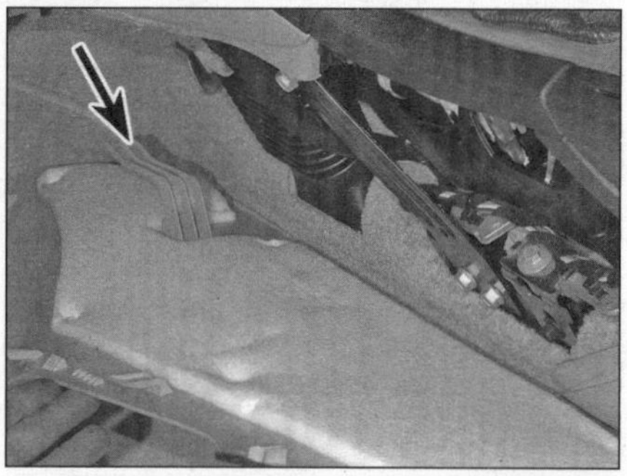

9.3b ... then slide the panel rearwards and downwards to disengage the hook (arrowed)

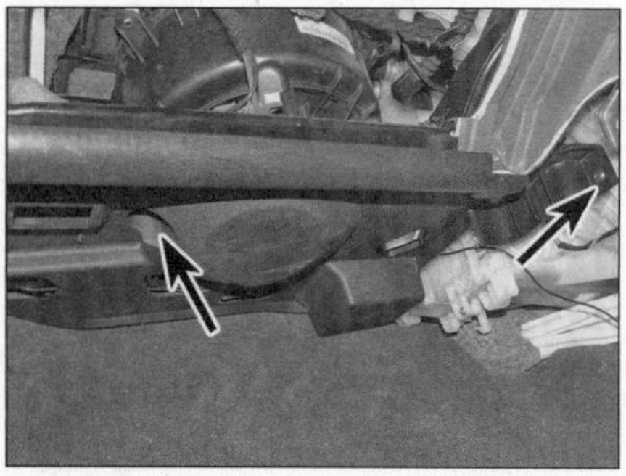

9.4 Lower facia panel screws (arrowed)

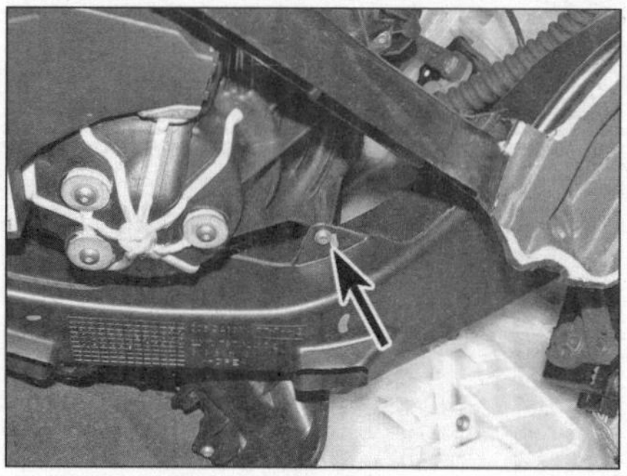

9.5 Lower air duct retaining screw (arrowed)

Precautions

11 When working on the air conditioning system, it is necessary to observe special precautions. If for any reason the system must be evacuated, entrust this task to a Saab dealer or a suitably-equipped specialist.

Warning: The refrigeration circuit contains a liquid refrigerant under pressure, and it is therefore dangerous to disconnect any part of the system without specialised knowledge and equipment. The refrigerant is potentially dangerous, and should only be handled by qualified persons. If it is splashed onto the skin, it can cause frostbite. It is not itself poisonous, but in the presence of a naked flame (including a cigarette) it forms a poisonous gas. Uncontrolled discharging of the refrigerant is dangerous, and potentially damaging to the environment. Do not operate the air conditioning system if it is known to be short of refrigerant, as this may damage the compressor.

9 Climate control system components – removal and refitting

Heater blower motor

Note: *Whenever any air conditioning component is disconnected or renewed the system should be recalibrated. Start the engine and press the 'Auto' and recirculation switches at the same time. The system will also automatically self calibrate after 40 drive cycles.*

Removal

1 Slide the passenger's seat fully rearwards.

2 Remove the glovebox as described in Chapter 11, Section 29.

3 Remove the passenger's side centre console forward side panel, by removing the fastener and sliding the panel downwards and rearwards **(see illustrations)**.

4 Undo the 2 retaining screws and remove the lower facia panel on the passenger's side **(see illustration)**. Disconnect the any wiring plugs as the panel is withdrawn.

5 Detach the lower air ducting and withdraw it through the glovebox aperture **(see illustration)**.

6 Disconnect the blower motor control unit wiring plug.

7 Undo the 7 retaining screws, release the clips, and lower the blower motor housing from position **(see illustration)**.

8 If necessary, transfer the control unit from the old motor to the new one. Note that if only the control module is at fault it is possible to remove it with the blower motor still in the vehicle **(see illustrations)**.

Refitting

9 Refitting is a reversal of removal but make sure that the wiring is clear of the fan before refitting the cover.

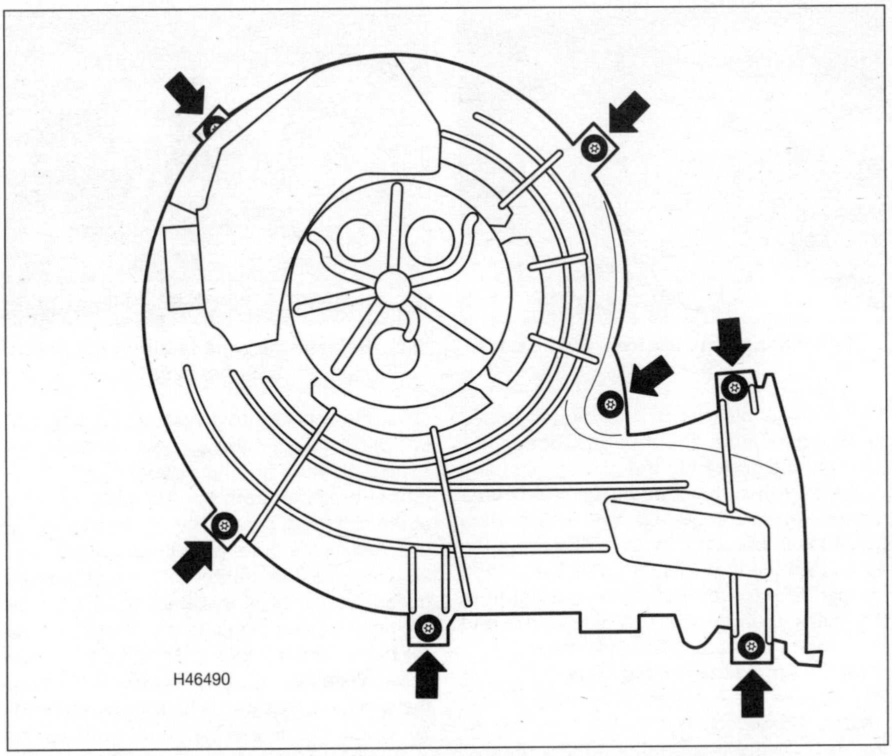

9.7 Undo the 7 Torx screws and remove the blower motor housing

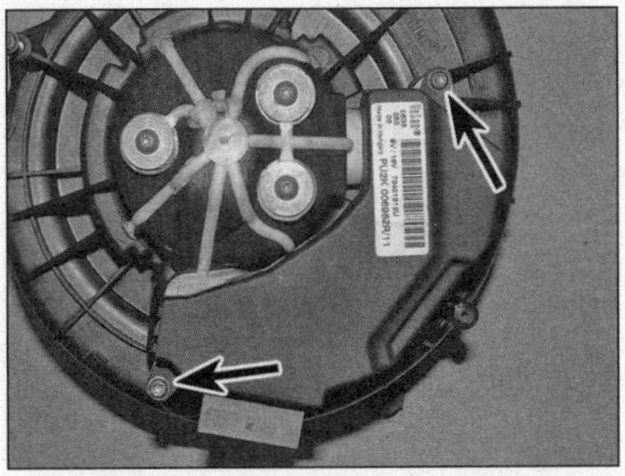

9.8a Heater blower motor control unit screws (arrowed)

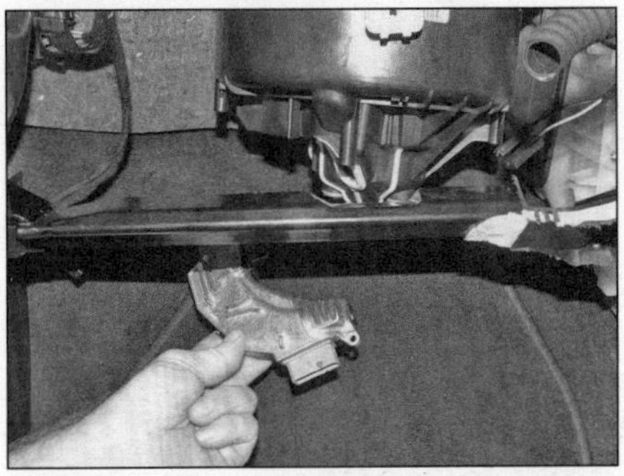

9.8b It is also possible to remove the control unit with the blower motor still in the vehicle

Heater matrix

Removal

10 Fit hose clamps to the heater hoses at the bulkhead or drain the cooling system as described in Chapter 1A, Section 27 or Chapter 1B, Section 28. Identify the hoses for position, then prise out the locking clips and disconnect them from the heater matrix **(see illustrations)**. Plug the stubs to prevent coolant spilling onto the floor when the matrix is removed from inside the car. To remove most of the coolant from the matrix, blow through one of the pipes and the coolant will escape from the other.

Caution: Antifreeze is poisonous.

11 Remove the glovebox as described in Chapter 11, Section 29.

12 Remove the passenger's (LHD) or driver's (RHD) side centre console forward side panel, by removing the fastener, and sliding the panel downwards and rearwards **(see illustrations 9.3a and 9.3b)**.

13 Undo the 2 Torx retaining screws and remove the lower facia panel on the passenger's side (LHD) or the driver's side (RHD) **(see illustration 9.4)**. Disconnect any wiring plugs as the panel is withdrawn. If removing the driver's side panel, slide off the cap, undo the 2 Torx screws and detach the diagnostic plug.

14 Undo the 3 screws and remove the matrix cover **(see illustrations)**.

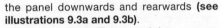

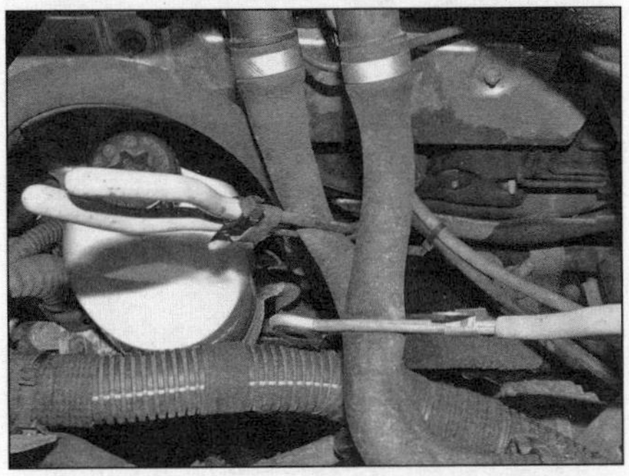

9.10a Use clamps on the heater hoses ...

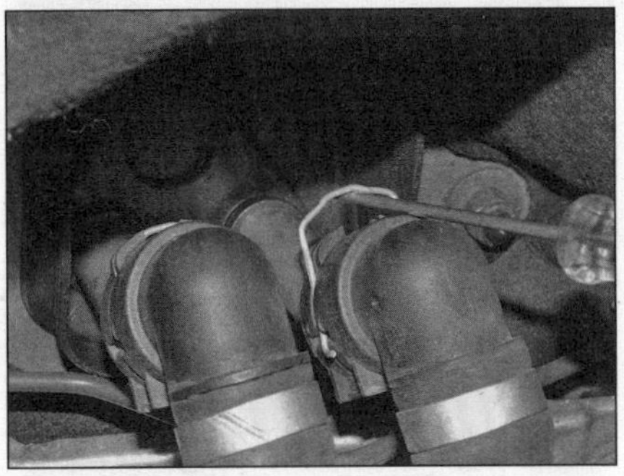

9.10b ... then prise out the locking clips ...

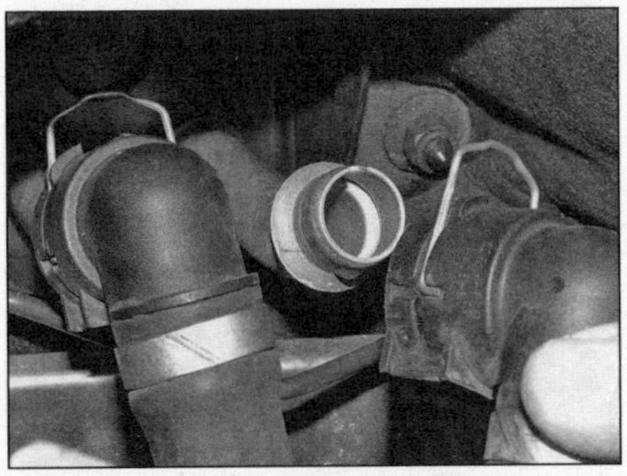

9.10c ... and disconnect the heater hoses

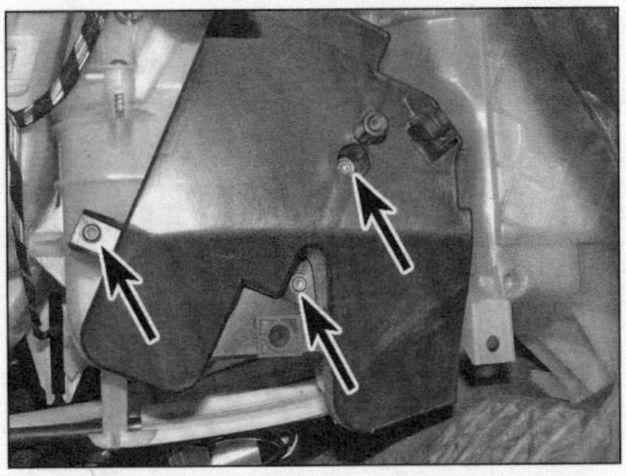

9.14a Undo the 3 Torx screws (arrowed) ...

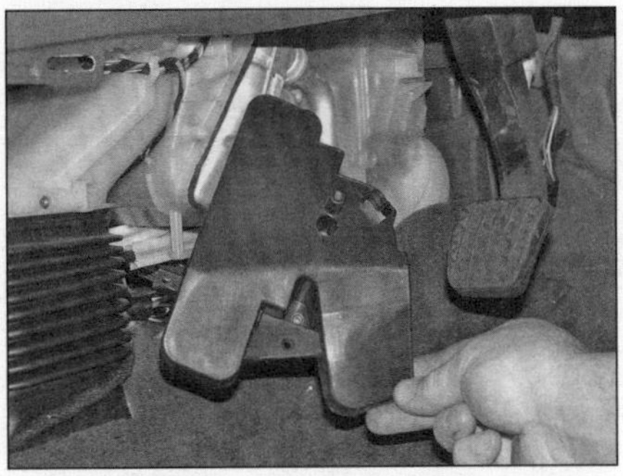

9.14b ... and remove the matrix cover

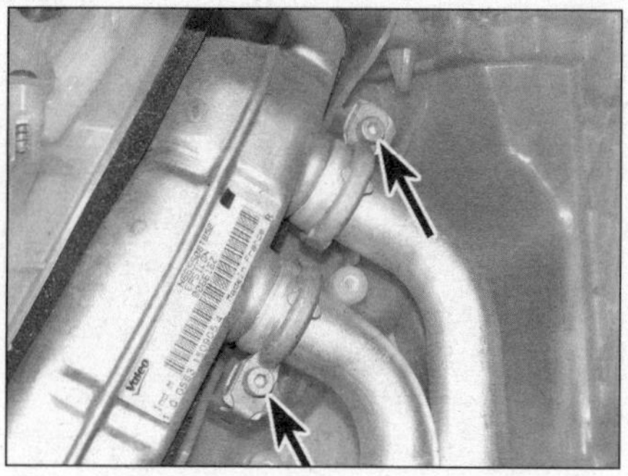

9.15 Use an Allen key to slacken the matrix pipe clamps (arrowed)

9.16 Slide the matrix from the heater housing

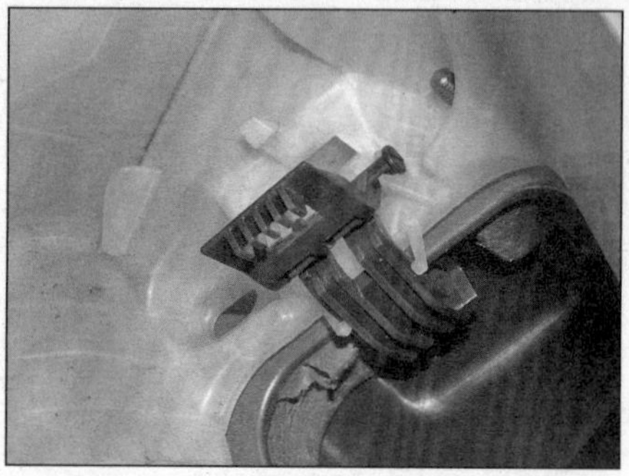

9.22 Release the clips securing the pollen filter housing

15 Place cloth rags beneath the matrix, then using an Allen key, release the clamps, and pull the two pipes from the heater matrix **(see illustration)**. Be prepared for fluid spillage.

16 Carefully slide the heater matrix from the housing **(see illustration)**.

Refitting

17 Refitting is a reversal of removal, but note the following points:

a) Renew the coolant pipe-to-matrix O-ring seals.

b) Fill the cooling system with reference to Chapter 1A, Section 27 or Chapter 1B, Section 28.

Evaporator

Removal

18 Have the refrigerant evacuated by a Saab dealer or suitably-equipped specialist.

19 Fit hose clamps to the heater hoses at the bulkhead. Identify the hoses for position, then prise out the locking clips and disconnect them from the heater matrix **(see illustrations 9.10a, 9.10b and 9.10c)**. Plug the stubs to prevent coolant spilling onto the floor when the matrix is removed from inside the car. To remove most of the coolant from the matrix, blow through one of the pipes and the coolant will escape from the other.

Caution: Antifreeze is poisonous.

20 Remove the wiper arms as described in Chapter 12, Section 11.

21 Remove the wiper motor as described in Chapter 12, Section 12.

22 Lift out the pollen filter, then release the clips and remove the filter housing **(see illustration)**.

23 Unscrew the nut and disconnect the refrigerant hoses at the bulkhead. Plug or cover the openings to prevent contamination.

24 Undo the 2 Allen screws, remove the expansion valve and nuts plate, then pull the rubber grommet from the A/C pipe aperture at the bulkhead, release the clips and slide up the plastic pipe guide **(see illustrations)**.

25 Remove the heater blower motor as described earlier in this Section, then undo the retaining bolt, and unclip the upper half of the heater blower motor housing from the side of the heater housing **(see illustration)**. Unclip the wiring harness as the housing is removed.

26 Undo the 8 screws, and remove the evaporator cover **(see illustration)**.

27 Carefully pull the evaporator from the housing **(see illustration)**.

Refitting

28 Refitting is a reversal of removal, but have the air conditioning system recharged

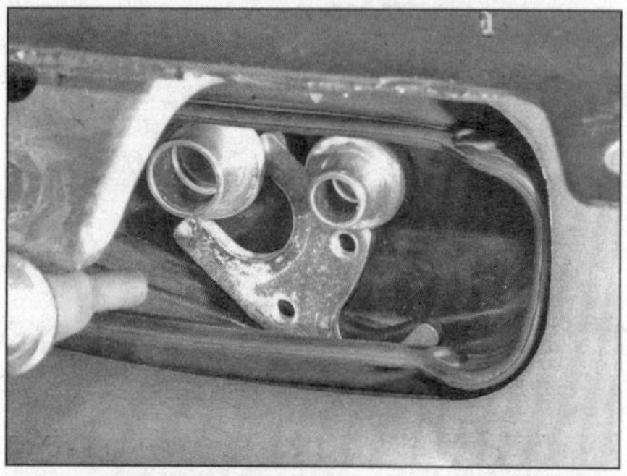

9.24a With the expansion valve removed, manoeuvre the nut plate from behind the pipe flanges ...

9.24b ... then pull the rubber grommet from the bulkhead ...

9.24c ... depress the clips (arrowed) ...

9.24d ... and slide the plastic pipe guide upwards and remove it

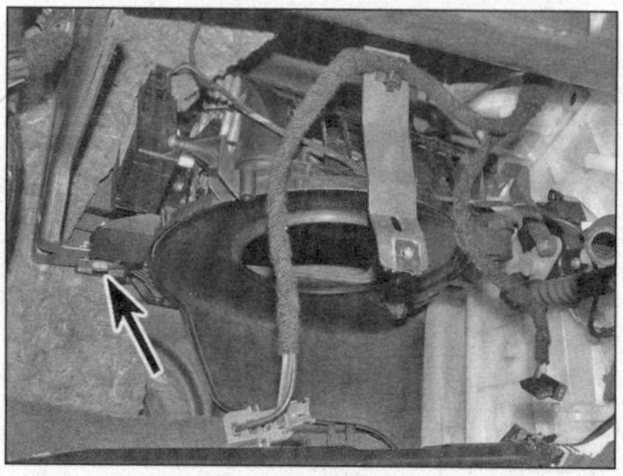

9.25 Heater blower motor upper housing retaining bolt (arrowed)

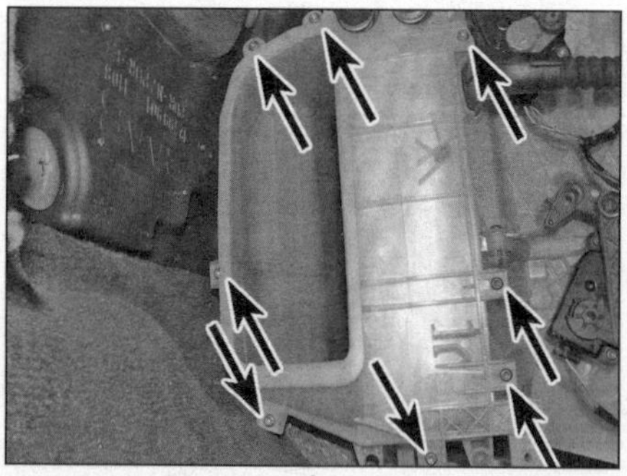

9.26 Undo the Torx screws (arrowed), remove the evaporator cover ...

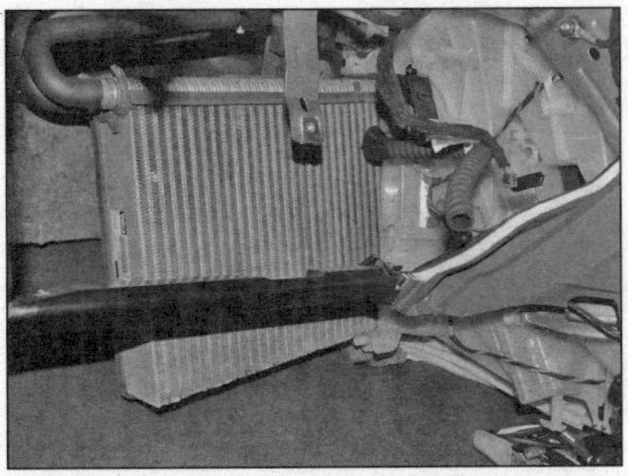

9.27 ... and pull the evaporator from the housing

9.28 Renew the O-ring seals on the air conditioning pipes

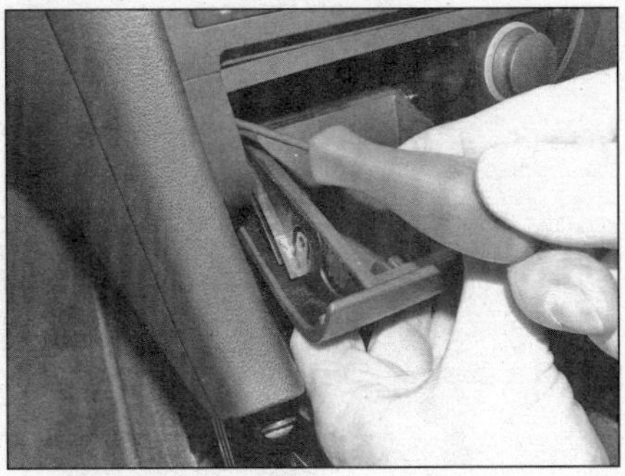

9.29a Release the compartment ...

9.29b ... and disconnect the wiring plug

9.30a Lift slightly and ...

9.30b ... pull the panel forward to release it

by a suitably-equipped specialist. Renew the air conditioning pipes sealing washers **(see illustration)**.

Control panel

Note: *If a new control unit is to be fitted, access to Saab's TECH2 diagnostic equipment is necessary to save various stored values, which will need to be transferred to the new unit. If necessary, entrust this task to a Saab dealer or suitably-equipped specialist.*

Removal

29 Using a small screwdriver release the storage compartment from below the control panel **(see illustrations)**.

30 Lift up slightly and pull the control unit from the facia **(see illustrations)**.

Caution: The control unit is extremely sensitive to static electricity. Earth yourself prior to disconnecting the wiring plugs by touching a metal part of the vehicle body.

31 Release the catch and disconnect the control unit wiring plugs **(see illustration)**. Do not touch the control unit terminal pins with bare fingers.

Refitting

32 Refitting is a reversal of removal. Note that if a new control unit has been fitted, the previously-stored values will need to be transferred using Saab's TECH2 diagnostic equipment.

Solar sensor

Removal

33 Using a blunt, flat-bladed tool, carefully prise the speaker grille from the centre of the facia **(see illustration)**.

34 Disconnect the wiring plug and release the LED anti-theft warning light **(see illustration)**.

35 Unclip the sensor from the speaker grille.

Refitting

36 Refitting is a reversal of removal.

Interior temperature sensor

Removal

37 Carefully prise off the rear section of the interior light console, followed by the centre and front sections.

38 Release the retaining clips and lift the sensor from the console. Disconnect the wiring plug as the sensor is withdrawn.

Refitting

39 Refitting is a reversal of removal.

Left-hand mixed air stepping motor

Removal

40 Remove the passenger's glovebox as described in Chapter 11, Section 29.

41 Remove the passenger's side centre console forward side panel, by removing the fastener, and sliding the panel downwards and rearwards **(see illustrations 9.3a and 9.3b)**.

9.31 Disconnect the wiring plugs

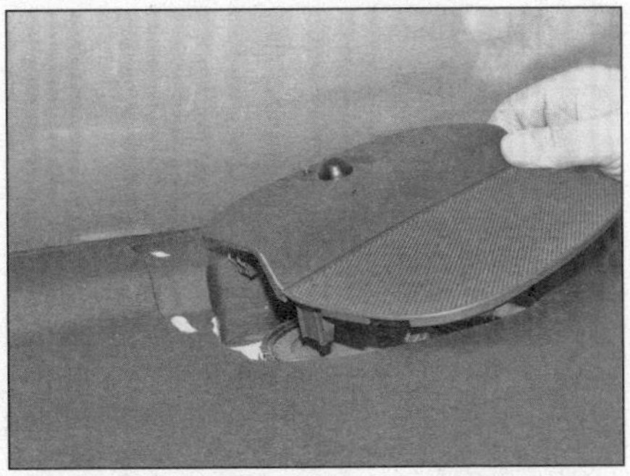

9.33 Prise up the centre speaker grille

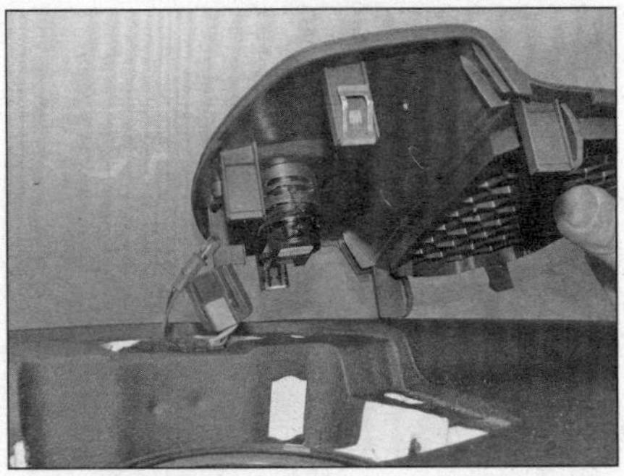

9.34 Release the LED and wiring plug

9.44 Left-hand mixed air stepping motor

42 Undo the 2 retaining screws and remove the lower facia panel on the passenger's side **(see illustration 9.4)**. Disconnect the any wiring plugs as the panel is withdrawn.
43 Remove the floor vent air duct through the glovebox aperture.
44 The left-hand mixed air stepping motor is the lower of the two motors. Disconnect the wiring plug, then undo the 2 screws and remove the motor. Disengage the motor lever from the flap link arm as the motor is withdrawn **(see illustration)**.

Refitting

45 Refitting is a reversal of removal, ensuring the lever arm engages correctly with the flap link arm.

Right-hand mixed air stepping motor

Removal

46 Remove the driver's side lower facia panel as described in Chapter 11, Section 26.
47 Remove the floor vent duct.
48 The right-hand mixed air stepping motor is the lower of the 3 motors. Undo the retaining screws, disconnect the wiring plug and remove the motor **(see illustration)**.

Refitting

49 Refitting is a reversal of removal.

Defrost air distribution flap stepping motor

Removal

50 Remove the passenger's side lower facia panel as described in Chapter 11, Section 26.

9.56 Floor distribution flap stepping motor

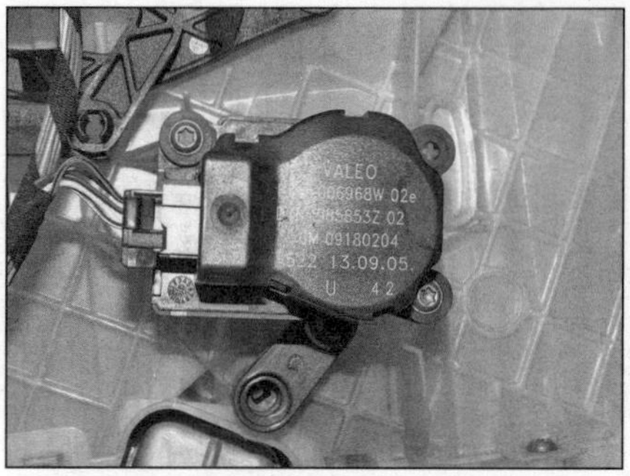

9.48 Right-hand mixed air stepping motor

51 Remove the floor vent air duct.
52 The defrost flap motor is the upper of the two motors. Undo the 2 retaining screws, lift out the motor and rotate it slightly to disengage the link arm **(see illustration)**. Disconnect the wiring plug as the motor is withdrawn.

Refitting

53 Refitting is a reversal of removal.

Floor air distribution flap stepping motor

Removal

54 Remove the driver's side lower facia panel as described in Chapter 11, Section 26.
55 Remove the floor vent air duct.
56 The floor air distribution flap stepping motor is the middle of the 3 motors. Undo the 2 screws and remove the motor **(see illustration)**. Disconnect the wiring plug as the motor is withdrawn.

Refitting

57 Refitting is a reversal of removal.

Air recirculation flap stepping motor

Removal

58 Remove the passenger's glovebox as described in Chapter 11, Section 29.
59 The motor is located on the end of the blower motor housing. Undo the retaining screws and remove the stepping motor. Disconnect the wiring plug as the motor is withdrawn **(see illustration)**.

9.59 Air recirculation flap stepping motor (arrowed)

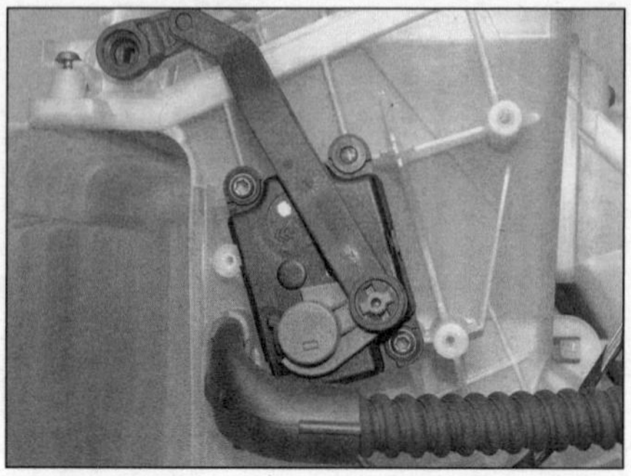

9.52 Defrost air distribution flap stepping motor

Refitting

60 Refitting is a reversal of removal, ensuring the motor lever engages correctly with the flap lever.

Expansion valve

Removal

61 Have the refrigerant circuit evacuated by a suitably-equipped specialist.
62 Remove the windscreen wiper motor as described in Chapter 12, Section 12.
63 Remove the pollen filter as described in Chapter 1A, Section 18 or Chapter 1B, Section 18, then release the clips and remove the housing **(see illustration 9.22)**.
64 Undo the nut and disconnect the air conditioning pipes at the bulkhead. Plug the openings to prevent contamination.
65 Undo the 2 retaining screws and remove the expansion valve. Plug the openings to prevent contamination.

Refitting

66 Refitting is a reversal of removal, noting the following points:
a) Renew the pipe connection's sealing washers.
b) Tighten the fasteners to the specified torque where given.
c) Have the refrigerant recharged by a suitably-equipped specialist.

Condenser

Removal

67 Have the refrigerant circuit evacuated by a suitably-equipped specialist.
68 Raise the front of the vehicle and support it securely on axle stands (see *Jacking and vehicle support*).
69 Remove the front bumper cover and the undershield from below the bumper – as described in Chapter 11, Section 6.
70 On diesel models remove the lower side cover **(see illustration)**. On petrol models remove the support bracket from the power steering cooler pipe.
71 Remove the right-hand headlight (as described in Chapter 11, Section 6) and then remove the air intake pipe **(see illustration)**
72 Remove the mounting screws from the receiver/drier.

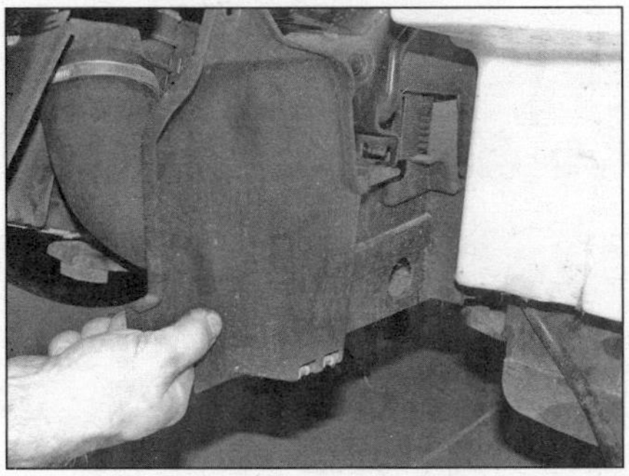

9.70 Remove the cover

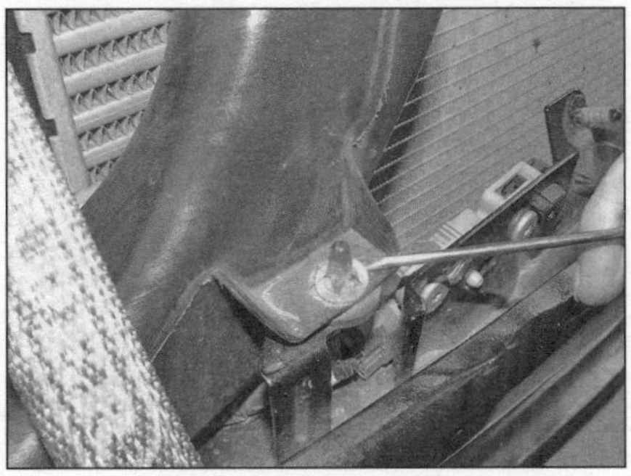

9.71 Prise free the crimp washer

9.74 Remove the mounting screws

73 Remove the upper and lower pipe connections from the condenser. Leave the pipes in position for the moment.

74 Remove the upper mounting screws **(see illustration)**

75 Pull the condenser free from the lower mounting brackets and gently ease the A/C pipes from the condenser as the condenser is lowered from the vehicle. Immediately plug the openings in the condenser and the A/C pipes.

Refitting

76 Refitting is a reversal of removal, noting the following points:

a) Renew the pipe connection's O-ring seals.

b) Tighten the fasteners to the specified torque where given.

c) Have the refrigerant recharged by a suitably-equipped specialist.

Compressor

Removal

77 Have the refrigerant circuit evacuated by a suitably-equipped specialist.

78 Raise the front of the vehicle and support it securely on axle stands (see *Jacking and vehicle support*). Undo the fasteners and remove the undershield beneath the radiator, and the one below the engine.

79 On Convertible models, undo the bolts and remove the front chassis reinforcement.

80 Remove the auxiliary drivebelt as described in Chapter 1A, Section 26 or Chapter 1B, Section 27.

81 On petrol models, undo the screws/clamps and remove the charge air pipe attached to the engine sump.

82 Disconnect the compressor wiring plug.

83 Undo the fastener and disconnect the refrigerant pipes from the compressor. Plug the openings to prevent contamination.

84 Undo the retaining bolts and remove the compressor **(see illustration)**.

85 If required, undo the nut and pull the drive pulley and clutch from the compressor **(see illustrations)**. When refitting the pulley/cover, measure the clearance between the cover and the pulley – the correct specification is 0.5 ± 0.15 mm. If necessary, adjust the clearance by adding or removing shims behind the cover.

Refitting

86 Refitting is a reversal of removal, noting the following points:

a) Renew the refrigerant pipe connection seals.

b) Tighten all fasteners to the specified torque where given.

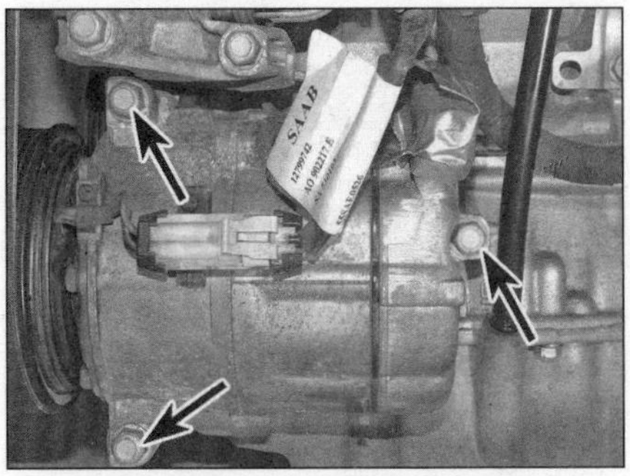

9.84 Compressor mounting bolts (arrowed)

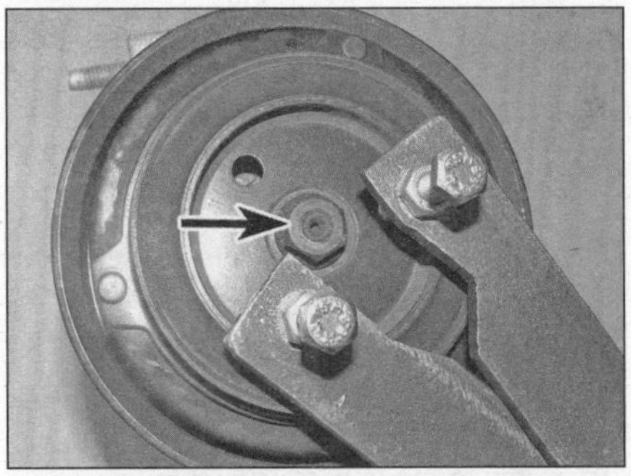

9.85a We used a homemade tool to hold the cover whilst slackening the nut (arrowed)

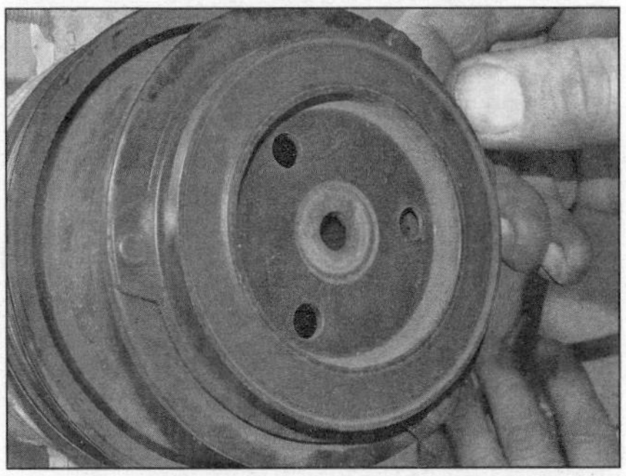

9.85b Remove the cover ...

9.85c ... and recover the shims behind it

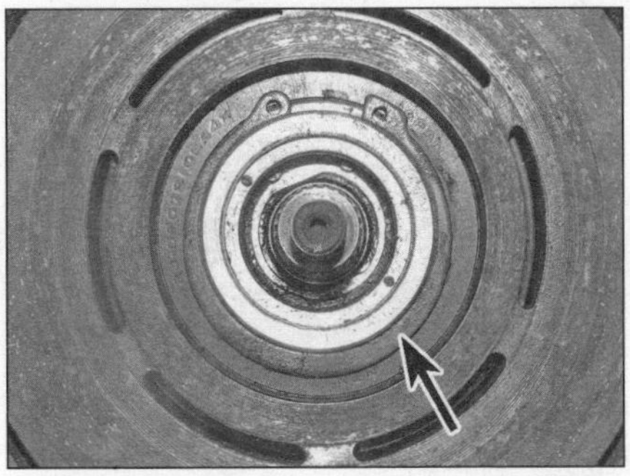

9.85d Remove the circlip (arrowed), and pull off the friction disc/pulley and bearing

9.85e The bearing is crimped into the pulley

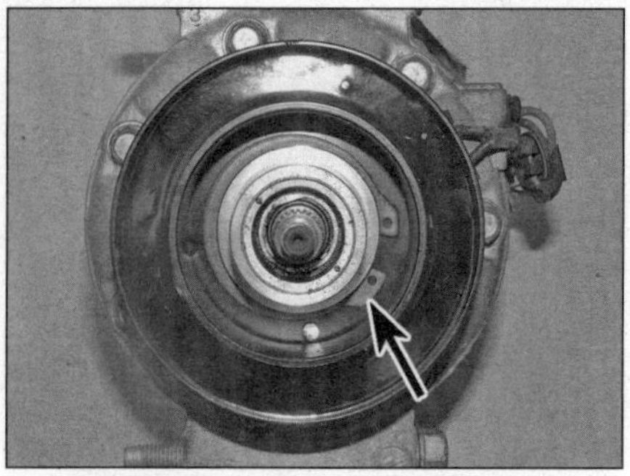

9.85f Remove the circlip (arrowed) and pull away the electromagnetic clutch

c) If the oil has drained from the compressor it should be filled with 70ml of the correct oil.
*d) New compressors are supplied filled with 135ml of oil – this is the maximum capacity of the entire system, so if only the compressor is renewed, drain off 70ml of oil (**Note:** Evacuating the system will have removed approximately 15ml).*
e) Have the refrigerant circuit recharged by a suitably-equipped specialist.

Receiver/drier – petrol models

Removal

87 Have the refrigerant circuit evacuated by a suitably-equipped specialist.
88 Raise the front of the vehicle and support it securely on axle stands (see *Jacking and vehicle support*). Undo the fasteners and remove the undershield beneath the radiator, and the one below the engine.
89 Remove the plastic cover on the top of the engine.
90 Undo the bolt and disconnect the refrigerant pipes from the receiver/drier located at the right-hand side of the intercooler. Plug the openings to prevent contamination.
91 Disconnect the turbocharger pipe from the intercooler, and move the pipe to one side.
92 Undo the retaining bolt and remove the right-hand radiator lower mounting **(see illustration 3.15)**.
93 Undo the screws and remove the receiver/drier **(see illustration)**.

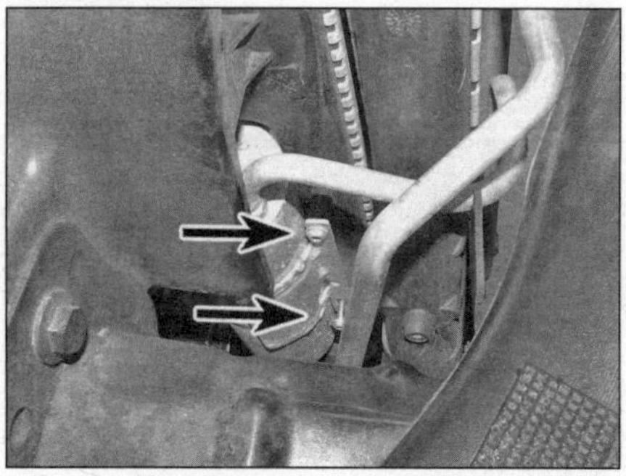

9.102 Remove the screws (arrowed)

9.93 Receiver/drier Torx mounting screws (arrowed)

Refitting

94 Refitting is a reversal of removal, noting the following points:
a) Renew the refrigerant pipe connection O-ring seal.
b) Tighten all fasteners to the specified torque where given.
c) Have the refrigerant circuit recharged by a suitably-equipped specialist.

Receiver/drier – diesel models

Removal – Z19DTR

95 Have the refrigerant circuit evacuated by a suitably-equipped specialist.
96 Raise the front of the vehicle and support it securely on axle stands (see *Jacking and vehicle support*). Undo the fasteners and remove the undershield beneath the radiator, and the one below the engine. Remove the plastic cover on the top of the engine.
97 With reference to Chapter 11, Section 6 remove the front bumper cover and then remove the right-hand headlight as described in Chapter 12, Section 6.
98 Disconnect the wiring plug from the airflow sensor and then remove the hose from the turbocharger intake **(see illustration)**.
99 Undo the bolt and disconnect the refrigerant pipe from the receiver/drier. Plug the opening to prevent contamination.
100 Working underneath the vehicle, remove upper and lower connector pipes from the condenser.
101 Remove the lower protective cover and (where fitted) remove the mounting bolt from the upper condenser pipe.

9.106 Turbocharger pipe mounting bolt (arrowed)

9.98 Remove the hose

102 Undo the 2 screws and lower the receiver/drier from place **(see illustration)**.

Removal – Z19DT and Z19DTH

103 Have the refrigerant circuit evacuated by a suitably-equipped specialist.
104 Raise the front of the vehicle and support it securely on axle stands (see *Jacking and vehicle support*).
105 Undo the fasteners and remove the undershield beneath the radiator, and the one below the engine.
106 Remove the turbocharger upper hose **(see illustration)**.
107 Unbolt and remove the A/C pipes from the receiver/drier.
108 Remove the intercooler hose **(see illustration)**.
109 Unbolt and then remove the receiver/drier.

Refitting

110 Refitting is a reversal of removal, noting the following points:
a) Renew the refrigerant pipe connection O-ring seal.
b) Tighten all fasteners to the specified torque where given.
c) Have the refrigerant circuit recharged by a suitably-equipped specialist.

10 Auxiliary heating system – general description

1 On some diesel models, an optional

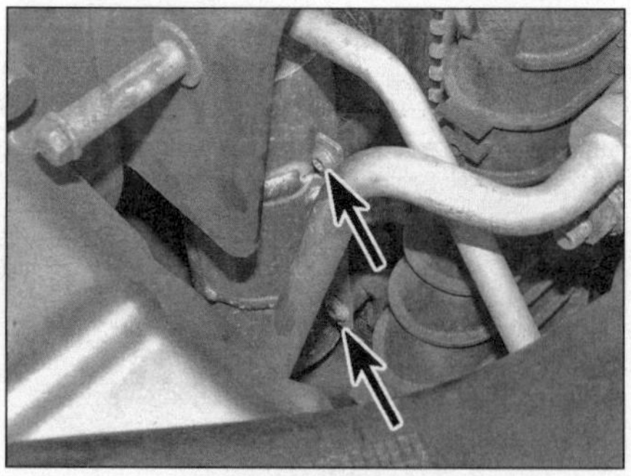

9.108 Receiver/drier mounting Torx screws (arrowed)

auxiliary heating system may be fitted which uses fuel from the fuel tank. The heater unit is mounted on the right-hand side of the bulkhead at the rear of the engine compartment, and heats coolant from the engine, both to heat the interior of the vehicle and to increase the temperature of the engine for improved starting. The unit is functional without the engine being started, although it may be activated when the engine is running to allow the engine to quickly reach normal operating temperature.

2 The auxiliary heater uses fuel from the fuel tank to provide a flame inside the heater unit which heats the coolant from the engine. A glow plug is used to ignite the fuel. Air for the heater is drawn through an intake pipe beneath the unit, and the exhaust gases are taken through an exhaust pipe beneath the vehicle floor.

3 The main components of the system are as follows:

a) Integrated control module.
b) Blower fan.
c) Glow plug.
d) Flame detector.
e) Temperature sensor.
f) Overheating protection circuit.
g) Relay.
h) Fuel pump, located in front of the fuel tank beneath the rear of the vehicle.

4 The system is controlled by a module which monitors outside temperature and engine coolant temperature. The heater will only start if the coolant temperature is below a nominal 80°C, and there is a minimum of 10 litres in the fuel tank. The heater operates at two levels: 2400 W and 5000 W, which are automatically selected by the module; the two outputs are achieved by different blower speeds.

5 Heater and control module faults are recorded and can be accessed using suitable diagnostic equipment.

Chapter 4 Part A:
Fuel and exhaust systems – petrol engine

Contents

Degrees of difficulty

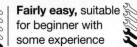

Easy, suitable for novice with little experience	**Fairly easy,** suitable for beginner with some experience	**Fairly difficult,** suitable for competent DIY mechanic	**Difficult,** suitable for experienced DIY mechanic	**Very difficult,** suitable for expert DIY or professional

Specifications

System type

All models	Saab Trionic T8 engine management system, sequential multipoint injection, with turbocharger and intercooler

Fuel pressure regulator

Opening fuel pressure	3.0 ± 0.1 bar

Fuel pump

Fuel pump capacity	700 ml per 30 secs at 3.0 bar

Charge air control valve

Resistance at 20°C	23 ohms

Fuel level sensor

Resistance:	
1.0 litre	249 ohms
8.0 litres	220 ohms
16.0 litres	178 ohms
24.0 litres	150 ohms
30.0 litres	126 ohms
40.0 litres	98 ohms
48.0 litres	70 ohms
56.0 litres	42 ohms
58.0 litres	40 ohms

Recommended fuel

All models	95 RON unleaded

Idle speed

All models	720 rpm, controlled by ECM (not adjustable)

Exhaust gas CO content

All models	Controlled by ECM (not adjustable)

Manifold absolute pressure (MAP) sensor

Supply voltage	5 volts
Pressure:	
-0.75 bar	0.5 volts
-0.50 bar	1.0 volts
-0.25 bar	1.5 volts
0 bar	2.0 volts
0.25 bar	2.5 volts
0.50 bar	3.0 volts
0.75 bar	3.5 volts
1.00 bar	4.0 volts

Atmospheric pressure sensor

Pressure:	
40 kPa	0.3 volts
60 kPa	1.6 volts
80 kPa	2.8 volts
100 kPa	4.1 volts
110 kPa	4.7 volts

Throttle body actuator

Resistance (pin 6 to 5)	1.13 ± 0.1 ohms
Control voltage	12 volts 600 Hz
Sensor 1 (pin 1 to 7):	
Throttle closed	0.065 to 1.09 volts
Fully open	3.93 to 4.775 volts
Sensor 2 (pin 4 to 2):	
Throttle closed	3.91 to 4.935 volts
Fully open	0.025 to 1.07 volts

Intake air temperature (IAC) sensor

Supply voltage	5 volts
Temperature:	
-30°C	4.74 volts
-10°C	4.33 volts
0°C	4.00 volts
20°C	3.13 volts
40°C	2.18 volts
60°C	1.39 volts
80°C	0.86 volts
90°C	0.67 volts

Crankshaft position sensor

Resistance (pins 1 and 2) at 20°C	860 ± 70 ohms
Sensor disc gap	0.4 to 1.4 mm

Fuel Injectors

Type:	
B207E and B207L	Siemens, blue, 2-hole
B207R	Siemens, green, 2-hole
Resistance at 20°C	12.0 ohms
Flow rating (at 3 bar fuel pressure):	
B207E and B207L	134 ± 5 ml/30 seconds
B207R	176 ± 7 ml/30 seconds
Maximum flow difference between injectors:	
B207E and B207L	10 ml
B207R	14 ml

Turbocharger

Type:	
B207E and B207L	Garrett GT2052s
Pressure	0.40 ± 0.03 bar
B207R	MHI TD04L-14T
Pressure	0.45 ± 0.03 bar
Wastegate preload (all types)	1.5 mm
Turbo shaft play (axial)	0.036 to 0.091 mm

Torque wrench settings

	Nm	lbf ft
Catalytic converter:		
Bolts	22	16
Nuts	25	18
Chassis reinforcement bolts (Convertible only)	50	37
Coolant temperature sensor	15	11
Exhaust manifold-to-cylinder head nuts*	24	18
Fuel rail bolts	10	7
Intake manifold	10	7
Oxygen sensor	40	30
Throttle body	10	7
Turbocharger to exhaust manifold	24	18
Turbocharger oil return pipe to turbo	15	11
Turbocharger oil supply pipe banjo bolt	28	21
Turbocharger oil supply pipe to cylinder block	28	21

** Do not re-use*

1 General information and precautions

The fuel supply system consists of a fuel tank mounted under the rear of the car (with an electric fuel pump immersed in it), a fuel filter, and the fuel feed and return lines. The fuel pump supplies fuel to the fuel rail, which acts as a reservoir for the four fuel injectors which inject fuel into the intake tracts. A fuel filter is incorporated in the feed line from the pump to the fuel rail to ensure that the fuel supplied to the injectors is clean. The filter is mounted adjacent to the fuel tank.

The engine management system is Saab Trionic type, incorporating sequential fuel injection and a separate ignition coil for each spark plug.

A cruise control system is fitted as standard equipment on most of the Saab models.

The turbocharger fitted is of a water-cooled type. Boost pressure is controlled by the Saab Trionic engine management.

Warning: Many of the procedures in this Chapter require the disconnection of fuel lines, which may result in some fuel spillage. Before carrying out any operation on the fuel system, refer to Section 5. See the precautions given in 'Safety first!' at the front of this manual and follow them implicitly. Petrol is a highly-dangerous and volatile liquid, and the precautions necessary when handling it cannot be overstressed.

2 Air cleaner assembly – removal and refitting

Removal

1 Disconnect the mass airflow meter wiring plug **(see illustration)**.

2 Slacken the clamp and disconnect the hose from the air filter cover.

3 Pull up the left-hand rear corner of the housing, then move the assembly to the left, and manoeuvre it from the engine compartment **(see illustration)**.

Refitting

4 Refitting is a reversal of removal.

3 Accelerator pedal – removal and refitting

Removal

1 Remove the driver's side lower facia panel as described in Chapter 11, Section 26.

2 Working in the driver's footwell, prise out the red locking catch and disconnect the accelerator pedal position sensor wiring plug.

3 Undo the 3 retaining nuts and remove the pedal assembly **(see illustration)**. Note that the position sensor is integral with the pedal assembly. No further dismantling is recommended.

Refitting

4 Refitting is a reversal of removal.

4 Engine management system – general information

The Saab Trionic T8 engine management system controls three functions of the engine from a single electronic control module (ECM). The three functions comprise the fuel injection system, ignition system, and the turbocharger boost control system. Details of the components related to the ignition function are given in Chapter 5B, Section 1.

The system is microprocessor-controlled, and the fuel system provides the correct amount of fuel necessary for complete combustion under all engine conditions. Data from various sensors is processed in the ECM, in order to determine the opening period of the fuel injectors for the exact amount of fuel to be injected into the intake manifold.

The system is of sequential type, where fuel is injected in sequence with the engine's firing order. Conventional sequential fuel injection systems requires a camshaft sensor, which works in conjunction with the crankshaft position sensor to indicate which cylinder at TDC is on its compression stroke and which is

2.1 Slide out the locking catch and disconnect the mass airflow sensor wiring plug

2.3 Pull the air filter assembly from the rubber mountings

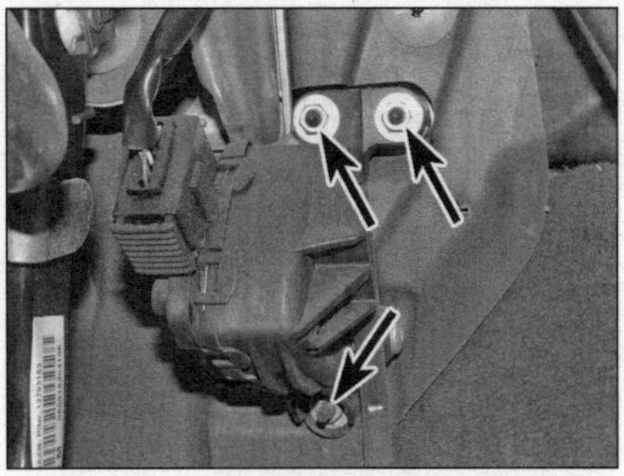

3.3 Accelerator pedal assembly retaining nuts (arrowed)

5.2 Undo the 3 Torx screws and remove the plastic cover (arrowed)

on its exhaust stroke. The Trionic system has no camshaft sensor, it determines each cylinder's stroke by applying a small direct current voltage across each spark plug. When a cylinder on its combustion stroke approaches TDC, this voltage causes an ionisation current to flow across the terminals of the spark plug, thus indicating which cylinder requires fuel injection and ignition next. Sequential control of the ignition timing to control combustion knock is achieved in the same manner (see Chapter 5B, Section 1).

When the ignition is initially switched on and after the fuel pump is operating, all the injectors operate simultaneously for a short period; this helps to minimise cold start cranking times.

The main components of the system are as follows:

ECM

• The electronic control module controls the entire operation of the fuel injection system, ignition system, cruise control and turbocharger boost control system.

Crankshaft position sensor

• The crankshaft position sensor provides a datum for the ECM to calculate the position of the crankshaft in relation to TDC. The sensor is triggered by a reluctor disc that rotates inside the crankcase.

Intake pressure/temperature sensor

• This sensor informs the ECM of the pressure and temperature of the intake air.

Manifold absolute pressure sensor

• The air pressure sensor informs the ECM of the pressure of the air in the hose between the intercooler and the throttle body.

5.3 Unscrew the plastic cap ...

Engine coolant temperature sensor

• The engine coolant temperature sensor informs the ECM of the engine temperature.

Mass airflow sensor

• Located on the right-hand front suspension turret. The engine load is measured by means of a hot-film type air mass flow meter. The meter houses a heated metal filament which is mounted in the flow of the air intake. The temperature reduction in the wire caused by the flow of air over it causes a change in electrical resistance, which is converted to a variable voltage output signal. Measuring air mass flow, rather than volume flow, compensates for the changes in air density encountered when driving on roads at different altitudes above sea level.

Accelerator pedal position sensor

• This sensor informs the ECM of the torque request from the driver.

Charge air (boost) control valve

• The boost pressure control valve (also referred to as the solenoid valve) is located on a bracket at the front of the cylinder head. It controls the operation of the turbocharger. Under certain conditions (eg, in 1st gear), boost pressure is reduced.

Fuel pressure regulator

• The regulator is connected to the end of the fuel rail on the intake manifold and regulates the fuel pressure to approximately 3.0 bars.

Fuel pump

• The fuel pump is housed in the fuel tank. The pump housing incorporates a separate feed pump which supplies the main fuel pump with pressurised fuel, free of air bubbles.

Injectors

• Each fuel injector consists of a solenoid-operated needle valve, which opens under the commands from the ECM. Fuel from the fuel rail is then delivered through the injector nozzle into the intake manifold.

Oxygen sensor

• The oxygen sensor provides the ECM with constant feedback on the oxygen content of the exhaust gases (see Chapter 4C, Section 1).

EVAP canister-purge valve

• The EVAP canister-purge valve is operated when the engine is started, to purge fuel accumulated in the canister. In order to allow the oxygen sensor to compensate for the additional fuel, the system is operated in short phases (see Chapter 4C, Section 1).

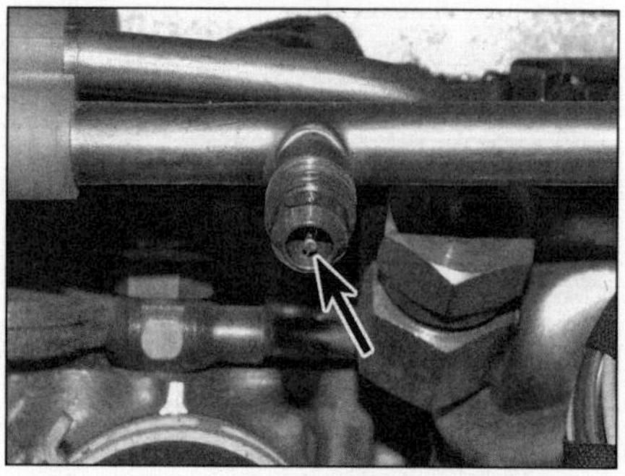

5.4 ... and depress the valve core to depressurise the fuel system

Ignition coils

• The ignition coils are fitted above each spark plug. Refer to Chapter 5B, Section 4 for further information.

Throttle body actuator

• No accelerator cable is fitted. Instead the throttle valve position is controlled by an electric motor, itself controlled by signals from the engine management ECM. The throttle body actuator also controls the idle speed.

'Check Engine' indicator

If the 'Check Engine' warning light comes on, the car should be taken to a Saab dealer or suitably-equipped specialist at the earliest opportunity. A flashing light indicates a potential catalytic converter damaging fault. The information panel in the instrument panel may also display: 'Reduced engine power. Contact service'. A complete test of the engine management system can then be carried out, using dedicated Saab diagnostic test equipment.

Saab have provided a further warning lamp (a spanner symbol) that will illuminate if a non emissions related fault is detected. Have the engine management system interrogated with Saab's TECH2 diagnostic equipment or other suitable diagnostic equipment at the earliest opportunity.

5 Fuel supply system – precautions and depressurisation

Note: *Refer to the Precautions at the end of Section 1 before proceeding.*

Warning: The following procedure will merely relieve the pressure in the fuel system – remember that fuel will still be present in the system components, and to take precautions accordingly before disconnecting any of them.

1 The fuel system referred to in this Section is defined as the tank-mounted fuel pump, the fuel filter, the fuel injectors, the fuel rail and the pressure regulator, and the metal pipes and flexible hoses connected between these components. All these contain fuel, which will be under pressure while the engine is running and/or while the ignition is switched on.

Warning: Residual fuel pressure may remain for some time after the ignition has been switched off, and must be relieved before any of these components are disturbed for servicing work.

2 Undo the 3 Torx screws and remove the plastic cover from the front, top of the engine **(see illustration)**.

3 Undo the plastic cap from the valve on the fuel supply pipe **(see illustration)**.

4 Hold a rag around the valve, then use a screwdriver to depress the valve core **(see illustration)**. Be prepared for fuel spillage.

6 Fuel pump – removal and refitting

Warning: Refer to the precautions given in Section 1, and the information detailed in the 'Safety first!' Section of this manual, before disturbing any component in the fuel supply system.

Note: *On all models, the fuel pump also incorporates the fuel level sensor.*

Removal

1 Remove the fuel tank (see Section 8).

2 Slide across the locking catch, depress the clip and disconnect the wiring plug from the cover **(see illustration)**.

3 Note their routing, then release the various fuel/breather pipes from the clips on the tank **(see illustration)**.

4 Make alignment marks between the maintenance cover and the tank, then carefully rotate the large retaining collar securing the cover to the tank anti-clockwise, then lift the cover **(see illustrations)**.

5 Lift the pump unit from the tank. Depress the release catch and disconnect the fuel hose from the pump at the quick-release coupling as the pump unit is lifted. Recover the sealing ring **(see illustrations)**.

Refitting

6 Fit a new seal to the fuel tank aperture, pressing it firmly into its recess.

7 Reconnect the fuel hose to the pump, and lower the pump into the tank. Ensure the locating lugs engage correctly **(see illustration)**.

8 Reconnect the pump wiring plug, and carefully refit the maintenance cover to the tank, ensuring the previously-made marks align.

9 With the cover correctly positioned, refit the retaining collar.

10 Reconnect the various fuel pipes and refit the fuel tank as described in Section 8.

7 Fuel level sensor – removal and refitting

1 Remove the fuel pump as described in the previous Section.

2 Depress the retaining clip and slide the sensor from the pump **(see illustration)**. Note that if the sensor is to be renewed, the sensor wires will need to be released from the connector on the underside of the pump cover.

3 Refitting is a reversal of removal.

6.2 Slide across the locking catch, depress the clip, and disconnect the wiring plug (arrowed)

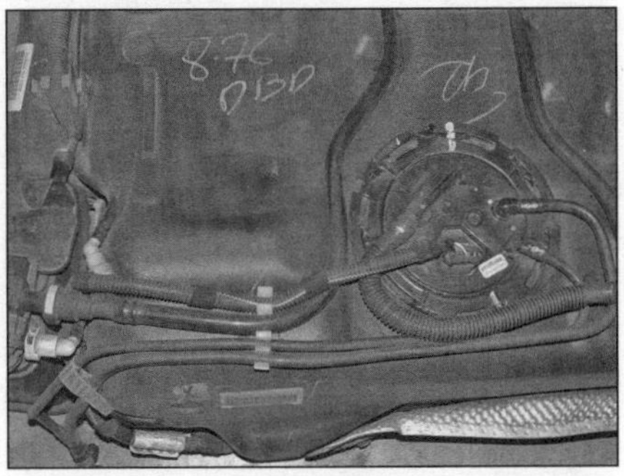

6.3 Release the hoses from the clips on the tank

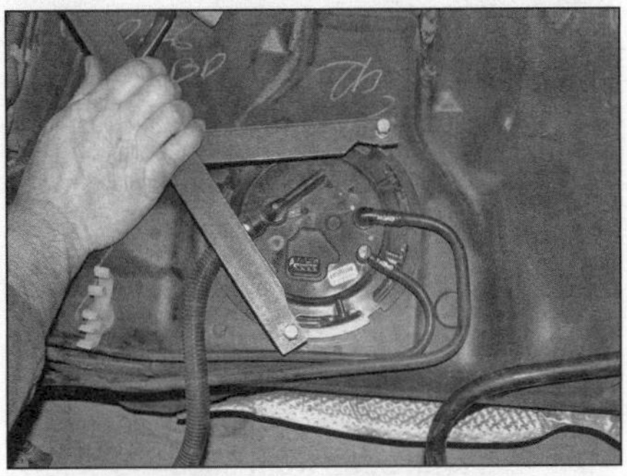

6.4a Rotate the collar anti-clockwise. We used a home-made tool fabricated from two lengths of steel bar with bolts at each end

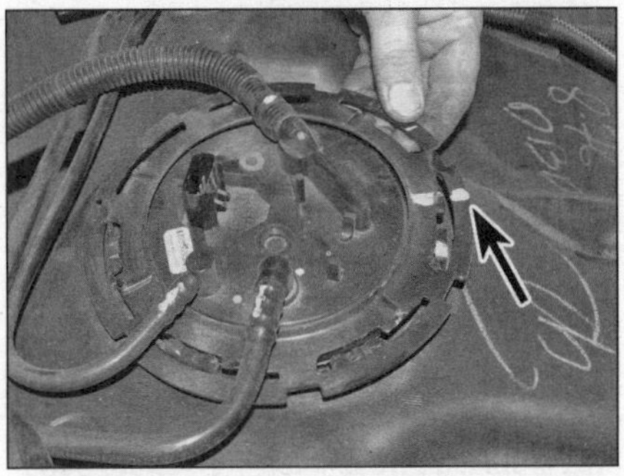

6.4b Note the alignment marks between the collar, cover, and tank (arrowed)

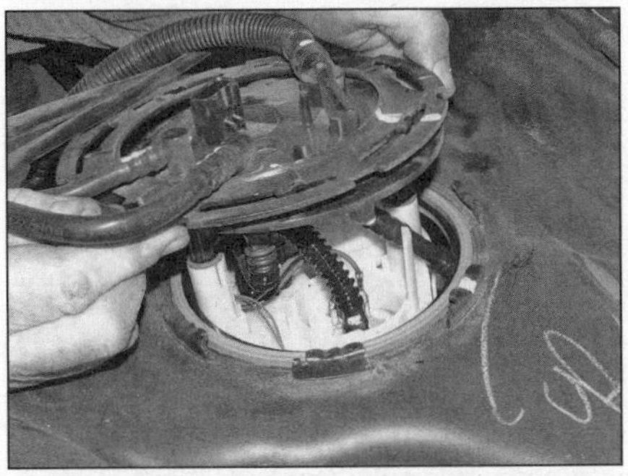

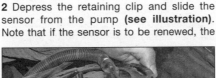

6.5a Lift the cover/pump assembly ...

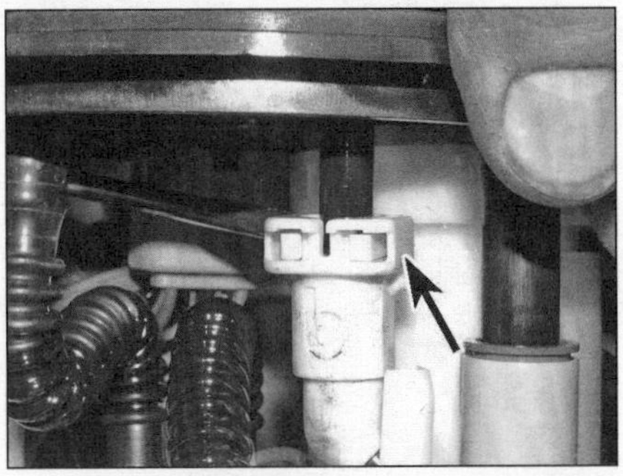

6.5b ... depress the release tab and disconnect the fuel hose (arrowed)

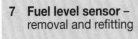

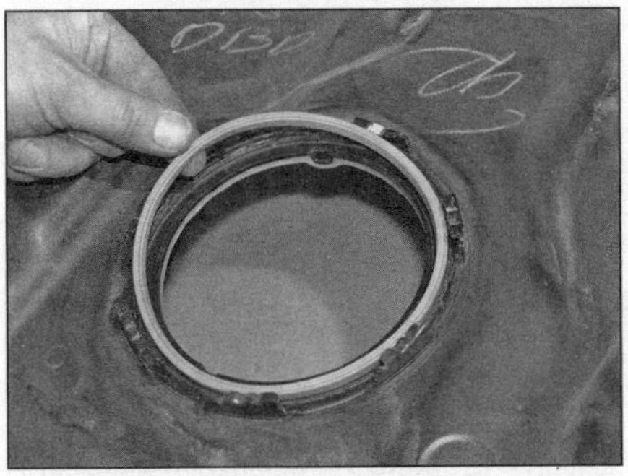

6.5c Recover the seal

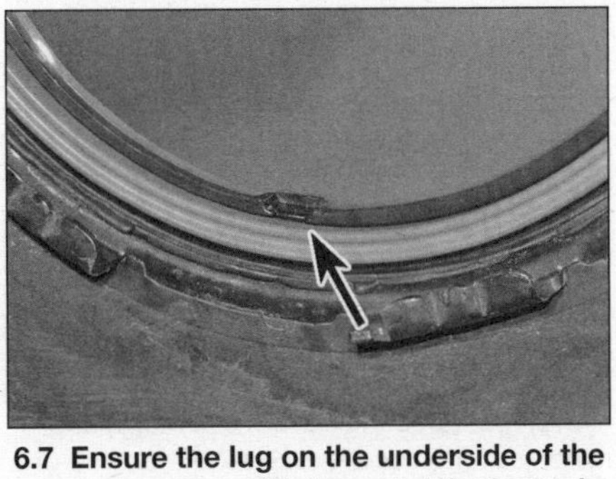

6.7 Ensure the lug on the underside of the cover engages with the notch in the tank rim (arrowed)

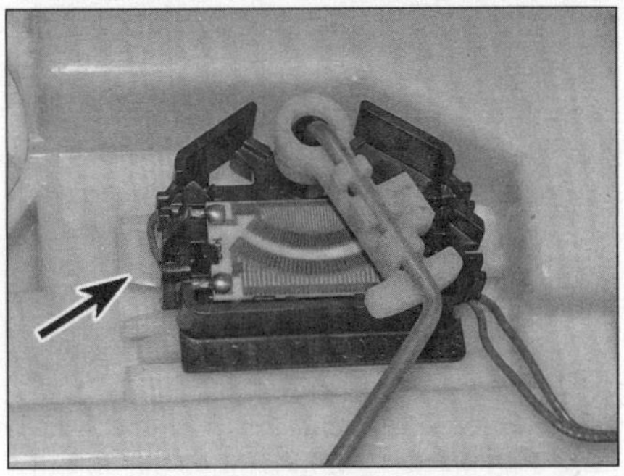

7.2 Depress the clip (arrowed) and slide the sensor from the pump

8.3 Slide out the red locking catch and disconnect the wiring plug in front of the tank

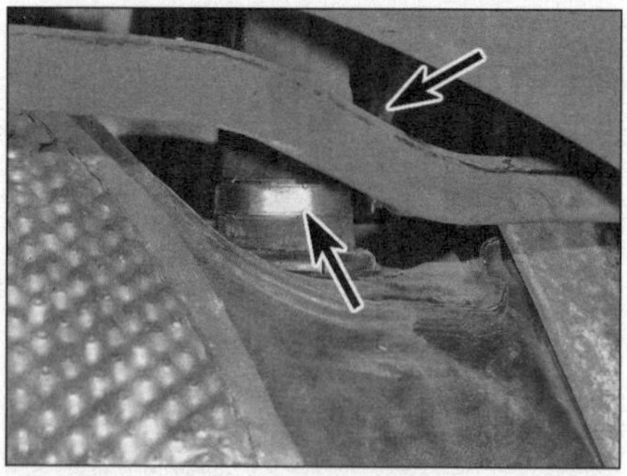

8.5 Fuel filler hose clamp (arrowed) – the breather hose coupling (arrowed) is above the anti-roll bar

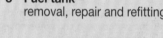

8 Fuel tank – removal, repair and refitting

Warning: Refer to the precautions given in Section 1, and the information detailed in the 'Safety first!' Section of this manual, before disturbing any component in the fuel supply system.

1 Before removing the fuel tank, it is preferable that all the fuel is first siphoned from the tank. Since a fuel tank drain plug is not provided, carry out the removal operation when the tank is almost empty.

Removal

2 Remove the complete exhaust system as described in Section 16.

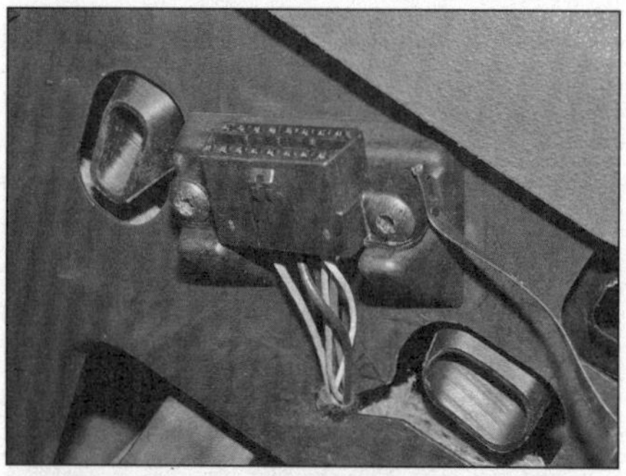

9.2 Pull off the cap to expose the 16-pin diagnostic connector under the driver's side of the facia

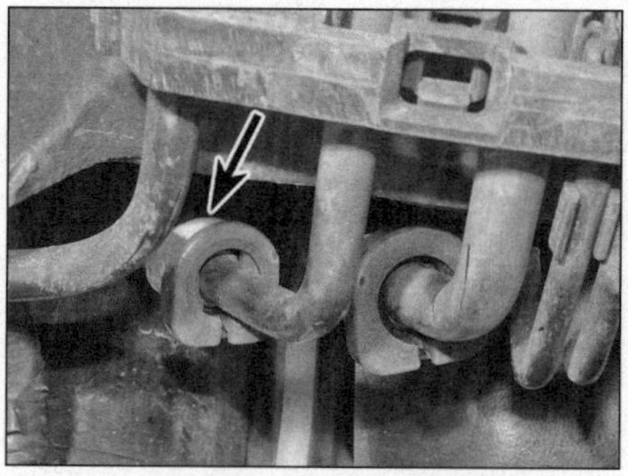

8.4a Depress the tab (arrowed) ...

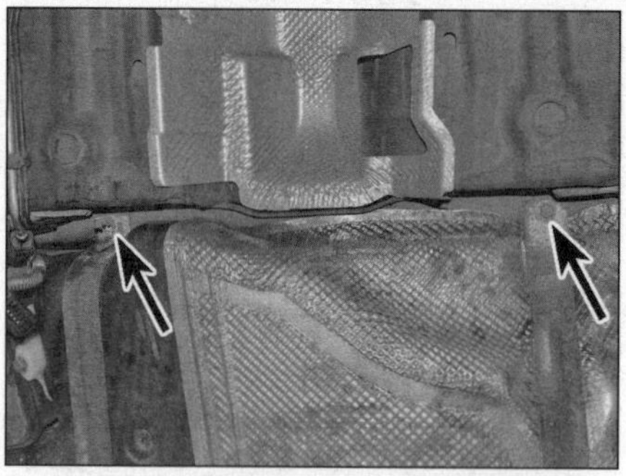

8.7 Fuel tank strap front securing bolts (arrowed)

3 Disconnect the fuel tank pump/level sensor wiring plug, and release it from the mounting bracket **(see illustration)**.

4 Depress the release catch, and disconnect the fuel supply and return hoses adjacent on the right-hand side of the tank, at the quick-release couplings **(see illustrations)**. Where applicable, disconnect the carbon canister coupling. Be prepared for fuel spillage.

5 At the rear of the tank, release the clamp, disconnect the filler hose and move it to one side, then depress the release catch and disconnect the breather hose at the quick-release coupling **(see illustration)**.

6 Position a trolley jack centrally beneath the fuel tank, with a plank of wood placed on the jack head. Raise the jack until it just starts to take the weight of the fuel tank.

7 Progressively undo the bolts securing the fuel tank support straps to their respective mounting brackets **(see illustration)**.

8 Slowly lower the fuel tank, then, with the help of an assistant, lower the fuel tank to the ground and remove it from under the car.

Repair

9 If the tank is contaminated with sediment or water, remove the fuel pump and wash the tank out with clean fuel. In certain cases, it may be possible to have small leaks or minor damage repaired. Seek the advice of a suitable specialist before attempting to repair the fuel tank.

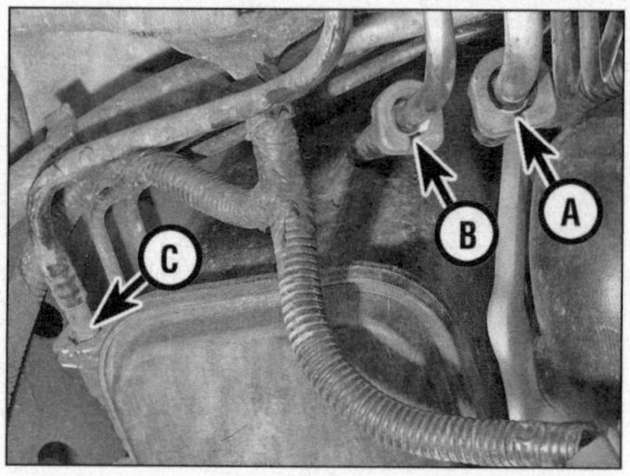

8.4b ... and disconnect the fuel supply (A), return (B) and the carbon canister hose (C)

Refitting

10 Refitting is a reversal of removal, noting the following points:

a) Inspect the O-rings at the fuel supply and return quick-release unions, adjacent to the fuel pump.

b) Ensure that all fuel lines and breather hoses are correctly routed and are not kinked or twisted.

c) Tighten the fuel tank support straps securely.

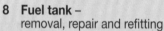

9 Engine management system – testing, checking and adjustment

1 If a fault appears to be present in the engine management system, first ensure that all the system wiring connectors are securely connected and free of corrosion. Then ensure that the fault is not due to poor maintenance – ie, check that the air cleaner filter element is clean, that the fuel filter has been renewed at the specified interval, and that the spark plugs and associated HT components are in good condition. Also check that the engine breather hoses are clear and undamaged. Finally, check that the cylinder compression pressures are correct, referring to Chapter 1A, 2A, and 5B for further information.

2 If these checks fail to reveal the cause of the problem, the car should be taken to a Saab dealer or suitably-equipped specialist for testing. A diagnostic connector is incorporated in the engine management system wiring harness, into which a suitable EOBD electronic diagnostic tester can be plugged. The tester will identify any faults detected by the engine management system ECM by interpreting fault codes stored in the ECM's memory. It also allows system sensors and actuators to be tested remotely without disconnecting them or removing them from the vehicle. This alleviates the need to test all the system components individually, using conventional test equipment. The diagnostic connector is located on the underside of the facia, on the driver's side of the vehicle **(see illustration)**.

3 Several low cost diagnostic tools are now available to the home mechanic, however it must be realised that these are generic tools that will only access mandatory EOBD codes.

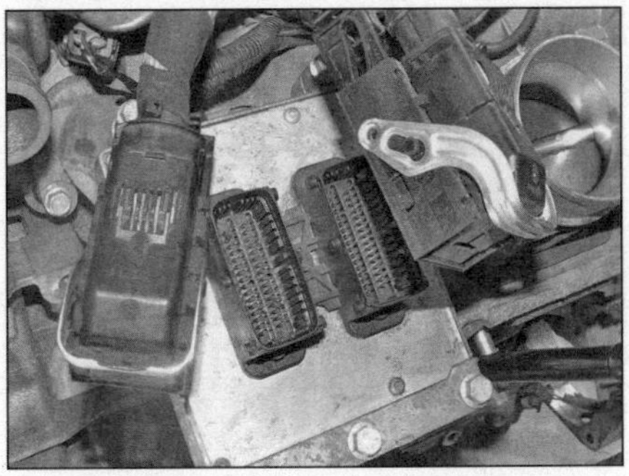

10.3 Lever over the catches and disconnect the ECM wiring plugs

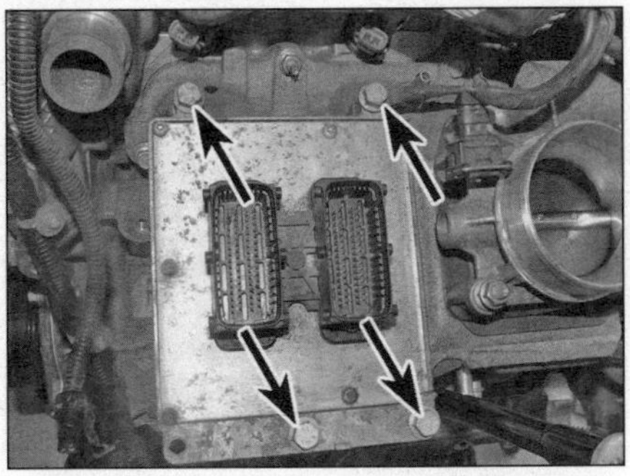

10.4 ECM retaining bolts (arrowed)

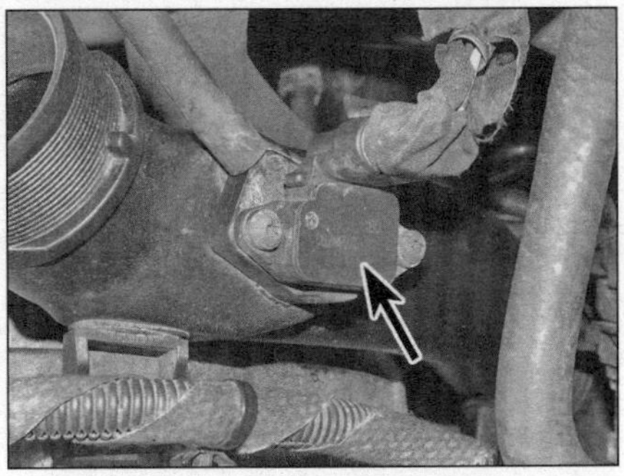

10.6 Intake air pressure/temperature sensor (arrowed)

These are emissions related fault codes only. The simple tools will display the fault code and provide a printed explanation of the meaning. The more expensive tools will display the fault code and its meaning. These tools may also give some limited access to other vehicle systems.

10 Engine management system components – removal and refitting

Warning: Refer to the precautions given in Section 1, and the information detailed in the 'Safety first!' Section of this manual, before disturbing any component in the fuel supply system.

Electronic Control Module (ECM)

Note: *If the ECM is to be renewed, various stored values must be extracted using Saab dedicated electronic diagnostic equipment, and reloaded once the new ECM is fitted. Entrust this task to a Saab dealer or suitably-equipped specialist.*

Caution: The ECM is extremely sensitive to static electricity. Earth yourself by touching a metal part of the vehicle body prior to starting work.

Removal

1 Ensure the ignition is turned off, and the steering lock engaged.

2 Remove the plastic cover from the top of the engine **(see illustration 5.2)**.

3 Release the catches, and carefully disconnect the wiring plugs from the ECM **(see illustration)**. Take care not to touch the terminal pins with bare fingers.

4 Undo the 4 retaining bolts and remove the ECM **(see illustration)**. Note the earth connection on one of the bolts.

Refitting

5 Refitting is a reversal of removal. Ensure that the wiring harness multiplug connectors are secured with the catches.

Intake air pressure/ temperature sensor

Removal

6 The sensor is located on the charge air pipe in the right-hand corner of the engine compartment. Disconnect the sensor wiring plug and vacuum pipe **(see illustration)**.

7 Undo the 2 retaining screws, remove the sensor, and recover the sealing washer.

Refitting

8 Refitting is a reversal of removal, but check and if necessary renew the sealing washer.

Throttle body/actuator

Removal

9 Ensure that the ignition switch is turned to the OFF position.

10 Remove the plastic cover from the top of the engine.

11 Release the clamp, disconnect the turbocharger delivery hose from the throttle body, and move it to one side **(see illustration)**.

12 Carefully bend up the bracket and detach the EVAP canister purge valve **(see illustration)**.

13 Disconnect the wiring plug from the throttle body.

14 Undo the 4 studs/bolts and remove the throttle body **(see illustration)**. Recover the O-ring seal.

Refitting

15 Refitting is a reversal of removal. Ensure that a new throttle body O-ring seal is fitted.

Manifold absolute pressure sensor

Removal

16 Remove the plastic cover from the top of the engine.

17 Disconnect the sensor wiring plug.

18 Undo the 2 bolts and remove the sensor, located on the left-hand side of the intake manifold. Recover the O-ring seal **(see illustration)**.

10.11 Turbocharger delivery hose (arrowed)

10.12 EVAP canister purge valve (arrowed)

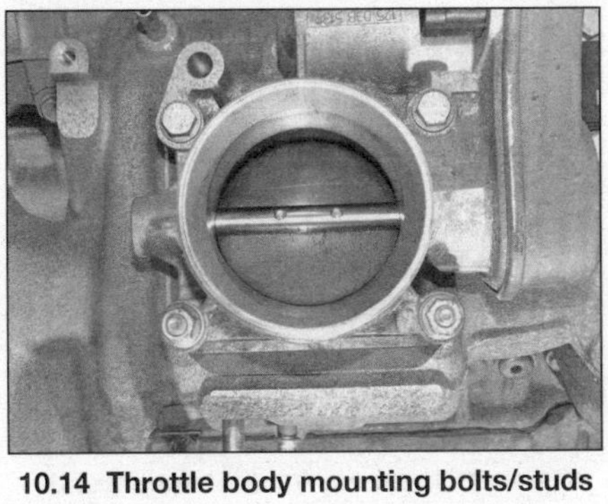

10.14 Throttle body mounting bolts/studs

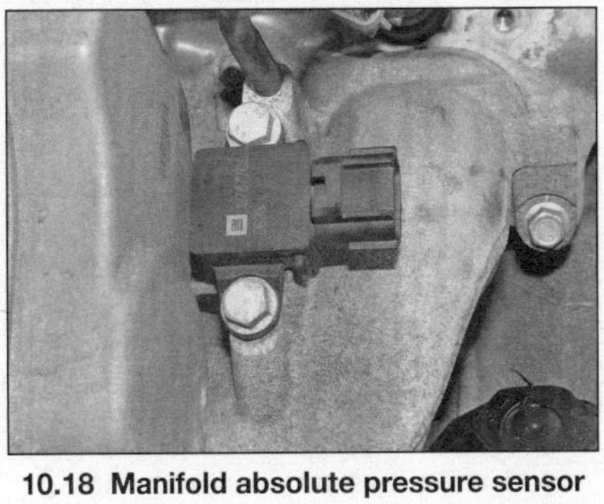

10.18 Manifold absolute pressure sensor

10.24 Atmospheric pressure sensor

10.28 Mass airflow sensor

10.34 Coolant temperature sensor

Refitting

19 Fit a new O-ring seal to the sensor, and lubricate it with a little petroleum jelly.

20 Refit the sensor to the manifold, and tighten the retaining screws securely.

21 Reconnect the sensor wiring plug.

22 Refit the plastic cover to the top of the engine.

Atmospheric pressure sensor

Removal

23 The pressure sensor is located adjacent to the left-hand end of the intake manifold.

24 Disconnect the wiring connector from the sensor, undo the 2 retaining screws, and recover the O-ring seal **(see illustration)**.

Refitting

25 Fit a new O-ring seal to the sensor, and apply a little petroleum jelly.

26 Refit the sensor, and tighten the retaining screws securely. Reconnect the wiring plug.

Mass airflow sensor

Removal

27 The mass airflow sensor is located on the right-hand side of the engine bay, and is fitted to the air ducting between the air filter housing and the turbocharger. Disconnect the sensor wiring plug **(see illustration 2.1)**.

28 Undo the 2 retaining screws and remove the sensor **(see illustration)**. Recover the O-ring seal.

Refitting

29 Fit a new O-ring seal to the sensor, and lubricate it with a little petroleum jelly.

30 Refit the sensor, tighten the retaining screws securely, and reconnect the wiring plug.

Coolant temperature sensor

Removal

31 The coolant temperature sensor is at the front right-hand corner of the engine. Ensure that the engine is completely cold, then release the pressure in the cooling system by removing and then refitting the expansion tank filler cap (see *Weekly checks*).

32 Remove the plastic cover at the top of the engine.

33 Unplug the wiring connector from the sensor.

34 Unscrew the sensor. Be prepared for some coolant loss **(see illustration)**.

Refitting

35 Clean the threads, then insert the sensor, and tighten it to the specified torque. Fit new sealing washer if necessary.

36 Ensure that the wiring connector is securely refitted.

37 Refit the plastic cover to the top of the engine.

38 Top-up the cooling system with reference to *Weekly checks*.

Crankshaft position sensor

Removal

39 The crankshaft position sensor is located on the front surface of the cylinder block, at the transmission end. Remove the plastic cover on the top of the engine.

40 Undo the retaining bolt and remove the sensor. Recover the O-ring seal and disconnect the wiring plug as the sensor is withdrawn **(see illustration)**.

Refitting

41 Fit a new seal to the sensor, and lubricate it with a little petroleum jelly.

42 Reconnect the wiring plug, then refit the sensor and tighten the retaining bolt securely.

43 Refit the plastic cover to the top of the engine.

Fuel supply rail, injectors and pressure regulator

Removal

44 Depressurise the fuel system as described in Section 5. Ensure that the ignition switch is then turned to the OFF position.

45 Remove the plastic cover from the top of the engine.

46 Disconnect the fuel supply and return pipes from the fuel rail **(see illustration)**. Plug the openings to prevent contamination. Be prepared for fuel spillage. Release the pipes from any retaining clips on the camshaft cover.

47 Undo the Torx screws and remove the cover over the ignition coils on the top of the engine.

48 Note their fitted positions, then disconnect the wiring plugs from the ignition coils, throttle body, coolant temperature sensor, CDM (combustion detection module) and the oxygen sensors.

49 Detach the harness ducting and move it one side **(see illustration)**.

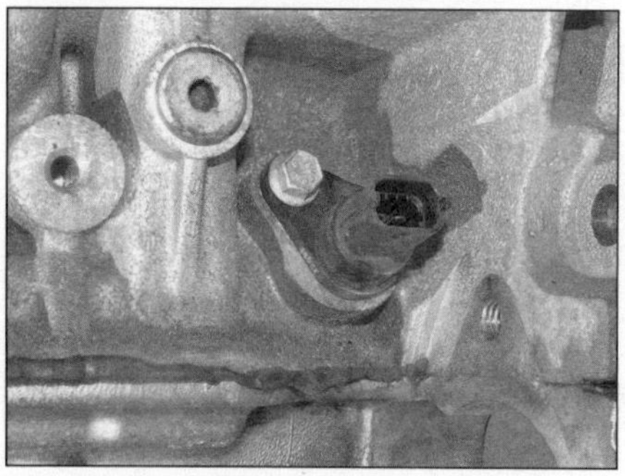

10.40 Crankshaft position sensor

10.46 Disconnect the fuel supply and return unions (arrowed)

10.49 Undo the nuts (arrowed) and remove the wiring ducting

10.50 Disconnect the regulator vacuum hose

50 Disconnect the vacuum hose from the fuel pressure regulator on the fuel rail **(see illustration)**.

51 Undo the 2 retaining bolts, and carefully pull the fuel rail and injectors upwards from place. Disconnect the injector wiring plugs by pulling out the blue lock tabs, and pressing down the black lock-tabs **(see illustrations)**. Plug the holes in the cylinder head to prevent contamination.

52 To remove the injectors from the fuel rail, press down the retaining clips and open them with a screwdriver. Recover the rubber O-ring seals and discard – new ones should be used on refitting **(see illustrations)**.

Refitting

53 Refitting is a reversal of the removal procedure, noting the following points:

*a) Fit new O-ring seal to the injectors, and seats: Blue for injector-to-fuel rail, black for the injector-to-seat, then apply a little clean engine oil to act as a lubricant **(see illustrations)**.*

b) Tighten the fuel rail bolts to the specified torque.

c) Ensure all electrical connections are secure, and the harness is routed as it was originally.

Charge air (boost) control valve

Removal

54 The valve is located at the rear of the engine compartment, adjacent to the turbocharger.

55 Unplug the wiring connector from the valve.

56 Press down the retaining clip and detach the valve from its mounting. Mark each of the hoses leading to the valve to identify their fitted positions, then release the clips and detach the hoses from the valve ports **(see illustration)**.

Refitting

57 Refitting is a reversal of removal. It is vitally important that the hoses are refitted to the correct ports on the boost control valve.

Wastegate valve

Removal

58 Remove the plastic cover from the top of the engine.

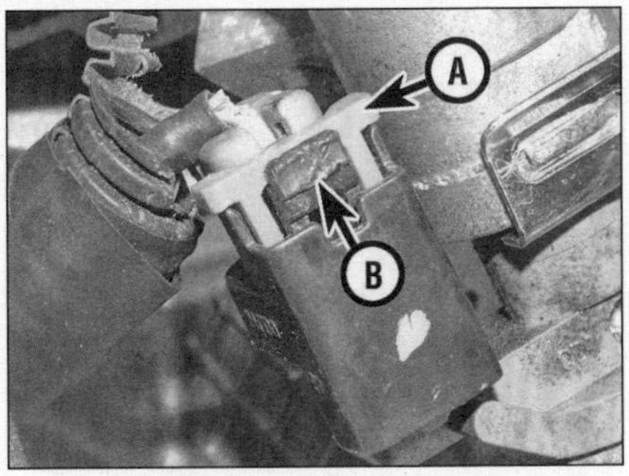

10.51a Prise out the block lock-tab (A) then depress the black lock-tab (B)

10.51b Fuel rail mounting studs/bolts (arrowed)

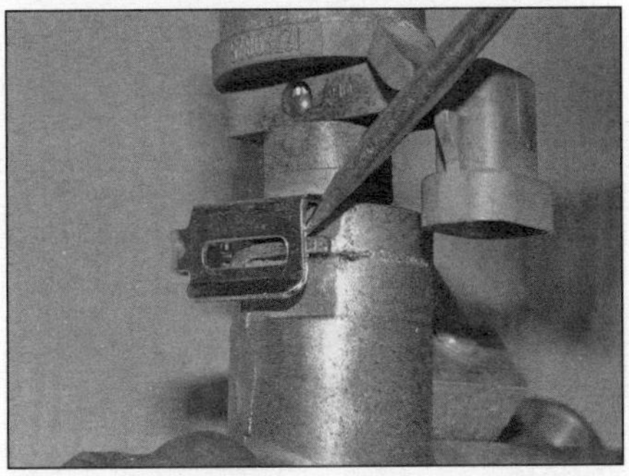

10.52a Carefully prise apart the retaining clip ...

10.52b ... and pull the injector from the fuel rail

59 The valve is located between the throttle body and the engine management ECM. Disconnect the wiring plug from the valve **(see illustration)**.

60 Release the retaining clip and detach the valve from its mounting. Note their fitted positions and disconnect the hoses as the valve is withdrawn.

Refitting

61 Refitting is a reversal of removal.

10.53a Renew the injector O-ring seals (arrowed) ...

10.53b ... and the seal on the injector seats (arrowed)

10.56 Charge air (boost) control valve

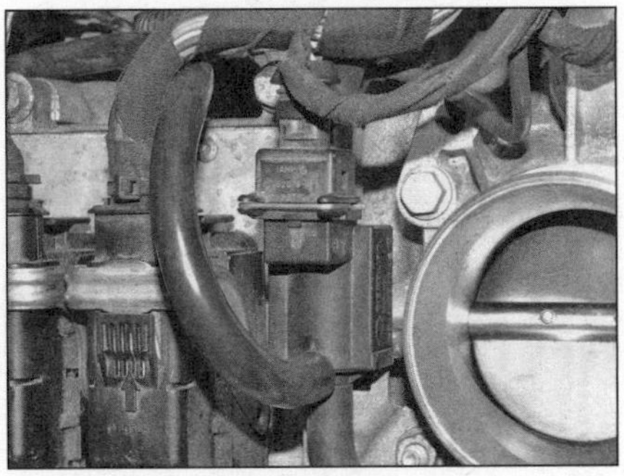

10.59 Wastegate valve

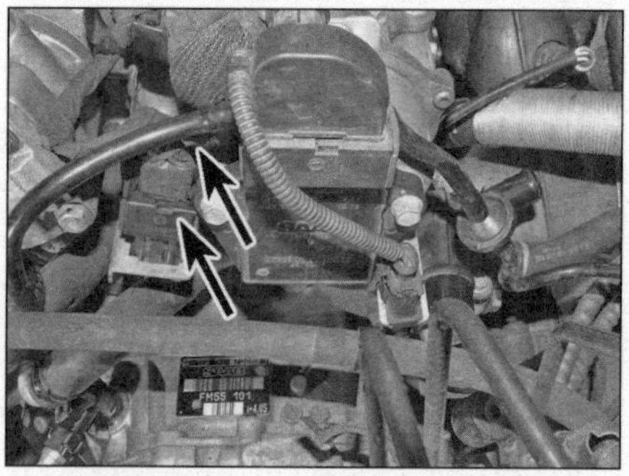

10.62 Oxygen sensor wiring plugs (arrowed)

10.64 Upper oxygen sensor

Oxygen (lambda) sensor

Upper sensor removal

62 Disconnect the sensor wiring plug **(see illustration)**.

63 Undo the bolts securing the heat shield over the turbocharger, the lift the heat shield from place to release the clip **(see illustration)**.

64 Unscrew the sensor from the top of the catalytic converter **(see illustration)**.

Lower sensor removal

65 Disconnect the sensor wiring plug **(see illustration 10.62)**.

66 Raise the front of the vehicle and support it securely on axle stands (see *Jacking and vehicle support*). On Convertible models, undo the bolts and remove the front chassis reinforcement **(see illustration)**.

67 Slacken the clamps, undo the retaining bolt and remove the turbocharger lower charge air pipe.

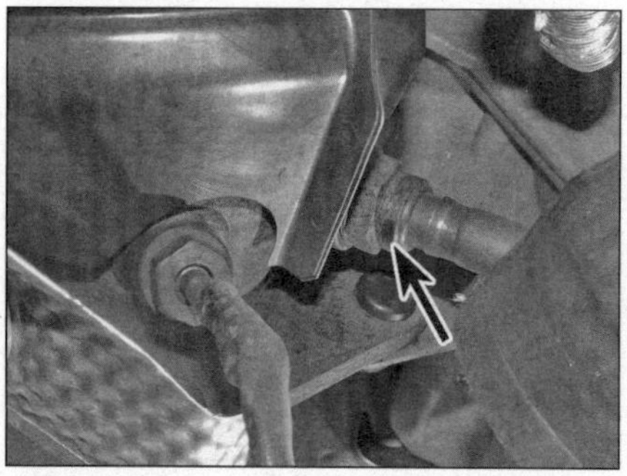

10.68 Lower oxygen sensor (arrowed)

10.63 Lift the heat shield upwards to release the clip (arrowed)

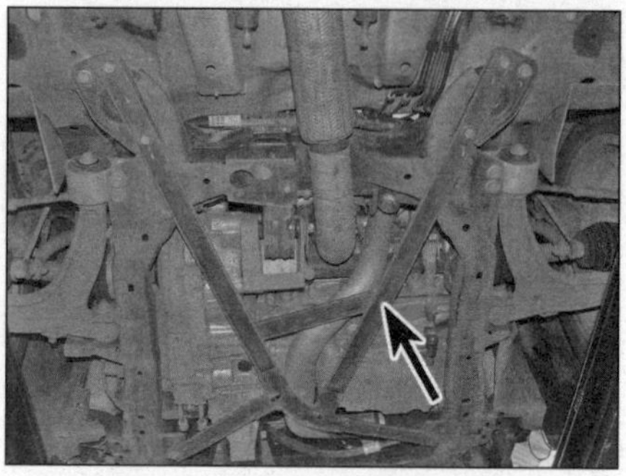

10.66 Front chassis reinforcement (arrowed) – Convertible models

68 Bend the corner of the heat shield slightly, then unscrew the sensor from the base of the catalytic converter **(see illustration)**.

Refitting

69 Refitting is a reversal of the removal procedure. Coat the threads of the sensor with a suitable high-temperature anti-seize grease, then refit and tighten it to the specified torque.

Power steering fluid pressure sensor

Removal

70 The sensor is fitted to the top of the power steering pump at the left-hand end of the cylinder head. Disconnect the sensor wiring plug **(see illustration)**.

71 Carefully unscrew the sensor from the pump.

Refitting

72 Refitting is a reversal of removal.

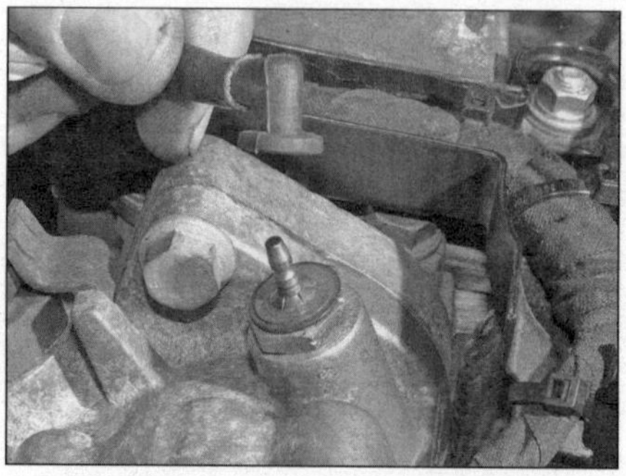

10.70 Pull the wiring plug from the power steering sensor

11 Turbocharger – description and precautions

Description

1 The turbocharger increases engine efficiency and performance by raising the pressure in the intake manifold above atmospheric pressure. Instead of the intake air being sucked into the combustion chambers, it is forced in under pressure. This leads to a greater charge pressure increase during combustion and improved fuel burning, which raises the thermal efficiency of the engine. Under these conditions, additional fuel is supplied by the fuel injection system, in proportion to the increased airflow.

2 Energy for the operation of the turbocharger comes from the exhaust gas. The gas flows through a specially-shaped housing (the turbine housing) and in so doing spins the turbine wheel. The turbine wheel is attached to a shaft, at the end of which is another vaned wheel known as the compressor wheel. The compressor wheel spins in its own housing, and compresses the intake air on the way to the intake manifold.

3 Between the turbocharger and the intake manifold, the compressed air passes through an intercooler. This is an air-to-air heat exchanger, mounted in front of the radiator and supplied with cooling air from the front grille and electric cooling fans. The temperature of the intake air rises due to the compression action of the turbocharger – the purpose of the intercooler is to cool the intake air again, before it enters the engine. Because cool air is denser than hot air, this allows a greater mass of air (occupying the same volume) to be forced into the combustion chambers, resulting in a further increase in the engine's thermal efficiency.

4 Boost pressure (the pressure in the intake manifold) is limited by a wastegate, which diverts the exhaust gas away from the turbine wheel in response to a pressure-sensitive actuator. The wastegate valve is controlled by the engine management system ECM, via an electronic boost control valve. The ECM opens and closes (modulates) the boost valve several times a second, which results in manifold vacuum being applied to the wastegate valve in a series of rapid pulses – the duty ratio of the pulses depends primarily on engine speed and load. The ECM monitors boost pressure via the manifold pressure sensor, and uses the boost control valve to maintain pressure at an optimum level throughout the engine speed range. If the ECM detects that combustion pre-ignition ('pinking' or 'knocking') is taking place, the boost pressure is reduced accordingly to prevent engine damage; see Chapter 5B, Section 1 for greater detail.

5 A boost bypass (wastegate) valve fitted in the airflow between the low-pressure supply and high-pressure delivery sides of the turbocharger compressor allows excess boost to be dumped into the intake air ducting when the throttle is closed at high engine speed (ie, during overrun or deceleration). This improves driveability by preventing compressor stall (and therefore reducing turbo 'lag'), and also by eliminating the surging that would otherwise occur when the throttle is reopened.

6 The turbo shaft is pressure-lubricated by an oil feed pipe from the main oil gallery. The shaft 'floats' on a cushion of oil and has no moving bearings. A drain pipe returns the oil to the sump. The turbine housing is water-cooled and has a dedicated system of coolant supply and return pipes.

Precautions

7 The turbocharger operates at extremely high speeds and temperatures. Certain precautions must be observed during servicing activities, to avoid injury to the operator or premature failure of the turbo.

- Do not operate the turbo with any of its parts exposed, or with any of its hoses removed. Foreign objects falling onto the rotating vanes could cause excessive damage, and (if ejected) personal injury.
- Do not race the engine immediately after start-up, especially if it is cold. Give the oil a few seconds to circulate.
- Always allow the engine to return to idle speed before switching it off – do not blip the throttle and switch off, as this will leave the turbo spinning without lubrication.
- Allow the engine to idle for a few minutes before switching off after a high-speed run. This will allow the turbine housing to cool before the coolant stops circulating under pressure.
- Observe the recommended intervals for oil and filter changing, and use a reputable oil of the specified quality. Infrequent oil changes, or use of inferior oil, can cause carbon formation on the turbo shaft, leading to subsequent failure.

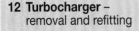

12 Turbocharger – removal and refitting

Note: *The exhaust system and turbocharger may still be hot, make sure the vehicle has cooled down before working on the engine.*

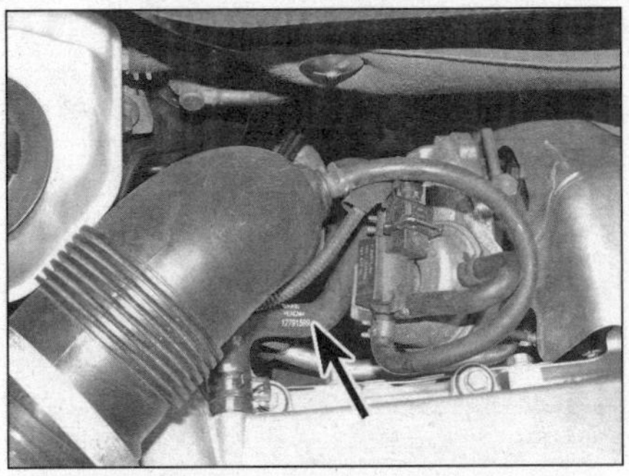

12.3 Release the clip and disconnect the ventilation hose (arrowed)

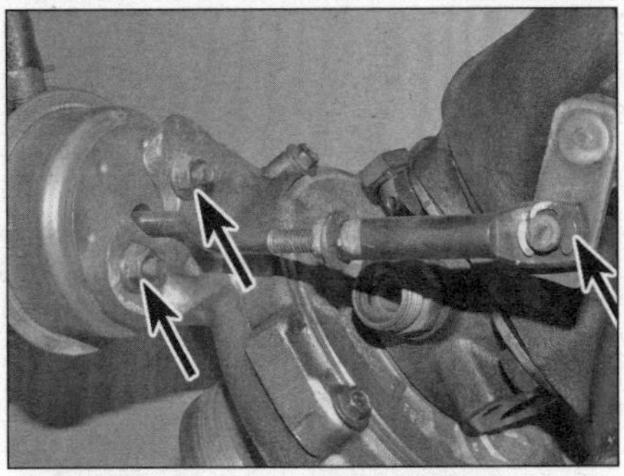

12.7 Control arm clip and vacuum unit nuts (arrowed)

12.9 Counter-hold the coolant port (arrowed) whilst slackening the union

12.10 Oil supply pipe banjo bolt (arrowed)

Removal

1 Apply the handbrake, then jack up the front of the car and support on axle stands (see *Jacking and vehicle support*). On Convertible models, undo the bolts and remove the front chassis reinforcement **(see illustration 10.66)**.

2 Remove the shield from beneath the radiator, then drain the cooling system as described in Chapter 1A, Section 27.

3 Remove the crankcase ventilation hose from the camshaft cover and turbocharger intake **(see illustration)**.

4 Remove the air cleaner assembly as describe in Section 2.

5 Remove the heat shield over the top of the turbocharger **(see illustration 10.63)**.

6 Note their fitted positions, and disconnect the solenoid valve hoses from the turbocharger.

7 Remove the clip securing the turbocharger control arm and remove the vacuum unit from the turbocharger **(see illustration)**.

8 Remove the catalytic converter as described in Section 16.

9 Disconnect the coolant pipe from the front of the turbocharger, and release the pipe from the cylinder head **(see illustration)**. Counter-hold the turbo coolant port to prevent it from coming loose.

10 Undo the bolt and disconnect the oil supply pipe from the top of the turbocharger. Recover the sealing washers, and plug the openings to prevent contamination **(see illustration)**.

11 Slacken the clamps, undo the retaining bolts and remove the lower charge air pipe **(see illustration)**.

12 Remove the heat shield over the steering rack.

13 Disconnect the coolant pipe from the turbocharger to the thermostat housing **(see illustration)**.

14 Undo the retaining screws and detach the oil return pipe from the turbocharger, then

12.11 Lower charge air pipe retaining bolts (arrowed)

12.13 Remove the coolant pipe (arrowed)

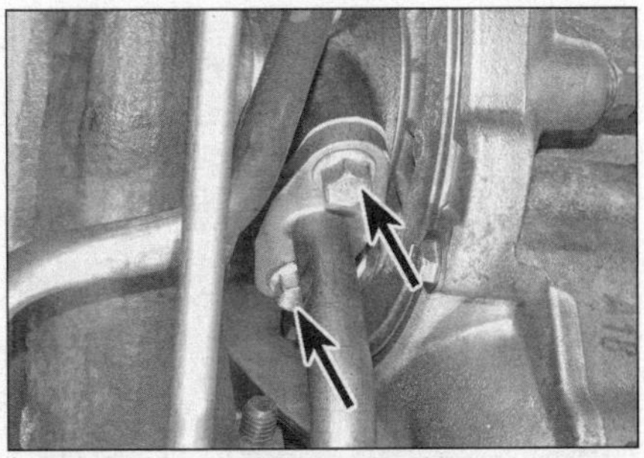

12.14a Undo the 2 screws securing the oil return pipe to the underside of the turbocharger (arrowed) ...

12.14b ... and pull the pipe from the block – renew the O-ring (arrowed) if necessary

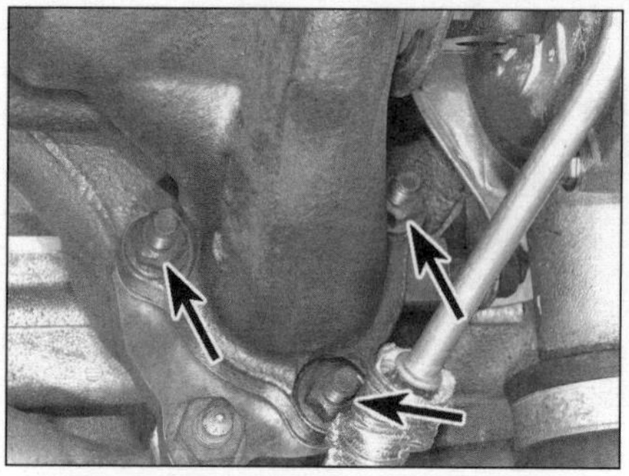

12.16a Turbocharger retaining nuts (arrowed)

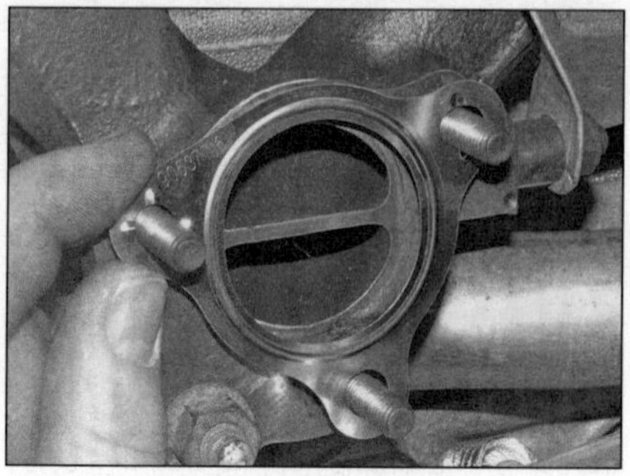

12.16b Renew the turbocharger-to-manifold gasket

disconnect the pipe from the cylinder block **(see illustrations)**. Take care not to bend the oil pipe excessively.

15 Disconnect the turbocharger oil supply pipe from the cylinder block.

16 Undo the 3 retaining nuts, and detach the turbocharger from the exhaust manifold. Lower the turbocharger from position **(see illustrations)**. Recover the gasket.

Refitting

17 Refitting is a reversal of removal, noting the following points:

a) Fill the turbocharger interchamber with clean engine oil, through the oil supply union on the turbocharger. This is important, as the turbocharger must have oil in it when the engine is started.

b) Thoroughly clean the exhaust manifold mating surface before refitting the turbocharger.

c) Renew all copper union sealing washers, O-ring seals and gaskets, where applicable.

d) Tighten all nuts, bolts and oil and coolant unions to the correct torque settings, where specified.

e) Apply a suitable high-temperature, anti-seize compound to the threads of the exhaust system-to-turbocharger and exhaust manifold-to-turbocharger studs and nuts.

f) Ensure that the charge air (boost) control valve hoses are refitted correctly to the turbocharger, wastegate actuator and air hose.

18 On completion, check that the radiator drain plug is tight, then refit the shield panel.

19 Lower the car to the ground, then check and if necessary top-up the engine oil level (see *Weekly checks*). If not already done, it is strongly recommended that the engine oil is changed before starting the engine if a new turbocharger has been fitted, as this will protect the turbo bearings during the 'running-in' period.

20 Refill the cooling system (see Chapter 1A, Section 27).

13 Intercooler – removal and refitting

Removal

1 Remove the battery cover and unclip the coolant pipe from the side of the cover.

2 Pull the washer fluid filler pipe upwards from place.

3 Remove the front bumper cover as described in Chapter 11, Section 6.

4 Remove the headlight upper retaining bolts, disconnect the bonnet release cable at the junction box adjacent to the fusebox at the left-hand side, then undo the bolts and remove the upper radiator crossmember/bonnet slam panel **(see illustration)**.

5 Remove the upper radiator cover **(see illustration)**.

6 Raise the front of the vehicle and support it securely on axle stands (see *Jacking and vehicle support*).

7 Remove the undershield beneath the radiator.

8 Remove the plastic covers, then slacken the clips and remove the hoses from both ends of the intercooler **(see illustrations)**.

9 Use cables-ties or straps to support the condenser from the vehicle body, then undo

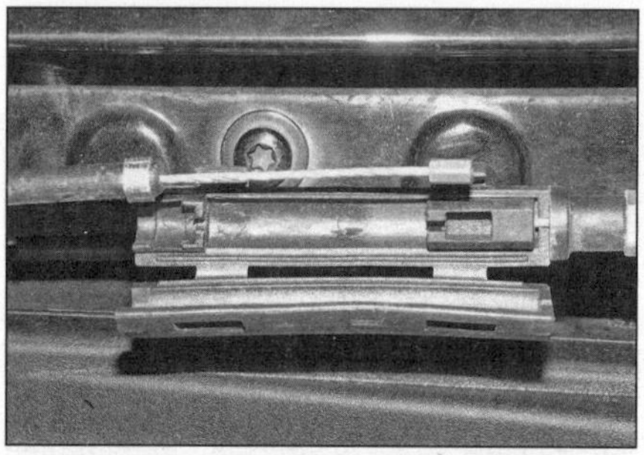

13.4 Open the junction box adjacent to the fusebox, and disconnect the bonnet release cable

13.5 Remove the plastic covers from the top of the radiator assembly

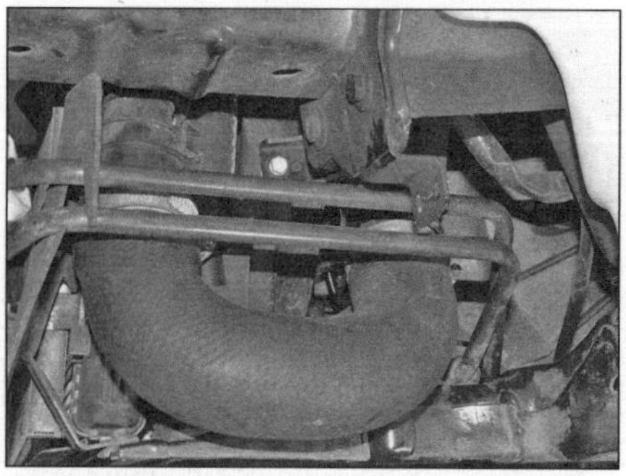

13.8a Right-hand intercooler pipe ...

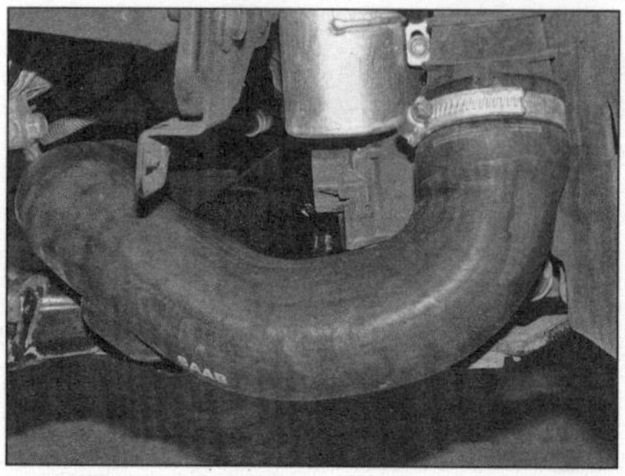

13.8b ... and left-hand intercooler pipe

13.9 Undo the Torx screw each end (arrowed) securing the condenser to the intercooler

the 2 screws securing the top of the condenser **(see illustration)**.

10 Undo the 2 screws securing the top of the intercooler **(see illustration)**.

11 Working underneath the vehicle, undo the radiator lower mounting screws **(see illustration)**.

12 Lift the intercooler slightly to disengage the hooks securing it to the radiator at the lower edge, then lower it from position.

Refitting

13 Refitting is a reversal of removal. To reduce the risk of the charge air hoses coming loose, clean the inside of the hoses with a solvent degreaser where they fit onto the intercooler.

14 Intake manifold – removal and refitting

Removal

1 Remove the engine management ECM as described in Section 10.

2 Refer to Section 10, and remove the throttle body/actuator from the intake manifold.

3 Undo the bolts and detach the support bracket from the underside of the manifold **(see illustration)**.

4 Disconnect the brake servo vacuum hose and breather hose from the intake manifold, then the two vacuum connections on the top side of the manifold **(see illustrations)**.

5 Undo the nut securing the wiring loom

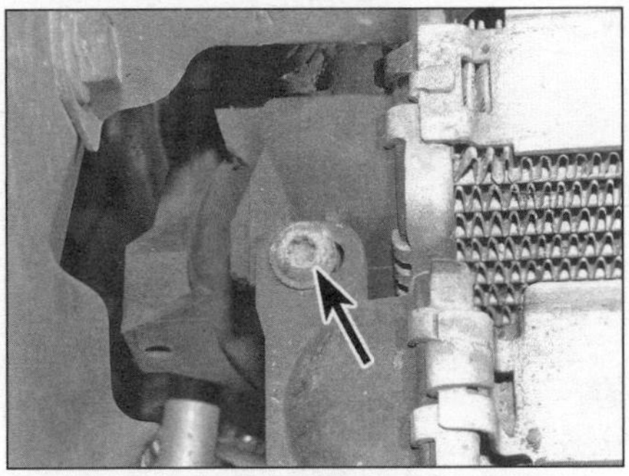

13.10 Undo the Torx screw each end (arrowed) securing the intercooler to the radiator

support bracket to the left-hand end of the intake manifold.

6 Prise up the blue locking tabs, pull out the lower edges of the black tabs, and disconnect the fuel injectors wiring plugs **(see illustration 10.51a)**.

7 Disconnect the vacuum hose from the boost pressure sensor, and the bypass valve hose, then remove the turbocharger solenoid valve and bracket from the front of the manifold.

8 Undo the bolt securing the oil level dipstick guide tube to the manifold.

9 Undo the bolts/nuts, and pull the manifold from the cylinder head **(see illustration)**. Recover the gasket from the cylinder head.

Refitting

10 Refitting is a reversal of removal. Fit a new gasket and ensure that the manifold retaining bolts are tightened to the specified torque.

13.11 Undo the Torx screw (arrowed) securing the radiator lower bracket each side

15 Exhaust manifold – removal and refitting

Removal

1 Remove the turbocharger as described in Section 12.

2 Undo the bolts/nut and remove the heat shield from the right-hand side of the exhaust manifold **(see illustration)**.

3 Unscrew and remove the exhaust manifold mounting nuts, and the bolt securing the manifold stay, then lift the manifold from the cylinder head. Discard the nuts, new ones must be fitted.

4 Remove the gaskets from the studs on the cylinder head **(see illustration)**.

14.3 Remove the bracket on the underside of the intake manifold

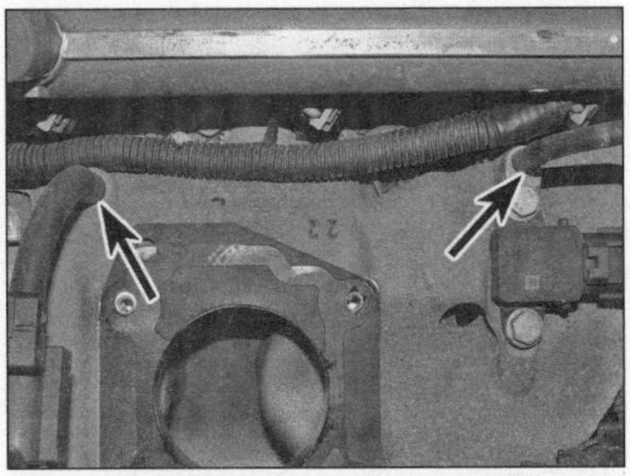

14.4a Two vacuum connections on the top of the manifold (arrowed)

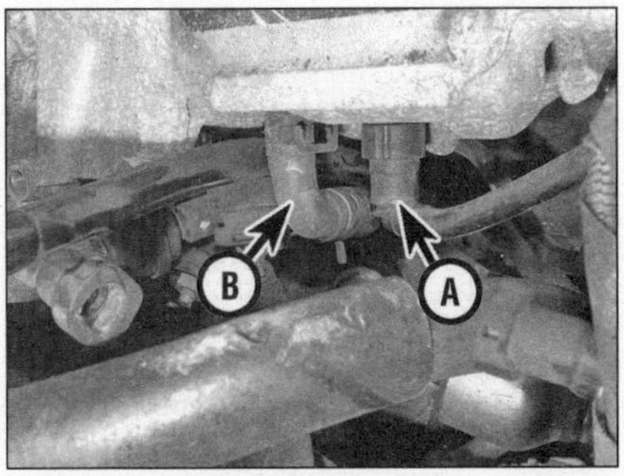

14.4b Servo hose (A) and breather hose (B) on the underside of the manifold

14.9 Intake manifold retaining bolts/nuts (arrowed)

15.2 Remove the heat shield from the manifold

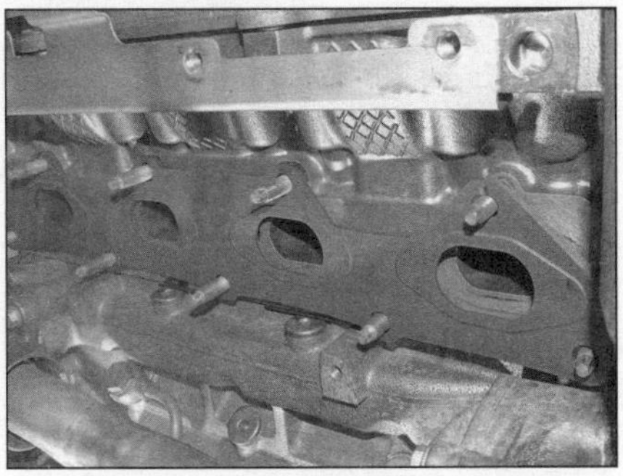

15.4 Renew the manifold gasket

16.6a Undo the nuts securing the front pipe to the catalytic converter (arrowed)

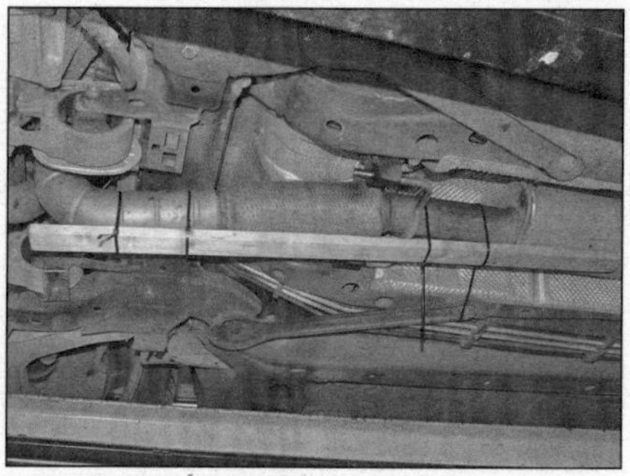

16.6b Use a length of wood strapped to the exhaust pipe to prevent damage to the flexible section

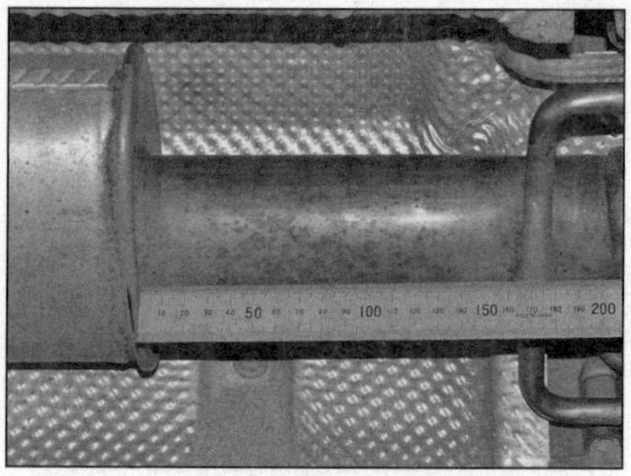

16.9 Cut the exhaust pipe 87 mm in front of the front silencer

Refitting

5 Clean the contact surfaces of the cylinder head and exhaust manifold.

6 Refit the exhaust manifold to the studs on the cylinder head together with a new gasket, then tighten the mounting nuts to the specified torque.

7 Refit the heat shield and manifold stay.

8 Refit the turbocharger with reference to Section 12.

16 Exhaust system – general information and component removal

General information

1 Originally, the factory-fitted system was one piece, but a new exhaust system consists of three sections:

a) The front pipe (incorporating a three-way catalytic converter).

b) The intermediate pipe incorporating the centre silencer.

c) The rear silencer (or silencers) and tailpipe.

2 The exhaust system sections are joined by flanges with internal flared tube ends, and no gaskets. The front pipe-to-manifold/turbocharger joint does have a gasket and is secured by studs and nuts. The front pipe and the connector pipes between the silencers are aluminium-plated. The silencers are made of chrome steel plate.

3 Two oxygen (lambda) sensors are fitted in the front pipe: one upstream of the catalytic converter, and one downstream of the catalytic converter.

4 On all models, the system is suspended throughout its entire length by rubber mountings.

Removal

Complete system

5 The exhaust system can be removed completely as one assembly.

6 Undo the 3 nuts securing the front pipe to the catalytic converter **(see illustrations)**.

7 Release the exhaust system from the rubber mountings and manoeuvre it from under the vehicle.

Front silencer

8 Raise the vehicle and support it securely on axle stands (see *Jacking and vehicle support*).

9 Use a hacksaw to cut the front pipe between the flexible section and the front silencer, 87 mm before the front silencer **(see illustration)**.

10 Cut the exhaust pipe 100 mm in front of the rear silencer **(see illustration)**.

11 Free the pipe from the rubber mountings, and manoeuvre it from under the vehicle.

Catalytic converter

Note: *The catalytic converter contains a fragile ceramic element, and should be handled with care to prevent internal damage.*

12 Remove the oxygen sensors as described in Section 10.

13 Remove the front pipe as described in paragraph 6 of this Section.

14 Remove the right-hand intermediate driveshaft as described in Chapter 8, Section 5.

15 Remove the nuts/bolts securing the catalytic converter support bracket **(see illustration)**.

16 Unscrew the nuts securing the catalytic converter to the turbocharger, then manoeuvre it from under the vehicle. Recover the gasket.

Rear silencer and tailpipe

17 Raise the rear of the vehicle and support it securely on axle stands (see *Jacking and vehicle support*).

18 Use a hacksaw to cut the exhaust pipe 100 mm before the rear silencer **(see illustration 16.10)**.

19 Unhook the mounting rubbers from the underbody, and lower the rear silencer and tailpipe to the ground.

Refitting

20 Each section is refitted by a reversal of the removal sequence, noting the following points:

a) Ensure that all traces of corrosion have been removed from the flared tube ends in the flanges, and renew the front pipe-to-turbocharger gasket.

b) Where the exhaust system was cut during removal, obtain joining sleeves from Saab dealers or a specialist, and join the new sections. If necessary, use a little exhaust system assembly paste between the sleeves and the pipes.

c) Inspect the rubber mountings for signs of damage or deterioration, and renew as necessary.

d) Refit the oxygen sensors with reference to Section 10.

e) Make sure that all rubber mountings are correctly located, and that there is adequate clearance between the exhaust system and underbody.

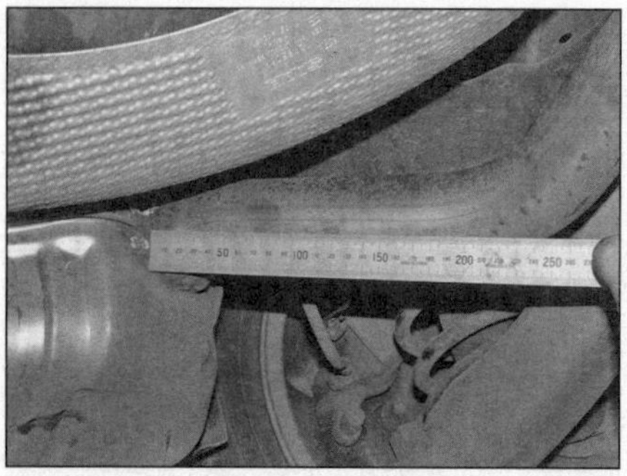

16.10 Cut the exhaust pipe 100 mm before the rear silencer

16.15 Remove the catalytic converter support bracket (arrowed)

Chapter 4 Part B:
Fuel and exhaust systems – diesel engines

Contents

Degrees of difficulty

Easy, suitable for novice with little experience	**Fairly easy,** suitable for beginner with some experience	**Fairly difficult,** suitable for competent DIY mechanic	**Difficult,** suitable for experienced DIY mechanic	**Very difficult,** suitable for expert DIY or professional

Specifications

Engine identification

Engine type	**Manufacturer's engine code**
SOHC 8-valve	Z19DT
DOHC 16-valve	Z19DTH and DTR

System type

All engines	Bosch EDC 16C9 high-pressure direct injection 'common-rail' system, electronically-controlled

Fuel system data

Firing order	1–3–4–2 (No 1 at timing belt end of engine)
Fuel system operating pressure	1600 bar at 2200 rpm
Idle speed	Controlled by ECM
Maximum speed	Controlled by ECM
High-pressure fuel pump:	
Type	Bosch CP1H
Fuel supply pump:	
Type	Electric, mounted in fuel tank
Delivery pressure	3.3 bar (maximum)
Injectors:	
Type	Bosch CRIP 1-MI
Injection holes (per injector)	6
Resistance	0.255 ± 0.04 ohms

Torque wrench settings

	Nm	lbf ft
Alternator bracket bolts	25	18
Camshaft sensor retaining bolt(s)	9	7
Catalytic converter clamp bolt	20	15
Crankshaft sensor retaining bolt	9	7
EGR valve pipe to exhaust manifold	25	18
Exhaust manifold nuts*	20	15
Exhaust front pipe-to-catalytic converter nuts*	20	15
Fuel injector clamp bracket nuts	25	18
Fuel pressure regulator to fuel rail	60	44
Fuel pressure sensor to fuel rail	70	52
Fuel rail retaining nuts/bolts	25	18
High-pressure fuel pipe unions:		
M12 union nuts	25	18
M14 union nuts	30	22
High-pressure fuel pump mounting bolts	25	18
Intake air sensor retaining bolt	9	7
Intake manifold bolts	25	18
Throttle body/housing bolts	9	7
Turbocharger oil return pipe bolts:		
M6 bolts	9	7
M8 bolts	25	18
Turbocharger oil supply pipe banjo union bolt	15	11

** Do not re-use*

1 General information and precautions

General information

1 These engines are fitted with a high-pressure direct injection system which incorporates the very latest in diesel injection technology. On this system, a high-pressure fuel pump is used purely to provide the pressure required for the injection system and has no control over the injection timing (unlike conventional diesel injection systems). The injection timing is controlled by the electronic control module (ECM) via the electrically-operated injectors. The system operates as follows.

2 The fuel system consists of a fuel tank (which is mounted under the rear of the car, with an electric fuel supply pump immersed in it), a fuel filter with integral water separator, a high-pressure fuel pump, injectors and associated components.

3 Fuel is supplied to the fuel filter housing which is located in the engine compartment. The fuel filter removes all foreign matter and water, and ensures that the fuel supplied to the pump is clean. Excess fuel is returned from the outlet on the filter housing lid to the tank via the fuel cooler. The fuel cooler is fitted to the underside of the vehicle and is cooled by the passing airflow to ensure the fuel is cool before it enters the fuel tank.

4 The fuel is heated to ensure no problems occur when the ambient temperature is very low. This is achieved by an electrically-operated fuel heater incorporated in the filter housing, the heater is controlled by the ECM.

5 The high-pressure fuel pump is driven at half-crankshaft speed by the timing belt. The high pressure required in the system (up to 1600 bar) is produced by the three pistons in the pump. The high-pressure pump supplies high-pressure fuel to the fuel rail, which acts as a reservoir for the four injectors. Since the pump has no control over the injection timing (unlike conventional diesel injection systems), this means that there is no need to time the pump when installing the timing belt.

6 The electrical control system consists of the ECM, along with the following sensors:

Accelerator pedal position sensor

- Informs the ECM of the accelerator pedal position, and the rate of throttle opening/closing.

Coolant temperature sensor

- Informs the ECM of engine temperature.

Airflow meter

- Informs the ECM of the amount of air passing through the intake duct.

Crankshaft sensor

- Informs the ECM of the crankshaft position and speed of rotation.

Camshaft sensor

- Informs the ECM of the positions of the pistons.

Intake air sensor

- Informs ECM of the intake air temperature and (boost) pressure in the intake manifold.

Fuel pressure sensor

- Informs the ECM of the fuel pressure present in the fuel rail.

ABS control unit

- Informs the ECM of the vehicle speed.

Particulate trap sensor

- Measures the differential pressure across the particulate filter, and informs the ECM when the filter is full.

Exhaust temperature sensor

- Informs the ECM of the exhaust gas temperature before and after the catalytic converters.

7 All the above signals are analysed by the ECM which selects the fuelling response appropriate to those values. The ECM controls the fuel injectors (varying the pulse width – the length of time the injectors are held open – to provide a richer or weaker mixture, as appropriate). The mixture is constantly varied by the ECM, to provide the best setting for cranking, starting (with either a hot or cold engine), warm-up, idle, cruising and acceleration.

8 The ECM also has full control over the fuel pressure present in the fuel rail via the high-pressure fuel regulator and third piston deactivator solenoid valve which are fitted to the high-pressure pump. To reduce the pressure, the ECM opens the high-pressure fuel regulator which allows the excess fuel to return direct to the tank from the pump. The third piston deactivator is used mainly to reduce the load on the engine, but can also be used to lower the fuel pressure. The deactivator solenoid valve relieves the fuel pressure from the third piston of the pump which results in only two of the pistons pressurising the fuel system.

9 The ECM also controls the exhaust gas recirculation (EGR) system, described in detail in Chapter 4C, Section 1, the pre/post-heating system (see Chapter 5A, Section 15), and the engine cooling fan.

10 The intake manifold is fitted with a butterfly valve arrangement to improve efficiency at low engine speeds. Each cylinder has two intake tracts in the manifold, one of which is fitted with a valve; the operation of the valve is controlled by the ECM via an electric motor actuator drive arrangement. At low engine speeds (below approximately 1500 rpm) the valves remain closed, meaning that air entering each cylinder is passing through only one of the two manifold tracts. At higher engine speeds, the ECM opens up each of the four valves allowing the air passing through the manifold to pass through both intake tracts.

11 A variable-vane turbocharger is fitted to all models except the twin turbo DTR engine. The turbocharger increases engine efficiency. It does this by raising the pressure in the intake manifold above atmospheric pressure. Instead of the air simply being sucked into the cylinders, it is forced in. Note that the turbocharger is integral with the exhaust manifold.

12 Between the turbocharger and the intake manifold, the compressed air passes through an intercooler. This is an air-to-air heat exchanger is mounted next to the radiator, and supplied with cooling air from the front of the vehicle. The purpose of the intercooler is to remove some of the heat gained in being compressed from the intake air. Because cooler air is denser, removal of this heat further increases engine efficiency.

13 Energy for the operation of the turbocharger comes from the exhaust gas. The gas flows through a specially-shaped housing (the turbine housing) and in so doing, spins the turbine wheel. The turbine wheel is attached to a shaft, at the end of which is another vaned wheel known as the compressor wheel. The compressor wheel spins in its own housing, and compresses the intake air on the way to the intake manifold. The turbo shaft is pressure-lubricated by an oil feed pipe from the main oil gallery. The shaft 'floats' on a cushion of oil. A drain pipe returns the oil to the sump. Boost pressure (the pressure in the intake manifold) is limited by a wastegate, which diverts the exhaust gas away from the turbine wheel in response to a pressure-sensitive actuator.

14 The twin turbo Z19DTR engine is fitted with a small turbocharger to provide power at low engines speeds and a large turbocharger to provide increased power (and economy) at higher engine speeds. Both turbochargers are conventional turbochargers fitted with wastegates. The turbochargers work in conjunction with each other. The output is controlled by the ECM and a mechanical diverter valve **(see illustration)**.

15 If certain sensors fail, and send abnormal signals to the ECM, the ECM has a back-up programme. In this event, the abnormal signals are ignored, and a pre-programmed value is substituted for the sensor signal, allowing the engine to continue running, albeit at reduced efficiency. If the ECM enters its back-up mode, a warning light on the instrument panel will illuminate, and a fault code will be stored in the ECM memory. This fault code can be read using suitable specialist test equipment plugged into the system's diagnostic socket. The diagnostic socket is located beneath the driver's side of the facia, above the pedals **(see illustrations)**.

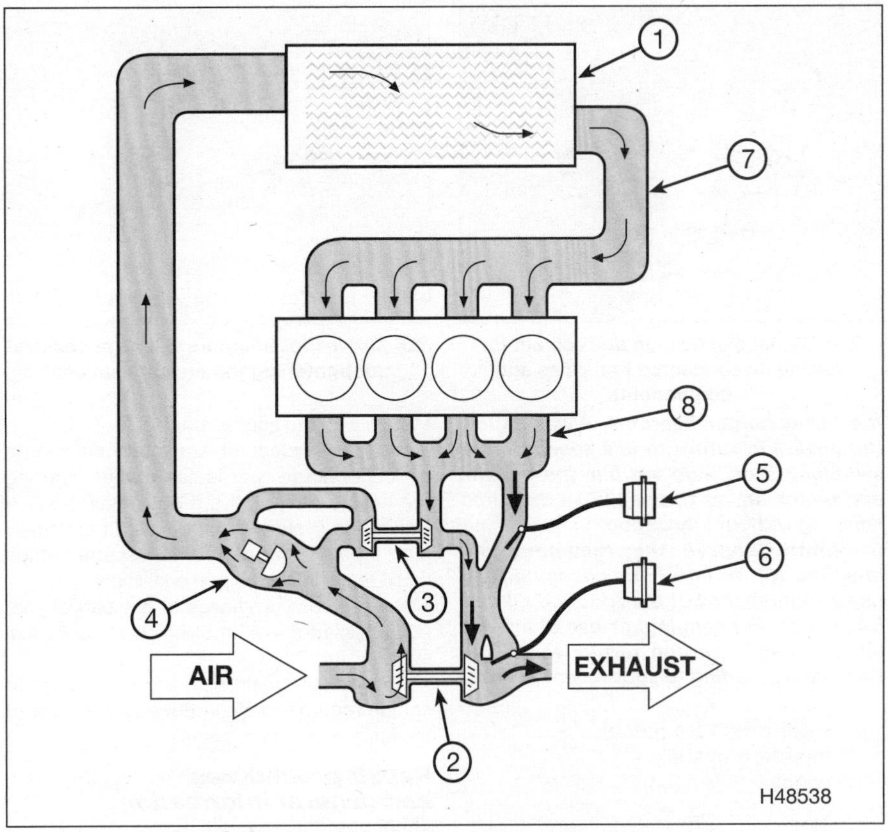

1.14 Turbocharger operation in the upper power range

1 *Intercooler*
2 *Low-pressure turbocharger*
3 *High-pressure turbocharger*
4 *Check valve*
5 *Wastegate control – high-pressure turbocharger*
6 *Wastegate control – low-pressure turbocharger*
7 *Inlet manifold*
8 *Exhaust manifold*

Warning: It is necessary to take certain precautions when working on the fuel system components, particularly the high-pressure side of the system. Before carrying out any operations on the fuel system, refer to the precautions given in 'Safety first!' at the beginning of this manual, and to any additional warning notes at the start of the relevant Sections.

Also refer to the additional information contained in Section 2.

Caution: Do not operate the engine if any of air intake ducts are disconnected or the filter element is removed. Any debris entering the engine will cause severe damage to the turbocharger.

Caution: To prevent damage to the turbocharger, do not race the engine immediately after start-up, especially if it is cold. Allow it to idle smoothly to give the oil a few seconds to circulate around

1.15a Pull of the plastic cap ...

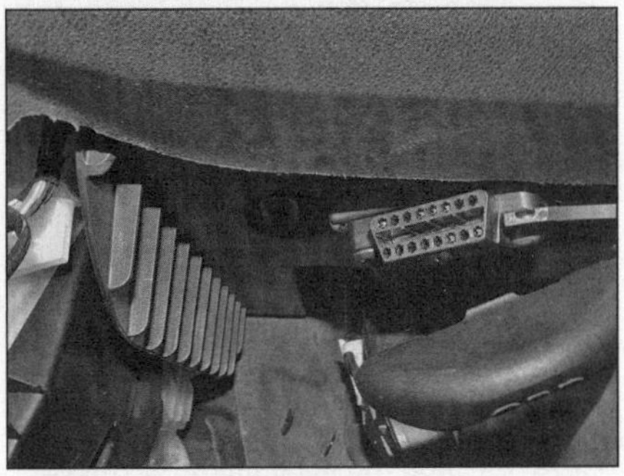

1.15b ... to expose the 16-pin diagnostic plug

2.4 Typical plastic plug and cap set for sealing disconnected fuel pipes and components

the turbocharger bearings. Always allow the engine to return to idle speed before switching it off – do not blip the throttle and switch off, as this will leave the turbo spinning without lubrication.

Caution: Observe the recommended intervals for oil and filter changing, and use a reputable oil of the specified quality. Neglect of oil changing, or use of inferior oil, can cause carbon formation on the turbo shaft, leading to subsequent failure.

2 High-pressure diesel injection system – special information

Warnings and precautions

1 It is essential to observe strict precautions when working on the fuel system components, particularly the high-pressure side of the system. Before carrying out any operations on the fuel system, refer to the precautions given in *Safety first!* at the beginning of this manual, and to the following additional information.

- Do not carry out any repair work on the high-pressure fuel system unless you are competent to do so, have all the necessary tools and equipment required, and are aware of the safety implications involved.
- Before starting any repair work on the fuel system, wait at least 30 seconds after switching off the engine to allow the fuel circuit to return to atmospheric pressure.
- Never work on the high-pressure fuel system with the engine running.
- Keep well clear of any possible source of fuel leakage, particularly when starting the engine after carrying out repair work. A leak in the system could cause an extremely high-pressure jet of fuel to escape, which could result in severe personal injury.
- Never place your hands or any part of your body near to a leak in the high-pressure fuel system.
- Do not use steam cleaning equipment or compressed air to clean the engine or any of the fuel system components.

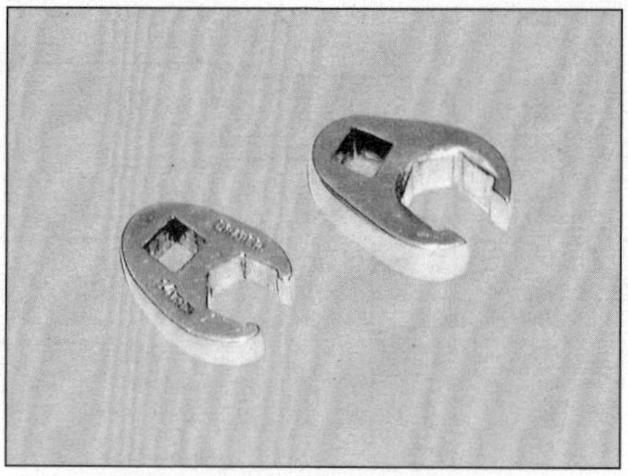

2.6 Crow-foot adapters will be necessary for tightening the fuel pipe unions

Repair procedures and general information

2 Strict cleanliness must be observed at all times when working on any part of the fuel system. This applies to the working area in general, the person doing the work, and the components being worked on.

3 Before working on the fuel system components, they must be thoroughly cleaned with a suitable degreasing fluid. Cleanliness is particularly important when working on the fuel system connections at the following components:

a) Fuel filter.
b) High-pressure fuel pump.
c) Fuel rail.
d) Fuel injectors.
e) High-pressure fuel pipes.

4 After disconnecting any fuel pipes or components, the open union or orifice must be immediately sealed to prevent the entry of dirt or foreign material. Plastic plugs and caps in various sizes are available in packs from motor factors and accessory outlets, and are particularly suitable for this application **(see illustration)**. Fingers cut from disposable rubber gloves should be used to protect components such as fuel pipes, fuel injectors and wiring connectors, and can be secured in place using elastic bands. Suitable gloves of this type are available at no cost from most petrol station forecourts.

5 Whenever any of the high-pressure fuel pipes are disconnected or removed, a new pipe(s) must be obtained for refitting.

6 The torque wrench settings given in the Specifications must be strictly observed when tightening component mountings and connections. This is particularly important when tightening the high-pressure fuel pipe unions. To enable a torque wrench to be used on the fuel pipe unions, crow-foot adapters are required. Suitable types are available from motor factors and accessory outlets **(see illustration)**.

3 Air cleaner assembly and intake ducts – removal and refitting

Removal

1 Slacken the clamp securing the air intake duct to the airflow meter, and disconnect the wiring plug from the airflow meter **(see illustrations)**.

2 Unclip the wiring harness from the side of the air cleaner housing **(see illustration)**.

3 Lift up the inner rear corner of the filter housing to release the mounting grommet. Move the filter housing toward the engine to disengage the front and rear mounting rubbers, then release the air intake duct at the front **(see illustration)**. Lift the filter housing out from the engine compartment.

4 The various air intake pipes/ducts linking the intercooler to the manifold and turbocharger can be disconnected and removed once the retaining clips have been slackened. In some cases it will be necessary to disconnect breather hoses, vacuum pipes and wiring connectors to allow the pipe/duct to be

3.1a Slacken the hose clamp (arrowed)

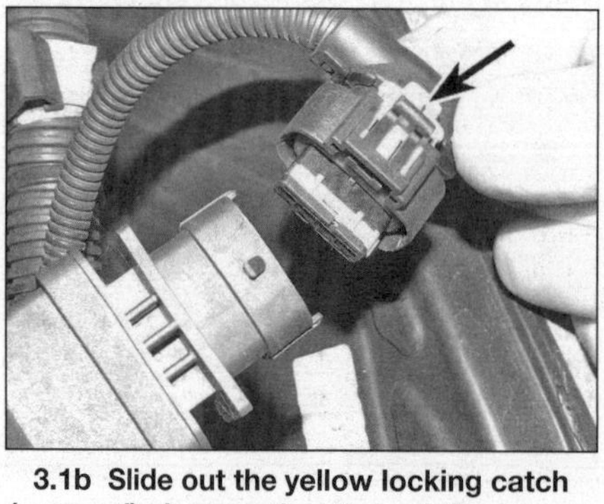

3.1b Slide out the yellow locking catch (arrowed), depress the clip and disconnect the airflow meter wiring plug

3.2 Unclip the wiring harnesses (arrowed)

removed; the pipe/duct may also be bolted to a support bracket.

Refitting

5 Refitting is the reverse of removal, making sure all the air intake ducts/hoses are securely reconnected.

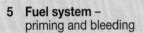

4 Accelerator pedal/ position sensor – removal and refitting

Refer to Chapter 4A, Section 3.

5 Fuel system – priming and bleeding

1 After disconnecting part of the fuel supply system or running out of fuel, it is necessary to prime the fuel system and bleed off any air which may have entered the system components, as follows.

2 Operate the fuel supply pump by switching on the ignition three times for approximately 15 seconds. The engine should now start. If it doesn't, wait a few minutes and repeat the procedure.

6 Fuel level sensor – removal and refitting

1 Remove the fuel tank as described in Section 8.

2 Note their fitted positions, then depress the release tabs and disconnect the fuel supply and return pipes from the pump maintenance cover **(see illustration)**. Where applicable disconnect the auxiliary heater fuel hose.

3 Disconnect the wiring plug from the maintenance cover.

4 Rotate the locking collar anti-clockwise, mark its fitted position, then lift the maintenance cover from place **(see illustrations)**. Reach under the cover and disconnect the fuel level sensor wiring plug.

5 Remove the maintenance cover sealing ring. A new one must be fitted.

3.3 Pull the up the left-hand rear corner of the housing, then pull it towards the engine

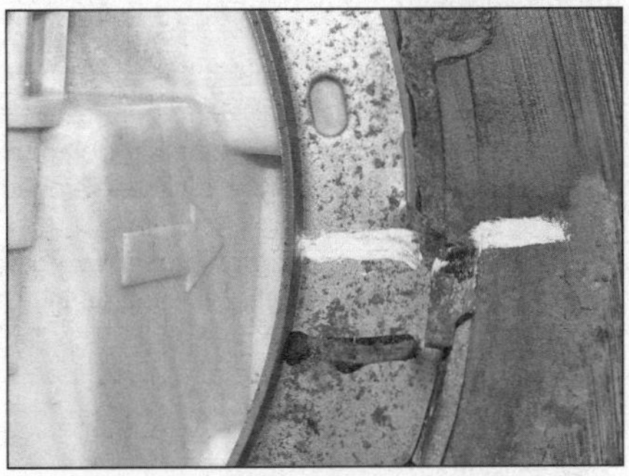

6.4a Make alignment marks between the locking collar, tank and maintenance cover ...

6 Press the retaining clip outwards and slide the level sensor upwards from the pump, and out of the fuel tank **(see illustrations)**.

7 Refitting is a reversal of removal, but fit a new maintenance cover sealing ring **(see illustration)**.

7 Fuel supply pump – removal and refitting

1 The diesel fuel supply pump is located in the same position as the fuel supply pump on petrol engine models, and the removal and refitting procedures are virtually identical. Refer to Chapter 4A, Section 6. On completion, bleed the fuel system as described in Section 5.

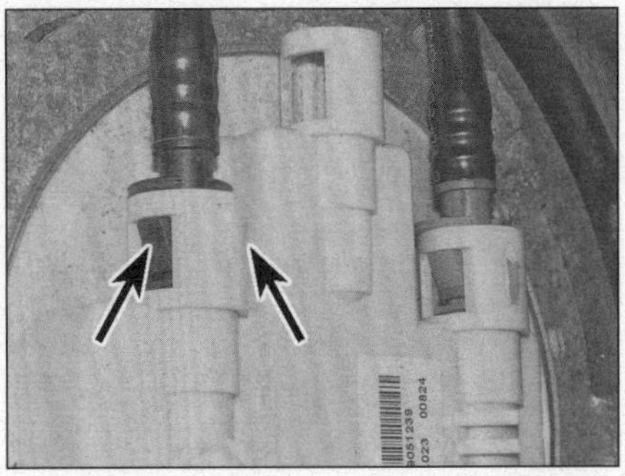

6.2 Squeeze together the clips (arrowed) and pull the fuel supply and return pipe from the cover

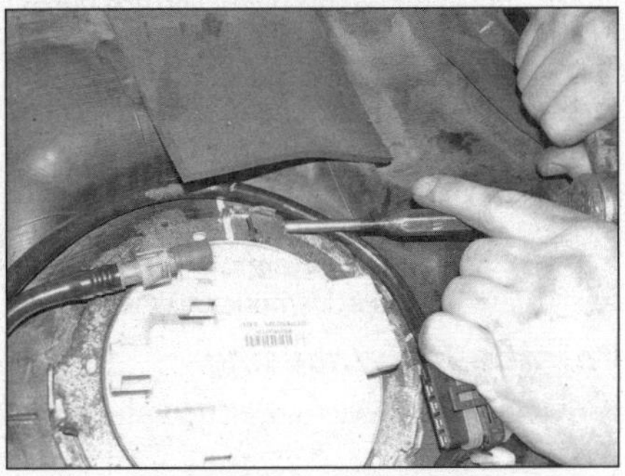

6.4b ... then unscrew the collar. We used a punch and hammer to gently rotate the collar anti-clockwise

8 Fuel tank – removal and refitting

1 Refer to Chapter 4A, Section 8, noting that there is no charcoal canister clipped to the tank.

2 On completion, bleed the fuel system as described in Section 5.

9 Injection system electrical components – removal and refitting

Airflow meter

1 Slacken the retaining clip securing the air

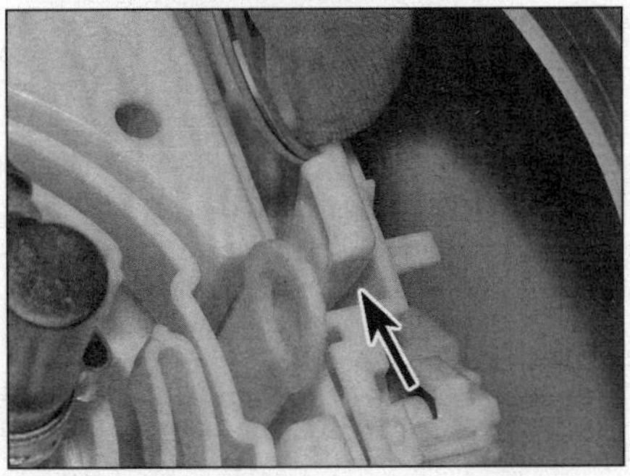

6.6a Press the clip (arrowed) outwards ...

6.6b ... and slide the sensor upwards

6.7 Always renew the cover sealing ring

9.6 Disconnect the charge air hose from the throttle body/housing, and intercooler charge air pipe

intake duct to the airflow meter and disconnect the duct **(see illustration 3.1a)**.

2 Disconnect the airflow meter wiring connector **(see illustration 3.1b)**.

3 Slacken the retaining clip and remove the airflow meter from the air cleaner housing lid.

4 Refitting is a reversal of removal, but ensure that the arrow on the airflow meter points toward the throttle body/housing when fitted.

Throttle body/housing

5 Remove the plastic cover from the top of the engine.

6 Release the retaining clip and disconnect the charge air hose from the throttle body/housing **(see illustration)**.

7 Disconnect the throttle body wiring plug.

8 Undo the three retaining bolts and remove the throttle body/housing from the intake manifold. Note the location of any wiring harness support brackets also secured by the retaining bolts.

9 Refitting is a reversal of removal, but thoroughly clean the mating faces and use a new gasket/seal. Tighten the retaining bolts to the specified torque.

Crankshaft sensor

10 The sensor is located at the rear of the cylinder block, below the starter motor **(see illustration)**. To gain access, firmly apply the handbrake, then jack up the front of the car and support it securely on axle stands (see *Jacking and vehicle support*).

11 Undo the retaining bolts and remove

9.10 The crankshaft sensor (arrowed) is located beneath the starter motor

the undershield from beneath the engine/transmission unit.

12 Wipe clean the area around the crankshaft sensor then disconnect the wiring connector.

13 Slacken and remove the retaining bolt and remove the sensor from the cylinder block. Recover the sealing ring.

14 Refitting is the reverse of removal, using a new sealing ring. Tighten the sensor retaining bolt to the specified torque.

Camshaft sensor

Z19DT engines

15 The camshaft sensor is located at the right-hand end of the cylinder head, behind the camshaft sprocket.

16 Remove the timing belt and camshaft sprocket as described in Chapter 2B, Section 7 and 8.

17 Undo the two bolts securing the camshaft sensor bracket to the cylinder head.

18 Disconnect the sensor wiring connector, undo the two bolts and remove the sensor.

19 Refit the sensor using the reverse of removal, tightening the retaining bolts to the specified torque, using a little thread-locking compound on the sensor bolts. Refit the camshaft sprocket and timing belt as described in Chapter 2B, Section 7 and 8.

Z19DTH and Z19DTR engines

20 The camshaft sensor is located at the right-hand end of the camshaft housing **(see illustration)**. To gain access, remove the plastic cover from the top of the engine.

21 Wipe clean the area around the camshaft sensor then disconnect the wiring connector.

22 Slacken and remove the retaining bolt and remove the sensor from the camshaft cover. Recover the sealing ring.

23 Refitting is the reverse of removal, using a new sealing ring. Tighten the sensor retaining bolt to the specified torque.

Coolant temperature sensor

24 The coolant temperature sensor is located on the thermostat housing on the left-hand end of the cylinder head. Partially drain the cooling system, disconnect the wiring plug and unscrew the sensor **(see illustration)**.

25 Refitting is a reversal of removal. Top-up the cooling system as described in *Weekly checks*.

Intake air pressure/temperature sensor

26 Remove the plastic cover from the top of the engine, then disconnect the wiring connector from the charge pressure sensor located in the centre of the intake manifold **(see illustration)**.

27 Slacken and remove the retaining bolt and remove the sensor from the manifold. Recover the sealing ring.

28 Refitting is the reverse of removal, using a new sealing ring. Tighten the sensor retaining bolt to the specified torque.

Fuel pressure regulator

Note: *On later engines and all Z19DTR engines the fuel pressure regulator is part of the high-pressure pump.*

29 Disconnect the battery negative terminal as described in Chapter 5A, Section 4.

30 Remove the plastic cover over the top of the engine.

31 On Z19DT engines, remove the fuel rail as described in Section 11.

32 On Z19DTH engines, disconnect the wiring connector from the fuel pressure regulator **(see illustration)**.

33 Remove the regulator from the fuel rail by unscrewing the inner nut (nearest the fuel rail) while counter-holding the regulator body with a second spanner. Be prepared for some loss of fuel.

9.20 Camshaft sensor location (arrowed) – Z19DTH engine

9.24 The coolant temperature sensor (arrowed) is located at the left-hand end of the cylinder head

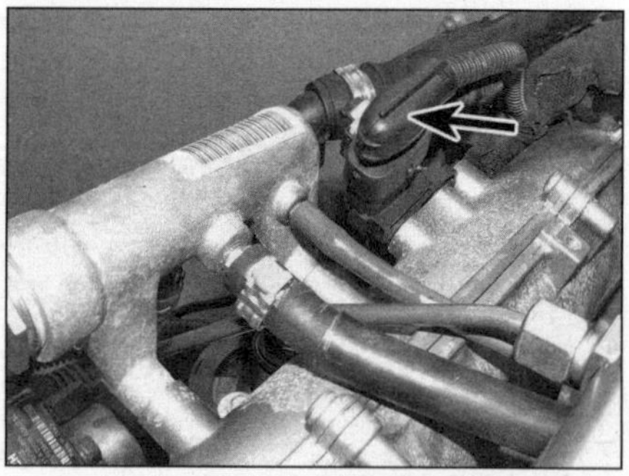

9.26 Disconnect the charge air pressure sensor wiring plug (arrowed)

9.32 Slide out the yellow locking catch, depress the clip and disconnect the fuel pressure regulator wiring plug

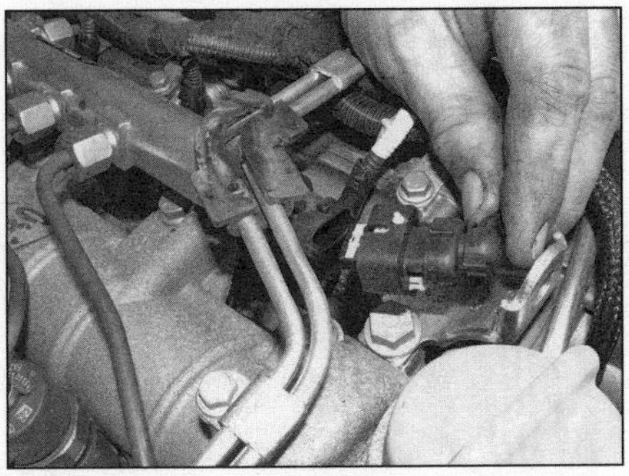

9.37 Disconnect the fuel pressure sensor wiring plug

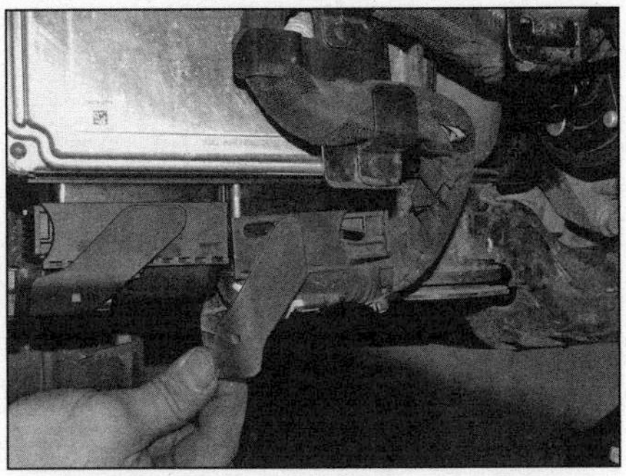

9.43a Pull out the locking clip, pull down the locking bar ...

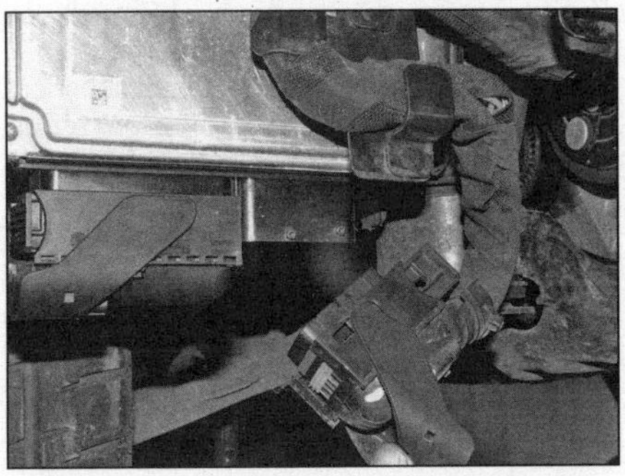

9.43b ... and disconnect the ECM wiring plugs

9.44 Undo the ECM bracket nuts (arrowed)

9.46 The turbocharger control solenoid (arrowed)

34 Refitting is the reverse of removal, tightening the regulator to the specified torque.

Fuel pressure sensor

35 Disconnect the battery negative terminal as described in Chapter 5A, Section 4.

36 Remove the plastic cover over the top of the engine.

37 Disconnect the wiring connector at the fuel pressure sensor **(see illustration)**.

38 Unscrew the sensor and remove it from the fuel rail. Be prepared for some loss of fuel.

39 Refitting is the reverse of removal, tightening the sensor to the specified torque.

Electronic control module (ECM)

Note: *If a new ECM is to be fitted, this work must be entrusted to a Saab dealer or suitably-equipped specialist as it is necessary to programme the new ECM after installation. This work requires the use of dedicated Saab diagnostic equipment or a compatible alternative.*

40 Disconnect the battery negative terminal as described in Chapter 5A, Section 4.

41 Firmly apply the handbrake, then jack up the front of the car and support it securely on axle stands (see *Jacking and vehicle support*). Remove the right-hand front roadwheel.

42 Undo the fasteners and remove the right-hand inner wing liner.

43 Release the locking clip, then open the locking bar and disconnect both wiring connectors from the ECM **(see illustrations)**. Release the wiring harness from its cable-ties.

44 Undo the 3 nuts securing the ECM mounting bracket **(see illustration)** and withdraw the ECM and mounting bracket from under the front wing.

45 Refitting is a reversal of removal.

Turbocharger boost pressure solenoids

Z19DT AND DTH engines

46 The turbocharger control solenoid is located above the radiator, attached to the underside of the bonnet slam panel **(see illustration)**.

47 Disconnect the wiring connector and the two vacuum hoses from the valve then undo the retaining nuts and remove the valve from its mounting bracket.

48 Refitting is the reverse of removal.

Z19DTR engines

49 The solenoid valves are located at the front of the engine compartment above the radiator.

50 Note the fitted positions of the solenoids **(see illustration)** and unplug the appropriate electrical connector.

51 Unbolt and lift out the solenoid mounting bracket.

52 Mark the position of the vacuum hoses and remove them as required.

53 Remove the single fixing bolt and remove the solenoid.

54 Refitting is a reversal of removal.

10 High-pressure fuel pump – removal and refitting

Warning: *Refer to the information contained in Section 2 before proceeding.*

Z19DT engines

Note: *A complete new set of high-pressure fuel pipes will be required for refitting.*

Removal

1 Disconnect the battery negative terminal (refer to Chapter 5A, Section 4).

2 Remove the plastic cover over the top of the engine.

3 Remove the timing belt and the

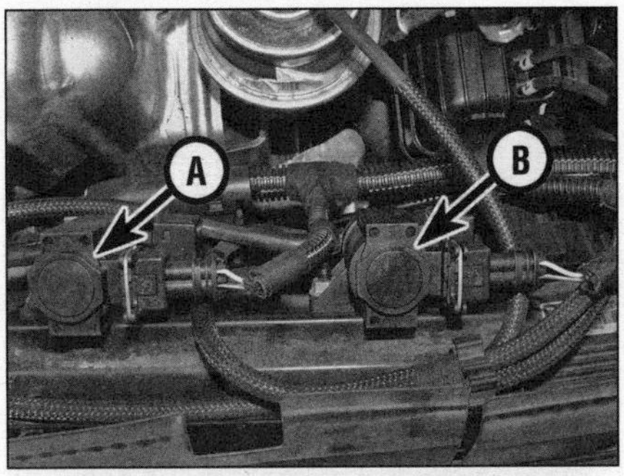

9.50 Note the position of the solenoids

A High-pressure (upper) turbocharger
B Low-pressure (lower) turbocharger

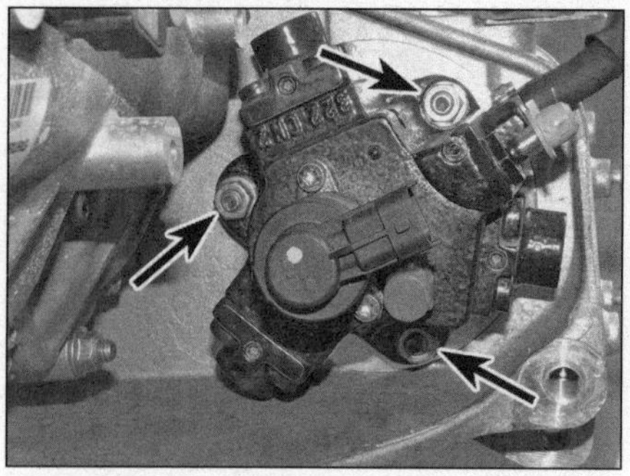

10.7a Unscrew the three retaining nuts (arrowed) ...

high-pressure fuel pump sprocket as described in Chapter 2B, Section 7 and 8.

4 Remove the fuel rail as described in Section 11.

5 Disconnect the fuel return hose quick-release fitting on the top of the high-pressure fuel pump. Suitably plug or cover the open unions to prevent dirt entry.

6 Disconnect the wiring connector from the high-pressure fuel pump.

7 Unscrew the three retaining nuts and remove the pump from the engine bracket **(see illustrations)**.

Caution: The high-pressure fuel pump is manufactured to extremely close tolerances and must not be dismantled in any way. No parts for the pump are available separately and if the unit is in any way suspect, it must be renewed.

10.7b ... and remove the high-pressure fuel pump from the engine bracket

Refitting

8 Refit the pump to the engine bracket and tighten the retaining bolts to the specified torque.

9 Reconnect the pump wiring connector and the fuel return hose quick-release fitting.

10 Refit the fuel rail as described in Section 11.

11 Refit the high-pressure fuel pump sprocket and the timing belt as described in Chapter 2B, Section 7 and 8.

12 Reconnect the battery negative terminal as described in Chapter 5A, Section 4.

13 Observing the precautions listed in Section 2, prime the fuel system as described in Section 5, then start the engine and allow it to idle. Check for leaks at the high-pressure fuel pipe unions with the engine idling. If satisfactory, increase the engine speed to 4000 rpm and check again for leaks. Take the car for a short road test and check for leaks once again on return. If any leaks are detected, obtain and fit a new high-pressure fuel pipe.

14 Refit the engine cover on completion.

Z19DTH and Z19DTR engines

Note: *A new fuel pump-to-fuel rail high-pressure fuel pipe will be required for refitting.*

Removal

15 Disconnect the battery negative terminal as described in Chapter 5A, Section 4.

16 Remove the plastic cover over the top of the engine.

17 Remove the timing belt and the high-pressure fuel pump sprocket as described in Chapter 2C, Section 6 and 7.

18 Release the retaining clips and disconnect the two fuel return hoses at the fuel return damping chamber **(see illustrations)**. Suitably plug or cover the open unions to prevent dirt entry.

10.18a Release the clips and disconnect the upper (arrowed) ...

10.18b ... and lower (arrowed) fuel return hoses at the damping chamber

19 Disconnect the injector leak-off pipe and the fuel return quick-release fitting, then undo the two bolts and remove the damping chamber. Suitably plug or cover the open unions to prevent dirt entry.

20 Disconnect the fuel supply hose quick-release fitting to the high-pressure fuel pump. Suitably plug or cover the open unions to prevent dirt entry **(see illustration)**.

10.20 Insert a release tool around the fuel pipe, and push it into the coupling to release the clips and disconnect the pipe

21 Disconnect the wiring connector from the high-pressure fuel pump.

22 Thoroughly clean the fuel pipe unions on the fuel pump and fuel rail. Using an open-ended spanner, unscrew the union nuts securing the high-pressure fuel pipe to the fuel pump and fuel rail. Counter-hold the union on the pump with a second spanner, while unscrewing the union nut **(see illustration)**. Withdraw the high-pressure fuel pipe and plug or cover the open unions to prevent dirt entry.

10.22 Unscrew the union nuts securing the high-pressure fuel pipe to the fuel pump and fuel rail

23 Unscrew the three retaining nuts and remove the pump from the engine bracket **(see illustrations 10.7a and 10.7b)**.

Caution: The high-pressure fuel pump is manufactured to extremely close tolerances and must not be dismantled in any way. No parts for the pump are available separately and if the unit is in any way suspect, it must be renewed.

Refitting

24 Refit the pump to the engine bracket and tighten the retaining bolts to the specified torque.

25 Remove the blanking plugs from the fuel pipe unions on the pump and fuel rail. Locate a new high-pressure fuel pipe over the unions and screw on the union nuts finger-tight at this stage.

26 Using a torque wrench and crow-foot adapter, tighten the fuel pipe union nuts to the specified torque. Counter-hold the unions on the pump with an open-ended spanner, while tightening the union nuts.

27 Reconnect the pump wiring connector and the fuel return hose quick-release fitting.

28 Refit the damping chamber and tighten the retaining bolts securely. Reconnect the injector leak-off pipe, and the two remaining fuel return hoses.
29 Refit the high-pressure fuel pump sprocket and the timing belt as described in Chapter 2C, Section 6 and 7.
30 Reconnect the battery negative terminal as described in Chapter 5A, Section 4.
31 Observing the precautions listed in Section 2, prime the fuel system as described in Section 5, then start the engine and allow it to idle. Check for leaks at the high-pressure fuel pipe unions with the engine idling. If satisfactory, increase the engine speed to 4000 rpm and check again for leaks. Take the car for a short road test and check for leaks once again on return. If any leaks are detected, obtain and fit a new high-pressure fuel pipe.
32 Refit the engine cover on completion.

11 Fuel rail – removal and refitting

Warning: Refer to the information contained in Section 2 before proceeding.

Note: *A complete new set of high-pressure fuel pipes will be required for refitting.*

Z19DT engines

Removal

1 Disconnect the battery negative terminal as described in Chapter 5A, Section 4.
2 Remove the plastic cover over the top of the engine.
3 Release the locking catches securing the wiring connectors to the four injectors, then disconnect the injector wiring.
4 Undo the two bolts at the top and the two bolts at the front, securing the plastic wiring trough to the intake manifold **(see illustrations)**. Move the wiring trough and injector wiring harness to one side.
5 Release the retaining clips and disconnect the two fuel return hoses at the fuel return damping chamber. Suitably plug or cover the open unions to prevent dirt entry.
6 Disconnect the injector leak-off pipe and the fuel return quick-release fitting, then undo the two bolts and remove the damping chamber. Suitably plug or cover the open unions to prevent dirt entry.
7 Thoroughly clean the fuel pipe unions on the fuel pump and fuel rail. Using an open-ended spanner, unscrew the union nuts securing the high-pressure fuel pipe to the fuel pump and fuel rail. Counter-hold the unions on the pump with a second spanner, while unscrewing the union nuts. Withdraw the high-pressure fuel pipe and plug or cover the open unions to prevent dirt entry.
8 Using two spanners, hold the unions and unscrew the union nuts securing the high-pressure fuel pipes to the fuel injectors. Unscrew the union nuts securing

11.4a Undo the two bolts at the top (arrowed) ...

the high-pressure fuel pipes to the fuel rail, withdraw the pipes and plug or cover the open unions to prevent dirt entry.
9 Disconnect the wiring connectors at the fuel pressure regulator and fuel pressure sensor, then undo the two nuts and remove the fuel rail.

Refitting

10 Refit the fuel rail and tighten the retaining nuts to the specified torque. Reconnect the fuel pressure regulator and fuel pressure sensor wiring connectors.
11 Working on one fuel injector at a time, remove the blanking plugs from the fuel pipe unions on the fuel rail and the relevant injector. Locate the new high-pressure fuel pipe over the unions and screw on the union nuts finger-tight. Tighten the union nuts to the specified torque using a torque wrench and crow-foot adapter. Counter-hold the union on the injector with an open-ended spanner, while tightening the union nut. Repeat this operation for the remaining three injectors.
12 Similarly, fit the new high-pressure fuel pipe to the fuel pump and fuel rail, and tighten the union nuts to the specified torque. Counter-hold the union on the pump with an open-ended spanner, while tightening the union nut.
13 Refit the damping chamber and tighten the retaining bolts securely. Reconnect the injector leak-off pipe, and the fuel return hoses.
14 Refit the wiring trough, and secure with the four retaining bolts. Reconnect the wiring connectors to the fuel injectors.

11.20 Unscrew the union nuts securing the high-pressure fuel pipes to the fuel rail and injectors

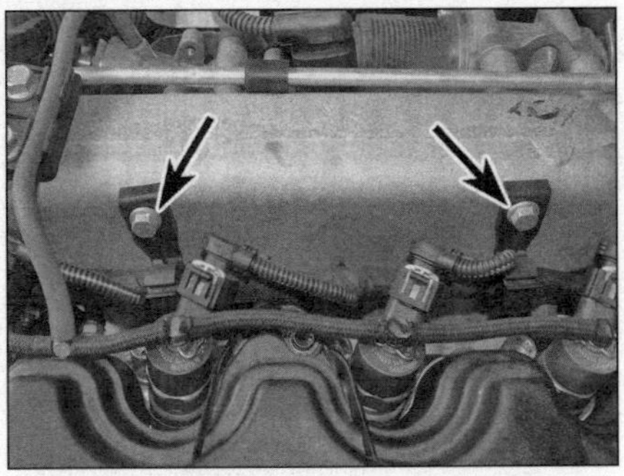

11.4b ... and the two bolts at the front (arrowed) and move the wiring harness trough to one side

15 Reconnect the battery negative terminal as described in Chapter 5A, Section 4.
16 Observing the precautions listed in Section 2, prime the fuel system as described in Section 5, then start the engine and allow it to idle. Check for leaks at the high-pressure fuel pipe unions with the engine idling. If satisfactory, increase the engine speed to 4000 rpm and check again for leaks. Take the car for a short road test and check for leaks once again on return. If any leaks are detected, obtain and fit a new high-pressure fuel pipe.
17 Refit the engine cover on completion.

Z19DTH and DTR engines

Removal

18 Disconnect the battery negative terminal as described in Chapter 5A, Section 4.
19 Remove the plastic cover over the top of the engine.
20 Thoroughly clean all the high-pressure fuel pipe unions on the fuel rail, fuel pump and injectors. Using two spanners, hold the unions and unscrew the union nuts securing the high-pressure fuel pipes to the fuel injectors. Unscrew the union nuts securing the high-pressure fuel pipes to the fuel rail, withdraw the pipes and plug or cover the open unions to prevent dirt entry **(see illustration)**.
21 Using an open-ended spanner, unscrew the union nuts securing the high-pressure fuel pipe to the fuel pump and fuel rail **(see illustration)**. Counter-hold the unions on the pump with a second spanner, while unscrewing the union nuts. Withdraw the

11.21 Unscrew the union nuts securing the high-pressure fuel pipe to the pump and fuel rail

11.22a Disconnect the fuel return hose ...

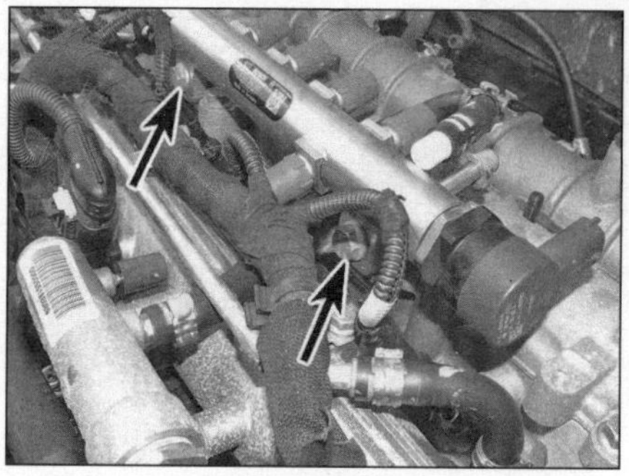

11.22b ... then undo the two bolts (arrowed) and remove the fuel rail

high-pressure fuel pipe and plug or cover the open unions to prevent dirt entry.

22 Disconnect the wiring connectors at the fuel pressure regulator and fuel pressure sensor, then release the clip and disconnect the fuel return hose. Undo the two bolts and remove the fuel rail **(see illustrations)**.

Refitting

23 Refit the fuel rail and tighten the retaining bolts to the specified torque. Reconnect the fuel pressure regulator and fuel pressure sensor wiring connectors, and reconnect the fuel return hose.

24 Working on one fuel injector at a time, remove the blanking plugs from the fuel pipe unions on the fuel rail and the relevant injector. Locate the new high-pressure fuel pipe over the unions and screw on the union nuts finger-tight. Tighten the union nuts to the specified torque using a torque wrench and crow-foot adapter. Counter-hold the union on the injector with an open-ended spanner, while tightening the union nut. Repeat this operation for the remaining three injectors.

25 Similarly, fit the new high-pressure fuel pipe to the fuel pump and fuel rail, and tighten the union nuts to the specified torque. Counter-hold the union on the pump with an open-ended spanner, while tightening the union nut.

26 Reconnect the battery negative terminal as described in Chapter 5A, Section 4.

27 Observing the precautions listed in Section 2, prime the fuel system as described in Section 5, then start the engine and allow it to idle. Check for leaks at the high-pressure fuel pipe unions with the engine idling. If satisfactory, increase the engine speed to 4000 rpm and check again for leaks. Take the car for a short road test and check for leaks once again on return. If any leaks are detected, obtain and fit a new high-pressure fuel pipe.

28 Refit the engine cover on completion.

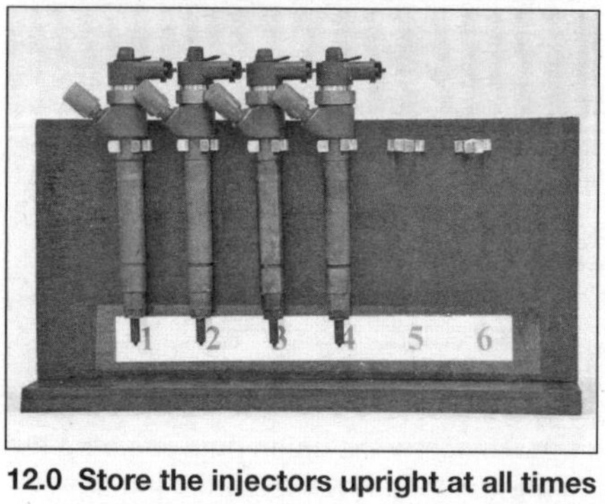

12.0 Store the injectors upright at all times

12 Fuel injectors – removal and refitting

Warning: Refer to the information contained in Section 2 before proceeding.

Z19DT engines

Note: *A new copper washer, retaining nut and high-pressure fuel pipe will be required for each removed injector when refitting.*

Note: *The injector is an extremely tight fit in the cylinder head, and it is likely that the special Saab puller (32 025 013) and adapter (32 025 012) or suitable alternatives, will be needed.*

Note: *Store the injectors vertically and in the correct order* ***(see illustration)****. If new injectors are fitted, note the code on the injector as this will be required to programme the injector to the engine using suitable diagnostic equipment. The engine may not start or will run inefficiently until the new injectors have been programmed.*

Removal

1 Disconnect the battery negative terminal as described in Chapter 5A, Section 4.

12.9 Remove the copper washer from the injector base

2 Remove the plastic cover over the top of the engine.

3 Release the locking catches securing the wiring connectors to the four injectors, then disconnect the injector wiring.

4 Undo the two bolts at the top and the two bolts at the front, securing the plastic wiring trough to the intake manifold **(see illustrations 11.4a and 11.4b)**. Move the wiring trough and injector wiring harness to one side.

5 Thoroughly clean the fuel pipe unions on the fuel rail and injector. Using two spanners, hold the unions and unscrew the union nut securing the high-pressure fuel pipe to the fuel injector. Unscrew the union nut securing the high-pressure fuel pipe to the fuel rail, withdraw the pipe and plug or cover the open unions to prevent dirt entry.

6 Disconnect the fuel leak-off hose connection at each injector by pushing in the locking clip and lifting out the hose fitting. Suitably plug or cap the leak-off hose union on each injector, and slip a plastic bag over the disconnected leak-off hose to prevent dirt entry.

7 Unscrew the retaining nut then remove the washer from the injector clamp bracket.

8 Withdraw the injector together with the clamp bracket from the cylinder head. If difficulty is experienced removing the injector, liberally apply penetrating oil to the base of the injector and allow time for the oil to penetrate. If the injector is still reluctant to free, it will be necessary to use a slide hammer engaged under the flange of the injector body casting, and gently tap free. If available, use Saab special tools 320 025 013, 32 025 012 and 83 90 270 or a suitable alternative for this purpose **(see illustrations 12.33a, 12.33b and 12.33c)**. Note that it is not possible to twist the injector from side-to-side to free them due to the design of the clamp bracket.

9 Once the injector has been removed, separate it from the clamp bracket and remove the copper washer from the injector base **(see illustration)**. The copper washer may have remained in place at the base of the injector orifice in the cylinder head. If so, hook it out with a length of wire.

10 Remove the remaining injectors in the same way.

11 Examine the injector visually for any signs of obvious damage or deterioration. If any defects are apparent, renew the injector.

Caution: The injectors are manufactured to extremely close tolerances and must not be dismantled in any way. Do not unscrew the fuel pipe union on the side of the injector, or separate any parts of the injector body. Do not attempt to clean carbon deposits from the injector nozzle or carry out any form of ultrasonic or pressure testing.

12 If the injectors are in a satisfactory condition, plug the fuel pipe union (if not already done) and suitably cover the electrical element and the injector nozzle.

13 Prior to refitting, obtain a new copper washer, a new retaining nut and new high-pressure fuel pipe for each injector.

12.28 Undo the two bolts (arrowed) and remove the breather pipe from the cylinder head

12.29a Slide out the locking catch ...

12.29b ... depress the clip and disconnect the injector wiring plugs

Refitting

14 Thoroughly clean the injector seat in the cylinder head, ensuring all traces of carbon and other deposits are removed.

15 Locate a new copper washer on the base of the injector.

16 Place the injector clamp bracket in the slot on the injector body and refit the injector to the cylinder head.

17 Fit the washer and the new injector clamp bracket retaining nut, and tighten the nut to the specified torque.

18 Remove the blanking plug from the fuel pipe union on the fuel rail and the injector. Locate the new high-pressure fuel pipe over the unions and screw on the union nuts. Take care not to cross-thread the nuts or strain the fuel pipe as it is fitted.

19 Tighten the fuel pipe union nuts to the specified torque using a torque wrench and crow-foot adapter **(see illustration 12.44)**. Counter-hold the union on the injector with an open-ended spanner, while tightening the union nut.

20 Repeat this procedure for the remaining injectors.

21 Refit the wiring trough, and secure with the four retaining bolts. Reconnect the wiring connectors to the fuel injectors.

22 Reconnect the leak-off hose fittings to the injectors by pushing in the locking clip, attaching the fitting, then releasing the locking clip. Ensure that each fitting is securely connected and retained by the clip.

23 Reconnect the battery negative terminal as described in Chapter 5A, Section 4.

24 Observing the precautions listed in Section 2, prime the fuel system as described in Section 5, then start the engine and allow it to idle. Check for leaks at the high-pressure fuel pipe unions with the engine idling. If satisfactory, increase the engine speed to 4000 rpm and check again for leaks. Take the car for a short road test and check for leaks once again on return. If any leaks are detected, obtain and fit a new high-pressure fuel pipe.

25 Refit the engine cover on completion.

Z19DTH and DTR engines

Note: *A new copper washer, retaining nut and high-pressure fuel pipe will be required for each injector when refitting*

Note: *The injector is an extremely tight fit in the cylinder head, and it is likely that the special Saab puller (32 025 013) and adapter (32 025 012) or suitable alternatives, will be needed.*

Note: *Store the injectors vertically and in the correct order* ***(see illustration 12.0)****. If new injectors are fitted, note the code on the injector as this will be required to programme the injector to the engine using suitable diagnostic equipment. The engine may not start or will run inefficiently until the new injectors have been programmed.*

12.30a Disconnect the fuel leak-off hose connection at each injector ...

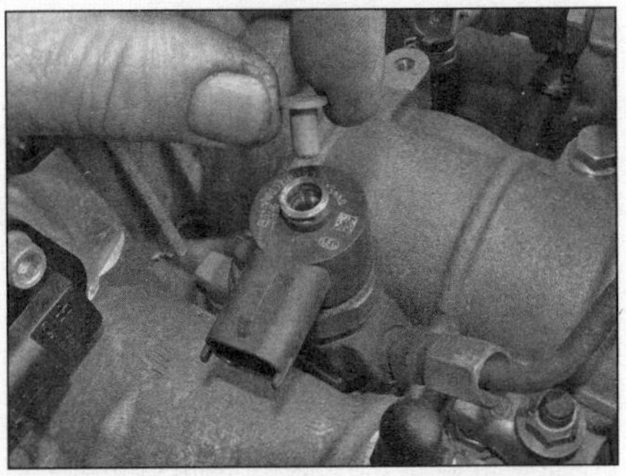

12.30b ... then plug or cap the leak-off hose union on each injector

Removal

26 Disconnect the battery negative terminal as described in Chapter 5A, Section 4.

27 Remove the plastic cover over the top of the engine.

28 Release the retaining clip securing the engine breather hose to the breather pipe adjacent to the engine oil dipstick. Undo the two bolts securing the breather pipe to the cylinder head, and disconnect the pipe from the hose **(see illustration)**.

29 Release the locking catches securing the wiring connectors to the four injectors, then disconnect the injector wiring **(see illustrations)**.

30 Disconnect the fuel leak-off hose connection at each injector by pushing in the locking clip and lifting out the hose fitting. Suitably plug or cap the leak-off hose union on each injector, and slip a plastic bag over the disconnected leak-off hose to prevent dirt entry **(see illustrations)**.

31 Thoroughly clean the fuel pipe unions on the fuel rail and injector. Using two spanners, hold the unions and unscrew the union nut securing the high-pressure fuel pipe to the fuel injector **(see illustration)**. Unscrew the union nut securing the high-pressure fuel pipe to the fuel rail, withdraw the pipe and plug or cover the open unions to prevent dirt entry.

32 Starting with injector No 1, unscrew the retaining nut then remove the washer from the injector clamp bracket **(see illustration)**.

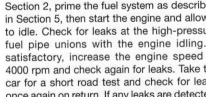

12.31 Counter-hold the injector union when unscrewing the high-pressure fuel pipe unions

12.32 Unscrew the injector clamp bracket retaining nut then remove the washer

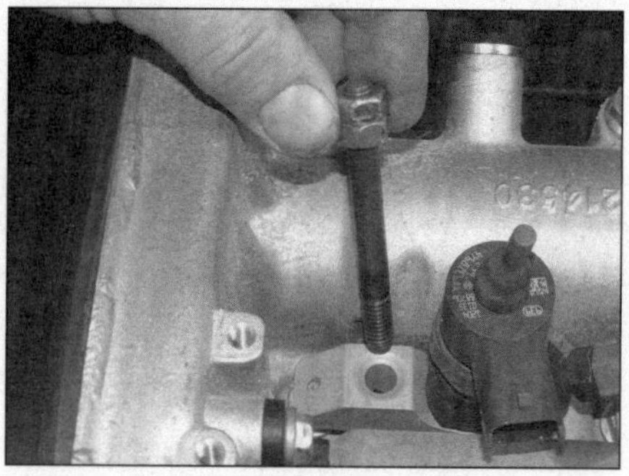

12.33a Remove the stud by locking 2 nuts together and then remove the yoke

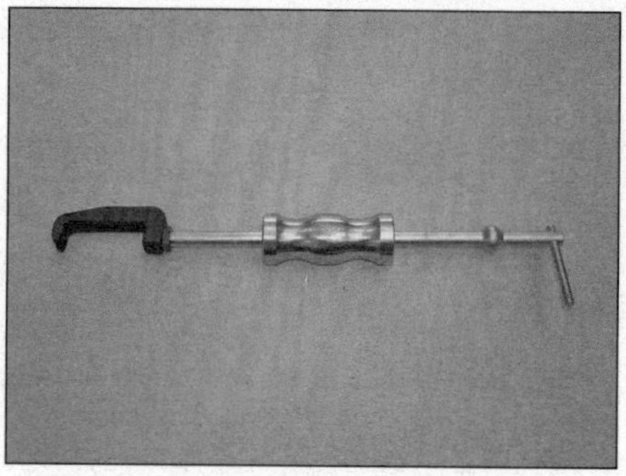

12.33b Suitable tools are available to ...

12.33c ... help remove a stuck injector

33 Withdraw the injector together with the clamp bracket from the cylinder head. If difficulty is experienced removing the injector, liberally apply penetrating oil to the base of the injector and allow time for the oil to penetrate. If the injector is still reluctant to free, it will be necessary to use a small slide hammer engaged under the flange of the injector body casting, and gently tap it free. If available, use Saab special tools 32 025 013, 32 025 012 and 83 90 270 or a suitable alternative for this purpose **(see illustrations)**. Note that it is not possible to twist the injector from side-to-side to free them due to the design of the clamp bracket.

34 Once the injector has been removed, separate it from the clamp bracket and remove the copper washer from the injector base **(see illustration)**. The copper washer may have remained in place at the base of the injector orifice in the cylinder head. If so, hook it out with a length of wire.

35 Remove the remaining injectors in the same way.

36 Examine the injector visually for any signs of obvious damage or deterioration. If any defects are apparent, renew the injector.

Caution: The injectors are manufactured to extremely close tolerances and must not be dismantled in any way. Do not unscrew the fuel pipe union on the side of the injector, or separate any parts of the injector body. Do not attempt to clean carbon deposits from the injector nozzle or carry out any form of ultrasonic or pressure testing.

37 If the injectors are in a satisfactory condition, plug the fuel pipe union (if not already done) and suitably cover the electrical element and the injector nozzle.

38 Prior to refitting, obtain a new set of copper washers, retaining nuts and high-pressure fuel pipes.

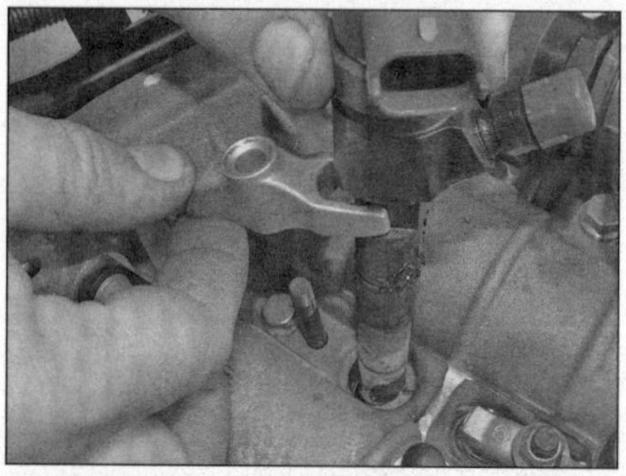

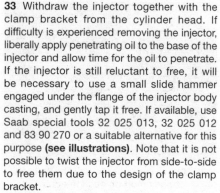

12.34 Once the injector has been removed, separate it from the clamp bracket

12.42a Fit the washer ...

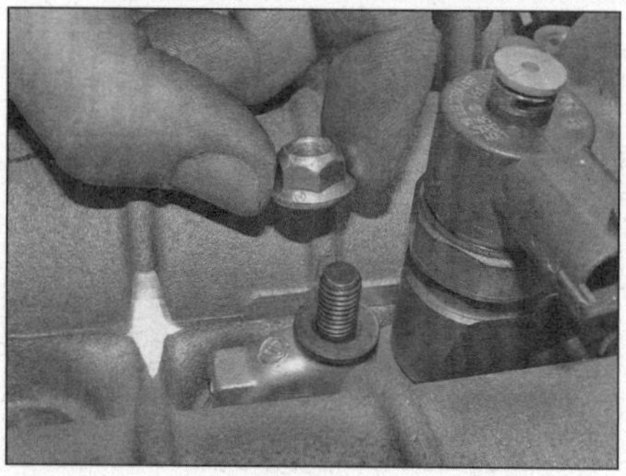

12.42b ... and the injector clamp bracket retaining nut

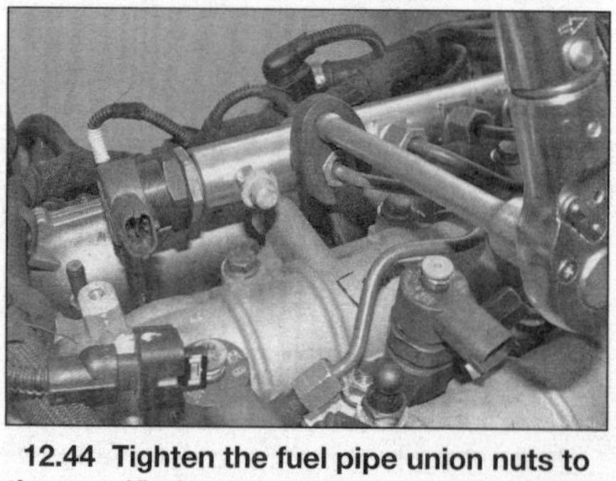

12.44 Tighten the fuel pipe union nuts to the specified torque using a torque wrench and crow-foot adapter

Refitting

39 Thoroughly clean the injector seat in the cylinder head, ensuring all traces of carbon and other deposits are removed.

40 Starting with injector No 4, locate a new copper washer on the base of the injector.

41 Place the injector clamp bracket in the slot on the injector body and refit the injector to the cylinder head.

42 Fit the washer and the injector clamp bracket retaining nut, and tighten the nut to the specified torque **(see illustrations)**.

43 Remove the blanking plug from the fuel pipe union on the fuel rail and the injector. Locate the new high-pressure fuel pipe over the unions and screw on the union nuts. Take care not to cross-thread the nuts or strain the fuel pipe as it is fitted.

44 Tighten the fuel pipe union nuts to the specified torque using a torque wrench and crow-foot adapter **(see illustration)**. Counter-hold the union on the injector with an open-ended spanner, while tightening the union nut.

45 Repeat this procedure for the remaining injectors.

46 Reconnect the leak-off hose fittings to the injectors by pushing in the locking clip, attaching the fitting, then releasing the locking clip. Ensure that each fitting is securely connected and retained by the clip.

47 Reconnect the wiring connectors to the fuel injectors.

48 Attach the engine breather hose to the breather pipe and secure with the retaining clip. Secure the breather pipe to the cylinder head with the two bolts securely tightened.

49 Reconnect the battery negative terminal as described in Chapter 5A, Section 4.

50 Observing the precautions listed in Section 2, prime the fuel system as described in Section 5, then start the engine and allow it to idle. Check for leaks at the high-pressure fuel pipe unions with the engine idling. If satisfactory, increase the engine speed to 4000 rpm and check again for leaks. Take the car for a short road test and check for leaks once again on return. If any leaks are detected, obtain and fit a new high-pressure fuel pipe.

51 Refit the engine cover on completion.

13 Intake manifold – removal and refitting

Z19DT engines

Removal

1 Disconnect the battery negative terminal as described in Chapter 5A, Section 4.

2 Remove the plastic cover over the top of the engine.

3 Drain the cooling system as described in Chapter 1B, Section 28.

4 Remove the exhaust gas recirculation (EGR) valve as described in Chapter 4C, Section 3.

5 Remove the high-pressure fuel pump as described in Section 10.

6 Undo the retaining bolt(s) to release the vacuum lines running over the top of the camshaft cover **(see illustration)**.

7 Remove the throttle body/housing as described in Section 9.

8 Disconnect the wiring connectors at the four glow plugs.

9 Undo the three retaining bolts and detach the vacuum reservoir from the rear of the cylinder block.

10 Release the retaining clips and disconnect the two coolant hoses at the EGR heat exchanger, and the adjacent hose at the thermostat housing.

11 Unscrew the nut and two bolts securing the coolant pipes to the starter motor bracket.

12 Release the clamp and disconnect the metal pipe from the EGR heat exchanger. Undo the retaining nut and bolt and remove the heat exchanger.

13 Remove the alternator as described in Chapter 5A, Section 7.

14 Undo the six bolts securing the alternator and high-pressure fuel pump mounting bracket to the cylinder block and cylinder head. There are five bolts securing the bracket to the block at the rear, and one securing the bracket to the head at the front.

15 Undo the nine retaining nuts and remove the intake manifold from the cylinder head studs. Recover the gasket.

Refitting

16 Thoroughly clean the intake manifold and cylinder head mating faces, then locate a new gasket on the intake manifold flange.

13.6 Undo the retaining bolt(s) to release the vacuum pipe from the camshaft cover

17 Locate the manifold in position and refit the retaining nuts. Diagonally and progressively tighten the nuts to the specified torque.

18 Refit the alternator and high-pressure fuel pump bracket and tighten the retaining bolts to the specified torque.

19 Refit the alternator as described in Chapter 5A, Section 7.

20 Refit the EGR heat exchanger and securely tighten the retaining nut and bolt. Reconnect the metal EGR pipe and secure with the retaining clamp.

21 Locate the coolant pipe on the starter motor bracket. Refit and securely tighten the retaining nut and bolts.

22 Reconnect the coolant hoses to the EGR heat exchanger and thermostat housing and secure with the retaining clips.

23 Attach the vacuum reservoir to the cylinder block, refit the three retaining bolts and tighten them securely.

24 Reconnect the wiring connectors to the glow plugs.

25 Refit the throttle body/housing as described in Section 9.

26 Refit the vacuum lines running over the top of the camshaft cover and reconnect the vacuum hoses.

27 Refit the high-pressure fuel pump as described in Section 10.

28 Refit the exhaust gas recirculation (EGR) valve as described in Chapter 4C, Section 3.

29 Refill the cooling system as described in Chapter 1B, Section 28.

30 Reconnect the battery negative terminal.

31 Observing the precautions listed in Section 2, prime the fuel system as described in Section 5, then start the engine and allow it to idle. Check for leaks at the high-pressure fuel pipe unions with the engine idling. If satisfactory, increase the engine speed to 4000 rpm and check again for leaks. Take the car for a short road test and check for leaks once again on return. If any leaks are detected, obtain and fit a new high-pressure fuel pipe.

32 Refit the engine cover on completion.

Z19DTH and Z19DTR engines

Removal

33 Disconnect the battery negative terminal as described in Chapter 5A, Section 4.

34 Remove the plastic cover over the top of the engine.

35 Remove the high-pressure fuel pump as described in Section 10.

36 Remove the exhaust gas recirculation (EGR) valve as described in Chapter 4C, Section 3.

37 Drain the cooling system as described in Chapter 1B, Section 28.

38 Release the clips and remove the turbocharger deliver hose from the throttle body.

39 Disconnect the coolant pipe, disconnect the level sensor wiring plug, then remove the coolant reservoir.

40 Disconnect the hose from the thermostat housing.

41 Undo the nuts securing the coolant pipe to the starter motor bracket, and bend the pipe away slightly **(see illustration)**.

42 Remove the oil separator and vacuum reservoir mounting bracket by undoing the two nuts above the vacuum reservoir, the bolt at the base of the vacuum reservoir, and the bolt at the right-hand side of the oil separator. Remove the mounting bracket complete with oil separator and vacuum reservoir **(see illustrations)**.

43 Undo the three bolts, release the hose clip, free the wiring harness and detach the coolant pipe from the intake manifold.

44 Screw two nuts onto the inner high-pressure fuel pump mounting stud. Lock the two nuts together and unscrew the stud from the engine bracket **(see illustration)**.

45 Disconnect the wiring connectors at the

13.41 Unscrew the nuts and free the wiring harness and coolant pipe from the starter motor bracket

13.42a Undo the two nuts (arrowed) above the vacuum reservoir ...

13.42b ... the bolt (arrowed) at the base of the vacuum reservoir ...

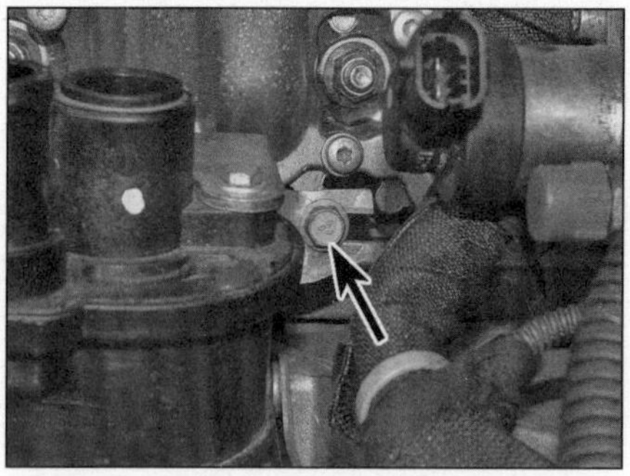

13.42c ... and the bolts (arrowed) on the right-hand side of the oil separator ...

13.42d ... then remove the mounting bracket complete with oil separator and vacuum reservoir

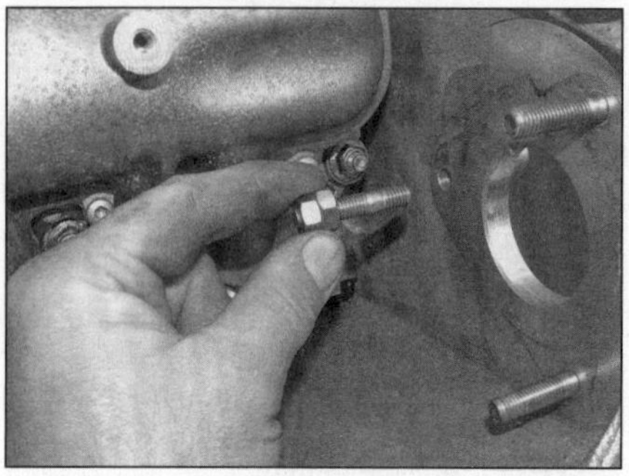

13.44 Lock two nuts together and unscrew the fuel pump stud from the engine bracket

13.46 Intake manifold retaining nuts (arrowed)

throttle body/housing, coolant temperature sensor, intake air sensor, fuel pressure sensor, and fuel pressure control valve.

46 Undo the nine retaining nuts and remove the intake manifold from the cylinder head studs **(see illustration)**. Recover the gasket (or gaskets on the Z19DTR engine).

47 With the manifold removed, if required, remove the throttle body/housing with reference to Section 9.

48 On the DTH engine the changeover flap actuator drive can be removed by disconnecting the drive motor actuating rod ball socket, and undoing the two stud bolts.

Refitting

49 If removed, refit the throttle body/housing with reference to Section 9, then refit the changeover flap actuator drive.

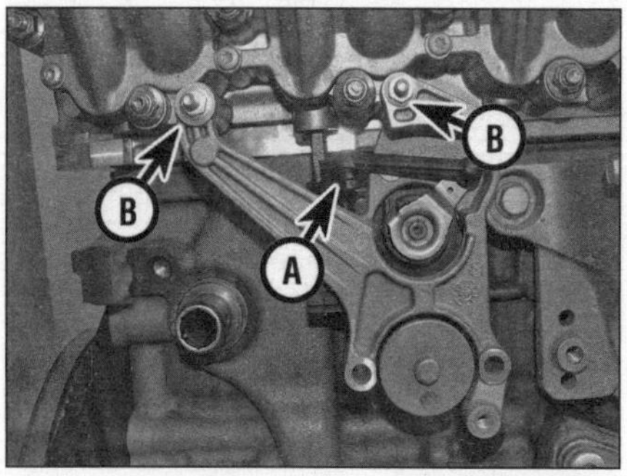

14.11 Disconnect the actuating rod ball socket (A), undo the two stud bolts (B) and remove the actuator drive

50 Thoroughly clean the intake manifold and cylinder head mating faces, then locate a new gasket(s) on the intake manifold flange.

51 Locate the manifold in position and refit the retaining nuts. Diagonally and progressively, tighten the nuts to the specified torque.

52 Reconnect the wiring connectors at the throttle body/housing and charge (boost) pressure sensor.

53 Refit the high-pressure fuel pump mounting stud, then remove the two nuts used to remove/refit the stud.

54 Refit the coolant pipe to the manifold, and secure with the three bolts tightened securely. Reconnect the coolant pipe and attach the wiring harness.

55 Refit the oil separator and vacuum reservoir mounting bracket. Refit and tighten the two bolts and two nuts, then reconnect the crankcase breather hoses.

56 Refit the coolant pipe and wiring harness to the starter motor bracket, then refit and tighten the two nuts.

57 Refit the exhaust gas recirculation (EGR) valve as described in Chapter 4C, Section 3.

58 Refit the high-pressure fuel pump as described in Section 10.

59 Reconnect the battery negative terminal as described in Chapter 5A, Section 4.

60 Observing the precautions listed in Section 2, prime the fuel system as described in Section 5, then start the engine and allow it to idle. Check for leaks at the high-pressure fuel pipe unions with the engine idling. If satisfactory, increase the engine speed to 4000 rpm and check again for leaks. Take the car for a short road test and check for leaks once again on return. If any leaks are detected, obtain and fit a new high-pressure fuel pipe.

61 Refit the engine cover on completion.

14 Intake manifold changeover flap actuator drive – removal and refitting

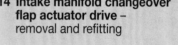

Note: *This only applies to Z19DTH engines.*

Removal

1 Disconnect the battery negative terminal as described in Chapter 5A, Section 4.

2 Remove the plastic cover over the top of the engine.

3 Remove the high-pressure fuel pump as described in Section 10.

4 Remove the exhaust gas recirculation (EGR) valve as described in Chapter 4C, Section 3.

5 Drain the cooling system as described in Chapter 1B, Section 28.

6 Release the clips and remove the turbocharger delivery hose from the throttle body.

7 Disconnect the coolant pipe, disconnect the level sensor wiring plug, then remove the coolant reservoir.

8 Disconnect the hose from the thermostat housing.

9 Undo the nuts securing the coolant pipe to the starter motor bracket, and bend the pipe away slightly **(see illustration 13.41)**.

10 Remove the oil separator and vacuum reservoir mounting bracket by undoing the two nuts above the vacuum reservoir, the bolt at the base of the vacuum reservoir, and the bolt at the right-hand side of the oil separator. Remove the mounting bracket complete with oil separator and vacuum reservoir **(see illustrations 13.42a to 13.42d)**.

11 Disconnect the drive motor actuating rod ball socket, and undo the 2 stud bolts **(see illustration)**.

12 Withdraw the assembly from the intake manifold and disconnect the wiring plug.

Refitting

13 Refitting is the reverse of removal.

15 Intercooler – removal and refitting

Removal

1 Remove the plastic cover from the top of the engine

2 Apply the handbrake, then jack up the front of the vehicle and support it on axle stands (see *Jacking and vehicle support*).

3 Remove the front bumper cover as described in Chapter 11, Section 6 and then remove the left-hand headlight as described in Chapter 12, Section 6.

4 Remove the battery cover.

5 Undo the bolt securing the air conditioning

pipe to the bonnet slam panel, then undo the bolts and remove the turbocharger control valve(s) **(see illustrations)**.

6 Undo the retaining bolts/nuts, disconnect the horn wiring plug, and remove the bonnet slam panel **(see illustrations)**. Lay the slam panel over the top of the engine.

7 Remove the 2 side covers from the lower section of the intercooler.

8 Slacken the retaining clips and remove the left-hand and right-hand lower charge air hoses from the intercooler and charge air pipes **(see illustrations)**.

9 Undo the upper bolt each side securing the condenser, then use straps or cable-ties to secure the condenser to the vehicle body **(see illustrations)**.

10 Undo the bolt each side securing the intercooler upper mounting brackets **(see illustration)**.

11 Unclip the plastic moulding from the top of the intercooler, lift the intercooler to disengage the lower lugs, then lower the intercooler and remove it from under the car **(see illustration)**.

Refitting

12 Refitting is the reverse of removal.

15.5a Undo the refrigerant pipe retaining bolt (arrowed) ...

15.5b ... and the 2 securing the turbo boost valve

15.6a Undo the bolts at the top of the slam panel (right-hand bolts arrowed) ...

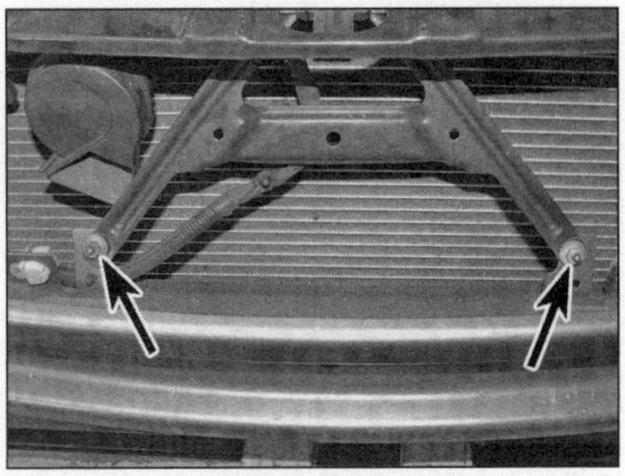

15.6b ... and the nuts in the centre (arrowed)

16 Turbocharger – description and precautions

Description

1 The turbocharger increases engine efficiency by raising the pressure in the intake manifold above atmospheric pressure. Instead of the air simply being sucked into the cylinders, it is forced in.

2 Energy for the operation of the turbocharger comes from the exhaust gas. The gas flows through a specially-shaped housing (the turbine housing) and, in so doing, spins the turbine wheel. The turbine wheel is attached to a shaft, at the end of which is another vaned wheel known as the compressor wheel. The

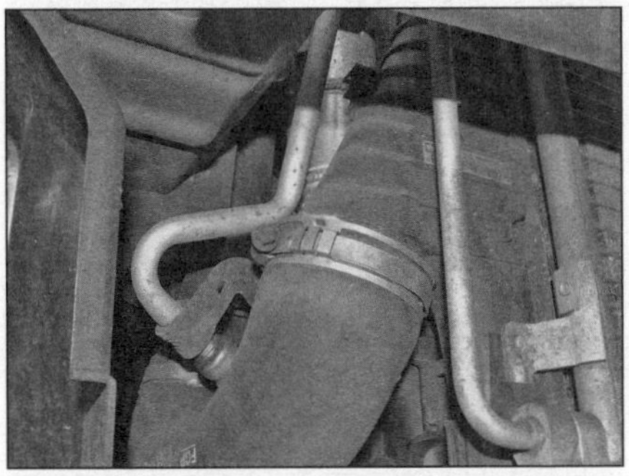

15.8a Slacken the clips and disconnect the right-hand ...

15.8b ... and left-hand intercooler hoses

15.9a Undo the condenser bolt each side (arrowed) ...

15.9b ... then suspend the condenser using cable-ties (or similar)

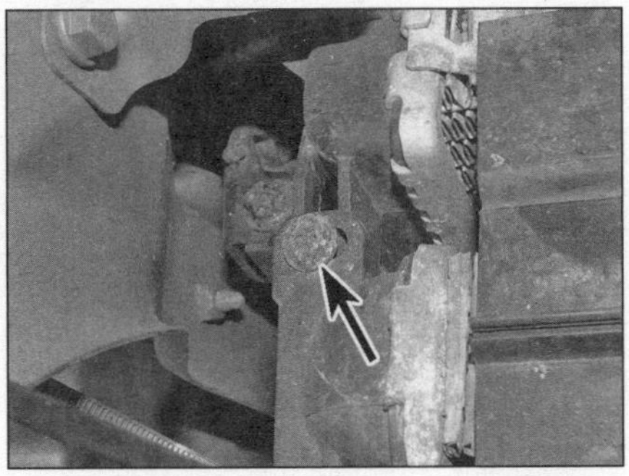

15.10 Remove the intercooler upper mounting bolt each side (arrowed)

15.11 Lift up and remove the plastic strip on the top of the intercooler

17.7 Undo the oil level dipstick tube bolt (arrowed)

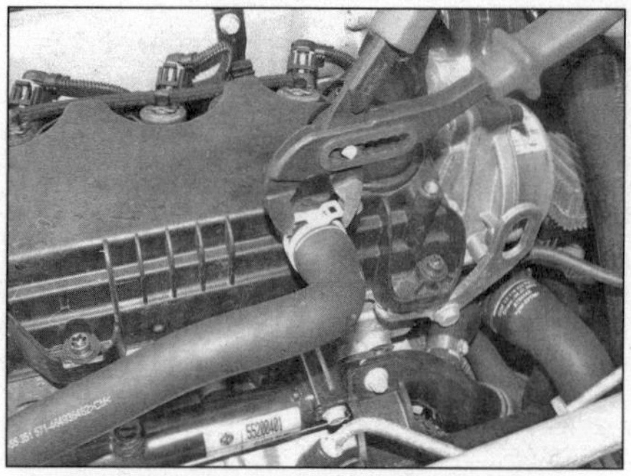

17.9 Release the retaining clip and disconnect the breather hose from the front of the camshaft cover

compressor wheel spins in its own housing, and compresses the intake air on the way to the intake manifold.

3 The turbocharger fitted to the Z19DT and Z19DTH engines operates on the principle of variable vane geometry. This type of turbocharger is often referred to as a variable nozzle turbine (VNT). At low engine speeds the vanes close to give less flow cross-section, then as the speed increases the vanes open to give an increased flow cross-section. This helps improve the efficiency of the turbocharger.

4 The position of the vanes in the VNT turbocharger is controlled by vacuum-driven actuator in response to commands from the engine management ECM via a solenoid in the vacuum line.

5 Two fixed vane turbochargers (and two wastegates) are fitted to the Z19DTR engine. The output of the turbochargers is controlled by the position of the wastegates and a mechanical diverter valve. The position of the wastegates is determined by the engine management ECM.

6 The turbo shaft is pressure-lubricated by an oil feed pipe from the main oil gallery. The shaft 'floats' on a cushion of oil. A drain pipe returns the oil to the sump.

Precautions

7 The turbocharger operates at extremely high speeds and temperatures. Certain precautions must be observed, to avoid premature failure of the turbo, or injury to the operator.

- Do not operate the turbo with any of its parts exposed, or with any of its hoses removed. Foreign objects falling onto the rotating vanes could cause excessive damage, and (if ejected) personal injury.
- Do not race the engine immediately after start-up, especially if it is cold. Give the oil a few seconds to circulate.
- Always allow the engine to return to idle speed before switching it off – do not blip the throttle and switch off, as this will leave the turbo spinning without lubrication.
- Allow the engine to idle for several minutes before switching off after a high-speed run.
- Observe the recommended intervals for oil and filter changing, and use a reputable oil of the specified quality. Neglect of oil changing, or use of inferior oil, can cause carbon formation on the turbo shaft, leading to subsequent failure.

17 Exhaust manifold and turbocharger – removal and refitting

Note: *New manifold retaining nuts, new gaskets for all disturbed joints, and new copper washers for the turbocharger oil supply pipe banjo union(s) will be required for refitting.*

Z19DT and Z19DTH engines

Removal

1 Disconnect the battery negative terminal as described in Chapter 5A, Section 4.

2 Remove the plastic cover from the top of the engine.

3 Firmly apply the handbrake, then jack up the front of the car and support it securely on axle stands (see *Jacking and vehicle support*). Undo the bolts and remove the engine undershield.

4 Drain the cooling system as described in Chapter 1B, Section 28.

5 Undo the fasteners and remove the front section of the exhaust pipe.

6 Undo the 2 nuts and remove the heat shield over the catalytic converter.

7 Undo the screw securing the oil level dipstick tube **(see illustration)**.

8 On Z19DTH engines, release the retaining clip securing the engine breather hose to the breather pipe adjacent to the engine oil dipstick. Undo the two bolts securing the breather pipe to the cylinder head, and disconnect the pipe from the hose.

9 On Z19DT engines, release the retaining clip and disconnect the breather hose from the front of the camshaft cover **(see illustration)**.

10 Remove the air cleaner assembly and air intake duct as described in Section 3.

11 Remove the turbocharger intake hose.

12 Remove the turbocharger delivery pipe from the throttle body and turbocharger.

13 Release the clip and disconnect the radiator top hose from the thermostat housing.

14 Disconnect the coolant hose between the reservoir and the manifold. Undo the mounting and remove the hose.

15 Disconnect the coolant hoses from the coolant pipe at the left-hand end of the engine, then remove the lower coolant hose from the coolant pipe.

16 Undo the 3 front bolts and wedge the upper timing cover away from the engine slightly.

17 Undo the 3 fasteners and remove the coolant pipe from the front of the engine.

18 Remove the heat shield at the front of the turbocharger **(see illustration)**.

19 Working underneath the vehicle, unscrew the temperature sensor from the catalytic converter (where fitted) **(see illustration)**.

20 Undo the catalytic converter lower mounting bolts, and bend the lower bracket down a little.

21 Undo the upper clamp securing the catalytic converter to the turbocharger, and lower the catalytic converter from place **(see illustrations)**.

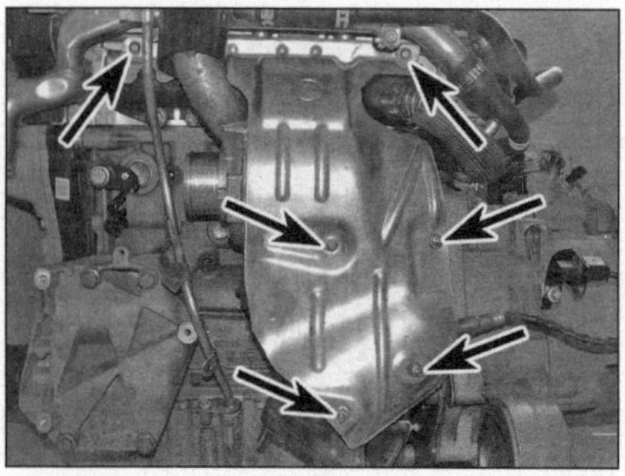

17.18 Heat shield retaining nuts and bolts (arrowed)

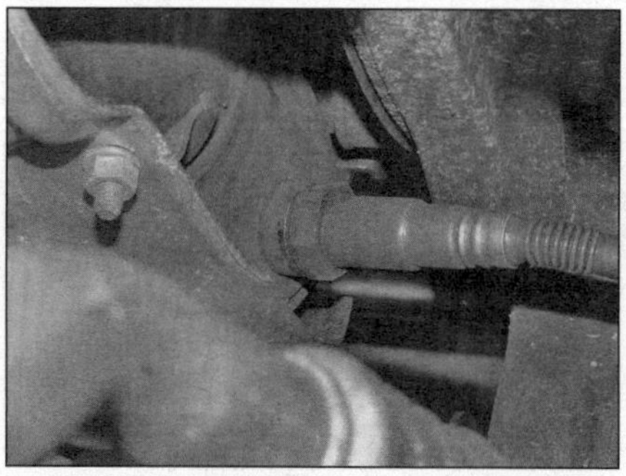

17.19 Unscrew the sensor from the catalytic converter

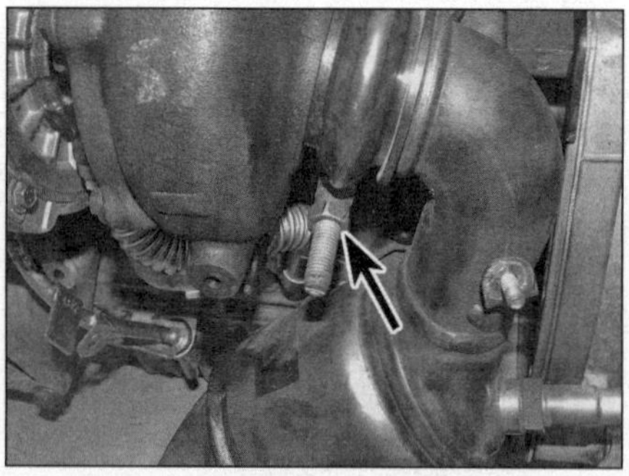

17.21a Unscrew the clamp bolt (arrowed) ...

17.21b ... and remove the catalytic converter

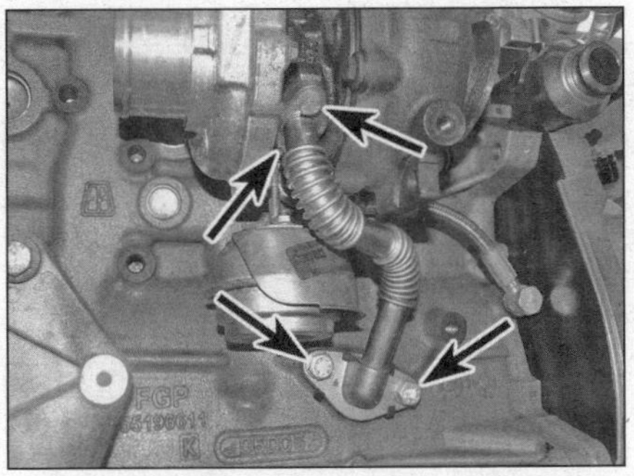

17.23 Unscrew the bolts (arrowed) securing the oil return pipe to the turbocharger and cylinder block

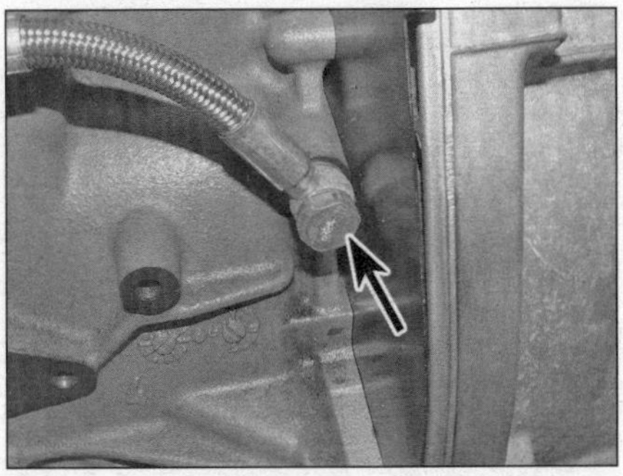

17.24 Unscrew the turbocharger oil supply banjo union (arrowed) and collect the two copper washers

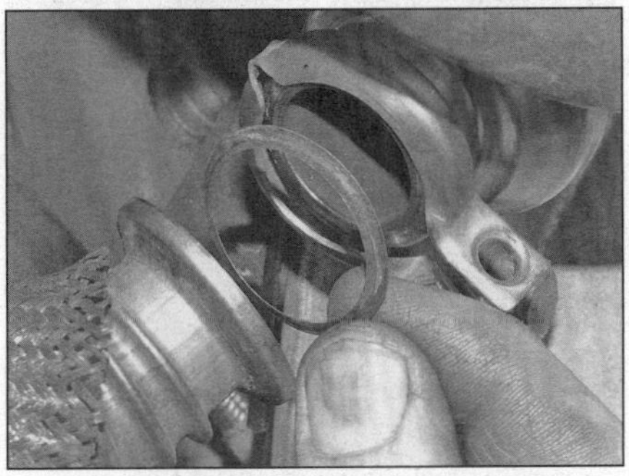

17.25 Release the EGR pipe clamp from the heat exchanger, separate the pipe and recover the gasket

17.26 Exhaust manifold retaining nuts (arrowed)

22 Disconnect the vacuum hose from the turbocharger wastegate actuator.

23 Unscrew the four bolts securing the oil return pipe to the turbocharger and cylinder block **(see illustration)**. Remove the pipe and recover the gaskets.

24 Unscrew the turbocharger oil supply pipe banjo union from the cylinder block and collect the two copper washers **(see Illustration)**.

25 Undo the retaining nut and bolt and release the metal EGR pipe clamp from the EGR valve heat exchanger. Separate the pipe from the heat exchanger and recover the gasket from the pipe fitting **(see illustration)**.

26 Unscrew the eight nuts securing the exhaust manifold to the cylinder head **(see illustration)**. Note that new nuts will be required for refitting. Withdraw the manifold and turbocharger assembly from the mounting studs, manipulate it sideways, and remove from under the car. Recover the gasket.

Refitting

27 Refitting is the reverse of removal, noting the following points.

- *a) Ensure all mating surfaces are clean and dry and renew all gaskets, seals and copper washers.*
- *b) Prime the turbocharger with fresh oil before refitting the oil supply pipe banjo bolt.*
- *c) Fit the new manifold nuts and tighten them evenly and progressively to the specified torque, working in a diagonal sequence.*
- *d) Tighten all other retaining nuts and bolts to the specified torque (where given).*
- *e) Refit the exhaust system as described in Section 18.*
- *f) On completion refill the cooling system as described in Chapter 1B, Section 28 and, if necessary, top-up the oil level as described in 'Weekly checks'.*
- *g) On starting the engine for the first time, allow the engine to idle for a few minutes before increasing the engine speed; this will allow oil to be circulated around the turbocharger bearings.*

Z19DTR engine

Removal

28 Remove the bonnet slam panel as described in Section 15 (paragraphs 1 to 6).

29 Raise the front of the vehicle (see *Jacking and vehicle support*) remove the deflector panel from below the radiator and remove the engine undershield. Drain the coolant from engine.

30 With reference to Chapter 3, Section 5 remove the cooling fans and to improve access remove the radiator. Access can be further improved by removing the intercooler as described in Section 15.

31 Remove the catalytic converter as described in Section 18.

32 Working from below, remove the oil drain hose, the lower oil feed pipe and the support bracket **(see illustrations)**. Recover the gaskets and copper washers.

33 Remove the upper heat shield **(see illustration)** the oil supply hose and the drain pipe from the upper turbocharger.

34 Disconnect any remaining vacuum hoses and then remove the dipstick **(see illustration)**.

35 Remove the fixing bolts from the crankcase

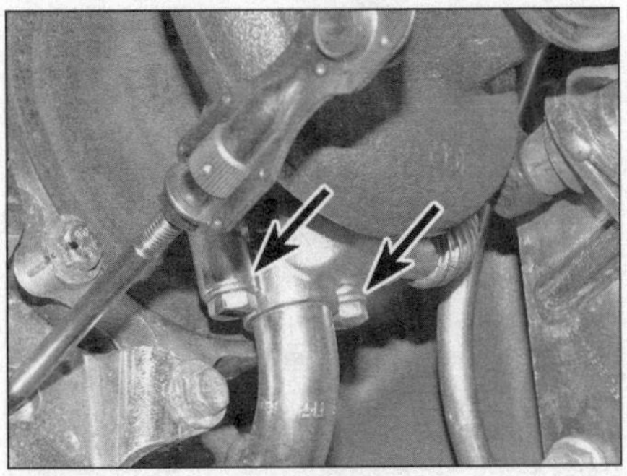

17.32a Remove the oil drain pipe bolts (arrowed) ...

17.32b ... the oil feed 'banjo' bolt ...

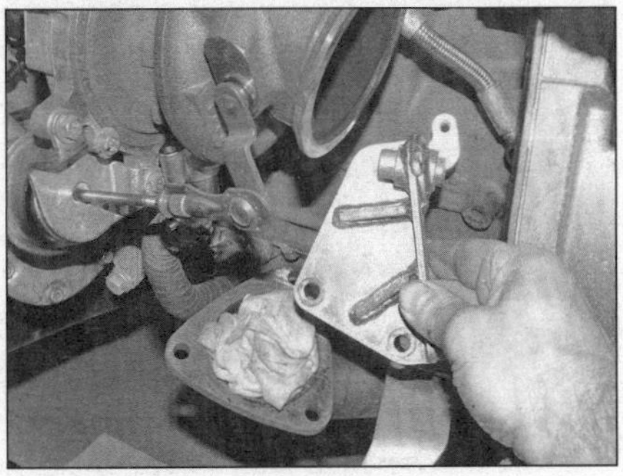

17.32c ... and the lower support bracket

17.33 Remove the upper heat shield

17.34 Remove the dipstick guide tube

17.36a Remove the hose ...

17.36b ... and recover the collar

17.37a Remove the manifold ...

17.37b ... and recover the gasket

ventilation pipe on the camshaft cover, disconnect the wiring plug and then remove the breather hose from the turbocharger inlet pipe.

36 Remove the inlet pipe from the turbocharger. Recover the collar **(see illustrations)**.

37 Remove the 9 manifold nuts and recover the special washers. Lift out the manifold and recover the gasket **(see illustrations)**.

38 With the manifold on the bench, remove the remaining banjo bolts form the oil supply pipes. The operation of the wastegates can be checked by manually operating them or by applying a vacuum to the control units. No further dismantling is recommended as Saab supply both turbochargers (complete with the exhaust manifold) as a single assembly. Individual turbochargers may be available from a specialist supply, but check with the supplier before dismantling further.

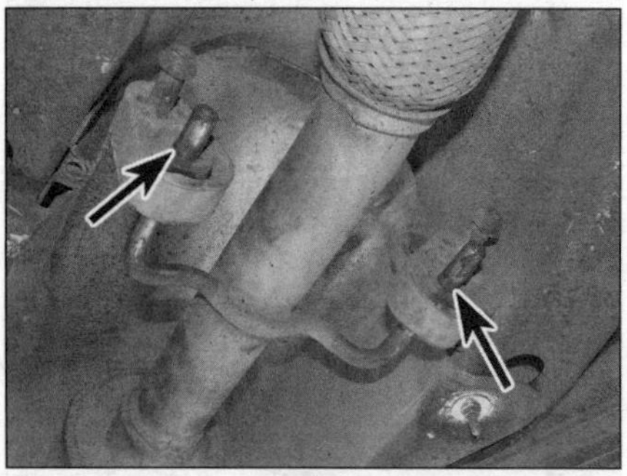

18.5 Spray penetrating oil over the exhaust rubber mounting blocks in the area arrowed

Refitting

39 Refitting is the reverse of removal, noting the following points.

a) Ensure all mating surfaces are clean and dry and renew all gaskets, seals and copper washers.
b) Prime the turbocharger with fresh oil before refitting the oil supply pipe banjo bolt.
c) Fit the special washers so that the internal sealis on the outside.
d) Fit the new manifold nuts and tighten them evenly and progressively to the specified torque, working in a diagonal sequence.
e) Tighten all other retaining nuts and bolts to the specified torque (where given).
f) Refit the exhaust system as described in Section 18.
g) On completion refill the cooling system as described in Chapter 1B, Section 28 and, if necessary, top-up the oil level as described in 'Weekly checks'.
h) On starting the engine for the first time, allow the engine to idle for a few minutes before increasing the engine speed; this will allow oil to be circulated around the turbocharger bearings.

18 Exhaust system – general information, removal and refitting

General information

1 Three different exhaust systems may be fitted dependent on model, market, etc. On some models a four-piece system is fitted, comprising a front catalytic converter, front pipe, particulate filter, and a rear pipe with silencer. On others, the particulate filter is replaced with a second catalytic converter/silencer. Post 2008 Z19DTR models feature a twin rear tail pipe system.

2 The front pipe is attached to the exhaust manifold/catalytic converter by a flange joint secured by nuts. The other exhaust sections are joined by overlap joints which are secured by clamps, or flange joints secured by nuts. The system is suspended throughout its entire length by rubber mountings.

3 The manufacturers specify that if any of the exhaust sections are separated, the clamps must be renewed. As the clamps are attached to the exhaust sections by means of a spot weld at manufacture, it will be necessary to use a suitable grinder to remove the spot weld.

Removal

Complete system

4 To remove the system, first jack up the front and rear of the car and support it securely on axle stands. Alternatively, position the car over an inspection pit or on car ramps. The help of an assistant will be needed. Undo the fasteners and remove the engine undershield.

5 Spray some penetrating oil over the exhaust rubber mounting blocks so that the mounting blocks will slide easily on the exhaust and underbody hangers **(see illustration)**.

6 Undo the two bolts securing the front pipe

18.7 Undo the 3 nuts (arrowed) and detach the front exhaust pipe from the catalytic converter

support bracket to the transmission bracket/ sump.

7 Undo the three retaining nuts and separate the exhaust front pipe from the exhaust manifold/catalytic converter, taking care to support the flexible section. **Note:** *Angular movement in excess of 10° can cause permanent damage to the flexible section.* Recover the gasket **(see illustration)**. Note that new nuts will be required for refitting.

8 Slide the front pipe rubber mounting blocks as far forward as possible. Move the exhaust system to the rear and disengage the front pipe hangers from the mounting blocks.

9 Move the exhaust system forward and disengage the intermediate pipe and tailpipe hangers from the rubber mounting blocks. Lower the system to the ground and slide it out from under the car.

Individual sections

10 Individual sections of the exhaust system can be removed by slackening the relevant clamp and releasing the exhaust from the rubber mountings.

11 Slacken and remove the nut from the relevant exhaust clamp retaining bolt. Apply liberal amounts of penetrating oil to the joint and tap around the joint and clamp with a hammer to free it. Twist the pipe to be removed in both directions while holding the adjacent pipe. Once the joint is free, pull the pipes apart.

12 Mark the position of the clamp on the pipe, so the new clamp can be fitted in the same position, then grind off the clamp retaining spot weld. Remove the clamp.

13 Where a twin rear silencer is fitted the system must be cut as shown **(see illustration)**. This will allow a sleeve type clamp to be fitted and the individual silencer renewed.

Catalytic converter

14 There maybe one or two catalytic

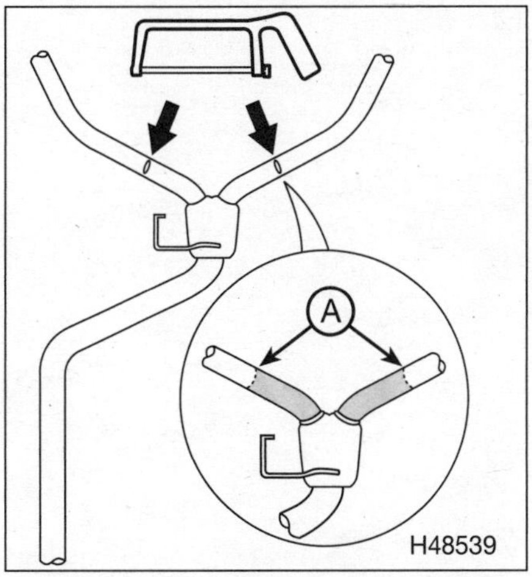

18.13 Cut the exhaust at point A, 130mm from the weld

converters, dependent on model, market, etc – one fitted between the exhaust manifold and the exhaust front pipe, and a second unit integral with the particulate filter.

15 Raise the front of the vehicle(see *Jacking and vehicle support*) and then remove the front section of the exhaust system.

16 Unbolt and remove the dipstick guide tube **(see illustration 17.34)**.

17 On the Z19DTH engine, remove the turbocharger hoses and remove the lower heat shield.

18 Drain the coolant from the radiator and then remove the radiator upper hose, lower hose and coolant pipe – DTH engines only.

19 Disconnect the wiring plug from temperature sensor and (where fitted) from the oxygen sensor.

20 Release the upper clamp **(see illustration)** remove the bottom mounting bracket and lower the converter from the vehicle.

Heat shield(s)

21 The heat shields are secured to the underside of the body by various nuts and threaded caps. Each shield can be removed once the relevant exhaust section has been removed. If a shield is being removed to gain access to a component located behind it, it may prove sufficient in some cases to remove the retaining nuts/caps, and simply lower the shield, without disturbing the exhaust system. If any of the threaded caps are damaged during removal, a suitable nut and washer can be used when refitting.

Particulate filter

22 Raise the vehicle and support it securely on axle stands (see *Jacking and vehicle support*).

18.20 Fit an extra nut to the clamp bolt to expand the clamp

23 Note their fitted positions, and disconnect the pressure sensor hoses from filter.

24 Unscrew the temperature sensor from the filter.

25 Undo the 3 nuts securing the filter to the front pipe. Note that new nuts will be required for refitting.

26 Undo the bolts securing the filter rear mounting bracket to the vehicle body.

27 Slacken the clamp and separate the rear exhaust pipe from the filter.

28 Release the filter from the rubber mountings and withdrawn it from under the vehicle.

29 Upon refitting, apply a little high-temperature anti-seize grease to the temperature sensor threads. Note that if a new particulate filter has been fitted, Saab diagnostic equipment must be connected to the vehicle's diagnostic plug to reset adaptation values in the engine management ECM. Entrust this task to a Saab dealer or suitably-equipped specialist.

Refitting

30 Refitting is a reversal of the removal sequence, noting the following points:

a) *Ensure that all traces of corrosion have been removed from the system joints and renew all disturbed clamps.*
b) *Inspect the rubber mountings for signs of damage or deterioration, and renew as necessary.*
c) *When refitting the front pipe to the manifold/catalytic converter, use a new gasket and new retaining nuts, and tighten the nuts to the specified torque.*
d) *Prior to tightening the exhaust system clamps, ensure that all rubber mountings are correctly located, and that there is adequate clearance between the exhaust system and vehicle underbody. Tighten the clamp bolt retaining nuts securely.*

Chapter 4 Part C: Emission control systems

Contents

Degrees of difficulty

Easy, suitable for novice with little experience	**Fairly easy,** suitable for beginner with some experience	**Fairly difficult,** suitable for competent DIY mechanic	**Difficult,** suitable for experienced DIY mechanic	**Very difficult,** suitable for expert DIY or professional

Specifications

Engine identification

Diesel engine type	**Manufacturer's engine code**
SOHC 8-valve	Z19DT
DOHC 16-valve	Z19DTH and DTR

Torque wrench settings

	Nm	**lbf ft**
Petrol engines		
Oxygen sensors	40	30
Diesel engines		
Exhaust gas recirculation (EGR) pipe bolts	25	18
Exhaust gas recirculation (EGR) valve bolts/nuts	25	18
Exhaust gas temperature sensors	45	33

1 General information

1 All petrol engine models use unleaded petrol and also have various other features built into the fuel system to help minimise harmful emissions. These include a crankcase emission control system, a catalytic converter, and an evaporative emission control system to keep fuel vapour/exhaust gas emissions down to a minimum.

2 The diesel engine models are also designed to meet strict emission requirements. All models are fitted with a crankcase emission control system, one or two catalytic converters, and a particulate filter (model and market dependent) to keep exhaust emissions down to a minimum. All models are also fitted with an exhaust gas recirculation (EGR) system to further decrease exhaust emissions.

3 The emission control systems function as follows.

Petrol engines

Crankcase emission control

4 To reduce the emission of unburned hydrocarbons from the crankcase into the atmosphere, the engine is sealed and the blow-by gases and oil vapour are drawn from inside the crankcase, through an oil separator, into the intake tract to be burned by the engine during normal combustion.

5 Under all conditions the gases are forced out of the crankcase by the (relatively) higher crankcase pressure; if the engine is worn, the raised crankcase pressure (due to increased blow-by) will cause some of the flow to return under all manifold conditions.

Exhaust emission control

6 To minimise the amount of pollutants which escape into the atmosphere, all models are fitted with a catalytic converter in the exhaust system. The system is of the closed-loop type, in which the oxygen sensors in the exhaust system provides the fuel injection/ignition system ECM with constant feedback, enabling the ECM to adjust the mixture to provide the best possible conditions for the converter to operate.

7 Two heated oxygen sensors are fitted to the exhaust system. The sensor nearest the engine (before the catalytic converter) determines the residual oxygen content of the exhaust gases for mixture correction. The sensor in the exhaust front pipe (after the catalytic converter) monitors the function of the catalytic converter to give the driver a warning signal if there is a fault.

8 The oxygen sensor's tip is sensitive to oxygen and sends the ECM a varying voltage signal depending on the amount of oxygen in the exhaust gases. Peak conversion efficiency of all major pollutants occurs if the intake air/fuel mixture is maintained at the chemically-correct ratio for the complete combustion of petrol of 14.7 parts (by weight) of air to 1 part of fuel (the 'stoichiometric' ratio). The sensor output voltage alters in a large step at this point, the ECM using the signal change as a reference point and correcting the intake air/fuel mixture accordingly by altering the fuel injector pulse width.

Evaporative emission control

9 To minimise the escape into the atmosphere of unburned hydrocarbons, an evaporative emissions control system is also fitted to all models. The fuel tank filler cap is sealed and a charcoal canister is mounted on the fuel tank. The canister collects the petrol vapours generated in the tank when the car is parked and stores them until they can be cleared from the canister (under the control of the fuel injection/ignition system ECM) via the purge valve into the intake tract to be burned by the engine during normal combustion.

10 To ensure that the engine runs correctly when it is cold and/or idling and to protect the catalytic converter from the effects of an

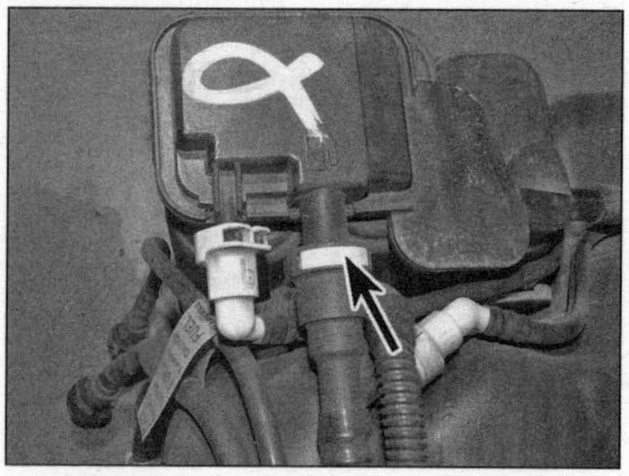

2.4 Depress the release tabs (arrowed) and disconnect the hoses from the carbon canister

over-rich mixture, the purge control valve is not opened by the ECM until the engine has warmed-up, and the engine is under load; the valve solenoid is then modulated on and off to allow the stored vapour to pass into the intake tract.

Diesel engines

Crankcase emission control

11 Refer to paragraphs 4 and 5.

Exhaust emission control

12 Post start heating of the glow plugs is used to raise the cylinder temperature as quickly as possible. The glow plugs are also energised as part of the diesel particulate filter (DPF) regeneration process, described below.

13 To minimise the level of exhaust pollutants released into the atmosphere, two catalytic converters are fitted in the exhaust system. On some models, the second catalytic converter is incorporated into a particulate filter.

14 The catalytic converter consists of a canister containing a fine mesh impregnated with a catalyst material, over which the hot exhaust gases pass. The catalyst speeds up the oxidation of harmful carbon monoxide, unburned hydrocarbons and soot, effectively reducing the quantity of harmful products released into the atmosphere via the exhaust gases.

15 The particulate filter is designed to trap soot particles. A pressure sensor measures the pressure drop across the filter, to inform the engine management ECM when the filter is full. The ECM then initiates filter regeneration. This process involves injecting extra fuel into the cylinders during the exhaust stroke. This fuel greatly raises the temperature of the exhaust gases, and burns off the soot trapped into the filter. This process is completely automatic, and takes approximately 15 minutes.

Exhaust gas recirculation system

16 This system is designed to recirculate small quantities of exhaust gas into the intake tract, and therefore into the combustion process. This process reduces the level of unburnt hydrocarbons present in the exhaust gas before it reaches the catalytic converter. The system is controlled by the injection system ECM, using the information from its various sensors, via the electrically-operated EGR valve.

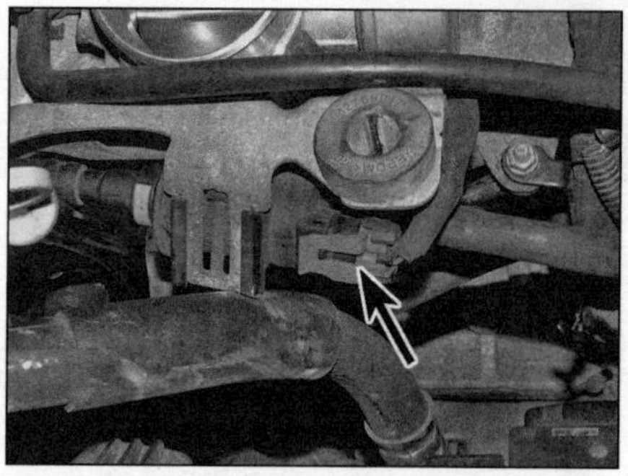

2.8 Disconnect the wiring plug from the purge valve (arrowed)

2 Petrol engine emission control systems – testing and component renewal

Crankcase emission control

1 The components of this system require no attention other than to check that the hose(s) are clear and undamaged at regular intervals.

Evaporative emission control system

Testing

2 If the system is thought to be faulty, disconnect the hoses from the charcoal canister and purge control valve and check that they are clear by blowing through them. Full testing of the system can only be carried out using specialist electronic equipment, which is connected to the engine management system diagnostic connector. If the purge control valve or charcoal canister are thought to be faulty, they must be renewed.

Charcoal canister renewal

3 The charcoal canister is located on the fuel tank. To gain access to the canister, remove the fuel tank as described in Chapter 4A, Section 8.

4 With the fuel tank removed, disconnect the vapour hose quick-release fittings at the charcoal canister **(see illustration)**.

5 Undo the retaining bolt and release the canister from its mounting bracket on the fuel tank. Remove the canister from the tank.

6 Refitting is a reverse of the removal procedure, ensuring the hoses are correctly and securely reconnected.

Purge valve renewal

7 Remove the plastic cover on the top of the engine. The valve is located at the front of the engine, just below the throttle body.

8 To renew the valve, ensure the ignition is switched off then depress the retaining clip and disconnect the wiring connector from the valve **(see illustration)**.

9 Disconnect the hoses from the valve, noting their correct fitted locations then unclip and remove the valve from the engine.

10 Refitting is a reversal of the removal procedure, ensuring the valve is fitted the correct way around and the hoses are securely connected.

Exhaust emission control

Testing

11 The performance of the catalytic converter can be checked only by measuring the exhaust gases using a good-quality, carefully-calibrated exhaust gas analyser.

12 If the CO level at the tailpipe is too high, the vehicle should be taken to a Saab dealer or engine diagnostic specialist so that the complete fuel injection and ignition systems, including the oxygen sensors, can be thoroughly checked using diagnostic equipment. This equipment will give an indication as to where the fault lies and the necessary components can then be renewed.

Catalytic converter renewal

13 Catalytic converter renewal is described in Chapter 4A, Section 16.

Oxygen sensor renewal

14 Oxygen sensor renewal is described in Chapter 4A, Section 10.

3 Diesel engine emission control systems – testing and component renewal

Crankcase emission control

1 The components of this system require no attention other than to check that the hose(s) are clear and undamaged at regular intervals.

Exhaust emission control

Testing

2 The performance of the catalytic converter(s) can be checked only by measuring the exhaust gases using a good-quality, carefully-calibrated exhaust gas analyser.

3 If the catalytic converter(s) is thought to be faulty, before assuming a fault, it is worth checking the problem is not due to a faulty injector(s). Refer to your Saab dealer or specialist for further information.

Catalytic converter renewal

4 Catalytic converter renewal is described in Chapter 4B, Section 18.

Particulate filter renewal

5 Particulate filter renewal is described in Chapter 4B, Section 18.

Particulate filter pressure sensor renewal

6 Remove the plastic cover from the top of the engine.

7 The sensor is located on the bulkhead at the left-hand side of the engine compartment. Disconnect the sensor wiring plug.

8 Note their fitted positions, then (where fitted) release the clips and disconnect the hoses from the sensor **(see illustrations)**.
9 Undo the screw and remove the sensor.
10 Refitting is a reversal of removal. Note that if a new sensor has been fitted, the engine management ECM adaptation values must be reset using Saab diagnostic equipment. Entrust this task to a Saab dealer or suitably-equipped specialist.

Exhaust gas temperature sensors

11 Two temperature sensors are fitted to the exhaust system. The front sensor is fitted in the inlet to the front catalytic converter, and the rear sensor is fitted into the front edge of the rear catalytic converter. To remove the sensor, raise the vehicle and support it securely on axle stands (see *Jacking and vehicle support*).
12 Remove the front right-hand roadwheel, and wheel arch liner.
13 Disconnect the sensor wiring plug.
14 Working underneath the vehicle, unscrew the sensor from the catalytic converter, and release the wiring from any retaining clips **(see illustrations)**.
15 Upon refitting the sensor, apply a little high-temperature anti-seize grease to the sensor threads, and tighten it to the specified torque.

Exhaust gas recirculation system

Testing

16 Comprehensive testing of the system can only be carried out using dedicated test equipment. If a fault is suspected, contact a Saab dealer or suitably-equipped local specialist who will have the necessary equipment.

EGR valve renewal – Z19DT engines

17 Remove the plastic cover over the top of the engine.
18 Disconnect the EGR valve wiring connector.
19 Undo the two bolts and disconnect the metal EGR pipe from the throttle body/housing. Recover the gasket.
20 Undo the two bolts securing the EGR heat exchanger metal pipe to the base of the valve.
21 Undo the three bolts securing the EGR valve to the intake manifold **(see illustration)**. Remove the valve together with the engine cover bracket.
22 Refitting is the reverse of removal using new gaskets and tightening the retaining bolts to the specified torque.

EGR valve renewal – Z19DTH engines

23 Remove the plastic cover from the top of the engine.
24 Disconnect the EGR valve wiring connector.
25 Unscrew the two bolts on the top of the valve and detach the metal EGR pipe flange from the base of the valve. Recover the gasket **(see illustration)**.
26 Unscrew the two nuts and two bolts securing the EGR valve to the intake manifold and lift off the engine cover bracket **(see illustration)**.

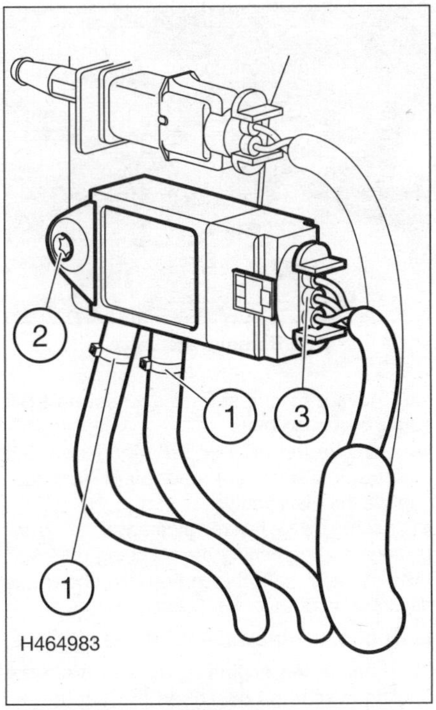

3.8a Particulate filter pressure sensor (DTH engines)
1 Delivery hoses
2 Retaining bolt
3 Wiring plug

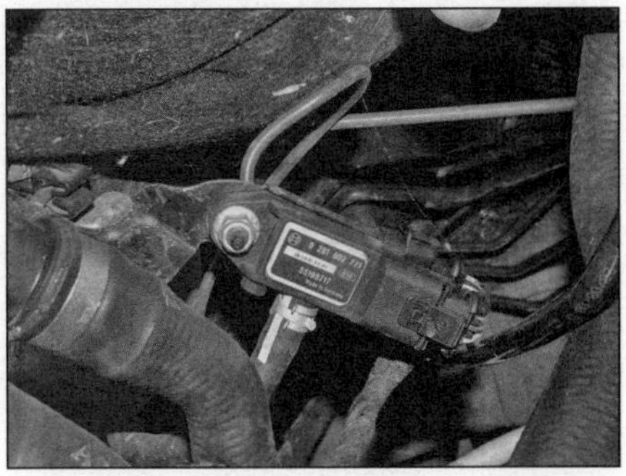

3.8b Particulate filter pressure sensor (DTR engines)

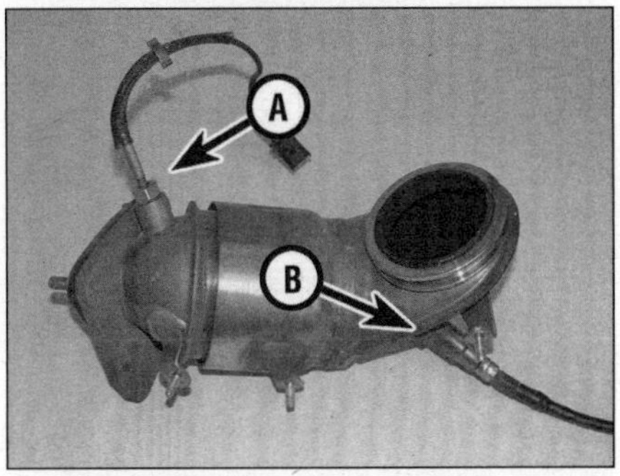

3.14a Front catalytic convertor exhaust gas temperature sensor
A Temperature sensor
B Oxygen sensor (DTR engines only)

3.14b Rear exhaust gas temperature sensor (arrowed)

3.21 EGR valve retaining bolts (arrowed)

3.25 Unscrew the two bolts, detach the metal EGR pipe flange and recover the gasket

3.26 Unscrew the two nuts and two bolts (arrowed) securing the EGR valve to the intake manifold

3.29 Remove the bolts (throttle body removed for clarity)

27 Refitting is the reverse of removal using new gaskets and tightening the retaining nuts and bolts to the specified torque.

EGR valve renewal – Z19DTR engines

28 Remove the plastic cover from the top of the engine.

29 Disconnect the wiring plug and remove the 2 bolts **(see illustration)**.

30 Remove the valve from the housing **(see illustration)**.

31 Refitting is the reverse of removal, but clean the mounting surfaces and use a suitable sealant on the mounting surfaces. Saab recommend Dow Corning Q3-1566, but any high-temperature resistant silicone sealer will be suitable.

EGR cooler renewal – Z19DT engines

32 Remove the engine cover and drain the cooling system as described in Chapter 1B, Section 28.

33 Release the hose clips and remove the turbocharger outlet hose.

34 Remove the return pipe from the EGR valve and throttle body. Recover the gasket.

35 Disconnect the wiring plugs from the EGR control valve and the throttle body.

36 Unbolt the supply pipe from the exhaust manifold.

37 Remove the coolant hoses and unbolt the pipe from the support brackets **(see illustration)**.

38 Disconnect the wiring plug from the coolant temperature sensor.

39 Disconnect the crankcase ventilation hose

3.30 Remove the valve

and move it to one side to access the EGR cooler mounting bolts.

40 Remove the EGR cooler mounting bolts and (anticipating some coolant spillage) remove the EGR cooler.

41 Refitting is the reverse of removal using new gaskets and tightening the retaining nuts and bolts securely. Refill the engine with coolant as described in Chapter 1B, Section 28.

EGR cooler renewal – Z19DTH engines

42 Remove the engine cover and drain the cooling system as described in Chapter 1B, Section 28.

43 Raise the front of the vehicle ((see *Jacking and vehicle support*) and remove the engine undershield.

44 Remove the turbocharger delivery pipe and then unclip the glow plug control module from the side of the battery. Move the module to the side and secure it to one side.

45 Release the spring clip from the thermostat coolant hose and move the hose to one side.

46 Remove the mounting bolt from the oil cooler coolant hose and then remove the hose. Remove the rear hose from the oil cooler.

47 Unbolt and remove the EGR cooler mounting bolts from the exhaust manifold and the EGR control valve. Recover the gaskets.

48 Remove the coolant pipe mounting bolts from the inlet manifold.

49 Remove the thermostat housing bolts from the cylinder head and move the housing to the side.

50 Disconnect the front cooler hose from the cooler and unbolt the cooler from the cylinder

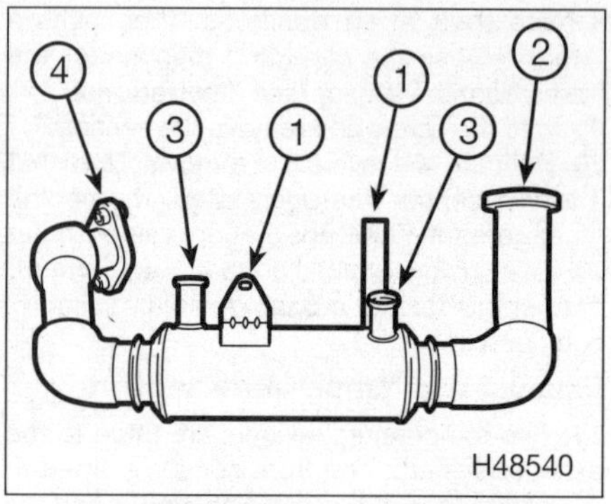

3.37 EGR cooler – Z19DT engine

1 Mounting points
2 Outlet pipe
3 Coolant hose connections
4 Inlet from exhaust manifold

head. Remove the cooler complete with the rear hose.

51 Refitting is the reverse of removal using new gaskets and tightening the retaining nuts and bolts securely. Refill the engine with coolant as described in Chapter 1B, Section 28.

EGR cooler – Z19DTR engines

52 Remove the engine cover and drain the cooling system as described in Chapter 1B, Section 28.

53 Raise the front of the vehicle ((see *Jacking and vehicle support*) and remove the deflector from behind the front bumper.

54 Working from below, remove the turbocharger outlet hose spring clips and single retaining bolt. Remove the hose.

55 Slacken the dipstick mounting bolt and then remove the upper section of the turbocharger outlet hose.

56 Remove the spring clips **(see illustration)** and release both coolant hoses from the thermostat housing.

57 Remove the wiring connectors from the throttle body, the coolant temperature sensor, the EGR solenoid and the EGR valve.

58 Remove the 3 upper an 2 lower bolts, recover the gaskets (noting their positions) and then remove the EGR return hose from the vehicle by rotating it as it is removed **(see illustration)**.

3.56 Release the spring clips

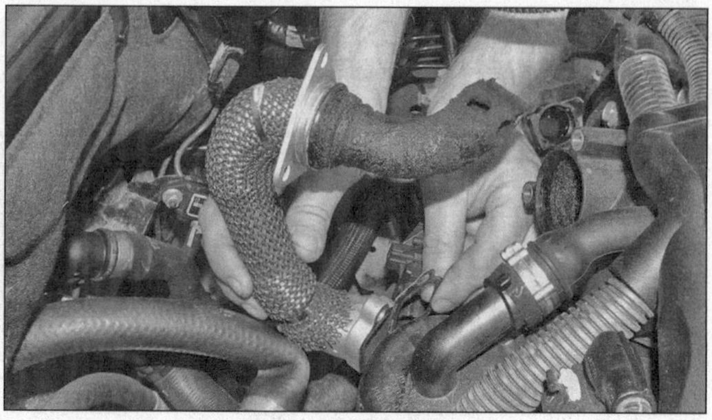

3.58 Remove the return hose

59 Remove the coolant hose from the EGR valve

60 Unbolt and remove the support bracket from the starter motor and then remove the single bolt from the gearbox.

61 Disconnect the vacuum hoses from the vacuum pump and EGR vacuum control. Note their positions and move them to one side **(see illustrations)**.

62 Unbolt the cooler and manoeuvre it from the engine bay **(see illustration)**.

63 If required the vacuum reservoir, the thermostat and the vacuum-controlled diverter valve can now be remove from the cooler **(see illustration)**.

64 Refitting is the reverse of removal using new gaskets and tightening the retaining nuts and bolts securely. Refill the engine with coolant as described in Chapter 1B, Section 28.

3.61a Remove the hose from the vacuum pump ...

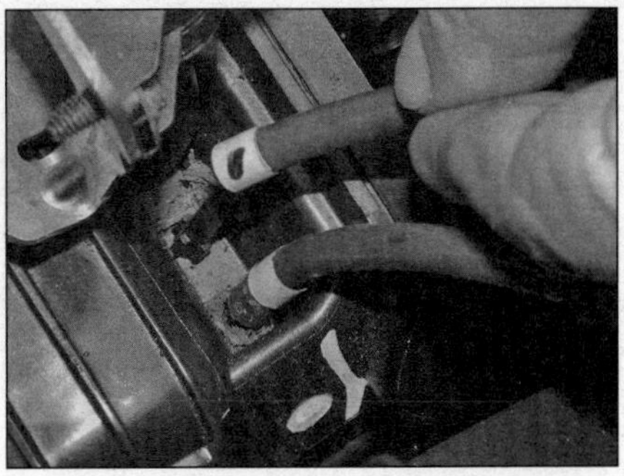

3.61b ... and the two hoses from the vacuum reservoir

3.62 Remove the complete EGR cooler assembly

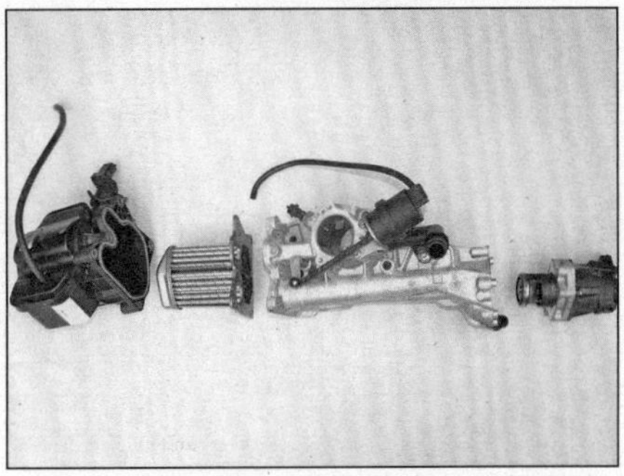

3.63 The component parts of the EGR cooler (DTR engines)

4 Catalytic converter – general information and precautions

1 The catalytic converter is a reliable and simple device which needs no maintenance in itself, but there are some facts of which an owner should be aware if the converter is to function properly for its full service life.

Petrol engines

a) DO NOT use leaded petrol or LRP in a car equipped with a catalytic converter – the lead will coat the precious metals, reducing their converting efficiency and will eventually destroy the converter.

b) Always keep the ignition and fuel systems well-maintained in accordance with the manufacturer's schedule.

c) If the engine develops a misfire, do not drive the car at all (or at least as little as possible) until the fault is cured.

d) DO NOT push- or tow-start the car – this will soak the catalytic converter in unburned fuel, causing it to overheat when the engine does start.

e) DO NOT switch off the ignition at high engine speeds.

f) DO NOT use fuel or engine oil additives – these may contain substances harmful to the catalytic converter.

g) DO NOT continue to use the car if the engine burns oil to the extent of leaving a visible trail of blue smoke.

h) Remember that the catalytic converter operates at very high temperatures. DO NOT, therefore, park the car in dry undergrowth, over long grass or piles of dead leaves after a long run.

i) Remember that the catalytic converter is FRAGILE – do not strike it with tools during servicing work.

j) In some cases a sulphurous smell (like that of rotten eggs) may be noticed from the exhaust. This is common to many catalytic converter-equipped cars and once the car has covered a few thousand miles the problem should disappear.

k) The catalytic converter, used on a well-maintained and well-driven car, should last for between 50 000 and 100 000 miles – if the converter is no longer effective it must be renewed.

Diesel engines

2 Refer to the information given in parts f, g, h, i and k of the petrol engines information given above.

Chapter 5 Part A: Starting and charging systems

Contents

Degrees of difficulty

Easy, suitable for novice with little experience	**Fairly easy,** suitable for beginner with some experience	**Fairly difficult,** suitable for competent DIY mechanic	**Difficult,** suitable for experienced DIY mechanic	**Very difficult,** suitable for expert DIY or professional

Specifications

Engine identification

Engine type	**Manufacturer's engine code**
2.0 litre (1998 cc) DOHC 16-valve petrol engine	B207E, L and R
1.9 litre (1910 cc) diesel engine:	
SOHC 8-valve	Z19DT
DOHC 16-valve	Z19DTH and DTR

General

System type	12 volt, negative earth

Battery

Type	Lead-acid, low-maintenance or 'maintenance-free' (sealed for life)
Battery capacity	60 or 85 amp-hour
Charge condition:	
Poor	12.5 volts
Normal	12.6 volts
Good	12.7 volts

Alternator

Type:	
Petrol engine	Bosch E6-14V 65 – 120A
Diesel engine	Denso 14V 70 – 130A
Rated voltage	14V
Slip-ring diameter:	
Minimum	15.4 mm
New	14.4 mm
Minimum brush protrusion from holder	7.5 mm
Output current:	
Bosch E6	
At 1800 rpm	65 amps
At 6000 rpm	120 amps
Denso:	
At 1800 rpm	70 amps
At 6000 rpm	130 amps

Starter motor

Type:	
Petrol engines	Delco
Diesel engines	Bosch DW 12V 0 001 109 015
Output:	
Petrol engines	1.8 kW
Diesel engines	2.0 kW
No of teeth on pinion:	
Petrol engines	11
Diesel engines	10
No of teeth on ring gear	135

Torque wrench settings

	Nm	lbf ft
Alternator bracket	25	18
Alternator mounting bolt:		
Petrol models	20	15
Diesel models:		
Z19DT:		
M8	25	18
M10	50	37
Z19DTH and DTR	60	44
Glow plugs	10	7
Oil pressure switch:		
Petrol models	18	13
Diesel models	30	22
Starter motor:		
Petrol models	47	35
Diesel models	24	18
Suspension lower balljoint pinch-bolt/nut	50	37

1 General information and precautions

General information

Because of their engine-related functions, the components of the starting and charging systems are covered separately from the body electrical devices such as the lights, instruments, etc (which are covered in Chapter 12). Refer to Chapter 5B, Section 1 for information on the ignition system.

The electrical system is of the 12 volt negative earth type. The battery fitted as original equipment is of low-maintenance or 'maintenance-free' (sealed for life) type. The battery is charged by the alternator, which is belt-driven from the crankshaft pulley. During the life of the car, the original battery may have been changed to a standard type battery.

The starter motor is of the pre-engaged type, incorporating an integral solenoid. On starting, the solenoid moves the drive pinion into engagement with the flywheel/driveplate ring gear before the starter motor is energised. Once the engine has started, a one-way clutch prevents the motor armature being driven by the engine until the pinion disengages from the ring gear.

Precautions

Further details of the various systems are given in the relevant Sections of this Chapter. While some repair procedures are given, the usual course of action is to renew the component concerned.

It is necessary to take extra care when working on the electrical system, to avoid damage to semi-conductor devices (diodes and transistors), and to avoid the risk of personal injury. In addition to the precautions given in *Safety first!* observe the following when working on the system:

- Always remove rings, watches, etc, before working on the electrical system. Even with the battery disconnected, capacitive discharge could occur if a component's live terminal is earthed through a metal object. This could cause a shock or nasty burn.
- Do not reverse the battery connections. Components such as the alternator, electronic control modules, or any other components having semi-conductor circuitry, could be irreparably damaged.
- If the engine is being started using jump leads and a slave battery, connect the batteries positive-to-positive and negative-to-negative (see *Jump starting*). This also applies when connecting a battery charger.

Caution: Never disconnect the battery terminals, the alternator, any electrical wiring, or any test instruments, when the engine is running.

- Do not allow the engine to turn the alternator when the alternator is not connected.
- Never 'test' for alternator output by 'flashing' the output lead to earth.
- Never use an ohmmeter of the type incorporating a hand-cranked generator for circuit or continuity testing.
- Always ensure that the battery negative lead is disconnected when working on the electrical system.
- Before using electric-arc welding equipment on the car, disconnect the battery, alternator, and components such as the fuel injection/ignition electronic control unit, to protect them from the risk of damage.

2 Electrical fault finding – general information

Refer to Chapter 12, Section 2.

3 Battery – testing and charging

Testing

Standard and low-maintenance battery

1 If the vehicle covers a small annual mileage, it is worthwhile checking the specific gravity of the electrolyte every three months, to determine the state of charge of the battery. Use a hydrometer to make the check, and compare the results with the following table. Note that the specific gravity readings assume an electrolyte temperature of 15°C; for every 10°C below 15°C, subtract 0.007. For every 10°C above 15°C, add 0.007. However, for convenience, the temperatures quoted in the following table are ambient (outdoor air) temperatures, above or below 25°C:

	Ambient temperature	
	Above 25°C	**Below 25°C**
Fully-charged	*1.210 to 1.230*	*1.270 to 1.290*
70% charged	*1.170 to 1.190*	*1.230 to 1.250*
Discharged	*1.050 to 1.070*	*1.110 to 1.130*

2 If the battery condition is suspect, first check the specific gravity of electrolyte in each cell. A variation of 0.040 or more between any cells indicates loss of electrolyte or deterioration of the internal plates.

3 If the specific gravity variation is 0.040 or more, the battery should be renewed. If the cell variation is satisfactory but the battery is discharged, it should be charged as described later in this Section.

Maintenance-free battery

4 In cases where a 'sealed for life' maintenance-free battery is fitted, topping-up and testing of the electrolyte in each cell is not possible. The condition of the battery can therefore only be tested using a battery condition indicator or a voltmeter.

5 A battery with a built-in charge condition indicator may be fitted. The indicator is located in the top of the battery casing, and indicates the condition of the battery from its colour. If the indicator shows green, then the battery is in a good state of charge. If the indicator turns darker, eventually to black, then the battery requires charging, as described later in this Section. If the indicator shows clear/yellow, then the electrolyte level in the battery is too low to allow further use, and the battery should be renewed. Do not attempt to charge, load or jump start a battery when the indicator shows clear/yellow.

All battery types

6 If testing the battery using a voltmeter, connect the voltmeter across the battery, and compare the result with those given in the Specifications under 'charge condition'. The test is only accurate if the battery has not been subjected to any kind of charge for the previous six hours, including charging by the alternator. If this is not the case, switch on the headlights for 30 seconds, then wait four to five minutes after switching off the headlights before testing the battery. All other electrical circuits must be switched off, so check (for instance) that the doors and tailgate or boot lid are fully shut when making the test.

7 If the voltage reading is less than 12.2 volts, then the battery is discharged. A reading of 12.2 to 12.4 volts indicates a partially-discharged condition.

8 If the battery is to be charged, remove it from the vehicle (Section 4) and charge it as described in the following paragraphs.

Charging

Note: *The following is intended as a guide only. Always refer to the manufacturer's recommendations (often printed on a label attached to the battery) before charging a battery.*

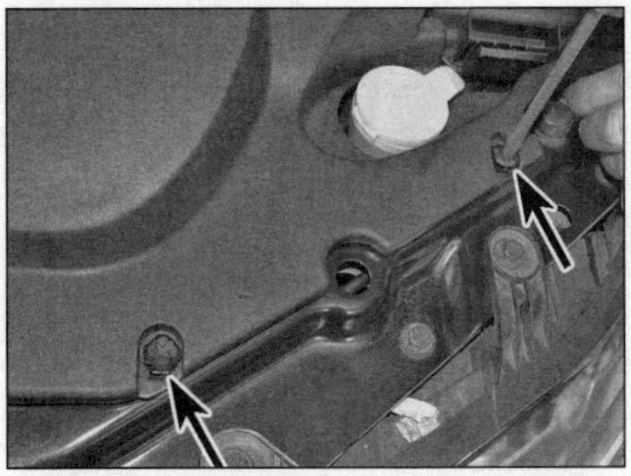

4.1a Rotate the fasteners (arrowed) anti-clockwise ...

Standard and low-maintenance battery

9 Charge the battery at a rate of 3.5 to 4 amps, and continue to charge the battery at this rate until no further rise in specific gravity is noted over a four hour period.

10 Alternatively, a trickle charger charging at the rate of 1.5 amps can safely be used overnight.

11 Specially rapid 'boost' charges which are claimed to restore the power of the battery in 1 to 2 hours are not recommended, as they can cause serious damage to the battery plates through overheating.

12 While charging the battery, note that the temperature of the electrolyte should never exceed 38°C.

Maintenance-free battery

13 This battery type requires a longer period to fully recharge than the standard type, the time taken being dependent on the extent of discharge, but it can take anything up to three days.

14 A constant-voltage type charger is required, to be set, where possible, to 13.9 to 14.9 volts with a charger current below 25 amps. Using this method, the battery should be usable within three hours, giving a voltage reading of 12.5 volts, but this is for a partially-discharged battery and, as mentioned, full charging can take considerably longer.

15 Use of a normal trickle charger should not be detrimental to the battery, provided excessive gassing is not allowed to occur, and the battery is not allowed to become hot.

4.2 Slacken the clamp nut

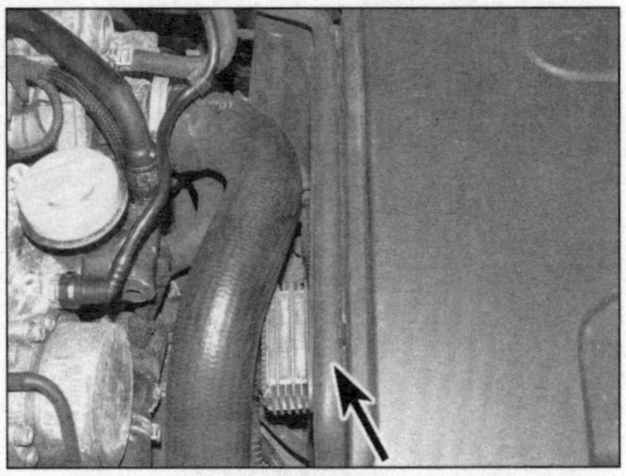

4.1b ... and unclip the coolant hose (arrowed)

4 Battery – disconnection, removal, refitting and reconnection

Disconnection and removal

1 The battery is located at the front left-hand side of the engine compartment. Rotate the 2 fasteners anti-clockwise, unclip the coolant hose, and remove the cover from the battery **(see illustrations)**.

2 Loosen the clamp nut and disconnect the lead at the negative (earth) terminal. Disconnect the lead at the positive terminal in the same way **(see illustration)**.

3 Unscrew the battery mounting clamp bolt located at the front of the battery, and remove the clamp **(see illustration)**.

4 Disconnect the battery drain hose (where applicable), then lift the battery out of the engine compartment (take care not to tilt it excessively).

5 To remove the battery tray on diesel models, release the clips and slide up the glow plug ECM from the side of the tray.

6 Depress the clips and slide up the fusible link junction box (where fitted) and bonnet switch from the side of the battery tray. On automatic transmission models, release the clip and slide the transmission control module (TCM) from the right-hand side of the battery tray **(see illustrations)**.

7 Undo the 3 T40 Torx screws and lift up the battery tray **(see illustration)**. Release any wiring harness clips as the tray is withdrawn.

4.3 Undo the battery clamp bolt (arrowed) and remove the clamp

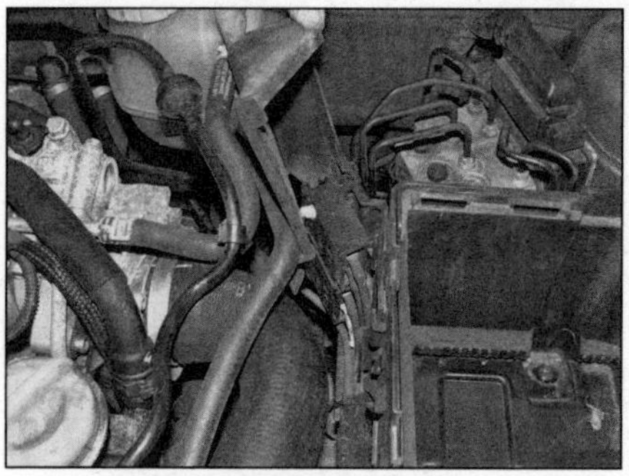

4.6a Slide up the cover ...

4.6b ... then press in the clip (arrowed) and slide up the fusible link junction box

4.6c On automatic transmission models, depress the clip (arrowed) and slide up the TCM from the battery tray

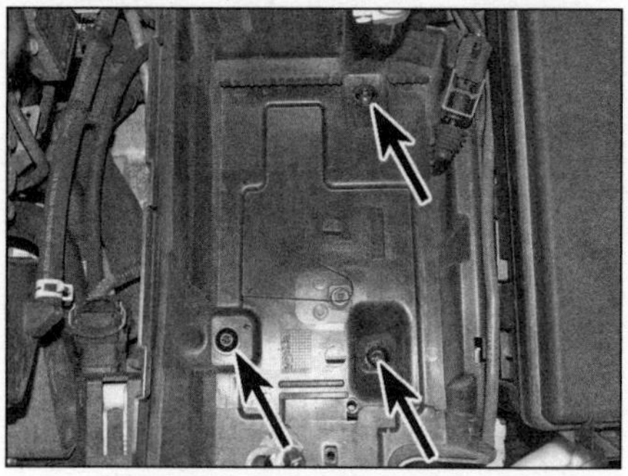

4.7 Battery tray Torx screws (arrowed)

Refitting and reconnection

8 Refitting is a reversal of removal. Smear petroleum jelly on the terminals after reconnecting the leads, and always reconnect the positive lead first, and the negative lead last.

9 After reconnection, it will be necessary to reset the clock, and date information as described in the owners handbook.

10 On vehicles fitted with the power window 'pinch protection' system, this must be reset. To do this:

1) Close all door and windows. Close the roof on Convertible models.
2) Remove and refit fuse number F5 in the facia fusebox.
3) Start the vehicle.
4) Keeping the button fully depressed, lower the window.
5) Fully raise the window and hold the button in the up position for at least 2 seconds.
6) Fully lower the window.
7) Fully raise the window and hold the switch in the up position for at least 2 seconds.
8) Release the switch and an audible beep will be heard to confirm that the programming is complete.
9) Repeat the procedure if no audible beep is heard.

11 On Convertible models, close the doors and the soft top, start the car, depress and hold the soft top close button until an audible signal, confirming the setting, is given.

12 All remotes should be re-synchronised by inserting them into the ignition lock. The vehicle must be driven at a speed greater than 11 mph and then stopped to ensure correct functioning of the steering column lock (SCL).

5 Charging system – testing

Note: *Refer to the warnings given in 'Safety first!' and in Section 1 of this Chapter before starting work.*

1 If the ignition/no-charge warning light does not come on when the ignition is switched on, first check the alternator wiring connections for security. If all is satisfactory a diagnostic check should be performed using Saabs dedicated test equipment (TECH2) or other suitable diagnostic equipment. The instrument panel does not contain a conventional bulb.

2 If the ignition warning light comes on when the engine is running, stop the engine. The SID (Saab Information Display) will also display a message. Check that the drivebelt is intact and correctly tensioned (see Chapter 1A, Section 26 or Chapter 1B, Section 27), and that the alternator connections are secure. If all is satisfactory, check the alternator brushes and slip-rings as described in Section 8. If the fault persists, the alternator should be taken to an auto-electrician for testing and repair, or else renewed.

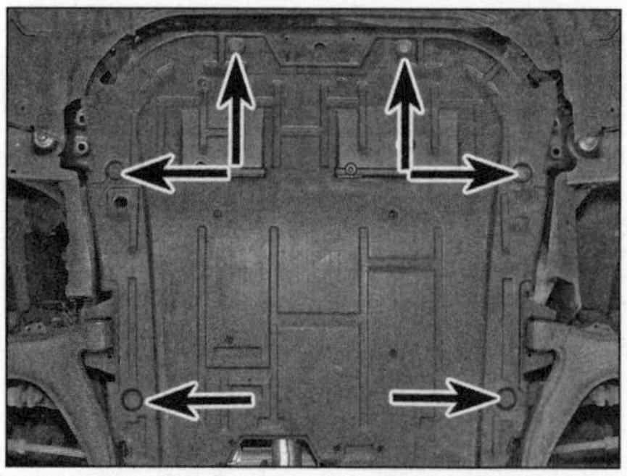

7.2 Undo the bolts (arrowed) and remove the engine undershield

3 If the alternator output is suspect even though the warning light functions correctly, the regulated voltage may be checked as follows.

4 Connect a voltmeter across the battery terminals, and start the engine.

5 Increase the engine speed until the voltmeter reading remains steady; the reading should be approximately 12 to 13 volts, and no more than 14 volts.

6 Switch on as many electrical accessories (eg, the headlights, heated rear window and heater blower) as possible, and check that the alternator maintains the regulated voltage at around 13 to 14 volts.

7 If the regulated voltage is not as stated, the fault may be due to worn brushes, weak brush springs, a faulty voltage regulator, a faulty diode, a severed phase winding, or worn or damaged slip-rings. The brushes and slip-rings may be checked (see Section 8), but if the fault persists, the alternator should be taken to an auto-electrician for testing and repair, or else renewed.

6 Alternator drivebelt – removal, refitting and tensioning

Refer to the procedure given for the auxiliary drivebelt in Chapter 1A, Section 26 or Chapter 1B, Section 27.

7 Alternator – removal and refitting

Removal

1 Remove the engine top cover. Disconnect the battery negative lead as described in Section 4 of this Chapter.

2 Apply the handbrake, then jack up the front of the vehicle and support it on axle stands (see *Jacking and vehicle support*). Remove the right-hand front roadwheel and the engine undershield **(see illustration)**.

3 Remove the right-hand front wing inner plastic moulding/wheel arch liner for access to the rear of the engine.

4 Remove the auxiliary drivebelt as described in Chapter 1A, Section 26 or Chapter 1B, Section 27.

Petrol models

5 Drain the cooling system as described in Chapter 1A, Section 27.

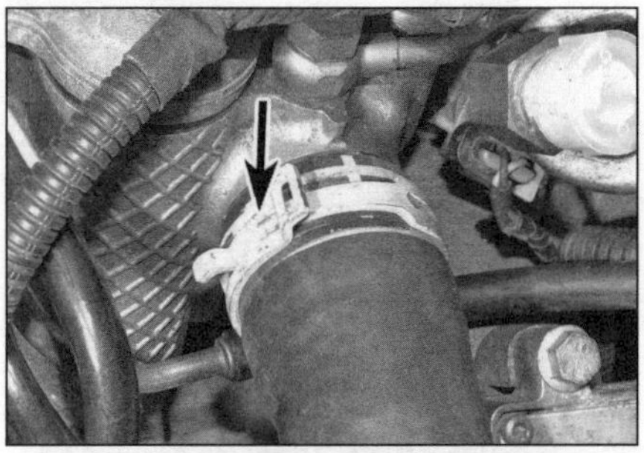

7.8 Release the clamp at each end (arrowed) and remove the coolant hose from the cylinder head to the radiator

6 Remove the engine management ECM as described in Chapter 4A, Section 10.

7 Remove the air cleaner assembly as described in Chapter 4A, Section 2.

8 Release the clips and disconnect the coolant hose from the engine and radiator **(see illustration)**. Move the hose assembly to one side.

9 Disconnect the vent hose from the throttle body air hose, and move the vent hose to one side.

10 Unscrew the nut and disconnect the two wires from the alternator terminals **(see illustration)**.

11 Unscrew and remove the mounting bolts, then rotate the alternator so the pulley is uppermost, and manoeuvre it upwards from the engine compartment **(see illustration)**.

Z19DT and Z19DTH diesel models

12 Remove the alternator upper mounting bolt (Z19DT) or bolts (Z19DTH) **(see illustration)**.

13 On the Z19DT and Z19DTH engines, remove the suspension right-hand lower arm balljoint pinch-bolt, and use a lever to lower the arm and balljoint from the hub carrier (see Chapter 10, Section 3). Use a block of wood to wedge the arm in the lowered position.

14 Tap the right-hand driveshaft from the support bearing, and push the driveshaft to one side.

15 Undo the nuts and disconnect the electrical connections from the rear of the alternator.

16 Undo the bolts, remove the alternator lower bracket (Z19DT), or lower mounting bolt (Z19DTH), and lower the alternator from the rear of the engine **(see illustration)**.

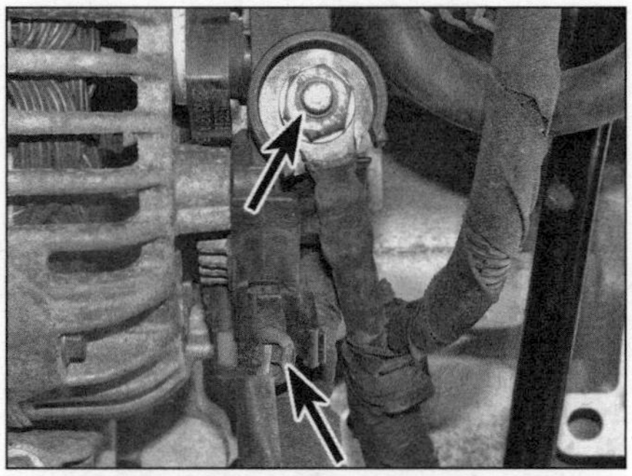

7.10 Alternator connections (arrowed)

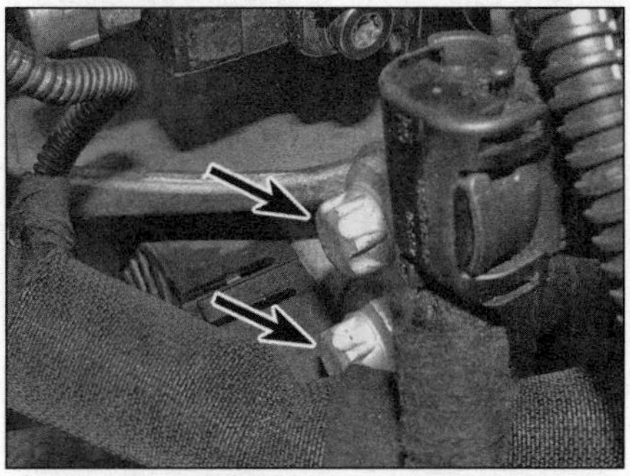

7.12 Alternator upper mounting bolts (arrowed) – Z19DTH engine

Z19DTR diesel models

17 If not already done so remove the air cleaner assembly as described in Chapter 4A, Section 3.

18 Disconnect the wiring harness support from above the injection pump and from the rear.

19 Remove the electrical connections from the rear of the alternator.

20 Remove the alternator upper mounting bolts.

21 Support the alternator and remove the lower bolt and then left the alternator up and remove it.

Refitting

22 Refitting is a reversal of removal, however, clean the alternator mounting points, and coat them with petroleum jelly to ensure a good electrical connection to the engine. Ensure that the alternator mountings are securely tightened, and refit the components referring to the relevant Chapters.

7.11 Alternator mounting bolts (arrowed)

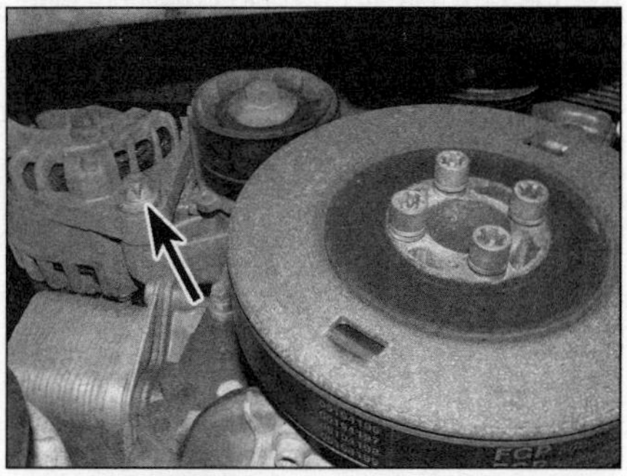

7.16 Alternator lower front mounting bolt (arrowed) – diesel engines

8 Alternator brushes and regulator – inspection and renewal

1 Remove the alternator (see Section 7).

2 Unscrew the 2 nuts and the screw securing the cover to the rear of the alternator **(see illustration)**.

3 Using a screwdriver, lever off the cover, and remove it from the rear of the alternator.

4 Unscrew and remove the three retaining screws, and remove the regulator/brushholder from the rear of the alternator **(see illustration)**.

5 Measure the protrusion of each brush from its holder, using a steel rule or vernier calipers **(see illustration)**. If less than 7.5 mm, a new regulator/brush assembly should be obtained.

8.2 Undo the nuts and screw (arrowed) securing the rear cover

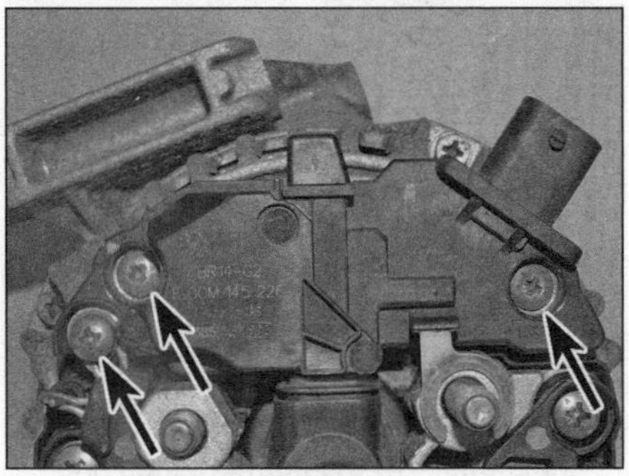

8.4 Undo the regulator/brushholder screws (arrowed)

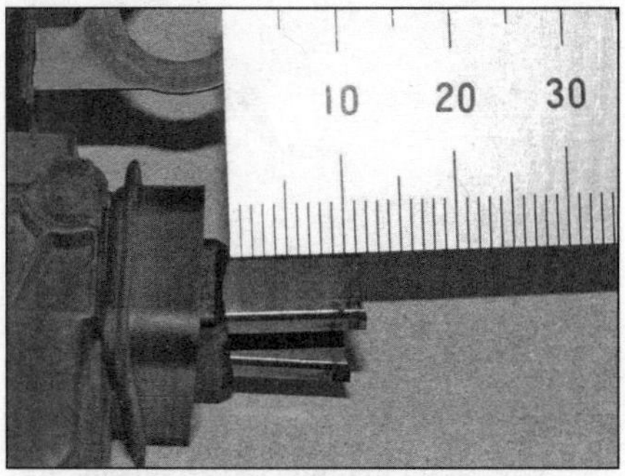

8.5 Measure the length of the brushes

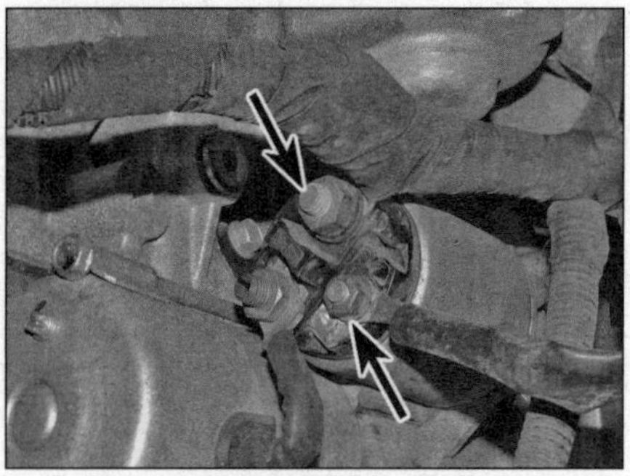

10.3 Undo the nuts (arrowed) and disconnect the wiring from the starter motor

10.4 Starter motor mounting bolts (arrowed)

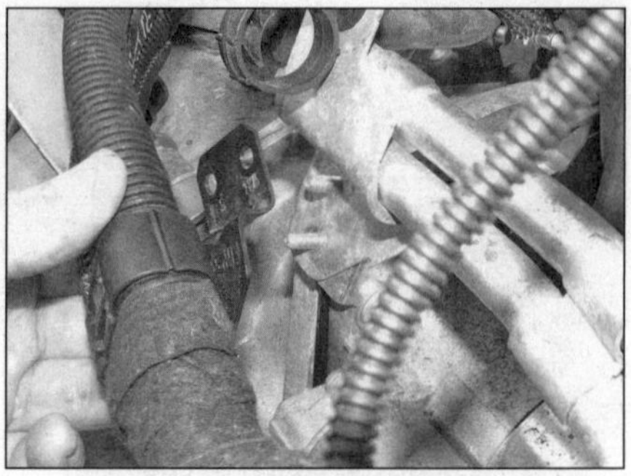

10.5 Undo the nuts and release the wiring harness from the support bracket

6 If the brushes are in good condition, clean them and check that they move freely in their holders.

7 Wipe clean the alternator slip-rings, and check them for signs of scoring or burning. It may be possible to have the slip-rings renovated by an electrical specialist.

8 Refit the regulator/brush holder assembly, and securely tighten the retaining screws.

9 Refit the cover, then insert and tighten the retaining screw and nut.

10 Refit the alternator with reference to Section 7.

9 Starting system – testing

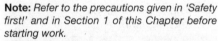

Note: *Refer to the precautions given in 'Safety first!' and in Section 1 of this Chapter before starting work.*

1 If the starter motor fails to operate when the ignition key is turned to the appropriate position, the following possible causes may apply:

a) The battery is faulty.

b) The electrical connections between the switch, solenoid, battery and starter motor are somewhere failing to pass the necessary current from the battery through the starter to earth.

c) The solenoid is faulty.

d) The starter motor is mechanically or electrically defective.

2 To check the battery, switch on the headlights. If they dim after a few seconds, this indicates that the battery is discharged – recharge (see Section 3) or renew the battery. If the headlights glow brightly, operate the starter on the ignition switch, and observe the lights. If they dim, this indicates that current is reaching the starter motor – therefore the fault must lie in the starter motor. If the lights continue to glow brightly (and no clicking sound can be heard from the starter motor solenoid), this indicates that there is a fault in the circuit or solenoid – see the following paragraphs. If the starter motor turns slowly when operated, but the battery is in good condition, then this indicates that either the starter motor is faulty, or that there is considerable resistance somewhere in the circuit.

3 If a fault in the circuit is suspected, disconnect the battery leads, the starter/solenoid wiring and the engine/transmission earth strap. Thoroughly clean the connections, and reconnect the leads and wiring, then use a voltmeter or test light to check that full battery voltage is available at the battery positive lead connection on the solenoid, and that the earth is sound.

4 If the battery and all connections are in good condition, check the circuit by disconnecting the wire from the solenoid terminal. Connect a voltmeter or test light between the wire end and a good earth (such as the battery negative terminal), and check that the wire is live when the ignition switch is turned to the start position. If it is, then the circuit is sound – if not, the circuit wiring can be checked as described in Chapter 12, Section 2.

5 The solenoid contacts can be checked by connecting a voltmeter or test light between the terminal on the starter side of the solenoid, and earth. When the ignition switch is turned to the start position, there should be a reading or lighted bulb, as applicable. If there is no reading or lighted bulb, the solenoid or contacts are faulty and the solenoid should be renewed.

6 If the circuit and solenoid are proved sound, the fault must lie in the starter motor. Begin checking the starter motor by removing it (see Section 10), and checking the brushes (see Section 11). If the fault does not lie in the brushes, the motor windings must be faulty. In this event, it may be possible to have the starter motor overhauled by a specialist, but check on the availability and cost of spares before proceeding, as it may prove more economical to obtain a new or exchange motor.

10 Starter motor – removal and refitting

Removal

1 The starter motor is located on the left-hand rear side (diesel models) or left-hand front side (petrol models) of the engine, and is bolted to the engine backplate and transmission. First remove the cover from the battery and disconnect the negative lead as described in Section 4 of this Chapter.

2 Apply the handbrake, then jack up the front of the car and support on axle stands (see *Jacking and vehicle support*). Undo the fasteners and remove the engine undershield **(see illustration 7.2)**.

Petrol models

3 Undo the nuts securing the starter motor electrical connections **(see illustration)**.

4 Unscrew the starter motor mounting bolts, then lower the starter motor from the engine compartment **(see illustration)**.

Diesel models

5 Working above the engine, remove the starter motor upper mounting bolts, and remove the bracket from the coolant pipe and wiring harness **(see illustration)**.

6 Note their fitted positions, then undo the nuts and detach the electrical connections from the starter motor **(see illustration)**.

7 Undo the lower mounting nut and detach

10.6 Undo the nuts (arrowed) and disconnect the starter solenoid wiring connectors

10.7 Unscrew the nut (arrowed) and disconnect the earth lead from the start motor stud bolt

the earth cable from the starter motor lower mounting stud **(see illustration)**.

8 Remove the starter motor lower mounting stud by using two nuts locked together.

9 Manoeuvre the starter motor from position.

Refitting

10 Refitting is a reversal of removal, but tighten the mounting bolts to the specified torque.

11 Starter motor – overhaul

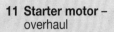

If the starter motor is thought to be suspect, it should be removed from the vehicle and taken to an auto-electrician for testing. Most auto-electricians will be able to supply and fit brushes at a reasonable cost. However, check on the cost of repairs before proceeding as it may prove more economical to obtain a new or exchange motor.

12 Ignition switch – removal and refitting

Refer to Chapter 12, Section 4.

13 Oil pressure warning light switch – removal and refitting

Removal

Petrol models

1 The switch is screwed into the front of the cylinder block, adjacent to the oil filter **(see illustration)**. To gain access to the switch, remove the plastic cover from the top of the engine.

2 Disconnect the wiring connector then unscrew the switch (using a 27 mm ring spanner or socket) and recover the sealing washer. Be prepared for oil spillage, and if the switch is to be left removed from the engine for any length of time, plug the switch aperture.

Diesel models

3 The switch is screwed into the oil filter

13.1 Oil pressure warning light switch – petrol engines

housing at the rear of the engine **(see illustration)**.

4 Firmly apply the handbrake, then jack up the front of the car and support it securely on axle stands (see *Jacking and vehicle support*).

5 Undo the bolts and remove the undershield from beneath the engine.

6 Disconnect the wiring connector then unscrew the switch and recover the sealing washer. Be prepared for oil spillage, and if the switch is to be left removed from the engine for any length of time, plug the switch aperture.

Refitting

7 Examine the sealing washer for signs of damage or deterioration and if necessary renew.

8 Refit the switch and washer, tightening it to the specified torque, and reconnect the wiring connector.

9 On diesel engine models, refit the engine undershield.

10 Lower the vehicle to the ground (where applicable) then check and, if necessary, top-up the engine oil as described in *Weekly checks*.

14 Oil level sensor – removal and refitting

Petrol models

Removal

1 The oil level sensor is located on the front face of the engine sump.

13.3 Oil pressure warning light switch (arrowed) – diesel engines

2 Remove the sump as described in Chapter 2A, Section 7.

3 Carefully prise of the circlip on the inside of the sump casing securing the connector **(see illustration)**.

4 Unscrew the retaining screws then ease the sensor out from the sump and remove it along with its sealing ring/washer. Discard the sealing ring/washer, a new one should be used on refitting **(see illustration)**.

Refitting

5 Refitting is the reverse of removal ensuring the wiring is correctly routed and securely reconnected. On completion refill the engine with oil (see Chapter 1A, Section 3).

Diesel models

Removal

6 The oil level sensor is located at the rear of the sump, beneath the crankshaft position sensor. Remove the sump as described in Chapter 2B, Section 13 or Chapter 2C, Section 13.

7 With the sump removed, slide off the retaining clip and free the sensor wiring connector from the sump **(see illustration)**.

8 Where fitted, undo the retaining bolts and remove the oil baffle plate from inside the sump **(see illustration)**.

9 Note the correct routing of the wiring then undo the retaining bolts and remove the sensor assembly from the sump **(see illustration)**. Check the wiring connector seal for signs or damage and renew if necessary.

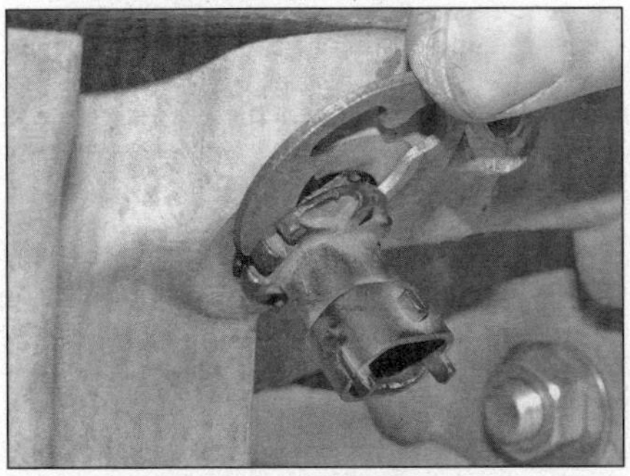

14.3 Slide off the retaining clip securing the sensor connector

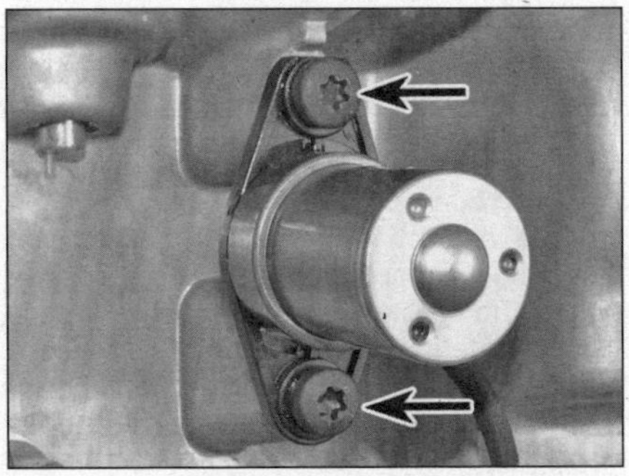

14.4 Oil level sensor Torx screws (arrowed)

14.7 Slide off the retaining clip (arrowed) and free the oil level sensor wiring connector from the sump

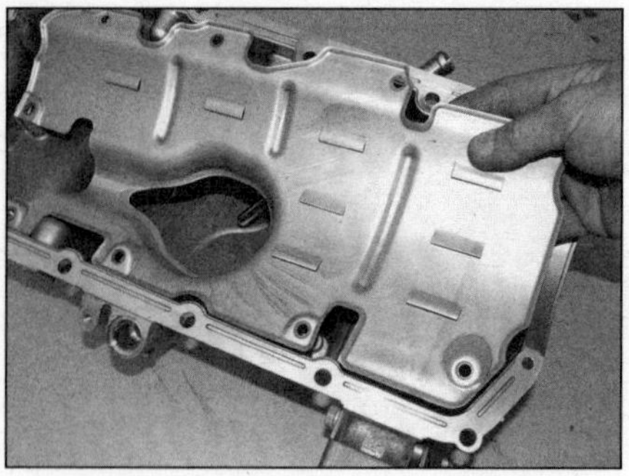

14.8 Where fitted, undo the retaining bolts and remove the oil baffle plate

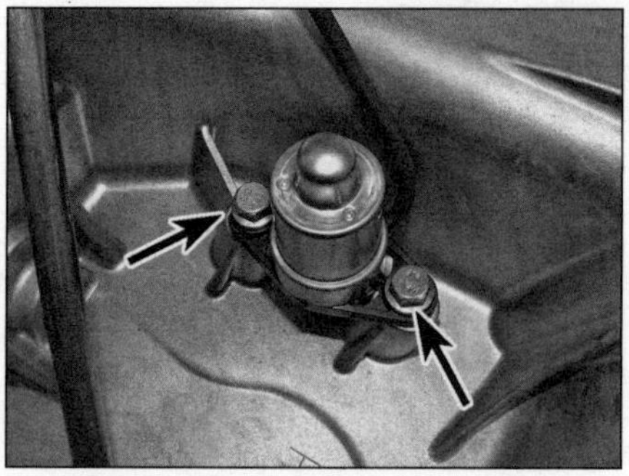

14.9 Undo the two bolts (arrowed) and remove the oil level sensor from the sump

Refitting

10 Prior to refitting, remove all traces of locking compound from the sensor retaining bolt and sump threads. Apply a drop of fresh locking compound to the bolt threads and lubricate the wiring connector seal with a smear of engine oil.

11 Fit the sensor, making sure the wiring is correctly routed, and securely tighten its retaining bolts. Ease the wiring connector through the sump, taking care not to damage its seal, and secure it in position with the retaining clip.

12 Ensure the sensor is correctly refitted then, where applicable, refit the oil baffle plate.

13 Refit the sump and refill the engine with oil (Chapter 1B, Section 3).

15 Pre/post-heating system – description and testing

Description

1 Each cylinder of the engine is fitted with a heater plug (commonly called a glow plug) screwed into it. The plugs are electrically-operated before and during start-up when the engine is cold. Electrical feed to the glow plugs is controlled via the pre/post-heating system control unit.

2 A warning light in the instrument panel tells the driver that pre/post-heating is taking place. When the light goes out, the engine is ready to be started. The voltage supply to the glow plugs continues for several seconds after the light goes out. If no attempt is made to start, the timer then cuts off the supply, in order to avoid draining the battery and overheating the glow plugs.

3 The glow plugs also provide a 'post-heating' function, whereby the glow plugs remain switched on after the engine has started. The length of time 'post-heating' takes place is also determined by the control unit, and is dependent on engine temperature.

4 The fuel filter is fitted with a heating element to prevent the fuel 'waxing' in extreme cold temperature conditions and to improve combustion. The heating element is an integral part of the fuel filter housing and is controlled by the pre/post-heating system control unit.

Testing

5 If the system malfunctions, testing is ultimately by substitution of known good units, but some preliminary checks may be made as follows.

6 Connect a voltmeter or 12 volt test lamp between the glow plug supply cable and earth (engine or vehicle metal). Make sure that the live connection is kept clear of the engine and bodywork.

7 Have an assistant switch on the ignition, and check that voltage is applied to the glow plugs. Note the time for which the warning light is lit, and the total time for which voltage is applied before the system cuts out. Switch off the ignition.

8 At an underbonnet temperature of 20°C, typical times noted should be approximately 3 seconds for warning light operation. Warning light time will increase with lower temperatures and decrease with higher temperatures.

9 If there is no supply at all, the control unit or associated wiring is at fault.

10 To locate a defective glow plug, disconnect the wiring connector from each plug.

11 Use a continuity tester, or a 12 volt test lamp connected to the battery positive terminal, to check for continuity between each glow plug terminal and earth. The resistance of a glow plug in good condition is very low (less than 1 ohm), so if the test lamp does not light or the continuity tester shows a high resistance, the glow plug is certainly defective.

12 If an ammeter is available, the current draw of each glow plug can be checked. After an initial surge of 15 to 20 amps, each plug should draw 12 amps. Any plug which draws much more or less than this is probably defective.

13 As a final check, the glow plugs can be removed and inspected as described in the following Section.

16 Glow plugs – removal, inspection and refitting

Caution: If the pre/post-heating system has just been energised, or if the engine has been running, the glow plugs will be very hot.

Removal

1 The glow plugs are located at the rear of the cylinder head above the intake manifold.

2 On Z19DT engines, remove the oil filler cap and unscrew the two bolts securing the plastic cover over the top of the engine. Release the engine breather hose, then lift off the cover and refit the oil filler cap. On Z19DTH and Z19DTR engines, remove the plastic cover by pulling it upwards off the mounting studs.

Z19DT engines

3 Disconnect the wiring plugs from the injectors, and detach the wiring harness from the intake manifold. Move the harness to one side.

4 Using a second spanner to counter-hold the fuel rail ports, undo the unions and remove the high-pressure fuel pipes from the injectors and the fuel rail. Note that the high-pressure fuel pipes must not be re-used. Obtain new ones.

All diesel engines

5 Pull the connectors from the glow plugs, then unscrew them using a 10 mm deep reach socket on the Z19DT engine and a 9 mm deep reach socket on all other diesel engines. Remove them from the cylinder head **(see illustration)**.

16.5 Unscrew the glow plugs and remove them from the cylinder head

Inspection

6 Inspect each glow plug for physical damage. Burnt or eroded glow plug tips can be caused by a bad injector spray pattern. Have the injectors checked if this type of damage is found.

7 If the glow plugs are in good physical condition, check them electrically using a 12 volt test lamp or continuity tester as described in the previous Section.

8 The glow plugs can be energised by applying 12 volts to them to verify that they heat up evenly and in the required time. Observe the following precautions.

a) Support the glow plug by clamping it carefully in a vice or self-locking pliers. Remember it will become red-hot.

b) Make sure that the power supply or test

lead incorporates a fuse or overload trip to protect against damage from a short-circuit.

c) After testing, allow the glow plug to cool for several minutes before attempting to handle it.

9 A glow plug in good condition will start to glow red at the tip after drawing current for 5 seconds or so. Any plug which takes much longer to start glowing, or which starts glowing in the middle instead of at the tip, is defective.

Refitting

10 Carefully refit the plugs and tighten to the specified torque. Do not overtighten, as this can damage the glow plug element. Push the electrical connectors firmly onto the glow plugs.

11 The remainder of refitting is a reversal of removal, checking the operation of the glow plugs on completion.

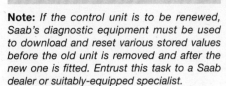

17 Pre/post-heating system control unit – removal and refitting

Note: *If the control unit is to be renewed, Saab's diagnostic equipment must be used to download and reset various stored values before the old unit is removed and after the new one is fitted. Entrust this task to a Saab dealer or suitably-equipped specialist.*

Note: *These electronic modules are very sensitive to static electricity. Before handling the unit, earth yourself by touching a bare metal part of the vehicle body.*

Removal

1 The control unit is located on the side of the battery box or on the slam panel adjacent to the battery. To improve access, slacken the clamps and remove the air intake duct between the intake manifold and intercooler.

17.2 Disconnect the glow plug control unit wiring plug (arrowed)

2 Disconnect the wiring plug from the control unit **(see illustration)**.

3 Unclip the control unit and slide it up and off the battery box.

Refitting

4 Refitting is a reversal of removal.

Chapter 5 Part B: Ignition system – petrol engines

Contents

Degrees of difficulty

Easy, suitable for novice with little experience	**Fairly easy,** suitable for beginner with some experience	**Fairly difficult,** suitable for competent DIY mechanic	**Difficult,** suitable for experienced DIY mechanic	**Very difficult,** suitable for expert DIY or professional

Specifications

System type

System type	Direct Ignition (DI) system incorporated in Saab Trionic T8 engine management system

Direct Ignition (DI) system

Ignition coils voltage	5 to 30 kV
Ignition timing	Pre-programmed in ECM
Firing order	1-3-4-2 (No 1 cylinder at timing chain end)

Torque wrench settings

	Nm	lbf ft
Ignition coils	12	9
Ignition discharge module	11	8
Spark plugs	27	20

1 General information

Direct ignition (DI) system

1 The Direct Ignition system is incorporated into the Saab Trionic engine management system. A single electronic control module (ECM) controls both the fuel injection and ignition functions. The system uses a separate HT coil for each spark plug, and the electronic control module monitors the engine by means of various sensors in order to determine the most efficient ignition timing.

2 The components of the system are a crankshaft position/speed sensor, combustion detection module (CDM) with one coil per plug, diagnostic socket, ECM, pressure sensor in the inlet manifold (to determine engine load), and a solenoid valve (to regulate the turbocharger operation).

3 During starting at a crankshaft speed in excess of 150 rpm, HT sparks are triggered in the cylinder pair with the pistons at TDC. Under difficult conditions, multi-sparking occurs during this period, to aid starting. The ECM determines in which cylinder combustion is taking place by monitoring the flow of current across the spark plug electrodes, and then uses this information to determine the firing.

4 From when the engine is stationary until it exceeds 500 rpm, the starting ignition timing at 20°C is 6° BTDC. At lower temperatures the ignition timing is advanced, and at higher temperatures, it's retarded. At higher engine speeds, the ECM regulates the ignition timing in accordance with the information received from the various sensors

5 When the ignition is switched off and the engine stops the main relay remains operational for a further 6 seconds. During this period, the Trionic control module earths all the trigger leads 210 times a second for 5 seconds, in order to burn off impurities from the spark plug electrodes.

6 Because the system does not use any HT leads, radio suppression must be incorporated in the spark plugs, so resistor-type plugs must always be used.

7 The direct ignition system uses the capacitive discharge method of producing an HT spark. Approximately 400 volts is stored in a capacitor, and at the time of ignition, this voltage is discharged through the primary circuit of the relevant coil. Approximately 30 000 volts is induced in the HT secondary coil, and this is discharged across the spark plug electrodes.

8 Should a fault occur in the system, a fault code is stored in the ECM. This code can only be accessed by a Saab dealer or specialist, using dedicated equipment.

9 Note that the starter motor must never be operated with the ignition module disconnected from the spark plugs but still connected to the wiring loom. This can cause irreversible damage to the module.

10 With the Saab Trionic system, the spark plugs themselves are used as knock sensors, instead of employing a separate knock detector in the cylinder block. It achieves this by applying a small, direct current voltage across each spark plug. When two cylinders approach TDC, this voltage causes an ionisation current to flow across the terminals of the spark plug in the cylinder under combustion; a high current indicates that knock is occurring thus indicating which cylinder requires ignition retardation. Sequential control of the fuel injection is achieved in the same manner (see Chapter 4A, Section 1).

11 A combustion detection module (CDM) is fitted to the left-hand end of the cylinder head, and carries out the initial processing of the ionising signals from each ignition coil. The CDM transmits the knock signal, and the combustion signals from cylinders 1 and 3 or 2 and 4.

3.1 Slide out the red locking catch (arrowed) and disconnect the wiring plug ...

2 Ignition system – testing

Warning: Voltages produced by an electronic ignition system are considerably higher than those produced by conventional ignition systems. Extreme care must be taken when working on the system with the ignition switched on. Persons with surgically-implanted cardiac pacemaker devices should keep well clear of the ignition circuits, components and test equipment. Refer to the precautions in Chapter 5A, Section 1, before starting work. Always switch off the ignition before disconnecting or connecting any component, and when using a multimeter to check resistances.

1 If a fault appears in the engine management system, first check that all wiring is secure and in good condition. If necessary, individual components of the Direct Ignition system may be removed for visual investigation as described later in this Chapter. Coils are best checked by substituting a suspect one with a known good coil, and checking if the misfire is cured.

2 Due to the location of the spark plugs beneath the ignition coils, it is not possible to easily check the HT circuit for faults. Further testing should be carried out by a Saab dealer or specialist, who will have equipment to access fault codes stored in the system ECM.

3.2 ... then undo the 2 bolts and remove the CDM

3 Combustion detection module – removal and refitting

Removal

1 Disconnect the wiring plug from the module located at the left-hand end of the cylinder head **(see illustration)**.

2 Undo the 2 bolts and remove the module **(see illustration)**.

Refitting

3 Refitting is a reversal of removal.

4 Ignition HT coils – removal and refitting

Removal

1 Undo the Torx screws and remove the cover from the top of the engine, between the camshafts **(see illustration)**.

2 Undo the retaining bolt and pull the coil upwards from the plug. Disconnect the wiring plug as the coil is withdrawn **(see illustrations)**.

Refitting

3 Refitting is a reversal of removal, tightening the coil retaining bolts to the specified torque.

5 Slotted rotor for crankshaft sensor – removal and refitting

Removal

1 The slotted rotor is located on the flywheel/driveplate end of the crankshaft. Remove the crankshaft as described in Chapter 2D, Section 10.

2 Using a Torx key, unscrew the four screws securing the slotted rotor to the crankshaft, then remove the rotor over the end of the crankshaft.

Refitting

3 Refitting is a reversal of removal. Note that the rotor can only be fitted in one position, since the bolt holes are unequally-spaced.

6 Ignition timing – general information

The ignition timing is preprogrammed into the system ECM, and cannot be adjusted or even checked with any accuracy. If the timing is thought to be incorrect, the car should be taken to a Saab dealer or specialist, who will have the necessary equipment to extract any fault codes stored in the ECM. For further information see Chapter 4A, Section 1.

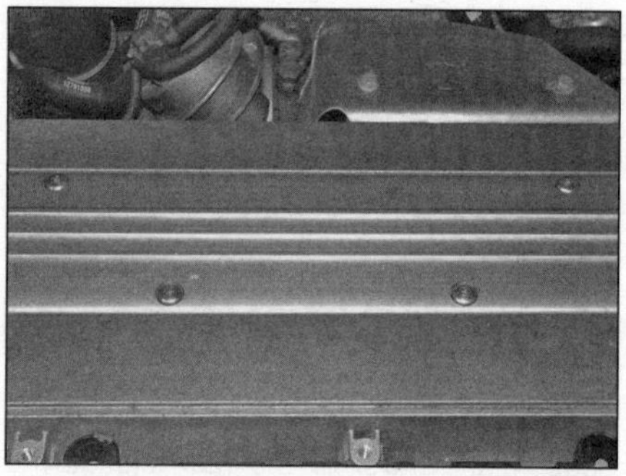
4.1 Undo the Torx screws and remove the cover

4.2a Undo the coil retaining bolt (arrowed)

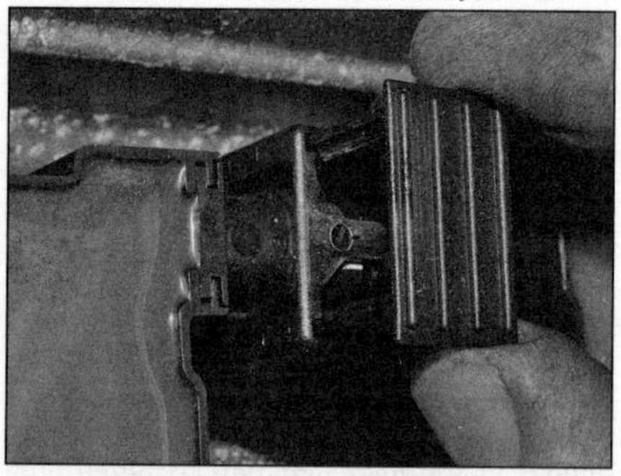
4.2b Lift the locking catch and disconnect the wiring plug

Chapter 6
Clutch

Contents

Degrees of difficulty

Easy, suitable for novice with little experience	**Fairly easy,** suitable for beginner with some experience	**Fairly difficult,** suitable for competent DIY mechanic	**Difficult,** suitable for experienced DIY mechanic	**Very difficult,** suitable for expert DIY or professional

Specifications

Type	Single dry plate with diaphragm spring, hydraulically-operated	
Friction disc		
Diameter	240 mm	
New lining thickness	7.3 mm	
Minimum thickness	5.5 mm	
Torque wrench settings	**Nm**	**lbf ft**
Brake master cylinder retaining nuts*	50	37
Clutch master cylinder retaining nuts	20	15
Pedal mounting bracket nuts*	20	15
Pressure plate retaining bolts	30	22
Release cylinder mounting screws	10	7
Vacuum servo unit stud bolts*	20	15

** Use new nuts/bolts*

1 General information

1 The clutch consists of a friction disc, a pressure plate assembly, and the hydraulic release cylinder (which incorporates the release bearing); all of these components are contained in the large cast-aluminium alloy bellhousing, sandwiched between the engine and the transmission.

2 The friction disc is fitted between the engine flywheel and the clutch pressure plate, and is allowed to slide on the transmission input shaft splines.

3 The pressure plate assembly is bolted to the engine flywheel. When the engine is running, drive is transmitted from the crankshaft, via the flywheel, to the friction disc (these components being clamped securely together by the pressure plate assembly) and from the friction disc to the transmission input shaft.

4 To interrupt the drive, the spring pressure must be relaxed. This is achieved using a hydraulic release mechanism which consists of the master cylinder, the release cylinder and the pipe/hose linking the two components. Depressing the pedal pushes on the master cylinder pushrod which hydraulically forces the release cylinder piston against the pressure plate spring fingers. This causes the springs to deform and releases the clamping force on the friction disc.

5 The clutch is self-adjusting and requires no manual adjustment.

6 The clutch pedal support and clutch pedal are one assembly and must be renewed as a complete unit. In the event of a frontal collision, the clutch pedal is released from its bearing in the support bracket to prevent injury to the driver's feet and legs (this also applies to the brake pedal). If an airbag has been deployed, inspect the clutch pedal assembly and if necessary renew the complete unit.

2 Clutch hydraulic system – bleeding

Warning: Hydraulic fluid is poisonous; wash off immediately and thoroughly in the case of skin contact, and seek immediate medical advice if any fluid is swallowed or gets into the eyes. Certain types of hydraulic fluid are flammable, and may ignite when allowed into contact with hot components; when servicing any hydraulic system, it is safest to assume that the fluid is flammable, and to take precautions against the risk of fire as though it is petrol that is being handled. Hydraulic fluid is also an effective paint stripper, and will attack plastics; if any is spilt, it should be washed off immediately, using copious quantities of fresh water. Finally, it is hygroscopic (it absorbs moisture from the air) – old fluid may be contaminated and unfit for further use. When topping-up or renewing the fluid, always use the recommended type, and ensure that it comes from a freshly-opened sealed container.

General information

1 The correct operation of any hydraulic system is only possible after removing all air from the components and circuit; this is achieved by bleeding the system.

2 The manufacturer's stipulate that the system must be initially bled by the 'back-bleeding' method using Saab special bleeding equipment. This entails connecting a pressure bleeding unit containing fresh brake fluid to the release cylinder bleed screw, with a collecting vessel connected to the brake fluid master

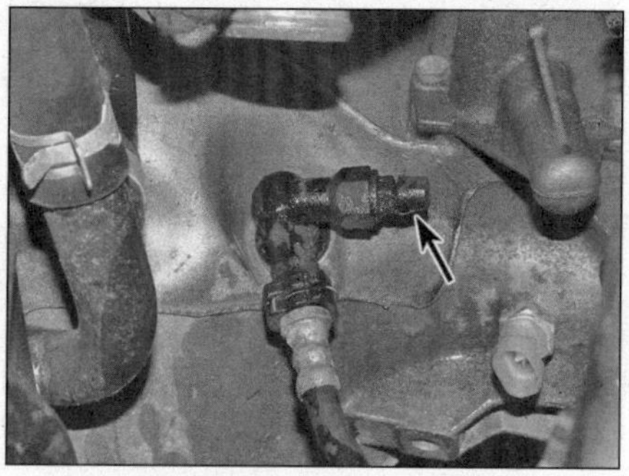

2.8 Clutch bleed screw (arrowed)

cylinder reservoir. The pressure bleeding unit is then switched on, the bleed screw is opened and hydraulic fluid is delivered under pressure, backwards, to be expelled from the reservoir into the collecting vessel. Final bleeding is then carried out in the conventional way.

3 In practice, this method would normally only be required if new hydraulic components have been fitted, or if the system has been completely drained of hydraulic fluid. If the system has only been disconnected to allow component removal and refitting procedures to be carried out, such as removal and refitting of the transmission (for example for clutch renewal) or engine removal and refitting, then it is quite likely that normal bleeding will be sufficient.

4 Our advice would therefore be as follows:

- *a) If the hydraulic system has only been partially disconnected, try bleeding by the conventional methods described in paragraphs 10 to 15, or 16 to 19.*
- *b) If the hydraulic system has been completely drained and new components have been fitted, try bleeding by using the pressure bleeding method described in paragraphs 20 to 22.*
- *c) If the above methods fail to produce a firm pedal on completion, it will be necessary to 'back-bleed' the system using Saab bleeding equipment, or suitable alternative equipment as described in paragraphs 23 to 28.*

5 During the bleeding procedure, add only clean, unused hydraulic fluid of the recommended type; never re-use fluid that has already been bled from the system.

2.27 A large syringe can be used to back-bleed bleed the system

Ensure that sufficient fluid is available before starting work.

6 If there is any possibility of incorrect fluid being already in the system, the hydraulic circuit must be flushed completely with uncontaminated, correct fluid.

7 If hydraulic fluid has been lost from the system, or air has entered because of a leak, ensure that the fault is cured before continuing further.

8 The bleed screw is located in the hose end fitting which is situated on the top of the transmission housing **(see illustration)**. On some models access to the bleed screw is limited and it may be necessary to jack up the front of the vehicle and support it on axle stands so that the screw can be reached from below, or remove the battery and battery box as described in Chapter 5A, Section 4, so that the screw can be reached from above.

9 Check that all pipes and hoses are secure, unions tight and the bleed screw is closed. Clean any dirt from around the bleed screw.

Bleeding procedure

Conventional method

10 Collect a clean glass jar, a suitable length of plastic or rubber tubing which is a tight fit over the bleed screw, and a ring spanner to fit the screw. The help of an assistant will also be required.

11 Unscrew the master cylinder fluid reservoir cap (the clutch shares the same fluid reservoir as the braking system), and top the master cylinder reservoir up to the upper (MAX) level line. Ensure that the fluid level is maintained at least above the lower level line in the reservoir throughout the procedure.

12 Remove the dust cap from the bleed screw. Fit the spanner and tube to the screw, place the other end of the tube in the jar, and pour in sufficient fluid to cover the end of the tube.

13 Have the assistant fully depress the clutch pedal several times to build-up pressure, then maintain it on the final down stroke.

14 While pedal pressure is maintained, unscrew the bleed screw (approximately one turn) and allow the compressed fluid and air to flow into the jar. The assistant should maintain pedal pressure and should not release it until instructed to do so. When the flow stops, tighten the bleed screw again, have the assistant release the pedal slowly, and recheck the reservoir fluid level.

15 Repeat the steps given in paragraphs 13 and 14 until the fluid emerging from the bleed screw is free from air bubbles. If the master cylinder has been drained and refilled allow approximately five seconds between cycles for the master cylinder passages to refill.

Using a one-way valve kit

16 As their name implies, these kits consist of a length of tubing with a one-way valve fitted, to prevent expelled air and fluid being drawn back into the system; some kits include a translucent container, which can be positioned so that the air bubbles can be more easily seen flowing from the end of the tube.

17 The kit is connected to the bleed screw, which is then opened.

18 The user returns to the driver's seat, depresses the clutch pedal with a smooth, steady stroke, and slowly releases it; this is repeated until the expelled fluid is clear of air bubbles.

19 Note that these kits simplify work so much that it is easy to forget the clutch fluid reservoir level; ensure that this is maintained at least above the lower level line at all times.

Pressure-bleeding method

20 These kits are usually operated by the reservoir of pressurised air contained in the spare tyre. However, note that it will probably be necessary to reduce the pressure to a lower level than normal; refer to the instructions supplied with the kit.

21 By connecting a pressurised, fluid-filled container to the clutch fluid reservoir, bleeding can be carried out simply by opening the bleed screw and allowing the fluid to flow out until no more air bubbles can be seen in the expelled fluid.

22 This method has the advantage that the large reservoir of fluid provides an additional safeguard against air being drawn into the system during bleeding.

'Back-bleeding' method

23 The following procedure describes the bleeding method using Saab equipment. Alternative equipment is available and should be used in accordance with the maker's instructions.

24 Connect the pressure hose (88 19 096) to the bleed screw located in the hose end fitting situated on the top of the transmission housing **(see illustration 2.8)**. Connect the other end of the hose to a suitable pressure bleeding device set to operate at approximately 2.0 bar.

25 Attach the cap (30 05 451) to the master cylinder reservoir, and place the hose in a collecting vessel.

26 Switch on the pressure bleeding equipment, open the bleed screw, and allow fresh hydraulic fluid to flow from the pressure bleeding unit, through the system and out through the top of the reservoir and into the collecting vessel. When fluid free from air bubbles appears in the reservoir, close the bleed screw and switch off the bleeding equipment.

27 An alternative method is to pressure bleed the clutch by using a large fluid-filled syringe and a length of screen washer hose (or similar). Ensuring that there are no air bubbles in the hose or syringe, connect the hose to the bleed screw, open the screw and use the syringe to push fluid up to the master cylinder **(see illustration)**. When the master cylinder is free of bubbles close the bleed nipple.

28 Disconnect the bleeding equipment from the bleed screw and reservoir.

29 If necessary carry out a final conventional bleeding procedure as described in paragraphs 10 to 15, or 16 to 19.

All methods

30 When bleeding is complete, no more bubbles appear and correct pedal feel is restored, tighten the bleed screw securely (do not overtighten). Remove the tube and spanner, and wash off any spilt fluid. Refit the dust cap to the bleed screw.

31 Check the hydraulic fluid level in the master cylinder reservoir, and top-up if necessary (see *Weekly checks*).

32 Discard any hydraulic fluid that has been bled from the system; it will not be fit for re-use.

33 Check the operation of the clutch pedal. If the clutch is still not operating correctly, air must still be present in the system, and further bleeding is required. Failure to bleed satisfactorily after a reasonable repetition of the bleeding procedure may be due to worn master cylinder/release cylinder seals.

3 Master cylinder – removal and refitting

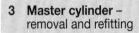

Note: *New master cylinder retaining nuts will be required for refitting.*

Removal

Right-hand drive models

1 Where fitted, remove the plastic cover over the top of the engine.

2 Release the clutch hydraulic pipe from the support clip(s) on the bulkhead.

3 Unscrew the brake/clutch hydraulic fluid reservoir filler cap, and top-up the reservoir to the MAX mark (see *Weekly checks*). Place a piece of polythene over the filler neck, and secure the polythene with the filler cap. This will minimise brake fluid loss during subsequent operations.

4 Remove all traces of dirt from the outside of the master cylinder and the brake/clutch hydraulic fluid reservoir, then position some cloth beneath the cylinder to catch any spilt fluid.

5 Extract the retaining clip and disconnect the hydraulic pipe from the connector on the end of the master cylinder **(see illustration)**. Plug the pipe end and master cylinder port to minimise fluid loss and prevent the entry of dirt.

6 Release the retaining clip (where fitted) and disconnect the fluid supply hose from the brake/clutch hydraulic fluid reservoir **(see illustration)**.

7 From inside the car, remove the lower facia panel on the driver's side as described in Chapter 11, Section 26.

8 Separate the clutch pedal from the master cylinder piston rod by releasing the retaining clip at the pedal. The clip may be released by pressing the retaining tabs together using screwdrivers, while at the same time pulling the clutch pedal rearwards **(see illustration)**. **Note:** *Do not remove the clip from the master cylinder piston rod, just release it from the pedal.*

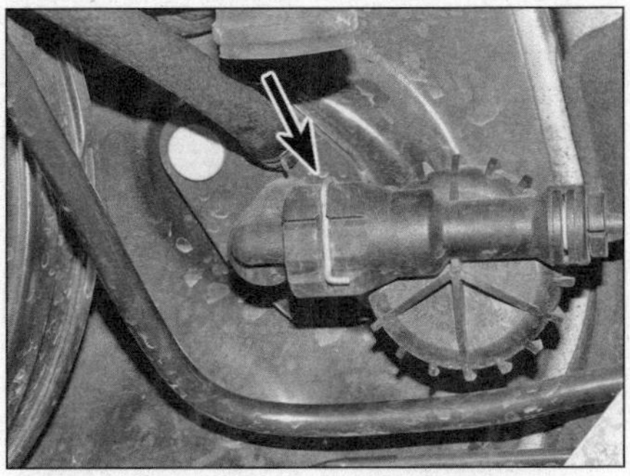

3.5 Prise out the clip (arrowed) and disconnect the pipe

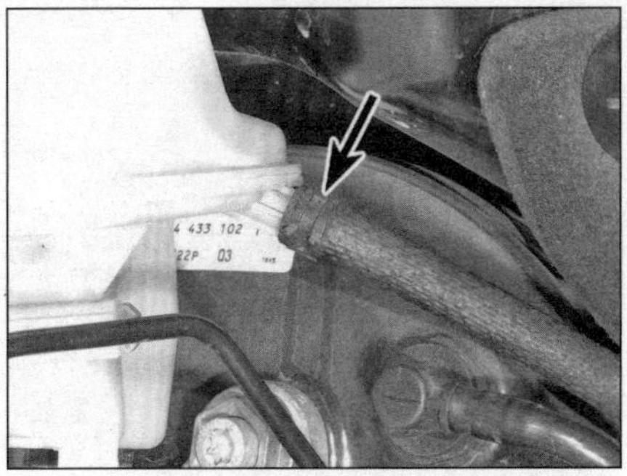

3.6 Release the clip (arrowed) and disconnect the hose

9 Unscrew the two nuts securing the master cylinder to the bulkhead, then return to the engine compartment and remove the master cylinder from the vehicle **(see illustration)**. If the master cylinder is faulty it must be renewed; overhaul of the unit is not possible.

Left-hand drive models

10 Remove the ABS hydraulic control unit as described in Chapter 9, Section 19.

11 Release the clutch hydraulic pipe from the two support clips beneath the battery box location.

12 Continue with the removal procedure as described in paragraphs 3 to 9.

Refitting

Right-hand drive models

13 Manoeuvre the master cylinder into position whilst ensuring that the piston rod and its retaining clip align correctly with the pedal. Fit the master cylinder retaining nuts and tighten them to the specified torque.

14 Push the master cylinder piston rod retaining clip into the clutch pedal, ensuring that the two lugs on the clip fully engage.

15 Refit the lower facia panel on the driver's side as described in Chapter 11, Section 26.

16 Connect the fluid supply hose to the brake/clutch hydraulic fluid reservoir and, where applicable, secure with the retaining clip.

17 Press the hydraulic pipe back into the connector on the end of the master cylinder and refit the retaining clip. Ensure that the retaining clip engages fully and the pipe is securely retained. Secure the pipe with the support clip(s).

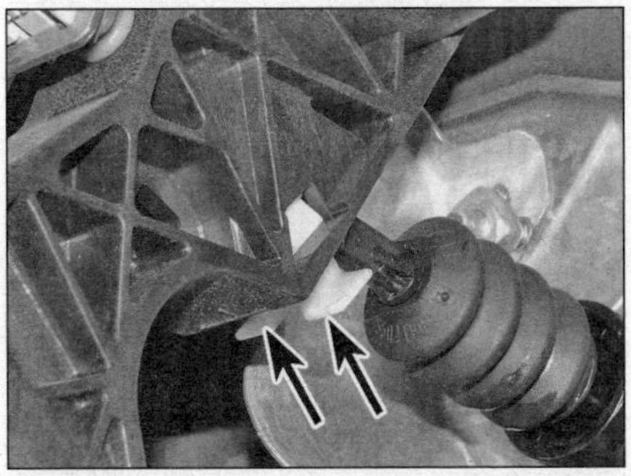

3.8 Squeeze together the tabs (arrowed) and pull the pedal rearwards

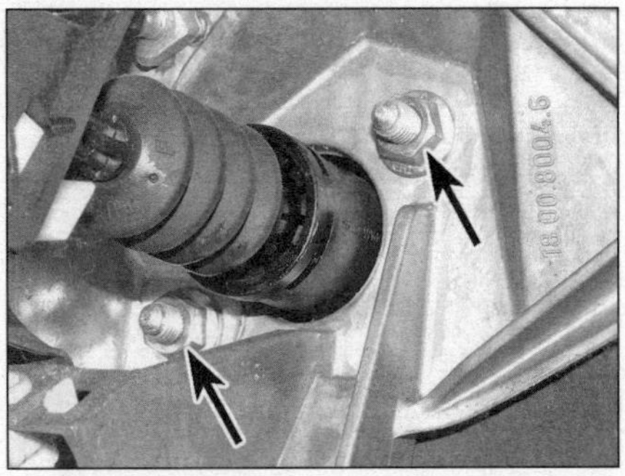

3.9 Undo the 2 nuts (arrowed) securing the master cylinder to the bulkhead

18 Bleed the clutch hydraulic system as described in Section 2, then refit the engine cover (where applicable).

Left-hand drive models

19 Carry out the operations described in paragraphs 13 to 18.

20 Refit the ABS hydraulic control unit as described in Chapter 9, Section 19.

4 Release cylinder – removal and refitting

Note: *Due to the amount of work necessary to remove and refit clutch components, it is usually considered good practice to renew the clutch friction disc, pressure plate assembly and release cylinder as a matched set, even if only one of these is actually worn enough to require renewal. It is also worth considering the renewal of the clutch components on a preventative basis if the engine and/or transmission have been removed for some other reason.*

Note: *Refer to the warning concerning the dangers of asbestos dust at the beginning of Section 5.*

Removal

1 Unless the complete engine/transmission unit is to be removed from the car and separated for major overhaul (see Chapter 2D, Section 4), the clutch release cylinder can be

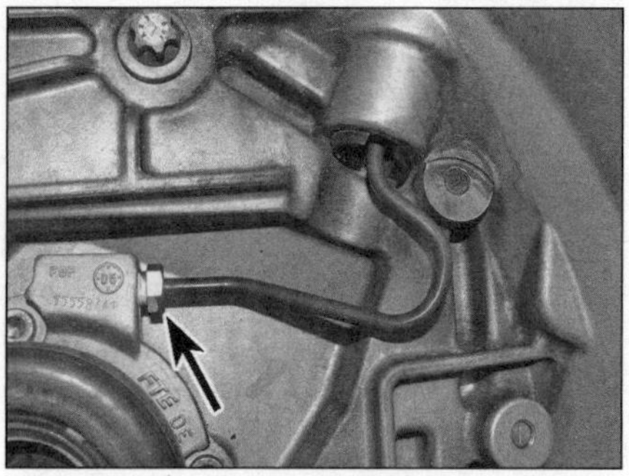

4.2 Clutch release cylinder hydraulic pipe union nut (arrowed)

reached by removing the transmission only, as described in Chapter 7A, Section 7.

2 Wipe clean the outside of the release cylinder then slacken the union nut and disconnect the hydraulic pipe **(see illustration)**. Wipe up any spilt fluid with a clean cloth.

3 Unscrew the three retaining screws and slide the release cylinder off the transmission input shaft **(see illustration)**. Whilst the cylinder is removed, take care not to allow any debris to enter the transmission unit.

4 The release cylinder is a sealed unit and cannot be overhauled. If the cylinder seals are leaking or the release bearing is noisy or rough in operation, then the complete unit must be renewed.

Refitting

5 Ensure the release cylinder and transmission mating surfaces are clean and dry.

6 Lubricate the release cylinder seal with a smear of transmission oil then carefully ease the cylinder along the input shaft and into position. Refit the release cylinder retaining screws with a little thread-locking compound and tighten them to the specified torque.

7 Reconnect the hydraulic pipe to the release cylinder, tightening its union nut securely.

8 Attach a 500 mm length of clear hose to the slave cylinder – screen washer hose is ideal – and then depress the slave cylinder. The cylinder will stay in the compressed position.

9 Carefully add brake fluid so that the hose is filled to about 350 mm. Connect a large syringe to the hose and force the fluid into the slave cylinder. The slave cylinder will move out at this point.

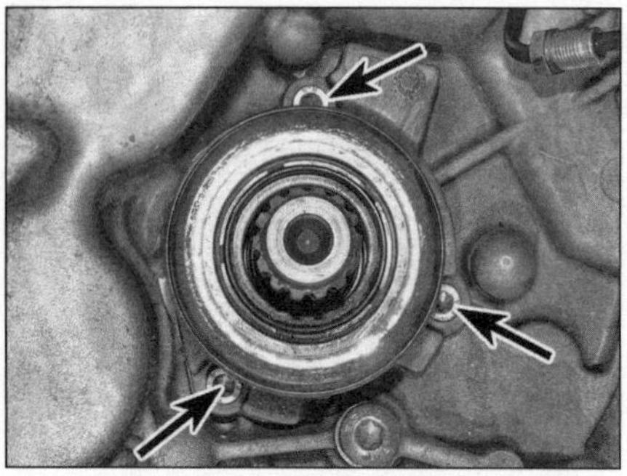

4.3 Clutch release cylinder retaining Torx screws (arrowed)

10 Remove the syringe and push the cylinder in to expel any air from the hose. Repeat the procedure until no air bubbles are present in the hose.

11 Remove the bleed hose and fit a sealing plug to the clutch slave cylinder outlet pipe.

12 Refit the transmission unit as described in Chapter 7A, Section 7.

13 Bleed the clutch hydraulic system as described in Section 2.

5 Clutch assembly – removal, inspection and refitting

Warning: Dust created by clutch wear and deposited on the clutch components may contain asbestos, which is a health hazard. DO NOT blow it out with compressed air, or inhale any of it. DO NOT use petrol or petroleum-based solvents to clean off the dust. Brake system cleaner or methylated spirit should be used to flush the dust into a suitable receptacle. After the clutch components are wiped clean with rags, dispose of the contaminated rags and cleaner in a sealed, marked container.

Removal

1 Unless the complete engine/transmission unit is to be removed from the car and separated for major overhaul (see Chapter 2D, Section 4), the clutch can be reached by removing the transmission as described in Chapter 7A, Section 7.

2 Before disturbing the clutch, use chalk or a marker pen to mark the relationship of the pressure plate assembly to the flywheel.

3 Progressively unscrew the pressure plate retaining bolts in diagonal sequence by half a turn at a time, until spring pressure is released and the bolts can be unscrewed by hand.

4 Remove the pressure plate assembly and collect the friction disc, noting which way round the disc is fitted. Note that Saab insist that the friction plate and pressure plate must be renewed together.

Inspection

Note: *Due to the amount of work necessary to remove and refit clutch components, it is usually considered good practice to renew the clutch friction disc, pressure plate assembly and release bearing as a matched set, even if only one of these is actually worn enough to require renewal. It is also worth considering the renewal of the clutch components on a preventative basis if the engine and/or transmission have been removed for some other reason.*

5 When cleaning clutch components, read first the warning at the beginning of this Section; remove dust using a clean, dry cloth, and working in a well-ventilated atmosphere.

6 Check the friction disc facings for signs of wear, damage or oil contamination. If the friction material is cracked, burnt, scored or damaged, or if it is contaminated with oil or grease (shown by shiny black patches), the friction disc must be renewed.

7 If the friction material is still serviceable, check that the centre boss splines are unworn, and that all the rivets are tight. If any wear or damage is found, the friction disc must be renewed.

8 If the friction material is fouled with oil, this must be due to an oil leak from the crankshaft oil seal, from the sump-to-cylinder block joint, or from the release cylinder assembly. Renew the crankshaft oil seal or repair the sump joint as described in Chapter 2A, 2B or 2C, before installing the new friction disc. The clutch release cylinder is covered in Section 4.

9 Check the pressure plate assembly for obvious signs of wear or damage; shake it to check for loose rivets, or worn or damaged fulcrum rings, and check that the drive straps securing the pressure plate to the cover do not show signs of overheating (such as a deep yellow or blue discoloration). If the diaphragm spring is worn or damaged, or if its pressure is in any way suspect, the pressure plate assembly should be renewed.

10 Examine the machined bearing surfaces of the pressure plate and of the flywheel; they should be clean, completely flat, and free from scratches or scoring. If either is discoloured from excessive heat, or shows signs of cracks, it should be renewed – although minor damage of this nature can sometimes be polished away using emery paper.

11 Check that the release cylinder bearing rotates smoothly and easily, with no sign of noise or roughness. Also check that the surface itself is smooth and unworn, with no signs of cracks, pitting or scoring. If there is any doubt about its condition, the clutch release cylinder should be renewed (it is not possible to renew the bearing separately).

Refitting

12 The clutch pressure plate is unusual, as there is a pre-adjustment mechanism to compensate for wear in the friction disc (this is termed by Saab as a self-adjusting clutch (SAC), which is slightly ambiguous as all clutches fitted to these models are essentially self-adjusting). However, this mechanism must be reset before refitting the pressure plate. A new plate may be supplied preset, in which case this procedure can be ignored. Note that new SAC clutches are supplied as a complete matched pair.

13 A large diameter bolt (M14 at least) long enough to pass through the pressure plate, a matching nut, and several large diameter washers, will be needed for this procedure. Mount the bolt head in the jaws of a sturdy bench vice, with one large washer fitted.

14 Offer the plate over the bolt, friction disc surface facing down, and locate it centrally over the bolt and washer – the washer should bear on the centre hub **(see illustration)**.

15 Fit several further large washers over the

bolt, so that they bear on the ends of the spring fingers, then add the nut and tighten by hand to locate the washers **(see illustration)**.

16 The purpose of the procedure is to turn the plate's internal adjuster disc so that the three small coil springs visible on the plate's outer surface are fully compressed. Tighten the nut just fitted until the adjuster disc is free to turn. Using a pair of thin-nosed, or circlip, pliers in one of the two windows in the top surface, open the jaws of the pliers to turn the adjuster disc anti-clockwise, so that the springs are fully compressed **(see illustrations)**.

17 Hold the pliers in this position, then unscrew the centre nut. Once the nut is released, the adjuster disc will be gripped in position, and the pliers can be removed. Take the pressure plate from the vice, and it is ready to fit.

18 On reassembly, ensure that the friction surfaces of the flywheel and pressure plate are completely clean, smooth, and free from oil or grease. Use solvent to remove any protective grease from new components.

19 Lightly grease the teeth of the friction disc hub with high melting-point grease. Do not apply too much, otherwise it may eventually contaminate the friction disc linings.

20 Locate the friction disc on the flywheel, making sure that the lettering 'transmission side' or 'Getriebeseite' points towards the transmission **(see illustration)**.

21 Refit the pressure plate assembly, aligning the marks made on dismantling (if the original pressure plate is re-used). Apply a little thread-locking compound then refit the pressure plate bolts, but tighten them only finger-tight so that the friction disc can still be moved **(see illustration)**.

22 The friction disc must now be centralised so that, when the transmission is refitted, its input shaft will pass through the splines at the centre of the friction disc.

23 Centralisation can be achieved by passing a screwdriver or other long bar through the friction disc and into the hole in the crankshaft. The friction disc can then be moved around until it is centred on the crankshaft hole. Alternatively, a clutch-aligning tool can be used to eliminate the guesswork; these can be obtained from most accessory shops **(see illustration)**.

24 When the friction disc is centralised, tighten the pressure plate bolts evenly and in a diagonal sequence to the specified torque setting.

25 Refit the transmission as described in Chapter 7A, Section 7.

5.14 Mount a large bolt and washer in a vice, then fit the pressure plate over it

5.15 Fit large washers and a nut to the bolt and hand-tighten

5.16a Tighten the nut until the spring adjuster is free to turn ...

5.16b ... then open the jaws of suitable pliers to compress the springs

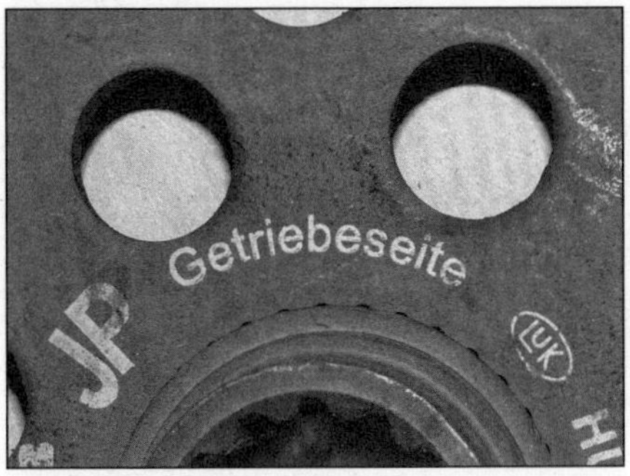

5.20 The lettering 'transmission side' or 'Getriebseite' on the friction disc must face towards the transmission

5.21 Fit the pressure plate assembly over the friction disc

5.23 Centralise the friction disc using a clutch aligning tool or similar

Chapter 7 Part A: Manual transmission

Contents

Degrees of difficulty

Easy, suitable for novice with little experience	**Fairly easy,** suitable for beginner with some experience	**Fairly difficult,** suitable for competent DIY mechanic	**Difficult,** suitable for experienced DIY mechanic	**Very difficult,** suitable for expert DIY or professional

Specifications

General

Type	Transversely-mounted, front-wheel-drive layout, with integral transaxle differential/final drive. Five or six forward speeds, one reverse, all with synchromesh

Torque wrench settings

Torque wrench settings	Nm	lbf ft
Anti-roll bar to subframe	18	13
Bellhousing-to-engine block bolts:		
M10	40	30
M12	70	52
Front chassis reinforcement bolts (Convertible only)	50	37
Front subframe bolts:		
Front:		
Stage 1	75	55
Stage 2	Angle-tighten a further 135°	
Rear:		
Stage 1	90	66
Stage 2	Angle-tighten a further 45°	
Left-hand oil seal retaining housing	24	18
Oil level, filler and drain plugs	50	37
Reversing light switch	20	15
Steering rack:		
Stage 1	50	37
Stage 2	Angle-tighten a further 60°	

2.4a Oil level/filler plug (arrowed) – 5-speed transmission

2.4b Oil filler plug (arrowed) – 6-speed transmission

1 General information

The manual transmission is mounted transversely in the engine bay, bolted directly to the engine. This layout has the advantage of providing the shortest possible drive path to the front wheels, as well as locating the transmission in the airflow through the engine bay, optimising cooling.

Drive from the crankshaft is transmitted from the clutch to the gearbox input shaft, which is splined to accept the clutch friction disc.

The pinions are in constant mesh with their corresponding driven gears, and are free to rotate independently of the gearbox shafts until a gear is selected. The difference in diameter and number of teeth between the pinions and gears provides the necessary shaft speed reduction and torque multiplication. Drive is then transmitted to the final drive gears/differential through the output shaft.

All gears are fitted with synchromesh, including reverse. When a gear is selected, the movement of the floor-mounted gear lever actuates a series of selector forks inside the gearbox, which are slotted onto the synchromesh sleeves. The sleeves, which slide axially over splined hubs, press baulk rings into contact with the respective gear/pinion. The coned surfaces between the baulk rings and the pinion/gear act as a friction clutch, progressively matching the speed of the synchromesh sleeve (and hence the gearbox shaft) with that of the gear/pinion. The dog teeth on the baulk ring prevent the synchromesh sleeve ring from meshing with the gear/pinion until their speeds are exactly matched; this allows gearchanges to be carried out smoothly, and greatly reduces the noise and mechanical wear caused by rapid gearchanges.

When reverse gear is engaged, an idler gear is brought into mesh between the reverse pinion and the teeth on the outside of the first/second speed synchromesh sleeve. This arrangement introduces the necessary speed reduction, and also causes the output shaft to rotate in the opposite direction, allowing the vehicle to be driven in reverse.

2 Transmission – draining and refilling

General information

1 The gearbox is filled with the correct quantity and grade of oil at manufacture. Although no specifically required by the manufacturer, it would be prudent to check the level regularly (where possible), and if necessary topped-up (see Chapter 1A, Section 22 or Chapter 1B, Section 24). However, there is no requirement to drain and renew the oil during the normal lifetime of the gearbox, unless repair or overhaul is carried out.

Draining

2 Take the car on a road test of sufficient length to warm the engine/transmission up to normal operating temperature; this will speed up the draining process, and any sludge and debris will be more likely to be drained out.

3 Park the car on level ground, switch off the ignition, and apply the handbrake firmly. For improved access, jack up the front of the car and support it securely on axle stands (see *Jacking and vehicle support*). **Note:** *The car must be lowered to the ground and parked on a level surface, to ensure accuracy when refilling and checking the oil level.* Undo the screws, and remove the engine undershield (where fitted).

4 Wipe clean the area around the filler plug, which is situated on the left-hand side of the transmission (5-speed) or the top front surface (6-speed). Unscrew the plug from the casing **(see illustrations)**.

5 Position a container with a capacity of at least 2.5 litres (ideally with a large funnel) under the drain plug **(see illustrations)**. The drain plug is located at the rear of the transmission, under the left-hand driveshaft (5-speed) or at the base of the housing (6-speed); use an Allen key to unscrew the plug from the casing (on 5-speed transmissions, a shortened 8 mm Allen key will be needed). Note that the drain plug contains an integral magnet, designed to catch the metal fragments produced as the transmission components wear. If the plug is clogged with a large amount of metal debris, this may be an early indication of component failure.

6 Allow all the oil to drain completely into the container. If the oil is still hot, take precautions against scalding. Clean both the filler and drain plugs thoroughly, paying particular attention to the threads.

Refilling

7 When the oil has drained out completely, clean the plug hole threads in the transmission casing. Coat the thread with thread-locking compound, and tighten it to the specified torque. If the car was raised for the draining operation, lower it to the ground.

8 When refilling the transmission, allow plenty of time for the oil level to settle completely before attempting to check it. Note that the car must be parked on a flat, level surface when checking the oil level. Use a funnel if necessary to maintain a gradual, constant flow and avoid spillage.

9 Refill the transmission with the specified grade and quantity of oil, then check the oil level as described in Chapter 1A, Section 22 or Chapter 1B, Section 24. If a large quantity flows out when the level checking plug is removed (5-speed only: no level plug is fitted to the 6-speed), refit both the filler and level plugs, then drive the car for a short distance so that the new oil is distributed fully around the transmission components. Recheck the level again upon your return.

10 On completion, fit the filler and level plugs with new sealing washers, and tighten them securely. Refit the engine undershield (where applicable).

2.5a Oil drain plug (arrowed) – 5-speed transmission

2.5b Oil drain plug (arrowed) – 6-speed transmission

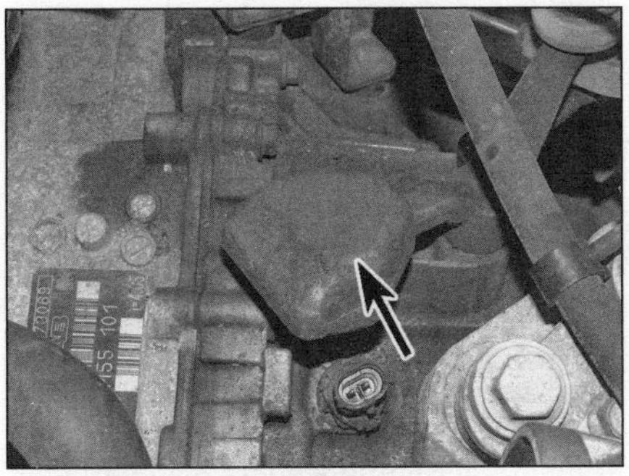

3.2 Rotate the uppermost lever (arrowed) fully clockwise

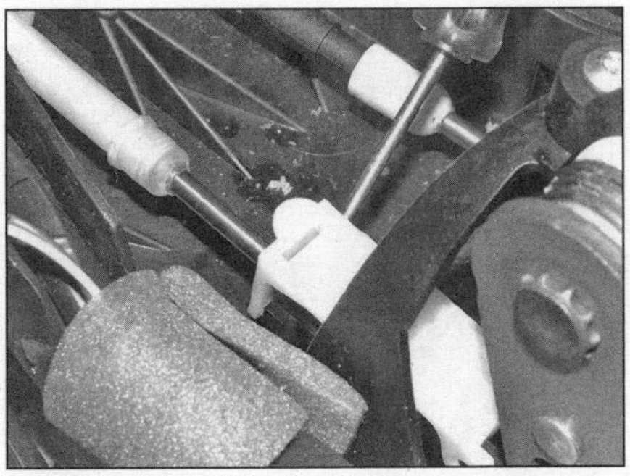

3.4a Lever the locking catch forwards ...

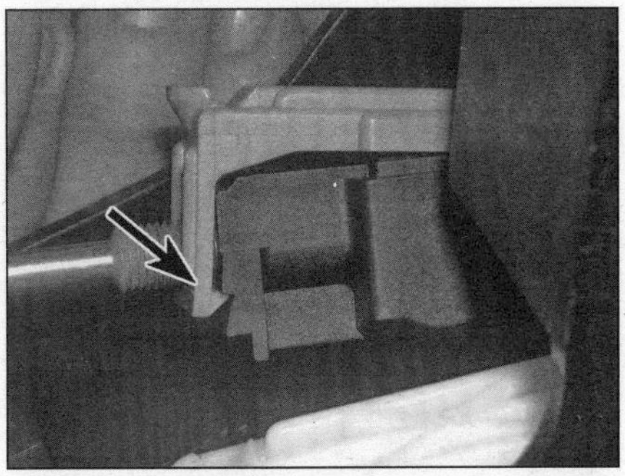

3.4b ... until the front edge lug (arrowed) rests on the notch

3 Gearchange cables – adjustment

1 If the action of the gearchange is stiff, slack or vague, the adjustment of the cables may be incorrect (also check the oil level and type is correct). The operations in the following paragraphs describe how to check and, if necessary, adjust the alignment.

5-speed transmission

2 Park the vehicle, apply the handbrake and switch off the ignition. Select 4th gear at the transmission end of the cables (uppermost lever fully clockwise) **(see illustration)**.

3 Starting at the rear, carefully prise up the gear lever gaiter and mounting frame to expose the gearchange lever housing.

4 Using a screwdriver, carefully lever the cable adjuster locking catch forward. An audible click means the adjustment locking catch has been released **(see illustrations)**. Repeat this procedure on the remaining cable.

5 Lift the gear lever adjusting sleeve, and use a pair of pliers to press in the two catches **(see illustration 3.13a)**. Allow the adjusting sleeve tab to engage in the adjusting notch at the rear of the housing **(see illustration)**.

6 Gently press a screwdriver against the crescent-shaped section of the adjustment catch. An audible click indicates the catch has engaged in the correct position **(see illustration)**. Repeat the procedure on the remaining cable.

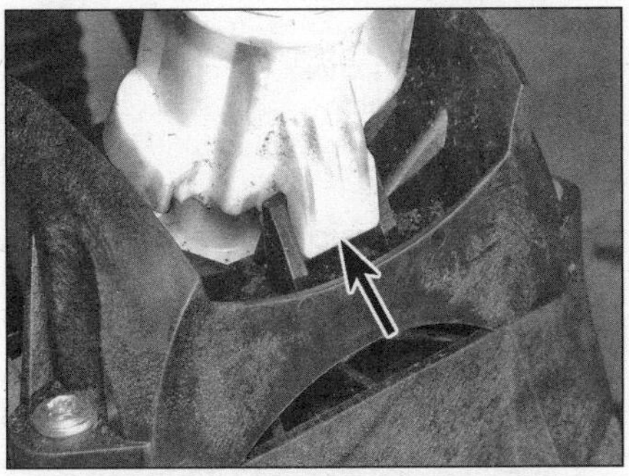

3.5 Position the adjusting sleeve tab (arrowed) in the notch at the rear

7 Lift the adjustment sleeve up into its normal position.

8 Check for correct operation of the gearchange assembly, and if satisfactory, refit the gear lever gaiter and mounting frame.

6-speed transmission

9 Engage neutral gear, then undo the fastener, slide the centre console side panel rearwards then downwards and remove it.

10 Lift the selector shaft slightly, and insert Saab tool No 87 92 335 into the hole in the shaft. In the absence of the special tool, a 5.0 mm drill bit will suffice **(see illustration)**.

11 Starting at the rear, carefully prise up the gear lever gaiter and mounting frame to expose the gearchange lever housing **(see illustration)**. Remove the rubber mat and panel in front of the mounting frame.

3.6 Press down the locking catch until it clicks into place

12 Using a screwdriver, carefully lever the cable adjuster slightly towards the gear lever. An audible click means the adjustment locking catch has been released **(see illustration)**. Repeat this procedure on the remaining cable.

13 Lift the gear lever adjusting sleeve, while pressing in the two catches using a pair of pliers (or two screwdrivers). Carefully lower the adjusting sleeve and allow the catch to engage in the recess in the gear lever housing **(see illustrations)**.

14 Use one finger to gently press the gear lever to the left, hold it in this position, and press a screwdriver down on the adjustment catch on the cable fitting. An audible click indicates the catch has engaged correctly

3.10 Insert a 5.0 mm drill bit (arrowed) through the hole in the bracket into the hole in the selector shaft

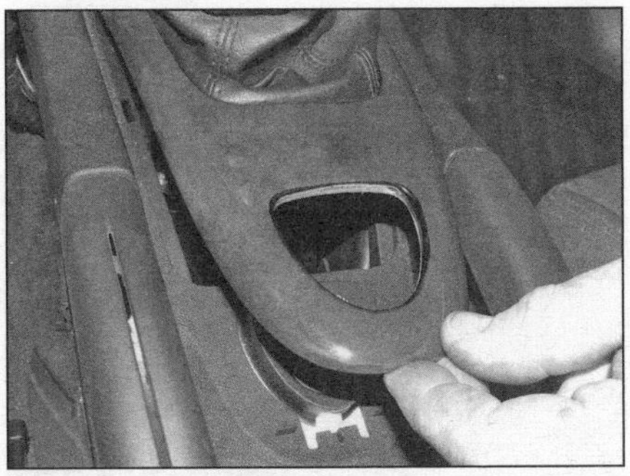

3.11 Starting at the rear, prise up and remove the gear lever surround trim panel

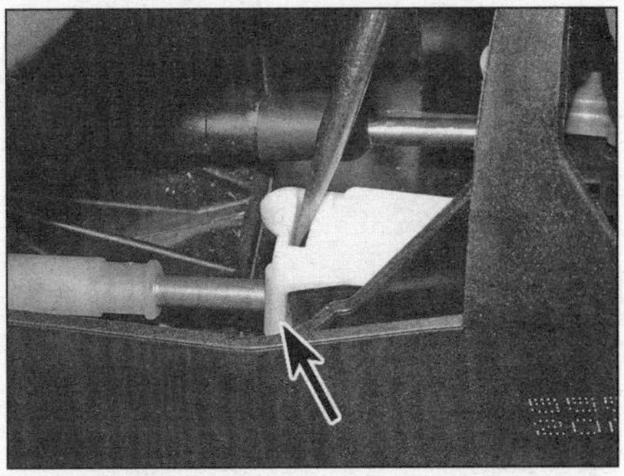

3.12 Insert a screwdriver, and pull the handle rearwards to lever the front section of the clip (arrowed) forwards to release it

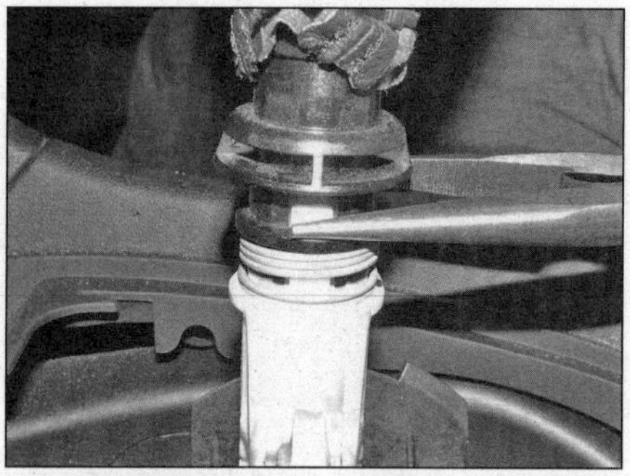

3.13a Squeeze together the retaining clips with pliers ...

3.14 Press the front edge of the clip downwards until it clicks into place

(see illustration). Repeat the procedure on the remaining cable.

15 Lift the adjusting sleeve to its normal position, and make sure the catches lock correctly.

3.13b ... lower the adjusting sleeve, and engage the catch with the recess (arrowed) in the housing

16 Remove the pin (drill bit) from the selector shaft, and check the operation of the gearchange assembly.

17 Refit the gear lever gaiter and mounting frame.

Both transmissions

18 Finally, road test the vehicle, and check that all gears can be obtained smoothly and precisely.

4 Gearchange cables – removal, inspection and refitting

Removal

1 Park the vehicle, switch off the ignition, and apply the handbrake.

2 Referring to Chapter 11, Section 27, remove the centre console, then remove the left-hand floor air duct.

3 Engage 4th gear (5-speed transmission) or neutral (6-speed transmission).

4 From the engine bay, use pliers to carefully prise the ends of the gearchange cables from the selector arms on the transmission **(see illustration)**.

5 Pull back the locking sleeves and detach the cables from the bracket on the transmission **(see illustration)**.

6 Carefully prise the rubber seal and plastic grommet from the engine compartment bulkhead.

7 Depress the catches and pull the outer cables from the gear lever housing **(see illustration)**. If necessary, lift the air duct slightly to access the cables.

8 Using a screwdriver, carefully lever the cable adjuster slightly towards the gear lever. An audible click means the adjustment locking catch has been released. Repeat this procedure on the remaining cable.

9 Carefully pull the cables out into the engine compartment.

Refitting

10 Insert the cable assembly through the aperture in the engine compartment.

11 Attach the cables to the gear lever and gear lever housing. The black and white cables correspond to the colour of the adjusters.

12 Refit the plastic grommet and rubber seal to the engine compartment bulkhead.

13 Fit the cable to the retainers on the transmission bracket, pull back the sleeves and allow them to lock the cables in place. The white cable attaches to the lower bracket, and the black one to the upper bracket.

14 Press the ends of the cables onto the selector levers.

15 Adjust the cables as described in Section 3.

5 Oil seals – renewal

Driveshaft oil seal

1 Remove the relevant driveshaft as described in Chapter 8, Section 2. If renewing the right-hand oil seal, remove the intermediate shaft as well as the driveshaft (Chapter 8, Section 5).

2 Refer to Section 2 and drain the transmission oil. Clean and refit the drain plug.

3 Using a suitable lever, prise the driveshaft oil seal out from the transmission housing **(see illustration)**, taking care not to damage the sealing surface. Discard the old seal.

4 Thoroughly clean the mating surfaces of the bearing housing/differential casing; take precautions to prevent debris entering the bearings of either assembly.

5 Carefully fit the new seal into the housing, ensuring that it is seated squarely. Use a suitable round spacer to drive the seal

4.4 Use pliers to prise the ends of the gearchange cables from the selector arms

4.5 Pull back the sleeves, and detach the outer cables from the bracket

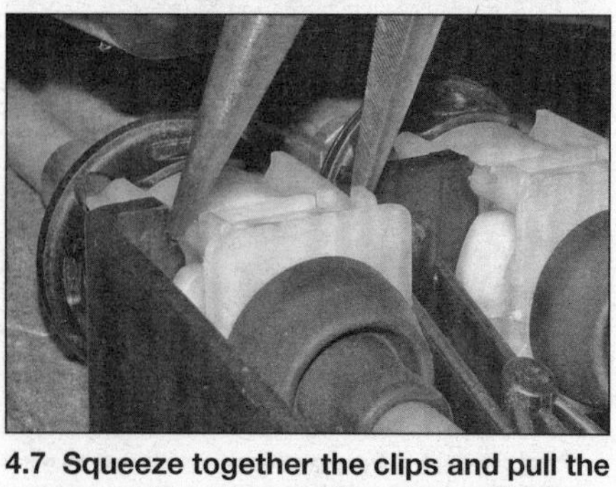

4.7 Squeeze together the clips and pull the outer cables upwards from the gear lever housing

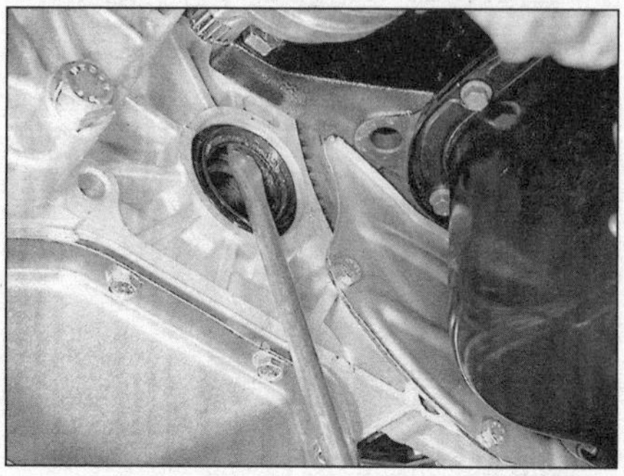

5.3 Prise out the driveshaft seal

squarely into the housing until its outer edge is flush with the housing **(see illustration)**.

6 Refer to Chapter 8, Section 2 and 5, and refit the driveshaft (and intermediate shaft and bearing assembly where applicable).

7 Refit the roadwheel, and lower the vehicle to the ground. Tighten the roadwheel bolts to the correct torque.

8 Refer to Section 2 and refill the transmission with oil of the correct grade.

Input shaft oil seal

9 The oil seal is part of the clutch release cylinder assembly and cannot be renewed separately, see Chapter 6, Section 4 for further information.

6 Reversing light switch – testing, removal and refitting

Testing

1 Unplug the wiring harness from the reversing light switch at the connector. The switch is located on the top of the transmission casing on both 5- and 6-speed transmissions **(see illustrations)**.

2 Connect the probes of a continuity tester, or a multimeter set to the resistance function, across the terminals of the reversing light switch.

3 The switch contacts are normally open, so with any gear other than reverse selected, the tester/meter should indicate an open circuit. When reverse gear is then selected, the switch contacts should close, causing the tester/meter to indicate continuity.

4 If the switch does not function correctly, or is intermittent in its operation, it should be renewed.

Removal

5 Unplug the wiring harness from the reversing light switch at the connector.

6 Unscrew the switch, recovering any washers that may be fitted; these must be refitted, to ensure that the correct clearance exists between the switch shaft and the reverse gear shaft.

Refitting

7 Refitting is a reversal of removal.

7 Transmission – removal and refitting

Note: *Refer to Chapter 2D, Section 4 for details on removal of the engine and transmission as a complete assembly.*

Removal

1 Apply the handbrake, then raise the front of the vehicle, support it securely on axle stands (see *Jacking and vehicle support*). Remove the front roadwheels. Remove the engine top

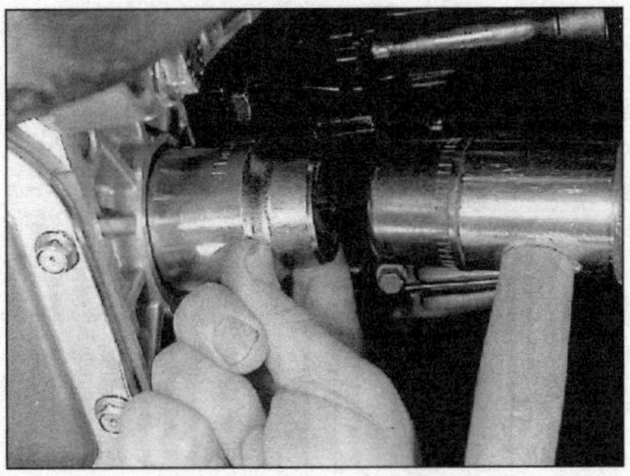

5.5 Use a socket as a tubular drift to drive the seal into place squarely

cover the engine transmission undershield.

2 Refer to Section 2 of this Chapter and drain the oil from the transmission. Refit and tighten the drain plug.

3 Remove the battery as described in Chapter 5A, Section 4, then undo the 3 bolts and remove the battery tray. Disconnect any wiring plugs as the tray is withdrawn.

4 Disconnect the earth cable from the transmission mounting, and disconnect the reversing light switch **(see illustration)**.

5 Prise the ends of the gearchange cables from the levers on the transmission, then undo the bolts and detach the cables and support bracket from the transmission casing **(see illustration)**.

6 Use a hose clamp to seal the hose, then pull out the retaining clip and disconnect the clutch hydraulic hose from the connection on the transmission housing (see Chapter 6, Section 2).

7 Remove the bolts securing the upper section of the transmission bellhousing to the engine.

8 Lift the coolant expansion tank from position and move it to one side.

9 Position a lifting beam across the engine bay, locating the support legs securely in the sills at either side, in line with the strut top mountings. Hook the jib onto the engine lifting eyelet and raise it, so that the weight of the engine is taken off the transmission mounting. Most people won't have access to an engine lifting beam, but it may be possible to hire one. Alternatively, an engine hoist may be used to support the engine, but when using this method, bear in mind that if the vehicle is lowered on its axle stands to adjust the working height, for example, then the hoist will have to be lowered accordingly, to avoid straining the engine mountings.

10 Remove the undershield beneath the radiator, then using straps or cable-ties, suspend the radiator from the vehicle bodywork. On Convertible models, undo the bolts and remove the front chassis reinforcement.

11 Undo the screws and remove the radiator lower mounting brackets from the front subframe **(see illustration)**.

12 Remove the front section of the exhaust system as described in Chapter 4A, Section 16 or Chapter 4B, Section 18.

13 Remove the engine torque rod from the subframe (see Chapter 2A, 2B or 2C).

14 Remove both driveshafts as described in Chapter 8, Section 2.

6.1a Reversing light switch (arrowed) – 6-speed transmissions

6.1b Reversing light switch (arrowed) – 5-speed transmissions

7.4 Detach the earth cable (arrowed)

7.5 Undo the bolts (arrowed) and remove the cable support bracket

7.11 Undo the Torx screw (arrowed) securing the lower radiator mounting bracket each side

15 Undo the nuts/bolts and detach the steering rack from the subframe. Do not allow the steering wheel to rotate at any point. Lock the steering wheel in the straight ahead position if necessary.

16 Release the power steering pipes from the clips securing them to the subframe.

17 Make alignment marks between the subframe and the vehicle body, then undo the mounting bolts/brackets, and lower the subframe slightly **(see illustrations)**.

18 Undo the bolts securing the anti-roll bar clamps, then lower the subframe.

19 Detach the earth lead from the left-hand end of the transmission casing **(see illustration)**.

20 Remove the rear torque rod brackets from the transmission housing.

21 Slacken the clamps, undo the retaining bolts and remove the charge air pipe under the engine.

22 Undo the remaining transmission bellhousing-to-engine bolts, leaving one bolt in place.

23 Undo the bolts securing the left-hand mounting to the transmission.

24 Using the cross-beam/engine hoist, lower the engine/transmission approximately 70 mm, then undo the remaining transmission-to-engine

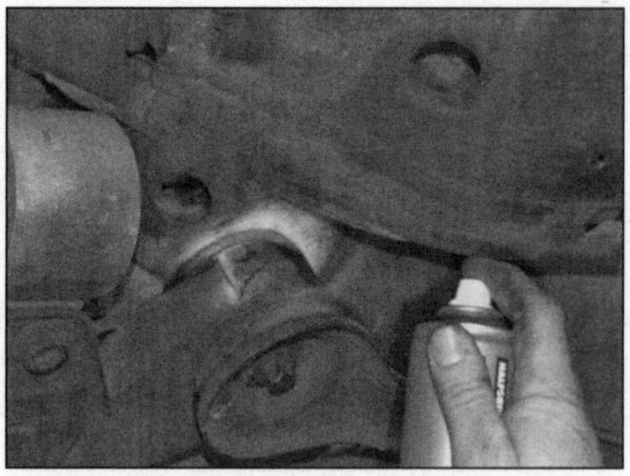

7.17a Make alignment marks around the subframe mountings – we used spray-on paint

bolt, slide the transmission from the engine and manoeuvre it from under the vehicle.

Caution: The transmission is very heavy, the help of an assistant is essential.

25 At this point with the transmission removed, it would be a good opportunity to check the clutch assembly, and renew it if necessary (see Chapter 6, Section 5).

Refitting

26 Refit the transmission by reversing the removal procedure, noting the following points:

- *a) Apply a smear of clutch assembly grease to the transmission input shaft. Do not apply an excessive amount, as there is a possibility of the clutch friction disc being contaminated.*
- *b) Refit the engine/transmission mountings with reference to Chapter 2A, 2B or 2C.*
- *c) Observe the specified torque wrench settings (where applicable) when tightening all nuts and bolts.*
- *d) Bleed the clutch hydraulic system, referring to Chapter 6, Section 2 for reference.*
- *e) On completion, if the transmission was drained, refill with the specified type and quantity of oil as described in Section 2.*

8 Transmission overhaul – general information

The overhaul of a manual transmission is a complex (and often expensive) engineering task for the DIY home mechanic to undertake, which requires access to specialist equipment. It involves dismantling and reassembly of many small components, measuring clearances precisely, and if necessary adjusting them by the selection shims and spacers. Internal transmission components are also often difficult to obtain, and in many instances extremely expensive. Because of this, if the transmission develops a fault or becomes noisy, the best course of action is to have the unit overhauled by a specialist repairer, or to obtain an exchange reconditioned unit.

Nevertheless, it is not impossible for the more experienced mechanic to overhaul the transmission, if the special tools are available and the job is carried out in a deliberate step-by-step manner, to ensure that nothing is overlooked.

The tools necessary for an overhaul include internal and external circlip pliers, bearing pullers, a slide hammer, a set of pin punches, a dial test indicator (dial gauge), and possibly a hydraulic press. In addition, a large, sturdy workbench and a vice will be required.

During dismantling of the transmission, make careful notes of how each component is fitted, to make reassembly easier and accurate.

Before dismantling the transmission, it will help if you have some idea of where the problem lies. Certain problems can be closely related to specific areas in the transmission, which can make component examination and renewal easier. Refer to *Fault finding* at the end of this manual for more information.

7.17b Then undo the front ...

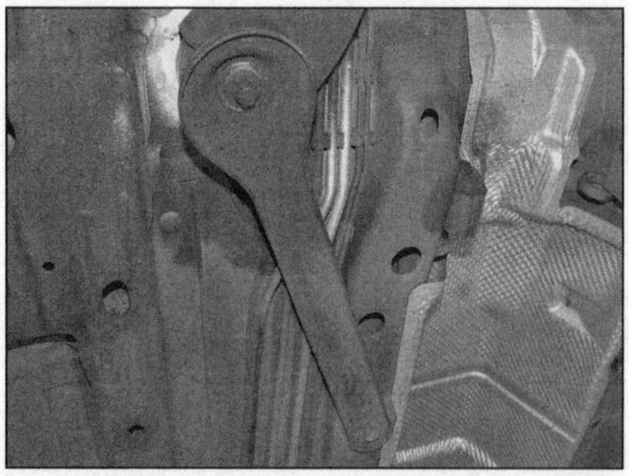

7.17c ... and rear subframe mounting bolts

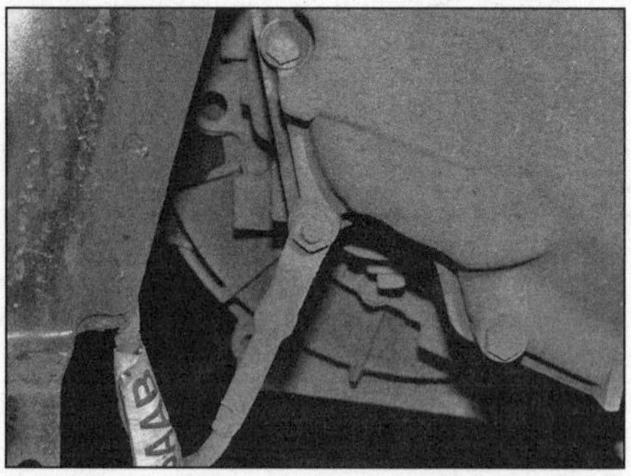

7.19 Detach the earth lead from the end of the transmission casing

Chapter 7 Part B: Automatic transmission

Contents

Degrees of difficulty

Easy, suitable for novice with little experience	**Fairly easy,** suitable for beginner with some experience	**Fairly difficult,** suitable for competent DIY mechanic	**Difficult,** suitable for experienced DIY mechanic	**Very difficult,** suitable for expert DIY or professional

Specifications

General

Designation	FA57 or AF40 (automatic transmission front-wheel-drive)	
Type:*		
FA57	Five-speed electronically-controlled automatic with manual Sentronic change function	
AF40	Six-speed electronically-controlled automatic with manual Sentronic change function	

** The type code is marked on a plate attached to the top of the transmission casing.*

Torque wrench settings	Nm	lbf ft
Anti-roll bar nuts	18	13
Engine-to-transmission unit bolts	70	52
Engine torque rod to subframe:		
Front	60	44
Rear	80	59
Front chassis reinforcement bolts (Convertible only)	50	37
Front subframe:		
Rear bracket bolts:		
Stage 1	90	60
Stage 2	Angle-tighten a further 45°	
Main bolts:		
Stage 1	75	55
Stage 2	Angle-tighten a further 135°	
Steering rack bolts:		
Stage 1	50	37
Stage 2	Angle-tighten a further 60°	
Torque converter-to-driveplate bolts	30	22
Torque rod bracket bolts	93	69
Transmission mounting bracket bolts	93	69

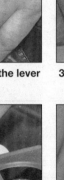

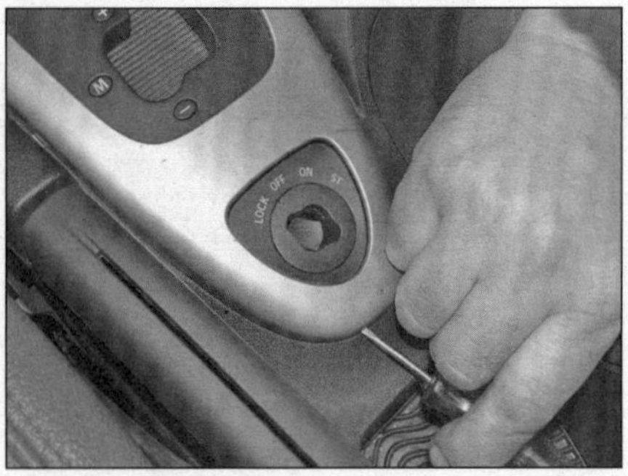

3.1a Starting at the rear, prise up the lever surround trim

3.1b The trim is hooked under at the front edge

3.3a Insert a screwdriver into the slot in the adjuster, and pull the handle rearwards ...

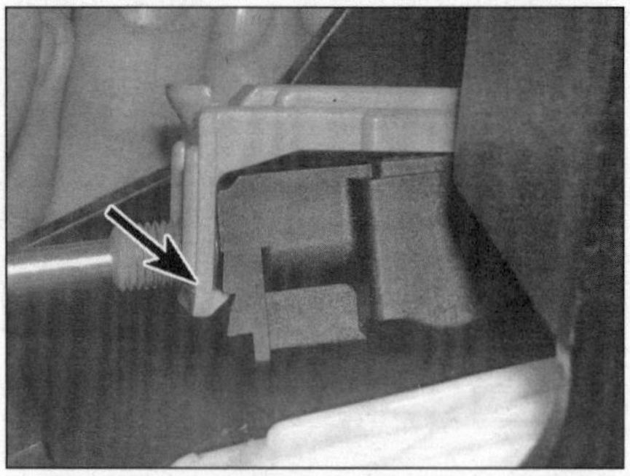

3.3b ... until the lug (arrowed) rests on the notch

1 General information

1 Automatic transmission is available as an option on all petrol models and the DOHC diesel models. The automatic transmission is an electronically-controlled five-speed (FA57) or six-speed (AF40) unit, incorporating a lock-up function. It consists mainly of a planetary gear unit, a torque converter with lock-up clutch, a hydraulic control system and an electronic control system. The unit is controlled by the electronic control module (ECM) via electrically-operated solenoid valves. The transmission unit also has a manual gearchange function (Sentronic) which allows sequential manual shift by moving the selector lever forwards or backwards, or on some models by depressing buttons on the steering wheel.

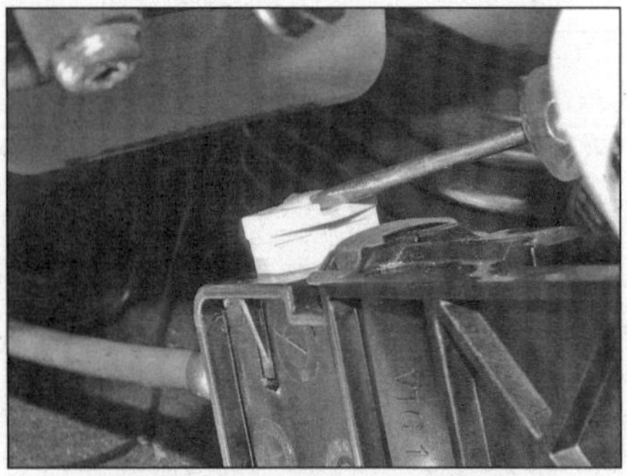

4.3 Lever up the outer cable clip

2 The torque converter provides a fluid coupling between engine and transmission, which acts as an automatic clutch, and also provides a degree of torque multiplication when accelerating.

3 The epicyclic geartrain provides one of the forward or reverse gear ratios, according to which of its component parts are held stationary or allowed to turn. The components of the geartrain are held or released by brakes and clutches which are activated by the control unit. A fluid pump within the transmission provides the necessary hydraulic pressure to operate the brakes and clutches.

4 Driver control of the transmission is by a centre console-mounted selector lever. The 'drive' D position, allows automatic changing throughout the range of all 5/6 gear ratios. An automatic kickdown facility shifts the transmission down a gear if the accelerator pedal is fully depressed.

5 Due to the complexity of the automatic transmission, any repair or overhaul work must be left to a Saab dealer or specialist with the necessary special equipment for fault diagnosis and repair. The contents of the following Sections are therefore confined to supplying general information, and any service information and instructions that can be used by the owner.

2 Transmission fluid – draining and refilling

Refer to the information given in Chapter 1A, Section 25 or Chapter 1B, Section 26.

3 Selector cable – adjustment

1 Starting at the rear, carefully prise up and remove the, and the plastic lever surround trim **(see illustrations)**.

2 Inside the vehicle, position the selector lever in the P (Park) position.

3 Using a flat-bladed screwdriver, carefully press down in the cable adjuster, and prise the screwdriver handle rearwards to move the front edge of the adjuster forwards **(see illustrations)**. An audible click indicates the adjustment catch has been released.

4 Working in the engine compartment, locate the lever on the transmission to which the selector cable is connected. Position the lever so that the transmission is set in the Park position.

5 With the handbrake in the off position, roll the car until the Park interlock engages.

6 Press down the cable adjuster to secure the cable.

7 Check the selector lever operates correctly.

8 Refit the trim surround and the rubber mat.

9 On completion, road test the vehicle to check the correct operation of the gearchange.

4 Selector cable – removal and refitting

Removal

1 Remove the centre console as described in Chapter 11, Section 27.

2 With the selector lever in position P, using a flat-bladed screwdriver, carefully press down in the cable adjuster, and prise slightly towards the lever **(see illustrations 3.3a and 3.3b)**. An audible click indicates the adjustment catch has been released.

3 Lift up the clip and detach the outer cable from the lever housing **(see illustration)**.

4 Working in the engine compartment, pull the rubber seal and plastic grommet the bulkhead where the cable passes through.

5 At the top of the transmission, pull the back the locking sleeve, and detach the outer cable from the bracket on the transmission **(see illustration)**.

6 Prise the end of the cable from the lever at the transmission **(see illustration)**.

7 Pull the cable through into the engine compartment.

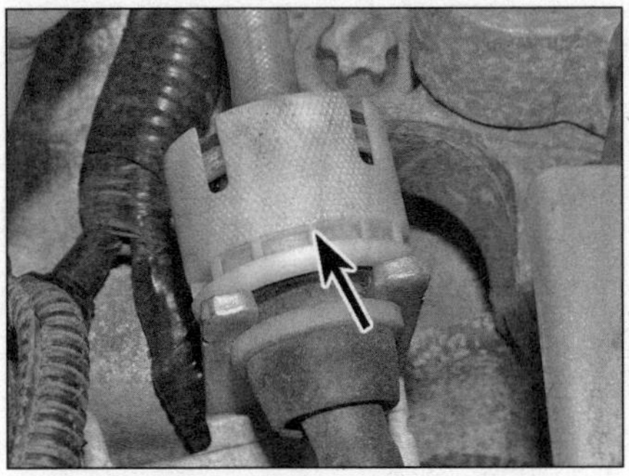

4.5 Pull the back the locking sleeve (arrowed)

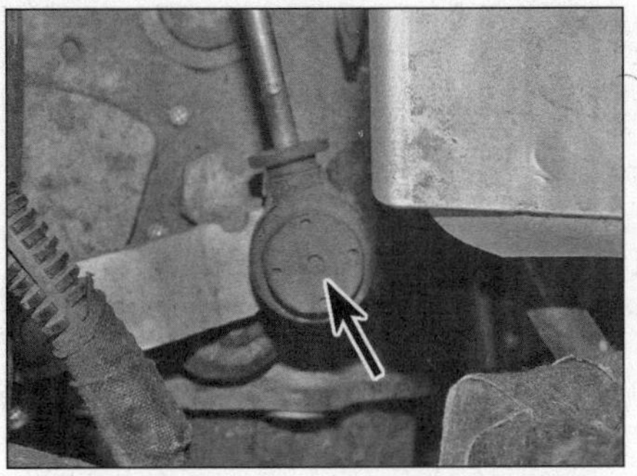

4.6 Prise the cable end fitting (arrowed) from the lever

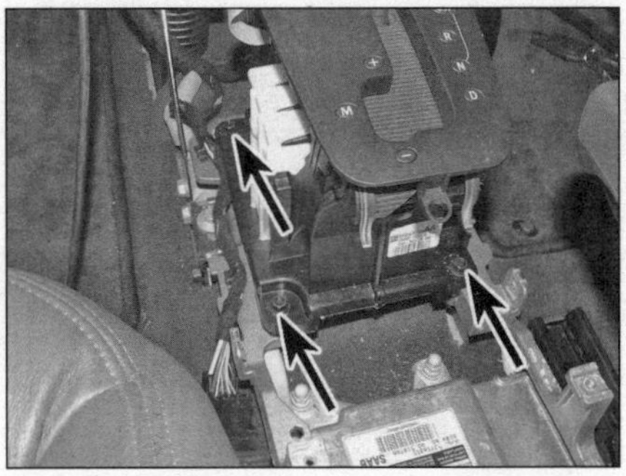

5.4 Selector lever housing retaining bolts (arrowed – 1 hidden)

Refitting

8 Refitting is a reversal of removal, noting the following points:

a) *Ensure the cable is correctly routed and located securely in the bulkhead.*

b) *Adjust the selector cable as described in Section 3.*

5 Selector lever assembly – removal and refitting

Removal

1 Remove the centre console, and the rear compartment air ducts, as described in Chapter 11, Section 27.

2 Detach the selector cable from the lever and housing as described in Section 4.

3 Disconnect the wiring plug from the selector housing.

4 Unscrew and remove the retaining bolts then lift the gear selector lever housing away from the floorpan **(see illustration)**.

5 Inspect the selector lever mechanism for signs of wear or damage.

Refitting

6 Refitting is a reversal of removal, but adjust the selector cable as described in Section 3.

6 Oil seals – renewal

Driveshaft oil seals

1 Remove the relevant driveshaft as described in Chapter 8, Section 2. If renewing the right-hand oil seal, remove the intermediate shaft as well as the driveshaft (Chapter 8, Section 5).

2 Using a suitable lever, prise the driveshaft oil seal out from the transmission housing, taking care not to damage the sealing surface. Discard the old seal.

3 Thoroughly clean the mating surfaces of the bearing housing and differential casing; take precautions to prevent debris entering the bearings of either assembly.

4 Carefully fit the new seal into the transmission housing, ensuring that it is seated squarely. Use a suitable round spacer to drive the seal squarely into the housing until its outer edge is flush with the housing.

5 Refer to Chapter 8, Section 2 and 5 and refit the driveshaft (and intermediate shaft and bearing assembly where applicable).

6 Refit the roadwheel, and lower the vehicle to the ground. Tighten the roadwheel bolts to the correct torque.

7 Refer to Chapter 1A, Section 26 or Chapter 1B, Section 27 and refill the transmission with fluid of the correct grade.

7 Fluid cooler – general information

The transmission fluid cooler is an integral part of the radiator assembly. Refer to Chapter 3, Section 3 for removal and refitting details. If the cooler is damaged the complete radiator assembly must be renewed.

8 Transmission control system electrical components – removal and refitting

Gear selector control module

Note: *If the module is to be renewed, stored values within the unit must be downloaded, and reloaded into the new module using Saab diagnostic equipment. Entrust this task to a Saab dealer or suitably-equipped specialist.*

1 Remove the centre console as described in Chapter 11, Section 27.

2 Undo the bolts and remove the right-hand facia support bracket, then remove the right-hand floor vent duct.

3 Before handling the module, earth yourself by touching a metal part of the vehicle body. Electronic modules are extremely sensitive to static electricity.

4 Release the clip and disconnect the wiring plug from the module.

5 Release the catch, and slide the control module forwards from position.

6 Refitting is a reversal of removal.

Transmission control module (TCM)

Note: *If the module is to be renewed, stored values within the unit must be downloaded, and reloaded into the new module using Saab diagnostic equipment. Entrust this task to a Saab dealer or suitably-equipped specialist.*

5-speed transmission

7 The TCM is located adjacent to the battery tray **(see illustration)**. Unclip the battery cover and unclip the cooling pipe.

8 Before handling the module, earth yourself by touching a metal part of the vehicle body. Electronic modules are extremely sensitive to static electricity.

9 Release the clips and disconnect the wiring plugs from the module **(see illustration)**.

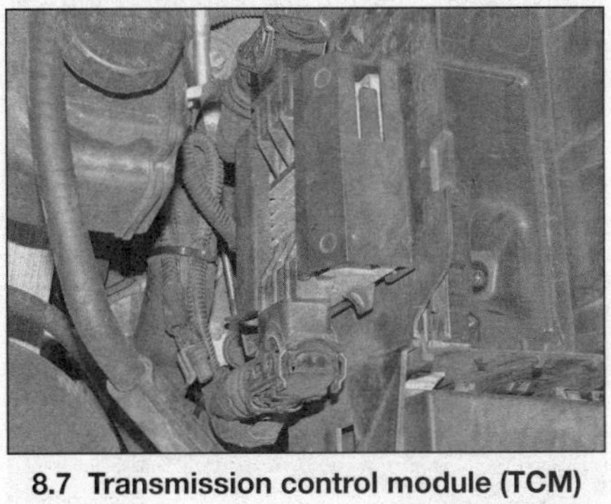

8.7 Transmission control module (TCM)

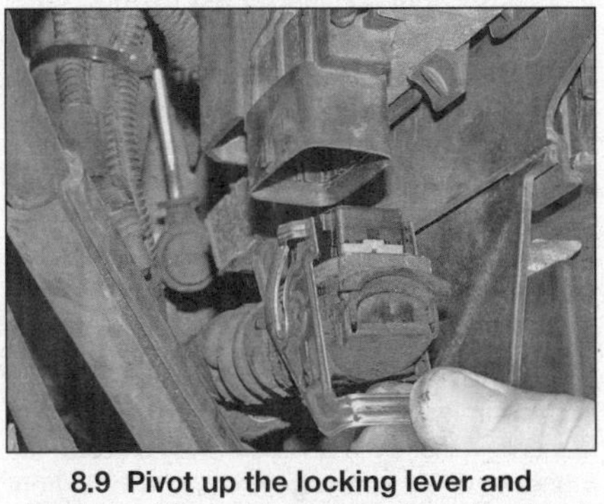

8.9 Pivot up the locking lever and disconnect the wiring plugs from the front and rear of the TCM

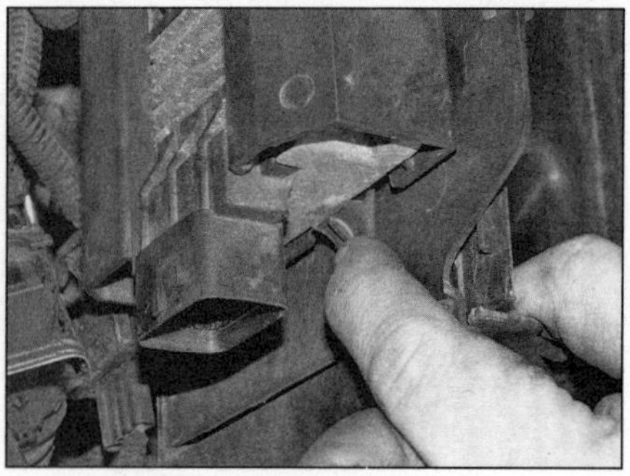

8.10a Depress the retaining clip ...

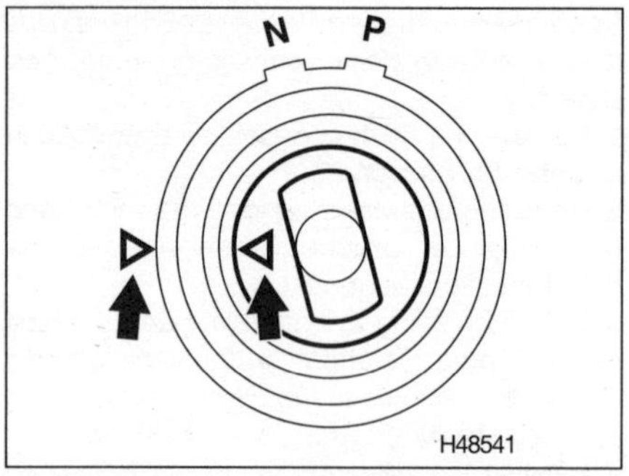

8.17 Align the index marks (arrowed)

10 Release the clips and remove the module **(see illustrations)**.

11 Refitting is the reverse of removal, ensuring that the wiring is securely reconnected.

6-speed transmission

12 The TCM is located on the top of the transmission casing. Ensure the selector lever is in position P. Slacken the clips and remove the turbocharger delivery pipe at the left-hand end of the cylinder head.

13 Before handling the module, earth yourself by touching a metal part of the vehicle body. Electronic modules are extremely sensitive to static electricity.

14 Pull out the pin, press down the lock disconnect the TCM wiring plug.

15 Slacken the nut securing the lever to the selector shaft, then select position N and pull the lever upwards off the shaft.

16 Undo the retaining bolts and lift the module straight up and off the selector shaft **(see illustration)**.

17 Refitting is the reverse of removal, ensuring that the inner rotating section aligns correctly **(see illustration)** and that the wiring is securely reconnected.

Shift lock solenoid

Manual release

18 If electrical power is lost, it will not be possible to move the selector lever as it is locked in position by the shift lock solenoid. In order to manually release the lever, carefully prise up the rubber mat in the storage compartment in front of the lever, followed by the lever surround trim **(see illustrations 3.1a and 3.1b)**.

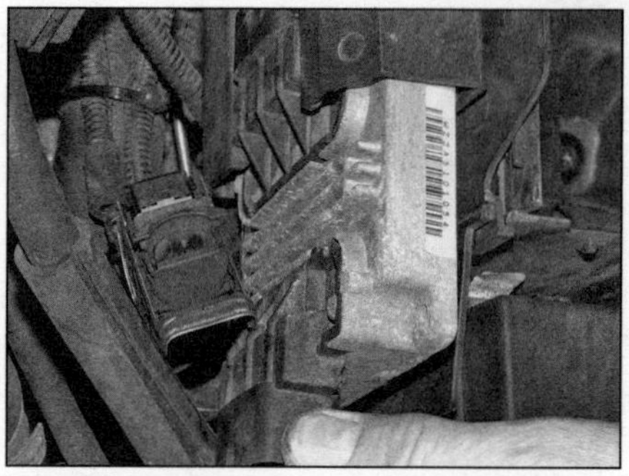

8.10b ... and slide the TCM from place

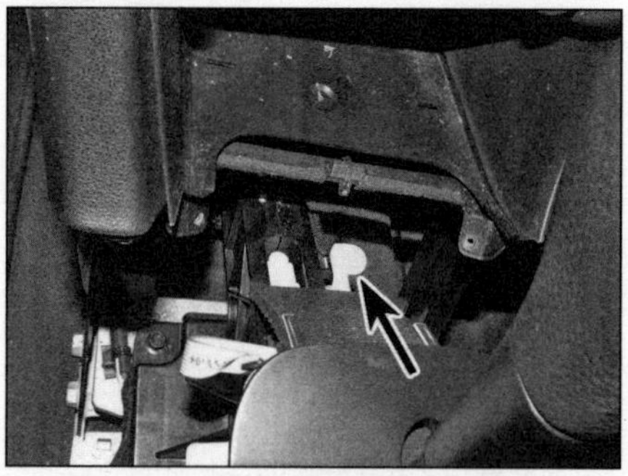

8.19 Depress the yellow catch lever (arrowed) to release the shift lock solenoid

19 Use a screwdriver to depress the yellow catch lever and move the selector lever to the desired position **(see illustration)**.

Removal and refitting

20 Undo the screw, then slide the centre console side panel rearwards to remove it.

21 Undo the 5 bolts and remove the right-hand side facia support bracket, then remove the right-hand floor vent duct.

22 Release the yellow retaining clip, disconnect the wiring plug and remove the solenoid.

23 Refitting is a reversal of removal.

9 Transmission – removal and refitting

Note: *This section describes removal of the transmission, leaving the engine in the car – refer to Chapter 2D, Section 4 for details*

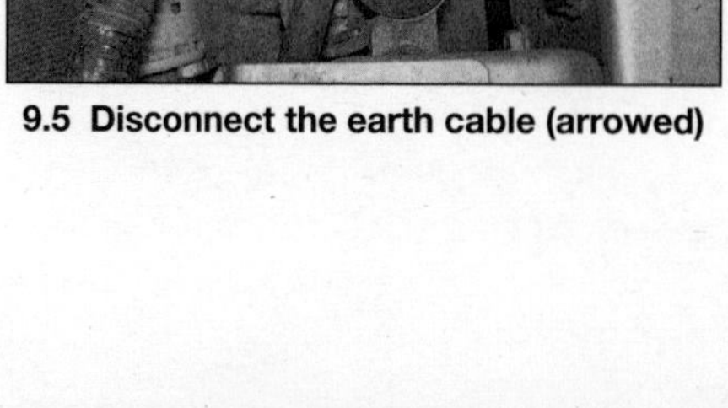

9.5 Disconnect the earth cable (arrowed)

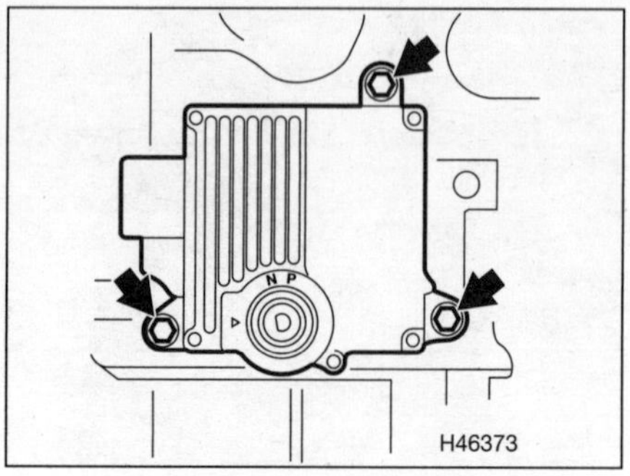

8.16 TCM mounting bolts (arrowed) – 6-speed transmission

of engine and transmission removal as a complete assembly. New fluid cooler union sealing rings will be required on refitting the transmission.

Removal

1 Apply the handbrake, then jack up the front of the vehicle and support it on axle stands (see *Jacking and vehicle support*). Place the selector lever in the N (Neutral) position. Remove both front roadwheels and the engine undershield.

2 Remove the plastic cover from the top of the engine.

3 Drain the transmission fluid as described in Chapter 1A, Section 26 or Chapter 1B, Section 27, then refit the drain plug and tighten it to the specified torque.

4 Remove the battery as described in Chapter 5A, Section 4, then undo the fasteners and remove the battery tray.

5 Disconnect the earth cable from the transmission **(see illustration)**.

6 Disconnect the selector cable from the transmission as described in Section 4.

7 Disconnect the breather hose (where fitted) from the top of the transmission unit.

8 Remove the upper bolts securing the transmission to the engine.

9 Unscrew the retaining bolt, then withdraw the dipstick and its tube from the transmission casing, and plug the open hole to prevent contamination.

10 Position a lifting beam across the engine bay, locating the support legs securely in the sills at either side, in line with the strut top mountings. Hook the jib onto the engine lifting eye and raise it, so that the weight of the engine is taken off the transmission mounting. Most people won't have access to an engine lifting beam, but it may be possible to hire one. Alternatively, an engine hoist may be used to support the engine, but when using this method, bear in mind that if the vehicle is lowered on its axle stands to adjust the working height, for example, then the hoist will have to be lowered accordingly, to avoid straining the engine mountings.

11 Use straps or cable-ties to suspend the radiator from the vehicle bodywork.

12 Undo the fasteners and remove the undershield beneath the radiator. On

Convertible models, undo the bolts and remove the front chassis reinforcement **(see illustration)**.

13 Undo the bolts and remove the radiator mounting brackets from the subframe.

14 Remove the complete exhaust system as described in Chapter 4A, Section 16 or Chapter 4B, Section 18.

15 Remove the front and rear engine torque rods.

16 Remove both driveshafts as described in Chapter 8, Section 2.

17 Undo the nuts securing the steering rack to the subframe.

18 Release the power steering fluid pipes from the retaining clips on the front subframe.

19 Undo the bolts securing the front subframe and rear mounting brackets.

20 Lower the front subframe slightly, then undo the bolts securing the anti-roll bar clamps to the subframe.

21 Undo the bolts and remove the front and rear torque rod brackets from the engine/transmission.

22 Remove the starter motor as described in Chapter 5A, Section 10.

23 Turn the driveplate as necessary to position the torque converter retaining bolts in the starter motor aperture, then unscrew and remove the bolts. **Note:** *As the transmission is removed, the torque converter must stay in the transmission bellhousing and not slide off the transmission shaft. Undo the plug and use a strip of metal to push the converter Into the transmission housing and jam it in place.*

24 Undo the nut and detach the transmission cooling hoses from the casing **(see illustration)**. Be prepared for fluid spillage. Plug the holes to prevent contamination.

25 Slacken the clips, undo the retaining bolts, and remove the charge air pipe under the engine.

26 Undo the remaining transmission-to-engine bolts. Leave one lower bolt in place.

27 Make alignment marks between the left-hand transmission mounting and the casing, then undo the bolts and remove the mounting.

28 Lower the engine/transmission assembly sufficiently that the engine of the transmission clears the lower side of the chassis leg, then undo the remaining bolt and slide the transmission from the engine.

Caution: The transmission is heavy. The help of an assistant will be necessary.

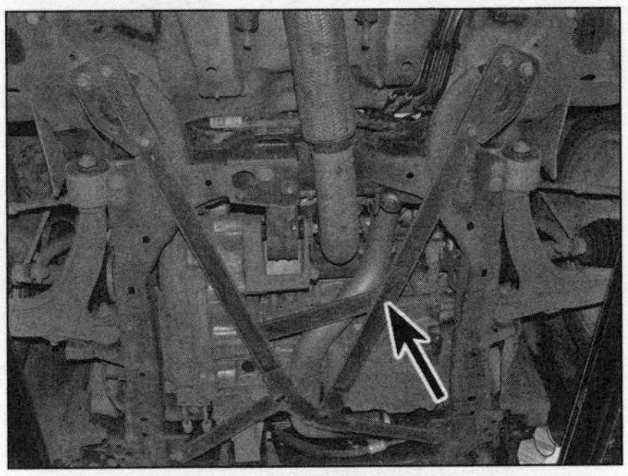

9.12 On Convertible models, undo the bolts and remove the front chassis reinforcement (arrowed)

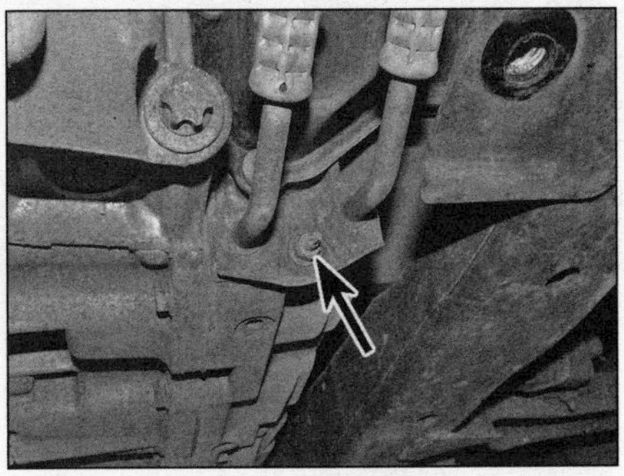

9.24 Undo the nut (arrowed) securing the cooling hoses

Refitting

29 The transmission is refitted by a reversal of the removal procedure, bearing in mind the following points.

a) *Remove all traces of old locking compound from the torque converter threads by running a tap of the correct thread diameter and pitch down the holes. In the absence of a suitable tap, use one of the old bolts with slots cut in its threads.*
b) *Ensure the engine/transmission locating dowels are correctly positioned and apply a smear of molybdenum disulphide grease to the torque converter locating pin and its centring bush in the end of the crankshaft.*
c) *Once the transmission is fully in position on the engine, refit the securing bolts and tighten them to the specified torque.*
d) *Apply thread-locking compound to the torque converter-to-driveplate bolts, then insert them and tighten them progressively to the specified torque.*
e) *Tighten all nuts and bolts to the specified torque (where given).*
f) *Renew the driveshaft oil seals (see Section 6) and refit the driveshafts as described in Chapter 8, Section 2.*
g) *Fit new sealing rings to the fluid cooler hose unions and ensure both unions are securely retained.*
h) *Ensure that all earth cables are securely refitted.*
i) *On completion, refill the transmission with the specified type and quantity of fluid as described in Chapter 1A, Section 26 or Chapter 1B, Section 27 and adjust the selector cable as described in Section 3.*

10 Transmission overhaul – general information

1 In the event of a fault occurring with the transmission, it is first necessary to determine whether it is of a mechanical or hydraulic nature, and to do this, special test equipment is required. It is therefore essential to have the work carried out by a Saab dealer or specialist if a transmission fault is suspected.

2 Do not remove the transmission from the car for possible repair before professional fault diagnosis has been carried out, since most tests require the transmission to be in the vehicle.

Chapter 8
Driveshafts

Contents

Degrees of difficulty

Easy, suitable for novice with little experience	**Fairly easy,** suitable for beginner with some experience	**Fairly difficult,** suitable for competent DIY mechanic	**Difficult,** suitable for experienced DIY mechanic	**Very difficult,** suitable for expert DIY or professional

Specifications

General

Driveshaft type	Steel shafts with outer constant velocity joints and inner tripod joints. Intermediate shaft from right-hand side of transmission to driveshaft
Lubrication (overhaul or repair only)	Use only special grease supplied in sachets with gaiter/overhaul kits; joints are otherwise prepacked with grease and sealed

Joint grease quantity

Outer joint	185 g
Inner joint:	
Automatic transmission	200 g
Manual transmission	185 g

Torque wrench settings

Torque wrench settings	Nm	lbf ft
Driveshaft/hub nut*	230	170
Front chassis reinforcement bolts (Convertible only)	50	37
Intermediate driveshaft bracket-to-engine bolts:		
Petrol models	47	35
Diesel models	20	15
Intermediate driveshaft bearing cover plate bolts	10	7
Lower suspension arm balljoint nut/bolt	50	37
Wheel bolts	110	81

** Do not re-use*

1 General information

Power is transmitted from the transmission final drive to the roadwheels by the driveshafts. The outer joints on all models are of 'constant velocity' (CV) type, consisting of six balls running in axial grooves. The driveshaft outer joints incorporate stub axles which are splined to the hubs located in the front suspension hub carriers. The inner 'universal' joints are designed to move in a smaller arc than the outer CV joints, and can also move axially to allow for movements of the front suspension. On automatic transmission models, they are of tripod type consisting of a three-armed 'spider' with needle bearings and outer race, splined to the driveshaft, and an outer housing with three corresponding cut-outs for the bearing races to slide in, whilst on manual transmission models, a CV type joint is fitted.

An intermediate shaft, with its own support bearing, is fitted between the transmission and right-hand driveshaft – a design which equalises driveshaft angles at all suspension positions, and reduces driveshaft flexing, improving directional stability under hard acceleration.

The universal and CV joints allow smooth transmission of drive to the wheels at all steering and suspension angles. The joints are protected by rubber gaiters, and are packed with grease to provide permanent lubrication. In the event of wear being detected, the joint can be renewed separately from the driveshaft. The joints do not require additional lubrication, unless they have been renovated or the rubber gaiters have been damaged, allowing the grease to become contaminated. Refer to Chapter 1A, Section 15 or Chapter 1B, Section 15 for details of checking the condition of the driveshaft gaiters.

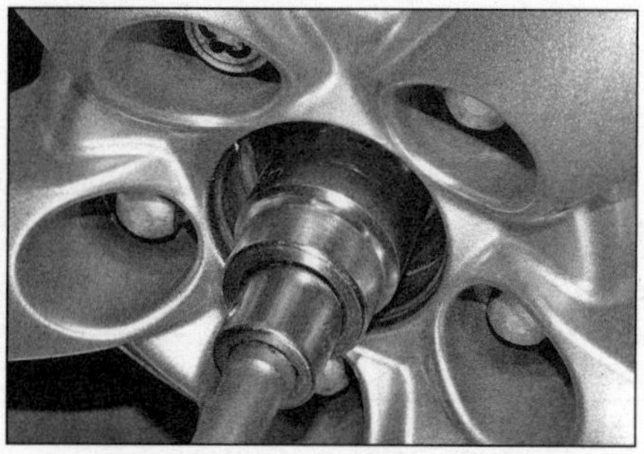

2.2 Prise out the wheel centre cap, then use a 32 mm socket to slacken the driveshaft nut

2.5a Undo the nut and remove the clamp bolt ...

2.5b ... then lever the control arm downwards

2 Driveshafts – removal and refitting

Removal

1 Park the vehicle on a level surface, apply the handbrake and chock the rear wheels.

2 Remove the wheel trim (or wheel centre cap for vehicles fitted with alloy wheels), then loosen the driveshaft nut, bearing in mind the high torque to which this nut is tightened – select a sturdy wrench and close-fitting socket to loosen it **(see illustration)**.

3 Apply the handbrake, then jack up the front of the vehicle and support it on axle stands (see *Jacking and vehicle support*). Remove the roadwheel. Undo the fasteners and remove the engine undershield (where fitted). On Convertible models, undo the bolts and remove the front chassis reinforcement. Note that the front chassis reinforcement bolts are shorter than the rear.

4 Unscrew and remove the driveshaft nut. Have an assistant apply the footbrake to prevent the driveshaft from rotating. Discard the driveshaft nut, a new one (normally supplied in the gaiter kit) must be fitted.

5 Unscrew the bolt, then lever the lower control arm downwards, detaching the balljoint from the hub carrier **(see illustrations)**. Press the lower control arm down as far as possible, and move the hub carrier/strut to one side. Take care not to damage the balljoint rubber boot, and do not strain the brake hoses and brake pad wear warning wiring.

6 Release the brake hose and ABS wiring harness from the strut bracket **(see illustration)**.

7 Using a mallet, carefully tap the driveshaft inwards from the splines in the hub while pulling out the bottom of the strut **(see illustration)**. If the driveshaft is reluctant to move, use a puller attached to the hub/carrier and push the driveshaft from place. If all else fails, remove the hub carrier complete with driveshaft, and press the driveshaft from the hub **(see illustration)**.

8 To remove the left-hand side driveshaft, position a container beneath the transmission to catch spilt oil, then pull out the driveshaft. The internal driveshaft circlip may be tight in the transmission side gear, in which case careful use of a lever against the transmission casing will be required. Lever against a block of wood to prevent damage to the casing, and take care not to damage the oil seal as the driveshaft is being removed **(see illustration)**. **Note:** *Pull only on the inner joint housing, not the driveshaft itself, otherwise the gaiter may be damaged.*

9 To remove the right-hand side driveshaft, use a soft metal drift (brass) to drive the outer driveshaft from the inner shaft.

Refitting

10 Where applicable, check the condition of the circlip on the inner end of the driveshaft and, if necessary, renew it **(see illustration)**.

11 Clean the splines on each end of the driveshaft and in the hub, and where applicable wipe clean the oil seal in the transmission casing. Check the oil seal and if necessary renew it as described in Chapter 7A, Section 5 or Chapter 7B, Section 6. Smear a little oil on the lips of the oil seal before fitting the driveshaft.

12 To refit the outer section of the right-hand driveshaft, lubricate the shaft splines with

2.6 Undo the bolt (arrowed) and detach the bracket from the strut

2.7a Pull the hub carrier outwards, and withdraw the driveshaft

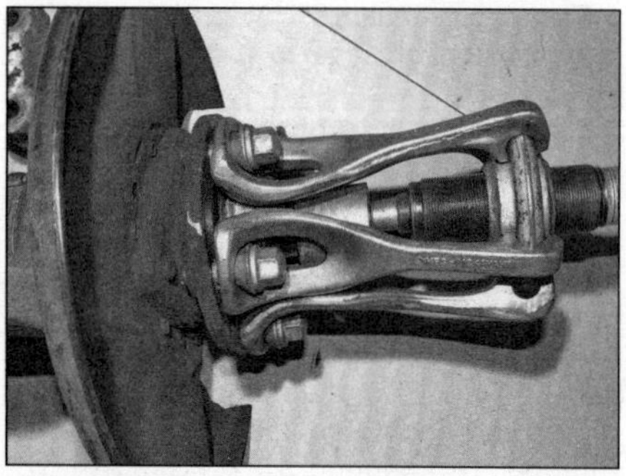

2.7b If necessary, use a puller to press the driveshaft from the hub

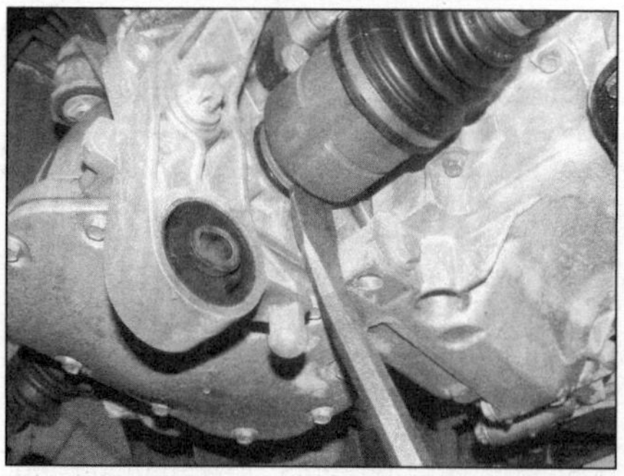

2.8 Use a lever to release the inner end of the driveshaft from the differential

2.10 Prise off the old circlip and fit a new one

assembly grease (Saab No 90 513 210), then locate the driveshaft into the intermediate shaft, and press in until the internal circlip engages the groove.

13 To refit the left-hand driveshaft, fit the outer end of the shaft into the wheel hub, then locate the inner end of the driveshaft into the transmission – turn the driveshaft as necessary to engage the splines. Press in the driveshaft until the internal circlip engages the groove. Check that the circlip is engaged by attempting to pull out the driveshaft with only moderate force.

14 Engage the outer end of the driveshaft with the splines in the hub, then press down the lower suspension arm and guide the bottom of the hub carrier onto the balljoint on the lower arm. Screw in the balljoint bolt and tighten the bolt to the specified torque.

15 Screw on the new driveshaft nut and tighten just moderately at this stage.

16 Refit the brake hose and ABS wiring harness to their retaining clips.

17 Check and if necessary top-up the transmission oil/fluid level with reference to Chapter 1A or 1B.

18 Refit the engine undershield and the front chassis reinforcement (where applicable).

19 Refit the roadwheel, then lower the vehicle to the ground and tighten the bolts to the specified torque.

20 Fully tighten the driveshaft nut to the specified torque, and refit the wheel trim/cap.

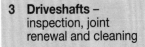

3 Driveshafts – inspection, joint renewal and cleaning

Inspection

1 If any of the checks described in Chapter 1A, Section 15 or Chapter 1B, Section 15 reveal apparent excessive wear or play, first check that the hub nut (driveshaft outer nut) is tightened to the specified torque. Repeat this check on the hub nut on the other side.

2 To check for driveshaft wear, road test the vehicle, driving it slowly in a circle on full steering lock (carry out the test on both left and right lock), while listening for a metallic clicking or knocking sound coming from the front wheels. An assistant in the passenger seat can listen for the sound from the nearside joint. If such a sound is heard, this indicates wear in the outer joint.

3 If vibration proportional to roadspeed is felt through the car when accelerating or on over-run, there is a possibility of wear in the inner joints. For a more thorough check, remove and dismantle the driveshafts where possible as described in the following sub-Sections. Refer to a Saab dealer for information on the availability of driveshaft components.

4 Continual noise from the area of the right-hand driveshaft, increasing with roadspeed, may indicate wear in the support bearing.

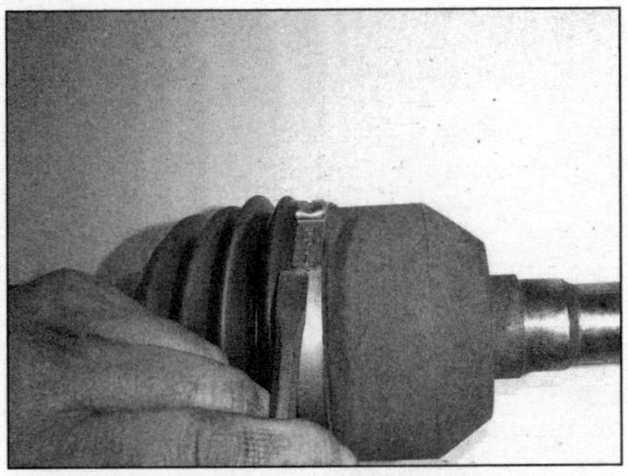

3.6 Use a chisel to release the gaiter clip

3.9 Use a soft drift to tap the joint hub from the shaft

Outer joint renewal

5 Remove the driveshaft as described in Section 2, then thoroughly clean it and mount it in a vice. It is important that foreign matter, such as dust and dirt, are prevented from entering the joint.

6 Release the large clip securing the rubber gaiter to the outer joint housing **(see illustration)**, then similarly release the small clip securing the rubber gaiter to the driveshaft. Note the fitted position of the gaiter.

7 Slide the rubber gaiter along the driveshaft, away from the joint, or cut it away from the shaft **(see illustration).** Scoop out as much of the grease as possible from the joint and gaiter.

8 Using a dab of paint, mark the outer joint and driveshaft in relation to each other to ensure correct refitting.

9 Use a hammer and soft drift to tap the joint hub from the splines **(see illustration)**.

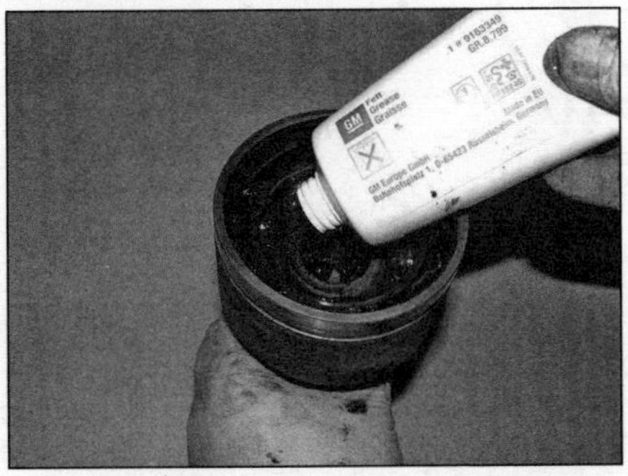

3.13 Work the grease into the joint

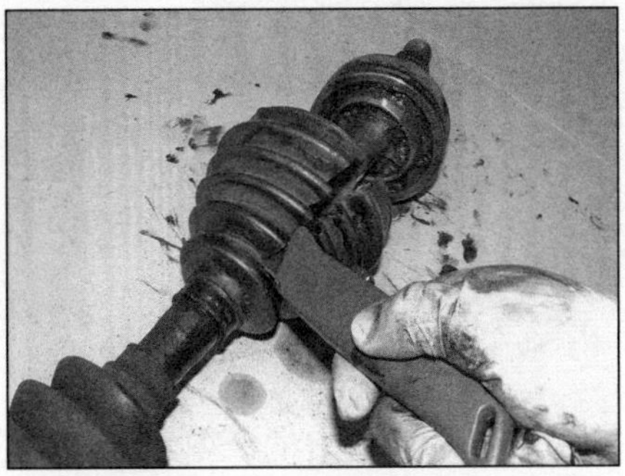

3.7 Cut the gaiter away from the shaft

3.11 Press the new circlip into the groove on the shaft

10 With the joint removed, slide the rubber gaiter (where still fitted) and small clip from the driveshaft. Check the rubber gaiter for cracks or slits, and renew it if necessary.

11 Thoroughly clean the splines of the driveshaft and outer joint, and also the rubber gaiter contact surfaces. If the joint has been contaminated with road grit or water, it must be dismantled and cleaned as described later in this Section. Renew the circlip on the shaft **(see illustration)**.

12 Locate the gaiter, together with small clip, on the outer end of the driveshaft. Smear a little grease onto the driveshaft to facilitate this.

13 Pack the joint with the specified quantity of grease, working it well into the cavities of the housing **(see illustration)**.

14 Locate the outer joint onto the driveshaft splines in its previously-noted position, and press it on until the internal circlip engages with the groove **(see illustration)**.

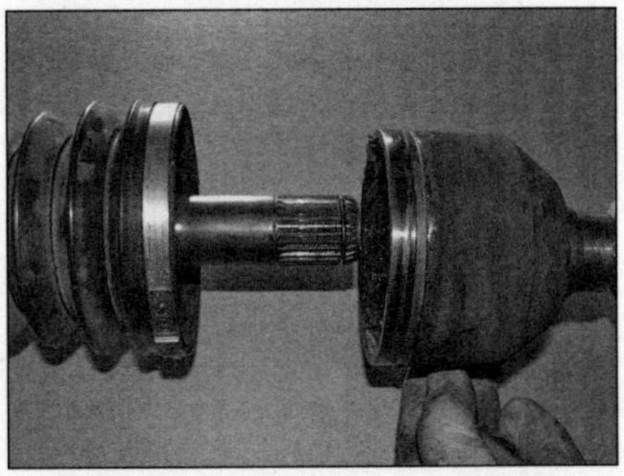

3.14 Tap the outer joint onto the end of the shaft, until the circlip engages

3.15a Secure the large gaiter retaining clip in position by crimping the sides, and compressing the raised section of the clip using pliers made for this purpose

3.15b The small inner retaining clip is secured in the same way

15 Reposition the rubber gaiter onto the joint outer housing in its previously-noted position, then refit the two clips. Tighten the clips securely **(see illustrations)**.
16 Refit the driveshaft with reference to Section 2.

Inner joint renewal

Manual transmission models

17 Remove the driveshaft as described in Section 2.
18 Release the clips securing the rubber gaiter to the driveshaft and inner joint housing. Note the fitted position of the gaiter, then slide the rubber gaiter along the driveshaft, away from the joint. Scoop out as much of the grease as possible from the joint and gaiter.
19 Using a dab of paint, mark the outer joint and driveshaft in relation to each other to ensure correct refitting.
20 Use a hammer and soft drift to tap the joint hub from the splines **(see illustration 3.9)**.
21 With the joint removed, slide the rubber gaiter and small clip from the driveshaft. Check the rubber gaiter for cracks or slits, and renew it if necessary.
22 Thoroughly clean the splines of the driveshaft and outer joint, and also the rubber gaiter contact surfaces. If the joint has been contaminated with road grit or water, it must be dismantled and cleaned as described later in this Section. Renew the circlip on the end of the shaft – a new one is supplied in the overhaul kit **(see illustration 3.11)**.
23 Locate the gaiter, together with small clip, on the end of the driveshaft. Smear a little grease onto the driveshaft to facilitate this.
24 Pack the joint with the specified quantity of grease, working it well into the cavities of the housing.
25 Locate the outer joint onto the driveshaft splines in its previously-noted position, and press it on until the internal circlip engages with the groove.
26 Reposition the rubber gaiter onto the joint outer housing in its previously-noted position, then refit the two clips. Tighten the clips securely **(see illustrations 3.15a and 3.15b)**.
27 Refit the driveshaft with reference to Section 2.

Automatic transmission models

28 Remove the driveshaft as described in Section 2.
29 Release the clips securing the rubber gaiter to the driveshaft and inner joint housing. Note the fitted position of the gaiter, then slide the rubber gaiter along the driveshaft, away from the joint. Scoop out as much of the grease as possible from the joint and gaiter.
30 Mark the driveshaft and joint housing in relation to each other, then slide the housing from the driveshaft. Take care not to disturb the rollers on the tripod **(see illustration)**
31 Mark the driveshaft and tripod in relation to each other using a centre-punch or dab of paint. Using circlip pliers, expand and remove the circlip from the end of the driveshaft, then use a hydraulic press to remove the tripod together with the needle roller bearings. Note that the chamfered edge of the tripod faces the centre of the driveshaft.
32 Slide the rubber gaiter and small clip from the driveshaft. Check the rubber gaiter for cracks or slits, and renew it if necessary.
33 Thoroughly clean the splines of the driveshaft and inner joint, and also the rubber gaiter contact surfaces. If the joint has been exposed to road grit or water, it should be thoroughly cleaned as described later in this Section. Check the condition of the circlip and renew it if necessary. Check that the three tripod bearings are free to rotate without resistance, and that they are not excessively worn.
34 Locate the gaiter, together with small clip, on the inner end of the driveshaft in its previously-noted position. Smear a little grease onto the driveshaft to facilitate this.
35 Locate the tripod on the driveshaft splines, chamfered edge first, making sure that the previously-made marks are aligned. Using a socket or metal tube, drive the tripod fully onto the driveshaft, then refit the circlip, making sure that it is correctly located in its groove.
36 Pack the tripod joint and inner joint housing with the specified quantity of grease, working it well into the bearings.
37 Locate the inner joint housing onto the tripod in its previously-noted position.

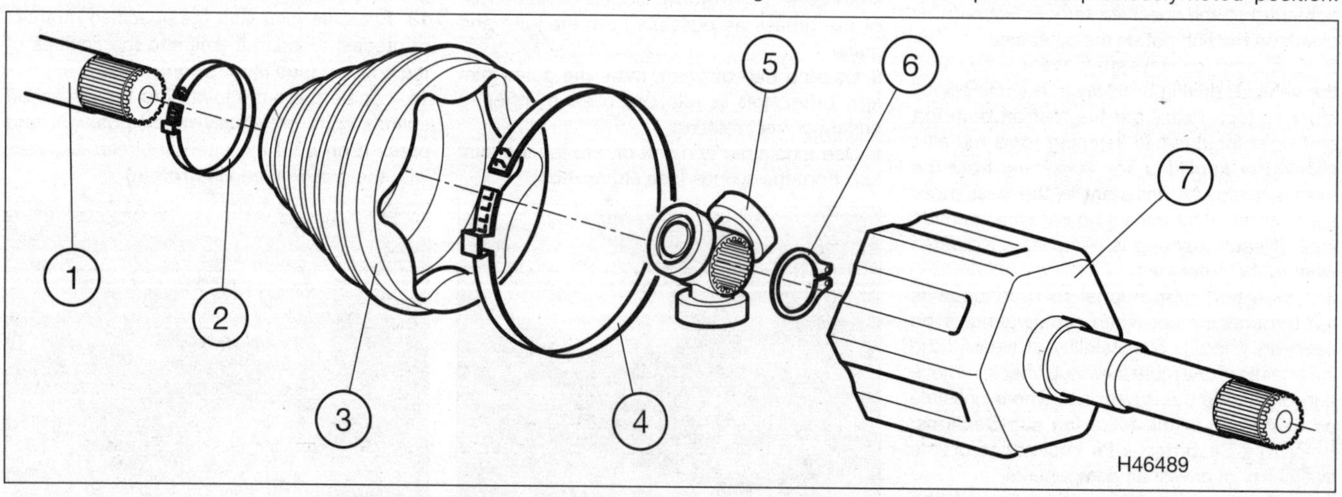

3.30 Driveshaft inner tripod joint details – automatic transmission models

1 *Driveshaft*
2 *Gaiter clip*
3 *Gaiter*
4 *Gaiter clip*
5 *Tripod joint rollers*
6 *Circlip*
7 *Joint housing*

Reposition the rubber gaiter onto the inner joint housing in its previously-noted position, then refit and tighten the clips. If crimp-type clips are being fitted, use a crimping tool to tighten them.

38 Refit the driveshaft with reference to Section 2.

Joint cleaning

39 Where a joint has been contaminated with road grit or water through a damaged rubber gaiter, the joint should be completely dismantled and cleaned. Remove the joint as described previously in this Section.

40 To dismantle the outer joint, mount it vertically in a soft-jawed vice, then turn the splined hub and ball cage so that the balls can be removed individually. Remove the hub followed by the ball cage.

41 The inner joint is dismantled during removal, and the tripod joint bearings should be washed in suitable solvent to remove all traces of grease.

42 Thoroughly clean the inner and outer joint housings, together with the ball-bearings, cages and hubs, removing all traces of grease and foreign matter.

43 To reassemble the outer joint, first insert the cage, followed by the splined hub. Manoeuvre the hub and carrier so that the balls can be inserted one at a time.

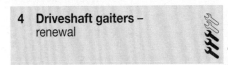

4 Driveshaft gaiters – renewal

1 Obtain a kit comprising new gaiters and retaining clips from a Saab dealer or motor factor.

2 Removal and refitting of the gaiters is described in Section 3.

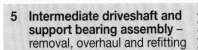

5 Intermediate driveshaft and support bearing assembly – removal, overhaul and refitting

Removal

1 On diesel models, to remove the intermediate shaft, remove the right-hand driveshaft as previously described, then undo the 3 bolts and pull the shaft from the transmission/ bearing housing **(see illustration)**.

2 To remove the intermediate shaft on petrol models, remove the right-hand driveshaft as previously described, then undo the 3 bolts securing the intermediate shaft bearing bracket to the cylinder block, and pull the shaft from the transmission **(see illustration)**.

Overhaul

Petrol models

3 Undo the 2 retaining bolts and remove the bearing cover plate **(see illustration)**.

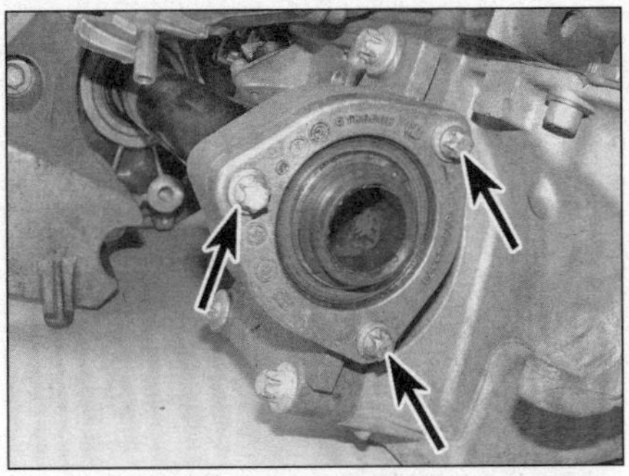

5.1 Intermediate shaft bearing housing retaining bolts (arrowed) – diesel models

5.2 Intermediate driveshaft bearing housing bolts (arrowed)

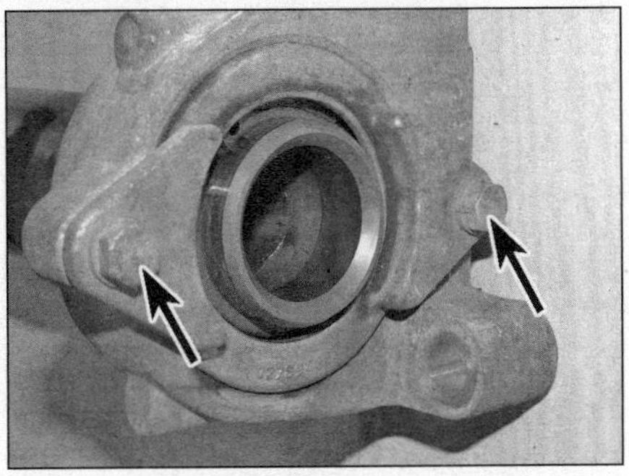

5.3 Undo the bearing cover plate screws (arrowed)

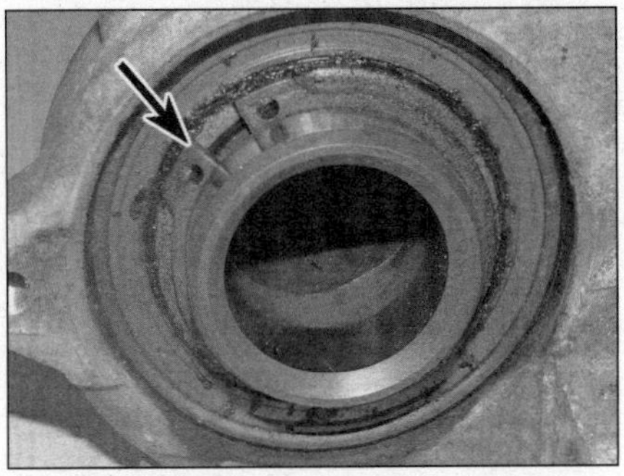

5.4 Remove the circlip (arrowed)

4 Remove the circlip securing the shaft in the bearing **(see illustration)**.

5 Press the shaft from the bearing, then press the bearing from the bracket **(see illustration)**.

6 Press the new bearing into the bracket, then press the shaft into the bearing. Secure the shaft with the circlip.

7 Fit the bearing cover plate and tighten the retaining bolts to the specified torque.

Diesel models

8 Remove the circlip on the end of the shaft **(see illustration)**.

9 Press the shaft from the bearing, then press the bearing from the bracket.

10 Press the new bearing into the bracket, then press the shaft into the bearing. Secure the shaft with the circlip.

Refitting

11 Refitting is a reversal of removal, but note the following additional points:

a) *Check the transmission oil seals and if necessary renew them with reference to Chapter 7A, Section 5 or Chapter 7B, Section 6.*
b) *Tighten all mounting nuts/bolts to the specified torque, where given.*
c) *Top-up the transmission oil/fluid with reference to Chapter 1A or 1B.*

5.5 Press the bearing from the shaft

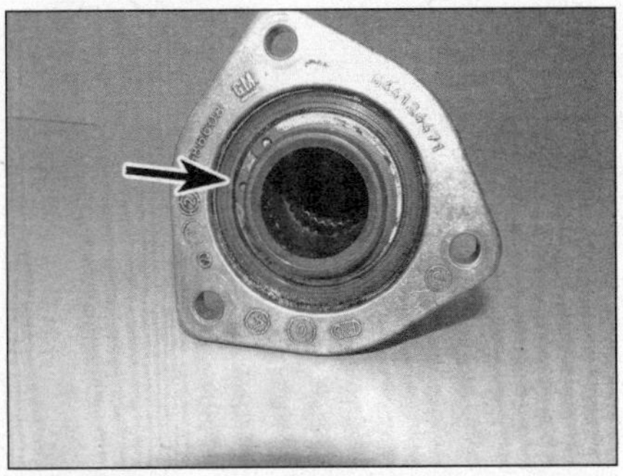

5.8 Extract the circlip (arrowed) securing the intermediate driveshaft in the bearing

Chapter 9
Braking system

Contents

Degrees of difficulty

Easy, suitable for novice with little experience	**Fairly easy,** suitable for beginner with some experience	**Fairly difficult,** suitable for competent DIY mechanic	**Difficult,** suitable for experienced DIY mechanic	**Very difficult,** suitable for expert DIY or professional

Specifications

General

Brake system type and layout:

Footbrake	Diagonally-split dual hydraulic circuits; front left/rear right and front right/rear left. Discs fitted front and rear, ventilated at the front. Single-piston, sliding calipers on front and rear. anti-lock braking system (ABS), traction control system (TCS), corning brake control (CBC) and electronic stability program (ESP) fitted as standard on all models
Handbrake	Lever and cable operation, acting on the pistons in the rear brake calipers

Front brakes

Discs:	
Type	Ventilated
Outside diameter	288, 302 or 314 mm
Thickness (new disc)	25 mm (288 mm dia.) or 28 mm (302 or 314 mm dia.)
Minimum thickness after grinding	23.5 mm (288 mm dia.) or 26.5 mm (302 or 314 mm dia.)
Minimum wear thickness	22.0 mm (288 mm dia.) or 25.0 mm (302 or 314 mm dia.)
Maximum run-out	0.08 mm
Maximum variation in disc thickness	0.015 mm
Calipers:	
Type	Single-piston, floating (FNG 57 or FNG 60)
Piston diameter	57.0 mm (FNG 57) or 60.0 mm (FNG 60)
Pads minimum friction material thickness	2.0 mm

Rear brakes

Discs:	
Type	Solid or ventilated
Outside diameter	278 mm (solid) or 292 mm (ventilated)
Thickness (new disc)	12 mm (solid) or 20 mm (ventilated)
Minimum thickness after grinding	10.5 mm (solid) or 18.5 mm (ventilated)
Minimum wear thickness	10.0 mm (solid) or 18.0 mm (ventilated)
Maximum run-out	0.08 mm
Maximum variation in disc thickness	0.015 mm
Calipers:	
Type	Single-piston, floating (FNC 38 or FNC 40)
Piston diameter	38.0 mm (FNC 38) or 40.0 mm (FNC 40)
Pads minimum friction material thickness	2.0 mm

ABS components

Clearance between sensor and tooth (not adjustable)	0.2 to 1.3 mm
Frequency	0 to 2000 Hz
Signal current, low:	
Nominal	7.0 mA
Min	5.6 mA
Max	8.4 mA
Signal current, high:	
Nominal	14.0 mA
Min	11.2 mA
Max	16.8 mA
Pulses per rotation	48

Torque wrench settings

	Nm	lbf ft
ABS hydraulic union nuts	15	11
ABS control unit to hydraulic unit	3	2
ABS hydraulic unit mounting nut	25	18
Bleed nipple	16	12
Brake caliper guide pins	28	21
Brake hose to caliper	40	30
Front brake caliper bracket to hub carrier:		
Stage 1	210	155
Stage 2	Angle-tighten a further 30°	
Master cylinder to servo	25	18
Rear brake caliper bracket to hub carrier:		
Stage 1	130	96
Stage 2	Angle-tighten a further 45°	
Roadwheel bolts	110	81
Servo to body	20	15
Vacuum pump mounting bolt:		
Petrol models	24	18
Diesel models	8	6

1 General information

Braking is achieved by a dual-circuit hydraulic system, assisted by a vacuum servo unit. All models have discs fitted at the front and rear. The front discs are ventilated, to improve cooling and reduce brake fade. Ventilated or solid discs may be fitted to the rear, depending on model.

The dual hydraulic circuits are diagonally-split; on LHD models, the primary circuit operates the front left and rear right brakes, and the secondary circuit operates the front right and rear left brakes. On RHD models, the circuits are the opposite. This design ensures that at least 50% of the vehicle's braking capacity will be available, should pressure be lost in one of the hydraulic circuits. Under these circumstances, the diagonal layout should prevent the vehicle from becoming unstable if the brakes are applied when only one circuit is operational.

Both the front and rear brake calipers are of floating single-piston type. Each caliper has two brake pads, one inboard and one outboard of the disc. During braking, hydraulic pressure forces the piston along its cylinder, and presses the inboard brake pad against the disc. The caliper body reacts to this effort by sliding along its guide pins, bringing the outboard pad into contact with the disc. In this manner, equal pressure is applied to each side of the disc by the brake pads. When the brake pedal is released, the hydraulic pressure drops and the piston seal retracts the piston from the brake pad.

The rear brake calipers incorporate the handbrake mechanism. When the handbrake lever is operated, the cable operates a lever on the caliper which forces the caliper piston against the brake pad via a pushrod. The pushrod incorporates and screw/rachet arrangement, which automatically adjusts the length of the pushrod, compensating for any brake pad wear, thus maintaining the handbrake lever position. Two handbrake cables are fitted, one for the left-hand side and one for the right-hand side.

On both petrol and diesel engine models, the brake vacuum servo unit uses engine intake manifold vacuum to boost the effort applied to the master cylinder by the brake pedal. The intake manifold vacuum is supplemented by a mechanical vacuum pump mounted on the left-hand end of the cylinder head and driven by the camshaft.

The anti-lock braking system (ABS) fitted as standard to all models prevents wheel lock-up under heavy braking, and not only optimises stopping distances, but also improves steering control. Electronic brake force distribution (EBD) is also incorporated into the ABS system. EBD optimises brake force distribution under normal braking conditions. By electronically monitoring the speed of each roadwheel in relation to the other wheels, the system can detect when a wheel is about to lock-up, before control is actually lost. The brake fluid pressure applied to that wheel's brake caliper is then decreased and restored ('modulated') several times a second until control is regained.

The system components comprise four wheel speed sensors, a hydraulic unit with integral electronic control unit (ECU), brake lines and a dashboard-mounted warning light. The four wheel sensors are mounted on the wheel hub carriers. Each wheel has a rotating toothed hub mounted on the driveshaft (front) or on the hub (rear). The wheel speed sensors are mounted in close proximity to these hubs. The teeth produce a voltage waveform whose frequency varies with the speed of the hubs. These waveforms are transmitted to the ECU, and used to calculate the rotational speed of each wheel. The ECU has a self-diagnostic facility, to inhibit the operation of the ABS if a fault is detected, lighting the dashboard-mounted warning light. The braking system will then revert to conventional, non-ABS operation. If the nature of the fault is not immediately obvious upon inspection, the vehicle must be taken to a Saab dealer or specialist, who will have the diagnostic equipment required to interrogate the ABS ECU electronically and pin-point the problem.

Most models feature a traction control system (TCS) and an electronic stability program (ESP) These systems use the basic ABS system, with an additional pump and valves fitted to the hydraulic actuator. A yaw sensor and a steering wheel angle sensor are also to vehicles that have ESP.

TCS is an anti-slip system. If wheel spin is detected at a speed below 30 mph, one of the valves opens, to allow the pump to pressurise the relevant brake, until the spinning wheel slows to a rotational speed corresponding to the speed of the vehicle. This has the effect of transferring torque to the wheel with most traction. At the same time, the throttle plate is closed slightly, to reduce the torque from the engine.

ESP functions by controlling engine torque and brake application in unexpected situations. By monitoring the various sensors the ESP can respond to a skid by applying one or more of the brakes. For example if the vehicle is understeering into a corner the brakes will be applied to the rear inside wheel. Cornering brake control (CBC) is also incorporated into the ESP system. CBC stabilises the vehicle in extreme situation when the driver is braking and cornering at the same time.

2 Hydraulic system – bleeding

Warning: Hydraulic fluid is poisonous; wash off immediately and thoroughly in the case of skin contact, and seek immediate medical advice if any fluid is swallowed or gets into the eyes. Certain types of hydraulic fluid are inflammable, and may ignite when brought into contact with hot components; when servicing any hydraulic system, it is safest to assume that the fluid is inflammable, and to take precautions against the risk of fire as though it is petrol that is being handled. Hydraulic fluid is also an effective paint stripper, and will attack plastics; if any is spilt, it should be washed off immediately, using copious quantities of fresh water. Finally, it is hygroscopic (it absorbs moisture from the air) – old fluid may be contaminated and unfit for further use. When topping-up or renewing the fluid, always use the recommended type, and ensure that it comes from a freshly-opened sealed container.

General

1 The correct operation of any hydraulic system is only possible after removing all air from the components and circuit; this is achieved by bleeding the system.

2 During the bleeding procedure, add only clean, unused hydraulic fluid of the recommended type; never re-use fluid that has already been bled from the system. Ensure that sufficient fluid is available before starting work.

3 If there is any possibility of incorrect fluid being already in the system, the brake components and circuit must be flushed completely with uncontaminated, correct fluid, and new seals should be fitted to the various components.

4 If hydraulic fluid has been lost from the system, or air has entered because of a leak, ensure that the fault is cured before proceeding further.

5 Park the vehicle over an inspection pit or on car ramps. Alternatively, apply the handbrake then jack up the front and rear of the vehicle and support it on axle stands (see *Jacking and vehicle support*). For improved access with the vehicle jacked up, remove the roadwheels.

6 Check that all pipes and hoses are secure, unions tight and bleed screws closed. Clean any dirt from around the bleed screws.

7 Unscrew the master cylinder reservoir cap, and top the master cylinder reservoir up to the MAX level line; refit the cap loosely, and remember to maintain the fluid level at least above the MIN level line throughout the procedure, otherwise there is a risk of further air entering the system.

8 There is a number of one-man, do-it-yourself brake bleeding kits currently available from motor accessory shops. It is recommended that one of these kits is used whenever possible, as they greatly simplify the bleeding operation, and also reduce the risk of expelled air and fluid being drawn back into the system. If such a kit is not available, the basic (two-man) method must be used, which is described in detail below.

9 If a kit is to be used, prepare the vehicle

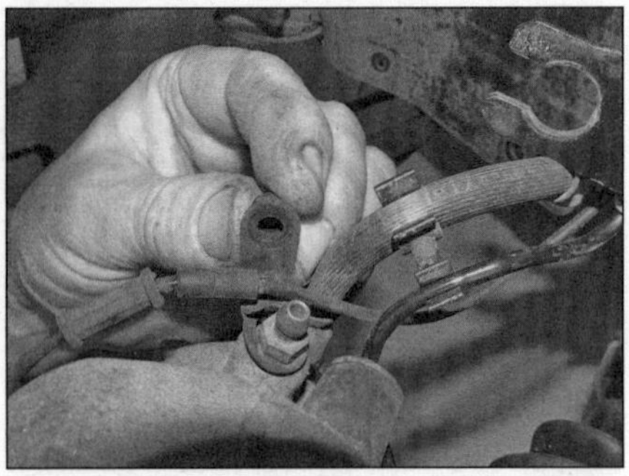

2.14 Remove the dust cap from the bleed screw

as described previously, and follow the kit manufacturer's instructions, as the procedure may vary slightly according to the type being used; generally, they are as outlined below in the relevant sub-section.

10 Whichever method is used, the same sequence must be followed (paragraphs 11 and 12) to ensure the removal of all air from the system.

Bleeding sequence

11 If the system has been only partially disconnected, and suitable precautions were taken to minimise fluid loss, it should only be necessary to bleed that part of the system (ie, the primary or secondary circuit).

12 If the complete system is to be bled, then it should be done working in the following sequence (**Note:** *On LHD models use opposite sides*):

a) Left-hand front brake.
b) Right-hand rear brake.
c) Right-hand front brake.
d) Left-hand rear brake.

Bleeding

Basic (two-man) method

13 Collect together a clean glass jar, a suitable length of plastic or rubber tubing which is a tight fit over the bleed screw, and a ring spanner to fit the screw. The help of an assistant will also be required.

14 Remove the dust cap from the first bleed screw in the sequence **(see illustration)**. Fit the spanner and tube to the screw, place the other end of the tube in the jar, and pour in sufficient fluid to cover the end of the tube.

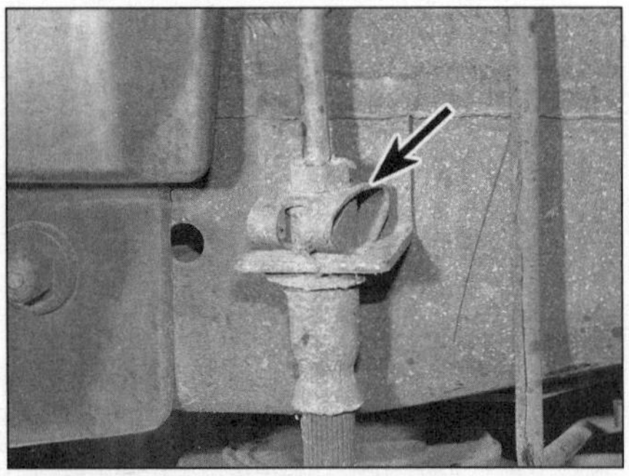

3.2a Brake pipe union spring clip (arrowed)

15 Ensure that the master cylinder reservoir fluid level is maintained at least above the MIN level mark throughout the procedure.

16 Have the assistant fully depress and release the brake pedal several times to build-up initial pressure in the system.

17 Unscrew the bleed screw approximately half a turn then have the assistant slowly depress the brake pedal down to the floor and hold it there. Tighten the bleed screw and have the assistant slowly release the pedal to its rest position.

18 Repeat the procedure given in paragraph 17 until the fluid emerging from the bleed screw is free from air bubbles. After every two or three depressions of the pedal, check the level of fluid in the reservoir and top-up if necessary.

19 When no more air bubbles appear, securely tighten the bleed screw, remove the tube and spanner, and refit the dust cap. Do not overtighten the bleed screw.

20 Repeat the procedure on the remaining screws in the sequence, until all air is removed from the system and the brake pedal feels firm again.

Using a one-way valve kit

21 As the name implies, these kits consist of a length of tubing with a one-way valve fitted, to prevent expelled air and fluid being drawn back into the system; some kits include a translucent container, which can be positioned so that the air bubbles can be more easily seen flowing from the end of the tube.

22 The kit is connected to the bleed screw, which is then opened. The user returns to the driver's seat, depresses the brake pedal with a smooth, steady stroke, and slowly releases it; this is repeated until the expelled fluid is clear of air bubbles.

23 Note that these kits simplify work so much that it is easy to forget the master cylinder reservoir fluid level; ensure that this is maintained at least above the MIN level line at all times.

Using a pressure-bleeding kit

24 These kits are usually operated by a reservoir of pressurised air contained in the spare tyre. However, note that it will probably be necessary to reduce the pressure to a lower level than normal; refer to the instructions supplied with the kit.

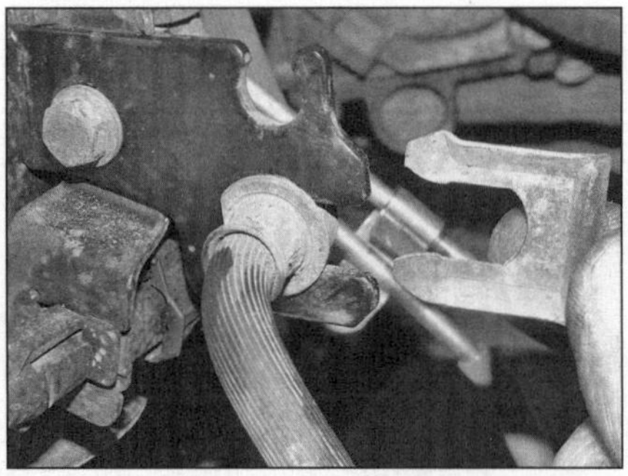

3.2b Pull out the spring clip

25 By connecting a pressurised, fluid-filled container to the master cylinder reservoir, bleeding can be carried out simply by opening each screw in turn (in the specified sequence), and allowing the fluid to flow out until no more air bubbles can be seen in the expelled fluid.

26 This method has the advantage that the large reservoir of fluid provides an additional safeguard against air being drawn into the system during bleeding.

27 Pressure-bleeding is particularly effective when bleeding 'difficult' systems, or when bleeding the complete system at the time of routine fluid renewal.

All methods

28 When bleeding is complete, and firm pedal feel is restored, wipe off any spilt fluid, securely tighten the bleed screws, and refit the dust caps.

29 Check the hydraulic fluid level in the master cylinder reservoir, and top-up if necessary (see *Weekly checks*).

30 Discard any hydraulic fluid that has been bled from the system; it will not be fit for re-use.

31 Check the feel of the brake pedal. If it feels at all spongy, air must still be present in the system, and further bleeding is required. Failure to bleed satisfactorily after a reasonable repetition of the bleeding procedure may be due to worn master cylinder seals.

3 Hydraulic pipes and hoses – renewal

1 If any pipe or hose is to be renewed, minimise fluid loss by first removing the master cylinder reservoir cap, then tightening it down onto a piece of polythene to obtain an airtight seal. The cap incorporates a level warning float and, alternatively, hose clamps can be fitted to flexible hoses to isolate sections of the circuit; metal brake pipe unions can be plugged (if care is taken not to allow dirt into the system) or capped immediately they are disconnected. Place a wad of rag under any union that is to be disconnected, to catch any spilt fluid.

2 If a flexible hose is to be disconnected, unscrew the brake pipe union nut before removing the spring clip which secures the hose to its mounting bracket **(see illustration)**. Where applicable, unscrew the banjo union bolt securing the hose to the caliper and recover the copper washers. When removing the front flexible hose, pull out the spring clip and disconnect it from the strut **(see illustration)**.

3 To unscrew union nuts, it is preferable to obtain a 'split' brake pipe spanner of the correct size; these are available from most motor accessory shops. Failing this, a close-fitting open-ended spanner will be required, though if the nuts are tight or corroded, their flats may be rounded-off if the spanner slips. In such a case, a self-locking wrench is often the only way to unscrew a stubborn union, but it follows that the pipe and the damaged nuts must be renewed on reassembly. Always clean a union and surrounding area before disconnecting it. If disconnecting a component with more than one union, make a careful note of the connections before disturbing any of them.

4 If a brake pipe is to be renewed, it can be obtained, cut to length and with the union nuts and end flares in place, from a dealer's parts shop. All that is then necessary is to bend it to shape, following the line of the original, before fitting it to the car. Alternatively, most motor accessory shops can make up brake pipes from kits, but this requires very careful measurement of the original, to ensure that the new one is of the correct length. The safest answer is usually to take the original to the shop as a pattern.

5 On refitting, do not overtighten the union nuts.

6 When refitting hoses to the calipers, always use new copper washers and tighten the banjo union bolts to the specified torque. Make sure that the hoses are positioned so that they will not touch surrounding bodywork or the roadwheels.

7 Ensure that the pipes and hoses are correctly routed, with no kinks, and that they are secured in the clips or brackets provided. After fitting, remove the polythene from the reservoir, and bleed the hydraulic system as described in Section 2. Wash off any spilt fluid, and check carefully for fluid leaks.

4 Front brake pads – renewal

Warning: Renew both sets of front brake pads at the same time – never renew the pads on only one wheel, as uneven braking may result. Note that the dust created by wear of the pads may contain asbestos, which is a health hazard. Never blow it out with compressed air, and don't inhale any of it. An approved filtering mask should be worn when working on the brakes. DO NOT use petrol or petroleum-based solvents to clean brake parts; use brake cleaner or methylated spirit only.

1 Apply the handbrake, then slacken the front roadwheel bolts. Jack up the front of the vehicle and support it on axle stands (see *Jacking and vehicle support*). Remove both front roadwheels.

2 One of two types of front brake caliper maybe fitted. For the most common caliper accompanying photos **(illustrations 4.2a to 4.2p)** for the pad renewal procedure. Where the second type of caliper differs follow the second set of photographs in conjunction with the first set **(see illustrations 4.2q to 4.2y)**. Be sure to stay in order and read the caption under each illustration, and note the following points:

a) New pads may have an adhesive foil on the backplates. Remove this foil prior to installation.

b) Thoroughly clean the caliper guide surfaces, and apply a little brake assembly grease (Molykote P37 or Copperslip).

c) When pushing the caliper piston back to accommodate new pads, keep a close eye on the fluid level in the reservoir.

Caution: Pushing back the piston causes a reverse-flow of brake fluid, which has been known to 'flip' the master cylinder rubber seals, resulting in a total loss of braking. To avoid this, clamp the caliper flexible hose and open the bleed screw – as the piston is pushed back, the fluid can be directed into a suitable container using a hose attached to the bleed screw. Close the screw just before the piston is pushed fully back, to ensure no air enters the system.

3 Depress the brake pedal repeatedly, until the pads are pressed into firm contact with the brake disc, and normal (non-assisted) pedal pressure is restored.

4 Repeat the above procedure on the remaining front brake caliper.

5 Refit the roadwheels, then lower the vehicle to the ground and tighten the roadwheel bolts to the specified torque.

6 Check the hydraulic fluid level as described in *Weekly checks*.

Caution: New pads will not give full braking efficiency until they have bedded-in. Be prepared for this, and avoid hard braking as far as possible for the first hundred miles or so after pad renewal.

4.2a Use screwdrivers to press the retaining spring away from the wheel hub, and detach it from the caliper

4.2b Prise out the rubber caps ...

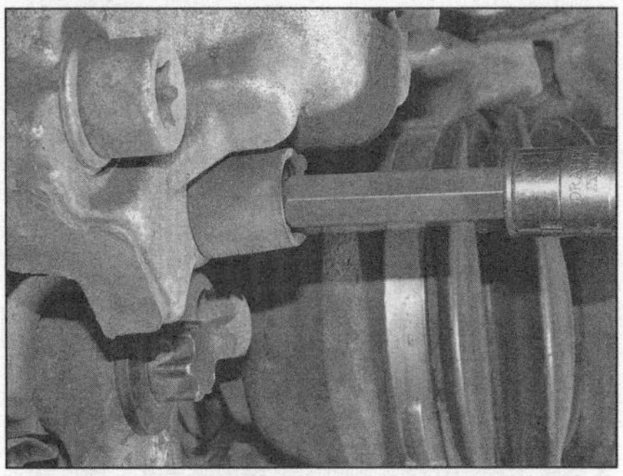

4.2c ... and use a 7 mm Allen bit/key to unscrew the upper and lower caliper guide pins

4.2d Lift away the caliper, complete with inner brake pad ...

4.2e ... then pull the outer pad from the caliper mounting bracket

4.2f Pull the inner pad from the caliper piston

4.2g Measure the thickness of the friction material – 2.0 mm is the minimum thickness

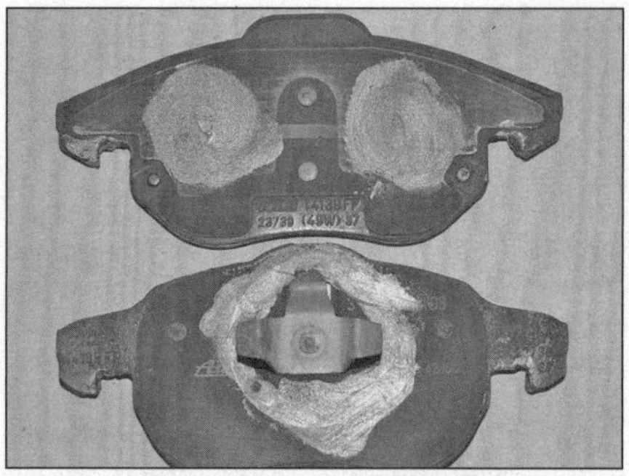
4.2h Apply a thin smear of high-temperature grease (Copperslip) to the rear of the brake pads as shown. Take care not to get any grease near the friction material

4.2i If new pads are being fitted, push the piston back into the caliper using a pad retraction tool or similar

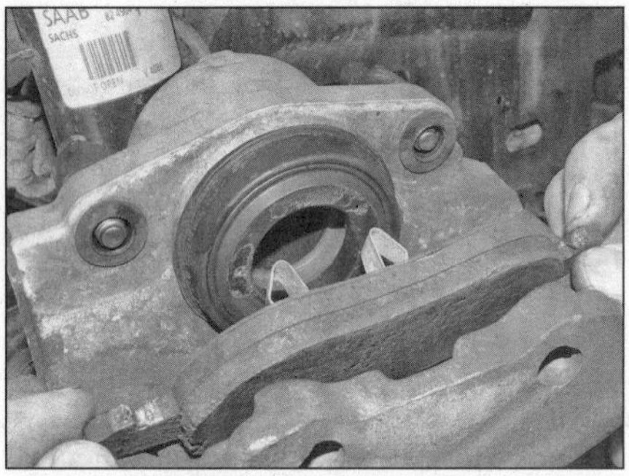
4.2j Clip the inner pad into the caliper piston

4.2k Fit the outer pad to the caliper bracket – friction material against the disc face ...

4.2l ... then fit the caliper over the pad, and into place on the caliper bracket

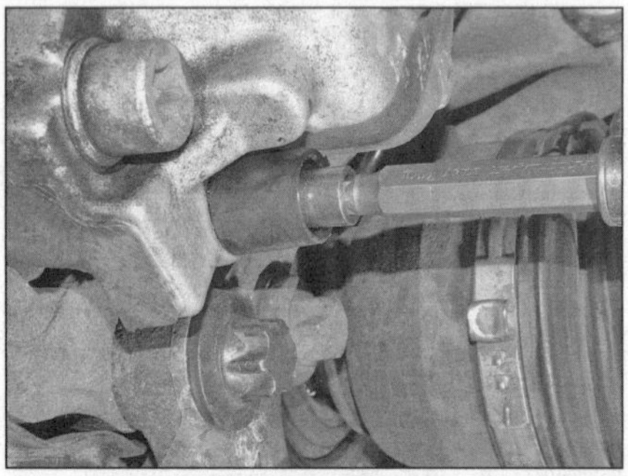
4.2m Screw the caliper guide pins into the bracket, and tighten them to the specified torque

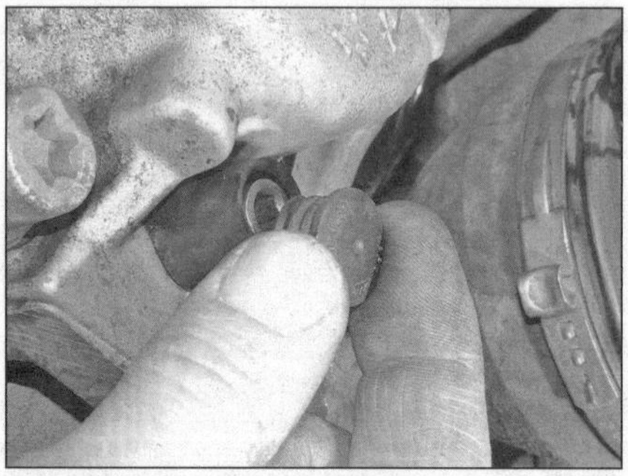
4.2n Refit the rubber caps

4.2o Fit the ends of the retaining spring against the caliper bracket lugs ...

4.2p ... then pull it away from the hub and engage the spring centre lugs with the holes in the caliper

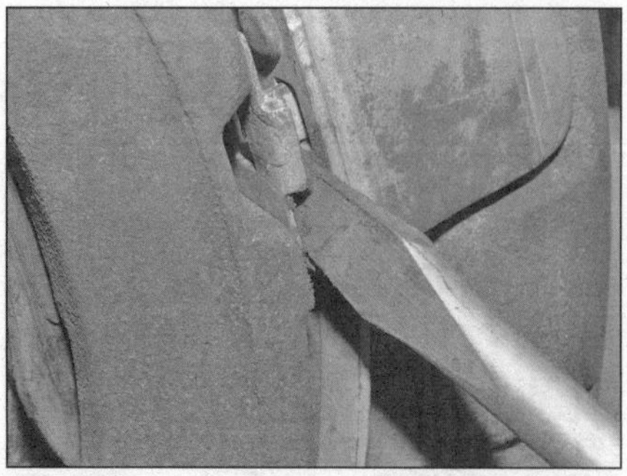
4.2q Release the spring on the alternative caliper

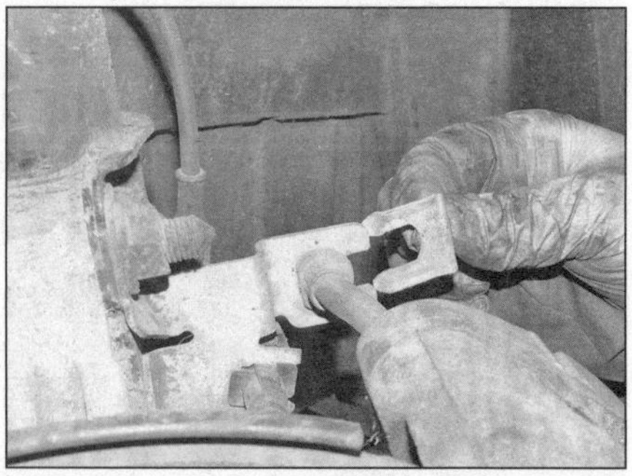
4.2r Remove the clip ...

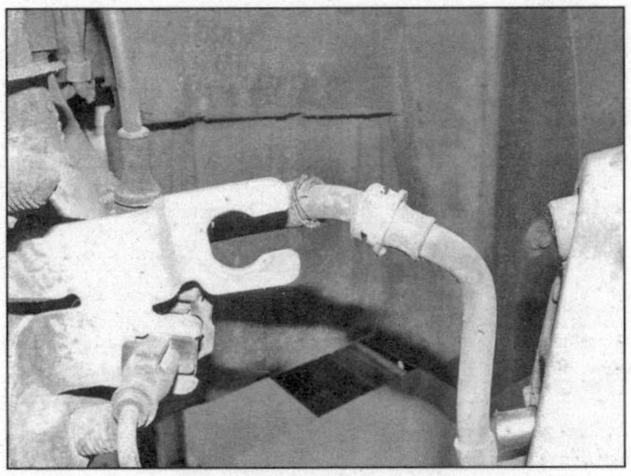

4.2s ... and release the brake hose from the support bracket

4.2t Remove the covers and then remove the upper and lower caliper guide pins

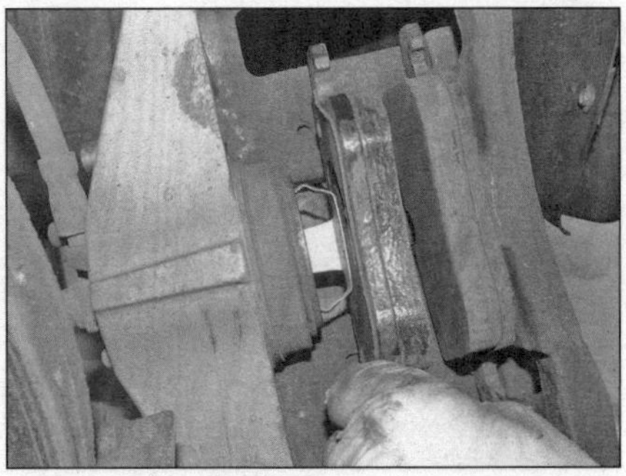

4.2u Lift of the caliper and remove the inner ...

4.2v ... and outer brake pads

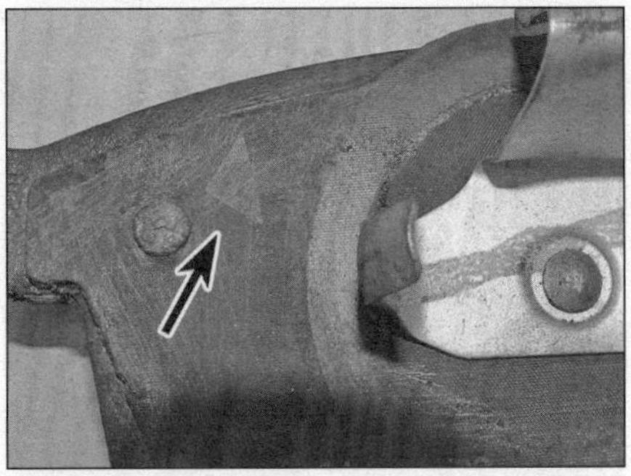

4.2w If new pads are fitted, push in the caliper (see illustration 4.2i) and fit the pads, noting the direction of rotation arrow on the pad (arrowed)

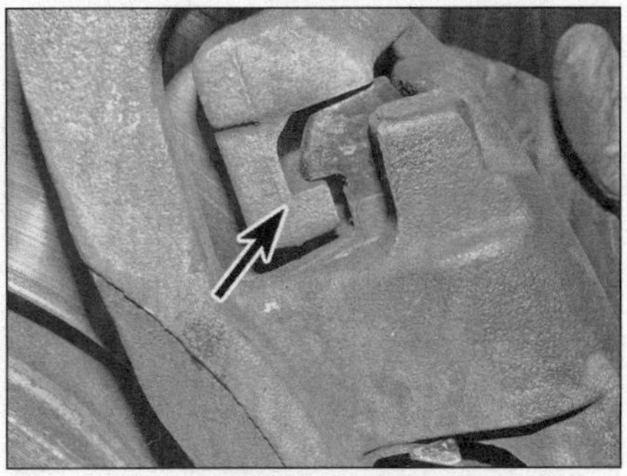

4.2x Fit the caliper, ensuring that the pads engage with the mounting bracket correctly (arrowed)

4.2y Refit the sliding pins and blanking plug and then refit the spring

5 Rear brake pads – renewal

Warning: Renew both sets of rear brake pads at the same time – never renew the pads on only one wheel, as uneven braking may result. Note that the dust created by wear of the pads may contain asbestos, which is a health hazard. Never blow it out with compressed air, and don't inhale any of it. An approved filtering mask should be worn when working on the brakes. DO NOT use petrol or petroleum-based solvents to clean brake parts; use brake cleaner or methylated spirit only.

1 Chock the front wheels, slacken the rear roadwheel bolts, then jack up the rear of the vehicle and support it on axle stands (see *Jacking and vehicle support*). Remove the rear wheels.

2 With the handbrake lever fully released, follow the accompanying photos **(see illustrations 5.2a to 5.2p)** for the pad renewal procedure. Be sure to stay in order and read the caption under each illustration, and note the following points:

a) *If re-installing the original pads, ensure they are fitted to their original positions.*

b) *Thoroughly clean the caliper guide surfaces and guide pins, and apply a little brake assembly grease (Molykote P37 or Copperslip).*

c) *If new pads are to be fitted, use a piston retraction tool to push the piston back and twist it clockwise at the same time – keep an eye on the fluid level in the reservoir whilst retracting the piston. Do not allow the rubber gaiter around the piston to revolve as the piston is rotated.*

Caution: Pushing back the piston causes a reverse-flow of brake fluid, which has been known to 'flip' the master cylinder rubber seals, resulting in a total loss of braking. To avoid this, clamp the caliper flexible hose and open the bleed screw – as the piston is pushed back, the fluid can be directed into a suitable container using a hose attached to the bleed screw. Close the screw just before the piston is pushed fully back, to ensure no air enters the system.

3 Depress the brake pedal repeatedly, until the pads are pressed into firm contact with the brake disc, and normal (non-assisted) pedal pressure is restored.

4 Repeat the above procedure on the remaining brake caliper.

5 If necessary, adjust the handbrake as described in Section 13.

6 Refit the roadwheels, then lower the vehicle to the ground and tighten the roadwheel bolts to the specified torque.

7 Check the hydraulic fluid level as described in *Weekly checks*.

Caution: New pads will not give full braking efficiency until they have bedded-in. Be prepared for this, and avoid hard braking as far as possible for the first hundred miles or so after pad renewal.

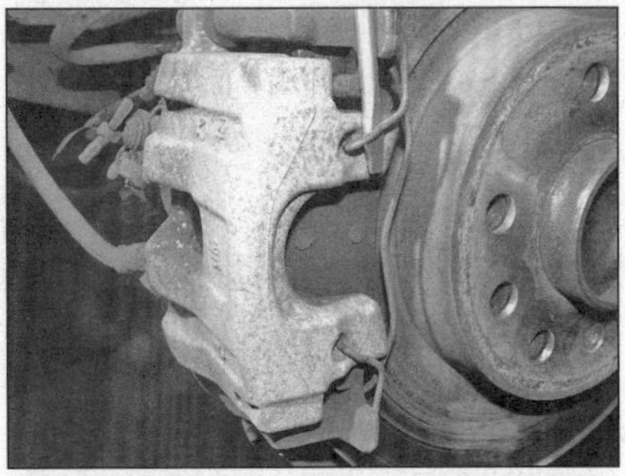

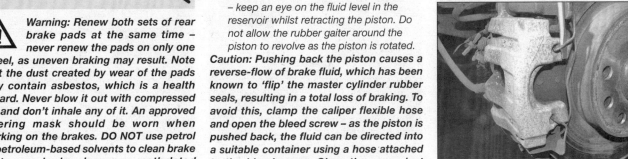

5.2a Prise off the retaining spring with a screwdriver

5.2b Pull out the rubber caps ...

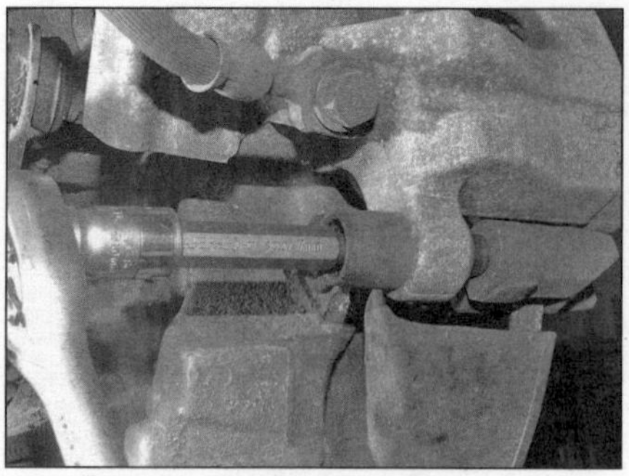

5.2c ... and undo the caliper guide pins at the top and bottom of the caliper

5.2d Lift the caliper from place (don't allow the weight of the caliper to hang on the hose)

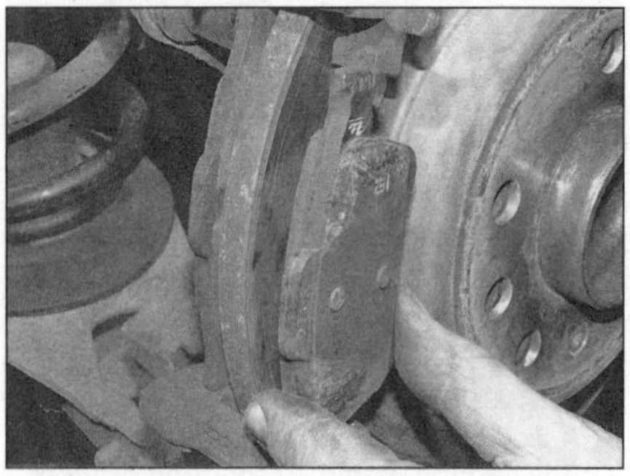

5.2e Remove the outer brake pad ...

5.2f ... followed by the inner pad

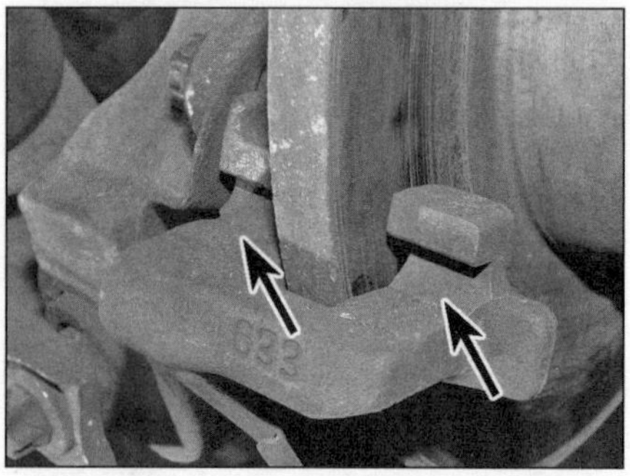

5.2g Use a wire brush to clean the pad mounting area of the caliper bracket (arrowed)

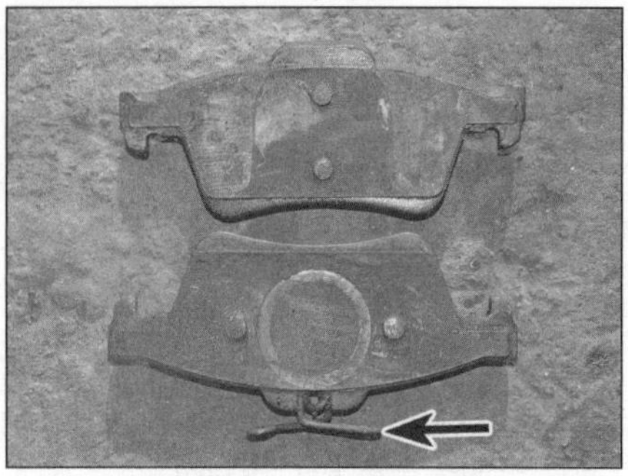

5.2h An anti-rattle spring is riveted to the inner pad (arrowed)

5.2i Fit the inner pad, friction side to the disc ...

5.2j Followed by the outer pad

5.2k If new pads are fitted, the caliper piston must be rotated clockwise, at the same time as being pushed back into the housing – use a piston retraction tool

5.2l Fit the caliper ...

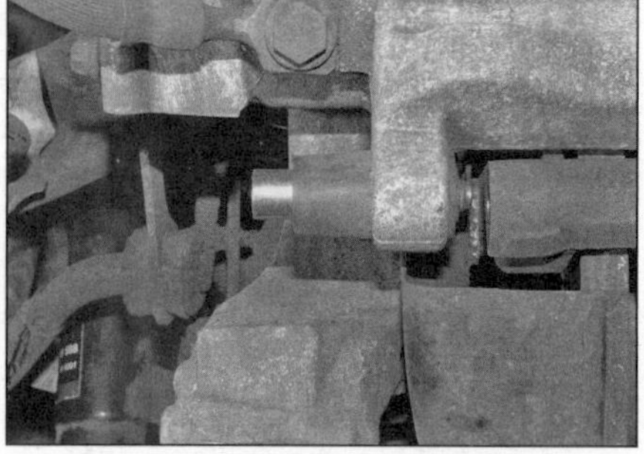

5.2m ... insert the guide pins ...

5.2n ... and tighten them to the specified torque

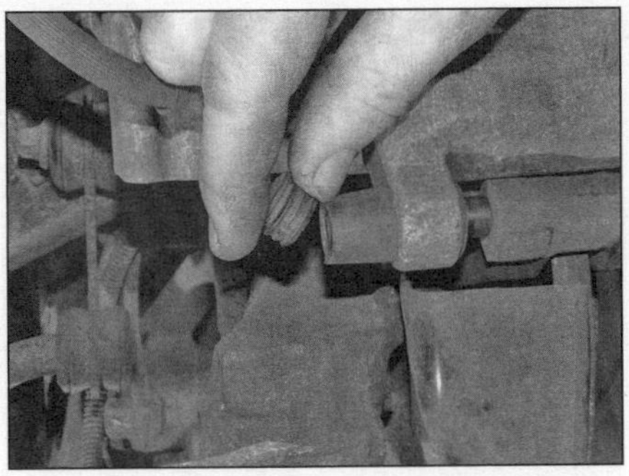

5.2o Refit the rubber caps ...

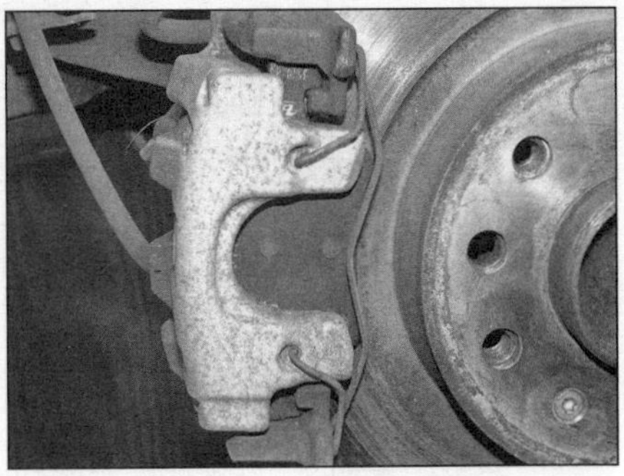

5.2p ... followed by the retaining spring

6 Front brake caliper – removal, overhaul and refitting

Removal

1 Apply the handbrake, then jack up the front of the vehicle and support it on axle stands (see *Jacking and vehicle support*). Remove the roadwheel.

2 Minimise fluid loss by first removing the master cylinder reservoir cap, then tightening it down onto a piece of polythene to obtain an airtight seal. Alternatively, use a brake hose clamp to clamp the flexible hose leading to the brake caliper.

3 Clean the area around the caliper brake hose union. Note the fitted angle of the hose (to ensure correct refitting), then unscrew and remove the union bolt and recover the copper sealing washer from each side of the hose union. Discard the washers; new ones must be used on refitting. Plug the hose end and caliper hole, to minimise fluid loss and prevent the ingress of dirt into the hydraulic system.

4 Remove the brake pads as described in Section 4, then remove the caliper from the vehicle.

5 If necessary, unbolt the caliper mounting bracket from the hub carrier **(see illustration)**.

Overhaul

6 With the caliper on the bench, clean away all external dirt and debris.

7 Prise out and remove the dust seal **(see illustration)**.

8 Withdraw the partially-ejected piston from the caliper body. The piston can be withdrawn by hand, if pushed out by applying compressed air to the brake hose union hole. Only low pressure compressed air should be used, such as is generated by a foot pump **(see illustration)**.

9 Carefully remove the piston seal from the caliper, taking care not to mark the caliper bore **(see illustration)**.

10 Thoroughly clean all components, using brake cleaning fluid, or methylated spirit. Never use mineral-based solvents such as petrol or paraffin, which will attach the hydraulic systems rubber components. Dry the components immediately using compressed air, or a clean lint-free cloth.

11 Check the caliper bore for scratches or corrosion. If in doubt, renew the components.

12 Soak the piston and the new seal in the clean hydraulic fluid. Smear clean fluid around the caliper bore.

13 Fit the new piston seal into the groove in the caliper bore using fingers only **(see illustration)**.

14 Fit the new dust seal to the piston, and fit the piston into the caliper bore using a twisting motion, ensuring the piston enters the bore squarely. Press the dust seal fully into the caliper body, and push the piston fully into the caliper bore.

Refitting

15 Locate the caliper mounting bracket on the hub carrier, then apply locking fluid to the threads of the mounting screws, insert them, and tighten to the specified torque.

16 Refit the brake pads as described in

6.5 Caliper bracket mounting Torx screws (arrowed)

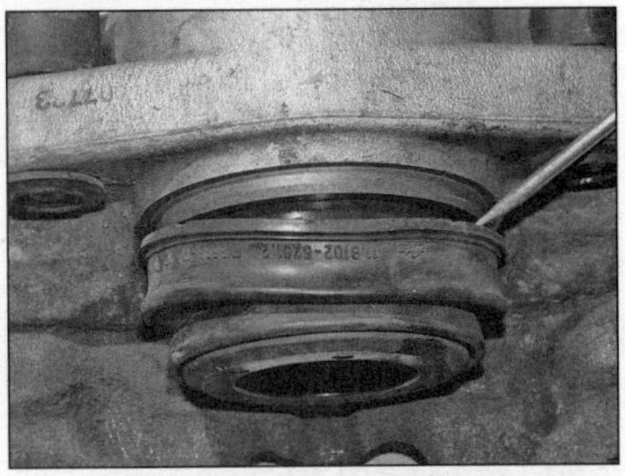

6.7 Prise off the dust seal

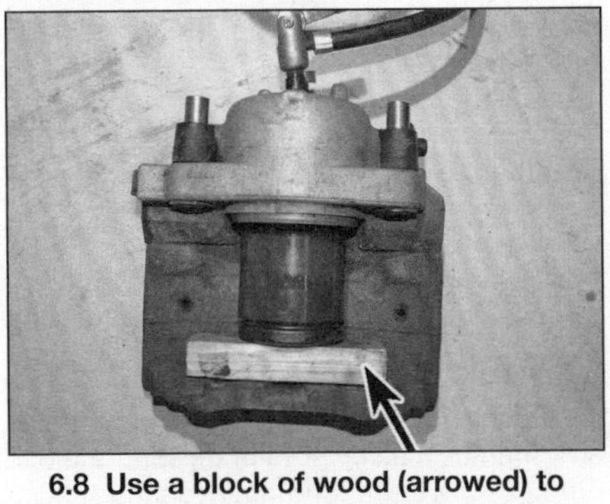

6.8 Use a block of wood (arrowed) to prevent damage to the piston or caliper when ejecting the piston

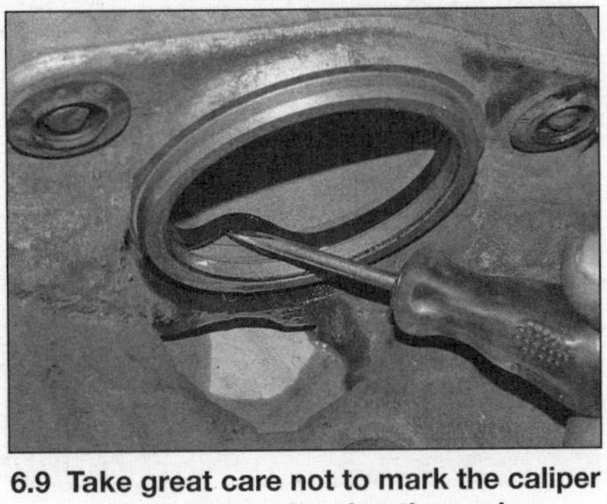

6.9 Take great care not to mark the caliper bore when removing the seal

6.13 Fit the new seal into the groove in the caliper bore

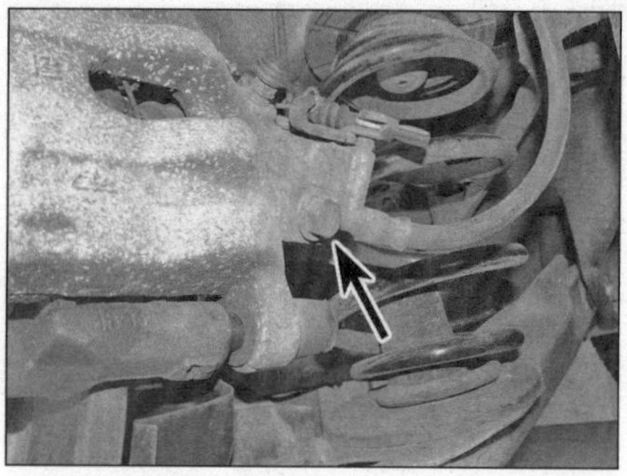

7.4 Rear brake hose union bolt (arrowed)

Section 4, together with the caliper which at this stage will not have the hose attached.

17 Position a new copper sealing washer on each side of the hose union, and connect the brake hose to the caliper. Ensure that the hose is correctly positioned against the caliper body lug, then install the union bolt and tighten securely.

18 Remove the brake hose clamp or the polythene, where fitted, and bleed the hydraulic system as described in Section 2. Note that, providing the precautions described were taken to minimise brake fluid loss, it should only be necessary to bleed the relevant front brake.

19 Refit the roadwheel, then lower the vehicle to the ground and tighten the roadwheel bolts to the specified torque.

7 Rear brake caliper – removal and refitting

Note: *No service parts are available for the rear caliper. If the caliper is faulty or leaking fluid it must be replaced with a new or exchange unit.*

Removal

1 Chock the front wheels, then jack up the rear of the vehicle and support on axle stands (see *Jacking and vehicle support*). Remove the roadwheel.

2 Slacken the handbrake cable adjusting nut, unhook the inner cable from the lever on the caliper, then detach the outer cable from the caliper bracket **(see illustration 14.6)**.

8.7 Use a micrometer to measure the thickness of the brake disc

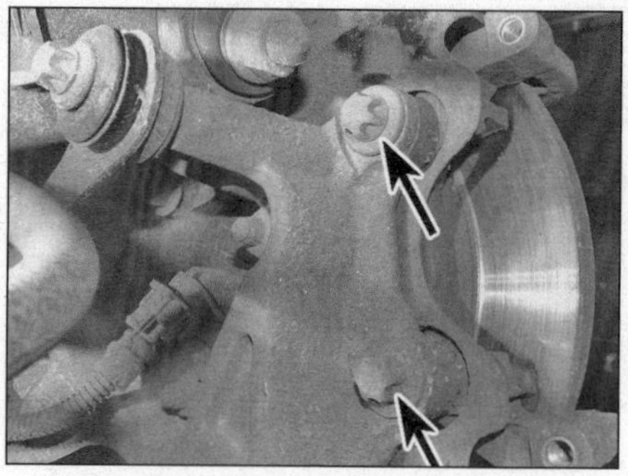

7.7 Caliper bracket mounting bolts (arrowed)

3 Minimise fluid loss by first removing the master cylinder reservoir cap, then tightening it down onto a piece of polythene to obtain an airtight seal. Alternatively, use a brake hose clamp on the flexible hose leading to the brake line on the rear axle.

4 Clean the area around the hydraulic hose union bolt, then loosen the bolt **(see illustration)**. Do not fully unscrew the bolt at this stage.

5 Remove the brake pads as described in Section 5.

6 Fully unscrew the union nut and disconnect the hydraulic line from the caliper, then withdraw the caliper from the disc. Tape over or plug the hydraulic line to prevent entry of dust and dirt.

7 If required, undo the 2 bolts and remove the caliper mounting bracket from the hub carrier **(see illustration)**.

Refitting

8 Locate the caliper mounting bracket on the hub carrier, then apply locking fluid to the threads of the mounting bolts, insert them, and tighten to the specified torque.

9 Reconnect the hydraulic hose to the caliper using new sealing washer each side of the banjo. Do not fully tighten the banjo bolt at this stage.

10 Refit the brake pads (see Section 5).

11 Fully tighten the hydraulic union bolt.

12 Remove the polythene, where fitted, and bleed the hydraulic system as described in Section 2. Note that, providing the precautions described were taken to minimise brake fluid loss, it should only be necessary to bleed the relevant rear brake.

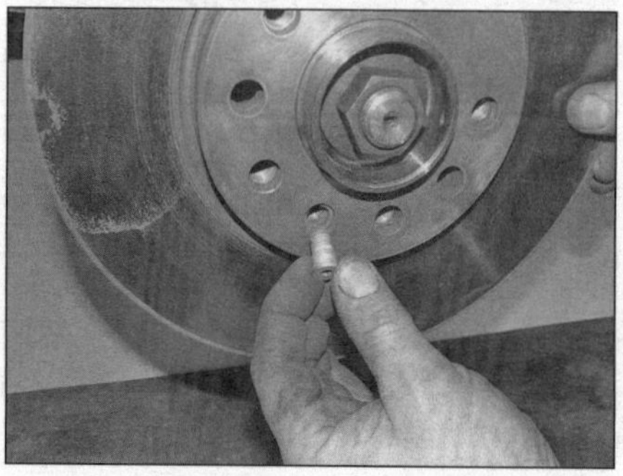

8.11 Undo the disc retaining screw

13 Adjust the handbrake as described in Section 13.

14 Refit the roadwheel, then lower the vehicle to the ground and tighten the roadwheel bolts to the specified torque.

8 Front brake disc – inspection, removal and refitting

Inspection

1 Apply the handbrake, then jack up the front of the vehicle and support it on axle stands (*see Jacking and vehicle support*). Remove both front roadwheels.

2 For an accurate check and for access to each side of the disc, the brake caliper should be unbolted and suspended to one side as described in Section 4.

3 Check that the brake disc securing screw is tight, then fit spacers approximately 10.0 mm thick to each of the roadwheel bolts, and refit and tighten the bolts. This will hold the disc in its normal running position.

4 Rotate the brake disc, and examine it for deep scoring or grooving. Light scoring is normal, but if excessive, the disc should be removed and either renewed or machined (within the specified limits) by an engineering works. The minimum thickness is given in the Specifications at the beginning of this Chapter.

5 Using a dial gauge, or a flat metal block and feeler blades, check that the disc run-out does not exceed the figure given in the Specifications.

6 If the disc run-out is excessive, remove the disc as described later, and check that the disc-to-hub surfaces are perfectly clean. Refit the disc and check the run-out again. If the run-out is still excessive, the disc should be renewed.

7 Using a micrometer check that the disc thickness is not less than that given in the Specifications. Take readings at several points around the disc **(see illustration)**.

8 Repeat the inspection on the other front brake disc.

Removal

9 Remove the roadwheel bolts and spacers used when checking the disc.

10 Remove the disc pads as described in Section 4, then tie the caliper to one side. Also remove the front brake caliper mounting bracket with reference to Section 6.

11 Remove the securing screw and withdraw the disc from the hub. If the screw is tight, use an impact driver to loosen it **(see illustration)**.

Refitting

12 Refitting is a reversal of removal, but make sure that the mating faces of the disc and hub are perfectly clean, and apply a little locking fluid to the threads of the securing screw before tightening it. If a new disc is being

9.7 Use a micrometer to measure the thickness of the disc

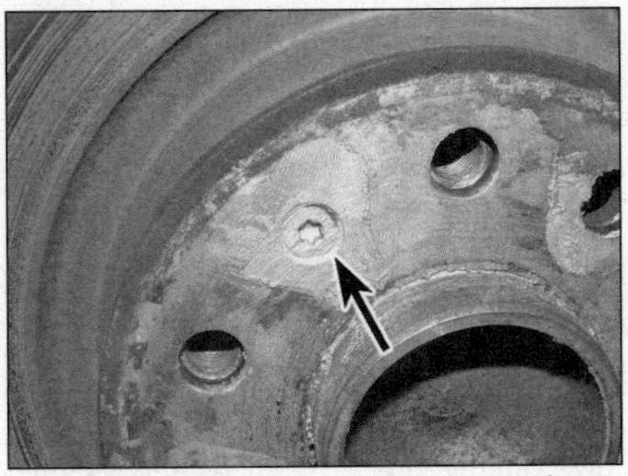
9.11a Undo the disc retaining Torx screw (arrowed) ...

9.11b ... and pull the disc from place

fitted, remove the protective coating from the surface, using an appropriate solvent. Refit the disc pads as described in Section 4, then refit the roadwheel and lower the vehicle to the ground.

9 Rear brake disc – inspection, removal and refitting

Inspection

1 Chock the front wheels, then jack up the rear of the vehicle and support on axle stands (see *Jacking and vehicle support*). Remove both rear roadwheels.

2 For an accurate check and for access to each side of the disc, remove the brake pads as described in Section 5, then suspend the brake caliper from the vehicle suspension/body to prevent any strain on the rubber hose.

3 Check that the brake disc securing screw is tight, then fit spacers approximately 10.0 mm thick to each of the roadwheel bolts, and refit and tighten the bolts. This will hold the disc in its normal running position.

4 Rotate the brake disc, and examine it for deep scoring or grooving. Light scoring is normal, but if excessive, the disc should be removed and either renewed or machined (within the specified limits) by an engineering works. The minimum thickness is given in the Specifications at the beginning of this Chapter.

5 Using a dial gauge, or a flat metal block and feeler blades, check that the disc run-out does not exceed the figure given in the Specifications.

6 If the disc run-out is excessive, remove the disc as described later, and check that the disc-to-hub surfaces are perfectly clean. Refit the disc and check the run-out again. If the run-out is still excessive, the disc should be renewed.

7 Using a micrometer check that the disc thickness is not less than that given in the Specifications. Take readings at several points around the disc **(see illustration)**.

8 Repeat the inspection on the other rear brake disc.

Removal

9 Remove the roadwheel bolts and spacers used when checking the disc.

10 Remove the caliper mounting bracket from the hub carrier as described in Section 7.

11 Remove the securing screw and withdraw the disc from the hub **(see illustrations)**.

Refitting

12 Refitting is a reversal of removal, but make sure that the mating faces of the disc and hub are perfectly clean, and apply a little locking fluid to the threads of the securing screw before tightening it. If a new disc is being fitted, remove the protective coating from the surface, using an appropriate solvent. Adjust the handbrake as described in Section 13, then refit the roadwheel and lower the vehicle to the ground.

10 Master cylinder – removal, overhaul and refitting

Removal

1 Exhaust the vacuum present in the brake servo unit by repeatedly depressing the brake pedal.

2 On left-hand drive models, move the coolant reservoir to one side – no need to disconnect the hoses.

3 Disconnect the wiring from the brake fluid level warning switch **(see illustration)**.

4 Siphon out the fluid from the reservoir. Alternatively, open any convenient bleed screw in the system, and gently pump the brake pedal to expel the fluid through a plastic tube connected to the bleed screw (see Section 2).

Warning: Do not siphon the fluid by mouth, as it is poisonous; use a syringe or an old poultry baster.

5 Place cloth rags beneath the master cylinder to catch spilt fluid.

6 On manual transmission models, disconnect the clutch hydraulic hose from the brake fluid reservoir.

7 On right-hand drive petrol models, remove the air intake hose.

8 On right-hand drive diesel models, remove the air filter assembly as described in Chapter 4B, Section 3.

9 Note the position of the brake lines, then unscrew the union nuts and move the lines to one side so that they are just clear of the master cylinder. Do not bend the brake lines excessively. If available, use a split spanner to unscrew the nuts, as they can be very tight. Tape over or plug the outlets of the brake lines and master cylinder.

10 Unscrew the mounting nuts and withdraw the master cylinder from the front of the vacuum servo. Wrap the master cylinder in cloth rags and remove it from the engine compartment. Take care not to spill fluid on the vehicle paintwork.

11 Undo the retaining bolt, and detach the reservoir from the master cylinder **(see illustration)**.

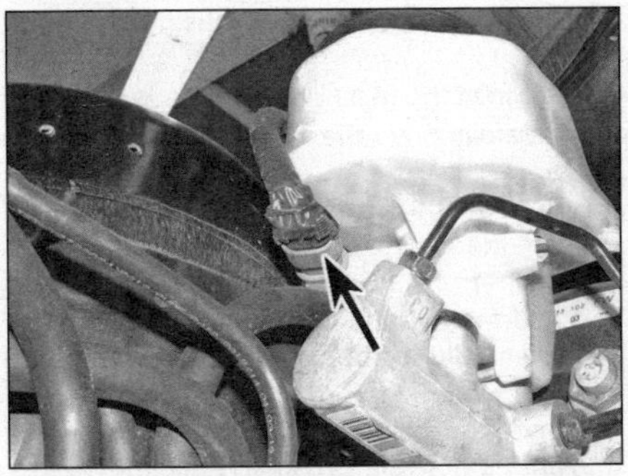
10.3 Disconnect the fluid level warning switch (arrowed)

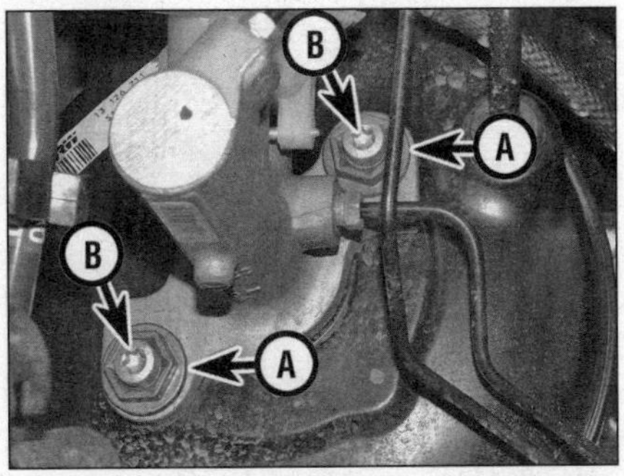

10.11 Master cylinder mounting nuts (A) and vacuum servo unit studs (B)

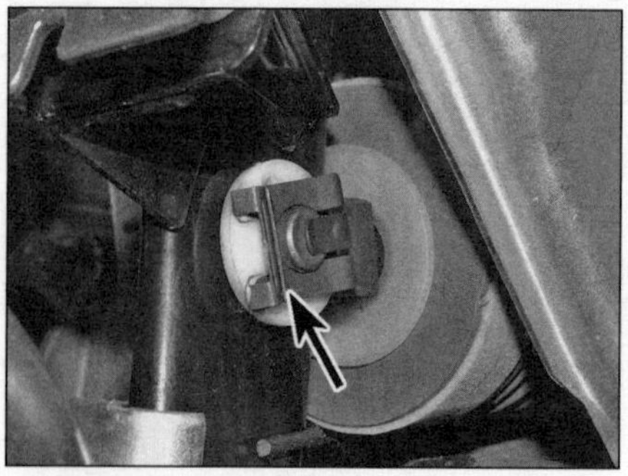

11.6 Lever up the edge of the clip (arrowed) and slide it from place

Overhaul

12 The only parts available to repair the master cylinder are the seals that locate the reservoir and the reservoir level sensor. If the cylinder itself is faulty, it must be renewed as a complete unit.

Refitting

13 Refit the reservoir to the master cylinder body, and tighten the retaining bolt (where applicable).
14 Ensure the mating surfaces are clean and dry then, fit the master cylinder to the studs on the vacuum servo unit, ensuring that the servo unit pushrod makes contact with the master cylinder pushrod. Apply thread-locking compound, and tighten the retaining nuts to the specified torque.
15 Remove the tape or plugs, and reconnect the brake lines to the master cylinder. Tighten the union nuts initially with fingers to prevent cross-threading, then fully tighten them with a spanner.
16 On manual transmission models, reconnect the clutch hydraulic hose to the brake fluid reservoir.
17 Fill the fluid reservoir with fresh brake fluid up to the MAX level mark.
18 Reconnect the wiring to the brake fluid warning switch.
19 On left-hand drive models, refit the coolant reservoir.
20 Bleed the hydraulic system as described in Section 2. Thoroughly check the operation of the braking system before using the vehicle on the road.
21 Refit the air intake hose or air cleaner assembly as applicable.

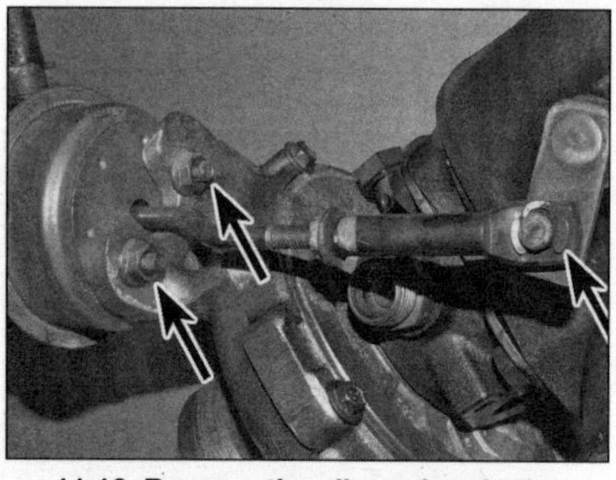

11.16 Remove the clip and undo the diaphragm unit nuts (arrowed)

11 Vacuum servo unit – testing, removal and refitting

Testing

1 To test the operation of the servo unit, with the engine off, depress the footbrake several times to dissipate the vacuum. Now start the engine, keeping the pedal firmly depressed. As the engine starts, there should be a noticeable 'give' in the brake pedal as the vacuum builds-up. Allow the engine to run for at least two minutes, then switch it off. The brake pedal should now feel normal, but further applications should result in the pedal feeling firmer, the pedal stroke decreasing with each application.
2 If the servo does not operate as described, first ensure the servo unit check valve allows air to pass in only one direction (servo-to-manifold/pump). If this appears to function correctly, the fault may lie with the servo unit itself. Repairs to the unit are not possible; if faulty, the servo unit must be renewed.

Right-hand drive models

Removal

3 Disconnect the battery negative lead as described in Chapter 5A, Section 4.
4 Remove the brake master cylinder as described in Section 10.
5 Remove the lower facia panel on the driver's side, as described in Chapter 11, Section 26.
6 Release the clip and remove the pin securing the servo pushrod to the brake pedal **(see illustration)**.
7 On petrol models, remove the air cleaner housing as described in Chapter 4A, Section 2.
8 Remove the crankcase ventilation hose from the turbo and cylinder head cover, then detach the turbocharger intake hoses.
9 Raise the front of the vehicle and support it securely on axle stands (see *Jacking and vehicle support*). On diesel models, undo the fasteners and remove the engine undershield.
10 Position a trolley jack under the engine, with a block of wood between the jack head and the sump. Take the weight of the engine.
11 Remove the right-hand engine mounting bolts and lower the engine approximately 30 mm.
12 On petrol models, remove the turbocharger heat shield.
13 Remove the bulkhead heat shield.
14 Carefully prise the vacuum hose from the servo.
15 Release the brake pipes from the retaining clips on the engine compartment bulkhead.
16 On petrol models, remove the retaining clip and remove the diaphragm unit from the turbo **(see illustration)**. Place the diaphragm unit to on side.
17 Undo the retaining bolt and move the coolant pipe at the cylinder head downwards approximately 20 mm.
18 Undo the 2 bolts securing the servo to the bulkhead, then manoeuvre the servo from position.

Refitting

19 Locate the servo unit on the bulkhead, then apply locking fluid to the threads of the upper mounting bracket bolts, insert and tighten them to the specified torque.
20 Inside the vehicle, connect the pushrod to the pedal, then insert the pivot pin and secure with the spring clip.
21 The remainder of refitting is a reversal of removal. On completion, start the engine and check for air leaks at the vacuum hose-to-servo unit connection. Check the operation of the braking system.

Left-hand drive models

Removal

22 Remove the ABS/TCS/ESP hydraulic unit as described in Section 19.
23 Remove the brake master cylinder as described in Section 10.
24 Remove the lower facia panel from the driver's side as described in Chapter 11, Section 26.
25 Release the retaining clip, and remove the clevis pin securing the servo pushrod to the brake pedal.
26 Raise the front of the vehicle and support it securely on axle stands (see *Jacking and vehicle support*). Undo the fasteners and remove the engine undershield.
27 Position a trolley jack under the transmission, with a block of wood between the jack head and the base of the transmission. Take the weight of the engine.
28 Remove the left-hand engine/transmission mounting bolts and lower the engine approximately 30 mm.
29 Carefully ease the vacuum hose from the servo.
30 Unscrew and remove the mounting bolts, then manoeuvre the servo from position.

Refitting

31 Locate the servo unit on the bulkhead with a new gasket, and at the same time engage the pushrod with the pedal. Apply some thread-locking compound and tighten the retaining bolts to the specified torque.
32 Inside the vehicle, connect the pushrod to the pedal, then insert the pivot pin and secure with the spring clip.
33 The remainder of refitting is a reversal of removal. On completion, start the engine and check for air leaks at the vacuum hose-to-servo unit connection. Check the operation of the braking system.

12 Vacuum pump – removal and refitting

Removal

Petrol models

1 The vacuum pump is bolted directly to the

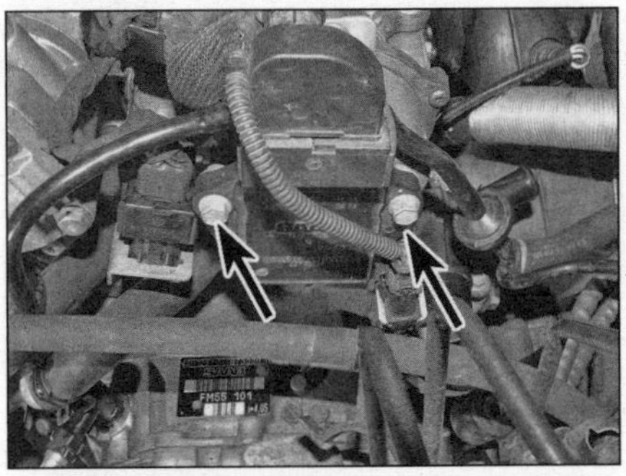
12.2 Undo the bolts (arrowed) and move aside the CDM

12.3 Depress the tab (arrowed) and disconnect the vacuum hose

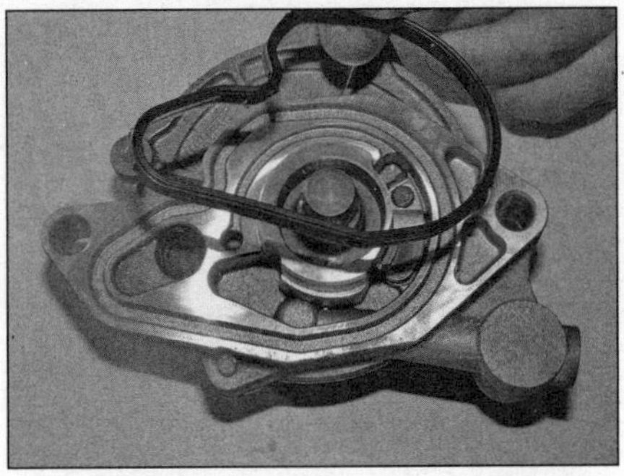
12.5 Renew the vacuum pump seal

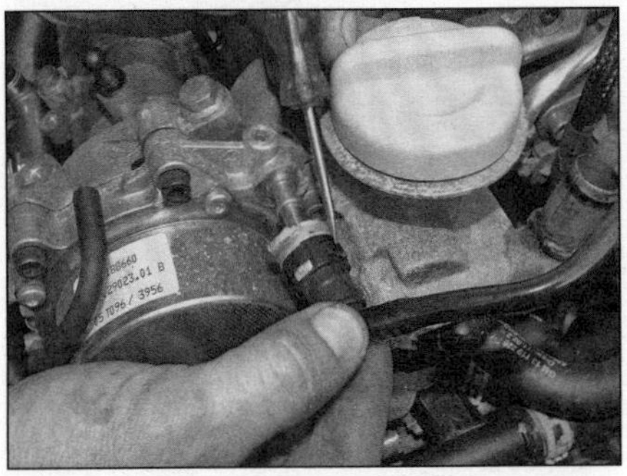
12.7a Disconnect the quick-release fitting and detach the servo unit vacuum hose ...

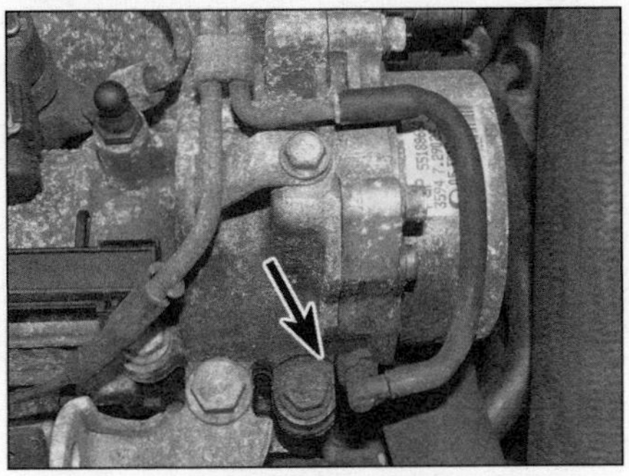
12.7b ... followed by the small vacuum hose (arrowed)

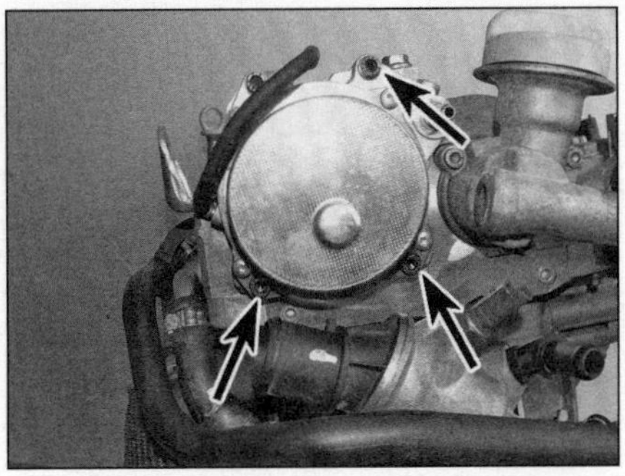
12.8 Vacuum pump retaining bolts (arrowed)

left-hand end of the cylinder head. First, undo the 3 Torx screws and remove the engine top cover.

2 Undo the 2 retaining bolts and move the CDM (combustion detection module) to one side **(see illustration)**.

3 Depress the release tab, and disconnect the vacuum hose from the pump **(see illustration)**.

4 Undo the 2 pump retaining bolts and move the bracket to one side.

5 Pull the pump from the end of the camshaft, and recover the O-ring seal. Be prepared for oil spillage. Discard all seals as new ones must be used for refitting **(see illustration)**.

Diesel models

6 The vacuum pump is bolted directly to the left-hand end of the cylinder head. First, pull the engine top cover upwards from place.

7 Depress the release tab, and disconnect the main vacuum hose from the pump. Disconnect the small vacuum hose also **(see illustrations)**.

8 Unscrew the mounting bolts, and withdraw the pump from the cylinder head **(see illustration)**.

9 Remove the O-ring from the groove in the pump. Discard the O-ring and obtain a new one.

Refitting

10 Refitting is a reversal of removal, but note the following additional points:

a) *Clean the mating faces of the pump and cylinder head, and fit new O-ring(s).*

b) *Position the pump drive dog so that it will engage with the slot in the end of the camshaft when refitted.*

c) *Tighten all nuts and bolts to the specified torque, where given.*

13 Handbrake – adjustment

1 It is normally only necessary to adjust the handbrake after dismantling or renewing the handbrake cables. First chock the front wheels, then jack up the rear of the vehicle and support on axle stands (see *Jacking and vehicle support*). Remove both rear wheels. Fully release the handbrake lever.

2 Check the distance between the caliper lever and the stop. It should be approximately 1.0 mm. If this is not the case, place a 1.0 mm feeler gauge between the lever and the stop on each side **(see illustration)**.

3 Working inside the vehicle, lift the armrest lid, and prise out the coin holder.

4 Tighten the adjusting bolt until the feeler gauges at the brake calipers become loose **(see illustration)**.

5 Refit the coin holder and close the armrest lid.

6 Firmly depress the brake pedal 3 times, then apply the handbrake and check both rear wheels are locked.

7 Release the lever and check that both wheels rotate freely.

8 On completion, lower the vehicle to the ground.

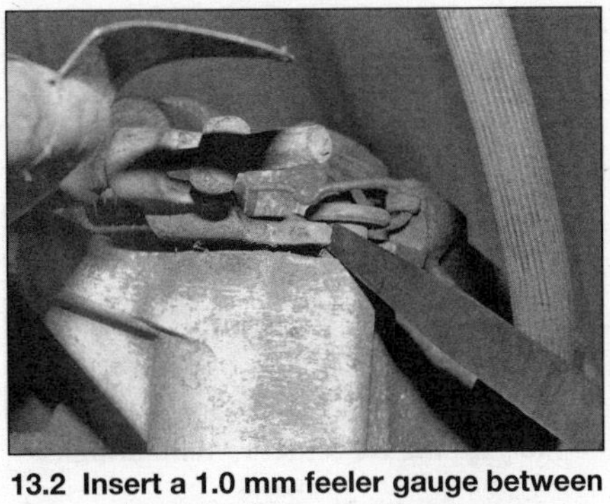
13.2 Insert a 1.0 mm feeler gauge between the cable lever and the stop

13.4 Handbrake adjusting bolt (arrowed)

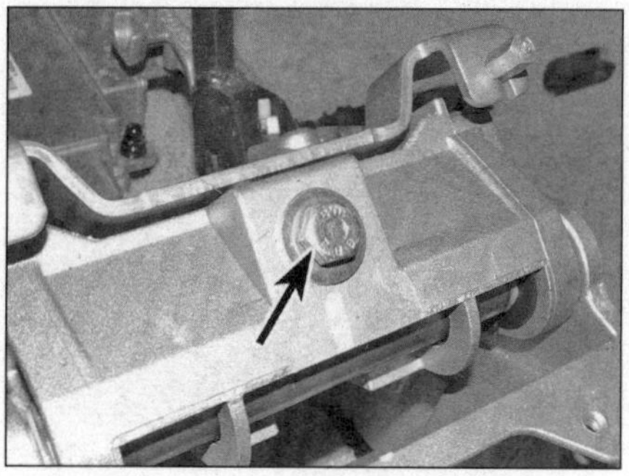

14.3a Slacken the adjuster bolt (arrowed) ...

14.3b ... disengage the cable end fitting from the plate ...

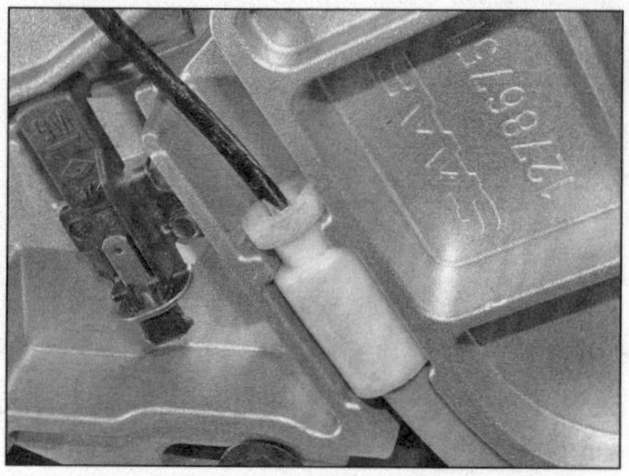

14.3c ... and the outer cable from the bracket

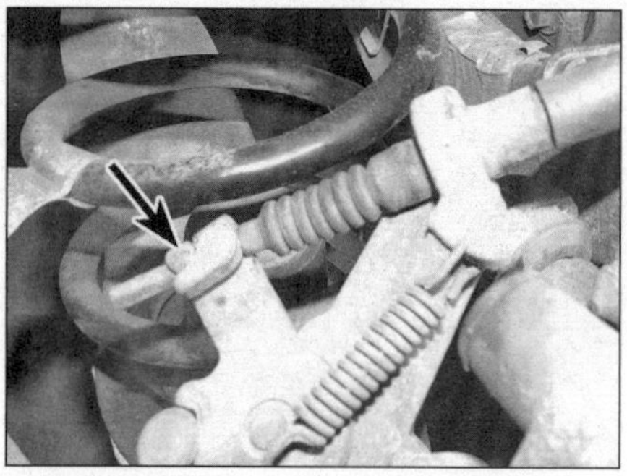

14.6 Pull the cable end fitting (arrowed) from the lever

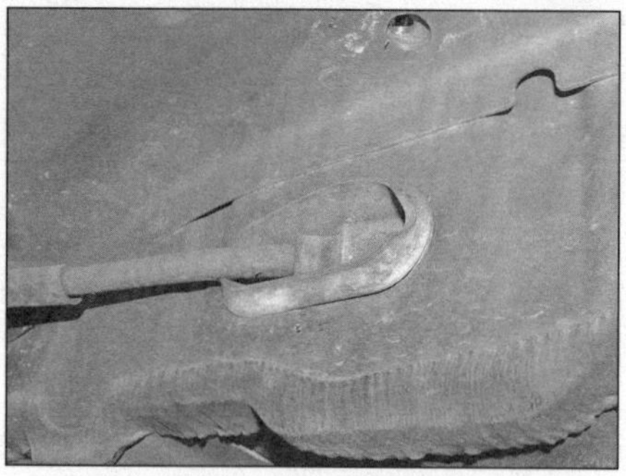

14.7 Prise out the rubber grommet

14 Handbrake cables – removal and refitting

Removal

1 First, chock the front wheels then jack up the rear of the vehicle and support on axle stands (see *Jacking and vehicle support*). Remove both rear roadwheels.

2 Remove the centre console as described in Chapter 11, Section 27.

3 Slacken the handbrake cable adjuster bolt, and detach the cable from the plate and the bracket **(see illustrations)**.

4 Remove the rear seat cushion as described in Chapter 11, Section 24.

5 Pull the carpet forward and release the handbrake cable from the clips on the floor.

6 Unhook the cable end fittings from the operating levers on the calipers, and pull the outer cable from the caliper bracket **(see illustration)**.

7 Release the cables from any retaining clips, prise out the rubber grommet and pull the cable from the vehicle **(see illustration)**.

8 Remove the remaining plastic ties and withdraw the cable components from under the vehicle.

Refitting

9 Refitting is a reversal of removal, but finally adjust the handbrake as described in Section 13.

15 Handbrake lever – removal and refitting

Removal

1 Remove the centre console as described in Chapter 11, Section 27.

2 Pull the rear air duct from place.

3 Slacken the handbrake cable adjusting bolt, and detach the cables from the brackets **(see illustrations 14.3a, 14.3b and 14.3c)**.

4 Mark the position of the front mounting nut on the lever assembly, then undo the retaining bolts/nuts and remove the lever assembly **(see illustration)**.

Refitting

5 Refitting is a reversal of removal, but finally adjust the handbrake as described in Section 13. Ensure the lever is the correct height in relation to the centre console before fitting the console side panels. If necessary, adjust the lever height by changing the washer beneath the lever. Tighten the handbrake lever mounting bolts securely.

16 Handbrake warning light switch – removal, testing and refitting

Removal

1 The handbrake ON warning light switch is mounted on the handbrake lever mounting bracket **(see illustration)**. Refer to Chapter 11, Section 27 and remove the centre console.

2 Disconnect the wiring from the switch.

3 Undo the mounting screw and remove the switch **(see illustration)**.

Testing

4 Connect a multimeter or battery test probe to the wiring contact and switch body.

15.4 Make the position of the front mounting nut (arrowed) before removing the handbrake bracket

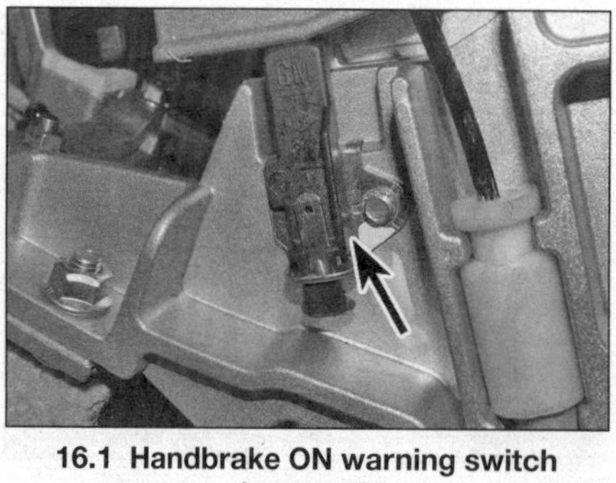

16.1 Handbrake ON warning switch (arrowed)

16.3 Handbrake ON warning switch retaining screw (arrowed) – viewed from the rear of the bracket

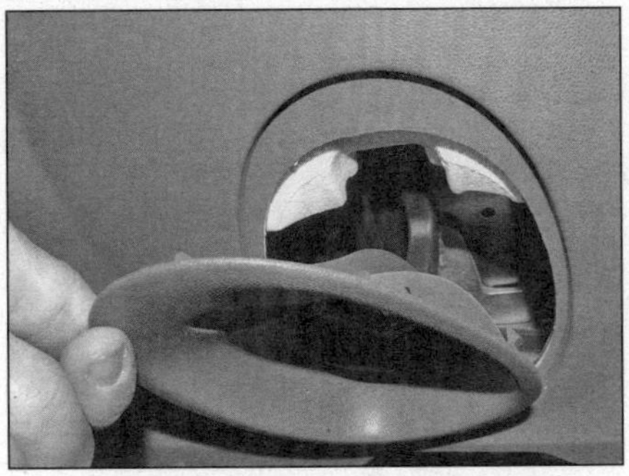

17.2 Prise out the steering column adjustment lever surround trim

5 With the switch plunger at rest, there should be continuity and the multimeter should read no resistance, or the test light should light. With the plunger depressed, there should be infinity resistance or the test light should be extinguished.

6 Failure to operate correctly may indicate corroded contacts or ultimately a faulty switch. Check that there is a 12 volt supply to the wiring with the ignition switched on. Renew the switch if necessary.

Refitting

7 Refitting is a reversal of removal.

17 Brake light switch – removal and refitting

Removal

1 Remove the driver's side lower facia panel as described in Chapter 11, Section 26.

2 Prise out and remove the steering column adjustment handle and trim surround **(see illustration).**

3 Depress the brake pedal and hold it down. **Note:** *In order to be able to depress the brake pedal sufficiently, there must be a vacuum in the brake servo. Either depress the pedal just after stopping the engine, or start the engine and depress the brake pedal.*

4 Pull out the switch pushrod and locking sleeve **(see illustration).**

5 Depress the locking clip and remove the switch **(see illustration).** Disconnect the wiring plug as the switch is withdrawn.

Refitting

6 Pull out the switch pushrod and locking sleeve.

7 Reconnect the switch wiring plug.

8 Depress the brake pedal as far as possible and hold it down. **Note:** *In order to be able to depress the brake pedal sufficiently, there must be a vacuum in the brake servo. Either depress the pedal just after stopping the engine, or start the engine and depress the brake pedal.*

9 Position the switch in the bracket, then press in the locking sleeve.

17.4 Prise the locking sleeve forward ...

10 Pull out the switch pushrod as far as possible, then release the pedal.

11 Refit the steering column adjustment handle and trim surround.

12 Refit the driver's side lower facia panel.

18 Anti-lock braking system (ABS) components – general information and fault finding

General information

1 The Anti-lock braking system (ABS) is managed by an electronic control unit (ECU), which has the capacity to monitor the status and condition of all the components in the system, including itself. If the ECU detects a fault, it responds by shutting down the ABS and illuminating the dashboard-mounted ABS warning light. Under these circumstances, conventional non-ABS braking is maintained. Note also that the warning light will be illuminated if the power supply to the ABS ECU is disconnected (eg, if the supply fuse blows).

2 If the ABS warning lights indicate a fault, it is very difficult to diagnose problems without the equipment and expertise to electronically 'interrogate' the ECU for fault codes. Therefore, this Section is limited firstly to a list of the basic checks that should be carried out to establish the integrity of the system.

3 If the cause of the fault cannot be immediately identified using the check list described, the only course of action open is to take the vehicle to a Saab dealer or specialist for examination. Dedicated test equipment is needed to interrogate the ABS ECU to determine the nature of the fault.

Basic fault finding checks

Brake fluid level

4 Check the brake fluid level (see *Weekly checks*). If the level is low, check the complete braking system for signs of leaks. Refer to Chapter 1A, Section 5 or Chapter 1B, Section 5 and carry out a check of the brake hoses and pipes throughout the vehicle. If no leaks are apparent, remove each roadwheel in turn, and check for leaks at the brake caliper pistons.

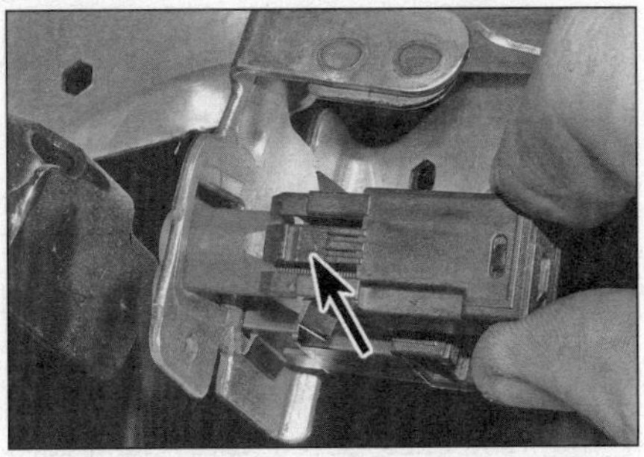

17.5 ... then depress the clip each side (arrowed) and pull the switch from the bracket

Fuses

5 The main fuses for the ABS/TCS/ESP are located in the instrument panel electrical centre (IPEC). Remove the end panel and pull out the relevant fuse. Visually check the fuse filaments; if it is difficult to see whether or not it has blown, use a multimeter to check the continuity of the fuse. If any of the fuses are blown, determine the cause before fitting a new one – if necessary, have the vehicle inspected by a Saab dealer or specialist.

Electrical connections and earthing points

6 The engine bay is a hostile environment for electrical connections, and even the best seals can sometimes be penetrated. Water, chemicals and air will induce corrosion on the connector's contacts and prevent good continuity, sometimes intermittently. Disconnect the battery negative cable, then check the security and condition of all connectors at the ABS hydraulic unit, situated on the left-hand side of the engine bay.

7 Unplug each connector, and examine the contacts inside. Clean any contacts that are found to be dirty or corroded. Avoid scraping the contacts clean with a blade, as this will accelerate corrosion later. Use a piece of lint-free cloth in conjunction with a proprietary cleaning solvent to produce a clean, shiny contact surface.

8 In addition, check the security and condition of the system electrical earthing point behind the ABS unit, attached to the suspension turret on the left-hand side of the engine compartment **(see illustration).**

18.8 Check the security of the earth connection (arrowed)

19 Anti-lock braking system (ABS) components – removal and refitting

Note: *If the ABS system is faulty, have it checked by a Saab dealer or specialist before removing any component.*

Front wheel sensor

1 The front wheel speed sensor is integral with the front wheel hub. Removal of the hub is described in Chapter 10, Section 2.

Rear wheel sensor

2 The rear wheel sensor is integral with the rear wheel hub. Removal of the hub is described in Chapter 10, Section 11.

ABS/TCS hydraulic/control unit

Note: *Before the hydraulic/control unit can be removed, the vehicles systems must be interrogated using specialist Saab diagnostic equipment (TECH 2), to reset and store various values, security codes, etc. If you do not have access to this equipment, entrust this task to a Saab dealer or specialist.*

Removal

3 Remove the battery and battery tray as described in Chapter 5A, Section 4.

4 Release the locking catch and disconnect the control unit wiring plug. Note that the unit is very sensitive to static electricity – earth yourself on the vehicle body prior to disconnect the wiring plug.

5 Note their fitted positions, then disconnect the brake pipes from the hydraulic unit. Be prepared for fluid spillage.

6 Remove the mounting bracket and earth connection from the suspension turret **(see illustration 18.8)**.

7 Lift up the unit, and undo the bolts securing the control unit. Pull the control unit from the hydraulic unit. If required, undo the bolts and detach the mounting bracket from the hydraulic unit.

Refitting

8 Refitting is a reversal of removal, but tighten the unit mounting nuts and the hydraulic brake pipe union nuts to the specified torque, and bleed the hydraulic system as described in Section 2. Once the procedure is complete, it may be necessary to reprogramme the control unit using Saab dedicated diagnostic equipment (TECH 2). If you do not have access to this equipment, entrust this task to a Saab dealer or specialist.

Chapter 10
Suspension and steering

Contents

Degrees of difficulty

Easy, suitable for novice with little experience	**Fairly easy,** suitable for beginner with some experience	**Fairly difficult,** suitable for competent DIY mechanic	**Difficult,** suitable for experienced DIY mechanic	**Very difficult,** suitable for expert DIY or professional

Specifications

General

Front suspension type	Independent with MacPherson struts and anti-roll bar. Struts incorporate gas-filled shock absorbers and coil springs. Aluminium lower control arms
Rear suspension type	Independent rear suspension with trailing arms, upper and lower transverse links, and a toe-in link
Steering type	Rack-and-pinion, hydraulic power assistance on all models

Wheel alignment (vehicle unladen with full tank)

Front:	
Toe-in:	
Angle	0.28° ± 0.08°
Dimension:	
16" wheels	2.0 ± 0.57 mm
17" wheels	2.2 ± 0.63 mm
18" wheels	2.4 ± 0.69 mm
Camber:	
Normal chassis	-0.8° ± 0.5°
Sport chassis	-0.9° ± 0.5°
Castor	2.90° ± 0.50°
Kingpin inclination	13.3°
Rear:	
Toe-in:	
Angle	0.12° ± 0.04°
Dimension:	
16" wheels	1.71 ± 0.57 mm
17" wheels	1.89 ± 0.63 mm
18" wheels	2.06 ± 0.69 mm
Camber:	
Normal chassis	-0.7° ± 0.3°
Sport chassis	-1.00° ± 0.3°

Wheels

Size	6.5 x 16, 7 x 17, 7.5 x 18	

Tyres

Size	216/55R16, 215/50R17, 225/45R17, 225/45R18	
Pressures	Refer to the end of *Weekly checks* on page 0•16	

Torque wrench settings

	Nm	lbf ft
Front suspension		
Anti-roll bar clamp bolts	18	13
Anti-roll bar link nuts	64	47
Driveshaft/hub nut*	230	170
Front chassis reinforcement bolts (Convertible only)	50	37
Hub to hub carrier:		
Stage 1	90	66
Stage 2	Angle-tighten a further 45°	
Lower arm:		
Front mounting to subframe:		
Stage 1	65	48
Stage 2	Angle-tighten a further 90°	
Outer balljoint-to-hub carrier nut*	50	37
Rear bush to arm:		
Stage 1	40	30
Stage 2	Angle-tighten a further 30°	
Rear bush to subframe:		
Stage 1	65	48
Stage 2	Angle-tighten a further 90°	
Shock absorber to hub carrier:*		
Stage 1	80	59
Stage 2	Angle-tighten a further 135°	
Shock absorber upper nut to strut mounting	105	77
Strut top mounting bolts	18	13
Subframe main mounting bolts:		
Stage 1	75	55
Stage 2	Angle-tighten a further 135°	
Subframe rear stay bolt:		
Stage 1	90	66
Stage 2	Angle-tighten a further 45°	
Rear suspension		
Anti-roll bar clamp bolts:		
15.2 mm diameter roll bar	18	13
16.7 mm diameter roll bar	31	23
Anti-roll bar link to hub carrier	53	39
Anti-roll bar outer mounting	53	39
Hub-to-hub carrier nuts:*		
Stage 1	50	37
Stage 2	Angle-tighten a further 30°	
Lower transverse link arm-to-subframe nut:*		
Stage 1	75	55
Stage 2	Angle-tighten a further 60°	
Lower transverse link arm to hub carrier:*		
Stage 1	75	55
Stage 2	Angle-tighten a further 90°	
Rear chassis reinforcement bolts (Convertible only):		
Front bolts	110	81
Rear bolts:		
Stage 1	75	55
Stage 2	Angle-tighten a further 135°	
Shock absorber bottom mounting	150	111
Shock absorber to upper mounting bracket	27	20
Shock absorber upper mounting bracket to body	53	39
Subframe to body:		
Stage 1	75	55
Stage 2	Angle-tighten a further 135°	
Toe-in link arm nuts:*		
Stage 1	75	55
Stage 2	Angle-tighten a further 60°	

Torque wrench settings (continued)

	Nm	lbf ft
Rear suspension (continued)		
Trailing arm front mounting to body:		
Stage 1	70	52
Stage 2	Angle-tighten a further 90°	
Trailing arm to front mounting:		
Stage 1	75	55
Stage 2	Angle-tighten a further 90°	
Trailing arm to hub carrier	150	111
Upper suspension arm to subframe:		
Stage 1	75	55
Stage 2	Angle-tighten a further 90°	
Upper suspension arm to hub carrier:		
Stage 1	125	92
Stage 2	Angle-tighten a further 135°	
Steering		
Hydraulic pipes to/from steering rack	28	21
Power steering pump delivery pipe	32	24
Power steering pump mounting bolts	22	16
Steering column bolts	24	18
Steering column universal joint pinch-bolt	30	22
Steering rack mounting bolts/nuts:		
Stage 1	50	37
Stage 2	Angle-tighten a further 60°	
Electro-hydraulic power steering delivery pipe	27	20
Electro-hydraulic power steering mounting bracket	7	5
Steering wheel	50	37
Track rod end to hub carrier	35	26
Track rod to steering rack:		
Stage 1	50	37
Stage 2	Angle-tighten a further 60°	
Wheels		
Roadwheel bolts	110	81

** Do not re-use*

1 General information

The front suspension is fully independent, utilising MacPherson struts and an anti-roll bar. The struts incorporate coil springs and gas-filled shock absorbers, and are attached to the hub carriers. The shock absorbers can be renewed separately from to the strut. The hub carriers are located on the outer ends of the lower arms by balljoints. The lower arms are attached to the subframe by rubber bushes, and the balljoints are integral with the lower arms. The front hubs are located in double race bearings and bolted to the hub carriers. The driveshafts are splined to the hubs and retained by single hub nuts and thrustwashers.

The rear suspension is fully independent, incorporating trailing arms connected by rubber bushes to the vehicle body, and bolted to the hub carriers at the rear. The trailing arms are manufactured from aluminium to reduce unsprung weight. Upper and lower transverse link arms are fitted between the rear subframe and the hub carrier. A toe-link arm is fitted between the rear of the hub carrier and the subframe to control rear wheel toe-in. An anti-roll bar is fitted between the trailing arms, and the rear subframe. The trailing arms pivot at their front extensions in rubber bushes located on the underbody, and gas-filled shock absorbers are fitted between the rear ends of the arms/hub carriers and mountings on the underbody. The rear coil springs are located between the lower arms and the underbody, and are supported at their upper ends in polyurethane seats and at the lower ends in rubber seats. The rear hubs and bearings are supplied as integral units which cannot be dismantled, and they are attached to the hub carriers by bolts. Each rear hub incorporates an internal ABS sensor to monitor the wheel speed.

A power-assisted, rack-and-pinion steering system is fitted to all models. The steering rack is essentially a hydraulic ram, which is actuated mechanically by a pinion gear, and hydraulically by pressurised hydraulic fluid, supplied by the power steering pump. The steering column transmits effort applied at the steering wheel to the pinion and a control valve, which manages the supply of hydraulic fluid to the steering rack. When the steering wheel is turned, the valve directs fluid to the appropriate side of the ram, assisting the movement of the rack. The inner ends of the track rods are attached to the rack at the centre of the steering gear, unlike the more conventional method of attaching them to the ends of the rack. The outer ends of the track rods are attached to the steering arms on the struts/hub carriers by balljoints. On petrol models the power steering pump is driven directly by the intake camshaft. On diesel models an electro-hydraulic system is fitted, where the pump is fitted to the steering rack assembly, and driven by an integral electric motor.

The design and mounting position of the steering column are such that, in the event of a head-on collision, it will absorb impact by crumpling longitudinally, and will also be deflected away from the driver.

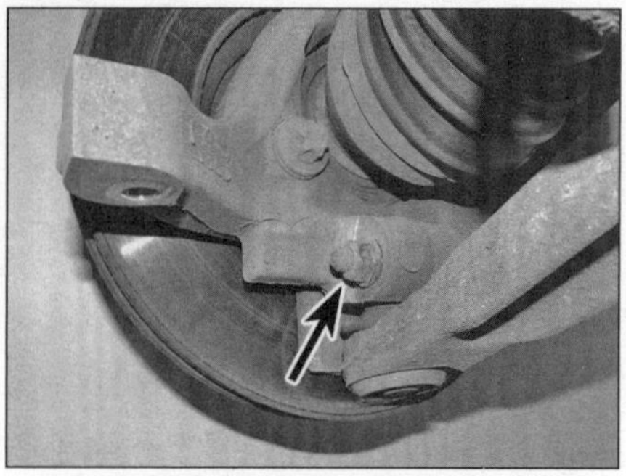
3.2a Unscrew the retaining nut (arrowed) ...

3.2b ... withdraw the pinch-bolt from the hub carrier ...

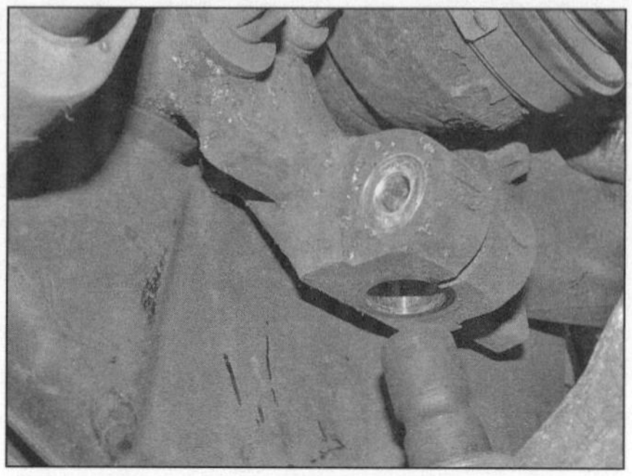
3.2c ... then lever the lower arm downwards to detach the balljoint shank

2 Front hub carrier – removal and refitting

Removal

1 Remove the hub and bearing assembly as described in Section 6.
2 Unscrew the nut and disconnect the track rod end from the hub carrier as described in Section 22.
3 Undo the nuts, remove the bolts and detach the hub carrier from the strut **(see illustration 4.4)**.

Refitting

4 Fit the hub carrier to the suspension strut, insert the bolts and tighten the nuts to the specified torque setting.
5 Re-attach the track rod end to the hub carrier and tighten the nut to the specified torque.
6 Refit the hub and bearing assembly as described in Section 6.

3 Front lower arm – removal, overhaul and refitting

Removal

1 Apply the handbrake, then jack up the front of the vehicle and support it on axle stands (see *Jacking and vehicle support*). Remove the roadwheel.
2 Undo the nut and remove the pinch-bolt securing the lower arm balljoint to the hub carrier, then using a lever, force the lower arm down, detaching the balljoint from the hub carrier **(see illustrations)**. Discard the nut, a new one must be fitted.
3 Undo the nut and withdraw the bolt securing the front of the arm to the subframe **(see illustration)**.
4 Slacken the bolt securing the rear bush to the arm **(see illustration)**.
5 Undo the 2 bolts securing the rear mounting bush to the subframe **(see illustration)**. Manoeuvre the arm from position.

Overhaul

6 It is not possible to renew the lower balljoint separately from the lower arm, although the balljoint rubber boot may be obtained separately. If the lower balljoint is worn excessively, the lower arm must be renewed complete.

Rear bush

7 There is no need to remove the arm to renew the rear bush. Remove the roadwheel on the appropriate side.
8 Undo the retaining bolts, note its fitted position and pull the bush from place. Soak the bush in releasing fluid if it's reluctant to move. Recover the conical washer.
9 Fit the conical washer to the suspension arm then fit the new bush. Apply a little thread-locking compound to the bush retaining bolt and insert it. Only finger-tighten the bolt at this stage, the bush must be able to rotate.
10 Position the rear bush on the subframe, and tighten the bolts to the specified torque.
11 Place a trolley jack under the outer end of the lower arm, raise the assembly until it's at 'normal' height. Hold the flat washer stationary with a pair of pliers and then tighten the bush retaining bolt to the specified torque.

Front bush

12 Remove the arm as described in this Section.
13 Press the bush from the arm. There are special Saab tools available for this task (KM-907-13, KM-508-3 and KM-508-4), or entrust this tack to a workshop equipped with a hydraulic press.
14 Press the new bush into position using the Saab tools or a hydraulic press.
15 Refit the suspension arm as described in this Section.

Refitting

16 Position the lower arm and refit the front mounting bolt finger-tight at this stage.
17 Fit the rear bush to the subframe, and tighten the retaining bolts to the specified torque.
18 Engage the suspension arm balljoint with the hub carrier, and raise the arm until the groove in the balljoint is visible through the pinch-bolt aperture. Insert the bolt, then tighten the new nut to the specified torque.
19 Place a trolley jack under the outer end of the suspension arm, and raise it until it's in the 'normal' position (the height it would be at with the wheel fitted and resting on the ground, taking the full weight of the vehicle).
20 Now tighten the suspension arm front and rear bushes retaining bolts to the specified torque.

3.3 Undo the nut (arrowed) securing the front of the arm

3.4 Slacken the rear bush bolt (arrowed)

3.5 Remove the rear mounting bolts

4.2 Use an open-ended spanner to counter-hold the anti-roll bar link balljoint shank

4.5 Upper mounting Torx screws

21 Refit the roadwheel, and tighten the bolts to the specified torque. It would be prudent to have the front wheel alignment checked at the earliest opportunity.

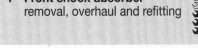

4 Front shock absorber – removal, overhaul and refitting

Removal

1 Raise the front of the vehicle and support it securely on axle stands (see *Jacking and vehicle support*). Remove the both front roadwheels.

2 Undo the nut securing the upper end of the anti-roll bar link to the suspension strut. Use an open-ended spanner on the flats of the balljoint to counter-hold the nut **(see illustration)**.

3 Detach the wheel speed sensor and brake hose from the bracket at the base of the strut **(see illustration)**.

4 Place a trolley jack under the outer end of the suspension arm, then undo the nuts and remove the bolts securing the hub carrier to the base of the strut. Note that the bolts are splined, and will not rotate. Detach the strut from the hub carrier **(see illustration)**.

5 Undo the 3 Torx screws securing the upper strut mounting to the vehicle body **(see illustration)**. Support the strut (it's heavy), and manoeuvre it from under the wheel arch.

Dismantling

6 Remove the strut from the car as described earlier in this Section.

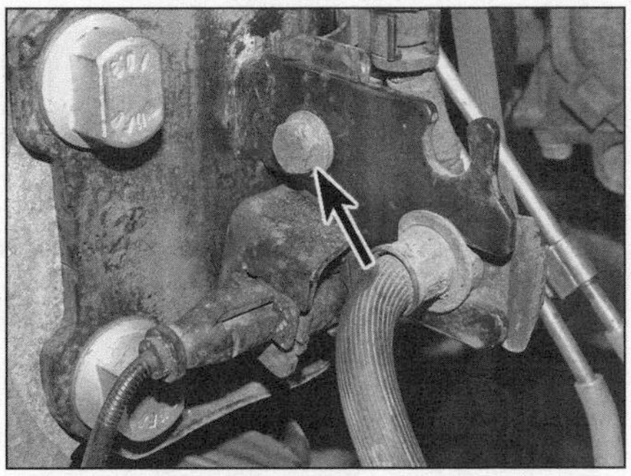
4.3 Undo the bolt and detach the bracket from the strut (arrowed)

4.7a Prise off the plastic cap ...

7 Prise off the protective cap, then slacken the strut mounting nut 1/2 a turn, while holding the protruding portion of the piston rod with an 8 mm Allen key **(see illustrations)**. Do not remove the nut at this stage.

8 Fit the spring compressors to coil springs, and tighten the compressors until the load is taken off the spring seats.

9 Remove the piston nut, mounting plate, upper spring seat/bearing, and gaiter followed by the spring. If required, remove the bump stop **(see illustrations)**.

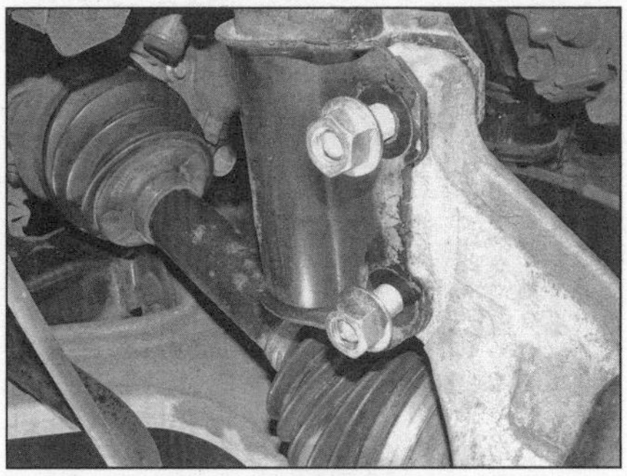
4.4 Undo the nuts and pull out the bolts securing the hub carrier to the strut

4.7b ... then counter-hold the piston rod with an 8 mm Allen key/bit, and undo the piston nut

4.9a Unscrew the piston nut ...

4.9b ... followed by the upper mounting plate ...

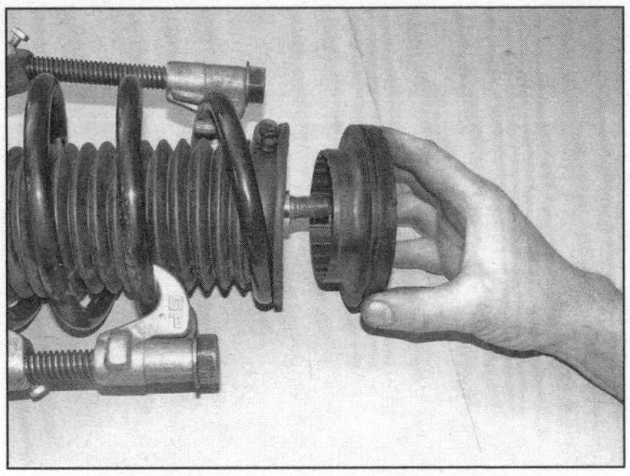
4.9c ... upper spring seat/bearing ...

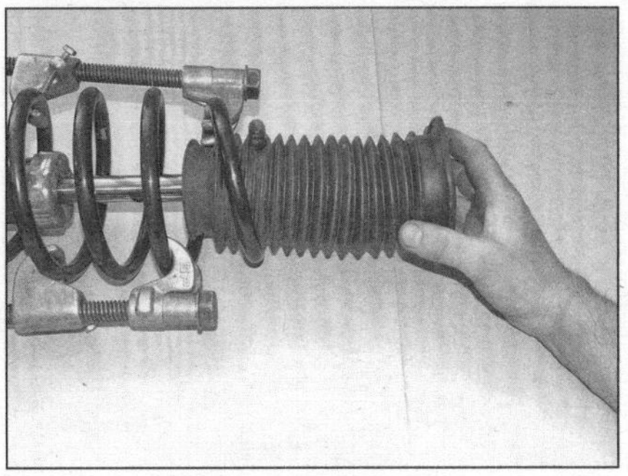
4.9d ... gaiter ...

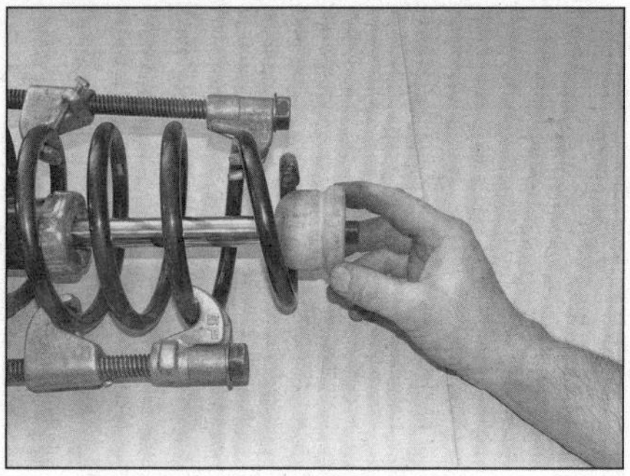

4.9e ... bump stop ...

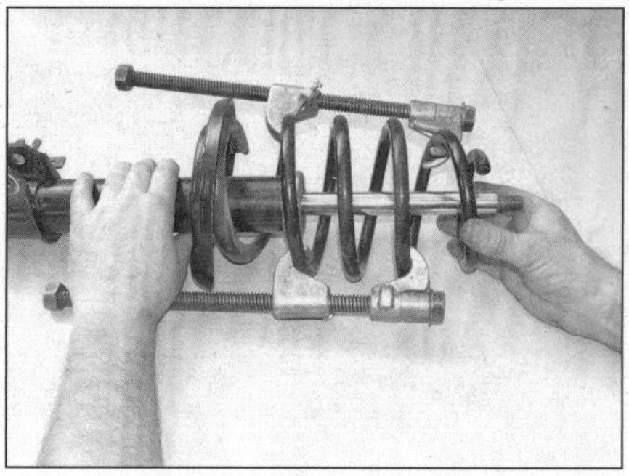

4.9f ... and spring

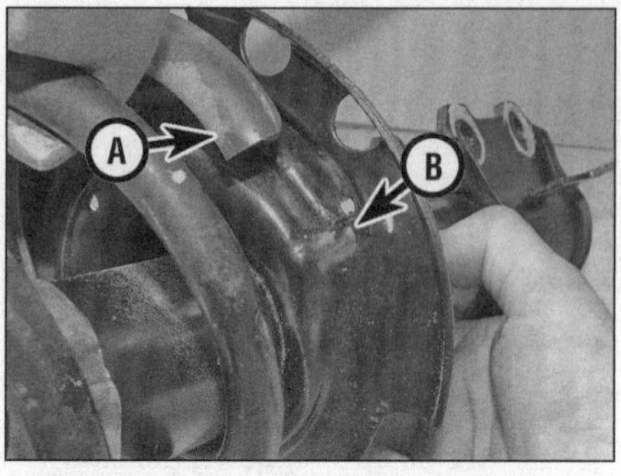

4.15 Ensure the lower end of the spring (A) locates against the raise stop (B)

Inspection

10 With the strut assembly now completely dismantled, examine all the components for wear, damage or deformation. Renew any of the components as necessary.

11 Examine the shock absorber for signs of fluid leakage, and check the strut piston for signs of pitting along its entire length. Test the operation of the shock absorber, while holding it in an upright position, by moving the piston through a full stroke and then through short strokes of 50 to 100 mm. In both cases, the resistance felt should be smooth and continuous. If the resistance is jerky, or uneven, or if there is any visible sign of wear or damage, renewal is necessary.

12 If any doubt exists about the condition of the coil spring, gradually release the spring compressor, and check the spring for distortion and signs of cracking. Since no minimum free length is specified by Saab, the only way to check the tension of the spring is to compare it to a new component. Renew the spring if it is damaged or distorted, or if there is any doubt as to its condition.

13 Inspect all other components for signs of damage or deterioration, and renew any that are suspect.

14 If a new shock absorber is being fitted, hold it vertically and pump the piston a few times to prime it.

Reassembly

15 Reassembly is a reversal of dismantling, but ensure that the spring is fully compressed before fitting. Make sure that the spring ends are correctly located in the lower seat, then tighten the new shock absorber upper mounting nut to the specified torque **(see illustration)**. Note that the upper mounting plate holes will only align with the holes in the inner wing in one position.

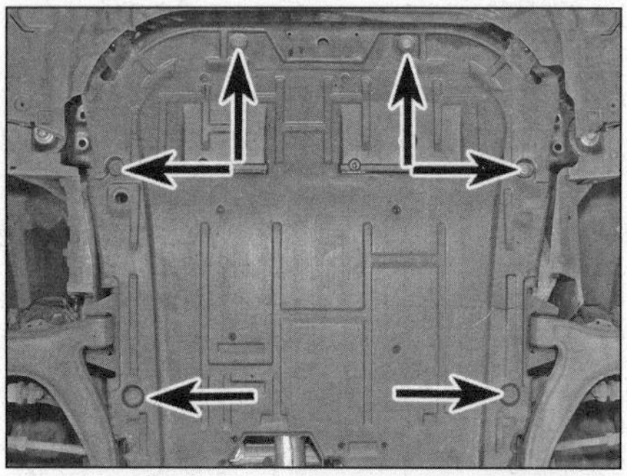

5.3a Undo the screws (arrowed) and remove the engine undershield

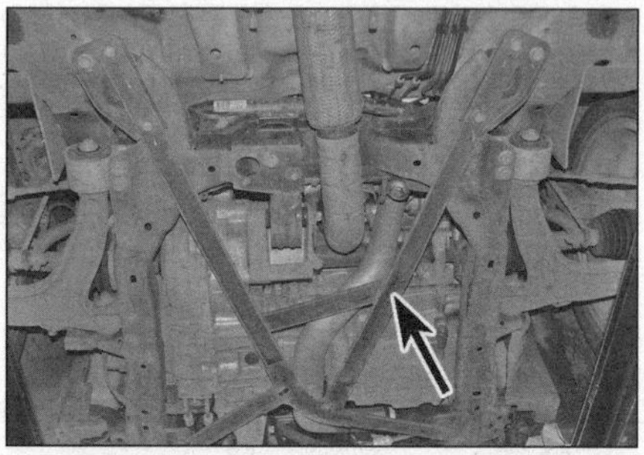

5.3b Undo the bolts and remove the front chassis reinforcement (arrowed) – Convertible models

5.5 Steering column universal joint pinch-bolt (arrowed)

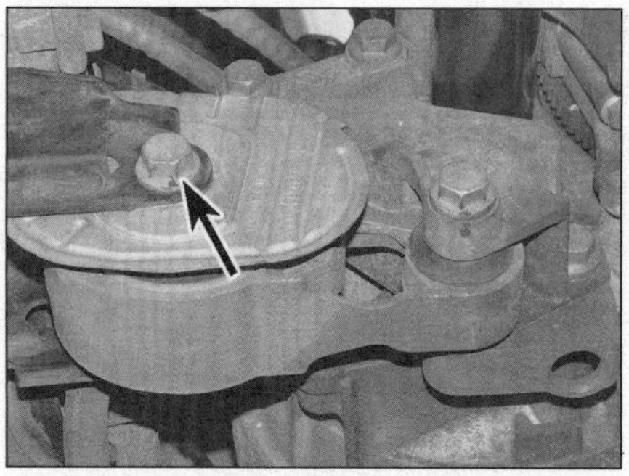

5.8a Left-hand rear torque arm bolt (arrowed) ...

Refitting

16 Refitting is a reversal of removal, noting the following points:

a) Use new nuts to secure the hub carrier to the base of the strut.

b) Tighten all fasteners to the specified torque where given.

c) Suspension struts must be changed in pairs. Always renew both sides.

5 Front anti-roll bar – removal, overhaul and refitting

Petrol models

Removal

1 Apply the handbrake, then jack up the front of the vehicle and support it on axle stands (see *Jacking and vehicle support*). Remove both roadwheels.

2 On LHD vehicles, remove the left-hand side front wheel arch liner, and on RHD vehicles, remove the right-hand side wheel arch liner.

3 Undo the fasteners and remove the engine undershield. On Convertible models, undo the bolts and remove the front chassis reinforcement **(see illustrations)**.

4 Remove the front section of the exhaust pipe as described in Chapter 4A, Section 16 or Chapter 4B, Section 18.

5 Undo the pinch-bolt and detach the universal joint at the base of the steering column from the steering rack pinion **(see illustration)**.

6 Undo the bolts and remove the heat shield from the steering rack.

7 Undo the nut and detach the track rod end from the hub carrier on the right-hand side (RHD vehicles) or left-hand side (LHD vehicles) as described in Section 22.

8 Undo the bolts securing the rear torque arms to the subframe **(see illustrations)**.

9 Make alignment marks between the subframe and body, then remove the rear subframe mounting bolts, and slacken the front mounting bolts a few turns. Pull the subframe down a little at the rear and hold it in this position using wooden wedges (or similar) between the subframe and the vehicle body **(see illustrations 23.11a to 23.11c)**.

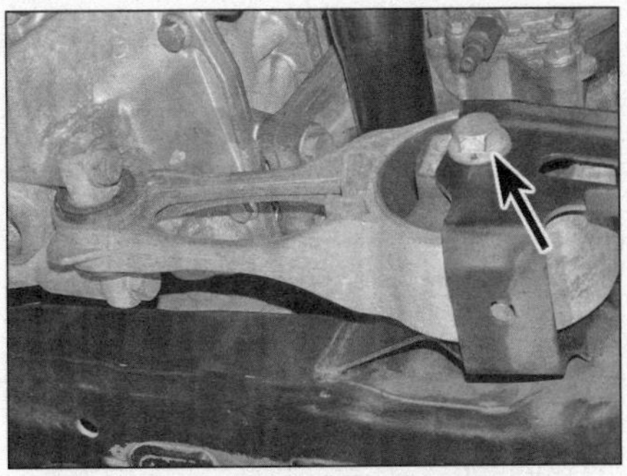

5.8b ... and right-hand rear torque arm bolt (arrowed) – petrol model

10 Undo the nuts securing the ends of the anti-roll bar to the link arms, using an open-ended spanner to counter-hold the balljoint shank as the nuts are undone **(see illustration)**.

11 Undo the bolts securing the anti-roll bar clamps to the subframe, and slide the anti-roll bar out between the subframe and the vehicle body **(see illustration)**.

12 Remove the split clamp mounting rubbers from the anti-roll bar.

Overhaul

13 Check the anti-roll bar and mountings for signs of wear and damage.

14 Check the split clamp mounting rubbers and renew them if necessary.

Refitting

15 Dip the split clamp mounting rubbers in soapy water and locate them on the anti-roll bar. Note that the opening of the bushes must face forwards.

16 Check that the mounting rubbers are in place then insert the anti-roll bar onto the subframe and locate the links in the end of the bar.

17 Fit the clamps and tighten the retaining bolts to the specified torque.

18 Lift the subframe up into position, aligning the previously-made marks, then insert the bolts and tighten all the subframe mounting bolts to the specified torque.

19 Tighten the subframe rear stay bolts to the specified torque.

20 The remainder of refitting is a reversal of removal.

Diesel models

Removal

21 Open the bonnet and remove the bumper cover upper mounting bolts.

22 Apply the handbrake, then jack up the front of the vehicle and support it on axle stands (see *Jacking and vehicle support*). Remove both roadwheels.

23 On Convertible models, undo the bolts and remove the front chassis reinforcement **(see illustration 5.3b)**.

24 Remove the engine undershield and partially remove the front section of the wing liners.

25 Using stout cord or suitable straps, secure the radiator assembly to the bonnet slam panel.

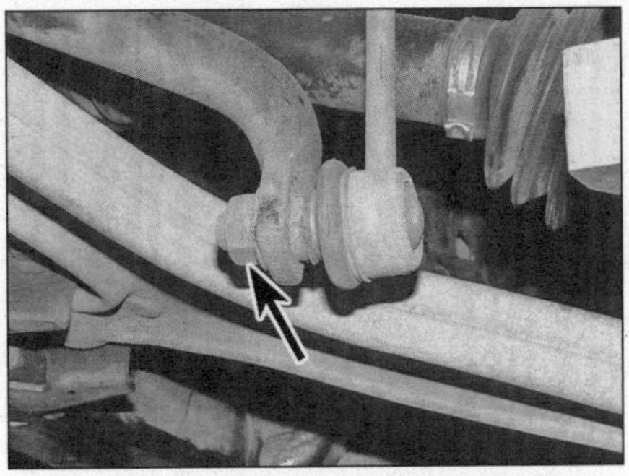

5.10 Undo the nut securing anti-roll bar to the link (arrowed)

26 Unbolt and remove the front section of the exhaust system and then remove the rear torque rod from the engine.

27 Unbolt the drop links from the anti-roll bar. A thin 17 mm spanner will be required to stop the balljoint from rotating.

28 Undo the pinch-bolt and detach the universal joint at the base of the steering column from the steering rack pinion.

29 Unclip the EHPS cable from the support clip and, on vehicles fitted with xenon headlights, disconnect the cable from the angle sensor.

30 Make alignment marks between the subframe and body. At this point the subframe must be supported with suitable jacks, so that it can be lowered at least 150 mm.

31 With the subframe supported, remove the 4 subframe mounting bolts and lower the subframe on the jacks.

32 Remove the anti-roll bar mounting clamps and then remove the anti-roll bar from the vehicle.

33 Remove the split clamp mounting rubbers from the anti-roll bar.

Overhaul

34 Check the anti-roll bar and mountings for signs of wear and damage.

35 Check the split clamp mounting rubbers and renew them if necessary. Given the amount of work involved in removing the anti-roll bar it would be prudent to renew the bushes.

Refitting

36 Dip the split clamp mounting rubbers in soapy water and locate them on the anti-roll bar. Note that the opening of the bushes must face forwards.

37 Check that the mounting rubbers are in place then insert the anti-roll bar onto the subframe and locate the links in the end of the bar.

38 Fit the clamps and tighten the retaining bolts to the specified torque.

39 Lift the subframe up into position, aligning the previously-made marks, then insert the bolts and tighten all the subframe mounting bolts to the specified torque.

40 The remainder of refitting is a reversal of removal.

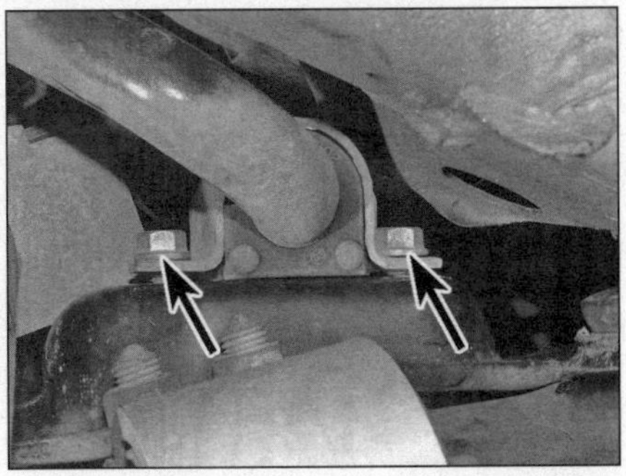

5.11 Anti-roll bar clamp bolts (arrowed)

6 Front hub bearing – renewal

1 Apply the handbrake, then jack up the front of the vehicle and support it on axle stands (see *Jacking and vehicle support*). Remove the roadwheel.

2 Fully unscrew and remove the hub nut. Have someone apply the footbrake to prevent the hub/driveshaft from turning.

3 Push the driveshaft inwards from the hub a little.

4 Undo the retaining screw and remove the ABS sensor harness and hose bracket from the strut/hub carrier.

5 Using a screwdriver, press the inner brake pad a little way into its cylinder so that the pads are clear of the disc.

6 Unscrew the caliper bracket mounting bolts, then withdraw the caliper and pads from the disc. Tie the caliper to one side taking care not to bend the hydraulic hose excessively.

7 Undo the screw and remove the brake disc.

8 Disconnect the wheel speed sensor wiring plug **(see illustration)**.

9 Undo the pinch-bolt and pull the suspension lower arm balljoint downwards and out from the hub carrier **(see illustrations 3.2a to 3.2c)**.

10 Pull the hub carrier outwards and the driveshaft from the hub.

11 Undo the 3 retaining screws and detach the hub from the hub carrier **(see illustration)**. Remove the brake shield from the hub.

6.8 Speed sensor wiring plug (arrowed)

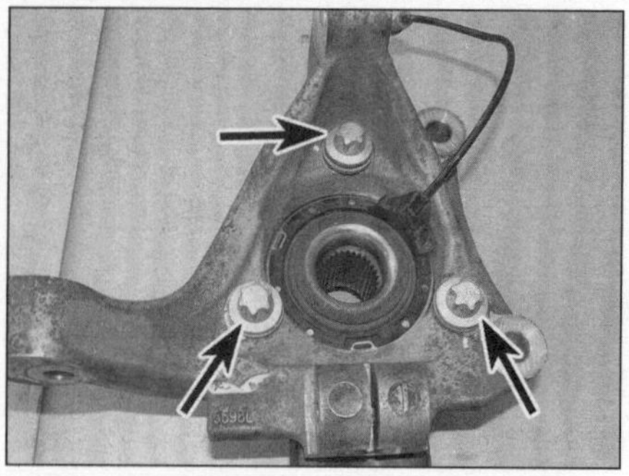

6.11 Undo the Torx screws securing the bearing assembly to the hub carrier (arrowed)

12 No further dismantling of the hub is possible. The hub and bearing must be renewed as a complete unit.

13 Ensure the contact faces of the hub carrier and hub are clean, then refit the brake shield and hub to the carrier. Make sure the wheel speed sensor cable is correctly positioned, then tighten the retaining bolts securely.

14 Insert the end of the driveshaft into the hub, and locate the lower arm balljoint into the base of the hub carrier. Refit the pinch-bolt and tighten the nut to the specified torque.

15 Refit the brake disc and caliper (see Chapter 9, Section 8 and 6).

16 Reconnect the wheel speed sensor plug, and fit the plug to the retaining bracket on the strut base.

17 Fit a new driveshaft/hub nut, prise out the centre cap, then refit the roadwheel.

18 Lower the vehicle to the ground, then tighten the driveshaft nut to the specified

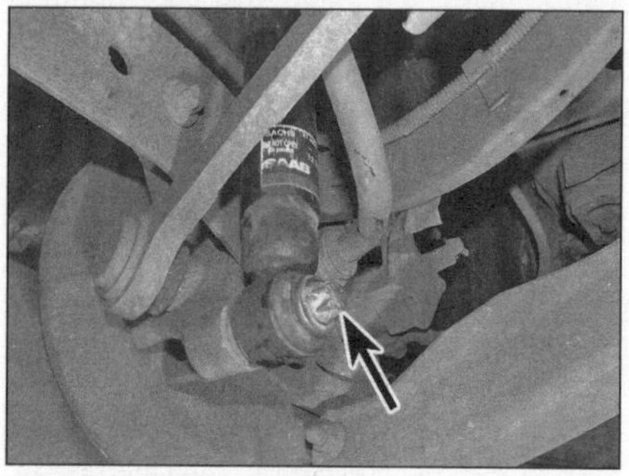

7.3 Shock absorber lower mounting screw (arrowed)

7.5 Undo the nut (arrowed) and pull the upper mounting from the shock absorber

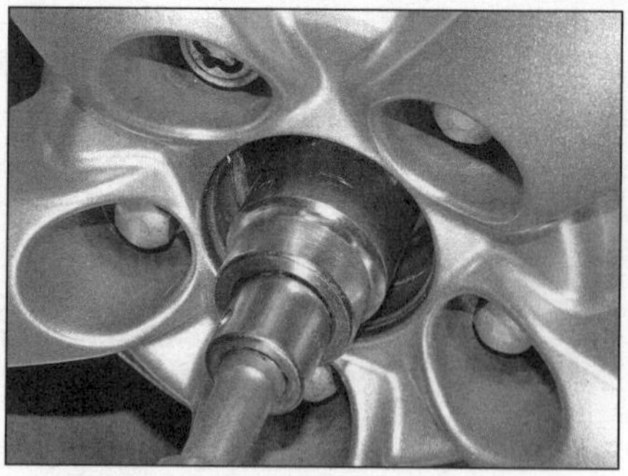

6.18 Prise out the centre cap and tighten the driveshaft nut with a 32 mm socket

torque with a socket and extension bar through the hole in the centre of the wheel **(see illustration)**.

19 Ensure the roadwheel bolts are correctly tightened, then press in the wheel centre cap.

7 Rear shock absorber – removal and refitting

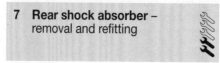

Note: *To ensure even handling, both rear shock absorbers must be renewed at the same time.*

Removal

1 Position the rear of the vehicle over an inspection pit or on car ramps. Alternatively, raise and support the rear of the vehicle (see *Jacking and vehicle support*), then remove the roadwheel and support the rear subframe with an axle stand or trolley jack on the appropriate side.

7.4 Shock absorber upper mounting screws (arrowed)

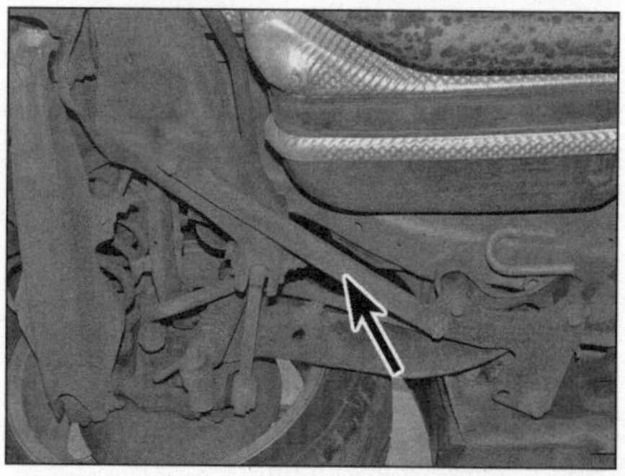

8.4 Rear chassis reinforcement (arrowed) – Convertible models

2 Place a trolley jack under the rear suspension hub carrier, and raise it to take the weight from the shock absorber.

3 Unscrew the rear shock absorber lower mounting Torx screw, and recover the washer and rubber bush **(see illustration)**.

4 Unscrew and remove the 3 retaining Torx screws securing the shock absorber upper mounting bracket, and manoeuvre the assembly from position **(see illustration)**.

5 Undo the nut and detach the upper mounting from the shock absorber **(see illustration)**.

6 Examine the rubber bushes for wear and damage. Note that the lower bush is not available as a separate part, if it is worn or damaged, both shock absorbers will require renewal.

Refitting

7 Refitting is a reversal of removal, but tighten the mounting bolts and nuts to the specified torque.

8 Rear anti-roll bar – removal and refitting

Removal

1 Chock the front wheels, then jack up the rear of the vehicle and support on axle stands positioned clear of the rear anti-roll bar (see *Jacking and vehicle support*). Remove both rear roadwheels.

2 On vehicles with tyre pressure monitoring, remove the right-hand rear wheel arch liner, and disconnect the signal detector wiring plug. Release the wiring harness from the retaining clips.

Convertible models

3 Undo the bolts and remove the centre tunnel chassis reinforcement plate.

4 Undo the bolts and remove the rear chassis reinforcement each side of the rear subframe **(see illustration)**.

All models

5 Remove the rear section of the exhaust system as described in Chapter 4A, Section 16 or Chapter 4B, Section 18.

6 Remove both rear brake calipers as described in Chapter 9, Section 7. Note there is no need to disconnect the brake fluid hose from the calipers – suspend the calipers from the vehicle body using straps/cable-ties, etc.

7 Undo the remove the screws securing the lower end of the shock absorbers to the hub carrier **(see illustration 7.3)**.

8 Prise open the box and disconnect the wheel speed sensors wiring plugs each side. Release the wiring harness from any retaining clips.

9 Place a trolley jack under the centre of the rear subframe, then remove the subframe mounting bolts.

10 Lower the subframe a maximum of 200 mm, and remove the coil springs each side.

11 Undo the bolts securing the anti-roll bar links to the hub carrier each side **(see illustration)**.
12 Undo the bolts securing the anti-roll bar clamps to the subframe and manoeuvre it rearwards between the subframe and body.
13 Examine the rubber clamp bushes for wear or damage, and renew where necessary.

Refitting

14 Manoeuvre the anti-roll bar into position, refit the clamps and apply a little thread-locking compound, and tighten the bolts to the specified torque.
15 The remainder of refitting is a reversal of removal, noting the following points:

a) *Refit the exhaust system as described in Chapter 4A, Section 16 or Chapter 4B, Section 18.*
b) *Refit the brake calipers as described in Chapter 9, Section 7.*
c) *Tighten all fasteners to the specified torque where given.*

9 Rear anti-roll bar bushes – renewal

1 Apply the handbrake, then jack up the front of the vehicle and support it on axle stands (see *Jacking and vehicle support*).
2 Undo the nuts securing the anti-roll bar links to the hub carriers **(see illustration 8.11)**.
3 Undo the bolts securing the anti-roll bar clamps to the subframe, pull the bar rearwards, remove the clamps, and remove the rubber bushes from the bar.
4 Apply a little silicone grease to the inside of the new bushes and fit them to the anti-roll bar.
5 Refit the clamps, and manoeuvre the anti-roll bar into position.
6 Apply a little thread-locking compound to the clamp bolts and tighten them to the specified torque.
7 Re-attach the anti-roll bar links to the hub carriers, and tighten the retaining nuts to the specified torque.
8 Lower the vehicle to the ground.

10 Rear coil spring – removal and refitting

Note: *To ensure equal ride heights on each side of the vehicle, both rear coil springs must be renewed at the same time.*

Removal

1 Slacken the roadwheel nuts, then chock the front wheels and raise the rear of the vehicle. Support it securely on axle stands (see *Jacking and vehicle support*). Remove the roadwheels.
2 Remove the brake caliper as described in Chapter 9, Section 7. Note there is no need to disconnect the brake fluid hose – suspend the caliper from the vehicle body using straps/cable-ties, etc.

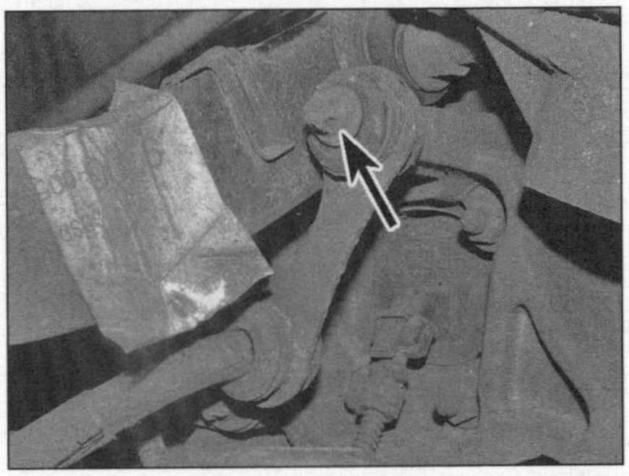

8.11 Remove the bolt (arrowed) securing the anti-roll bar link

3 Attach spring compressors to the spring and compress the spring. Saab specify tool No 88 18 791. Alternative spring compressors may be available **(see illustration)**.
4 Lift out the spring from its location.
5 Examine all the components for wear or damage, and renew as necessary.

Refitting

6 Refit the rubber seats to the spring **(see illustration)**.
7 Refit the compressed spring onto the seat in the lower control arm.
8 Release and remove the spring compressor.
9 Refit the brake caliper as described in Chapter 9, Section 7.
10 Refit the roadwheels, lower the vehicle to the ground, and tighten the wheel bolts to the specified torque.

11 Rear hub carrier – removal and refitting

Removal

1 Slacken the roadwheel nuts, then chock the front wheels and raise the rear of the vehicle. Support it securely on axle stands (see *Jacking and vehicle support*). Remove the roadwheels.
2 Remove the brake disc as described in Chapter 9, Section 9.
3 Disconnect the wheel speed sensor wiring plug **(see illustration 12.2)**.
4 Undo and remove the nut securing the toe-link arm to the hub carrier **(see illustration 13.35)**.
5 Place a trolley jack under the lower transverse link arm and take the weight.
6 Unscrew the bolt securing the lower transverse link arm to the hub carrier **(see illustration 13.24b)**.
7 Undo the bolts securing the base of the shock absorber to the hub carrier.
8 Undo the bolt and detach the anti-roll bar link from the hub carrier **(see illustration 8.11)**.
9 Undo the bolt and detach the upper transverse link arm from the hub carrier **(see illustration 13.19a)**.
10 Undo the 3 retaining bolts and detach the hub carrier from the trailing link arm.
11 If required, undo the 4 bolts and detach the hub and brake shield from the hub carrier.

Overhaul

12 Check the hub carrier bushes for wear and damage. If necessary, press out the old bushes. Special Saab tools are available (No KM 906-61-62 and KM 906-63-64), or use an hydraulic press.
13 Press in the new bushes using the same method.

Refitting

14 If removed, refit the hub assembly and brake disc shield to the hub carrier using new nuts, then tighten them to the specified torque.
15 Reconnect the toe-in link and finger-tighten the new nut.
16 Re-attach the upper transverse link arm with a new nut – finger-tight only.
17 Re-attach the anti-roll bar link to the hub carrier and tighten the bolt to the specified torque.
18 Reconnect the trailing arm to the hub carrier, and tighten the bolts to the specified torque.
19 Refit the lower shock absorber mounting and tighten the bolt to the specified torque.
20 Tighten the toe-in link arm nut to the specified torque.
21 Tighten the upper transverse link arm nut to the specified torque.
22 Reconnect the lower transverse link arm to the hub carrier and tighten the bolt to the specified torque.
23 The remainder of refitting is a reversal of removal.

10.3 Attach spring compressors to the rear coil spring

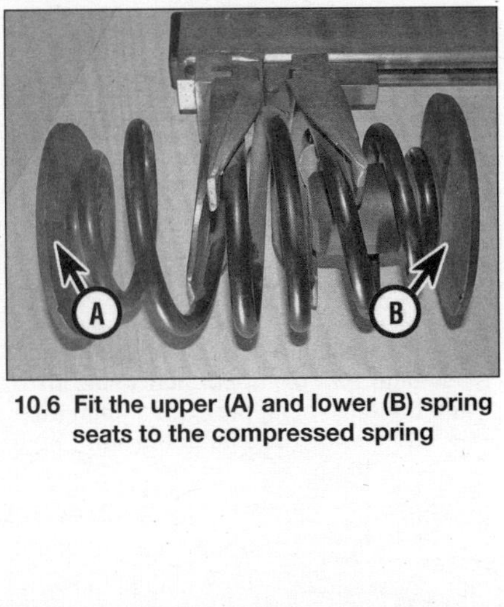

10.6 Fit the upper (A) and lower (B) spring seats to the compressed spring

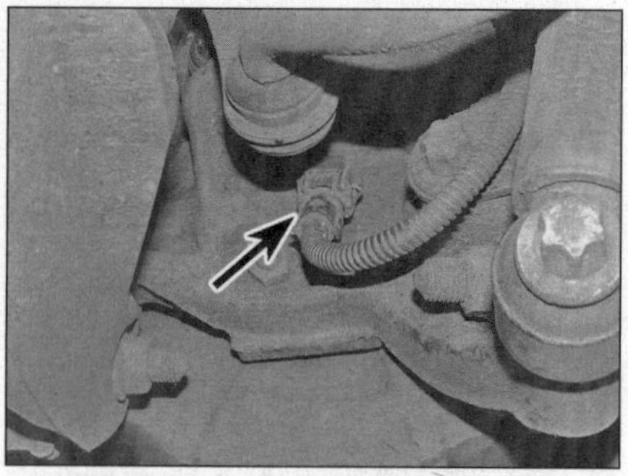

12.2 Disconnect the wheel speed sensor wiring plug (arrowed)

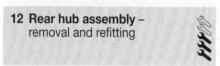

12 Rear hub assembly – removal and refitting

Removal

1 Remove the rear brake disc as described in Chapter 9, Section 9. Suspend the caliper from the vehicle bodywork using cable-ties/straps, etc. Do not allow any strain to be placed on the brake hose.

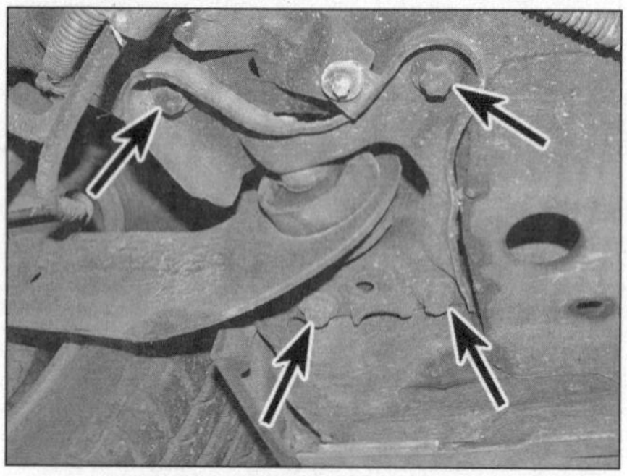

13.7 Trailing arm front mounting bracket bolts (arrowed)

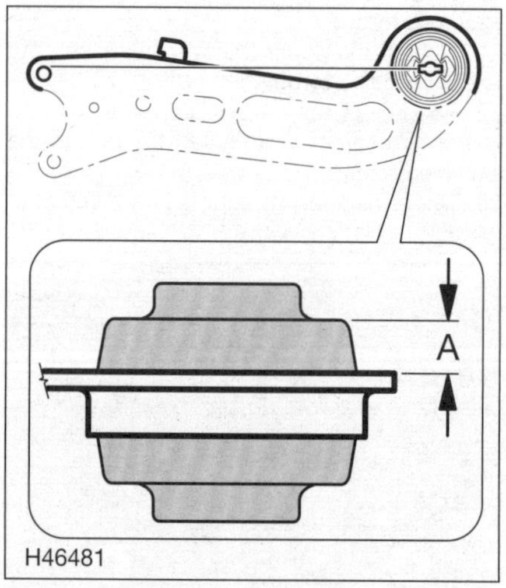

13.11 The trailing arm bush elongated hole must align with the upper hole in the arm, and the bush must protrude 14 mm (A) above the flat side of the arm

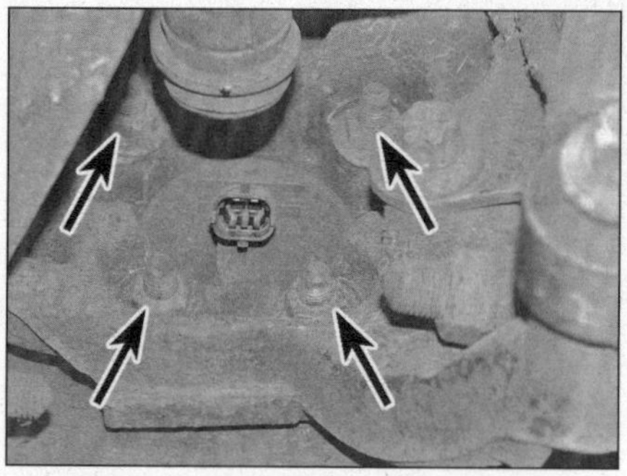

12.3 Undo the 4 nuts (arrowed) and remove the hub/brake shield assembly

2 Disconnect the wheel speed sensor wiring plug **(see illustration)**.

3 Undo the 4 nuts and remove the hub and brake disc shield **(see illustration)**.

4 The bearing and wheel speed sensor are integral with the hub. If faulty the complete assembly must be renewed.

Refitting

5 Clean the contact surfaces of the hub, and hub carrier.

6 Locate the brake shield on the hub studs, then locate the assembly on the hub carrier and tighten the new nuts to the specified torque.

7 Reconnect the wheel speed sensor wiring plug.

8 Refit the brake disc as described in Chapter 9, Section 9.

13 Rear suspension link arms – removal and refitting

Trailing arm

Removal

1 Slacken the relevant roadwheel nuts, then chock the front wheels and raise the rear of the vehicle. Support it securely on axle stands (see *Jacking and vehicle support*). Remove the relevant roadwheel.

2 On Convertible models, undo the bolts and remove the rear chassis reinforcement each side of the rear subframe **(see illustration 8.4)**.

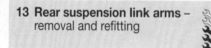

3 Release the wheel speed sensor wiring harness from the clips on the trailing arm.

4 Release the handbrake cable from the clips on the trailing arm.

5 Place a trolley jack under the hub carrier, and take the weight off the shock absorber.

6 Undo the shock absorber lower mounting bolt.

7 Undo the 4 bolts securing the trailing arm front bracket to the vehicle body **(see illustration)**.

8 Undo and remove the bolts securing the trailing arm to the hub carrier.

9 Lower the trailing arm from place, then if required, undo the nut and bolt and remove the front mounting bracket.

10 To renew the bush, use a suitable tubular spacer and press the bush from the arm using a hydraulic press.

Refitting

11 If the bush has been removed, press the new bush into place so the elongated hole in the bush aligns with the top hole at the end of the arm. The bush should protrude 14 mm above the flat side of the arm **(see illustration)**.

12 Grip the arm in a vice, then refit the mounting bracket to the front, only finger-tighten the nut/bolt at this stage.

13 Align the mounting bracket as shown **(see illustration)** then tighten the nut and bolt to the specified torque.

14 Position the trailing arm and fit the bolts securing the bracket to the vehicle body, and the bolts securing the hub carrier to the arm. Tighten the bolts to the specified torque.

15 The remainder of refitting is a reversal of removal.

Upper transverse link arm

Removal

16 Raise the rear of the vehicle and support it securely on axle stands (see *Jacking and vehicle support*). Remove the relevant roadwheel.

17 With reference to Chapter 9, Section 14, slacken the handbrake cable adjustment, detach the cable from the brake caliper, and unclip it from the upper transverse link arm.

18 Unclip the wheel speed sensor wiring harness from the arm.

19 Undo the bolts securing the arm to the rear subframe and the hub carrier, and manoeuvre it from position **(see illustrations)**.

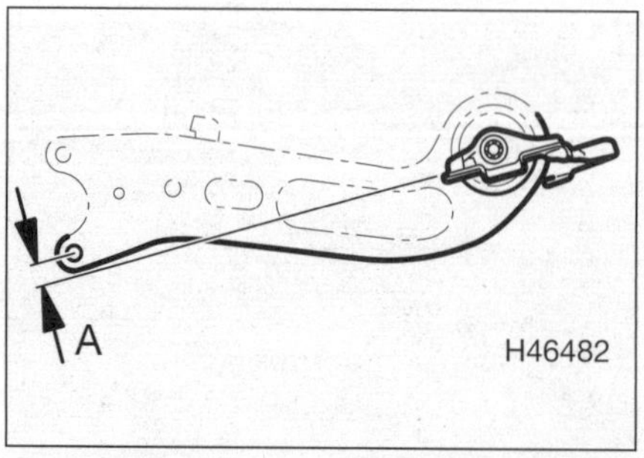

13.13 Position the front mounting bracket so the centre line is 20 mm (A) below the centre of the lower mounting hole

13.19a Upper link arm outer bolt (arrowed) ...

13.19b ... and inner bolt (arrowed)

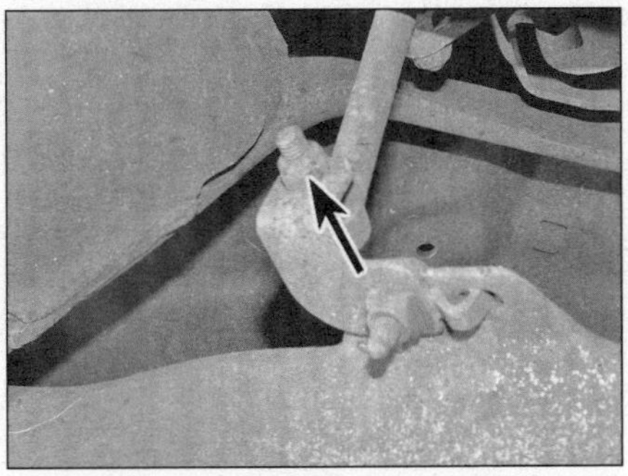

13.22 Undo the nut (arrowed) and detach the suspension level sensor arm

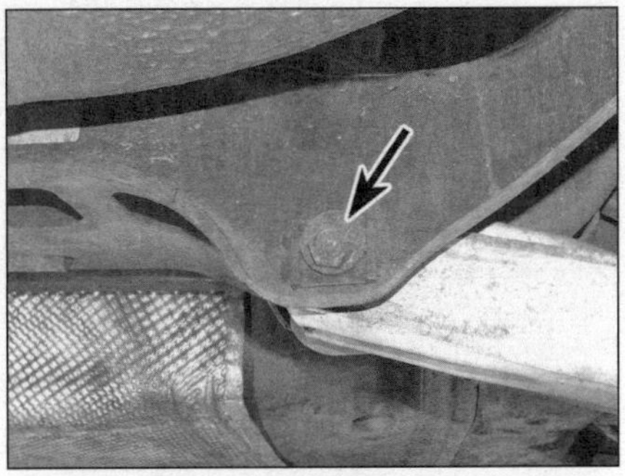

13.24a Make alignment marks between the eccentric washer (arrowed) and the subframe

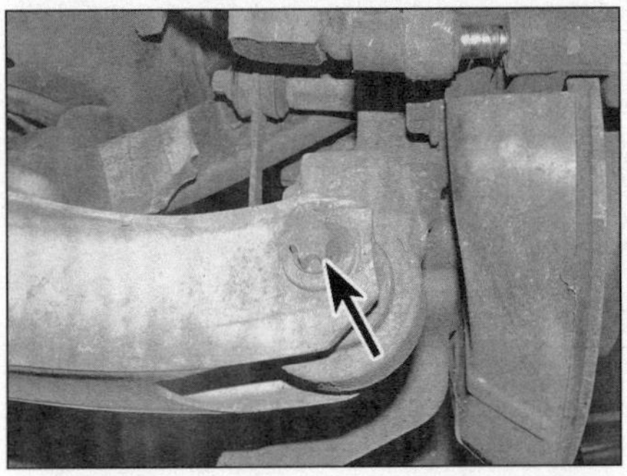

13.24b Lower arm outer bolt (arrowed)

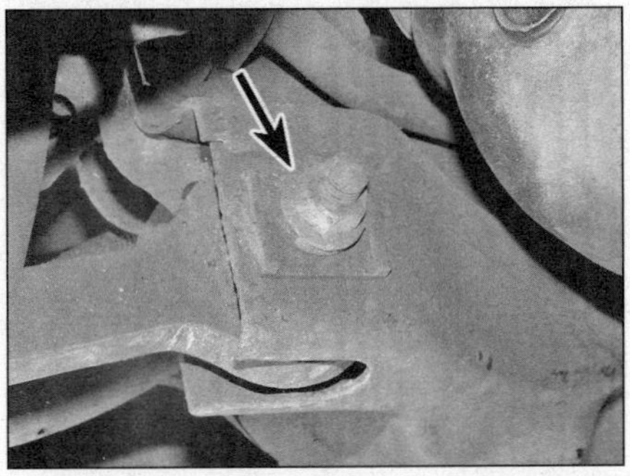

13.34 Make alignment marks between the eccentric washer (arrowed) and the subframe

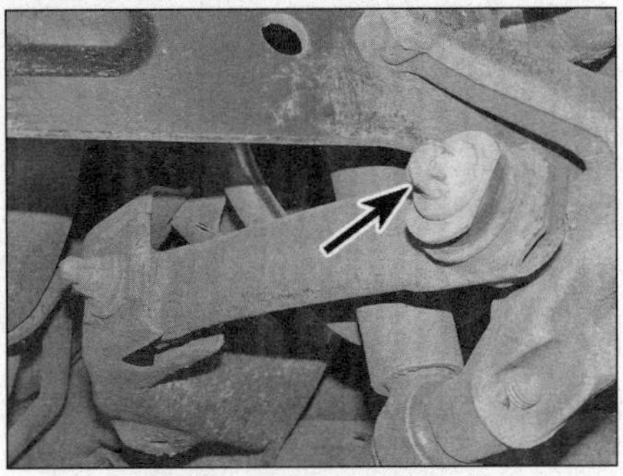

13.35 Toe-in link arm outer bolt (arrowed)

Refitting

20 Refitting is a reversal of removal, remembering to tighten the bolts to the specified torque.

Lower transverse link arm

Removal

21 Raise the rear of the vehicle and support it securely on axle stands (see *Jacking and vehicle support*). Remove the relevant roadwheel.

22 If removing the left-hand lower arm on models with xenon headlights, remove the level sensor from the arm **(see illustration)**.

23 Place a trolley jack opposite the spring under the lower arm, and support the weight of the spring.

24 Make alignment marks between the eccentric washer and the rear subframe at the inner end of the arm, then unscrew the outer bolt securing the arm to the hub carrier **(see illustrations)**. Use the jack to slowly lower the arm and withdrawn the spring.

25 Undo the inner mounting bolt and remove the arm. Discard the nut, a new one must be fitted.

Refitting

26 Align the inner end of the arm and insert the mounting bolt, aligning the previously-made marks. Fit the new nut, but only finger-tighten it at this stage.

27 Refit the spring and raise the arm to the 'normal' position with a trolley jack.

28 Screw-in the outer mounting bolt and tighten the nut to the specified torque.

29 Tighten the inner mounting bolt/nut to the specified torque. Ensure the marks still align.

30 Remove the jack, refit the level sensor (where applicable), and refit the roadwheel.

31 It is recommended that the vehicle be checked for wheel alignment at the earliest opportunity.

Toe-in link arm

Removal

32 Raise the rear of the vehicle and support it securely on axle stands (see *Jacking and vehicle support*). Remove the relevant roadwheel.

33 Disconnect the wheel speed sensor wiring plug.

34 Make alignment marks between the link arm inner mounting bolt eccentric washer and the rear subframe, then undo the nut and remove the bolt **(see illustration)**.

35 Undo the outer bolt and remove the link arm **(see illustration)**.

Refitting

36 Position the link arm, and insert the inner and outer mounting bolts.

37 Align the previously-made marks between the inner bolt eccentric washer and the rear subframe, then fit the nuts and tighten the inner and outer nuts to the specified torque.

38 Reconnect the wheel speed sensor wiring plug and refit the roadwheel.

39 It is recommended that the vehicle be checked for wheel alignment at the earliest opportunity.

14 Steering wheel – removal and refitting

Removal

1 Remove the driver's airbag module from the steering wheel as described in Chapter 12, Section 21.

Caution: Observe the safety instructions meticulously.

2 Ensure the wheel is in the straight-ahead position, then unscrew and remove the steering wheel retaining bolt using an Allen key **(see illustration)**. Mark the steering wheel and column in relation to each other with a dab of paint.

3 Disconnect the wiring plug, then carefully ease the steering wheel from the column splines **(see illustration)**.

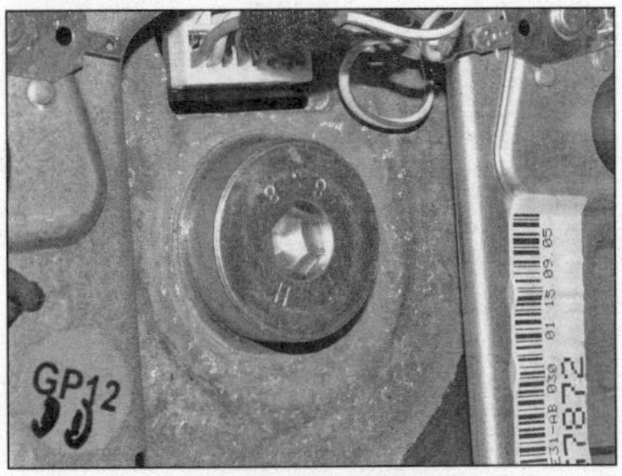

14.2 Use an Allen key to undo the steering wheel bolt

Caution: Do not use a hammer or mallet to tap the steering wheel from the splines, as this may damage the collapsible inner column.

Refitting

4 Locate the steering wheel on the column splines with the previously-made marks aligned.

5 Apply a little thread-locking compound, then refit the retaining bolt and tighten the nut to the specified torque.

6 Reconnect the wiring plug.

7 Refit the driver's airbag module with reference to Chapter 12, Section 21.

15 Steering column – removal and refitting

Removal

1 Remove the steering wheel as described in Section 14.

2 Unclip the gaiter from the front of the column integration module.

3 Release the 2 clips and slide the column integration module up from the column **(see illustration)**.

Caution: Electronic control modules are extremely sensitive to static electricity. Before touching any module, earth yourself by touching a metal part of the vehicle body.

4 Disconnect the wiring plug from the column integration module **(see illustration)**.

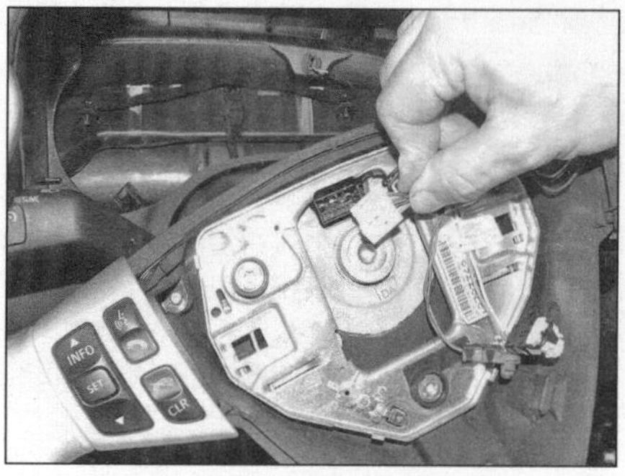

14.3 Disconnect the wiring plug

5 Remove the gaiter from the instrument panel.

6 Remove the main instrument unit as described in Chapter 12, Section 9.

7 Remove the driver's side lower facia panel as described in Chapter 11, Section 26.

8 Remove the floor air duct under the driver's side of the facia.

9 Prise down and remove the cover around the steering column adjustment lever **(see illustration)**.

10 At the bottom of the steering column, unscrew and remove the universal joint clamp bolt **(see illustration)**.

11 Disconnect the wiring plug from the steering column lock, and release the wiring harness from any retaining clips on the column.

12 Unscrew and remove the column lower mounting bolt **(see illustration)**. On manual transmissions, depress the clutch pedal to access the bolt.

13 Unscrew and remove the upper mounting bolts located beneath the instrument panel, then withdraw the steering column from the bulkhead bracket **(see illustration)**.

Refitting

14 Locate the steering column, hook the upper part onto the facia bracket at the top, fit the bolts, then tighten them to the specified torque. On manual transmissions, depress the clutch pedal to access the lower bolt.

15 Engage the universal joint on the bottom of the column with the steering rack pinion shaft, making sure that the bolt hole is aligned with the cut-out in the shaft. Apply a little thread-locking compound to the threads and tighten it to the specified torque.

16 The remainder of refitting is a reversal of removal.

16 Power steering hydraulic system – bleeding

Note: *The power steering hydraulic system must be bled if any part of the system has been disconnected.*

1 Remove the fluid reservoir filler cap, and top-up to the maximum level mark with fluid of the specified type and grade; refer to Chapter 1A, Section 12 or Chapter 1B, Section 12 for guidance.

Conventional power steering (engine-driven pump)

2 Park the vehicle on a level surface and apply the handbrake.

15.3 Release the 2 clips (arrowed) and slide the CIM up the steering column

15.4 Slide out the red locking catch and disconnect the wiring plug

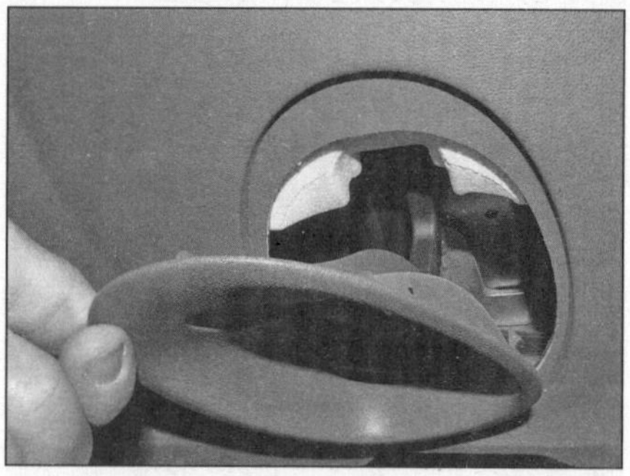

15.9 Prise down the trim around the column adjustment lever

15.10 Undo the universal joint pinch-bolt (arrowed)

15.12 Steering column lower mounting bolt (arrowed)

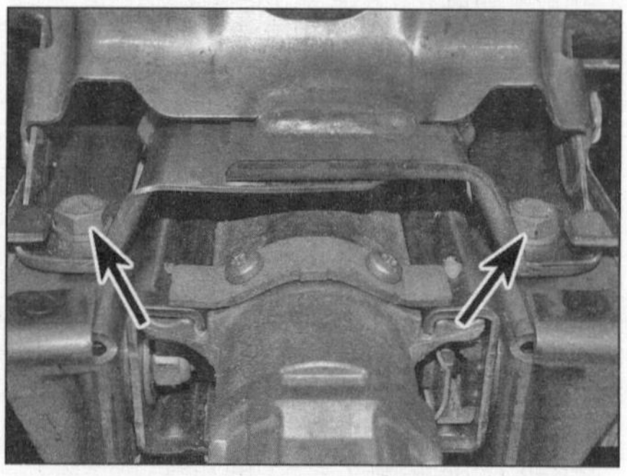

15.13 Steering column upper mounting bolts (arrowed)

3 Without turning the steering wheel, start the engine and allow it to run for 5 seconds – no more.
4 Check, and if necessary, top-up the power steering reservoir.
5 Start the engine again, and let it run until no more air bubbles appear in the fluid reservoir. Any abnormal noise from the pump indicates that air is still present in the system.
6 Once all traces of air have been purged from the power steering hydraulic system, stop the engine and allow the system to cool. Finally, check that the fluid level is up to the maximum mark on the reservoir, and top-up if necessary.

Electro-hydraulic power steering

7 Start the engine, allow it to run for 5 seconds and turn it off. Pause for a few seconds, then repeat this procedure twice more.
8 Start the engine, and turn the steering wheel from lock-to-lock 5 times.
9 Switch off the engine and recheck the fluid level in the reservoir. Top-up if necessary.

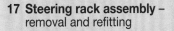

17 Steering rack assembly – removal and refitting

Conventional power steering (engine-driven pump)

Removal

1 Apply the handbrake, then jack up the front of the vehicle and support it on axle stands (see *Jacking and vehicle support*). Remove both front roadwheels and the engine undershield.
2 Clamp the steering rack return hose using a hose clamp.
3 Undo the clamp bolt and detach the pipe from the bracket on the top of the steering rack.
4 Ensure the steering wheel and front wheels are in the straight-ahead position and engage the steering lock.
5 On Convertible models, undo the bolts and remove the front chassis reinforcement **(see illustration 5.3b)**.
6 Detach the track rod ends from the hub carriers as described in Section 22.
7 Undo the nuts and detach the anti-roll bar links from the anti-roll bar **(see illustration 5.10)**.
8 At the bottom of the steering column, unscrew and remove the clamp bolt and slide the universal joint from the steering rack pinion shaft **(see illustration 5.5)**.
9 Detach the front section of the exhaust pipe from the catalytic converter with reference to Chapter 4A, Section 16 or Chapter 4B, Section 18.
10 Undo the bolts and remove the rear torque rod from the engine/transmission and subframe.
11 Place a trolley jack under the rear of the subframe, then remove the subframe rear mounting bolts, and slacken the front ones a few turns.
12 Lower the rear of the subframe a little, then undo the bolts securing the anti-roll bar clamps to the subframe.

17.14 Steering rack mounting bolts (arrowed)

13 Place a container under the steering rack, then undo the unions and detach the fluid delivery and return pipes from the steering rack. Be prepared for fluid spillage.
14 Undo and remove the steering rack mounting bolts/nuts, then raise the anti-roll bar as high as possible, and manoeuvre the steering rack out through the left-hand wheel arch **(see illustration)**.

Refitting

15 Refitting is a reversal of removal, but note the following additional points.

a) Lubricate the bulkhead rubber with a little petroleum jelly.
b) Fit new O-ring seals where necessary.
c) Tighten all nuts and bolts to the specified torque where given.
d) Engage the universal joint on the bottom of the column with the steering rack pinion shaft, making sure that the bolt hole is aligned with the cut-out in the shaft and the alignment marks are adjacent as previously noted. Apply a little thread-locking compound to the threads prior to fitting the pinch-bolt.
e) Fill the power steering system with the specified hydraulic fluid and bleed the system with reference to Section 16.
f) Have the front wheel alignment checked at the earliest opportunity (see Section 25).

Electro-hydraulic power steering

Removal

16 Ensure the steering wheel and front wheels are in the straight-ahead position and engage the steering lock.

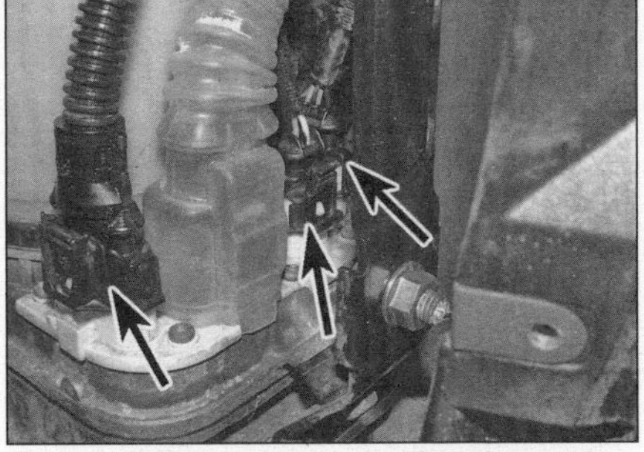

17.23 Disconnect the wiring plugs (arrowed) from the EHPS supply unit

17.22 Undo the steering column universal joint pinch-bolt (arrowed – viewed through the wheel arch aperture)

17 Apply the handbrake, then jack up the front of the vehicle and support it on axle stands (see *Jacking and vehicle support*). Remove both front roadwheels and the engine undershield.
18 Remove the undershield beneath the radiator.
19 On Convertible models, undo the bolts and remove the front chassis reinforcement **(see illustration 5.3b)**
20 Remove the front section of the exhaust system as described in Chapter 4A, Section 16 or Chapter 4B, Section 18.
21 Undo the bolts and remove the rear engine torque rod.
22 At the bottom of the steering column, unscrew and remove the clamp bolt and slide the universal joint from the steering rack pinion shaft **(see illustration)**. Mark the shaft and column if necessary to ensure correct refitting.
23 Disconnect the wiring plugs from the EHPS motor **(see illustration)** and where fitted disconnect the wiring plug from steering angle sensor.
24 Detach the track rod ends from the hub carriers as described in Section 22.
25 Release the steering rack gaiter clamps and slide the gaiters off the main rack body.
26 Using a crows-foot spanner unbolt and remove both track rods.
27 Unbolt the combined EHPS reservoir and pump from the steering rack.
28 Place a suitable container below the vehicle and then unbolt the power steering supply and return pipes from the steering rack **(see illustration)**.

17.28 Hydraulic supply and return pipe connections (arrowed) on the side of the EHPS supply unit

18.1 Disconnect the pressure sensor wiring plug

18.2 Undo the fluid delivery pipe banjo bolt

29 Remove the steering rack nuts, bolts and washers. Lift the pump assembly from the steering rack and manoeuvre the rack from the vehicle.

30 No further dismantling is recommended. Due to the complexity and the need for special tools, have any fault investigated by a Saab dealer or specialist.

Refitting

31 Refitting is a reversal of removal, but note the following additional points.

a) Fit new O-ring seals where necessary.

b) Tighten all nuts and bolts to the specified torque where given.

c) The track rods are handed and should be marked L or R. When correctly fitted they will curve slightly backwards.

d) Engage the universal joint on the bottom of the column with the steering rack pinion shaft, making sure that the bolt hole is aligned with the cut-out in the shaft and the alignment marks are adjacent as previously noted. Apply a little thread-locking compound to the threads prior to fitting the pinch-bolt.

e) Fill the power steering system with the specified hydraulic fluid and bleed the system with reference to Section 16.

f) Have the front wheel alignment checked at the earliest opportunity (see Section 25).

18.3 Release the clip and disconnect the fluid return hose

18 Power steering pump – removal and refitting

Conventional power steering (engine-driven pump)

Removal

1 Disconnect the pressure sensor wiring plug **(see illustration)**.

2 Undo the bolt and disconnect the delivery pipe from the pump. Recover the sealing washers and be prepared for fluid spillage **(see illustration)**.

3 Release the clip and disconnect the fluid return hose from the reservoir **(see illustration)**. Be prepared for fluid spillage.

4 Undo the retaining bolts and remove the pump. Recover the gasket/seal **(see illustrations)**.

Refitting

5 Refitting is a reversal of removal, but note the following additional points.

a) Tighten all nuts and bolts to the specified torque where given.

b) Fit the pump with a new gasket/seal.

c) Fill the hydraulic system with fluid and bleed it as described in Section 16.

18.4a Undo the pump mounting bolts (upper bolt arrowed)

18.4b Renew the seal

Electro-hydraulic power steering

Removal

6 Disconnect the battery negative (earth) cable before starting work.

7 Jack up and support the front of the vehicle (see *Jacking and vehicle support*).

8 Remove the engine undershield and then remove the 2 front nuts from the rubber mounting pad.

9 On left-hand drive models disconnect the wiring plug and remove all 4 of the EHPS mounting nuts.

10 Place a suitable container below the EHPS unit and lower the vehicle to the ground.

11 Unhook the coolant reservoir and secure it to one side. Disconnect the brake fluid level sensor wiring plug and (where fitted) unbolt the pressure sensor bracket for the particle filter.

12 Release the coolant hoses from the support bracket and move them to one side.

13 On right-hand drive models disconnect the wiring plug from the EHPS unit and remove the remaining mounting nuts.

14 To avoid the spillage of power steering fluid the reservoir must be emptied at this point.

15 Move the EHPS unit forward and remove the supply and return hoses.

16 Lift the EHPS unit from the engine bay.

Refitting

17 Refitting is a reversal of removal, but note the following additional points.

a) Tighten all nuts and bolts to the specified torque where given.

b) Fit new o-ring seals to the supply and return pipes.

c) Check the condition of the EHPS mountings and renew them if necessary.

d) Fill the hydraulic system with fluid and bleed it as described in Section 16.

19 Electro-hydraulic power steering control module – general information

The electro-hydraulic power steering (EHPS) control module is integral with the power steering unit, and cannot be renewed separately. If the steering system should develop a fault, have the system's self-diagnosis facility interrogated using Saab's TECH2 diagnostic equipment, before removing the steering rack assembly.

Once the unit has been renewed, the vehicle variant details and possibly the latest software will need to be loaded into the control module. This is only possible using Saab's diagnostic equipment, and therefore should be entrusted to a Saab dealer or suitably-equipped specialist.

20 Steering angle sensor – removal and refitting

Removal

1 The steering angle sensor is fitted to the steering rack pinion housing on models with EHPS. To remove the sensor, depress the retaining clip and disconnect the wiring plug from the sensor.

2 Undo the 2 retaining bolts, and pull the sensor from the housing.

Refitting

3 Ensure the sensor and steering rack housing mating surfaces are clean.

4 Check the sensor seal is in good condition and correctly located, then refit the sensor to the housing, and tighten the bolts securely.

5 Reconnect the sensor wiring plug.

6 If the sensor has been renewed the sensor will need calibrating using Saab's TECH2 diagnostic (or other suitable) equipment. Most generic diagnostic equipment that covers Saab vehicles will be capable of performing this task.

21 Steering rack rubber gaiter – renewal

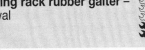

1 Remove the track rod end on the side concerned as described in Section 22. Unscrew the locknut from the track rod.

2 Release the two clips and peel off the gaiter **(see illustration)**.

3 Clean out any dirt and grit from the inner end of the track rod and (when accessible) the rack.

4 Wrap insulating tape around the track rod threads to protect the new gaiter whilst installing.

5 Refit the track rod end locknut.

6 Refit the track rod end as described in Section 22.

22 Track rod end – removal and refitting

1 Loosen the appropriate front wheel nuts. Chock the rear wheels, then jack up the front of the vehicle and support it on axle stands (see *Jacking and vehicle support*). Remove the appropriate front roadwheel.

2 Counter-hold the track rod end, and slacken the track rod end locknut by half a turn **(see illustration)**. If the locknut is now left in this position, it will act as a further guide for refitting.

3 Unscrew the track rod end balljoint nut, using a spanner to counter-hold the balljoint shank. Separate the balljoint from the hub carrier with a proprietary balljoint separator,

21.2 Release the clips (arrowed) at each end of the gaiter

then remove the nut and disengage the balljoint from the arm **(see illustration)**.

4 Unscrew the track rod end from the track rod, counting the number of turns needed to remove it. Make a note of the number of turns, so that the tracking can be reset (or at least approximated) on refitting.

Refitting

5 Screw the track rod end onto the track rod by the same number of turns noted during removal. Note that the track rod ends are marked L or R, indicating which side they are fitted to.

6 Engage the balljoint in the hub carrier. Tighten the nut to the specified torque.

7 Counter-hold the track rod and tighten the locknut.

8 Refit the front wheel, lower the car and tighten the wheel bolts in a diagonal sequence to the specified torque.

9 Have the front wheel alignment checked at the earliest opportunity (see Section 25).

23 Front subframe – removal and refitting

Removal

1 Apply the handbrake, then raise the front of the vehicle, support it securely on axle stands (see *Jacking and vehicle support*). Remove the front roadwheels. Remove the engine top cover the engine transmission undershield.

2 Position a lifting beam across the engine bay, locating the support legs securely in the

22.3 Release the balljoint tapered shank using a universal balljoint separator

22.2 Slacken the track rod end locknut (arrowed)

sills at either side, in line with the strut top mountings. Hook the jib onto the engine lifting eyelet and raise it, so that the weight of the engine is taken off the transmission mounting. Most people won't have access to an engine lifting beam, but it may be possible to hire one. Alternatively, an engine hoist may be used to support the engine, but when using this method, bear in mind that if the vehicle is lowered on its axle stands to adjust the working height, for example, then the hoist will have to be lowered accordingly, to avoid straining the engine mountings.

3 Remove the undershield beneath the radiator, then using straps or cable-ties, suspend the radiator from the vehicle bodywork. On Convertible models, undo the bolts and remove the front chassis reinforcement **(see illustration 5.3b)**.

4 Undo the screws and remove the radiator lower mounting brackets from the front subframe **(see illustration)**. Where applicable, detach the power steering cooler brackets from the radiator brackets.

5 Remove the complete exhaust system as described in Chapter 4A, Section 16 or Chapter 4B, Section 18.

6 Remove the engine torque rod(s) from the subframe (see Chapter 2A, 2B or 2C).

7 Undo the bolts, and lever down both lower suspension arms from the base of the hub carriers.

8 Undo the nuts/bolts and detach the steering rack from the subframe **(see illustration 17.14)**.

9 Release the power steering pipe clips from the subframe.

10 Disconnect the wiring plug, then release

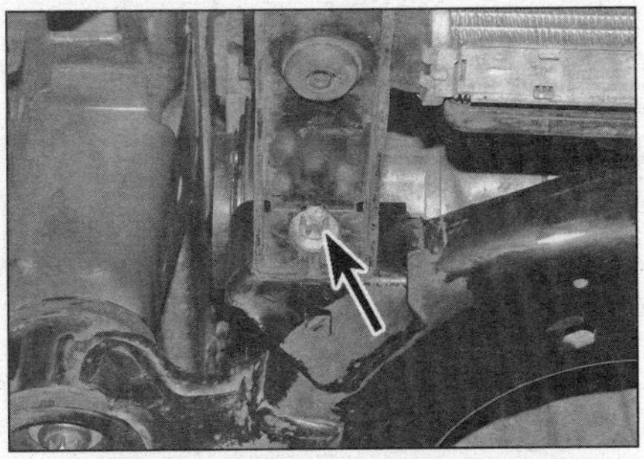

23.4 Undo the Torx screw (arrowed) securing the radiator lower mounting bracket each side

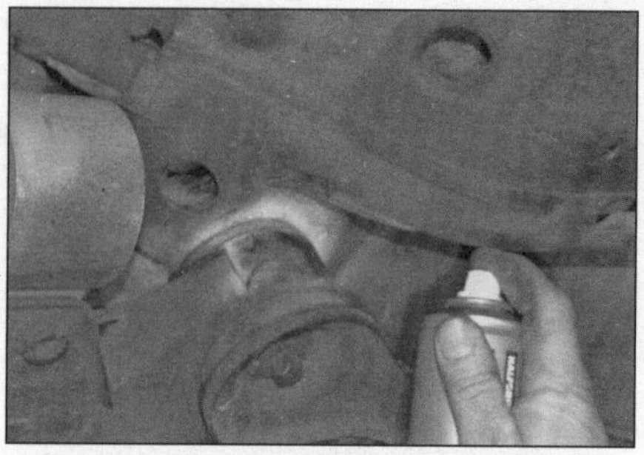

23.11a We used spray paint to make alignment marks around the subframe mountings

23.11b Undo the front subframe mounting bolts ...

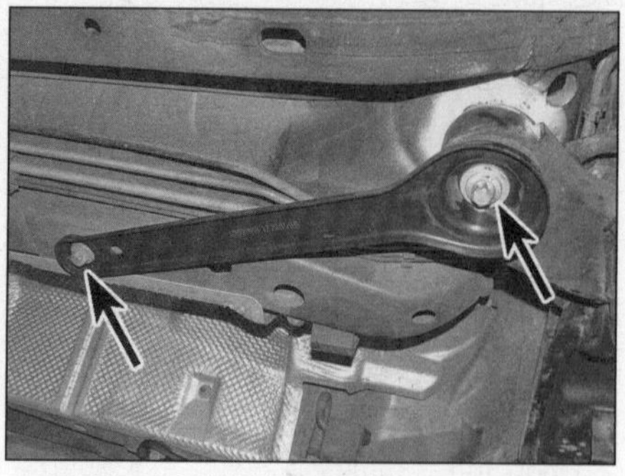

23.11c ... and the rear mounting bolts (arrowed)

the clips securing the level sensor wiring (where fitted) to the subframe.

11 Make alignment marks between the subframe and the vehicle body, then undo the mounting bolts/brackets, and lower the subframe slightly **(see illustrations)**.

12 Undo the bolts securing the anti-roll bar clamps, then lower the subframe.

Refitting

13 Refitting is a reversal of removal. Remember to align the previously-made marks, and tighten the bolts to the specified torque.

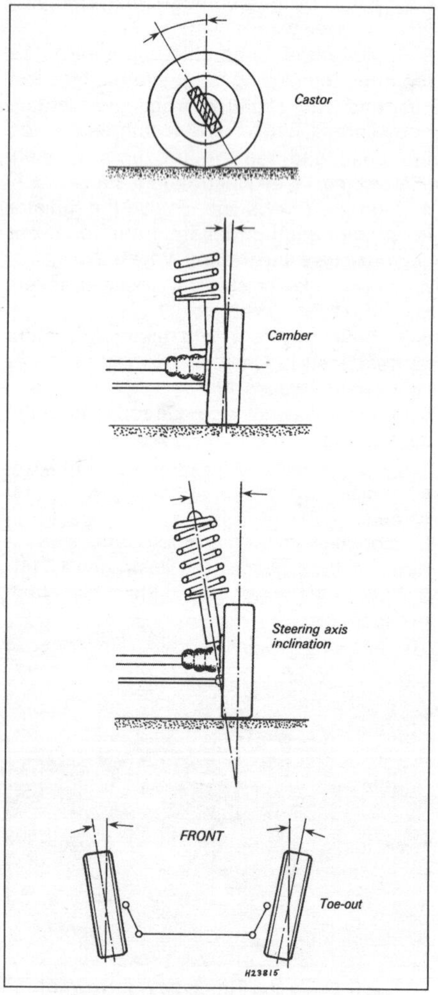

25.1 Front steering and suspension geometry

24 Rear subframe – removal and refitting

Removal

1 Raise the rear of the vehicle and support it securely on axle stands (see *Jacking and vehicle support*). Remove both rear roadwheels.

2 On vehicles fitted with a tyre pressure monitoring system (TPMS) remove the right-hand wing liner and disconnect the wiring plug from the sensor.

3 With reference to Chapter 9, Section 7, remove both rear calipers and hang them securely from the brake hose support bracket.

4 Unclip the handbrake cables from the control arms on both sides and then disconnect the wiring plug from the ABS sensors.

5 Remove the rear springs as described in Section 10.

6 Disconnect the shock absorbers at the lower mounting bolts.

7 On Convertible models unbolt and remove the reinforcement struts from the rear subframe.

8 Mark precisely the position of the subframe in relation to the vehicle body.

9 Position a suitable trolley jack beneath the subframe. Support the subframe on the jack and remove the subframe mounting bolts.

10 With the aid of an assistant lower the subframe on the trolley jack. Free the handbrake cables completely as the jack is lowered.

Refitting

11 Refitting is a reversal of removal. Remember to align the previously-made marks, and tighten the bolts to the specified torque.

25 Wheel alignment and steering angles – general information

1 A car's steering and suspension geometry is defined in four basic settings – all angles are expressed in degrees (toe settings are also expressed as a measurement); the relevant settings are camber, castor, steering axis inclination, and toe setting **(see illustration)**. On the models covered by this manual, only the front and rear wheel toe settings are adjustable.

2 Camber is the angle at which the front wheels are set from the vertical when viewed from the front or rear of the car. Negative camber is the amount (in degrees) that the wheels are tilted inward at the top from the vertical.

3 The front camber angle is adjusted by slackening the steering knuckle-to-suspension strut mounting bolts and repositioning the hub carrier assemblies as necessary.

4 Castor is the angle between the steering axis and a vertical line when viewed from each side of the car. Positive castor is when the steering axis is inclined rearward at the top.

5 Steering axis inclination is the angle (when viewed from the front of the vehicle) between the vertical and an imaginary line drawn through the front suspension strut upper mounting and the control arm balljoint.

6 Toe setting is the amount by which the distance between the front inside edges of the roadwheels (measured at hub height) differs from the diametrically opposite distance measured between the rear inside edges of the roadwheels. Toe-in is when the roadwheels point inwards, towards each other at the front, while toe-out is when they splay outwards from each other at the front.

7 The front wheel toe setting is adjusted by altering the length of the steering track rods on both sides. This adjustment is normally referred to as the tracking.

8 The rear wheel toe setting is adjusted by rotating the upper transverse link or toe-in link arms mounting bolts in the subframe. The bolt incorporates an eccentric washer, and the pivot point for the link varies as the bolt is rotated.

9 All other suspension and steering angles are set during manufacture, and no adjustment is possible. It can be assumed, therefore, that unless the vehicle has suffered accident damage, all the preset angles will be correct.

10 Special optical measuring equipment is necessary to accurately check and adjust the front and rear toe settings and front camber angles, and this work should be carried out by a Saab dealer or similar expert. Most tyre-fitting centres have the expertise and equipment to carry out at least a front wheel toe setting (tracking) check for a nominal charge.

Chapter 11
Bodywork and fittings

Contents

Section number

Degrees of difficulty

Easy, suitable for novice with little experience	**Fairly easy,** suitable for beginner with some experience	**Fairly difficult,** suitable for competent DIY mechanic	**Difficult,** suitable for experienced DIY mechanic	**Very difficult,** suitable for expert DIY or professional

Specifications

Soft top hydraulic fluid

Type	Refer to *Lubricants and fluids* on page 0•16
Capacity	0.6 litres

Torque wrench settings

Torque wrench settings	Nm	lbf ft
Front seat belt:		
Saloon and Estate models:		
Reel	37	27
Height adjuster	37	27
Buckle	45	33
Convertible models:		
Reel	47	35
Anchorage	47	35
Buckle	39	29
Front seat mounting screws	30	22
Passenger airbag	9	7
Passenger airbag safety band bolt	9	7
Rear seat belt:		
Saloon and Estate models:		
Reel	37	27
Floor anchorage	37	27
Centre belt inertia reel	45	33
Centre seat belt carrier	37	27
Strap guide	37	27
Convertible models:		
Reel	47	35
Strap guide	47	35
Lower anchorage	47	35
Buckle	45	35
Soft top mounting nuts	28	21

1 General information

The vehicle's body is constructed from pressed-steel sections that are either spot-welded or seam-welded together. The overall rigidity of the body is increased by the use of stiffening beams built into the body panels, steel flanges in the window and door openings, and the application of adhesive in fixed glass joints.

The front subframe assembly provides mounting points for the engine/transmission unit and front suspension, and the steering gear is bolted to the bulkhead. The front wings are also bolted on, rather than welded on, allowing accident damage to be repaired easily.

The vehicle's underside is coated with polyester underseal and an anti-corrosion compound. This treatment provides protection against the elements, and also serves as an effective sound insulation layer. The cabin, luggage area and engine compartment are also lined with bituminous felt and other sound-insulating materials, to provide further noise damping.

All models are fitted with electric windows at the front and rear. The window glass is raised and lowered by an electric motor, directly operating a scissor-action regulator.

Central locking is fitted to all models, and is actuated from the driver's or passenger's door lock. It operates the locks on all four doors, the tailgate or the boot lid, and the fuel filler cap. The lock mechanisms are actuated by servo motor units, and the system is controlled by an electronic control module (ECM).

2 Maintenance – bodywork and underframe

The general condition of a vehicle's bodywork is the one thing that significantly affects its value. Maintenance is easy, but needs to be regular. Neglect, particularly after minor damage, can lead quickly to further deterioration and costly repair bills. It is important also to keep watch on those parts of the vehicle not immediately visible, for instance the underside, inside all the wheel arches, and the lower part of the engine compartment.

The basic maintenance routine for the bodywork is washing – preferably with a lot of water, from a hose. This will remove all the loose solids which may have stuck to the vehicle. It is important to flush these off in such a way as to prevent grit from scratching the finish. The wheel arches and underframe need washing in the same way, to remove any accumulated mud which will retain moisture and tend to encourage rust. Paradoxically enough, the best time to clean the underframe and wheel arches is in wet weather, when the mud is thoroughly wet and soft. In very wet weather, the underframe is usually cleaned of large accumulations automatically, and this is a good time for inspection.

Periodically, except on vehicles with a wax-based underbody protective coating, it is a good idea to have the whole of the underframe of the vehicle steam-cleaned, engine compartment included, so that a thorough inspection can be carried out to see what minor repairs and renovations are necessary. Steam-cleaning is available at many garages, and is necessary for the removal of the accumulation of oily grime, which sometimes is allowed to become thick in certain areas. If steam-cleaning facilities are not available, there are one or two excellent grease solvents available, which can be brush-applied; the dirt can then be simply hosed off. Note that these methods should not be used on vehicles with wax-based underbody protective coating, or the coating will be removed. Such vehicles should be inspected annually, preferably just prior to Winter, when the underbody should be washed down, and any damage to the wax coating repaired. Ideally, a completely fresh coat should be applied. It would also be worth considering the use of such wax-based protection for injection into door panels, sills, box sections, etc, as an additional safeguard against rust damage, where such protection is not provided by the vehicle manufacturer.

After washing paintwork, wipe off with a chamois leather to give an unspotted clear finish. A coat of clear protective wax polish will give added protection against chemical pollutants in the air. If the paintwork sheen has dulled or oxidised, use a cleaner/polisher combination to restore the brilliance of the shine. This requires a little effort, but such dulling is usually caused because regular washing has been neglected. Care needs to be taken with metallic paintwork, as special non-abrasive cleaner/polisher is required to avoid damage to the finish. Always check that the door and ventilator opening drain holes and pipes are completely clear, so that water can be drained out. Brightwork should be treated in the same way as paintwork. Windscreens and windows can be kept clear of the smeary film which often appears, by the use of proprietary glass cleaner. Never use any form of wax or other body or chromium polish on glass.

3 Maintenance – upholstery and carpets

Mats and carpets should be brushed or vacuum-cleaned regularly, to keep them free of grit. If they are badly stained, remove them from the vehicle for scrubbing or sponging, and make quite sure they are dry before refitting. Seats and interior trim panels can be kept clean by wiping with a damp cloth. If they do become stained (which can be more apparent on light-coloured upholstery), use a little liquid detergent and a soft nail brush to scour the grime out of the grain of the material. Do not forget to keep the headlining clean in the same way as the upholstery. When using liquid cleaners inside the vehicle, do not over-wet the surfaces being cleaned. Excessive damp could get into the seams and padded interior, causing stains, offensive odours or even rot. If the inside of the vehicle gets wet accidentally, it is worthwhile taking some trouble to dry it out properly, particularly where carpets are involved. Do not leave oil or electric heaters inside the vehicle for this purpose.

4 Minor body damage – repair

Minor scratches

If the scratch is very superficial, and does not penetrate to the metal of the bodywork, repair is very simple. Lightly rub the area of the scratch with a paintwork renovator, or a very fine cutting paste, to remove loose paint from the scratch, and to clear the surrounding bodywork of wax polish. Rinse the area with clean water.

Apply touch-up paint to the scratch using a fine paint brush; continue to apply fine layers of paint until the surface of the paint in the scratch is level with the surrounding paintwork. Allow the new paint at least two weeks to harden, then blend it into the surrounding paintwork by rubbing the scratch area with a paintwork renovator or a very fine cutting paste. Finally, apply wax polish.

Where the scratch has penetrated right through to the metal of the bodywork, causing the metal to rust, a different repair technique is required. Remove any loose rust from the bottom of the scratch with a penknife, then apply rust-inhibiting paint, to prevent the formation of rust in the future. Using a rubber or nylon applicator, fill the scratch with bodystopper paste. If required, this paste can be mixed with cellulose thinners, to provide a very thin paste which is ideal for filling narrow scratches. Before the stopper-paste in the scratch hardens, wrap a piece of smooth cotton rag around the top of a finger. Dip the finger in cellulose thinners, and quickly sweep it across the surface of the stopper-paste in the scratch; this will ensure that the surface of the stopper-paste is slightly hollowed. The scratch can now be painted over as described earlier in this Section.

Dents

When deep denting of the vehicle's bodywork has taken place, the first task is to pull the dent out, until the affected bodywork almost attains its original shape. There is little point in trying to restore the original shape completely, as the metal in the damaged area will have stretched on impact, and cannot be reshaped fully to its original contour. It is better to bring the level of the dent up to a point which is about 3 mm below the level of the surrounding bodywork. In cases where the dent is very shallow anyway, it is not worth trying to pull it out at all. If the underside of the dent is accessible, it can be hammered out gently from behind, using a mallet with a wooden or plastic head. Whilst doing this, hold a suitable block of wood firmly against the outside of the panel, to absorb the impact from the hammer blows and thus prevent a large area of the bodywork from being 'belled-out'.

Should the dent be in a section of the bodywork which has a double skin, or some other factor making it inaccessible from behind, a different technique is called for. Drill several small holes through the metal inside the area – particularly in the deeper section. Then screw long self-tapping screws into the holes, just sufficiently for them to gain a good purchase in the metal. Now the dent can be pulled out by pulling on the protruding heads of the screws with a pair of pliers.

The next stage of the repair is the removal of the paint from the damaged area, and from an inch or so of the surrounding 'sound' bodywork. This is accomplished most easily by using a wire brush or abrasive pad on a power drill, although it can be done just as effectively by hand, using sheets of abrasive paper. To complete the preparation for filling, score the surface of the bare metal with a screwdriver or the tang of a file, or alternatively, drill small holes in the affected area. This will provide a really good 'key' for the filler paste.

To complete the repair, see the Section on filling and respraying.

Rust holes or gashes

Remove all paint from the affected area, and from an inch or so of the surrounding 'sound' bodywork, using an abrasive pad or a wire brush on a power drill. If these are not available, a few sheets of abrasive paper will do the job most effectively. With the paint removed, you will be able to judge the severity of the corrosion, and therefore decide whether to renew the whole panel (if this is possible) or to repair the affected area. New body panels are not as expensive as most people think, and it is often quicker and more satisfactory to fit a new panel than to attempt to repair large areas of corrosion.

Remove all fittings from the affected area, except those which will act as a guide to the original shape of the damaged bodywork (eg headlamp shells etc). Then, using tin snips or a hacksaw blade, remove all loose metal and any other metal badly affected by corrosion. Hammer the edges of the hole inwards, in order to create a slight depression for the filler paste.

Wire-brush the affected area to remove the powdery rust from the surface of the remaining metal. Paint the affected area with rust-inhibiting paint; if the back of the rusted area is accessible, treat this also.

Before filling can take place, it will be necessary to block the hole in some way. This can be achieved by the use of aluminium or plastic mesh, or aluminium tape.

Aluminium or plastic mesh, or glass-fibre matting is probably the best material to use for a large hole. Cut a piece to the approximate size and shape of the hole to be filled, then position it in the hole so that its edges are below the level of the surrounding bodywork. It can be retained in position by several blobs of filler paste around its periphery.

Aluminium tape should be used for small or very narrow holes. Pull a piece off the roll, trim it to the approximate size and shape required, then pull off the backing paper (if used) and stick the tape over the hole; it can be overlapped if the thickness of one piece is insufficient. Burnish down the edges of the tape with the handle of a screwdriver or similar, to ensure that the tape is securely attached to the metal underneath.

Filling and respraying

Before using this Section, see the Sections on dent, deep scratch, rust holes and gash repairs.

Many types of bodyfiller are available, but generally speaking, those proprietary kits which contain a tin of filler paste and a tube of resin hardener are best for this type of repair. A wide, flexible plastic or nylon applicator will be found invaluable for imparting a smooth and well-contoured finish to the surface of the filler.

Mix up a little filler on a clean piece of card or board – measure the hardener carefully (follow the maker's instructions on the pack), otherwise the filler will set too rapidly or too slowly. Using the applicator, apply the filler paste to the prepared area; draw the applicator across the surface of the filler to achieve the correct contour and to level the surface. As soon as a contour that approximates to the correct one is achieved, stop working the paste – if you carry on too long, the paste will become sticky and begin to 'pick-up' on the applicator. Continue to add thin layers of filler paste at 20-minute intervals, until the level of the filler is just proud of the surrounding bodywork.

Once the filler has hardened, the excess can be removed using a metal plane or file. From then on, progressively-finer grades of abrasive paper should be used, starting with a 40-grade production paper, and finishing with a 400-grade wet-and-dry paper. Always wrap the abrasive paper around a flat rubber, cork, or wooden block – otherwise the surface of the filler will not be completely flat. During the smoothing of the filler surface, the wet-and-dry paper should be periodically rinsed in water. This will ensure that a very smooth finish is imparted to the filler at the final stage.

At this stage, the 'dent' should be surrounded by a ring of bare metal, which in turn should be encircled by the finely 'feathered' edge of the good paintwork. Rinse the repair area with clean water, until all of the dust produced by the rubbing-down operation has gone.

Spray the whole area with a light coat of primer – this will show up any imperfections in the surface of the filler. Repair these imperfections with fresh filler paste or bodystopper, and once more smooth the surface with abrasive paper. If bodystopper is used, it can be mixed with cellulose thinners, to form a really thin paste which is ideal for filling small holes. Repeat this spray-and-repair procedure until you are satisfied that the surface of the filler, and the feathered edge of the paintwork, are perfect. Clean the repair area with clean water, and allow to dry fully.

The repair area is now ready for final spraying. Paint spraying must be carried out in a warm, dry, windless and dust-free atmosphere. This condition can be created artificially if you have access to a large indoor working area, but if you are forced to work in the open, you will have to pick your day very carefully. If you are working indoors, dousing the floor in the work area with water will help to settle the dust which would otherwise be in the atmosphere. If the repair area is confined to one body panel, mask off the surrounding panels; this will help to minimise the effects of a slight mis-match in paint colours. Bodywork fittings (eg chrome strips, door handles etc) will also need to be masked off. Use genuine masking tape, and several thicknesses of newspaper, for the masking operations.

Before commencing to spray, agitate the aerosol can thoroughly, then spray a test area (an old tin, or similar) until the technique is mastered. Cover the repair area with a thick coat of primer; the thickness should be built up using several thin layers of paint, rather than one thick one. Using 400 grade wet-and-dry paper, rub down the surface of the primer until it is really smooth. While doing this, the work area should be thoroughly doused with water, and the wet-and-dry paper periodically rinsed in water. Allow to dry before spraying on more paint.

Spray on the top coat, again building up the thickness by using several thin layers of paint. Start spraying at the top of the repair area, and then, using a side-to-side motion, work downwards until the whole repair area and about 2 inches of the surrounding original paintwork is covered. Remove all masking material 10 to 15 minutes after spraying on the final coat of paint.

Allow the new paint at least two weeks to harden, then, using a paintwork renovator or a very fine cutting paste, blend the edges of the paint into the existing paintwork. Finally, apply wax polish.

Plastic components

With the use of more and more plastic body components by the vehicle manufacturers (eg bumpers. spoilers, and in some cases major body panels), rectification of more serious damage to such items has become

6.2a Undo the screws (arrowed) securing the wheel arch liner to the bumper ...

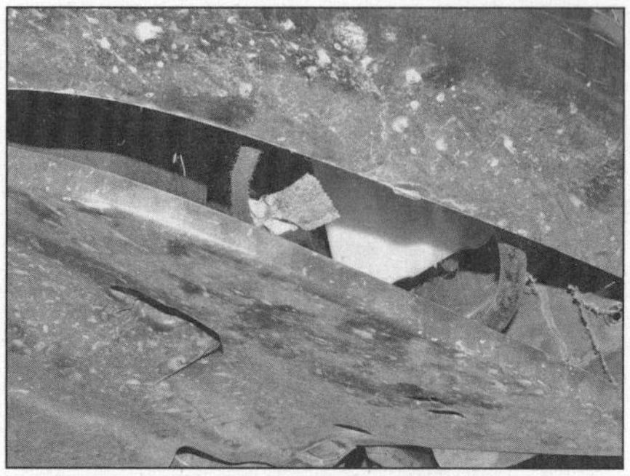

6.2b Lower the corner section ...

6.2c ... disconnect the wiring plug ...

6.2d ... and remove the headlight washer hose

a matter of either entrusting repair work to a specialist in this field, or renewing complete components. Repair of such damage by the DIY owner is not really feasible, owing to the cost of the equipment and materials required for effecting such repairs. The basic technique involves making a groove along the line of the crack in the plastic, using a rotary burr in a power drill. The damaged part is then welded back together, using a hot air gun to heat up and fuse a plastic filler rod into the groove. Any excess plastic is then removed, and the area rubbed down to a smooth finish. It is important that a filler rod of the correct plastic is used, as body components can be made of a variety of different types (eg polycarbonate, ABS, polypropylene).

Damage of a less serious nature (abrasions, minor cracks etc) can be repaired by the DIY owner using a two-part epoxy filler repair. Once mixed in equal, this is used in similar fashion to the bodywork filler used on metal panels. The filler is usually cured in twenty to thirty minutes, ready for sanding and painting.

If the owner is renewing a complete component himself, or if he has repaired it with epoxy filler, he will be left with the problem of finding a suitable paint for finishing which is compatible with the type of plastic used. At one time, the use of a universal paint was not possible, owing to the complex range of plastics encountered in body component applications. Standard paints, generally speaking, will not bond to plastic or rubber satisfactorily, but suitable paints to match any plastic or rubber finish, can be obtained from dealers. However, it is now possible to obtain a plastic body parts finishing kit which consists of a pre-primer treatment, a primer and coloured top coat. Full instructions are normally supplied with a kit, but basically, the method of use is to first apply the pre-primer to the component concerned, and allow it to dry for up to 30 minutes. Then the primer is applied, and left to dry for about an hour before finally applying the special-coloured top coat. The result is a correctly-coloured component, where the paint will flex with the plastic or rubber, a property that standard paint does not normally possess.

5 Major body damage – repair

Where serious damage has occurred, or large areas need renewal due to neglect, it means that complete new panels will need welding-in, and this is best left to professionals. If the damage is due to impact, it will also be necessary to check completely the alignment of the bodyshell, and this can only be carried out accurately by a dealer using special jigs. If the body is left misaligned, it is primarily dangerous, as the car will not handle properly, and secondly, uneven stresses will be imposed on the steering, suspension and possibly transmission, causing abnormal wear, or complete failure, particularly to such items as the tyres.

6 Front bumper – removal and refitting

Removal

1 Apply the handbrake, then jack up the front of the vehicle and support it on axle stands (see *Jacking and vehicle support*).

2 Undo the screws and detach the wheel arch liners from the rear ends of the bumper. On the left-hand side, lower the pivoting section of the panel and disconnect the wiring plug and (where fitted) the headlight washer hose **(see illustrations)**. Plug or clamp the washer hose.

3 Remove the remaining bolts from the panel.

4 Press in the centre pins, and lever out the plastic expansion rivets securing the top edge of the bumper to the bonnet slam panel. Remove the Torx head screws **(see illustrations)**.

5 With the aid of an assistant, pull out the rear upper edges of the bumper **(see illustration)**

6.4a Push in the centre pins and prise out the plastic rivets at the top of the bumper ...

6.4b ... and remove the Torx head screws

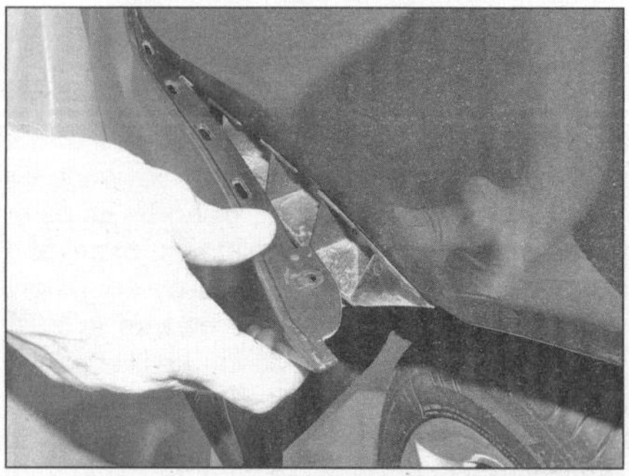

6.5 Prise free the edge of the bumper cover

to release the clips on each side, then slide the bumper forwards and manoeuvre it from the vehicle.

Refitting

6 Lift the bumper into position.
7 Insert the screws securing the bumper to the wheel arch liners and tighten them securely.
8 Reset **(see illustration)** and then refit the plastic expansion rivets at the top edge of the bumper, and press the centre pins down. Fit the Torx headed screws.
9 Refit the radiator undershield, and reconnect any wiring plugs/washer tubes.
10 Lower the vehicle to the ground.

7 Rear bumper – removal and refitting

Removal

Estate models

1 Raise the rear of the vehicle and support it securely on axle stands (see *Jacking and vehicle support*).
2 Undo the 2 nuts securing the underside of the bumper in the centre **(see illustration)**.
3 Remove the 3 screws each side securing the wheel arch liner to the bumper **(see illustration 7.9)**. Where applicable, undo the screws securing the mudguard first.
4 Raise the tailgate and remove the rear lamp assemblies as described in Chapter 12, Section 6. Insert a screwdriver under the bumper retaining clip, and lever the screwdriver to release the clip **(see illustration)**. Repeat on the remaining side.
5 On models with SPA (parking assistance system), disconnect the wiring plug at the base of the side hatch aperture.
6 Pull the front, top edges of the bumper outwards from the retaining clips, release the clips at the base of the tailgate aperture, then with the help of an assistant, manoeuvre the bumper rearwards **(see illustration)**.

Saloon models

7 Raise the rear of the vehicle and support it securely on axle stands (see *Jacking and vehicle support*).
8 Undo the 2 nuts securing the underside of the bumper in the centre **(see illustration 7.2)**.
9 Remove the 3 screws each side securing the wheel arch liner to the bumper **(see illustration)**.
10 Working in the luggage compartment, open the side hatch, then undo the rear light retaining nuts, disconnect the wiring plug and remove the rear lights **(see illustration)**. Repeat on the remaining side.
11 On models with SPA (parking assistance system), disconnect the wiring plug adjacent to the rear light aperture on the passenger's side, then release the rubber grommet and pull the wiring harness through **(see illustration)**.
12 On some models, the bumper is secured by 2 screws under the rear light apertures. Undo and remove the screws. On other models release the locking tab **(see illustration)**.
13 Pull the front, top edges of the bumper outwards from the retaining clips, then with the help of an assistant, manoeuvre the bumper rearwards **(see illustration)**.

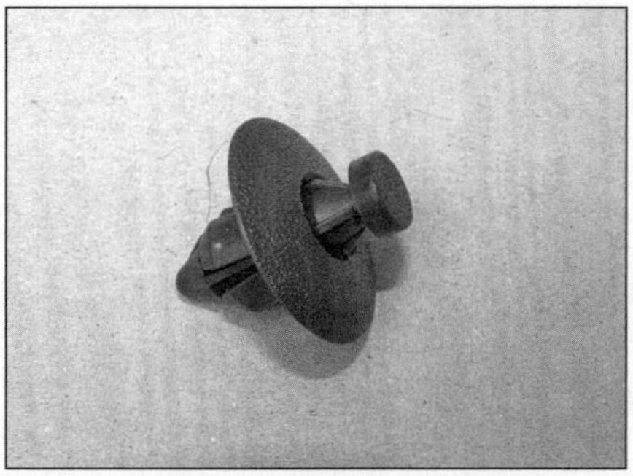

6.8 The centre peg correctly positioned for refitting

7.2 Rear bumper retaining nuts (arrowed)

7.4 Release the bumper from the retaining clip

7.6 Release the locking tabs at the front edges of the bumper cover

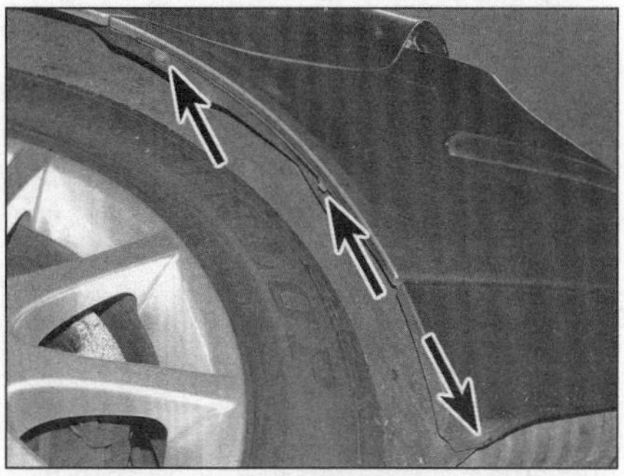

7.9 Bumper-to-wheel arch liner screws (arrowed)

7.10 Remove the rear lights

7.11 Disconnect the wiring plug (arrowed) and push the grommet through (arrowed) – models with SPA

7.12 Release the tab

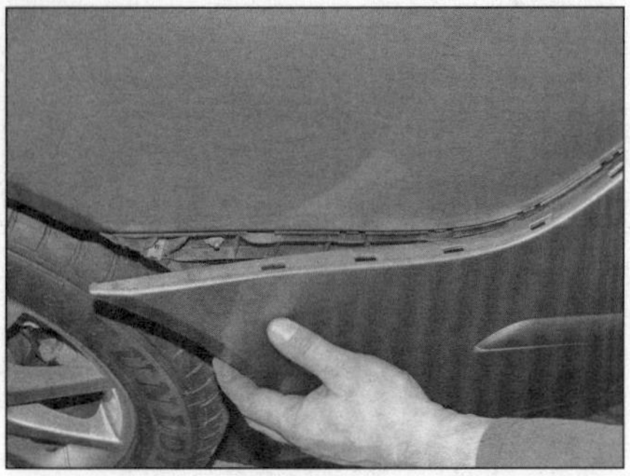

7.13 Pull out the front, top edges of the bumper

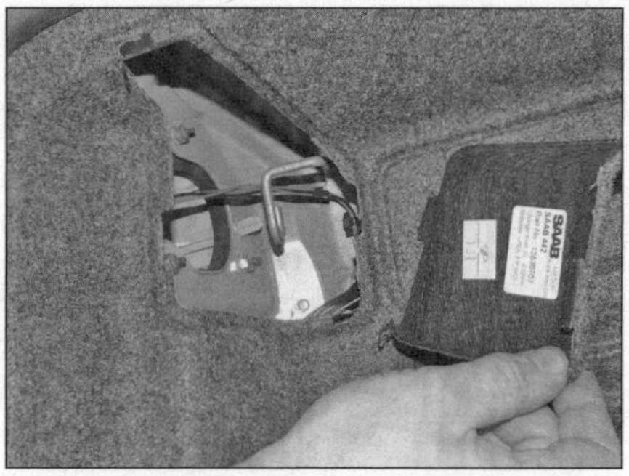

7.17a Remove the access panels ...

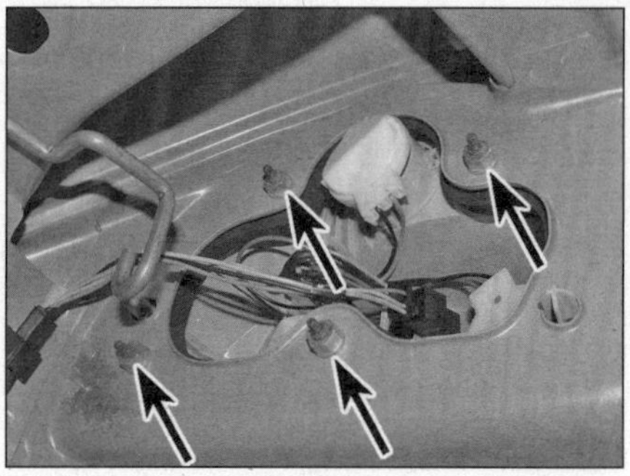

7.17b ... and undo the 4 nuts securing the rear lights (arrowed)

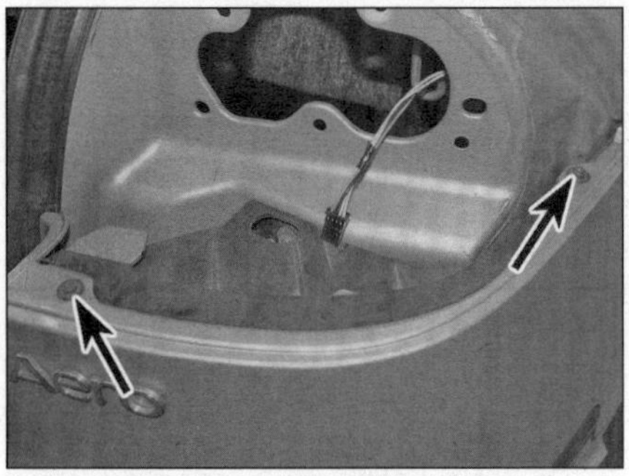

7.18 Undo the screws under the light apertures (arrowed)

Convertible models

14 Raise the rear of the vehicle and support it securely on axle stands (see *Jacking and vehicle support*).

15 Undo the 2 nuts securing the underside of the bumper in the centre **(see illustration 7.2)**.

16 Remove the 3 screws each side securing the wheel arch liner to the bumper **(see illustration 7.9)**.

17 Working in the luggage compartment, open the side hatch, then undo the rear light retaining nuts, disconnect the wiring plug and remove the rear lights **(see illustrations)**. Repeat on the remaining side.

18 Undo the 2 screws under the rear light apertures **(see illustration)**.

19 Pull the front, top edges of the bumper outwards from the retaining clips, then with the help of an assistant, manoeuvre the bumper rearwards **(see illustration)**.

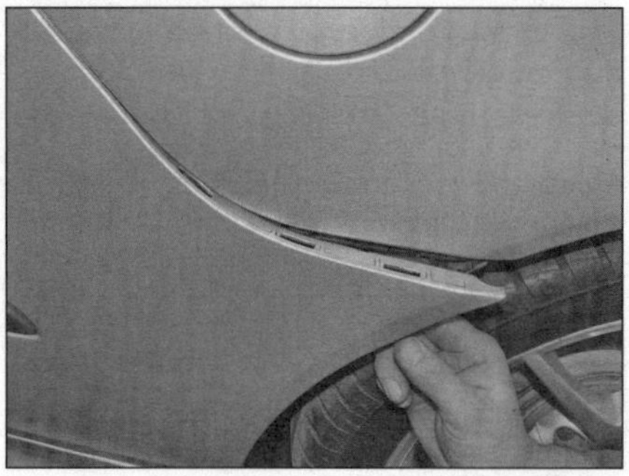

7.19 Pull the top edges of the bumper from the wing

Refitting

20 Lift the bumper into position and slide it forwards. Make sure the bumper engages correctly with the side brackets. Check for correct positioning by looking beneath the bumper.

21 The remainder of refitting is a reversal of removal.

8 Bonnet and struts – removal and refitting

Bonnet

⚠ ***Warning: It is essential to enlist the help of an assistant for this operation.***

Removal

1 With the bonnet open, place some cloth rags or card between the rear edge of the bonnet and the windscreen valance.

2 Release the lower edge of the bonnet sound insulation panel **(see illustration)**.

3 Disconnect the washer tube at the connector.

4 Where fitted, pull the cover from the hinges. Have the assistant support the bonnet open.

5 Disconnect the struts from the bonnet by prising out the retaining clips with a screwdriver, then pulling off the struts **(see illustration 8.10)**. Lower the struts onto the front wings.

6 Using a pencil, mark the position of the hinges on the bonnet.

7 While the assistant supports the bonnet, unscrew and remove the hinge bolts **(see illustration)**. Carefully lift the bonnet from the vehicle and place in a safe position, taking care not to damage the paintwork.

Refitting

8 Refitting is a reversal of removal. When first closing the bonnet, lower it slowly and check that the striker is aligned with the lock. Also check that the bonnet is positioned centrally between the front wings. If necessary, loosen the bolts and reposition the bonnet on the hinges before fully closing the bonnet. Tighten the bolts on completion. Check that the front of the bonnet is level with the front wings, and if necessary screw the rubber stops located in the front corners of the engine compartment in or out.

Struts

Removal

9 Open the bonnet. If removing just one strut,

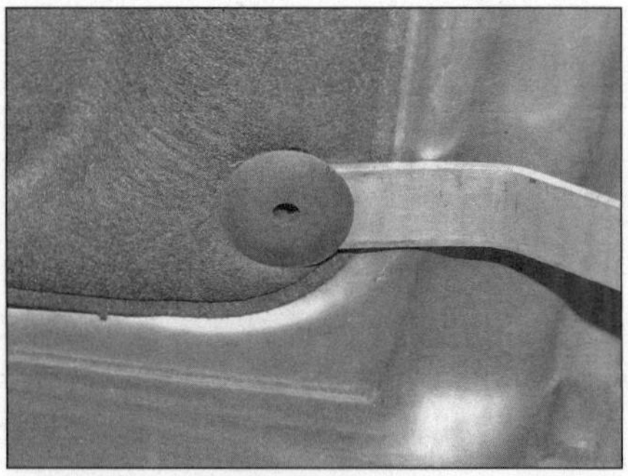

8.2 Prise out the clips at the lower edge of the bonnet panel

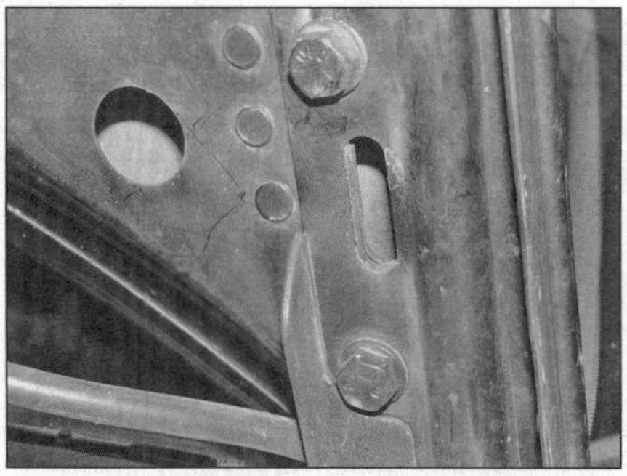

8.7 Bonnet hinge bolts

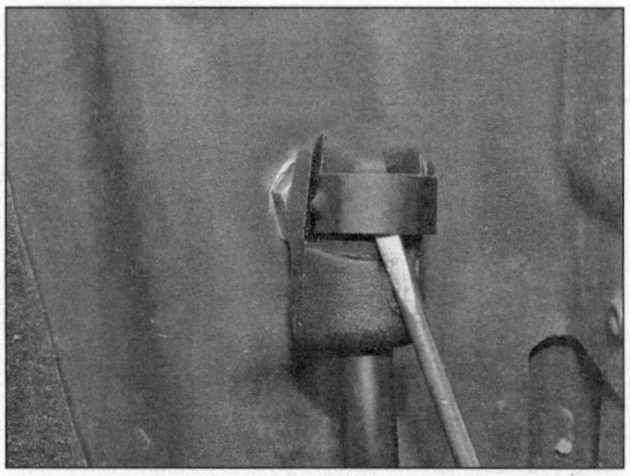

8.10 Prise the clip from the top of the strut

the remaining strut will hold the bonnet up, however if removing both struts an assistant will be required to hold the bonnet open. Alternatively, use a length of wood to prop the bonnet open.

10 Using a screwdriver, prise the spring clip from the top of the strut and disconnect the strut **(see illustration)**.

11 Disconnect the bottom of the strut by prising out the spring clip.

Refitting

12 Refitting is a reversal of removal.

9 Bonnet release cable and lever – removal and refitting

Removal

1 With the bonnet open, unclip the release cable from the inner wing adjacent to the fusebox, and prise open the coupling housing **(see illustration)**. Separate the two halves of the release cable.

2 Remove the clips and prise up the right-hand corner of the scuttle trim panel in front of the windscreen.

3 Remove the driver's side lower facia panel as described in Section 26.

4 Remove the driver's footwell kick panel.

5 Remove the bonnet release lever using two screwdrivers to prise free the locking tabs each side **(see illustration)**.

6 Tie a length of string to the inner end of the cable as an aid to refitting the cable correctly. Withdraw the cable assembly through the bulkhead and remove from the passenger compartment. Untie the string and leave it through the bulkhead.

Refitting

7 Tie the string to the cable and wrap adhesive tape around the end of the cable to assist it through the bulkhead. Pull the cable through into the engine compartment and untie the string.

8 Press the release lever firmly into place inside the vehicle, and reposition the carpet.

9 Refit the kick panel and driver's side lower facia panel.

10 Refit the scuttle trim panel and secure the retaining clips.

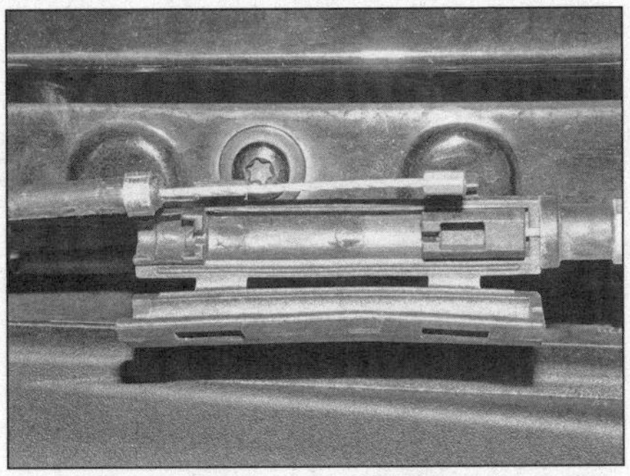

9.1 Open the housing and disconnect the bonnet release cable

11 Reconnect the cable halves at the coupling housing.

12 Clip the coupling into position.

13 Close the bonnet and check that the cable operates the release spring correctly.

10 Bonnet lock – removal and refitting

Removal

1 With the bonnet open, slacken the outer cable clamp **(see illustration)**.

2 Lever the cable free at the left-hand side and then use pliers to pull the cable free from the right-hand lock **(see illustrations)**.

3 Undo the bolts securing the bonnet lock to the slam panel **(see illustration)**.

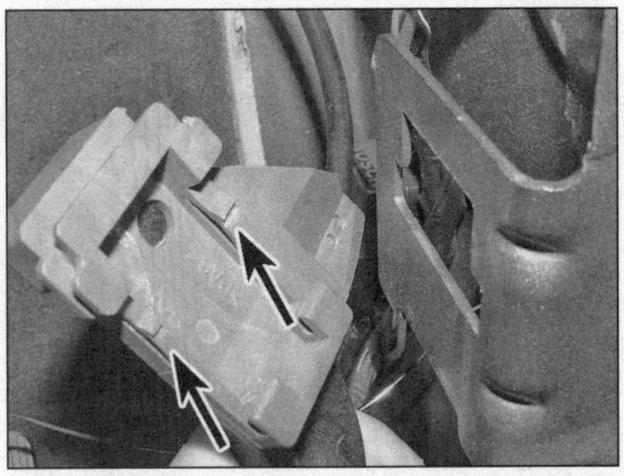

9.5 Depress the 2 clips (arrowed) and slide the release handle and bracket downwards from the bracket

Refitting

4 Refitting is a reversal of removal.

11 Doors – removal, refitting and adjustment

Front

Removal

1 Open the door and disconnect the wiring plug located between the door and A-pillar **(see illustration)**.

2 Unbolt the check strap from the A-pillar **(see illustration)**.

3 Mark the position of the hinge plates on the door in relation to each other **(see illustration)**.

10.1 Slacken the clamp

10.2a Release the cable at the left-hand side ...

10.2b ... and pull it free at the right-hand side

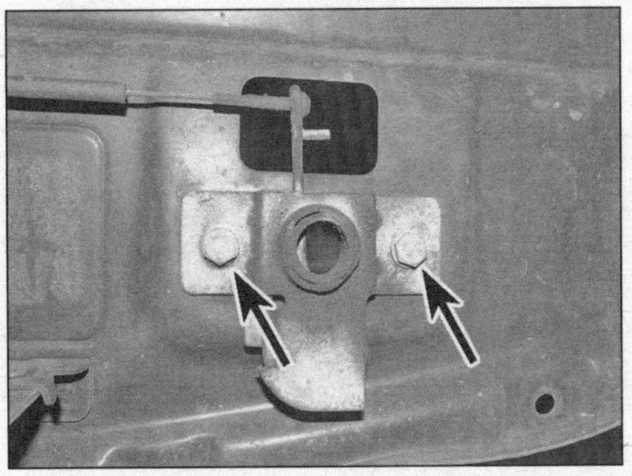

10.3 The bonnet lock bolts (arrowed) are on the underside of the slam panel

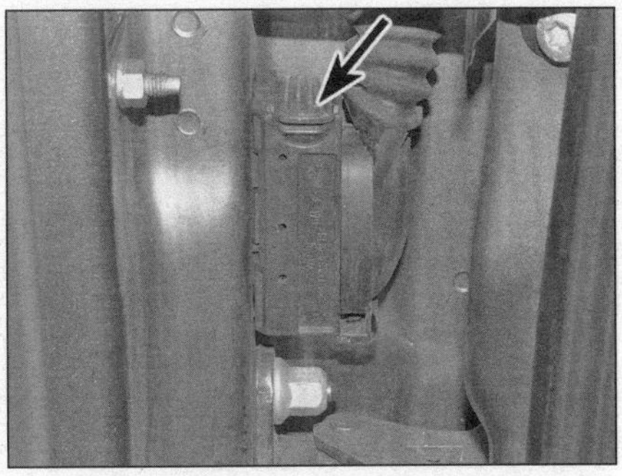

11.1 Prise up the locking catch (arrowed) and disconnect the wiring plug

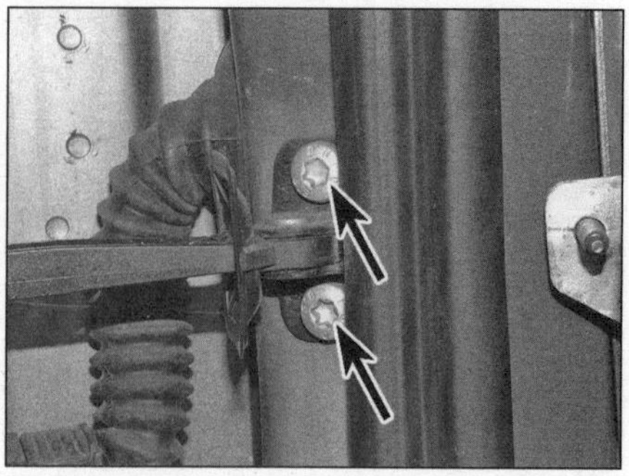

11.2 Undo the check strap Torx screws

4 With the help of an assistant, unscrew the mounting nuts and withdraw the door from the vehicle. Take care not to damage the paintwork.

Refitting and adjustment

5 Refitting is a reversal of removal. Check that the door lock aligns correctly with the striker on the B-pillar, and that the gap between the door and surrounding bodywork is equal when the door is shut. If necessary, the striker may be adjusted slightly by loosening it. Tighten it on completion. Slacken the hinge bolts/nuts, reposition the door, then tighten the bolts/nuts securely.

6 On vehicles fitted with the power window 'pinch protection' system, this must be reset. Cars with the pinch protection system have 2 position window switches fitted. To reset the system:

a) Close all door and windows. Close the roof on Convertible models.

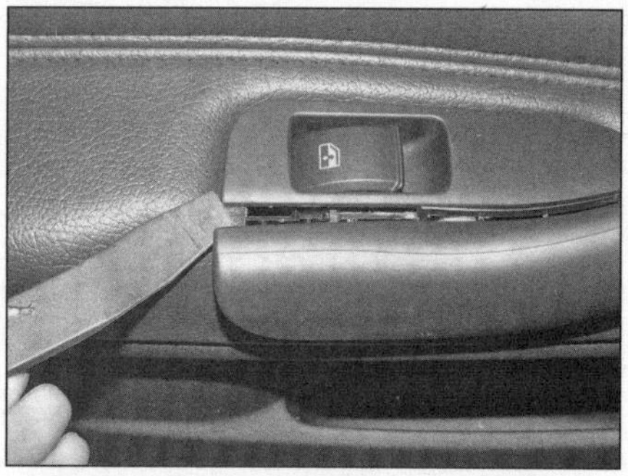

12.1a Carefully lever the handle cover from place ...

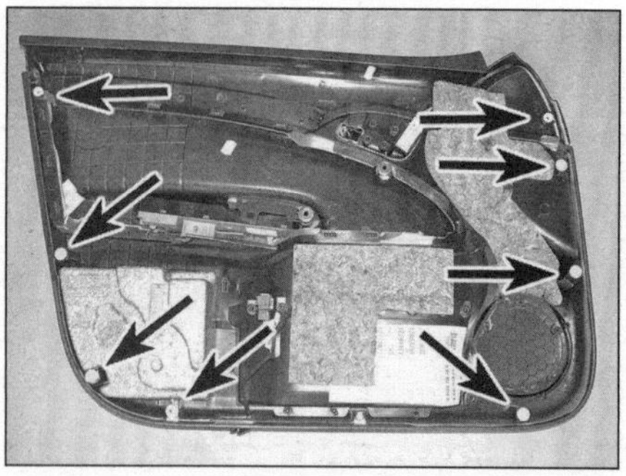

12.2 Door panel retaining clips (arrowed) – front door panel

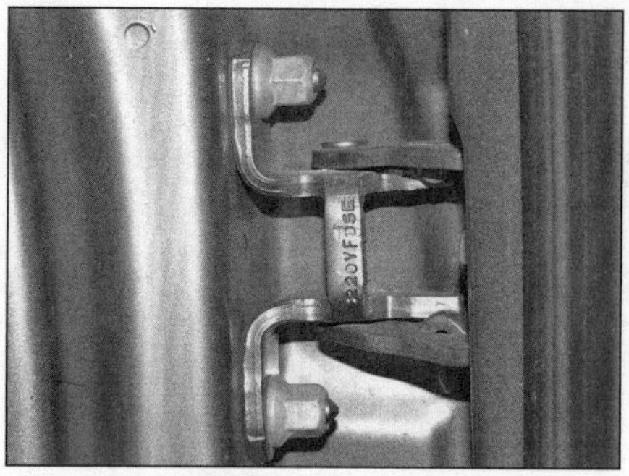

11.3 Door hinge nuts

b) Remove and refit fuse number F5 in the facia fusebox.
c) Start the vehicle.
d) Keeping the button fully depressed, lower the window.
e) Fully raise the window and hold the button in the up position for at least 2 seconds.
f) Fully lower the window.
g) Fully raise the window and hold the switch in the up position for at least 2 seconds.
h) Release the switch and an audible beep will be heard to confirm that the programming is complete.
i) Repeat the procedure if no audible beep is heard.

Rear

Removal

7 Open the front and rear doors on the relevant side.

8 Disconnect the wiring plug at the door edge.

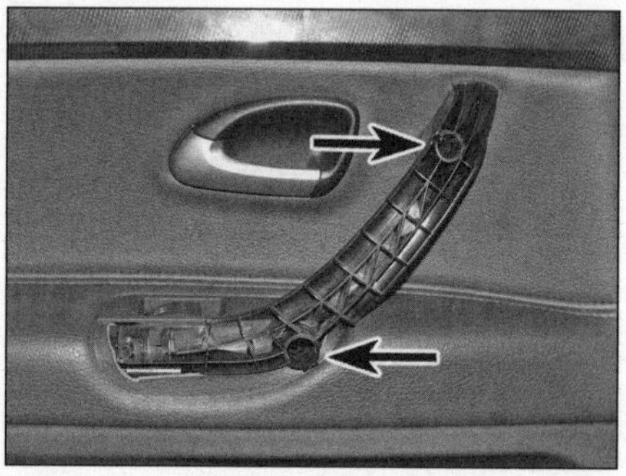

12.1b ... and undo the 2 screws (arrowed)

12.3 Lift the door trim panel upwards to free the top edge

9 Unbolt the check strap from the pillar.

10 Mark the position of the hinge plates on the B-pillar brackets in relation to each other.

11 With the help of an assistant, unscrew the mounting nuts and withdraw the door from the vehicle. Take care not to damage the paintwork.

Refitting and adjustment

12 Refitting is a reversal of removal, but tighten the mounting nuts securely. Check that the door lock aligns correctly with the striker on the C-pillar, and that the gap between the door and surrounding bodywork is equal when the door is shut. If necessary, the striker may be adjusted slightly by loosening it. Tighten it on completion. To adjust the position of the door, loosen the hinge bolts/nuts, reposition the door and tighten the nuts/bolts securely.

12 Door inner trim panel – removal and refitting

Removal

Saloon and Estate models

1 Carefully prise the door pull handle cover from place, then undo the 2 screws exposed **(see illustrations)**.

2 Using a wide-bladed screwdriver, carefully prise out the clips securing the trim panel to the door **(see illustration)**. Take care not to damage the trim panel or break the clips by prising as near to the clip positions as possible.

3 With the clips released, lift the trim panel upwards to free the top edge **(see illustration)**.

4 Disconnect the cable from the interior door release handle, then note their fitted positions and disconnect the switch wiring plugs **(see illustration)**.

5 If necessary unscrew the speaker, and carefully remove the membranes from the door **(see illustration)**.

Convertible models

6 Undo the screw, then pull the mirror base cover upwards to release the clips and disconnect the wiring plug **(see illustrations)**.

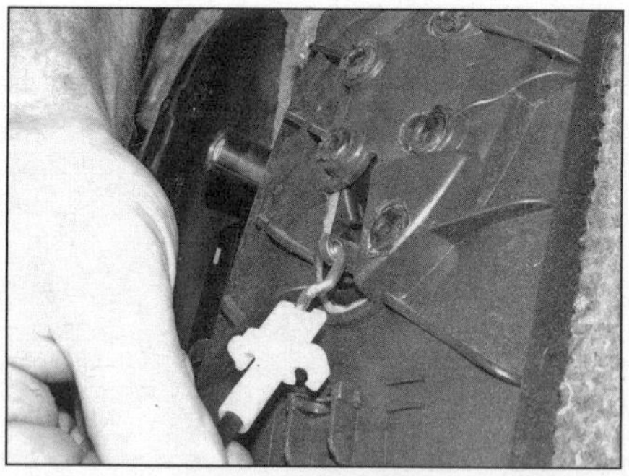

12.4 Disconnect the interior door handle release cable

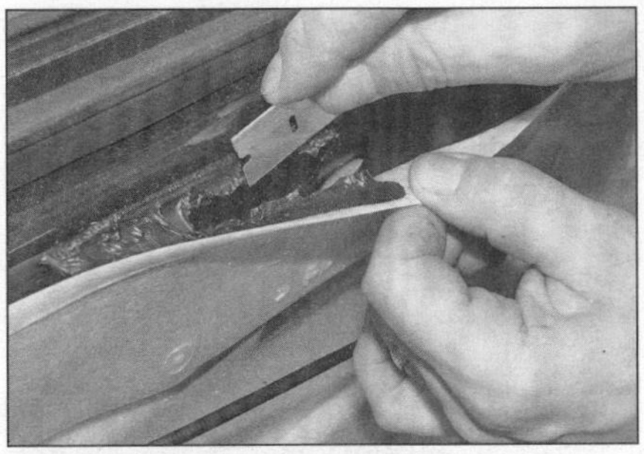

12.5 Use a scalpel or sharp knife to cut through the sealant between the door and membrane

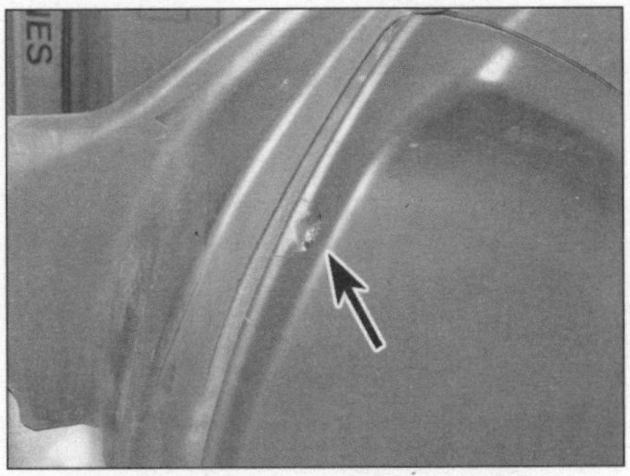

12.6a Undo the screw (arrowed) ...

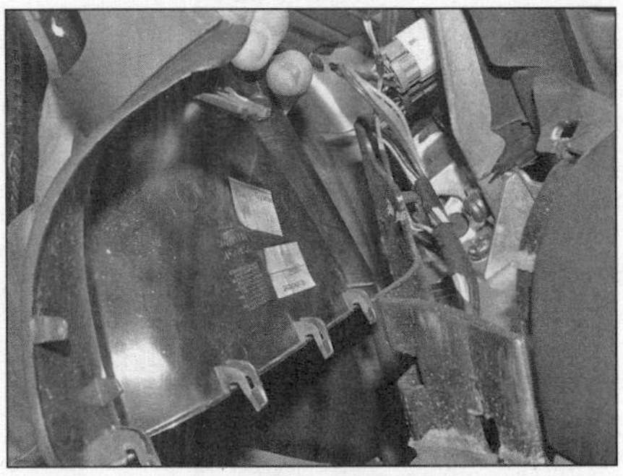

12.6b ... and lift up the mirror base cover

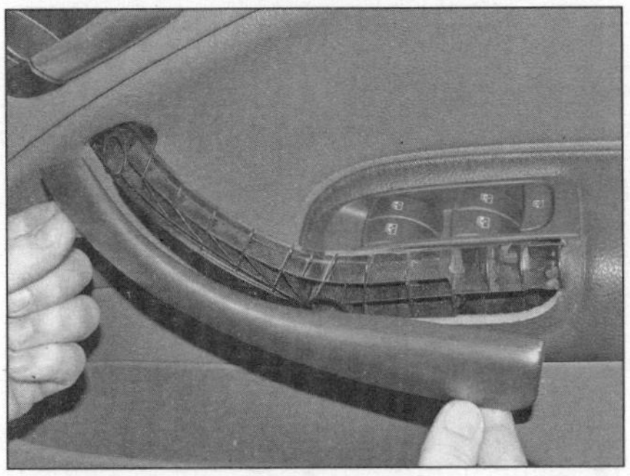

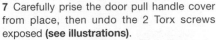

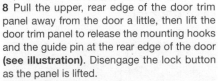

12.7a Carefully pull the cover from the handle ...

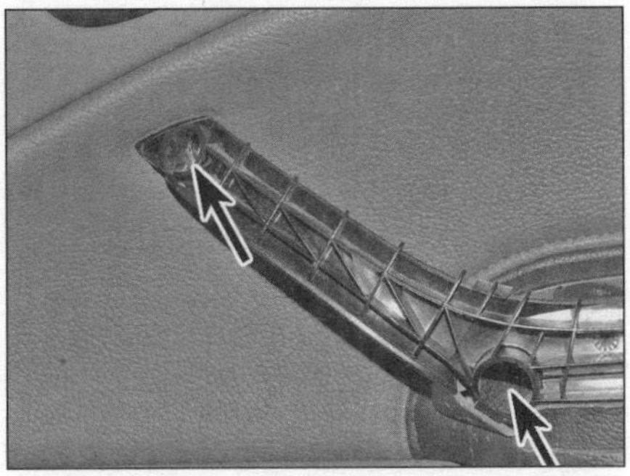

12.7b ... then undo the 2 screws (arrowed)

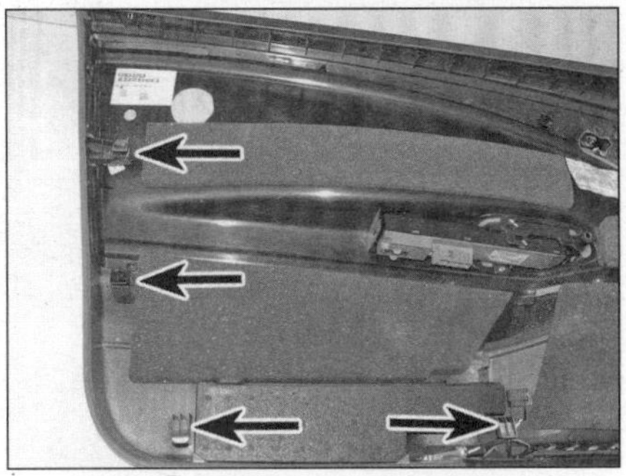

12.8 Door inner trim panel hooks (arrowed) – Convertible models

7 Carefully prise the door pull handle cover from place, then undo the 2 Torx screws exposed **(see illustrations)**.

8 Pull the upper, rear edge of the door trim panel away from the door a little, then lift the door trim panel to release the mounting hooks and the guide pin at the rear edge of the door **(see illustration)**. Disengage the lock button as the panel is lifted.

9 Unclip the outer cable, then disengage the interior door release handle cable.

10 Disconnect the wiring plug(s) and remove the door trim panel. If required, carefully remove the weatherproof membrane from the door panel **(see illustration)**.

Refitting

11 Refitting is a reversal of removal.

12 After refitting (and where fitted) carry out the 'pinch protection' calibration as described in Section 11.

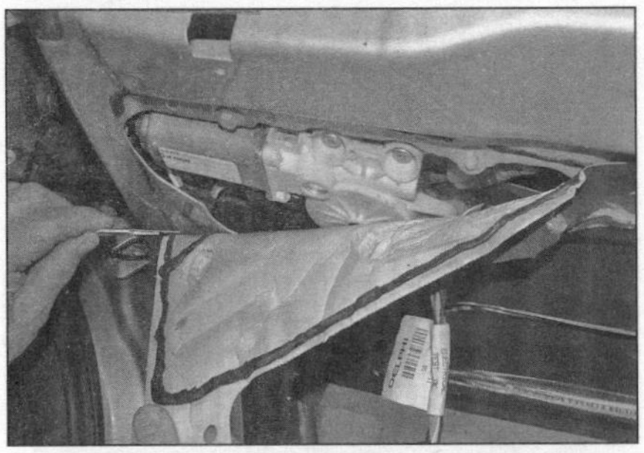

12.10 Use a sharp knife or scalpel to cut through the sealant between the membrane and the door frame

13 Door handle and lock components – removal and refitting

Interior door handle

1 The interior door release handle is integral with the door trim panel, and cannot be renewed separately (see Section 12).

Front door lock

Saloon and Estate models

2 Given the simplicity of removing the door handle, the easiest way to remove the lock is to remove it complete with the inner section of the outer door handle. Note that it is also possible to remove the lock with the outer handle still in the door.

3 With the window closed, remove the door trim and membranes (see Section 12).

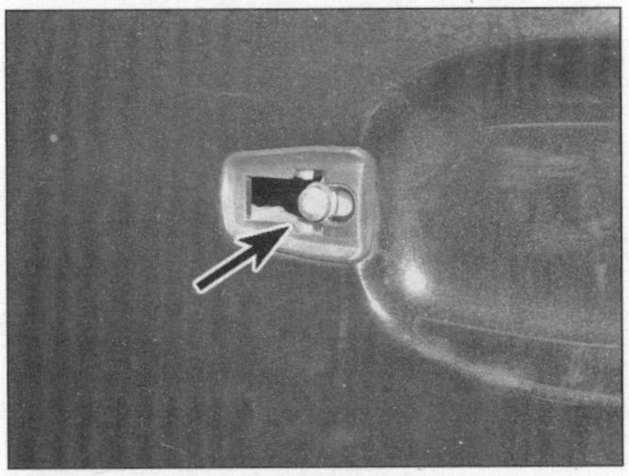

13.6 Slacken, but do not remove the screw (arrowed)

4 On vehicles fitted with a lock guard, undo the screws and remove the guard.

5 Remove the outer door handle as described below in paragraphs 28 to 31.

6 With the outer handle removed, slacken the inner frame locking screw **(see illustration)**.

7 Undo the 3 screws securing the lock to the door frame. Slide the inner section of the outer handle from the outer door skin **(see illustration)**.

8 Lower the inner section of the handle and the lock far enough to access and remove the wiring plug **(see illustrations)**. Unhook the lock button cable.

9 Manoeuvre the lock from the door, unhook the lock from the inner section of the outer handle and disconnect the cable for the door inner release handle **(see illustrations)**.

10 Refitting is a reversal of removal, however before refitting the door trim, make sure that the lock operates correctly.

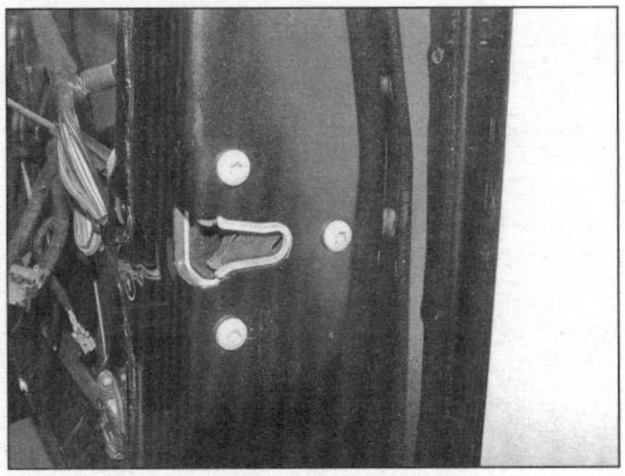

13.7 Lock retaining Torx screws

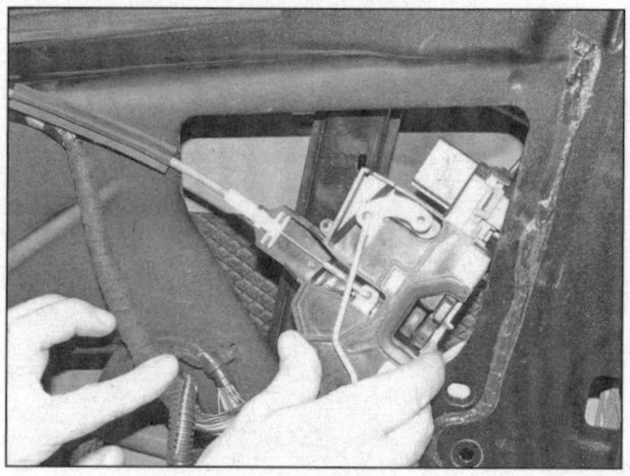

13.8a Lower the lock ...

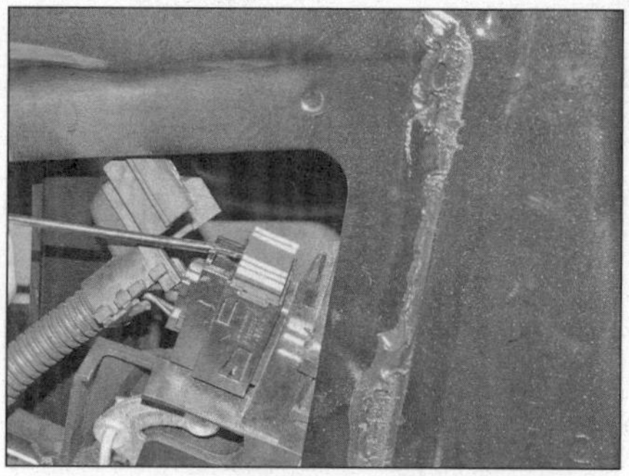

13.8b ... release the wiring plug locking plate ...

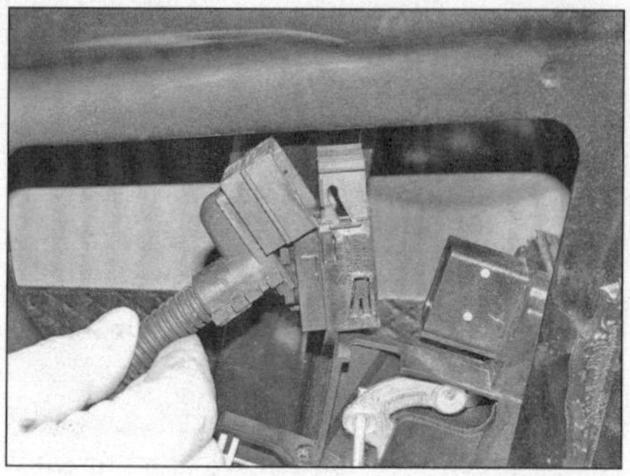

13.8c ... and disconnect the wiring plug

13.9a Lift the catch and unhook the link rod

Convertible models

11 If removing the driver's side lock, remove the door glass as described in Section 14. If removing the passenger's side lock, raise the door window to the highest position.

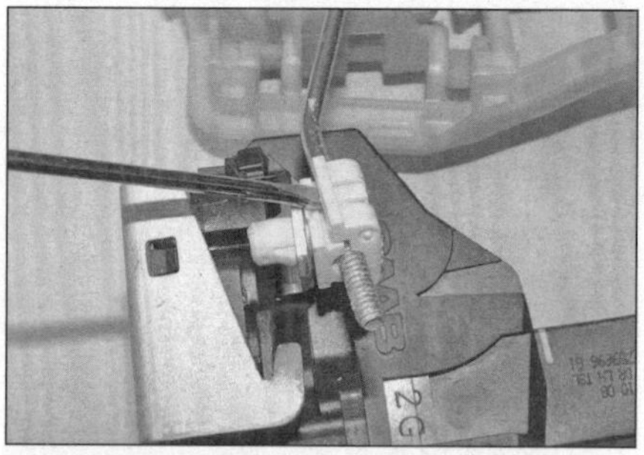

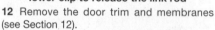

13.9b If removing the lock assembly with the outer handle in place, lever open the lower clip to release the link rod

12 Remove the door trim and membranes (see Section 12).

13 On vehicles fitted with a lock guard, undo the screws and remove the guard.

14 Undo the 3 screws securing the lock to the door frame **(see illustration)**.

15 Slacken the lock cylinder retaining nut (where fitted).

16 If removing the driver's door lock, rotate the lock cylinder anti-clockwise, pull it from the handle and disconnect the lock rod.

17 Move the lock forwards, and disengage the rod from the exterior handle **(see illustrations)**.

18 Manoeuvre the lock from its place, complete with inner handle cable and lock button rod. Release the cover and disconnect the wiring plug as the lock is withdrawn **(see illustrations)**.

19 Detach the interior door release handle cable from the lock if required **(see illustration)**.

20 Refitting is a reversal of removal, however before refitting the door trim, make sure that the lock operates correctly.

Rear door lock

21 Remove the door outer handle (as

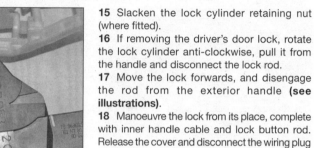

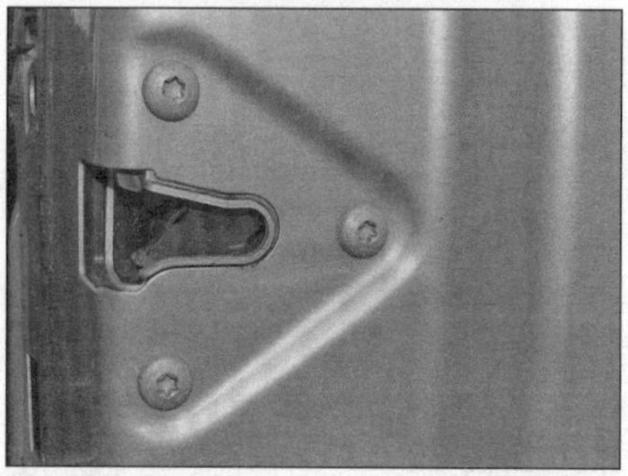

13.14 Undo the 3 screws securing the lock to the door frame

13.17a Disengage the exterior handle rod from the lock ...

13.17b ... by prising open the cover ...

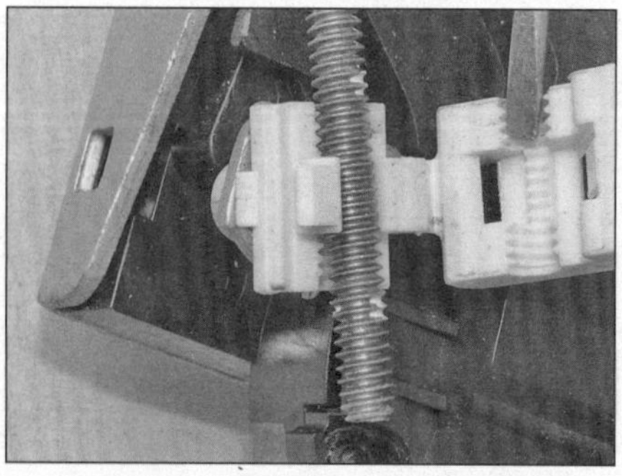

13.17c ... and releasing the rod

13.18a Slide off the cover ...

13.18b ... then pull out the red locking catch and disconnect the wiring plug

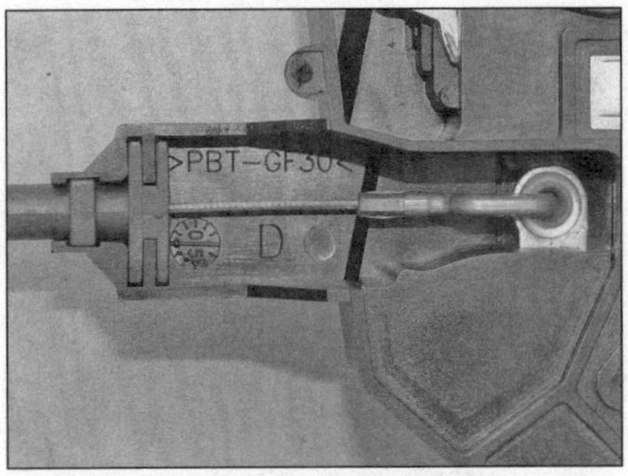

13.19 Detach the interior release handle cable from the lock

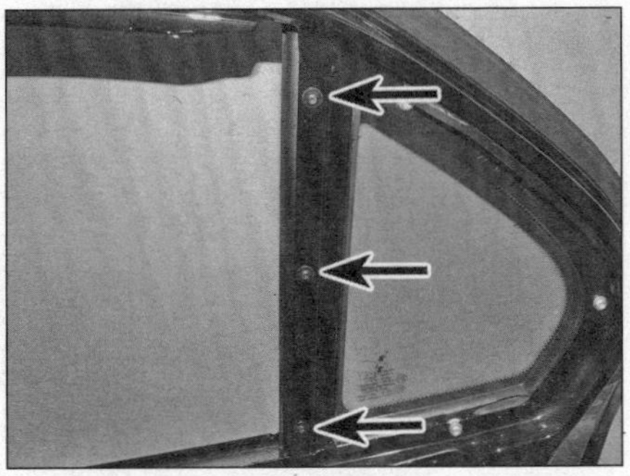

13.22a Undo the 3 screws at the top (arrowed) ...

13.22b ... and the one at the base of the channel (arrowed)

described in paragraphs 28 to 31) and then remove the window glass as described in Section 14. Note that it is also possible to remove the lock with the outer handle still in the door.

22 Undo the 4 rear glass channel retaining Torx screws **(see illustrations)**.

23 Prise out and remove the rubber window channel from the window frame, and remove the rear glass channel **(see illustration)**.

24 Undo and remove the 3 Torx screws securing the door lock to the rear of the door frame **(see illustration)**. With the outer handle removed, slacken the inner frame locking screw **(see illustration 13.6)**.

25 Lower the lock and outer handle inner frame. Release the wiring harness from the retaining clips, and manoeuvre the lock from position **(see illustrations)**.

26 With the assembly removed release the cables and unhook the lock from the handle **(see illustrations 13.9a and 13.9b)**.

27 Refitting is a reversal of removal, however before refitting the door trim, make sure that the lock operates correctly.

Door exterior handle

Saloon and Estate models

28 The removal procedure is the same for all 4 doors, but note that the front left-hand door has a key cylinder fitted.

29 Pull the door handle outwards and release the locking bolt. A small (T15) Torx key will be required for the front left-hand door. The handle will remain in the pulled out position when the locking bolt has be slackened sufficiently **(see illustrations)**.

30 With the handle still pulled out, release the smaller section of the handle assembly and then remove the main section **(see illustrations)**. If required the cover can be removed from the key cylinder (left-hand front door only).

31 Refitting is a reversal of removal.

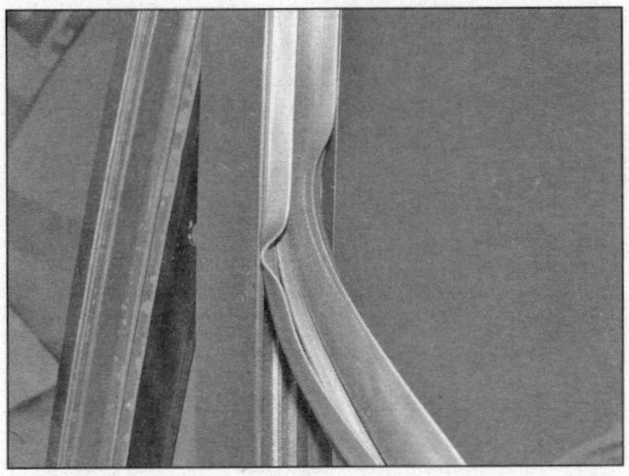

13.23 Prise out the rubber from the glass channel

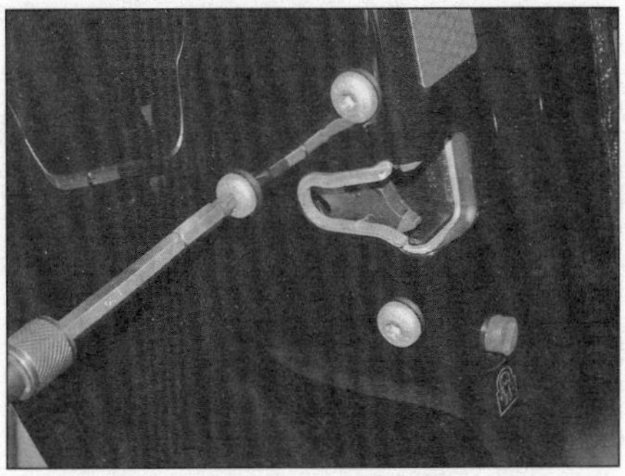

13.24 Undo the lock retaining Torx screws

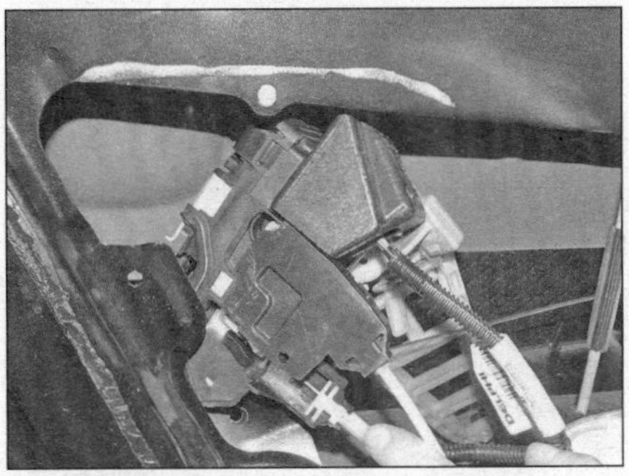

13.25a Lower the lock assembly ...

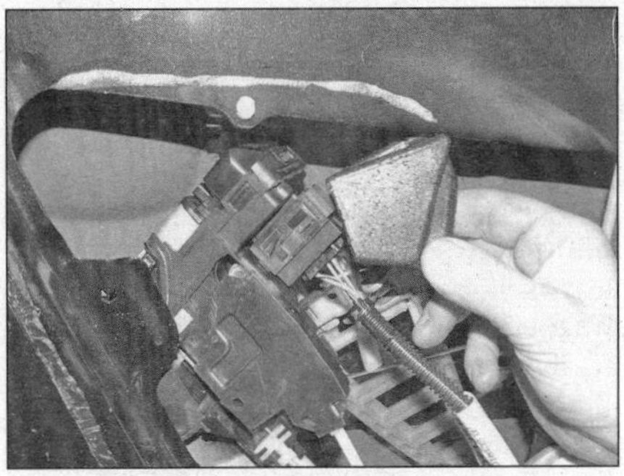

13.25b ... remove the cover ...

13.25c ... and disconnect the wiring plug

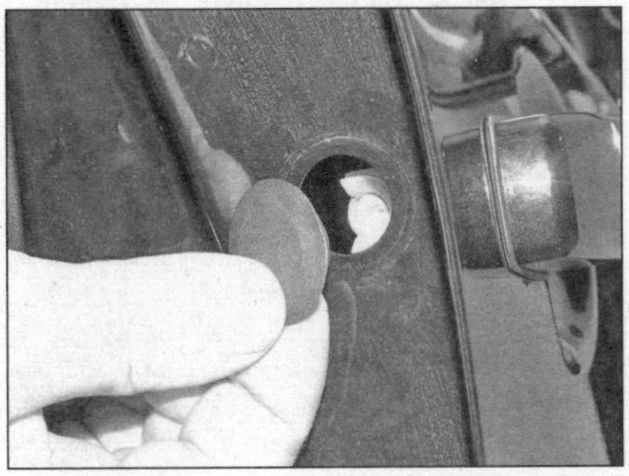

13.29a Remove the blanking plug ...

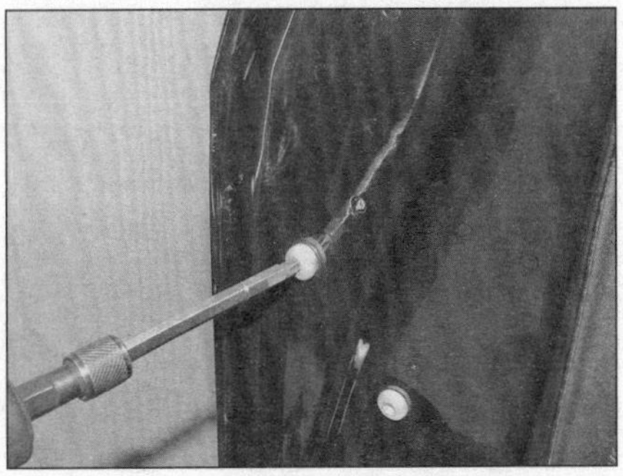

13.29b ... or bolt

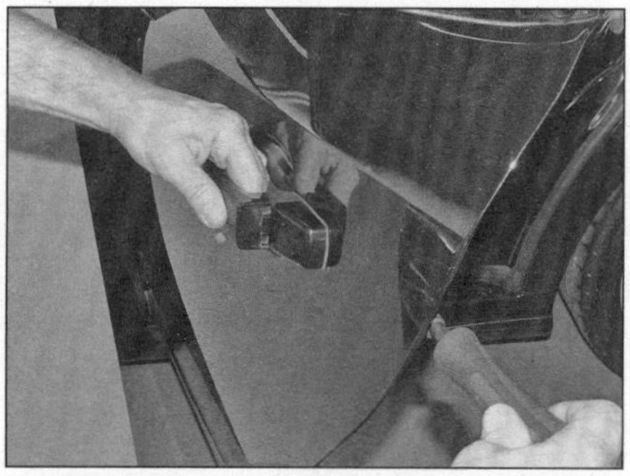

13.29c Pull out the handle and release the bolt

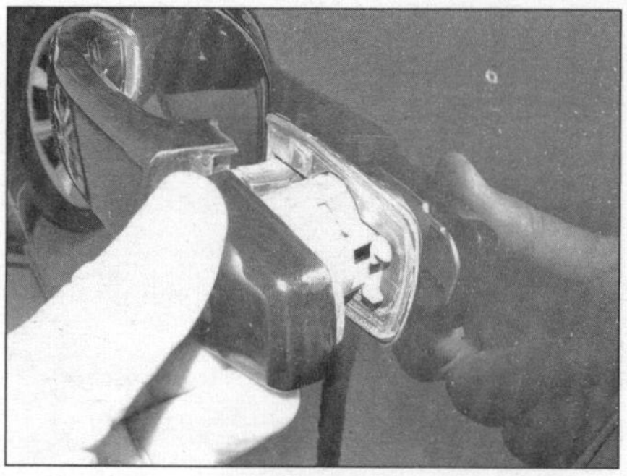

13.30a Remove the smaller section of the handle ...

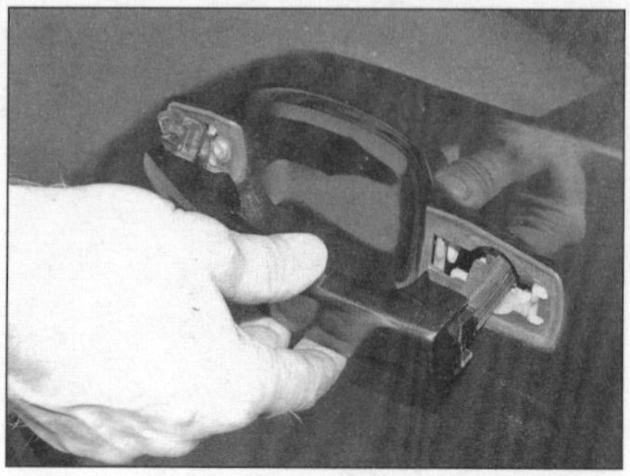

13.30b ... and then slide out and unhook the handle

13.39 Exterior handle retaining nuts (arrowed)

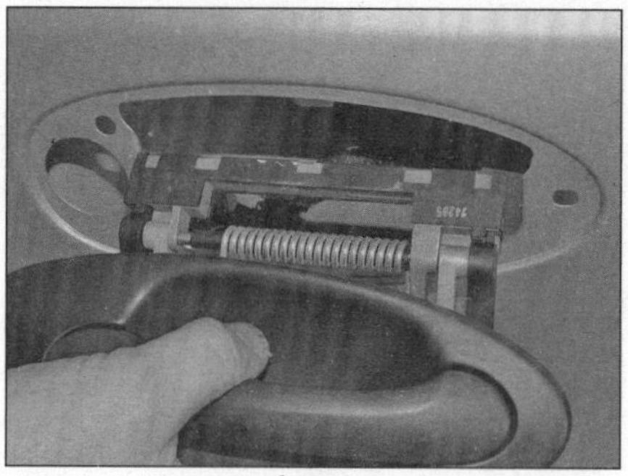

13.40 Lower the exterior handle from the door skin

13.45 Lift up the cover, prise up the red locking catch and disconnect the wiring plug

Convertible models

32 If removing the left-hand side handle, remove the door glass as described in Section 14. If removing the right-hand side handle, raise the door window to the highest position.

33 Remove the door trim and membranes (see Section 12).

34 On vehicles fitted with a lock guard, undo the screws and remove the guard.

35 Release the clip, open the cover and detach the handle rod from the plastic clip on the lock lever **(see illustrations 13.17a, 13.17b and 13.17c)**.

36 Slacken the lock cylinder retaining nut (where fitted).

37 If removing the driver's door handle, rotate the lock cylinder anti-clockwise, pull it from the handle and disconnect the lock rod.

38 Undo the 2 retaining nuts and remove the reinforcement plate (where fitted) behind the exterior handle.

39 Undo the 3 nuts securing the handle to the door frame **(see illustration)**.

40 Pull out the lower edge of the exterior handle, then lower it so the mechanism clears the door skin, then lift it to feed the lock rod through the aperture **(see illustration)**.

41 Refitting is a reversal of removal.

Key cylinder

Convertible models

42 Remove the door glass as described in Section 14.

43 Remove the door trim and membranes (see Section 12).

44 On vehicles fitted with a lock guard, undo the screws and remove the guard.

45 Release the cover and detach the handle rod from the clip **(see illustration)**.

46 Undo the 3 bolts securing the lock to the door frame **(see illustration 13.14)**.

47 Slacken the lock cylinder retaining nut.

48 Rotate the lock cylinder anti-clockwise, pull it from the handle and disconnect the lock rod.

49 Refitting is a reversal of removal.

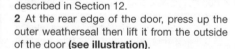

14 Door/side window glass – removal and refitting

Front door

Saloon and Estate models

1 Lower the window about 5 cm, then remove the inner door trim panel and membranes as described in Section 12.

2 At the rear edge of the door, press up the outer weatherseal then lift it from the outside of the door **(see illustration)**.

3 Slacken the window clamp bolts **(see illustration)**.

4 Carefully lift the rear of the window and withdraw it from the outside of the door.

5 Refitting is a reversal of removal.

Convertible models

6 Fully lower the window, then raise it approximately 10 cm.

7 Remove the door trim panel and weather membrane as described in Section 12.

8 Undo the 3 Torx screws and remove the door mirror assembly **(see illustration 20.3)**.

9 Carefully prise out the fixing plugs at the rear section, then starting at the rear, prise the outer weatherstrip from between the door and window **(see illustrations)**.

10 Carefully prise up the inner weatherstrip

14.2 Prise up the outer weatherstrip from the door

14.3 Slacken the window clamp bolts (arrowed)

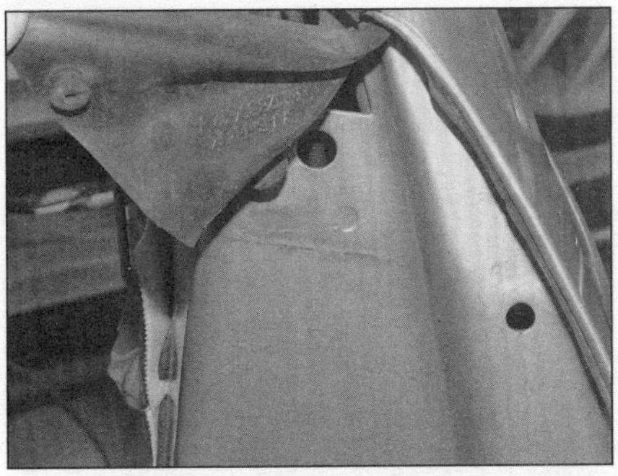

14.9a Pull the weatherstrip plugs from the door ...

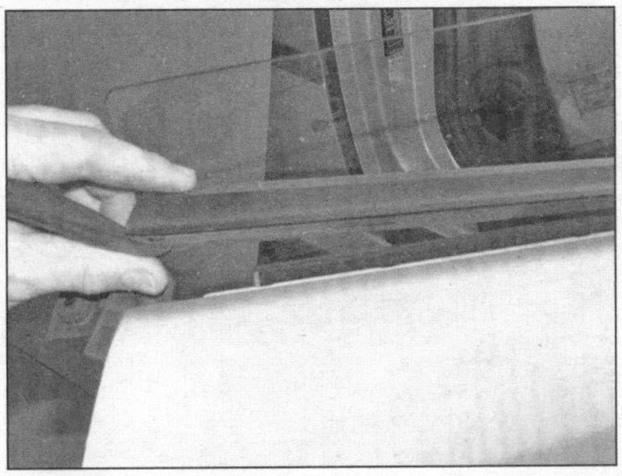

14.9b ... then starting at the rear, lift the outer weatherstrip from place

14.10 Prise up the inner weatherstrip

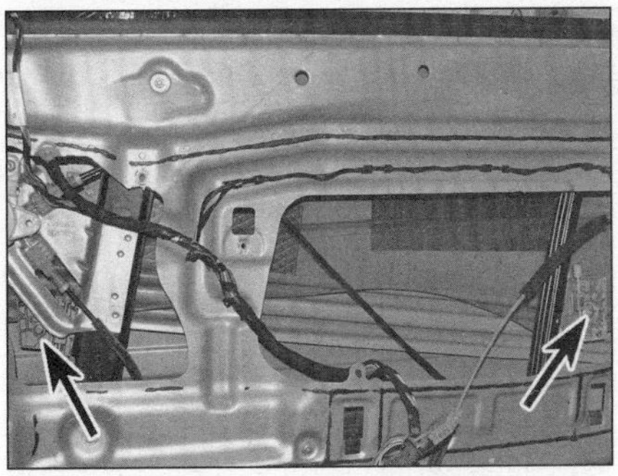

14.11 Window retaining screws (arrowed)

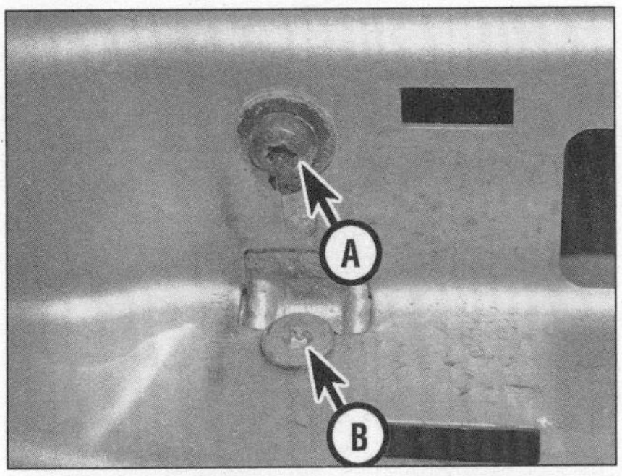

14.12a Locking screw (A) and fixing screw (B) at the lower edge of the door

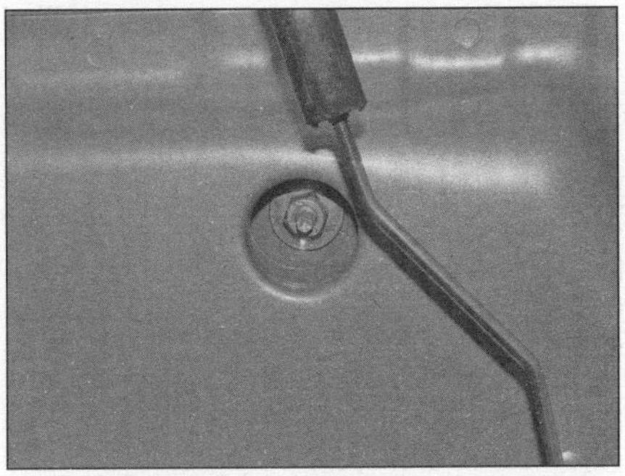

14.12b Upper rear fixing stud

between the door and window **(see illustration)**.

11 Make alignment marks around the rear screw, then undo the rear and slacken the front screw securing the window to the regulator mechanism, then lift the window from the door **(see illustration)**.

12 Refitting is a reversal of removal. Check the operation of the window, and if necessary, prise out the plastic grommet on the lower edge of the door frame, and adjust the position of the window regulator assembly by slackening the locking screw, then rotating the adjusting screw. Further adjustment is by adjusting the upper rear fixing stud position, and fore-and-aft window position can be adjusted by slackening the rear window clamp screw **(see illustrations)**.

Rear door

13 Fully lower the window, then remove the inner door trim panel and membranes as described in Section 12.

14 Carefully prise away the centre part of the window frame cover, followed by the front lower part, and then remove the rest of the frame cover **(see illustrations)**.

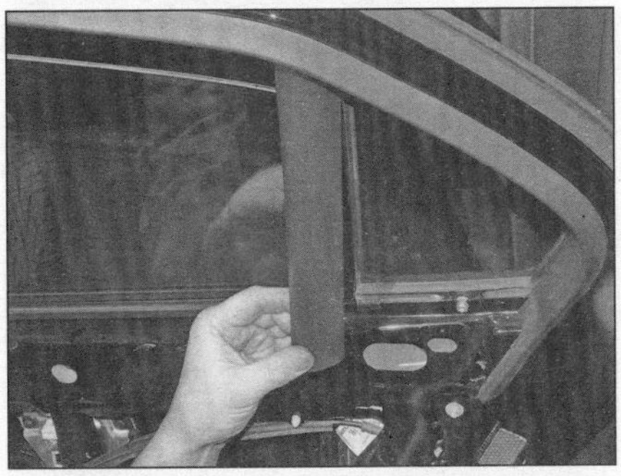

14.14a Pull away the centre part of the frame cover ...

15 Prise up the inner weatherseal from the door, starting from the rear **(see illustration)**.

16 Prise up the outer weatherseal from the door **(see illustration)**.

17 Carefully remove the U-shaped moulding

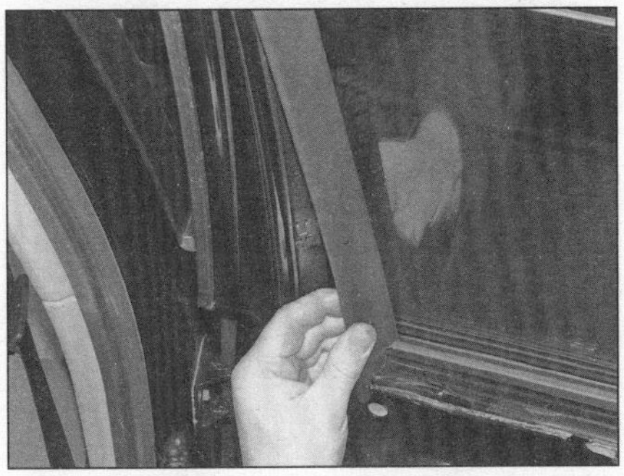

14.14b ... the front part ...

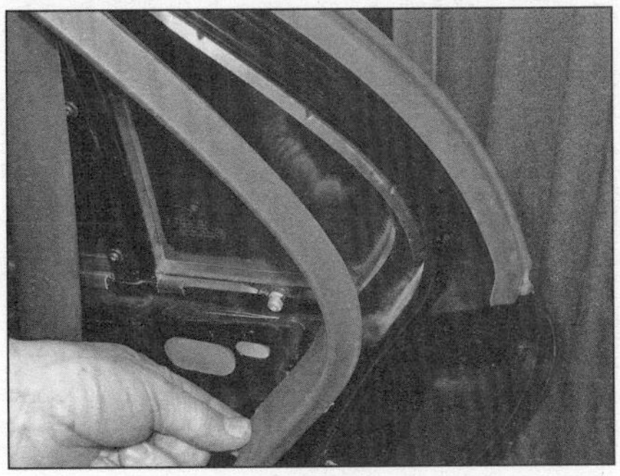

14.14c ... and the rear part

14.15 Prise up the inner weatherstrip ...

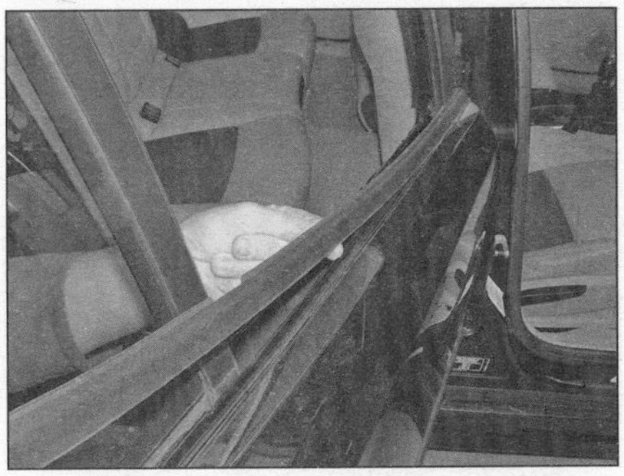

14.16 ... and the outer weatherstrip

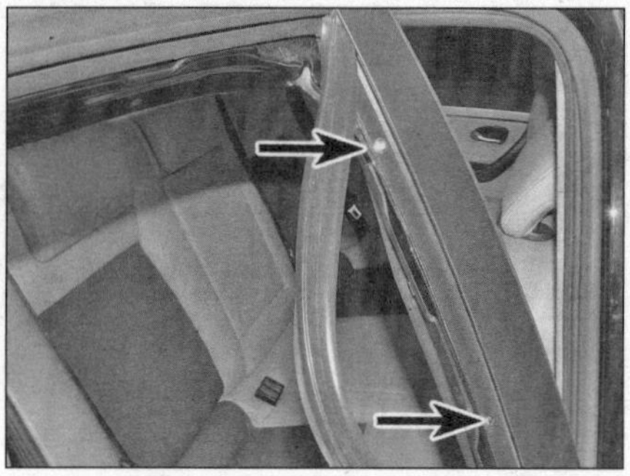

14.17 Prise out the rubber strip, undo the 2 screws (arrowed) ...

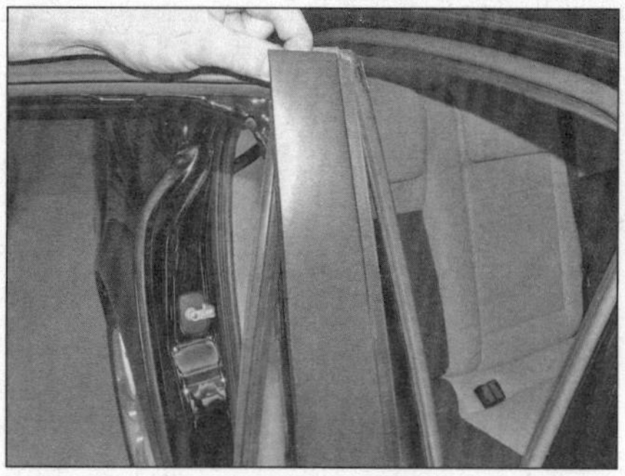

14.18 ... and remove the glass channel

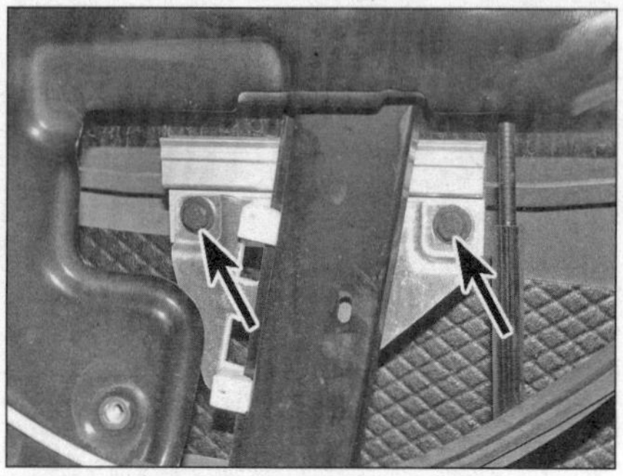

14.19 Window clamp bolts (arrowed)

from the front glass channel, and undo the screws **(see illustration)**.

18 Lift away the glass channel (see illustration).

19 Raise the window a little to access the clamping bolts. Undo the bolts and lift out the window **(see illustration)**.

20 Refitting is a reversal of removal. Check the function of the window before refitting the door trim.

Rear side window

Convertible

21 Lower the window approximately 6 cm.

22 Remove the rear seat backrest and cushion as described in Section 24.

23 Remove the rear side trim panel as described in Section 26.

24 Carefully prise up and remove the window outer weatherstrip **(see illustration)**.

25 Remove the insulation, and undo the 3 upper window regulator screws **(see illustrations)**.

26 Fold down the waterproof membrane, then prise out the rubber grommet, and slacken the lower window regulator nut **(see illustration)**.

27 Disconnect the wiring plug from the window lift motor **(see illustration)**.

28 Lift the window and regulator from their place **(see illustration)**.

29 If required, undo the window regulator screws and detach the window **(see illustrations)**.

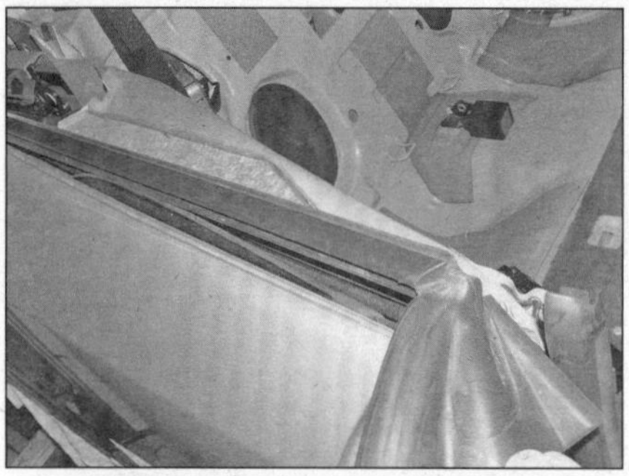

14.24 Prise up the window outer weatherstrip

14.25a Remove the insulation (arrowed) ...

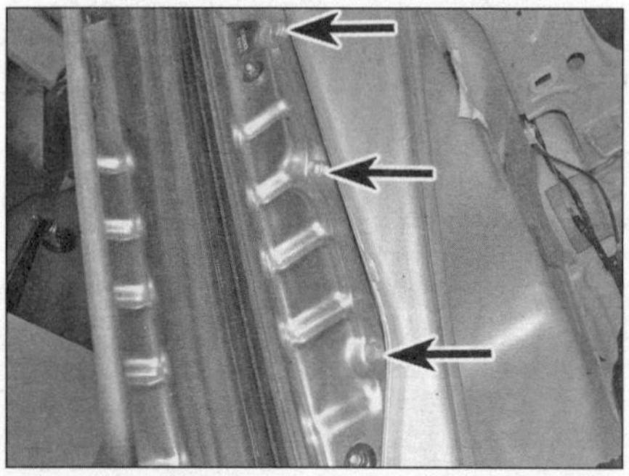

14.25b ... then undo the window regulator screws (arrowed)

14.26 Prise out the grommet, and slacken the regulator nut (arrowed)

14.27 Pull out the red locking catch and disconnect the wiring plug (arrowed)

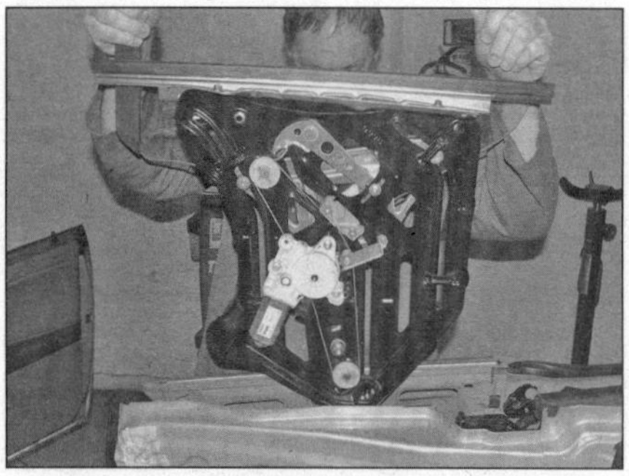

14.28 Lift the window and regulator from the side panel

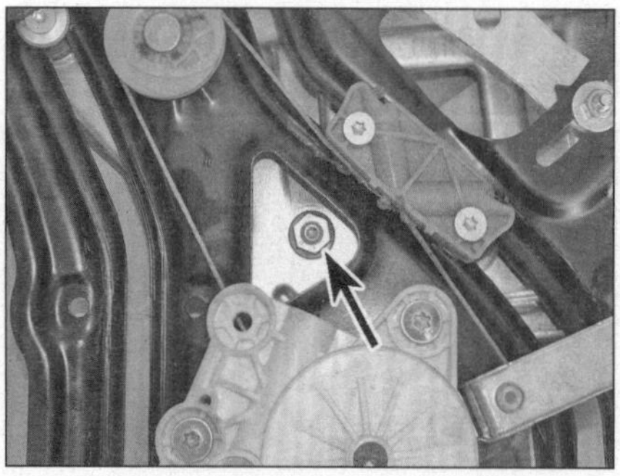

14.29a Undo the nut (arrowed) ...

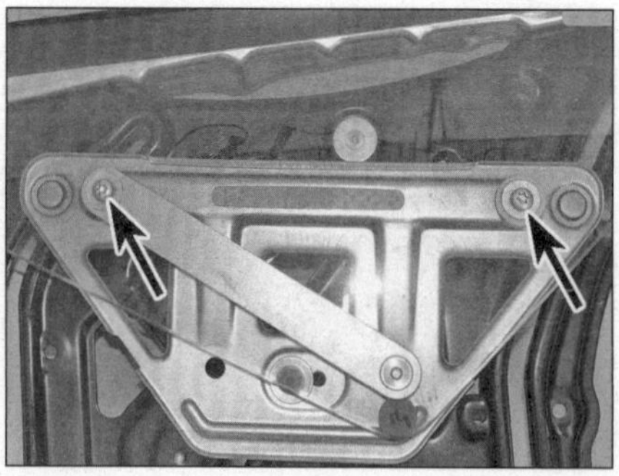

14.29b ... and screws (arrowed) to detach the window glass

30 Refitting is a reversal of removal. Check that there is a gap of approximately 23 ± 1 mm between the rear edge of the side window sealing moulding and the rear edge of the front window, when closed. The surface of the side window should align exactly with the surface of the door window **(see illustration)**.

31 If adjustment is necessary, the forward/rearward position can be altered by slackening the two upper, and one lower nut securing the window regulator, and moving the window to the required position **(see illustrations)**.

32 To adjust the side-to-side position, remove the rubber grommet, slacken the lower window regulator mounting nut, and adjust the screw inwards or outwards as appropriate **(see illustration 14.31a)**. Tighten the locknut. The plastic screws are used to adjust the height setting, and the in/out studs are used to adjust the inclination.

33 To adjust the closing height of the window, slacken the nut on the window regulator arm, then adjust the side window height by moving the arm **(see illustration)**. Note that each mark on the arm is the equivalent of 1.0 mm vertical movement of the window. Tighten the nut when finished.

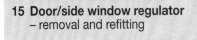

15 Door/side window regulator – removal and refitting

Note: *Whenever any of the power window components are removed the 'pinch protection' function (where fitted) must be synchronised as follows:*

a) Close all door and windows. Close the roof on Convertible models.
b) Remove and refit fuse number F5 in the facia fusebox.
c) Start the vehicle.
d) Keeping the button fully depressed, lower the window.
e) Fully raise the window and hold the button in the up position for at least 2 seconds.
f) Fully lower the window.
g) Fully raise the window and hold the switch in the up position for at least 2 seconds.
h) Release the switch and an audible beep will be heard to confirm that the programming is complete.
i) Repeat the procedure if no audible beep is heard.

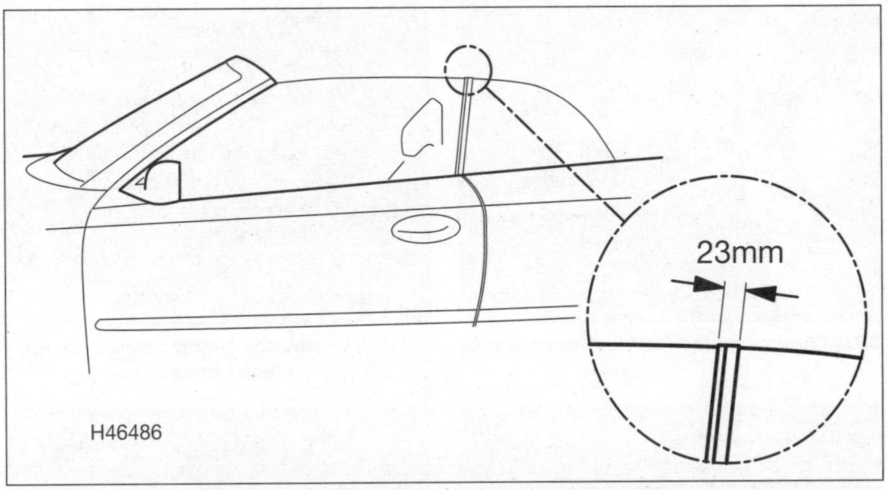

14.30 The gap between the rear edge of the side window sealing moulding and the rear edge of the front window should be 23 ± 1 mm

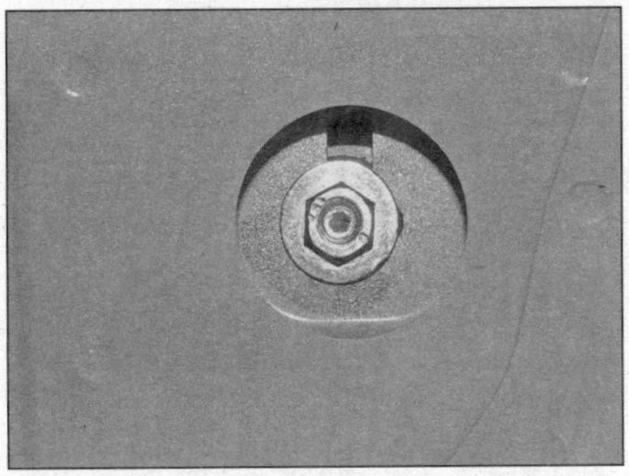

14.31a Lower regulator mounting nut ...

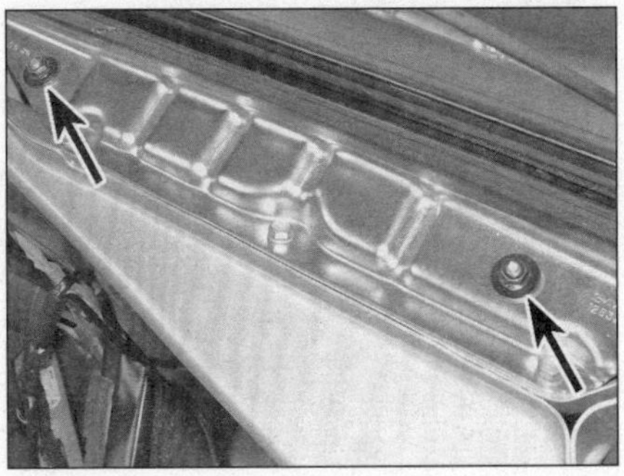

14.31b ... and upper mounting nuts (arrowed)

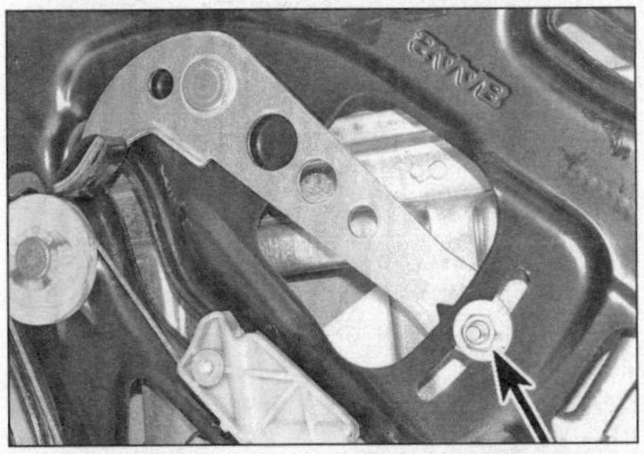

14.33 Slacken the nut (arrowed) and move the arm to adjust the closing height of the window

Front door window

Saloon and Estate models

1 Open the window approximately 5 cm, then remove the inner door trim panel and membranes as described in Section 12.

2 Starting at the rear, carefully prise up and remove the outer weatherstrip between the window and door frame **(see illustration 14.2)**.

3 Slacken the window clamp bolts **(see illustration 14.3)**, then lift the window and secure it in place using tape **(see illustration)**.

4 Undo the window regulator mounting nuts **(see illustration)** and release the upper cable from the retaining clip.

5 Undo the window motor wiring plug, and manoeuvre the regulator assembly from the door.

6 If necessary, unbolt the motor from the regulator **(see illustration)**.

7 Refitting is a reversal of removal. Ensure the window mounting rubbers are correctly positioned in the regulator **(see illustration)**.

Convertible models

8 Remove the front door window as described in Section 14.

9 Undo the 2 Torx screws and remove the vibration damper from the base of the door frame **(see illustration)**.

15.3 Tape the window to the frame

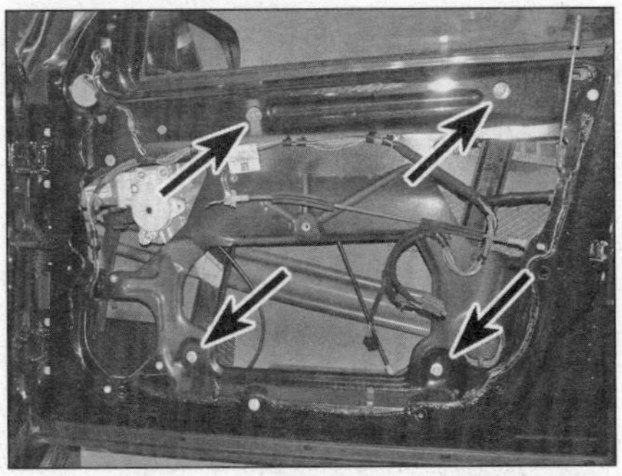

15.4 Window regulator mounting nuts (arrowed)

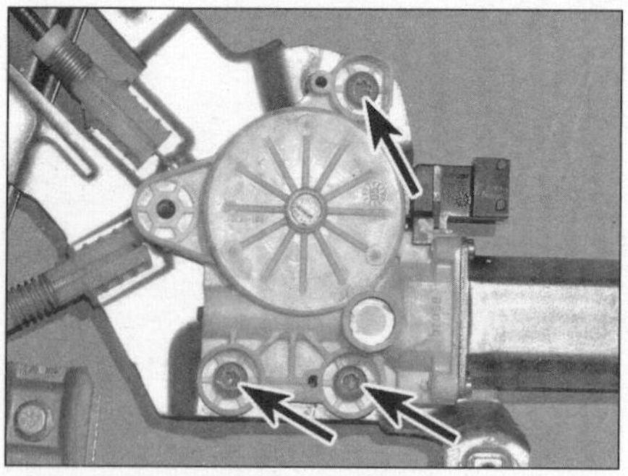

15.6 Window motor Torx screws (arrowed)

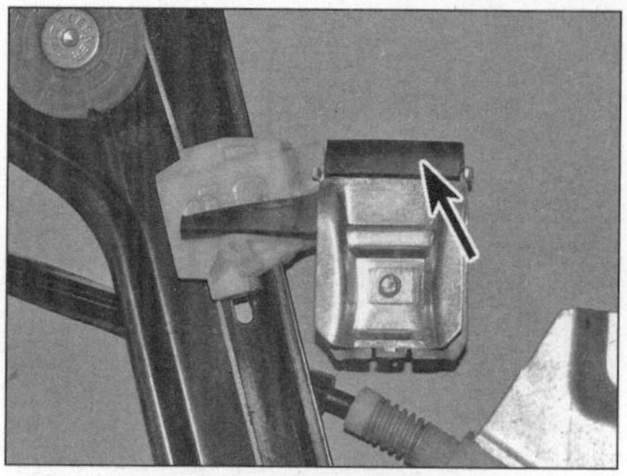

15.7 Ensure the clamp rubbers are in place (arrowed)

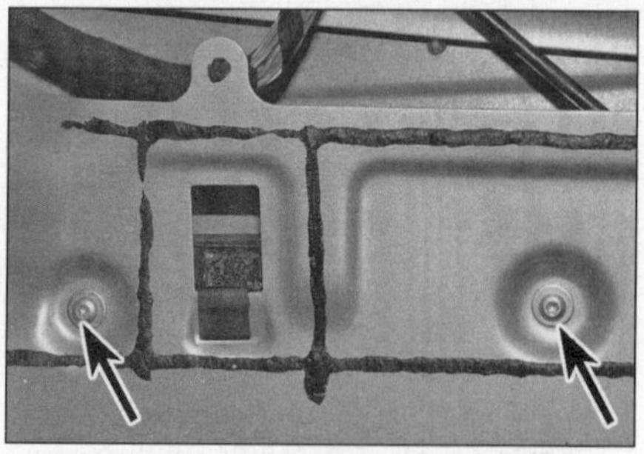

15.9 Undo the 2 screws (arrowed) and remove the vibration damper/polystyrene block from the base of the door

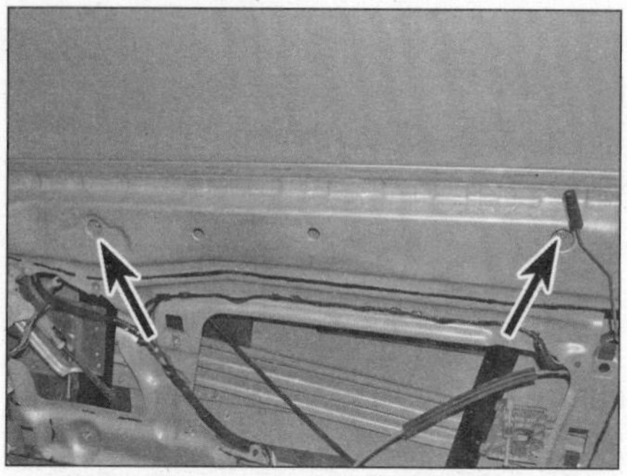

15.11a Window regulator upper retaining bolts (arrowed) ...

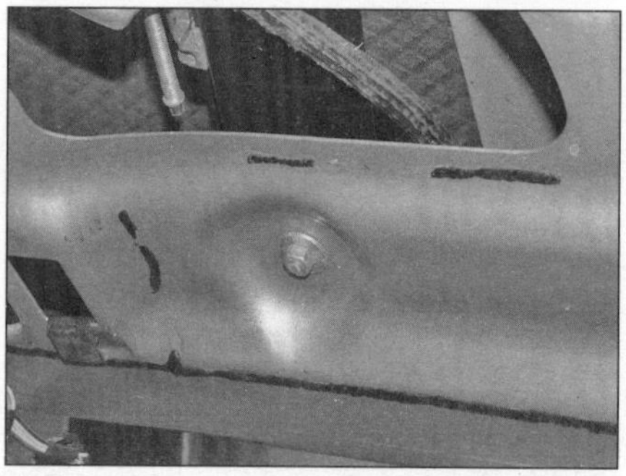

15.11b ... lower rear nut ...

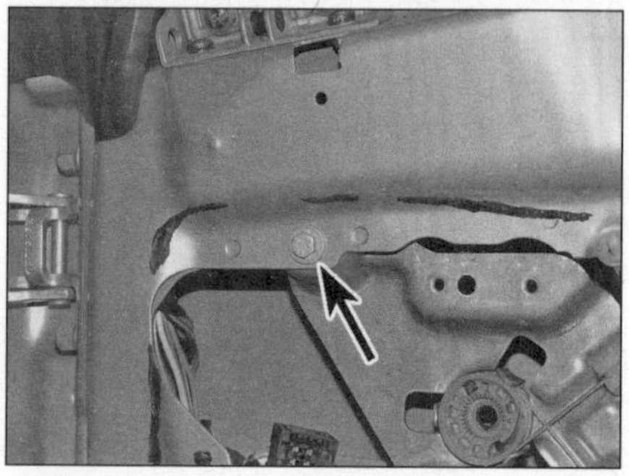

15.11c ... upper front bolt (arrowed) ...

10 Undo the 3 Torx screws and pull the window motor from the regulator **(see illustration 19.2)**. Disconnect the wiring plug as the motor is withdrawn.

11 Prise out the plastic cover at the lower edge of the door, then undo the regulator retaining nuts/bolts **(see illustrations)**. Make alignment marks around the screw heads prior to undoing them.

12 Release the upper cable clip, then manoeuvre the regulator from the door.

13 Refitting is a reversal of removal.

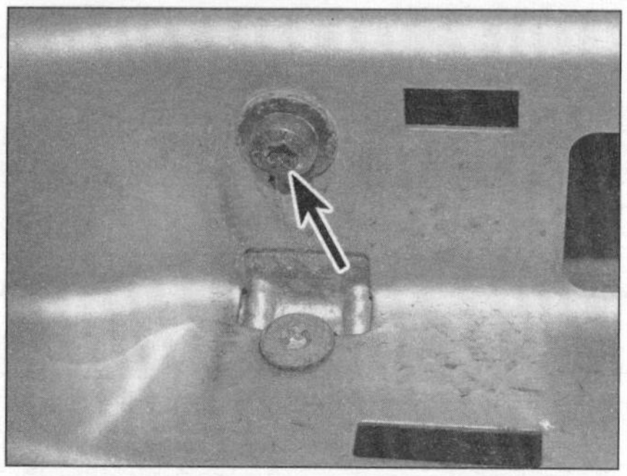

15.11d ... and lower bolt (arrowed)

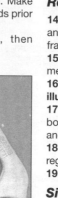

15.18 Motor retaining bolts (arrowed)

16.3a Remove the blanking grommets to access ...

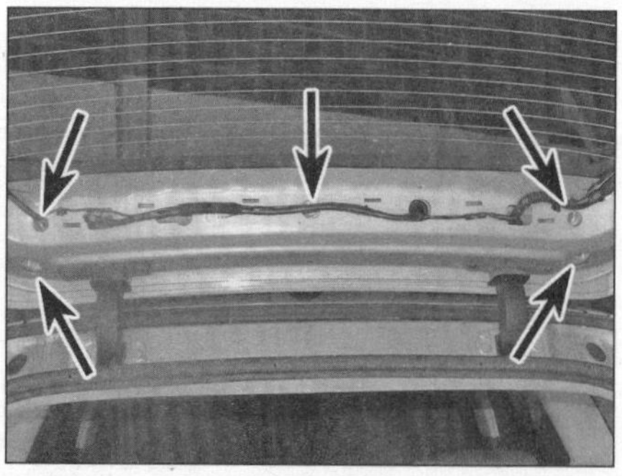

16.3b ... the rear spoiler retaining nuts (arrowed)

Rear door window

14 Open the window approximately 10 cm, and use masking tape to secure it to the door frame.

15 Remove the inner door trim panel and membranes as described in Section 12.

16 Undo the window clamp bolts **(see illustration 14.19)**.

17 Undo the window regulator mounting bolts/nuts, disconnect the motor wiring plug and manoeuvre the assembly from the door.

18 If necessary, unbolt the motor from the regulator **(see illustration)**.

19 Refitting is a reversal of removal.

Side window – Convertible models

20 Removal of the side window regulator is part of the window glass removal described in Section 14.

16 Tailgate/boot lid and support struts – removal and refitting

Tailgate

1 With the tailgate open, carefully prise away the hinge trim panel from above the rear window **(see illustration 26.54)**.

2 Pull the tailgate window side trim panels inwards to release the clips **(see illustration 26.55)**.

3 Prise out the rubber grommets, and undo the rear spoiler retaining nuts **(see illustrations)**.

4 Close the tailgate and lift the spoiler from place. Disconnect the wiring plug and washer tube as the spoiler is withdrawn.
5 Remove the luggage compartment side trim panel as described in Section 26.
6 Remove the seals and cable ducts from the tailgate hinges **(see illustration)**.
7 Note their fitted positions, then disconnect the various wiring plugs and earth cables from the tailgate. Release the wiring harness from the retaining clips.
8 Remove the load grille mountings from the headlining.
9 Rotate the clips 90°, pull them from place, then lower the rear section of the headlining.
10 Remove the wiring harness retainer, prise open the locking clip and detach the harness from the retainer.
11 Disconnect the washer tube at the quick-release coupling.
12 Make alignment marks between the tailgate hinge bolts and the vehicle bodywork, and place thick cardboard (or similar) between the roof and the tailgate to protect the paintwork.
13 Undo the tailgate mounting bolts, and with the help of an assistant, remove the tailgate.
14 Refitting is a reversal of removal. Check that the tailgate closes properly and is located centrally within the body aperture. Adjustment is possible by lowering the headlining and loosening the hinge bolts. Check that the striker enters the lock centrally, and if necessary loosen the striker screws to adjust its position.

Boot lid

15 Undo the 2 Torx screws and remove the boot lid inner handle **(see illustration)**.
16 Press in the centre pins, and prise out the 9 boot lid trim panel retaining clips **(see illustration 26.61)**.
17 Note their fitted positions, disconnect the boot lid wiring plugs, and release the wiring harness from the retaining clips. Pull the harness from the boot lid.
18 Mark the position of the boot lid on the hinges, then, with the help of an assistant, unscrew the bolts and remove the boot lid **(see illustration)**.
19 Refitting is a reversal of removal.

Support struts

Tailgate

20 In order to renew the tailgate support struts, the headlining must be lowered at the rear. Remove the load grille support brackets from the headlining each side.
21 Rotate the headlining clips at the rear 90° and remove them.
22 Lower the rear of the headlining and support it to prevent it hanging down and creasing, etc.
23 Prise off the retaining clips and remove the support struts.
24 Refitting is a reversal of removal.

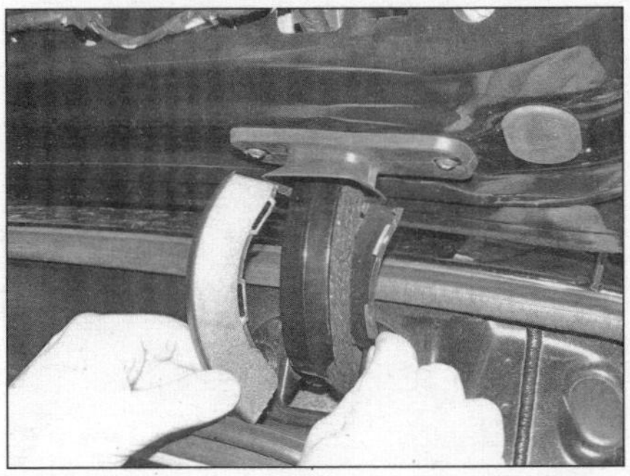

16.6 Remove the ducting from the tailgate hinges

16.18 Boot lid hinge bolts (arrowed)

Boot lid – Convertible

25 Open the boot, and prise the retaining clips from the ends of the struts **(see illustration)**.
26 With an assistant supporting the boot lid, pull the struts from place.
27 Refitting is a reversal of removal.

Boot lid springs – Saloon

28 Remove the access flap and then partially remove the side trim.
29 Wearing gloves unhook the spring and remove it.
30 Refitting is a reversal of removal. Note that the spring has a choice of positions. Select the position that supports the boot lid in the open position. Adjust both springs equally.

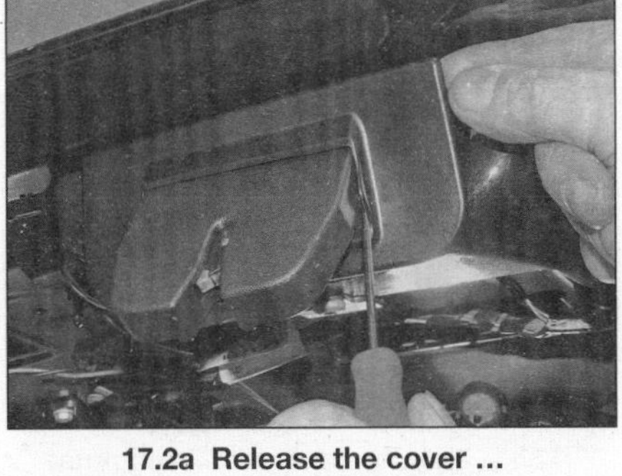

17.2a Release the cover ...

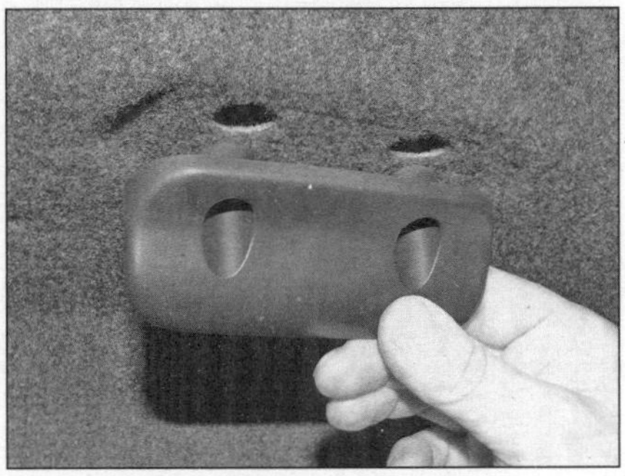

16.15 Remove the handle

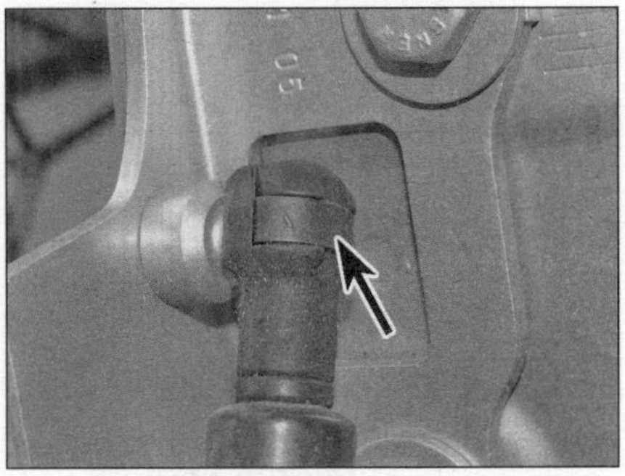

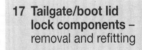

16.25 Prise the clip from the strut (arrowed)

17 Tailgate/boot lid lock components – removal and refitting

Tailgate lock

1 Remove the tailgate trim panel as described in Section 26.
2 Undo the 3 retaining screws, and remove the lock assembly **(see illustrations)**. Disconnect the lock wiring plug as it's withdrawn.
3 Refitting is a reversal of removal.

Boot lid lock

4 Remove the boot lid trim panel as described in Section 26.

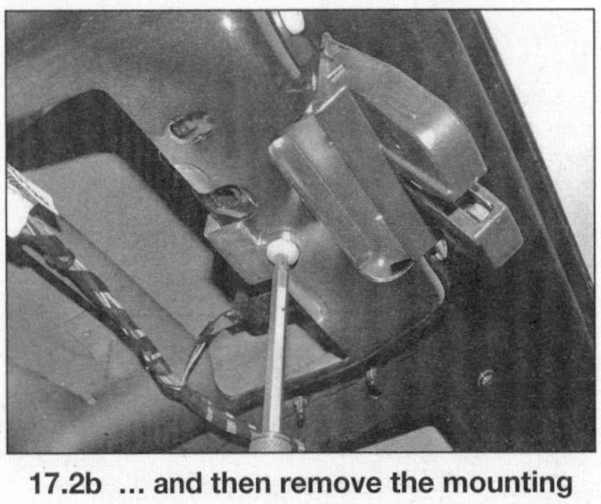

17.2b ... and then remove the mounting screws

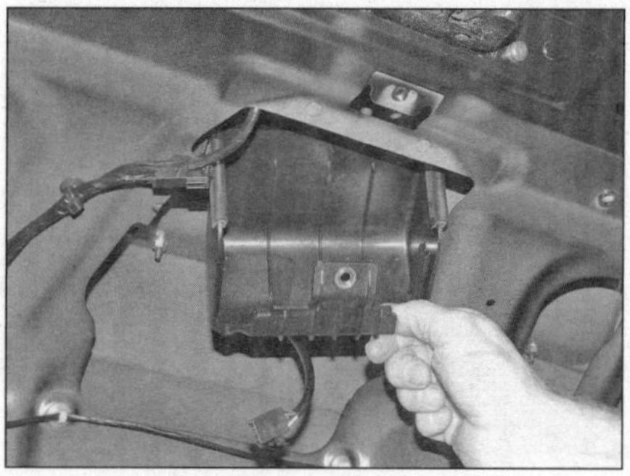

17.5 Remove the lock cover

17.6a Lower the lock ...

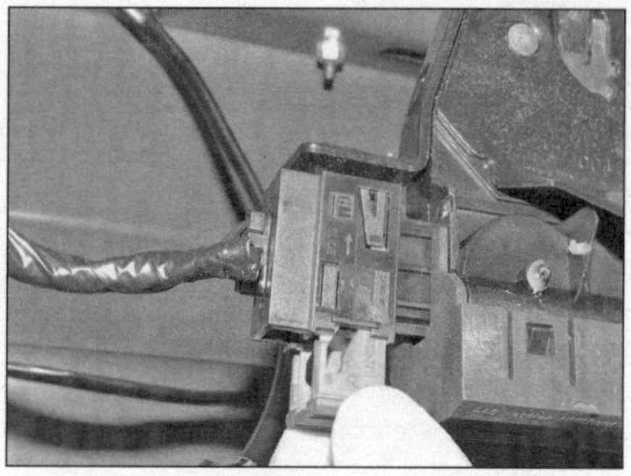

17.6b ... and slide out the red locking catch. Disconnect the wiring plug

17.7a Prise off the cover ...

17.7b ... and detach the operating cable – Convertible models

5 Remove the lock cover **(see illustration)**.

6 Remove the remaining Torx screws and withdraw the lock assembly. Disconnect the wiring plug as the lock is withdrawn **(see illustrations)**.

7 On Convertible models, prise off the cover and detach the operating cable **(see illustrations)**.

8 Refitting is a reversal of removal.

Boot lid lock cylinder – Convertible models

9 Remove the boot lid trim panel as described in Section 26.

10 Undo the 2 retaining nuts, and remove the cylinder cover **(see illustration)**.

11 Pull the out the cylinder and disengage the operating cable **(see illustration)**.

12 Refitting is a reversal of removal.

Tailgate release button

13 Remove the tailgate trim panel as described in Section 26.

14 Disconnect the wiring plugs, then remove the rear speakers **(see illustration)**.

15 Undo the 4 nuts securing the handle moulding to the tailgate, then disconnect the wiring plug **(see illustration)**.

16 Remove the handle.

17 If required, release the catch and detach the microswitch.

18 Refitting is a reversal of removal.

Boot lid release button

19 Remove the boot lid light units as described in Chapter 12, Section 7.

20 Undo the 4 retaining nuts and disconnect the handle wiring plug **(see illustration)**.

21 Remove the button/number plate light assembly.

22 If required, release the catch and detach the microswitch **(see illustrations)**.

23 Refitting is a reversal of removal.

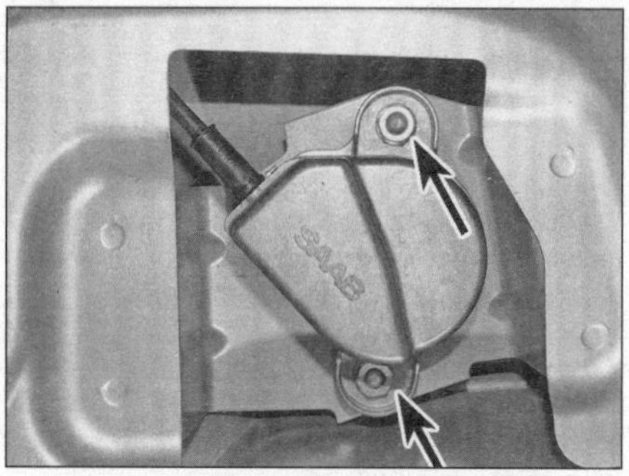

17.10 Cylinder cover retaining nuts (arrowed)

17.11 Disengage the cable from the lock cylinder

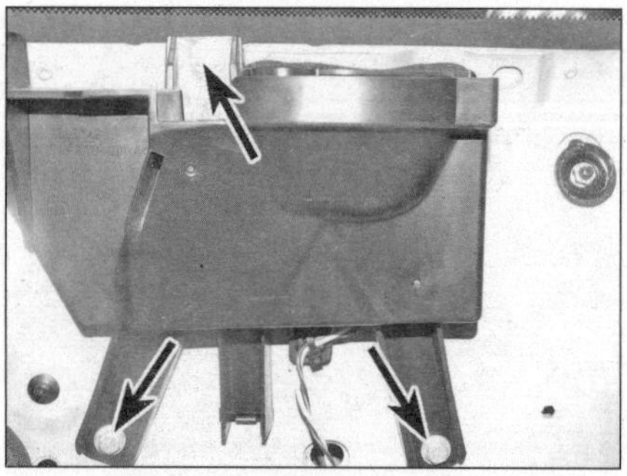

17.14 Tailgate speaker retaining screws (arrowed)

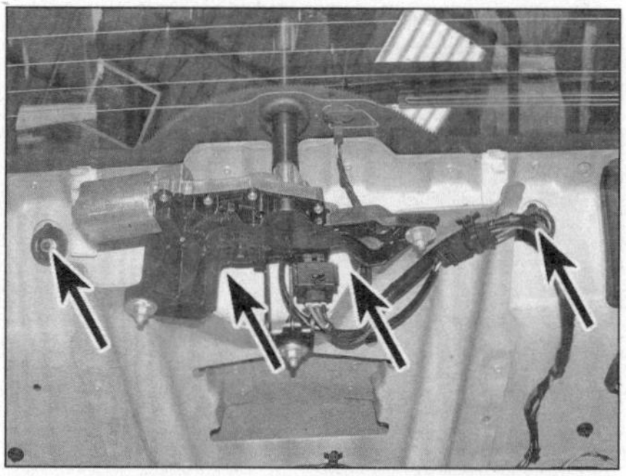

17.15 Tailgate handle retaining nuts (arrowed – inner nuts obscured)

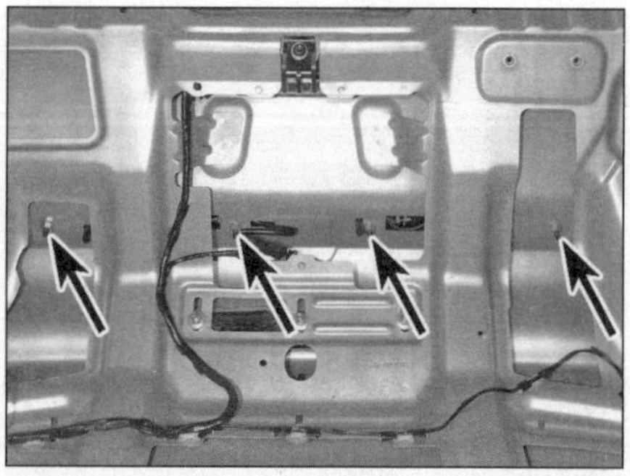

17.20 Undo the 4 retaining nuts (arrowed)

18 Central locking system components – removal and refitting

Central locking motors

1 The motors are integral with the lock assemblies. Removal and refitting of the motors is included in the lock procedure described in Section 13 or 17.

Lock switches

2 The lock switches are integral with the lock assemblies. Removal and refitting of the locks is described in Section 13 or 17.

Door control modules

3 The door control modules (fitted to each door) control the operation of the electric windows, door mirrors, courtesy lighting at the base of the door, and the function of the central locking motors within the door locks. All the door modules are networked together, and share information with all the other modules on the network.

4 To remove a module, first remove the door trim panel as described in Section 12.

Caution: The modules are extremely sensitive to static electricity. Prior to touching the module, 'earth' yourself by briefly touching a bare metal part of the vehicle body or engine.

5 Undo the retaining screw, release the clips and remove the module from the door trim.

6 Refitting is a reversal of removal. Note that if a new module has been fitted, it may be necessary to have the software reprogrammed using dedicated Saab diagnostic equipment. Entrust this task to a Saab dealer or suitably-equipped specialist.

19 Electric window motor – removal and refitting

Door window motor

Removal

1 Remove the door trim panel and waterproof membrane as described in Section 12.

2 Undo the 3 retaining screws, and remove the motor **(see illustration)**. Disconnect the wiring plug as the motor is withdrawn.

Refitting

3 Refitting is a reversal of removal. Carry out the synchronising of the 'pinch protection' function as described at the start of Section 15.

Rear side window motor – Convertible models

Removal

4 Remove the rear side trim panel as described in Section 26.

5 Carefully peel away the waterproof membrane, then undo the 3 retaining screws and remove the motor **(see illustration)**. Disconnect the wiring plug as the motor is withdrawn.

17.22a Release the clip ...

17.22b ... and remove the microswitch

Refitting

6 Refitting is a reversal of removal. Carry out the synchronising of the 'pinch protection' function as described at the start of Section 15.

20 Exterior door mirror and glass – removal and refitting

Mirror

Saloon and Estate models

1 Remove the door inner trim panel as described in Section 12.

2 Remove the plastic cover in the corner of the window frame **(see illustration)**. Disconnect the mirror wiring plug.

3 Undo the 3 Torx screws and withdraw the mirror from the outside of the door **(see illustration)**.

4 Refitting is a reversal of removal.

Convertible models

5 Undo the retaining screw, then pull up and remove the door mirror base cover **(see illustrations 12.6a and 12.6b)**. Disconnect the mirror wiring plugs, then undo the 3 retaining screws and remove the mirror assembly.

6 Refitting is a reversal of removal.

Glass

7 Fold the mirror forwards at the top, and angle the glass outwards as far as possible.

8 Using a wide-bladed screwdriver, unhook the retaining clip from the back of the mirror glass **(see illustration)**.

19.2 Door window motor Torx screws (arrowed)

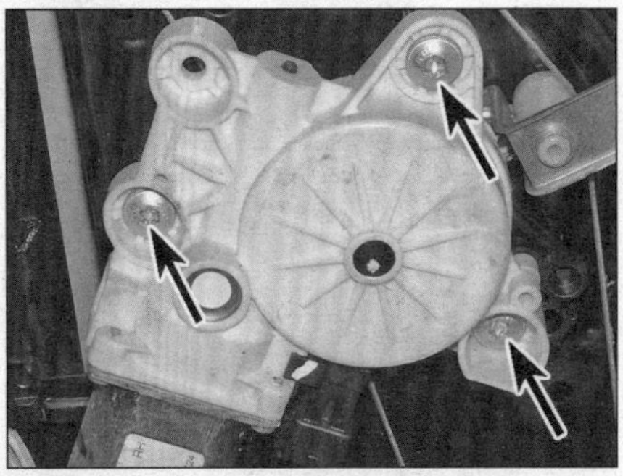

19.5 Rear side window motor Torx screws (arrowed) – Convertible models

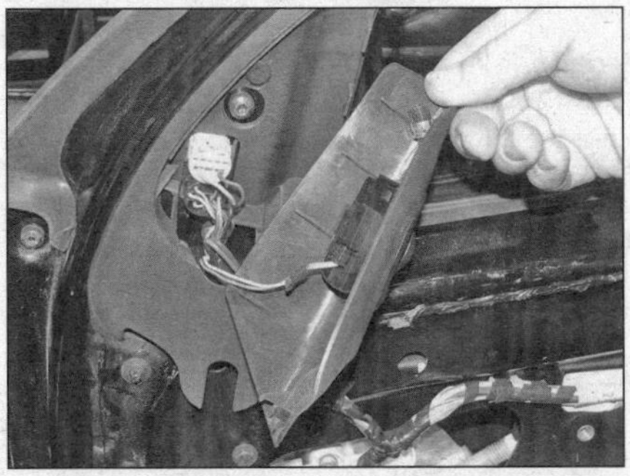

20.2 Carefully pull the cover from the window frame

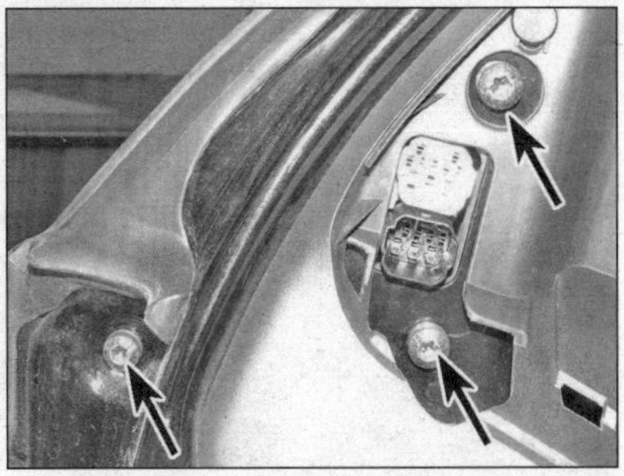

20.3 Mirror mounting Torx screws (arrowed)

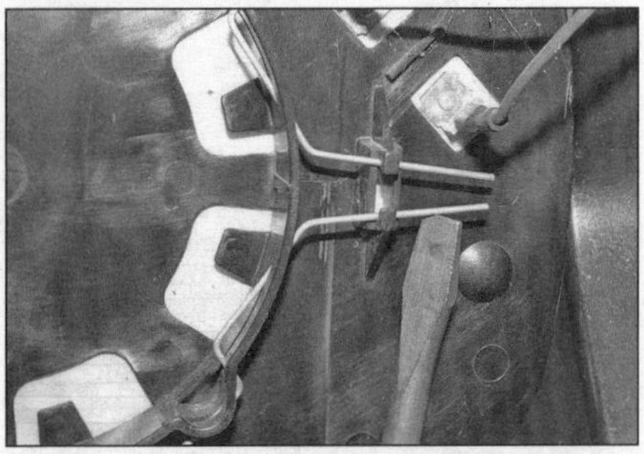
20.8 Insert a screwdriver behind the glass and release the clips (shown with the glass removed for clarity)

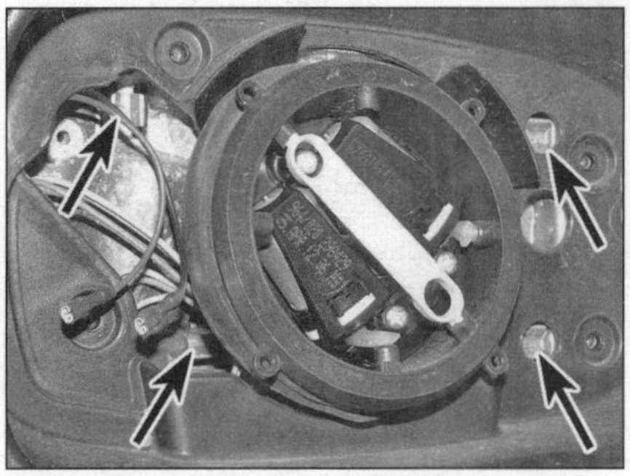
20.13a Release the 4 clips (arrowed) ...

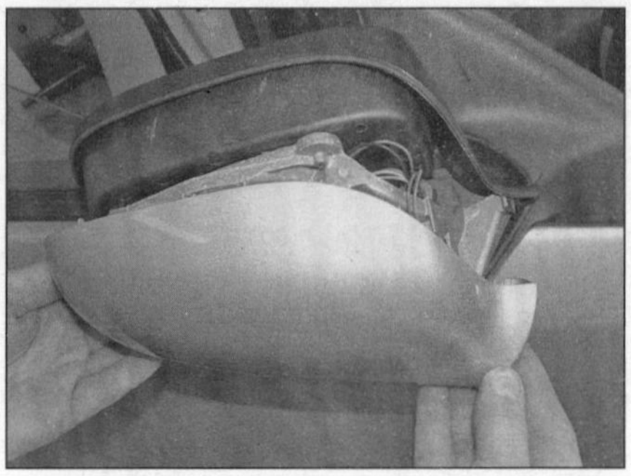
20.13b ... and pull the cover forwards

9 Disconnect the heater wires.
10 Reconnect the wiring.
11 Using a wad of cloth rag, press the mirror into position until the clip engages.

Mirror cover

12 Remove the mirror glass as previously described.
13 Release the 4 clips and pull off the mirror cover **(see illustrations)**.
14 Press the cover into place.
15 The remainder of refitting is a reversal of removal.

Mirror motor

16 Remove the door mirror glass as previously described.
17 Undo the 3 retaining screws, and lift out the motor **(see illustration)**. Disconnect the wiring plug as the motor is withdrawn.
18 Refitting is a reversal of removal.

21 Windscreen, rear window and fixed windows – general information

1 The windscreen, rear window glass and fixed side windows are bonded in position with a special adhesive. Renewal of such fixed glass is a complex, messy and time-consuming task, which is beyond the scope of the home mechanic; without the benefit of extensive practice, it is difficult to attain a secure, waterproof fit. Furthermore, the task carries a high risk of accidental breakage – this applies especially to the laminated glass windscreen. In view of this, owners are strongly advised to entrust work of this nature to a Saab dealer, or one of the many specialist windscreen fitters.

22 Sunroof assembly – removal and refitting

1 Due to the complexity of the tilt/slide sunroof mechanism, considerable expertise is required to repair, renew or adjust the sunroof components successfully. Removal of the sunroof or drive motor first requires that the headlining be removed, which is a tedious operation, not to be undertaken lightly (see Section 26). Therefore, it is recommended that any problems related to the sunroof are referred to a Saab dealer or specialist.

23 Body exterior fittings – removal and refitting

Badges and trim mouldings

1 Side trim panels, rubbing strips, and bonnet, boot lid and tailgate emblems are all secured in place by adhesive tape or nuts.
2 To remove the fittings from the bodywork, select an implement to use as a lever that will not damage the paintwork, such as a plastic spatula, or a filling knife wrapped in PVC tape. On items secured with adhesive tape, it will help if heat is applied from a heat gun.
3 Insert the lever between the top edge of the fitting and the bodywork, and carefully prise it away.
4 Progressively pull the lower edge of the fitting away from the bodywork, allowing the adhesive tape to peel off.
5 Clean the bodywork surface, removing all traces of dirt and the remains of any adhesive tape.
6 Peel the backing strip from the new fitting. Offer it up to its mounting position, top edge first, and press the stud fixings into their holes. Smooth the lower edge of the fitting into place, then press down on it firmly to ensure that the tape adheres along its whole length.

Wheel arch liners

7 The wheel arch liners are secured by means of 10 screws and nuts. First apply the handbrake, then jack up the relevant end of the vehicle and support it on axle stands (see *Jacking and vehicle support*). Remove the relevant roadwheel.
8 Note their fitted positions, undo the screws/nuts, and remove the liner **(see illustration)**.
9 Refitting is a reversal of removal.

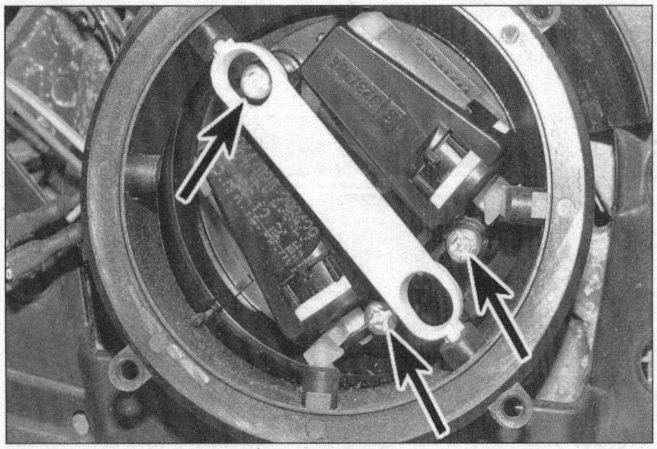
20.17 Mirror motor screws (arrowed)

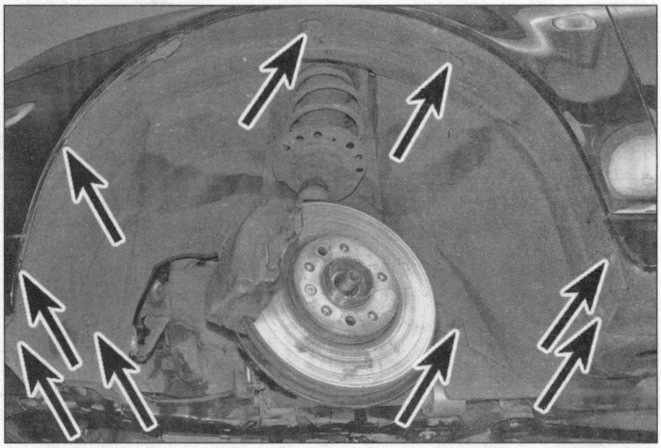
23.8 Wheel arch liner retaining screws and nut (arrowed)

24.3 Remove the bolt from the seat belt lower anchorage

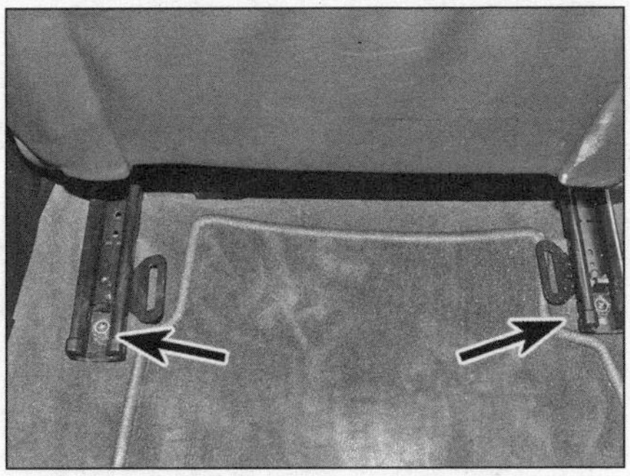

24.4 Undo the Torx screws at the rear of the seat rails (arrowed)

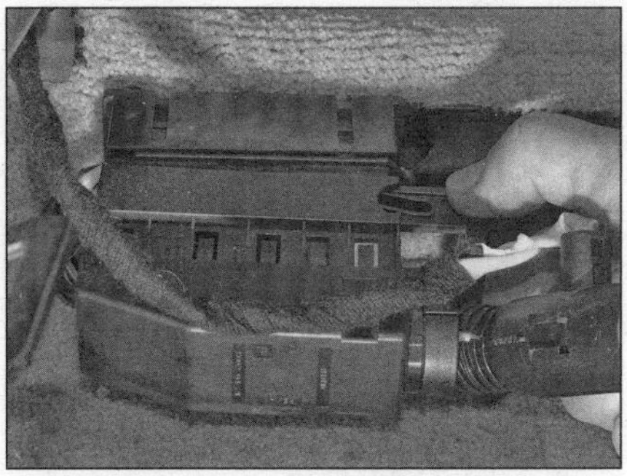

24.5 Slide out the locking catch and disconnect the seat wiring plug

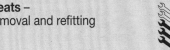

24 Seats – removal and refitting

Front seat

Saloon and Estate models

1 Raise the seat to its highest, forward-most position.

2 Disconnect the battery negative lead as described in Chapter 5A, Section 4, then wait at least 3 minutes before recommencing work to allow any residual electrical charge to dissipate.

3 Where fitted prise off the plastic cover, then undo the bolt securing the belt outer mounting to the seat **(see illustration)**.

4 Undo the 2 Torx screws securing the rear of the seat rails to the vehicle body **(see illustration)**.

5 Tip the seat forwards a little, and disconnect the seat wiring plugs **(see illustration)**.

6 Pull the seat backwards to unhook the front mountings, and manoeuvre it from the cabin.

7 Refit the seat into position, ensuring the front hooks locate correctly into their brackets. Apply a little thread-locking compound, then fit the rear mounting screws and tighten them to the specified torque.

Convertible models

8 Fully retract the soft top.

9 Move the seat to the rearmost and highest position.

10 Undo the seat front mounting Torx screws. On vehicles fitted with electrically-operated seats use a screwdriver on the rear mounting bolt to block the movement of the seat whilst moving the seat backwards for a few seconds.

11 Move the seat to the front and remove the rear mounting screws.

12 Ensure the ignition switch is in the off position, then disconnect the wiring plug under the rear of the seat, and manoeuvre the seat from the cabin.

13 Refit the seat into position and reconnect the wiring plug.

14 Apply a little thread-locking compound, then fit and tighten the rear mounting screws to their specified torque.

15 Slide the seat to the rear, then apply a little thread-locking compound and tighten the screws to the specified torque.

16 On vehicles with electrically-operated seats a fault code may be generated. Once all work is completed turn the ignition on – do not start the vehicle – and leave the ignition on for at least one minute. Should any fault codes be generated during this procedure, have them deleted using Saab (or suitable) diagnostic equipment. Once deleted, they should not re-occur.

Rear seat cushion

Saloon and Estate models

17 Grip the front edge of the seat cushion, and pull it sharply upwards **(see illustration)**.

18 Lift the rear of the seat forwards and upwards, then manoeuvre it from the cabin. If required, depress the 2 clips and slide the cup holder from the cushion **(see illustration)**.

19 Refitting is a reversal of removal.

Convertible models

20 Fully open the soft top.

21 Undo the 2 screws at the front lower edge of the cushion, then lift the cushion from place, releasing the retaining clips **(see illustrations)**.

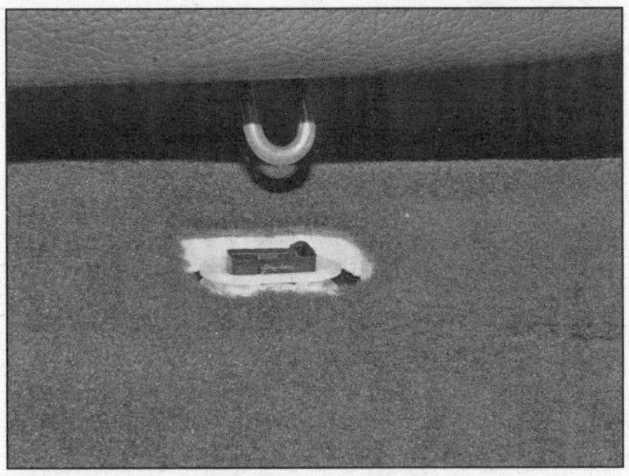

24.17 Release the seat cushion

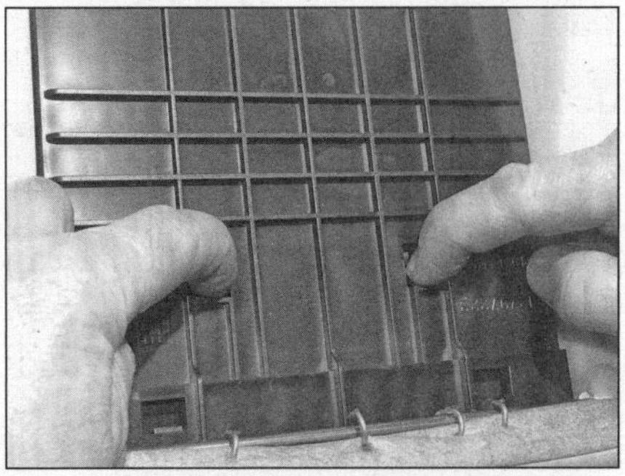

24.18 Depress the clips and slide the cup holder from place

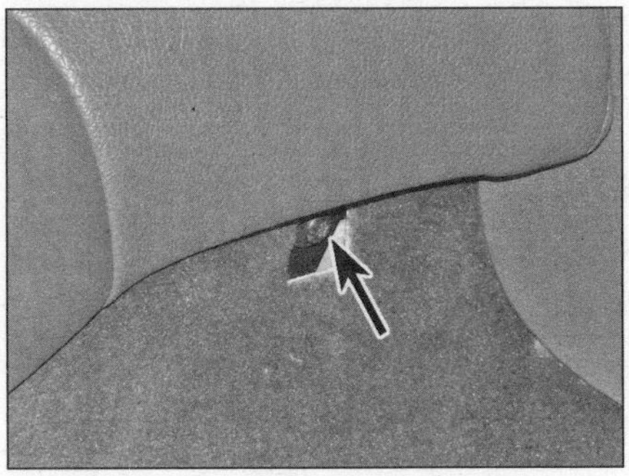

24.21a Undo the screw each side (arrowed) ...

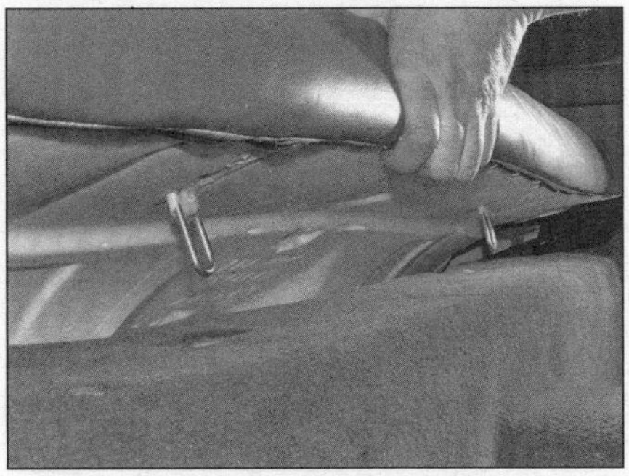

24.21b ... and pull the seat cushion upwards ...

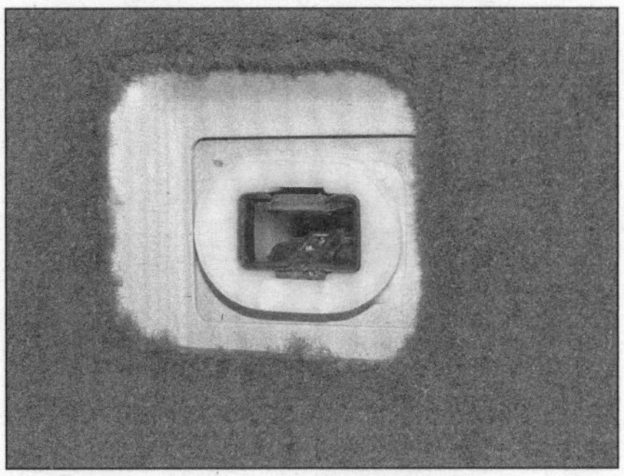

24.21c ... from the clips

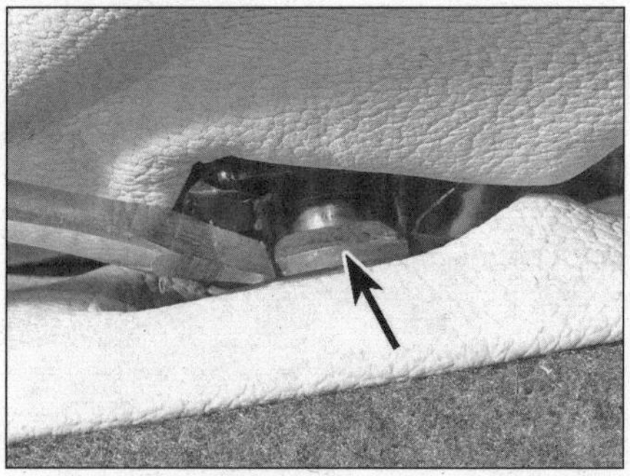

24.26 Use a screwdriver to press the collar (arrowed) towards the seat backrest

Note that it's quite likely the retaining clips will be damaged by the removal procedure – ensure new ones are available.

22 Refitting is a reversal of removal.

Rear seat backrest

40% section

23 Remove the rear seat cushion as previously described.

24 If the 60% backrest is to be removed, undo the nut and detach the centre lower belt anchorage.

25 Fold the rear seat backrest forwards.

26 Press back the collar on the outer mounting, then lift up the outer edge of the 40% backrest **(see illustration)**. Press in the side panel upholstery whilst the backrest is lifted to prevent damage.

27 Angle the backrest forwards/upwards, and pull it from the central guide pin.

28 Refitting is a reversal of removal.

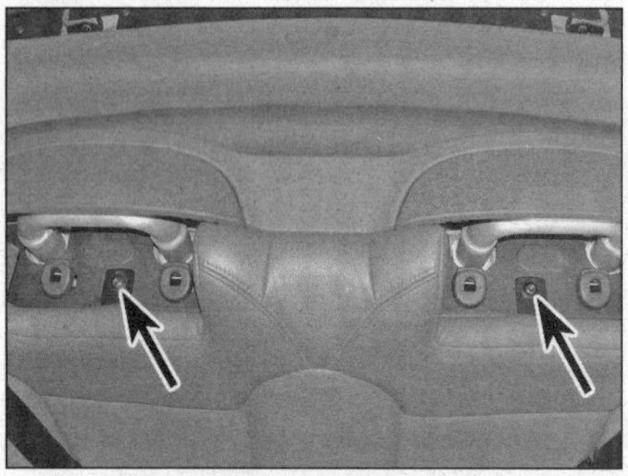

24.36 Undo the backrest upper securing Torx screws (arrowed)

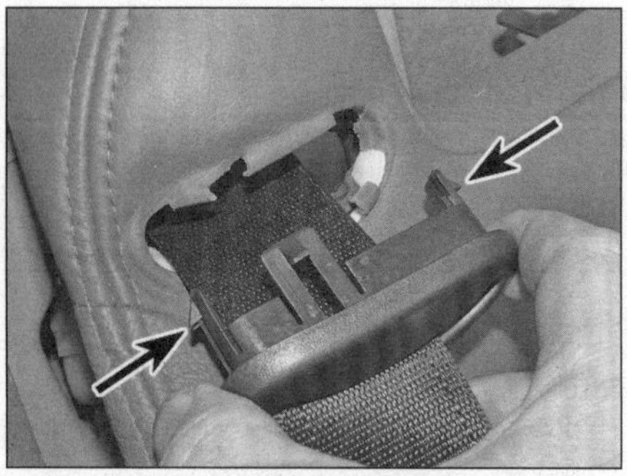

24.37b Depress the clips (arrowed) and detach the seat belt guide ...

24.31 Recover the plastic washer (arrowed)

60% section

29 Remove the 40% section rear seat backrest as described earlier.

30 Press back the collar on the outer mounting, then lift up the outer edge of the remaining backrest **(see illustration 24.26)**. Press in the side panel upholstery whilst the backrest is lifted to prevent damage.

31 Angle the backrest forwards/upwards, and release it from the central bracket. Recover the plastic washer **(see illustration)**.

32 Refitting is a reversal of removal.

Convertible models

33 Remove the rear seat cushion as described in this Section.

34 Undo the bolts securing the lower left- and right-hand seat belt anchorages.

35 Depress the catches, and pull the rear head restraints from the backrest **(see illustration)**.

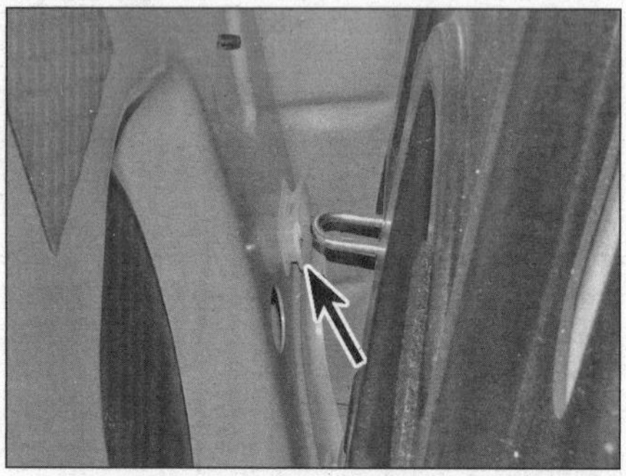

24.37a Pull the backrest from the plastic retaining clips (arrowed)

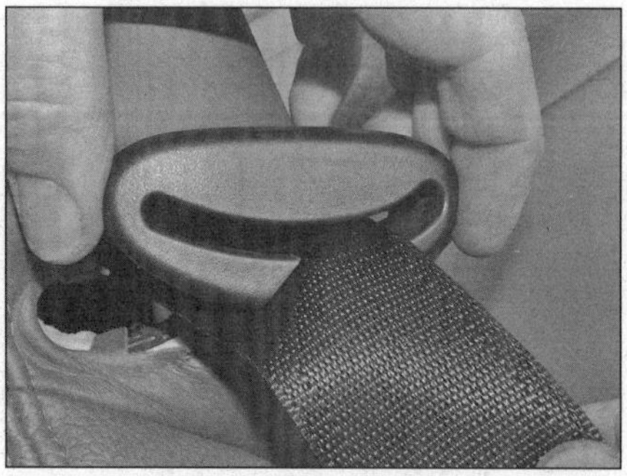

24.37c ... then feed the belt through the split in the guide

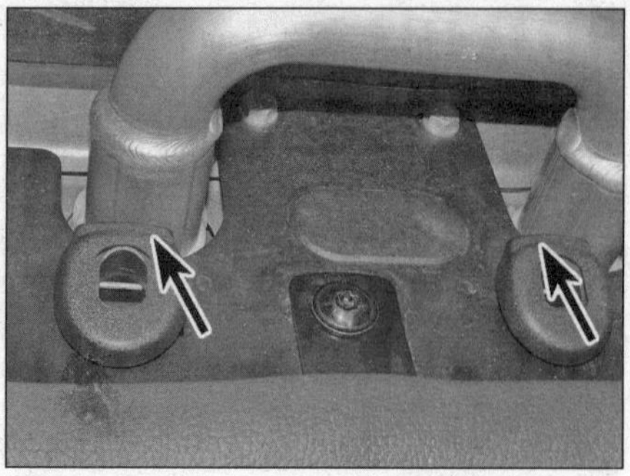

24.35 Depress the clips (arrowed) and pull the headrests upwards

36 Remove the backrest cushion upper securing screws **(see illustration)**.

37 Pull the lower edge of the backrest forwards a little to release the lower retaining clips, remove the seat belt guides from the backrest. Pull the seat belts out of the guides and remove the backrest **(see illustrations)**. Note that the backrest maybe extremely reluctant to release from the clips – it's quite likely the clips will be damaged during the procedure.

38 Refitting is a reversal of removal, but tighten the seat belt mounting bolts to the specified torque.

25 Seat belts – removal and refitting

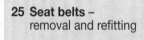

Warning: If the vehicle has been involved in an accident which caused the seat belt pretensioners to be activated, the complete seat belt must be renewed.

Front belts

Saloon and Estate models

1 Disconnect the battery negative lead as described in Chapter 5A, Section 4. Wait at least 3 minutes for any residual electrical energy to dissipate before recommencing work.

2 Remove the belt from the seat **(see illustration 24.3)** and then remove the B-pillar trim as described in Section 26.

3 Undo the bolts and remove the seat belt guide from the pillar **(see illustration)**.

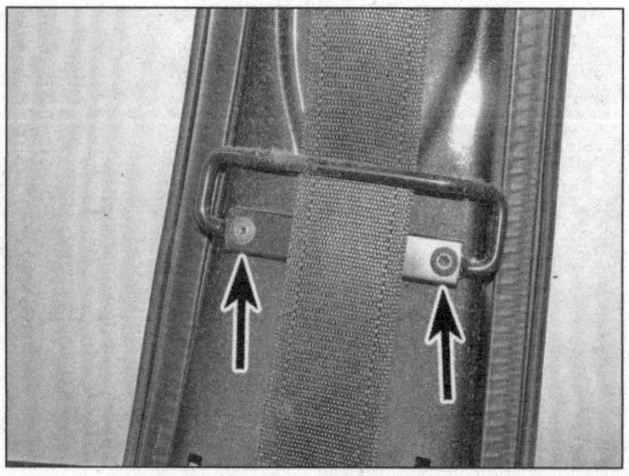

25.3 Seat belt guide bolts (arrowed)

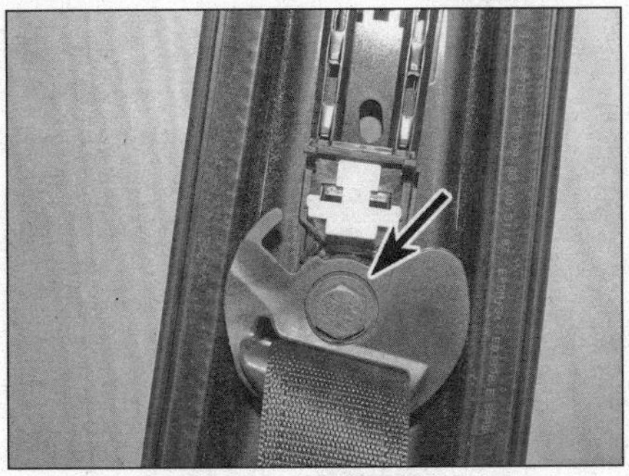

25.4 Undo the height adjuster bolt

4 Undo the retaining bolt and detach the height adjuster assembly **(see illustration)**.
5 Undo the inertia reel retaining bolts, prise up the locking clip, disconnect the wiring plug and remove the inertia reel **(see illustrations)**.
6 Refitting is a reversal of removal, but apply a little thread-locking compound, and tighten the mounting bolts to the specified torque.

Convertible models

7 This is an involved task that requires the removal of the seat cover. Remove the front seat as described in Section 24.
8 Remove the backrest pocket by prising the lower edge outwards to release the clips, then lifting it from place **(see illustration)**.
9 Undo the 2 screws at the base of the backrest cover **(see illustration)**.
10 Lift the tilt release handle, undo the Torx screw, then pull the belt plastic cover straight up **(see illustrations)**.
11 Undo the backrest cover upper screws, and slide the backrest cover downwards to remove it **(see illustration)**.
12 Prise out the two plastic clips and unclip the rear lower plastic cover **(see illustration)**.
13 Undo the screw and push forward the plastic casing **(see illustration)**.
14 Prise out the locking catch and disconnect the wiring plug on the base of the inertia reel.
15 Undo the bolt and lift the inertia reel from place **(see illustrations)**.
16 Undo the 2 Torx screws securing the upper seat belt guide **(see illustration)**.

25.5a Inertia reel mounting bolts (arrowed)

25.5b Prise out the locking clip and disconnect the wiring plug

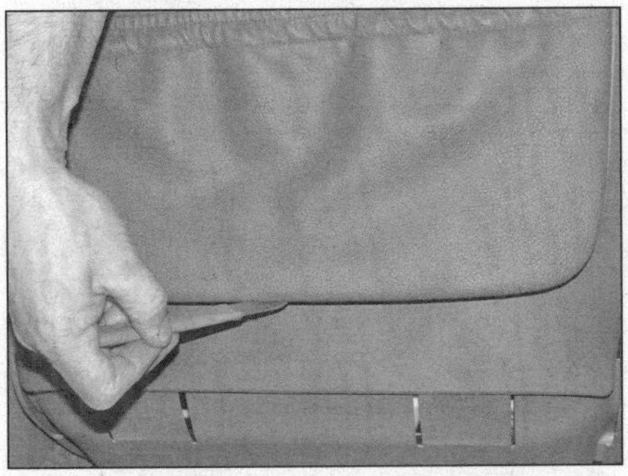

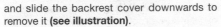

25.8 Prise out the lower edge, and lift the backrest pocket upwards

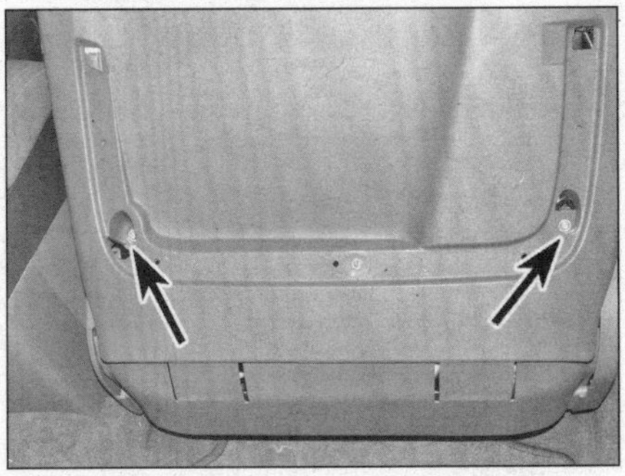

25.9 Undo the 2 screws at the base of the cover (arrowed)

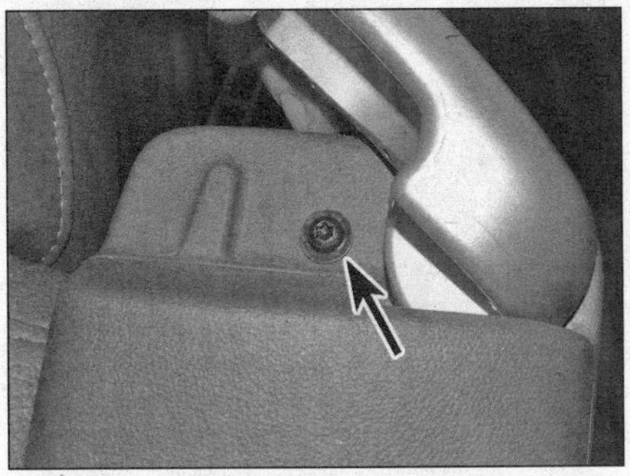

25.10a Undo the screw (arrowed) ...

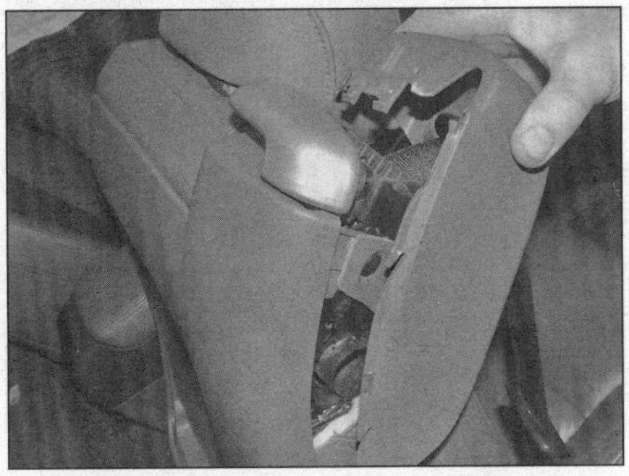

25.10b ... and lift the cover straight up

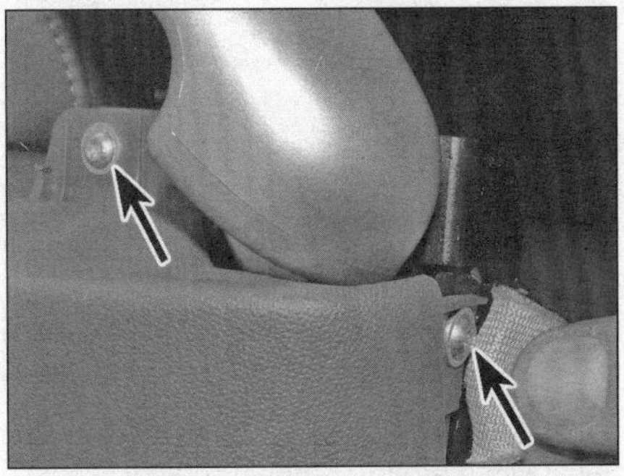

25.11 Undo the two screws (arrowed) and slide the backrest cover downwards

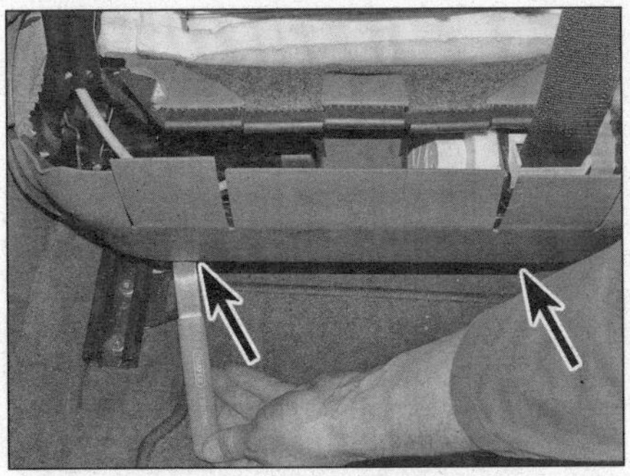

25.12 Use a flat-bladed tool to prise out the 2 plastic clips (arrowed)

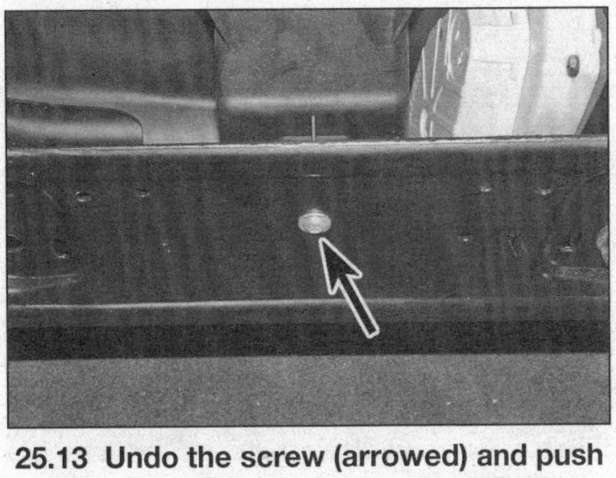

25.13 Undo the screw (arrowed) and push the plastic panel forwards for access to the inertia reel

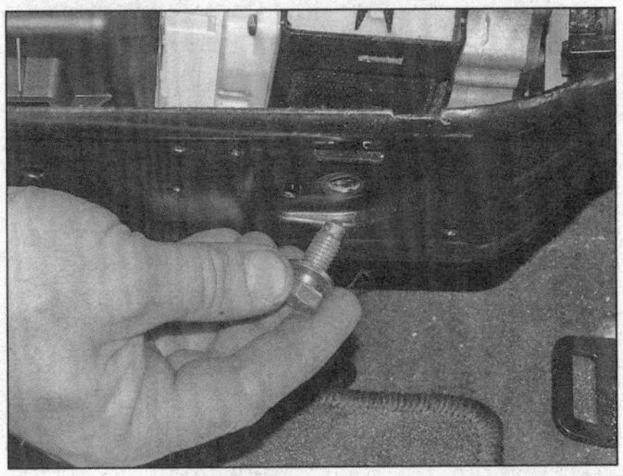

25.15a Undo the inertia reel retaining bolt ...

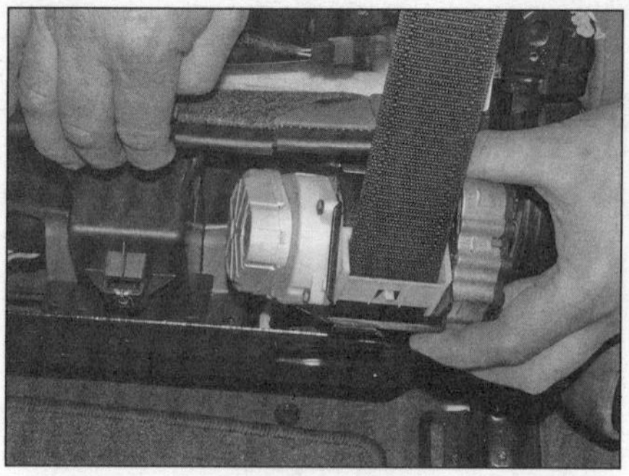

25.15b ... and lift the reel from place

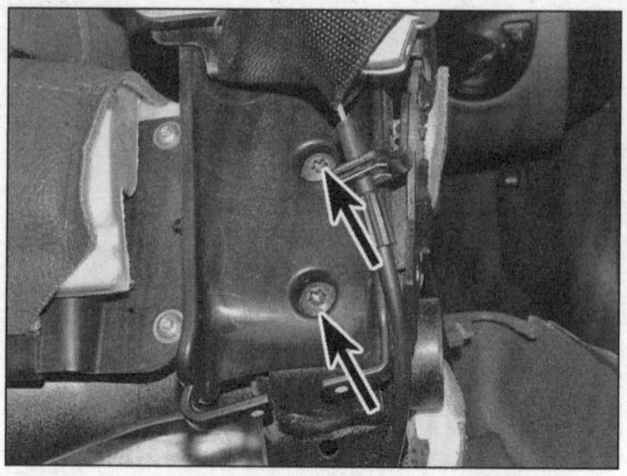

25.16 The upper seat belt guide is retained by 2 Torx screws (arrowed)

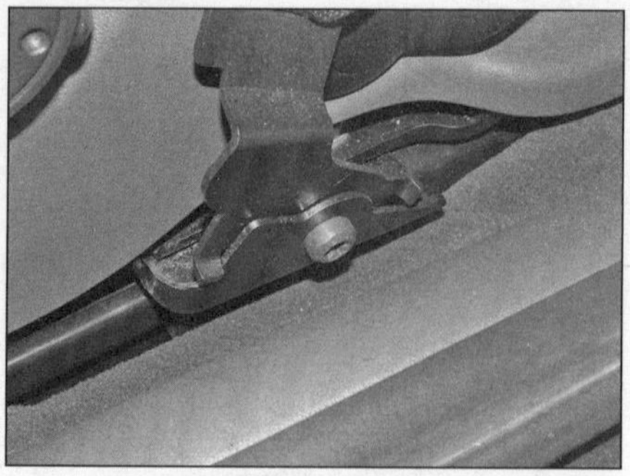

25.17 Undo the seat belt lower anchorage

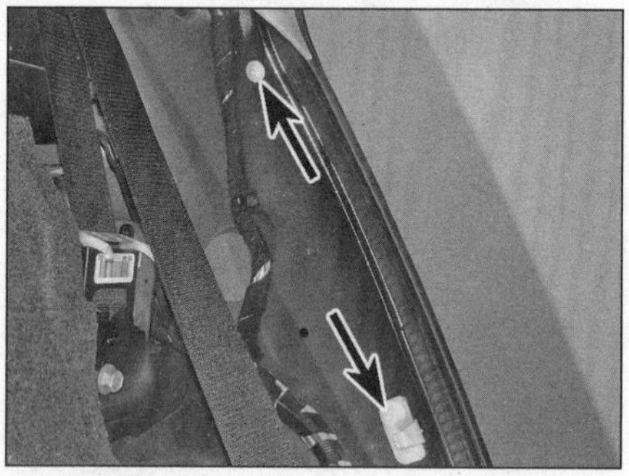

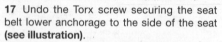

25.21a The side bolster is held by a clip at the top (arrowed), a hook midway (arrowed) ...

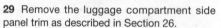

25.21b ... locates in a bracket at the base ...

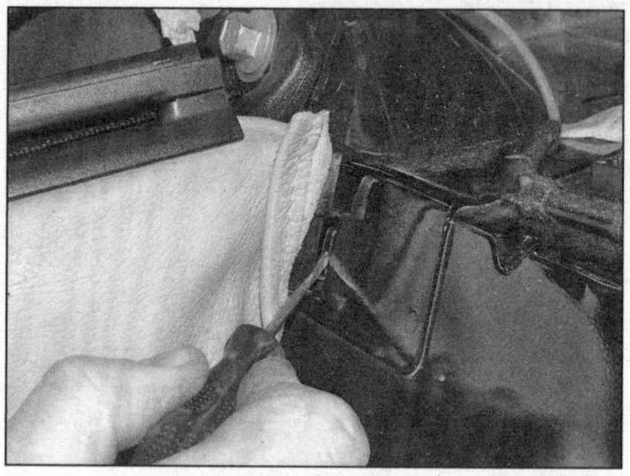

25.21c ... and is clipped at the top

17 Undo the Torx screw securing the seat belt lower anchorage to the side of the seat **(see illustration)**.

18 Feed the seat belt through the plastic assembly, and remove the assembly.

19 Refitting is a reversal of removal, but tighten the mounting bolts to the specified torque.

Rear outer belts

Saloon models

20 Remove the C-pillar trim panel as described in Section 26.

21 Remove the side bolster trim panel. On some vehicles the bolster is secured by a cable-tie at the top outer edge. Most vehicles feature a clip fixing. There is also a clip at the top inner edge, and a hook midway up the outer edge. Unclip the top half of the seat belt guide trim **(see illustrations)**.

22 Remove the upper seat belt guide.

23 Pull out the locking piece, and disconnect the inertia reel wiring plug **(see illustration)**.

24 Undo the inertia reel and lower anchorage bolts, and remove the seat belt assembly **(see illustration)**.

25 Refitting is a reversal of removal, but tighten the mounting bolts to the specified torque.

Estate models

26 Remove the C-pillar trim panel as described in Section 26.

27 Remove the rear seat as described in Section 24.

28 Prise out the plastic rivets, then remove the side bolster trim panel by pulling it upwards to release the clips **(see illustration 26.40)**.

29 Remove the luggage compartment side panel trim as described in Section 26.

30 Remove the lower belt anchorage bolt/nut.

31 Undo the retaining bolts and manoeuvre the inertia reel from the vehicle **(see illustrations)**.

32 Refitting is a reversal of removal, but tighten the mounting bolts to the specified torque.

25.23 Prise up the yellow locking clip and disconnect the wiring plug

25.24 Seat belt inertia reel and upper seat belt guide bolts (arrowed)

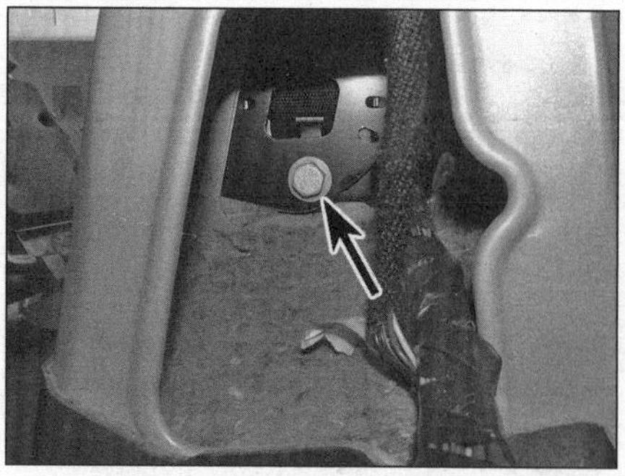

25.31a Rear seat belt front-facing retaining bolt (arrowed) ...

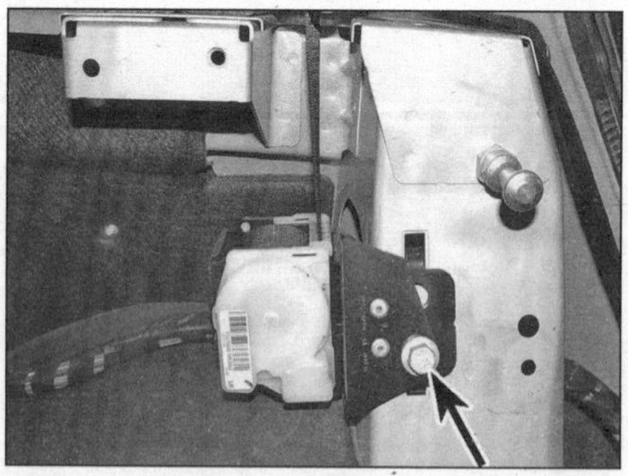

25.31b ... and inward-facing retaining bolt (arrowed)

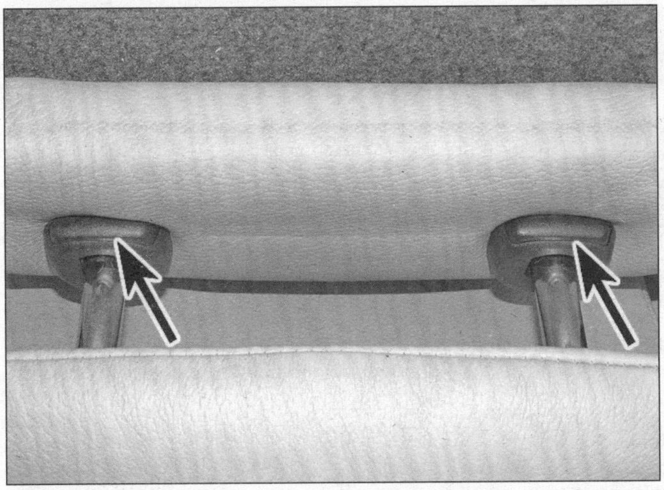

25.34 Depress the clips and pull the headrest from the backrest (arrowed)

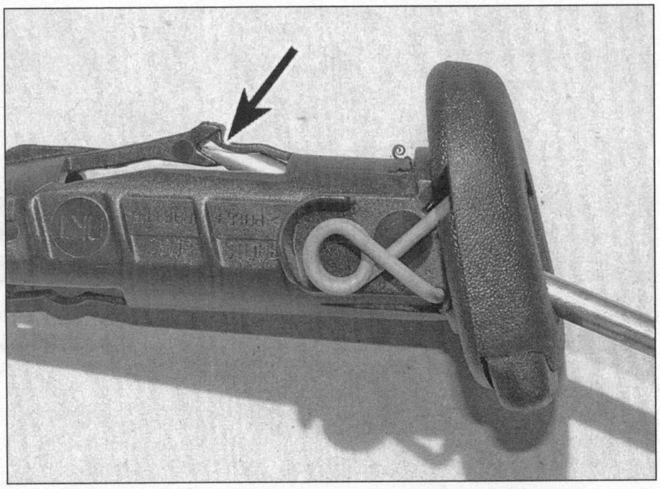

25.35 Engage a screwdriver with the clip (arrowed) then lever the clip into the sleeve

Rear centre belts

Saloon and Estate models

33 Remove the rear seat cushions and backrests as described in Section 24.

34 Depress the clips and pull the head restraints from the 60% backrest **(see illustration)**.

35 Using a screwdriver, release the clip and pull the headrest sleeves from the backrest **(see illustration)**.

36 On Estate models, remove the backrest lock plastic covers by releasing the 4 clips and pulling it upwards.

37 Unclip the seat belt guide from the top of the backrest **(see illustration)**.

38 Unclip the upper section and sides of the rear upholstery from the backrest **(see illustration)**.

39 Carefully fold the trim over top of the backrest, and pull the foam piece away to access the inertia reel **(see illustration)**.

40 Remove the belt carrier from the backrest frame, then undo the retaining bolt and remove the inertia reel **(see illustrations)**.

41 Refitting is a reversal of removal, but tighten the mounting bolts to the specified torque.

Rear belts

Convertible models

42 Open the soft top and remove the rear seat backrest as described in Section 24.

43 Ensure the ignition key is in the OFF

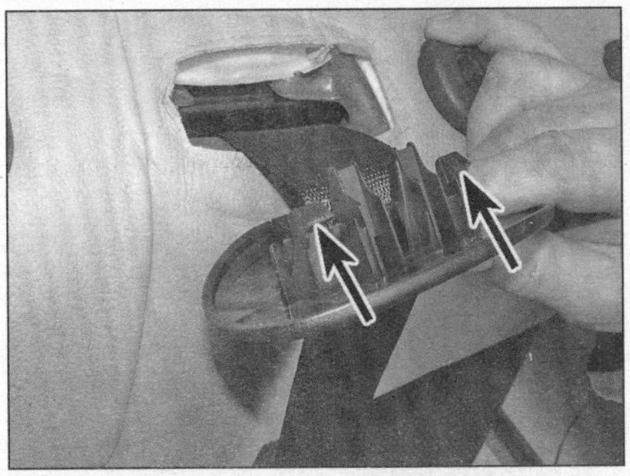

25.37 Depress the clips (arrowed) and pull the seat belt guide from place

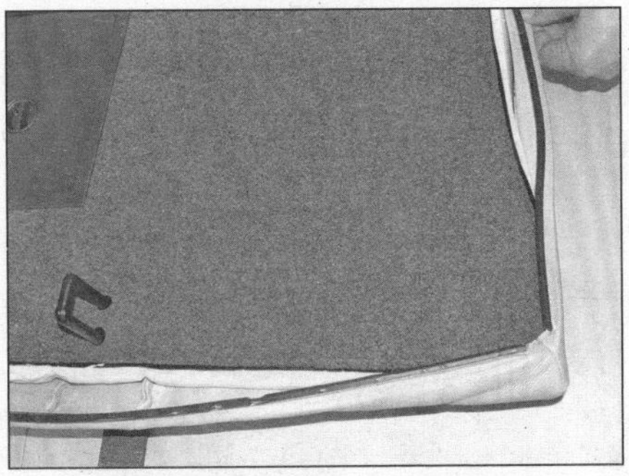

25.38 The upholstery pulls out of the channels in the backrest

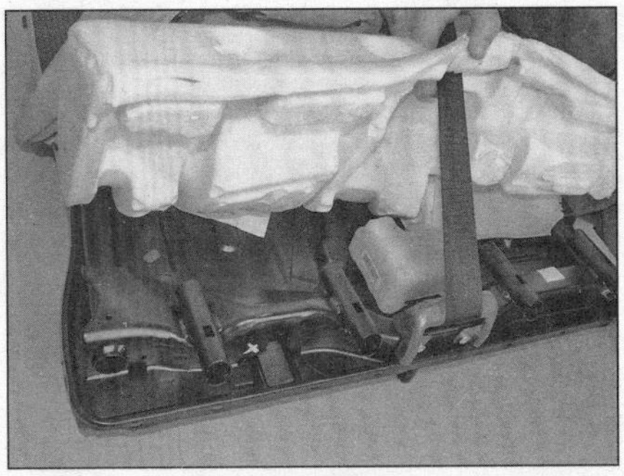

25.39 Pull the trim and foam away from the backrest

25.40a Undo the Torx screws and remove the belt carrier ...

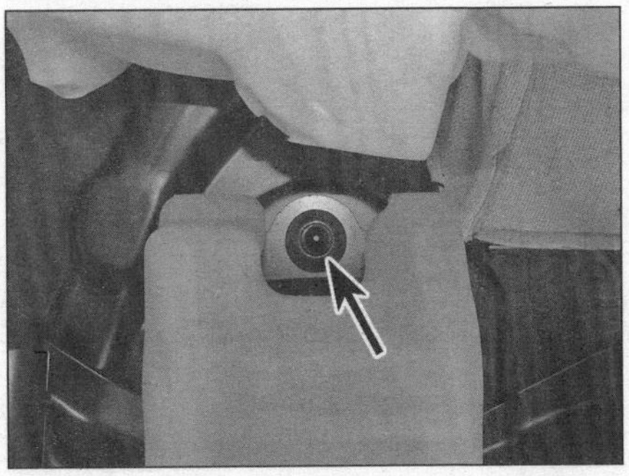

25.40b ... then undo the nut (arrowed) ...

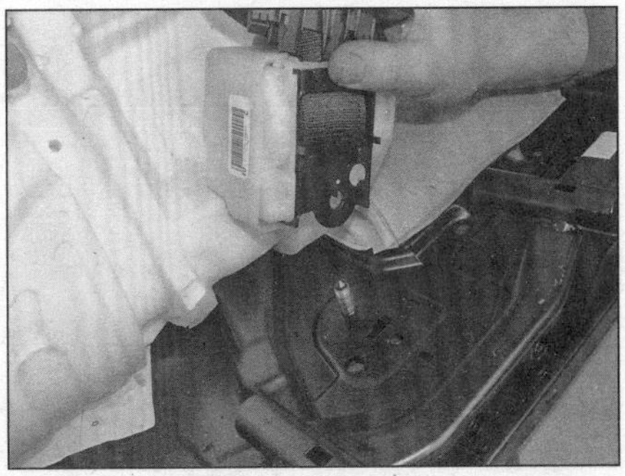

25.40c ... and remove the inertia reel

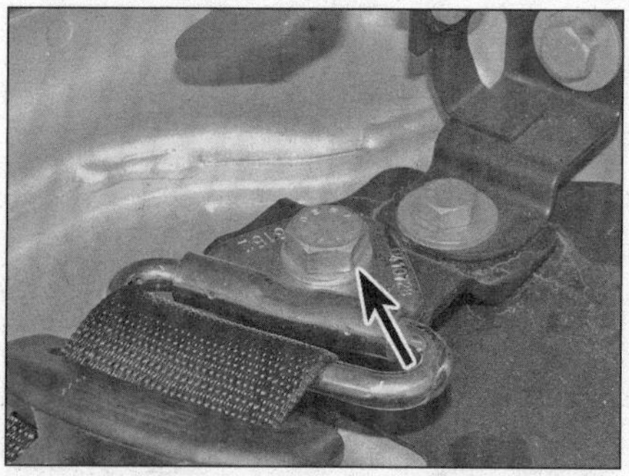
25.43 Undo the bolt (arrowed) and detach the seat belt upper guide

position, then remove the belt upper guide **(see illustration)**.

44 Undo the inertia reel retaining bolt and manoeuvre the reel from the recess **(see illustration)**.

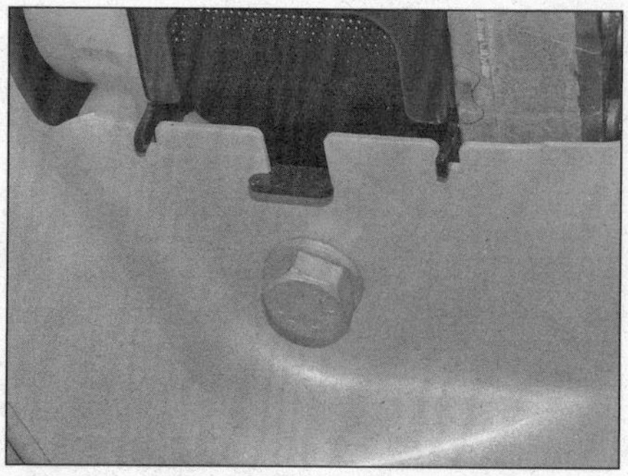
25.44 Undo the inertia reel mounting bolt

45 Disconnect the wiring plug as the reel is withdrawn **(see illustration)**.

46 Refitting is a reversal of removal, but tighten the mounting bolts to the specified torque.

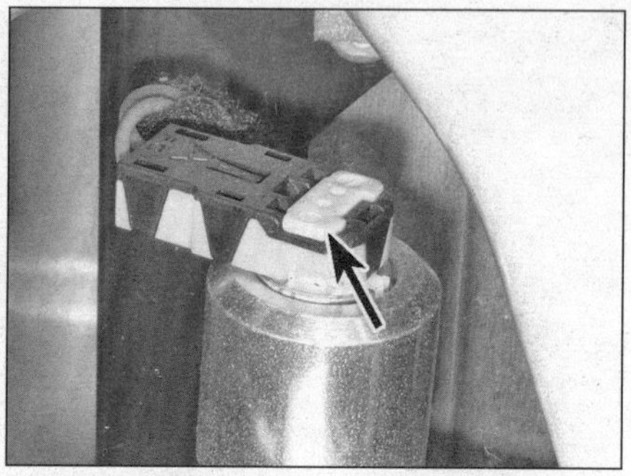
25.45 Prise up the yellow locking clip (arrowed), and pull the wiring plug upwards

26 Interior trim panels – removal and refitting

A-pillar trim panels

Saloon and Estate models

1 Open the relevant front door, and prise out the AIRBAG emblem from the top of the pillar trim **(see Illustration)**.

2 Undo the screw in the emblem recess.

3 Starting at the top edge, pull the trim away from the pillar **(see illustration)**.

4 To refit, offer the panel up to its mounted position, and apply firm pressure over each press-stud until it engages. Tighten the retaining screws securely.

Convertible models

5 Open the soft top and remove both front sunvisors as described later in this Section.

6 Carefully prise the interior light assembly down from the windscreen frame upper trim **(see illustration)**. Disconnect the wiring plug, but note that the light will remain attached to the sunvisor harness.

7 Pull down the mirror base cover, then undo the three screws and remove the interior mirror **(see illustrations)**. Disconnect any wiring plugs as the mirror is withdrawn.

8 Pull the windscreen trim panel downwards at the front edge, then pull it back to release it **(see illustration)**.

9 Pull the A-pillar trim at the top edge to release it from the pillar **(see illustration)**.

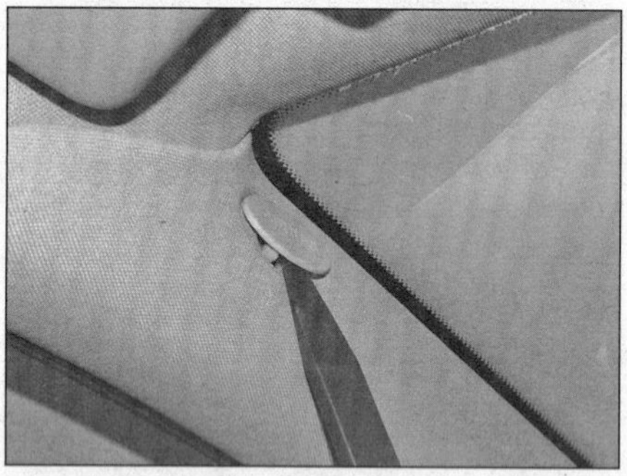
26.1 Prise out the AIRBAG emblem and undo the screw

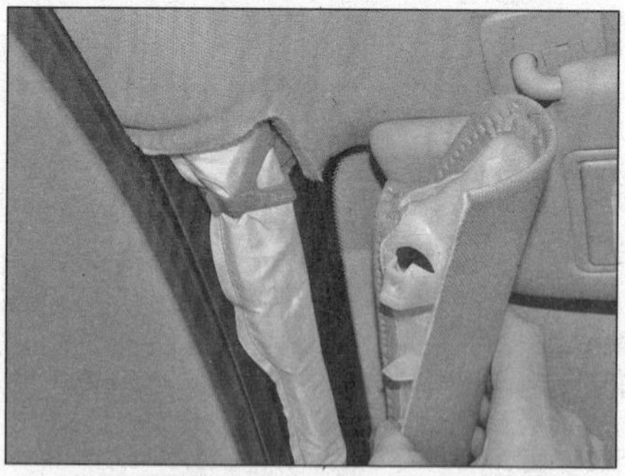
26.3 Release the panel

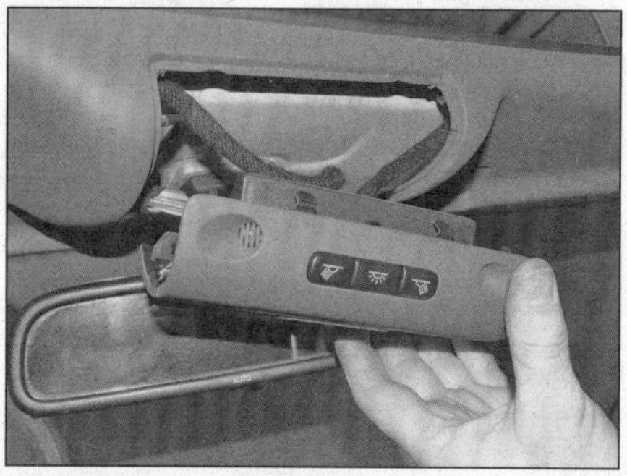
26.6 Pull down the rear edge and remove the interior light

26.7a Pull down the plastic cover ...

26.7b ... then undo the 3 screws and remove the interior mirror

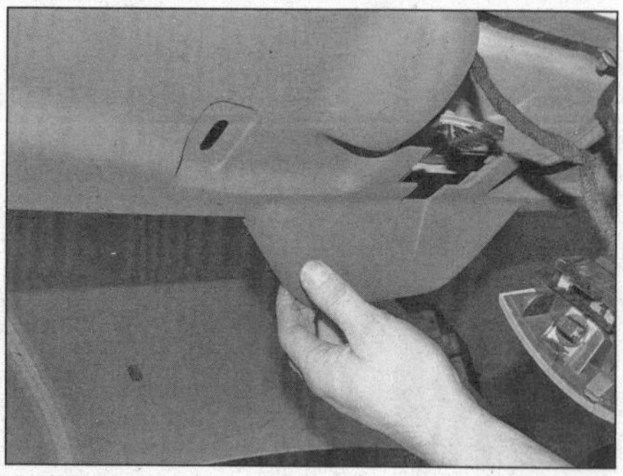
26.8 Pull the front edge of the windscreen trim panel downwards a little

26.9 Pull the A-pillar trim from place – note the lugs at the base of the trim (arrowed)

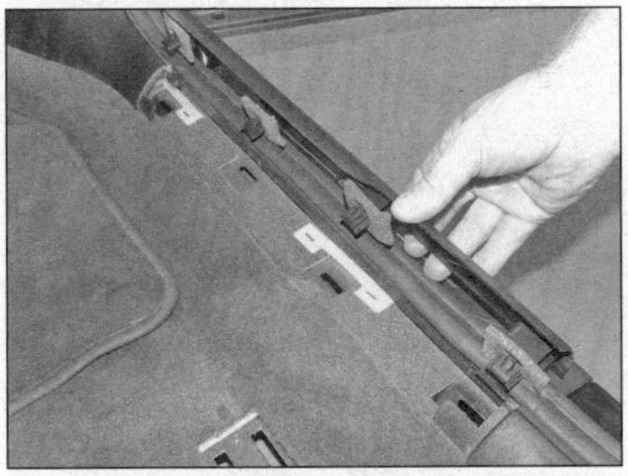

26.14 Pull the sill trim panels straight up to release the clips

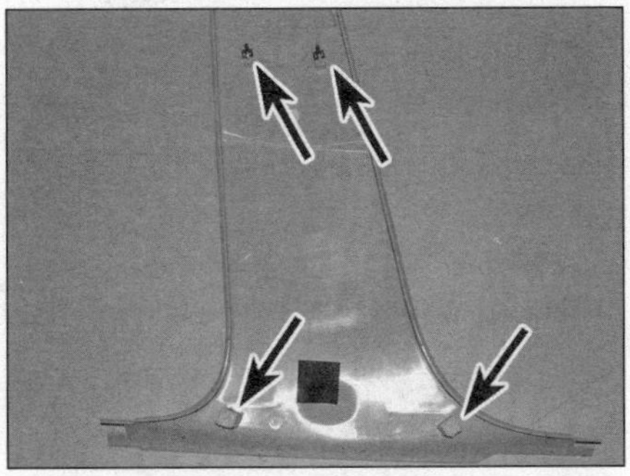

26.15a Pull the lower edge of the B-pillar trim to release the clips (arrowed)

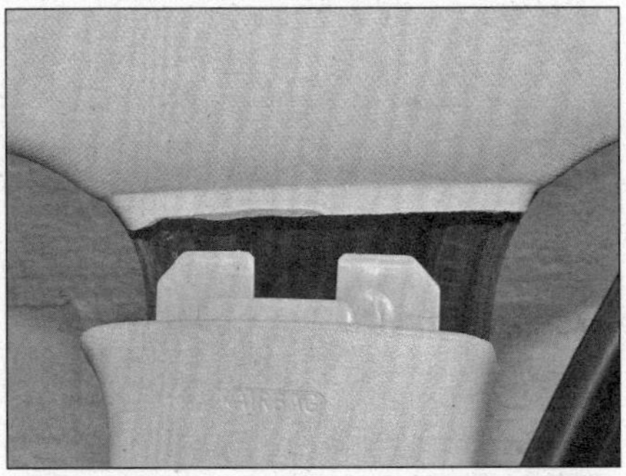

26.15b Note how the lugs at the top of the B-pillar trim engage behind the headlining

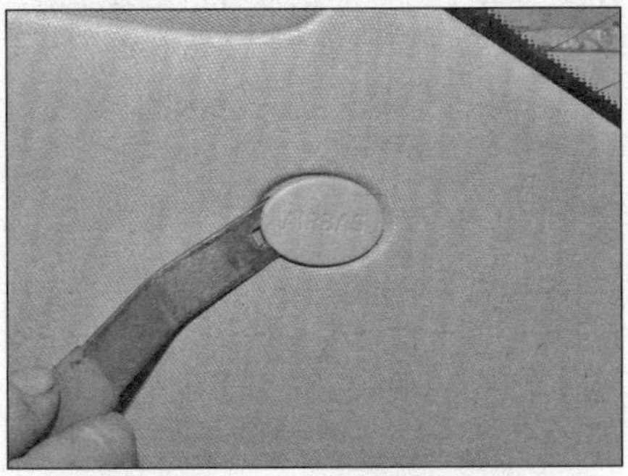

26.19 Prise out the AIRBAG emblem

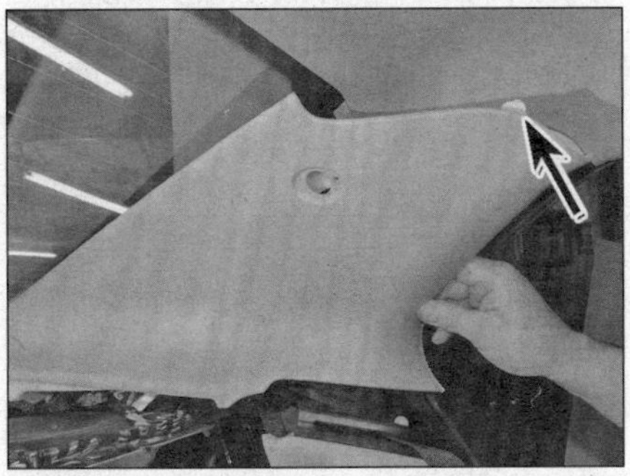

26.22 Note the lug at the top of the C-pillar trim (arrowed)

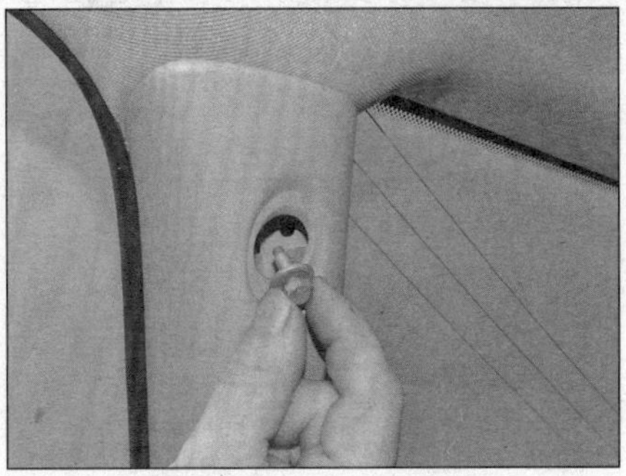

26.23 Remove the bolt

Disconnect any wiring plugs as the panel is withdrawn.

10 Refitting is a reversal of removal. Ensure the rubber mouldings are in place and renew any trim fasteners that are damaged.

B-pillar trim panels

11 Move the front seat fully forwards, and tip the backrest forwards.

12 Remove the cover, then undo the seat belt lower anchorage bolt **(see illustration 24.3)**.

13 Remove the rear seat cushion as described in Section 24.

14 Pull the front and rear door sill trim panels straight up to release the retaining clips **(see illustration)**.

15 Adjust the seat belts to the lowest height position, then pull the lower edge of the B-pillar trim away from the pillar, then pull the trim downwards to release it **(see illustrations)**.

16 Feed the seat belt through the opening in the trim as it's withdrawn.

17 Refitting is a reversal of removal.

C-pillar trim panels

Saloon models

18 Remove the parcel shelf as described later in this Section.

19 Prise out the AIRBAG emblem **(see illustration)** and slacken the bolt in the recess. Slacken the bolt sufficiently to allow it to be removed complete with the expansion nut that fits into the bodywork.

20 Using a wide-bladed screwdriver, carefully prise the trim panel away from the C-pillar.

21 Withdraw the panel from inside the vehicle.

22 Refitting is a reversal of removal, noting how the lug at the top of the panel engages with the headlining **(see illustration)**.

Estate models

23 Fold down the rear seat backrest, then prise out the AIRBAG emblem from the top of the pillar trim and undo the screw **(see illustration)**.

24 Remove the trim panel by pulling it upwards and away from the pillar.

25 Refitting is a reversal of removal.

Rear side trim panel

Convertible models

26 Operate the soft top so that it is fully open.

27 Remove the rear seat cushion and backrest as described in Section 24.

28 Carefully prise out the trim panel speaker grille, then undo the 2 panel retaining screws in the aperture **(see illustrations)**.

29 Lift up the trim panel, ensure the rubber weatherstrips at the top and front of the panel remain in place.

30 Disconnect and unclip the speaker cables, and disconnect the door module wiring plug(s).

31 Refitting is a reversal of removal, ensuring the door rubber weatherstrips are correctly positioned against the side trim panel **(see illustration)**.

26.28a Carefully prise away the speaker grille ...

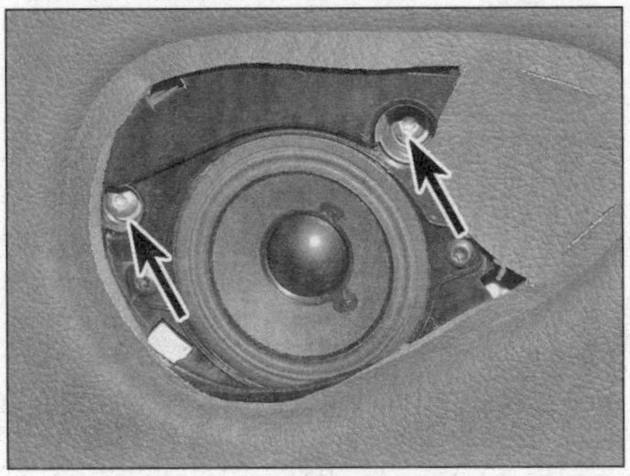

26.28b ... then undo the trim screws (arrowed)

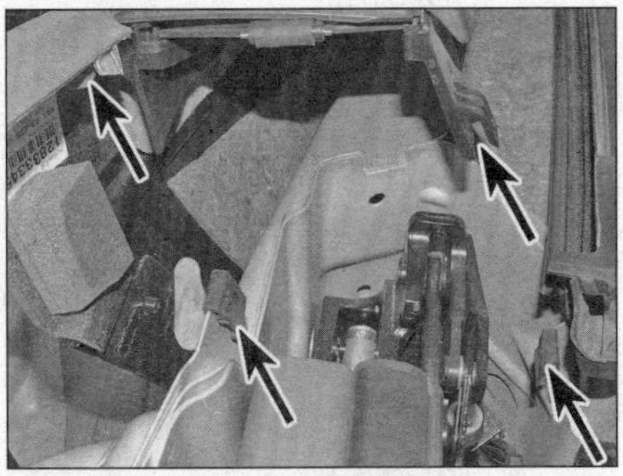

26.31 On refitting, ensure the hooks engage correctly over the rubber fittings (arrowed)

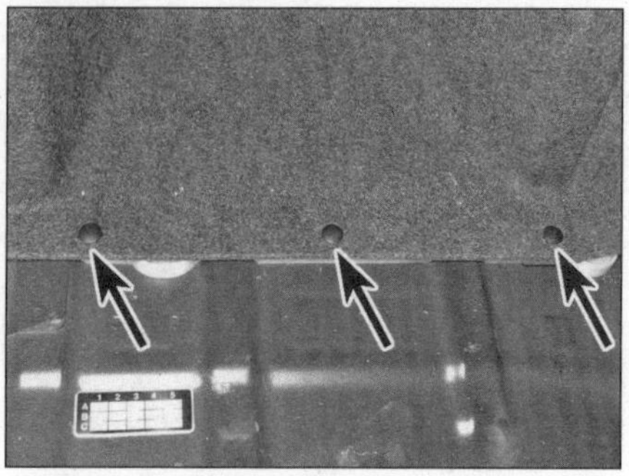

26.36 Prise out the clips securing the side cover

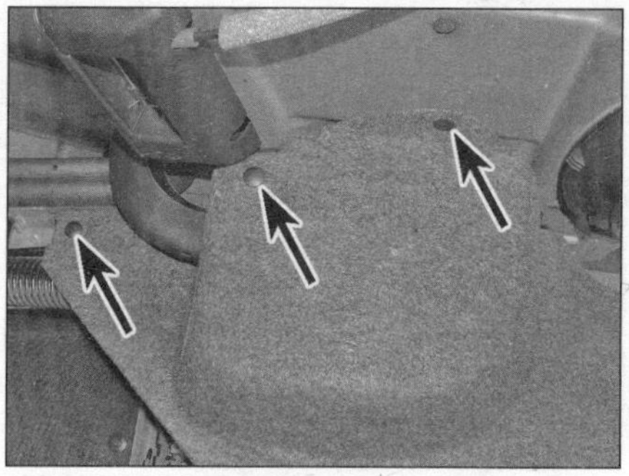

26.37a Prise out the 3 clips at the upper edge (arrowed) ...

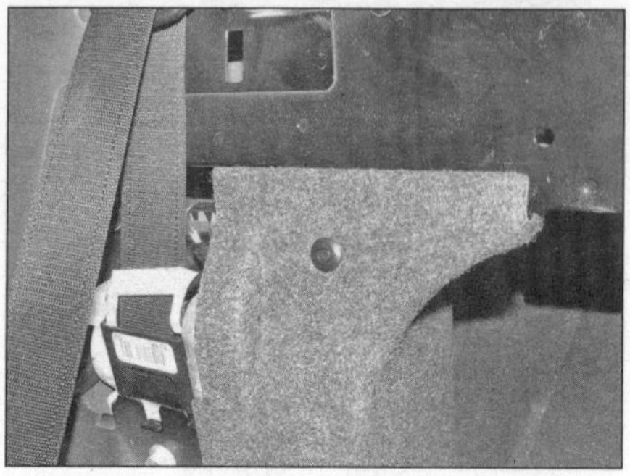

26.37b ... then push in the centre pin and prise out the rivet at the front

Luggage area side trim panel

Saloon models

32 Remove the rear seat backrest as described in Section 24.

33 Release luggage compartment floor panel.

34 Remove the plastic expansion rivets from the parcel shelf **(see illustration 26.71)**.

35 Remove the side bolster trim panel. On some vehicles this panel is secured by a cable-tie at the top outer edge, on some there is a clip. There is also a clip at the top inner edge, and a hook at the lower edge up the outer edge **(see illustrations 25.21a, 25.21b and 25.21c)**.

36 Prise out the 3 clips and remove the luggage compartment inspection cover **(see illustration)**.

37 Prise out the 4 clips, and remove the side trim panel **(see illustrations)**.

38 Refitting is a reversal of removal.

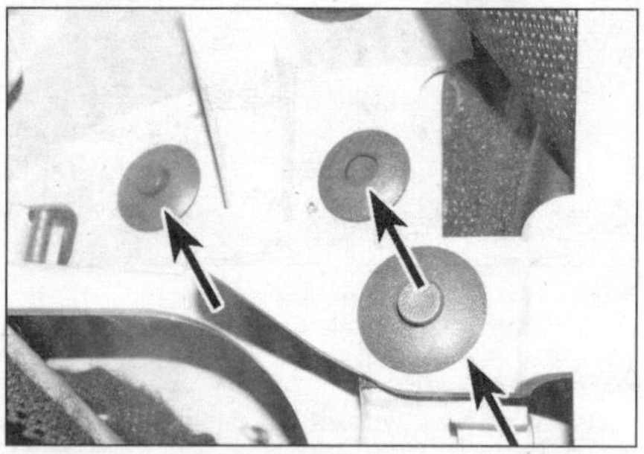

26.40 Push in the centre pins, and prise out the plastic rivets at the top of the side bolster (arrowed)

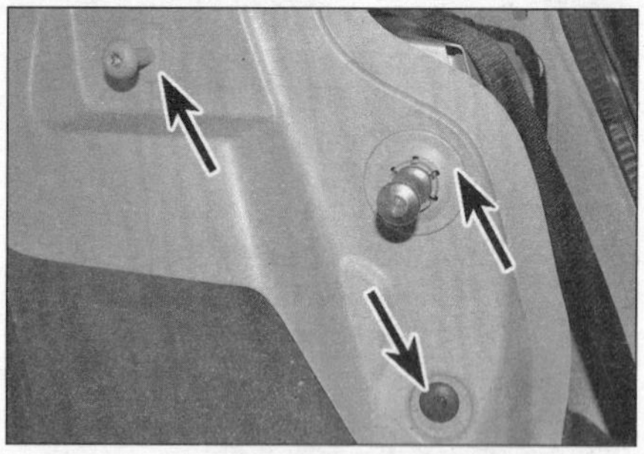

26.41 Remove the plastic expansion rivet, prise off the clip, and unscrew the cover stud (arrowed)

Estate models

39 Remove load area cover and then remove the C-pillar trim panel as described earlier in this Section.

40 Remove the side bolster trim panel by removing the 3 clips at the top, then pulling it upwards **(see illustration)**.

41 Push in the centre pin, prise out the plastic expansion rivet, undo the cover stud, and remove the clip from the front edge of the side trim panel **(see illustration)**.

42 Prise out the cover in the centre of the luggage stowage rings, and undo the retaining Torx screw **(see illustration)**.

43 Prise out the luggage compartment light and disconnect the wiring plug.

44 Pull the side trim panel inwards to release the 6 retaining clips and manoeuvre it from the vehicle **(see illustration)**.

45 Refitting is a reversal of removal.

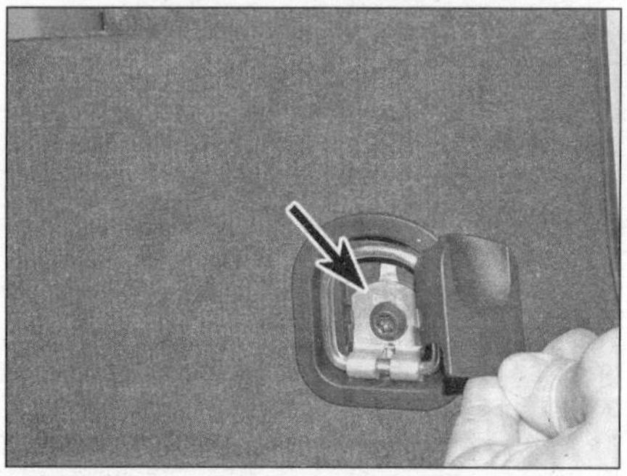

26.42 Undo the Torx screw in the centre of the luggage stowage ring (arrowed)

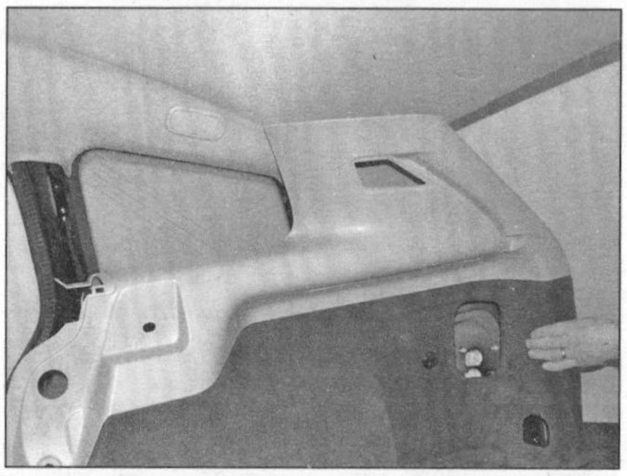

26.44 Remove the panel

Convertible models

46 Ensure the soft top is closed, then open the boot lid and remove the floor panel.

47 Push in the centre pins, then remove the plastic expansion rivets securing the boot sill trim panel. Pull the panel straight up to release the retaining clips **(see illustrations)**.

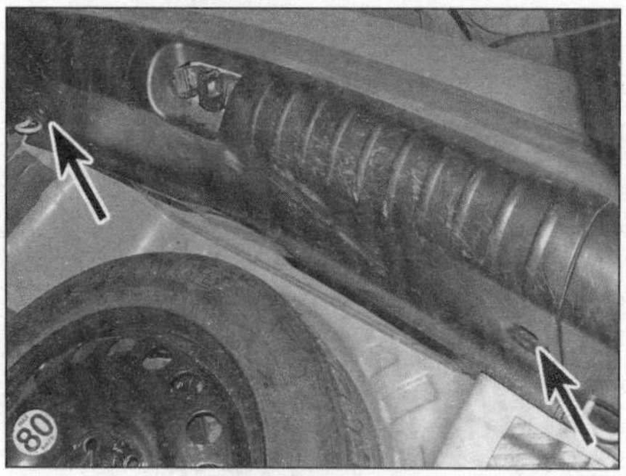

26.47a Push in the centre pins, and prise out the clips (arrowed) ...

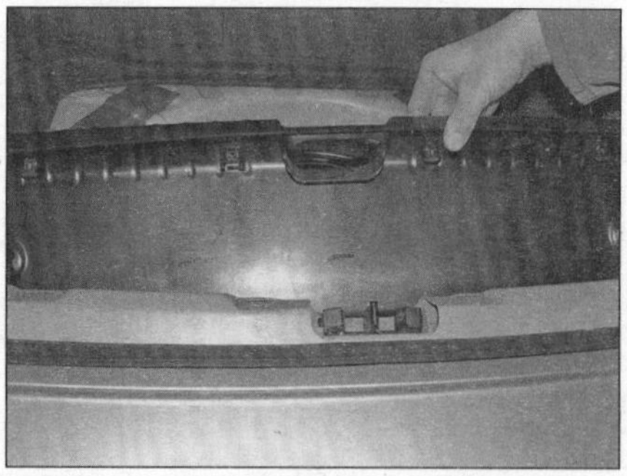

26.47b ... then pull the sill trim straight upwards

26.48 Prise out the clip and remove the side trim (arrowed)

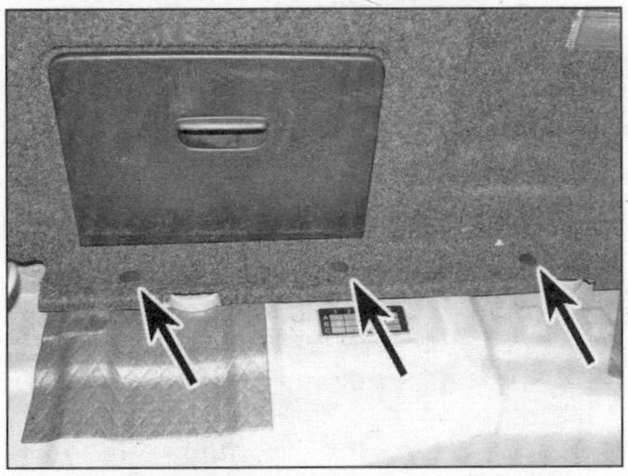

26.49a Prise out the 3 clips on the left-hand panel (arrowed) ...

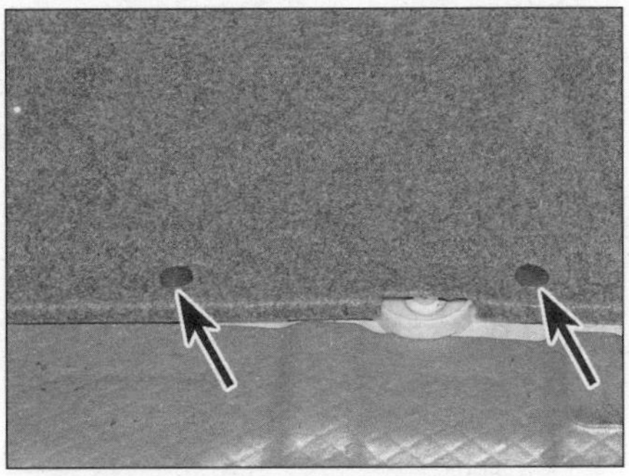

26.49b ... or 2 clips on the right-hand panel (arrowed) ...

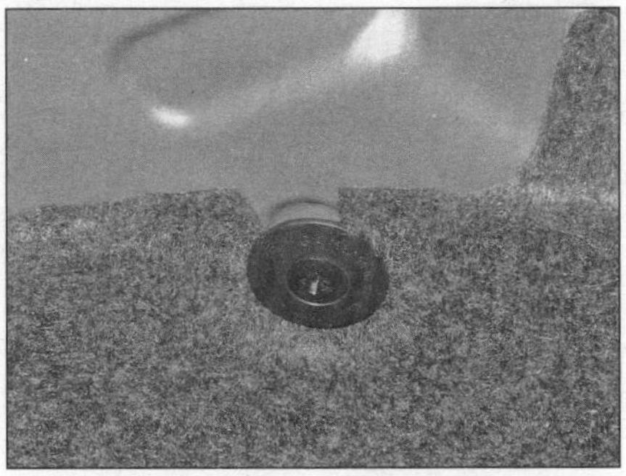

26.49c ... then unscrew the clip at the top (both sides)

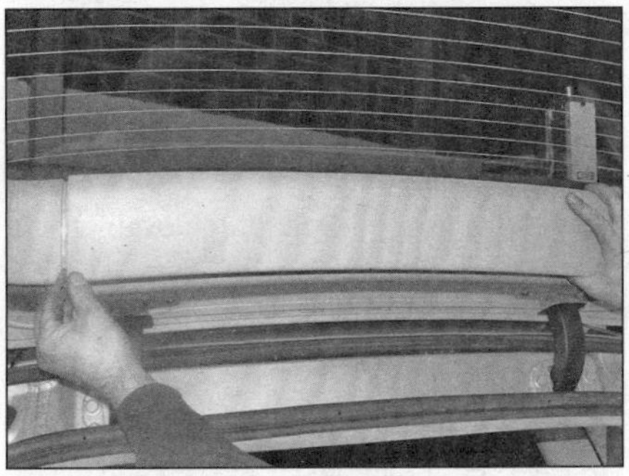

26.54 Pull the tailgate upper trim panel away to release the clips

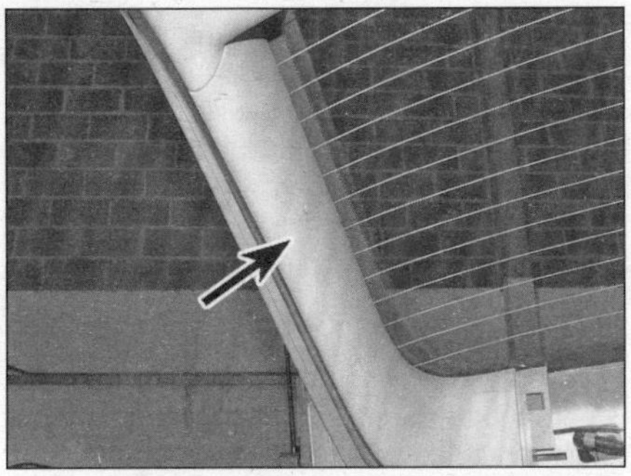

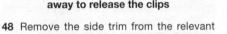

26.55 Pull the side trim panels inwards to release the clips (arrowed)

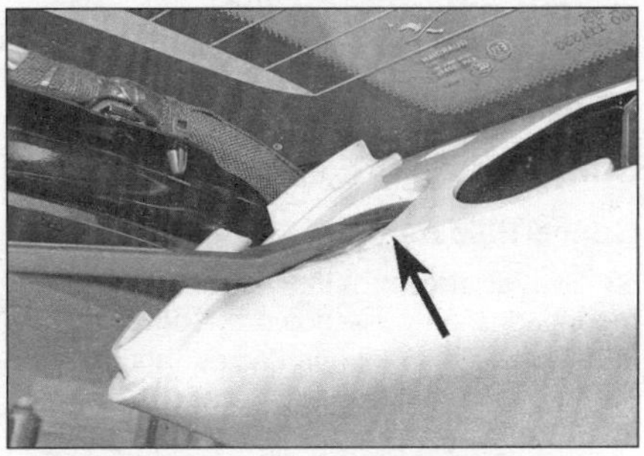

26.57 Push in the centre pins and prise out the plastic rivets in the speaker grille apertures (arrowed)

48 Remove the side trim from the relevant side of the boot lid aperture **(see illustration)**.

49 Prise out the 3 clips (left-hand side) or 2 clips (right-hand side) at the base of the panel, and undo the screw and remove the expanding rivet at the top edge **(see illustrations)**.

50 Manoeuvre the side trim panel from place. Where applicable, disconnect the light unit wiring plug as the panel is withdraw.

51 Refitting is a reversal of removal.

Headlining

52 The headlining is clipped to the roof, and can be withdrawn only once all fittings such as grab handles, sunvisors, sunroof, fixed window glass, and related trim panels have been removed and the relevant sealing strips have been prised clear.

53 Note that headlining removal and refitting requires considerable skill and experience if it is to be carried out without damage, and is therefore best entrusted to a dealer or automotive upholstery specialist.

Tailgate trim panel

54 Open the tailgate, and carefully pull the trim panel above the rear window to release the retaining clips **(see illustration)**.

55 Pull the window side trims inwards and detach them from the main trim panel **(see illustration)**.

56 Prise out the speaker grilles from the main trim panel.

57 Lever out the plastic clips in the speaker grille apertures **(see illustration)**.

58 Undo the 2 Torx screws at the lower edge of the main trim panel, and then pull the panel away from the tailgate to release the 8 push-in clips **(see illustration)**.

59 Ensure the clips are in place on the back of the tailgate trim panel. The remainder of refitting is a reversal of removal.

Boot lid trim panel

60 Open the boot lid, undo the 2 Torx screws and remove the pull-down handle **(see illustration 16.15)**.

61 Push in the centre pins, prise out the plastic clips and remove the panel **(see illustration)**. Note that on some models, the boot lid panel is

26.58 Pull the tailgate panel away to release the push-in clips (right-hand clips arrowed)

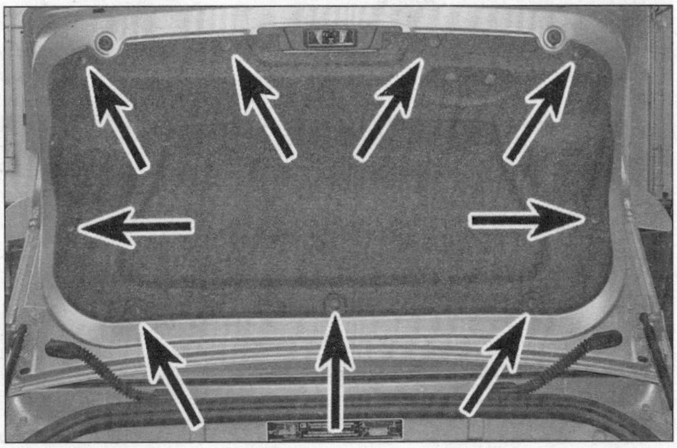

26.61 Push in the centre pins and prise out the clips (arrowed)

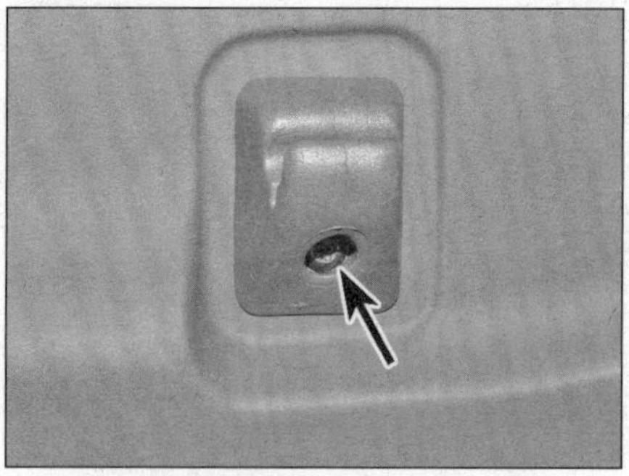

26.63 Sunvisor inner mounting screw (arrowed) – Convertible models

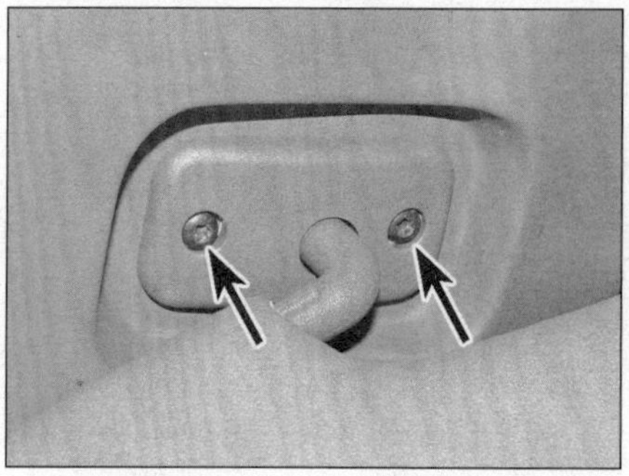

26.64 Sunvisor outer mounting screws (arrowed) – Convertible models

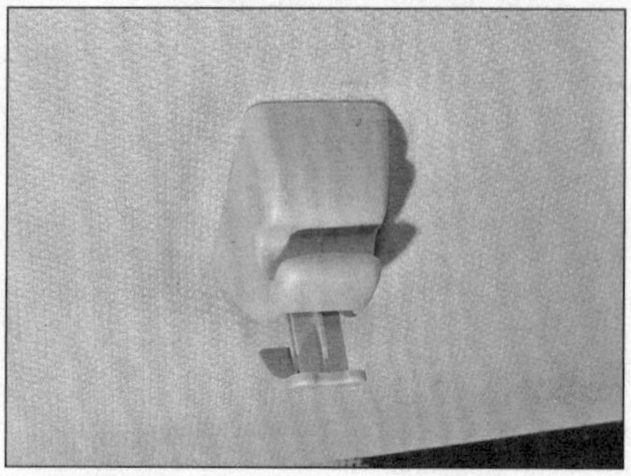

26.66a Prise down the cover/plug to remove the inner mounting ...

further secured by 2 push-in clips – simply pull the panel from place.

62 Refitting is a reversal of removal.

Sunvisors

Convertible models

63 Swivel the sunvisor out of the inner mounting, then prise down the cover (where fitted), undo the mounting screw, and remove the inner mounting **(see illustration)**.

64 Prise down the cover (where fitted). Undo the outer mounting screw and remove the outer mounting **(see illustration)**. Disconnect the wiring plug as the sunvisor is removed.

65 Refitting is a reversal of removal.

Saloon and Estate models

66 Prise down the cover/plug securing the mounting **(see illustrations)**.

67 To remove the outer mounting, use 2 small screwdrivers to release the clips and pull the mounting downward. To disconnect the wiring plug, remove the grab handle and A-pillar trim, pull down the headlining a little, reach up and disconnect the wiring plug.

68 To remove the inner mounting, push the mounting forwards and pull down the rear edge.

69 To refit the mountings, carefully pull down the front edge of the headlining, position the retaining plates with the large clip to the front (inner mounting), or the clip towards the front (outer mounting), then push the mounting into place, and press the cover/plug upwards **(see illustrations)**.

Parcel shelf

Saloon models

70 Fold down the rear seat backrest.

71 Push in the centre pins, and prise out the 3 plastic expansion rivets from the front edge of the parcel shelf **(see illustration)**.

72 Pull the parcel shelf from position. If require the rear seat back locking catches can now be removed.

73 Refitting is a reversal of removal, ensure the lugs at the rear of the shelf located correctly with the mountings.

Lower facia panel

Driver's side

74 Undo the fastener and pull the centre console side panel rearwards **(see illustration 27.1b)**.

75 Remove the diagnostic socket from the facia panel, then undo the 2 screws and lower the panel from place **(see illustration)**.

76 Disconnect the wiring plug as the panel is withdrawn.

77 Refitting is a reversal of removal.

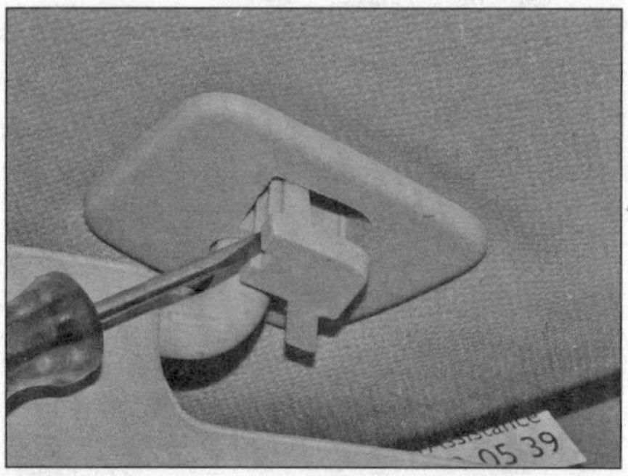

26.66b ... or outer mounting

26.69a The retaining plate for the inner mounting ...

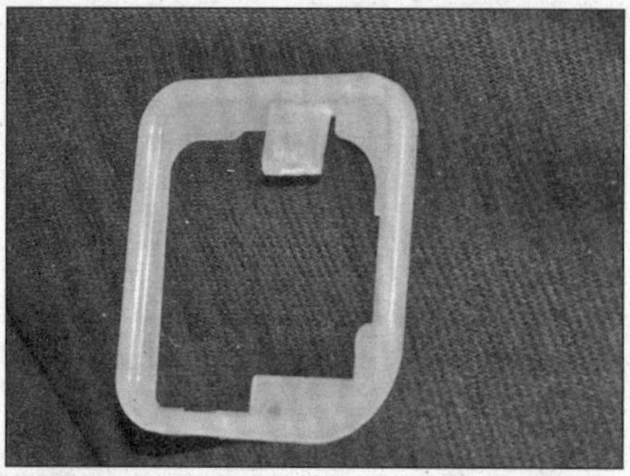

26.69b ... and outer mounting

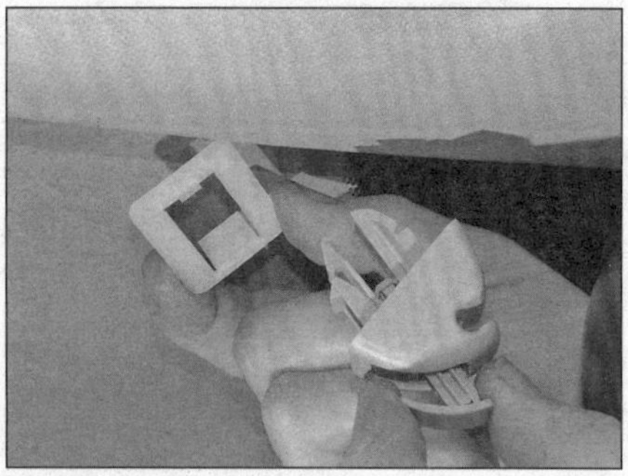

26.69c Slide the mounting plate into place above the headlining

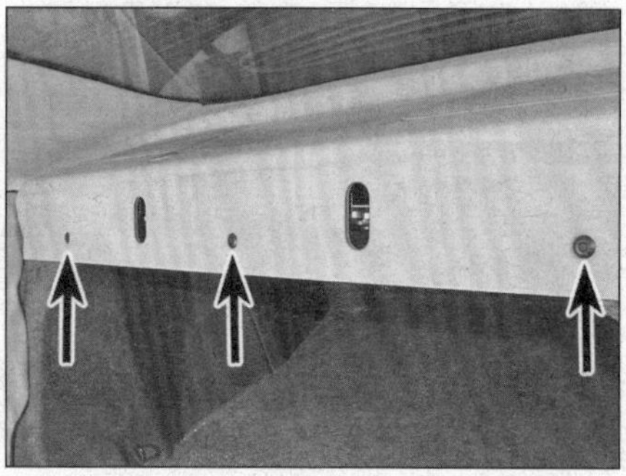

26.71 Push in the centre pins and prise out the parcel shelf rivets (arrowed)

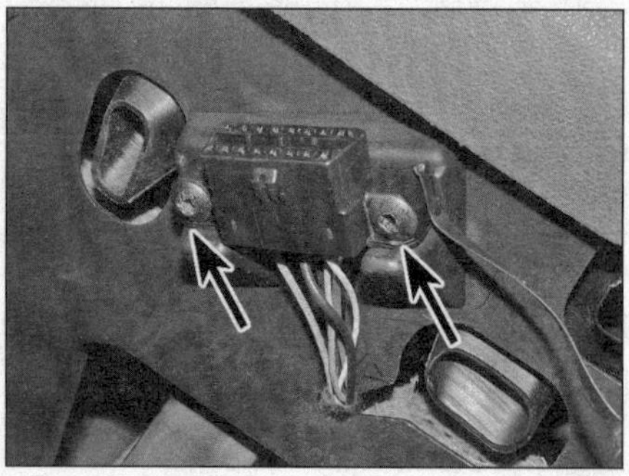

26.75 Undo the 2 Torx screws (arrowed) securing the diagnostic plug

Passenger's side

78 Undo the fastener and pull the centre console side panel rearwards **(see illustration 27.1b)**.
79 Undo the two screws, pull down the front edge, and disengage the hook at the rear of the panel **(see illustration)**.
80 Disconnect the wiring plug as the panel is withdrawn.
81 Refitting is a reversal of removal.

Grab handles

82 Prise out the plastic cover/plug at each end of the grab handle **(see illustration)**.
83 Pull the grab handle from place **(see illustration)**.
84 Refitting is a reversal of removal.

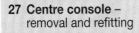

27 Centre console – removal and refitting

Removal

1 Undo the fasteners and remove both front side panels from the centre console **(see illustrations)**.
2 Pull the cover at the rear of the console straight back to release the retaining clips **(see illustration)**.
3 Slide the rear side panels rearwards from the console **(see illustration)**.
4 Remove the mat from in front of the gear lever and (starting at the rear) carefully prise up and remove the lever surround trim **(see illustration)**.

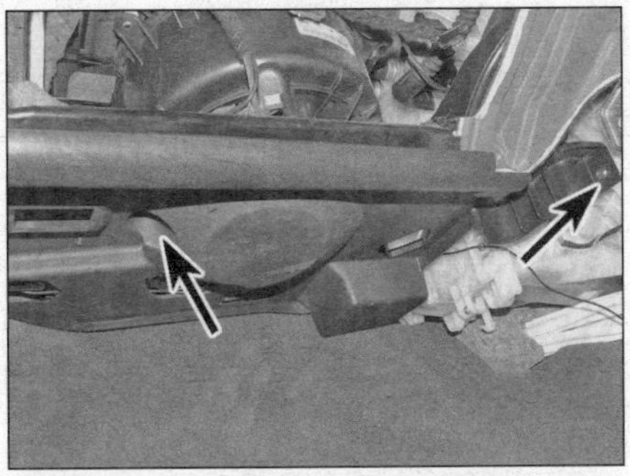

26.79 Undo the 2 screws (arrowed) securing the passenger's side lower facia panel

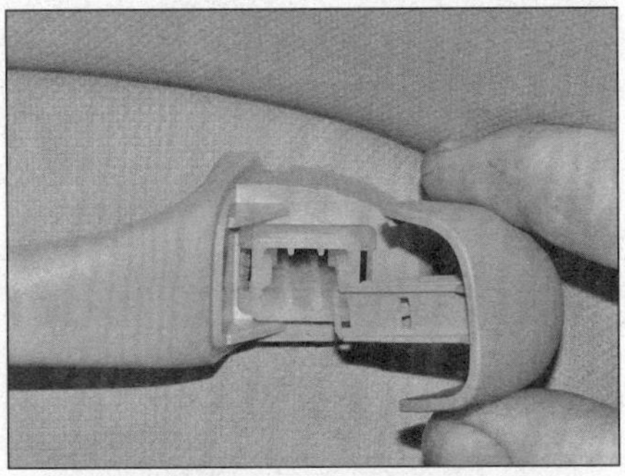

26.82 Prise out the cover/plugs ...

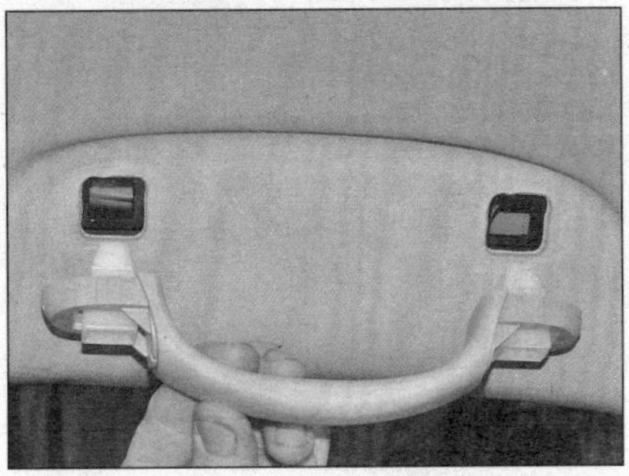

26.83 ... and remove the grab handle

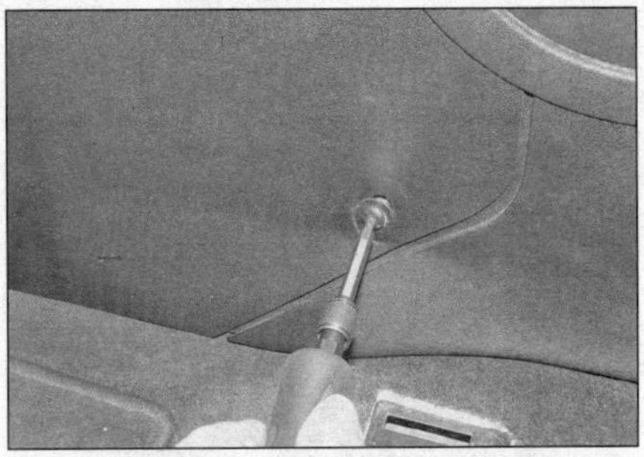

27.1a Where fitted, prise off the cap, and remove the Torx screw at the rear of the side panel

5 On manual transmission models, release the clips and detach the gaiter and frame from the surround trim **(see illustration)**.
6 On automatic transmission models, undo the Torx screw, lift the rear of the selector lever display panel, and slide out the retaining frame **(see illustrations)**.
7 Carefully prise out the plastic cover under the handbrake lever **(see illustration)**.
8 Remove the cover on the passenger's side,

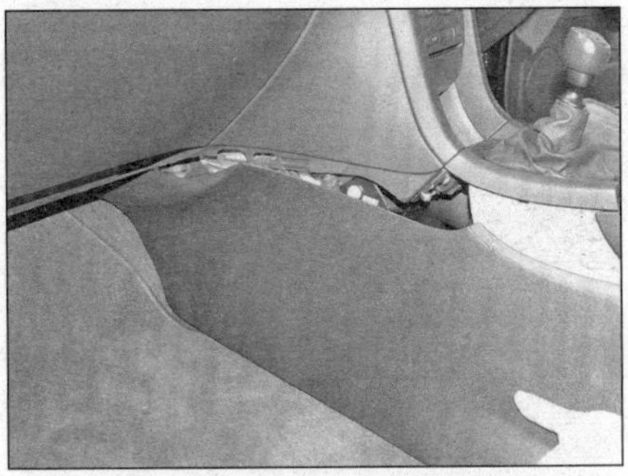

27.1b Pull the side panel rearwards to remove it

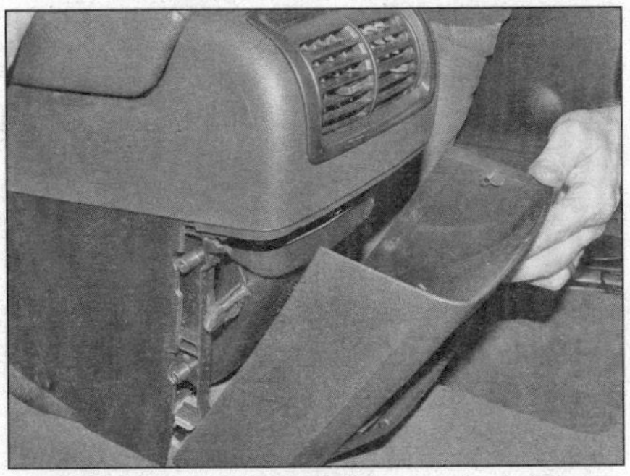

27.2 Pull the console rear cover straight backwards

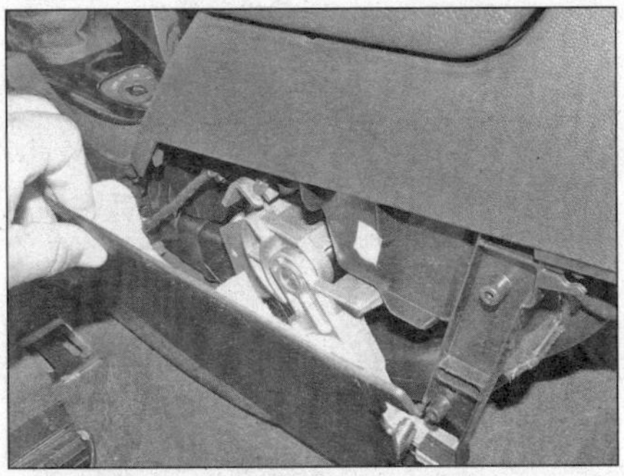

27.3 Remove the rear side panels

27.4 Starting at the rear, prise up and remove the gear lever surround trim panel

27.5 Unclip the gear lever gaiter/frame from the trim

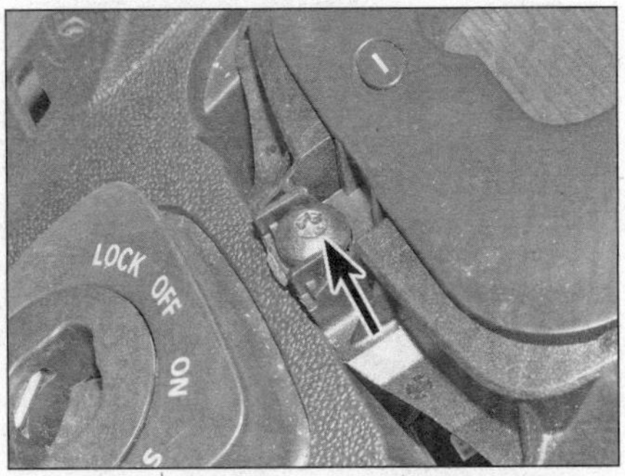

27.6a On automatic transmission models, undo the screw (arrowed) ...

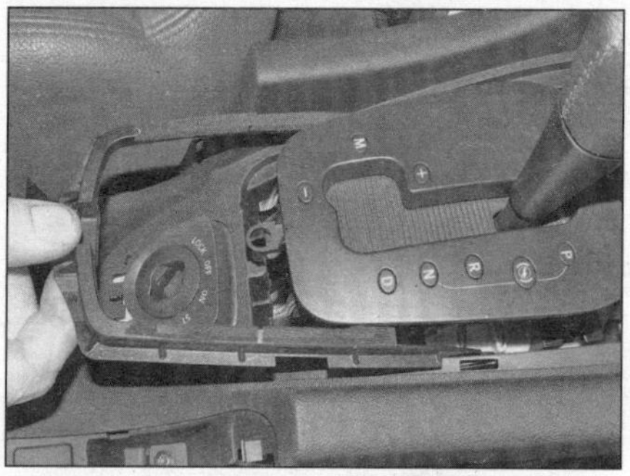

27.6b ... and slide out the retaining frame

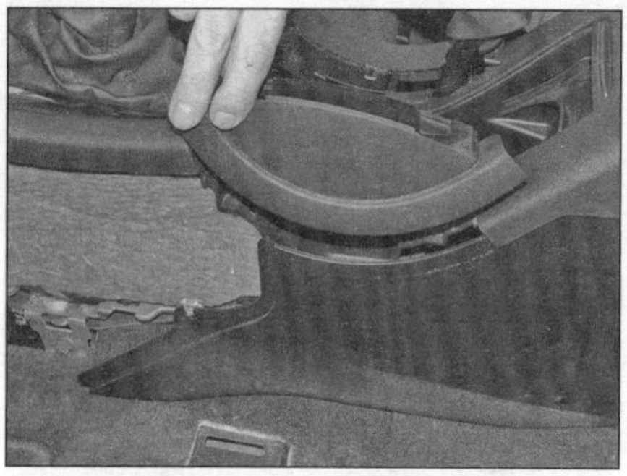

27.8a Lift up the cover ...

then undo the 2 Torx screws and remove the compartment **(see illustrations)**.

9 Lift up the rubber mat in the storage box, and undo the 2 retaining screws **(see illustration)**.

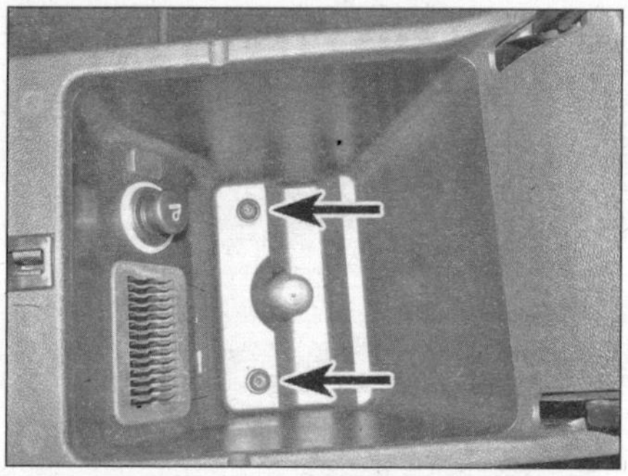

27.9 Undo the 2 Torx screws in the storage box (arrowed)

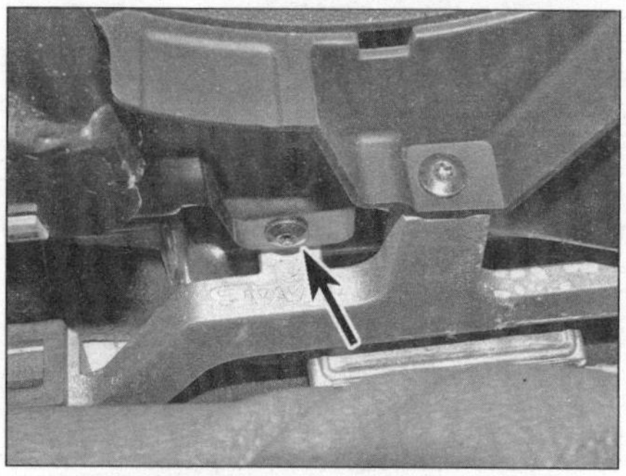

27.10c On some models, remove the screw each side (arrowed)

27.7 Prise up the panel beneath the handbrake lever

27.8b ... and undo the 2 Torx screws

10 Undo the 2 screws at the front of the console, and the 2 screws at the middle **(see illustrations)**. On some models, also remove the two Torx screws each side midway along the console **(see illustration)**.

27.10a Undo the 2 Torx screws at the front of the console (arrowed) ...

27.11a Lift the air duct from its mountings, and pull it rearwards

11 Apply the handbrake, detach the air duct from the mounting at the rear of the console, and manoeuvre the console upwards and rearwards **(see illustrations)**. If required the remaining heating ducts can now be removed. Disconnect any wiring plugs as the console is withdrawn.

Refitting

12 Refitting is a reversal of removal.

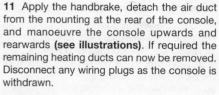

28 Facia assembly – removal and refitting

Warning: ECMs are extremely sensitive to static electricity. Earth yourself by touch a bare-metal part of the vehicle before touching an ECM.

Removal

1 Position the front seat in the rearmost setting, then disconnect the battery negative (earth) lead as described in Chapter 5A, Section 4.

2 Remove the A-pillar trim panels on both sides as described in Section 26.

3 Carefully prise the speaker grilles from the facia, then undo the screws and lift out the speaker(s) **(see illustrations)**. Disconnect the wiring plugs as the speakers are withdrawn.

4 Remove the centre air vents as described in Chapter 12, Section 9. Follow the instructions exactly to avoid damaging the vents. Remove the audio unit **(see illustration)**. Disconnect the wiring plug as the unit is withdrawn.

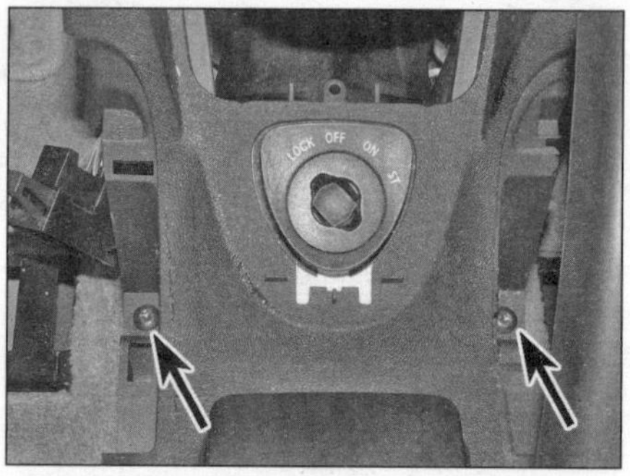

27.10b ... and the screw each side (arrowed)

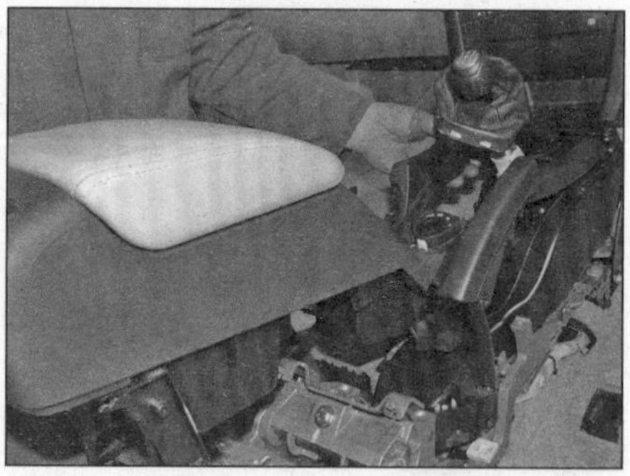

27.11b Lift the rear of the console and manoeuvre it from place

28.3a Prise out the speaker grilles at each end and at the centre of the facia ...

28.3b ... then undo the screws and lift out the speakers

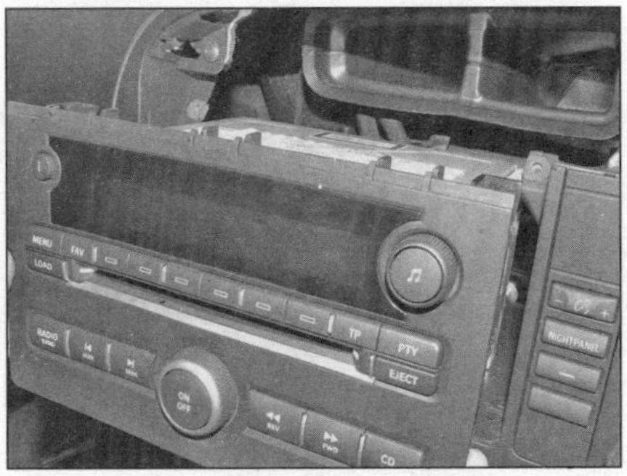

28.4 Remove the audio unit

5 Carefully prise away the trim panels at the ends of the facia, and remove the 2 retaining nuts behind the panels **(see illustrations)**.

6 Remove the steering wheel as described in Chapter 10, Section 14.

7 Carefully prise the gaiter from the back of the CIM (column integration module), then release the 2 clips and slide the module up and over the end of the steering column. Disconnect the wiring plug as the module is removed **(see illustrations)**. Use insulation tape to prevent the airbag contact unit from being accidentally rotated.

8 Remove the instrument panel as described in Chapter 12, Section 9.

9 Remove the climate control panel as described in Chapter 3, Section 9.

10 Release the clips and remove the front cup holder **(see illustration)**.

11 Pull out the storage compartment in front of the gearchange lever, and undo the 4 nuts in the centre aperture **(see illustrations)**.

12 Remove the passenger's glovebox as described in Section 29.

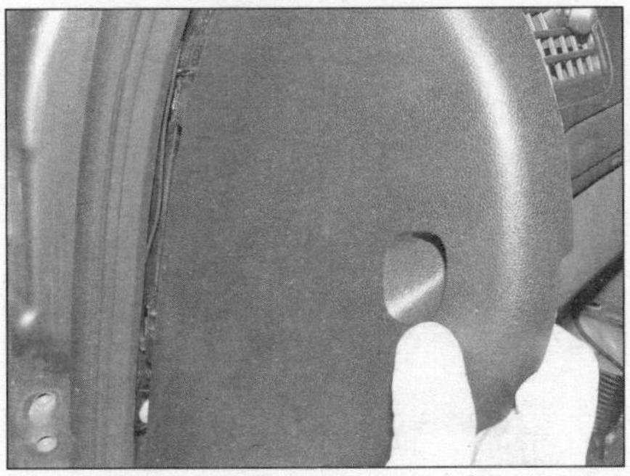

28.5a Prise away the facia end panels ...

28.5b ... then undo the 2 nuts each end (arrowed)

13 Undo the bolt(s) securing the passenger's airbag to the facia crossmember, and disconnect the wiring plug **(see illustrations)**.

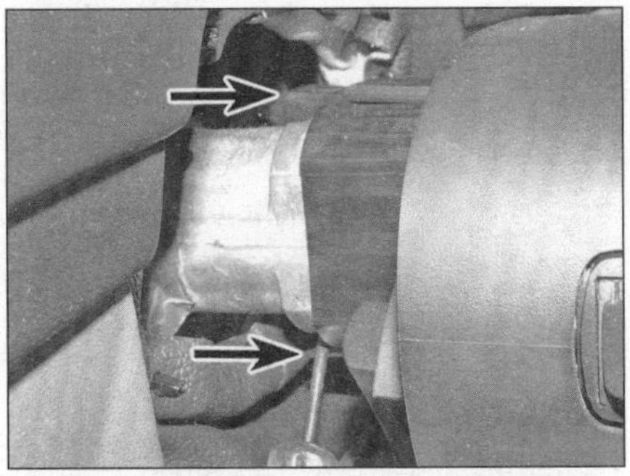

28.7a Release the clips (arrowed) ...

28.7b ... prise up the red locking catch and disconnect the wiring plug ...

28.7c ... then pull the CIM over the end of the steering column

28.10 Depress the clips (arrowed) and pull the cup holder from the facia

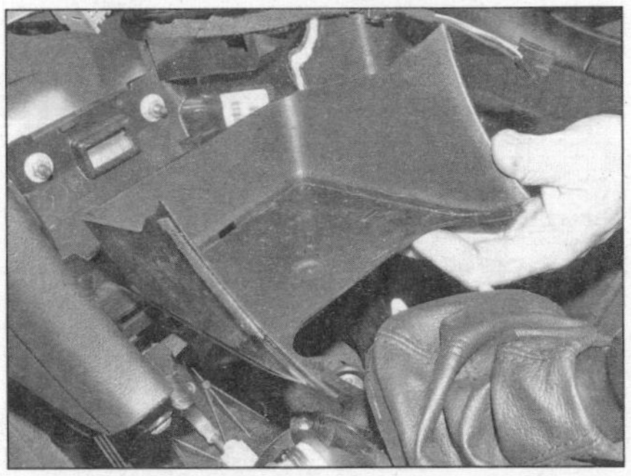

28.11a Release the clips in the base of the storage compartment and pull it from place

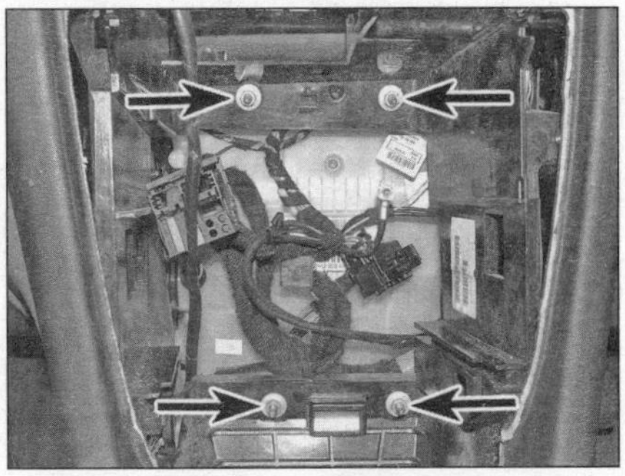

28.11b Undo the 4 nuts in the centre aperture (arrowed)

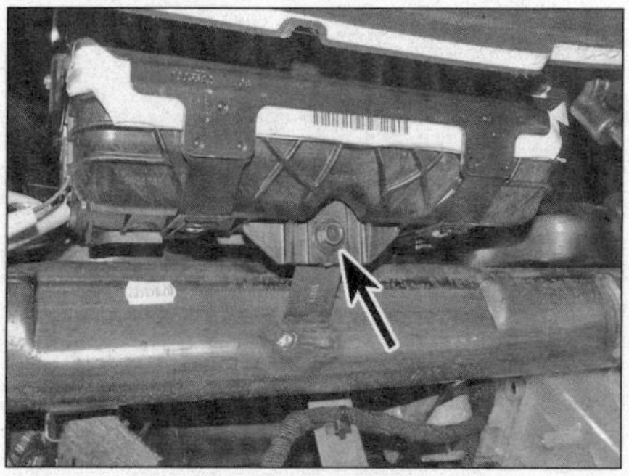

28.13a Undo the passenger's airbag bolt (arrowed)

28.13b Prise out the locking clips (arrowed) and disconnect the airbag wiring plugs

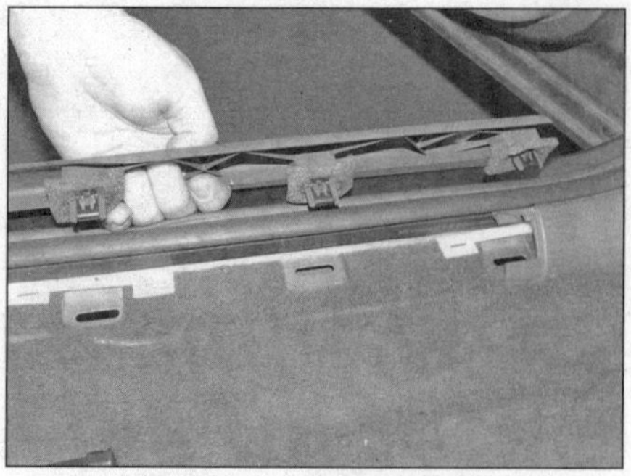

28.14a Pull the sill trim panel straight upwards to release the clips

28.14b Pull the kick panel inwards to release the clips

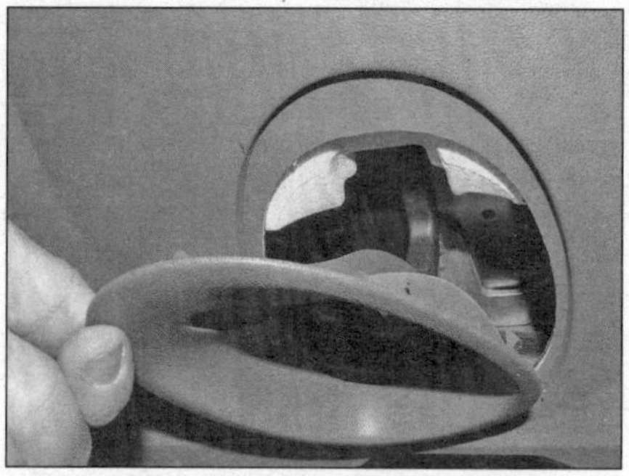

28.16 Prise down the steering column lever trim

28.20 Remove the facia

14 Pull the front door sill trim panels upwards to release the retaining clips, then remove the footwell kickpanels **(see illustrations)**.

15 Remove the centre console as described in Section 27.

16 Using a screwdriver, prise down and remove the steering column adjustment lever surround trim **(see illustration)**.

17 Disconnect the light switch wiring plug.

18 Detach the temperature sensors from the driver's and passenger's side air vents.

19 Undo the screws and remove the driver's side and passenger's side lower facia panels **(see illustration 26.79)**. Disconnect any wiring plugs as the panels are withdrawn.

20 With the help of an assistant, carefully withdraw the facia from the bulkhead and withdraw from the car. Feed the wiring plugs through the facia as it is withdrawn **(see illustration)**.

Refitting

21 Refitting is a reversal of removal.

29 Glovebox – removal and refitting

Removal

1 With the glovebox open, undo the Torx mounting screws – 3 inside the glovebox, and 2 underneath **(see illustrations)**.

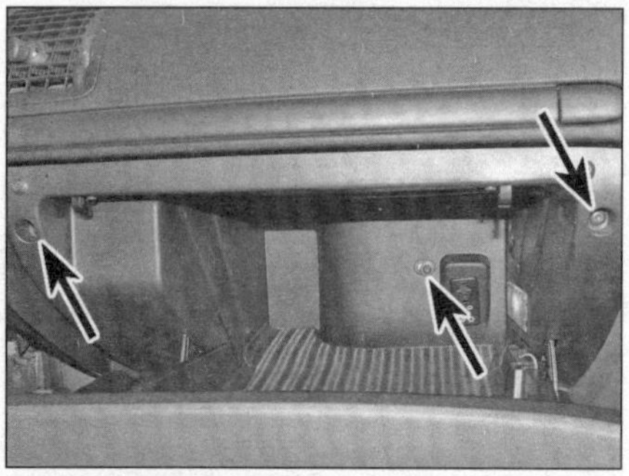

29.1a Undo the 3 Torx screws in the glovebox (arrowed) ...

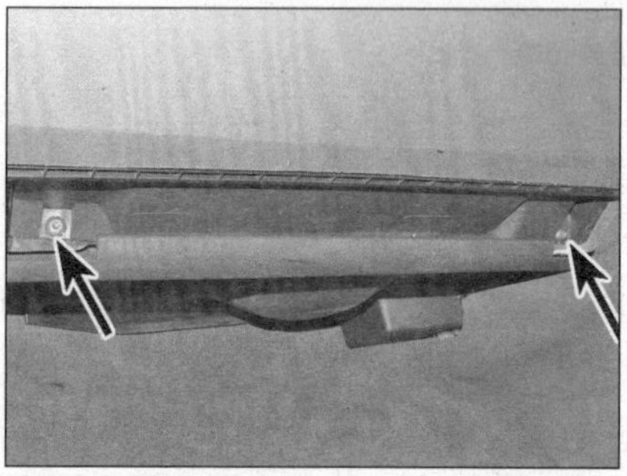

29.1b ... and the 2 underneath (arrowed)

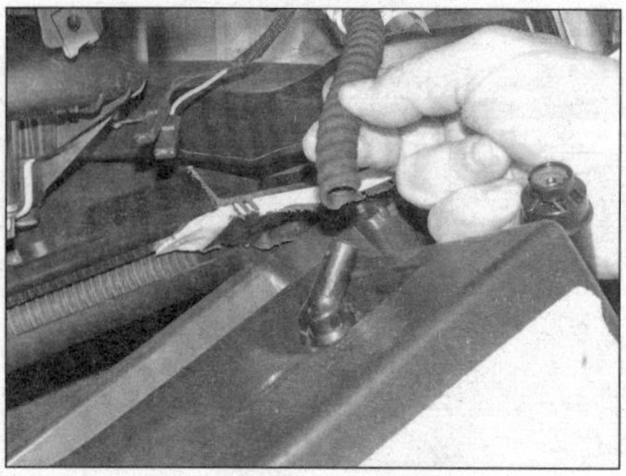

29.3 Disconnect the cooling hose

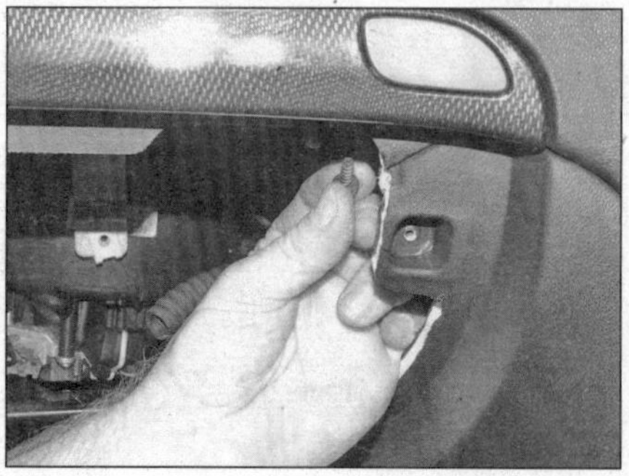

29.4a Remove the screw from the rear ...

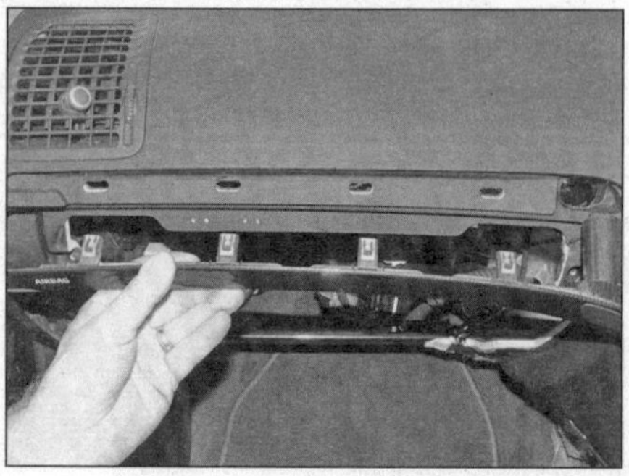

29.4b ... and prise off the trim

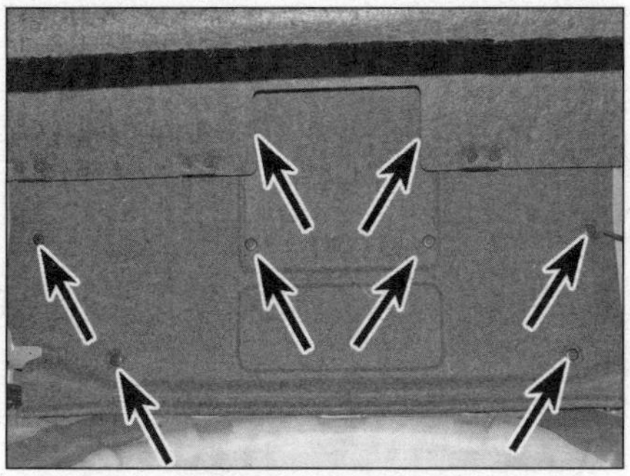
31.3 Prise out the 8 clips (arrowed) and remove the panel

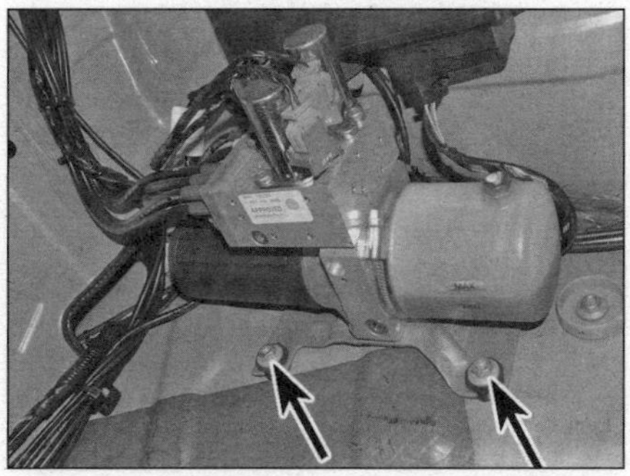
31.4 The hydraulic unit is secured by 2 nuts at the front (arrowed) and 1 nut behind

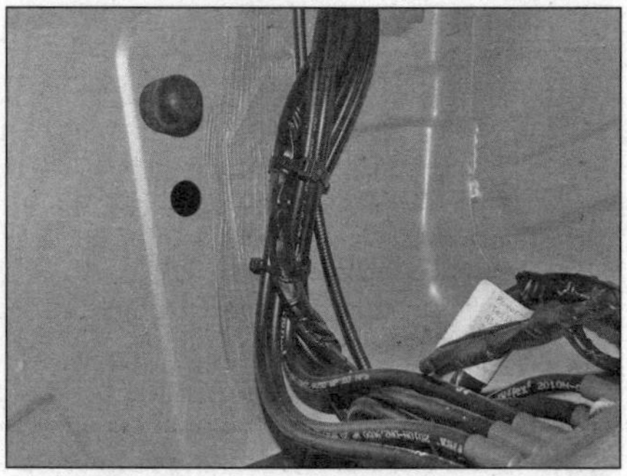
31.5a Release the hydraulic hose retaining clips on the right-hand side ...

2 Lift out the glovebox and disconnect the light unit wiring plug.
3 Disconnect the cooling hose as the glovebox is withdrawn **(see illustration)**.
4 If required the glovebox catch can also be removed. Remove the hidden screw and prise off the trim piece **(see illustrations)**.

Refitting

5 Refitting is a reversal of removal.

30 Soft top – general information

The Convertible soft top is raised and lowered by an electrically-operated hydraulic unit together with seven hydraulic cylinders. The system is controlled by a module which monitors the action progress in stages by means of sensors, and sanctions subsequent actions in the hydraulic unit. The soft top bows are manufactured from magnesium. Any malfunction of the soft top will generate a trouble code and a corresponding message will appear on the Saab Information Display on the instrument panel.

The module also operates the side windows in the doors and rear panel. Before opening the soft top, the windows are opened a small distance, then after the top has been closed, the windows assume their normal closed position. This is to ensure the upper edges of the windows are positioned on the inside of the soft top to prevent rain entry.

In the event of failure of the soft top, the car should be taken to a Saab dealer or specialist who will use a special diagnostic tool to pin-point the problem area. If the soft top operates normally to a particular stage, then stops, it is likely that one of the sensors is at fault. Failure of the hydraulic system may be due to lack of fluid or a faulty hydraulic unit motor.

31 Soft top complete assembly – removal and refitting

Note: *This procedure describes removal of the complete soft top assembly including hydraulic unit and cylinders.*

Note: *Retrieve the soft top emergency opening tool from the vehicle's tool kit before commencing this operation (see the vehicle handbook).*

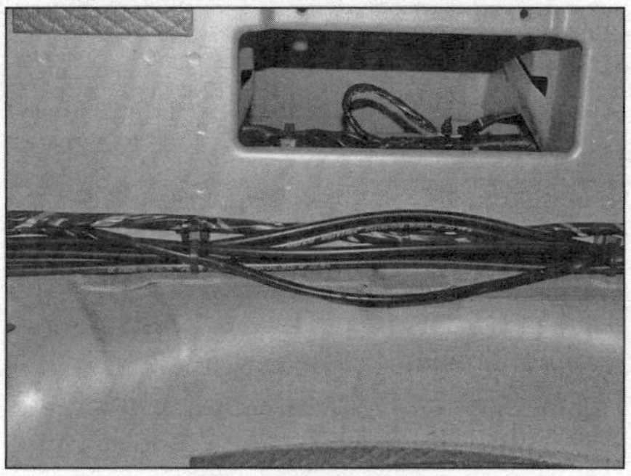
31.5b ... the centre ...

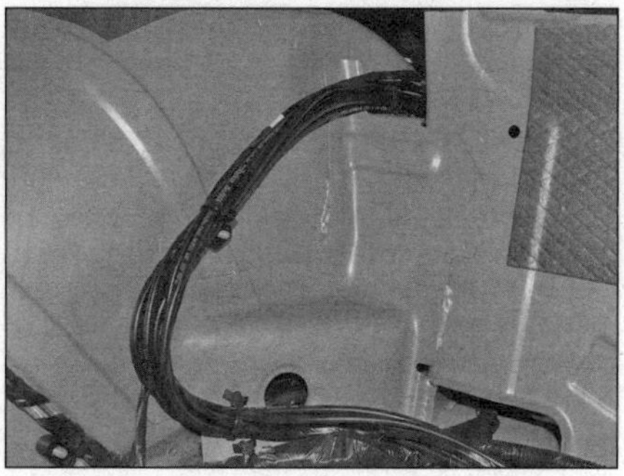
31.5c ... and the left-hand side

Removal

1 Remove the rear seat as described in Section 24 of this Chapter.
2 Remove the rear side trim and luggage compartment trim panels as described in Section 26 of this Chapter.
3 Prise up the centre pins, and lever out the 8 plastic expansion rivets securing the luggage compartment front trim panel. Remove the trim panel **(see illustration)**.
4 Undo the 3 nuts securing the hydraulic unit **(see illustration)**.
5 Trace the hoses from the hydraulic unit, note their fitted positions, then release the hose retaining clips **(see illustrations)**.
6 Close the boot, and open the soft top cover. Raise the 6th bow and support it in position using a length of wood **(see illustration)**.
7 Undo the front nuts securing the soft top storage, and the three Torx screws securing the storage floor to the drive lever at the right-hand side **(see illustration)**.
8 Unhook the side bands (where fitted), detach the front of the soft top storage floor and place it in the luggage compartment.
9 Disconnect the heated rear window wiring plug.
10 Disconnect the soft top control module blue wiring plug **(see illustration)**.
11 Unhook the cable from the soft top storage drive, then undo the 2 bolts, prise

31.6 Support the 6th bow with a suitable length of wood

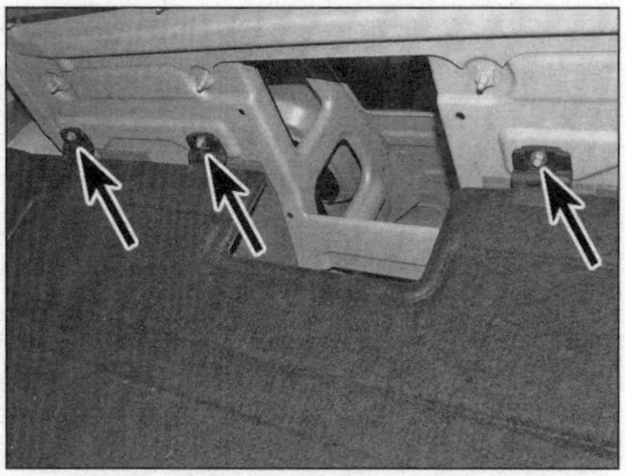
31.7 Remove the storage floor front nuts (arrowed)

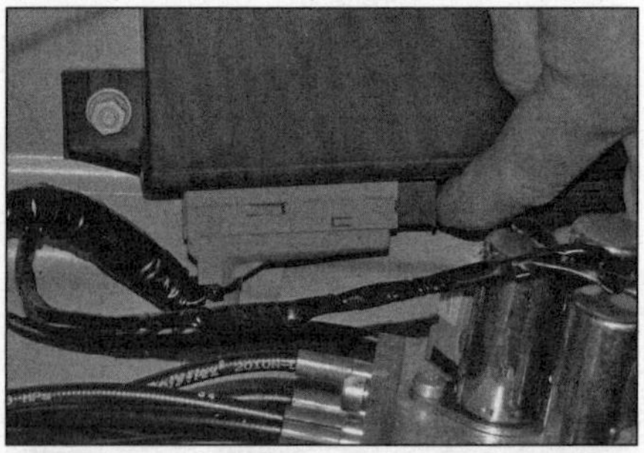

31.10 Slide out the red locking catch and disconnect the blue connector from the control module next to the hydraulic unit

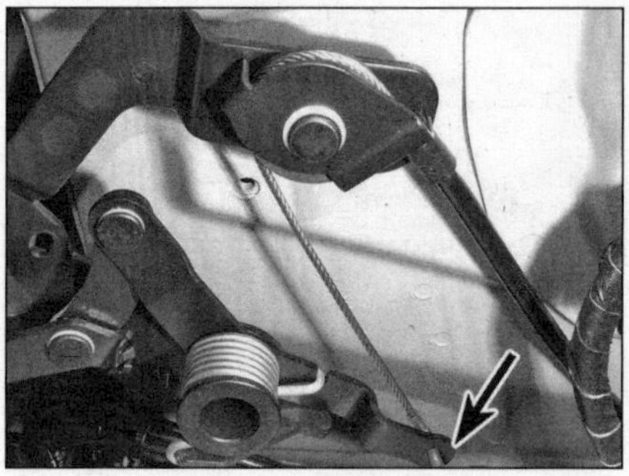

31.11a Unhook the cable (arrowed) from the lever ...

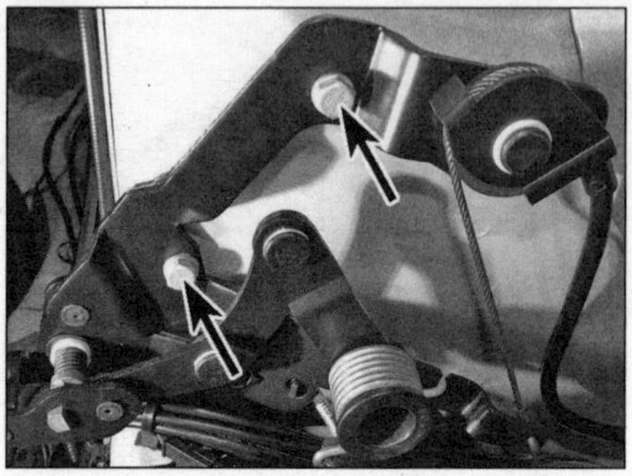

31.11b ... undo the two bolts (arrowed) ...

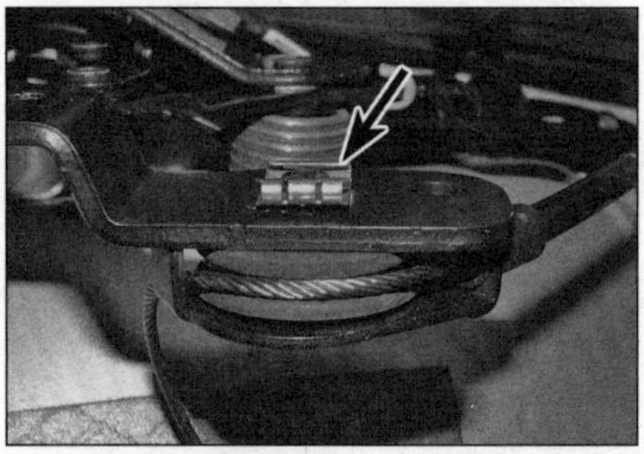

31.11c ... prise off the retaining clip (arrowed), then slide out the pulley and detach the cable

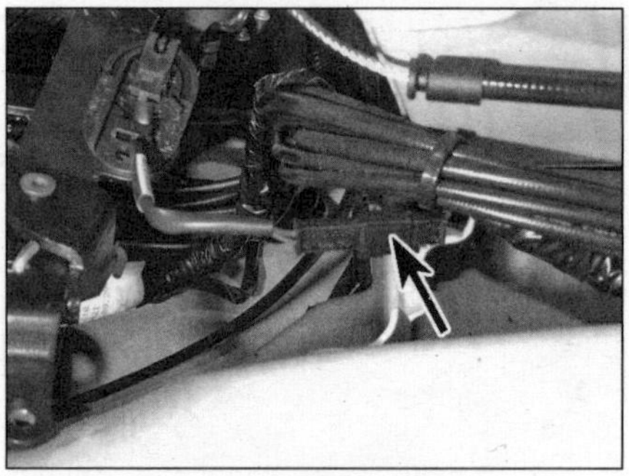

31.12 Disconnect the storage drive position sensor (arrowed)

off the retaining clip, undo the idler pulley and unhook the cable from the holder **(see illustrations)**.

12 Disconnect the soft top storage drive position sensor, and suspend the drive from the luggage hook **(see illustration)**.

13 Remove the cable-ties securing the hydraulic hoses to the body and soft top cover hinges.

14 Disconnect the soft top cover hinge position sensors.

15 Prise off the retaining clip and remove the pin securing the hydraulic cylinder to the soft top cover each side, and unclip the pin at the other end of the cylinders. Recover the washers **(see illustrations)**.

16 Lift away the hydraulic cylinders from the soft top cover hinge on each side.

17 Make alignment marks around the bolt head, then undo the soft top outer mounting bolts (1 each side), then remove the length of wood and lower the 6th bow **(see illustration)**.

18 Make alignment marks around the bolt heads, then remove the soft top inner mounting bolts each side. Recover any shims/washer under the mounting bracket **(see illustration)**.

19 Using the emergency soft top opening tool from the vehicle's tool kit, release the 1st bow latch **(see illustration)**.

20 With the assistance of at least 3 other people, lift the soft top, hydraulic unit, hoses

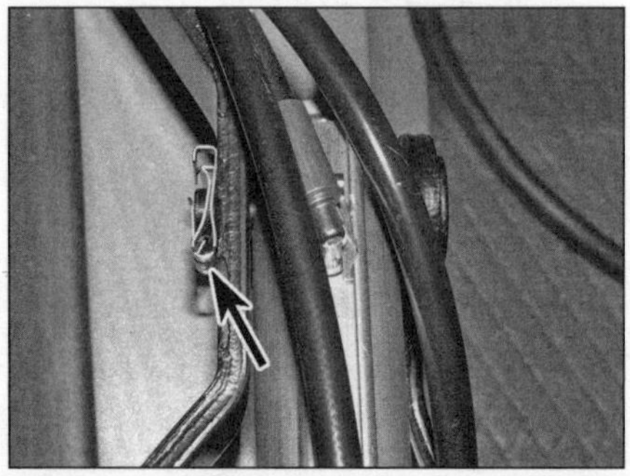

31.15a Prise out the clip (arrowed) and slide out the pin at one end of the cylinder ...

31.15b ... then unclip the other end

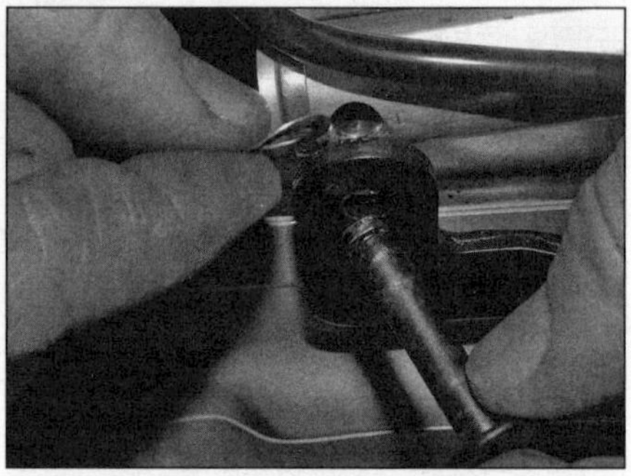

31.15c Don't overlook the washer between the cylinder and bracket

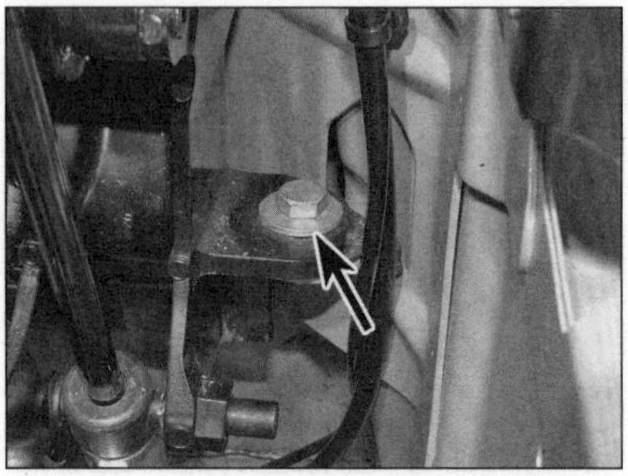

31.17 Soft top outer mounting bolt (arrowed)

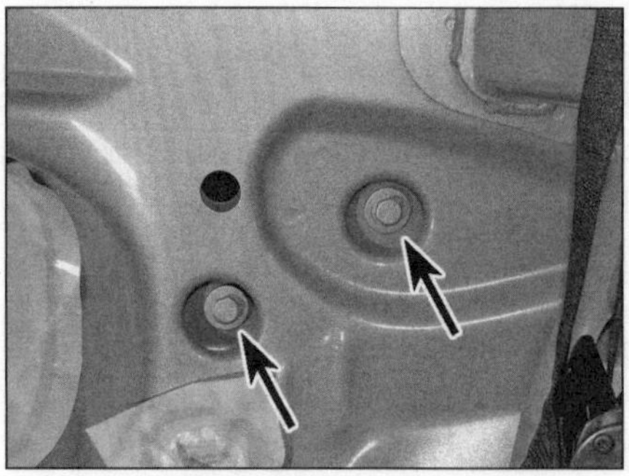

31.18 Make alignment marks around the soft top inner mounting bolt heads (arrowed)

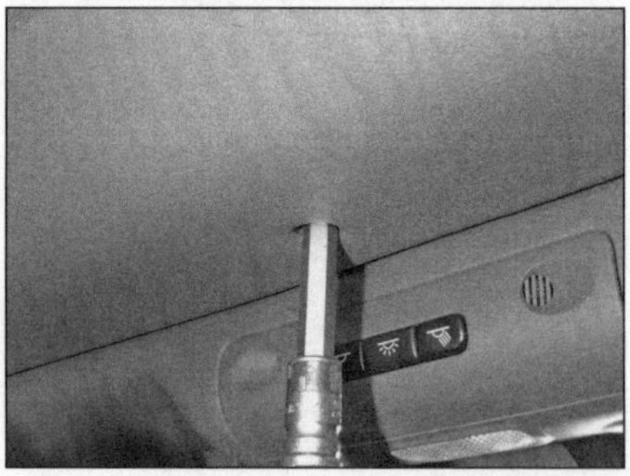

31.19 Use the soft top emergency opening tool, or an Allen key

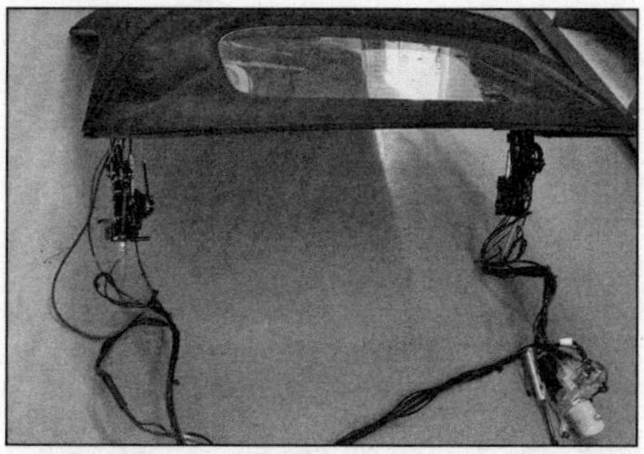

31.20 Lift the soft top off as a complete assembly with the hydraulic unit, pipes and cylinders

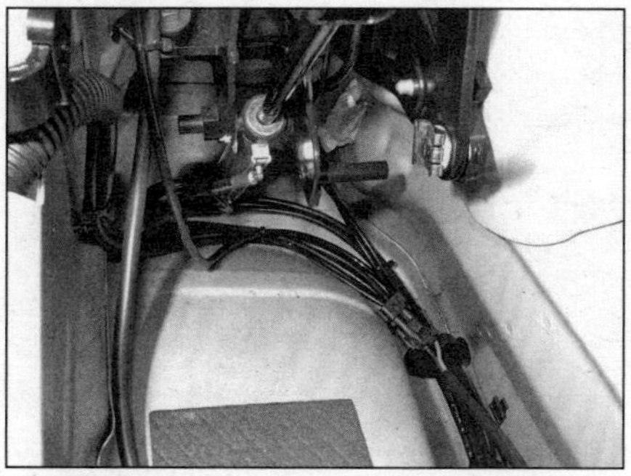

31.22 Ensure the hoses/pipes are routed behind the soft top mounting brackets

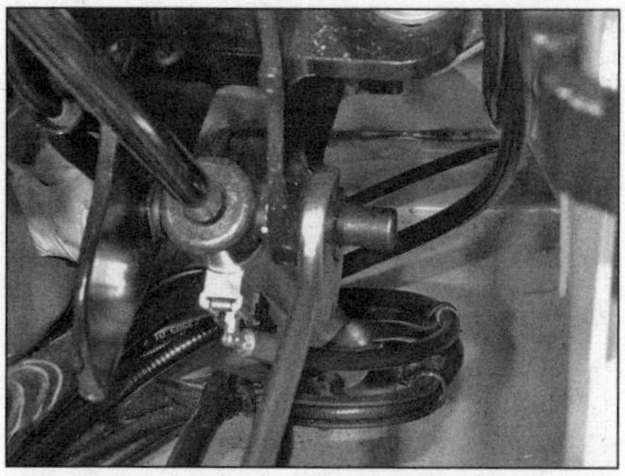

31.25a Using a spanner on the hexagonal section, press down ...

and 2 soft top cover cylinders from the vehicle **(see illustration)**. Take great care not to damage the hydraulic cylinders.

Refitting

21 Before refitting the soft top, ensure it's in the 'closed' position with the 6th bow open.

22 Lift the soft top, hydraulic unit and cylinders into position. Ensure the hoses are located behind the soft top brackets **(see illustration)**.

23 Support the 6th bow with a suitable length of wood, then lock the 1st bow to the windscreen frame using the emergency soft top opening tool. In the absence of the tool, use an 8 mm Allen key.

24 Refit the bolts securing the soft top brackets to the vehicle body, but only finger-tighten them at this stage. Ensure any shims/washers removed are fitted to their original positions.

25 Using a 17 mm spanner, press down gently on the soft top mechanism hexagon section, until the gap between the mechanism and the bracket stop disappears **(see illustrations)**.

26 Hold the spanner in this position, and tighten the soft top brackets retaining bolts securely. Repeat this operation on the remaining side.

27 The remainder of refitting is a reversal of removal, but note the following additional points:

a) Refit the hydraulic hoses in their original positions, and secure with cable-ties.

b) If adjustment of the soft top is required, the vehicle must be taken to a Saab dealer or suitably-equipped specialist who will have the jigs necessary to carry out the work.

c) If the system display unit indicates any soft top fault codes, a Saab dealer or specialist must erase them using a diagnostic tool.

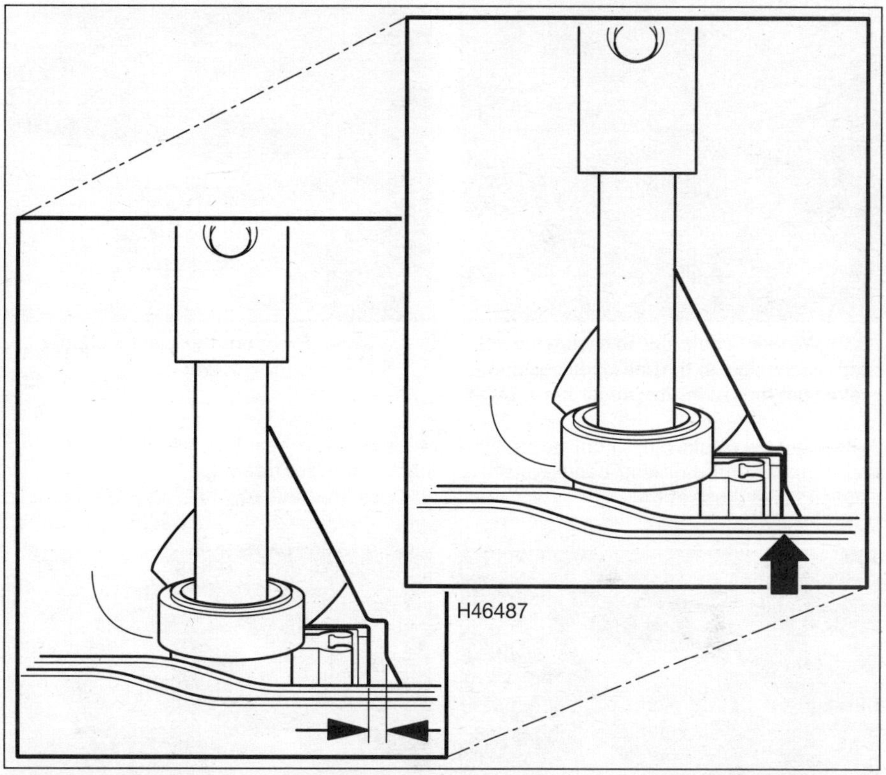

31.25b ... until the gap (arrowed) between the mechanism and the bracket disappears

32 Soft top covering – removal and refitting

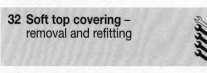

Note: *Extra care must be taken during the following procedure to prevent damage to the covering while it is being fitted.*

Removal

1 Operate the soft top to its fully open position, but leave the soft top cover open.

2 Undo the 9 retaining screws, remove the cover plate, then pull the cover plate rearwards and remove it along with the insulation piece **(see illustrations)**.

32.2a Undo the cover plate screws ...

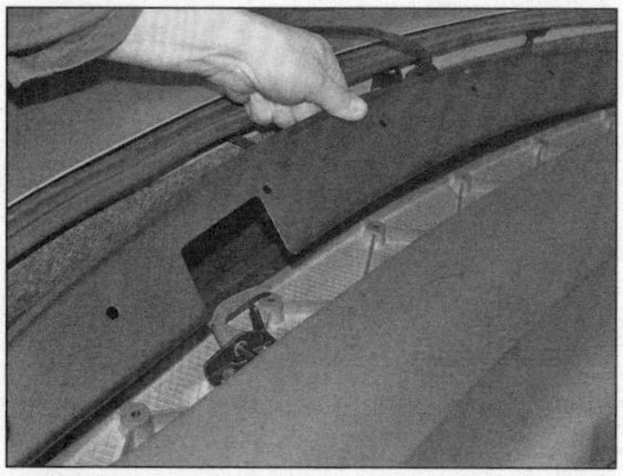

32.2b ... then remove the cover plate ...

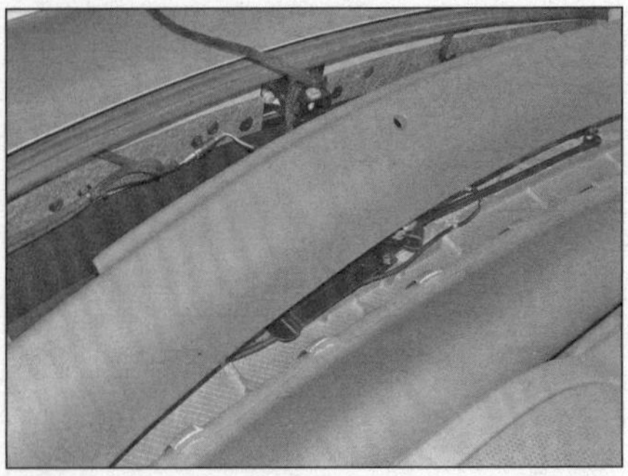

32.2c ... along with the insulation piece

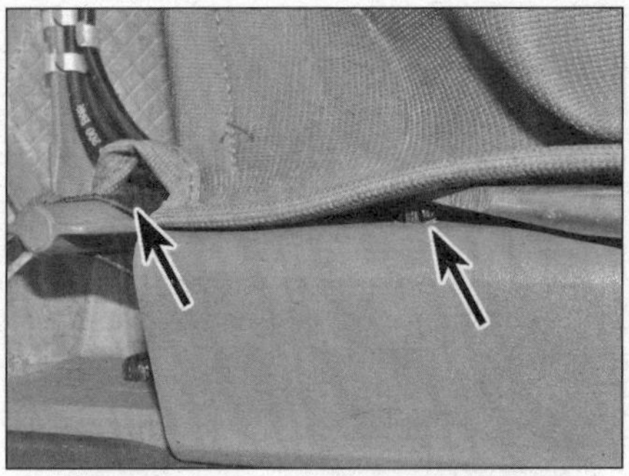

32.3 Prise out the plastic plugs, and release the eyelets (arrowed)

32.4 Unclip the headlining from the hooks (arrowed)

32.5 We used cable-ties to secure the soft top mechanism in the half-open position – make sure the cable-ties are strong enough!

32.6a Prise out the plastic clips (arrowed) ...

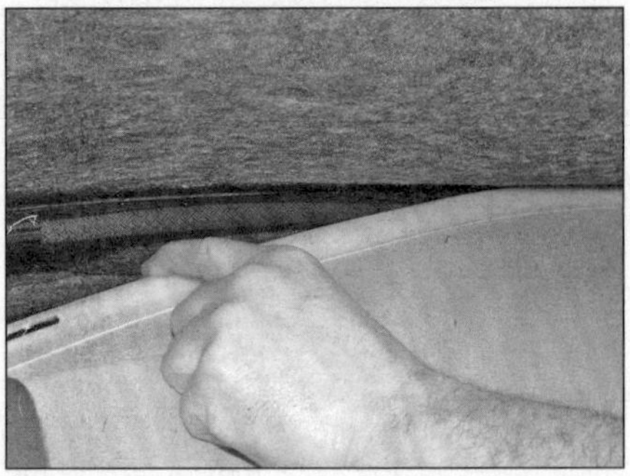

32.6b ... and unclip the headlining holder from the bow

3 Prise out the plastic plugs from the 1st bow, and unhook the headlining band eyelets at each end **(see illustration)**.

4 Detach the headlining from the 1st bow hooks **(see illustration)**.

5 Open the soft top half-way. Secure it in this position using Saab tool No 82 93 847 or fabricate an equivalent **(see illustration)**.

6 Prise out the plastic clips securing the headlining to the 2nd bow, then pull the headlining plastic holder from the 2nd bow **(see illustrations)**.

7 Prise out the plastic clips securing the headlining to the 3rd bow, then pull the headlining plastic holder from the 3rd bow.

8 Pull the headlining forward out of the mounting on each side and detach it from the rear rails **(see illustration)**.

9 Pull the headlining rubber straps out of the attaching eyelets **(see illustration)**.

10 Prise out the plastic clips securing the headlining to the 4th bow, then pull the headlining plastic holder from the 4th bow.

11 Remove the support tool/cable-tie and close the soft top.

12 Raise the 6th bow and support it in this position using a suitable length of wood or similar.

13 Release the plastic headlining clip and pull the headlining edging from the 6th bow groove **(see illustrations)**. Remove the support and lower the 6th bow.

14 Open the soft top half-way and secure it in position using Saab tool No 82 93 847 **(see illustration 32.5)**.

15 Pull the fabric strips from the 2nd, 3rd, 4th and 5th bows **(see illustration)**.

16 Unhook the insulation from the 1st bow.

17 Undo the Velcro fastener from the linkage system for the front rail.

18 Pull the outer fabric from the underside of

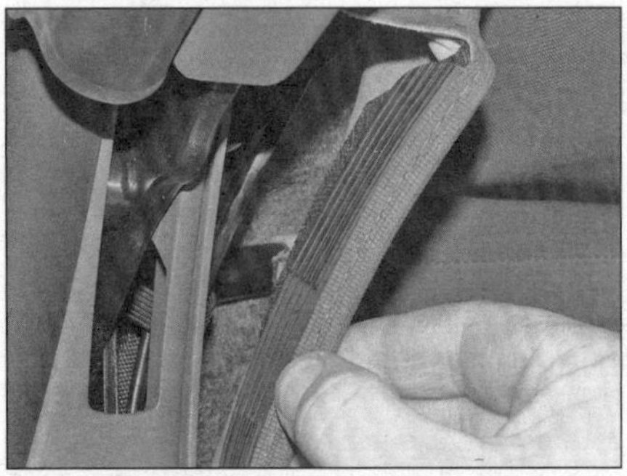

32.8 Pull the from the rear mounting rails each side

32.9 Detach the elastic headlining straps each side

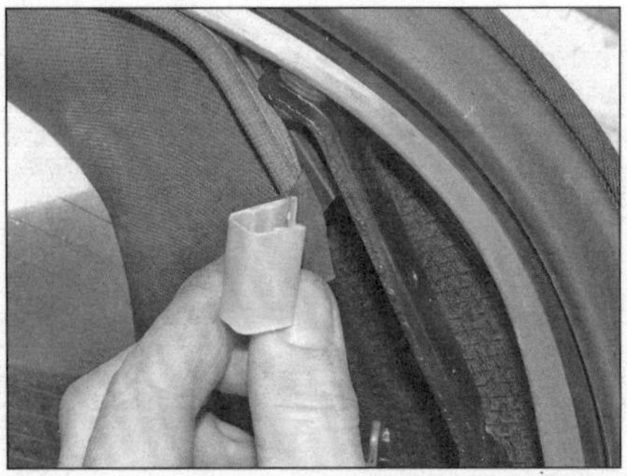

32.13a Release the headlining plastic clips ...

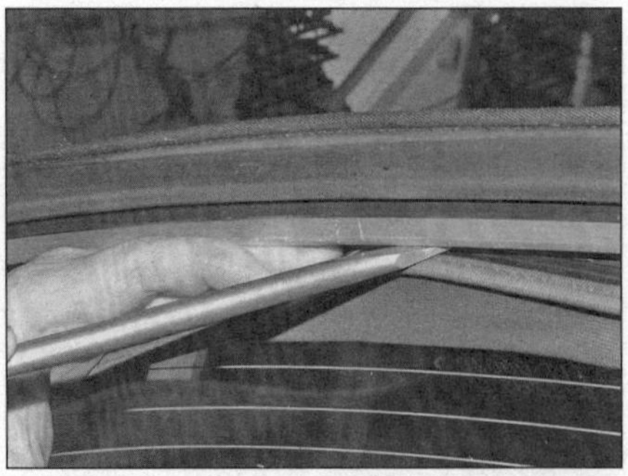

32.13b ... then carefully prise the edging strip securing the headlining to the 6th bow

32.15 Pull the fabric strips securing the insulation to the bows

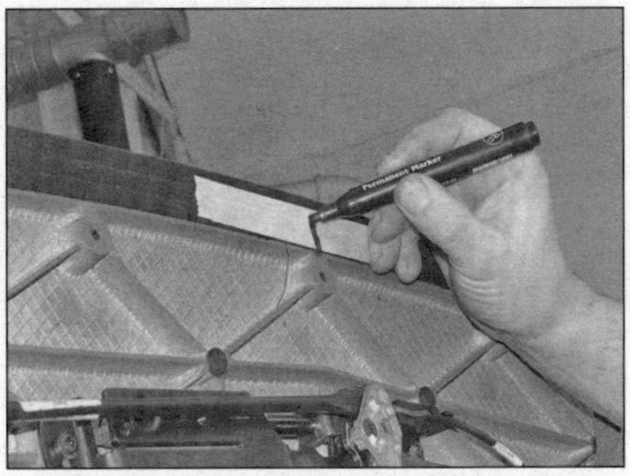

32.18a If the cover is to be refitted, mark the centre position

32.18b Pull the outer cover from the 1st bow ...

the 1st bow, releasing it from the double-sided adhesive tape, then unhook the tensioning cables from the 1st bow. Pull the old adhesive tape from place. **Note:** *If the covering is to be refitted, mark the centre position of the fabric at the 1st bow before removing it **(see illustrations).***

19 Remove the rear rail seals, by pulling them out from the U-shaped rails. Start at the top, unhook the top part of the seal from the mounting and leave it hanging **(see illustrations)**.

20 Remove the soft top support tool, raise the 6th bow and support it in position.

21 Pull out the 6th bow locking strip from the mounting groove, then prise out the outer roof edging strip from the 6th bow **(see illustrations)**.

22 Remove the soft top support tool, open the soft top half-way, and support it in position.

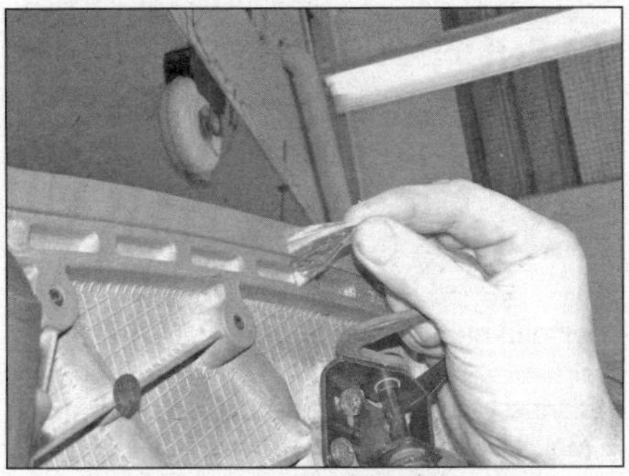

32.18c ... then pull away the old double-sided tape

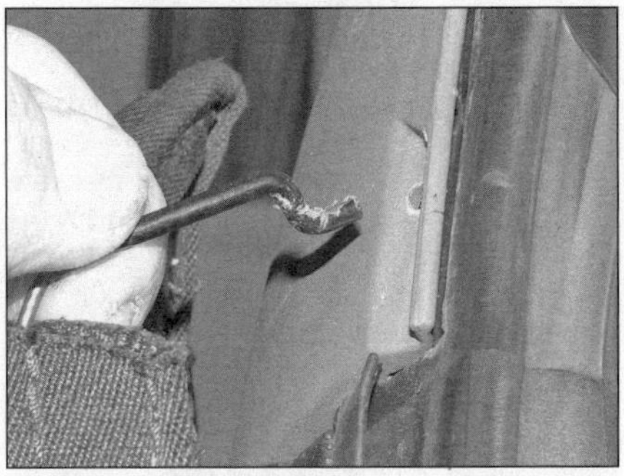

32.18d Unhook the tensioning cables from the 1st bow

23 Unhook the outer roof attaching profiles from the rear rails **(see illustration)**.

24 Release the Velcro fasteners from the rear rails.

25 Unhook the tension cables from the rear rails **(see illustration)**.

26 Remove the soft top support tool and close the soft top.

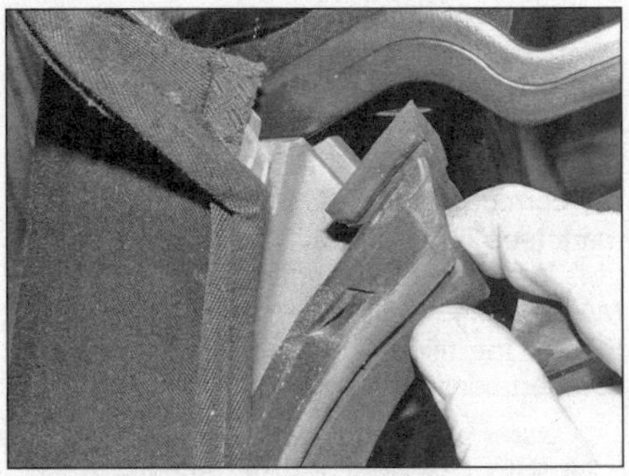

32.19a Pull out the top of the rear rail seals ...

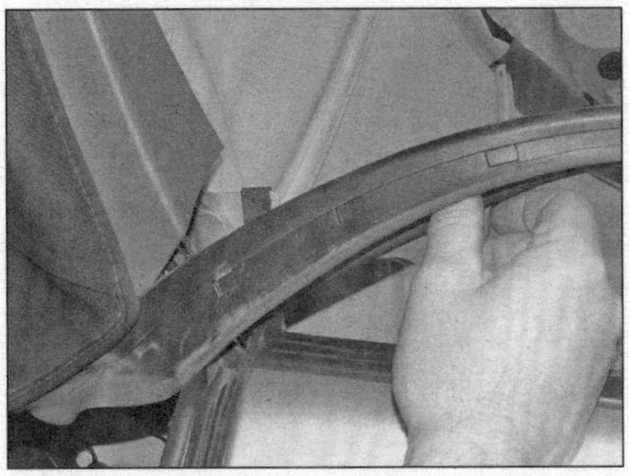

32.19b ... and leave them to hang

32.21a Pull the locking strip from the 6th bow ...

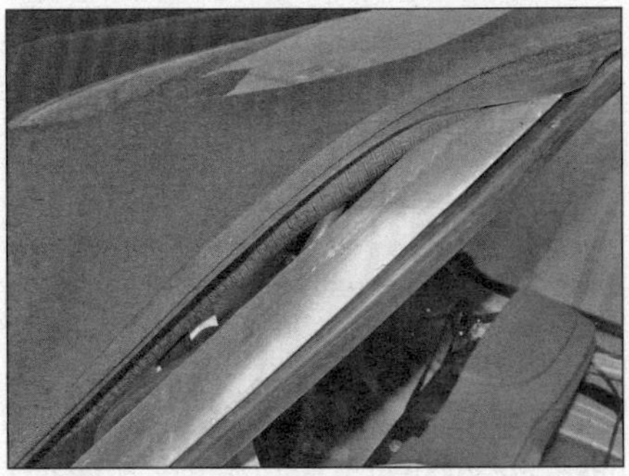

32.21b ... then prise out the roof edging strip

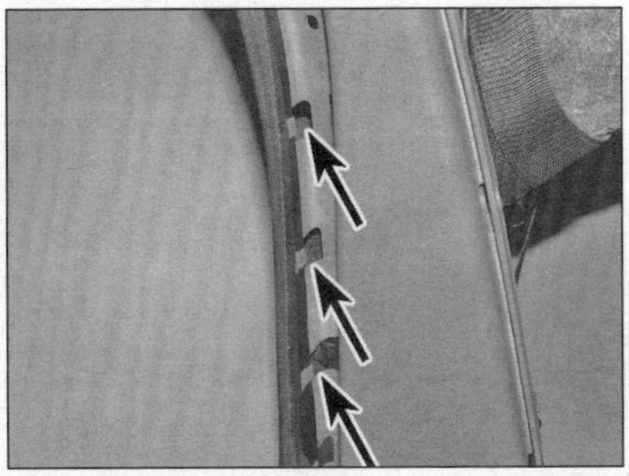

32.23 Unhook the outer roof from the clips (arrowed)

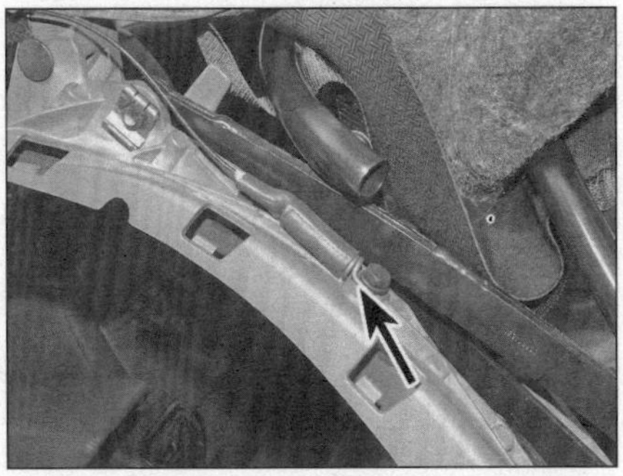

32.25 Detach the tensioning cables from the rails (arrowed)

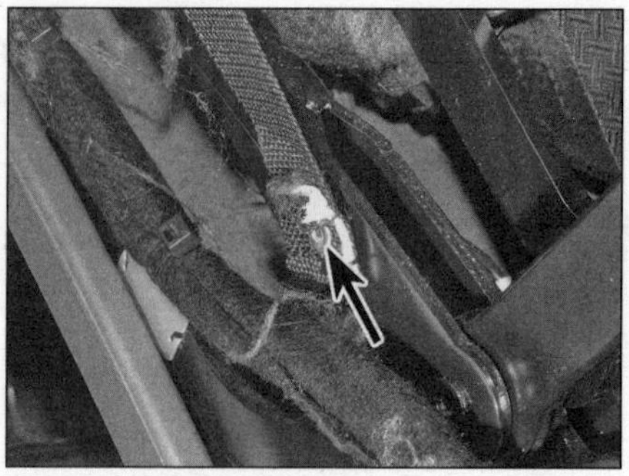

32.27 Drill out the rear window strap rivets (arrowed)

27 Drill out the rivets securing the rear window guide straps **(see illustration)**.

28 Disconnect the heated rear window wiring plug.

29 Remove the cable-ties from the rear window mounting frame, then undo the window frame Torx screws each side, pull out the straps from the insulation pocket, and with an assistant, lift the outer roof complete with rear window from the vehicle **(see illustration)**.

30 Renewal of the rear window is a specialist task and should be entrusted to a Saab dealer, specialist, or windscreen renewal company.

Refitting

31 Refitting is a reversal of removal.

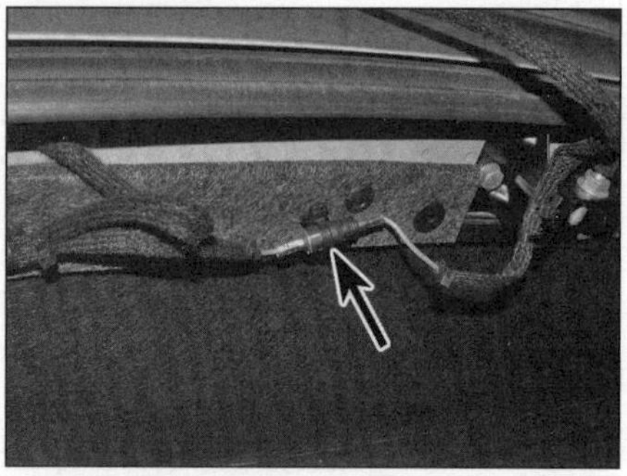

33.2 Disconnect the aerial connector (arrowed)

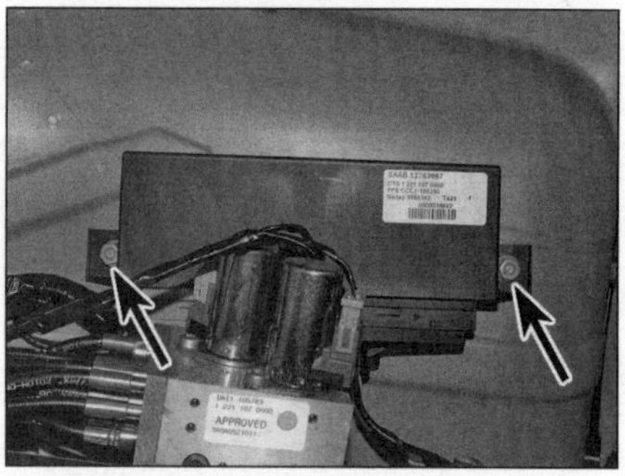

34.2 Undo the module retaining nuts (arrowed)

32.29 Undo the window frame Torx screw each side (arrowed)

33 Soft top cover – removal and refitting

Removal

1 Operate the soft top so that the cover is open and nearly vertical.

2 Squeeze together the retaining lugs and disconnect the aerial connector **(see illustration)**.

3 Make alignment marks between the cover and the mounting brackets, then undo the bolts and remove the soft top cover **(see illustration)**.

Refitting

4 Refitting is a reversal of removal. If necessary the position of the cover can be adjusted by slackening the hinge bolts and repositioning the cover.

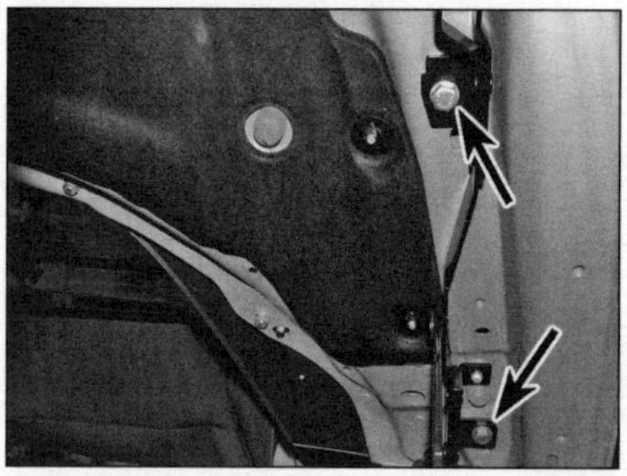

33.3 Undo the soft top cover mounting bracket bolts (arrowed)

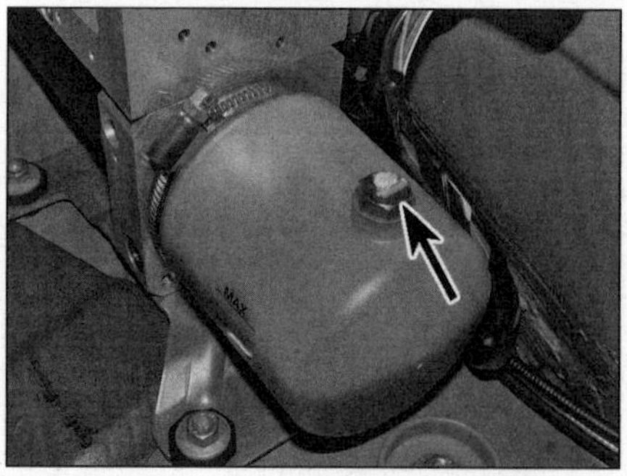

35.4 Undo the reservoir filler plug (arrowed)

34 Soft top control module – removal and refitting

Caution: Electronic control modules are extremely sensitive to static electricity. Before touching the module, earth yourself by touching a bare metal part of the vehicle body or engine.

Removal

1 Fully raise the soft top, then remove the luggage compartment side trim panel on the right-hand side as described in Section 26.

2 Undo the 2 nuts securing the control module, and disconnect the wiring plug as the module is withdrawn **(see illustration)**.

Refitting

3 Refitting is a reversal of removal. Note that if a new control module has been fitted, it may need to be programmed prior to use. Entrust this task to a Saab dealer or suitably-equipped specialist.

35 Soft top hydraulic system – checking oil level

Caution: Only use the correct fluid (see 'Lubricants and fluids').

1 Fully raise the soft top.

2 Remove the right-hand side luggage compartment side trim panel as described in Section 26.

3 Use a flashlight to check the hydraulic fluid level. The fluid level should be between the MIN and MAX marks.

4 To top-up the fluid level, remove the filler plug from the top of the reservoir, and add the correct specification fluid up to the MAX mark **(see illustration)**. Note that the amount of fluid required to raise the level from MIN to MAX is 65 ml.

5 Refit the filler plug, and refit the luggage compartment side trim panel.

36 Soft top hydraulic system – bleeding

1 Check and if necessary top-up the hydraulic fluid level as described in Section 35.

2 Open and close the soft top manually 4 or 5 times, then check the fluid level again.

3 Using the soft top emergency opening tool in the vehicle's tool kit, open the 1st bow latch 4 or 5 times **(see illustration 31.19)**.

4 Manually open and close the soft top 4 or 5 times, then check the fluid level again.

5 The soft top hydraulic system is now bled. If the soft top still fails to operate correctly, have the system's self-diagnosis facility interrogated by a Saab dealer or suitably-equipped specialist.

Chapter 12
Body electrical system

Contents

Degrees of difficulty

Easy, suitable for novice with little experience	**Fairly easy,** suitable for beginner with some experience	**Fairly difficult,** suitable for competent DIY mechanic	**Difficult,** suitable for experienced DIY mechanic	**Very difficult,** suitable for expert DIY or professional

Specifications

General

System type	12 volt negative earth

Bulbs

	Watts
Ashtray illumination	1.2
Brake lights	21 PR21W (red)
Cigarette lighter illumination	1.2
Direction indicators	21 PY21W (yellow)
Foglight:	
Front	35 H8
Rear	21 PR21W (red)
Glovebox light	10 R10W festoon
Headlights:	
Dipped beam:	
Halogen headlights	55 H7
Xenon headlights	35 D2S
Main beam:	
Halogen headlights	65 H9
Xenon headlights	55 H7
Interior light	10 R10W festoon
Luggage compartment light	10 R10W festoon
Number plate	5 R5W festoon
Reading lights:	
Front	5 W5W wedge
Rear	4 T4W
Reversing light	21 P21W
Side repeater light	5 WY5W wedge
Sidelights	LED array (not renewable)
Tail lights	21 PR21W (red)

Torque settings

	Nm	lbft
Airbag control module	10	7
Impact sensors:		
Front side	9	7
Side	6	4
Passenger's airbag nuts (top and bottom edges)	10	7
Wiper arm nuts	20	15

1 General information and precautions

General information

The electrical system is of the 12 volt negative earth type and comprises a 12 volt battery, an alternator with integral voltage regulator, a starter motor and related electrical accessories, components and wiring.

Electronic control modules/units are provided for the following systems (see Section 19):

a) Engine management.
b) Glow plug control.
c) Automatic transmission.
d) Climate control.
e) Airbag control module (ACM).
f) Electric seat control.
g) ABS/TC/ESP control.
h) Main instrument panel.
i) Soft top control (STS).
j) Door control modules.
k) Parking assistance (SPA).
l) Automatic headlight levelling.
m) Column integration module (CIM).
n) Body control module (BCM).
o) Infotainment control.
p) Power steering control.
q) Alarm control module (ACM).
r) Rear electrical centre (REC).
s) Ignition switch module (ISM).
t) Steering column lock (SCL).

All modules can communicate with each other via the serial data bus – often referred to as the 'can-bus' (for 'controller area network'). The communications network is itself divided into a high speed power train (P-bus) network for fast communication between critical systems and a low speed instrument network (I-bus) for communication between non-critical systems, such as the power windows for example. The column integrated module (CIM) acts as a getaway between the high and low speed networks.

A diagnostic socket is provide to allow access to any fault codes stored in the system **(see illustration)**. The socket or DLC (data link connector) is also used to program any new control modules using the dealer tool (Tech 2) or other suitable equipment.

All models feature a passive immobiliser and most models are fitted with an anti-theft alarm system consisting of sensors on the doors, tailgate and bonnet. A glass breakage sensor is also fitted in the interior light on the front of the headlining. The system is controlled by a central electronic control module which operates the warning horn.

While some repair procedures are given, the usual course of action is to renew a defective component.

Precautions

It is necessary to take extra care when working on the electrical system to avoid damage to semi-conductor devices (diodes and transistors) and to avoid the risk of personal injury. Certain procedures must be followed when removing the SRS components. In addition to the precautions given in *Safety first!* at the beginning of this Manual, observe the following when working on the system:

- Always remove rings, watches, etc, before working on the electrical system. Even with the battery disconnected, capacitive discharge could occur if a component's live terminal is earthed through a metal object. This could cause a shock or nasty burn.
- Do not reverse the battery connections. Components such as the alternator, fuel injection/ignition system ECM, or any other having semi-conductor circuitry could be irreparably damaged.
- Do not allow the engine to turn the alternator when the alternator is not connected.
- Always ensure that the battery negative lead is disconnected when working on the electrical system.
- Before using electric-arc welding equipment on the vehicle, disconnect the battery, alternator and components such as the fuel injection/ignition system ECM to protect them.

2 Electrical fault finding – general information

Note: *Refer to the precautions given in 'Safety first!' and in Section 1 of this Chapter before starting work. The following tests relate to testing of the main electrical circuits, and should not be used to test delicate electronic circuits (such as anti-lock braking systems), particularly where an electronic control module (ECM) is involved.*

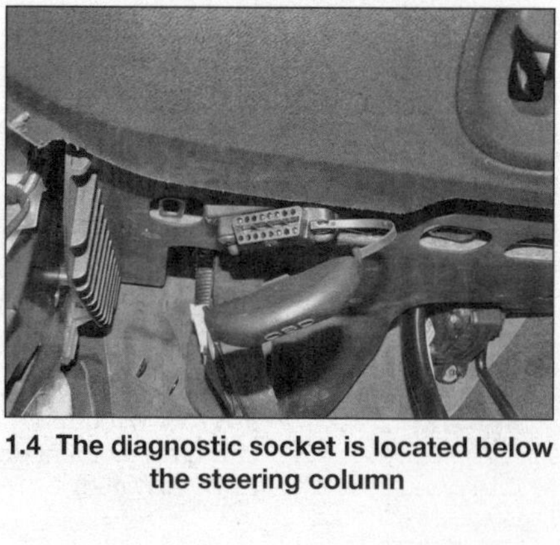

1.4 The diagnostic socket is located below the steering column

General

1 A typical electrical circuit consists of an electrical component, any switches, relays, motors, fuses, fusible links or circuit breakers related to that component, and the wiring and connectors which link the component to both the battery and the chassis. To help to pin-point a problem in an electrical circuit, wiring diagrams are included at the end of this Chapter.

2 Before attempting to diagnose an electrical fault, first study the appropriate wiring diagram, to obtain a more complete understanding of the components included in the particular circuit concerned. The possible sources of a fault can be narrowed down by noting whether other components related to the circuit are operating properly. If several components or circuits fail at one time, the problem is likely to be related to a shared fuse or earth connection.

3 Electrical problems usually stem from simple causes, such as loose or corroded connections, a faulty earth connection, a blown fuse, a melted fusible link, or a faulty relay (refer to Section 3 for details of testing relays). Visually inspect the condition of all fuses, wires and connections in a problem circuit before testing the components. Use the wiring diagrams to determine which terminal connections will need to be checked, in order to pin-point the trouble-spot.

4 The basic tools required for electrical fault finding include: a circuit tester or voltmeter (a 12 volt bulb with a set of test leads can also be used for certain tests), a self-powered test light (sometimes known as a continuity tester), an ohmmeter (to measure resistance), a battery and set of test leads, and a jumper wire, preferably with a circuit breaker or fuse incorporated, which can be used to bypass suspect wires or electrical components. Before attempting to locate a problem with test instruments, use the wiring diagram to determine where to make the connections.

5 To find the source of an intermittent wiring fault (usually due to a poor or dirty connection, or damaged wiring insulation), an integrity test can be performed on the wiring, which involves moving the wiring by hand, to see if the fault occurs as the wiring is moved.

It should be possible to narrow down the source of the fault to a particular section of wiring. This method of testing can be used in conjunction with any of the tests described in the following sub-Sections.

6 Apart from problems due to poor connections, two basic types of fault can occur in an electrical circuit - open-circuit, or short-circuit.

7 Open-circuit faults are caused by a break somewhere in the circuit, which prevents current from flowing. An open-circuit fault will prevent a component from working, but will not cause the relevant circuit fuse to blow.

8 Short-circuit faults are caused by a 'short' somewhere in the circuit, which allows the current flowing in the circuit to 'escape' along an alternative route, usually to earth. Short-circuit faults are normally caused by a breakdown in wiring insulation, which allows a feed wire to touch either another wire, or an earthed component such as the bodyshell. A short-circuit fault will normally cause the relevant circuit fuse to blow. **Note:** *A short-circuit that occurs in the wiring between a circuit's battery supply and its fuse will not cause the fuse in that particular circuit to blow. This part of the circuit is unprotected - bear this in mind when fault finding on the vehicle's electrical system.*

Finding an open-circuit

9 To check for an open-circuit, connect one lead of a circuit tester or voltmeter to either the negative battery terminal or a known good earth.

10 Connect the other lead to a connector in the circuit being tested, preferably nearest to the battery or fuse.

11 Switch on the circuit, bearing in mind that some circuits are live only when the ignition switch is moved to a particular position.

12 If voltage is present (indicated either by the tester bulb lighting or a voltmeter reading, as applicable), this means that the section of the circuit between the relevant connector and the battery is problem-free.

13 Continue to check the remainder of the circuit in the same fashion.

14 When a point is reached at which no voltage is present, the problem must lie between that point and the previous test point with voltage. Most problems can be traced to a broken, corroded or loose connection.

Finding a short-circuit

15 To check for a short-circuit, first disconnect the load(s) from the circuit (loads are the components which draw current from a circuit, such as bulbs, motors, heating elements, etc).

16 Remove the relevant fuse from the circuit, and connect a circuit tester or voltmeter to the fuse connections.

17 Switch on the circuit, bearing in mind that some circuits are live only when the ignition switch is moved to a particular position.

18 If voltage is present (indicated either by the tester bulb lighting or a voltmeter reading, as applicable), this means that there is a short-circuit.

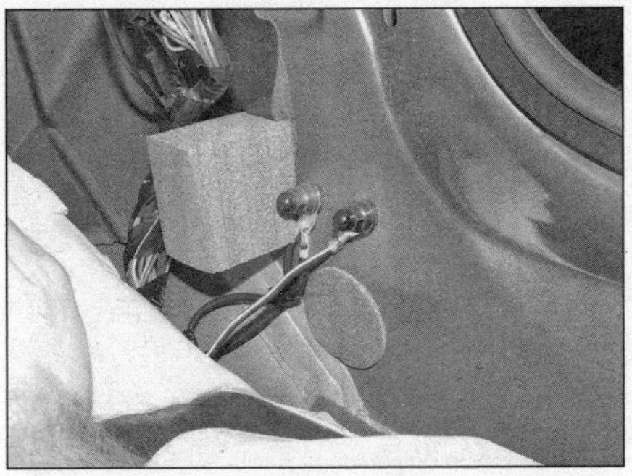

2.20a Earth connections at the right-hand side footwell

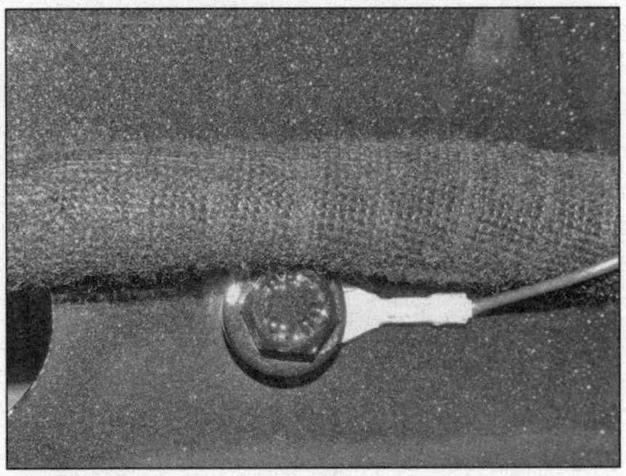

2.20b Earth connection on the Estate tailgate

19 If no voltage is present, but the fuse still blows with the load(s) connected, this indicates an internal fault in the load(s).

Finding an earth fault

20 The battery negative terminal is connected to 'earth' - the metal of the engine/transmission and the car body - and most systems are wired so that they only receive a positive feed, the current returning via the metal of the car body. This means that the component mounting and the body form part of that circuit. Loose or corroded mountings can therefore cause a range of electrical faults, ranging from total failure of a circuit, to a puzzling partial fault. In particular, lights may shine dimly (especially when another circuit sharing the same earth point is in operation), motors (eg, wiper motors or the radiator cooling fan motor) may run slowly, and the operation of one circuit may have an apparently-unrelated effect on another. Note that on many vehicles, earth straps are used between certain components, such as the engine/transmission and the body, usually where there is no metal-to-metal contact between components, due to flexible rubber mountings, etc **(see illustrations)**.

21 To check whether a component is properly earthed, disconnect the battery (as described in Chapter 5A, Section 4), and connect one lead of an ohmmeter to a known good earth point. Connect the other lead to the wire or earth connection being tested. The resistance reading should be zero; if not, check the connection as follows.

22 If an earth connection is thought to be faulty, dismantle the connection, and clean back to bare metal both the bodyshell and the wire terminal, or the component's earth connection mating surface. Be careful to remove all traces of dirt and corrosion, then use a knife to trim away any paint, so that a clean metal-to-metal joint is made. On reassembly, tighten the joint fasteners securely; if a wire terminal is being refitted, use serrated washers between the terminal and the bodyshell, to ensure a clean and secure connection. When the connection is remade, prevent the onset of corrosion in the future by applying a coat of petroleum jelly or silicone-based grease, or by spraying on (at regular intervals) a proprietary ignition sealer or a water-dispersant lubricant.

3 Fuses and relays - general information

Fuses

1 Fuses are designed to break an electrical circuit when a predetermined current limit is reached, in order to protect the components and wiring which could be damaged by excessive current flow. Any excessive current flow will be due to a fault in the circuit, usually a short-circuit (see Section 2).

2 The fuses are located either in the fusebox located on the left-hand end of the facia (the instrument panel electrical centre - IPEC) in the fusebox located in the left-hand front of the engine compartment (the underbonnet electrical centre - UEC), or on the left-hand side of the luggage compartment (the rear electrical centre - REC). Relays and control modules are also incorporated into the fuse boxes.

3 Access to the facia fusebox is gained by opening the left-hand front door and releasing the plastic cover. The engine compartment fusebox is opened by opening the bonnet and unclipping the plastic cover, and the luggage compartment fusebox by releasing the clip and folding the panel down **(see illustrations)**.

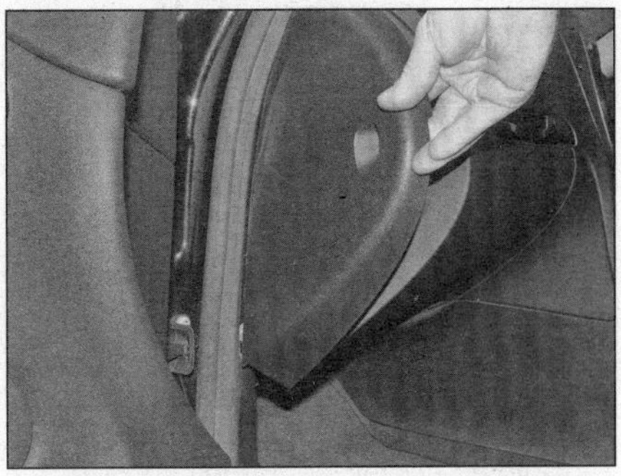

3.3a Pull open the facia end panel ...

3.3b ... to access the passenger compartment fusebox

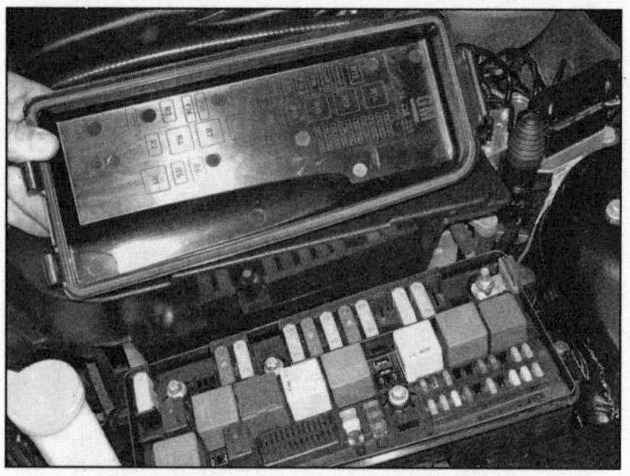

3.3d The engine compartment fusebox is located next to the battery

4 To remove a fuse, use the plastic tool provided in the fusebox to pull the fuse from its socket **(see illustration)**.

5 Inspect the fuse from the side, through the transparent plastic body – a blown fuse can be recognised by its melted or broken wire.

6 Spare fuses are provided in the blank terminal positions in the fusebox.

7 Before renewing a blown fuse, trace and rectify the cause, and always use a fuse of the correct rating.

Caution: Never substitute a fuse of a higher rating, or make temporary repairs using wire or metal foil; more serious damage, or even a fire, could result.

8 Note that the fuses are colour-coded, as described below – refer to the wiring diagrams for details of the fuse ratings and the circuits protected.

Colour	Rating
Brown	5A
Red	10A
Blue	15A
Yellow	20A
Clear	25A
Green	30A

9 In addition to the system fuses, Maxi fuses are also located in the fuseboxes. Their purpose is to protect certain areas of the car's electrical wiring, each including more than one electrical component. These are rated much higher than a normal fuse. Their ratings are as follows:

Colour	Rating
Orange	40A (maximum)
Blue	60A (maximum)

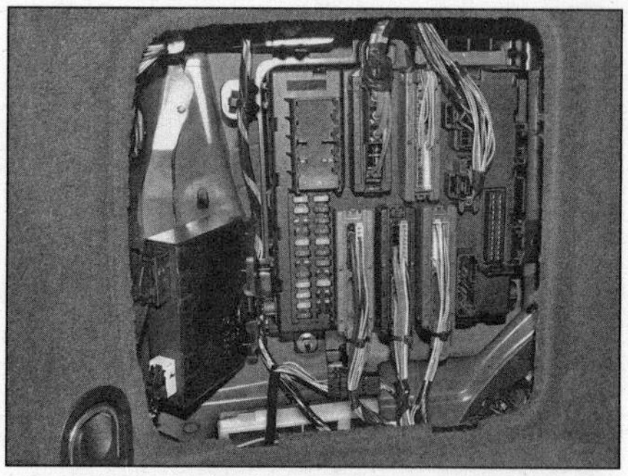

3.3c Open the cover to access the luggage compartment fusebox (Estate model)

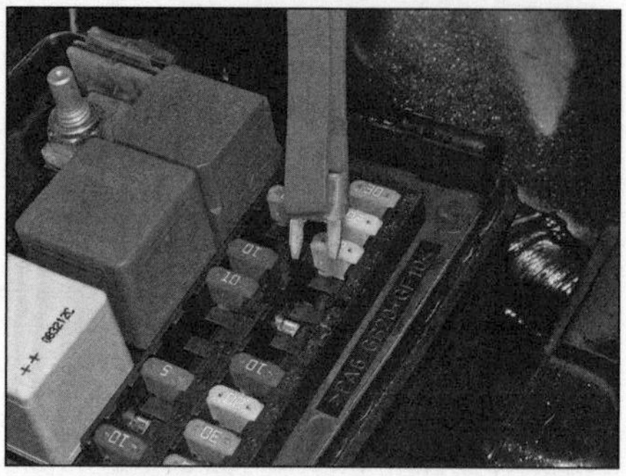

3.4 Use the tool provided on the inside of the facia fusebox cover to pull out a fuse

10 In addition, fusible links are fitted alongside the battery in the engine compartment. The fuses protect different areas of the vehicles electrical system, and are rated much higher that normal or Maxi fuses. Failure of a fusible link indicates a major problem with the electrical system, and it is recommended that the problem is entrusted to a Saab dealer or auto-electrician.

Relays

11 A relay is an electrically-operated mechanical switch, which is used for the following reasons:

a) A relay can switch a heavy current remotely from the circuit in which the current is flowing, therefore allowing the use of lighter-gauge wiring and switch contacts.

b) A relay can receive more than one control input, unlike a mechanically-operated switch.

c) A relay can have a timer function.

12 The main relays are located in all three fuseboxes. Lift off the cover for access to the relays.

13 If a circuit or system that is controlled by a relay develops a fault and the performance of the relay is in doubt, switch on the system in question. In general, if the relay is functioning, it should be possible to hear it 'click' as it is energised. If this is found to be the case, then it is probable that the fault lies with the system's components or wiring. If the relay cannot be heard to energise, then either the relay is not receiving a main supply or switching voltage, or the relay itself is faulty. Verification can be carried out by the substitution of a known good unit, but be careful – while some relays are identical in appearance and operation, others look similar but perform different functions – ensure that the substitute relay is of exactly the same type.

14 To remove a relay, first ensure that the relevant circuit is switched off. The relay can then simply be pulled out from the socket, and pushed back into position.

4 Switches and controls – removal and refitting

Ignition switch module (ISM)

1 Remove the centre console as described in Chapter 11, Section 27.

Caution: All ECMs are extremely sensitive to static electricity. Before touching the ignition switch module, earth yourself by touching a bare metal part of the vehicle body or engine/transmission.

2 Release the 4 retaining clips and remove the module from the underside of the console **(see illustration)**.

3 Refitting is a reversal of removal.

4.2 Depress the clips (arrowed) on the side, and pull out the ignition switch

Column integration module (CIM)

4 Remove the steering wheel as described in Chapter 10, Section 14.

Caution: All ECMs are extremely sensitive to static electricity. Before touching the ignition switch module, earth yourself by touching a bare metal part of the vehicle body or engine/transmission.

5 Pull the gaiter from the facia and slide it over the CIM **(see illustration)**.

6 Use masking tape to secure the clock spring in position and then release the 2 retaining clips and pull the module from the steering column **(see illustrations)**.

7 Disconnect the wiring plug from the rear of the module, and release the harness clip **(see illustration)**.

8 Refitting is a reversal of removal, but note the following:

a) If the clock spring has rotated, align the

4.5 Release the gaiter

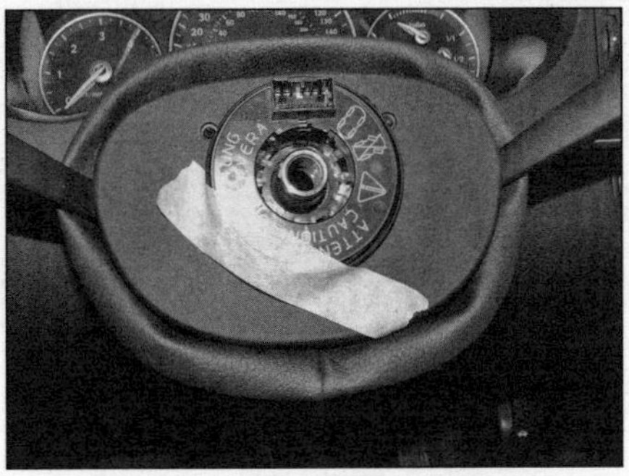

4.6a Secure the clock spring ...

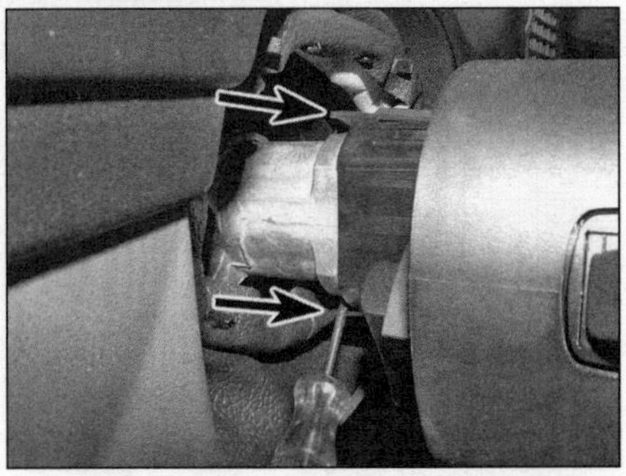

4.6b ... and then release the 2 clips (arrowed) and slide the CIM up the column

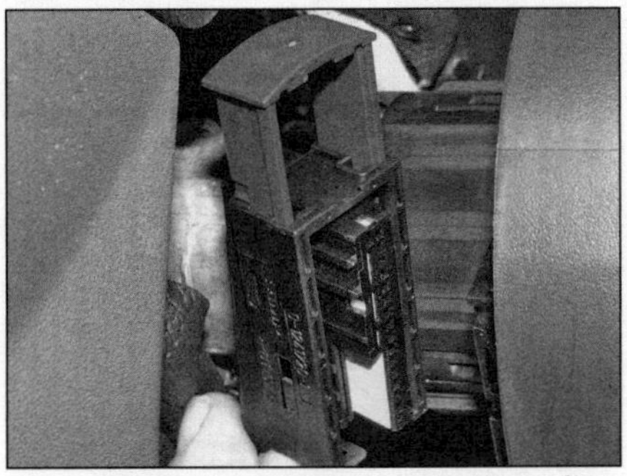

4.7 Slide up the red locking catch and disconnect the wiring plug

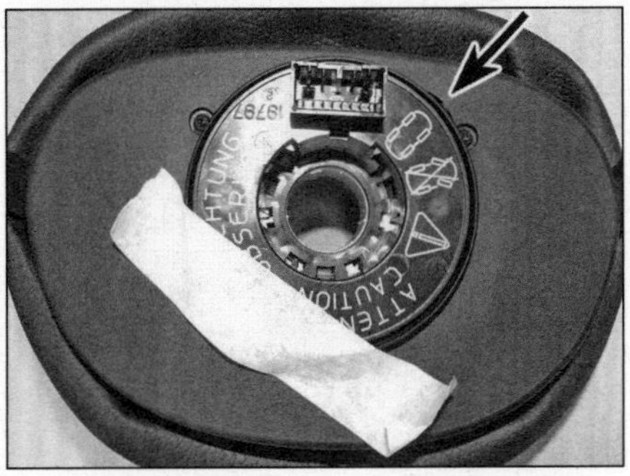

4.8 Align the index mark (arrowed)

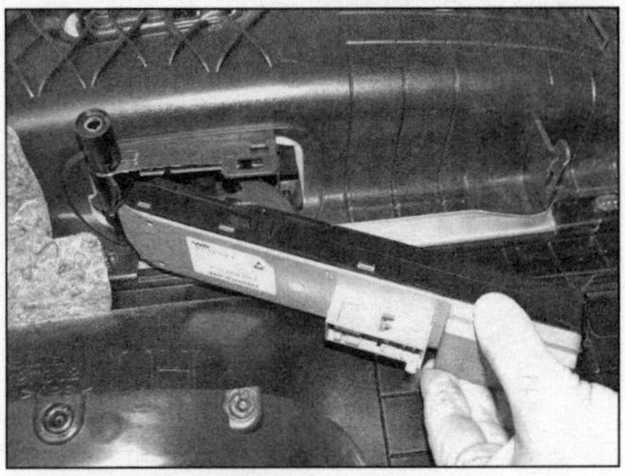

4.10 Release the clips at the rear and remove the door switch module

pointer with the fixed mark on the CIM ***(see illustration)****. The wheels must be in the straight-ahead position when aligning the pointer.*

b) If a new module has been fitted, it will be necessary to have it programmed prior to use. Entrust this task to a Saab dealer or suitably-equipped specialist.

c) It is possible to fit a used CIM, but this must have been divorced (with suitable diagnostic equipment) from the donor vehicle.

d) The vehicle will not start until the new CIM has been programmed.

Window switches/ control module

9 Remove the appropriate door inner trim panel as described in Chapter 11, Section 12. ***Caution: All ECMs are extremely sensitive to static electricity. Before touching the ignition switch module, earth yourself by touching a bare metal part of the vehicle body or engine/transmission.***

10 Remove the door trim panel Torx screw (Convertible driver's door only), then release the clips and remove switch/module. Start with the clip at the rear first **(see illustration)**.

11 Refitting is a reversal of removal. Note that if a new module has been fitted, it will be necessary to have it programmed prior to use. Entrust this task to a Saab dealer or suitably-equipped specialist.

Interior lighting control

12 Carefully prise the lens and front cover from the interior light unit behind the interior rear view mirror **(see illustration)**.

13 Undo the 2 Torx screws and remove the centre cover from the interior light unit **(see illustration)**.

14 Release the clips with a small screwdriver and remove the switches **(see illustration)**.

15 Refitting is a reversal of removal.

Foglight switches

16 Both the front and rear foglights are operated by switches which are integral with the main lighting switch. Removal of the switch is described later in this Section.

Lighting switch

17 Remove the end panel from the facia on the driver's side.

18 Access the rear of the switch from the end of the facia, release the retaining clips and push the light switch from position. If this proves difficult, remove the vent from above

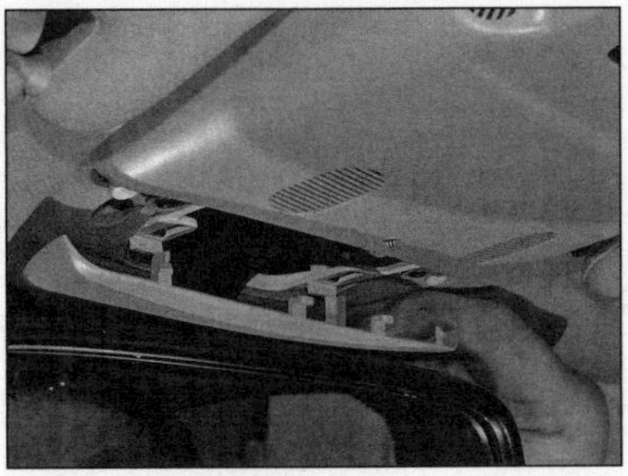

4.12 Pull down the cover behind the interior mirror

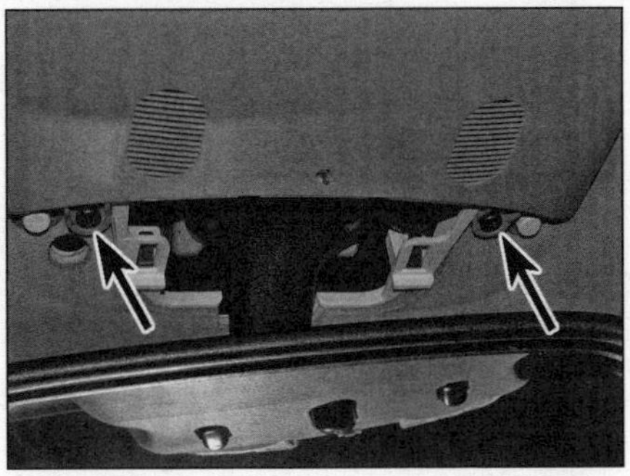

4.13 Undo the 2 Torx screws (arrowed)

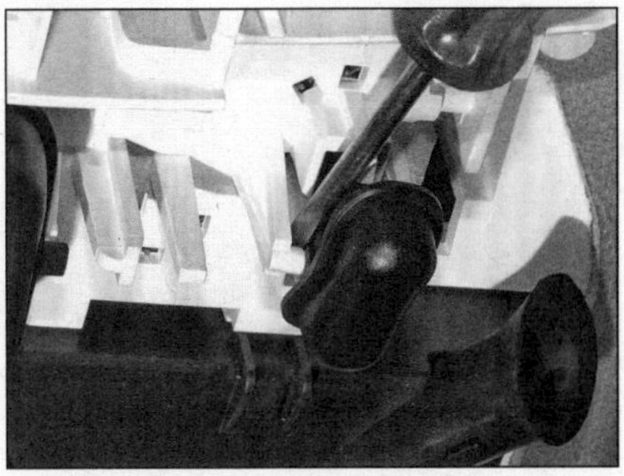

4.14 Release the clip and remove the switch

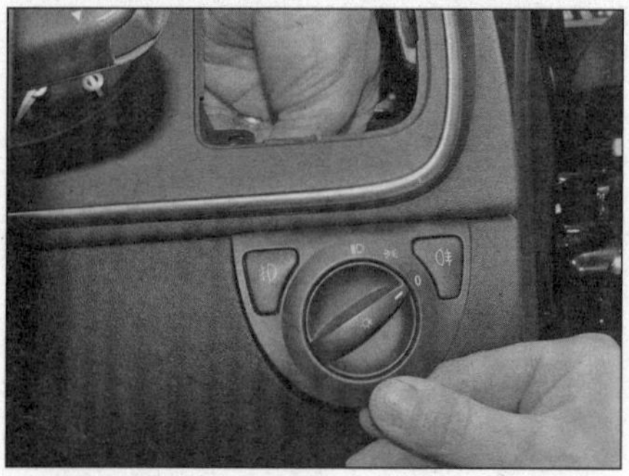

4.18a Push the switch out from the rear ...

4.18b ... noting the position of the upper ...

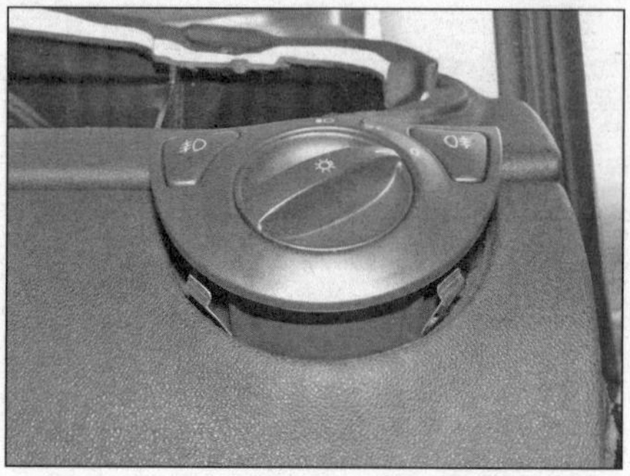

4.18c ... and lower retaining spring clips

4.22 Prise down the handle trim

4.23a Prise forwards the locking sleeve ...

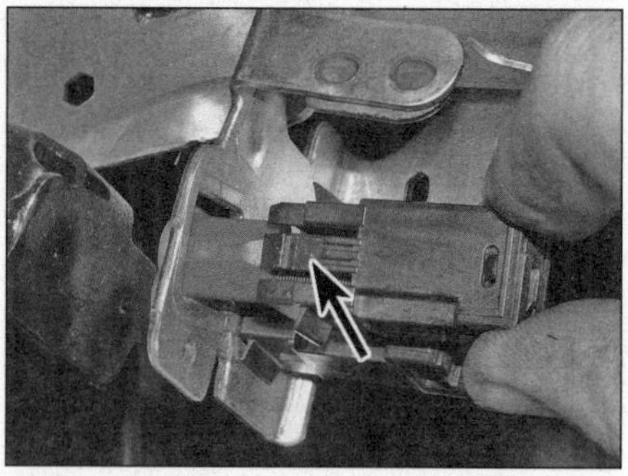

4.23b ... then depress the clip (arrowed) each side, and pull the switch from the bracket

the switch and access the rear of the switch this way **(see illustrations)**.

19 Disconnect the wiring plug as the switch is withdrawn.

20 Refitting is a reversal of removal.

Brake light switch

21 Remove the driver's side lower facia panel as described in Chapter 11, Section 26.

22 Prise down and remove the steering column adjustment handle surround trim **(see illustration)**.

23 Depress the brake pedal, then pull out the switch pushrod and locking sleeve, depress the clips and pull the switch from position **(see illustrations)**. Note that it must be possible to depress the brake pedal a little – if necessary, start the engine to build-up servo vacuum.

24 Refitting is a reversal of removal.

Hazard warning light switch

25 The hazard warning light switch is integral the climate control panel – refer to Chapter 3, Section 9.

Electric door mirror switch

26 Carefully prise the switch from the cover on the front door **(see illustration)**. Note that on some early models the switch may be glued in position. This makes removal extremely difficult.

27 Disconnect the wiring.

28 Refitting is a reversal of removal. If the switch was glued into position, remove all traces of the adhesive and refit the switch using a suitable adhesive.

Door courtesy light switch

29 The function of the courtesy light switch is contained within the door lock assembly. Removal of the lock is described in Chapter 11, Section 13.

Handbrake switch

30 Remove the centre console as described in Chapter 11, Section 27.

31 Disconnect the wiring plug from the switch.

32 Undo the screw and remove the switch **(see illustrations)**.

33 Refitting is a reversal of removal.

Clutch pedal switch

34 Remove the driver's side lower facia panel as described in Chapter 11, Section 26.

35 Carefully prise the steering wheel adjustment lever surround trim from the steering column shroud **(see illustration 4.22)**.

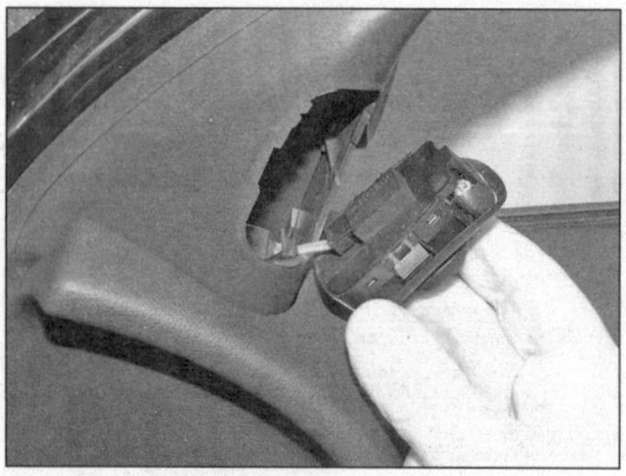

4.26 Prise the switch from the cover

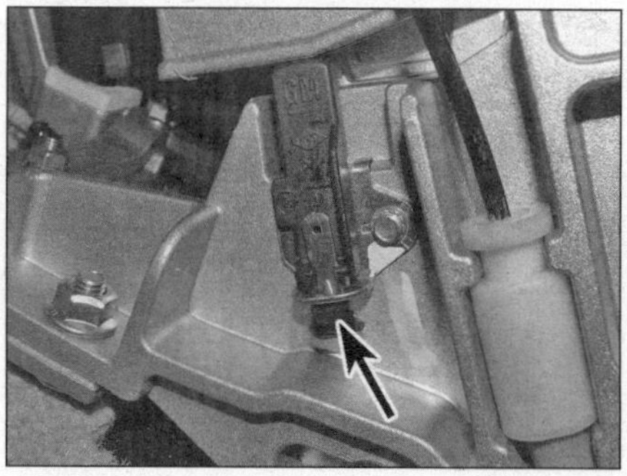

4.32a The handbrake warning switch (arrowed) ...

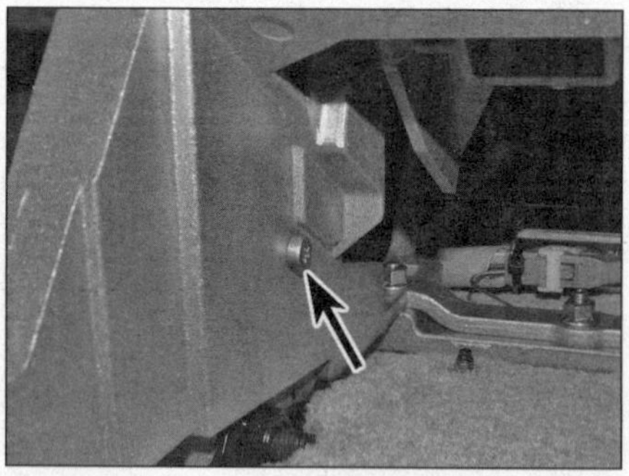

4.32b ... is secured by a single Torx screw (arrowed)

36 Depress the clutch pedal, pull out the switch pushrod and locking sleeve, then release the 2 retaining clips and pull the switch from position **(see illustration)**.
37 Disconnect the wiring plug as the switch is withdrawn.
38 To refit the switch, pull out the switch pushrod and locking sleeve **(see illustration)**.
39 Depress the clutch pedal, and push the switch into place.
40 Push in the locking sleeve, and pull out the pushrod. Release the pedal and refit the facia panel.

Reversing light switch

41 Removal and refitting of the reversing light switch is described in Chapter 7A, Section 6.

Sunroof switch

42 Using a flat-bladed tool, carefully prise the front interior light lens and front cover from place.
43 Undo the 2 screws and remove the centre cover from the interior light assembly.
44 Release the clips and remove the switch.
45 Disconnect the wiring plug as the switch is withdrawn.
46 Refitting is a reversal of removal.

Heated rear window switch

47 The heated rear window switch is integral with the climate control unit – refer to Chapter 3, Section 9.

Steering wheel switches

48 Remove the driver's airbag from the steering wheel as described in Section 21.
49 Undo the retaining Torx screw and pull the switches from the steering wheel **(see illustration)**. Disconnect the wiring plug from the right-hand switch gear as it's removed. Note that the switches are supplied as an assembly with the interconnecting wiring loom **(see illustration)**.
50 Refitting is a reversal of removal.

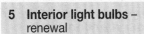

5 Interior light bulbs – renewal

Instrument panel

1 The instrument panel is illuminated by a number of LEDs. These are not renewable. Should a fault develop with the panel lighting, have the system's self-diagnosis facility interrogated using Saab test equipment before condemning the unit.

Interior lights

Front roof lights

2 Pull down the rear edge and remove the lens from the interior light **(see illustration)**.
3 Pull the wedge type bulb from the bulbholder **(see illustration)**.
4 Fit the new bulb using a reversal of the removal procedure.

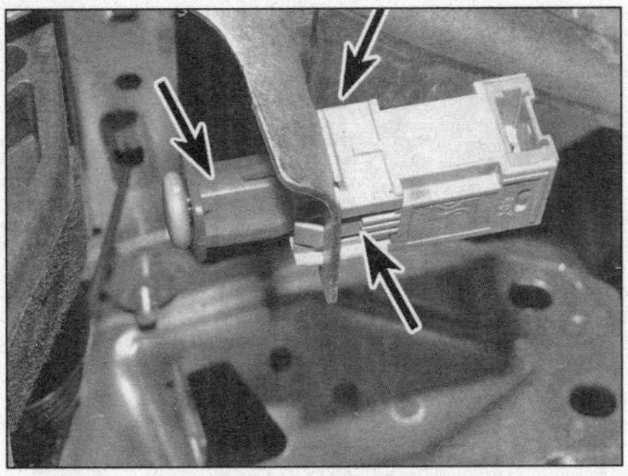

4.36 Pull out the locking sleeve and depress the clips (arrowed)

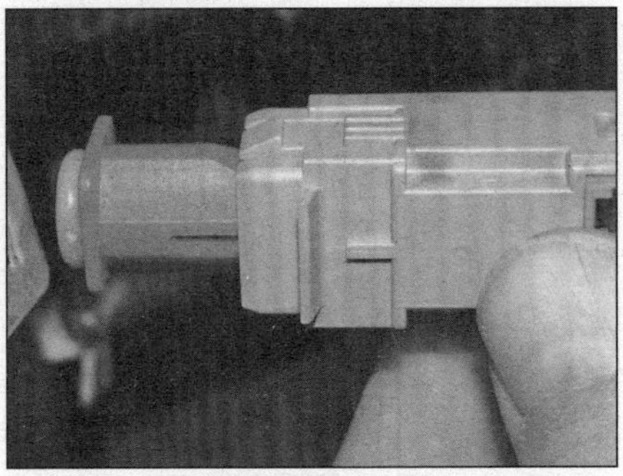

4.38 Pull out the locking sleeve before refitting the switch

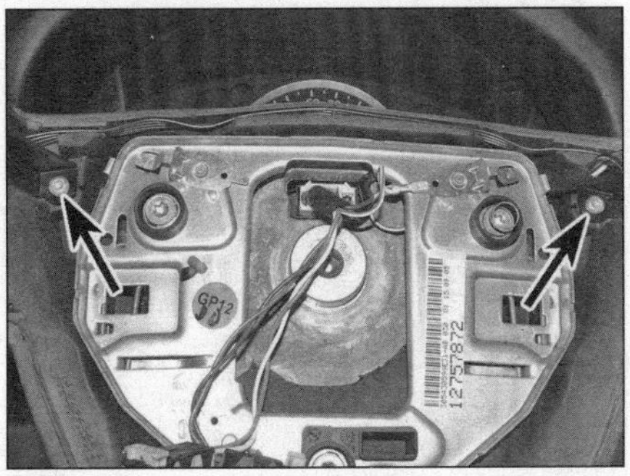

4.49a Undo the steering wheel switch Torx screws (arrowed)

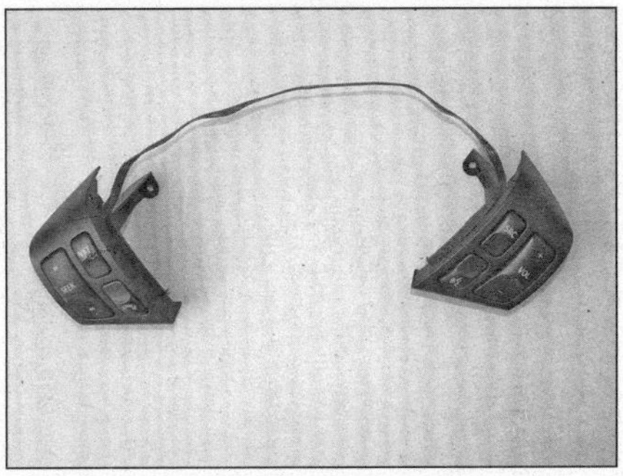

4.49b The steering wheel switches are supplied as an assembly, complete with the wiring loom

Rear roof lights

5 Pull the rear edge of the lens/cover down from the interior light **(see illustration)**.
6 Remove the reading light bulbs by pushing and twisting, or prise the interior light festoon bulb from the contacts **(see illustration)**.
7 Fit the new bulb(s) using a reversal of the removal procedure.

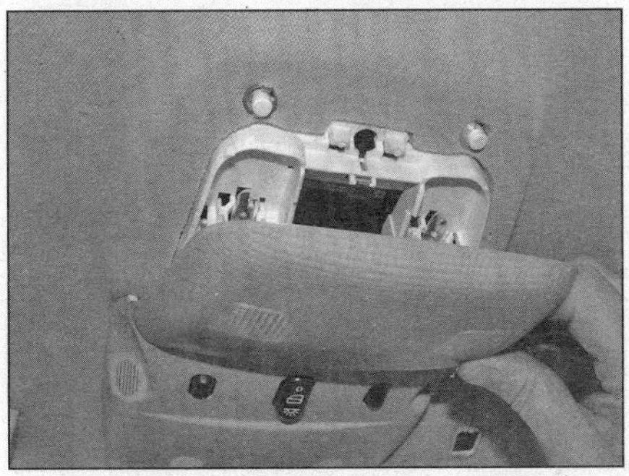

5.2 Pull down the rear edge of the lens ...

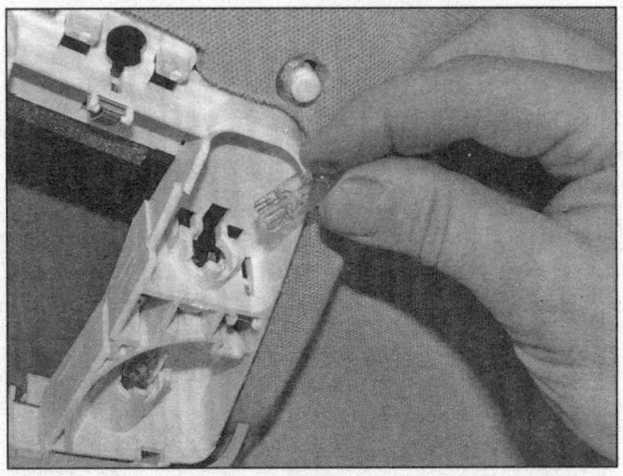

5.3 ... then pull the wedge bulb from place

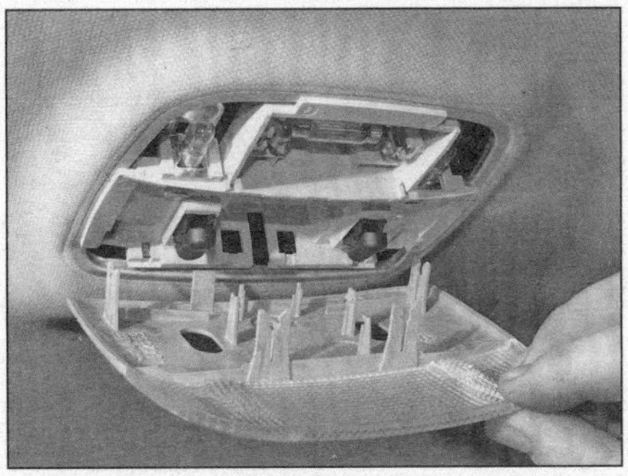

5.5 Pull the down the rear edge of the centre light lens

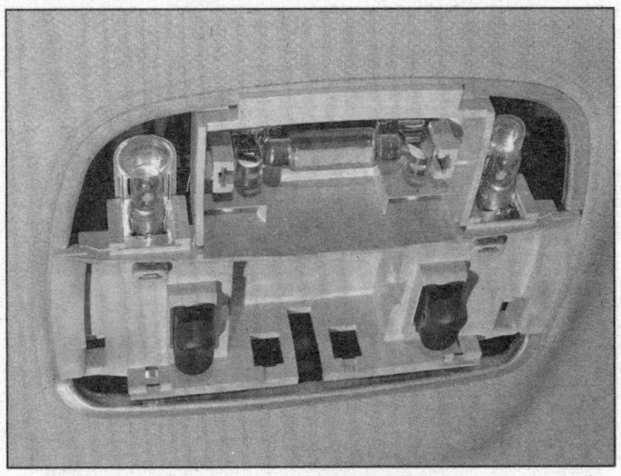

5.6 The reading light bulbs push-and-twist, and the interior light bulb pulls from place

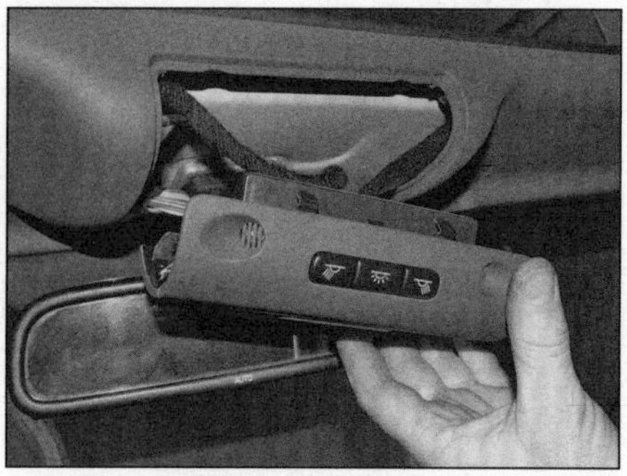

5.8a Pull the down the rear edge first

5.8b Release the clips and disconnect the wiring plug

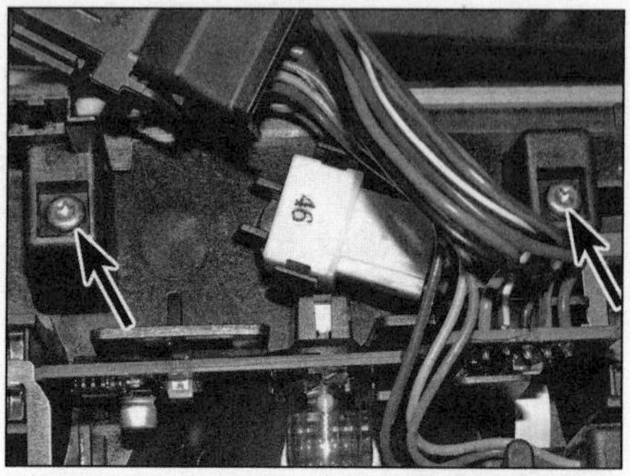

5.9a Undo the 2 screws (arrowed) and remove the lens ...

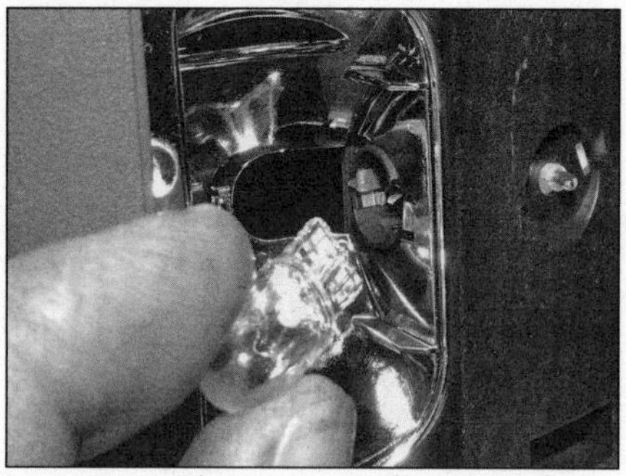

5.9b ... then pull the bulb from the holder

5.12a Twist the bulbholder anti-clockwise

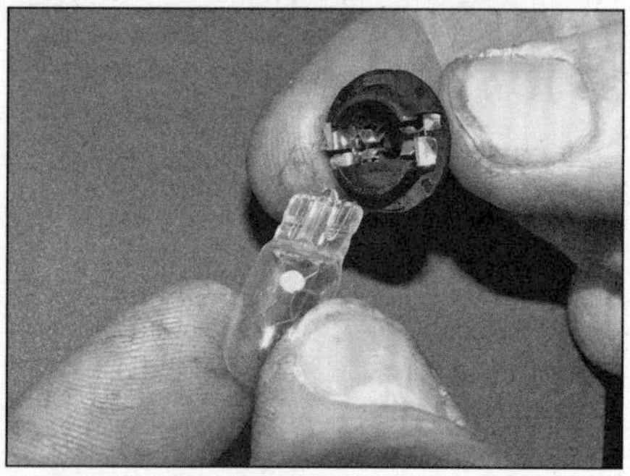

5.12b Pull the bulb from the holder

Roof light – Convertible models

8 Starting at the rear, carefully prise down the light assembly, then release the clips and detach the electrical connector **(see illustrations)**.

9 Undo the 2 retaining screws, lower the lens assembly and then pull the wedge type bulb to remove it from the bulbholder **(see illustrations)**.

10 Fit the new bulb using a reversal of the removal procedure.

Reading light – Convertible models

11 Starting at the rear edge, carefully prise down the light assembly. The bulbs are accessed from the rear of assembly.

12 Twist the bulbholder anti-clockwise and pull the bulbholder from the light. Pull the wedge bulb from the holder **(see illustrations)**.

13 Fit the new bulb using a reversal of the removal procedure.

Air conditioning/ climate control illumination

14 The air conditioning/climate control panel is illuminated by non-renewable LEDs.

Glovebox/luggage compartment/ courtesy/floor illumination

15 Carefully prise the light unit from position **(see illustrations)**.

16 Pull the bulb from the contacts **(see illustrations)**.

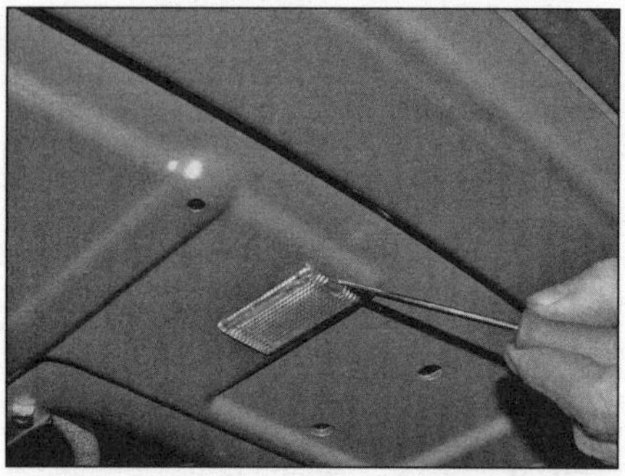

5.15a Prise the light unit from place

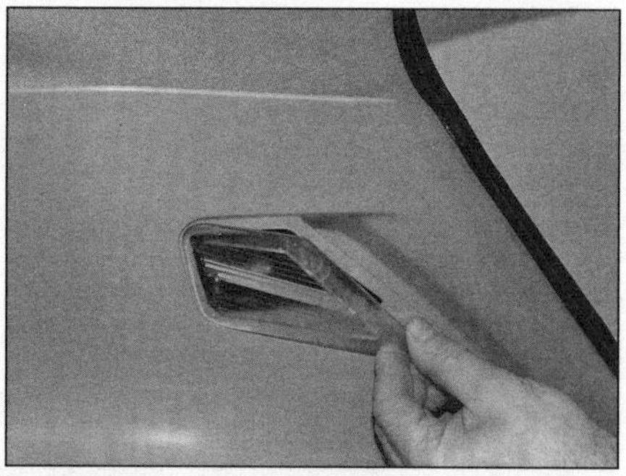

5.15b The Estate model uses a slightly different lamp

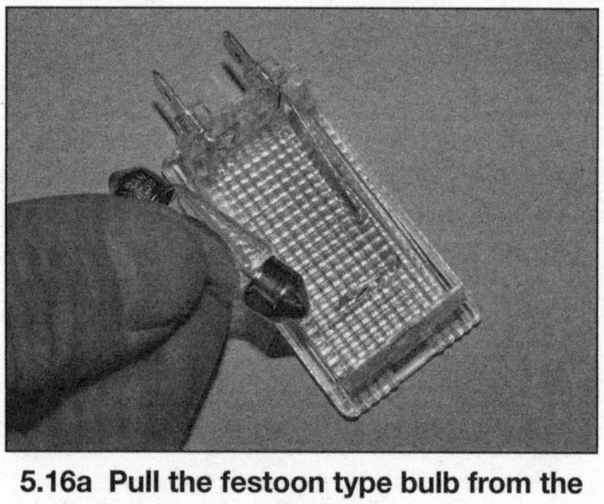

5.16a Pull the festoon type bulb from the contacts ...

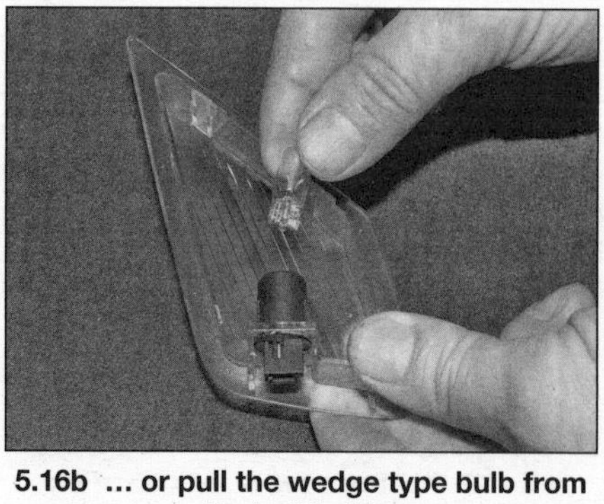

5.16b ... or pull the wedge type bulb from the bulbholder

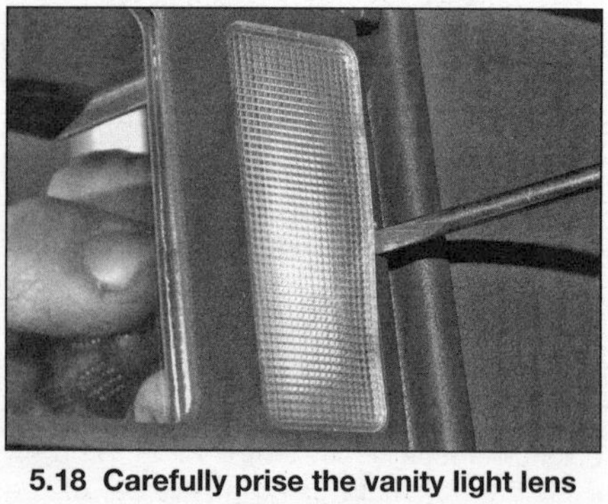

5.18 Carefully prise the vanity light lens from place

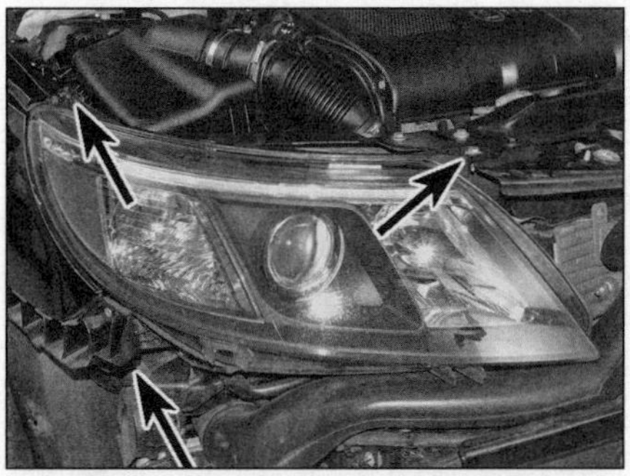

6.2 Undo the 2 upper bolts and the single lower bolt (arrowed)

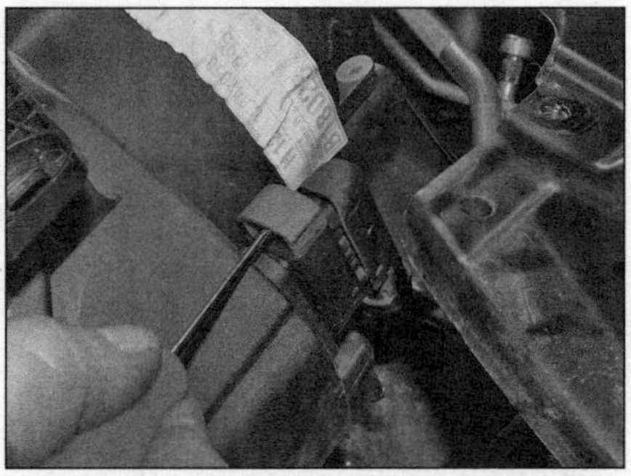

6.4 Prise up the blue locking catch and disconnect the wiring plug

6.5 Screw the adjuster fully home

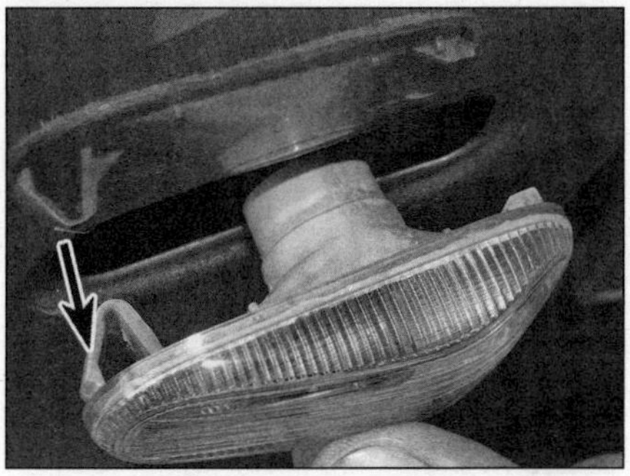

6.6 Press the side repeater against the spring clip (arrowed)

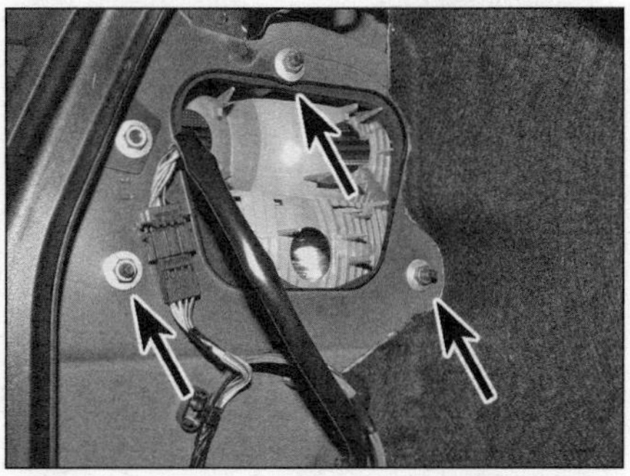

6.10 Rear light retaining nuts (arrowed)

6.13 Boot lid mounted light retaining nuts (arrowed)

17 Fit the new bulb using a reversal of the removal procedure.

Vanity lighting

18 Use a small screwdriver to carefully prise the lens from the light unit **(see illustration)**.

19 Pull the wedge type bulb from the bulbholder.

20 Fit the new bulb using a reversal of the removal procedure.

6 Exterior light units – removal and refitting

Headlight

1 Remove the front bumper cover as described in Chapter 11, Section 6.

2 Undo the headlight upper and lower retaining bolts **(see illustration)**.

3 Manoeuvre the headlight from place.

4 Disconnect the wiring plug as the headlight is withdrawn **(see illustration)**.

5 Refitting is a reversal of removal, but ensure that the lower adjustable screw is screwed in fully before refitting the headlight **(see illustration)**.

Side repeater light

6 Carefully press the light forwards against the tension of the plastic clip, then release the rear of the light from the front wing **(see illustration)**.

7 Rotate the bulbholder anti-clockwise and pull it from the lens.

8 Refitting is a reversal of removal,

Rear light cluster – Saloon models

Rear wing mounted lights

9 Open the boot lid, and open the side hatch.

10 Remove the 3 retaining nuts **(see illustration)**, and remove the light unit. Disconnect the wiring plug as the unit is withdrawn.

11 Refitting is a reversal of removal.

Boot lid mounted lights

12 Remove the boot lid trim panel as described in Chapter 11, Section 26.

13 Undo the 2 retaining nuts, disconnect the wiring plug, and remove the light unit **(see illustration)**.

14 Refitting is a reversal of removal.

Rear light cluster – Estate models

15 Prise out the luggage compartment light unit, and undo the upper retaining nut **(see illustration)**.

16 Prise out the access panel, then undo the 3 retaining nuts and remove the light unit **(see illustrations)**. Disconnect the wiring plug as the unit is withdrawn.

17 Refitting is a reversal of removal.

6.15 Access the upper retaining nut with a socket and long extension bar

6.16a Access to the lamp mounting bolts is limited ...

6.16b ... so consider removing the trim to gain access to the fixings (arrowed)

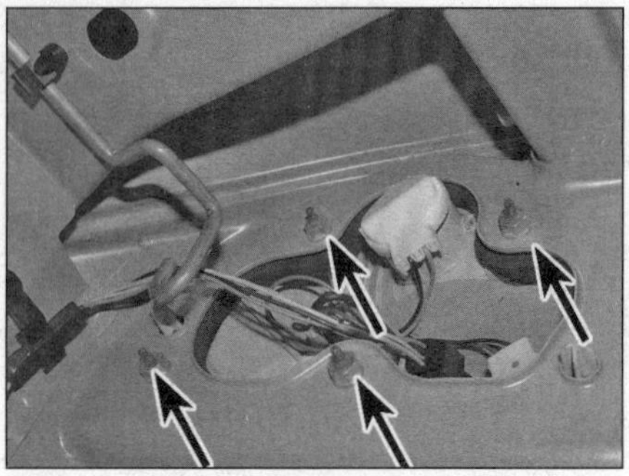

6.19 Rear light unit retaining nuts (arrowed) – Convertible models

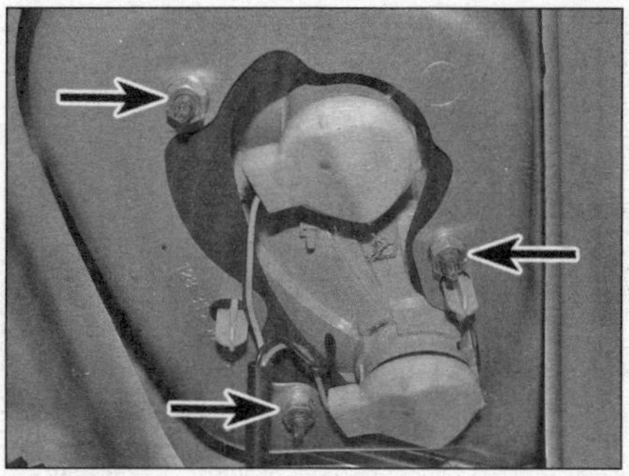

6.23 Boot lid light retaining nuts (arrowed) – Convertible models

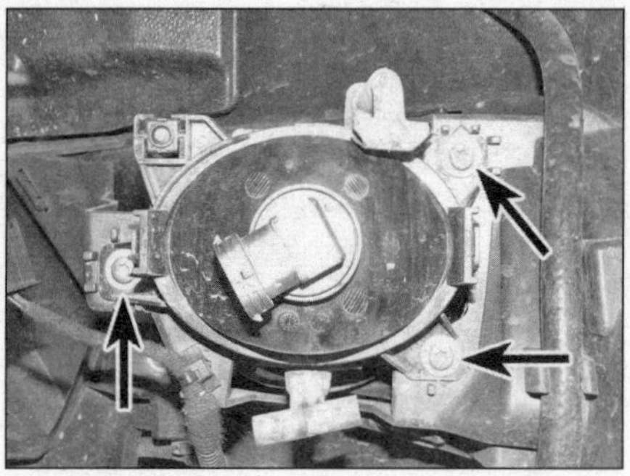

6.26 Foglight retaining nuts (arrowed)

Rear light cluster – Convertible models

Rear wing mounted lights

18 Remove the cover from the luggage compartment side trim panel behind the rear light cluster.

19 Undo the 4 retaining nuts and remove the light unit **(see illustration)**. Disconnect the wiring plug as the unit is withdrawn.

20 Refitting is a reversal of removal.

Boot lid mounted lights

21 Remove the boot trim panel as described in Chapter 11, Section 26.

22 Disconnect the light unit wiring plug, and release the loom from any clips.

23 Undo the 3 retaining nuts and remove the light unit **(see illustration)**.

24 Refitting is a reversal of removal.

Front foglight

25 Remove the bumper cover as described in Chapter 11, Section 6.

26 Undo the 3 foglight retaining screws, and disconnect the wiring plug **(see illustration)**.

27 Remove the foglight.

28 Refitting is a reversal of removal. If required, the aim of the foglight can be adjusted by means of the screw in the lower grille **(see illustration)**.

Number plate light

29 The lamps are part of the tailgate/boot release assembly.

30 Undo the Torx screws and withdraw the lens from the number plate light. then prise the lens from the tailgate/boot lid.

31 Remove the tailgate/boot trim as described in Chapter 11, Section 26, remove the 4 mounting bolts, disconnect the wiring plug and remove the complete assembly.

32 Refitting is a reversal of removal.

High-level brake light

Saloon models

33 Pull down the rear edge, and carefully remove the lamp cover from the screen **(see illustration)**.

34 Disconnect the wiring plug, pull out the 2 catches, and remove the light unit **(see illustration)**.

35 Refitting is a reversal of removal.

Estate models

36 Pull the upper trim panel above the rear window from the tailgate **(see illustration)**.

37 Pull the window side trims inwards to release the retaining clips.

38 Remove the 2 rubber plugs, then undo the 5 nuts securing the spoiler to the tailgate **(see illustrations)**.

6.28 Front foglight adjustment screw (arrowed)

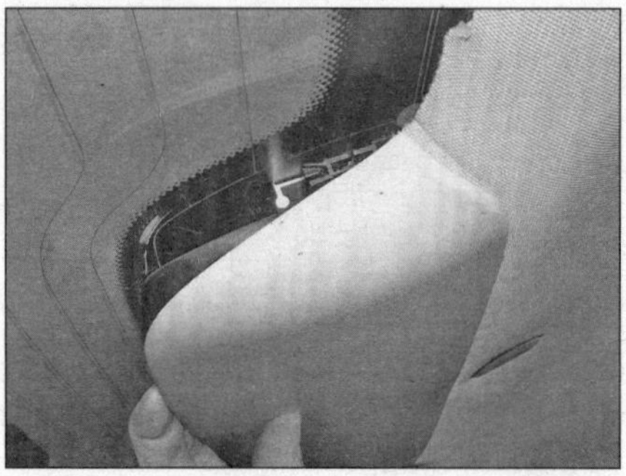

6.33 Pull down the rear edge and remove the light cover

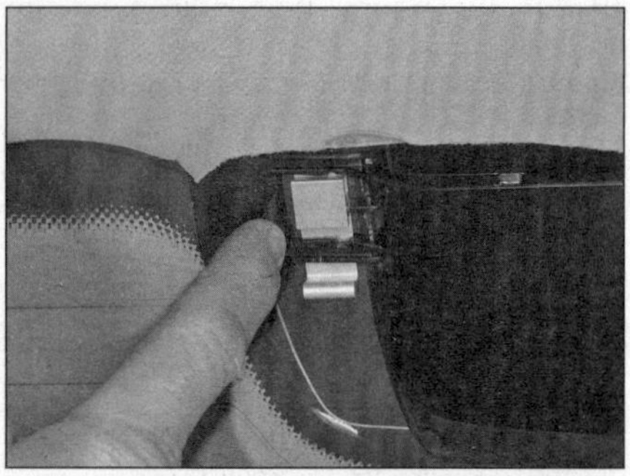

6.34 Slide out the clip each side

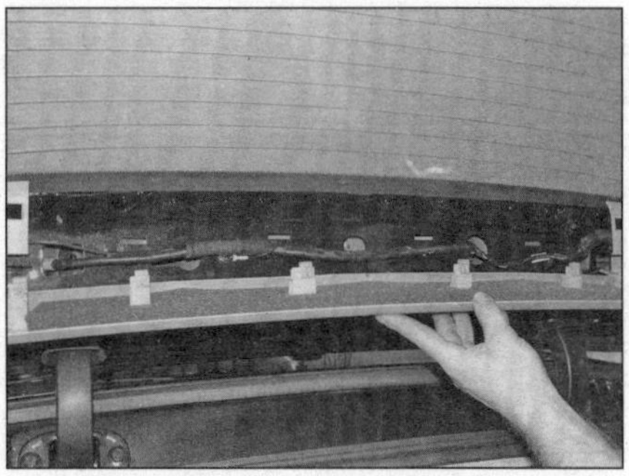

6.36 Pull the tailgate upper trim panel away to release the clips

6.38a Remove the blanking plugs ...

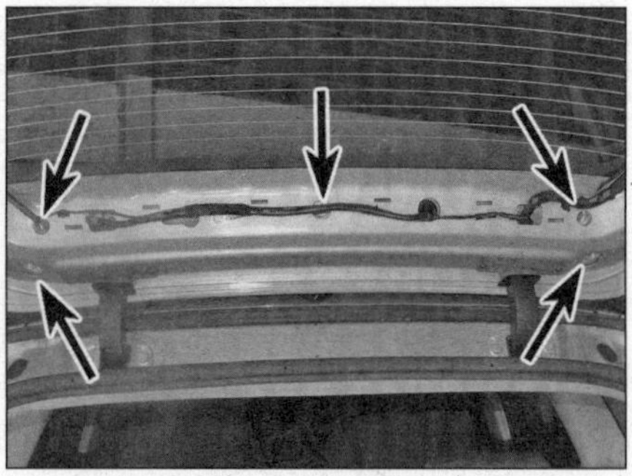

6.38b ... and then remove the retaining nuts (arrowed)

39 Disconnecting the wiring plug and washer tube. Lift the spoiler from the tailgate.

40 Undo the 2 Torx screws and remove the brake light **(see illustration)**.

41 Refitting is a reversal of removal.

Convertible models

42 Remove the boot lid trim panel as described in Chapter 11, Section 26.

43 Disconnect the wiring plug, undo the 3 nuts and remove the light unit **(see illustration)**.

44 Refitting is a reversal of removal.

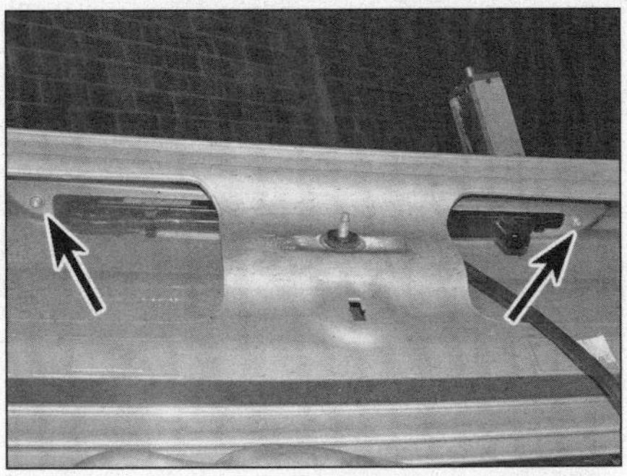

6.40 High-level brake light Torx screws (arrowed)

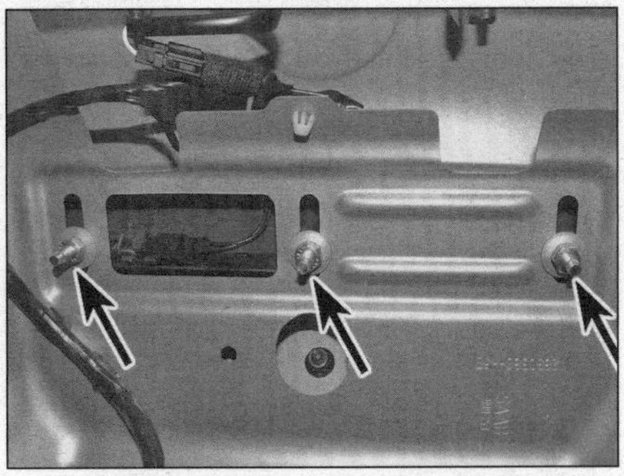

6.43 High-level brake light retaining nuts (arrowed) – Convertible models

7 Exterior light bulbs – renewal

1 Whenever a bulb is renewed, note the following points:

a) Remember that, if the light has just been in use, the bulb may be extremely hot.

b) Do not touch the bulb glass with the fingers, as this can result in early failure or a dull reflector.

c) Always check the bulb contacts and holder, ensuring that there is clean metal-to-metal contact between the bulb and its live and earth. Clean off any corrosion or dirt before fitting a new bulb.

d) Ensure that the new bulb is of the correct rating.

Main beam and halogen headlight dipped beam

Left-hand headlight

2 Lift aside the coolant hose and wiring loom from alongside the battery cover **(see illustration)**.

3 Rotate the 2 fasteners 90° anti-clockwise and remove the battery cover **(see illustration)**.

4 If renewing the dipped beam bulb, pull the washer fluid filler pipe from place **(see illustration)**.

5 Detach the air inlet pipe from the lower battery cover.

Both headlights

6 Pull off the cover from the rear of the headlight **(see illustration)**.

7 Rotate the bulbholder anti-clockwise and pull it from the reflector **(see illustration)**.

8 Pull the bulb from the holder, taking care not to touch the glass with bare fingers **(see illustration)**.

9 Fit the new bulb using a reversal of the removal procedure.

Xenon headlight dipped beam

Warning: Xenon headlight bulbs operate at high voltage. Before starting this procedure, ensure the ignition is turned off, and wait at least 5 minutes for any residual electrical charge to dissipate.

Caution: Xenon bulbs are pressurised to approximately 7.0 bar. Wear protective goggles and gloves before starting this procedure.

10 Remove the headlight as described in Section 6.

11 Undo the 2 retaining screws and remove the ballast unit **(see illustration)**.

12 Remove the plastic cover from the rear of the headlight **(see illustration)**.

13 Disconnect the wiring plug.

14 Rotate the bulb anti-clockwise and remove it from headlight **(see illustration)**.

7.2 Unclip the coolant hose and loom (arrowed)

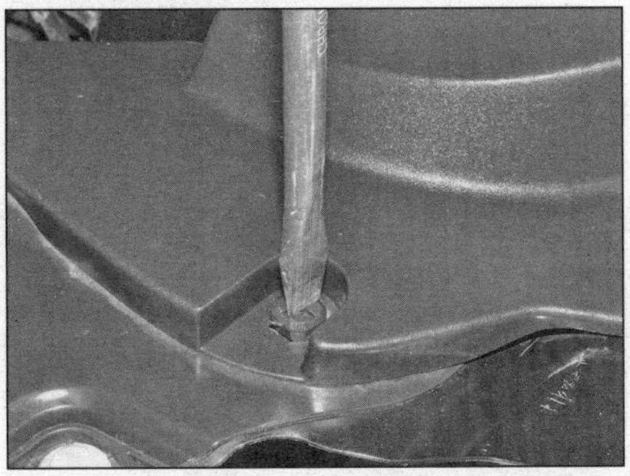

7.3 Rotate the battery cover fasteners 90° anti-clockwise

7.4 Pull up the washer filler pipe from behind the left-hand headlight

7.6 Pull the cover from the rear of the headlight

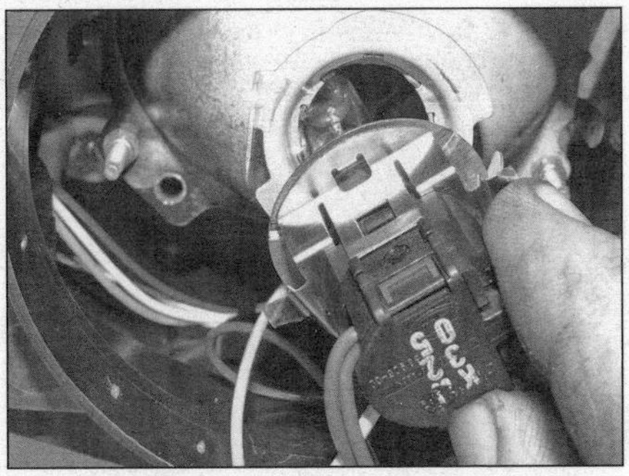

7.7 Rotate the bulbholder anti-clockwise and pull it from the reflector

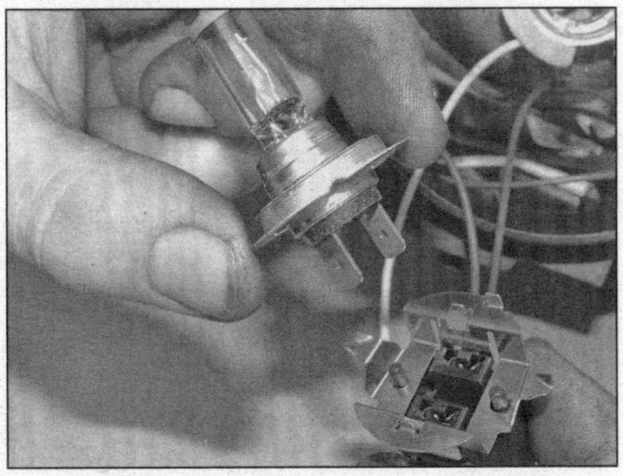

7.8 Pull the bulb from the holder

7.11 Undo the 2 Torx screws (arrowed) and remove the ballast unit

7.12 Remove the bulb cover

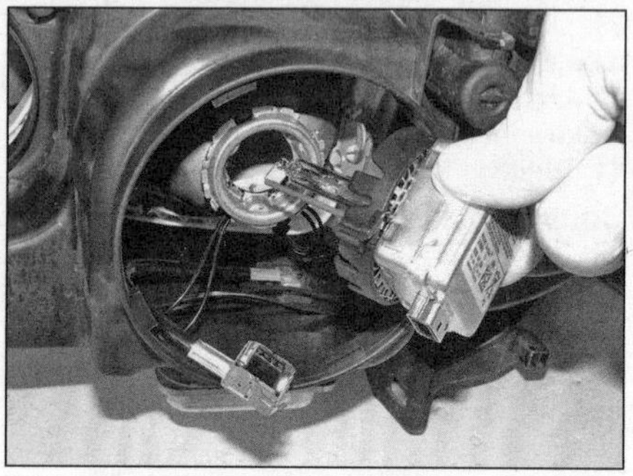

7.14 Remove the bulb

15 Fit a new bulb using a reversal of the removal procedure.

Front sidelight

16 Illumination for the front sidelights is provided by a series of LEDs (light emitting diodes). If a fault develops with the sidelights the headlight must be renewed as a complete unit (as described in Section 6).

Front direction indicator

17 If renewing the left-hand side sidelight bulb, carry out the procedures described in paragraphs 2 to 5 of this Section.

18 With difficulty reach the bulbholder and twist it anti-clockwise to remove it **(see illustration)**. A pair of pliers can be used to remove the bulbholder if necessary.

19 Depress and twist the bulb to remove it from the bulbholder **(see illustration)**.

20 Fit the new bulb using a reversal of the removal procedure.

Side repeater lights

21 Carefully press the light forwards against the tension of the plastic clip, then release the rear of the light from the front wing **(see illustration 6.6)**.

22 Twist the bulbholder and remove the lens unit, then pull out the wedge type bulb **(see illustrations)**. Do not allow the wiring to drop into the space behind the wing.

23 Fit the new bulb using a reversal of the removal procedure.

Rear light cluster – Saloon models

Wing mounted lights

24 Open the boot lid, release the clip and remove the access panel from the side trim panel.

25 Lift the retaining clip and pull the bulbholder assembly from the light unit **(see illustrations)**.

26 Depress and twist the relevant bulb and remove it from the bulbholder.

27 Fit the new bulb using a reversal of the removal procedure.

Boot lid mounted lights

28 Undo the 2 screws securing the grab handle to the inside of the boot lid, push in the centre pins, prise out the rivets, and remove the boot lid trim panel.

29 Release the retaining clip and remove the bulbholder assembly **(see illustration)**.

30 Depress and twist the relevant bulb and remove it from the bulbholder.

31 Fit the new bulb using a reversal of the removal procedure.

7.18 Twist indicator bulbholder anti-clockwise and pull it from the headlight

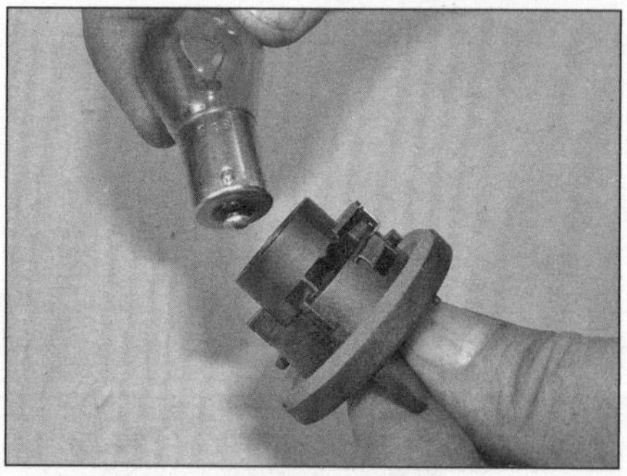

7.19 Push and twist the bulb to release it

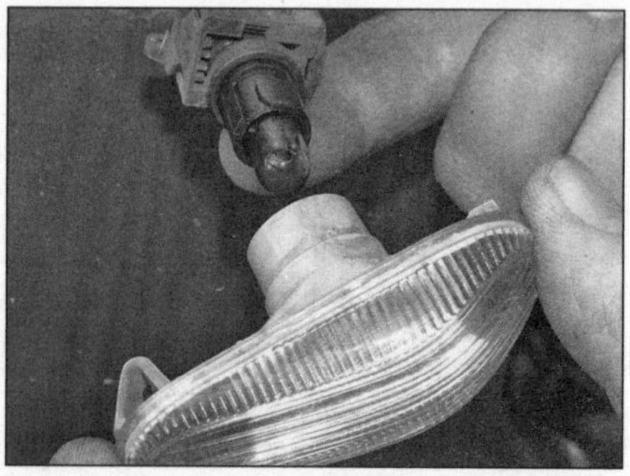

7.22a Twist the bulbholder anti-clockwise, remove it from the lens ...

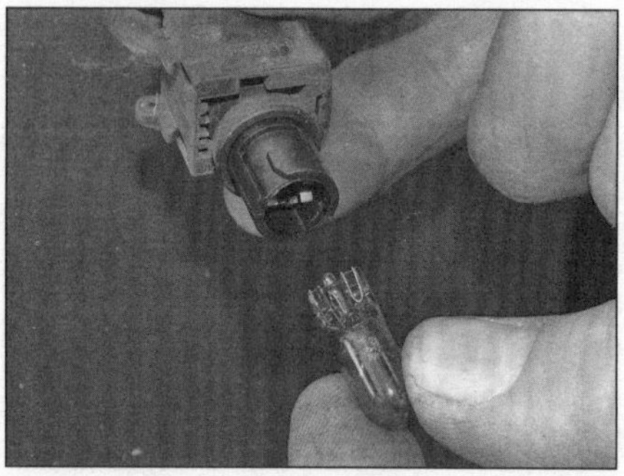

7.22b ... then pull the bulb from the holder

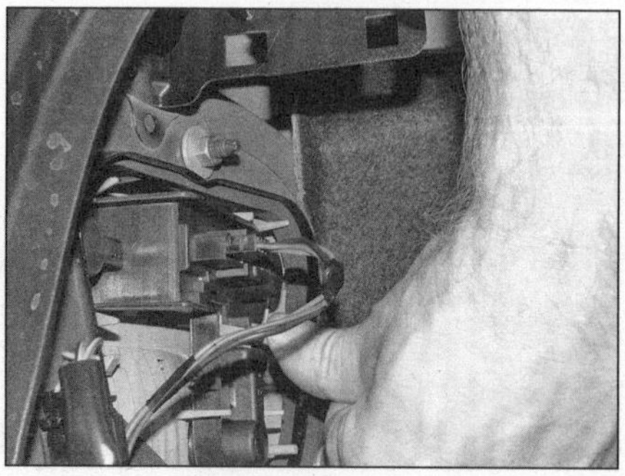

7.25a Lift the clip ...

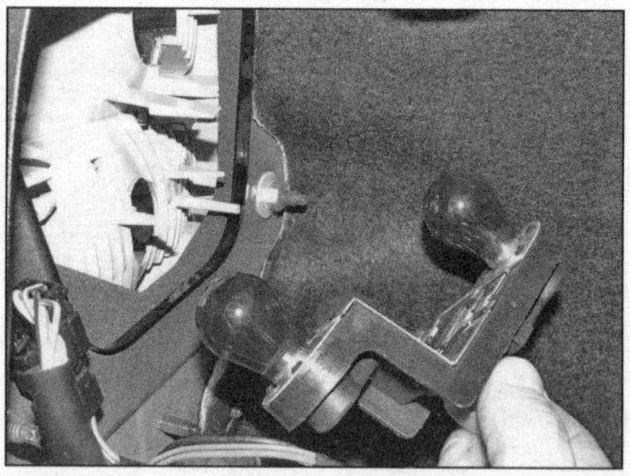

7.25b ... and remove the bulbholder

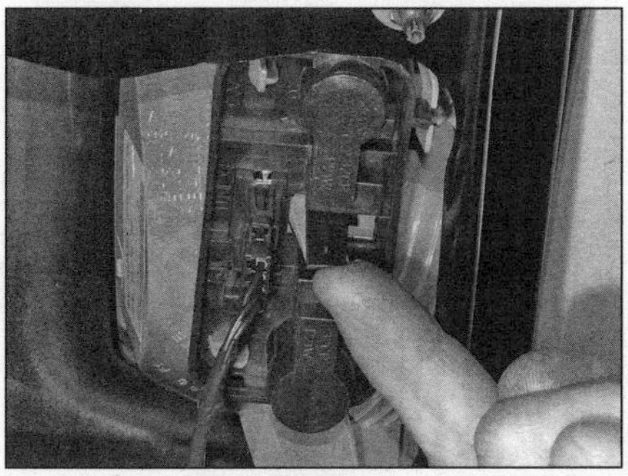
7.29 Lift the clip and remove the bulbholder

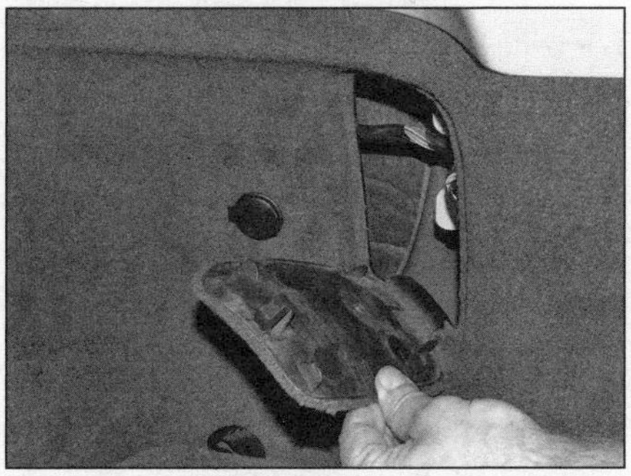
7.32 Remove the access panel

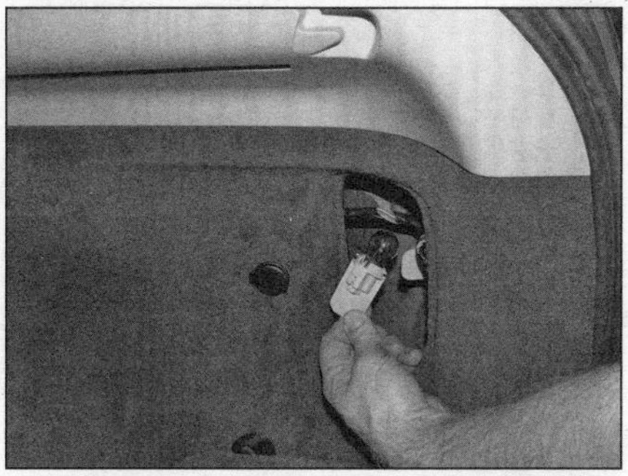
7.33 Rotate and remove the bulbholder

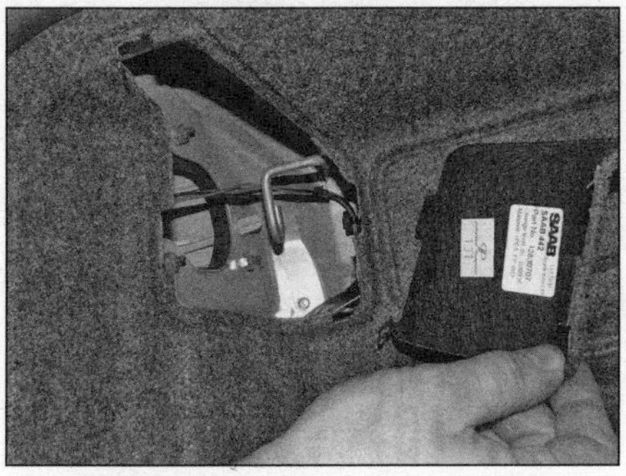
7.36 Remove the access panel

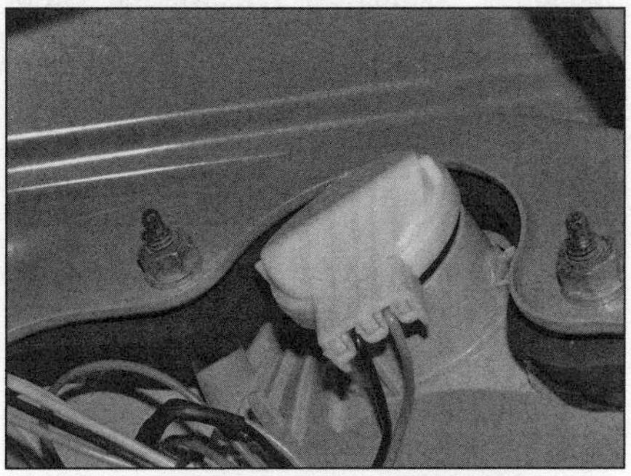
7.37 Rotate the bulbholder anti-clockwise ...

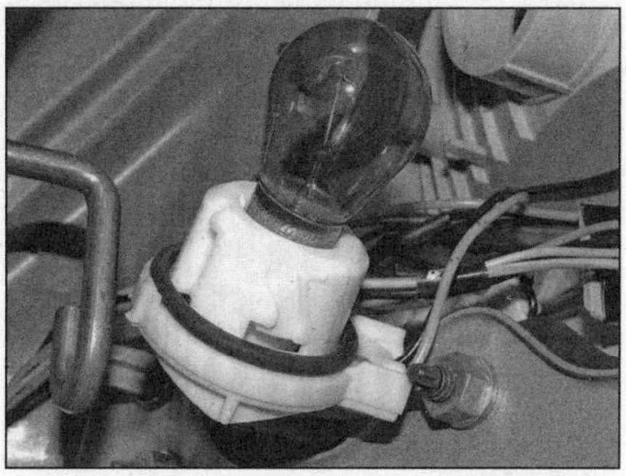
7.38 ... then depress and twist the bulb anti-clockwise to remove it

Rear light cluster – Estate models

32 Open the tailgate and remove the access panel from the luggage compartment side trim panel **(see illustration)**.

33 Rotate the relevant bulbholder anti-clockwise and pull it from the light unit **(see illustration)**.

34 Depress and twist the relevant bulb and remove it from the bulbholder.

35 Fit the new bulb using a reversal of the removal procedure.

Rear light cluster – Convertible models

Wing mounted lights

36 Remove the access panel from the luggage compartment side trim panel **(see illustration)**.

37 Rotate the relevant bulbholder anti-clockwise and pull it from the light unit **(see illustration)**.

38 Depress and twist the relevant bulb and remove it from the bulbholder **(see illustration)**.

39 Fit the new bulb using a reversal of the removal procedure.

Boot lid mounted lights

40 Remove the boot lid trim panel as described in Chapter 11, Section 26.

41 Rotate the relevant bulbholder anti-clockwise and pull it from the light unit **(see illustration)**.

42 Depress and twist the relevant bulb and remove it from the bulbholder.

43 Fit the new bulb using a reversal of the removal procedure.

Front foglight

44 Undo the screw securing the lower spoiler shield to the wheel arch liner, and pull the shield down.

45 Disconnect the wiring plug **(see illustration)**

46 Rotate the bulbholder and remove it from the foglight **(see illustration)**. Do not touch the glass with your fingers.

47 Fit the new bulb using a reversal of the removal procedure.

Number plate light

48 Undo the Torx screws and withdraw the lens from the number plate light **(see illustration)**.

49 Pull out the festoon bulb **(see illustration)**.

50 Fit the new bulb using a reversal of the

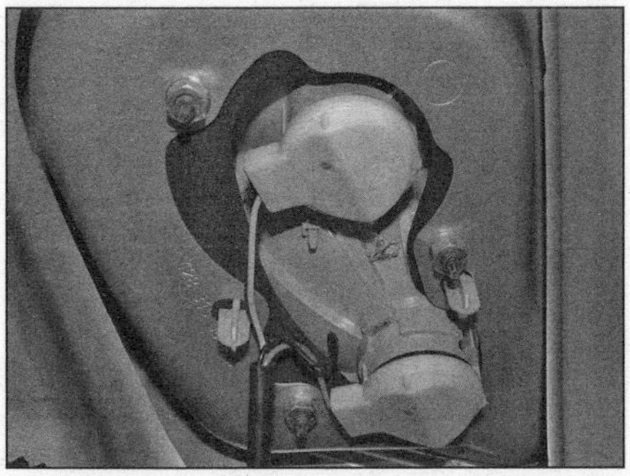
7.41 Rotate the bulbholder anti-clockwise

7.45 Disconnect the wiring plug

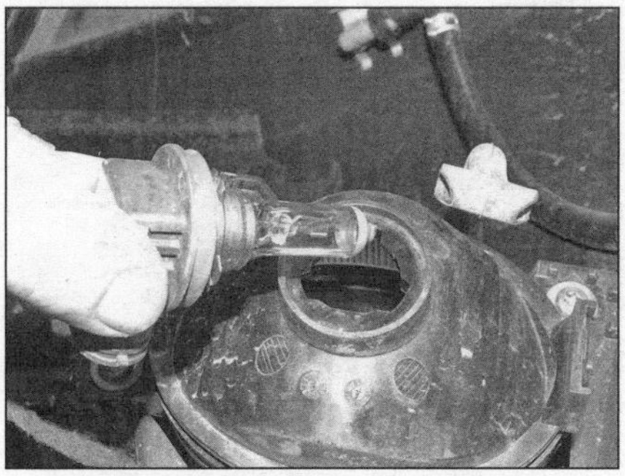
7.46 Remove the bulbholder

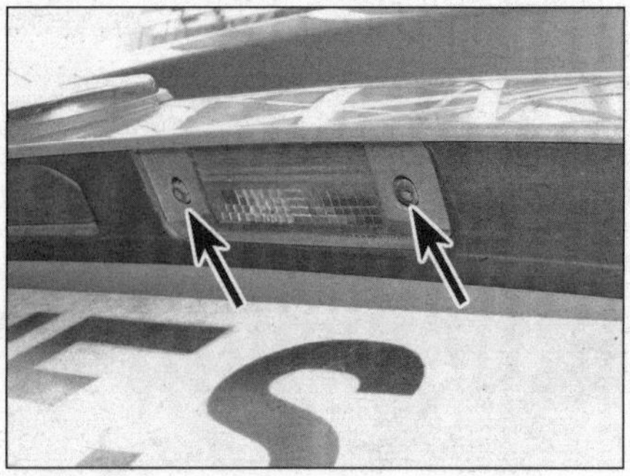

7.48 Undo the 2 Torx screws (arrowed) ...

removal procedure, ensuring the rubber seal is correctly fitted.

High-level brake light

51 On all models, the high-level brake lights are illuminated by LEDs, and are not renewable. If the LEDs fail, the complete light unit must be renewed as described in Section 6.

8 Headlight beam adjustment – general information

1 Accurate adjustment of the headlight beam is only possible using optical beam-setting equipment, and this work should therefore be carried out by a Saab dealer or suitably-equipped workshop. In an emergency, it is possible to adjust the headlights by turning the screws located on the rear of the headlight **(see illustration)**.

2 All models have a headlight beam

7.49 ... and pull the number plate light festoon bulb from its contacts

adjustment control, which allows the aim of the headlights to be adjusted to compensate for variation in the vehicle's payload.

3 On models with xenon the headlights are controlled by sensors on the front suspension, on models with halogen headlights, the aim is altered by means of facia mounted switch, which controls electric adjuster motors located in the rear of the headlight assemblies. The switch should be positioned as follows, according to the load being carried in the vehicle:

Switch position	Vehicle load
1	Up to 3 occupants in rear seats, up to 30 kg in luggage.
2	Up to 3 occupants in rear seats, up to 80 kg in luggage.
3	Up to 5 occupants, luggage area full, towing caravan/trailer.

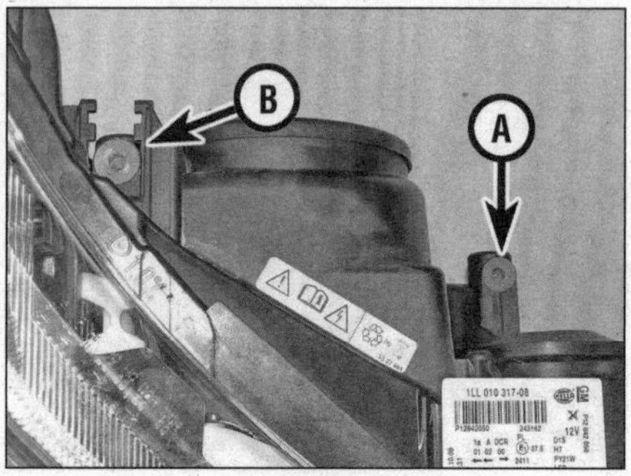

8.1 Headlight vertical adjustment (A) and horizontal adjustment (B)

9 Instrument panel – removal and refitting

Note: *If the instrument panel is to be renewed, have the systems stored values extracted, then reprogrammed into the new unit using dedicated diagnostic equipment (TECH 2) by a Saab dealer or a suitably-equipped specialist.*

Removal

1 Using several small screwdrivers through the air vent grilles, release the hooks and remove the centre- and right-hand air vents from each side of the instrument panel **(see illustrations)**. Locate the screwdrivers exactly as shown, as failure to do so will result in the front section of the vent separating from the main body of the vent. If the front section becomes separated the movable vanes of the vent will collapse and whilst it is possible to rebuild the vent it is a complicated mechanism that requires time and patience to repair.

2 Undo the 2 Torx screws and pull the infotainment control panel from place **(see illustrations)**. Disconnect the wiring plug as the panel is withdrawn.

3 Reach through the aperture, squeeze the retaining clips together, and starting at the top, push the switch panel from the facia **(see illustration)**. Disconnect the wiring plug as the panel is withdrawn.

4 Undo the 7 screws and pull the instrument panel surround trim from place **(see illustrations)**. Where applicable, disconnect the wiring plugs as the trim is removed.

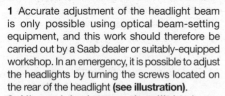

9.1a Locate the small screwdrivers exactly as shown on the top ...

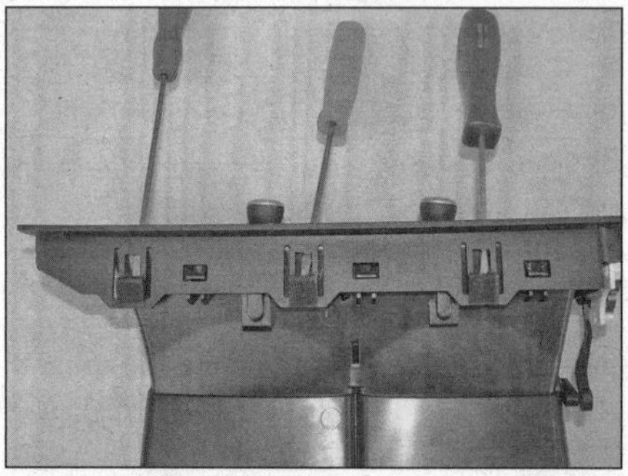

9.1b ... and the bottom of the centre vent

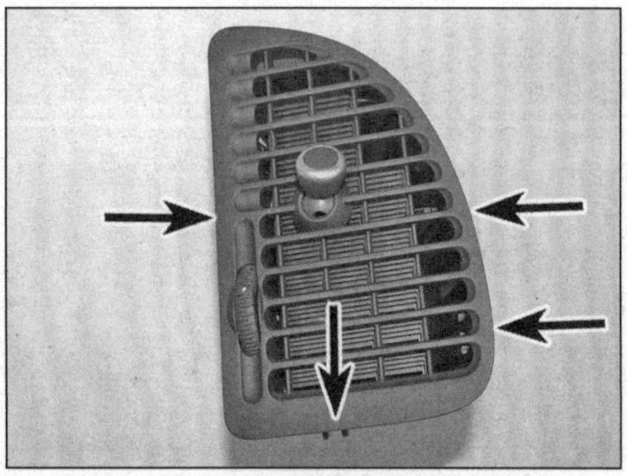

9.1c On the side vent locate the screwdriver(s) at the points shown ...

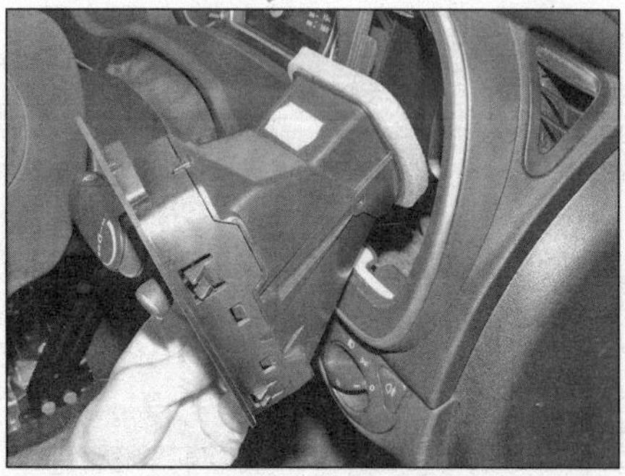

9.1d ... and remove the vent

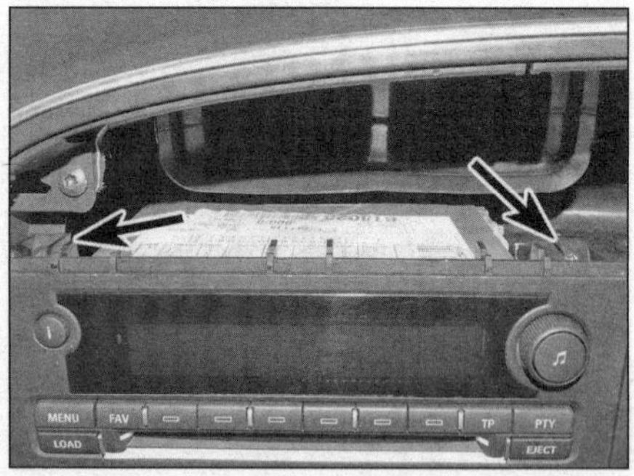

9.2a Remove the Torx screws (arrowed) ...

9.2b ... lift up and then pull the unit forward to release it

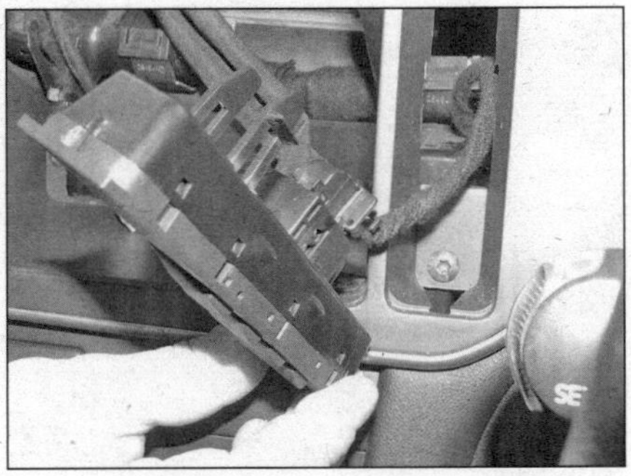

9.3 Remove the switch panel

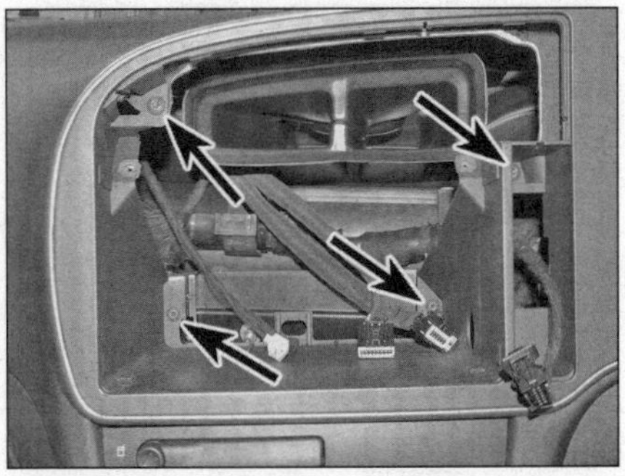

9.4a Undo the 4 Torx screws (arrowed) on the left ...

5 Undo the instrument panel mounting screws, pull it forward and disconnect the wiring plug **(see illustrations)**.

Caution: All modules are extremely sensitive to static electricity. Before touching the instrument panel, earth yourself by touching a bare metal part of the vehicle body or engine/transmission.

6 Manoeuvre the panel from the facia.

Refitting

7 Refitting is a reversal of removal.

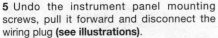

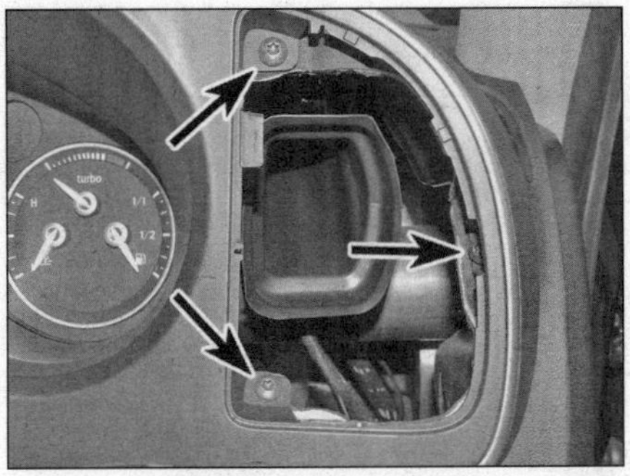

9.4b ... and the 3 on the right-hand side (arrowed)

9.4c Remove the panel

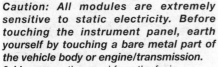

10 Horn – removal and refitting

Removal

1 To access the low tone horn **(see illustration)**, remove the front bumper cover as described in Chapter 11, Section 6.

2 To access the high tone horn **(see illustration)** jack up and support the front of the vehicle (see *Jacking and vehicle support*) and partially remove the right-hand end of the splash shield from below the front bumper.

3 Disconnect the wiring from the appropriate horn.

4 Unscrew the bracket mounting bolt and lift the horn assembly from place.

Refitting

5 Refitting is a reversal of removal.

9.5a Remove instrument cluster Torx screws (arrowed) ...

9.5b ... and remove the panel

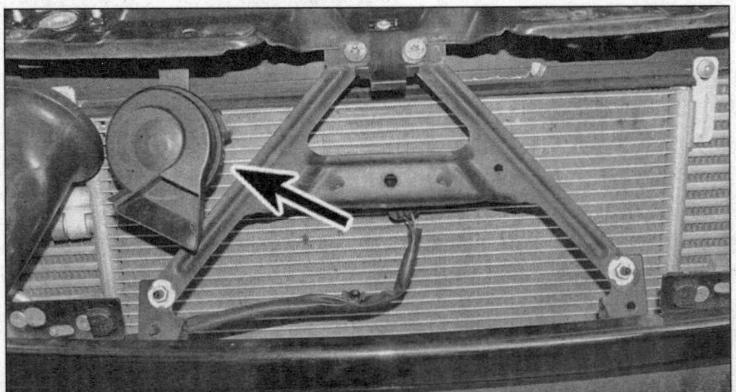

10.1 The low tone horn (arrowed)

10.2 The high tone horn

11.2 Prise up the cover ...

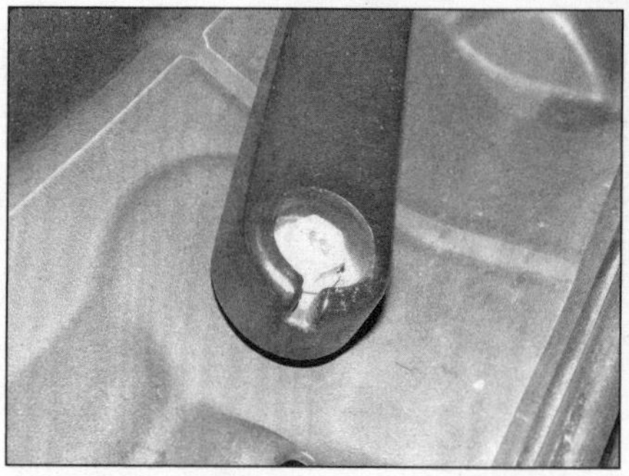

11.3 ... then undo the spindle nut

11.4 If necessary, use a puller to remove the arm from the spindle

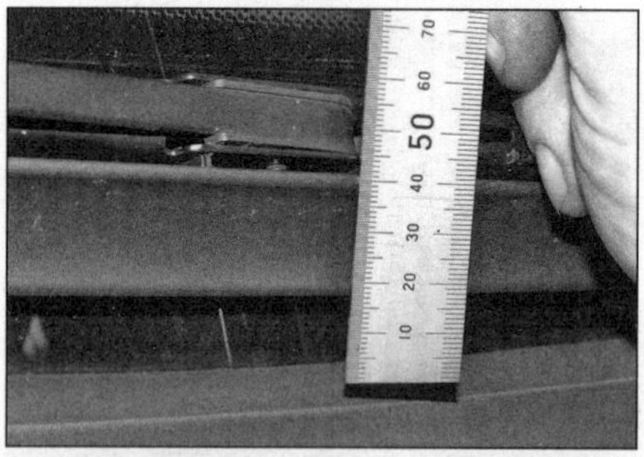

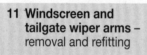

11.5 Set the arms so the distance between the arm mounting and the scuttle trim panel is 45 mm

11.8 Lift up the cover, and unscrew the wiper arm nut

11.9 Special pullers are available to aid removal of the wiper arm

11 Windscreen and tailgate wiper arms – removal and refitting

Windscreen wiper arm

Removal

1 Make sure that the windscreen wipers are at their rest positions. Use a piece of tape to mark the position on the windscreen.

2 Using a screwdriver, prise up the cover from the windscreen wiper arm **(see illustration)**.

3 Unscrew the nut securing the wiper arm to the shaft **(see illustration)**.

4 Ease the arm from the shaft by carefully rocking it side-to-side. If necessary, use a small 2-legged puller (or one specifically designed for the task) to remove the arm **(see illustration)**.

Refitting

5 Refitting is a reversal of removal. If the position of the arms has been lost, set the arms so the distance between the arm mounting in the blade and the scuttle trim panel is 45 mm on both the driver's and passenger's side **(see illustration)**.

Tailgate wiper arm

Removal

6 Make sure that the wiper is at its rest position.

7 Lift up the cover at the base of the tailgate wiper arm.

8 Unscrew the nut securing the wiper arm to the shaft **(see illustration)**.

9 Ease the arm from the shaft by carefully rocking it side-to-side. If necessary, use a small 2-legged puller to remove the arm **(see illustration)**.

Refitting

10 Align the wiper arm with the marks provided in the tailgate glass and tighten the fixing nut to the specified torque.

12 Windscreen and tailgate wiper motor and linkage – removal and refitting

Windscreen wiper motor

Removal

1 Remove the wiper arms as described in Section 11.

2 Pull the weatherstrip from the bulkhead **(see illustration)**.

3 Release the clips and remove the scuttle panel trim **(see illustrations)**.

4 Press up the catch and detach the wiring plug from the bracket, then disconnect the

12.2 Pull the rubber weatherstrip from the bulkhead

12.3a Push in the centre pins and remove the clips at each end ...

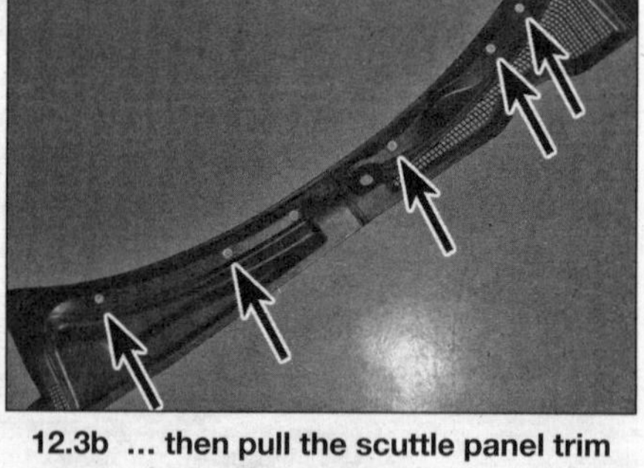

12.3b ... then pull the scuttle panel trim upwards to release the retaining clips (arrowed)

motor wiring plug. Where fitted, cut and remove the cable-tie from the wiring loom.

5 Unscrew the 4 mounting bolts and manoeuvre the wiper motor and linkage from the bulkhead **(see illustrations)**.

6 If required, undo the bolts/nuts and detach the motor from the linkage **(see illustration)**.

Refitting

7 Refitting is a reversal of removal. Renew the cable-tie if one was fitted to the wiring loom.

Tailgate wiper motor

Removal

8 Remove the tailgate trim panel as described in Chapter 11, Section 26.

9 Remove the wiper arm (see Section 11).

10 Disconnect the wiring from the wiper motor.

11 Unscrew the mounting nuts and lower the wiper motor from the tailgate, while guiding the shaft through the rubber grommet **(see illustration)**.

12 If necessary, remove the grommet.

Refitting

13 Refitting is a reversal of removal.

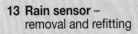

13 Rain sensor – removal and refitting

Saloon and Estate models

1 Using a blunt, flat-bladed tool, carefully prise away the cover from the rain sensor.

2 Disconnect the wiring plug from the sensor.

3 Release the clamps and remove the sensor.

4 Refitting is a reversal of removal.

Convertible models

5 Open the soft-top and remove the sunvisors as described in Chapter 11, Section 26.

6 Carefully prise the interior light unit from place, and disconnect the main wiring plug **(see illustrations 5.9a and 5.9b)**. Note the unit will hang from the wires from the sunvisors.

7 Pull down the plastic cover, then undo the 3 screws and remove the interior mirror assembly **(see illustrations)**.

8 Starting at the front edge, pull the windscreen trim panel downwards, then rearwards **(see illustration)**.

9 Disconnect the rain sensor wiring plug.

10 Release the clamps and remove the sensor **(see illustration)**.

11 Refitting is a reversal of removal.

14 Windscreen, tailgate and headlight washer system – removal and refitting

Removal

Reservoir

1 The washer fluid reservoir and pump are located beneath the front left-hand wing. For access to them, remove the front bumper cover.

2 Note their fitted positions, and disconnect the various hoses and wiring plugs from the pumps/level sensor **(see illustrations)**.

3 Undo the 3 retaining nuts and remove the reservoir **(see illustration)**. Note that the front

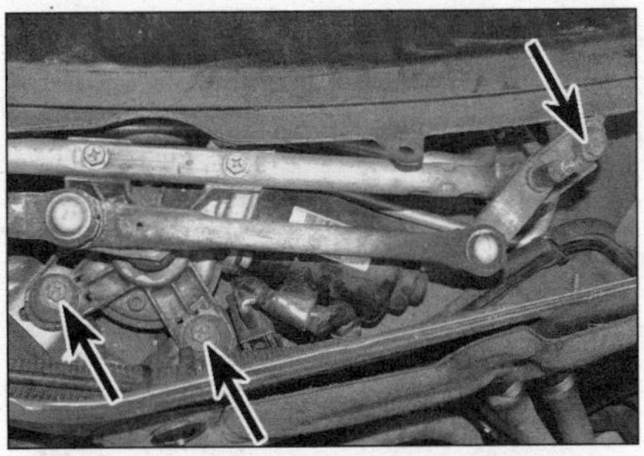

12.5a The windscreen wiper motor is secured by 3 bolts towards the centre (arrowed) ...

12.5b ... and one at the edge (arrowed)

12.6 Undo the bolts/nut and detach the motor from the linkage (arrowed)

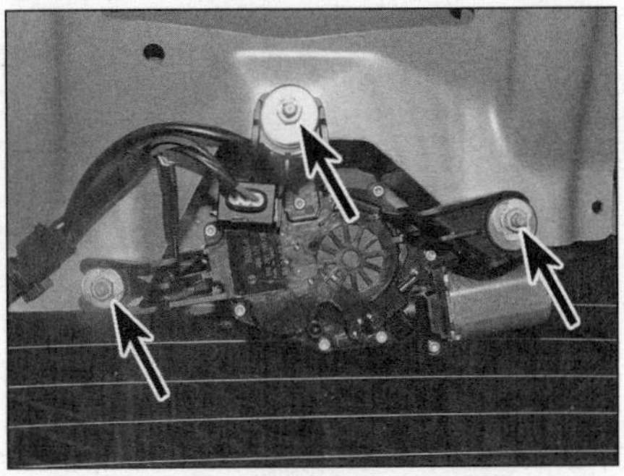

12.11 Wiper motor mounting nuts (arrowed)

13.7a Pull down the plastic cover ...

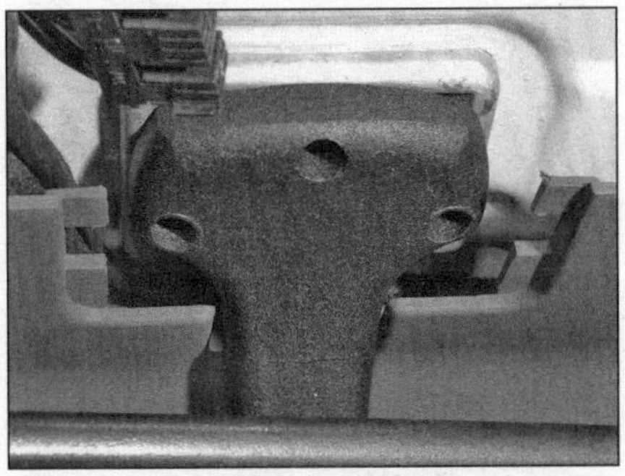

13.7b ... then undo the 3 mirror mounting screws

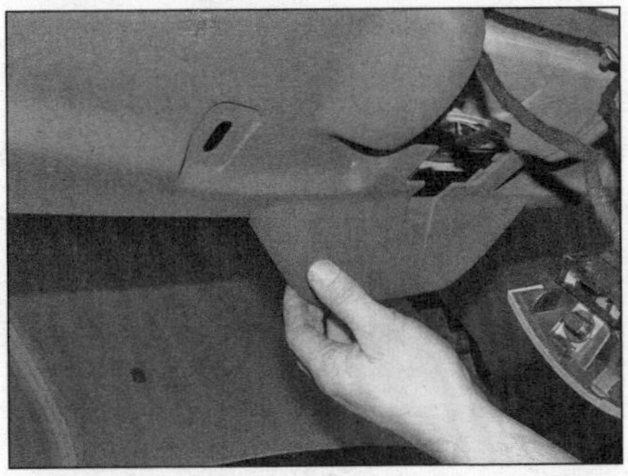

13.8 Pull the front edge of the windscreen trim panel downwards

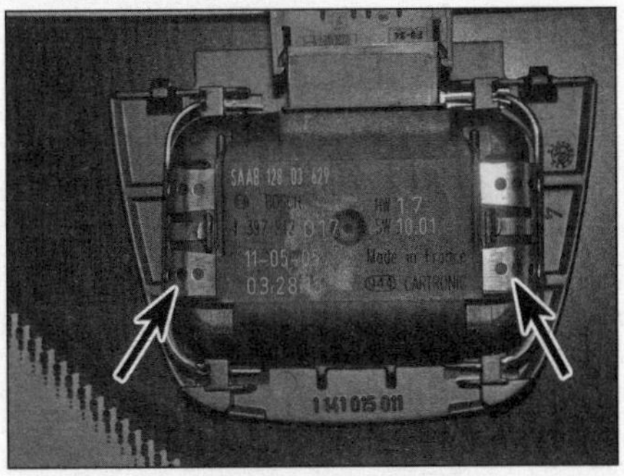

13.10 Prise open the clamps and remove the sensor (arrowed)

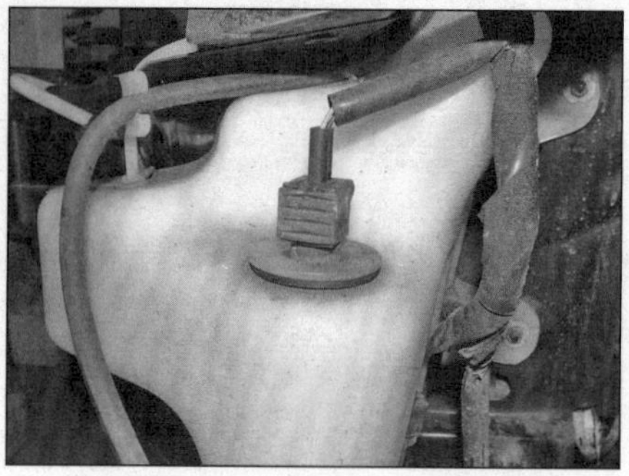

14.2a Washer reservoir level sensor

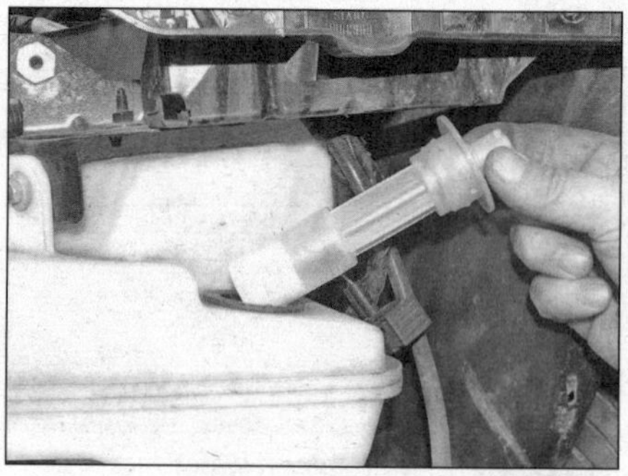

14.2b The sensor can be removed with the reservoir in situ

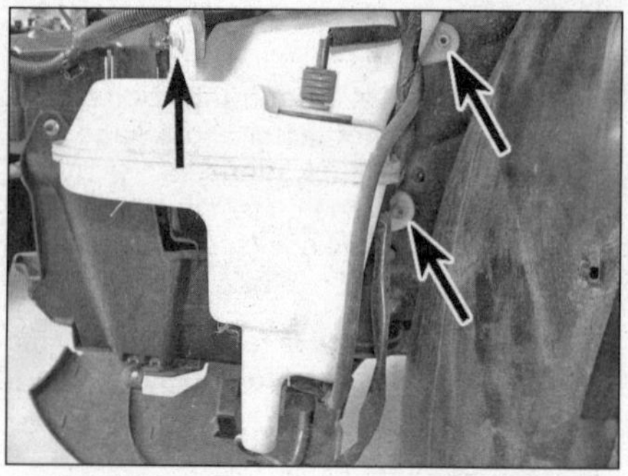

14.3 Remove the mounting nuts (arrowed)

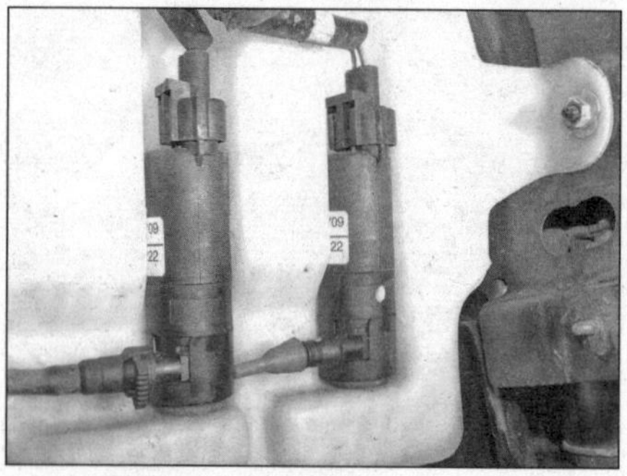

14.6 Pull the washer pumps from the grommets

14.8 Prise out the clips and fold up the bonnet insulation panel

and rear windscreen jets are supplied from the same reservoir.

Pumps

4 Raise the front of the vehicle and support it securely on axle stands (see *Jacking and vehicle support*). Remove the left-hand front roadwheel.

5 Undo the screws and remove the left-hand front wheel arch liner.

6 Pull the pump from the reservoir **(see illustration)**. Be prepared for fluid spillage.

7 Disconnect the washer hose and wiring plug from the pump.

Windscreen washer jets

8 Open the bonnet, prise out the retaining clips, and fold up the base of the bonnet insulation panel **(see illustration)**.

9 Disconnect the hose from the base of the jet, then depress the clip and pull the jet from the bonnet **(see illustrations)**.

Tailgate washer jet

10 Remove the high-level brake light from the tailgate as described in Section 6.

11 Expand the retaining clips and pull the jet from the light unit **(see illustrations)**.

12 Disconnect the washer hose.

Headlight washer jets

13 Remove the front bumper cover as described in Chapter 11, Section 6.

14.9a Disconnect the hose from the base of the jet ...

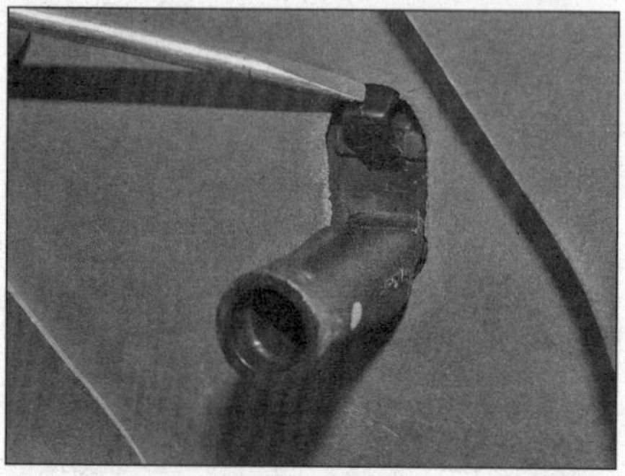

14.9b ... then depress the clip and remove the jet

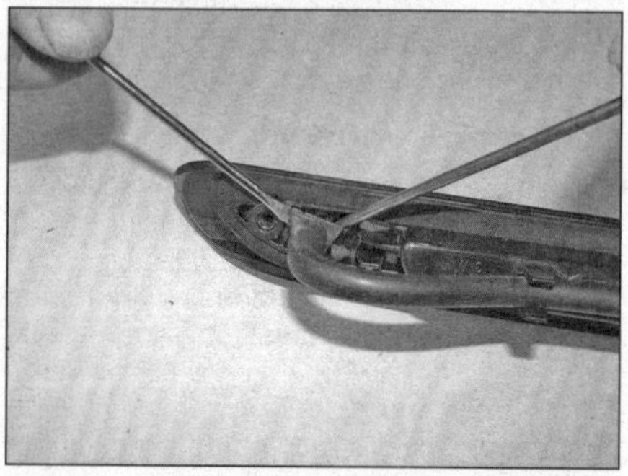

14.11a A pair of screwdrivers are used to release ...

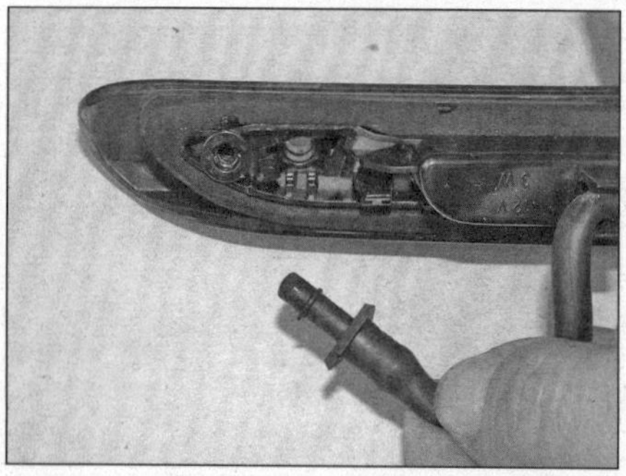

14.11b ... and then remove the washer jet

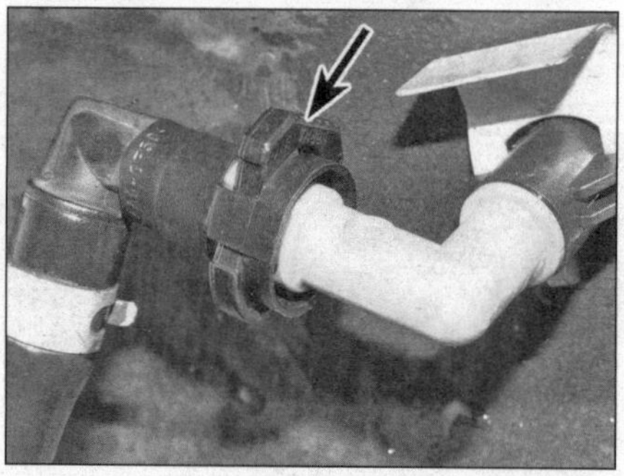

14.14 Depress the catch (arrowed) and disconnect the hose

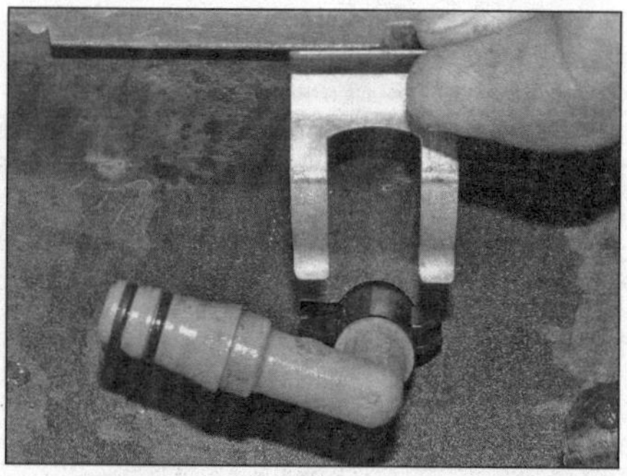

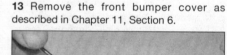

14.15a Slide up the clip and pull the washer jet from the bumper

14 Disconnect the washer hose from the jet **(see illustration)**.
15 Slide out the clip and detach the washer jet **(see illustrations)**.

Refitting

16 Refitting is a reversal of removal.

15 Infotainment system – component removal and refitting

Caution: All modules are extremely sensitive to static electricity. Before touching any module, earth yourself by touching a bare metal part of the vehicle body or engine/transmission.

Note: *If any infotainment module is to be renewed, have the systems stored values extracted, then reprogrammed into the new unit using dedicated diagnostic equipment (TECH 2) by a Saab dealer or suitably-equipped specialist.*

Removal

Audio unit

1 Using a small screwdriver through the air vent grilles, release the hooks and remove the centre vent **(see illustrations 9.1a and 9.1b)**.
2 Undo the 2 screws and pull the audio unit from place **(see illustrations 9.2a and 9.2b)**. Disconnect the wiring plug as the panel is withdrawn.

Amplifier – Estate models

3 Lift up and remove the luggage compartment floor cover. Note that models fitted with the Bose audio system may have an additional amplifier fitted in the spare wheel well.
4 Remove the rear kick panel.
5 Remove the lower and side trim panels from the left-hand side of the luggage compartment (as described in Chapter 11, Section 26).
6 Undo the retaining bolts and lift the amplifier from place. Disconnect the wiring plug as the amplifier is withdrawn.

Amplifier – Saloon models

7 Remove the trim panel from the left-hand side of the boot.
8 Undo the retaining nuts and lift the amplifier

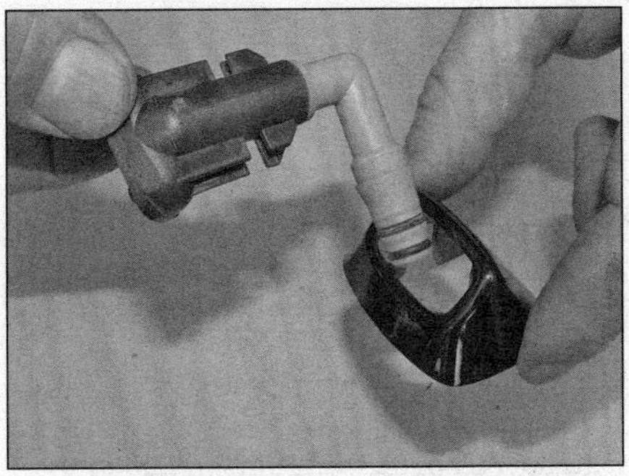

14.15b Remove the trim piece from the jet

from place **(see illustration)**. Disconnect the wiring plug as the amplifier is withdrawn.

Amplifier – Convertible models

9 Remove the left-hand side panel trim as described in Chapter 11, Section 26.
10 On models fitted with a dual amplifier audio system, insert Saab tool No 84 71 203 into each side of the amplifier. Release the retaining clips and pull the amplifier from the bracket. Disconnect the wiring plug as the amplifier is withdrawn.
11 On models with a single amplifier (or after the upper amplifier has been removed) undo the mounting bolts and then disconnect the amplifier wiring plug
12 Undo the retaining bolt and detach the amplifier from the bracket.

Satellite navigation head unit

13 On models fitted with a satellite navigation system (Sat-Nav) the audio unit is replaced by the Sat-Nav display. Removal follows the same procedure as removing the audio unit – see this Section.

Satellite navigation radio receiver

14 All models fitted with Sat-Nav also have a separate radio receiver fitted. On the 4- and 5-door models the receiver is located next to the audio unit amplifier in the left-hand side of the luggage area. On the Convertible model the amplifier is located on the right-hand side of the load area.
15 To remove the receiver, remove the appropriate trim panel (as described in Chapter 11, Section 26 and above).

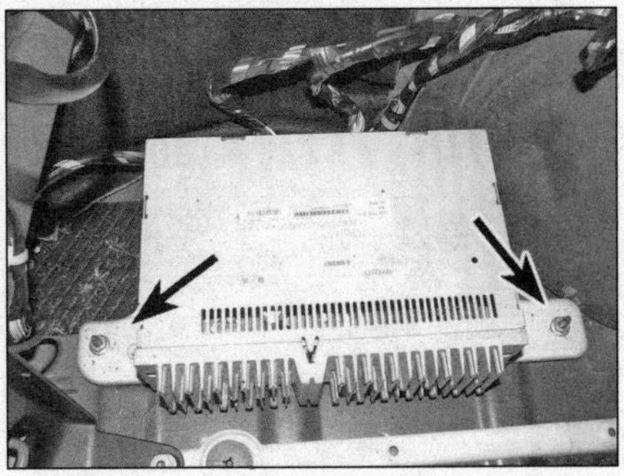

15.8 Remove the mounting nuts (arrowed)

Disconnect the wiring plug and then unbolt the unit.

Refitting

16 Refitting is a reversal of removal.

16 Loudspeakers – removal and refitting

Facia mounted speakers

1 Using a screwdriver carefully prise out the grille from the relevant speaker **(see illustration)**.
2 Using a Torx key, undo the screws securing the speaker in the facia, and carefully lift it out **(see illustrations)**.
3 Disconnect the wiring and tape it to the facia to prevent it dropping down inside.
4 Refitting is a reversal of removal.

Front door mounted speaker

5 Remove the door inner trim panel. On Convertible models remove the waterproof membrane as described in Chapter 11, Section 12.
6 Peel back the foam insulation, undo the mounting screws, then withdraw the speaker and disconnect the wiring **(see illustrations)**.
7 Refitting is a reversal of removal.

Rear speakers

Saloon models

8 Remove the appropriate speaker grille **(see illustration)**.

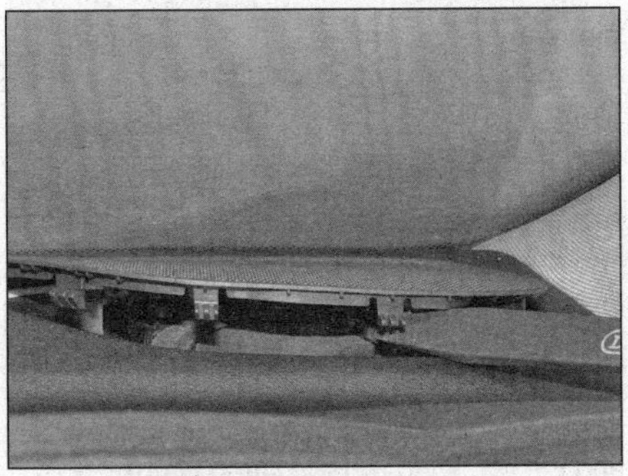

16.1 Prise up the speaker grille

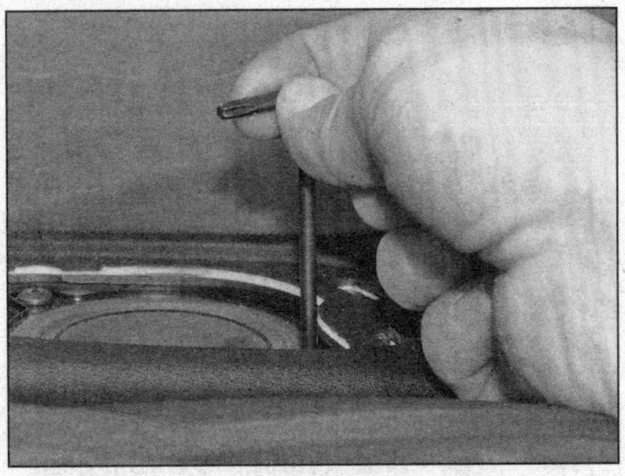

16.2a Undo the speaker Torx screws

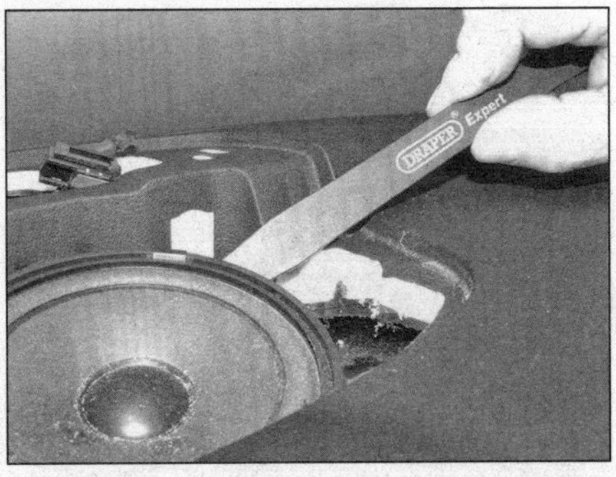

16.2b The centre speaker can be levered out. There are no screw fixings

16.6a Door speaker Torx screws (arrowed)

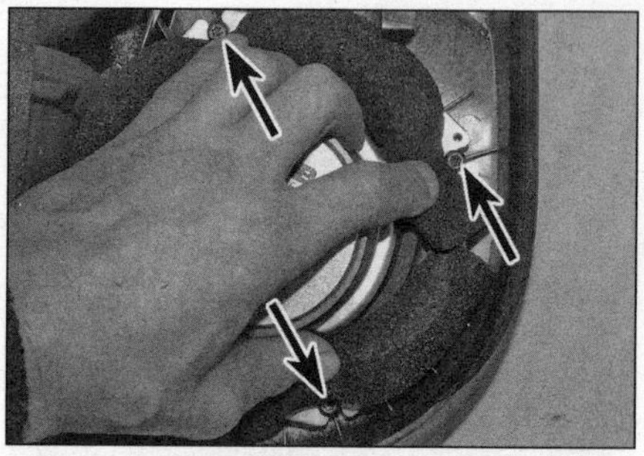

16.6b Pull back the foam, and undo the speaker retaining screws (arrowed) – Convertible models

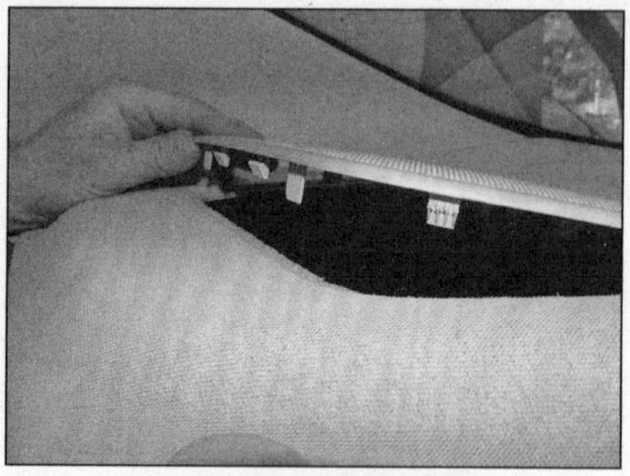

16.8 Remove the grille

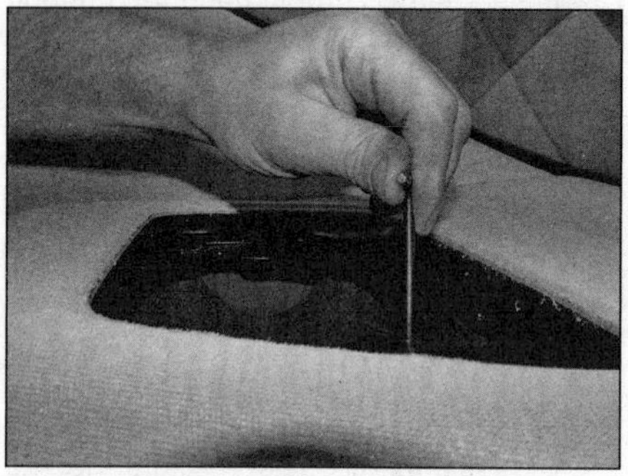

16.9 Remove the Torx fixings

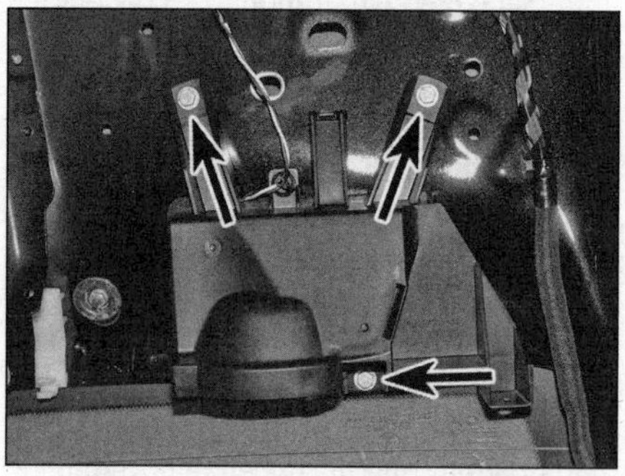

16.15a Tailgate speaker mounting retaining screws (arrowed)

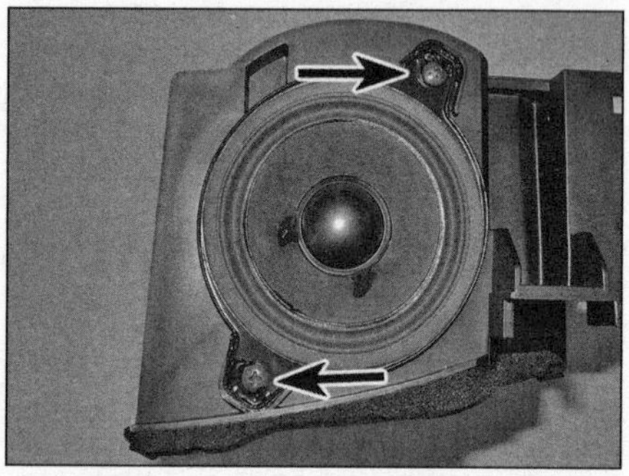

16.15b Remove the screws (arrowed)

9 Use a Torx key to release the screws and lift the speaker from position **(see illustration)**. Disconnect the wiring plug as the speaker is withdrawn.

10 Refitting is a reversal of removal.

Estate models – woofer

11 Lift up the luggage compartment floor panel.

12 Disconnect the speaker wiring plug, and remove the speakers.

13 Refitting is a reversal of removal.

Estate models – tailgate speaker

14 Remove the tailgate trim panel as described in Chapter 11, Section 26.

15 Undo the 3 retaining screws and lift off the speaker mounting bracket. Disconnect the wiring plug and remove the speaker from the bracket **(see illustrations)**.

16 Refitting is a reversal of removal.

Convertible models – woofer

17 Remove the rear seat backrest as described in Chapter 11, Section 24.

18 Undo the retaining nuts and lift out the speaker. Disconnect the wiring plug as the speaker is withdrawn.

19 Refitting is a reversal of removal.

Convertible models – side panel speaker

20 Remove the relevant rear side panel trim as described in Chapter 11, Section 26.

21 Undo the retaining screws and detach the speaker from the panel trim.

22 Refitting is a reversal of removal.

17.6a Remove the nut ...

17 Aerial and aerial amplifier – removal and refitting

Aerial – general information

1 On Saloon models the aerial is incorporated into the rear window glass. It comprises 2 separate circuits – one for AM reception and one for FM reception.

2 Estate models have a the AM/FM aerial located in the right-hand rear side glass. Some models also feature an additional FM aerial in the left-hand rear side glass.

3 If a fault develops with the aerial, the appropriate piece of glass will require renewal and, as all the glass is bonded to the bodywork, this work is best entrusted to a Saab dealer or glass renewal specialist.

4 Convertible models feature a traditional aerial located on the right-hand side of the soft top cover.

17.6b ... and disconnect the wiring plug (arrowed) as the base is lowered from the vehicle

Aerial removal – Convertible models

5 Open the Convertible roof, but stop the process so that the roof cover leaves the base of the aerial accessible.

6 Unscrew the mast, lift up the cover and remove the mounting nut. Disconnect the wiring plug as the base is removed **(see illustrations)**.

Aerial amplifier removal

Note: *On Convertible models, the amplifier is integral with the base of the aerial.*

Saloon models

7 Remove the right-hand C-pillar trim panel as described in Chapter 11, Section 26.

8 Disconnect the wiring plugs from the amplifier and the rear window **(see illustration)**.

9 Undo the 2 retaining nuts and remove the amplifier.

Estate models

10 Remove the C-pillar trim, the side bolster and rear side trim as described in Chapter 11, Section 26.
11 Disconnect the wiring plugs from the amplifier and the rear window.
12 Undo the retaining nuts and remove the amplifier. Repeat the procedure on the opposite side for models fitted with aerial in both rear side glasses.

Refitting

13 Refitting is a reversal of removal.

18 Heated front seat components – general information

Certain models are fitted with thermostatically-regulated heated front seats. Individual control switches are provided for each seat, which allow the heating element temperature to be set to one of three levels, or switched off completely.

Two heating elements are fitted to each seat – one in the backrest, and one in the seat cushion. Access to the heating elements can only be gained by removing the upholstery from the seat – this is an operation which should be entrusted to a Saab dealer or upholstery specialist.

19 Electronic control modules/units – general information

Caution: All modules are extremely sensitive to static electricity. Before touching any module, earth yourself by touching a bare metal part of the vehicle body or engine/transmission.

Note: *If any module is to be renewed, have the systems stored values extracted, then reprogrammed into the new unit using dedicated diagnostic equipment (TECH 2) by a Saab dealer or suitably-equipped specialist.*

1 The control modules for the various electronic systems are located as follows:

Anti-lock braking system (ABS)

- Left-hand rear of the engine compartment.

Automatic/manual climate control (ACC/MCC)

- Beneath the audio unit on the facia.

Automatic xenon headlight leveling

- Behind the left-hand headlight unit.

Automatic transmission

- Top of the transmission casing.

Body control module

- Facia electrical fusebox.

Convertible soft top control (STC)

- On the right-hand rear wheel arch.

Electrically-adjustable door mirrors with memory (PMM)

- In the driver's door.

Column integrated module (CIM)

- On the steering column

Electrically-adjustable driver's seat with memory

- Beneath the driver's seat cushion.

Electro-hydraulic power steering system

- Power steering rack, behind the engine.

Engine management

- Petrol models – on the front side of the engine.
- Diesel models – right-hand side wheel arch, behind the liner.

Diesel glow plugs

- Right-hand side of the slam panel beside the battery box.

Ignition switch module (ISM)

- Between the front seats.

Combustion detection module (CDM)

- Left-hand end of the cylinder head.

Supplementary control system

- Beneath the centre console.

Traction control/EPS system

- Integral with the ABS modulator, left-hand rear of the engine compartment.

20 Anti-theft alarm system components – removal and refitting

Electronic (body) control module

Caution: All modules are extremely sensitive to static electricity. Before touching any module, earth yourself by touching a bare metal part of the vehicle body or engine/transmission.

Note: *If any module is to be renewed, have the systems stored values extracted, then reprogrammed into the new unit using dedicated diagnostic equipment (TECH 2) by a Saab dealer or suitably-equipped specialist.*

Removal

1 Remove the driver's side (LHD models), or passenger's side (RHD) lower facia panel as described in Chapter 11, Section 26.

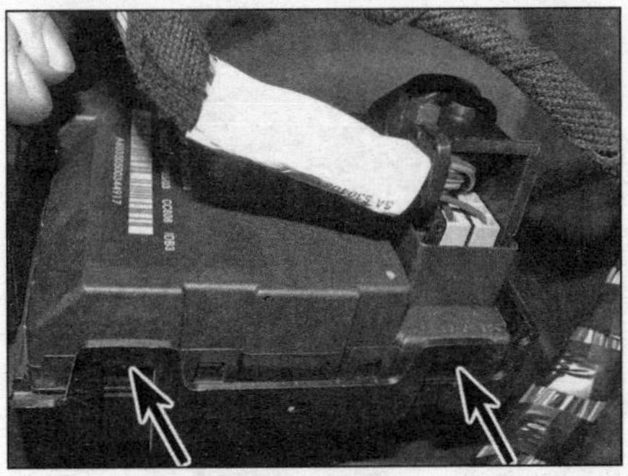

20.3 Anti-theft module lower retaining clips (arrowed)

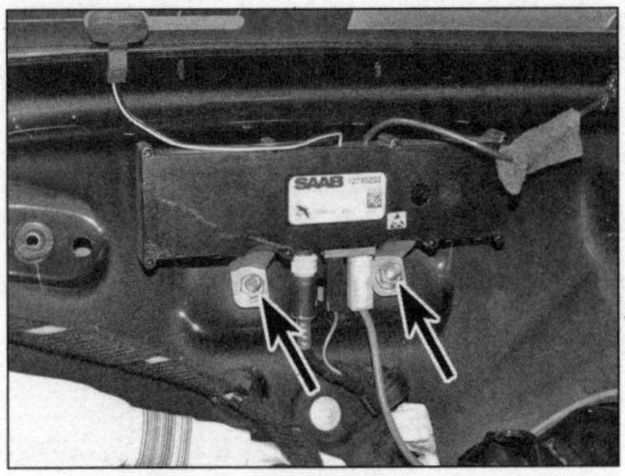

17.8 Aerial amplifier retaining nuts (arrowed)

2 Release the locking catch and disconnect the module wiring plug.
3 Release the 4 clips and remove the module **(see illustration)**.

Refitting

4 Refitting is a reversal of removal.

Volumetric sensor

Removal – Saloon and Estate models

5 Carefully remove the cover from the rear of the front interior light.
6 Remove the switch panel cover from the interior light.
7 Release the clips and remove the sensor **(see illustration)**. Disconnect the sensor wiring plug as it's withdrawn.

Removal – Convertible models

8 Carefully remove the interior light from the windscreen frame.
9 Release the 2 clips and remove the sensor. Disconnect the wiring plug as the sensor is withdrawn.

Refitting

10 Refitting is a reversal of removal.

Siren

Removal – Saloon models

11 The siren is located behind the right-hand side luggage compartment side trim panel. Remove the panel as described in Chapter 11, Section 26.
12 Undo the 2 retaining bolts **(see**

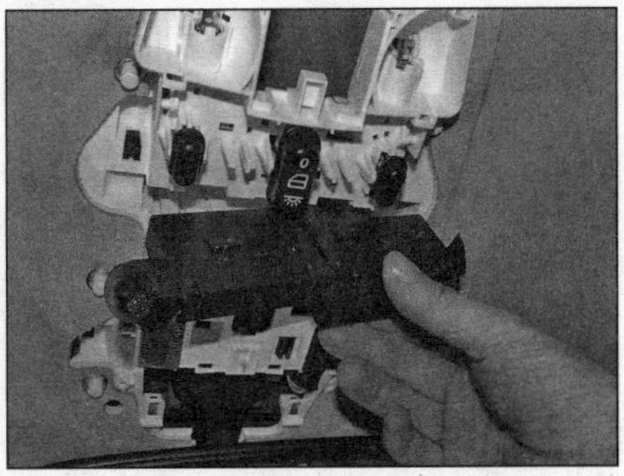

20.7 Unclip the sensor

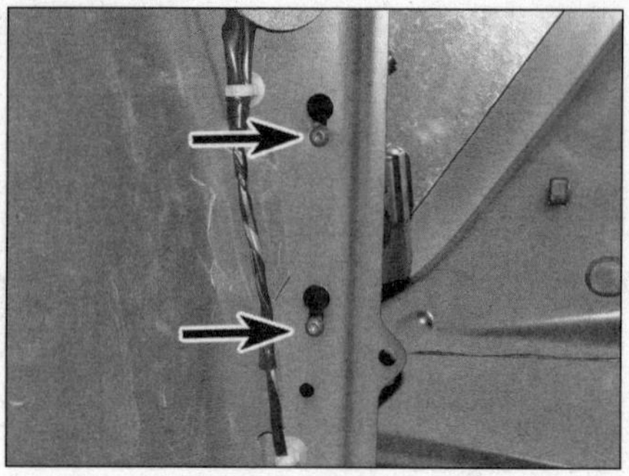

20.12 The alarm siren mounting screws (arrowed)

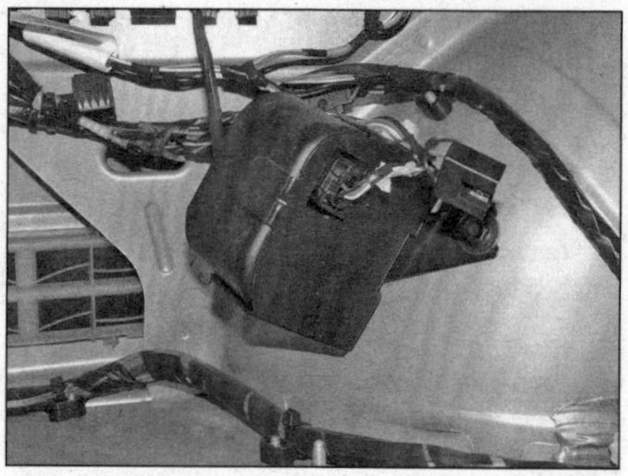

20.16 Anti-theft siren – Convertible models

illustration), disconnect the wiring plug and remove the siren.

Removal – Estate models

13 The siren is located behind the right-hand side luggage compartment side panel. Remove the C-pillar panel and the side panel as described in Chapter 11, Section 26.

14 Undo the 2 retaining bolts, disconnect the wiring plug and remove the siren.

Removal – Convertible models

15 The siren is located behind the left-hand side luggage compartment side trim panel. Remove the panel as described in Chapter 11, Section 26.

16 Disconnect the siren wiring plug, then depress the retaining catch and remove the siren **(see illustration)**.

Refitting

17 Refitting is a reversal of removal.

21 Supplementary restraint system (SRS) components – removal and refitting

Caution: All modules are extremely sensitive to static electricity. Before touching any module, earth yourself by touching a bare metal part of the vehicle body or engine/transmission.

The operation of the SRS is managed by an airbag control module (ACM). When the vehicle's ignition switch is turned on, the ACM performs self-test checks of the system's components; if a fault is detected, the ACM records it in memory as a fault code. Following this, the ACM illuminates the instrument panel mounted SRS warning light. If this should occur, the vehicle should be taken to a Saab dealer or specialist for examination. Dedicated test equipment is needed to interrogate the SRS ACM, firstly to determine the nature and incidence of the fault, and secondly to clear the stored fault code, thus preventing the fault from being displayed by the warning light once the fault has been rectified.

For safety reasons, owners are strongly advised against attempting to diagnose problems with the SRS using standard workshop equipment. The information in this Section is therefore limited to those components in the SRS which must occasionally be removed to gain access to other components on the vehicle.

Warning: A number of additional precautions must be observed when working on vehicles with airbags/SRS:

- ***Disconnect the battery negative lead, and wait at least 1 minute for any residual electrical energy to dissipate before starting any of these procedures.***
- ***Do not attempt to splice into any of the electric cables in the SRS wiring harness.***
- ***Avoid hammering or causing any harsh vibration at the front of the vehicle, particularly in the engine bay, as this may trigger the crash sensors and activate the SRS.***
- ***Do not use ohmmeters or any other device capable of supplying current on any of the SRS components, as this may cause accidental detonation.***
- ***Airbags (and seat belt tensioners) are classed as pyrotechnical (explosive) devices, and must be stored and handled according to the relevant laws in the country concerned. In general, do not leave these components disconnected from their electrical wiring any longer than is absolutely necessary; in this state they are unstable, and the risk of accidental detonation is introduced. Rest a disconnected airbag with the metal bracket facing downwards, away from flammable materials – never leave it unattended.***

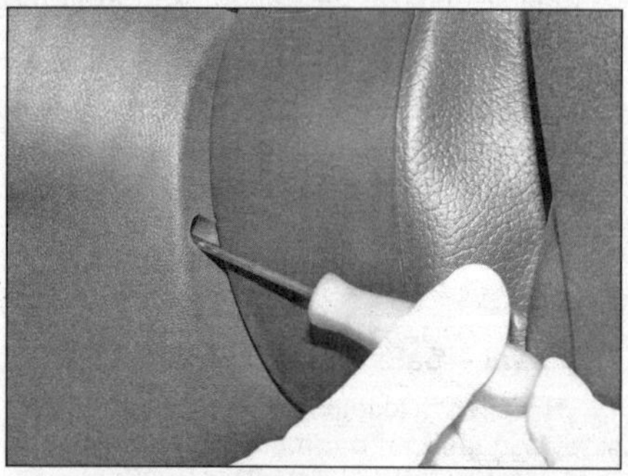

21.3a Insert a flat-bladed screwdriver through the hole ...

21.3b ... and release the airbag clip (arrowed)

Driver's airbag

Removal

1 Ensure the front wheels are in the 'straight-ahead' position.

2 Put the steering wheel in its rearmost position.

3 Turn the steering wheel 45° in one direction, then insert a flat-bladed screwdriver into the hole in the front face of the steering wheel boss, and push the airbag retaining clip in towards the centre to release it **(see illustrations)**.

4 Now turn the steering wheel 45° from 'straight-ahead' in the other direction, and release the remaining airbag clip.

5 Carefully lift the airbag from the steering wheel, then prise up the locking elements and disconnect the wiring plugs **(see illustrations)**.

6 Rest the airbag in a safe place with the metal bracket facing downwards.

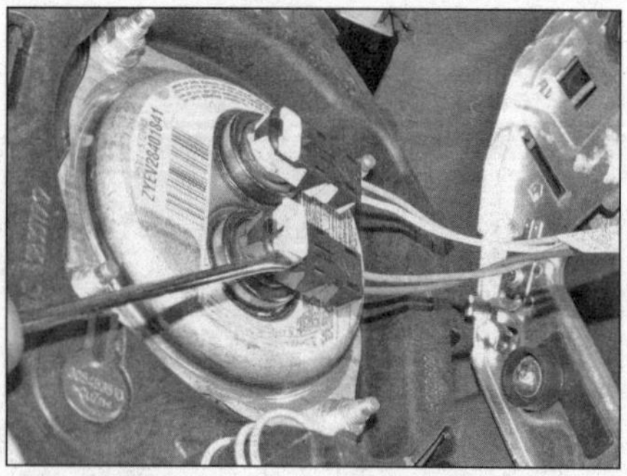

21.5a Prise up the locking elements ...

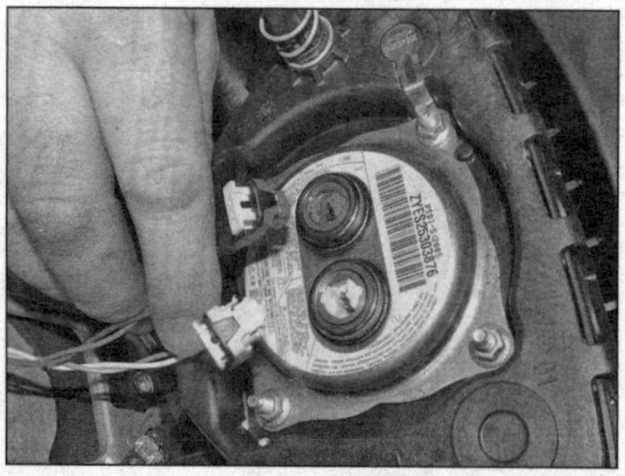

21.5b ... and pull the wiring plugs from the airbag

Refitting

7 Locate the airbag over the steering wheel and reconnect the wiring plugs and press down the locking elements.

8 Lower the airbag into the steering wheel, then push it into place to engage the clips.

9 Reconnect the battery negative lead (see Chapter 5A, Section 4), switch on the ignition, wait at least 10 seconds, and check that the SRS warning light goes out. If not, the control module probably has a fault code stored in it and it will be necessary to have a Saab dealer or suitably-equipped specialist check the system.

Passenger's airbag

Removal

10 Disconnect the battery negative lead as described in Chapter 5A, Section 4, then wait at least 1 minute for any residual electrical energy to dissipate before proceeding.

11 The removal of the passenger airbag requires partial removal of the facia.

12 With reference to Chapter 11, remove the floor console, the A-pillar trim, the facia end panel, the lower facia panel and the glovebox.

13 With reference to Section 15, remove the audio unit and then remove the heating control panel (as described in Chapter 3, Section 9).

14 Remove the centre and end facia mounting bolts, as described in Chapter 11, Section 28 and then remove the lower airbag mounting bolt.

15 Disconnect the wiring plug from the airbag.

16 To remove the airbag the facia panel must be pulled slightly away from the A-pillar on the passenger's side.

17 Remove the remaining mounting bolts and carefully lower the airbag from the facia **(see illustration)**.

18 Rest the airbag in a safe place with the metal bracket facing downwards.

Refitting

19 Position the airbag in the facia and tighten the nuts to the specified torque. Make sure that there are no loose objects between the facia and airbag.

20 The remainder of refitting is a reversal of removal. Reconnect the battery negative lead (see Chapter 5A, Section 4), switch on the ignition, wait at least 10 seconds, and check that the SRS warning light goes out. If not, the control module probably has a fault code stored in it and it will be necessary to have a Saab dealer or suitably-equipped specialist check the system.

Side airbags

21 The airbags are fitted into the seats. Removal of the airbags requires removal of the seat upholstery. This is an involved task, requiring patience and experience. Consequently, we recommend this tack is entrusted to a Saab dealer or specialist.

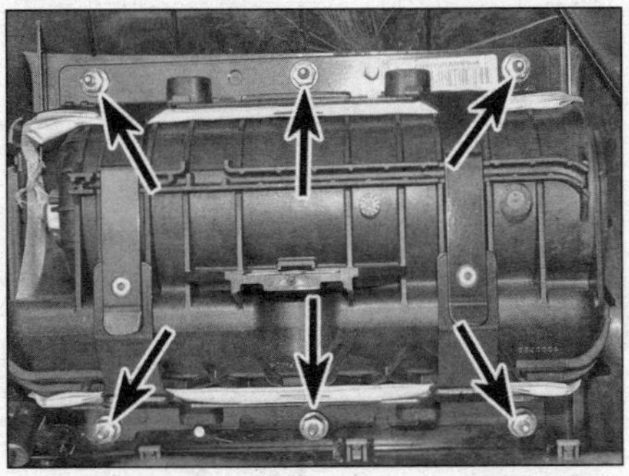

21.17 Passenger's airbag mounting nuts (arrowed)

Head airbag/curtain

22 Renewal of the head airbag/curtain requires the removal of the complete headlining. This is an involved task, requiring patience and experience. Consequently, we recommend this tack is entrusted to a Saab dealer or specialist.

Impact sensors

Front

23 Disconnect the battery negative lead as described in Chapter 5A, Section 4, then wait at least 1 minute for any residual electrical energy to dissipate before proceeding.

24 Remove the front bumper cover as described in Chapter 11, Section 6.

25 Disconnect the sensor wiring plug.

26 Slacken the 2 retaining screws, press in the clip and manoeuvre the sensor from position **(see illustration)**.

27 Refit the sensor using a reversal of the removal procedure, tightening the retaining screws to the specified torque. Reconnect the battery.

Side, front (Saloon and Estate models)

28 Disconnect the battery negative lead as described in Chapter 5A, Section 4, then wait at least 1 minute for any residual electrical energy to dissipate before proceeding.

29 Remove the B-pillar trim panel as described in Chapter 11, Section 26.

30 Fold back the carpet to expose the sensor.

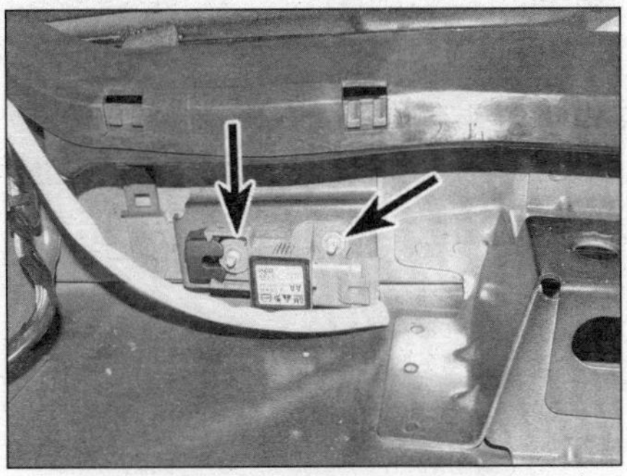

21.31 Side impact sensor screws (arrowed)

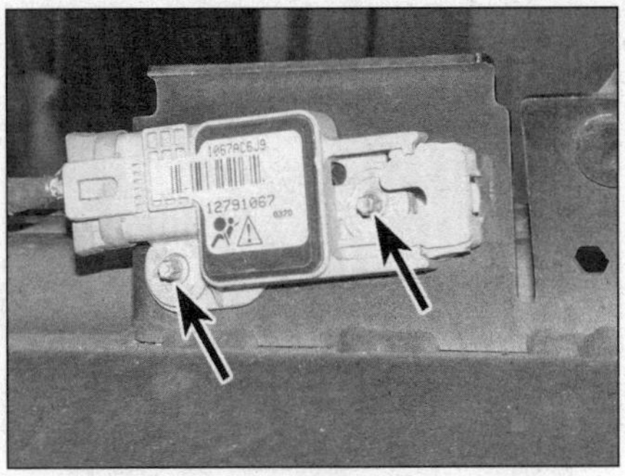

21.26 Front impact sensor screws (arrowed)

31 Slacken the 2 retaining screws, press in the clip/slide the sensor forwards and manoeuvre the sensor from position **(see illustration)**. Disconnect the wiring plug as the sensor is withdrawn.

32 Refit the sensor using a reversal of the removal procedure, tightening the retaining screws to the specified torque. Reconnect the battery.

Side, rear (Saloon and Estate models)

33 Disconnect the battery negative lead as described in Chapter 5A, Section 4, then wait at least 1 minute for any residual electrical energy to dissipate before proceeding.

34 Remove the rear seat cushion as described in Chapter 11, Section 24.

35 Pull the rear door sill trim panel upwards from position.

36 Disconnect the sensor wiring plug.

37 Slacken the 2 retaining screws, press in the clip/slide the sensor and manoeuvre the sensor from position **(see illustration)**.

38 Refit the sensor using a reversal of the removal procedure, tightening the retaining screws to the specified torque. Reconnect the battery.

Side (Convertible models)

39 Disconnect the battery negative lead as described in Chapter 5A, Section 4, then wait at least 1 minute for any residual electrical energy to dissipate before proceeding.

40 With the seat in its forward-most position, remove the rear seat cushion as described in Chapter 11, Section 24.

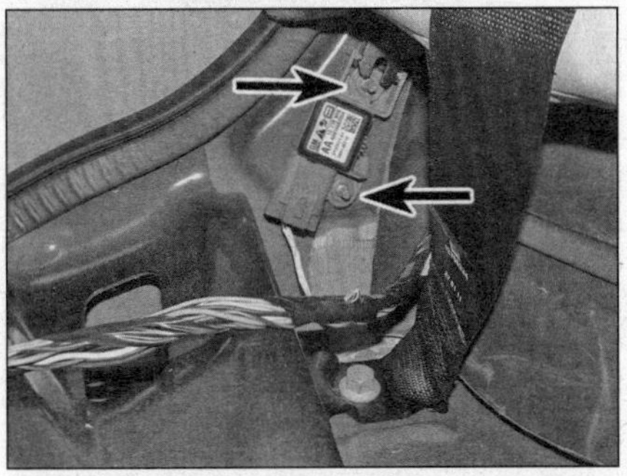

21.37 Undo the 2 screws (arrowed) and remove the side impact sensor – Estate model

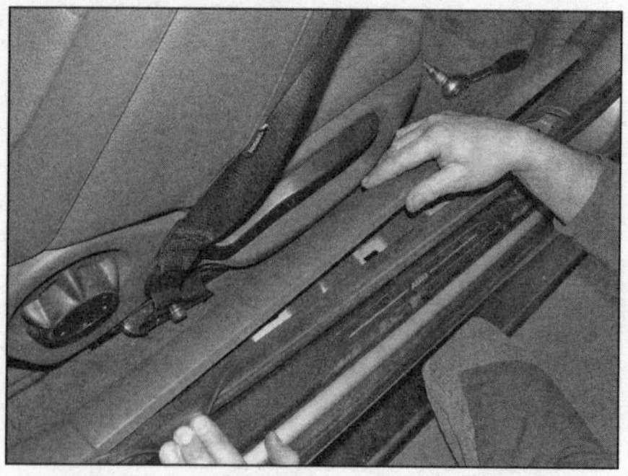

21.41 Pull the sill trim panel upwards to release the clips

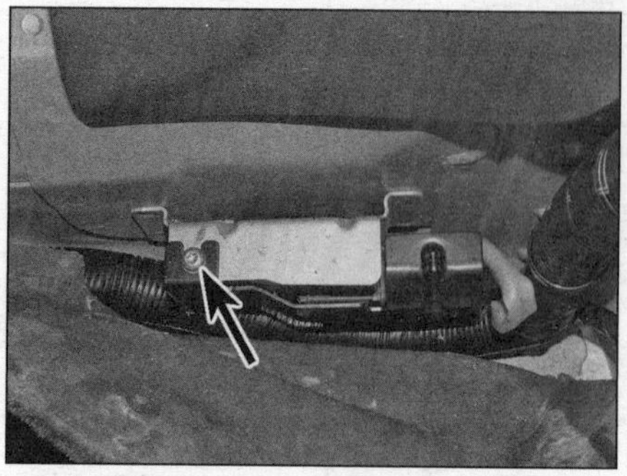

21.42 Undo the protective plate retaining screw (arrowed)

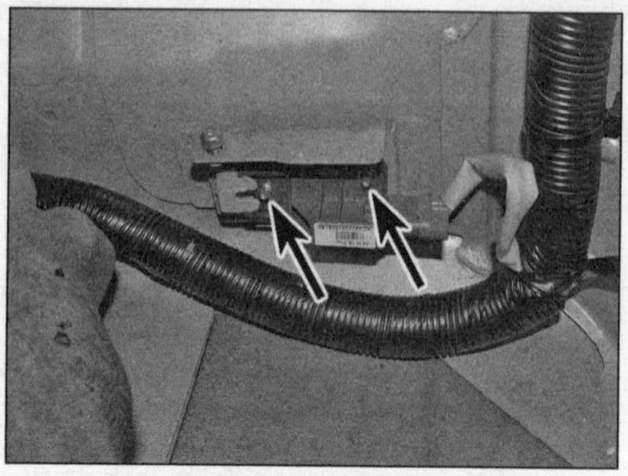

21.43 Side impact sensor screws (arrowed)

41 Pull the door sill trim panel upwards from position **(see illustration)**.

42 Pull back the carpet, then undo the screw and remove the protective plate over the sensor **(see illustration)**.

43 Slacken the 2 retaining screws and manoeuvre the sensor from position **(see illustration)**. Disconnect the sensor wiring plug as it's withdrawn.

44 Refit the sensor using a reversal of the removal procedure, tightening the retaining screws to the specified torque. Reconnect the battery.

Airbag control module (ACM)

Note: *If a new electronic control module is fitted, it must be reprogrammed by a Saab dealer or suitably-equipped specialist.*

Removal

45 Disconnect the battery negative lead as described in Chapter 5A, Section 4, then wait at least 1 minute for any residual electric energy to dissipate before commencing.

46 Remove the centre console as described in Chapter 11, Section 27.

47 Disconnect the wiring from the ACM.

48 Unscrew the nuts and remove the ACM from inside the car **(see illustration)**. Note which way round the ACM is fitted, as it will not work if fitted incorrectly. The arrow on the module must face to the front of the vehicle.

Refitting

Warning: Do not connect the control module before it's fitted.

49 Refitting is a reversal of removal. Tighten the retaining nuts securely. Reconnect the battery negative lead (see Chapter 5A, Section 4), switch on the ignition, wait at least 10 seconds, and check that the SRS warning light goes out. If not, the control module probably has a fault code stored in it and it will be necessary to have a Saab dealer or suitably-equipped specialist check the system.

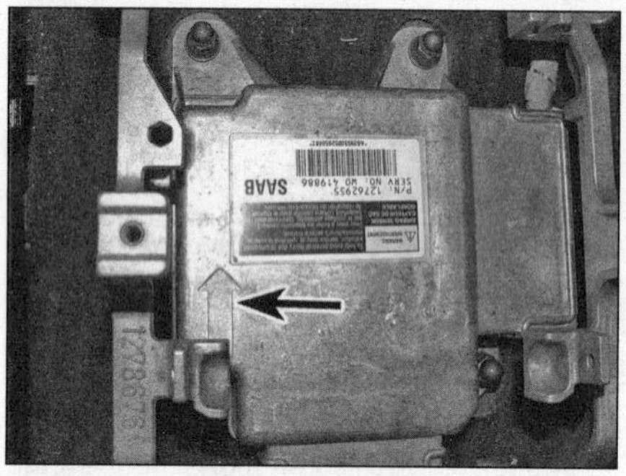

21.48 The arrow on the ECM must point to the front of the vehicle (arrowed)

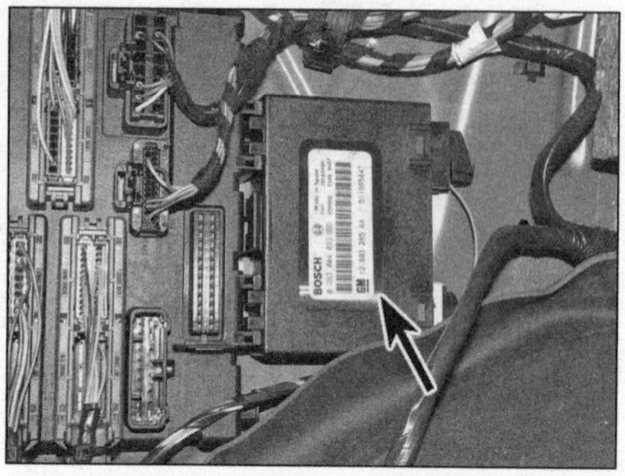

22.2 Parking assistance module (arrowed)

22 Parking assistance module – removal and refitting

Removal

1 Remove the left-hand side luggage compartment trim panel as described in Chapter 11, Section 26.

2 Disconnect the wiring plugs, then release the clip and detach the module from the rear fusebox **(see illustration)**.

3 To remove the sensors, remove the bumper cover as described in Chapter 11, Section 7, then disconnect the wiring plug, release the retaining clips and pull the sensor from the bumper **(see illustrations)**.

22.3a Disconnect the wiring plug ...

22.3b ... and pull the sensor from the bumper

Refitting

4 Refitting is a reversal of removal.

SAAB 9-3 wiring diagrams

Diagram 1

WARNING: This vehicle is fitted with a supplemental restraint system (SRS) consisting of a combination of driver (and passenger) airbag(s), side impact protection airbags and seatbelt pre-tensioners. The use of electrical test equipment on any SRS wiring systems may cause the seatbelt pre-tensioners to abruptly retract and airbags to explosively deploy, resulting in potentially severe personal injury. Extreme care should be taken to correctly identify any circuits to be tested to avoid choosing any of the SRS wiring in error.
For further information see airbag system precautions in body electrical systems chapter.
Note: The SRS wiring harness can normally be identified by yellow and/or orange harness or harness connectors.

Key to symbols

Solenoid actuator 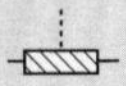

Heating element 

Earth point & location 

Wire colour (red with yellow tracer) 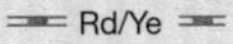

Dashed outline denotes part of a larger item, containing in this case an electronic or solid state device 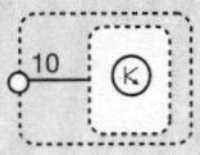

Bulb 

Switch 

Fuse/fusible link 

Resistor 

Variable resistor 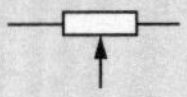

Variable resistor 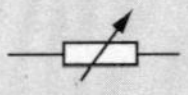

Wire splice, soldered joint, or unspecified connector 

Connecting wires 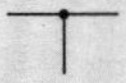

Diode 

Light-emitting diode 

Item number 

Motor/pump 

Earth locations

E1	LH front inner wing, near headlight
E2	In luggage compartment below LH light cluster
E3	Under centre console
E4	On engine control unit
E5	Under LH front seat
E6	LH front inner wing, near headlight
E7	On LH engine mount
E8	In luggage compartment below RH light cluster
E9	LH front inner wing, near headlight
E10	LH front inner wing, near headlight
E11	RH front inner wing near headlight
E12	At base of LH 'A' pillar
E13	At base of LH 'A' pillar
E14	At base of LH 'A' pillar
E15	At base of RH 'A' pillar
E16	At base of RH 'A' pillar
E17	At LH end of dashboard crossmember
E18	At centre of dashboard crossmember
E19	At centre of dashboard crossmember
E20	In steering wheel
E21	In steering wheel
E22	By Soft Top control unit
E23	LH 'C' pillar

Fusebox in front of battery

Fuse	Rating	Circuit protected
F1	60A	Air pump for secondary air
F2	20A	Fuel pump, oxygen sensors
F3	10A	A/C compressor
F4	30A	Engine management main relay

R1	Air pump relay for secondary air
R2	A/C compressor relay
R3	Oxygen sensors
R4	Engine management main relay

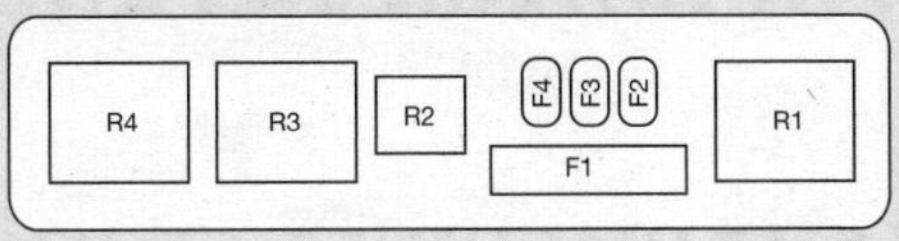

Engine fusebox 4

Fuse	Rating	Circuit protected
F1	30A	Engine management control unit (Diesel)
F2	10A	Engine management control unit (petrol), transmission control unit
F3	20A	Horn
F4	10A	Engine management control unit
F5	-	Spare
F6	10A	A/T selector lever
F7	-	Spare
F8	5A	Vacuum pump relay for brake system
F9	-	Spare
F10	-	Spare
F11	-	Spare
F12	10A	Rear washer pump
F13	10A	A/C compressor (Diesel)
F14	-	Spare
F15	30A	Headlight washer pump
F16	30A	RH front side light, RH direction indicator, RH main beam, LH dipped beam, front LH foglight
F17	30A	Front wiper motor low speed
F18	30A	Front wiper motor high speed
F19	20A	Fuel filter (Diesel)
F20	10A	Headlight levelling
F21	-	Spare
F22	30A	Front washer pump
F23	-	Spare
F24	20A	Extra lighting
F25	20A	Audio amplifier
F26	30A	LH front side light, LH direction indicator, LH main beam, RH dipped beam, front RH foglight

F27-F37 Maxifuse

R1	Windscreen washer relay
R2	A/C air compressor relay (Diesel)
R3	Spare
R4	Preheater relay (Diesel)
R5	Extra lighting relay
R6	Horn relay
R7	Engine management main relay
R8	Starter relay
R9	Front wiper relay
R10	Rear washer relay
R11	Ignition relay
R12	Front wiper low/high speed relay
R13	Spare
R14	Headlight washer relay
R15	Spare
R16	Spare

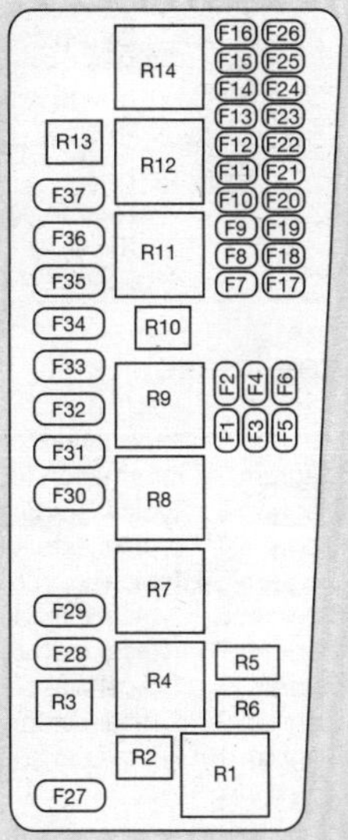

H33763

SAAB 9-3 wiring diagrams

Diagram 2

Passenger fusebox 5

Fuse	Rating	Circuit protected
F1	15A	Steering wheel lock
F2	5A	Steering column control unit, ignition switch
F3	10A	CD player, phone, SID
F4	10A	Main instrument display panel, climate control, air conditioning
F5	7.5A	Front door control units, shift lever control unit
F6	7.5A	Stop light switch
F7	20A	Passenger compartment fusebox, fuel filler flap
F8	30A	Front passenger door control unit
F9	10A	Passenger compartment fusebox
F10	30A	Accessory socket, trailer socket
F11	15A	Diagnostic connector
F12	15A	Interior lighting, glovebox light
F13	30A	Accessories
F14	20A	Audio, infotainment control panel
F15	30A	Driver's door control unit
F16	-	Spare
F17	-	Spare
F18	7.5A	Manual climate control
F19	-	Spare
F20	7.5A	Manual headlight levelling switch
F21	7.5A	Phone, brake pedal switch, clutch pedal switch, manual climate control
F22	30A	Cigar lighter
F23	40A	Blower motor
F24	7.5A	Airbag control unit
F25	-	Spare
F26	5A	Yaw sensor
F27	-	Spare

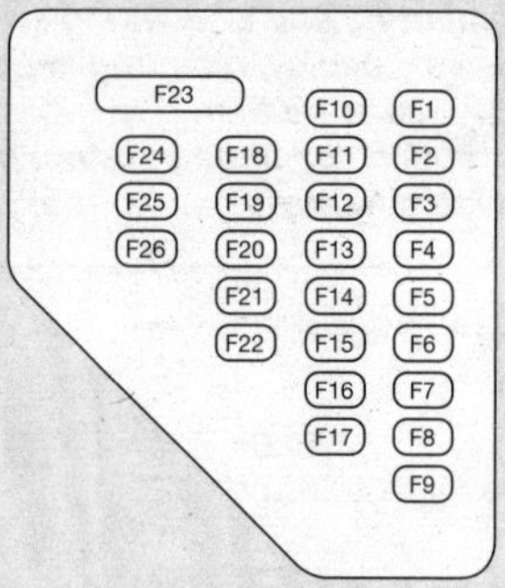

Rear fusebox 18

Fuse	Rating	Circuit protected
F1-F5	Maxifuse	
F6	30A	LH rear door control unit
F7	30A	RH rear door control unit
F8	20A	Trailer
F9	-	Spare
F10	30A	High level stop light, trailer lighting, rear lighting, direction indicators, reversing lights, luggage compartment lighting
F11	-	Spare
F12	-	Spare
F13	-	Spare
F14	15A	Rear wiper
F15	15A	LH heated seat
F16	15A	RH heated seat
F17	7.5A	Automatic interior mirror, rain sensor
F18	15A	Sunroof
F19	7.5A	Telematic control unit
F20	7.5A	DVD player
F21	7.5A	Rear door control unit, parking assistance control unit
F22	30A	Sound system amplifier
F23	-	Spare
F24	10A	Alarm, CD changer
F25	30A	Driver's electric seat
F26	30A	Rear foglight, number plate lighting, luggage compartment lighting, trailer lighting, rear lighting, stop lights, direction indicators, reversing lights

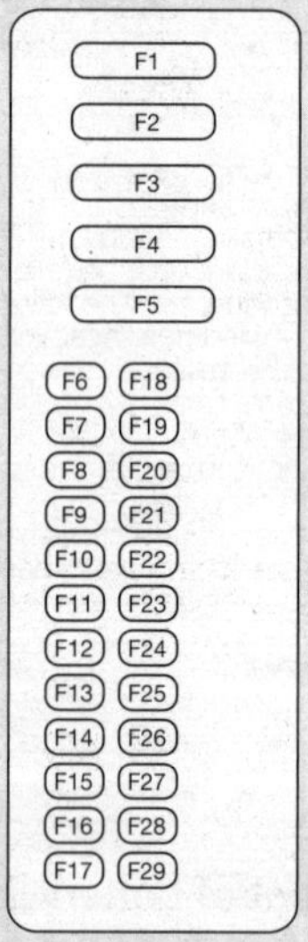

Key to circuits

Diagram 1	Information for wiring diagrams
Diagram 2	Information for wiring diagrams
Diagram 3	Typical starting, charging, engine cooling fan, horn & ignition
Diagram 4	Typical side, tail, number plate & headlights, foglights, direction indicator & hazard warning lights
Diagram 5	Typical stop & reversing lights, trailer socket, headlight levelling (models with xenon headlights)
Diagram 6	Typical interior lighting, heared rear window, headlight levelling (models with halogen headlights)
Diagram 7	Typical manual & automatic climate control
Diagram 8	Typical wash/wipe, electric mirrors & audio system
Diagram 9	Typical central locking
Diagram 10	Typical electric windows

H33764

Wire colours

Bk	Black	**Pk**	Pink
Bn	Brown	**Rd**	Red
Bu	Blue	**Vt**	Violet
Gn	Green	**Wh**	White
Gy	Grey	**Ye**	Yellow
Or	Orange		

Key to items

1 Battery
2 Alternator
3 Starter motor
4 Engine fusebox
  R6 = Horn relay
  R8 = Starter relay
  R11 = Ignition relay
5 Passenger fusebox
6 Ignition switch control unit
7 Steering column lock unit
8 Steering column control unit
9 Engine management control unit
10 Engine coolant temperature sensor
11 Engine cooling fan
12 Engine cooling fan relay
13 Horn
14 Horn switch

Diagram 3

H33765

Typical ignition circuit

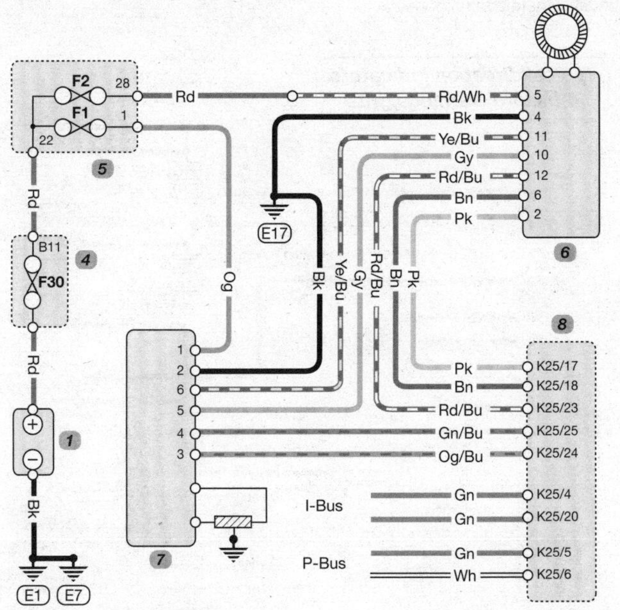

Typical starting & charging

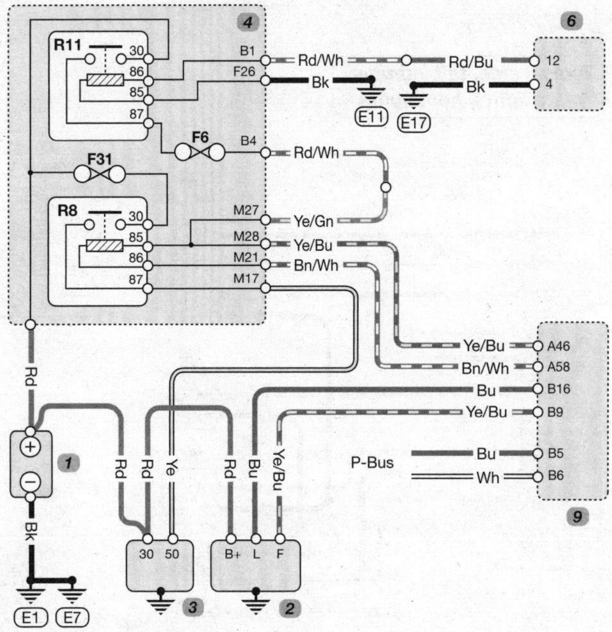

Typical engine cooling fan

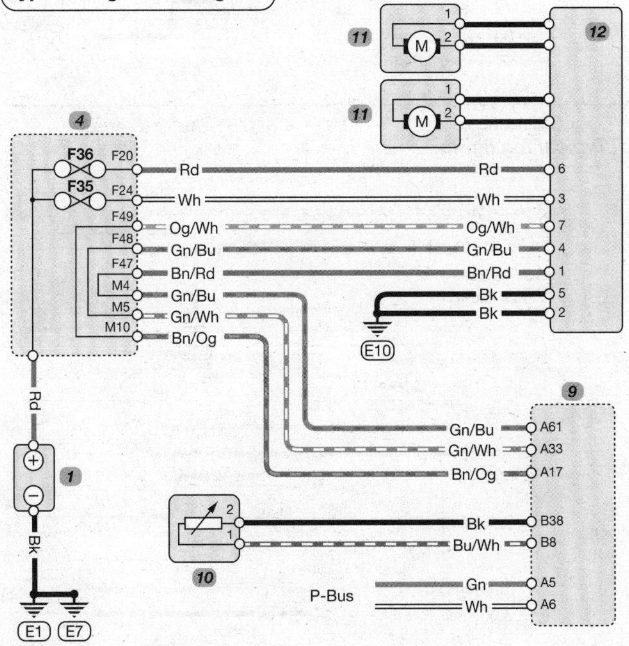

Typical horn

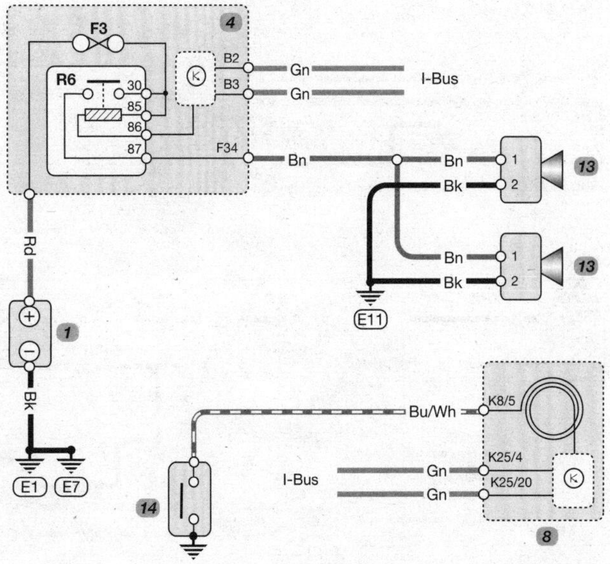

Wire colours

Bk Black **Pk** Pink
Bn Brown **Rd** Red
Bu Blue **Vt** Violet
Gn Green **Wh** White
Gy Grey **Ye** Yellow
Or Orange

Key to items

4 Engine fusebox
5 Passenger fusebox
18 Rear fusebox
19 Light switch
  a = side/headlight switch
  b = front foglight switch
  c = rear foglight switch
20 Tailgate handleswitch/number plate light
21 LH side marker light
22 RH side marker light
23 LH headlight
  a = parking light
  b = main beam
  c = dip beam
  d = main beam dimming solenoid
  e = xenon light ballast
  f = xenon light ignition transformer
  g = xenon light
  h = direction indicator
24 RH headlight (as above)
25 LH rear light
  a = tail light
  b = stop/tail light
  c = direction indicator
26 RH rear light (as above)
27 Manual climate control panel
28 Automatic climate control unit
29 LH indicator side repeater
30 RH indicator side tepeater
31 LH front fog light
32 RH front fog light
33 RH fog/reversing light
  a = fog light

Diagram 4

H33766

Typical side, tail, number plate lights, headlights

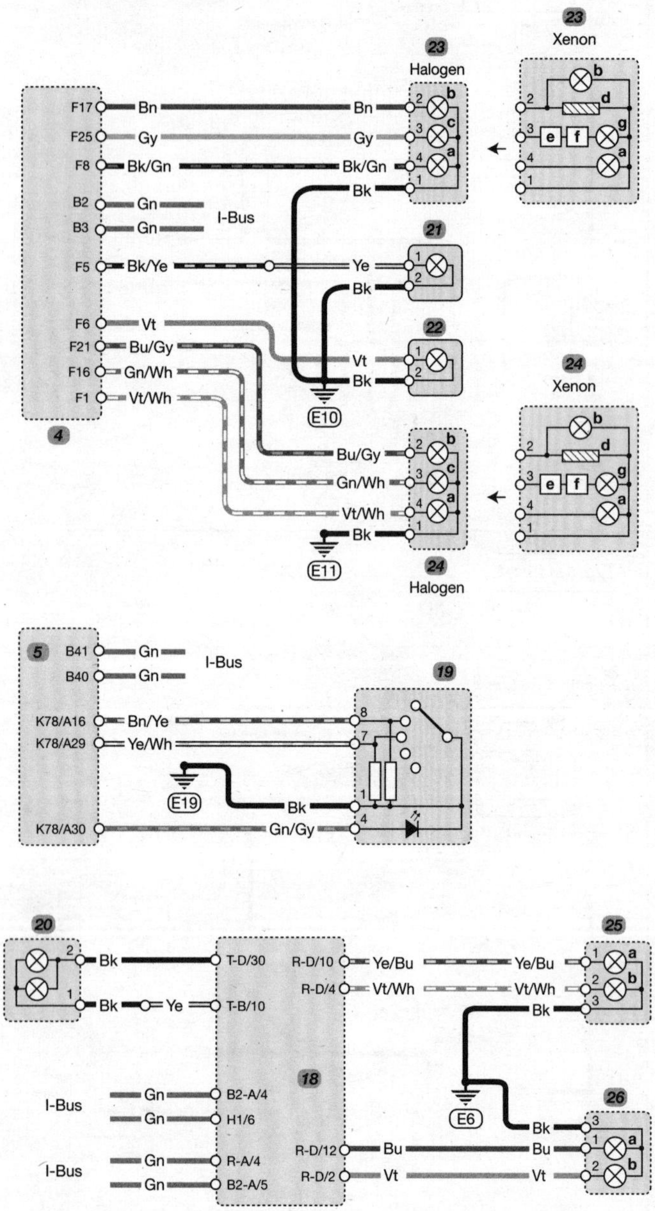

Typical direction indicators & hazard warning lights

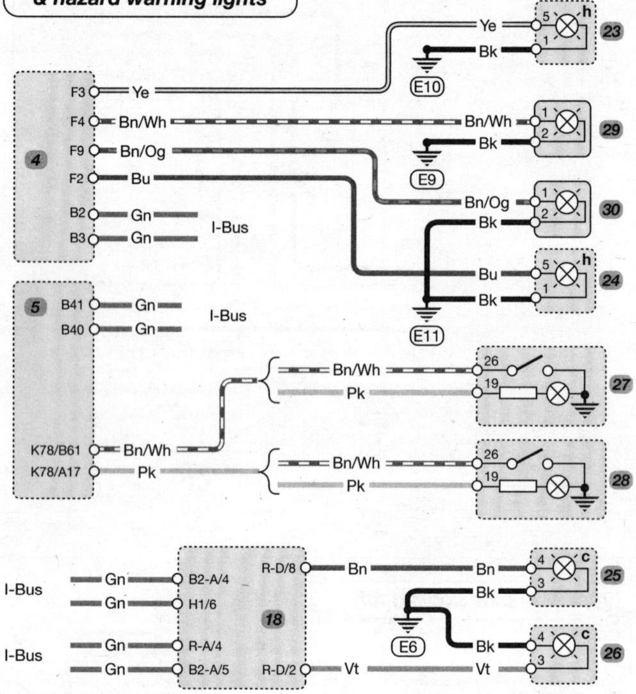

Typical fog lights

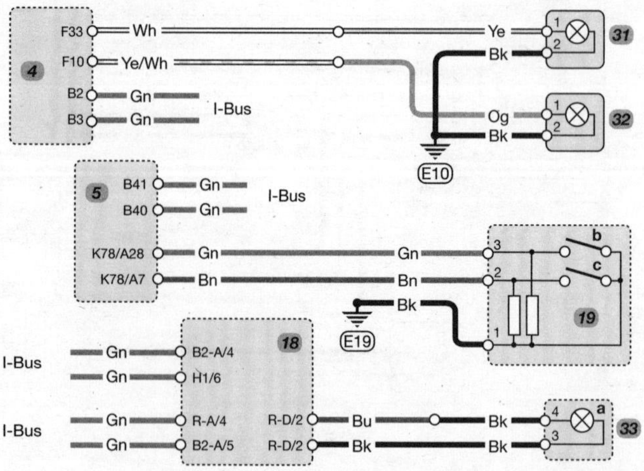

Diagram 5

Wire colours

Bk	Black	**Pk**	Pink
Bn	Brown	**Rd**	Red
Bu	Blue	**Vt**	Violet
Gn	Green	**Wh**	White
Gy	Grey	**Ye**	Yellow
Or	Orange		

Key to items

1 Battery
4 Engine fusebox
  R11 = ignition relay
5 Passenger fusebox
  R1 = trailer relay
6 Ignition switch control unit
18 Rear fusebox
  a = trailer control unit
23 LH headlight
  i = headlight levelling motor
24 RH headlight
  (as above)
25 LH rear light
  b = stop/tail light
  d = stop light
26 RH rear light
  (as above)
33 RH fog/reversing light
  b = reversing light
34 LH fog/reversing light
  b = reversing light
35 Reversing light switch
  (manual transmission)
36 Transmission control unit
37 Stop light switch
38 Transmission range switch
39 High level stop light
40 Trailer socket
41 Headlight levelling control
42 Front load angle sensor
43 Rear load angle sensor

H33767

Typical stop & reversing lights

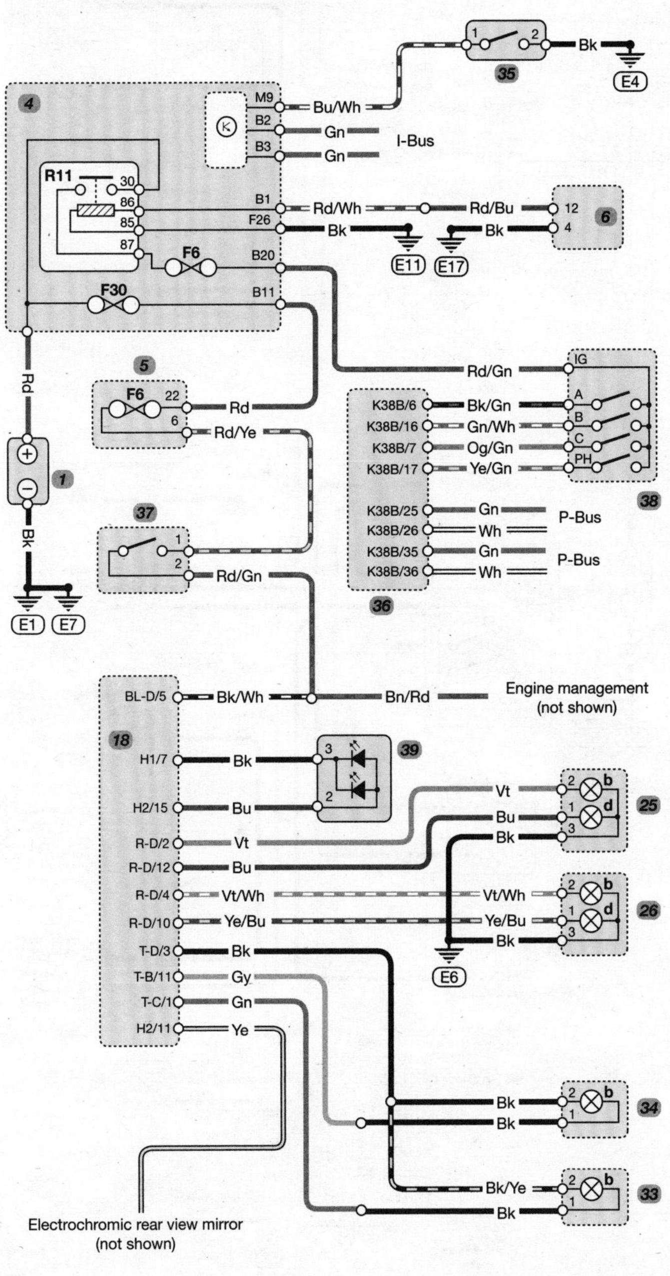

Typical trailer socket

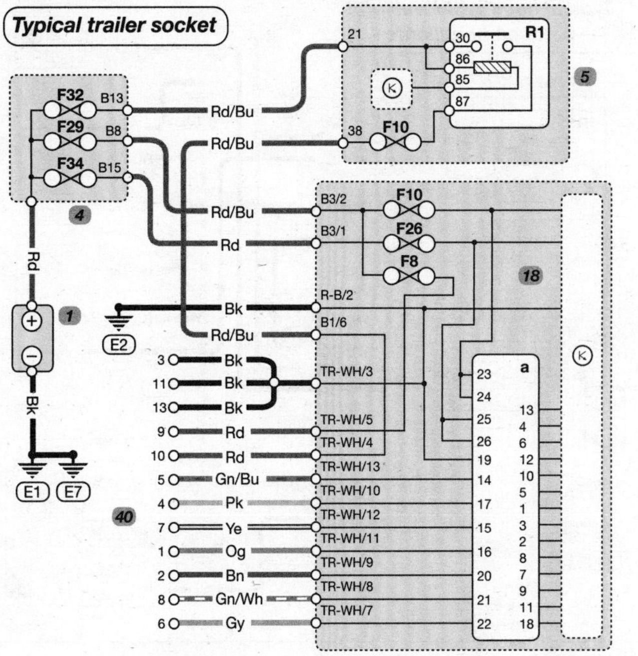

Typical headlight levelling - xenon headlights

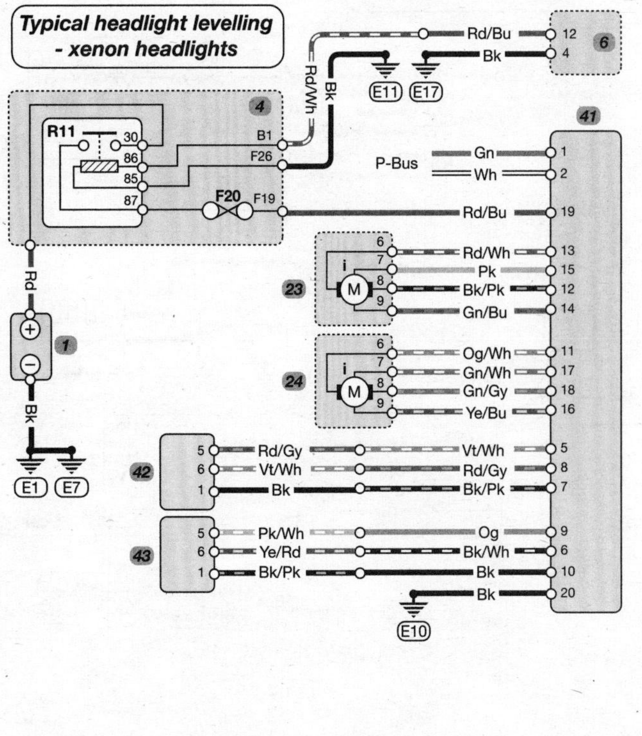

Diagram 6

Wire colours

Bk	Black	**Pk**	Pink
Bn	Brown	**Rd**	Red
Bu	Blue	**Vt**	Violet
Gn	Green	**Wh**	White
Gy	Grey	**Ye**	Yellow
Or	Orange		

Key to items

1 Battery
4 Engine fusebox
  R11 = ignition relay
5 Passenger fusebox
  R2 = ignition relay
6 Ignition switch control unit
18 Rear fusebox
  R4 = heated rear window relay
19 Light switch
  d = headlight levelling switch
23 LH headlight
  i = headlight levelling motor
24 RH headlight
  (as above)
27 Manual climate control panel
28 Automatic climate control unit
45 Front roof light
46 Rear roof light
47 LH vanity mirror light
48 RH vanity mirror light
49 LH footwell light
50 RH footwell light
51 Glove box light/switch
52 Luggage compartment light
53 Luggage compartment light switch/tailgate lock motor
54 Driver's door control unit
55 Passenger's door control unit
56 LH front door courtesy light
57 RH front door courtesy light
58 Heated rear window
59 Antenna amplifier
60 Antenna filter

H33768

Typical headlight levelling - halogen headlights

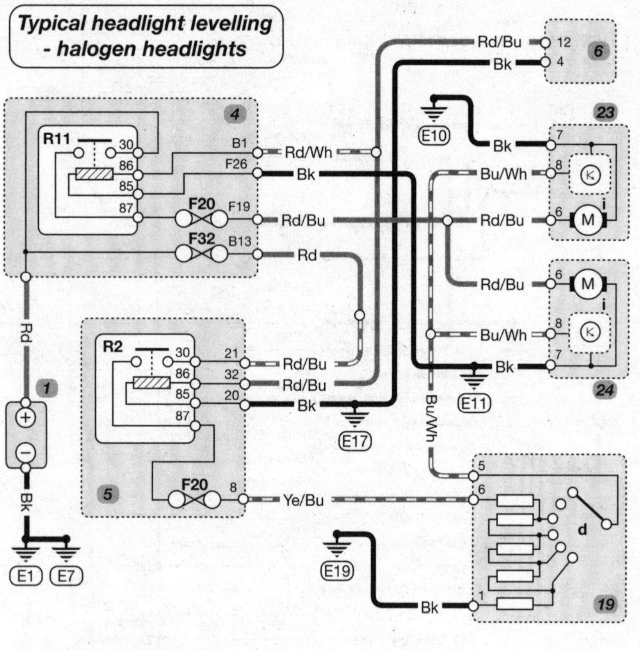

Typical heated rear window

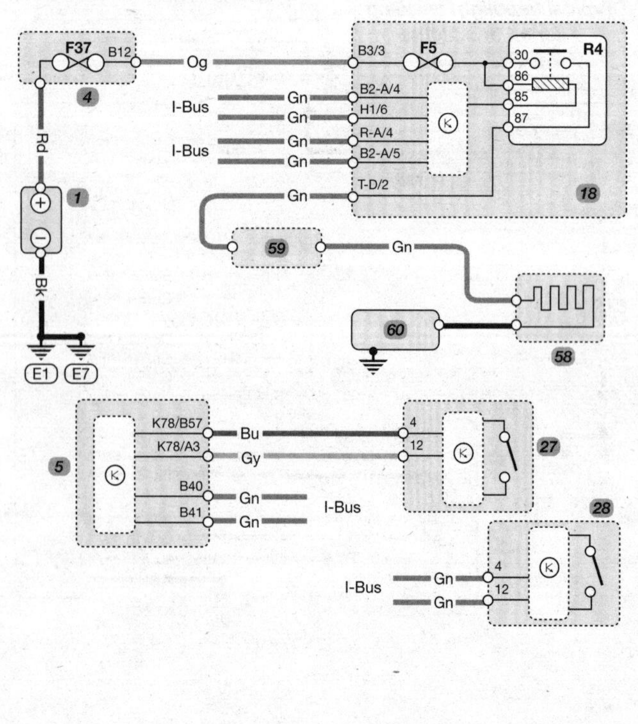

Typical interior lighting

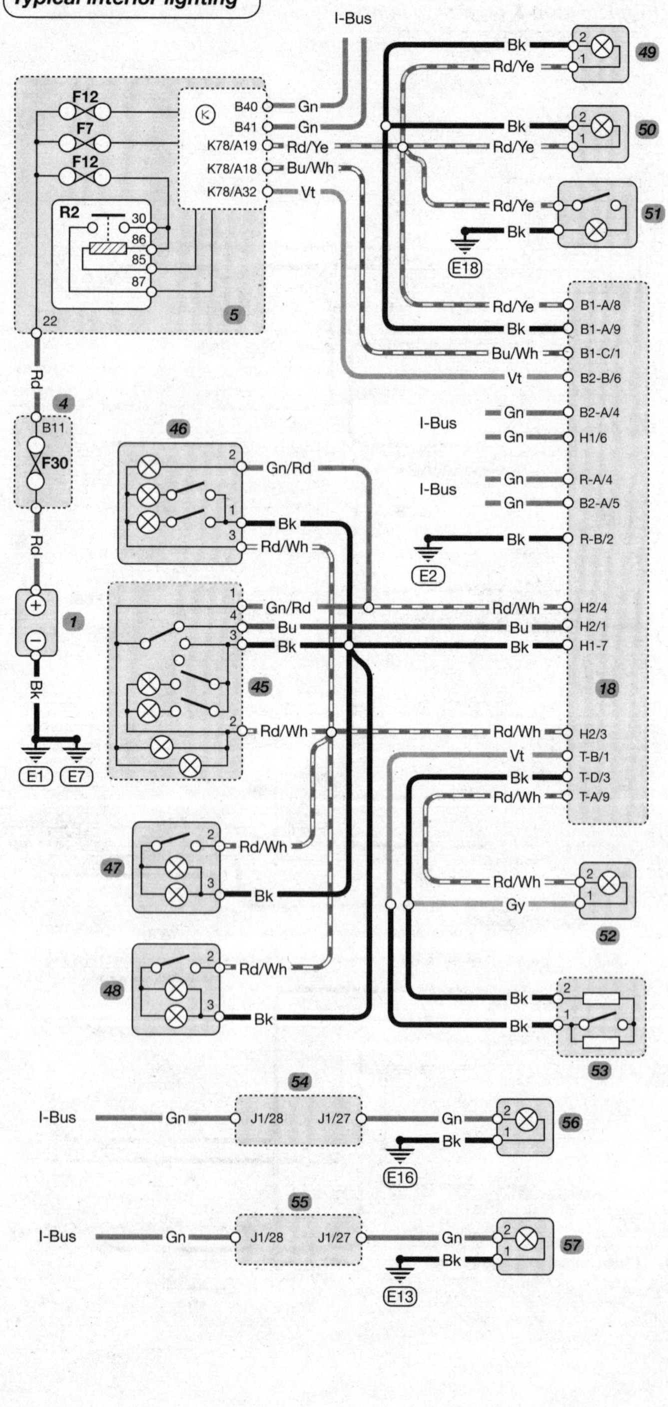

Diagram 7

Wire colours

Bk	Black	**Pk**	Pink
Bn	Brown	**Rd**	Red
Bu	Blue	**Vt**	Violet
Gn	Green	**Wh**	White
Gy	Grey	**Ye**	Yellow
Or	Orange		

Key to items

1 Battery
4 Engine fusebox
5 Passenger fusebox
R1 = trailer lighting relay
R2 = ignition relay
6 Ignition switch control unit
27 Manual climate control panel
28 Automatic climate control unit
45 Front roof light
63 Blower fan control unit
64 Blower fan
65 Air recirculation flap motor
66 Air distribution flap motor
67 Air mixing flap motor
68 Outside air temperature sensor
70 Sun sensor
71 Floor air distribution motor
72 Defroster air distribution motor
73 LH air mixing damper motor
74 RH air mixing damper motor
75 RH air distribution motor
76 LH air duct temperature sensor
77 RH air dust temperature sensor
78 LH floor temperature sensor
79 RH floor temperature sensor

H33769

Typical manual climate control

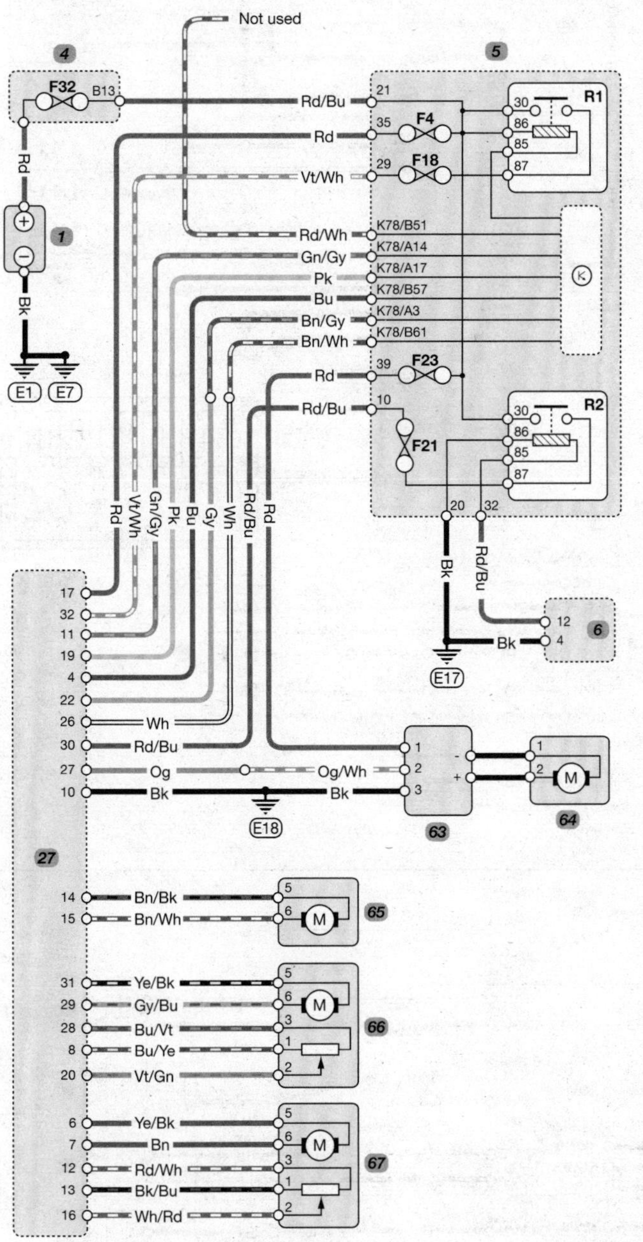

Typical automatic climate control

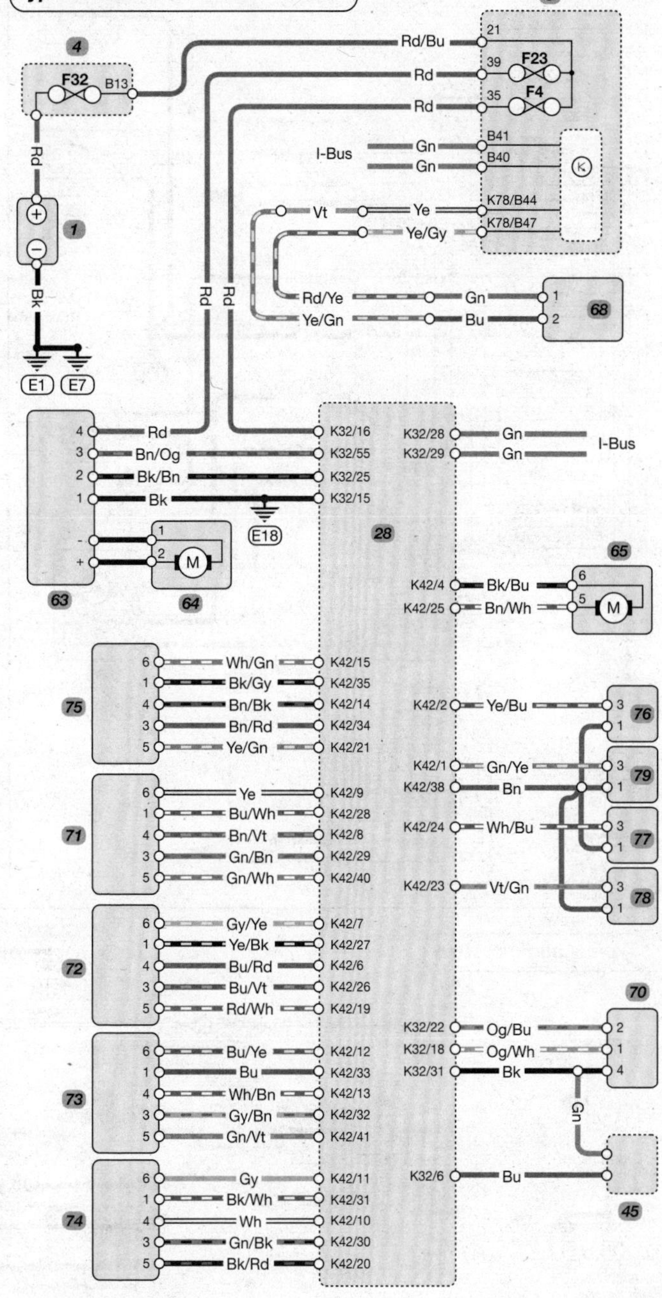

Diagram 8

Wire colours

Bk	Black	**Pk**	Pink
Bn	Brown	**Rd**	Red
Bu	Blue	**Vt**	Violet
Gn	Green	**Wh**	White
Gy	Grey	**Ye**	Yellow
Or	Orange		

Key to items

1 Battery
4 Engine fusebox
  R1 = windscreen washer relay
  R9 = front wiper relay
  R12 = wiper hi/lo speed relay
  R14 = headlight washer relay
8 Steering column control unit
  a = intermittent wiper delay
  b = wiper switch
54 Driver's door control unit
55 Passenger's door control unit
58 Heated rear window
59 Antenna amplifier
60 Antenna filter
85 Wiper motor
86 Headlight washer pump
87 Windscreen washer pump
88 Washer fluid level switch
89 LH dashboard speaker
90 RH dashboard speaker
91 LH rear speaker
92 RH rear speaker
93 Audio unit
94 Driver's door mirror switch
95 Driver's door mirror assembly
96 Passenger's door mirror assembly

H33770

Typical wash/wipe

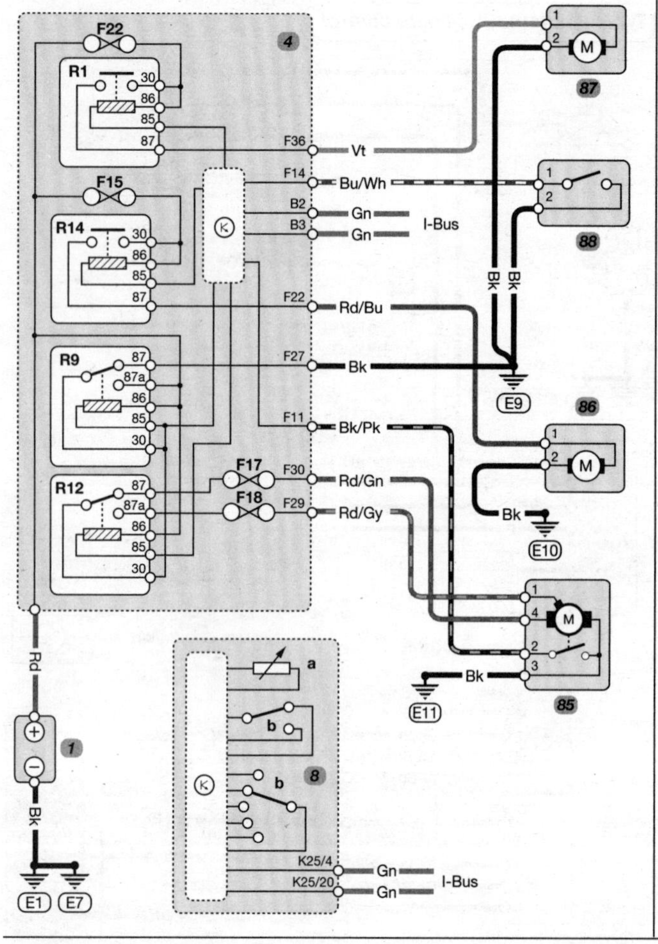

Typical electric mirrors

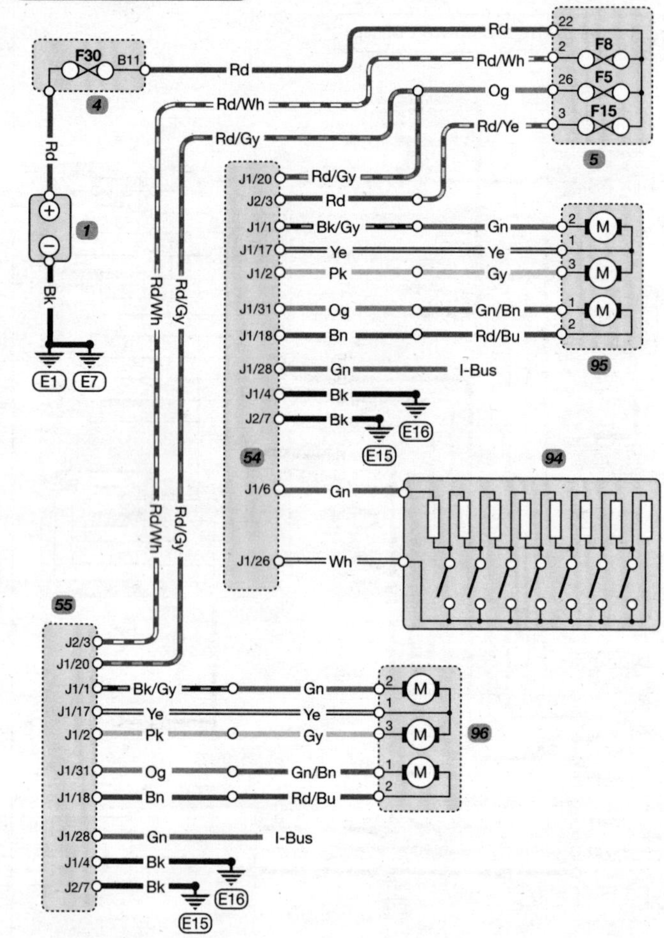

Typical audio system

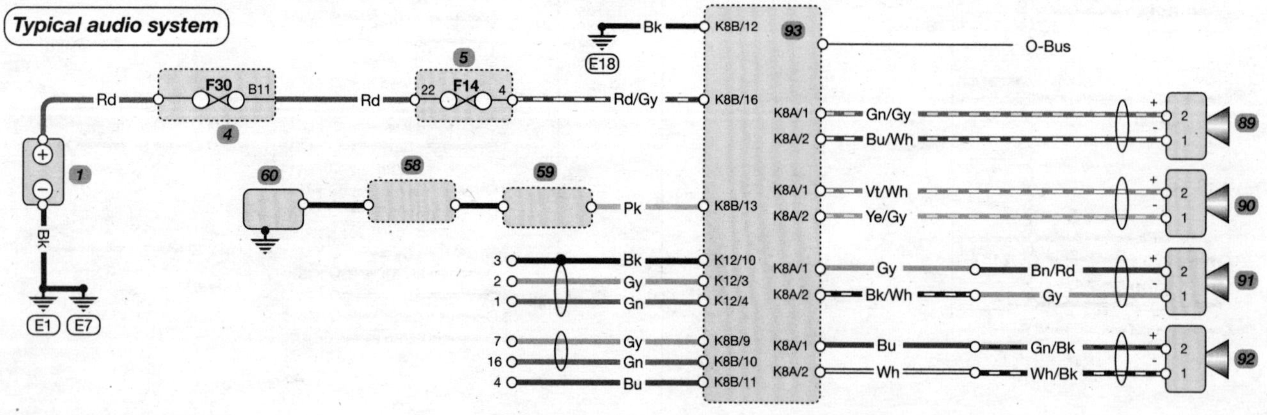

Diagram 9

Wire colours

Bk	Black	**Pk**	Pink
Bn	Brown	**Rd**	Red
Bu	Blue	**Vt**	Violet
Gn	Green	**Wh**	White
Gy	Grey	**Ye**	Yellow
Or	Orange		

Key to items

1 Battery
4 Engine fusebox
5 Passenger fusebox
18 Rear fusebox
R7 = tailgate release relay
20 Tailgate handle switch/number plate light
53 Luggage compartment light switch/ tailgate lock motor
54 Driver's door control unit
55 Passenger's door control unit
100 LH front door lock
101 LH rear door lock
102 RH front door lock
103 RH rear door lock
104 LH rear door control unit
105 RH rear door control unit
106 Tailgate switch (driver's door)
107 Driver's locking switch (driver's door)
108 Passenger's locking switch (passenger's door)
109 Fuel filler flap lock motor
110 Tailgate handle switch

H33771

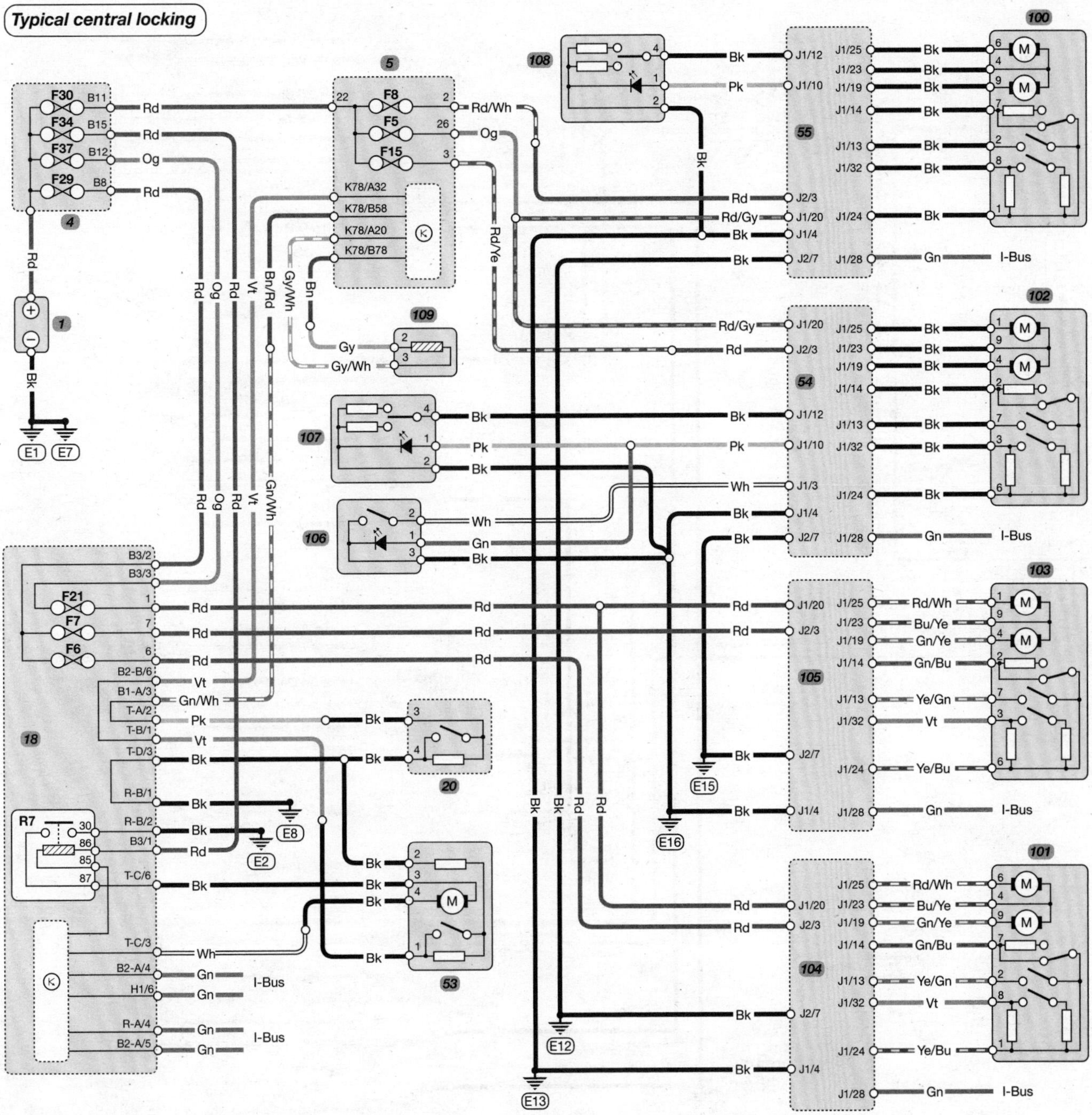

Wire colours

Bk	Black	**Pk**	Pink
Bn	Brown	**Rd**	Red
Bu	Blue	**Vt**	Violet
Gn	Green	**Wh**	White
Gy	Grey	**Ye**	Yellow
Or	Orange		

Key to items

1 Battery
4 Engine fusebox
5 Passenger fusebox
8 Steering column control unit
18 Rear fusebox
54 Driver's door control unit
55 Passenger's door control unit
104 LH rear door control unit
105 RH rear door control unit
112 LH front window motor
113 LH rear window motor
114 RH front window motor
115 RH rear window motor

Diagram 10

H33772

Typical electric windows

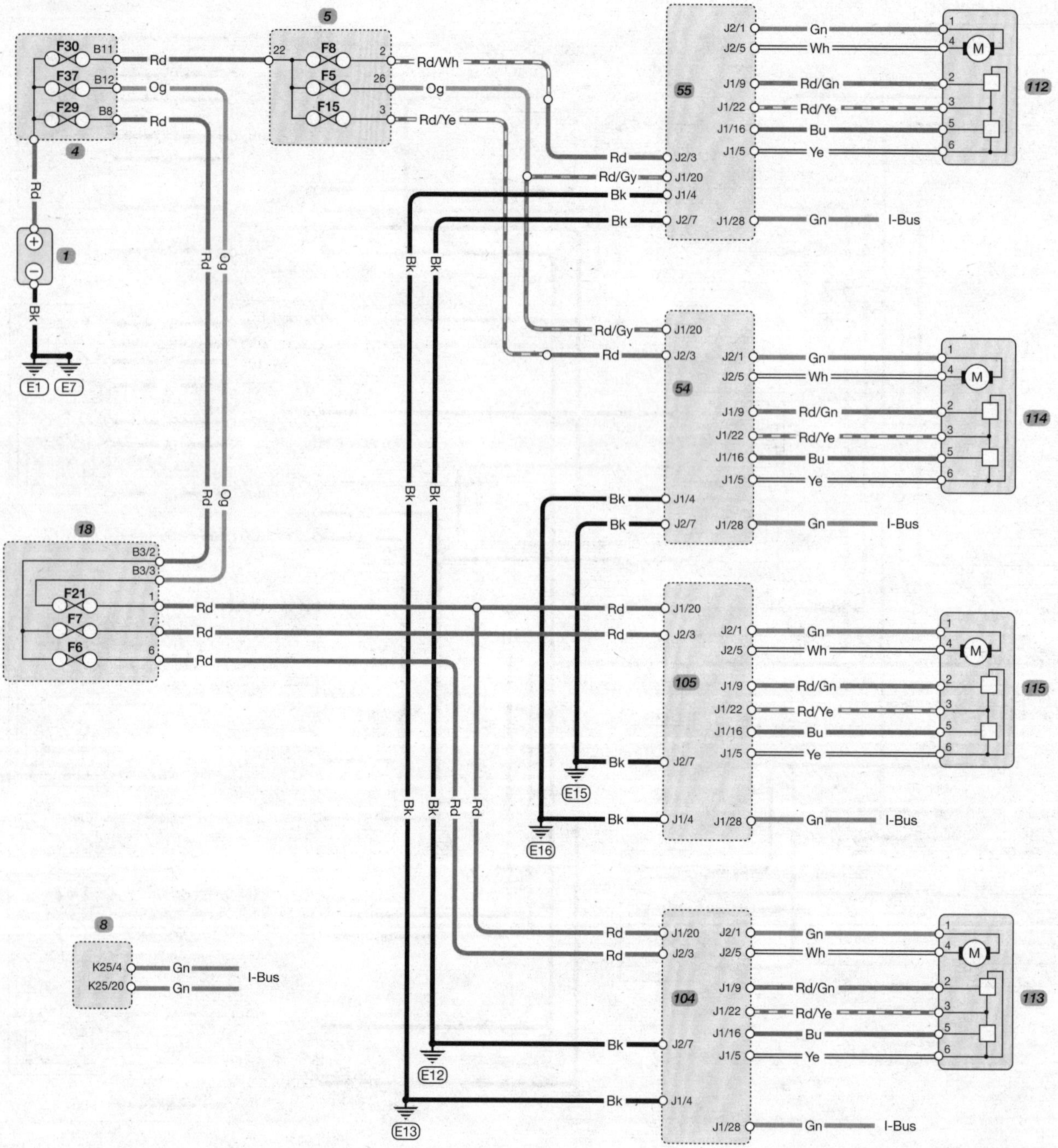

Dimensions and weights

Note: *All figures are approximate, and vary according to model. Refer to manufacturer's data for exact figures.*

Dimensions

Overall length:	
Saloon and Convertible	4635 mm
Estate (Sport wagon)	4654 mm
Overall width (including wing mirrors)	2038 mm
Maximum height	1539 mm
Wheelbase	2675 mm
Track width:	
Front	1524 mm
Rear	1506 mm
Ground clearance (at max weight)	120 mm
Turning circle diameter:	
Wall-to-wall	11.4 m

Weights

Kerb weight	1440 to 1825 kg
Maximum axle load:	
Front	1125 kg
Rear	1125 kg
Maximum roof rack load	100 kg
Maximum towing weight:	
Unbraked trailer	750 kg
Braked trailer	1600 kg

Fuel economy

Although depreciation is still the biggest part of the cost of motoring for most car owners, the cost of fuel is more immediately noticeable. These pages give some tips on how to get the best fuel economy.

Working it out

Manufacturer's figures

Car manufacturers are required by law to provide fuel consumption information on all new vehicles sold. These 'official' figures are obtained by simulating various driving conditions on a rolling road or a test track. Real life conditions are different, so the fuel consumption actually achieved may not bear much resemblance to the quoted figures.

How to calculate it

Many cars now have trip computers which will display fuel consumption, both instantaneous and average. Refer to the owner's handbook for details of how to use these.

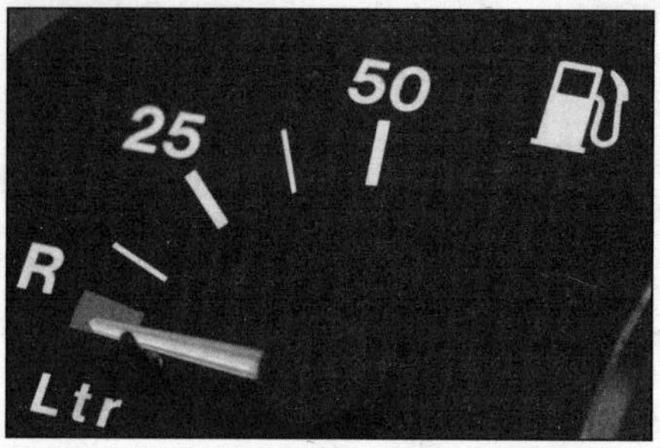

To calculate consumption yourself (and maybe to check that the trip computer is accurate), proceed as follows.

1. Fill up with fuel and note the mileage, or zero the trip recorder.
2. Drive as usual until you need to fill up again.
3. Note the amount of fuel required to refill the tank, and the mileage covered since the previous fill-up.
4. Divide the mileage by the amount of fuel used to obtain the consumption figure.

For example:

Mileage at first fill-up (a) = 27,903
Mileage at second fill-up (b) = 28,346
Mileage covered (b - a) = 443
Fuel required at second fill-up = 48.6 litres

The half-completed changeover to metric units in the UK means that we buy our fuel in litres, measure distances in miles and talk about fuel consumption in miles per gallon. There are two ways round this: the first is to convert the litres to gallons before doing the calculation (by dividing by 4.546, or see Table 1). So in the example:

48.6 litres ÷ 4.546 = 10.69 gallons
443 miles ÷ 10.69 gallons = 41.4 mpg

The second way is to calculate the consumption in miles per litre, then multiply that figure by 4.546 (or see Table 2).

So in the example, fuel consumption is:

443 miles ÷ 48.6 litres = 9.1 mpl
9.1 mpl x 4.546 = 41.4 mpg

The rest of Europe expresses fuel consumption in litres of fuel required to travel 100 km (l/100 km). For interest, the conversions are given in Table 3. In practice it doesn't matter what units you use, provided you know what your normal consumption is and can spot if it's getting better or worse.

Table 1: conversion of litres to Imperial gallons

litres	1	2	3	4	5	10	20	30	40	50	60	70
gallons	0.22	0.44	0.66	0.88	1.10	2.24	4.49	6.73	8.98	11.22	13.47	15.71

Table 2: conversion of miles per litre to miles per gallon

miles per litre	5	6	7	8	9	10	11	12	13	14
miles per gallon	23	27	32	36	41	46	50	55	59	64

Table 3: conversion of litres per 100 km to miles per gallon

litres per 100 km	4	4.5	5	5.5	6	6.5	7	8	9	10
miles per gallon	71	63	56	51	47	43	40	35	31	28

Maintenance

A well-maintained car uses less fuel and creates less pollution. In particular:

Filters

Change air and fuel filters at the specified intervals.

Oil

Use a good quality oil of the lowest viscosity specified by the vehicle manufacturer (see *Lubricants and fluids*). Check the level often and be careful not to overfill.

Spark plugs

When applicable, renew at the specified intervals.

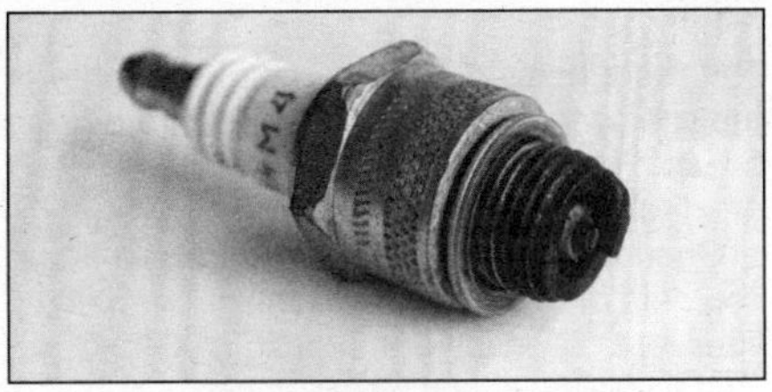

Tyres

Check tyre pressures regularly. Under-inflated tyres have an increased rolling resistance. It is generally safe to use the higher pressures specified for full load conditions even when not fully laden, but keep an eye on the centre band of tread for signs of wear due to over-inflation.

When buying new tyres, consider the 'fuel saving' models which most manufacturers include in their ranges.

Driving style

Acceleration

Acceleration uses more fuel than driving at a steady speed. The best technique with modern cars is to accelerate reasonably briskly to the desired speed, changing up through the gears as soon as possible without making the engine labour.

Air conditioning

Air conditioning absorbs quite a bit of energy from the engine – typically 3 kW (4 hp) or so. The effect on fuel consumption is at its worst in slow traffic. Switch it off when not required.

Anticipation

Drive smoothly and try to read the traffic flow so as to avoid unnecessary acceleration and braking.

Automatic transmission

When accelerating in an automatic, avoid depressing the throttle so far as to make the transmission hold onto lower gears at higher speeds. Don't use the 'Sport' setting, if applicable.

When stationary with the engine running, select 'N' or 'P'. When moving, keep your left foot away from the brake.

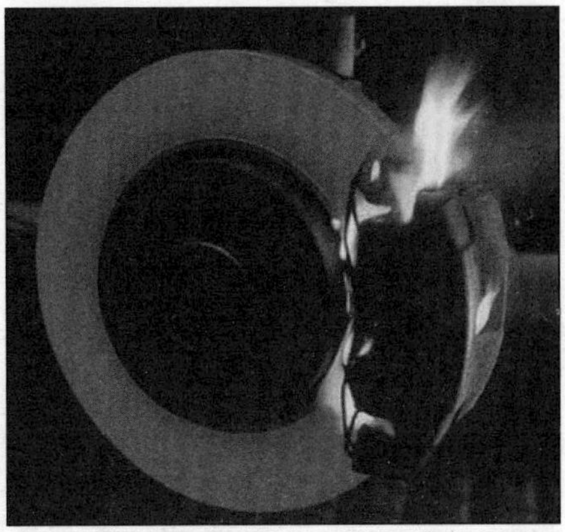

Braking

Braking converts the car's energy of motion into heat – essentially, it is wasted. Obviously some braking is always going to be necessary, but with good anticipation it is surprising how much can be avoided, especially on routes that you know well.

Carshare

Consider sharing lifts to work or to the shops. Even once a week will make a difference.

Electrical loads

Electricity is 'fuel' too; the alternator which charges the battery does so by converting some of the engine's energy of motion into electrical energy. The more electrical accessories are in use, the greater the load on the alternator. Switch off big consumers like the heated rear window when not required.

Freewheeling

Freewheeling (coasting) in neutral with the engine switched off is dangerous. The effort required to operate power-assisted brakes and steering increases when the engine is not running, with a potential lack of control in emergency situations.

In any case, modern fuel injection systems automatically cut off the engine's fuel supply on the overrun (moving and in gear, but with the accelerator pedal released).

Gadgets

Bolt-on devices claiming to save fuel have been around for nearly as long as the motor car itself. Those which worked were rapidly adopted as standard equipment by the vehicle manufacturers. Others worked only in certain situations, or saved fuel only at the expense of unacceptable effects on performance, driveability or the life of engine components.

The most effective fuel saving gadget is the driver's right foot.

Journey planning

Combine (eg) a trip to the supermarket with a visit to the recycling centre and the DIY store, rather than making separate journeys.

When possible choose a travelling time outside rush hours.

Load

The more heavily a car is laden, the greater the energy required to accelerate it to a given speed. Remove heavy items which you don't need to carry.

One load which is often overlooked is the contents of the fuel tank. A tankful of fuel (55 litres / 12 gallons) weighs 45 kg (100 lb) or so. Just half filling it may be worthwhile.

Lost?

At the risk of stating the obvious, if you're going somewhere new, have details of the route to hand. There's not much point in achieving record mpg if you also go miles out of your way.

Parking

If possible, carry out any reversing or turning manoeuvres when you arrive at a parking space so that you can drive straight out when you leave. Manoeuvering when the engine is cold uses a lot more fuel.

Driving around looking for free on-street parking may cost more in fuel than buying a car park ticket.

Premium fuel

Most major oil companies (and some supermarkets) have premium grades of fuel which are several pence a litre dearer than the standard grades. Reports vary, but the consensus seems to be that if these fuels improve economy at all, they do not do so by enough to justify their extra cost.

Roof rack

When loading a roof rack, try to produce a wedge shape with the narrow end at the front. Any cover should be securely fastened – if it flaps it's creating turbulence and absorbing energy.

Remove roof racks and boxes when not in use – they increase air resistance and can create a surprising amount of noise.

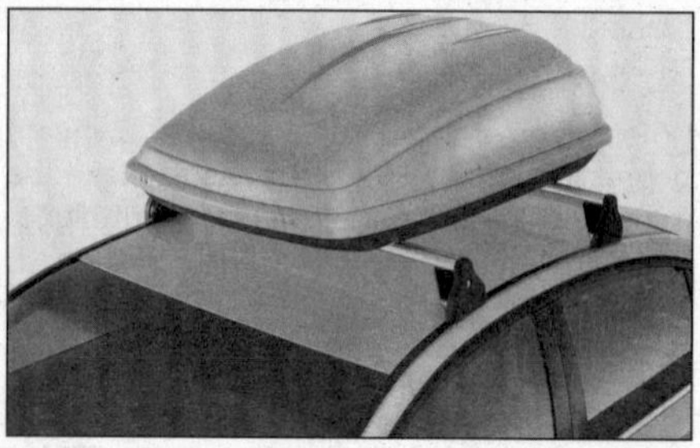

Short journeys

The engine is at its least efficient, and wear is highest, during the first few miles after a cold start. Consider walking, cycling or using public transport.

Speed

The engine is at its most efficient when running at a steady speed and load at the rpm where it develops maximum torque. (You can find this figure in the car's handbook.) For most cars this corresponds to between 55 and 65 mph in top gear.

Above the optimum cruising speed, fuel consumption starts to rise quite sharply. A car travelling at 80 mph will typically be using 30% more fuel than at 60 mph.

Supermarket fuel

It may be cheap but is it any good? In the UK all supermarket fuel must meet the relevant British Standard. The major oil companies will say that their branded fuels have better additive packages which may stop carbon and other deposits building up. A reasonable compromise might be to use one tank of branded fuel to three or four from the supermarket.

Switch off when stationary

Switch off the engine if you look like being stationary for more than 30 seconds or so. This is good for the environment as well as for your pocket. Be aware though that frequent restarts are hard on the battery and the starter motor.

Windows

Driving with the windows open increases air turbulence around the vehicle. Closing the windows promotes smooth airflow and

reduced resistance. The faster you go, the more significant this is.

And finally . . .

Driving techniques associated with good fuel economy tend to involve moderate acceleration and low top speeds. Be considerate to the needs of other road users who may need to make brisker progress; even if you do not agree with them this is not an excuse to be obstructive.

Safety must always take precedence over economy, whether it is a question of accelerating hard to complete an overtaking manoeuvre, killing your speed when confronted with a potential hazard or switching the lights on when it starts to get dark.

Conversion factors

Length (distance)

Inches (in)	x 25.4	= Millimetres (mm)	x 0.0394	= Inches (in)
Feet (ft)	x 0.305	= Metres (m)	x 3.281	= Feet (ft)
Miles	x 1.609	= Kilometres (km)	x 0.621	= Miles

Volume (capacity)

Cubic inches (cu in; in^3)	x 16.387	= Cubic centimetres (cc; cm^3)	x 0.061	= Cubic inches (cu in; in^3)
Imperial pints (Imp pt)	x 0.568	= Litres (l)	x 1.76	= Imperial pints (Imp pt)
Imperial quarts (Imp qt)	x 1.137	= Litres (l)	x 0.88	= Imperial quarts (Imp qt)
Imperial quarts (Imp qt)	x 1.201	= US quarts (US qt)	x 0.833	= Imperial quarts (Imp qt)
US quarts (US qt)	x 0.946	= Litres (l)	x 1.057	= US quarts (US qt)
Imperial gallons (Imp gal)	x 4.546	= Litres (l)	x 0.22	= Imperial gallons (Imp gal)
Imperial gallons (Imp gal)	x 1.201	= US gallons (US gal)	x 0.833	= Imperial gallons (Imp gal)
US gallons (US gal)	x 3.785	= Litres (l)	x 0.264	= US gallons (US gal)

Mass (weight)

Ounces (oz)	x 28.35	= Grams (g)	x 0.035	= Ounces (oz)
Pounds (lb)	x 0.454	= Kilograms (kg)	x 2.205	= Pounds (lb)

Force

Ounces-force (ozf; oz)	x 0.278	= Newtons (N)	x 3.6	= Ounces-force (ozf; oz)
Pounds-force (lbf; lb)	x 4.448	= Newtons (N)	x 0.225	= Pounds-force (lbf; lb)
Newtons (N)	x 0.1	= Kilograms-force (kgf; kg)	x 9.81	= Newtons (N)

Pressure

Pounds-force per square inch (psi; lbf/in^2; lb/in^2)	x 0.070	= Kilograms-force per square centimetre (kgf/cm^2; kg/cm^2)	x 14.223	= Pounds-force per square inch (psi; lbf/in^2; lb/in^2)
Pounds-force per square inch (psi; lbf/in^2; lb/in^2)	x 0.068	= Atmospheres (atm)	x 14.696	= Pounds-force per square inch (psi; lbf/in^2; lb/in^2)
Pounds-force per square inch (psi; lbf/in^2; lb/in^2)	x 0.069	= Bars	x 14.5	= Pounds-force per square inch (psi; lbf/in^2; lb/in^2)
Pounds-force per square inch (psi; lbf/in^2; lb/in^2)	x 6.895	= Kilopascals (kPa)	x 0.145	= Pounds-force per square inch (psi; lbf/in^2; lb/in^2)
Kilopascals (kPa)	x 0.01	= Kilograms-force per square centimetre (kgf/cm^2; kg/cm^2)	x 98.1	= Kilopascals (kPa)
Millibar (mbar)	x 100	= Pascals (Pa)	x 0.01	= Millibar (mbar)
Millibar (mbar)	x 0.0145	= Pounds-force per square inch (psi; lbf/in^2; lb/in^2)	x 68.947	= Millibar (mbar)
Millibar (mbar)	x 0.75	= Millimetres of mercury (mmHg)	x 1.333	= Millibar (mbar)
Millibar (mbar)	x 0.401	= Inches of water (inH_2O)	x 2.491	= Millibar (mbar)
Millimetres of mercury (mmHg)	x 0.535	= Inches of water (inH_2O)	x 1.868	= Millimetres of mercury (mmHg)
Inches of water (inH_2O)	x 0.036	= Pounds-force per square inch (psi; lbf/in^2; lb/in^2)	x 27.68	= Inches of water (inH_2O)

Torque (moment of force)

Pounds-force inches (lbf in; lb in)	x 1.152	= Kilograms-force centimetre (kgf cm; kg cm)	x 0.868	= Pounds-force inches (lbf in; lb in)
Pounds-force inches (lbf in; lb in)	x 0.113	= Newton metres (Nm)	x 8.85	= Pounds-force inches (lbf in; lb in)
Pounds-force inches (lbf in; lb in)	x 0.083	= Pounds-force feet (lbf ft; lb ft)	x 12	= Pounds-force inches (lbf in; lb in)
Pounds-force feet (lbf ft; lb ft)	x 0.138	= Kilograms-force metres (kgf m; kg m)	x 7.233	= Pounds-force feet (lbf ft; lb ft)
Pounds-force feet (lbf ft; lb ft)	x 1.356	= Newton metres (Nm)	x 0.738	= Pounds-force feet (lbf ft; lb ft)
Newton metres (Nm)	x 0.102	= Kilograms-force metres (kgf m; kg m)	x 9.804	= Newton metres (Nm)

Power

Horsepower (hp)	x 745.7	= Watts (W)	x 0.0013	= Horsepower (hp)

Velocity (speed)

Miles per hour (miles/hr; mph)	x 1.609	= Kilometres per hour (km/hr; kph)	x 0.621	= Miles per hour (miles/hr; mph)

Fuel consumption*

Miles per gallon, Imperial (mpg)	x 0.354	= Kilometres per litre (km/l)	x 2.825	= Miles per gallon, Imperial (mpg)
Miles per gallon, US (mpg)	x 0.425	= Kilometres per litre (km/l)	x 2.352	= Miles per gallon, US (mpg)

Temperature

Degrees Fahrenheit = (°C x 1.8) + 32

Degrees Celsius (Degrees Centigrade; °C) = (°F - 32) x 0.56

* *It is common practice to convert from miles per gallon (mpg) to litres/100 kilometres (l/100km), where mpg x l/100 km = 282*

Spare parts are available from many sources, including maker's appointed garages, accessory shops, and motor factors. To be sure of obtaining the correct parts, it will sometimes be necessary to quote the vehicle identification number. If possible, it can also be useful to take the old parts along for positive identification. Items such as starter motors and alternators may be available under a service exchange scheme – any parts returned should be clean.

Our advice regarding spare parts is as follows.

Officially appointed garages

The demise of Saab as a car manufacturer has lead to a unique situation with the supply of genuine parts. Whilst no genuine parts are available from the original company, a new company (Saab Automobile Parts AB) have purchased the assets and tooling from the original Saab company. At the time of writing over 84% of the parts required to repair a Saab 9-3 were available. The new company is backed by the Swedish state and is determined to provide new 'genuine' parts for all models.

Saab Automobile Parts AB have also set up a new 'Approved' repair network to allow all owners to purchase genuine parts. The network of approved garages also have all the specialist diagnostic tools to carry out repairs beyond the scope of the home mechanic. Many of the approved garages will of course have been former official Saab dealers.

This network is the best source of parts which are peculiar to your car, and which are not otherwise generally available (eg, badges, interior trim, certain body panels, etc).

Accessory shops

These are very good places to buy materials and components needed for the maintenance of your car (oil, air and fuel filters, light bulbs, drivebelts, greases, brake pads, tough-up paint, etc). Components of this nature sold by a reputable shop are of the same standard as those used by the car manufacturer.

Besides components, these shops also sell tools and general accessories, usually have convenient opening hours, charge lower prices, and can often be found close to home. Some accessory shops have parts counters where components needed for almost any repair job can be purchased or ordered.

Motor factors

Good factors will stock all the more important components which wear out comparatively quickly, and can sometimes supply individual components needed for the overhaul of a larger assembly (eg, brake seals and hydraulic parts, bearing shells, pistons, valves). They may also handle work such as cylinder block reboring, crankshaft regrinding, etc.

Engine reconditioners

These specialise in engine overhaul and can also supply components. It is recommended that the establishment is a member of the Federation of Engine Re-Manufacturers, or a similar society.

Tyre and exhaust specialists

These outlets may be independent, or members of a local or national chain. They frequently offer competitive prices when compared with a main dealer or local garage, but it will pay to obtain several quotes before making a decision. When researching prices, also ask what 'extras' may be added – for instance fitting a new valve and balancing the wheel are both commonly charged on top of the price of a new tyre.

Other sources

Beware of parts or materials obtained from market stalls, car boot sales or similar outlets. Such items are not invariably sub-standard, but there is little chance of compensation if they do prove unsatisfactory. In the case of safety-critical components such as brake pads, there is the risk not only of financial loss, but also of an accident causing injury or death.

Second-hand components or assemblies obtained from a car breaker can be a good buy in some circumstances, but his sort of purchase is best made by the experienced DIY mechanic.

Vehicle identification

Modifications are a continuing and unpublicised process in vehicle manufacture, quite apart from major model changes. Spare parts manuals and lists are compiled upon a numerical basis, the individual vehicle identification numbers being essential to correct identification of the component concerned.

When ordering spare parts, always give as much information as possible. Quote the car model, year of manufacture, body and engine numbers as appropriate.

- The vehicle identification number (VIN) or chassis number appears in several places on the vehicle **(see illustrations)**:

a) Stamped on the bulkhead at the rear of the engine compartment.
b) Printed on a plate, attached to the top of the facia, behind the windscreen.
c) Printed on a label at the base of the left-hand B-post.

- The engine number is stamped on the front left-hand side of the cylinder block.
- The transmission number is printed on a plate, attached to the front/top of the transmission casing.
- The paint codes are printed on a label attached to passenger's glovebox lid, next to the tyre pressure chart.

The VIN is stamped in to the bulkhead at the rear of the engine compartment ...

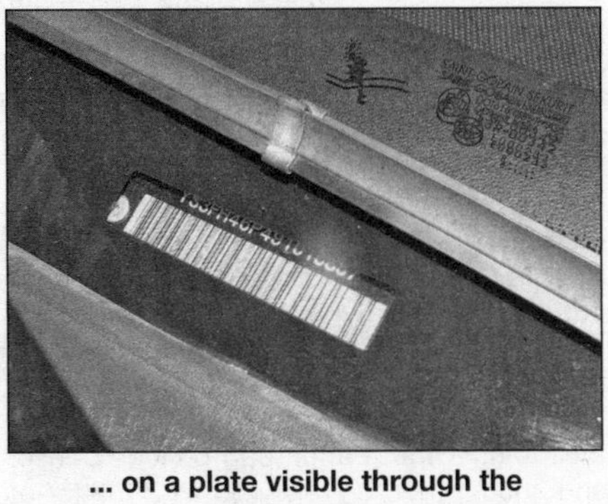

... on a plate visible through the windscreen ...

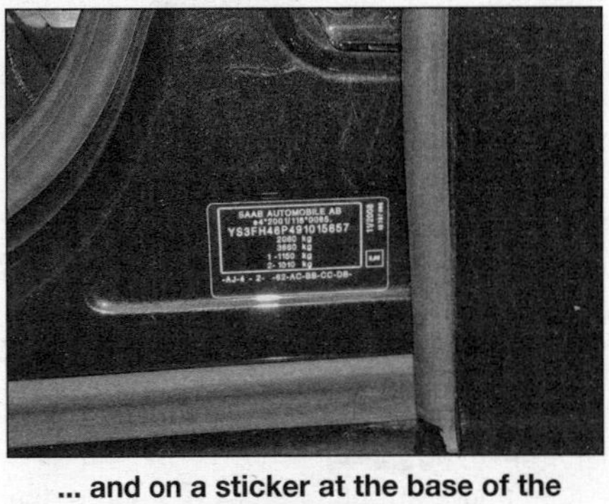

... and on a sticker at the base of the left-hand B-post

Whenever servicing, repair or overhaul work is carried out on the car or its components, observe the following procedures and instructions. This will assist in carrying out the operation efficiently and to a professional standard of workmanship.

Joint mating faces and gaskets

When separating components at their mating faces, never insert screwdrivers or similar implements into the joint between the faces in order to prise them apart. This can cause severe damage which results in oil leaks, coolant leaks, etc upon reassembly. Separation is usually achieved by tapping along the joint with a soft-faced hammer in order to break the seal. However, note that this method may not be suitable where dowels are used for component location.

Where a gasket is used between the mating faces of two components, a new one must be fitted on reassembly; fit it dry unless otherwise stated in the repair procedure. Make sure that the mating faces are clean and dry, with all traces of old gasket removed. When cleaning a joint face, use a tool which is unlikely to score or damage the face, and remove any burrs or nicks with an oilstone or fine file.

Make sure that tapped holes are cleaned with a pipe cleaner, and keep them free of jointing compound, if this is being used, unless specifically instructed otherwise.

Ensure that all orifices, channels or pipes are clear, and blow through them, preferably using compressed air.

Oil seals

Oil seals can be removed by levering them out with a wide flat-bladed screwdriver or similar implement. Alternatively, a number of self-tapping screws may be screwed into the seal, and these used as a purchase for pliers or some similar device in order to pull the seal free.

Whenever an oil seal is removed from its working location, either individually or as part of an assembly, it should be renewed.

The very fine sealing lip of the seal is easily damaged, and will not seal if the surface it contacts is not completely clean and free from scratches, nicks or grooves. If the original sealing surface of the component cannot be restored, and the manufacturer has not made provision for slight relocation of the seal relative to the sealing surface, the component should be renewed.

Protect the lips of the seal from any surface which may damage them in the course of fitting. Use tape or a conical sleeve where possible. Where indicated, lubricate the seal lips with oil before fitting and, on dual-lipped seals, fill the space between the lips with grease.

Unless otherwise stated, oil seals must be fitted with their sealing lips toward the lubricant to be sealed.

Use a tubular drift or block of wood of the appropriate size to install the seal and, if the seal housing is shouldered, drive the seal down to the shoulder. If the seal housing is unshouldered, the seal should be fitted with its face flush with the housing top face (unless otherwise instructed).

Screw threads and fastenings

Seized nuts, bolts and screws are quite a common occurrence where corrosion has set in, and the use of penetrating oil or releasing fluid will often overcome this problem if the offending item is soaked for a while before attempting to release it. The use of an impact driver may also provide a means of releasing such stubborn fastening devices, when used in conjunction with the appropriate screwdriver bit or socket. If none of these methods works, it may be necessary to resort to the careful application of heat, or the use of a hacksaw or nut splitter device. Before resorting to extreme methods, check that you are not dealing with a left-hand thread!

Studs are usually removed by locking two nuts together on the threaded part, and then using a spanner on the lower nut to unscrew the stud. Studs or bolts which have broken off below the surface of the component in which they are mounted can sometimes be removed using a stud extractor.

Always ensure that a blind tapped hole is completely free from oil, grease, water or other fluid before installing the bolt or stud. Failure to do this could cause the housing to crack due to the hydraulic action of the bolt or stud as it is screwed in.

For some screw fastenings, notably cylinder head bolts or nuts, torque wrench settings are no longer specified for the latter stages of tightening, "angle-tightening" being called up instead. Typically, a fairly low torque wrench setting will be applied to the bolts/nuts in the correct sequence, followed by one or more stages of tightening through specified angles.

When checking or retightening a nut or bolt to a specified torque setting, slacken the nut or bolt by a quarter of a turn, and then retighten to the specified setting. However, this should not be attempted where angular tightening has been used.

Locknuts, locktabs and washers

Any fastening which will rotate against a component or housing during tightening should always have a washer between it and the relevant component or housing.

Spring or split washers should always be renewed when they are used to lock a critical component such as a big-end bearing retaining bolt or nut. Locktabs which are folded over to retain a nut or bolt should always be renewed.

Self-locking nuts can be re-used in non-critical areas, providing resistance can be felt when the locking portion passes over the bolt or stud thread. However, it should be noted that self-locking stiffnuts tend to lose their effectiveness after long periods of use, and should then be renewed as a matter of course.

Split pins must always be replaced with new ones of the correct size for the hole.

When thread-locking compound is found on the threads of a fastener which is to be re-used, it should be cleaned off with a wire brush and solvent, and fresh compound applied on reassembly.

Special tools

Some repair procedures in this manual entail the use of special tools such as a press, two or three-legged pullers, spring compressors, etc. Wherever possible, suitable readily-available alternatives to the manufacturer's special tools are described, and are shown in use. In some instances, where no alternative is possible, it has been necessary to resort to the use of a manufacturer's tool, and this has been done for reasons of safety as well as the efficient completion of the repair operation. Unless you are highly-skilled and have a thorough understanding of the procedures described, never attempt to bypass the use of any special tool when the procedure described specifies its use. Not only is there a very great risk of personal injury, but expensive damage could be caused to the components involved.

Environmental considerations

When disposing of used engine oil, brake fluid, antifreeze, etc, give due consideration to any detrimental environmental effects. Do not, for instance, pour any of the above liquids down drains into the general sewage system, or onto the ground to soak away. Many local council refuse tips provide a facility for waste oil disposal, as do some garages. You can find your nearest disposal point by calling the Environment Agency on 08708 506 506 or by visiting www.oilbankline.org.uk.

OIL CARE
FOLLOW THE CODE

Note: It is illegal and anti-social to dump oil down the drain. To find the location of your local oil recycling bank, call 08708 506 506 or visit www.oilbankline.org.uk.

The jack supplied with the vehicle tool kit should only be used for changing the roadwheels – see *Wheel changing* at the front of this manual. When carrying out any other kind of work, raise the vehicle using a hydraulic trolley jack, and always supplement the jack with axle stands positioned under the vehicle jacking points.

When using a trolley jack or axle stands, always position the jack head or axle stand head under, or adjacent to one of the relevant wheel changing jacking points under the sills. Use a block of wood between the jack or axle stand and the sill – the block of wood should have a groove cut into it, in which the welded flange of the sill will locate **(see illustrations)**.

Do not attempt to jack the vehicle under the rear axle, floorpan, engine sump, automatic transmission sump, or any of the suspension components.

The jack supplied with the vehicle locates in the jacking points on the underside of the sills – see *Wheel changing* at the front of this manual. Ensure that the jack head is correctly engaged before attempting to raise the vehicle.

Never work under, around, or near a raised vehicle, unless it is adequately supported in at least two places.

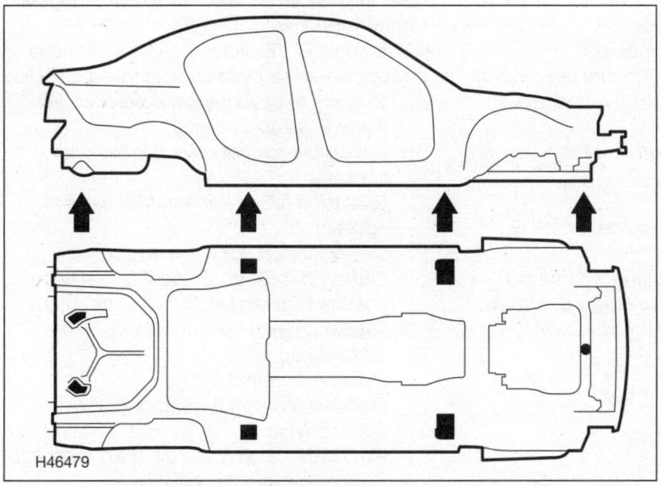

Jacking points for hydraulic jack (arrowed)

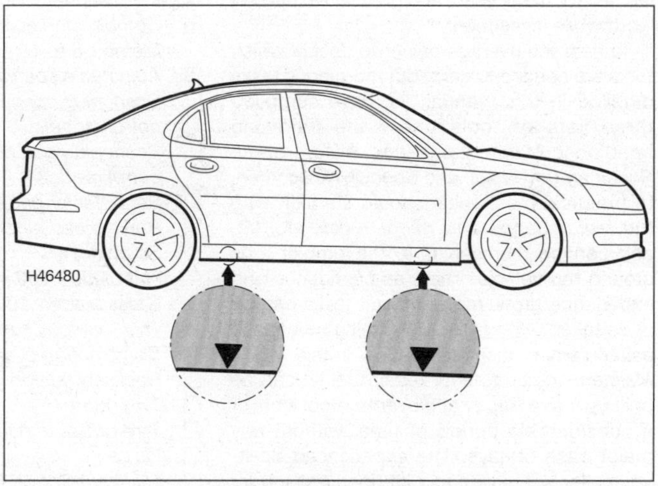

Wheel changing jacking points are identified by triangular indentations in the sills

Disconnecting the battery

Caution: After reconnecting the battery, the anti-pinch function of the electric windows will not be reinstated until the windows have been reprogrammed. This could potentially cause severe pinching injuries (see Chapter 5A, Section 4).

Whenever the battery is to be disconnected (see Chapter 5A, Section 4), first note the following points to ensure there are no unforeseen consequences. Several of the systems require battery power to be available at all times (permanent live). This is either to ensure their continued operation (such as the clock) or to maintain electronic memory settings which would otherwise be erased.

a) *Firstly, on any vehicle with central door locking, it is a wise precaution to remove the key from the ignition, and to keep it with you. This avoids the possibility of the key being locked inside the car, should the central locking engage when the battery is reconnected.*

b) *The engine management system ECM is of the 'self-learning' type, meaning that, as it operates, it adapts to changes in operating conditions, and stores the optimum settings found (this is especially true for idle speed settings). When the battery is disconnected, these 'learned' settings are lost, and the ECM reverts to the base factory settings. When the engine is restarted, it may idle and run roughly until the ECM has 'relearned' the best settings. To further this 'learning' process, take the car for a road test of at least 15 minutes' duration, covering as many engine speeds and loads as possible, and concentrating on the 2000 to 4000 rpm range. On completion, let the engine idle for at least 10 minutes, turning the steering wheel occasionally and switching on high-current-draw equipment such as the heater fan or heated rear window. If the engine does not regain its normal performance, have the system checked for faults by a Saab dealer or suitably-equipped garage.*

c) *When reconnecting the battery, turn the sidelights on for a few minutes before attempting to start the vehicle.*

d) *After the battery has been reconnected, the electric windows positions must be reprogrammed as described in Chapter 5A, Section 4.*

e) *When reconnecting the battery the vehicle must be driven at a speed greater than 11 mph and then brought to a stop to enable the CIM (column integrated module) and steering lock to function correctly.*

f) *All available remote controls must be synchronised by placing them in the ignition lock.*

Devices known as 'memory-savers' or 'code-savers' can be used to avoid some of the above problems. Precise details of use vary according to the device used. Typically, it is plugged into the cigarette lighter socket, and is connected by its own wiring to a spare battery; the vehicle battery is then disconnected from the electrical system, leaving the memory-saver to pass sufficient current to maintain audio unit security codes, and other memory values, and also to run permanently-live circuits such as the clock.

Warning: Some of these devices allow a considerable amount of current to pass, which can mean that many of the vehicle's systems are still operational when the main battery is disconnected. If a memory-saver is used, ensure that the circuit concerned is actually 'dead' before carrying out any work on it.

Introduction

A selection of good tools is a fundamental requirement for anyone contemplating the maintenance and repair of a motor vehicle. For the owner who does not possess any, their purchase will prove a considerable expense, offsetting some of the savings made by doing-it-yourself. However, provided that the tools purchased meet the relevant national safety standards and are of good quality, they will last for many years and prove an extremely worthwhile investment.

To help the average owner to decide which tools are needed to carry out the various tasks detailed in this manual, we have compiled three lists of tools under the following headings: *Maintenance and minor repair, Repair and overhaul*, and *Special*. Newcomers to practical mechanics should start off with the *Maintenance and minor repair* tool kit, and confine themselves to the simpler jobs around the vehicle. Then, as confidence and experience grow, more difficult tasks can be undertaken, with extra tools being purchased as, and when, they are needed. In this way, a *Maintenance and minor repair* tool kit can be built up into a *Repair and overhaul* tool kit over a considerable period of time, without any major cash outlays. The experienced do-it-yourselfer will have a tool kit good enough for most repair and overhaul procedures, and will add tools from the *Special* category when it is felt that the expense is justified by the amount of use to which these tools will be put.

Maintenance and minor repair tool kit

The tools given in this list should be considered as a minimum requirement if routine maintenance, servicing and minor repair operations are to be undertaken. We recommend the purchase of combination spanners (ring one end, open-ended the other); although more expensive than open-ended ones, they do give the advantages of both types of spanner.

- ☐ *Combination spanners:*
  Metric - 8 to 19 mm inclusive
- ☐ *Adjustable spanner - 35 mm jaw (approx.)*
- ☐ *Spark plug spanner (with rubber insert) - petrol models*
- ☐ *Spark plug gap adjustment tool - petrol models*
- ☐ *Set of feeler gauges*
- ☐ *Brake bleed nipple spanner*
- ☐ *Screwdrivers:*
  Flat blade - 100 mm long x 6 mm dia
  Cross blade - 100 mm long x 6 mm dia
  Torx - various sizes (not all vehicles)
- ☐ *Combination pliers*
- ☐ *Hacksaw (junior)*
- ☐ *Tyre pump*
- ☐ *Tyre pressure gauge*
- ☐ *Oil can*
- ☐ *Oil filter removal tool (if applicable)*
- ☐ *Fine emery cloth*
- ☐ *Wire brush (small)*
- ☐ *Funnel (medium size)*
- ☐ *Sump drain plug key (not all vehicles)*

Repair and overhaul tool kit

These tools are virtually essential for anyone undertaking any major repairs to a motor vehicle, and are additional to those given in the *Maintenance and minor repair* list. Included in this list is a comprehensive set of sockets. Although these are expensive, they will be found invaluable as they are so versatile - particularly if various drives are included in the set. We recommend the half-inch square-drive type, as this can be used with most proprietary torque wrenches.

The tools in this list will sometimes need to be supplemented by tools from the *Special* list:

- ☐ *Sockets to cover range in previous list (including Torx sockets)*
- ☐ *Reversible ratchet drive (for use with sockets)*
- ☐ *Extension piece, 250 mm (for use with sockets)*
- ☐ *Universal joint (for use with sockets)*
- ☐ *Flexible handle or sliding T "breaker bar" (for use with sockets)*
- ☐ *Torque wrench (for use with sockets)*
- ☐ *Self-locking grips*
- ☐ *Ball pein hammer*
- ☐ *Soft-faced mallet (plastic or rubber)*
- ☐ *Screwdrivers:*
  Flat blade - long & sturdy, short (chubby), and narrow (electrician's) types
  Cross blade – long & sturdy, and short (chubby) types
- ☐ *Pliers:*
  Long-nosed
  Side cutters (electrician's)
  Circlip (internal and external)
- ☐ *Cold chisel - 25 mm*
- ☐ *Scriber*
- ☐ *Scraper*
- ☐ *Centre-punch*
- ☐ *Pin punch*
- ☐ *Hacksaw*
- ☐ *Brake hose clamp*
- ☐ *Brake/clutch bleeding kit*
- ☐ *Selection of twist drills*
- ☐ *Steel rule/straight-edge*
- ☐ *Allen keys (inc. splined/Torx type)*
- ☐ *Selection of files*
- ☐ *Wire brush*
- ☐ *Axle stands*
- ☐ *Jack (strong trolley or hydraulic type)*
- ☐ *Light with extension lead*
- ☐ *Universal electrical multi-meter*

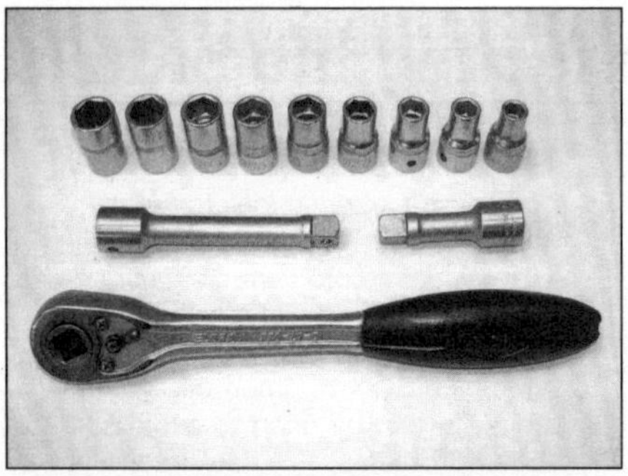

Sockets and reversible ratchet drive

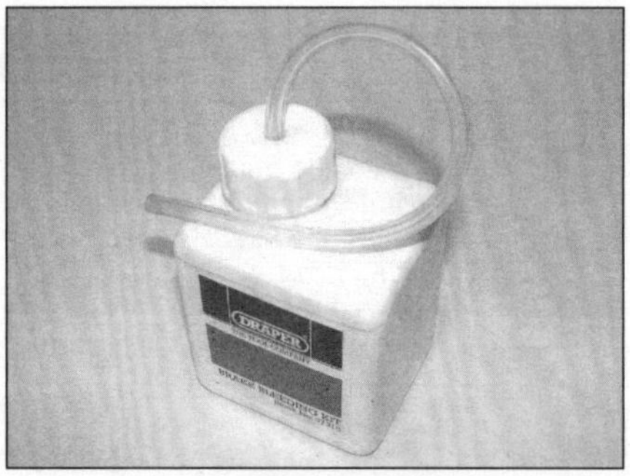

Brake bleeding kit

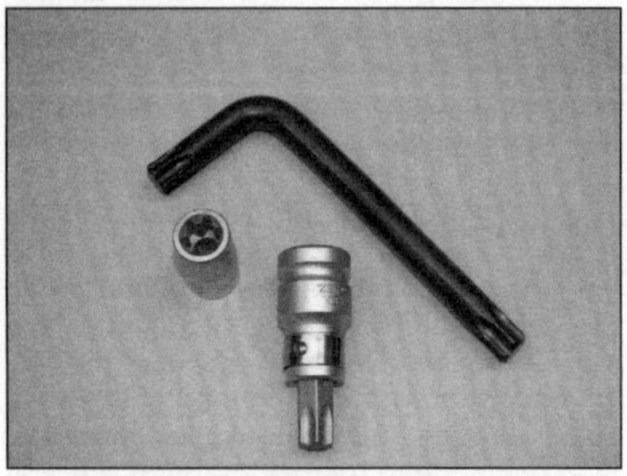

Torx key, socket and bit

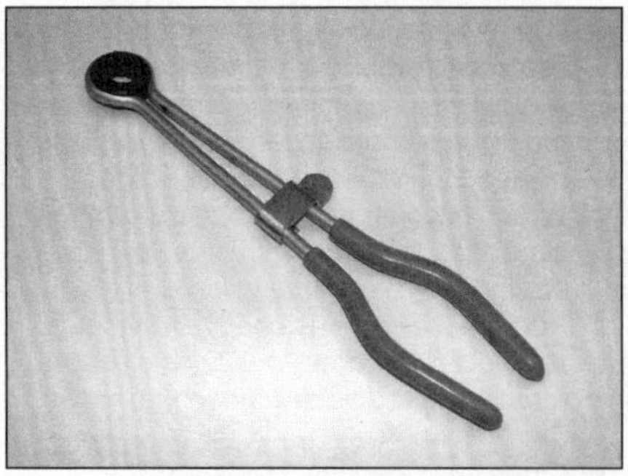

Hose clamp

Angular-tightening gauge

Special tools

The tools in this list are those which are not used regularly, are expensive to buy, or which need to be used in accordance with their manufacturers' instructions. Unless relatively difficult mechanical jobs are undertaken frequently, it will not be economic to buy many of these tools. Where this is the case, you could consider clubbing together with friends (or joining a motorists' club) to make a joint purchase, or borrowing the tools against a deposit from a local garage or tool hire specialist.

The following list contains only those tools and instruments freely available to the public, and not those special tools produced by the vehicle manufacturer specifically for its dealer network. You will find occasional references to these manufacturers' special tools in the text of this manual. Generally, an alternative method of doing the job without the vehicle manufacturers' special tool is given. However, sometimes there is no alternative to using them. Where this is the case and the relevant tool cannot be bought or borrowed, you will have to entrust the work to a dealer.

☐ *Angular-tightening gauge*
☐ *Valve spring compressor*
☐ *Valve grinding tool*
☐ *Piston ring compressor*
☐ *Piston ring removal/installation tool*
☐ *Cylinder bore hone*
☐ *Balljoint separator*
☐ *Coil spring compressors (where applicable)*
☐ *Two/three-legged hub and bearing puller*
☐ *Impact screwdriver*
☐ *Micrometer and/or vernier calipers*
☐ *Dial gauge*
☐ *Tachometer*
☐ *Fault code reader*
☐ *Cylinder compression gauge*
☐ *Hand-operated vacuum pump and gauge*
☐ *Clutch plate alignment set*
☐ *Brake shoe steady spring cup removal tool*
☐ *Bush and bearing removal/installation set*
☐ *Stud extractors*
☐ *Tap and die set*
☐ *Lifting tackle*

Buying tools

Reputable motor accessory shops and superstores often offer excellent quality tools at discount prices, so it pays to shop around.

Remember, you don't have to buy the most expensive items on the shelf, but it is always advisable to steer clear of the very cheap tools. Beware of 'bargains' offered on market stalls, on-line or at car boot sales. There are plenty of good tools around at reasonable prices, but always aim to purchase items which meet the relevant national safety standards. If in doubt, ask the proprietor or manager of the shop for advice before making a purchase.

Care and maintenance of tools

Having purchased a reasonable tool kit, it is necessary to keep the tools in a clean and serviceable condition. After use, always wipe off any dirt, grease and metal particles using a clean, dry cloth, before putting the tools away. Never leave them lying around after they have been used. A simple tool rack on the garage or workshop wall for items such as screwdrivers and pliers is a good idea. Store all normal spanners and sockets in a metal box. Any measuring instruments, gauges, meters, etc, must be carefully stored where they cannot be damaged or become rusty.

Take a little care when tools are used. Hammer heads inevitably become marked, and screwdrivers lose the keen edge on their blades from time to time. A little timely attention with emery cloth or a file will soon restore items like this to a good finish.

Working facilities

Not to be forgotten when discussing tools is the workshop itself. If anything more than routine maintenance is to be carried out, a suitable working area becomes essential.

It is appreciated that many an owner-mechanic is forced by circumstances to remove an engine or similar item without the benefit of a garage or workshop. Having done this, any repairs should always be done under the cover of a roof.

Wherever possible, any dismantling should be done on a clean, flat workbench or table at a suitable working height.

Any workbench needs a vice; one with a jaw opening of 100 mm is suitable for most jobs. As mentioned previously, some clean dry storage space is also required for tools, as well as for any lubricants, cleaning fluids, touch-up paints etc, which become necessary.

Another item which may be required, and which has a much more general usage, is an electric drill with a chuck capacity of at least 8 mm. This, together with a good range of twist drills, is virtually essential for fitting accessories.

Last, but not least, always keep a supply of old newspapers and clean, lint-free rags available, and try to keep any working area as clean as possible.

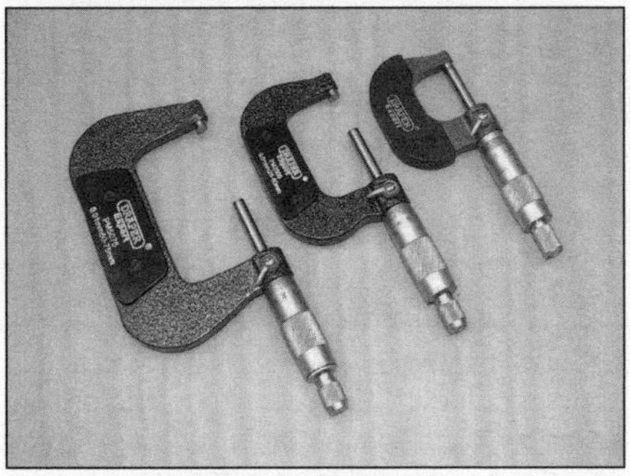

Micrometers

Dial test indicator ("dial gauge")

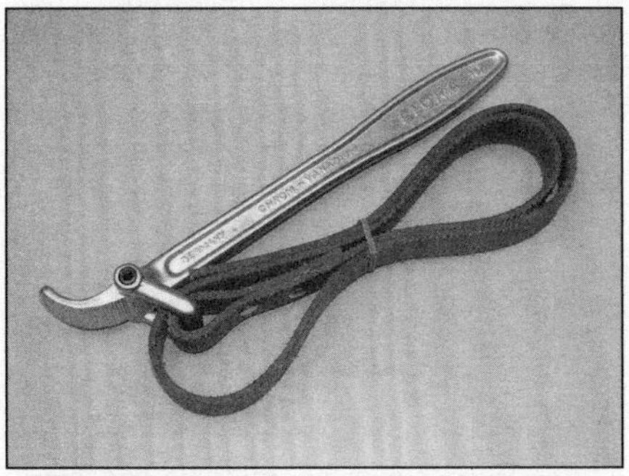

Oil filter removal tool (strap wrench type)

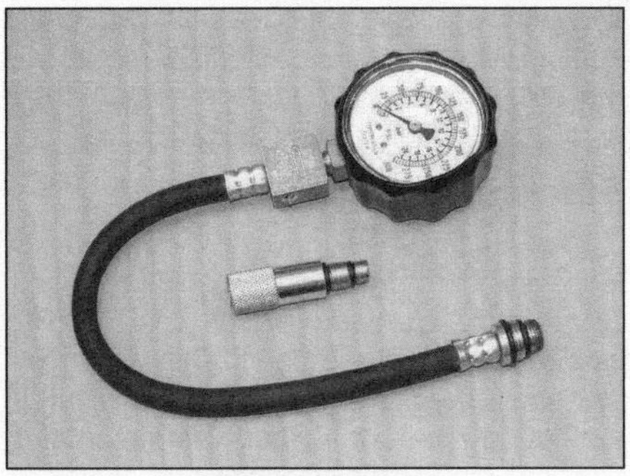

Compression tester

Bearing puller

MOT test checks

This is a guide to getting your vehicle through the MOT test. Obviously it will not be possible to examine the vehicle to the same standard as the professional MOT tester. However, working through the following checks will enable you to identify any problem areas before submitting the vehicle for the test.

It has only been possible to summarise the test requirements here, based on the regulations in force at the time of printing. Test standards are becoming increasingly stringent, although there are some exemptions for older vehicles.

An assistant will be needed to help carry out some of these checks.

The checks have been sub-divided into four categories, as follows:

1 Checks carried out **FROM THE DRIVER'S SEAT**

2 Checks carried out **WITH THE VEHICLE ON THE GROUND**

3 Checks carried out **WITH THE VEHICLE RAISED AND THE WHEELS FREE TO TURN**

4 Checks carried out on **YOUR VEHICLE'S EXHAUST EMISSION SYSTEM**

1 Checks carried out FROM THE DRIVER'S SEAT

Handbrake (parking brake)

□ Test the operation of the handbrake. Excessive travel (too many clicks) indicates incorrect brake or cable adjustment.

□ Check that the handbrake cannot be released by tapping the lever sideways. Check the security of the lever mountings.

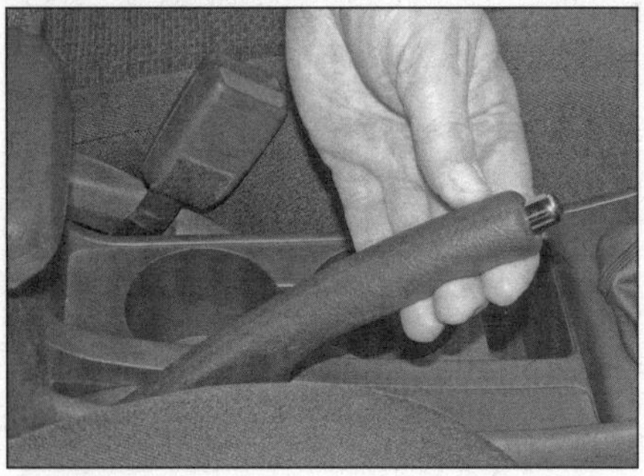

□ If the parking brake is foot-operated, check that the pedal is secure and without excessive travel, and that the release mechanism operates correctly.

□ Where applicable, test the operation of the electronic handbrake. The brake should engage and disengage without excessive delay. If the warning light does not extinguish when the brake is disengaged, this could indicate a fault which will need further investigation.

Footbrake

□ Depress the brake pedal and check that it does not creep down to the floor, indicating a master cylinder fault. Release the pedal, wait a few seconds, then depress it again. If the pedal travels nearly to the floor before firm resistance is felt, brake adjustment or repair is necessary. If the pedal feels spongy, there is air in the hydraulic system which must be removed by bleeding.

□ Check that the brake pedal is secure and in good condition. Check also for signs of fluid leaks on the pedal, floor or carpets, which would indicate failed seals in the brake master cylinder.

□ Check the servo unit (when applicable) by operating the brake pedal several times, then keeping the pedal depressed and starting the engine. As the engine starts, the pedal will move down slightly. If not, the vacuum hose or the servo itself may be faulty.

Steering wheel and column

□ Examine the steering wheel for fractures or looseness of the hub, spokes or rim.

□ Move the steering wheel from side to side and then up and down. Check that the steering wheel is not loose on the column, indicating wear or a loose retaining nut. Continue moving the steering wheel as before, but also turn it slightly from left to right.

□ Check that the steering wheel is not loose on the column, and that there is no abnormal movement of the steering wheel, indicating wear in the column support bearings or couplings.

□ Check that the ignition lock (where fitted) engages and disengages correctly.

□ Steering column adjustment mechanisms (where fitted) must be able to lock the column securely in place with no play evident.

Windscreen, mirrors and sunvisor

□ The windscreen must be free of cracks or other significant damage within the driver's field of view. (Small stone chips are acceptable.) Rear view mirrors must be secure, intact, and capable of being adjusted.

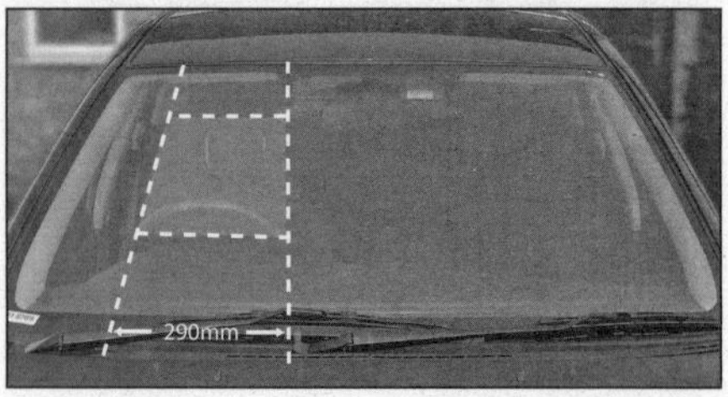

□ The driver's sunvisor must be capable of being stored in the "up" position.

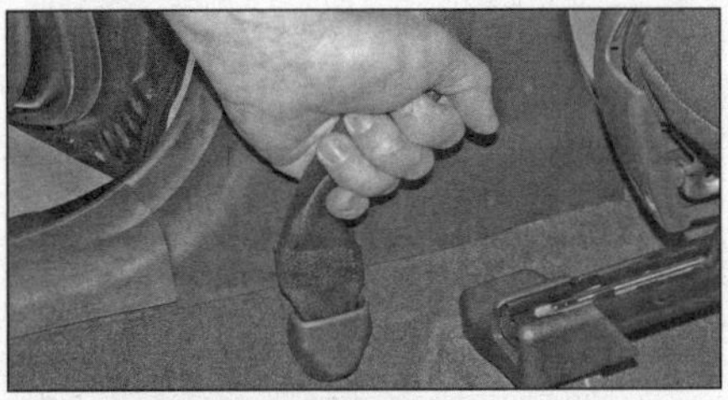

Seat belts and seats

Note: *The following checks are applicable to all seat belts, front and rear.*

☐Examine the webbing of all the belts (including rear belts if fitted) for cuts, serious fraying or deterioration. Fasten and unfasten each belt to check the buckles. If applicable, check the retracting mechanism. Check the security of all seat belt mountings accessible from inside the vehicle, ensuring any height adjustable mountings lock securely in place.

☐Seat belts with pre-tensioners, once activated, have a "flag" or similar showing on the seat belt stalk. This, in itself, is not a reason for test failure.

☐The front seats themselves must be securely attached and the backrests must lock in the upright position.

Doors

☐Both front doors must be able to be opened and closed from outside and inside, and must latch securely when closed.

Bonnet and boot/tailgate

☐The bonnet and boot/tailgate must latch securely when closed.

2 Checks carried out WITH THE VEHICLE ON THE GROUND

Vehicle identification

☐Number plates must be in good condition, secure and legible, with letters and numbers correctly spaced – spacing at (A) should be 33 mm and at (B) 11 mm. At the front, digits must be black on a white background and at the rear black on a yellow background. Other background designs (such as honeycomb) are not permitted.

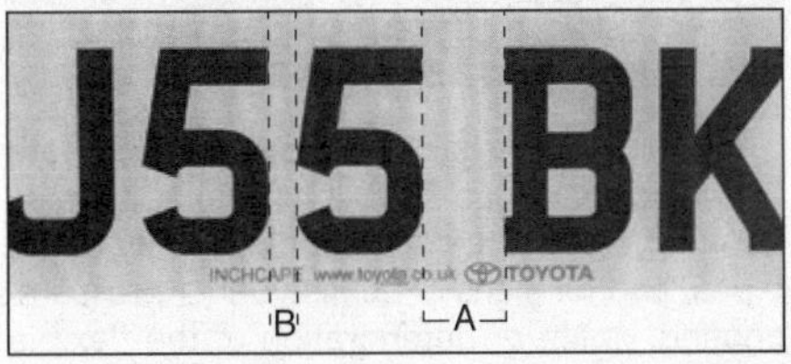

☐The VIN plate and/or homologation plate must be permanently displayed and legible.

Electrical equipment

☐Switch on the ignition and check the operation of the horn.

☐Check the windscreen washers and wipers, examining the wiper blades; renew damaged or perished blades. Also check the operation of the stop-lights.

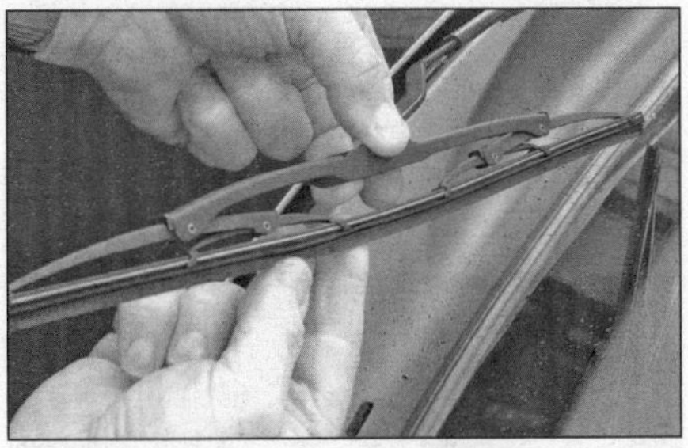

☐Check the operation of the sidelights and number plate lights. The lenses and reflectors must be secure, clean and undamaged.

☐Check the operation and alignment of the headlights. The headlight reflectors must not be tarnished and the lenses must be undamaged.

☐Switch on the ignition and check the operation of the direction indicators (including the instrument panel tell-tale) and the hazard warning lights. Operation of the sidelights and stop-lights must not affect the indicators - if it does, the cause is usually a bad earth at the rear light cluster. Indicators should flash at a rate of between 60 and 120 times per minute – faster or slower than this could indicate a fault with the flasher unit or a bad earth at one of the light units.

☐Check the operation of the rear foglight(s), including the warning light on the instrument panel or in the switch.

☐The warning lights must illuminate in accordance with the manufacturer's design. For most vehicles, the ABS and other warning lights should illuminate when the ignition is switched on, and (if the system is operating properly) extinguish after a few seconds. Refer to the owner's handbook.

Footbrake

☐Examine the master cylinder, brake pipes and servo unit for leaks, loose mountings, corrosion or other damage. If ABS is fitted, this unit should also be examined for signs of leaks or corrosion.

☐The fluid reservoir must be secure and the fluid level must be between the upper (**A**) and lower (**B**) markings.

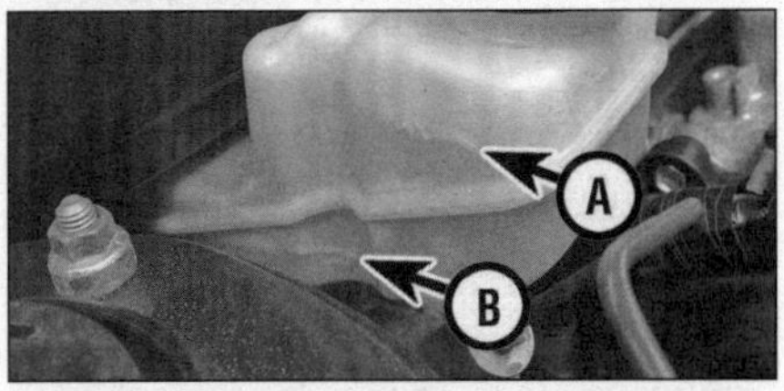

☐Inspect both front brake flexible hoses for cracks or deterioration of the rubber. Turn the steering from lock to lock, and ensure that the hoses do not contact the wheel, tyre, or any part of the steering or suspension mechanism. With the brake pedal firmly depressed, check the hoses for bulges or leaks under pressure.

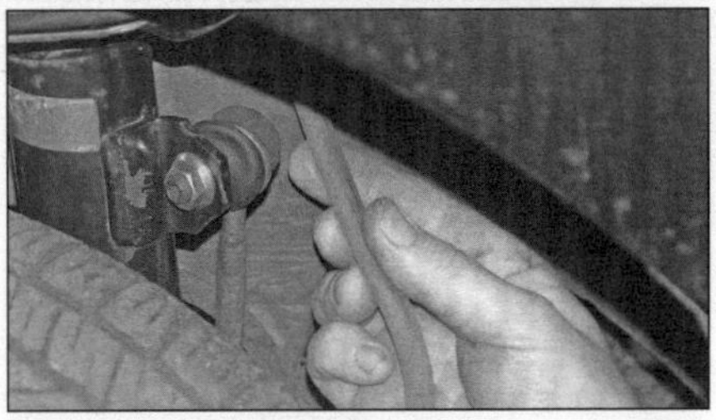

Steering and suspension

☐Have your assistant turn the steering wheel from side to side slightly, up to the point where the steering gear just begins to transmit this movement to the roadwheels. Check for excessive free play between the steering wheel and the steering gear, indicating wear or insecurity of the steering column joints, the column-to-steering gear coupling, or the steering gear itself.

☐Have your assistant turn the steering wheel more vigorously in each direction, so that the roadwheels just begin to turn. As this is done, examine all the steering joints, linkages, fittings and attachments. Renew any component that shows signs of wear or damage. On vehicles with power steering, check the security and condition of the steering pump, drivebelt and hoses.

☐Check that the vehicle is standing level, and at approximately the correct ride height.

Shock absorbers

☐Depress each corner of the vehicle in turn, then release it. The vehicle should rise and then settle in its normal position. If the vehicle continues to rise and fall, the shock absorber is defective. A shock absorber which has seized will also cause the vehicle to fail.

Exhaust system

□ Start the engine. With your assistant holding a rag over the tailpipe, check the entire system for leaks. Repair or renew leaking sections.

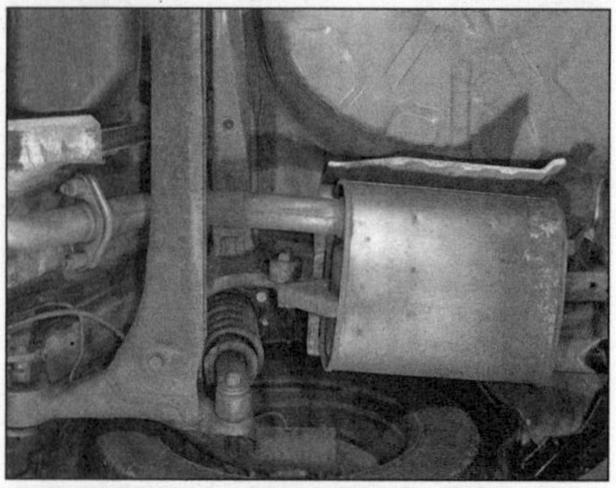

3 Checks carried out WITH THE VEHICLE RAISED AND THE WHEELS FREE TO TURN

Jack up the front and rear of the vehicle, and securely support it on axle stands. Position the stands clear of the suspension assemblies. Ensure that the wheels are clear of the ground and that the steering can be turned from lock to lock.

Steering mechanism

□ Have your assistant turn the steering from lock to lock. Check that the steering turns smoothly, and that no part of the steering mechanism, including a wheel or tyre, fouls any brake hose or pipe or any part of the body structure.

□ Examine the steering rack rubber gaiters for damage or insecurity of the retaining clips. If power steering is fitted, check for signs of damage or leakage of the fluid hoses, pipes or connections. Also check for excessive stiffness or binding of the steering, a missing split pin or locking device, or severe corrosion of the body structure within 30 cm of any steering component attachment point.

Front and rear suspension and wheel bearings

□ Starting at the front right-hand side, grasp the roadwheel at the 3 o'clock and 9 o'clock positions and rock gently but firmly. Check for free play or insecurity at the wheel bearings, suspension balljoints, or suspension mount-ings, pivots and attachments.

□ Now grasp the wheel at the 12 o'clock and 6 o'clock positions and repeat the previous inspection. Spin the wheel, and check for roughness or tightness of the front wheel bearing.

□ If excess free play is suspected at a component pivot point, this can be confirmed by using a large screwdriver or similar tool and levering between the mounting and the component attachment. This will confirm whether the wear is in the pivot bush, its retaining bolt, or in the mounting itself (the bolt holes can often become elongated).

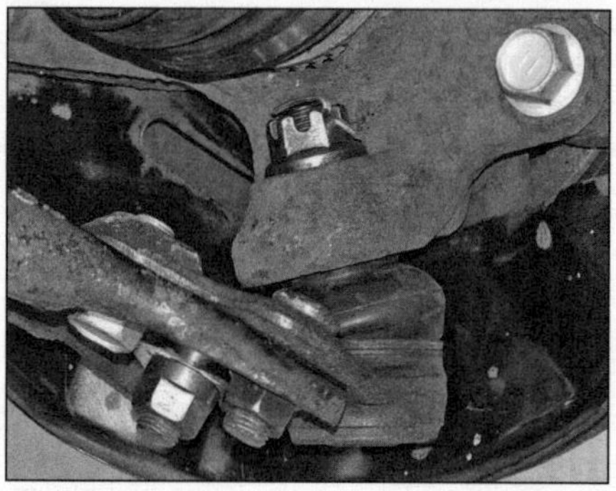

□ Carry out all the above checks at the other front wheel, and then at both rear wheels.

Springs and shock absorbers

□ Examine the suspension struts (when applicable) for serious fluid leakage, corrosion, or damage to the casing. Also check the security of the mounting points.

□ If coil springs are fitted, check that the spring ends locate in their seats, and that the spring is not corroded, cracked or broken.

□ If leaf springs are fitted, check that all leaves are intact, that the axle is securely attached to each spring, and that there is no deterioration of the spring eye mountings, bushes, and shackles.

□ The same general checks apply to vehicles fitted with other suspension types, such as torsion bars, hydraulic displacer units, etc. Ensure that all mountings and attachments are secure, that there are no signs of excessive wear, corrosion or damage, and (on hydraulic types) that there are no fluid leaks or damaged pipes.

□ Inspect the shock absorbers for signs of serious fluid leakage. Check for wear of the mounting bushes or attachments, or damage to the body of the unit.

Driveshafts (fwd vehicles only)

□ Rotate each front wheel in turn and inspect the constant velocity joint gaiters for splits or damage. Also check that each driveshaft is straight and undamaged.

Braking system

□ If possible without dismantling, check brake pad wear and disc condition. Ensure that the friction lining material has not worn excessively, (A) and that the discs are not fractured, pitted, scored or badly worn (B).

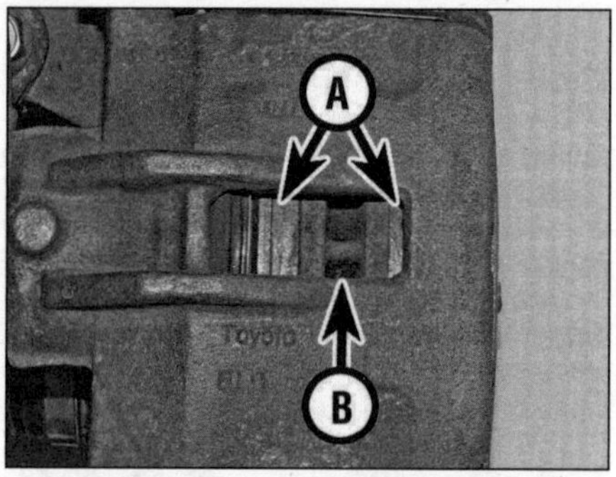

□ Examine all the rigid brake pipes underneath the vehicle, and the flexible hose(s) at the rear. Look for corrosion, chafing or insecurity of the pipes, and for signs of bulging under pressure, chafing, splits or deterioration of the flexible hoses.

□ Look for signs of fluid leaks at the brake calipers or on the brake backplates. Repair or renew leaking components.

□ Slowly spin each wheel, while your assistant depresses and releases the footbrake. Ensure that each brake is operating and does not bind when the pedal is released.

☐ Examine the handbrake mechanism, checking for frayed or broken cables, excessive corrosion, or wear or insecurity of the linkage. Check that the mechanism works on each relevant wheel, and releases fully, without binding.

☐ It is not possible to test brake efficiency without special equipment, but a road test can be carried out later to check that the vehicle pulls up in a straight line.

Fuel and exhaust systems

☐ Inspect the fuel tank (including the filler cap), fuel pipes, hoses and unions. All components must be secure and free from leaks. Locking fuel caps must lock securely and the key must be provided for the MOT test.

☐ Examine the exhaust system over its entire length, checking for any damaged, broken or missing mountings, security of the retaining clamps and rust or corrosion.

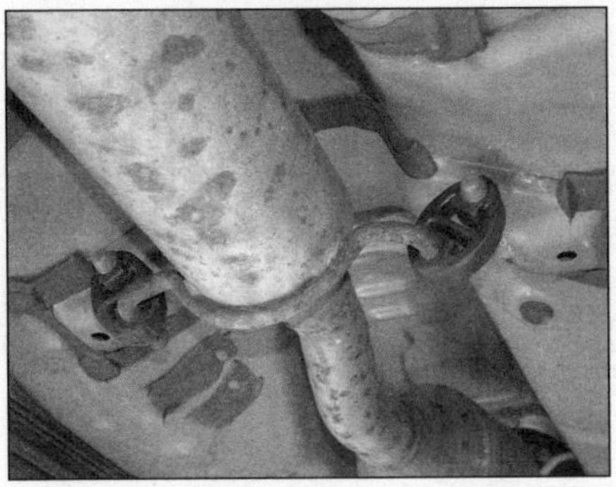

Wheels and tyres

☐ Examine the sidewalls and tread area of each tyre in turn. Check for cuts, tears, lumps, bulges, separation of the tread, and exposure of the ply or cord due to wear or damage. Check that the tyre bead is correctly seated on the wheel rim, that the valve is sound and properly seated, and that the wheel is not distorted or damaged.

☐ Check that the tyres are of the correct size for the vehicle, that they are of the same size and type on each axle, and that the pressures are correct.

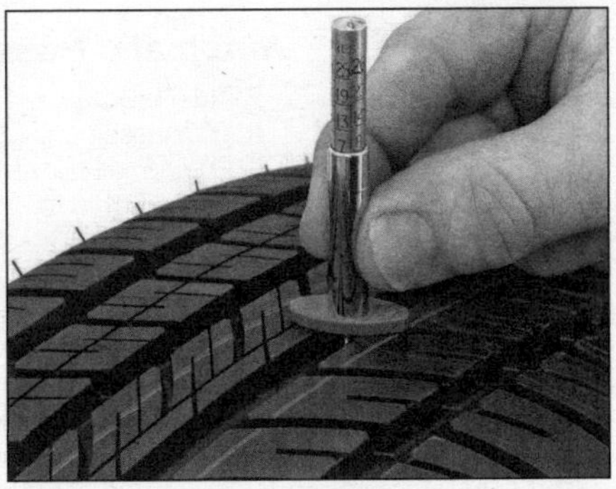

☐ Check the tyre tread depth. The legal minimum at the time of writing is 1.6 mm over the central three-quarters of the tread width. Abnormal tread wear may indicate incorrect front wheel alignment or wear in steering or suspension components.

☐ If the spare wheel is fitted externally or in a separate carrier beneath the vehicle, check that mountings are secure and free of excessive corrosion.

Body corrosion

☐ Check the condition of the entire vehicle structure for signs of corrosion in load-bearing areas. (These include chassis box sections, side sills, cross-members, pillars, and all suspension, steering, braking system and seat belt mountings and anchorages.) Any corrosion which has seriously reduced the thickness of a load-bearing area (or is within 30 cm of safety-related components such as steering or suspension) is likely to cause the vehicle to fail. In this case professional repairs are likely to be needed.

☐ Damage or corrosion which causes sharp or otherwise dangerous edges to be exposed will also cause the vehicle to fail.

Towbars

☐ Check the condition of mounting points (both beneath the vehicle and within boot/ hatchback areas) for signs of corrosion, ensuring that all fixings are secure and not worn or damaged. There must be no excessive play in detachable tow ball arms or quick-release mechanisms.

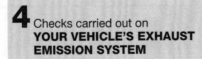

4 Checks carried out on YOUR VEHICLE'S EXHAUST EMISSION SYSTEM

Petrol models

☐ The engine should be warmed up, and running well (ignition system in good order, air filter element clean, etc).

☐ Before testing, run the engine at around 2500 rpm for 20 seconds. Let the engine drop to idle, and watch for smoke from the exhaust. If the idle speed is too high, or if dense blue or black smoke emerges for more than 5 seconds, the vehicle will fail. Typically, blue smoke signifies oil burning (engine wear); black smoke means unburnt fuel (dirty air cleaner element, or other fuel system fault).

☐ An exhaust gas analyser for measuring carbon monoxide (CO) and hydrocarbons (HC) is now needed. If one cannot be hired or borrowed, have a local garage perform the check.

CO emissions (mixture)

☐ The MOT tester has access to the CO limits for all vehicles. The CO level is measured at idle speed, and at 'fast idle' (2500 to 3000 rpm). The following limits are given as a general guide:

At idle speed – Less than 0.5% CO
At 'fast idle' – Less than 0.3% CO
Lambda reading – 0.97 to 1.03

☐ If the CO level is too high, this may point to poor maintenance, a fuel injection system problem, faulty lambda (oxygen) sensor or catalytic converter. Try an injector cleaning treatment, and check the vehicle's ECU for fault codes.

HC emissions

☐ The MOT tester has access to HC limits for all vehicles. The HC level is measured at 'fast idle' (2500 to 3000 rpm). The following limits are given as a general guide:

At 'fast idle' – Less then 200 ppm

☐ Excessive HC emissions are typically caused by oil being burnt (worn engine), or by a blocked crankcase ventilation system ('breather'). If the engine oil is old and thin, an oil change may help. If the engine is running badly, check the vehicle's ECU for fault codes.

Diesel models

☐ The only emission test for diesel engines is measuring exhaust smoke density, using a calibrated smoke meter. The test involves accelerating the engine at least 3 times to its maximum unloaded speed.

Note: *On engines with a timing belt, it is VITAL that the belt is in good condition before the test is carried out.*

☐ With the engine warmed up, it is first purged by running at around 2500 rpm for 20 seconds. A governor check is then carried out, by slowly accelerating the engine to its maximum speed. After this, the smoke meter is connected, and the engine is accelerated quickly to maximum speed three times. If the smoke density is less than the limits given below, the vehicle will pass:

Non-turbo vehicles: 2.5m-1
Turbocharged vehicles: 3.0m-1

☐ If excess smoke is produced, try fitting a new air cleaner element, or using an injector cleaning treatment. If the engine is running badly, where applicable, check the vehicle's ECU for fault codes. Also check the vehicle's EGR system, where applicable. At high mileages, the injectors may require professional attention.

Engine
- ☐ Engine fails to rotate when attempting to start
- ☐ Engine rotates, but will not start
- ☐ Engine difficult to start when cold
- ☐ Engine difficult to start when hot
- ☐ Starter motor noisy or excessively-rough in engagement
- ☐ Engine starts, but stops immediately
- ☐ Engine idles erratically
- ☐ Engine misfires at idle speed
- ☐ Engine misfires throughout the driving speed range
- ☐ Engine hesitates on acceleration
- ☐ Engine stalls
- ☐ Engine lacks power
- ☐ Engine backfires
- ☐ Oil pressure warning light illuminated with engine running
- ☐ Engine runs-on after switching off
- ☐ Engine noises

Cooling system
- ☐ Overheating
- ☐ Overcooling
- ☐ External coolant leakage
- ☐ Internal coolant leakage
- ☐ Corrosion

Fuel and exhaust systems
- ☐ Excessive fuel consumption
- ☐ Fuel leakage and/or fuel odour
- ☐ Excessive noise or fumes from the exhaust system

Clutch
- ☐ Pedal travels to floor – no pressure or very little resistance
- ☐ Clutch fails to disengage (unable to select gears)
- ☐ Clutch slips (engine speed increases, with no increase in vehicle speed)
- ☐ Judder as clutch is engaged
- ☐ Noise when depressing or releasing clutch pedal

Manual transmission
- ☐ Noisy in neutral with engine running
- ☐ Noisy in one particular gear
- ☐ Difficulty engaging gears
- ☐ Jumps out of gear
- ☐ Vibration
- ☐ Lubricant leaks

Automatic transmission
- ☐ Fluid leakage
- ☐ Transmission fluid brown, or has burned smell
- ☐ Engine will not start in any gear, or starts in gears other than Park or Neutral
- ☐ General gear selection problems
- ☐ Transmission slips, shifts roughly, is noisy, or has no drive in forward or reverse gears

Driveshafts
- ☐ Vibration when accelerating or decelerating
- ☐ Clicking or knocking noise on turns (at slow speed on full-lock)

Braking system
- ☐ Vehicle pulls to one side under braking
- ☐ Noise (grinding or high-pitched squeal) when brakes applied
- ☐ Excessive brake pedal travel
- ☐ Brake pedal feels spongy when depressed
- ☐ Excessive brake pedal effort required to stop vehicle
- ☐ Judder felt through brake pedal or steering wheel when braking
- ☐ Pedal pulsates when braking hard
- ☐ Brakes binding

Steering and suspension
- ☐ Vehicle pulls to one side
- ☐ Wheel wobble and vibration
- ☐ Excessive pitching and/or rolling around corners, or during braking
- ☐ Wandering or general instability
- ☐ Excessively-stiff steering
- ☐ Excessive play in steering
- ☐ Lack of power assistance
- ☐ Tyre wear excessive

Electrical system
- ☐ Battery will not hold a charge for more than a few days
- ☐ Ignition/no-charge warning light remains illuminated with engine running
- ☐ Ignition/no-charge warning light fails to come on
- ☐ Lights inoperative
- ☐ Instrument readings inaccurate or erratic
- ☐ Horn inoperative, or unsatisfactory in operation
- ☐ Windscreen/tailgate wipers inoperative, or unsatisfactory in operation
- ☐ Windscreen/tailgate washers inoperative, or unsatisfactory in operation
- ☐ Electric windows inoperative, or unsatisfactory in operation
- ☐ Central locking system inoperative, or unsatisfactory in operation

Introduction

The vehicle owner who does his or her own maintenance according to the recommended service schedules should not have to use this section of the manual very often. Modern component reliability is such that, provided those items subject to wear or deterioration are inspected or renewed at the specified intervals, sudden failure is comparatively rare. Faults do not usually just happen as a result of sudden failure, but develop over a period of time. Major mechanical failures in particular are usually preceded by characteristic symptoms over hundreds or even thousands of miles. Those components which do occasionally fail without warning are often small and easily carried in the vehicle.

With any fault-finding, the first step is to decide where to begin investigations. Sometimes this is obvious, but on other occasions, a little detective work will be necessary. The owner who makes half a dozen haphazard adjustments or replacements may be successful in curing a fault (or its symptoms), but will be none the wiser if the fault recurs, and ultimately may have spent more time and money than was necessary. A calm and logical approach will be found to be more satisfactory in the long run. Always take into account any warning signs or abnormalities that may have been noticed in the period preceding the fault – power loss, high or low gauge readings, unusual smells, etc – and remember that failure of components such as fuses or spark plugs may only be pointers to some underlying fault.

The pages which follow provide an easy-reference guide to the more common problems which may occur during the operation of the vehicle. These problems and their possible causes are grouped under headings denoting various components or systems, such as Engine, Cooling system, etc. The general Chapter which deals with the problem is also shown in brackets; refer to the relevant part of that Chapter for system-specific information. Whatever the fault, certain basic principles apply. These are as follows:

Verify the fault. This is simply a matter of being sure that you know what the symptoms are before starting work. This is particularly important if you are investigating a fault for someone else, who may not have described it very accurately.

Don't overlook the obvious. For example, if the vehicle won't start, is there fuel in the tank? (Don't take anyone else's word on this particular point, and don't trust the fuel gauge either!) If an electrical fault is indicated, look for loose or broken wires before digging out the test gear.

Cure the disease, not the symptom. Substituting a flat battery with a fully-charged one will get you off the hard shoulder, but if the underlying cause is not attended to, the new battery will go the same way. Similarly, changing oil-fouled spark plugs for a new set will get you moving again, but remember that the reason for the fouling (if it wasn't simply an incorrect grade of plug) will have to be established and corrected.

Don't take anything for granted. Particularly, don't forget that a 'new' component may itself be defective (especially if it's been rattling around in the boot for months), and don't leave components out of a fault diagnosis sequence just because they are new or recently-fitted. When you do finally diagnose a difficult fault, you'll probably realise that all the evidence was there from the start.

Diesel fault diagnosis

The majority of starting problems on small diesel engines are electrical in origin. The mechanic who is familiar with petrol engines but less so with diesel may be inclined to view the diesel's injectors and pump in the same light as the spark plugs and distributor, but this is generally a mistake.

When investigating complaints of difficult starting for someone else, make sure that the correct starting procedure is understood and is being followed. Some drivers are unaware of the significance of the preheating warning light – many modern engines are sufficiently forgiving for this not to matter in mild weather, but with the onset of winter, problems begin.

As a rule of thumb, if the engine is difficult to start but runs well when it has finally got going, the problem is electrical (battery, starter motor or preheating system). If poor performance is combined with difficult starting, the problem is likely to be in the fuel system. The low-pressure (supply) side of the fuel system should be checked before suspecting the injectors and high-pressure pump. The most common fuel supply problem is air getting into the system, and any pipe from the fuel tank forwards must be scrutinised if air leakage is suspected. Normally the pump is the last item to suspect, since unless it has been tampered with, there is no reason for it to be at fault.

Engine

Engine fails to rotate when attempting to start

- ☐ Battery terminal connections loose or corroded (see *Weekly checks*).
- ☐ Battery discharged or faulty (Chapter 5A).
- ☐ Broken, loose or disconnected wiring in the starting circuit (Chapter 5A).
- ☐ Defective starter solenoid or switch (Chapter 5A).
- ☐ Defective starter motor (Chapter 5A).
- ☐ Starter pinion or flywheel ring gear teeth loose or broken (Chapters 2A, 2B, 2C and 5A).
- ☐ Engine earth strap broken or disconnected (Chapter 5A).

Engine rotates, but will not start

- ☐ Fuel tank empty.
- ☐ Battery discharged (engine rotates slowly) (Chapter 5A).
- ☐ Battery terminal connections loose or corroded (see *Weekly checks*).
- ☐ Ignition components damp or damaged – petrol models (Chapter 5B).
- ☐ Broken, loose or disconnected wiring in the ignition circuit – petrol models (Chapter 5B).
- ☐ Worn, faulty or incorrectly-gapped spark plugs – petrol models (Chapter 1A).
- ☐ Preheating system faulty – diesel models (Chapter 5A).
- ☐ Fuel injection system faulty – petrol models (Chapter 4A).
- ☐ Air in fuel system – diesel models (Chapter 4B).
- ☐ Major mechanical failure (eg camshaft drive) (Chapter 2).

Engine difficult to start when cold

- ☐ Battery discharged (Chapter 5A).
- ☐ Battery terminal connections loose or corroded (see *Weekly checks*).
- ☐ Worn, faulty or incorrectly-gapped spark plugs – petrol models (Chapter 1A).
- ☐ Preheating system faulty – diesel models (Chapter 5A).
- ☐ Fuel injection system faulty – petrol models (Chapter 4A).
- ☐ Other ignition system fault – petrol models (Chapters 1A and 5B).
- ☐ Low cylinder compressions (Chapter 2A, 2B or 2C).

Engine difficult to start when hot

- ☐ Air filter element dirty or clogged (Chapter 1A or 1B).
- ☐ Fuel injection system faulty – petrol models (Chapter 4A).
- ☐ Low cylinder compressions (Chapter 2).

Starter motor noisy or excessively-rough in engagement

- ☐ Starter pinion or flywheel ring gear teeth loose or broken (Chapters 2A, 2B, 2C and 5A).
- ☐ Starter motor mounting bolts loose (Chapter 5A).
- ☐ Starter motor internal components worn or damaged (Chapter 5A).

Engine starts, but stops immediately

- ☐ Loose or faulty electrical connections in the ignition circuit – petrol models (Chapters 1A and 5B).
- ☐ Vacuum leak at the throttle body or inlet manifold – petrol models (Chapter 4A).
- ☐ Blocked injector/fuel injection system fault – petrol models (Chapter 4A).

Engine idles erratically

- ☐ Air filter element clogged (Chapter 1A or 1B).
- ☐ Vacuum leak at the throttle body, inlet manifold or associated hoses – petrol models (Chapter 4A).
- ☐ Worn, faulty or incorrectly-gapped spark plugs – petrol models (Chapter 1A).
- ☐ Uneven or low cylinder compressions (Chapter 2).
- ☐ Camshaft lobes worn (Chapter 2A, 2B or 2C).
- ☐ Timing chain incorrectly fitted (Chapter 2A).
- ☐ Timing belt incorrectly fitted (Chapter 2B or 2C).
- ☐ Blocked injector/fuel injection system fault – petrol models (Chapter 4A).
- ☐ Faulty injector(s) – diesel models (Chapter 4B).

Engine misfires at idle speed

- ☐ Worn, faulty or incorrectly-gapped spark plugs – petrol models (Chapter 1A).
- ☐ Vacuum leak at the throttle body, inlet manifold or associated hoses – petrol models (Chapter 4A).
- ☐ Blocked injector/fuel injection system fault – petrol models (Chapter 4A).
- ☐ Faulty injector(s) – diesel models (Chapter 4B).
- ☐ Uneven or low cylinder compressions (Chapter 2A, 2B or 2C).
- ☐ Disconnected, leaking, or perished crankcase ventilation hoses (Chapter 4C).

Engine (continued)

Engine misfires throughout the driving speed range

- ☐ Fuel filter choked (Chapter 1A or 1B).
- ☐ Fuel pump faulty, or delivery pressure low – petrol models (Chapter 4A).
- ☐ Fuel tank vent blocked, or fuel pipes restricted (Chapter 4A or 4B).
- ☐ Vacuum leak at the throttle body, inlet manifold or associated hoses – petrol models (Chapter 4A).
- ☐ Worn, faulty or incorrectly-gapped spark plugs – petrol models (Chapter 1A).
- ☐ Faulty injector(s) – diesel models (Chapter 4B).
- ☐ Faulty ignition coil – petrol models (Chapter 5B).
- ☐ Uneven or low cylinder compressions (Chapter 2).
- ☐ Blocked injector/fuel injection system fault – petrol models (Chapter 4A).

Engine hesitates on acceleration

- ☐ Worn, faulty or incorrectly-gapped spark plugs – petrol models (Chapter 1A).
- ☐ Vacuum leak at the throttle body, inlet manifold or associated hoses – petrol models (Chapter 4A).
- ☐ Blocked injector/fuel injection system fault – petrol models (Chapter 4A).
- ☐ Faulty injector(s) – diesel models (Chapter 4B).

Engine stalls

- ☐ Vacuum leak at the throttle body, inlet manifold or associated hoses – petrol models (Chapter 4A).
- ☐ Fuel filter choked (Chapter 1A or 1B).
- ☐ Fuel pump faulty, or delivery pressure low – petrol models (Chapter 4A).
- ☐ Fuel tank vent blocked, or fuel pipes restricted (Chapter 4A or 4B).
- ☐ Blocked injector/fuel injection system fault – petrol models (Chapter 4A).
- ☐ Faulty injector(s) – diesel models (Chapter 4B).

Engine lacks power

- ☐ Timing chain/belt incorrectly fitted or tensioned (Chapter 2).
- ☐ Fuel filter choked (Chapter 1A or 1B).
- ☐ Fuel pump faulty, or delivery pressure low – petrol models (Chapter 4A).
- ☐ Uneven or low cylinder compressions (Chapter 2).
- ☐ Worn, faulty or incorrectly-gapped spark plugs – petrol models (Chapter 1A).
- ☐ Vacuum leak at the throttle body, inlet manifold or associated hoses – petrol models (Chapter 4A).
- ☐ Blocked injector/fuel injection system fault – petrol models (Chapter 4A).
- ☐ Faulty injector(s) – diesel models (Chapter 4B).
- ☐ Brakes binding (Chapters 1A, 1B and 9).
- ☐ Clutch slipping (Chapter 6).

Engine backfires

- ☐ Timing chain/belt incorrectly fitted or tensioned (Chapter 2).
- ☐ Vacuum leak at the throttle body, inlet manifold or associated hoses – petrol models (Chapter 4A).
- ☐ Blocked injector/fuel injection system fault – petrol models (Chapter 4A).

Oil pressure warning light illuminated with engine running

- ☐ Low oil level, or incorrect oil grade (*Weekly checks*).
- ☐ Faulty oil pressure sensor (Chapter 5A).
- ☐ Worn engine bearings and/or oil pump (Chapter 2D).
- ☐ High engine operating temperature (Chapter 3).
- ☐ Oil pressure relief valve defective (Chapter 2D).
- ☐ Oil pick-up strainer clogged (Chapter 2).

Engine runs-on after switching off

- ☐ Excessive carbon build-up in engine (Chapter 2D).
- ☐ High engine operating temperature (Chapter 3).
- ☐ Fuel injection system faulty – petrol models (Chapter 4A).

Engine noises

Pre-ignition (pinking) or knocking during acceleration or under load

- ☐ Ignition timing incorrect/ignition system fault – petrol models (Chapters 1A and 5B).
- ☐ Incorrect grade of spark plug – petrol models (Chapter 1A).
- ☐ Incorrect grade of fuel (Chapter 4A or 4B).
- ☐ Vacuum leak at the throttle body, inlet manifold or associated hoses – petrol models (Chapter 4A).
- ☐ Excessive carbon build-up in engine (Chapter 2D).
- ☐ Blocked injector/fuel injection system fault – petrol models (Chapter 4A).

Whistling or wheezing noises

- ☐ Leaking inlet manifold or throttle body gasket – petrol models (Chapter 4A).
- ☐ Leaking exhaust manifold gasket or pipe-to-manifold joint (Chapter 4A or 4B).
- ☐ Leaking vacuum hose (Chapters 4A, 4B, 5 and 9).
- ☐ Blowing cylinder head gasket (Chapter 2).

Tapping or rattling noises

- ☐ Worn valve gear or camshaft (Chapter 2D).
- ☐ Ancillary component fault (coolant pump, alternator, etc) (Chapters 3, 5, etc).

Knocking or thumping noises

- ☐ Worn big-end bearings (regular heavy knocking, perhaps less under load) (Chapter 2D).
- ☐ Worn main bearings (rumbling and knocking, perhaps worsening under load) (Chapter 2D).
- ☐ Piston slap (most noticeable when cold) (Chapter 2D).
- ☐ Ancillary component fault (coolant pump, alternator, etc) (Chapters 3, 5, etc).

Cooling system

Overheating

- ☐ Insufficient coolant in system (*Weekly checks*).
- ☐ Thermostat faulty (Chapter 3).
- ☐ Radiator core blocked, or grille restricted (Chapter 3).
- ☐ Electric cooling fan or thermostatic switch faulty (Chapter 3).
- ☐ Inaccurate temperature gauge sender unit (Chapter 3).
- ☐ Airlock in cooling system (Chapter 3).
- ☐ Expansion tank pressure cap faulty (Chapter 3).

Overcooling

- ☐ Thermostat faulty (Chapter 3).
- ☐ Inaccurate temperature gauge sender unit (Chapter 3).

External coolant leakage

- ☐ Deteriorated or damaged hoses or hose clips (Chapter 1A or 1B).
- ☐ Radiator core or heater matrix leaking (Chapter 3).
- ☐ Pressure cap faulty (Chapter 3).
- ☐ Coolant pump internal seal leaking (Chapter 3).
- ☐ Coolant pump-to-block seal leaking (Chapter 3).
- ☐ Boiling due to overheating (Chapter 3).
- ☐ Core plug leaking (Chapter 2D).

Internal coolant leakage

- ☐ Leaking cylinder head gasket (Chapter 2).
- ☐ Cracked cylinder head or cylinder block (Chapter 2).

Corrosion

- ☐ Infrequent draining and flushing (Chapter 1A or 1B).
- ☐ Incorrect coolant mixture or inappropriate coolant type (see *Weekly checks*).

Fuel and exhaust systems

Excessive fuel consumption

- ☐ Air filter element dirty or clogged (Chapter 1A or 1B).
- ☐ Fuel injection system faulty – petrol models (Chapter 4A).
- ☐ Faulty injector(s) – diesel models (Chapter 4B).
- ☐ Ignition timing incorrect/ignition system faulty – petrol models (Chapters 1A and 5B).
- ☐ Tyres under-inflated (see *Weekly checks*).

Fuel leakage and/or fuel odour

- ☐ Damaged or corroded fuel tank, pipes or connections (Chapter 4A or 4B).

Excessive noise or fumes from the exhaust system

- ☐ Leaking exhaust system or manifold joints (Chapters 1A, 1B and 4).
- ☐ Leaking, corroded or damaged silencers or pipe (Chapters 1A, 1B and 4).
- ☐ Broken mountings causing body or suspension contact (Chapter 4A or 4B).

Clutch

Pedal travels to floor – no pressure or very little resistance

- ☐ Air in hydraulic system/faulty master or slave cylinder (Chapter 6).
- ☐ Faulty hydraulic release system (Chapter 6).
- ☐ Broken clutch release bearing (Chapter 6).
- ☐ Broken diaphragm spring in clutch pressure plate (Chapter 6).

Clutch fails to disengage (unable to select gears)

- ☐ Air in hydraulic system/faulty master or slave cylinder (Chapter 6).
- ☐ Faulty hydraulic release system (Chapter 6).
- ☐ Clutch disc sticking on gearbox input shaft splines (Chapter 6).
- ☐ Clutch disc sticking to flywheel or pressure plate (Chapter 6).
- ☐ Faulty pressure plate assembly (Chapter 6).
- ☐ Clutch release mechanism worn or incorrectly assembled (Chapter 6).

Clutch slips (engine speed increases, with no increase in vehicle speed)

- ☐ Faulty hydraulic release system (Chapter 6).
- ☐ Clutch disc linings excessively worn (Chapter 6).
- ☐ Clutch disc linings contaminated with oil or grease (Chapter 6).
- ☐ Faulty pressure plate or weak diaphragm spring (Chapter 6).

Judder as clutch is engaged

- ☐ Clutch disc linings contaminated with oil or grease (Chapter 6).
- ☐ Clutch disc linings excessively worn (Chapter 6).
- ☐ Faulty or distorted pressure plate or diaphragm spring (Chapter 6).
- ☐ Worn or loose engine or gearbox mountings (Chapter 2A or 2B).
- ☐ Clutch disc hub or gearbox input shaft splines worn (Chapter 6).

Noise when depressing or releasing clutch pedal

- ☐ Worn clutch release bearing (Chapter 6).
- ☐ Worn or dry clutch pedal pivot (Chapter 6).
- ☐ Faulty pressure plate assembly (Chapter 6).
- ☐ Pressure plate diaphragm spring broken (Chapter 6).
- ☐ Broken clutch friction plate cushioning springs (Chapter 6).

Manual transmission

Noisy in neutral with engine running

- ☐ Input shaft bearings worn (noise apparent with clutch pedal released, but not when depressed) (Chapter 7A).*
- ☐ Clutch release bearing worn (noise apparent with clutch pedal depressed, possibly less when released) (Chapter 6).

Noisy in one particular gear

- ☐ Worn, damaged or chipped gear teeth (Chapter 7A).*

Difficulty engaging gears

- ☐ Clutch faulty (Chapter 6).
- ☐ Worn or damaged gear linkage (Chapter 7A).
- ☐ Worn synchroniser units (Chapter 7A).*

Jumps out of gear

- ☐ Worn or damaged gear linkage (Chapter 7A).
- ☐ Worn synchroniser units (Chapter 7A).*
- ☐ Worn selector forks (Chapter 7A).*

Vibration

- ☐ Lack of oil (Chapter 1A or 1B).
- ☐ Worn bearings (Chapter 7A).*

Lubricant leaks

- ☐ Leaking oil seal (Chapter 7A).
- ☐ Leaking housing joint (Chapter 7A).*
- ☐ Leaking input shaft oil seal (Chapter 7A).*

**Although the corrective action necessary to remedy the symptoms described is beyond the scope of the home mechanic, the above information should be helpful in isolating the cause of the condition, so that the owner can communicate clearly with a professional mechanic.*

Automatic transmission

Note: *Due to the complexity of the automatic transmission, it is difficult for the home mechanic to properly diagnose and service this unit. For problems other than the following, the vehicle should be taken to a dealer service department or automatic transmission specialist. Do not be too hasty in removing the transmission if a fault is suspected, as most of the testing is carried out with the unit still fitted.*

Fluid leakage

☐ Automatic transmission fluid is usually dark in colour. Fluid leaks should not be confused with engine oil, which can easily be blown onto the transmission by airflow.

☐ To determine the source of a leak, first remove all built-up dirt and grime from the transmission housing and surrounding areas using a degreasing agent, or by steam-cleaning. Drive the vehicle at low speed, so airflow will not blow the leak far from its source. Raise and support the vehicle, and determine where the leak is coming from. The following are common areas of leakage:

a) Oil pan (Chapter 1A, 1B and 7B).
b) Dipstick tube (Chapter 1A, 1B and 7B).
c) Transmission-to-fluid cooler pipes/unions (Chapter 7B).

Transmission fluid brown, or has burned smell

☐ Transmission fluid level low, or fluid in need of renewal (Chapter 1A, 1B and 7B).

Engine will not start in any gear, or starts in gears other than Park or Neutral

☐ Incorrect starter/inhibitor switch adjustment (Chapter 7B).
☐ Incorrect selector cable adjustment (Chapter 7B).

General gear selection problems

☐ Chapter 7B deals with checking and adjusting the selector cable on automatic transmissions. The following are common problems which may be caused by a poorly-adjusted cable:

a) Engine starting in gears other than Park or Neutral.
b) Indicator panel indicating a gear other than the one actually being used.
c) Vehicle moves when in Park or Neutral.
d) Poor gear shift quality or erratic gear changes.

☐ Refer to Chapter 7B for the selector cable adjustment procedure.

Transmission will not downshift (kickdown) with accelerator pedal fully depressed

☐ Low transmission fluid level (Chapter 1A or 1B).
☐ Incorrect selector cable adjustment (Chapter 7B).

Transmission slips, shifts roughly, is noisy, or has no drive in forward or reverse gears

☐ There are many probable causes for the above problems, but the home mechanic should be concerned with only one possibility – fluid level. Before taking the vehicle to a dealer or transmission specialist, check the fluid level and condition of the fluid as described in Chapter 1A, 1B or 7B, as applicable. Correct the fluid level as necessary, or change the fluid and filter if needed. If the problem persists, professional help will be necessary.

Driveshafts

Vibration when accelerating or decelerating

☐ Worn inner constant velocity joint (Chapter 8).
☐ Bent or distorted driveshaft (Chapter 8).
☐ Worn intermediate bearing – where applicable (Chapter 8).

Clicking or knocking noise on turns (at slow speed on full-lock)

☐ Worn outer constant velocity joint (Chapter 8).
☐ Lack of constant velocity joint lubricant, possibly due to damaged gaiter (Chapter 8).

Braking system

Note: *Before assuming that a brake problem exists, make sure that the tyres are in good condition and correctly inflated, that the front wheel alignment is correct, and that the vehicle is not loaded with weight in an unequal manner. Apart from checking the condition of all pipe and hose connections, any faults occurring on the anti-lock braking system should be referred to a Saab dealer for diagnosis.*

Vehicle pulls to one side under braking

- ☐ Worn, defective, damaged or contaminated front or rear brake pads on one side (Chapters 1A, 1B and 9).
- ☐ Seized or partially-seized front or rear brake caliper piston (Chapter 9).
- ☐ A mixture of brake pad lining materials fitted between sides (Chapter 9).
- ☐ Brake caliper mounting bolts loose (Chapter 9).
- ☐ Worn or damaged steering or suspension components (Chapters 1A, 1B and 10).

Noise (grinding or high-pitched squeal) when brakes applied

- ☐ Brake pad friction lining material worn down to metal backing (Chapters 1A, 1B and 9).
- ☐ Excessive corrosion of brake disc – may be apparent after the vehicle has been standing for some time (Chapters 1A, 1B and 9).
- ☐ Foreign object (stone chipping, etc) trapped between brake disc and shield (Chapters 1A, 1B and 9).

Excessive brake pedal travel

- ☐ Faulty master cylinder (Chapter 9).
- ☐ Air in hydraulic system (Chapter 9).
- ☐ Faulty vacuum servo unit (Chapter 9).
- ☐ Faulty vacuum pump – diesel models (Chapter 9).

Brake pedal feels spongy when depressed

- ☐ Air in hydraulic system (Chapter 9).
- ☐ Deteriorated flexible rubber brake hoses (Chapters 1A, 1B and 9).
- ☐ Master cylinder mountings loose (Chapter 9).
- ☐ Faulty master cylinder (Chapter 9).

Excessive brake pedal effort required to stop vehicle

- ☐ Faulty vacuum servo unit (Chapter 9).
- ☐ Disconnected, damaged or insecure brake servo vacuum hose (Chapters 1A, 1B and 9).
- ☐ Faulty vacuum pump – diesel models (Chapter 9).
- ☐ Primary or secondary hydraulic circuit failure (Chapter 9).
- ☐ Seized brake caliper piston (Chapter 9).
- ☐ Brake pads incorrectly fitted (Chapter 9).
- ☐ Incorrect grade of brake pads fitted (Chapter 9).
- ☐ Brake pad linings contaminated (Chapter 9).

Judder felt through brake pedal or steering wheel when braking

- ☐ Excessive run-out or distortion of brake disc(s) (Chapter 9).
- ☐ Brake pad linings worn (Chapters 1A, 1B and 9).
- ☐ Brake caliper mounting bolts loose (Chapter 9).
- ☐ Wear in suspension or steering components or mountings (Chapters 1A, 1B and 10).

Pedal pulsates when braking hard

- ☐ Normal feature of ABS – no fault

Brakes binding

- ☐ Seized brake caliper piston(s) (Chapter 9).
- ☐ Incorrectly-adjusted handbrake mechanism (Chapter 9).
- ☐ Faulty master cylinder (Chapter 9).

Rear wheels locking under normal braking

- ☐ Rear brake pad linings contaminated (Chapters 1A, 1B and 9).
- ☐ Rear brake discs warped (Chapters 1A, 1B and 9).

Steering and suspension

Note: *Before diagnosing suspension or steering faults, be sure that the trouble is not due to incorrect tyre pressures, mixtures of tyre types, or binding brakes.*

Vehicle pulls to one side

- ☐ Defective tyre (see *Weekly checks*).
- ☐ Excessive wear in suspension or steering components (Chapters 1A, 1B and 10).
- ☐ Incorrect front wheel alignment (Chapter 10).
- ☐ Accident damage to steering or suspension components (Chapters 1A, 1B and 10).

Wheel wobble and vibration

- ☐ Front roadwheels out of balance (vibration felt mainly through the steering wheel) (Chapter 10).
- ☐ Rear roadwheels out of balance (vibration felt throughout the vehicle) (Chapter 10).
- ☐ Roadwheels damaged or distorted (Chapter 10).
- ☐ Faulty or damaged tyre (*Weekly checks*).
- ☐ Worn steering or suspension joints, bushes or components (Chapters 1A, 1B and 10).
- ☐ Wheel bolts loose (Chapter 1A, 1B and 10).

Excessive pitching and/or rolling around corners, or during braking

- ☐ Defective shock absorbers (Chapters 1A, 1B and 10).
- ☐ Broken or weak coil spring and/or suspension component (Chapters 1A, 1B and 10).
- ☐ Worn or damaged anti-roll bar or mountings (Chapter 10).

Wandering or general instability

- ☐ Incorrect front wheel alignment (Chapter 10).
- ☐ Worn steering or suspension joints, bushes or components (Chapters 1A, 1B and 10).
- ☐ Roadwheels out of balance (Chapter 10).
- ☐ Faulty or damaged tyre (*Weekly checks*).
- ☐ Wheel bolts loose (Chapter 10).
- ☐ Defective shock absorbers (Chapters 1A, 1B and 10).

Excessively-stiff steering

- ☐ Seized track rod end balljoint or suspension balljoint (Chapters 1A, 1B and 10).
- ☐ Broken or incorrectly adjusted auxiliary drivebelt (Chapter 1A or 1B).
- ☐ Incorrect front wheel alignment (Chapter 10).
- ☐ Steering gear damaged (Chapter 10).

Excessive play in steering

- ☐ Worn steering column universal joint(s) (Chapter 10).
- ☐ Worn steering track rod end balljoints (Chapters 1A, 1B and 10).
- ☐ Worn steering gear (Chapter 10).
- ☐ Worn steering or suspension joints, bushes or components (Chapters 1A, 1B and 10).

Lack of power assistance

- ☐ Broken or incorrectly-adjusted auxiliary drivebelt (Chapter 1A or 1B).
- ☐ Incorrect power steering fluid level (*Weekly checks*).
- ☐ Restriction in power steering fluid hoses (Chapter 10).
- ☐ Faulty power steering pump (Chapter 10).
- ☐ Faulty steering gear (Chapter 10).

Tyre wear excessive

Tyres worn on inside or outside edges

- ☐ Tyres under-inflated (wear on both edges) (*Weekly checks*).
- ☐ Incorrect camber or castor angles (wear on one edge only) (Chapter 10).
- ☐ Worn steering or suspension joints, bushes or components (Chapters 1A, 1B and 10).
- ☐ Excessively-hard cornering.
- ☐ Accident damage.

Tyre treads exhibit feathered edges

- ☐ Incorrect toe setting (Chapter 10).

Tyres worn in centre of tread

- ☐ Tyres over-inflated (*Weekly checks*).

Tyres worn on inside and outside edges

- ☐ Tyres under-inflated (*Weekly checks*).
- ☐ Worn shock absorbers (Chapter 10).

Tyres worn unevenly

- ☐ Tyres/wheels out of balance (*Weekly checks*).
- ☐ Excessive wheel or tyre run-out (Chapter 10).
- ☐ Worn shock absorbers (Chapters 1A, 1B and 10).
- ☐ Faulty tyre (*Weekly checks*).

Electrical system

Note: *For problems associated with the starting system, refer to the faults listed under 'Engine' earlier in this Section.*

Battery will not hold a charge for more than a few days

- ☐ Battery defective internally (Chapter 5A).
- ☐ Battery electrolyte level low – where applicable (*Weekly checks*).
- ☐ Battery terminal connections loose or corroded (*Weekly checks*).
- ☐ Auxiliary drivebelt worn – or incorrectly adjusted, where applicable (Chapter 1A or 1B).
- ☐ Alternator not charging at correct output (Chapter 5A).
- ☐ Alternator or voltage regulator faulty (Chapter 5A).
- ☐ Short-circuit causing continual battery drain (Chapters 5 and 12).

Ignition/no-charge warning light remains illuminated with engine running

- ☐ Auxiliary drivebelt broken, worn, or incorrectly adjusted (Chapter 1A or 1B).
- ☐ Internal fault in alternator or voltage regulator (Chapter 5A).
- ☐ Broken, disconnected, or loose wiring in charging circuit (Chapter 5A).

Ignition/no-charge warning light fails to come on

- ☐ Warning light bulb blown (Chapter 12).
- ☐ Broken, disconnected, or loose wiring in warning light circuit (Chapter 12).
- ☐ Alternator faulty (Chapter 5A).

Lights inoperative

- ☐ Bulb blown (Chapter 12).
- ☐ Corrosion of bulb or bulbholder contacts (Chapter 12).
- ☐ Blown fuse (Chapter 12).
- ☐ Faulty relay (Chapter 12).
- ☐ Broken, loose, or disconnected wiring (Chapter 12).
- ☐ Faulty switch (Chapter 12).

Instrument readings inaccurate or erratic

Fuel or temperature gauges give no reading

- ☐ Faulty gauge sender unit (Chapters 3 and 4A or 4B).
- ☐ Wiring open-circuit (Chapter 12).
- ☐ Faulty gauge (Chapter 12).

Fuel or temperature gauges give continuous maximum reading

- ☐ Faulty gauge sender unit (Chapters 3 and 4A or 4B).
- ☐ Wiring short-circuit (Chapter 12).
- ☐ Faulty gauge (Chapter 12).

Horn inoperative, or unsatisfactory in operation

Horn operates all the time

- ☐ Horn contacts permanently bridged or horn push stuck down (Chapter 12).

Horn fails to operate

- ☐ Blown fuse (Chapter 12).
- ☐ Cable or cable connections loose, broken or disconnected (Chapter 12).
- ☐ Faulty horn (Chapter 12).

Horn emits intermittent or unsatisfactory sound

- ☐ Cable connections loose (Chapter 12).
- ☐ Horn mountings loose (Chapter 12).
- ☐ Faulty horn (Chapter 12).

Windscreen/tailgate wipers inoperative, or unsatisfactory in operation

Wipers fail to operate, or operate very slowly

- ☐ Wiper blades stuck to screen, or linkage seized or binding (*Weekly checks* and Chapter 12).
- ☐ Blown fuse (Chapter 12).
- ☐ Cable or cable connections loose, broken or disconnected (Chapter 12).
- ☐ Faulty relay (Chapter 12).
- ☐ Faulty wiper motor (Chapter 12).

Wiper blades sweep over too large or too small an area of the glass

- ☐ Wiper arms incorrectly positioned on spindles (Chapter 12).
- ☐ Excessive wear of wiper linkage (Chapter 12).
- ☐ Wiper motor or linkage mountings loose or insecure (Chapter 12).

Wiper blades fail to clean the glass effectively

- ☐ Wiper blade rubbers worn or perished (*Weekly checks*).
- ☐ Wiper arm tension springs broken, or arm pivots seized (Chapter 12).
- ☐ Insufficient windscreen washer additive to adequately remove road film (*Weekly checks*).

Electrical system (continued)

Windscreen/tailgate washers inoperative, or unsatisfactory in operation

One or more washer jets inoperative

- ☐ Blocked washer jet (Chapter 12).
- ☐ Disconnected, kinked or restricted fluid hose (Chapter 12).
- ☐ Insufficient fluid in washer reservoir (*Weekly checks*).

Washer pump fails to operate

- ☐ Broken or disconnected wiring or connections (Chapter 12).
- ☐ Blown fuse (Chapter 12).
- ☐ Faulty washer switch (Chapter 12).
- ☐ Faulty washer pump (Chapter 12).

Washer pump runs for some time before fluid is emitted from jets

- ☐ Faulty one-way valve in fluid supply hose (Chapter 12).

Electric windows inoperative, or unsatisfactory in operation

Window glass will only move in one direction

- ☐ Faulty switch (Chapter 12).
- ☐ Faulty motor (Chapter 11).

Window glass slow to move

- ☐ Regulator seized or damaged, or in need of lubrication (Chapter 11).
- ☐ Door internal components or trim fouling regulator (Chapter 11).
- ☐ Faulty motor (Chapter 11).

Window glass fails to move

- ☐ Blown fuse (Chapter 12).
- ☐ Faulty relay (Chapter 12).
- ☐ Broken or disconnected wiring or connections (Chapter 12).
- ☐ Faulty motor (Chapter 11).

Central locking system inoperative, or unsatisfactory in operation

Complete system failure

- ☐ Blown fuse (Chapter 12).
- ☐ Faulty relay (Chapter 12).
- ☐ Broken or disconnected wiring or connections (Chapter 12).
- ☐ Faulty motor (Chapter 11).

Latch locks but will not unlock, or unlocks but will not lock

- ☐ Faulty switch (Chapter 12).
- ☐ Broken or disconnected latch operating rods or levers (Chapter 11).
- ☐ Faulty relay (Chapter 12).
- ☐ Faulty motor (Chapter 11).

One solenoid/motor fails to operate

- ☐ Broken or disconnected wiring or connections (Chapter 12).
- ☐ Faulty motor (Chapter 11).
- ☐ Broken, binding or disconnected lock operating rods or levers (Chapter 11).
- ☐ Fault in door lock (Chapter 11).

A

ABS (Anti-lock brake system) A system, usually electronically controlled, that senses incipient wheel lockup during braking and relieves hydraulic pressure at wheels that are about to skid.
Air bag An inflatable bag hidden in the steering wheel (driver's side) or the dash or glovebox (passenger side). In a head-on collision, the bags inflate, preventing the driver and front passenger from being thrown forward into the steering wheel or windscreen.
Air cleaner A metal or plastic housing, containing a filter element, which removes dust and dirt from the air being drawn into the engine.
Air filter element The actual filter in an air cleaner system, usually manufactured from pleated paper and requiring renewal at regular intervals.

Air filter

Allen key A hexagonal wrench which fits into a recessed hexagonal hole.
Alligator clip A long-nosed spring-loaded metal clip with meshing teeth. Used to make temporary electrical connections.
Alternator A component in the electrical system which converts mechanical energy from a drivebelt into electrical energy to charge the battery and to operate the starting system, ignition system and electrical accessories.

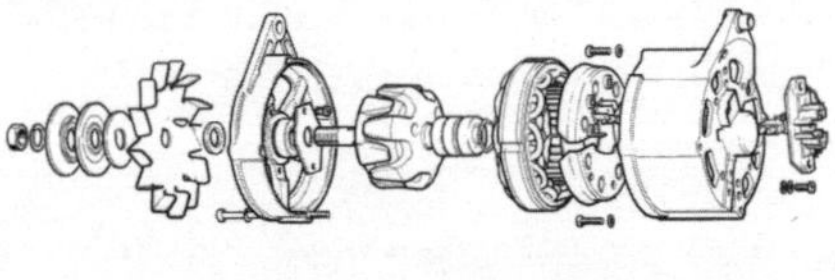

Alternator (exploded view)

Ampere (amp) A unit of measurement for the flow of electric current. One amp is the amount of current produced by one volt acting through a resistance of one ohm.
Anaerobic sealer A substance used to prevent bolts and screws from loosening. Anaerobic means that it does not require oxygen for activation. The Loctite brand is widely used.
Antifreeze A substance (usually ethylene glycol) mixed with water, and added to a vehicle's cooling system, to prevent freezing of the coolant in winter. Antifreeze also contains chemicals to inhibit corrosion and the formation of rust and other deposits that would tend to clog the radiator and coolant passages and reduce cooling efficiency.
Anti-seize compound A coating that reduces the risk of seizing on fasteners that are subjected to high temperatures, such as exhaust manifold bolts and nuts.

Anti-seize compound

Asbestos A natural fibrous mineral with great heat resistance, commonly used in the composition of brake friction materials. Asbestos is a health hazard and the dust created by brake systems should never be inhaled or ingested.
Axle A shaft on which a wheel revolves, or which revolves with a wheel. Also, a solid beam that connects the two wheels at one end of the vehicle. An axle which also transmits power to the wheels is known as a live axle.

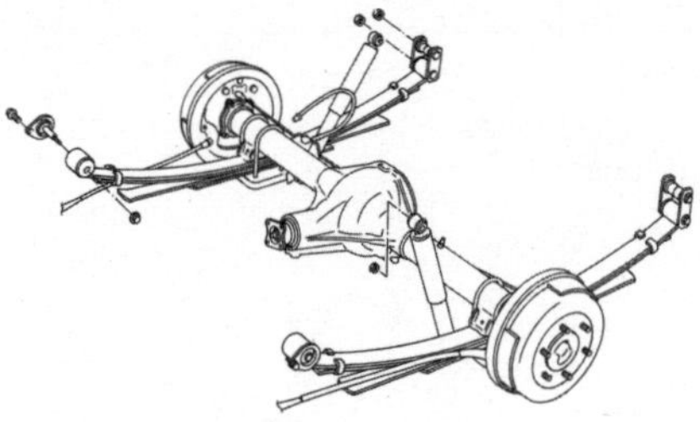

Axle assembly

Axleshaft A single rotating shaft, on either side of the differential, which delivers power from the final drive assembly to the drive wheels. Also called a driveshaft or a halfshaft.

B

Ball bearing An anti-friction bearing consisting of a hardened inner and outer race with hardened steel balls between two races.

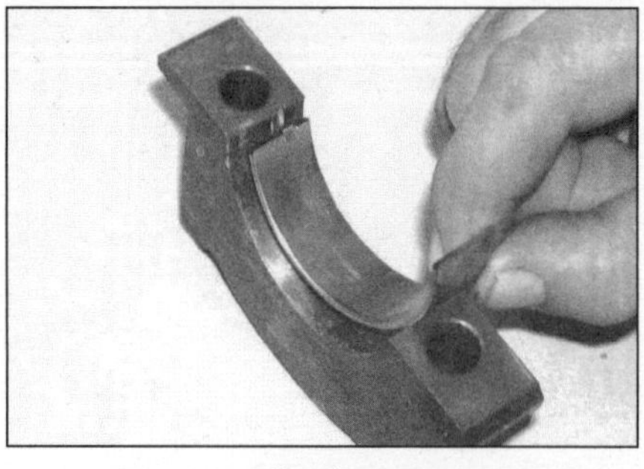

Bearing

Bearing The curved surface on a shaft or in a bore, or the part assembled into either, that permits relative motion between them with minimum wear and friction.
Big-end bearing The bearing in the end of the connecting rod that's attached to the crankshaft.
Bleed nipple A valve on a brake wheel cylinder, caliper or other hydraulic component that is opened to purge the hydraulic system of air. Also called a bleed screw.

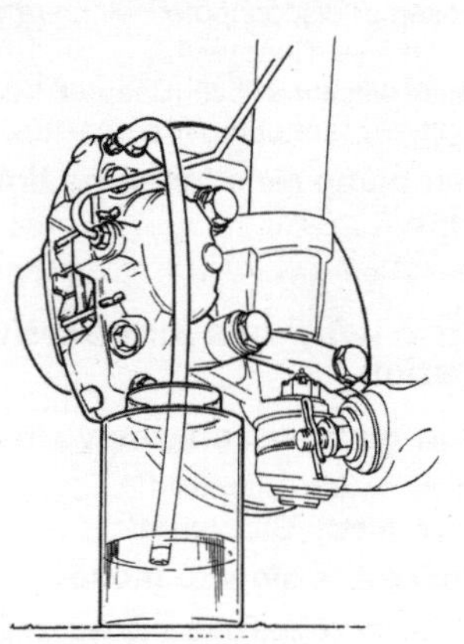

Brake bleeding

Brake bleeding Procedure for removing air from lines of a hydraulic brake system.
Brake disc The component of a disc brake that rotates with the wheels.
Brake drum The component of a drum brake that rotates with the wheels.
Brake linings The friction material which contacts the brake disc or drum to retard the vehicle's speed. The linings are bonded or riveted to the brake pads or shoes.
Brake pads The replaceable friction pads that pinch the brake disc when the brakes are applied. Brake pads consist of a friction material bonded or riveted to a rigid backing plate.
Brake shoe The crescent-shaped carrier to which the brake linings are mounted and which forces the lining against the rotating drum during braking.
Braking systems For more information on braking systems, consult the *Haynes Automotive Brake Manual*.
Breaker bar A long socket wrench handle providing greater leverage.
Bulkhead The insulated partition between the engine and the passenger compartment.

C

Caliper The non-rotating part of a disc-brake assembly that straddles the disc and carries the brake pads. The caliper also contains the hydraulic components that cause the pads to pinch the disc when the brakes are applied. A caliper is also a measuring tool that can be set to measure inside or outside dimensions of an object.

Camshaft A rotating shaft on which a series of cam lobes operate the valve mechanisms. The camshaft may be driven by gears, by sprockets and chain or by sprockets and a belt.

Canister A container in an evaporative emission control system; contains activated charcoal granules to trap vapours from the fuel system.

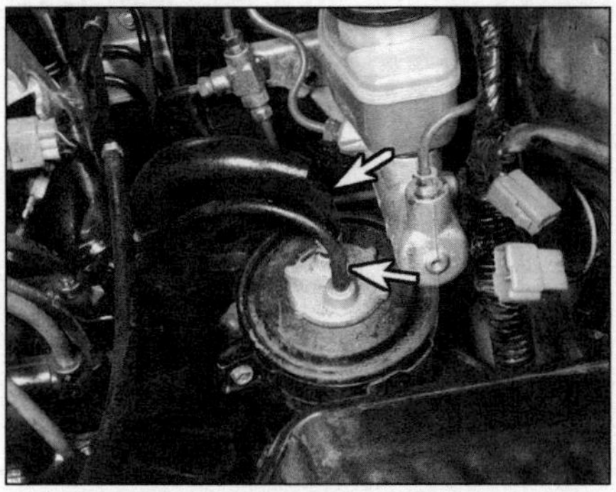
Canister

Carburettor A device which mixes fuel with air in the proper proportions to provide a desired power output from a spark ignition internal combustion engine.

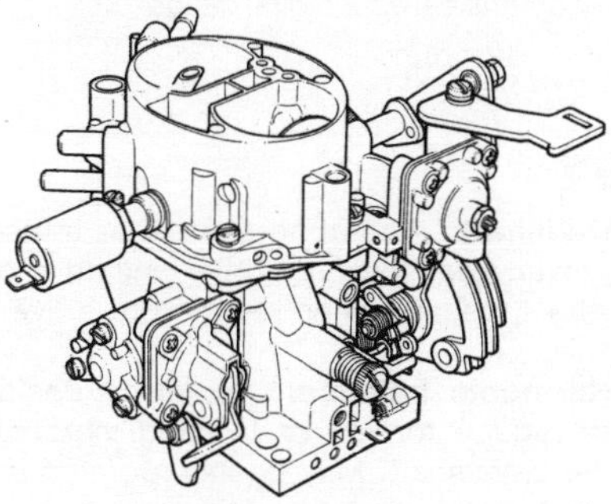
Carburettor

Castellated Resembling the parapets along the top of a castle wall. For example, a castellated balljoint stud nut.

Castellated nut

Castor In wheel alignment, the backward or forward tilt of the steering axis. Castor is positive when the steering axis is inclined rearward at the top.

Catalytic converter A silencer-like device in the exhaust system which converts certain pollutants in the exhaust gases into less harmful substances.

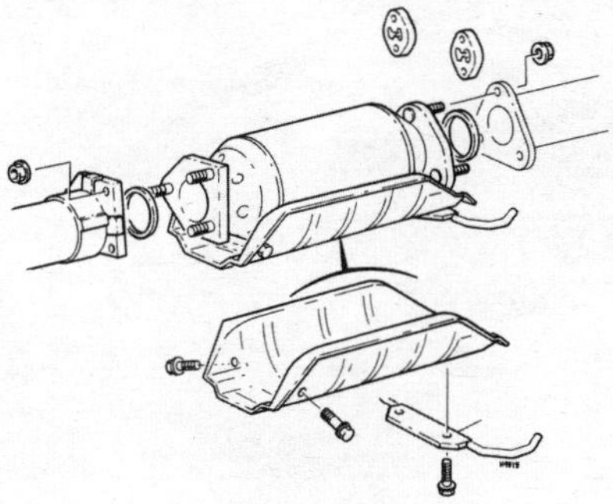
Catalytic converter

Circlip A ring-shaped clip used to prevent endwise movement of cylindrical parts and shafts. An internal circlip is installed in a groove in a housing; an external circlip fits into a groove on the outside of a cylindrical piece such as a shaft.

Clearance The amount of space between two parts. For example, between a piston and a cylinder, between a bearing and a journal, etc.

Coil spring A spiral of elastic steel found in various sizes throughout a vehicle, for example as a springing medium in the suspension and in the valve train.

Compression Reduction in volume, and increase in pressure and temperature, of a gas, caused by squeezing it into a smaller space.

Compression ratio The relationship between cylinder volume when the piston is at top dead centre and cylinder volume when the piston is at bottom dead centre.

Constant velocity (CV) joint A type of universal joint that cancels out vibrations caused by driving power being transmitted through an angle.

Core plug A disc or cup-shaped metal device inserted in a hole in a casting through which core was removed when the casting was formed. Also known as a freeze plug or expansion plug.

Crankcase The lower part of the engine block in which the crankshaft rotates.

Crankshaft The main rotating member, or shaft, running the length of the crankcase, with offset "throws" to which the connecting rods are attached.

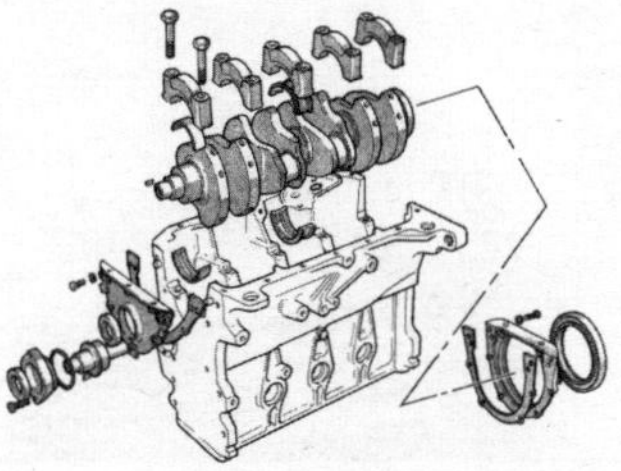
Crankshaft assembly

Crocodile clip See Alligator clip

D

Diagnostic code Code numbers obtained by accessing the diagnostic mode of an engine management computer. This code can be used to determine the area in the system where a malfunction may be located.

Disc brake A brake design incorporating a rotating disc onto which brake pads are squeezed. The resulting friction converts the energy of a moving vehicle into heat.

Double-overhead cam (DOHC) An engine that uses two overhead camshafts, usually one for the intake valves and one for the exhaust valves.

Drivebelt(s) The belt(s) used to drive accessories such as the alternator, water pump, power steering pump, air conditioning compressor, etc. off the crankshaft pulley.

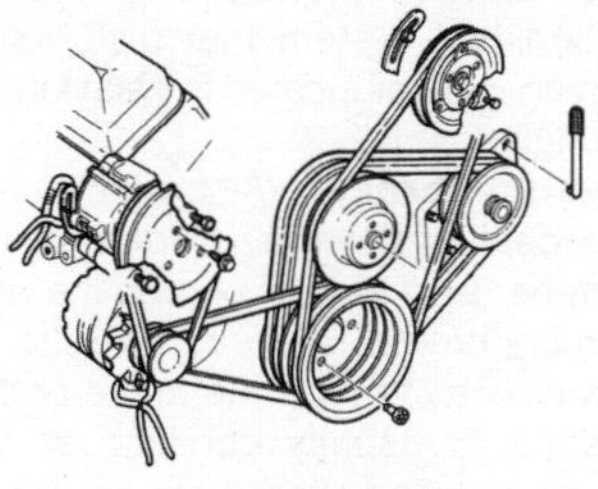
Accessory drivebelts

Driveshaft Any shaft used to transmit motion. Commonly used when referring to the axleshafts on a front wheel drive vehicle.

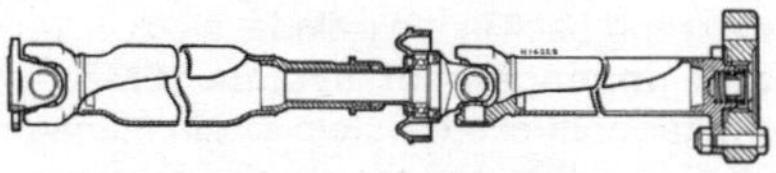
Driveshaft

Drum brake A type of brake using a drum-shaped metal cylinder attached to the inner surface of the wheel. When the brake pedal is pressed, curved brake shoes with friction linings press against the inside of the drum to slow or stop the vehicle.

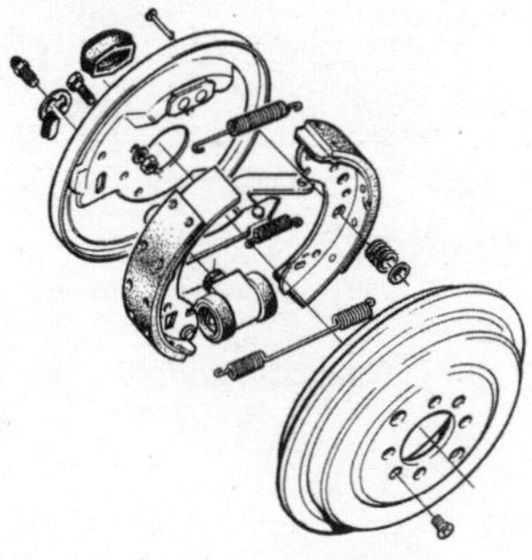
Drum brake assembly

E

EGR valve A valve used to introduce exhaust gases into the intake air stream.

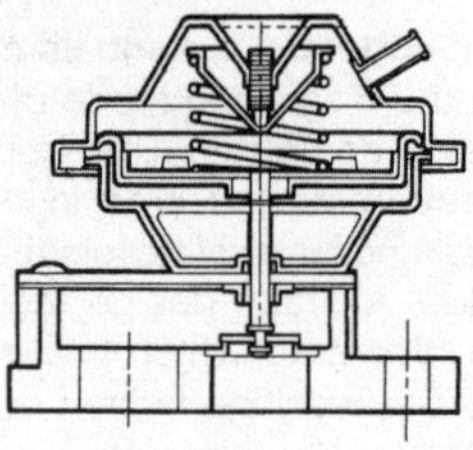

EGR valve

Electronic control unit (ECU) A computer which controls (for instance) ignition and fuel injection systems, or an anti-lock braking system. For more information refer to the Haynes Automotive Electrical and Electronic Systems Manual.

Electronic Fuel Injection (EFI) A computer controlled fuel system that distributes fuel through an injector located in each intake port of the engine.

Emergency brake A braking system, independent of the main hydraulic system, that can be used to slow or stop the vehicle if the primary brakes fail, or to hold the vehicle stationary even though the brake pedal isn't depressed. It usually consists of a hand lever that actuates either front or rear brakes mechanically through a series of cables and linkages. Also known as a handbrake or parking brake.

Endfloat The amount of lengthwise movement between two parts. As applied to a crankshaft, the distance that the crankshaft can move forward and back in the cylinder block.

Engine management system (EMS) A computer controlled system which manages the fuel injection and the ignition systems in an integrated fashion.

Exhaust manifold A part with several passages through which exhaust gases leave the engine combustion chambers and enter the exhaust pipe.

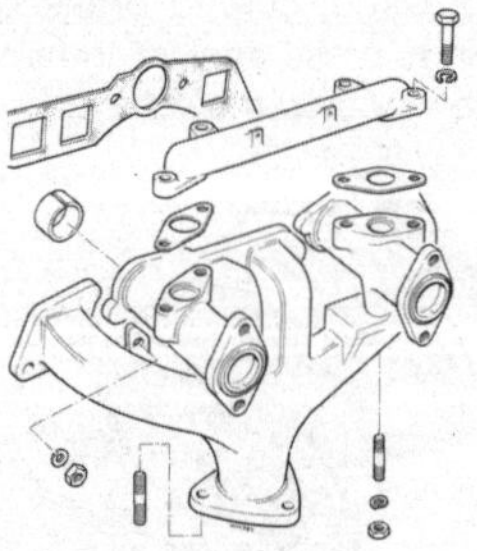

Exhaust manifold

F

Fan clutch A viscous (fluid) drive coupling device which permits variable engine fan speeds in relation to engine speeds.

Feeler blade A thin strip or blade of hardened steel, ground to an exact thickness, used to check or measure clearances between parts.

Feeler blade

Firing order The order in which the engine cylinders fire, or deliver their power strokes, beginning with the number one cylinder.

Flywheel A heavy spinning wheel in which energy is absorbed and stored by means of momentum. On cars, the flywheel is attached to the crankshaft to smooth out firing impulses.

Free play The amount of travel before any action takes place. The "looseness" in a linkage, or an assembly of parts, between the initial application of force and actual movement. For example, the distance the brake pedal moves before the pistons in the master cylinder are actuated.

Fuse An electrical device which protects a circuit against accidental overload. The typical fuse contains a soft piece of metal which is calibrated to melt at a predetermined current flow (expressed as amps) and break the circuit.

Fusible link A circuit protection device consisting of a conductor surrounded by heat-resistant insulation. The conductor is smaller than the wire it protects, so it acts as the weakest link in the circuit. Unlike a blown fuse, a failed fusible link must frequently be cut from the wire for replacement.

G

Gap The distance the spark must travel in jumping from the centre electrode to the side electrode in a spark plug. Also refers to the spacing between the points in a contact breaker assembly in a conventional points-type ignition, or to the distance between the reluctor or rotor and the pickup coil in an electronic ignition.

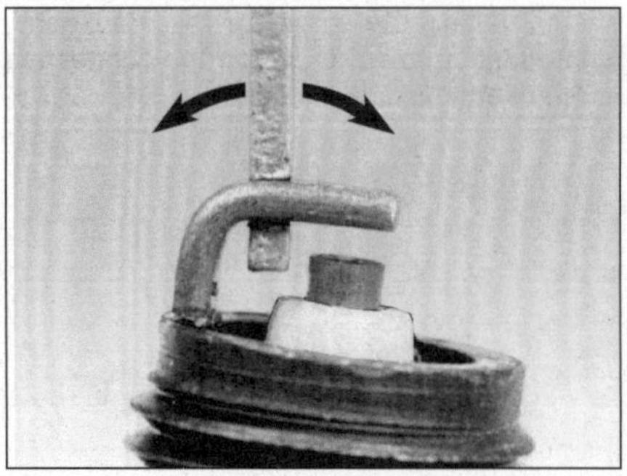

Adjusting spark plug gap

Gasket Any thin, soft material - usually cork, cardboard, asbestos or soft metal - installed between two metal surfaces to ensure a good seal. For instance, the cylinder head gasket seals the joint between the block and the cylinder head.

Gasket

Gauge An instrument panel display used to monitor engine conditions. A gauge with a movable pointer on a dial or a fixed scale is an analogue gauge. A gauge with a numerical readout is called a digital gauge.

H

Halfshaft A rotating shaft that transmits power from the final drive unit to a drive wheel, usually when referring to a live rear axle.

Harmonic balancer A device designed to reduce torsion or twisting vibration in the crankshaft. May be incorporated in the crankshaft pulley. Also known as a vibration damper.

Hone An abrasive tool for correcting small irregularities or differences in diameter in an engine cylinder, brake cylinder, etc.

Hydraulic tappet A tappet that utilises hydraulic pressure from the engine's lubrication system to maintain zero clearance (constant contact with both camshaft and valve stem). Automatically adjusts to variation in valve stem length. Hydraulic tappets also reduce valve noise.

I

Ignition timing The moment at which the spark plug fires, usually expressed in the number of crankshaft degrees before the piston reaches the top of its stroke.

Inlet manifold A tube or housing with passages through which flows the air-fuel mixture (carburettor vehicles and vehicles with throttle body injection) or air only (port fuel-injected vehicles) to the port openings in the cylinder head.

J

Jump start Starting the engine of a vehicle with a discharged or weak battery by attaching jump leads from the weak battery to a charged or helper battery.

L

Load Sensing Proportioning Valve (LSPV) A brake hydraulic system control valve that works like a proportioning valve, but also takes into consideration the amount of weight carried by the rear axle.

Locknut A nut used to lock an adjustment nut, or other threaded component, in place. For example, a locknut is employed to keep the adjusting nut on the rocker arm in position.

Lockwasher A form of washer designed to prevent an attaching nut from working loose.

M

MacPherson strut A type of front suspension system devised by Earle MacPherson at Ford of England. In its original form, a simple lateral link with the anti-roll bar creates the lower control arm. A long strut - an integral coil spring and shock absorber - is mounted between the body and the steering knuckle. Many modern so-called MacPherson strut systems use a conventional lower A-arm and don't rely on the anti-roll bar for location.

Multimeter An electrical test instrument with the capability to measure voltage, current and resistance.

N

NOx Oxides of Nitrogen. A common toxic pollutant emitted by petrol and diesel engines at higher temperatures.

O

Ohm The unit of electrical resistance. One volt applied to a resistance of one ohm will produce a current of one amp.

Ohmmeter An instrument for measuring electrical resistance.

O-ring A type of sealing ring made of a special rubber-like material; in use, the O-ring is compressed into a groove to provide the sealing action.

O-ring

Overhead cam (ohc) engine An engine with the camshaft(s) located on top of the cylinder head(s).

Overhead valve (ohv) engine An engine with the valves located in the cylinder head, but with the camshaft located in the engine block.

Oxygen sensor A device installed in the engine exhaust manifold, which senses the oxygen content in the exhaust and converts this information into an electric current. Also called a Lambda sensor.

P

Phillips screw A type of screw head having a cross instead of a slot for a corresponding type of screwdriver.

Plastigage A thin strip of plastic thread, available in different sizes, used for measuring clearances. For example, a strip of Plastigage is laid across a bearing journal. The parts are assembled and dismantled; the width of the crushed strip indicates the clearance between journal and bearing.

Plastigage

Propeller shaft The long hollow tube with universal joints at both ends that carries power from the transmission to the differential on front-engined rear wheel drive vehicles.

Proportioning valve A hydraulic control valve which limits the amount of pressure to the rear brakes during panic stops to prevent wheel lock-up.

R

Rack-and-pinion steering A steering system with a pinion gear on the end of the steering shaft that mates with a rack (think of a geared wheel opened up and laid flat). When the steering wheel is turned, the pinion turns, moving the rack to the left or right. This movement is transmitted through the track rods to the steering arms at the wheels.

Radiator A liquid-to-air heat transfer device designed to reduce the temperature of the coolant in an internal combustion engine cooling system.

Refrigerant Any substance used as a heat transfer agent in an air-conditioning system. R-12 has been the principle refrigerant for many years; recently, however, manufacturers have begun using R-134a, a non-CFC substance that is considered less harmful to the ozone in the upper atmosphere.

Rocker arm A lever arm that rocks on a shaft or pivots on a stud. In an overhead valve engine, the rocker arm converts the upward movement of the pushrod into a downward movement to open a valve.

Rotor In a distributor, the rotating device inside the cap that connects the centre electrode and the outer terminals as it turns, distributing the high voltage from the coil secondary winding to the proper spark plug. Also, that part of an alternator which rotates inside the stator. Also, the rotating assembly of a turbocharger, including the compressor wheel, shaft and turbine wheel.

Runout The amount of wobble (in-and-out movement) of a gear or wheel as it's rotated. The amount a shaft rotates "out-of-true." The out-of-round condition of a rotating part.

S

Sealant A liquid or paste used to prevent leakage at a joint. Sometimes used in conjunction with a gasket.

Sealed beam lamp An older headlight design which integrates the reflector, lens and filaments into a hermetically-sealed one-piece unit. When a filament burns out or the lens cracks, the entire unit is simply replaced.

Serpentine drivebelt A single, long, wide accessory drivebelt that's used on some newer vehicles to drive all the accessories, instead of a series of smaller, shorter belts. Serpentine drivebelts are usually tensioned by an automatic tensioner.

Serpentine drivebelt

Shim Thin spacer, commonly used to adjust the clearance or relative positions between two parts. For example, shims inserted into or under bucket tappets control valve clearances. Clearance is adjusted by changing the thickness of the shim.

Slide hammer A special puller that screws into or hooks onto a component such as a shaft or bearing; a heavy sliding handle on the shaft bottoms against the end of the shaft to knock the component free.

Sprocket A tooth or projection on the periphery of a wheel, shaped to engage with a chain or drivebelt. Commonly used to refer to the sprocket wheel itself.

Starter inhibitor switch On vehicles with an automatic transmission, a switch that prevents starting if the vehicle is not in Neutral or Park.

Strut See MacPherson strut.

T

Tappet A cylindrical component which transmits motion from the cam to the valve stem, either directly or via a pushrod and rocker arm. Also called a cam follower.

Thermostat A heat-controlled valve that regulates the flow of coolant between the cylinder block and the radiator, so maintaining optimum engine operating temperature. A thermostat is also used in some air cleaners in which the temperature is regulated.

Thrust bearing The bearing in the clutch assembly that is moved in to the release levers by clutch pedal action to disengage the clutch. Also referred to as a release bearing.

Timing belt A toothed belt which drives the camshaft. Serious engine damage may result if it breaks in service.

Timing chain A chain which drives the camshaft.

Toe-in The amount the front wheels are closer together at the front than at the rear. On rear wheel drive vehicles, a slight amount of toe-in is usually specified to keep the front wheels running parallel on the road by offsetting other forces that tend to spread the wheels apart.

Toe-out The amount the front wheels are closer together at the rear than at the front. On front wheel drive vehicles, a slight amount of toe-out is usually specified.

Tools For full information on choosing and using tools, refer to the *Haynes Automotive Tools Manual*.

Tracer A stripe of a second colour applied to a wire insulator to distinguish that wire from another one with the same colour insulator.

Tune-up A process of accurate and careful adjustments and parts replacement to obtain the best possible engine performance.

Turbocharger A centrifugal device, driven by exhaust gases, that pressurises the intake air. Normally used to increase the power output from a given engine displacement, but can also be used primarily to reduce exhaust emissions (as on VW's "Umwelt" Diesel engine).

U

Universal joint or U-joint A double-pivoted connection for transmitting power from a driving to a driven shaft through an angle. A U-joint consists of two Y-shaped yokes and a cross-shaped member called the spider.

V

Valve A device through which the flow of liquid, gas, vacuum, or loose material in bulk may be started, stopped, or regulated by a movable part that opens, shuts, or partially obstructs one or more ports or passageways. A valve is also the movable part of such a device.

Valve clearance The clearance between the valve tip (the end of the valve stem) and the rocker arm or tappet. The valve clearance is measured when the valve is closed.

Vernier caliper A precision measuring instrument that measures inside and outside dimensions. Not quite as accurate as a micrometer, but more convenient.

Viscosity The thickness of a liquid or its resistance to flow.

Volt A unit for expressing electrical "pressure" in a circuit. One volt that will produce a current of one ampere through a resistance of one ohm.

W

Welding Various processes used to join metal items by heating the areas to be joined to a molten state and fusing them together. For more information refer to the *Haynes Automotive Welding Manual*.

Wiring diagram A drawing portraying the components and wires in a vehicle's electrical system, using standardised symbols. For more information refer to the *Haynes Automotive Electrical and Electronic Systems Manual*.

Note: *References throughout this index are in the form* **"Chapter number" • "Page number"**. *So, for example, 2C•15 refers to page 15 of Chapter 2C.*

Note: *References throughout this index are in the form* **"Chapter number" • "Page number"**. *So, for example, 2C•15 refers to page 15 of Chapter 2C.*

Note: *References throughout this index are in the form* **"Chapter number" • "Page number"**. *So, for example, 2C•15 refers to page 15 of Chapter 2C.*

Note: *References throughout this index are in the form* "**Chapter number**" • "**Page number**"*. So, for example, 2C•15 refers to page 15 of Chapter 2C.*

Note: *References throughout this index are in the form* **"Chapter number" • "Page number"**. *So, for example, 2C•15 refers to page 15 of Chapter 2C.*

Note: *References throughout this index are in the form* **"Chapter number" • "Page number"***. So, for example, 2C•15 refers to page 15 of Chapter 2C.*